Twentieth-Century Literary Criticism

Archive Volume

Guide to Gale Literary Criticism Series

When you need to review criticism of literary works, these are the Gale series to use:

If the author's death date is: **You should turn to:**

After Dec. 31, 1959
(or author is still living)

CONTEMPORARY LITERARY CRITICISM

for example: Jorge Luis Borges, Anthony Burgess,
William Faulkner, Mary Gordon,
Ernest Hemingway, Iris Murdoch

1900 through 1959

TWENTIETH-CENTURY LITERARY CRITICISM

for example: Willa Cather, F. Scott Fitzgerald,
Henry James, Mark Twain, Virginia Woolf

1800 through 1899

NINETEENTH-CENTURY LITERATURE CRITICISM

for example: Fyodor Dostoevsky, Nathaniel Hawthorne,
George Sand, William Wordsworth

1400 through 1799

LITERATURE CRITICISM FROM 1400 TO 1800
(excluding Shakespeare)

for example: Anne Bradstreet, Daniel Defoe,
Alexander Pope, François Rabelais,
Jonathan Swift, Phillis Wheatley

SHAKESPEAREAN CRITICISM

Shakespeare's plays and poetry

Antiquity through 1399

CLASSICAL AND MEDIEVAL LITERATURE CRITICISM

for example: Dante, Homer, Plato, Sophocles, Vergil,
the Beowulf Poet

Gale also publishes related criticism series:

CHILDREN'S LITERATURE REVIEW

This series covers authors of all eras who have written for
the preschool through high school audience.

SHORT STORY CRITICISM

This series covers the major short fiction writers of all nationalities
and periods of literary history.

POETRY CRITICISM

This series covers poets of all nationalities, movements, and periods of
literary history.

ISSN 0276-8178

Volume 30

Twentieth-Century Literary Criticism

Archive Volume

**Excerpts from Criticism of Various Topics
in Twentieth-Century Literature, including Literary
and Critical Movements, Prominent Themes and
Genres, Anniversary Celebrations, and Surveys
of National Literatures**

**Paula Kepos
Dennis Poupard
Editors**

**Marie Lazzari
Thomas Ligotti
Joann Prosyniuk
Associate Editors**

 Gale Research Inc. • *DETROIT* • *LONDON*

Paula Kepos, Dennis Poupard, *Editors*

Marie Lazzari, Thomas Ligotti, Joann Prosyniuk, *Associate Editors*

Keith E. Schooley, Laurie Sherman, *Senior Assistant Editors*

Sandra Liddell, Timothy Veeser, *Assistant Editors*

Denise Michelwicz Broderick, Susan Miller Harig, Debra A. Wells, *Contributing Assistant Editors*

Jeanne A. Gough, *Permissions & Production Manager*
Lizbeth A. Purdy, *Production Supervisor*
Cathy Beranek, Christine A. Galbraith, Suzanne Powers, Kristine E. Tipton,
Lee Ann Welsh, *Editorial Assistants*
Linda M. Pugliese, *Manuscript Coordinator*
Maureen A. Puhl, *Senior Manuscript Assistant*
Donna Craft, Jennifer E. Gale, *Manuscript Assistants*

Victoria B. Cariappa, *Research Supervisor*
Maureen R. Richards, *Research Coordinator*
Mary D. Wise, *Senior Research Assistant*
Joyce E. Doyle, Kevin B. Hillstrom, Karen D. Kaus, Eric Priehs, Filomena Sgambati, *Research Assistants*

Janice M. Mach, *Text Permissions Supervisor*
Kathy Grell, *Text Permissions Coordinator*
Mabel E. Gurney, *Research Permissions Coordinator*
Josephine M. Keene, *Senior Permissions Assistant*
H. Diane Cooper, Anita Lorraine Ransom, Kimberly F. Smilay, *Permissions Assistants*
Melissa A. Brantley, Denise M. Singleton, Sharon D. Valentine, Lisa M. Wimmer, *Permissions Clerks*

Patricia A. Seefelt, *Picture Permissions Supervisor*
Margaret A. Chamberlain, *Picture Permissions Coordinator*
Pamela A. Hayes, Lillian Tyus, *Permissions Clerks*

Mary Beth Trimper, *Production Manager*
Laura McKay, *Production Assistant*

Arthur Chartow, *Art Director*
Linda A. Davis, *Production Assistant*

Laura Bryant, *Production Supervisor*
Louise Gagné, *Internal Production Associate*

The paper used in this publication meets the minimum requirements
of American National Standard for Information Sciences—Permanence
Paper for Printed Library Materials, ANSI Z39.48-1984. ∞™

Since this page cannot legibly accommodate all the copyright notices,
the Appendix constitutes an extension of the copyright notice.

Library of Congress Catalog Card Number 76-46132
ISBN 0-8103-2412-1
ISSN 0276-8178

10 9 8 7 6 5 4 3 2

Printed in the United States of America.

Published simultaneously in the United Kingdom
by Gale Research International Limited
(An affiliated company of Gale Research Inc.)

Contents

Preface

The study of literature embraces many disciplines, including history, sociology, psychology, and philosophy. To fully comprehend a literary work, it is often necessary to understand the history and culture of the author's nation, the literary movements the author belonged to or disdained, the political passions and social concerns of the author's era, or themes common to the literature of the author's nation. Thus, to gain a fuller perspective on an author, a student often needs to examine a great many social, historical, and literary factors.

Many schools reflect the necessity for such a broad view of literature by including historical and thematic surveys in their curricula. In these courses, themes that recur throughout many works of literature are examined, the literary tempers of various historical eras are assessed, and literary and critical movements are defined. Increasingly, comparative literature courses and thematic surveys of foreign literature are being offered by colleges and universities, introducing students to the most significant literature of many nations. In order to provide important information on the variety of topics encountered by the general reader or student of literature, *Twentieth-Century Literary Criticism (TCLC)* has extended its scope by creating the *TCLC* Archive volumes. Once a year, *TCLC* devotes an entire volume to criticism of literary topics that cannot be addressed by our regular format.

Scope of the Series

TCLC is designed to serve as an introduction to the authors of the period 1900 through 1959 and to the most significant commentators on these authors. Since a vast amount of relevant critical material confronts the student, *TCLC* presents significant passages from the most important published criticism to aid students in the location and selection of critical commentary. *TCLC* is a companion series to *Contemporary Literary Criticism (CLC)*, which excerpts criticism on current writing. Because of the difference in time span under consideration (*CLC* considers authors who were still living after 1959), there is no duplication of material between *CLC* and *TCLC*.

Standard volumes of *TCLC* comprise surveys of the careers of fifteen to twenty authors representing a variety of nationalities. The authors selected include the most important writers of the era 1900 to 1959, as well as lesser-known figures whose significant contributions to literary history are important to the study of twentieth-century literature. Each author entry represents a historical survey of the critical response to that author's work: some early criticism is presented to indicate initial reactions, later criticism is selected to represent any rise or decline in the author's reputation, and current retrospective analyses provide students with the latest views. Every attempt is made to identify and include excerpts from seminal essays on each author's work.

Scope of the Archive Volumes

The *TCLC* Archive volumes enhance the usefulness of the series by examining literary topics that cannot be covered under the author approach used in the rest of the series. Such topics include literary movements, prominent themes or subjects in twentieth-century literature, literary reaction to political and historical events, studies of significant eras in literary history, prominent literary anniversaries, and examinations of the literatures of cultures that are often overlooked by English-speaking readers. *TCLC* 30, for example, examines the following seven topics: the body of literature produced by exiles from Nazi Germany; the New York Intellectuals, a group of writers and thinkers whose diverse and far-reaching accomplishments include contributions to the development of literary Modernism, leftist political theory, and, in recent years, the neoconservative movement in American politics; travel writing and supernatural fiction, two genres that experienced their "golden age" during the early twentieth century and have undergone a resurgence in the last two decades; the oral and written literature of twentieth-century Nigeria; Russian Symbolism, the movement that initiated the last great flourishing of Russian culture before the imposition of official Soviet literary doctrines and whose works have achieved renewed prominence under the liberalization policies of Mikhail Gorbachev; and Surrealism, an international movement in literature and the arts whose accomplishments have influenced virtually every area of modern art and culture.

The subjects of Archive entries are chosen for their usefulness and timeliness; the length of each entry is determined by the importance of the subject and the amount of criticism available in English. Subjects considered in Archive volumes are restricted as much as possible to the period 1900 to 1959. For this reason, we discuss only literary movements and subjects that saw their greatest influence in this period. In some cases this means that we will include discussion of authors who are covered in *CLC* or in *Nineteenth-Century Literature Criticism (NCLC)*. For example, many of the writers of the Surrealist movement lived into the era covered by the *CLC* series (post-1959), yet the movement was born and had its greatest influence in the period covered by *TCLC* (1900-1959). To ensure a complete discussion of Surrealism, the editors have included criticism of all important authors associated with the movement, regardless of death dates. However, we have not duplicated criticism already published in the other series.

Organization of the Book

This Archive volume includes excerpted criticism on seven topics. Each subject entry consists of the following elements:

- The *introduction* briefly defines the subject of the entry and provides social and historical background information important to an understanding of the criticism.

- The *criticism* is arranged thematically. Entries commonly begin with general surveys of the subject or essays providing historical or background information, followed by essays that develop particular aspects of the topic. For example, the entry devoted to Surrealism begins with essays detailing the history and formative influences of the movement and excerpts from the first and second Surrealist Manifestos. These are followed by a section on the philosophic, aesthetic, and political principles of the Surrealists and by sections devoted to Surrealist poetry, fiction, drama, film, and plastic arts. The entry concludes with an essay evaluating the extent to which the Surrealists achieved their ultimate ambitions. Each section has a separate title heading and is identified with a page number in the table of contents for easy reader access.

  The critic's name is given at the beginning of each piece of criticism; when an unsigned essay is later attributed to a critic, the critic's name appears in brackets at the beginning of the excerpt and in the bibliographic citation. Anonymous essays are headed by the title of the journal in which they appeared. Many critical essays in *TCLC* contain translated material to aid users. Unless otherwise noted, translations within brackets are by the editors; translations within parentheses are by the author of the excerpt.

- Critical essays are prefaced by *explanatory notes* providing the reader with information about both the critic and the criticism that follows. Included are the critic's reputation, individual approach to literary criticism, and particular expertise in the subject under discussion. Also noted are the relative importance of a work of criticism, the scope of the excerpt, and the growth of critical controversy or changes in critical trends regarding the subject. In some cases, these notes cross-reference the work of critics who agree or disagree with each other.

- A complete *bibliographical citation* designed to facilitate location of the original essay or book by the interested reader follows each piece of criticism.

- *Illustrations* throughout the entry include portraits of the authors under discussion, important manuscript pages, magazine covers, dust jackets, movie stills, reproductions of artwork, maps, and photographs of people, places, and events important to the topic.

- The *additional bibliography* appearing at the end of each subject entry suggests further reading on the subject, in some cases including essays for which the editors could not obtain reprint rights. The bibliography also includes anthologies of creative writing pertaining to the subject.

An appendix lists the sources from which material in each volume has been reprinted. It does not, however, list every book or periodical consulted in the preparation of a volume.

Cumulative Indexes

Each volume of *TCLC*, including the Archive volumes, contains a cumulative author index listing all authors who have appeared in the following Gale series: *Contemporary Literary Criticism, Twentieth-Century Literary Criticism, Nineteenth-Century Literature Criticism, Literature Criticism from 1400 to 1800,* and *Classical and Medieval Literature Criticism.* Archive entries devoted to a single author, such as the entry on James Joyce's *Ulysses* in *TCLC* 26, are listed in this index. Also included are cross-references to the Gale series *Short Story Criticism, Children's Literature Review, Authors in the News, Contemporary Authors, Contemporary Authors Autobiography Series, Dictionary of Literary Biography, Concise Dictionary of American Literary Biography, Something about the Author, Something about the*

Author Autobiography Series, and *Yesterday's Authors of Books for Children.* The index, which lists birth and death dates when available, is particularly valuable for those authors who are identified with a certain period but whose death date causes them to be placed in another, or for those authors whose careers span two periods. For example, F. Scott Fitzgerald is found in *TCLC,* yet a writer often associated with him, Ernest Hemingway, is found in *CLC.*

Each *TCLC* Archive volume also includes a cumulative nationality index which lists all authors who have appeared in regular *TCLC* volumes, arranged alphabetically under their respective nationalities, as well as Archive entries devoted to particular national literatures.

Titles discussed in the Archive entries are not included in the *TCLC* cumulative title index.

Acknowledgments

No work of this scope can be accomplished without the cooperation of many people. The editors especially wish to thank the copyright holders of the criticism in this volume, the permissions managers of many book and magazine publishing companies for assisting us in securing reprint rights, and Anthony Bogucki for assistance with copyright research. We are also grateful to the staffs of the Detroit Public Library, the Library of Congress, the University of Michigan Library, the Wayne State University Library, and the University of Detroit Library for making their resources available to us.

Suggestions Are Welcome

In response to suggestions, several features have been added to *TCLC* since the series began, including explanatory notes to excerpted criticism, a cumulative index to authors in all Gale literary criticism series, entries devoted to criticism on a single work by a major author, and more extensive illustrations.

Readers who wish to suggest authors or topics to appear in future volumes, or who have other suggestions, are cordially invited to write the editors.

Authors to Be Featured in Forthcoming Volumes

Mikhail Artsybashev (Russian novelist)—Artsybashev was notorious for works promoting the principles of anarchic individualism and unrestrained sensuality. His erotic novel *Sanin* produced an international sensation and inspired cults dedicated to the destruction of social convention.

Henri Bergson (French philosopher)—One of the most influential philosophers of the twentieth century, Bergson is renowned for his opposition to the dominant materialist thought of his time and for his creation of theories that emphasize the supremacy and independence of supra-rational consciousness.

Edgar Rice Burroughs (American novelist)—Burroughs was a science fiction writer who is best known as the creator of Tarzan. His *Tarzan of the Apes* and its numerous sequels have sold over thirty-five million copies in fifty-six languages, making Burroughs one of the most popular authors in the world.

Samuel Butler (English novelist and essayist)—Butler is best known for *The Way of All Flesh,* an autobiographical novel that is both a classic account of the conflict between father and son and an indictment of Victorian society.

Willa Cather (American novelist and short story writer)—In her works, Cather combined knowledge of Nebraska with an artistic expertise reminiscent of the nineteenth-century literary masters to create one of the most distinguished achievements of twentieth-century American literature. She has been compared to Gustave Flaubert and Henry James for her sensibility, emphasis on technique, and high regard for the artist and European culture, and to the "lost generation" of Ernest Hemingway and F. Scott Fitzgerald for her alienation from modern American society.

Anton Chekhov (Russian dramatist and short story writer) Praised for his stylistic innovations in both fiction and drama as well as for his depth of insight into the human condition, Chekhov is the most significant Russian author of the generation to succeed Leo Tolstoy and Fyodor Dostoevsky. *TCLC* will devote an entry to Chekhov's plays, focusing on his dramatic masterpieces *The Seagull, Uncle Vanya, Three Sisters,* and *The Cherry Orchard.*

Stephen Crane (American novelist and short story writer) Crane was one of the foremost realistic writers in American literature. *TCLC* will devote an entry to his masterpiece, *The Red Badge of Courage,* in which he depicted the psychological complexities of fear and courage in battle.

Theodore Dreiser (American novelist)—A prominent American exponent of literary Naturalism and one of America's foremost novelists, Dreiser was the author of works commended for their powerful characterizations and strong ideological convictions.

Thomas Hardy (English novelist)—Considered one of the greatest novelists in the English language, Hardy is best known for his portrayal of characters who are subject to social and psychological forces beyond their control. *TCLC* will devote an entry to *The Mayor of Casterbridge,* a tragedy of psychological determinism in which Hardy introduced his belief that "character is fate."

Vicente Huidobro (Chilean poet)—Huidobro was among the most influential South American poets of the twentieth century for his formulation of *creacionismo,* a poetic theory that regarded poetry not as an imitation of nature but as an original creation.

William James (American philosopher and psychologist)—One of the most influential figures in modern Western philosophy, James was the founder of Pragmatism, a philosophy that rejected abstract models of reality in an attempt to explain life as it is actually experienced.

Nikos Kazantzakis (Greek novelist)—Kazantzakis was a controversial Greek writer whose works embodied Nietzschean and Bergsonian philosophical ideas in vividly portrayed characters, the most famous of which was the protagonist of *Zorba the Greek.*

Thomas Mann (German novelist)—Mann is credited with reclaiming for the German novel an international stature it had not enjoyed since the time of the Romantics. *TCLC* will devote an entry to his novel *Buddenbrooks,* a masterpiece of Realism which depicts the rise and fall of a wealthy Hanseatic family.

George Orwell (English novelist and essayist)—Designated the "conscience of his generation" by V. S. Pritchett, Orwell is the author of influential novels and essays embodying his commitment to personal freedom and social justice. *TCLC* will devote an entry to Orwell's first major popular and critical success, *Animal Farm,* a satirical fable in which Orwell attacked the consequences of the Russian Revolution while suggesting reasons for the failure of most revolutionary ideals.

Marcel Proust (French novelist)—Proust's multivolume *A la recherche du temps perdu (Remembrance of Things Past)* is among literature's works of highest genius. Combining a social historian's chronicle of turn-of-the-century Paris society, a philosopher's reflections on the nature of time and consciousness, and a psychologist's insight into a tangled network of personalities, the novel is acclaimed for conveying a profound view of all human existence.

Joseph Roth (Austrian novelist)—A chronicler of the last years of the Austro-Hungarian Empire, Roth is best known for his novels *Radetzky March, Job,* and *Flight without End.*

George Saintsbury (English critic)—Saintsbury has been called the most influential English literary historian and critic of the late nineteenth and early twentieth centuries.

Ernest Thompson Seton (American naturalist and author) Best known as the founder of the Boy Scouts of America, Seton was the author of twenty-five volumes of animal stories for children as well as books on woodcraft and natural history.

Italo Svevo (Italian novelist)—Svevo's ironic portrayals of the moral life of the bourgeoisie, which characteristically demonstrate the influence of the psychoanalytic theories of Sigmund Freud, earned him a reputation as the father of the modern Italian novel.

Mark Twain (American novelist)—Considered the father of modern American literature, Twain combined moral and social satire, adventure, and frontier humor to create such perenially popular books as *The Adventures of Tom Sawyer, The Adventures of Huckleberry Finn,* and *A Connecticut Yankee in King Arthur's Court.*

Thorstein Veblen (American economist and social critic) Veblen's seminal analyses of the nature, development, and consequences of business and industry—as well as his attack on bourgeois materialism in *The Theory of the Leisure Class*—distinguished him as one of the foremost American economists and social scientists of the twentieth century.

William Butler Yeats (Irish poet, dramatist, and essayist) Yeats is considered one of the greatest poets in the English language. Although his interest in Irish politics and his visionary approach to poetry often confounded his contemporaries and set him at odds with the intellectual trends of his time, Yeats's poetic achievement stands at the center of modern literature.

Additional Authors to Appear in Future Volumes

Abbey, Henry 1842-1911
Abercrombie, Lascelles 1881-1938
Adamic, Louis 1898-1951
Ade, George 1866-1944
Agustini, Delmira 1886-1914
Akers, Elizabeth Chase 1832-1911
Aldrich, Thomas Bailey 1836-1907
Aliyu, Dan Sidi 1902-1920
Allen, Hervey 1889-1949
Archer, William 1856-1924
Arlen, Michael 1895-1956
Austin, Alfred 1835-1913
Bahr, Hermann 1863-1934
Bailey, Philip James 1816-1902
Barbour, Ralph Henry 1870-1944
Benjamin, Walter 1892-1940
Bennett, James Gordon, Jr. 1841-1918
Berdyaev, Nikolai Aleksandrovich 1874-1948
Beresford, J(ohn) D(avys) 1873-1947
Binyon, Laurence 1869-1943
Bishop, John Peale 1892-1944
Blake, Lillie Devereux 1835-1913
Blest Gana, Alberto 1830-1920
Blum, Léon 1872-1950
Bodenheim, Maxwell 1892-1954
Bowen, Marjorie 1886-1952
Byrne, Donn 1889-1928
Caine, Hall 1853-1931
Cannan, Gilbert 1884-1955
Carducci, Giosuè 1835-1907
Carswell, Catherine 1879-1946
Churchill, Winston 1871-1947
Conner, Ralph 1860-1937
Corelli, Marie 1855-1924
Croce, Benedetto 1866-1952
Crofts, Freeman Wills 1879-1957
Cruze, James (Jens Cruz Bosen) 1884-1942
Curros, Enríquez Manuel 1851-1908
Dall, Caroline Wells (Healy) 1822-1912
Daudet, Léon 1867-1942
Delafield, E.M. (Edme Elizabeth Monica de la Pasture) 1890-1943
Deneson, Jacob 1836-1919
Diego, José de 1866-1918
Douglas, (George) Norman 1868-1952
Douglas, Lloyd C(assel) 1877-1951
Dovzhenko, Alexander 1894-1956
Drinkwater, John 1882-1937
Durkheim, Émile 1858-1917
Duun, Olav 1876-1939
Eaton, Walter Prichard 1878-1957
Eggleston, Edward 1837-1902
Erskine, John 1879-1951
Fadeyev, Alexander 1901-1956

Ferland, Albert 1872-1943
Field, Rachel 1894-1924
Flecker, James Elroy 1884-1915
Fletcher, John Gould 1886-1950
Fogazzaro, Antonio 1842-1911
Francos, Karl Emil 1848-1904
Frank, Bruno 1886-1945
Frazer, (Sir) George 1854-1941
Freud, Sigmund 1853-1939
Fröding, Gustaf 1860-1911
Fuller, Henry Blake 1857-1929
Futabatei Shimei 1864-1909
Gamboa, Federico 1864-1939
Glaspell, Susan 1876-1948
Glyn, Elinor 1864-1943
Golding, Louis 1895-1958
Gould, Gerald 1885-1936
Guest, Edgar 1881-1959
Gumilyov, Nikolay 1886-1921
Gyulai, Pal 1826-1909
Hale, Edward Everett 1822-1909
Hansen, Martin 1909-1955
Hernández, Miguel 1910-1942
Hewlett, Maurice 1861-1923
Heyward, DuBose 1885-1940
Hope, Anthony 1863-1933
Ilyas, Abu Shabaka 1903-1947
Imbs, Bravig 1904-1946
Ivanov, Vyacheslav Ivanovich 1866-1949
James, Will 1892-1942
Jammes, Francis 1868-1938
Johnson, Fenton 1888-1958
Johnston, Mary 1870-1936
Jorgensen, Johannes 1866-1956
King, Grace 1851-1932
Kirby, William 1817-1906
Kline, Otis Albert 1891-1946
Kohut, Adolph 1848-1916
Kuzmin, Mikhail Alexseyevich 1875-1936
Lamm, Martin 1880-1950
Leipoldt, C. Louis 1880-1947
Lima, Jorge De 1895-1953
Locke, Alain 1886-1954
López Portillo y Rojas, José 1850-1903
Louys, Pierre 1870-1925
Lucas, E(dward) V(errall) 1868-1938
Lyall, Edna 1857-1903
Machar, Josef Svatopluk 1864-1945
Mander, Jane 1877-1949
Maragall, Joan 1860-1911
Marais, Eugene 1871-1936
Masaryk, Tomas 1850-1939
Mayor, Flora Macdonald 1872-1932
McClellan, George Marion 1860-1934

Mikszáth, Kálmán 1847-1910
Mirbeau, Octave 1850-1917
Mistral, Frédéric 1830-1914
Monro, Harold 1879-1932
Moore, Thomas Sturge 1870-1944
Móricz, Zsigmond 1879-1942
Morley, Christopher 1890-1957
Morley, S. Griswold 1883-1948
Murray, (George) Gilbert 1866-1957
Nansen, Peter 1861-1918
Nobre, Antonio 1867-1900
O'Dowd, Bernard 1866-1959
Ophuls, Max 1902-1957
Orczy, Baroness 1865-1947
Oskison, John M. 1874-1947
Ostaijen, Paul van 1896-1928
Owen, Seaman 1861-1936
Page, Thomas Nelson 1853-1922
Parrington, Vernon L. 1871-1929
Paterson, Andrew Barton 1864-1941
Peck, George W. 1840-1916
Phillips, Ulrich B. 1877-1934
Pinero, Arthur Wing 1855-1934
Powys, T. F. 1875-1953
Prévost, Marcel 1862-1941
Quiller-Couch, Arthur 1863-1944
Ramos, Graciliano 1892-1953
Randall, James G. 1881-1953
Rappoport, Solomon 1863-1944
Read, Opie 1852-1939
Reisen (Reizen), Abraham 1875-1953
Remington, Frederic 1861-1909
Reyes, Alfonso 1889-1959
Riley, James Whitcomb 1849-1916
Rinehart, Mary Roberts 1876-1958
Ring, Max 1817-1901
Rivera, José Eustasio 1889-1928
Rozanov, Vasily Vasilyevich 1856-1919
Saar, Ferdinand von 1833-1906
Sabatini, Rafael 1875-1950
Sakutaro, Hagiwara 1886-1942
Sanborn, Franklin Benjamin 1831-1917
Sánchez, Florencio 1875-1910
Santayana, George 1863-1952
Sardou, Victorien 1831-1908
Schickele, René 1885-1940
Seabrook, William 1886-1945
Shestov, Lev 1866-1938
Shiels, George 1886-1949
Singer, Israel Joshua 1893-1944
Södergran, Edith Irene 1892-1923
Solovyov, Vladimir 1853-1900
Sorel, Georges 1847-1922
Spector, Mordechai 1859-1922
Squire, J(ohn) C(ollings) 1884-1958
Stavenhagen, Fritz 1876-1906

Stockton, Frank R. 1834-1902
Subrahmanya Bharati, C. 1882-1921
Sully-Prudhomme, René 1839-1907
Sylva, Carmen 1843-1916
Talvik, Heiti 1904-1947?
Taneda Santoka 1882-1940
Thoma, Ludwig 1867-1927
Tomlinson, Henry Major 1873-1958
Totovents, Vahan 1889-1937
Tozzi, Federigo 1883-1920
Tuchmann, Jules 1830-1901

Turner, W(alter) J(ames) R(edfern)
   1889-1946
Upward, Allen 1863-1926
Vachell, Horace Annesley 1861-1955
Van Dyke, Henry 1852-1933
Villaespesa, Francisco 1877-1936
Wallace, Edgar 1874-1932
Wallace, Lewis 1827-1905
Walsh, Ernest 1895-1926
Webster, Jean 1876-1916

Whitlock, Brand 1869-1927
Wilson, Harry Leon 1867-1939
Wolf, Emma 1865-1932
Wood, Clement 1888-1950
Wren, P(ercival) C(hristopher) 1885-
   1941
Yonge, Charlotte Mary 1823-1901
Yosano Akiko 1878-1942
Zecca, Ferdinand 1864-1947
Zeromski, Stefan 1864-1925

Readers are cordially invited to suggest additional authors to the editors.

German Literature in Exile

INTRODUCTION

On January 30, 1933, Adolf Hitler was appointed Chancellor of Germany. On February 27 a fire that the Nazis claimed was set by the Communist Party nearly destroyed the building that housed the *Reichstag,* or German parliament. This incident became a pretext for Hitler to suspend the civil liberties guaranteed by the German constitution, call for emergency elections, gain control of the *Reichstag,* and institute political persecution against Jews, members of the political Left, and all intellectuals who did not affirm Nazi ideology. By March, Thomas Mann, Alfred Döblin, and many other scholars and writers had been forced to resign from the Prussian Academy of the Arts. On May 10, the Nazis staged book burnings at most German universities, destroying priceless copies of the Bible as well as the works of Karl Marx, Sigmund Freud, Albert Einstein, Sinclair Lewis, Emile Zola, Fyodor Dostoevsky, Thomas Mann, and many other writers; during the twelve years of their rule the Nazis banned a total of twelve thousand books. It became almost impossible for a German writer to publish anything but Nazi propaganda within the confines of Germany, and many writers, fearing arrest and internment in concentration camps for their published beliefs, fled Germany along with thousands of other refugees from political or ethnic persecution.

Historians recognize two waves of emigration from Germany. The first lasted from 1933 to 1938, as the Nazis gained control over increasingly large segments of German life and began persecuting those whom they perceived as their enemies, including all Jews and anyone closely associated with a Jew. The majority of writers who were either expelled from Germany or voluntarily emigrated during this period settled in Switzerland, France, Austria, Britain, and other European countries, while a number of Communist writers migrated to the Soviet Union, and a few writers traveled to the United States. The second wave of emigration began in 1939, when Austria was annexed by Germany and the whole of Europe became embroiled in war. Exiled Germans fled to Israel, China, South Africa, Australia, and, in large numbers, to North and South America, especially the United States.

The position of exiled writers in non-German-speaking countries was often precarious. Cut off from publication in their native land, only those with established international reputations, such as Thomas Mann, were able to publish in their own language. While some trade publishers, small presses, and periodicals were established to print works in German, most exiled writers were able to have their work published only in translation, or not at all. Since writers, in contrast to visual artists and composers, depend on language as their medium of expression, many qualities that were applauded in a German writer's work were untranslatable and others were of a distinctly German perception that did not appeal to non-German publishers. Unable to support themselves by their chosen profession, many German writers were forced to take menial jobs which they considered demeaning. While some continued to labor at manuscripts that they knew would remain unpublished, at least until after the war, others gave up their literary work entirely.

German exiles in the United States were also faced with an inevitable clash between German and American culture. They were offended by the banality of American popular culture, amused by American intellectual naiveté in many areas, and puzzled by the circumspect and evasive nature of American speech. While many exiles settled in New York, the most commercially successful of the writers were those who traveled to Los Angeles and worked in the motion picture industry. These were able to support themselves by writing, but many deplored the clichéd scripts they were expected to produce. The exiles' sense of alienation was often exacerbated by their status as natives of an aggressor nation.

The nature and unity of German exile literature and its relationship to the German literary tradition is disputed among critics. The exiles emigrated from both Germany and Austria; they settled in diverse places over the entire world; and they displayed an extreme variance in subject matter, literary forms and techniques, and artistic quality. As a result, some critics have questioned the usefulness of the term "German exile literature," contending that the diversity of exile writing makes the term meaningless except as a historical designation. Others, however, maintain that the experience of exile carries enough psychological import to distinguish the émigré writers as a loose but decidedly identifiable group. Similar debate has surrounded the relation of exile literature to the writing of the "inner emigration"—a number of writers who remained in Germany and wrote in protest of the Nazi regime. While some exiles, notably Thomas Mann, contended that no writing of any significance was written within Germany during the years of the Third Reich, and that exile writing therefore constituted the essence of German literature during the war years, other critics have argued that the exiles, having been cut off from their native land, could not be included in, let alone constitute the major part of, the mainstream of German literature. Nonetheless, since the majority of German literary works of significant merit composed during the war years were written by exiled authors, most critics agree that the German literary tradition was in fact continued outside Germany.

The literature of the German exile was composed in circumstances of great psychological and sometimes physical hardship, yet a number of writings were produced during the years of the Third Reich that honorably carried on the rich tradition of German literature: Thomas Mann's *Joseph und seine Brüder* (*Joseph and His Brothers*), Hermann Broch's *Der Tod des Vergil* (*The Death of Virgil*), and Bertolt Brecht's *Leben des Galilei* (*Galileo*) were all composed in exile. The legacy of these compositions, written in defiance of extreme adversity, is a testimony to the determination and talent of the writers of the German exile.

THE WRITER AND THE NAZI STATE

SANDER L. GILMAN

[Gilman is an American educator and critic. In the following essay he examines the effect of politics on German literature

1

during the years of Nazi rule, recounting the persecution of writers by the government, mass emigration of intellectuals, and development of an "inner emigration," as well as tracing trends in German literature both within and without Germany.]

When it all began, it seemed it would pass quickly. When the Reichstag burned at the end of February 1933, it was obvious that it would not. At the beginning of 1933, Thomas Mann (1875-1955), Germany's first and only winner in the interwar period of the Nobel Prize for literature, was touring France and the Low Countries lecturing on the "sufferings and greatness of Richard Wagner." Ernst Toller (1893-1939), the author who had headed the Bavarian Soviet during its short-lived existence in 1918, was also out of Germany. The Bavarian folk-writer Oskar Maria Graf (1899-1967) was on a lecture tour as well when the Reichstag burned. None returned to Germany.

Heinrich Mann (1871-1950), Thomas Mann's brother and the chairman of the Section for Literature of the Prussian Academy, quietly packed a suitcase, took his umbrella, and left for France on February 21. Six days later, when the Reichstag burned, the floodgates opened and the leading German intellectuals fled. On February 28 the playwright-poet Bertolt Brecht (1898-1956) left Berlin for Prague; the novelists Johannes R. Becher (1891-1958), Alfred Döblin (1878-1957), and Bruno Frank (1887-1945), and the poet Karl Wolfskehl (1869-1948), and the communist publicist Willi Münzenberg (1889-1940) fled the same day. On March 1, 1933, Alfred Polgar (1873-1955), the drama critic, and Berthold Viertel (1885-1953), the novelist, left; on March 2, the poet Max Herrmann-Neisse (1886-1941); on March 3, the dramatist Friedrich Wolf (1880-1953); on March 4, the writers Alfred Wolfenstein (1883-1945) and Gabriele Tergit (b. ca. 1900); on March 5, the editor and essayist Theodor Lessing (1872-1933); on March 8, the publisher and writer Harry Graf Kessler (1868-1937); on March 10, Leonhard Frank (1882-1961), the novelist, and Leopold Schwarzschild (1891-1950), the liberal editor; on March 12, Alfred Kantorowicz (1899-1979), the publicist, and Thomas Mann's daughter, Erika (1905-1969), herself an established actress; on March 13, Thomas Mann's son Klaus (1906-1949), the novelist; on March 14, the novelist Arnold Zweig (1887-1968). The list of those who fled continued until the rupture of German intellectual life had drained the "spirit of Weimar" from the "New Germany."

The new exiles were, however, the lucky ones. The novelist Anna Seghers (1900-1983), the newspaperman Egon Erwin Kisch (1885-1948), the writers Manès Sperber (b. 1905) and Karl August Wittfogel (b. 1896), all spent time in jail, and writers such as the Marxists Willi Bredel (1901-1964) and Ludwig Renn (1899-1979) spent between one and two years in prison. Even less lucky were those writers who were seen to be direct opponents of the new regime. The writers and publicists Erich Baron, Erich Mühsam (1878-1934), and Klaus Neukrantz (1895-1941) all died in the Nazi prisons or newly created concentration camps. The editor and essayist Carl von Ossietzky (1888-1938), arrested and tortured by the Gestapo, the new German political police, was awarded the 1936 Nobel Prize for peace while still in the camp at Papenburg-Esterwegen. Ossietzky was released from the camp but remained under house arrest in a sanatorium in Berlin until he died of the results of his imprisonment in 1938.

It was not merely writers who fled, nor was it the writers alone who were imprisoned and tortured. Liberal intellectuals, and later conservative opponents of the "Thousand Year Reich,"

as well as Jews, all felt the hatred of the regime. But writers held a special place in the fanaticism of the Nazis. In the struggle for public opinion during the Weimar Republic writers, editors, and publishers of the center and left were felt to be the enemy of the right. The various political tendencies all had their publishing houses, news services, newspapers, as well as authors who wholeheartedly supported one party or another. On the right the press czar was Alfred Hugenberg (1865-1951), who, among other things, owned the major German film studio; on the left was Willi Münzenberg, editor of the *Workers' Illustrated News* and head of the Marxist news service. The ideological struggle between right and left was carried out in the media, and the media became identified with this struggle.

Adolf Hitler, in his programmatic statement of Nazi goals *Mein Kampf* (*My Struggle,* 1925/1926), commented over and over again on the power of the press and the writer in society. Hitler attacked the "so-called 'freedom of the press,'" arguing that the state "must make sure of this instrument of public education." But the press and the writer were not simply the enemies of the "new order." They were the tool of the Jews: "The state authorities either cloak themselves in silence or, what usually happens, in order to put an end to the Jewish press campaign, they persecute the unjustly attacked, which in the eyes of such an official ass, passes as the preservation of state authority and the safeguarding of law and order." Hitler's charge of a Jewish conspiracy against their enemies has, of course, a very specific focus. Hitler, in the preface to his work, sees the rationale for writing it as the need "to destroy the foul legends about my person dished up in the Jewish press." The press accounts of Hitler's abortive coup attempt in 1923 had been for the most part comic. Hitler struck out against the press as the tool of his "hidden enemy," the Jews. The power of this association between the Jew as the enemy and the press (and writers) as his ally in attacking the Germans illustrates the conflation of images the Nazis used to present the image of the writer. His importance was all out of proportion to his role, as he was manipulated by a greater and hidden power. Here the vilification of the opposition becomes a metaphysical condemnation as agents of demonic forces of all who oppose Hitler.

The political implications of the Nazis' image of the writer as the mouthpiece of the Jews can be seen in the first list of Germans whose citizenship was revoked. On August 23, 1933, this list appeared; on it stood Willi Münzenberg, Leopold Schwarzschild, Heinrich Mann, Ernst Toller, Kurt Tucholsky (1890-1935), and the novelist Lion Feuchtwanger (1884-1958). Indeed, in all the lists of those who had their German citizenship revoked (which continued until 1939, with over 8,000 individuals listed), the proportion of writers was extraordinarily high. In addition, the Nazis' creation of the Reich Cultural Organization in September 1933 marked the establishment of a new definition of the writer within German society: the supporter, rather than the opponent, of established order.

The elimination of most writers of international status from Germany did not create an intellectual vacuum. For within the structure of the literary world of the Weimar Republic there had been a large number of writers who were either advocates of the right or whose ideological position permitted them to function under the new literary codes. Rooted in the intellectual conservatism of the late nineteenth century, these writers defined themselves as the "conservative revolution" against the cosmopolitanism and experimentalism of the Weimar Republic. Writers such as Wilhelm Pleyer (1901-1974), with his

A Nazi book-burning at the University of Berlin in 1933. By permission of Ullstein Bilderdienst.

novels of German-speaking peasants in Czechoslovakia, Hans Grimm (1875-1959), with his evocations of the lost German colonies in Africa, and Ernst Jünger (b. 1895), with his bittersweet novels of the glories of World War I, all contributed to the intellectual opposition to a literature that was seen as sterile, proletarian, city-based, and Jewish. All of these writers, as well as many other conservative thinkers, saw in the purification of German intellectual life their chance to create a new German literature. But one must also stress that this desire to be liberated from that which they viewed as the ''disease of internationalism'' and to see ''literature as the intellectual locus of the nation'' (so ran Hugo von Hofmannsthal's programmatic essay of 1927) had been the wish of many conservative writers following World War I. Writers such as Hofmannsthal (1874-1929), had he lived, would have been excluded from this ''new community'' on racial grounds. Other conservative writers who had wished for a ''third Reich,'' such as Stefan George (1868-1933), made a conscious decision in 1933 not to collaborate with the reality of the Third Reich as created by the Nazis.

Perhaps the best pragmatic example of the tensions of the first year after the Nazis' assumption of power can be found in their restructuring of the Section for Literature in the Prussian Academy. During the Weimar Republic its chairman had been the liberal writer Heinrich Mann, who saw as its prime goal the restructuring of the function of literature in the republican state.

To this end the Section for Literature sponsored a new history textbook for the schools of the Weimar Republic. Even before the Ministry for Propaganda was formed under the direction of the Ph.D. in German literature and failed novelist Joseph Goebbels, the conservative president of the Prussian Academy, Max von Schilling, had demanded from all the members of the Academy oaths of loyalty to the new regime. Thomas Mann, Alfred Döblin, and Ricarda Huch (1864-1947) resigned immediately in protest. Ten more writers of international reputation, including Franz Werfel (1890-1945), Jakob Wassermann (1873-1934), and the pacifist René Schickele (1883-1940), were excluded after the Enabling Act of May 23, 1933, placed the Academy under the overall direction of Goebbels. But the other members of the section, including Gerhart Hauptmann (1862-1946), signed. Eventually replacing Heinrich Mann as chairman was Hanns Johst, the author of *Schlageter* (1933), a play dedicated to Adolf Hitler and commemorating the execution of a German nationalist during the French occupation of the Ruhr in 1923. But even within the newly reorganized section on literature, the identification of conservative writers with the new regime was not total. Among the new members proposed by Goebbels for the section on literature was Ernst Jünger, whose glorifications of war had placed him at the forefront of conservative literature during the 1920s. Jünger informed the president of the Prussian Academy that he refused election because of his sense of the role of the writer as individual rather than as part of any collective voice.

The writers who found themselves in exile in France, Austria, the Netherlands, and Czechoslovakia, despite their heterogeneous political and aesthetic views, focused on their opposition to the Third Reich. Most thought of their exile as short-term and were convinced that the sound intelligence of the German people coupled with their own propagandistic opposition would soon topple the government and restore the Republic. Bertolt Brecht, sitting in exile in Denmark, admonished his readers in his poem "On the Designation Emigrant" ("Über die Bezeichnung Emigranten") that one should stay "close to the borders / waiting for the day of return." The focus on the inner political workings of the Nazi state as well as the sense of a temporary exile permitted many writers to absolve themselves of responsibility for any active opposition to the state. Only a few writers, such as Jan Petersen (1906-1969), drifted into the political underground in Germany, remaining to actively organize whatever opposition forces remained. In 1935 he appeared at the First International Writers' Congress in Paris and reported on life in Nazi Germany, wearing a black mask to disguise himself; he quickly became one of the cultural heroes of the literary opposition to the Nazis as the "Man with the Black Mask."

The opposition to the Nazis for the most part took literary form. Through the newly created publishing houses, such as Willi Münzenberg's Edition du Carrefour, or new lines in established houses, such as the liberal Querido Press in Amsterdam, a broad spectrum of works by exiled writers began to appear in Germany for distribution illegally in Nazi Germany and to the growing exile community in Europe. What is striking about this literature is that it paralleled the development of the new literature of Nazi Germany in its selection of literary genres, modes of presentation, and tone. Actually, this should not be so surprising, as both the fascist and antifascist traditions continued propagandistic models for the function of literature in society that had been well established in the Weimar Republic.

Three major thematic or genre traditions can be observed in both the official literature within Germany and the writings of the exiled opponents of the regime. First was the use of volumes of popularized documents as a means of commenting on contemporary events. The most widely read of these early works of documentary montage was the 1933 *Brown Book on the Reichstag Fire and Hitler Terrorism (Braunbuch über Reichstagsbrand und Hitlerterror),* compiled by Willi Münzenberg's exile publishing house as a means of countering the anticommunist propaganda associated with the trial of those accused of having started the Reichstag fire. The quasi-official Nazi publishing houses, such as the Franz Eher Press in Munich, brought out similar compilations of documents on the Jewish press.

But even more striking is the second parallel, the search for historical models of contemporary events as a means of examining the rise of the Nazis. What would seem on the surface a flight from exactly the type of pseudo-objectivity implied by the documentary reveals itself to be merely the fictionalization of documentary evidence. The most successful work of this genre that appeared during the period immediately following the Nazi seizure of power was Lion Feuchtwanger's *The Family Oppenheim (Die Geschwister Oppenheim,* 1933), a study of a Jewish middle-class family in the period immediately before the Nazi takeover. The attempt to examine a Jewish family as paradigmatic for the blindness of the German middle class proved to be controversial, even among the German writers who supported Feuchtwanger's views. For indeed the abrupt

rise of Nazi power also meant the establishment of anti-Semitism as an official policy of the state, and many writers "discovered" the Jewish identity only when they were labeled as "Jewish." On the side of the fascist writers, the interest in the period immediately before 1933 continued as a justification for the new regime. On April 13, 1933, Richard Euringer's (1891-1953) *German Passion 1933 (Deutsche Passion, 1933;* 1933) was broadcast throughout Germany as a literary sign of the transition. Euringer's radio-play is a pseudometaphysical recreation of the post-World War I era in mock-classical style. It serves much the same function as such novels as *The Family Oppenheim,* to situate the present political situation within the continuum of political history, at least as perceived in 1933.

The conservative tradition that became established as the primary mode of literary expression within Germany and the liberal tradition of those writers who found themselves in opposition to the new regime in 1933 also shared one final common tradition, that is, the tone of their literary works. The polarity of political discourse in the 1920s had so destroyed the possibility of writing outside polemic that the harsh, condemnatory tone of personal vituperation was heard on both sides of the literary discourse. Coming from the supporters of the "New Order," with their training in the anti-Semitic tradition of Dietrich Eckardt (1868-1923) and Julius Streicher (1885-1946), this does not come as a surprise. But that the tone of many early antifascist works reflected not an understanding of the implications of such rhetoric but its incorporation makes many of these early works quite problematic. Klaus Mann's 1936 novel *Mephisto,* based on the career of the actor-director Gustaf Gründgens (1899-1963), exhibits not only Mann's personal animus against Gründgens as an individual and a type (the opportunistic supporter of whatever regime is in power) but also many of the racist attitudes of prefascist Germany. Mann's portrayal of the hero's black mistress especially echoes distinctly fascist racism. The tone of Mann's diatribe is found in many works of the first few years, especially once the illusion vanished that the Nazi terror would be swept away in the course of a normal change in government.

The initial phase of reaction by writers both within and without Germany following the Nazi assumption of power ended by the end of 1936. By then it had become evident that the Nazis had no intention of sharing power even with their conservative political allies and that they were certainly not going to vanish from the scene. With the laws concerning the nature of German citizenship promulgated in 1935 it also became evident that both Jews and politically unwelcome writers were not going to be able to function, even marginally, within the Nazi state. Immediately after the Nazi seizure of power major writers such as Thomas Mann and René Schickele, although themselves in exile, continued to publish within Germany, but this became more and more difficult with the solidification of power within the state. Writers in exile began to consider the establishment of a unified front to oppose the Nazi state.

In December 1935 a group of German intellectuals spanning the spectrum from orthodox communists, such as Johannes R. Becher, to independents, such as Lion Feuchtwanger, published the first appeal to the Germans that came from all political tendencies. On June 9, 1936, the planning committee for a unified political opposition was constituted under the direction of Heinrich Mann. The intellectual organs of the exile community had begun to reveal a common opposition to the Nazis. No longer was it the communists or the socialists or, indeed, the exiled conservative opposition alone; all of these groups began to consider themselves as elements in a common struggle against international facism.

The debates within the exile community on the nature of fascism revealed how superficially the German exiles understood the nature of the historical process that had led to the rise of Hitler. Their discussion, like the polemics written in 1933, attempted to pinpoint specific historical errors, and they saw these errors in the mirror of literature. The most evident and naive attempt to place the blame for the rise of the Nazi mentality is seen in the so-called expressionism debate that raged among Marxist exiles in the Moscow-based periodical *Das Wort* (The Word) during 1937 and 1938. The primary participants in this debate were the playwright Bertolt Brecht and the Hungarian Marxist theorist Georg Lukács (1885-1971). The debate began with the publication of an essay by Klaus Mann on the poet Gottfried Benn (1886-1956), whose personal views on racism made him acceptable to the Nazis during the period of their coalescence of power. Klaus Mann saw in Benn's flirtation with the Nazis the result of the expressionists' vitalism and stress on the irrational. Alfred Kurella (1895-1975) stated the case even more baldly in a subsequent issue of *Das Wort:* "We can see today who the intellectual children of expressionism are and where its spirit led—to fascism."

The view that the expressionists, such as Benn, Arnolt Bronnen (1895-1959), and Hanns Johst, were in some manner preprogrammed for their later movement to fascism and that Marxist writers, such as Johannes R. Becher, Bertolt Brecht, and Friedrich Wolf, moved to the left in spite of their roots in expressionism became the touchstone of the debate. It became the duty of the exile writers, according to Kurella, to abandon the experimentalism and self-absorption of expressionism. This meant, of course, the move to realism. As the debate in the late 1920s concerning the role of realism (or the "new realism") in social change had been a natural reaction to the experimentalism of the expressionists, it was no surprise that the answer to the pathology of expressionism, with its natural progression to fascism, was realism.

Lukács had already, in 1934, stressed the flight from reality of the expressionists and seen in realism the only possible tool for combating the fascist mentality. In June 1938 Lukács published an essay on realism in *Das Wort* in which he stated that "political unity, nearness to the true nature of the people and true realism" are the three central tenets of oppositional literature. This naive attempt to see in modes of narrative the truth or falsity of political values, to trace the roots of fascism to styles of staging or experiments in form—in general to give literature or culture the determining role in political history—was understood even by Lukács's contemporaries as a superficial means of establishing the official Soviet version of "socialist realism" as the true creed of the progressive. Bertolt Brecht, in a series of unpublished essays of the period, and the philosopher Ernst Bloch (1885-1977), both questioned this assumption. The static, formalistic criteria of the expressionism debate were revealed by Brecht and Bloch to be little more than the imposition on literature of yet another external set of determinants. Literature had become a surrogate for political life. Since the writers in exile could affect neither the political world of Nazi Germany nor that of their exile, they fled into that world in which they had complete control, the world of letters. The impotence of the German intellectual in exile can be measured by the importance given the expressionism debate.

The belief that literary traditions determined political direction was in no way limited to the exiles. As early as 1933 Paul Kluckhohn (1886-1957), one of the most respected academic critics in Germany, published his programmatic essay on "the conservative revolution in contemporary letters." This was paralleled by a series of conservative literary histories that saw the sole salvation of Germany as an intellectual and cultural entity, not in the pluralism of the Weimar Republic, but in a monolithic, homogeneous literature "of the people [*Volk*]." This conservatism was often, but not always, linked to a negative image by which the "people," the source of all virtue and truth in letters, was defined. And this negative image was that of the Jew, who became the embodiment of "cosmopolitanism," of "asphalt literature," of "internationalism," of "degenerate literary experimentalism."

Drawing on the mix of populist (*völkisch*) and racist literary criticism present in the works of critics such as Adolf Bartels (1862-1945), who spent most of his career as a critic determining the racial and therefore (at least in his mind) the intellectual pedigree of German writers, racist literary theory became paramount in Germany. What is most fascinating is that it drew on conservative tendencies in literary scholarship that, as seen from their roots in the 1920s, did not seem inherently racist. Parallel to Bartels was the Austrian critic Josef Nadler (1884-1963), who wrote a "literary history of German lands and tribes" in which he attempted to determine the particular nature of, for example, Austrian as opposed to Prussian literature, just as elsewhere critics were trying to differentiate American from British letters. Nadler's *völkisch* literary history was quickly subsumed under the more general tradition of a quasi-official literary criticism, which again differentiated between positive literature, i.e., the various strains of *völkisch* writing, and Jewish writing (which often was not written by Jews). Just as there developed a German physics to counter the work of Albert Einstein, so too there developed a German criticism. Because of the nativistic bias in literary criticism, which exists even today, "German criticism" sounds more benign than does "German physics." It is not. It led to work such as that by Johannes Alt (b. 1896), which attempts to determine with "scientific" precision the true nature of Jewish letters.

But the movement from *völkisch* to racist literary theory is not as difficult to understand as the movement of existential literary theory from the realm of abstract philosophy to racist literary segregation. Martin Heidegger's (1889-1976) own strong support of the Nazi movement was not merely a personal aberration; rather it grew quite naturally out of his preoccupation with the existential essence of the literary text. His literary disciples, primarily Hermann Pongs (1889-1979), placed existential literary criticism squarely in the service of the new state. Pongs was able to write in a programmatic essay on the "new duties of literary scholarship," published in 1937, that "more populist power and populist spirit can be found in the rough, archetypal prose of Paul Ernst [1866-1933] than from the linguistic suppleness of the lost bourgeoisie of Thomas Mann." Here the very nature of the description carries racist tones. For "linguistic suppleness" is a code phrase for "Jewish falsity of language," for their manipulation of German to their own ends, while "rough" and "archetypal" point toward the *Volk* with their truthful, pure use of language. The racism of such a view of language is clear. Here the goal of literary theory, as in the so-called expressionism debate is the placing of blame, the creation of scapegoats. It also stresses the importance of the written word for the Nazis as a means of presenting their "revolution" as one with legitimate intellectual credentials. Unlike the exiles' debate about the origin of literary fascism, the racist theories of German literary criticism led to the burning of books throughout Germany on the night of May 10, 1933, and as Heine had written a hundred years before, "Where books are burned, people too can be burned."

Between March 11, 1938, and August 23, 1939, political events in Europe radically altered the nature and role of the exiled writer writing in German. On March 11, 1938, Germany annexed Austria. German writers who had found a home in Austria, which shared a common literary language with Germany, as well as those who had settled in Prague, which fell to the Germans in March 1939, fled once again. In September 1939 a nonaggression pact was signed by Stalin and Hitler, which isolated the German intellectuals who had found refuge in the Soviet Union. Indeed, many German exiles who were viewed as dangerous to order in the Soviet Union were summarily turned over to the Nazis and vanished into concentration camps. A similar fate befell Carola Neher (1900-1942), Bertolt Brecht's Polly in the original *Threepenny Opera* (*Dreigroschenoper,* 1928), who was interned in a Soviet labor camp and shot in 1942. By the end of August 1939, war was seen to be inevitable. The Nazi invasion of Poland on September 1, and the subsequent invasion of Western Europe destroyed whatever refuge the German exiles had found in Europe. They fled, if they could, or like Walter Benjamin (1892-1940), the German social theorist, committed suicide as a means of escaping the Nazi advance.

Flight from Europe was also flight from the organs of literary expression that had developed to state the position of the exiles. The publishing houses in France and the Netherlands were closed (although the S. Fischer Press managed to relocate to neutral Sweden), and the journals ceased publication. Much of this suppression was undertaken with the active support of the powers in the now conquered nations of Western Europe. The French government under Pétain, which established itself at Vichy, promulgated laws that disenfranchised Jewish exiles and other nonnatives quite independently of any German pressure. Feelings against the exiles were quite negative, at least on the part of the conservative anti-Semitic leaders of the "new" France.

Flight to the rest of the world was difficult, if not impossible. The sense of despair that engulfed the intellectual exiles, cut off from their potential reading public and robbed of any direct link with their language, can be measured in one of the major works to come out of this period, Anna Seghers's novel *Transit (Transit).* Published in 1944, the novel chronicles the reactions of a group of refugees in the summer of 1940 who attempt to flee the German invasion of France and find themselves in the port of Marseille. The struggle for a visa to escape the Nazis becomes the focus of the lives of all the characters. The loss of personal identity, the overriding importance of that small piece of stamped paper, the visa, which determines one's identity as much as one's fate, becomes the central theme of the novel. The fate of the hero, who assumes one identity after another as he acquires different sets of papers, and his eventual decision to abandon his flight to join the French Resistance constitute the idealized answer to the exiles' feeling of having abandoned the fight against the menace of the Nazis. Seghers herself found refuge in Mexico, where this novel was first published in Spanish.

Seghers's fate, and the fate of her novel, can stand as emblematic of some of the problems faced by other writers who fled France, the Soviet Union, the Netherlands, or Denmark following the German invasion. They were forced to abandon

a literary infrastructure of journals and presses and established, if illegal, links to daily life in Germany. They were, moreover, forced to abandon their language and attempt to function in a world that spoke English or Spanish and for which German did not exist as a cultural second tongue. Writers fled to the United States, to Great Britain, to Mexico, indeed as far away as to New Zealand. Exile had become real, as it had become exile not only from Germany but from continental Europe.

In Germany itself major changes had come about as the passage of time had given an ever greater sense of legitimacy to the Nazi regime. Without a doubt, the major international event that provided the Nazi leadership with the label of international respectability was the Olympic Games of 1936, held in Berlin. As Nazi official propaganda, the games, and the resulting film made by Leni Riefenstahl (b. 1902), a product of the conservative Hugenberg studios of the 1920s, served to provide the Germans with a model for public entertainment. German sports activities during the 1920s, especially in the Sports palace in Berlin, had already acquired the image of a public spectacle. Through the influence of Dietrich Eckardt the Nazis began to exploit the idea of public spectacle as a means of achieving the uniform support of the masses. Through the creation of populist public theater, the *Thingspiel,* as well as the creation of pseudopublic events, such as party congresses, the Nazis were able to manipulate large numbers of people. By the use of film, the official agencies of party propaganda were able to extend their reach into every town; and by the use of radio, they were present at every hearth.

The solidification of power in Germany also meant that some of the more tenuous agreements with intellectuals allied with the Nazis were abrogated. Gottfried Benn, whose quirky racism, similar to that of the American poet Ezra Pound, had enabled him to be used by the Nazis, was quickly returned to the rubbish heap of writers viewed as "swinish." Even major figures such as Hans Grimm, the author of the quintessential colonial novel, *People Without Space* (*Volk ohne Raum,* 1926), broke at least partially with the regime. What developed out of the older traditions within Germany was a new, party-oriented literature.

The conservative literary traditions in Germany before 1933 have been generally classified as "blood and earth" literature (*Blut-und-Boden-Literatur*). Writers such as Wilhelm von Polenz (1861-1903), who glorified the peasant and vilified the city-dweller, were succeeded by an entire generation of writers during the 1930s and 1940s who seemed able to generate an endless stream of paeans to the German peasant. Joseph Georg Oberkofler's (1889-1962) novel *The Forest Preserve* (*Der Bannwald,* 1939), with its mythic reconstruction of German social conflicts and the most popular novel of the 1930s, Josefa Berens-Totenohl's (1891-1969) *The Secret Court* (*Der Femhof,* 1934), with its stress on the irrational, are typical. The use of historical fiction and drama, which serve in the works of older writers such as Hans Friedrich Blunck (1888-1961) or Erwin Guido Kolbenheyer (1878-1962) as the historiographic foundation for a new German literary mythology, was paralleled by the exile writers' attempts to present historical analogies to the rise of Nazism. These included the brilliant tetralogy *Joseph and His Brothers* (*Joseph und seine Brüder*), published between 1933 and 1943, on which Thomas Mann worked during the majority of his years in exile, as well as his brother Heinrich Mann's series of novels on the life and times of King Henri IV of France. The idea of the novel as a cryptohistory of the present day was used by writers both within and without Germany. Within Germany such attempts to adapt older literary forms had a pragmatic purpose in the daily life of the German people. They served to change the Germans' sense of history, wiping out the entire period from the Treaty of Versailles to the rise of the Nazis. The role of such novels outside Germany was less evident, and although in retrospect their value as flashes of historical illumination can be seen, contemporary writers were doubtful of their efficacy in documenting the horrors of the Nazi regime. Younger writers, such as Klaus Mann, sought contemporary events, such as those presented in his novel of exile, *The Volcano* (*Der Vulkan,* 1939), rather than historical analogies.

Within Germany the passage of time brought forth a series of younger writers who contributed pure party literature. Poets such as Heinrich Anacker (1901-1940), Hans Baumann (b. 1914), and the head of the Hitler Youth, Baldur von Schirach (1907-1974), contributed volume after volume of salutes to the new state. Schirach is typical of those writers who combined false pathos with propaganda, as in his poem "Hitler":

> You are many thousands behind me
> and you are me and I am you.
>
> I have not lived an idea
> which has not beaten in your heart.
>
> And when I speak words, I know none
> that is not one with your will.
>
> For you are me and I am you,
> and we all believe, Germany, in you.

Such a text, in thousands of variations, can be found in the numerous volumes of hack poetry written by and for party functionaries. Poetry had become the servant of the state, glorifying the leader and identifying itself as the one true voice of the people. One major writer who saw himself in this role was the poet Josef Weinheber (1892-1945), whom many of his contemporaries viewed as the natural heir of Stefan George. George, who had emigrated to Switzerland and died there in 1933, never acknowledged the Nazis' expressions of interest in him. With Weinheber they acquired a major poetic voice who saw the Nazi dictatorship as the creation of a natural order. Weinheber's early lyric, full of the pathos of a world in collapse, gave way to the crudest glorifications of the heroism of the fascist state.

If the passage of years enabled party poetry to flourish within Germany, it also drove some writers who remained within Germany ever further into what became designated after 1945 as their "inner emigration." Mainly conservative writers, they remained in Germany, where their public existed. Often their writing was intended for a future generation and was consigned for the present to the recesses of a desk drawer. Poets such as Oskar Loerke (1884-1941) and Wilhelm Lehmann (1882-1968) sought poetic refuge in nature poetry but also kept running commentaries on their hidden intent in diaries and letters. Some of the conservative writers, such as Ernst Wiechert (1887-1950), wound up in more or less direct opposition to the state. Wiechert, for example, was sent to a concentration camp for opposing the arrest of Pastor Martin Niemöller. While in the camp he was able to have his works, viewed by the party and state as exemplary presentations of the universal values that opposed the "asphalt civilization," placed in the camp library. Younger writers, such as Marie Luise Kaschnitz (1901-1974), Elisabeth Langgässer (1899-1950), and Eugen Gottlob Winkler (1912-1936), were able to publish their conservative, but not oppositional, writings in the few literary journals, such as the

Deutsche Rundschau (German Review), that would still accept nonfascist literature.

At least one clearly liberal writer, the satirist Erich Kästner (1899-1974), whose works were banned by the Nazis, remained in Germany during the Third Reich. Forbidden to earn his living by writing, he turned out hack works under a series of pseudonyms. When, however, the official film company of the Reich wanted to celebrate its twenty-fifth anniversary with a film of the tales of the fabulous liar Baron von Münchhausen, they were forced to allow Kästner a "special permit" to write the film, which appeared in 1942. A few writers used the literary traditions of the conservative mode of literature for hidden, oppositional purposes. Reinhold Schneider's (1903-1958) 1938 novel *Las Casas Before Charles V* (*Las Casas vor Karl V*) centers on the racist persecution of the Indians by the Spanish conquistadors. The king is moved to action by the monk's plea, which illustrates to no small degree the chasm between the reality of racism (and the nature of the leader) in fact and in the wish-dreams of fiction.

No work of the "inner emigration" was better accepted by the official state reviewers than Werner Bergengruen's (1892-1964) novel *A Matter of Conscience* (*Der Grosstyrann und das Gericht*). Bergengruen was a Baltic German, whose works were widely accepted within Germany as part of the conservative wave of appreciation for writers who represented the border Germans (*Auslandsdeutschtum*). These writers were seen as outposts of German culture abroad, often in exactly those lands, such as Bohemia and Moravia or the Baltic region, where German hegemony was to be established by military means. In 1935 Bergengruen published his novel of the murder of a functionary in a Renaissance city-state and the involvement in the murder of the ruler. The official party newspaper, the *Völkischer Beobachter* (*Populist Observer*), heralded it as the "Führer-novel of the Renaissance." By 1940 it had sold 182,000 copies. The work, a thinly veiled attack on the totalitarian state, used the device of the historical novel to its full advantage. It showed the inner corruption of the state, the flaws of any leadership that claims an absolute right to rule. The polis had been seen as the highest good. Yet in Bergengruen's novel the murder of the functionary, shown to have been committed by the ruler of the city-state for "reasons of national security," reveals the center of the state to be corrupt. The immediate references in the novel are clear. They are to the Röhm putsch of 1934, which revealed the rotten inner circle of Hitler's "SA" ("Storm Troopers") to the world. The novel lent itself to two possible interpretations. One, which was seen and accepted by the state, was the need for a strong leader who could undertake even murder for the good of the state; the other presented such an action on the part of a Christian leader as unthinkable and self-condemnatory. This inherent ambiguity enabled those who wished to read into the novel a negative critique of contemporary events to do so; for those who saw in it only historical escapism, the contemporary analogies could easily be overlooked.

Parallel structures of ambiguity can be found coded into other novels of the period, such as Ernst Jünger's *On the Marble Cliffs* (*Auf den Marmorklippen*) of 1939. But this ambiguity could also have a negative side. Karl Aloys Schenzinger's (1886-1962) party novel *Hitleryouth Quex* (*Der Hitlerjunge Quex,* 1932), a hagiography commemorating the murder of a fascist youth group member by the Communists, was banned after extensive distribution because the central figure seemed to have some inner doubt about his sacrifice—an ambiguity impossible in a novel about contemporary events in the Third

Reich. In the historical novel, such as Jochen Klepper's (1903-1942) 1937 novel of the life of Frederick the Great, *The Father (Der Vater)*, just such ambiguity was permitted. For Klepper, Prussia became the true German state and Frederick the true ruler, with the implied contrast to the Nazi regime, which itself wished to claim Prussia as its model. Bergengruen survived the war, Klepper did not. He committed suicide with his Jewish wife and their daughter, sensing their eventual fate.

Within Germany there was also a small nucleus of writers who joined the active underground opposition to the regime. Jan Petersen, "the Man with the Black Mask," assumed the leadership of the Organization of Proletarian-Revolutionary Writers in 1933. By 1935 this organization of Marxist opponents of the regime had been infiltrated and destroyed by the Nazis. Such organizations circulated literally millions of broadsides and pamphlets, the latter often disguised as cookbooks or tracts on hygiene. They contained not only straightforward documentation of the realities of Nazism but also literary texts aimed at exposing the horrors of German fascism. In 1936, according to the Gestapo's own figures, 1,643,200 such texts were seized, more than 70 percent stemming from the various communist underground organizations. Poets such as Albrecht Haushofer (1903-1945), whose *Moabit Sonnets (Moabiter Sonette, 1946)* were found in his hand after he was executed by the Nazis for his participation in the abortive July 20, 1941, attempt to assassinate Hitler, were published in this manner. Haushofer, whose father's concept of a "space to live" *(Lebensraum)* had been adopted as Nazi ideological jargon, felt himself drawn to the antifascist opposition. Like many other conservative writers, he saw the corruption of the German language as indicative of corruption in the German soul. Their organizations attempted to create alternatives to the existing state, none of which succeeded in altering the ongoing policies of the Nazis. Of the oppositional groups perhaps the most interesting was the Schulze-Boysen/Harnack group, labeled by the Gestapo as the "red band," which consisted of communist as well as conservative writers and thinkers. Beginning in 1941 this group published the illegal periodical *Die innere Front* (The Inner Front). Its members included the writer Adam Kuckhoff (1887-1943) and the novelist Günther Weisenborn (1902-1969). By 1943 the group had been discovered by the Nazis and forty-nine of its members, including Kuckhoff, had been executed.

The inner-German opposition to the Nazis, in terms of both political and literary strategies, was a failure to some extent because of the factionalization of the opposition groups. In the late 1930s the Communists, under the direction of Stalin, abandoned the antifascist struggle, only to assume it again once the Soviet Union had been attacked. The conservative writers either ceased to write or melted into the background, writing the type of nature poetry that was so protean that it could function both under the Nazis and later under the occupying forces and eventually assume the primary direction of German letters once the Federal Republic was created. Few joined the opposition. But this state of affairs was paralleled within other nations in Europe under fascist domination. Neither in the occupied countries nor in the fascist states was a unified intellectual opposition to the Nazis to be found until Nazi domination began to wane. Exceptions to this acquiescence, such as the great Danish poet Kai Munk (1898-1944), who was murdered by the Nazis, prove as difficult to find outside Germany as within its borders.

On January 20, 1942, members of the Nazi hierarchy met at a villa on Berlin's Wannsee Lake and formalized the Third Reich's plan for the "final solution to the Jewish problem."

Jews had been brought into concentration camps in ever-increasing numbers since 1933. Often the Germans were aided in their "removal" by anti-Semites and fascists of the occupied countries. By 1942 the rate of death through "natural" causes—typhus, malnutrition, and so on—was not great enough for the Nazis, and a plan for the systematic destruction of the Jews of Europe, as well as other groups, such as Gypsies, homosexuals, and Jehovah's Witnesses, was begun. Six million Jews died in the concentration camps, such as Buchenwald, and in the death camps, such as Auschwitz. Among them were poets such as Gertrud Kolmar (1894-1943), Arthur Silbergleit (1881-1944), and Gertrud Kantorowicz (1876-1945). Nelly Sachs (1891-1970), the joint recipient of the 1966 Nobel Prize for literature, was rescued from a concentration camp in 1940 only through the intercession of the Swedish government.

Most remarkably, young writers began to express themselves in the camps. Often all that is left of their memories is a fragment of a poem smuggled out from the camps. Such is the case of Friedrich Karl Pick, who is known only from a tiny notebook with the title "A Few Thoughts About Theresienstadt—On 9.1.43," which was found in the papers of a Czechoslovakian refugee going to Israel. In the camps the need for sanity, for a sense of stability, often drove young writers to search for the most stable, conservative forms to express the horrors they were living. The use of strict meter, of classical poetic form, of traditional images, was a means of grasping the sanity of the schoolroom that had existed before the corruption of literature and art by the Nazis. The thirteen-year-old Ruth Klüger (b. 1931), who survived Theresienstadt, wrote the following poem in Auschwitz in 1944:

> Daily behind the barracks
> I see smoke and fire.
> Jew, bend your back,
> No one can escape *that*.
> Do you not see in the smoke
> A distorted face?
> Does it not call out, full of mockery and sarcasm:
> Five million I now contain!
> Auschwitz lies in my hand,
> Everything, everything will be consumed.
>
> Daily, behind the barbed wire
> The sun rises purple,
> But its light seems empty and hollow
> When the other flame appears.
> For the warm light of life
> has had no meaning in Auschwitz.
> Look into the red flame:
> The only truth is the furnace.
> Auschwitz lies in his hand,
> Everything, everything will be consumed.
>
> Some have lived full of horror
> faced with threatening danger.
> Today he looks with equanimity,
> offering up his life.
> Everyone is depressed by suffering,
> No beauty, no joy,
> Life, sun are gone,
> And the furnace glows.
> Auschwitz lies in his hand,
> Everything, everything will be consumed.
>
> Don't you hear the moans and the groaning
> As from someone who is dying?
> And between them bitter mockery,
> The furnace's horrid song:
> No one has yet outrun me,
> No one, no one will I spare.

And those who build me as a grave
I will consume at last.
Auschwitz lies in my hand,
Everything, everything will be consumed.

The totality of destruction, the blackness of a vision obscured by the foul-smelling clouds belching from the crematoria smokestacks, is cast in this remarkable poem in formal, controlled terms. How different from the radical experimentalism of Paul Celan's (1920-1970) "Fugue of Death" ("Todes-fuge"), written retrospectively in 1945. Ruth Klüger survived the death camps, which claimed the lives of her father and brother, and emigrated to the United States, where she now teaches literature.

The literature of the camps survived as fragmentary documents, buried in gardens, hidden in mattresses, smuggled out in the minds and memories of the survivors. The more extensively published and preserved production of the exile writers, who had fled their refuges in 1938, 1939, and 1940 as the Nazi menace advanced, provided a more comprehensive context for their work. Rather than fragmentary texts and snippets of poems, the exile communities in Britain, the United States, Canada, Australia, and New Zealand provided a new, English-language context and inspiration for their writings. Some, such as Thomas Mann, who arrived in the United States in 1939 for an extended exile, had long-established American contacts, translators, and publishers. His brother Heinrich was not as lucky. Although the final volume of Heinrich Mann's life of Henri IV was published to great critical acclaim in 1939, it proved to be the last volume of Mann's works to appear in English. The author, accompanied by his wife, the popular author Lion Feuchtwanger, Franz and Alma Werfel, and Golo Mann, Thomas Mann's author-son who had just escaped a Vichy internment camp, crossed the Pyrenees on foot in the fall of 1940 in order to reach neutral Portugal and a ship that would eventually take them to New York. In New York and later in California, where he settled, Heinrich Mann lived for the most part on the bounty of his younger brother.

This final period of exile for the German liberal establishment also coincided with the beginning of the end of the Nazi domination of Germany and Europe. The exile writers had begun to see their exile as the material for their literary creations. Their gaze was not fixed on Germany, their ears were not constantly attuned to the inner-German situation. They began to sense the need to create a new literature that reflected their own experience but that used a radically new means of achieving an expression denied the now corrupt German language. A series of works evolved out of the productive interaction between the literature of their new hosts and the problems they still saw as central to their creative endeavors.

Such work was the major play of Bertolt Brecht's California exile, *The Life of Galileo* (*Das Leben des Galilei*), which premiered in the Zurich playhouse in September 1943. The play and its productions present an excellent case study of the life and creativity of the exile writers during the final years of their English-speaking exile. Brecht's dramatized life of the Renaissance scientist was his first play to treat distant history. All of his dramatic works to that point either had treated contemporary events or were set in the immediate past. Part of this shift was due to the search for historical analogies, as found in the works of Thomas and Heinrich Mann; but more than that, Brecht's role in the Hollywood film colony of the 1940s determined his choice of material as well as his per-

spective. For Brecht wrote the play with the British film actor Charles Laughton in mind for the title role. Laughton had starred in a series of historical films during the 1930s, the best known of which was *The Private Life of Henry VIII*, and Brecht wished to capture the strengths of Laughton's characterization of the "great man" under stress. Laughton in fact collaborated on the English version of the play between 1944 and its American premiere in 1947.

But even more than Laughton's character, his role as an expatriate British actor paralleled Brecht's sense of distance, which was reflected in the play. For the central motif of Brecht's play is the trials of the exile. Galileo is, at least at the beginning of the drama, a more or less voluntary exile; by the play's close he is the captive of the church (and his family), which monitors his very thoughts. This is not Brecht's mirror of Nazi Germany. His work had come far from his fixation on the inner workings of the Nazi state, as in his *Private Life of the Master Race* (*Furcht und Elend des Dritten Reiches,* 1938). What Brecht incorporated in the sense of isolation was the Marxist exile's impression of life in the wartime United States. With the Federal Bureau of Investigation (FBI) monitoring the daily life of the left-wing exile community, with spies from their own ranks reporting on their every statement, it must have seemed to Brecht that his exile in the United States was quite like Galileo's Italy, full of cabals. This theme was coupled with the issue of the responsibility of the scientist, a prefiguring of the questioning surrounding the beginning of the atomic age and the bombing of Japan in 1945. Galileo is the peripatetic scientist, driven to ask difficult, perhaps unanswerable ques-

Bertolt Brecht. Reproduced by permission of Robert Boyers, editor of Salmagundi.

tions in a world that believes itself to be in the possession of absolute truth. The exile, seeing himself as a marginal man, is in much the same position. Brecht's drama, with its American inspiration, its Swiss premiere, its British collaborator, and its Renaissance setting, is in many ways the true product of the American exile of the German intellectual. Those who were able to integrate the American experience, at least to a limited degree, into their work were able to cope creatively with their new environments. This group included Brecht; Max Reinhardt (1873-1943), the theater director; Kurt Weill (1900-1950), the composer; Peter Lorre (1904-1964), the actor; and Felix Salten (1869-1947), the author of *Bambi* and innumerable film scripts. Other writers and intellectuals were more or less destroyed by their exile, turning inward and romanticizing the Germany that remained in their fantasy.

Brecht's work for the theater, with its complex theoretical framework and its intent to educate as well as entertain, was perhaps the greatest achievement of the Marxist exiles. The conservative wing of the exile community also produced a series of major literary works during the last four years of the Third Reich. Two of the greatest works of twentieth-century fiction drew on the exile experience. Hermann Broch's (1886-1951) *The Death of Virgil* (*Der Tod des Vergil*, 1945) drew on the reconstruction of the thoughts of the dying and exiled Virgil cast in the form of an interior monologue. By far the greatest contribution of Broch's creation was its fusion of classical, psychological, and political themes into a work of truly international status. The other great novel to come out of the exile community at the end of the war was Thomas Mann's *Dr. Faustus*, the story of the German composer Adrian Leverkühn as told by a slightly obtuse friend. The story, published in 1947, reconstructed the inner life of the quintessential German artist, representing that which Germany claimed as its greatest gift to the world—German culture—as it regressed from creativity to irrational primitiveness. Mann used the life of the German philosopher Friedrich Nietzsche as his primary model but incorporated into the figure of the composer many traits and views of recognizable contemporaries. Casting the entire work in the form of a biography written by a pedant, Mann gave the novel his own ironic touch, distancing himself from the German misery through his vantage point as an exile. *Dr. Faustus* and *Galileo* are the two sides of the exile's image of the world. Neither would have been possible without the rich literary and intellectual tradition in which the exiles found themselves while in the last stages of their diaspora.

Cultural life and literary production during the period from 1933 to 1945 was most probably the most fragmented in the tradition of German letters. The scattering of the exile writers and thinkers throughout the civilized world, the regimentation of cultural life within the German state, the mass murder of the concentration and death camps, had no parallel in Western experience. German intellectual life after 1945 was marked with the stigma of the Nazi period. This inheritance has remained the primary focus of German letters in the post-war era. (pp. 276-96)

Sander L. Gilman, "Literature in German, 1933-1945," in Contemporary Germany: Politics and Culture, *Charles Burdick, Hans-Adolf Jacobsen, Winfried Kudszus, eds., Westview Press, 1984, pp. 276-96.*

DEFINING GERMAN EXILE LITERATURE

WILLIAM K. PFEILER

[*In the following excerpt, Pfeiler surveys critical classification of German literature in exile in an attempt to define its nature and to determine its relationship to the whole of German literature.*]

Speaking of a German Literature in Exile, one may ask: How is this literature to be defined? What is meant by it? The answer could be simply this: German literature in general is the body of writing in the German language; it is differentiated by the character of its creators, who, by native endowment, tradition, environment and numerous other factors, some not always easily comprehended in rational terms, give substantial expression to their reactions to the world about or within them. Literature in Exile is a part of the German Literature and is, above all, a *formale Kategorie*. It is the literature created by authors who were forced or chose to leave their native land and who continued their work in German no matter where they might find themselves. Of course, the writing done in exile assumed features which reflected the specific circumstances of their existence. But it is part and parcel of German literature as a whole. The domicile of a writer is not and never was a decisive, qualitative criterion concerning his belonging to a certain literature.

While this statement may have the naive charm of simplicity, it should not be taken as more than it claims to be. The character of exile literature, as that of any literature, is complex and has given rise to lively theoretical discussions. As Thomas Mann pointed out early, the boundary line between "emigrated" and "non-emigrated" literature cannot be drawn easily, but it certainly does not coincide with territorial boundaries.

Attempts to come to definitional terms about the literature in exile started early. . . . [Here] some of the efforts toward analyzing and clarifying it may be recounted.

In 1934, the Dutch writer Menno ter Braak, in an article *"Emigranten-Literatur,"* called to task exiled writers and critics, who in their indulgence in *adoration mutuelle*, failed in what the objective of a true literature in exile should be. He denied that there was anything "essential" in practically any literature, and doubted that literature per se expresses "values of life"; it rather presents a distortion of them, owing to the process of artistic shaping. In many respects, German literature before Hitler's reign had been a concern of the *literati* only, and the impression was now that the emigrants simply "continue their business." The new situation was, if different at all, noticeable only in the choice of *Motive*. Yet these were not decisive criteria in a valid appraisal of literature. A rousing indignation as, for instance, that of Ernst Toller was more welcome than "smooth literature." Writers regard their own work rather naively, in that they take their disguises, their gestures, their "airs" as essence, and thus no surprise should be registered when the writers who had been driven out of their land now developed *Kritiklosigkeit* into a complex. In the necessity of defending himself against degrading calumny, against the Nazi idiocy that palmed itself off as mysticism, the writer necessarily resorted to defensive armor and weapons, and this well-understandable fact made him supersensitive to any criticisms toward himself and his colleagues in a similar position. Hence the mutual gushing praise observed in the reviews of works of emigrants. But the *Emigrantenliteratur* should be more than a perpetuation of the old modes and attitudes. The refugee writer should get a firmer grasp of his European mission and not permit the domineering influences that were generated by the fight against the false mysticism of the blood-and-soil idolatry. Criticism should have as its standard the genius of great personalities, not the smooth skill of the literary craftsman.

The article stirred up a vigorous response. Erich Andermann, in his refutation of the charges, arrived at some formulations which seem to have validity beyond the discussion at the time. The implicit premise of ter Braak that the grievous experience of the refugee writers should have had a stimulating rather than a paralyzing effect was unacceptable, aside from the fact that there was no such intellectual-spiritual (*geistige*) entity as *Emigrantenliteratur*. The common experience of exile, to which its participants were led by far from uniform reasons, created at best a "community of fate" and nothing more. To challenge this heterogeneous group to a fulfillment of a European mission would first require a specific clarification of this term. Meanwhile, what else could reasonably be expected from the writers other than the continuation of the work begun at home? A certain leniency in criticism of their books was imperative under the extreme jeopardy of publishing in foreign lands. At home, adverse judgments could be absorbed and, indeed, with profit, because of the vast audience an author potentially enjoyed there; however, any adverse criticism in exile might mean the death knell not only for an author's work but for his very physical existence.

Ludwig Marcuse, one of the most prolific and vigorous writers of the exile, . . . also rejected the reference to an *Emigrantenliteratur* because, as a generic concept, it was void of a "deeper, factual justification." He called this literature the sum of all books by authors writing in German who either *could* or *would* not work at home under Hitler's rule. There was no correlation between the commonly shared fact of living in exile and literary communality. He rightly raised the question: Why should a writer outside of Germany not continue his earlier work in the same spirit and manner as he had done before? It speaks for his intellectual solidness and integrity when he does so. The fact was that the world view of the exiled writer stood the acid test of uprooting and transposition, while, on the other hand, the attitude of many authors remaining at home in Germany had to undergo radical changes if they wanted to stay in good health.

Another reaction to ter Braak came from Hans Sahl. He went beyond Andermann's assertion that the writer's task was to cultivate the German language and be the guardian of the true German spirit. Sahl asked for more lucid and more obligating challenges; he insisted that categories other than the aesthetic ought to be used to determine the value of existence of a literature; it could be reduced to a common denominator just as little as the whole of the emigration from Nazi rule. He felt certain that this exile literature would bring forth what any literature would: the good, the trifling and the bad and, yes, maybe even something truly great. This, however, was not the salient point. The decisive question to be asked was: Is a sense, a meaning, being found for or given to the phenomenon of emigration? Certain works published had already attempted to give an answer to this question. The expatriated German literature would overcome the geographic distance from its native soil by proximity of the spirit; and it would assist in the building of a new Germany by everywhere securing cadres of her true representatives.

In challenging the free writers to tasks clearly outside the concept of an art per se, Sahl touched upon a theme that . . . was to engage considerable attention of writers and critics during the years of exile. Book after book, as well as significant articles in periodicals, appeared in German, a fact which gave substance to the claim that the center of the German cultural sphere might not necessarily be any longer found inside the territorial boundaries of Germany but had shifted outside the borders of the Reich. (pp. 5-8)

The first two noteworthy attempts for a general comprehension of this, by now, great body of literature in terms of serious categories and interpretative literary history appeared about five years after the exile began in 1933.

Odd Eidem, a young Norwegian writer who, from the start, had followed the events with sympathetic concern, wrote a study which, in a mainly sociologically determined approach, found the common denominator of the *Emigrantenliteratur* in the "universal unfortunate political fate" of its representatives. He saw a militant literature emerging as the mouthpiece of an enslaved and silenced Germany, a literature that would become the standard-bearer in the fight for freedom. As such, it concerned even non-Germans to a high degree.

The primary objective of Eidem's study was to describe this fight. After briefly outlining the collapse of the Weimar Republic, the taking over of power by the Nazis and the initial effects on the cultural life of the nation, Eidem submitted to the reader not only a generally sympathetic picture of the fate of the exiled authors, but he also desired to have their situation and struggle comprehended in terms of history. In this manner, he presented the *Emigrantenliteratur* as a historical phenomenon. While wholly aware of the heterogeneity of the exile literature (always referred to as *Emigrantenliteratur*), Eidem arrived at some semblance of order by giving special consideration to three distinct groups. The chapter on Jewish nationalism pointed out that the Jewish people constituted the largest component among the exiles; their writings were mainly of a polemic and confessional character. The national-conscious Jews could clearly be recognized as a separate group, an assertion against which the critic Werner Türk pointed to the indubitable fact that, for example, Arnold Zweig and Alfred Döblin not only were Jewish ideologists but also very definitely, and "above all," German authors. In another chapter, Eidem dealt with the socialist writers of the emigration. Since the "essential" part of German refugees consisted of persons who had left for political reasons, the socialist writers gave more adequate expression to the general mentality of the German emigration. Their characteristic trait was optimism, despite the extraordinarily heartbreaking conditions under which they had to do their writing.

The non-socialist, individualistic authors were discussed by Eidem in a chapter entitled "The Emigrant Writer and History." These lacked the firm intellectual-spiritual (*geistig*) basis which the writers of the other two groups could claim. The individualists had turned to history in order to find parallels for the contemporary situation. Biographies and historical novels were therefore preponderantly their domain. It might be of interest to note that Eidem included in his list of exiled writers some Austrians, who did not have to go into banishment until a few months later.

The preliminary character of Eidem's mainly sociological appraisal was recognized by the critics; it was frankly conceded even by the author himself when, for example, he named Lion Feuchtwanger as one who would fit into each of his three classes of writers. However, Eidem's pioneering essay was the first serious and informative introduction to the intellectual and political currents and points of view prevalent within the literature of the German refugees. Its drawback was that the author's eagerness to give a view of contemporary German history in vividly presented book summaries resulted in an unevenness of presentation not commensurate with the importance of the individual writers and the specific literary merits of their works.

The literary situation in Germany before 1933 as he saw it was the starting point of Alfred Döblin's almost debonair survey of the German literature in exile, an essay that claimed as its core a "dialogue between politics and art." From what is called a "historical point of view," Döblin perceived three great contemporary "classes" in German literature since 1900; first there were the feudalists, the agrarian and expansive-bourgeois conservatives whose gaze was turned backward and who were inclined toward "classicism." Then we would find the humanists with liberal, progressive and conciliatory middle-class tendencies. Finally, the intellectual-revolutionary group would come into view, alert to the present but with accents often quite contradictory. There were either political and non-political rationalists or mystics beholden to no definite political creed. This group especially represented the younger generation.

Such, then, was the situation in 1933. When, at that time, German Literature broke apart, the question was: Did this happen along lines predetermined according to the above grouping of the literary forces? The answer of Döblin was: in part, yes. The conservatives found in Nazism much to their liking. To be sure, the Caliban manners of the new masters thoroughly startled them, and Nazi reality had little in common with their own dreams of a new Reich shaped according to the romantic ideas of a Richard Wagner. Yet most of the "conservatives," if "racially" in the clear, stayed home.

Harder hit were the humanists. Their nature revolted against totalitarianism and dictatorship; to them *Gleichschaltung,* coordination, seemed, of course, out of the question. But was this so with all of them? Quite a few were scions of the well-to-do middle class who liked their comfort—and would not the realm of ideas and ideals always be free? So many remained at home and learned to hold their tongues, for they long since had become incapable of straightforward, honest hatred and hostility anyway. Those who did not succumb were pushed out or left on their own, branded by the Nazis as liberals, reactionaries and *Judenknechte.* In consequence, many of the authors of the cultured middle class were found abroad.

The class of intellectual revolutionaries was sharply torn asunder. There were those who shared with the conservatives the contempt for the liberal and humanist ideas that had "grown stale"; again, others had a certain affinity toward the mystic and the irrational. The rightist radicals among the *Geistesrevolutionäre* swung, for a while at least, into the Nazi orbit. However, the exodus of leftists occurred in great numbers.

The result of the break-up of German literature in 1933 was, then, that inside the Third Reich the conservatives and feudalists, rightist radicals and a few, very few, cryptohumanists carried on, even though they were under constant pressure. Abroad were found, besides a few splinter elements of group one, the block of the humanists and the greater part of the intellectual revolutionaries. The question of "aryan or non-aryan" was, of course, an important factor not to be forgotten.

After its severance from the Reich, the German literature abroad was by no means a torso. No matter how indigent and handicapped in innumerable ways the authors might have been, they continued to develop and grow in their craft. They were not necessarily "leftist" when they insisted on working "as they pleased." Freedom was indispensable for creative literary work; if it was denied, true art had to die. Literature in exile was free, yet Döblin contended that this fact in itself gave but a modicum of encouragement. Like cultures of bacteria, the writers had been transplanted into a different, and highly dubious, new "nutrient solution." Free German-writing authors had only parts of Switzerland and Russia for an immediate clientele, in addition to sporadic readers in Holland, Scandinavia and the U.S.A. But there was more to the exile than this material shrinkage of an audience. A writer in his native country absorbed, according to Döblin, consciously or unconsciously, the thousand impacts and vibrations of his fellow countrymen, which induced in him an ever-changing field of tension and would call forth an energy that made him grow and prosper in his art. How different the situation in exile! A total change in the environment brought almost complete social isolation, and even the close circle of his friends and "fellows in fate" was of little help because they, too, were involved in the same compulsive process of desperately trying to come to terms with a new world.

If this sad plight would now lead an observer, continued Döblin, to expect with apprehension a creeping anemia of the German literature abroad, his alarm would be groundless. In vain would future historians look for signs of weakness as a mark of this literature. Each in his individual way, most writers in exile went about their task with courage, with loyalty to themselves and their calling. Exile was more than a crushing blow of fate; it was the acid test for a man to prove his mettle. As the banishment dragged on and on, as it turned more and more into a long and wearisome march through waste and desert lands, the character was steeled and the work continued, even if it meant the the critical tapping of irreplaceable reserves. The suffering, the strength and greatness of this literature thrown out of its native land was worthy of songs of high praise. It was, Döblin stated, German literature, not just a "literature of emigrants."

This literature now became subject to attacks from various quarters, not to mention the absolute and vicious hostility of the Nazis. The primary politically minded people levelled the charge against it that its preoccupation with historic topics of past ages and of various climes ignored the burning issues of the day, and that it thus turned into a kind of escape from reality. The answer that literature might very well deal with peoples and epochs of the past and yet in doing so report passionately on the burning issues of the present was brushed aside; the imperious demand was made that literature in general, and especially this one of the exile, should not deal with aesthetic or psychological questions of a private nature, but stress political and social values above all. The response of Döblin was that the writers produced and did whatever was in their might and talent; they continued, each one individually, as they had done at home, spinning the thread of their work. The deepest misery in exile could not change the basic facts of their existence which were the indispensable presuppositions and conditions for all art and literature. They worked at long range; they were concerned with man and the world in their totality; and they had to follow their own creative impulses. The "practical man" and the "political man" may counter: You writers own a weapon of greatest force, the living word. Do not use it in artful play while the world seems doomed to perish; use it to give direction and aim to the forces that will heal the world, else your art may go hang.

The confrontation of these views is, or course, a simplification and, at the same time, is overelaborated in its formulation. An artist, a writer, truly could not and should not cultivate "private" concerns to the exclusion of considerations of vital communal interest. He has, indeed, to put up with some curtailment of the self-sovereignty as an artist and examine his position. But fundamentally this was the artist's—Döblin's—answer.

"Each artist, each writer, carries the community in which he lives along into his deepest solitude. Through language, judgments, images and concepts the community has a share in the artist's creative process. The writer is by no means struck dumb when in his solitude. He carries on innumerable 'conversations' all around, merging with them his inspiration." Isolation or communal contact was therefore not a question for an author, but the problem was, what kind of society has generated the directive force even into his most private sphere.

Many German writers, in contrast to French authors, had carried only wretched miniature editions of their society into their solitude, showing a very low degree of communality spirit, *Gesellschaftlichkeit*. There were determining predelections for the abstract and morally arrogant (and stupid) contempt for the everyday life, the *Alltag*; instead, "eternal problems" were the exclusive concern; the interest in the fullness of human life for which Goethe once had raised his voice had gone by the board. A short circuit into mysticism often took place, a *Kurzschluss in die Mystik*.

The secularization of German literature, a process somewhat parallel to the gradual lowering of political barriers, had been infinitely slow. But pushing too hard in this direction had led to another short circuit, that one into the ephemeral problems of the day and into party politics, a danger to which French and English literature also had begun to succumb. Tolstoy and Gorki, Flaubert and Keller were able through their work to stir up a sense of social awareness because their hearts gave truth and completeness to their stories, not party platforms and a desire to accommodate politicians. It was ridiculous and provoking to Döblin when theoreticians, critics and writers solicited in exile the creation of antifascist works. The writers ought to be left strictly alone in their work. They were *The German Literature* abroad, and they should not tolerate indoctrination by politicians. It was they who continued the free German literature and they had to be on guard not to fall prey to compulsory neuroses. Cliques of the German political parties, irresponsible and detestable, had tried in exile to elbow their way into literary criticism. For their own selfish purposes they began to classify "friendly" and "hostile" authors, and they also singled out those to be ruined by the "silent treatment."

The sensible attitude, so Döblin continued, would be to encourage free German writers to aim at a closer attachment to society and to have them develop a spirit of communality, *Gemeinschaft*. An author would find far deeper satisfaction if he would enter the complex web of human relations, rather than explore his own private sphere to the point of exhaustion. But no political program could animate the working toward such a goal, only the slow-working impact of personal experience. Political formulae and manifestos are intellectual abstractions; in the field of art they amount at best to labels and slogans and nothing more.

The world was a world of horror, and even if the authors could not help but be incorrigible glorifiers and lovers of life and would never give up that which they knew was its depth and magic, more than heretofore they would have to deal with the "tiger face" of the world, whose features were composed of evil, harshness and war. Insignificant as he may have felt, the writer had to put greater trust in the "gentle and great" power of art and the creative word, and be convinced that he was the guardian of a fire through which the "tiger" had to be tamed and conquered. His field was the world and not just the drawing rooms of the—after all not so—mighty ones. While he himself kept aloof from politics and the struggles for power, inasmuch as they are manifested in society as well as in private lives, he had to recognize the forces at work and react to them positively through his creative art.

In concluding the theoretical discussion of the literature in exile, Döblin wanted to make it clear that his negative criticism was mainly aimed at the contempt of "reality" and of "the human community"; he wanted to score the clinging to bloodless phantoms and abstractions that posed as *Mystik* but were, in fact, only indications of hollowness, disillusionment and degeneration. Religion, genuine *Mystik*, was part of the creative basis of a new humanity, and literature was to share in the great process of recovery and restitution in the degree to which it penetrated into the ancient core of life from whence radiated all the forces of creation.

In the second part of Döblin's book, about forty writers pass in review, among them, naturally, the best known. Brief samples of some of their works illustrate the points Döblin wanted to make. His comments are presented in a style that is as compact as it is elegant and fluent, if not without caprice. The impression left by Döblin is that the body of literature created by the German writers abroad was true German literature in its proper sense; it was not a questionable branch to be stigmatized by derogatory overtones which, intended or not, would brand it inferior and illegitimate.

A vigorous brief against classifying the work of authors in exile as a "literature of emigrants" was presented by Hermann Kesten in the same year in which Döblin's study appeared. Point by point he examined and rejected the arguments in favor of using qualifying terms for the literature produced abroad, although he recognized that Hitler's murderous persecution of the free spirit resulted from the start in a "double-entry bookkeeping" concerning literature. A Chinese wall arose between the censored and the free book. Numerically the greater part of writers, of course, remained in the Third Reich, but nowhere do quantitative terms mean less than in the realm of the spirit. A very significant group of authors went into exile or returned to their homelands: Switzerland, Austria, Czechoslovakia. A magnificent and prospering literature turned its back for a while on a dishonored motherland. Yet there did not run a truly deep schism between the Nazi-corralled literature and the *Emigrantenliteratur*. Neither exile nor membership in the Reich's official chamber of writers separated *die "beiden deutschsprachigen Literaturen"* (sic), the two German-language literatures. Along with writers of genius and character, scoundrels and amateurs also went into exile, and within the Reich remained upright patriots and charming talents beside "chained dogs" and lick-spittles. The dividing line between the living free German literature and the National-Socialist *Gräberliteratur*, the literature of the tombs, ran straight through the Reich and through the exile as it did through those free countries where German was the mother tongue or one of the mother tongues.

No German *Emigrationsliteratur* existed, according to Kesten, in the sense in which this word was often employed, either in a hateful attitude or with a benevolent intent. Nobody had succeeded in postulating one single valid and unifying principle by which the term ''literature of emigrants'' could be justified. For what, besides the German language, had the writers of the emigration in common? Certainly not German citizenship nor the place of domicile. Or should, perhaps, the fact that their works were banned in Germany unite them? Hermann Hesse was still published there, and Thomas Mann was until recently; they were humanists both and deadly enemies of Nazism, but Otto Strasser, whose work clearly revealed fascist tendencies, was banned also. Were perhaps the inner and external factors of exile a common denominator? The great divergencies in the fate of many proved this argument illusionary. The firmly stated conclusion of Kesten was that no common character for the *Emigrationsliteratur* existed, just as there was none for the literature in the Reich. The fact of exile or the banishment of his works did not create a literary postulate and criterion for judging a writer. The exile left traces as did any experience, but no single experience was sufficient in itself to have art and literature named after or classified by it, nor was any experience significant enough to require it.

In a review of Döblin's study especially aimed at what he considered the questionable and faulty application of sociological principles, Ferdinand Lion shared with Kesten the thesis that style and form immanent to the artistic creation had to provide the evaluating criteria; they afforded the drawing of much sharper lines of demarcation than a social grouping into feudalists, humanists and revolutionaries—if a classification of literature was possible at all in the desire for getting a grasp of the creative spirit in terms of rational comprehension. Contrary to Kesten, however, Lion ''cannot get rid of a feeling that one deals with a compact body that is fighting and feels *solidarisch*.'' In literature, the decision about a new intellectual-spiritual German existence, and hence a new definitional category, could be made only when a ''new style'' would make an appearance. Caution was advisable for the history of the European Mind abounds in quickly succeeding theses, antitheses and syntheses of styles which, in fact, mark the caesuras of the Mind's ''real revolutions.'' The magic formula of such a ''new style'' might be created even by someone who was still in the camp of the opposition, maybe now living within the Reich, but whom to welcome into exile would be an honor. Lion acknowledged by inference the oneness of German literature in its essence, although he was aware that there was a body of literature outside the Reich even if a common denominator for it was lacking. (pp. 8-16)

The concept of a German literature in exile . . . refers to a specific body of writing and as such is first of all a term of reference. It embraces works of high and low quality; it is the creation of a host of writers of most divergent genius, talents, tendencies and beliefs. Their fate as writers in exile, when viewed in the light of history, was not as unique as it might seem at first. The portent of exile could almost be called a professional hazard for many masters of the pen. A long and proud record from the days of the Greeks and Romans up to modern times tells the story of authors whom tyranny had driven from their native soil and forced onto the ''battlefield of exile.'' (p. 19)

William K. Pfeiler, ''German Literature Outside the Third Reich,'' in his German Literature in Exile: The Concern of the Poets, *University of Nebraska, 1957, pp. 1-23.*

LIFE IN EXILE

ANTHONY HEILBUT

[*In the following excerpt, Heilbut recounts the difficulties met by German writers in the United States and discusses the experiences and writings of several prominent exiled authors.*]

Exaggerating only slightly, Thomas Mann wrote in 1941 that ''all of German literature had settled in America.'' The arrival went largely unnoticed, with the single exception of Mann himself. For while Americans were welcoming foreign musicians and filmmakers, the writers saw that far from shaping and cultivating a popular audience, they were losing even their émigré readers. This made them the unhappiest of refugee artists: the ultimate vindication of their talents, evident in the numerous scholarly studies of *Exilliteratur,* occurred long after it could have made any difference. But the truth is that the writers' influence on this country was real. As much as any group that was more visible, they set the tone for other émigrés.

They did so initially with a special confidence. As Thomas Mann's son Klaus put it after surveying his fellow refugees, ''There is only one homogeneous group and representative minority, the writers.'' They alone had sensed, almost at once, the danger represented by Hitler, not least because they had perceived his rape of the German language. The exodus united members of disparate religious and political groups, as well as experimental and traditional stylists. What linked them, as Klaus Mann saw, was ''the political mission to warn an unaware and drowning world.'' The veterans of Berlin, Prague, Vienna, and Paris were thus forced to combine the barely compatible roles of artist and Cassandra. It was a hard job with meager rewards. As if Hitler were exacting his revenge, the boldest political witnesses would also suffer the greatest professional losses. Their political observations had been rooted in the German language, and the network of linguistic associations proved almost impossible to transport. Yet, while they embodied failure, they were temperamentally disinclined, at least for a period, to indulge in self-pity.

The writers defended themselves by holding to the cocky, impious tone that had once been a generational style. The German idiom ''*Er gibt den Ton an*'' (''He sets the tone'') applies particularly to those writers who continued to assert the skepticism and irreverence of their youth. Not that sentimental novels didn't sell well to some émigrés, or that a roll call of the names of Holocaust victims at the annual *Jahrzeit* services of a German Jewish congregation would not evoke massive outbursts of weeping. But along with the predictable notes sounded in their exile—elegiac, melancholy, baffled—the characteristic assertiveness of their emigration remained to guarantee that all was not lost. Hitler had not conquered a group that could still say no to everything. Appropriately, the best writers provided few consolations and employed a narrative voice that was bracing rather than embracing.

The irreverence was salutary: Walter Mehring reported that his *Berliner Schnauze* saw him through the worst days of emigration. It was not only the Berliners who agreed that the best way of approaching a monstrous history was through satire and parody. Even the magisterial Thomas Mann delighted in such play: he once said that another writer wrote exactly the way he did but meant it *seriously*. There were other signs of disrespect for traditional material. As émigrés became literary athletes engaged in prodigious feats of quotation, the writers rummaged everywhere in search of an appropriate slant or image. This eclecticism invited accusations of plagiarism and blasphemy. Brecht admitted that emigration had made them scoundrels, but he defended his friend Hanns Eisler's pastiches of classical music: "Well, it may be that as an exile, he is not in a position to lug so much stuff around with him."

Few refugee writers in America suffered as harshly as the impoverished émigré poet Else Lasker-Schüler, who spent her first days in Switzerland, sleeping on park benches and begging for food (admittedly the slightly demented Lasker-Schüler enjoyed such occasions). A parallel case was Robert Musil, also in Switzerland. Mrs. Musil had American relatives, but they could not provide the affidavit necessary for emigration. The consummate master of irony and distance now grew desperate for public recognition. A friend says he was obsessed with the trivia of social ritual. When a local literary society refused to admit him, he fought for membership "as though his life depended on it." He spoke wistfully of best-sellers and book promotions. At least two guests remember his railing about the impossibility of emigration: "If I go to North America, Thomas Mann is there. If I go to South America, I will meet Stefan Zweig." In 1943 Musil died while performing gymnastics, as if limbering up for the flight.

In America the lack of funds diminished everyone. Artists found themselves dependent on the whim of sponsors. Brecht's poems were copied and privately circulated, a sort of Stalinist samizdat; the venerated Richard Beer-Hofmann's last publication was subsidized by a wealthy émigré. Hermann Broch's novel depended on prepublication subscriptions solicited by Helen and Kurt Wolff. Commercial assignments and/or academic fellowships at least sustained writers like Brecht and Broch. The editor of a leading Dresden newspaper ended his days as a New York watchmaker. Johannes Urzidil, a lion of Czech literary circles, supported his family in the forties with leatherwork.

While there was a spirit of camaraderie among most of the film directors, the writers' community was riddled with feuds and hostility. Not surprisingly, the most famous were also the most attacked. Franz Werfel's colleagues frequently condemned him for supporting the Austrian clericofascist Schuschnigg, who had helped destroy the anti-Fascist Austrian labor movement. (Schuschnigg arrived in this country in 1947, and taught at St. Louis University for many years.) Werfel's flirtations with Catholicism climaxed in the lugubrious *Song of Bernadette*. Werfel's friend Thomas Mann ridiculed his "snobbish Catholicism and unpalatable belief in miracles." In the end, however, Mann could not stay angry with Werfel, whom he saw as "basically a figure out of opera." Though Werfel never officially converted from Judaism, some readers found traces of anti-Semitism in his last works. Another famous writer, Erich Maria Remarque, was condemned both for his aloofness from the émigré colony and for his silence during the war years that he spent in Switzerland. Franz Schoenberner joked that Remarque must know nothing about émigré life or he wouldn't have a character spend enough money on liquor and cabarets in a day to support other refugees for a fortnight.

Throughout the thirties, whether living in France or attending the international conferences of anti-Fascist writers, Lion Feuchtwanger was a symbol of literary resistance: together with the ill-fated Ernst Toller, he headed the German-speaking branch of PEN.... [His] camp behavior was not universally well regarded. Other émigrés attacked his style or his salon Stalinism. In the United States he continued to socialize with left-wingers while residing in impeccable comfort: "The political

climate here is terrible, but the climate is good, and I remain optimistic that man will advance toward reason." This spirit won him many American fans, including Richard Milhous Nixon, but not all refugees were persuaded.

Thomas Mann was excoriated on all sides. His supplicants became his enemies. Some refugees recalled his initial attempts to retain a German audience; conversely, others accused him of being too unforgiving toward the Germans. Still others simply disliked his style; missing the spirit of parody, they found him egregiously middlebrow. The émigré novelist Alfred Döblin's contempt for Mann seems to have kept him happily enraged for years. In 1928 he referred snidely to Mann as his "colleague" for "stylistic beauties"; in another letter, he called him an "opportunist." Döblin once received a fellowship recommendation from Mann, and accepted his congratulations on his sixty-fifth birthday. But he was soon back on the prowl, insisting that Mann symbolized the moribund in literature. Mann himself wrote of Döblin, "He would like to kill me, for that is really the sense behind his claim that I *am* dead."

Success was everyone's aim, and it came occasionally, but usually in forms that were not satisfying. During the thirties and early forties many émigrés had supported themselves by turning out historical novels. Some were potboilers; others, like Stefan Zweig's historical fictions, *gemütlich* middlebrow entertainments, good for a few tears and a little education. Yet others, such as Heinrich Mann's two novels about King Henry IV of France, could be read as coded references to the present. The witty Berlin writer Kurt Hiller accused such writers of retreating into the past, and offered a set of outlandish historical subjects: "Pippin the In-Between, Rameses IV, and Melanie the Unusual of Paphlagonia." But historical vagaries transport better than local color, and though it was hardly planned that way, such novels provided a useful preparation for the Hollywood that homogenized all historical periods.

During the war years, movies were made from the novels of Vicki Baum, Lion Feuchtwanger, Franz Werfel, Bruno Frank, Martin Gumpert, Alfred Neumann, Erich Maria Remarque, Hans Habe, Stefan Heym, and Ernst Toller. There were also best-sellers written by émigrés, and Thomas Mann, Franz Werfel, and Stefan Zweig maintained their audiences. On a less exalted level, popular writers stayed popular. Emil Ludwig's middlebrow biographies satisfied a readership that later welcomed James Michener and John Gunther, while a large audience still hankered for the urbane kitsch of Vicki (*Grand Hotel*) Baum, who lived in the California hills, supported less successful refugees, and admonished all newcomers, "Don't be afraid." A more unusual popular success was Curt Riess. As New York correspondent for *Paris-Soir,* he had developed a colloquial, quasi-fictional approach. In the manner of later participant journalists, he wrote such series as *I Was a G-Man* and *I Was a Racketeer.* Riess was a cynic and hustler, but the chameleon air of his journalism was peculiarly appropriate to the refugee. He made a career out of the mobility and flux that were the normal conditions of émigré lives. How different from Riess were the refugee lawyers, engineers, and sociologists who could have written books entitled "I Was a Frenchman," "I Was a Butler," "I Was a Janitor," "I Was a Cook"?

There was a writers' community of sorts, and not all of it was German-speaking. English writers like W. H. Auden, Stephen Spender, and Christopher Isherwood were close to émigré circles. After all, Auden was Thomas Mann's son-in-law (he had married Erika Mann in order to provide her with a passport), while in England Isherwood was to write *Prater Violet*, a novel about an émigré filmmaker, a character inspired by Berthold Viertel. Once in California, Isherwood joined the circle of bohemians, radicals, and homosexuals that convened at the home of Viertel's wife. In New York, American writers like Upton Sinclair (whose works had helped inspire the youthful radicals) and Theodore Dreiser socialized with other émigrés; Dorothy Thompson and the English novelist Bryher provided many introductions. New German-American literary careers opened up. Hans Sahl and Walter Mehring translated several American plays into German for émigré little theaters, while Hermann Kesten translated American novels for the Foreign Council on Books under the Office of War Information.

Yet there was about all this something desperate and even disreputable. Gifted artists, preoccupied with petty tribal squabbles, counted themselves lucky to find hack assignments. Serious work did not find a public. One émigré, Klaus Mann, speculated that the real problem was the absence of a language sufficiently flexible to render unprecedented events: "The refugee writer will have to find a new vocabulary, a new set of rhythms and devices, a new medium to articulate his sorrows and emotions, his protests and his progress." The refugee writer needed the liberating perspective of a new language as much for himself as for a world "drowsing and unaware." Klaus Mann thought that an American journal would be the appropriate literary hybrid. It wasn't, it failed after twelve issues, but what other forum would have been better, or truer to the refugee writers as a community?

That Klaus Mann should conceive of such a magazine bespoke his prominent position in literary circles, as well as his particular affection for American life. If the action was quixotic, Klaus was the right man to perform it. Klaus, Thomas Mann's oldest son, lived the life of a Mann character, frequently to his father's annoyance. In the late twenties he and his sister Erika had become the very types of spoiled bohemian socialites, engaging in all forms of the avant-garde, from surrealism to expressionism. Klaus liked to move between the domains of "world literature" and "the underworld." He shared his uncle Heinrich's Francophilia, and a concomitant irreverence for German pomp. As a homosexual, he could go beyond Heinrich in exploring the night world of large cities. (pp. 261-66)

An illustrious list of editorial advisers graced the journal he inaugurated in 1941. He first thought of calling it *Cross-Roads* but rejected the title as ambivalent, and chose the more straight-forward *Decision*. Exile literature needed rejuvenation; exile writers needed an audience; the aims of literature and propaganda would be met in *Decision*. In the first issue, Mann wrote, "The most distinguished representatives of European literature in America are doomed to perish unless they have contact with the vigor and youth of American literature."

Decision will be a "mouthpiece for European refugees," he said. As such, it will be irreverent and opinionated. Also in the initial issue, Mann waged a typical refugee attack on the American infatuation with "facts, just facts." But he went other critics like Adorno or Lowenthal one better, in both wit and perspicacity. In an analysis of the popular radio program "Information Please," he noted that "knowledge for its own sake" was a nineteenth-century monster, peculiarly European, dolled up in New York fashions. In another article, Aldous Huxley sounded a similar note: there is "a general over-estimation of facts and under-estimation of concepts and ideas." Along with his call for a new language for the refugee, Klaus Mann demanded a new epistemology, larger than the mere acquisition of facts but not abstract to the point of political quietism.

In different issues, *Decision* saluted several refugee groups. German writers were represented most often, but special issues were devoted to English, French, and Italian literature. Through his relationship to Auden, Mann recruited such distinguished English writers as Christopher Isherwood, who provided an obituary of Virginia Woolf, and E. M. Forster. But the magazine was always manifestly an American journal; it printed Sherwood Anderson's last work, stories by Eudora Welty, and Carson McCullers's comparison of Southern fiction and Russian realism.

Because the refugees had a new subject and audience, *Decision* was interested particularly in refugee responses to American culture. In its first issue, Franz Werfel paid homage to Poe and Whitman: Werfel loved Whitman for showing him that there was no subject too "commonplace" for poetry; in a reformulation of the Wordsworth-Coleridge split, he lauded Poe for discovering the exotic in the familiar. Werfel sounded like a French structuralist when he celebrated in Poe "the cabala of the consonants and the demons that dwell in the vowels." Klaus Mann wrote paeans of praise to Whitman as an American match for Socrates himself in his uniting of the erotic and the metaphysical. Mann also paid rigorous attention to current best-sellers. Anne Morrow Lindbergh had begun publishing her diaphanous musings. Mann was not charmed; he found them insidious pieces of Nazi propaganda, for they advocated a passive withdrawal to nature. He spoke as an insulted European when he criticized her glorification of an "American October" unique to this continent: Is your October the same in Detroit, Seattle, and Florida? he questioned sarcastically. He was much more sympathetic to the American women Gertrude Stein and Carson McCullers, and imagined an amusing conversation between the "well-preserved aunt" and her "delicate niece," with Stein perhaps scoring the nicer critical points.

Turning to unknown writers, Klaus Mann juxtaposed the attempts of American surrealists—he had long since broken with his French surrealist comrades—and a new young writer, Paul Goodman. He recognized in Goodman the "revolutionary conservative" temperament of a Goethe. Goodman, for some reason, was not pleased with Mann's approval. But Mann's judgment of Goodman's polymath achievements and his perpetual debts to romanticism seem to have been strikingly prophetic.

With refugees so well launched in Hollywood, *Decision* paid movies the tribute of taking them seriously. Erich von Stroheim, in an article for the journal, wrote that he had been the first to present a realistic cinematic depiction of sexual desire; he also wrote that he was dismayed by the new film *Citizen Kane*. Richard Plant observed that, on the whole, American films were quite as good as European: we merely saw Europe's best and least representative works. Klaus himself analyzed anti-Nazi films in Hollywood. Once, he said, in a German film directed by Richard Oswald, militarism had been properly indicted, but Hollywood reduced the plight of anti-Fascists to something "too idyllic, too private, too sentimental, too conventional." (Virtually at the same time, Lowenthal and Arnheim were noting the same flaws in magazine biographies and radio dramas.) In a devastating attack on Fritz Lang's *Man Hunt*, he accused the director of "venturing on the most appalling topic of human history with the shabby tricks of Wild West and gangster thrillers." Here was justification for a true refugee complaint: American culture could diminish the most talented émigré artists.

A few of *Decision*'s political essays remain timely. Klaus's younger brother Golo used a review of Emil Lederev's economics as a pivot for an attack on Marxism and dismissed such terms as "capitalist," "socialist," and "revolutionary" as obsolete, while paying patriotic homage to the "permanent revolution" of America. This argument would be echoed by many conservative émigrés after the war. (Recently, Golo Mann was a supporter of Franz Josef Strauss, the conservative West German candidate for chancellor—a stand one cannot imagine shared by his father, uncle, or brother.) In the final issue of *Decision*, a Trinidadian analyzed the potential for black fascism, and pointed out that the separatist Marcus Garvey had negotiated with the Ku Klux Klan. A Harvard historian alluded to the debate between Rosa Luxemburg and Lenin that had split the German Left in World War I, and echoed Lenin's argument that it was possible to fight a socialist war on the imperialists' side—an academic restatement of the debate between Stalinists and Trotskyists.

Klaus's sophisticated sense of politics was reflected in the work he printed. In an early issue was a poem by a new Warner Brothers screenwriter, "Bert Brecht." This is the famous "Yes I Live in a Dark Age," an acknowledgment of his generation's moral failures and an implicit plea for mercy: "We wanted to make our soil ready for kindness . . . think of us kindly." On one occasion, *Decision* demonstrated by focusing on Ernst Toller, the hero of Munich 1919, that among the victims of emigration were the writers themselves. Toller was not happy in America. His low estimation of the culture had been evident in his play *Mary Baker Eddy,* written even before he reached the country, in which Eddy is sexually obsessed and a secret ally of the town bosses against the workers. For a while in New York he received flattering publicity, and kept busy raising funds for orphans of the Spanish Civil War. But the public interest in Toller and his cause dwindled. After his suicide, *Decision* printed an obituary by Hermann Kesten, a young writer who had helped organize the rescue of the writers stranded in Marseilles, in which he wrote, "What grotesque adventures lie behind us German émigré writers. We have lost our people and our market, our publishers, newspapers, theaters, homes, bank accounts, passports, papers, our manuscripts and our friends. . . . One and all, we were prophets, for we knew about Hitler and Germany, we foresaw the future, predicted the war. . . . No-one listened to us, no-one believed us." And then, to arrive, "see the same processes at work" and not dare to speak "because one is an alien"; no wonder Toller killed himself. Kesten's lament was a synopsis of many lives. World War II had not yet begun, and already their story could be told, as if they were all dead men.

The man of letters, Klaus Mann said, had become a "political": whatever his subject matter, the change in his fortunes had specific political implications. It was no longer a question of finding an adequate prose style in German or English when language itself, the writer's privileged sphere of interest, had been subverted. In a manner that resembled the analyses of Orwell or Adorno (or of the New School authors of *Nazi Deutsch*), Klaus Mann wrote in *Decision* that the "function of the word is no longer to inform, to clarify, to reveal, but to confuse." He asked: What is left when language has become the instrument of a "disquieting state of schizophrenic confusion"? Unlike other writers like Adorno or the New School authors who also recorded the social damages of *Nazi Deutsch*, Mann extended his analysis of "the word" into a political editorial in which he attacked the English (for their devotion to Bank of England economics rather than to political morality)

Hannah Arendt. Reproduced by permission of Robert Boyers, editor of Salmagundi.

and the Russians (the Kremlin needed to recover the integrity of Dimitroff, the Communist who stood up to Nazi prosecutors after the Reichstag fire). Prophetic again, he anticipated the postwar confrontations: the Allies' coalitions must not conceal a plot to usher in world revolution, or an encirclement of the Soviet Union. Mann wrote as if he knew that the distortions of language are coterminous with the confusions of politics—and that both are "schizophrenic."

Klaus loved America. After the failure of *Decision*, he served in the American Army. But transcending the parochial prejudices and moral restrictions of all national groups, he remained an internationalist. In his autobiography he defied the philistines: "My moral consciousness is not affected by the sex taboos of bourgeois or proletarian society . . . or by the hateful slogans of nationalism." Some years later Hannah Arendt would draw a similar connection between political and sexual outsiders, and recently neoconservatives and fundamentalist Christians have waged a right-wing attack on the homosexual's lack of commitment to family and country. Klaus Mann would have been the perfect man to answer Norman Podhoretz and Jerry Falwell. But in 1950 he committed suicide. He had made many earlier attempts, though for a brief period during the war he had come to realize that suicide was "pompous and obsolete."

Klaus had in his favor youth, a facile social manner, and a command of American language and culture. Still he left no mark on this country's literature. So it should hardly be surprising that much older men fared no better, particularly the crew that toiled—or, more likely, didn't toil—in the Hollywood studios. They may once have seen themselves as modernists and radicals, members of an international vanguard; exile revealed them as custodians of a humanist legacy, eccentric but all too European.

The political commitment was indisputable. Heinrich Mann arrived in 1940 at age sixty-nine, after having been for decades the symbol of socialist humanism. During World War I, his scathing depictions of German philistines and the Gallic lucidity of his prose had distinguished him from his brother Thomas with his orotund verbal flourishes and muddleheaded nationalism. Thomas mistook their political disagreements for sibling rivalry. When he detected unflattering personal references in an essay of Heinrich's, his brother responded, "There is no 'I' in my public utterances, and for that reason also no brother." In bouts of miffed feelings as in political argument, Heinrich's dignity did not fail him.

The two brothers had achieved a personal and political rapprochement during the twenties. But it was Heinrich who presided over conferences of anti-Fascist writers during the thirties, just as he had served on a "soviet of brain workers" during the 1918-19 Munich revolution. In 1933, rising above the self-destructive quarrels of the German Left, he joined Kaethe Kollwitz in pleading for a reconciliation of the Social Democrats and Communists. Shortly after the election of Hitler, he published a series of dialogues, *Scenes from Nazi Life,* that anticipated Brecht's later plays, as well as a devastating essay in his nephew Klaus's magazine *Die Sammlung,* which asserted that Hitler's gangsterism was evident in his assault on the German language. "Future generations" would have to be "cleansed in their vocabulary from the words peace, justice, and truth." By erasing the words and the values they represented, Hitler might succeed in snatching the Germans' children from them. This was too bold a literary analysis for other German writers; brother Thomas, Alfred Döblin, and Stefan Zweig all disavowed the article, though they got the message soon enough. As the noblest and most prophetic of anti-Fascist writers, Heinrich Mann became, in Ludwig Marcuse's words, "the Hindenburg of the emigration."

After his arrival in America, Heinrich wrote for *Decision* an essay in which he recalled the cultural issues that had dominated his thinking for over thirty years. "The pattern is always the same: the worthwhile goes down in France—the great King, or the Republic, his distant successor [Mann's late work *Henry, King of France,* presents the French king as "laying the foundation for the first democracy"]—and at once the Germans get the elbow room needed to commit excesses, as is their custom, and exercise their calling which is destruction." Mann had noted all this in a novel: "*Der Untertan* was devoured and did not change a thing." Yet once again he found himself laughing at his destructive countrymen—"They have become a horror; and yet in my eyes, they remain the grotesque figures they were when I met them."

This last observation is one of the recurrent notes of émigré literature; it is repeated by the Mann brothers, Brecht, and even Hannah Arendt in her later dissections of Adolf Eichmann's prose. The Germans are horrible, horrifying—and also terribly funny, as ridiculous as they are grotesque. Such gallows humor, smacking of the cabarets or the Berlin streets, also characterized the left-wing politics of writers like Leonhard Frank and Alfred Döblin, other Hollywood émigrés. Frank too was a socialist humanist: the title of his autobiography *Links ist wo das Herz ist* (literally, "Left is where the heart is") sounds like oom-pah-pah Marxism. He enjoyed big-city life: friends remember him in Paris during the thirties, snarling like a Berlin cabdriver, making fun of everything.

The more dour Döblin was also the most spiritually peripatetic of émigrés, a man for whom exile was an enduring condition. The son of a working-class family, he practiced medicine for many years while turning out fiction, essays, and articles. The constant attitude in his work was an identification with suffering humanity, prompted either by political principles or by an almost masochistic delight in his capacity to withstand hardship. This was accompanied by so many shifts in philosophy and politics that in the thirties some fellow exiles dubbed him *Konfusionsrat* (counsel of confusion). Always sympathetic to the Left (in exile he wrote a three-volume study of Rosa Luxemburg) though often anti-Marxist, Döblin was briefly a Zionist and eventually converted to Catholicism, arguing that he had become what evangelists call "a completed Jew."

Döblin was assertively contemporary in his manner. He championed a "Berlin program" for writers, one that stressed kinetic movement, a cinematic sensibility, and vernacular discourse; Walter Benjamin said that "he speaks with the city's voice." His most famous novel, *Alexanderplatz Berlin* (1929), is the story of a one-armed Berlin laborer, Franz Biberkopf, and his prostitute lover, Mieze. The book is crammed with statistics, road signs, headlines, advertising slogans, popular song lyrics. The language is always resolutely simple and colloquial, often with the singsong rhythms and rhymed phrases of an agitprop anthem.

There was a similarly advanced urban sensibility expressed in Leonhard Frank's work. While Döblin at times resembles a Berlin James Joyce (although he derived his stream-of-consciousness passages from Dadaism and expressionism), Frank's *Carl and Anna* reads like a Berlin version of D. H. Lawrence's romantic mysticism. An army veteran assumes his buddy's identity and succeeds in convincing the man's wife that he is really her husband. Their love affair is described as a "nature film," compact of blood knowledge and nonverbal understandings; the two find themselves in an "unfathomable" but eminently erotic mystical state. The novel's American edition appeared with the kind of apology that once graced Lawrence's novels: "clean . . . informed by an almost religious purity."

With their gift for the vernacular and the erotic, Frank and Döblin seemed well equipped to write in the American popular style. Heinrich Mann's craft appeared to be more forbidding. Yet early in the century he had exhibited a similar mastery, first in *Professor Unrat,* the source of the Josef von Sternberg-Marlene Dietrich film *The Blue Angel,* and even more in *Der Untertan* (*The Subject*). The latter novel's hero, Diederich, is an arriviste, something of a Teutonic Flem Snopes. By ignoring all humanist values and carrying nationalist pieties to absurd extremes, he manages to become rich, marry well, and defeat the grand old man of his town. Diederich is at once terrifying and pathetic. Anticipating writers as varied as Hermann Broch or Erik Erikson, Mann depicted his protofascist villain initially as a lonely and fearful child.

Der Untertan, published in 1912, foreshadowed some of the major cultural issues of the emigration: one character becomes an actor, insisting that "the representative man of this era is the actor," but gives up the stage after moving to tears a police officer who had earlier fired on striking workers (compare the perpetual amazement that admirers of Beethoven or Brahms could also run concentration camps). Someone observes that capitalists like Diederich buy off their employees with just enough goods to prevent a real class war—an observation central to the essays of Herbert Marcuse.

These were not literary snobs. Granting their great ages—Mann arrived at sixty-nine, Döblin at sixty-three—they would still seem to have had the equipment for the movie studios. Döblin had constructed his fiction cinematically; scholars have found cinematic techniques in Heinrich Mann's late writings. Döblin enjoyed popular art; unlike some of his fellow California exiles he felt that "entertainment music" liberated people's lives and that elitist critics simply didn't want them to be happy.

At least at first, Döblin attempted to hustle himself a position in the literary marketplace. On November 5, 1942, his wife wrote to the publisher B. W. Huebsch, acknowledging that her husband's previous writings might have appeared inaccessible—"I understand it only since we are living here"—but that his newest work had something that would truly satisfy everyone: "From this book which I am presenting you now, runs a stream of life, giving as life itself: knowledge, understanding, truth, dreams, love, tears and smiles. . . ." She begged Huebsch not to sell the American audience short—"Please do not underestimate the American people, they do not only like funnies, love-stories or detective tales." But Huebsch, though sympathetic, felt that this work also was too specifically German in scope and scale.

Yet how such men must have hated their periods of Hollywood underemployment, what Alfred Neumann called "$100-a-week charity." Döblin loathed his Hollywood assignments; he contributed to such war films as *Mrs. Miniver* and *Random Harvest,* but complained in a letter that "One does nothing, absolutely nothing." In 1942 Heinrich Mann wrote his nephew, "Here one drags one's life along without particular necessity. No one asks you to give evidence of your presence. . . . One must not be discouraged. We are more or less buried with the debris of a decrepit humanity which is nevertheless in world rebellion." As for his work: "I see a film and say something. Actually I could say something without having seen it." Bad as the jobs were, losing them was worse. Heinrich Mann was poor; he wrote his sister-in-law, "Don't open the door, unless creditors aren't behind me." After his death, there appeared reports of his haunting the offices of Hollywood studios. Döblin wrote a friend, "It is simply *fatal* for an author to have no money and to live on subsidies, as I and others are doing."

Döblin and Frank, at least, managed to escape after the war's end. Döblin returned to work with propaganda forces in Germany. He left America, having accomplished little besides the composition of his journal of European exile, *Fateful Journey* (*Schicksalsreise*), but without recriminations. Like Brecht, he admired the natives' friendliness and physical grace. He noted their "robust business sense and the curiously easy and superficial religiosity that belongs to this society." En route to Europe, Döblin composed a short poem bidding farewell to America, with the assurance that he loved her even though she did not want him. (By the end of his life, Döblin's audience had so shrunk that he was forced to publish his last novel in East Germany. In 1951 he wrote Ludwig Marcuse that his manuscripts were being ignored, "just as in Hollywood," and within two years, he had "emigrated a second time," this time to France.)

Leonhard Frank also returned, publishing in Germany a novel, *Mathilde,* that he had started in Hollywood. This is an unsettling combination of intellectual humanism and Frank's patented sexual mysticism, the first represented by a historian who becomes a RAF pilot, the second by his farm-girl wife; while her husband participates in the political present, Mathilde remains an almost prehistorical figure, drawing him back to the period when they were "wedded by nature." Nothing in the novel smacks of Hollywood.

For all his mystical high jinks, Frank retained his Berlin humor. In his autobiography he joined émigrés of such disparate personality as Albert Ehrenstein and Max Horkheimer in condemning a consumer culture responsible for "*Gefühlsarmut*" (poverty of feeling). So, indeed, the Left was where the heart was: a political decision needed to be heartfelt. After all, how else could one prove, as one of his titles naïvely proclaimed, that *Der Mensch ist gut*?

Heinrich Mann did not live to return to Europe. His last years were terrible ones. He had married a Berlin bargirl, Nellie Kroeger. Shades of *The Blue Angel,* she publicly humiliated her old husband, smashed up cars, and eventually committed suicide. Despite everything, the old man kept writing. In 1946, in honor of his seventy-fifth birthday, Thomas described his brother's punctilious work habits, citing the clear Roman script and steel pen as anachronisms. Thomas went on to praise the prophetic language of Heinrich's autobiography: "the prose's condensed and intellectually resilient plainness makes it appear to me as the language of the future, the idiom of the new world." This gracious tribute, with its implicit condemnation of his own style, must have warmed his brother, but it could not make up for a lost public. In 1949 Heinrich wrote a friend, "In fifty years, I have not been so completely disregarded as now."

By 1948 some German Communists had revived interest in *Der Untertan,* but Mann objected that "it's the wrong kind of discovery. . . . I don't want to survive as the author of an editorial in novel form." Heinrich Mann's autobiography revealed enough of his old Stalinist sympathies to endear him to the East German literary bureaucrats—despite the book's praise of Roosevelt, Churchill, and de Gaulle—and they invited him to return. Eventually funds were raised for the trip, but he died in March of 1950, a month before his planned departure. In one of his last letters, he surveyed a decade that had been reduced for him to a ceaseless pursuit of funds and added, "If we had no need of dollars, we would laugh. At least let me smile."

After Heinrich's death, Thomas paid a final tribute to his brother's mastery of a New World idiom: "It was so moving to see in his fiction and essays how a highly cultivated, austere and brilliant mind sought plainness, strove to reach social community and the common people, without the slightest surrendering of his aristocratic quality." All émigré writers would applaud this ambition, and see in Heinrich's case a ringing example of its failure; Heinrich's New World idiom ended along with Klaus's wish for a new refugee prose. A decade earlier in *Decision,* Heinrich wrote that he had derived from French literature the notion that "life ought to be a novel." The balances of his own life were already clear and he could acknowledge the fiction because "the ending satisfies if and when the truth was fought for." The coda to that "novel," the final years in Hollywood, would render the estimable ending anticlimactic.

Despite the abysmal conditions of literary exile, at least one writer as poverty-stricken and fatalistic as the rest was able to produce a masterpiece. This was Hermann Broch, who may have had the curious advantage of not living in Hollywood, where the general malaise seemed to demoralize everyone. Broch comprehended the extremes of Middle European intellectual temperament. He was so prodigiously devoted to humanist culture that he could spend years composing his masterpiece, *The Death of Virgil (Der Tod des Vergil)*. But Broch was also a political witness; part of the *Virgil* was written in a Nazi prison cell, and the book was completed in America, where the exigencies of health, money, and language made his work seem a quixotic comment on the general hopelessness of exile. Before Broch turned to ancient Rome, he had already portrayed the decline of German society; his first novel, *The Sleepwalkers (Die Schlafwandler;* 1931, published in English a year later), looked forward to Nazi terror as the culmination of an era of unreason: Hannah Arendt asserted that Broch was the first author to figure out the "radical atomization" of modern life.

The scholarly Broch was enough a product of his generation to imagine a more coherent future elsewhere. There are times when Esch, the doomed anarchist of *The Sleepwalkers,* feels "that there is a region in his head that is America, a region that is none other than the site of the future in his head, and yet that cannot exist so long as the past keeps breaking in so boundlessly into the future. . . ." Broch's tragedy was that America, "the site of the future," produced neither the breakthrough to a transcendent vision nor a sympathetic public. Here was a man with a scholarly command of the modern sciences, from physics to psychoanalysis, and with a literary reach from the abstract to the sensual that was always tinged with melancholy. Yet everything—in the times, in his intellectual tradition, in his own complicated self—conspired against him; as he had forecast, "the wrecked and annihilated overwhelm[ed] the new."

Broch was the son of a wealthy Austrian textile manufacturer, and he worked in the family business throughout his youth. In his forties he resumed his education with studies in mathematics, philosophy, and psychology. He studied with the Vienna Circle positivists, and immersed himself in science, although the spiritual undercurrents in his fiction have been identified by Hannah Arendt, his most loving reader, as "essentially Christian." Broch prepared a script for a movie on Einstein's relativity theory; he also planned six movies on scientists to combat the 1930s anti-intellectualism (a ridiculous mathematics teacher in Broch's *The Guiltless [Die Schuldlosen]* attacks Einstein's theories). Einstein helped facilitate Broch's entrance into the country, and the two later became friends.

Broch was also a modern city man, deeply affected by Freud's work. In a devastating analysis of Viennese kitsch worthy of Karl Kraus, Broch reiterated his belief that culture and politics were indivisible. He observed a world in which adult concerns were imperfect suppressions of childhood terrors. He valued Kafka and Hugo von Hofmannsthal for discovering, by stylistically discrete routes, the center of modern consciousness in "that symbolization of helplessness itself . . . the child."

The Sleepwalkers drew upon all his preoccupations as well as the novels of Mann and Joyce (who, for Broch, had brought "all aesthetic elements under the dominion of the ethical"). Broch is a profounder thinker than either Joyce or Mann. He may also be a less talented novelist, but his works of fiction are so fused with historical and philosophical speculations that

the term "novel" as applied to any of his fictional writings may not be adequate. Hannah Arendt noted after the 1945 publication of Broch's *Death of Virgil* that Broch resembled Proust in his "fondness for the world" and also Kafka in his recognition that the hero as individual had been replaced by "man as such." Thus the real life of Virgil was no more than the occasion for a treatise on art and humanity.

The Sleepwalkers is not so formidable a work as the novel on Virgil. Of its three main figures, only the last, Hugenau, seems without individual traits, and this lack is a deliberate comment on the dehumanizing times in which he lives. The novel covers the period from 1888 to 1918. Far more than Mann's *Der Untertan*, it sees politics as the surrogate for unconscious desires. Broch's characters are consumed by homosexual panic and an almost lustful need for a powerful parent. Each is more mindless than the last; the least conscious of all, Hugenau, is a murderer without guilt, because he is without memory.

Broch collapses Hugenau's pathology into the general mindlessness: "War is war, *l'art pour l'art*, in politics there is not room for compunction, business is business,—all these signify the same thing . . . that uncanny, I might almost say that metaphysical lack of consideration for consequences, that ruthless logic directed on the object and on the object alone, which looks neither to the right nor to the left; and this, all this, is the style of thinking that characterizes our age." In Broch's difficult but coherent vision, nationalism, capitalism, academic art, and kitsch all exemplify the same failure to investigate consequences.

Broch stayed in Vienna until the late thirties. During a very brief imprisonment by the Gestapo, he began to work on his *Virgil*. After his arrival in America he depended on grants and university fellowships; even his novel's publication was partially subsidized. More than any other émigré writer he is remembered for his unceasing generosity and kindness. Arendt recalls that in a circle in which distress was "ubiquitous," it was always Broch who "took care of everything." One of his translators, Jean Starr Untermeyer, says that in his last years Broch would go about on swollen feet collecting money for poorer friends. He himself was then living in shabby students' digs.

With perhaps undue optimism, he placed his confidence for American success in the *Virgil*. Stefan Zweig, after reading the manuscript, had warned him that the work was untranslatable, but Broch was sufficiently impressed by Jean Starr Untermeyer's translations of Rilke's *Duino Elegies* to contact her. Though Untermeyer still recalls him as the signal influence on her life, Broch at first exhibited that combination of haughtiness and desperation that could make émigrés appear monstrous. In an early meeting he despaired over the universal atmosphere of death. She replied in a note, rather platitudinously, that "death-in-life" was the real danger. Broch had no time for such "kitsch." He informed her that if she lacked his "poetic strengths," she would endanger his "whole American future." And when she objected to his arrogance, he answered, "You act like a spoiled child who says I'm not appreciated." Once again, the curiously European directness offended an American; conversely, of course, émigrés complained that the natives were not straightforward enough—no wonder a blunt assertion struck them as tactless. Only later did Untermeyer recognize that the harsh tone confirmed Broch's trust in her: since *she* was a mature artist, she could take criticism.

Although he continued to serve his fellow refugees, Broch was also concerned with American problems. During the war years, he worked on a study of mass psychology in addition to *Virgil*. Distressed by the race riots in Detroit, not to mention the anti-Semitism that had driven him from Europe, he submitted to the United Nations a "bill of duties." He told one correspondent that he expected his next "work of a politico-psychological nature" to be of "definitely greater importance" than the *Virgil*.

The *Virgil* is an extraordinarily long and difficult telling of the Roman poet's last days. There are vivid passages depicting the carnival excesses of Roman street life as well as Virgil's memories of the courtesans and shepherds he has loved. But there are endless declamations—one sentence runs for twelve pages—on art and responsibility. Virgil wishes to disown his art for many reasons, and each is subjected to Talmudic or Jesuitical exegesis. Broch, at his most despairing, felt himself completely alienated from the humanity he meant to serve and removed from the human being he was when he began to write. He wrote the Germanist Hermann J. Weigand that "The three years spent in polishing up the *Virgil* have in large measure blurred for me the experience of the cognition of death such as I had divined it." He credited his American supporters with pushing him to finish the exhausting work. "I came over to America with the unfinished *Virgil* and I have experienced the confidence and helpfulness of so many people and institutions that I had to keep my promise. . . ."

European readers immediately recognized the importance of the *Virgil*, that here was a novel that evoked their recent lives as much as the chaos of Virgil's last days. Appropriately, the book received a front-page review in *The New York Times*. It was Broch's bad luck—"my perpetual fate"—that the review was published during a truckers' strike. Perhaps no mass market existed for Broch's work, but the strike augured a lack of attention that confirmed his sense of isolation. Writing in *The Nation*, a still-unknown Hannah Arendt stressed the book's immediate relevance: "When the night arrived, Broch woke up. He awoke to a reality which so overwhelmed him that he translated it immediately into a dream, as is fitting for a man roused at night"; Arendt's own prose rhythms pay homage to Broch and Kafka. In a plaintive note, she observed that those "greedy with self-idolatry" were "excluded from all true community, which is based on helpfulness." Arendt's own work leaves little doubt that "helpfulness" in the "community" refers to the circuit of refugee assistance, to which she and Broch donated so much time.

Alvin Johnson recognized Broch's integrity. "Mann gave us a stone," he wrote Broch, "but you gave us bread." Einstein read the *Virgil* and found himself "steadfastly resisting" the book's implications: "The book shows me clearly what I fled from when I sold myself body and soul to Science—the flight from the I and WE to the IT" (although . . . Einstein was no slave to abstractions). With all this affirmation, Broch must have known he was loved and honored. Yet he saw himself, almost like Virgil, betrayed by physical desires and neuroses. He wrote Edith Jonas Levy after receiving an analysis of his handwriting: "In my feeling, I wasted my life, and doubtless my neurotic compulsions have a large part in causing this failure. However there are other reasons, and I am wondering whether and why the analyst didn't mention them; it is the whole field of drives and instincts (the field of the 'it') which was a real battleground for me." Perhaps no tribute could assuage his self-doubts.

Hermann Broch. Reproduced by permission of Robert Boyers, editor of Salmagundi.

Broch's last years were cursed by illness, financial worries, and public indifference. In 1950 the Austrian PEN Club almost nominated him for a Nobel Prize, but Broch proved to be equally unattractive to the Stalinist and clericofascist (Catholic) members. His deepening depression alarmed his American friends. Edith Jonas Levy suggested that Alvin Johnson reopen Broch's Nobel candidacy, but Levy and Johnson then learned that Broch's backers would have to be former prizewinners in literature. Broch, who had once feared for "his whole American future," now trembled at the elusive prospect of world recognition. Once more reduced to scuffling about, he would sit with Mrs. Levy and compose lists of writers to solicit for recommendations.

Broch exhibited a Kafkaesque embarrassment before his American friends. When Hermann Hesse replied to Johnson that he was too ill to write a word, Broch despaired over *Johnson's* humiliation. Johnson, "this wonderful old man," was not disturbed. He wrote Thomas Mann, pleading for a commitment to Broch, a message that was a bit insulting to Mann, as well as patronizing to Broch, with its implication that only a Nobel Prize could revive his drooping spirits. Mann replied, "I regret that his condition leads him to believe 'I never will consider him worth my backing.' What hypochondria! Good heavens, I am sure I need his 'backing' more than he does mine." Mann noted that the committee had also bypassed Joyce and Kafka, that Broch's works were considered "abstruse and sophistical" in many quarters, that even he felt that Broch's achievement was not "fully ripened." Withal, he allowed the use of his name. Broch didn't win. His status as a world-class novelist would be secured only after his death in 1951 in a New Haven lodging house. Broch was a cardiac patient, yet he lugged a heavy suitcase up three flights of stairs. Some friends suspect it was a form of suicide. (pp. 268-85)

The history of the exiled writers in America is a disheartening one. Perhaps they could have exhibited a deeper curiosity about American life; why weren't there more émigré novels about New York or Los Angeles, two cities they knew well? Yet something new came out of the émigré experience, a style that tested, confirmed, and moved beyond the assumptions of earlier modernists.

Immediately new was the subject. The great "I" that inhabited the heart of Western literature had disappeared. In part, this absence was a legacy of modernism; as Adorno noted, even Proust, the most subjective of writers, "decomposed the subjective mind." It was also a political reaction to the capitalist excesses of individualism: Walter Benjamin once said, "I write well because I seldom use 'I.'" Most profoundly, the sense of individual identity was blurred by the common experiences of exile, and some, such as Arendt, applauded this change. Alfred Döblin remembered a similar loss, though he was less happy about it: "I was never less 'I'" than during the flight from the Nazis. The move from the "I" to the "we" was purchased at the cost of a consoling warmth, but the chilly tone of the plural pronoun helped avoid the bathos that threatened the most heartfelt personal testimony.

As the traditional subject evaporated, the very conception of past and present began to blur. In 1945, reviewing Broch's *Virgil,* Hannah Arendt revealed a Berliner's impatience with the mind-set that "puts before us the alternative between going ahead and going backward, an alternative which appears so devoid of sense precisely because it still presupposes an unbroken chain of continuity." For writers like Arendt, history was a fraud, not merely in the phony objectivity of its method (historians were no more pleased with her cavalier use of data), but in its assumption that events moved in linear sequence. Arendt often cited William Faulkner's statement that the past was not over, it was not even past. She believed with her mentor Walter Benjamin that the past was a vast wasteland populated by victims still calling for redemption. The past had to be lived through, its issues fully confronted and finally settled before one could start living in some hypothetical present.

To render the new sense of self and time, the writers needed a new style. Various literary pronouncements were offered. Some were specifically grammatical, such as Mehring's analysis of Proust's "subjunctive of doubt" or Broch's assertion that the sentence suspends time by placing "subject and object in a relationship of simultaneity"—yet another reduction of the subject's autonomy, as well as a statement that was implicitly dialectical. While not many others investigated the conventions of grammar, the émigré writers as a whole were irritated with discrete literary forms.

The obvious exponent of such a cavalier attitude toward prose styles was the traditional man of letters. He could write about anything, leaping between forms, although his favored one was the essay. Yet the essayistic style developed by émigré writers is qualitatively different, both in the variety of forms they employed and in the urgency of their procedure. Above all, in keeping with the skeptical tone, this style demanded a resolute questioning of everything—the discipline, the form, the boundary, the sequence, the observers themselves.

At a particularly dramatic point in *Joseph in Egypt,* Thomas Mann apologizes for his discursive speculations: "When does a commentator set himself up in competition with his text?" The irony is deliberate. Mann presumes that literature today is possible only when the writer competes with his material and its reflection in himself. The result is fiction that resembles the essay, the literary manifestation of what Robert Musil called "decisive thought" rising above the lunacy of modern life and, for writers like Mann, helping to impose order on the chaos of emigration. For, finally, history and politics constitute the text that émigré writers must contend with. What they achieve with words is no simple aesthetic transcendence; theirs is not a French structuralist's linguistic legerdemain. Rather, with Teutonic solemnity, they aim for an intellectual advance that will enable them to organize data in a way that reflects the simultaneous changes in politics and the psyche. This approach keeps them in touch with the historical moment; it allows a style as manifold and diffuse as modern life while granting, virtually in its procedure alone, a control that almost no person alive could achieve, much less a deracinated writer in competition with his text.

Political events had undercut the old literary certainties and rendered literary decorum almost obscene. Regarding the traditional boundaries of genre as unsupportable, Arendt praised Broch for diminishing the status of the "made-up" in his fiction. Broch had no patience with *l'art pour l'art,* although his own seductive rhythms have been viewed as self-indulgent.

The Anglo-American academy, however, decreed that literary manners called for a faithfulness to genre and a modesty of tone, not the essayistic, heavily didactic style of émigré literature. In America the essayistic fiction of Musil and Broch went without readers, and Thomas Mann's most discursive and innovative work of fiction, *Doctor Faustus,* elicited an equivocal response. . . . These writers' audiences and imitators would not be found for years, and then only in Europe.

Some of their émigré interpreters fared better in this country. Perhaps because they addressed American issues, the works of writers like Arendt and Adorno ultimately succeeded in becoming models of academic prose. Yet one might say that they did so by standing the form of essayistic fiction—hybrid to begin with—on its head. Even as they assimilated the fictional sensibilities of writers like Kafka and Broch, Arendt and Adorno employed devices confounding enough in the fiction they admired—elliptical speculation, a surreal fragmentation of focus—in discursive essays that they prepared for stolid scholarly journals. Often, as a flickering code signaling to the initiated, these highly abstruse thinkers leavened their work with the familiar irreverence of the émigré skeptic.

In Arendt's work, an anecdote can yield a perception that will, almost magically, expand into an elaborate diagnosis that skips over disciplinary borders, and makes no apologies to the frontier guards she declines to recognize. Adorno—like Arendt, so confirmed in his manner that he approached self-caricature—continued to punctuate detailed, metaphysical arguments with whimsical conceits, as if a droning pedant were to leap an octave and imitate a wise-cracking adolescent. Thus, in the midst of a philosophical attack on George Lukács, Adorno suddenly compared the Hungarian's most recent work to an ice cream sundae shimmering in a state between thaw and refreeze.

On a less abstruse level, émigré writers were pitiless in examining all kinds of social and political rhetoric. One could forgive Bruno Bettelheim many sins for the power with which he demolished certain clichés: from the description of Helen Keller's nurse as a "miracle-worker" although no "miracle" was possible for Keller (one of the happiest instances of a refugee squeezing all the untruth out of an American idiom), to his attack on a movie in which a Nazi guard gives a gun to a concentration camp inmate and orders him to shoot his friend (as Bettelheim notes, any sane inmate would have turned the gun on his captor). Adorno was similarly horrified when thoughtless artists used the Holocaust as an occasion for slapstick. He condemned Charlie Chaplin's *The Great Dictator* for presenting the unlikely situation of a Jewish girl satirizing the Nazi authorities, when in reality such behavior would have ensured her death. At their best, Brecht and Arendt are full of such moments. These writers can sweep away a mess of idiocies with the broom of good sense. In the presence of the émigrés' common wisdom, arguments about methodology become insignificant.

A generation of young American academics has acquired the Adorno method and now produces essays that read like botched translations from the German. Hannah Arendt's ferreting out of the moral and political origins of social commonplaces preceded many similar investigations by cultural critics like Susan Sontag and Renata Adler, while political scientists have benefited from her distinctive vocabulary. Today, German novelists like Günter Grass acknowledge Döblin and Thomas Mann as their literary ancestors.

Although the writers who suffered through years in Hollywood did not share the spectacular successes of émigré directors, in retrospect it is clear how much the two groups had in common. Above all, there is that icy, rigorous tone. Outside perhaps of Ophuls, none of the great émigré directors offered the invigorating consolations associated with the most admired American ones. And even Ophuls's spectacles, like those of Sirk or Lang, Wilder or Preminger, cast a shadow over the reality they depict by embedding it in doubt, despair, and the fatal passage of time. In the use of aesthetic means to explode conventional film values and epistemologies can be found mirror images of the writers' procedure. *"Er gibt den Ton an"*: was it Brecht who set the tone? Or the directors? Or Musil or Broch or the later, liberated Thomas Mann? No matter. The characteristic tone of emigration distinguished them all. Only on the page, however, could it be expressed so directly, without charm or kitsch, and without the involvement of American performers or settings to temper its foreignness. (pp. 292-97)

> *Anthony Heilbut, "'Er Gibt den Ton An',"* in his Exiled in Paradise: German Refugee Artists and Intellectuals in America, from the 1930s to the Present, *The Viking Press, 1983, pp. 261-97.*

JOHN WILLET

[*Willet is an English drama and art critic, biographer, dramatist, and translator. In the following excerpt, he discusses German writers exiled in England. Translations in brackets are by Gerhard Hirschfeld.*]

In England, unlike France or Russia or America, there was never a coherent nucleus of German literature in exile, just individual exiled writers who remained more or less displaced. This was partly because the exiled publishing houses—Querido, Bermann-Fischer, Carrefour and the rest—were all based elsewhere apart from Wieland Herzfelde's Malik-Verlag, which was only technically registered in London, c/o Margaret Mynatt

and the foreign book department of Selfridge's store. Nor did we house any of the major anti-Nazi magazines, such as *Mass und Wert, Internationale Literatur, Das Wort, Die Sammlung, Die Neue Weltbühne* and other more or less miraculous survivals. After 1933 the *Schutzverband deutscher Schriftsteller* had set itself up in Paris and the library of exiled publications which it gathered there fell, like Paris itself, into the hands of the Nazis in 1940. There was the international PEN whose secretary, Herman Ould, was certainly sympathetic to the German writers (and himself translated Toller's plays); and an anti-Nazi German section of that body was founded by Ernst Toller, Rudolf Olden and Herrmann-Neisse. There were some active and efficient émigré booksellers, such as Hans Preiss, near the British Museum, Joseph Suschitzky, formerly at Swiss Cottage, and Dr. Fritz Homeyer and Miss Eva Dworetsky in the foreign department of J. and E. Bumpus (who no longer exist). Martin Schor at the London Library saw to that institution's exceptionally good holding of modern German books. But generally the exiled writers were left without either a local outlet or a spiritual home. There was the *Freier Deutscher Kulturbund,* presided over by, among others, Oskar Kokoschka but largely run by the Communists; there was the rival *Gruppè unabhängiger Autoren* which Kurt Hiller set up, but which remained relatively obscure. Cafés, let alone literary cafés, were virtually unknown—thus Jakob Hegner, writing wistfully to America from London in 1940: "In der neuen Welt wird es wieder eine alte Mampe-Stube geben. Hier gab es und gibt es nichts dergleichen—wenigstens nicht für unsereinen." ["There will be another old *Mampe-stube* in the New World. There is not and never has been anything of that sort here—at least not for the likes of us."] Only Elias Canetti, bulging briefcase under his arm, could somehow turn the ordinary English teashop into such.

The writers were thrown back on themselves, and not all of them were happy there. They were lost among the disorderly subtleties of the language—the "feuchtklimatische, wolkengefächelte englische Sprache," ("damp-aired, cloud-caressed English language"), as the Prague German poet Rudolf Fuchs called it in his late *Gedichte aus London*—they missed what Hermann-Neisse, in another posthumous volume, termed "Die Kleinigkeiten, die nicht viel bedeuten", ("The little things that do not count for much"), like large porcelain stoves or civilised drinking hours; they were dumbfounded by our political complacency. Once again, from Herrmann-Neisse's unfinished cycle "Zwischenzeit."

> Da klang, was wir erzählten, übertrieben,
> man lauschte zweifelnd, wenn auch wohlgesinnt:
> man war noch immer Gentleman geblieben,
> als welcher jede letzte Schlacht gewinnt.
>
> [What we told them sounded exaggerated,
> Well-meaning as they were, they listened sceptically:
> They were, after all, still the *gentleman*
> Who always wins the last battle.]

Much the same depression seized even so successful a writer as Stefan Zweig, who had had a second home in London since well before the fall of Austria and whose sales in English translation were comparable with those of Feuchtwanger and Thomas Mann. He too looked backwards to more congenial times and forward to nothing much but his own death. And indeed Fuchs and Herrmann-Neisse died in England in the early 1940s, aged respectively fifty-two and fifty-five, while Zweig killed himself, aged sixty, after moving on to Brazil in mid-1940. "London ist jetzt für mich furchtbar geworden," he told Hermann Kesten on the eve of the war, seit sich die ganze Emigration hierher wendet und zwar ihre letzte und ich darf wohl sagen, schlechteste Welle—alle jene, die nicht von Deutschland fortwollten, alle Schriftsteller, die nie wirklich Schriftsteller waren. Ausser Körmendi [a Hungarian novelist], Fülop-Miller [author of *Geist und Gesicht des Bolschewismus*], Robert Neumann, Zarek und Friedenthal machen fast alle im billigen Radikalismus und agitieren gegeneinander. Wie bei jedem Zersetzungsprozes bilden sich in der Emigration notwendigerweise giftige und stinkige Gase. . . .

["London has become unbearable for me . . . since the whole of the emigration descended on it—the last, and I dare say worst wave what's more: all those who did not want to leave Germany, all the writers who were never real writers. Apart from Körmendi (a Hungarian novelist), Fülop-Miller (author of *The Mind and Face of Bolshevism*), Robert Neumann, Zarek and Friedenthal, they are almost all cheap radicals agitating against each other. Poisonous and foul gases are as natural a part of the emigration as of any other process of decay. . . ."]

Of this handful of writers of whom Zweig approved, Robert Neumann was exceptional in that he learnt to write in English—an English of a somewhat idiosyncratic sort, but none the less readable for that—and also became an adviser to a London publishing house: Hutchinson's. Richard Friedenthal too (who was later Zweig's literary executor) had a very perceptive understanding of his insular hosts, about whom he wrote both amusingly and accurately—and without any kind of self-pity—in his postwar novel *Die Welt in der Nusschale*, the nutshell in this case being the internment camp on the Isle of Man to which so many assorted members of the emigration were sent in 1940. Indeed Friedenthal, an upright and apparently nonpolitical Prussian who emigrated of his own free choice, in due course settled in London even though his great post-war successes—the Goethe and Luther biographies—were primarily with German publishers. Finally, unmentioned in Zweig's list and some ten years younger than these two writers, Elias Canetti too was . . . genuinely at home in England, where his massive and complex prewar Viennese novel *Die Blendung* (*Auto-da-fé*) had a great critical success in 1946 in Dame Veronica Wedgwood's translation. Alone among the writers of the emigration he had a perceptible influence on our own literature, since it was largely he who persuaded Iris Murdoch to publish her first novel *Under the Net*. Its successor *The Flight from the Enchanter* is dedicated to him.

Others came and went without leaving much mark on their surroundings: Kurt Hiller, Karl Otten, Hans Rehfisch, Felix Braun, Jan Petersen from the Communist underground within Germany. Brecht made two brief visits in 1934 and 1936, during the second of which he established some slight contact with our own anti-Nazi writers (inviting Auden, for instance, to come and see him in Denmark). To these trips we owe a handful of poems of which "Der Kalendonische Markt" with its echoes of Kipling is the most attractive and "Die Hölle der Enttäuscher" ("The Hell of the Disenchanters") the most intriguing: was it the Londoners or the emigrants themselves who "had crumbled under threats"? and could be seen to "show one another their letters of credit / And point at the many stamps and signatures / Using their thumb to cover the places / Where the year had been scratched out." We also have Hanns Eisler's recollection of his visit with Brecht to Stefan Zweig's comfortable apartment, where the two men gave their host a personal rendition of their new song "Von der belebenden Wirkung des Geldes" ("On the Stimulating Impact of Cash"),

ill-manneredly emphasising its relevance to their immediate surroundings in St John's Wood. This not uncharacteristic bit of "Schärfe" or (by English standards) wanton aggressiveness may help to explain the older writer's growing distaste for "Radikalismus."

Radical writers, however, have the enormous advantage in such circumstances—a psychological as well as a literary advantage—of always looking forward. They are too busy with the future, and with the meaning of what is going on around them, to be able to lament a past which their readers may see as hopelessly foreign or remote. And so the outstanding émigré author for us was, until his sad death in 1983, a man who shared much of Brecht's background and political interests, even though he had turned against the Communist Party soon after coming here and now anathema to the extreme left. This was of course Arthur Koestler, the former Berlin journalist and collaborator of Willi Münzenberg in Paris who, with the publication of *Darkness at Noon* in December 1940, became a major English novelist. Koestler's great strength was that he had not merely been close to, or had himself experienced, the desperately extreme situations of which he wrote, but was able to bring them home to English readers. He wrote without overstatement; he had a nice sense of irony and a good eye for the comic or curious detail; his most minor characters were often vividly and understandingly sketched. Moreover he knew how to construct a story; the different episodes, flashbacks and reflections were well balanced and economically set down. And he thought for himself, not along a party line. All these are qualities which would anyway carry over into a translation, but on top of that he was remarkably lucky in the translator of that first novel, the sculptor Daphne Hardy, for her English had just the right unobtrusive momentum, and from then on his works all appeared as original English books.

Koestler's clarity, like his all-consuming curiosity, sprang from his journalistic training; the emigration also brought England other central-European journalists of whom the finest was probably Rudolf Olden, who was drowned when the ship carrying him to America went down in 1940. Many of these people worked (as did Friedenthal and Hans Flesch, an eminent radio producer, some of whose novels appeared under the name "Vincent Brun") for the wartime BBC or for the officially-backed weekly *Die Zeitung*, among them being Peter de Mendelssohn, his wife Hilde Spiel and Sebastian Haffner who was to hold a leading position on *The Observer* for some years after the war. Three had been outstanding theatre critics in glittering, republican Berlin: Alfred Kerr, Lutz Weltmann and Monty Jacobs. Another, Frank Warschauer, had been an early friend of Brecht's. Heinrich Fraenkel ran the chess column in the *New Statesman*. But the only one to make a lasting impression on the face of British journalism was the former editor of the *Münchner Illustrierte*, Stefan Lorant, whose work for the Hulton Press papers *Picture Post* and *Lilliput* set a new standard for photo-journalism and the intelligent juxtaposition of pictures with text. It was these two journals that featured the drawings of Erich Kästner's chief illustrator, Walter Trier, and introduced the British magazine public to the work of John Heartfield who a few years earlier had been laying out the exiled *Arbeiter-Illustrierte-Zeitung* for Willi Münzenberg. As for book production proper, it remained as yet virtually untouched by the German influence. Like the whole business of publishing it would only seriously begin to reflect the impact of the emigration once the emigration itself was at an end. (pp. 198-202)

John Willett, *"The Emigration and the Arts," in* Exile in Great Britain: Refugees from Hitler's Germany, *edited by Gerhard Hirschfeld, Berg Publishers, 1984, pp. 195-217.*

HENRY PACHTER

[*Pachter is a German-born American historian, nonfiction writer, and critic. In the following excerpt, he describes his experiences as an exiled writer and the state of German refugee literary circles in the United States and Europe.*]

Being an exile is not a matter of needing a passport; it is a state of mind. I discovered this but gradually. In the beginning I did not experience exile as a universal mode of existence. I still attributed my stance entirely to the specific and, so it seemed, transitory phenomenon of Hitler. We all felt that Hitler was something extra-ordinary, irregular, unforeseeable and, if rightly considered, impossible. According to the German philosophy which still was most commonly accepted and to which the Marxists also paid their tribute, this unthinkable phenomenon had no right to, and therefore did not, exist. Not really. Ernst Cassirer, the philosopher who was to be my neighbor in New York, once expressed it in a classical way which I repeat every year for my undergraduates' edification: "You know, Mr. Pachter, this Hitler is an error (Irrtum) of History; he does not belong in German history at all. And therefore he will perish." This is what all decent people felt at the time. But History cared not for human decency—or German philosophy for that matter.

While I still felt that History owed us a rectification of her mistakes—a faith on which hinged our confidence in the eventual triumph of anti-Fascism—yet I delivered my message that Hitler would last five years and that the condition of our rebirth was recognition of our defeat. They almost lynched me. Bertolt Brecht said: "How can you maintain that we suffered a defeat when we did not even fight?" He was capable of such sophistries on behalf of the Party, and I never found out whether he believed them or whether he really was an unpolitical person. But other comrades' answers were no better; all the has-beens expressed the fervent belief that nothing had happened to debunk their prophets. None of the political groups that met in somber backrooms of a brasserie or bistro to deliberate the fate of the world knew its own fate yet. Each was trying to prove to the others that its special brand of Marxism should have been followed and that others should not have betrayed the cause. There is nothing as inconsequential as émigré *querelles,* and in the midst of all that activity I soon felt more isolated than I had been in Nazi Berlin. I formed an alliance with Arkadj Gurland, who also had managed to be alienated from all groups and who was prepared to start thinking anew—that is if he was not reading whodunits, which he considered an appropriate occupation for us.

Many of us, indeed, fell silent. The myth that exile produces Dantes, Marxes, Bartoks and Avicennas certainly is not justified in the mass. More often exile destroys talent, or it means the loss of the environment that nourished the talent morally, socially and physically. Even the musicians, whose idiom one might suppose is both personal and international, were surprised to find out how little their values were appreciated in a culture next door. Only the few who already had world-famous names were able to carry on—living on reduced royalties, but not reduced to starting from scratch; yet, even in this category we have Thomas Mann's comically pathetic complaint that he

had to live in a hotel room! Lucky also were those young enough to claim that their studies had been interrupted: benevolent committees provided the means for them to complete their education, and some endured hunger for the opportunity of a new start in intellectual life. But for most of us a new country meant more than a new language. Few found jobs in their field, and most not even jobs that might be termed tolerable. No one had a working permit, and the kind of work one could do illegally was poorly paid, never steady, and often demeaning. The more pleasant opportunities were "nègre" ("ghosting"), i.e. a dentist, lawyer, engineering consultant, research chemist etc. did the job of a Frenchman who lent his name and took most of the pay. Many of the jobs I had were fraudulent, ridiculous or repulsive. Having been taught by my puritanical father that work ennobles, I now learned that work can be more degrading than anything else. People who once had taken money for granted shared my feelings. One day Rudolf Hilferding, former Finance Minister and author of *Das Finanzkapital,* asked me with a sigh: "Did you ever have to work for a living?"

Each of us solved this problem in his own way, and not all did so honorably. Many had to rely on their wives, who could always find maids' jobs; but over this, many marriages broke. Others made an art of persuading backers and committees that we had a claim on their respect and money: even those of us who had not produced a line yet represented that thin veneer of culture which stood between Western civilization and the new barbarians. Our physical and moral survival depended on this high-class form of extortion, and the piratical attitude we developed toward moneyed institutions prepared us for the games we later had to play with American foundations. We may even have helped to develop the art of thinking up research projects and writing outlines which has now become the mark of the academic operator in the Western world. (I suspect this because the percentage of German problems in American research, notably in the 'forties and 'fifties, far exceeded our share in the academic population.) While one could not beat the Nazis one could still analyze them—hoping in one act to keep the question of the century before the public eye and to justify one's existence.

It is no exaggeration to say that at that time we needed the Nazis as our *raison d'être.* They had become our obsession. Their omnipotence could not be illustrated more poignantly than by the way Nazism or Fascism affected our professional careers. Erich Fromm, a psychologist, wrote *Escape from Freedom;* Theodor Adorno, who had sparked the modern interest in Kierkegaard and was interested in the sociology of music, instead studied *The Authoritarian Personality*; Hannah Arendt, a gifted philosopher with little talent for politics, gave us the book on the origins of totalitarianism; Ernst Kris, Freud's co-editor of *Imago,* studied Nazi propaganda; Ernst Cassirer, who detested the entire area of politics and statecraft, nevertheless had to write *The Myth of the State.* Remote fields like philology were raked over in efforts to discover strands of Nazi ideology in early German literature or in the structure of the German language. Having published an analysis of Nazi grammar, I was deeply touched when after the war I discovered that two scholars inside Germany had collected evidence of totalitarian corruption of the German language—a handsome example of parallel ideas among internal and external exiles. (How even the purest of sciences had been affected became apparent only much later when it was revealed that Einstein, Meitner, Bohr, Bethe and other pacifists had contributed to the development of the atomic bomb.)

Unfortunately, the Nazis were not alone in debasing the German language. We the pure ones, the bearers and preservers of German culture, became guilty of something worse: our language froze at the point of emigration, or it even became poorer for want of a dialogue with the people who create and develop speech every day. The sweet preciousness of the past which some of the famous among us cultivated was no substitute for living communion. By observing my Russian and Italian friends I had seen what happens to people who are reduced to in-breeding as émigrés. (The Russian newspaper in Paris even refused to use the simplified spelling the Bolsheviks had introduced.) Were we similarly dated? We were writing about ghosts, writing for ghosts, and gradually becoming ghosts.

It was even worse when one decided to abandon German. Working in a language which is not the language of one's dreams is to miss many over- and undertones, ambiguities and poetic notions, the spontaneousness and even the silences. Dimensions of thought and feeling must be replaced by a technique of significations, using spoken words in prefabricated, studied sequences which threaten to impoverish that which they ought to enrich. Few succeeded in becoming creative writers in their second language, though they learned to express their ideas precisely in a technical Esperanto.

Observation: uneducated people quickly learn to make small talk in canned phrases. Intellectuals learn slowly and tend to speak "translatese," painfully aware that it is one flight below the level they would like to inhabit intellectually.

The exile literature of those days is deeply steeped in the experience of defeat, of emigration, of the breakdown of hope. Alfred Döblin's *Babylonische Wanderung*, Thomas Mann's *Joseph*, Anna Segher's *Seventh Cross*, Ernest Glaeser's *Last Civilian*, Erich Maria Remarque's *Three Comrades* (as well as his later *Arch of Triumph* and Franz Werfel's *Jacobowsky and the Colonel*) offer glimpses of the new outlook. Thomas Mann probably was unaffected in his Olympian serenity; he continued to write for an imaginary cosmopolitan audience. Anna Seghers on her part knew others for whom she wrote: the comrades of the Communist International. But Döblin told me that he did not know his audience any longer and was afraid his art might suffer from it; he then made a deliberate effort to find an audience: he wrote a Rosa Luxemburg trilogy. Brecht, likewise, gave me a long, angry and didactic speech on the necessity for the writer to be in good standing with the Party. "Stalin?" he exclaimed contemptuously in answer to my objection; "fifty years from now the communists will have forgotten who Stalin was. But I want them to read and produce Brecht; therefore I must not alienate myself from the Party now."

It was, of course, not a question of having a publisher (which Brecht ironically called "the inner question") but of knowing that one was writing for a culture with a future; that no matter how gloomy its present content, one's play or novel would hold out hope for those to whom it addressed itself. Writers who had lost this faith, or no longer believed that their audience shared their faith, foundered and their style deteriorated. Some of the older writers who no longer knew which values they defended fell silent. Some younger ones who had given promises were stopped in their tracks for want of an audience or a sympathetic environment. The only German writer to achieve world stature in exile was Hermann Broch; most of those who had gained it before failed to sustain their excellence. But we shall never know how many good writers were broken by the shattering experience of loneliness. No unpublished master-

works emerged from secret drawers after the fall of the Third Reich. Joseph Roth died of drinking absinthe. Ernst Glaeser broke down and returned to Nazi Germany (where he became a hack, and after the war drank himself to death). In a moving letter to Walter Hasenclever, Kurt Tucholsky relates how someone asked Nitti, whose cabinet Mussolini overthrew: "What are you doing in Paris?" He answered: "I am waiting." Tucholsky comments: "I would not want to be like him." Both Tucholsky and Hasenclever took their lives. The same sense of futility caused the suicides of Stefan Zweig, Walter Benjamin, Klaus Mann, Ernst Weiss and Ernst Toller.

Many who tried to avoid failure met regularly in the German Exile Writers' Club and assured each other that German culture was where they were and that Hitler could not suppress German literature. Other writers, we heard, had little circles in Prague, at the Cote d'Azur, in London, in New York and even in Hollywood—though it also was reported that in this latter place they were unhappy or ineffective and received stipends rather than remuneration for services rendered. In Paris, at least, the indignities of our miserable life were compensated by the knowledge that our exile had significance. The closeness of refugee circles might give us a rather dim view of our leaders' human qualities; but as carriers of the great European heritage we saw ourselves, ten feet tall, bestriding the theatre of history.

This sense of our mission received an enormous boost when the Communist International held its Seventh World Congress in 1934. After a long period of sterility, Stalin—for his own reasons, of course—returned to the humanistic and democratic wellsprings of Marxism. As he sought a rapprochement with the Western powers, he launched the Popular Front slogan and issued the "Trojan Horse" directive: his propagandists engaged in a vast campaign of cultural mobilization, organized writers' congresses against Fascism, created magazines and promoted fellow-traveling enterprises. Reputable publishing houses which previously had been denounced as purveyors of mass deception now were infiltrated as vehicles of mass enlightenment; bourgeois culture, which so far had been an object for derision, now became the heritage which the proletariat was to bring to new flowering. The refugee writers, more dependent and more malleable, eagerly seized the opportunities this well-heeled conspiracy opened to them and, knowingly or unknowingly, provided the core of the alliance whose outer fringes encompassed Aldous Huxley and Julien Benda. In these circles it was easy to meet André Gide, Aragon, Malraux, Nizan, Georges Friedman and others. Though Gide was soon to voice his disappointment with the Soviet Union, it is fair to say that staying close to the Communist Party did no harm to some lesser literary reputations at that time.

The German writers, indoctrinated and disciplined by our club, constituted a sort of cadre for this campaign. Our meetings were graced by appearances of Heinrich Mann, Arthur Koestler, Erich Reger and Alfred Döblin; but our discussions were dominated by the commissars and conducted in the style of the Moscow Writers' Club. Manes Sperber—then an editor of Gallimard publishers and now an important figure in Paris literary circles—bravely tried to stem the tide of party literature by emphasizing that art must speak to the deeper emotions too; but Alfred Kantorowicz remained plagued by the knowledge that his mediocrity condemned him to remain a partisan writer and a liar. After the war he acted as East Germany's literary pope for a while, but eventually he had to seek asylum in the West.

Another staunch defender of the party line was then Arthur Koestler. Later he boasted that he had an anti-Soviet play hidden in his desk; but at that time his job and his fame depended on the party, and the only time we met we clashed rather vehemently. Despite his ''Spanish Testament,'' which at the time was a deeply moving document, I still think that he is no more than an intelligent reporter. After he broke with the Communists, he found a comfortable niche in the liberal establishment and retired to his private ivory tower. But his later writings betray an acute awareness of the problem with which I am concerned here: what it means to be a refugee cannot be described in the simple terms of finding a job and adjusting to foreign customs. It is a way of being, constantly lingering between arrival and departure. No one has told it better than Koestler. (pp. 16-22)

Henry Pachter, ''On Being an Exile: An Old-Timer's Personal and Political Memoir,'' in The Legacy of the German Refugee Intellectuals, *edited by Robert Boyers, Schocken Books, 1972, pp. 12-51.*

THOMAS MANN

[*A German man of letters, Mann singlehandedly raised the German novel to an international stature it had not enjoyed since the time of the Romantics. Like his contemporaries James Joyce and Marcel Proust, Mann keenly reflected the intellectual currents of his age, particularly the belief that European realism was no longer an adequate means of expression in a sophisticated and complex century. Yet while Joyce and Proust expressed this predicament through the form of their writing, Mann maintained the outward convention of realistic fiction, emphasizing an ironic vision of life and a deep, often humorous, sympathy for humanity. In the following lecture, first delivered at the Writers' Congress held at the University of California in 1943, Mann articulates the conflict between the German exile writer's love of his native country and abhorrence of the atrocities of the Nazi state.*]

It was a splendid and generous decision on the part of the heads of this Congress that, in the course of the discussions of the problems of the writer in wartime, the literary exiles should also have their say and should be invited to express their opinions concerning the relation of the emigrant intellectuals to their own country in this war and, looking into the future, after this war. But I do not know whether to be pleased that this task has been assigned to me; these are painful and complicated matters about which I am to write—experiences which one can scarcely communicate in words to you who, in these times, live with your own people, in complete harmony with them, in unshakable faith in their cause, and are permitted to fight enthusiastically for that cause. This perfectly natural good fortune is denied us; not the enthusiasm, only the battle is ours. We also battle; these times permit no one to retreat to an ivory tower, to an existence of a peaceful cult of beauty. But it is our destiny to carry on this battle against our own land and its cause of whose corruptness we are convinced; against the land whose speech is the spiritual material in which we work, against the land in whose culture we are rooted, whose tradition we administer, and whose landscape and atmosphere should be our natural shelter.

You will say to me: ''We are all fighting for the same cause, the cause of humanity. There is no distinction between you and us.'' Certainly, but it is your good fortune to be able to identify yourselves more or less with the cause of your people, of your fighting forces, of your government, and when you see the emblem of American sovereignty, the Stars and Stripes,

you are perhaps not naïvely patriotic enough that your heart beats with pride in your throat and that you break into loud hurrahs. You are critical people and you know that these colors must conceal many human weaknesses and inadequacies and perhaps even corruption and yet you look upon this emblem with a feeling of home, with sympathy and confidence, with calm pride and heartfelt hopes, while we ————. You can scarcely conceive the feelings with which we look upon the present national emblem of Germany, the swastika. We do not look upon it, we look away. We would rather look at the ground or at the sky, for the sight of the symbol under which our people are fighting for their existence, or rather delude themselves that they are fighting for that existence, makes us physically ill. I speak as a German; the Italians may have similar feelings at the sight of their national fasces. You do not know how horribly strange, how detestable, how shocking it is for us to see the swastika-ornamented entrance to a German consulate or embassy. Here I have this experience only in the cinema; but when I lived in Zürich I often came into the neighborhood of the house of the German representative with the ominous flag upon it, and I confess that I always made a wide detour as one would about a den of iniquity, an outpost of murderous barbarism, extending into the realm of a friendly civilization under whose protection I lived.

German—a great name, a word which carries with it hundreds of homely and respected, pleasant and proud associations. And now, this word, a name of terror and of deadly wilderness, into which even our dreams do not dare to transport us. Whenever I read that some unhappy person has been ''taken to Germany,'' as were recently the party leaders from Milan who had signed the anti-Fascist manifesto, or as was Romain Rolland, who is said to be in a German concentration camp, cold shudders run up and down my back. To be ''taken to Germany'' is the worst. To be sure, Mussolini has also been taken to Germany but I doubt whether even he is happy under Hitler's protection.

What an abnormal, morbid condition, abnormal and morbid for anyone, but especially for the writer, the bearer of a spiritual tradition, when his own country becomes the most hostile, the most sinister foreign land! And now I wish to think not only

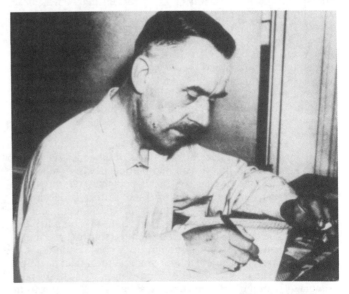

Thomas Mann writing in his diary in 1939. Princeton University Library. Caroline Newton Collection of Thomas Mann.

of us out here in exile, I finally wish to remember also those people who are still there, the German masses, and to think of the cruel compulsion which destiny has forced upon the German spirit. Believe me, for many there the fatherland has become as strange as it has for us; an "inner emigration" of millions is there awaiting the end just as we. They await the end, that is the end of the war, and there can be only one end. The people in Germany, in spite of their strangled isolation, are well aware of it, and yet they long for it, in spite of their natural patriotism, in spite of their national conscience. The ever-present propaganda has deeply impressed upon their consciousness the pretended permanently destructive results of a German defeat, so that in one part of their being they cannot avoid fearing that defeat more than anything else in the world. And yet there is one thing which many of them fear more than a German defeat, that is a German victory; some only occasionally, at moments which they themselves regard as criminal, but others with complete clarity and permanently although with pangs of conscience. Imagine that you were forced with all your wishes and hopes to oppose an American victory as a great misfortune for the entire world; if you can imagine that you can place yourself in the position of these people. This attitude has become the destiny of uncounted Germans and it is my deep conviction that this destiny is particularly and unimaginably tragic. I know that other nations have been put into the position of wishing for the defeat of their government for their own sake and for the sake of the general future. But I must insist that in view of the all-too-great credulousness and innate loyalty of the German character the dilemma in this case is especially acute, and I cannot resist a feeling of deepest resentment against those who have forced the German love of country into such a position.

These people have been deluded and seduced into crimes that cry to high heaven. They have begun to atone for them and they will atone even more severely; it cannot be otherwise; common morality or, if you wish, divine justice demands it. But we out here, who saw disaster coming, we, who, ahead of our compatriots intoxicated by a fraudulent revolution, ahead of all the rest of the world, were convinced that the Nazi rule could never bring anything except war, destruction and catastrophe, we see no great difference between that which these scoundrels have done to us and what they have done to our people at home. We hate the destroyers and we long for the day which rids the world of them. But with very few exceptions we are far from being victims of a wretched emigrant hatred against our own land and we do not desire the destruction of our people. We cannot completely deny their responsibility, for somehow man is responsible for his being and doing; but misfortune is a milder and more understanding word than guilt and we feel that it is more appropriate to speak of misfortune and error than of crime.

To my own surprise I became conscious of the indestructibility of the bands which link a man and particularly an intellectual to his home, to the mother soil of his personal culture, when, soon after the outbreak of the war the British Broadcasting Corporation gave me an opportunity to speak to my fellow countrymen with my own voice from time to time. It is no easy fate to be completely severed from the spiritual and moral life of the nation into which one has been born. Emigration in our days has assumed a much more radical form than in earlier times. The exile of Victor Hugo, for example, was child's play compared with ours. To be sure, he sat as an outcast far from Paris on his island in the ocean, but the spiritual link between him and France was never broken. What he wrote was printed

in the French press; his books could be bought and read at home. Today exile is a total exile, just as war, politics, world, and life have become total. We are not only physically far from our country but we have been radically expelled from its life both in the purpose and, at least for the present, in the effects of our exile. Our books are outlawed, just as we ourselves are; they exist only in translations, in fact, since the conquest of the European continent by the enemy, they exist only in English. We can count ourselves fortunate that it is still so, that that which we produce exists at all, for every writer will feel with us what it means to exist only as a literary shadow, to live only a translated and denatured life. The English broadcast gave me the only opportunity in these years to break the stupid ban, to exert a direct and original effect in German speech rhythm behind the backs of the dictators; and I have used this opportunity with the greatest satisfaction and have tried once a month to inform those people over there of their situation, to speak to them for their own good and to appeal to their consciences as impressively as possible.

This unfortunately weak and uncertain contact with the people at home I owe to the war; and it is true that without the war those of us who sought refuge in strange lands would have lost all but the most nebulous feeling for our land. Through the war, however, it has again come into more attainable proximity and we now live in hopes of an end of this estrangement. Did we therefore wish for this war? I know that this prejudice existed against us, that we were looked upon as warmongers in a time when the world was still trying to win peace by flattery from the Fascist dictators. We were given to understand that the world could not go to war "pour vos beaux yeux," and I know that even today there still lurks a certain resentment in the regard of many for us, born of the feeling that people who wished the war are in some manner responsible for it. But it is not true that we wished the war. We only knew that it would come without fail if the march of Fascism were not interrupted, and we knew it at a time when that was not only possible but easy. We knew that appeasement was the surest means of bringing about the war. Indeed we have suffered from the unwillingness of the world to grasp the fact that domestic and foreign policies are one and the same, and that the sort of policies which the Nazis carried on in their own land were already war even though at the time in domestic form. It required no prophetic gift to see that, one needed only to be a German.

Now that the war is here we support it with all our hearts and stand firmly on the side of the nations who, for the honor of humanity, had to undertake the difficult and costly struggle. Their final victory is our most urgent prayer, not because we expect revenge against the land which exiled us, but because the defeat of Nazi Germany is the only means of bringing back our country into the community of civilized nations, of taking from the name Germany the horror which now clings to it and of returning to us the spiritual fatherland.

It is an entirely different question whether we intend to take up again our former life in our fatherland after its liberation, no matter how that liberation may occur. This question can only be answered individually, and the answers would vary according to personal circumstances. If I ask myself I must say: No. The idea of returning to Germany, to be reinstated into my property, and to regard these ten years, or how many they may be, as a mere interlude, this thought is far from me and appears to me quite impossible. It is now too late for me, and I say to myself that at my age it is of no consequence in what place one completes the life's work which, on the whole, is already established and which in a certain sense is already history. I am now on the point of becoming an American citizen just as my grandchildren who were born here and are growing up here, and my attachment to this country has already progressed so far that it would be contrary to my sense of gratitude to part from it again. To spend a few months every year in Switzerland where I lived five memorable years would be sufficient for my character as a European. As for Germany, all my wishes would be fulfilled if it were again spiritually open to me and if my work, so closely linked to the German language, again had access there.

Many emigrants may have a similar view with regard to a return home. Many have taken root in the lands of their refuge, have built up a new life and will not wish to start over again. Others perhaps, especially younger ones, await nothing more longingly than the historic moment when the bells will call them back to their home. With the first airplane, with the first ship, with the first train, they will hasten home, anxious to serve as cultural or political leaders in the new Germany. Equipped with the experiences which they have collected in the years of their cosmopolitan life and which have broadened their horizons, they can indeed be very useful to their country; for what Germany needs most is fresh air from the outside, knowledge and understanding of a world in which it has long been alone.

But those who renounce the return home will also have their responsibility and their mission for Germany, for Europe, and for the world. In any case it is an advantage today and a historically appropriate position to be a citizen of two worlds. The world wishes to become unified. Humanity faces the alternative of lacerating itself in one destructive war after another and of seeing civilization perish, or of agreeing upon a form of life which is based upon the idea of union and coöperation, in which the entire world is regarded as the common home of all and in which all are granted a similar right to the enjoyment of its fruits. In such a world and in preparation for such a world it is of small importance to be a German, an American, or an Englishman, in short to be a national in spirit, experience, language, and feeling. The old word "Weltbürger," which, for a time, appeared old-fashioned, will again become honorable, and it is a German word.

We are writers and we claim to be psychologists enough to recognize that this monstrous German attempt at world domination, which we now see ending catastrophically, is nothing but a distorted and unfortunate expression of that universalism innate in the German character which formerly had a much higher, purer, and nobler form and which won the sympathy and admiration of the world for this important people. Power politics destroyed this universalism and brought about its downfall, for whenever universalism becomes power politics then humanity must arise and defend its liberty. Let us trust that German universalism will find the way to its old place of honor, that it will forever renounce the wanton ambition of world conquest and again prove itself as world sympathy, world understanding, and spiritual enrichment.

How closely connected are liberty and peace, and how closely connected the liberty of Germany and peace of the world! We emigrants are deeply ashamed when we think of the sufferings and sacrifices which the world has had to undergo on account of the errors of Germany, but all the more inspiring is the thought that Germany's liberty will be the peace of the world. (pp. 339-44)

Thomas Mann, "The Exiled Writer's Relation to His Homeland," in Writers' Congress by Thomas Mann and others, University of California Press, 1944, pp. 339-44.

GUY STERN

[*Stern is a German-born professor and critic of German language and literature. In the following excerpt, he discusses cooperation between Jewish and Christian writers in exile from Germany.*]

It can be argued that five characteristics defined the interaction between German Jews and Christians during the exile years. For one, collaboration between the two groups continued as before, but now with an increased and pervasive, if respectful, awareness of each other's different patrimony. When thousands of German writers, from poets to essayists, from belletristic authors to journalists, left Germany, it became clear that literary life in exile—no matter how much the refugees wished it to be otherwise—could be sustained unaltered in only the rarest of cases. The ingenuous, natural relationship that had often marked the interaction between German Christians and German Jews in their professional encounters subtly shifted. Where Jews and Christians had previously collaborated or worked together, minimally cognizant of their differences, this naturalness and acceptance became often impossible in the face of the strident propagandizing of Nazi racism. In refuting the Nazis' pseudoscience—in mere reaction to it—the subject of similarities and differences between Christians and Jews was raised despite the disinclination to do so on the part of the well intentioned. In consequence, respect and appreciation of each other's background, frequently implicit and spontaneous in the past, now often became explicit and conscious.

One aspect of interaction in the field of literature may be taken as symptomatic. Ever since the eighteenth century, when Gotthold Ephraim Lessing and Moses Mendelssohn collaborated in the editing of the *Briefe, die neueste Literatur betreffend,* up to Karl von Ossietzki's and Kurt Tucholsky's joint editorship of the *Weltbühne,* there had existed a mutually beneficial, complementary working relationship between German Jews and Christians in the editorship of journals and magazines. But in these relationships, the religious or ethnic background of each collaborator, *qua* collaborator, was ignored or considered fortuitous. In the entire editorial correspondence of the *Neue Merkur,* for example, which for several years united the Jew Efraim Frisch and the Protestant Wilhelm Hausenstein, there is at most an accidental and insignificant mention of their different backgrounds. My subsequent interviews confirmed that this was simply not a topic of their conversations. This ingenuousness continued to characterize Ferdinand Lion's and Klaus Mann's joint venture of editing the exile journal *Mass und Wert.* While Klaus Mann's correspondence, recently made accessible to scholars, does contain occasional antisemitic, if jocular, remarks, Mann does not jibe at Lion or his Jewish collaborators and, in fact, ignores such externalia.

But, in interviewing the German-Jewish author Robert Jungk in the summer of 1983, I gained the impression that a heightened awareness of each other's background characterized the behavior of the editorial staff of another exile magazine, *Die Flaschenpost,* published in Switzerland. It involved, at various times, the Protestant Arnold Künzli, a Swiss writer . . . and several Jewish writers, including Jungk. Each knew (and respectfully commented upon) the other's affiliation, down to the fact that Alfons Rosenberg, one of the editors, had converted from Judaism to Catholicism. Here and elsewhere the former spontaneity had been replaced by a more conscious behavior.

The same attitude of respectful awareness can be sensed where Jewish and Christian writers collaborated on a book, even as late as 1947. In the foreword to the anthology *Verboten und Verbrannt,* Alfred Kantorowicz stresses his feelings of respect for the "inner immigration"; later in the book his Christian collaborator, Richard Drews, is identified as one of its representatives. The anthology itself is marked by a careful balance of excerpts by Jewish and non-Jewish writers. Similarly, when Wilhelm Sternfeld corresponded with the Deutsche Bibliothek in search of a collaborator for the *Exil-Lexikon,* one of the earliest bio-bibliographical tools for the study of exile literature, he asked for a "German" library scientist. That undoubtedly meant, in the context of the time, a German Christian.

My second point is closely related to the first. Even a random enumeration of literary circles in exile reveals the same type of mix, crossing religious lines, as had existed in the German or Austrian homelands. With a greater sensitivity than they had often shown at home, the exiles provided mutual support for one another—ranging from criticism of each other's works to financial help—while all the while more conscious of each other's religion. In New York, a group loosely conjoined around the husband-and-wife writers and collaborators Hertha Pauli and E. B. Ashton (Ernst Basch), themselves an example of a mixed marriage, included the Jews Walter Mehring and, on a transient basis, Paul Frischauer, and the Christians George Grosz and Lucy Sabsay, a film editor. As a member of the group, more spectator than participant, I noticed the tact and restraint that characterized the conversations when the ethnic or religious background of a fellow exile was under discussion. George Grosz, whose correspondence is not without highly ambivalent remarks toward Jews, was far more restrained during these gatherings.

Whatever we know of the Yorkville round table of Oskar Maria Graf, which included the Jewish writer-editor Manfred Georg, or the circle around Thomas Mann, to which such Jewish writers as Alfred Neumann, Bruno Frank, and Lion Feuchtwanger belonged, the same conscious goodwill seems to have prevailed. In Mexico City, Anna Seghers, Egon Erwin Kisch, Bruno Frei, and other socialists, Jews and non-Jews, collaborated on journals and newspapers and met frequently for literary and political discussions. But we can infer that here, too, ingeniousness had given way to awareness. Bruno Frei, in a recent essay, significantly called for a creation or restoration of naturalness as an antitoxin to antisemitism: "An incessant education and self-education toward unself-consciousness [*zum Selbstverständnis*] will become necessary. . . . The relationship of Jews and non-Jews must become as natural, as unencumbered by the past, as that of Allemanians to Friesians."

Third, literary works increasingly accentuated interreligious relationships. The problem of intermarriages or liaisons, though not a new subject in German literature, became far more frequent. This accentuation was to be expected, of course, in works set in Germany or German-occupied countries—such as Ferdinand Bruckner's *Die Rassen.* More significant, the subject also occurs quite often in works about exiles or exile situations. It is as if the assimilation of the Jews and the related problem of intermarriages, once they were halted in Nazi Germany, forced a reexamination of attitudes even upon those who had escaped the enforcement of the Nuremberg Laws.

Yet these works vary in their resolutions. In Solomon Dembitzer's unpublished novel, *Das Mädchen aus Flandern,* the strain of living in an inhospitable New York breaks apart the Jewish protagonist's relationship with his Christian fiancée. Hans Habe, on the other hand, in his first novel, *Drei über die Grenze,* depicts how a relationship between a young Jewish refugee woman and a Christian political exile is sustained and strengthened by the shared experience of flight and exile. Similarly, a self-sacrificing Christian gives a young Jewish couple a chance to establish a new life in Mexico in Erich Maria Remarque's *Liebe deinen Nächsten.* Also in a remarkable novel by Horst Schade, *Ein Engel war mit mir: Ein Tatsachenroman,* a Christian girl from the Silesian town of Gleiwitz helps the Jewish hero escape across the border. In the autobiographical sequel, *Denn Dämmerung herrscht auf der Welt,* the Christian protagonist leaves Germany with his Jewish fiancée, later his wife, to emigrate to Palestine. His experience as bohemian, boxer, and free-lance writer enables him to survive the struggle for daily existence, and his robust health helps him overcome injuries from the rifle shot of an Arab terrorist. With the understanding of his wife, he masters the challenges and confrontations of being a Christian among Jews in an emerging State of Israel. It appears equally symptomatic that a Jewish writer, Carl Seelig, wrote an epilogue to *Ein Engel war mit mir* and aided in its publication.

Conversely, exiled Jewish writers in their belletristic works singled out Christians *as Christians* for particular acts of nobility. Alfred Kerr's poem "Helmuth von Gerlach," for example, begins with an implicit recognition of that exile's background: "Verächter seiner Väter Sitten / Zog er in eine fremde Welt" ("Despiser of his fathers' customs / He wandered to a foreign world").

My fourth observation is that where Christians and Jews joined in efforts at help and rescue of the persecuted or of exiles, they stressed their impartiality and, if they showed preferences, they would lean over backwards, Christians often championing Jewish writers and Jewish writers their Christian colleagues. Clearly the collaborations of German-Jewish and German-Christian writers in those apocalyptic times were not confined to literary concerns or creations, and writers of all persuasions joined in this humanitarian mission. It is to the credit of many that they programmatically eschewed appeals or actions preferential to helping one or the other group. Most surprising in tracing these efforts is the fact that they disprove the assumption often put forth in exile studies, but particularly in East Germany, that writers persecuted as Jews did not join forces with those persecuted as political opponents of the Nazis, be they Jews or Christians. While clashes did abound, as Alfred Kantorowicz details in his autobiographies, there were also remarkable acts of mutual support. Wherever possible, victims of religious and political persecution joined together for sheer survival, even when outright antipathies had previously existed among them.

In certain groups, the composition of the leadership alone, perhaps by design, reflected mutual support among Jews and Christians. In the United States the American Guild for German Cultural Freedom subsidized writers, secured sponsors for affidavits, and occasionally acted as contact to publishers. It relied heavily, of course, on American dignitaries and intellectuals for its board members and officers, but its European Council, with Thomas Mann as chairman, consisted of an illustrious cadre of German Christians and Jews: R. A. Berman-Hoellriegel, Lion Feuchtwanger, Bruno Frank, Leonard Frank, Sigmund Freud, Bronislav Hubermann, Otto Klemperer, Emil

Lederer, Heinrich Mann, Father Georg Moenius, Robert Musil, Alfred Neumann, Rudolph Olden, Max Reinhardt, René Schickele, Erwin Schroedinger, Paul J. Tillich, Ernst Toch, Ernst Toller, Fritz von Unruh, Veit Valentin, and Franz Werfel.

This council was led, from the beginning, by Prince Hubertus zu Loewenstein as general-secretary. Its statement of purpose (1937), probably drafted by Peter de Mendelssohn, explicitly states that the humanitarian problem it seeks to address is not "circumscribed to any area or class [of persecuted]." And Prince zu Loewenstein, in an interview in 1983, added, "We political immigrants never gave recognition to the differences either among religions or among emigrants for political or ethnic reasons—neither before, nor at that time, nor now."

A similar though far more Marxist-oriented organization in England, the Free German League of Culture in Great Britain, espoused identical principles: "The path of all refugees from Germany, whether they be Jews or non-Jews, is a common one in our fight against Hitler-Fascism." The organization's executive council included both German Jews and Christians, such as John Heartfield and Johanna Klopstock, and solicited and—surprisingly—gained support from communist writers like Bodo Uhse, after the war a party functionary and feature writer for the German Democratic Republic. In 1942 the Free German League devoted a special issue of its magazine, *Unser ist der Morgen,* to the eradication of antisemitism. Uhse concluded his article by asking for a common effort to defeat Hitler, because his defeat alone could end the suffering of Jews in Europe. Jan Petersen, likewise a non-Jewish communist, wrote the foreword: "A free Germany is unimaginable without the complete removal of the injustices that victimize the Jews. . . . The fight for the restoration of equal rights of all mankind, regardless of religious or racial affiliation, must form an essential part of the German people's struggle for freedom. Even more surprising, another contributor to this special issue was Alexander Abusch. Although he later became an instrument of Stalinist suppression, he contributed an extremely sensitive article on the spiritual and intellectual richness of German Jewry. It is idle to ask whether it was sincere; it served the purpose of presenting a united front in behalf of the oppressed German Jews, especially the intelligentsia. Given the appeal by Abusch, it is only to be expected that the far less dogmatic, if leftist, Jew Arnold Zweig, then living in Palestine, should declare his solidarity with Jews of all political persuasions. Zweig described himself as "equally oppressed . . . by the cruelties inflicted upon the Left. But in the main this book [of mine] is a declaration in behalf of the Jews." In the lengthy epilogue to the postwar reissue of the book authorized by Zweig, Achim von Borries emphasized Zweig's loyalty to Judaism: "As he remained a Jew as a German, he also remained a Jew as a Marxian Socialist."

There were also, much to their credit, Jewish organizations that tried to help non-Jewish exiles. The German-Jewish Club of New York, later the New York World Club, while primarily a form and forum of Jewish self-help in such matters as job procurement, also served some Christian exiles, among them Kurt Kersten. And, according to Hans Steinitz, its publication the *New York Aufbau* drew upon "non-Jewish journalists and members of the editorial staff in large numbers." To find validation for Steinitz's assertion, one need only to recall that the *Aufbau* offered a first American foothold to Fritz von Unruh, published Oskar Maria Graf immediately after his arrival in America, and gave editorial positions to Siegfried Anhäuser, a German-Christian editor and former member of the German

parliament, and to the postwar political writer Gert Niers. In England, Jewish communities no doubt repeatedly heeded the plea of Dr. Ignaz Maybaum of Berlin, a prominent immigrant rabbi, who enjoined his fellow Jews to aid intellectuals of both religions, because "the world of tomorrow has need of the Christian intellectual who is a Christian and of the Jewish intellectual who is a Jew." In turn, the archbishop of Canterbury wrote the foreword to one of Maybaum's books, *Man and Catastrophe.*

There are also many instances in which individual writers bent over backward to rescue others of different religious persuasions. Most notable among them was, of course, Thomas Mann. In the past Mann—as is now well known—had flirted with antisemitism—and not only in his *Betrachtungen eines Unpolitischen* (1918). But in his lecture "The Decline of European Jewry," delivered in San Francisco in July 1943, he singled out Jewish writers for defense and approbation. He pointed to the contributions of Jewish artists, musicians, and scientists, and he closed with a moving appeal in behalf of the persecuted Jews: "May this hall, this meeting radiate waves of compassion, of indignation and of our determination to help, which will reach perhaps and frighten the murderers of right and humanity, but above all may they move those who have the power and the means to alleviate the suffering of our time!" Mann also wrote recommendations and forewords for Jewish writers, even when he might have had reservations about the work, in order to help them succeed. A long-forgotten novel by Frederick Hollander (b. Friedrich Hollaender), for example, received an almost lyrical tribute in Mann's preface:

> I have read this book with genuine delight and I am happy for the opportunity to congratulate both the author and the publisher before it release for this extraordinary and beautiful work. It is a splendid novel, new, tense with life, courageous, and artistically entertaining, written in a visible, vigilant, and colorful English, in the rhythmical charms of which one can sense the musicianship of the author.

Henrich Mann was no less eloquent than his brother in his intercession on behalf of German-Jewish writers and intellectuals. In an appeal written in France and intended to encourage revolution agains the Nazis, he also invoked the injustice done to German-Jewish writers: "[Hitler] drove creative, talented people out of Germany. . . . The Jews had contributed very heavily to German intellectual life. They had done their duty beyond their numerical representatives. That alone was reason enough to be persecuted by a despot who has set naked tyranny as his only goal and purpose."

Paul Tillich, from his religious and ethical convictions, reminded his Christian listeners, even when making an appeal for help for non-Jews via the American Christian Committee for Refugees from Germany, of the historic plight of the Jews: "God separates men, if He elects them. He separates Israel from the nations and makes her an exile in Egypt, in Babylon, in the Hellenic, in the Roman Empire, and now in the occidental world and its nations."

German-Jewish writers showed a similar spirit of generosity and altruism. One example among many will suffice. It could happen that two former rivals or enemies, whether or not such antagonisms were nurtured in part by a Jewish-Christian conflict, forgot such antipathies once they were in exile. The Jewish director Max Reinhardt, unfavorably disposed toward his rival Erwin Piscator when both were in pre-1933 Germany, became supportive to the point of self-denial when both were exiles. In May 1939, when Piscator had just arrived in America, Reinhardt, already somewhat more established, supplied him with a letter of recommendation in which he unselfishly declared, "One is even fully justified in saying that the last phase of development of the German theatre, before the beginning of the so called [*sic*] Third Reich, bears your name."

Similarly Alfred Kerr, in his capacity as president of the PEN Club in Exile, stressed time and again that the common exile fate united them all. As his notes for his agendas and short addresses show, he frequently used his forum to solicit aid for German-Christian writers. "Perhaps," he recorded, "we together can do something for Kurt Kersten who is still a prisoner in the South of France." The full extent, however, to which Christian exiles were helped by Jews—of course not by German Jews alone and certainly not only by German-Jewish writers— can be gauged by an editorial that accompanied the printing of Paul Tillich's speech in the *Presbyterian Tribune* of October 29, 1936:

> There are [among the refugees from Germany] 14,000 Christian exiles, and these 14,000 have received woefully inadequate help. In most instances such help as has been given was contributed by Jews. . . . [At the meeting addressed by Dr. Tillich] profound gratitude was expressed that relief had in many instances been extended to Christian refugees by Jewish organizations, despite their crushing responsibilities for refugees of their own faith.

Finally, a new cooperation between German-Jewish writers and German-Christian writers of the postwar generation has developed in the more recent past. It has often been claimed, and correctly so, that Jewish exile writers were not particularly welcomed back by the German book trade, by the German reading public, or by their colleagues after 1945. But it is fair to add that exceptions abound. The socialist Friedrich Oppler has repeatedly reminded the German government of its obligations to Germany's postwar Jews: "Every state, unless it is one with a Hitlerian ideology, must be interested in bringing about the true integration [of those Jews] who wish it and are capable of it." Erich Lüth, drama critic and an admirer of the exiled Erwin Piscator, expressed similar sentiments, but also made a special plea for German-Jewish writers and intellectuals: "We want to renew the remembrance of great Jews in the world and in Germany and do everything to be able to profit from the insights of Jewish men and women, scholars, and poets."

Among the newly established fiction writers of postwar Germany, several raised their championship of works by Jewish exiles to the level of a personal crusade. Three examples will illustrate the point. Ingeborg Drewitz, well-known lyricist and novelist, has reviewed, in a long succession, every book from the pen of a German-Jewish author, both newly published, and republished, and she has used her position as a publisher's reader to advance the careers of others, among them Jean Améry, H. G. Adler, Ulrich Becher, Alfred Döblin, Irmgard Keun, Nelly Sachs, who became a personal friend, and Hans Sahl. Drewitz explains her missionary zeal as follows: "And then, after 1945, came the avid eagerness—more than curiosity—to get to these unknown works." She also details her friendships with several of these authors and explains how those friendships prompted her to use her presidency of the PEN Club in their behalf: "To prepare exhibitions, to get [the exiled writers] invited, to investigate possibilities for their return was for me one of the most noble tasks among my work and my respon-

sibilities to the Writers Club and it accompanied my work as a reviewer."

Similarly Horst Bienek has championed the rediscovery of German-Jewish writers. In his so-called Silesian Trilogy he has deliberately included Jewish writers who once lived in Silesia, even unearthing some completely forgotten, such as Alphons Silbergleit, a poet and short story writer who died in a concentration camp. In addition, Bienek became, for a while, a kind of unpaid literary agent for Hermann Kesten, whose descriptions of the literary world he particularly admired. At last Bienek was able to convince the Ullstein-Verlag to publish Kesten's works in their entirety.

Heinrich Böll, for his part, has appointed himself—to use his word—the "minesweeper" for Germany, which, in his opinion, is still mined with antisemitism. Therefore he reviews books and encourages radio and television series that are likely to dispel prejudices. He most clearly defines his intent in a foreword to a reprint edition of Heinz Liepman's *Das Vaterland* (1933, 1981): "May this book remind younger readers how much of Germany was driven out of Germany." It is important to add that Drewitz, Bienek, and Böll do not stand alone. (pp. 151-62)

> Guy Stern, *"German-Jewish and German-Christian Writers: Cooperation in Exile," in* The Jewish Response to German Culture: From the Enlightenment to the Second World War, *edited by Jehuda Reinharz and Walter Schatzberg, University Press of New England, 1985, pp. 150-63.*

SURVEYS OF EXILE LITERATURE

H. M. WAIDSON

[*Waidson is an English educator and critic specializing in German and Swiss literature. In the following excerpt, he discusses the novels written in exile by Thomas Mann, Heinrich Mann, Alfred Döblin, Hermann Broch, Franz Werfel, Carl Zuckmeyer, Oskar Maria Graf, Hermann Kesten, Erich Maria Remarque, Theodor Plievier, and Hans Henny Jahnn.*]

In a letter from Switzerland, of 13 March 1933, Thomas Mann explained how political developments in Germany now impelled him to remain outside his homeland, and what an abrupt change this would bring about in his personal life:

> I am too good a German, too closely bound to the cultural traditions and the language of my country, for the thought of exile over years or even a lifetime not to have a hard, fateful significance for me. Yet we have been forced to look around for a new basis of living. . . . At 57 such a loss of normal existence, to which one had become accustomed and in which one was beginning to become a little stiff, may not be an insignificant matter.

For the time being the Manns settled in Switzerland, Thomas Mann's major creative writing being now devoted to *Joseph und seine Brüder (Joseph and his Brethren)*, 1933-43, a novel of an individual's development to a yet more consistent extent than *Der Zauberberg (The Magic Mountain)*, 1924, that other major novel in which the author could be seen as expressing a positive, indeed "representative," attitude to the outlook of the Weimar Republic. After settling in the United States, the work of *Joseph und seine Brüder* continued, while concurrently

Mann gave a lot of time and energy to the assistance of fellow-refugees and to other forms of public activity, as his letters illustrate. Contacts with France and Czechoslovakia, for instance, were kept up as long as possible, and in the United States he made repeated efforts to obtain asylum, or more favourable living conditions, for those who were exiled with him. From 1940 onwards Heinrich Mann was also living in California, at no great distance from his brother.

As he was approaching the end of *Joseph und seine Brüder* in 1942, Mann recorded the "fun" which this task had given him. At that time he wrote about himself and his habits with humour and with a recognition of the "bürgerlich" elements which he was again to stress in "Meine Zeit." He cannot accept (7 October 1941) that his life has been a hard one: "You call my life 'hard,' but I cannot feel it as such. In principle I feel it gratefully as a *happy, blessed* life—I say 'in principle,' for it is not a question naturally of all kind of suffering, darkness and danger not being present in such a life, but of its basis being gay, so to speak sunny...." His work and the preoccupation generally with art are seen here as a matter for enjoyment, not suffering: "I am an artist, that is, someone who wishes to entertain himself—one should not put on a solemn expression about this.... No, there can be no question of suffering in art." it was at this time that Mann was turning over in his mind the possibility of taking up the theme of *Doktor Faustus*. Once he had begun writing this novel, the author soon became aware of the "serious mood" it produced in him, and looked back to it soon after he had finished it (12 December 1947) as a kind of autobiography, "a work which has cost me more and has consumed me more deeply than any earlier one."

It became one of the most discussed novels when it appeared in Germany in 1947, making a challenging impact by its use of the Faust story as a means not only of probing the problems of the artistic vocation but also of linking these problems with the role of Germany in world politics up to and including the period of the Second World War. It is the biography of a fictitious musician, but it unfolds a personality that ends in sterility and decay, not stability and maturity; the artistic temperament here is not adapted to the requirements of living in society, as was the case with Joseph, but becomes increasingly turned in upon itself. The demonic forces swamp the "flickering flame of the spirit." Thomas Mann no longer puts a confident case for reason and worldly wisdom, but is an impassioned, comminatory prophet. The life-story of Adrian Leverkühn allows the author to recapitulate moods and tendencies in German society as he experienced them in the years before his own exile in 1933. Born in 1885, Adrian grows up in a middle-German small-town environment which represents a link with the experience of nineteenth-century German regionalism. His theological studies allow for satire at the expense of religious institutions, both Lutheran and Catholic, which are represented by teachers who are more interested in demonology than saintliness. Adrian's choice of music as his specialization is a fatal step towards complicity with the devil. His preoccupation with musical composition is pursued persistently throughout the First World War, the period of inflation, and the most hopeful years of the Weimar Republic; his indifference to social and political issues contrasts with the attitude of his author. The group of prosperous, cultured Bohemians who are his friends in and around Munich are shown as equally remote from the problems of their time, unless they have leanings to the extreme nationalism of the Kridwiss circle. With considerable liveliness Thomas Mann reconstructs the Germany he knew, so that *Doktor Faustus* includes documented reconstruction of previous epochs of German life.

The central chapter of the novel is a dialogue with the devil in which Adrian becomes aware that he has bough the ectasies of artistic creativity and also the depth of depression with a pact that has been signed not in blood, but in venereal infection. Modelled on Ivan's confrontation with the devil in Dostoievsky's *The Brothers Karamazov*, this scene may be regarded as a delusion of Adrian's fevered mind rather than as the consequence of a corporeal manifestation. Mann's work is almost always kept within the bounds of everyday realism, but occasionally delusion and fantasy allow for a new dimension, in this pact scene as also, for instance, in the hypnotic suggestive powers of Cipolla in *Mario und der Zauberer (Mario and the Magician)*, 1930, a Novelle which in its criticism of Italian Fascism anticipates *Doktor Faustus*. The price Adrian has to pay for inspiration derived from pride is complete isolation: "You may not love.... Your life is to be cold—therefore you may not love anyone." By temperament Adrian is cool and undemonstrative, retreating from emotional contact with others, an uncommitted observer in all things except musical composition. But he twice tries to break the devil's bargain, when normal, simple human affection impels him to overcome the austerity of icy aestheticism. On both occasions it is a Swiss influence that kindles in him these warmer feelings. Adrian's love for Marie Godeau is shy and tentative, and his own clumsiness loses her to his friend Rudi Schwerdtfeger; disaster supervenes with Rudi's assassination in a Munich tram, and Marie feels she can have no more contact with Adrian and his circle. This somewhat novelettish episode is less impressive than Adrian's affection for his nephew Nepomuk, the child of his sister who has married a Swiss optician. Adrian develops a spontaneous fondness for the five-year-old boy, being much affected by his innocence and Swiss-German talk. His feeling for the child is much more purely affectionate than that of Aschenbach for Tadzio in *Der Tod in Venedig (Death in Venice)*, 1913, and it is more appealing than that between Cornelius and his infant daughter in *Unordnung und frühes Leid (Disorder and Early Sorrow)*, 1926. But Nepomuk is unpredictably stricken with cerebro-spinal meningitis, and Adrian is confronted with the problem of suffering and evil in stark terms; as he watches the child die in the midst of intense pain, he is beset by pity and indignation, like Ivan Karamazov when he too is considering the sufferings of children, and Adrian ascribes his nephew's death to the machinations of the devil. The latter chapters of the novel are told with an increasing momentum, and the reader is hurtled along at a quick pace until the catastrophe of Adrian's collapse, while he is ostensibly expounding his latest composition, "Dr. Faustus' Lament," to his friends. If *Der Zauberberg* and *Joseph* are novels of individual development, *Doktor Faustus* might be seen as an "Anti-Bildungsroman," a parody and reversal of the didactic optimism of this traditional German novel form.

In his treatment of the Faust theme, Mann deliberately ignores Goethe's version in order to adhere more closely to the original conception of Faust in the chap-book of 1587. Thus Thomas Mann implies a rejection of the Faustian man, and a differing interpretation from that of Goethe who in the "Prologue in Heaven" causes the Lord to bless Faust's striving as being ultimately to a good end. Faust, the wanderer, the eagle, the amoral embodiment of sheer energy and curiosity, should be saved, as Goethe interpreted the legend; in order to make the legend apposite to his twentieth-century interpretation, Mann preferred to leave aside Goethe's approach to Faust. Adrian's life is in part based on incidents from Nietzsche's biography, such as the visit to the brothel in Leipzig, the relationship with the prostitute Esmeralda, the subsequent feverish creative activity alternating with intense depression, and the final ten years of mental collapse. In the essay "Nietzches Philosophie im Lichte unserer Erfahrung" ("Nietzsche's Philosophy in the Light of Contemporary Events"), 1947, Mann expresses his disagreement with Nietzsche on two issues. The latter assumed that reason was threatening to extinguish instinct, whereas, says Mann, the reverse is true, for the forces of unreason have never been more violent and dangerous than in the mid-twentieth century. If Nietzsche assumed that Morality was the enemy of instinctive life, Mann asserts that the real opposites are ethics and aesthetics; it would then not be morality, but beauty that would be linked to death and destruction. While taking care to acknowledge Nietzsche's dislike of nationalism and anti-Semitism, Mann does maintain a faith in the middle-class, enlightenment values which Nietzsche attacked. As a composer, Adrian Leverkühn is faced with a sense of crisis owing to the conviction that the resources of diatonic harmony have largely been exhausted, rather on the lines of the feeling that the narrative methods of nineteenth-century realism in the novel might be threatened by as yet incalculable forms of experimentation. Adrian's music teacher, Wendell Kretschmar, expounds Beethoven's last piano sonata, which is presented as an example of a demonic German lack of formal self-control breaking through the sonata form; it is impressive, but disastrous, says Mann, and anticipates romanticism in music, the chromaticism of Wagner, and the subsequent dissolution of traditional musical harmony. "Why must it seem to me as if almost all, in fact, all methods and devices of the art are today only still of use for purposes of parody?," Adrian asks. He becomes an atonal composer, and in order to have anything original to say musically, he is dependent on the devil's help.

Adrian is thus to contain Faust, Nietzsche, the spirit of German music, and indeed the German national character as a whole. In an essay "Deutschland und die Deutschen" (1947), Thomas Mann develops generalizations about the association of music, the demonic and German nature which are part of the mod underlying *Doktor Faustus:* "The Germans are people of the Romantic Counter-Revolution against the philosophical intellectualism and rationalism of the Age of Enlightenment—of a revolt of music against literature, of mysticism against clarity."

The narrator of the novel, Dr. Serenus Zeitblom, a teacher of Classics, has been Adrian's devoted admirer and famulus from schooldays onwards. Like Settembrini in *Der Zauberberg,* he can be discursively pedagogic, but at the same time he can speak for his author. After Adrian's death in 1940, the year of Hitler's most intoxicating triumphs, Zeitblom begins collecting biographical material about his friend and writes down the life-story between May 1943 and the last days of the Third Reich two years later. Adrian's pact and decline are shown as parallel to Germany's fortunes in the course of the last two years of the war. There seems little hope at the end of *Doktor Faustus,* but there are alternatives to despair. The final high cello note of "Dr. Faustus' Lament" is intended to bear positive significance; and even if Adrian himself is lost, Zeitblom, his other self, has survived, so that the voice of Liberal humanism may yet be heard. (pp. 14-20)

[Thomas Mann's] elder brother Heinrich Mann (1871-1950) clearly shared many experiences with the more widely celebrated Thomas. Already before the First World War Heinrich Mann had become an admirer of the French tradition of rationalism and liberalism, and after 1914 the brothers were estranged for some years on account of their differing loyalties during that period. They came together in their support for the

Weimar Republic, and both left Germany in 1933. Shortly before the beginning of the Second World War Heinrich Mann lived in France, an important literary product of this time being the extended biographical novel *Henri Quatre* (1935-38), a mellow tribute to the French king who is seen as an embodiment of humane values. The two novels of Heinrich Mann which appeared after 1945, while he was resident in the United States, also have French associations, though neither work is as satisfying as *Henri Quatre. Der Atem (Breath),* 1949, centres upon the mysterious figure of Lydia Kowalski, in particular upon the last hours of her life which coincide with the outbreak of war in 1939; the scene is Nice and its neighbourhood. Lydia was once a great lady, but her husband took his life in May 1914 and her lover Fernand deserted her and left her impoverished. She has been a factory-worker since, but now pays a daily visit to a Nice bank in the forlorn expectation that money will be there for her. On the morning of this particular day her breathing is difficult and she more than once collapses; but a series of adventures befall her, linking her fate with political intrigues and clashes between representatives of industrialism and proletariat, while at the same time she receives the affection and respect of simple people, who see her as one of themselves and yet also as a great lady from another era and place. In a sequence of happenings that is unexpected, she moves from street to bank and bank-manager's flat, from hotel bedroom to gambling casino, and from night-club to the death-bed scenes at the hotel. A fortune is won, but it can have little meaning for her now. The novel proliferates into various subsidiary actions, and contains much that is bizarre, though the heroine is presented as having a grandeur that transcends the limitations and follies of her surroundings. *Empfang bei der Welt (Reception for the World),* 1956, devotes its main, central section to the description of a fashionable reception, attended largely by wealthy business-men and by people from the world of opera. It has been organized by Arthur, an opera agent, who hopes to raise funds for the establishment of an opera-house. The earlier mood of the assembly, one of self-absorbed hardness, yields to an interlude of relaxed amiability before most of the guests disperse; the final stages of the party, for the few that remain, contain elements of the gross and grotesque. It is a cosmopolitan atmosphere, with snatches of dialogue in French and other languages. Although the grotesque elements have at times a threatening quality, the satire is resolved into a fairy-tale idyllic finale. Arthur's father Balthasar dies at the age of ninety in his wine-cellar where he keeps his hidden hoard of gold: "'The first time that I really enjoyed my life was when I could play the poor man and hide my gold.'" The old man's fate and testament bring the young couple, Arthur's son André and Stephanie, to a full realization of their love for each other. They propose to reject the fortune bequeathed to them and to transfer it to Melusine, Stephanie's mother and a bank director, and to Arthur, who have likewise confirmed their affection for one another after the reception. If those who are older feel an emotional need for money and complicated living, the young lovers can tolerate, even sympathize with this need, without sharing it.

In 1933 Alfred Döblin (1878-1957) left Germany and shortly afterwards settled in France, though with the German occupation of France in 1940 he moved again, this time to the United States; he came back to Germany for a time after the end of the war, with an official position in the French Zone. During his years of exile from Germany Döblin was working on the novel *November 1918,* which was completed in 1943 and published in 1948-50. The action of this work is centred on the events of the winter 1918-19, concentrating principally on the stormy days of the revolution in Berlin. Döblin clearly has no regrets here for the passing of the old pre-war civilization, and the hero of his work is the revolution itself rather than any of the individuals participating in it. The president, Ebert, and the leader of the Freikorps, Noske, are shown in a poor light by comparison with the Spartacist leaders Rosa Luxemburg and Karl Liebknecht, whom the author wishes to vindicate. The narration of these public political events is less satisfying than the action which describes the attempt of an ex-army officer to return to his pre-war occupation as a schoolmaster, his conversion to the Spartacist cause and his subsequent years of anonymous pilgrimage. This novel is comparable to Jules Romains's *Les Hommes de bonne volonté* or John Dos Passos's *U.S.A.* in the attempt to present the wide range of a large city by means of a series of parallel actions which are linked mainly by the context of their time and place. In spite of many gripping incidents the work is hardly convincing as a whole, and is less compelling than *Berlin Alexanderplatz*. Döblin's last novel *Hamlet oder Die lange Nacht nimmt ein ende (Hamlet, or The Long Night Comes to an End)*, written 1945-6, and published 1956, has as its initial theme the homecoming of a young man after severe injury of body and mind in the war; the centre of narrative interest, however, moves from Edward to his parents Gordon and Alice Allison. The setting is for the most part a family house in the English countryside and it is predominantly an English cultural environment which is presented to the reader. In its form the work is reminiscent of Boccaccio's *Decameron* or Goethe's *Unterhaltungen deutscher Ausgewanderten (Entertainments of German Emigrés)*; at a time of crisis and uncertainty a group of people agree to present stories orally to each other. The father, a professional writer, makes the suggestion, and their medical adviser hopes that the entertainment will act as a form of therapy. In this respect some success is achieved, since with the passing of the novel's time Edward is restored to balance and well-being; but with his recovery comes the collapse of his parents' relationship to one another, indeed the breakdown of their stability. The possessive mother is particularly vulnerable, but so too is Gordon, the father whose good intentions have been much misunderstood. The inset-stories have implications for the issues at stake in the main narrative; at the same time they provide points of reference to archetypal prefigurations, as in the stories of Pluto and Persephone, of Theodora, of the troubador Jaufie, and of Lear. Edward's uncle, James Mackenzie, at one point sees Edward as going the way of a Hamlet "to whom the task of action was given not by the ghost of a dead father, but by his own morbid inner impulse, just as are imagination and empirical experience"; Gordon Allison says: "To have imagination means to experience complete reality."

The search for totality of experience had been expressed by Hermann Broch (1886-1951) mainly on the social plane in the trilogy *Die Schlafwandler (The Sleepwalkers)*, 1931-2. He wrote an essay "James Joyce und die Gegenwart" ("James Joyce and the Present"), 1936, in honour of Joyce's birthday, and in the epilogue to *Die Schuldlosen (The Innocent Ones)*, 1950, he endowed Leopold Bloom with a representative significance extending well beyond the confines of *Ulysses*. In this epilogue Broch has indicated something of his approach to fiction, summing up what he considered to be the function of the novel. The novel, he says, must depict a "world totality," increasingly difficult though this is as the world becomes more complex and incoherent. This totality must not be on one plane only, since the novelist need not be limited by the naturalist convention, but should include the moral and metaphysical. Can the novel have a social purpose, he asks. Only the con-

verted will be convinced, scepticism may say; but nevertheless the purpose of art is to be moral—it is to be "Läuterung," purification, and Broch cites Goethe's *Faust*.

Der Tod des Vergil (The Death of Virgil), 1945, took shape as a short story in 1937; the author left Austria in 1938 and lived subsequently in the United States, where this material was developed into a novel. This record of the last eighteen hours of Virgil's life is a vast interior monologue that reflects the sensations and thoughts of a highly sensitive and intelligent man who knows that he is dying; the monologue is only interrupted by conversation that the poet himself hears or takes part in. The work covers a whole range of experience, from the crudity of the drunken revellers in the street outside to the most abstract expressions of the poet's quest for truth; it carries within it a wide historical synthesis, and Broch himself has said that the parallels between the first pre-Christian century and his own time are deliberate. On his death-bed the poet wants to destroy the manuscript of his *Aeneid;* art is not enough, and moreover his has been an art that has allowed itself to be subordinated to ends that he now considers unworthy. In his last hours Virgil sees his own life and its problems in a new light. There is a highly wrought scene between the emperor Augustus and the poet which brings the human issues of the work to a dramatic climax, the outcome of which is Virgil's presentation of his epic as a gift to Augustus from motives of loving self-sacrifice.

For all Broch's conscious affinities to James Joyce in his experimental technique, there is an important difference between their approaches. Broch's writing expresses firm ethical beliefs which separate him from Joyce's outlook, as expressed in Stephen Dedalus's "I will not serve." There is nothing parodistic in the Salvation Army scenes or in Esch's Bible study in *Die Schlafwandler; Die unbekannte Größe (The Unknown Quantity)*, 1933, preaches the futility of the search for knowledge if this is divorced from the developed heart. The didactic element is present too in *Die Schuldlosen*, with its castigation of indifference and of refusal to assume moral and political responsibility. *Die Schuldlosen* is an interesting, if uneven experiment. The author has taken a number of his early sketches and tales, written in the first place independently of each other, and has added to them new stories with the aim, imperfectly realized, of bringing the whole into one coherent narrative. This "novel in eleven stories" is a series of tales which can be taken as separate works, but which are also to be read as consecutive sections of a whole work. Like *Die Schlafwandler* it covers three periods of time, 1913, 1923, and 1933, as the earlier novel had its three sections, 1888, 1903, and 1918. Behind the surface reality of the middle-class sphere in which the action is unfolded there looms a complex scaffolding of symbolism.

Broch's *Der Versucher (The Tempter)*, as edited and published after the author's death by Felix Stössinger in 1953, is on the broad scale of *Die Schlafwandler* and *Der Tod des Vergil*. It is set in an Austrian Alpine community, and its action may be assumed to take place during the period when Broch was first working on it, the years 1934-6. It is interesting that after *Der Tod des Vergil* and *Die Schuldlosen* Broch went on to make more use of traditional narrative methods, and this last novel shows clearly his control over action, suspense, and characters conceived in these terms. A remote and largely primitive village populace succumbs to the oratory of a vagrant fanatic; in a wave of mass hysteria this man's influence reaches its height in the committing of a ritual murder. The action is seen through the eyes of the village doctor, a middle-aged man who has forsaken eminence in the city for the obscurity of general practice in this out-of-the-way spot; he is a complex figure, one of the community of rough peasants and their familiar confident, and yet separated from them by his work and background. As a three-dimensional novel of village life *Der Versucher* has something of the vitality and grandeur of Jeremias Gotthelf's narratives of Bernese country life—in particular the theme of healing recalls the issues of the Swiss author's *Anne Bäbi Jowäger*; however, Gotthelf's peasant families have a norm of Christian belief which is lacking here, for the weakness of the Church's influence in this village is one of the factors which permit the tempter to lead it astray. Broch combines straightforward narrative with visions and monologues indicative of primitive, tellurian forces. His protagonist says:

> Our life is dreaming and waking at once, and if the chill wind of dreams occasionally blows into that world which we call reality—and it does so more often than we think—this reality becomes sometimes strangely illuminated and deep like a landscape after a cool shower of rain, or like speech which all at once is no longer a mere string of words telling of things that have happened in some shapeless limbo, but which has been breathed upon by a higher reality and has suddenly gained the power to portray things as they are with life and warmth.

The rhapsodic evocation of subconscious perspectives of symbolic depth does not wholly blend with the straightforward depiction of people and action in terms of common-sense realism. The different layers of perception remain disparate, so that the problem of combining them in an artistic whole is still unsolved. This last novel of Broch's is nevertheless fascinating and powerful.

Franz Werfel (1890-1945) turned to novel writing after making his name in the vanguard of the Expressionist movement primarily with verse and drama. He left Austria for France in 1938, and from there went to the United States. Religious themes had already played some part in his work before the success of *Das Lied von Bernadette (The Song of Bernadette)*, 1941, made this story of the healing at Lourdes a best-seller. His last novel was a vision of life 100,000 years ahead, *Sternder Ungeborenen (Star of the Unborn)*, 1946. Its picture of the future is more circumstantial than that of Hesse's *Das Glasperlenspiel*, though less poetic and refined in style. Werfel speculates freely on the details of possible intellectual and technical developments, such as inter-planetary travel. In its Californian background, its spiritualistic framework, and its general approach to intellectual problems, *Stern der Ungeborenen* has something of Aldous Huxley's *Time Must Have a Stop* and the earlier *Brave New World*. The author portrays a world-state which has been in existence in its present highly developed and comfortable way for many centuries. Life is longer, but the world population is smaller, and each individual is more precious and more delicate. This civilization, with its abundance of amenities, is, however, threatened with collapse through the extension of the "jungle" reservations, tracts of land inhabited by primitives of a twentieth-century type. The "astromental" world is finally overrun by the jungle dwellers, and for the most part its inhabitants choose suicide when faced by this situation. Werfel's portrayal of an over-refined civilization that collapses before a new assertion of instinctive vitality is undoubtedly compelling.

Carl Zuckmayer (born 1896) although more widely known as a dramatist, has been writing prose fiction as well as plays since the 1920s. He had to give up the home of his choice near Salzburg in 1938, and spent the war years in the United States. The vitality and down-to-earth humour which Zuckmayer has at his disposal is revealed in the tale *Der Seelenbräu* (1945), which gives a picture of incidents from life in an Austrian village community. The local priest is jocularly known as "Seelenbräu(tigam)," "bridegroom of the soul," on account of his rendering of a popular item of religious music; his counterpart and rival in the neighbourhood is the village publican, a personality representing in particular the pleasures of food and drink. *Die Fastnachtsbeichte (Carnival Confession)*, 1959, is written in a mood of sombre seriousness, where the starkness of the action contrasts with the apparent gaiety of the setting, Carnival time in 1913 in Mainz, a city which was closely associated with the author's youthful background. It is a story of the uneasy relationship between past guilt and the seeming stability of the present. Adelbert Panezza, "Carnival Prince" for the time being, is a prosperous owner of a saw-mill, a brick factory, and a vineyard in a village near Mainz. The shortcomings of his earlier life, especially in his attitude to his illegitimate son, are issues that he has to contend with again after the son's return to Mainz and his murder on Carnival-Saturday. Guilt is, however, by no means limited to one central figure, and the author's skilful exposition maintains tension throughout. The restless movements of masked revellers emphasize further the problems of dissociating appearance and reality.

Oscar Maria Graf (1894-1967) published in *Unruhe um einen Friedfertigen (Unrest about a Peaceable Man)*, 1947, a novel centring upon a Bavarian country community during the period extending from shortly before the First World War until 1933. The "peaceable man" is a shoemaker who comes with wife and one son to settle in a village where he hopes to be able to make his living in peace. His wife's death and his son's precipitate emigration to America confirm his desire to avoid involvement in any of the private or public events that take place around him. The rural locality is, however, shown as affected by the political and economic issues of the day, from the deprivations of war-time to the uncertainties of the revolutionary period in Bavaria after 1918, from the interlude of the inflation, when the farmers enjoy unprecedented but often unstable prosperity, to the first months of 1933. If the shoemaker Kraus is for the most part an onlooker, two younger men become leading figures and enemies in the political conflicts that flare up intermittently, but dangerously, in the area. Silvan, the Nazi, can triumph in 1933, while Ludwig, a Left Wing supporter, escapes to Austria after great difficulties, and subsequently to America. Although considerable stress is laid on the political issues, there is careful and loving portrayal of village life, with a varied gallery of figures that are characterized with robust vigour.

Graf's "novel of a future," *Die Eroberung einer Welt (The Conquest of a World)*, 1948, was written in America before the end of the Second World War. The story envisages a chaotic situation at the conclusion of the Third World War which is eventually resolved by the establishment of a humane world government. His "New York novel," *Die Flucht ins Mittelmäßige (Flight into the Mediocre)*, 1959, directs attention to a group of German-speaking expatriates living in New York in the post-war period and to some of the problems of living as part of this "diaspora." Martin Ling, a widower in his late fifties, is the central figure. Episodes from his earlier years in Germany and, as a refugee, in Czechoslovakia are recalled, while further inset material is provided by the stories which

Oskar Maria Graf. By permission of Ullstein Bilderdienst.

Ling recounts at the social evenings of the Kumians. Eventually persuaded to start writing stories for publication, Ling finds success, and therewith a problematic transformation of his personality. His relationship with another writer who has gained popularity is compared, by one of his friends, to that of Faust with Mephistopheles. Within a fairly short time Ling finds himself estranged from many of those he previously knew, and after catastrophes befalling those around him, for some of which he feels accountable, he gives up writing, declaring: "I want to live like anyone else, like one of the crowd. Simply to live and to be ordinary, nothing else, nothing at all!" This novel is a sympathetic and graphic presentation of some aspects of middle age, depicting the stresses of living and of being urged to creativity in an environment that in the last resort is not home. Martin Ling, like Ludwig in *Unruhe um einen Friedfertigen* after his emigration to the United States, has suffered from his forcible uprooting from the environment of his earlier life, "a man between the past and the uncomprehended present."

Hermann Kesten's *Die Zwillinge von Nürnberg (The Twins of Nürnberg)*, 1947, combines comedy with political satire. It follows the chief public events and moods of the two periods described, the two years after the end of the First World War and the years 1938-45. Everything that happens in the complicated but neatly contrived plot is within the bounds of reason, but only just. The twins Primula and Uli get married, the former to an ex-officer who later becomes an official in Goebbels's ministry, the latter to a writer who has to emigrate to Paris because of his humanitarian ideals. Primula becomes the mother of twin boys, both of whom later turn against the Nazi outlook. The last chapters, depicting both the life of German emigrants in Paris and the conditions in Germany shortly before the outbreak of war in 1939, are more serious in tone than the earlier part of the book. The final chapter shows with great effect the confrontation of Primula, still loyal to the outlook of wartime Germany, with her son Alexander, now a lieutenant in the American army, over the ruins of Nürnberg in 1945. This novel excels in the skill of its management of plot and dialogue. *Die fremden Götter (The Strange Gods)*, 1949, takes as its main theme the conflict between a father and his daughter over religious loyalties. Schott has become a firm believer in the orthodox Jewish faith of his fathers, but Luise has accepted the Roman Catholic faith taught her in the convent where she was looked after during those war years when her parents were in a concentration camp. The setting is the south of France. After a series of comedy-style adventures Luise is to marry the young man of her choice, though her father is by no means reconciled to this situation.

Im Westen nichts Neues (Nothing New in the West, English translation published as *All Quiet On the Western Front)*, 1929, established the popular reputation of Erich Maria Remarque (1898-1970) and became one of the most widely read novels about the First World War. His *Arc de Triomphe* (1946), the story of a German refugee surgeon in Paris just before the last war, has been a best-seller too. In *Der Himmel hat keine Günstlinge (Heaven Has No Favourites)*, 1961, Remarque writes a love-story concerning a motor racing-driver and a sufferer from tuberculosis; backgrounds in Switzerland, France, and Italy are lightly and efficiently sketched in. *Die Nacht von Lissabon (The Night in Lisbon)*, 1962, is a sympathetic evocation of the plight of German refugees from National Socialism. A man who calls himself Schwarz decides to give his long sought-after permit to emigrate from Europe to America to a fellow refugee in Lisbon. In the course of a night in 1942 he explains his reasons to the latter and thereby unfolds the story of his adventures between Germany and France after 1933, his internment in September 1939 and his flight southwards after the German occupation of France had begun.

Theodor Plievier (1892-1955) completed shortly before his death a trilogy which is a large-scale epic of the war between Germany and Russia and its aftermath. His manner of composition hardly applies to fiction in the normal sense, for there is so much emphasis on documentation and the narration of tactical movements that few of the many characters receive individual treatment. This is particularly the case with the first two volumes of the work. *Stalingrad* (1945) surveys the events leading to the defeat of the Germans in Stalingrad in January 1943. Its sequel *Moskau* (1952) takes as its starting-point the first days of the German invasion of Russia in 1941, and culminates in the approach of the fateful Russian winter as the Germans stand before Moscow. Plievier had unique facilities for collecting the material for his work; as a refugee from Germany in 1933, he made his way to Russia, and was allowed to observe the scene and sift documents of this piece of history. The events of the war in the east are told as a vivid and detailed piece of reporting in the naturalist manner. The impetus behind Plievier's writing turns from political theory to a more universal sympathy and pity. In *Moskau* a German whose life has been spared by Russian partisans reflects:

> Germans and Russians lay frozen in the snow.
>
> What had they wanted? What had their rules intended with them? They wanted to decide the fate of Europe.

> Not for the first time. . . . Charles XII was ruined on the fields of Poltava. The French musketeers of Napoleon failed. The German grenadiers now lay on the same frozen earth. Europe remained unborn, and the peoples on either side of the bloody wound are suffering hopelessly. . . .

The words of an old Russian man offer prophetic meaning to the despairing German: "'The earth has been given to men from God's hands without any frontiers. . . . The whole earth belongs to all, entirely!'" *Berlin* (1954), the longest of the three parts of the work, brings the novel to its conclusion. As an imaginative work it is the most satisfactory part of the whole, for Plievier brings to life the city of Berlin and the surrounding Eastern Zone with a vigour and variety of treatment that make fascinating reading. There is much that must be autobiographical in this novel which traces the fortunes of Berlin from the last days of Hitler in April 1945 through the early days of Russian occupation until it concludes with the abortive rising of June 1953; after holding an official post in the East, Plievier went to the West in 1947. There is an impressive picture of Berlin burning and of Hitler's final phase, before the narrative moves on to showing for the most part the struggles of a politician who tries to administer just government in the Eastern Zone, and the life of German prisoners of war in Russian hands.

The major work of Hans Henny Jahnn (1894-1959) is the novel *Fluß ohne Ufer (River without Banks)* which he was writing during his exile on Bornholm from 1933 onwards. The title indicates the theme: the river of life, or the stream of consciousness, which is a demonic, elemental force knowing no control. Jahnn's hero learns to identify himself with the raw, teeming life of sailors' quarters in South American and African ports and the bleaker poverty of a Norwegian coastal community. Gustav Anias Horn loses his fiancée when the *Lais,* a ship with a mysterious freight, goes down, and the memory of this catastrophe throws his whole life out of course. He refuses to see his parents again or to assume normal social responsibilities, but in perverse friendship with the man who murdered his fiancée lives first among half-castes and negroes and later in isolation in Scandinavia. A rebel against all traditional usages, he is passionately indignant at the injustice of race and class distinctions. A cultured handful of white folk in America and Europe may be in fact the conscious mind of humanity, but let them beware of their dependence on the inarticulate but vast and vital mass of mankind who are beneath them. If materialism is taken to be the right interpretation of the world, all life is equally holy, and if all life is holy, then life's fulfilment in the present should not be distorted by the memory of past failures. it is the paradox of Horn's life that as a man of forty-nine he is haunted by the shadows of a catastrophe that befell the ship *Lais* twenty-seven years before, although he has so strenuously been trying to live for the moment and to deny the validity of any code that would compel him to assume a responsibility which he resents. *Fluß ohne Ufer* is, like Mann's *Doktor Faustus* and Broch's *Der Tod des Vergil,* in part a "Künstlerroman," a novel about an artist. Horn gradually realizes his potentialities as a musician and composer (Jahnn refers in an essay "Über den Anlaß" ("Concerning the Cause"), 1954, to his admiration for the Danish composer Carl Nielsen). Characteristically enough, it is a pianola in a seedy South American hotel that makes the young man thrill to the discovery of a new talent. This work has eruptive violence and nightmarish qualities. Horn preserves the body of his dead friend and keeps the coffin as a piece of house-furniture. After his murder at the hands of Ajax von Uchri, the latter assumes the identity of Horn's dead friend Tutein

and enters into a relationship with Horn's adolescent son Nikolaj, who has been brought up in the family of the horsedealer Egil Bohn. The *Epilog* (1961), edited by Walter Muschg after the author's death, is not completed, but is a substantial narrative of events taking place in the months following the murder of Horn. The boy Nikolaj becomes confirmed in his musical vocation, while Ajax von Uchri develops a concern for the boy's development. In the *Epilog* Jahnn brings forward a number of episodes centring upon more peripheral figures: the relationship of Gemma Bohn to her children, Xavier Faltin's organization of the memorial concert of Horn's music and his subsequent illness and death, Faltin's children, and the adolescent development of Nikolaj's half-brothers Asger and Sverre.

The incident at the opening of the second book of *Die Niederschrift des Gustav Anias Horn (The Account of Gustav Anias Horn)* is indicative of one recurrent set of motifs in Jahnn's work and in part of his manner:

> I was deeply stirred. I will relate it briefly: I heard out of a heap of loosely piled-up dry pine twigs the beating of the wings of a big insect. I came close and recognized a dragon-fly which was fluttering anxiously in the open lattice-work of the small branches. It was not possible to recognize at once why the creature did not seek freedom, which seemed so easy to attain. It pushed against the ground with its head. It did not seem to recognize its surroundings. I bent down and now saw that a number of ants were spraying acid over the dragon-fly's great netted eyes; others were biting with their mandibles into those very eyes. I quickly stepped in to liberate the creature. It was too late. It had already been blinded, or partially blinded. It fell, beating its wings, to earth. . . . It died within a minute of over-strain, having succumbed to a heart-attack or to the unimaginable pain of blinding.

The maiming and destruction of the good and beautiful is seen as something horrifying but inevitable. In the *Epilog* Faltin's son Frode, a biologist, is haunted by the cruelty and destruction which he sees as built into natural life; if nature has no place for pity, "the awareness and acknowledgement of the pain of others," man can develop this quality. Lyrical moods and idyllic moments frequently appear as part of the texture of Jahnn's style, as well as other incidents of stark ferocity.

The short novel *Die Nacht aus Blei (The Night of Lead),* 1956, is a terse, closely woven piece of writing that is dominated by an atmosphere of the incalculable and apparently inevitable, concentrated within a few hours of a night in an unknown city that becomes increasingly solitary and dark. The protagonist Matthieu fails to make contact with whatever may lie behind the one illuminated window he first sees. He is reluctant to make advances to Franz and Elvira, while his subsequent meeting with Andreas ("Anders," his double at an earlier time of life) leads finally to his witnessing the latter's death in his underground cellar, when the last light, a flickering candle, goes out. In utter darkness and knowing no way out of the enclosing cellar, Matthieu nevertheless sense the returning presence of the "dark angel" who had left him at the beginning of the story. With few requisites here, Jahnn has given compelling shape to a vision of life and death. (pp. 23-37)

H. M. Waidson, "'We Have Been Forced to Look Around for a New Basis of Living . . .'" in his The Modern German Novel: 1945-1965, *second edition, Oxford University Press, London, 1971, pp. 14-37.*

THOMAS A. KAMLA

[In the following excerpt, Kamla examines various political and artistic approaches to the subject of exile in novels written about the exodus from Germany.]

Matthias Wegner introduces the exile novel in the closing chapter of his book on exile literature [*Exil und Literatur: Deutsche Schriftsteller im Ausland 1933-1945*]. His analyses of Lion Feuchtwanger's *Exil*, Anna Seghers' *Transit*, Klaus Mann's *Der Vulkan*, and Walter Hasenclever's *Die Rechtlosen* are undertaken to promote further comparative investigation into a body of novels reflecting a clearly defined theme, one in which the exile of German intellectuals in 1933 becomes historically identifiable. . . . Wegner's conception of the exile novel embraces a certain typology; it excludes many novels written between 1933 and 1945 which might only allude to or treat peripherally the exile situation, and restricts itself instead to those taking this condition as their primary subject matter, in which the problem of uprootedness is not the result of a timeless, existential predicament but of a specific historical phenomenon, namely the rise of the Third Reich.

In this type of novel there emerges the perpetual fugitive who lacks official identity and is always hounded by bureaucratic agents; there are the resigned and despairing, the uprooted languishing in nostalgia; there are the politically defiant whose protests are motivated either by contempt, a sense of democratic humanism, or a collective ideology; there are also the hopeful whose brief optimism is sustained by love and a selfless readiness to give; and there are the aesthetes and anarchist revolutionaries who denounce all forms of society, be they totalitarian or democratic.

Many of these figures, if divorced from the sociopolitical setting against which they are cast, could be interpreted as embodiments of a timeless exile condition. According to Wegner's definition, however, the fictional characters portrayed in the novels which concern us share an experience that brings art into a direct relationship with historical reality. In his analyses of the novels mentioned above, he establishes a method for further study into the way writers with different styles and social views might approach this reality.

The political character of the writer's new environment, which plays a significant role in any novel dealing with the Nazi-perpetrated exile, becomes conspicuously problematical, for example, in those cases where authors cater to the left but still adhere to traditional artistic precepts. In Klaus Mann's *Flucht in den Norden* (1934), Hans Habe's *Drei über die Grenze* (1937), and Lion Feuchtwanger's *Exil* (1940) the writer in each case purports to come to terms with the political demands of exile by incorporating into his work a communist who functions either as a contrast figure to the political indecisiveness of the West, or as a stabilizing element amidst the disillusioned and factionalized emigrant population. The fact that these writers create characters who are isolated revolutionaries, without a collective following, stems from their unwillingness or inability as liberal humanists to develop the full implications of their ideological shift. Both Mann and Feuchtwanger had sympathized with the Soviet Union as an ideological deterrent to the spread of militant Nazism. The nonintervention policy of the West in the thirties, the indulence accorded Germany as a potential counterthreat to the Soviet Union, and the presence of nationalist factions identifying with Hitler's regime explain these writers' emotional, but certainly not dogmatic, attraction to a nation that was preparing for the inevitable showdown.

As an "Ermutigung" ["encouragement"] to an emigration he considered to be "zerfahren und verfahren" ["in a hopeless confusion"], Habe portrays a revolutionary representing a collective, antifascist effort which, as he emphasizes in a later comment, bore no connection with the Popular Front movement dominating the communist exile scene in the 1930s.

In all three of these novels we detect a tendency on the part of each author to isolate his character from a Weltanschauung rooted in collective reality; this results in a discrepancy between form and content which is only aggravated by the writer's attempt to actualize his craft in the service of a political mission which he presumes to be Marxist, given the ideological premise on which he is operating. In *Flucht in den Norden* one would expect, going on this premise, a confrontation to arise between the communist heroine Johanna and the conservative Scandinavian family with whom she resides. Yet any political views voiced in her presence become totally one-sided. While Johanna might predictably have responded to them in a manner consistent with her political background in Germany, here she either evades the issues or disagrees on merely emotional impulse. The image conveyed of Johanna as the story unfolds clashes with the one evoked through flashbacks, where she is described as a member of a student communist group forced into exile in the wake of Nazi oppression. Johanna is to join her comrades in Paris after a brief recuperation with her classmate's family in an unspecified Scandinavian country far removed from any communist activity. There she becomes involved in a passionate love affair which prolongs her stay and causes her to neglect her political obligations toward her fellow communists in France. However, when she does come to understand the reason for her exile, she represses this awareness; periodic realization of the political nature of her flight and disregard of the revolutionary mission of fellow exiles do not form an integral part of the novel's action, but are concealed instead in reminiscences and feelings of guilt. Thus her commitment to a political cause remains passive; she never asserts herself against the views of her hosts which sympathize with the nationalist fervor erupting in Germany.

Klaus Mann's penchant for intimate psychological study, as evidenced in his portrayal of Johanna, ultimately serves as an artistic justification for eschewing a confrontation between the forces of progress and reaction. A literary tradition based on the principle of individual creative expression (to which Mann belongs) must preclude the systematic depiction of an exiled leftist as an effective counterforce to nationalist undercurrents outside Germany. Mann is caught up in the predicament of the literary artist who, at this crucial time in history, perceives as keenly as any other humanistic writer the urgency of confronting ideological issues in exile. But the difficulty in reconciling this purpose with his own creative impulse comes through quite clearly in his novel. That Mann takes an extreme position by attempting to create a revolutionary as his leading character is explained in large part by his sympathy for the Soviet Union at a time when the democracies were taking an irresolute political stance toward the Third Reich. This sympathy led to his presence, soon after the completion of *Flucht in den Norden,* at the First Congress of Soviet Writers in Moscow in the summer of 1934. The situation of the non-Marxist writer vacillating between the extremes of social commitment and individual freedom in artistic expression explains Mann's ambivalent impressions of this convention, and provides a revealing testimony to the problem with which he had to grapple in the novel.

In contrast to the remote, untypical exile setting of Klaus Mann's work, Hans Habe undertakes in *Drei über die Grenze* to hold up to the entire exile population a mirror reflecting its politically ambivalent physiognomy. Since most exiles have not achieved a sense of mission through their escape from Nazi Germany, and continue to indulge their private whims as though nothing had really changed, Habe implants in their midst a lone communist who functions as a unifying catalyst for the discordant emigrant population. Like Klaus Mann, Habe introduces a revolutionary more out of sympathy for the strength of an ideology resolute enough to combat Nazism than for the ideology itself, which presupposes a following. Averse to the dialectical materialism of class struggle, he envisions in the figure of an individual proletarian a socializing spirit on purely humanistic grounds, one which transcends the dehumanizing tendencies of party line dogma. Habe's motives for creating an undogmatic communist are both aesthetic and critical. He himself could never submit to the rigid authoritarianism of a revolutionary doctrine. In his autobiography he states: "I soon discovered that there exists an unbridgeable gulf between Marxism and the Muses: the Communists see in anything poetic—or, indeed in anything human—a threat to their principles." To bridge this gulf Habe strips his communist hero Richard Sergius of the "inhuman" attributes of his political allegiance by depicting him as a Christianized Marxist. The reification of individual humanity and the spiritualization of collective materialism implicit in this dialectic enable Habe to strike a politically tendentious tone in the novel without compromising an aesthetics of humanity aimed more at the individual than the amorphous masses. It is thus not surprising that he refrains from drawing a picture of a communist political arena in exile. By characterizing Sergius as a lone wolf, segregated from a united front of the proletariat (a stance which, in reality, was inconceivable for a communist exile), Habe can idealize the collective spirit of the political left without advocating a revolutionary sectarian program in opposition to his concept of liberal humanism directed at the masses.

The case of the liberal writer whose literary heritage prevents him from reconciling creative expression with the political demands of the day seems, at first glance, not applicable to Lion Feuchtwanger's situation in 1938-39, the years that saw the completion of the major portion of *Exil*. In his essay *Moskau 1937* he outlines a position which, unlike Klaus Mann's dilemma, no longer vacillates between the extremes of individual feeling and social conscience. This conflict, which Feuchtwanger's hero Sepp Trautwein faces unresolved in the novel, may have been felt by the author before he embarked for the Soviet Union. Subsequently, however, he renounced any further allegiance to a tradition which continued to uphold the ideals of bourgeois individualism at a time when such ideals had waned in the face of fascist tyranny.

The widely held opinion that Trautwein's indecision directly mirrors the author's own situation is an oversimplification and tends to ignore other textual characteristics. By arguing this way one inevitably removes the problem from the time frame of the novel (1935) and places it within the framework of Feuchtwanger's later works. Critics see the antagonism between Trautwein and his son as typical of the author's own predicament during the complete writing process. Yet, whereas Trautwein's son Hanns was only just preparing to embark for the Soviet Union, his creator had already returned. It seems improbable that Feuchtwanger would intentionally transpose his own conflict to 1935, when it was presumably resolved by the time he had returned from the Soviet Union in 1937. Furthermore, the creation of a musician, rather than a writer, as the leading character, makes a direct autobiographical link less compelling.

One peripheral figure does emerge, however, whose Soviet visit and professional interests constitute, as Hans Mayer correctly points out, "ein regelrechtes . . . Selbstportrait" ["a genuine self-portrait"] of Feuchtwanger himself. In the writer Jacques Tüverlin, Feuchtwanger is juxtaposing a figure from the post-1937 period to the events of the novel in 1935. Tüverlin, who in the first two parts of Feuchtwanger's *Wartesaal* trilogy was experiencing a crisis situation à la Sepp Trautwein, appears in *Exil* as a writer who had supposedly achieved a synthesis through his conversion to Marxism. By transcending the immediate time frame of the novel, Feuchtwanger introduces in the person of Tüverlin another historical perspective altogether, one which reflects his ideological position at the end of the decade. But this position, as it relates to character portrayal, is a dubious one, for Tüverlin functions only *marginally* in the novel; he is not a representative figure. In effect, Feuchtwanger produces a socially disengaged Marxist whose nonactive role precludes a direct interaction with the subject matter.

Feuchtwanger sets out to expose the political ineptitudes of the emigration without integrating a counterargument into his work. His sympathetic treatment of the Marxist writer Tüverlin implies a disaffection for the problem of Trautwein, but the break was not a conclusive one, regardless of his ideological predilections after 1937. Through his creation of Tüverlin, Feuchtwanger occupies a pseudosocialist ivory tower that only emphasizes the timeliness of Trautwein's conflict. Whereas most critics feel that Feuchtwanger was consciously voicing his own dilemma in Trautwein's wavering attitude toward individual freedom and a collective ideology, it would seem that the novelist was operating under the delusion that he had overcome it. Needless to say, the problem still exists in *Exil* despite the author's apparent unawareness of it, as indicated by his air of detached superiority to the events described. The connection with Trautwein had suggested an earlier conflict; the more immediate affinity with Tüverlin represents Feuchtwanger's position after 1937, intimating a resolution of the problem of artistic autonomy which, as the novel's structure reveals, actually remains unresolved.

Each of the three novels discussed above shows one way in which the exiled writer attempts to cope with the political demands of his new environment. On the other hand, most liberal writers treating the exile scene were not inclined to the left. Some chose merely to recount the common experiences which accentuate the condition of uprootedness. Without attempting to color their setting by radical ideology, these writers drew true-to-life characters whose actions exemplify the psychological and material strains experienced by exiles victimized by a grotesque network of bureaucratic red tape.

In Irmgard Keun's *Kind aller Länder* (1938) and Erich Maria Remarque's *Liebe deinen Nächsten* (1941) the respective writers set out to expose the economic and internal political inequities which determine the motivations of a large segment of the German exile community. The situation of the liberal writer in exile appears less problematical in this kind of portrayal. Since Keun and Remarque confront reality as it is, without trying to politicize it by flirting with an antibourgeois ideology quite alien to their literary backgrounds, they succeed in revealing that quality of "Wahrheit" ["truth"] which Hans Mayer sees as sorely lacking in the exile novel. In Keun's case, the creative distance needed to render an objective impression of a highly personal experience is achieved through the device of a child-narrator. Keun sees in the naiveté of the child a capacity for truthful observation. Although the author's own status as an exile writer is embodied in the figure of the child's father, she is still able to distance herself from this person by employing a narrative perspective less directly affected by the overriding problems hampering the writing process. By allowing her fictitious narrator to tell the story of the difficulties involved in eking out an existence by the use of one's pen, Keun creates an image of the exile writer that is representative of a whole generation of young, relatively unknown literary artists.

In *Liebe deinen Nächsten,* Remarque addresses himself to those complications in an emigrant's life stemming from his inability to claim legal asylum. A German "exile novel" would hardly be deserving of the name if it failed to take into account the unsolicitous attitude of many "humanitarian" host countries. For the most part, the democratic governments were unsympathetic to the plight of nameless exiles, a stance which often led to a mockery of justice when an outcast's desperate attempt to establish roots became a legal issue. *Leibe deinen Nächsten* illustrates the difficult problems existing among nations faced with an unprecedented influx of exiles. The novel's central theme, that of the vagabond expatriate, suggests that the only "domicile" remaining for a persecuted emigrant is the border itself. This theme illuminates the contradictions inherent in bureaucracies which made a pretense of justice by clinging to the letter of the law as it pertained to illegal entry.

Through Remarque's exposure of these contradictions one acquires a sense of perspective toward the German emigration of 1933; whereas, on the one hand, it was engendered by a dictatorship, on the other it was, in a manner of speaking, actually perpetuated by the democracies. Homelessness thus became a way of life for those exiles unable to prove their identity as German emigrés, although such a status was in most cases obvious to the various host countries. Remarques's realistic treatment of the exile environment manifests itself in the objective manner in which he portrays the reactions of legal functionaries to the emigrant problem. He does not arbitrarily depict them in an unfavorable light merely because the bureaucracies they represent made existence almost impossible for illegal exiles; instead, he perceptively draws a distinction between the bureaucratic callousness that emanates from genuine socioeconomic burdens and the indifference that is the result of the political regime operating the bureaucracy.

In other words, Remarque recognizes the internal problems facing the governments as they tried to control the emigrant population in their respective territories. He therefore sees the greatest contradiction between the principle of humanity and its pratical application in those countries whose governments were *democratically* structured, namely Czechoslovakia, Switzerland, and France (during Léon Blum's ministry). Austria, on the other hand, did not, even before the annexation by Germany, display so strong a discrepancy between the spirit and letter of the law owing to its influential fascist population. In this country exiled outcasts were, as the novel shows, hounded not only by an insensitive officialdom—which was the case in all countries—but were also baited by a decidedly hostile government. In *Liebe deinen Nächsten* one of the more realistic exile scenes unfolds. Here Remarque is describing not so much the problems of exile as such, as he is those of the exile country. The quasi-existentialist manifestations of the state of exile (e.g.,

uprootedness, alienation, lack of identity) thus take on concrete meaning through the particular sociopolitical setting that induced them.

In *Arc de Triomphe* (1946), however, Remarque's tone and attitude are so drastically different from those of the earlier novel that the reader is almost tempted to recheck the title page to confirm identical authorship. Here the format is no longer that of a realistic cross-section of exiles in conflict with an antagonistic milieu. Dominating the exile scene, instead, is a morbidly depressing character study of a single emigrant's private encounters in the bistros, morgues, and brothels of Parisian society. In contrast to *Liebe deinen Nächsten,* affectation and sensationalism prove to be the stylistic rule rather than the exception. Remarque does not resort to flamboyant display and intimate character analysis merely for the sake of digression, as is occasionally the case in *Liebe deinen Nächsten;* in *Arc de Triomphe* it becomes the underlying artistic principle, whereby the predominance of private entanglements and trivial conversation sheds little light on the actual exile theme.

As we turn to other novels we see that the writer may, at times, indeed alter concrete reality, mold it to his wishes as an escape device, or transcend it completely without reducing the pertinence of his work as it relates to the exile condition. Any of these approaches to his material can constitute an artistic means by which he seeks to understand his new existence.

In Bruno Frank's *Der Reisepass* (1937), for example, the author attempts to preserve, indeed ennoble, humanity at a time when barbarism was threatening to dominate all of Europe. Rather than politicize humanitarian ideals by defiant protest against the despoilers of German culture, Frank envisions the emigrant scene as a sanctuary in which cultural treasures can be nurtured unhampered by the reign of tyranny enveloping the homeland. His hero, whom we see initially as a member of a paramilitary resistance group inside Nazi Germany, retreats from any further political involvement after he goes into exile, a state which allows him to resume undisturbed his research on historical luminaries, extolling their timeless virtues as a cultural countermeasure to the current wave of obscurantism. In the idealized portrayal of his prince-hero, Frank creates during a period of upheaval an atmoshere of order and harmony which conveys those ideals of humanity and decency unspoiled by the blood and soil ideology infecting all spheres of cultural activity at home. The motto fervently upheld by most humanistic writers in exile, "preservation of the German spirit" (*Bewahrung des deutschen Geistes*), seems appropriate as a description of Frank's artistic motivation in *Der Reisepass.* Instead of confronting the exile population critically, as Habe and Feuchtwanger had done, or treating it as a springboard for political opposition, he molds his new existence into a humanistic cultural haven which, by implication, is itself a form of protest since its very perpetuation by a German writer defies the corrupting tendencies inherent in Nazi cultural policy.

The "escapist" inclinations evolving from a writer's exile experience assume rather unsual form in Renée Brand's *Niemandsland* (1940), where the author acts as both realistic interpreter of events and creative idealist. In the novel's two realms of existence—an exile-related one in which Brand unmasks the inhumanity of the would-be host nations, and an idyllic one in which she fashions her own poetic reality—both a political and autonomous narrative point of view are employed with equal justification. Brand's no-man's-land, a strip of terrain enclosed by barbed wire fencing, evokes an illusion of both freedom and confinement. While no country (for the time being) will encroach on this area in order not to violate its political neutrality, no "imprisoned" exiled inhabitant is at liberty to go beyond it. Hence a certain structural logic exists for invoking an idyllic past when Brand's no-man's-land is viewed in terms of the freedom of action and thought of which only its "citizens" may partake. In a manner of speaking, no-man's-land is segregated from the outside world: where the one is fenced in, the other is fenced out. It therefore reveals an identity uninfluenced by anything going on beyond the confines of the fence. When the author, in turn, addresses the political implications of the captivity-freedom dualism, she does so with the eye of the realist, denouncing those nations responsible for creating a no-man's-land in the first place. From this critical perspective, she depicts the neutral terrain (here the resemblance to Remarque's border as a kind of "domicile" in *Liebe deinen Nächsten* becomes readily apparent) as an outgrowth of inhuman legal restrictions which allow stranded refugees to suffer simply because they are unable to identify themselves to border officials. In *Niemandsland* interacting authorial views come into play, the one based on a politically confining reality, the other on the limitless reality of the mind. Both are produced by the dualistic nature of the setting.

The theme of freedom and confinement is evident also in Walter Hasenclever's *Die Rechtlosen* (MS 1940; publ. 1963). The characters, prisoners in a French internment camp, find in the realm of intellectual activity the only vestige of freedom left for them. As in Brand's novel, the image of a dual world is also evoked here by the one outside the prison and the one within. Hasenclever frequently refers to the community atmosphere of the internment camp as opposed to the aimless, unbridled existence led by those who are supposedly free on the outside. The concept of freedom takes on special meaning in light of this twofold form of existence. Who is actually free? The interned intellectuals who, in the midst of physical captivity, engage in abstract debates about the future of mankind, or those who are physically free but captives of their own irrational instincts and petty indulgences? With war looming in the background, Hasenclever makes a virtue of necessity. He seems to prefer the intellectual autonomy born of the crisis situation to the "normal" reality prevailing outside the camp. Paradoxically, the world of the internment camp provides his autobiographical narrator with that element of freedom unobtainable under more fortunate circumstances. The irrational impulses determining the present course of events are momentarily suspended in an "ideal" environment divorced from the anarchistic one outside. By creating within the internment camp a pseudoidyllic setting in which the intellectual elite acquire a kind of stoic immunity to their confinement, Hasenclever relates to the exile scene in a manner reminiscent of Brand's dual narrative posture in *Niemandsland*. This scene, set in late 1939 as man's irrational instincts were about to be unleashed, takes on mythical dimensions in the course of the debates, symbolizing ultimately the universal conflict between spirit (freedom) and nature (captivity) which Hasenclever perceives in society as a whole.

The writer's mixed reaction to the exile condition, seen in his factual and fictional handling of the subject matter, also emerges in Klaus Mann's *Der Vulkan* (1939). Mann's attempt in *Flucht in den Norden* to mesh a hitherto individualistic conception of literary art with an ideological shift to the left is abandoned in the later novel. The subtitle of *Der Vulkan*, "Roman unter Emigranten," is applicable to those episodes which, without any ideological bias on the part of the narrator, simply chronicle the activities of the homeless within the exile environment.

Cartoon from the magazine Simplicissimus, *1925. Klaus Mann is saying to Thomas Mann: "You know, of course, Papa, that geniuses never have highly gifted sons. Therefore, you are no genius." Simplicissimus Verlag GmbH.*

The detailed psychological and religious-philosophical scenes, on the other hand, are products of Mann's artistic temperament and reflect a narrative attitude that receives its creative impulse not from immediate social and political conditions, but from European literary masters who regard the intellect as the molder of one's own reality. What is noteworthy about Mann's twofold narrative point of view in *Der Vulkan*—that of objective chronicler and subjective aesthete—is his theoretical program concerning art and politics around 1938, when he began writing the novel. Mann's brief flirtation with the cultural politics of the Soviet Union had produced only a momentary conflict between the social conscience and subjective freedom of the individual; by the late thirties he had taken the position that these facets of the writer's personality are to be kept in their proper place. In *Der Vulkan*, he reveals this position by repeatedly stepping out of his role as sensitive artist and recounting objectively the typical problems besetting the emigration and, departing from this detached posture, by drawing characters who embody his creative assumptions. Proceeding on the basis of Mann's theoretical postulates, one cannot really speak of a discrepancy between form and content in this particular writer's treatment of the exile when he subscribes, in principle, to the absolute sovereignty of creative expression, as exemplified in such figures as Martin, Marcel, and above all Kikjou.

In deference to the argument that a direct relationship between aesthetic theory and practice does not necessarily hold true for all writers, we must of course turn to the work itself to determine the tenability of a writer's views. When applied to *Der Vulkan* do these views suggest an intimely perpetuation of an art for art's sake disposition, or do they have historical relevance to the period at hand? Is the supposed discrepancy between creative freedom and political conscience, which Matthias Wegner sees as typical not only of Mann's confrontation with exile but that of other writers, really an issue in *Der*

Vulkan, or does the problem lie elsewhere—in the political lethargy of the West, for example?

Indeed, this latter point is given sufficient treatment in the novel to suggest a justification for Mann's subjective preoccupation with such an eccentric figure as Kikjou. In his characterization of Marion von Kammer, the author points out the ineffectiveness of political art in a society unwilling to stand up to the threat of Nazi domination. The fact that Marion's recitations are unable to inspire resistance is not due to deficiencies in her art but to an unresponsive public. In creating his artist-heroine, Mann does not betray a conflict between aesthetic pleasure and social action, between freedom of intellect and political reality. These perspectives are not sensed as incompatible by Marion; on the contrary, they are quite compellingly interrelated. It is not the artist's fault if the message goes unheeded.

In those scenes depicting a confrontation between an ominous reality and a humanistic literary heritage, *Der Vulkan* sheds unusual light on the situation of the liberal artist in exile. Here a figure emerges who succeeds in adapting her intellectual heritage to the exigencies of the moment. She has achieved a balance between political commitment and bourgeois art, yet this achievement is destined for failure. In Marion's role as a defiant, humanistic artist, the problem of creative expression and empirical reality is not equivalent to a discrepancy between form and content (as it was in Mann's portrayal of a "bourgeois communist" in *Flucht in den Norden*), but to a problem whose origin lies in the international state of political apathy prevailing at the moment. An exiled artist's failure to receive public resonance for her efforts to influence change does not necessarily mean she is unable to reconcile timeless humanistic values with sociopolitical topicality. Such a figure is quite conscious of the necessity for commitment when she can relate her literary heritage to the demands of the time.

In his portrayal of Marion, therefore, it becomes apparent that Klaus Mann can integrate the aesthetic aspects of the intellect into a politically tendentious cause if he so chooses. In drawing this character, he departs from his theoretical "ivory tower" and, through Marion's recitations, renders classical examples of humanistic literature in a political context in order to demonstrate their *ineffectiveness* among the public for whom their activistic message is intended. Mann's penchant for artistic autonomy thus constitutes a reaction to the "apolitical" international scene forming the backdrop of the novel. And so it is not Marion who embodies Mann's *creative* intention but Kikjou, an erotic-mystical figure who appears in *Der Vulkan* neither as an artist nor as a German emigrant. A native of Brazil, his Bohemian existence in Paris emerges independent of the Hitler exile. As a result, the politics-art issue plays no direct role in the development of this character—a fact which enables Mann to explore the complexities of the human psyche without having to objectify them in the framework of social consciousness or political polemic.

If one were to point out a theme common to most of these novels, it would have to center on the problem of humanity and how it is defined in the context of the exile experience. In Konrad Merz's *Ein Mensch fällt aus Deutschland* (1936), however, the author employs, at times, such loathsome metaphors that one is initially at a loss to explain just how he relates to his exile situation at a time when most humanistic novelists were, in the act of writing, defending the dignity of language and thought against their gross misrepresentation at home. The rebellious, anarchistic spirit of German expres-

sionism, with which Merz had identified himself earlier in the century, erupts in a violent form of polemic which appears to reflect nothing but blunt retaliation, devoid of any rational insight whatsoever. One is tempted upon a first reading to dismiss the novel as a frustrated expression of uprootedness, followed by a senseless vilification of the uncivilized nation responsible for putting the protagonist in such a situation.

Yet, whereas much of the dehumanized imagery stemming from the more radical sectors of expressionistic writing may have seemed too anarchistic at the time, its employment as a vehicle of protest against an actual barbaric oppressor had special significance after 1933. Merz's strategy for coping with the exile situation and its Nazi perpetrators does not derive from the language of the humanist; rather, his frustration and indignation are conveyed through an imagery directly related to the ugly reality prevailing. The exposure of a vulgar ideology by an appropriately strong idiom is a more cogent form of polemic than one rooted in the spirit of humanism, a concept totally foreign to the Nazi mentality to begin with. Images of excrement, blood, filth, decay—all reflective of the more revolutionary, antitraditional aspects of literary expressionism— now appear in a context related to the peculiar reality (Nazi bestiality) underlying them. Thus, whereas some liberal writers approach the exile scene from incongruous narrative perspectives, unable to deal with a turbulent reality through a traditional mode of literary expression, Konrad Merz employs a narrative form which, in its relation to content, is more appropriate to the current situation than to the period of its genesis in pre-World War I Germany. Although the smug conventionality and false idealism of Wilhelminian society were perhaps not so reprehensible as to warrant the type of violent reaction seen in much of expressionistic literature at the time, the degenerate character of Nazi society certainly was.

The relationship between form and content becomes a less crucial issue, of course, in those exile novels which regard sociopolitical reality as a determinant of artistic creation. The communist exile novel reveals situations which differ markedly from those seen in works originating in the liberal camp, situations which provide an insight into typical ideological problems encountered by the politically engaged writer. The Marxist writer's alliance with the Soviet Union, and the ideological crises emanating from this affiliation during the Popular Front years and subsequent to the Hitler-Stalin nonaggression pact, are among the more decisive factors contributing to a leftist's literary assessment of the exile experience. In Fritz Erpenbeck's *Emigranten* (1939), Friedrich Wolf's *Zwei an der Grenze* (1938), and Anna Seghers' *Transit* (1943), we receive a fairly representative impression of the changing reactions to Moscow and the international political scene up to the outbreak of war.

Erpenbeck's novel, a product of the pre-Popular Front period, reflects the sectarian policy of the Communist International in mustering a united front of the proletariat against reactionary tyranny. Erpenbeck advances the position of the more dogmatic communist exiles who lived in the Soviet Union and never openly conflicted with directives laid down by the ideological homeland, which insisted on retaining political leadership in the right against fascism and denounced as traitors any communist exiles suspected of revisionist leanings. Whereas, in the early years of exile, other Marxists living outside the Soviet Union recognized the necessity of a rapprochement with Social Democrats and nonparty liberals in a collective effort to combat Nazism, Erpenbeck, who completed *Emigranten* in the Soviet Union in the wake of Stalin's purges, describes an exile scene in Prague in which an uncompromising revolutionary commitment asserts itself in the Marxist camp. His exiled Marxists continue to perpetuate the cleavage that had divided the two major socialist parties in Weimar Germany. A revolutionary front from below, augmented by a mass initiation of noncommunist workers into party ranks, is formed for the purpose of rendering the Social Democratic leadership impotent. In *Emigranten,* Erpenbeck depicts the early exile as an arena for solidifying the proletariat in its historical path to socialism. By isolating the workers from the influence of "social fascists" and other "capitalist liberals" in exile, he espouses the position adhered to in high communist circles that the revolution is close at hand and that only a mobilization from the left can bring about the downfall of a reactionary regime.

Like Erpenbeck, Robert Groetzsch was a Social Democrat who fled to Czechoslovakia and then to the Soviet Union after Hitler's rise to power. In his novel *Wir suchen ein Land* (1936), Groetzsch shows that the polarization of the two leading parties was hardly a one-sided affair, induced only by the communist camp. In many respects the Social Democrats in exile were more fearful of communist influence than were the liberal nonpartisans. Both socialist parties had traditionally claimed to constitute the true leadership of the working class, and mutual enmities became even more exacerbated in exile. Groetzsch's novel, portraying proletarian workers in a somewhat idyllic setting on the Czech frontier, must be viewed as a reaction to the kind of political activity initiated by Erpenbeck's workers in Prague. Groetzsch isolates his proletarians from any possible influence by the opposing party, "socializing" them in a rural environment more reminiscent of a Rousseauistic community than an antagonistic class society.

The novels by Erpenbeck and Groetzsch present a contrasting ideological picture of the early political emigration. Where the former unites his workers from below (revolutionary socialism), the latter does so from above ("liberal" socialism). A comparison of these novels shows that the exile scene for political escapees in Prague was but an extension of the ideological antagonisms that had characterized the political arena in the Weimar Republic.

In Friedrich Wolf's novel it becomes clear that not all exiled communist writers considered Moscow's political strategy to be in the best interests of the German nation. *Zwei an der Grenze,* a product of the Popular Front era, betrays feelings not totally in line with the spirit of this movement, which had its inception in the Soviet Union. In his novel, Wolf defends a revolutionary ideology on the national level only, and concerns himself with that group which, in present reality, exemplifies this ideology, namely the proletariat in conflict. The contrast between a nation (the Soviet Union) which had realized the revolution and one which was struggling to realize it (an oppressed Germany) crystallizes in the hero's vehement denunciation of an existence divorced from the problems at home. Ideologically, exile meant to many expatriated German Marxists a temporary home in the Soviet Union. Wolf's, or his narrator's, disgust for anything resembling an exile status constitutes a subtle attack on the host country of exiled communists and of the author himself.

The problem of activity versus passivity or, in ideological terms, of a dynamic revolutionary theory versus the mere lip service accorded it, finds a direct parallel in the dichotomy between a native home versus a "home" in exile. It is understandable that the author argues his case here with some caution. The crucial chapter, entitled "Einsamkeit," reads like a miniature

roman à clef and does not openly reveal the object of Wolf's diatribe. It becomes apparent that, by confining the conflict to Prague and the Czech-German border, Wolf consciously avoids a direct confrontation with Soviet policy, thereby creating the impression that his hero's impatience with party politics is limited to the local scene. One will recall that Wolf lived in the Soviet Union throughout most of his exile, and that any open venting of the source of his discontent—which appeared to stem from the undermining of the Popular Front effort by Stalin's purges—would have made his position in Moscow rather precarious.

The exile condition for the communist writer had even more serious implications in Anna Seghers' *Transit*. The republican cause in Spain had failed; the Moscow trials had triggered ideological panic among rank-and-file communist exiles; Hitler's militant expansion had swallowed up Austria and Czechoslovakia; the Stalin-Hitler pact had precipitated the demise of the Popular Front campaign; and now wartime conditions prevailed in most of Western Europe. By 1940, historical events had shown that antifascist efforts to thwart the wave of Nazi tyranny had proved unsuccessful. The communist writer still in France (second only to the Soviet Union as a refuge for the left) who wished to adopt the exile theme in the novel, was faced with a disjointed reality which made impractical the incorporation of any sort of ideological confrontation. In *Transit,* which depicts the flight of refugees from Marseille in the wake of the German invasion, Seghers resorts to the only source of material remaining at her disposal—the chaos of reality itself.

Without a viable ideological model to draw on for revolutionary inspiration (in view of the Soviet Union's isolationism) or an appropriate historical setting upon which to construct a collective opposition to militant fascism, Seghers must confront her fragmented milieu with artistic suppositions which themselves are fragmented. In a setting dominated by Nazi disorder, she can no longer employ a method of writing which postulates a dialectic process in social conflict. Seghers' debate with Georg Lukács in 1938 and 1939 over a writer's creative method establishes the theoretical tenor of the process which was to become a reality for the author in 1940 and 1941. In her correspondence with Lukács, she needed only the raw material to exemplify her aesthetic principles. Throughout her debate such expressions as "Splitterchen" and "Bruchteil" ["splinter" and "fragment"] appear regularly, characterizing both her artistic conception of reality and her personal relationship to it in view of the uprootedness created by an exile that was on the verge of dissolving into "Nazi order," the term poignantly used by the bandmaster in *Transit* to describe the disorder in Marseille.

Seghers discloses her position on artistic creation at a time when the uncertainties of a socialism modelled after that of the Soviet Union were already beginning to surface. Thus exile not only prompted her to outline her artistic postulates; it also brought about the expression of a creative posture quite appropriate to the situation at hand. In other words, Seghers formulates in her letters, however unsystematically, a kind of aesthetics of exile which was to be incorporated about a year later in her novel *Transit*. In this work there are several interacting elements: art and reality, personal experience and objective detachment, and an absurd exile milieu and a rational nonexile one. These elements interact, reflecting the novel's structural peculiarity as well as the author's own predicament at the moment.

In closing with this novel, we have shown that the complexity of the exile experience as well as the differences in background and philosophy perforce elicited a variety of reactions to the problem of homelessness and its attendant difficulties in mustering a united opposition to Nazi tyranny. Hans Mayer is quite correct in observing the lack of a "gemeinsamer Erlebniszusammenhang" ["common context of experience"] in the exile novel; but the requirement of a common experience is an inadequate criterion for determining the relevance and authenticity of this type of prose fiction, since the very backgrounds of these writers will cause them to relate to this experience not commonly, but in different ways. (pp. 395-413)

> Thomas A. Kamla, "The German Exile Novel during the Third Reich: The Problem of Art and Politics," in German Studies Review, Vol. III, No. 2, May, 1980, pp. 395-413.

OSCAR CAEIRO

[*In the following excerpt from an essay examining German and Spanish literature in exile, Caeiro discusses the work of German poets in Latin America.*]

It is a well known fact that Hitler's persecutions in Germany and the Civil War in Spain forced many intellectuals to leave their respective countries. Among those intellectuals were the cultivators of the lyric genre, the poets. These men, concerned with developing the qualitative aspect of language, its vertical dimension, played a predominant role among the Spanish exile group, as Juan Larrea noted quite some time ago. Similarly, among the German literary refugees, the poets also constituted a significant segment and were, according to Klaus Mann, forced into exile not only because of external pressures and political censure, but also because the atmosphere of the country had become unbearable to those who sought "to be intellectually creative." (p. 181)

Various journals, in different parts of Latin America, allowed exiled German writers to address those in that geographic area who knew their language. *Das andere Deutschland/La otra Alemania* was published in Buenos Aires by August Siemsen from 1937 to 1949 with the declared aim of "enlightenment concerning fascism." *Das freie Deutschland/Alemania libre* was first published in Mexico in 1941 and continued until 1946. *Deutsche Blätter/Ojas Alemanas* was published by Udo Rukser and Albert Theile in Santiago, Chile, between 1943 and 1946. It was circulated throughout the Americas and earned acclaim as "the most important voice of exile" because of its intellectual stature.

Deutsche Blätter, through both the classical and modern models proposed or remembered with admiration and the compositions of the exiles themselves, gives some indication of the role played by lyric poetry in the intellectual life of the German exiles in Latin America. In June, 1943, for example, this magazine paid tribute to Hölderlin. There is a connection between the texts by Hölderlin selected for that occasion and the condition of exile itself. This is perceptible in "Die Heimat" ("Native Soil"), one of the poems selected, in which the theme is the return from faraway islands after having experienced both joy and suffering. Hermann Hesse's "Ode an Hölderlin," included in the tribute, also seems to be an expression of that shared "eternal homesickness." The centennial of the birth of Paul Verlaine was commemorated with texts by Stefan Zweig and the translation by Paul Zech of a poem titled "Mirakel," which in the tone of a romance deals with war, the effect of

which is characterized with the words "A new heart was bestowed upon me...." The same Paul Zech, in another issue of the journal, remembers Else Lasker-Schüler encomiastically by paraphrasing a psalm of the Biblical exile in these terms: those who are seated by the banks of the river and weep and have hanged their harps from the willows will know how to appreciate the refined poetry of this German-Jewish poetess in whom the Goethean tradition and Jewish inspiration find resonance. Rainer Maria Rilke, an exceptional man and poet, also was the subject of a tribute by Zech, who saw him as a brilliant artist and as a prophet of the inner life. Hölderlin, Hesse, Verlaine, Lasker-Schüler, and Rilke form a constellation brought together not by chance but by a clear preference for consummate poetry able to express deeply felt emotions and to rescue the values of spirit. The exiles, in contrast with the barbarity entrenched in the homeland, again discover these deep springs from which to drink during their forced uprooting.

But *Deutsche Blätter* did not limit its selection of poetry to renowned poets of the past. It also strove to gauge the exile poets' own inner conditions. From different Latin American countries, exiled poets sent in their contributions. In July, 1943, Paul Zech offered four sonnets. The first of these is a somber lament that begins:

> Was it an excess, hardly bearable,
> that which injured us during the decade
> of wandering, so that we always continue to question,
> leaning exhausted against a foreign tree . . .

Although the poet refers to his own experience, his reference to inordinate pain brings Hölderlin to mind. A Germanic instinct directs the poet's attention to the tree, but the adjective "foreign" underscores the distance of this land from his own. The second sonnet by Zech concerns the lapacho trees, and it would seem that in them that which is foreign loses its harshness: "they are easier on us now, than ever was a space in this foreign country."

"The Falls of Iguassú," the third sonnet, expresses the profound awe produced by the grandiose natural spectacle of the falls; but the inner voices are not stilled. It is as though the impact of the encounter with the American land was not able to blot out the feeling of nostalgia: "But within, shouting voices raged."

Many poems raise moral issues. In "Strophes of Contemplation," a poem published in 1945, Zech observes with the reconciling tone of a moralist: "To praise yourself as just is easier than reinhabiting a guilty house...." He preaches the need to be at peace with oneself and insists that all destruction only serves to delay the inevitable. Exile has not taught him how to hate, but rather to appreciate the enduring values. From Mexico, Gustav Regler published a poem in 1944 that evokes, with an admonitory intent, the horrors of the concentration camps. The title of this poem is "Children of the Ghetto." Deliverance, as a vision of Zion, illuminates the somber destiny of the interned Jewish children. An infantile and fantastic interpretation of death, horrorless, with Biblical allusions, characterizes "Jacob's Ladder," a poem published by Regler in 1946. This poet is characterized by his preoccupation with persecution, cruelty, and death. Wolfram Dietrich (Mauricio Boersner), on the other hand, reflects a different intent. In "Das deutsche Jahr," a cycle of poems sent from Caracas, this poet seeks to evoke the quintessences of German culture, following, month by month, the progression of the calendar. Allusions to exile and to the political reality creep into some of these compositions. The one for October, devoted to Nietzsche, points to the discovery of the New World: "Forward! It is time to discover an America." The compositions for November, which refer to Luther and Schiller, pose the problems of freedom, law, and the need to rely only on God. (pp. 182-85)

The concrete examples of individual poets will illustrate the pilgrimages and the poetic themes and motifs outlined above. To begin . . . , some additional light will first be shed on Paul Zech (1881-1946). After having been jailed in Germany, his homeland, he went abroad in 1933, settling in Argentina, where he died without fulfilling his desire "to see Germany again and to be active there once more." The poems collected in his book *Neue Welt: Verse der Emigration* (1939, *The New World*) enable us to glimpse the course he followed from the moment he fled his homeland and through his subsequent encounter with the Ibero-American reality and a certain involvement with it. As Wm. K. Pfeiler has pointed out, these poems give evidence that "his integrity and creative power suffered no impairment in exile." The poems, most of which are sonnets, are characterized, in effect, by their sustained formal rigor and the authenticity of the feelings expressed.

Zech's exile began when he left a homeland ruled by crime and injustice, "where the earth blushes." Nevertheless, time and again, his thoughts turned to the past: "As the tide cannot be held by my hand / the word flows on and returns to the Fatherland." He also clung to the hope that Germany would again be free. His feelings oscillated between repudiation of the political situation and a nostalgia full of expectations. Zech was one of the German poets who allowed himself to be won enthusiastically by his South American surroundings; but nostalgia for the homeland continued to be the essential aspect of his poetry. This is clearly expressed in the XXXIVth sonnet of the "Die argentinischen Sonette" ("The Argentinian Sonnets"), which begins by denying: "Not the orange, that one may pluck from any tree . . . ," and then, in the tercet, explains:

> The foreign land has not freed us from lostness,
> but the homeland which we, mutely,
> only learned to love when we had to say: No!
>
> *(Neue Welt)*

"In the utterly foreign world," that beloved "home" blossoms with greater strength and beauty each passing day. The poet believes that even in the midst of those terrible days, the "righteous three" who would justify forgiveness can still be found.

A reference to trees and forests as poetic motifs is inevitable. In 1920, many years before his exile, Zech had published a book of poems titled *Der Wald* (*The Forest*) in which he represented—as Oskar Loerke has commented—the eternal law opposed to the mechanical civilization. This theme reappears in the poetry he wrote in exile. Perhaps as a symbol of his own personal destiny, he wrote: "No longer can a tree be so empty in autumn," so stripped had it become. Perhaps the forest brings back to him memories of the homeland and of its dead, memories he cannot elude in exile. He thought he had forgotten, but: "They overtake us, they're already there / where forests still appear as clouds to us."

Some of the poems in *Neue Welt* constitute poetic efforts to become involved with the American reality. Mythological American characters are evoked: Zupáy, the Quechua demon, leaps ahead of the rider through the passes to enclose him in a deadly circle. Another poem attempts to capture the mood of the round-up, along with the dances and music that mark this activity. Local words are intermingled with the German verses: "chacarera," "poncho," "pampero." The poet is se-

duced by what Esteban Echeverría called "the virgin, grandiose American nature," by the forests "which never saw a human trace . . ." and by the spectacle of cattle so numerous they have never been counted. This intact, unique, unedited reality repeatedly forces upon him the locution "noch nie" ("never"). His German verses reveal the awe that was evident from the beginning in the accounts of discoverers and *conquistadores*. And at a given moment he feels that the song rising in his throat and boiling in his blood is inadequate:

> Leave your lyre outside, because song from it
> does not fit here with tree and bird
> and this thunder-dark background.

The encounter with the Latin American reality awoke in Werner Bock motifs similar to those found in Zech (and perhaps even Goethe). Bock (1839-1962), who following the family tradition, had forged a brilliant university career and had participated as an officer in the First World War, went into exile in 1939. He arrived in Buenos Aires and settled there. In 1951, he published a selection of his poetry in a book titled *Tröstung* (*Consolation*). The initial shock of his exile is revealed in the poem "An meine Enkel" ("To My Descendents"): he, a man deeply rooted in the life and culture of Germany, suddenly, by decree of cruelly adverse circumstances, is no longer considered a German. The rejection is complete when he has to leave, as he expresses in an atmosphere in his poem "Abschied von Deutschland" ("Departure from Germany"): "Germany, your own child denies you." From the very beginning his poetry portrays this solitary, perhaps narcissistic, self that with great difficulty seeks to heal the wound opened up by being uprooted from its native soil. In the poem "Am Kamin" ("At the Fireplace"), contemplating the burning logs, the poet thinks about his own life: he too was a "young sprout, sprung from the forest floor," he grew, he knew the twilight and the morning fog. And then came the day when he was torn away from his native soil. He found himself compelled to mature, to flower next to the abyss:

> What you did was for my benefit,
> Into another plot of soil I could
> sink my half-dead roots.
>
> The energy of the young world flows through the branch,
> Spring in autumn: as I blossom once more,
> Glowing colorful my day wanes.

The tragic uprooting came to be seen as a blessing, because he was able to nurture himself with the energy of the young world. Several poems in this book, in effect, show how, through the encounter with another person, a "you" of intimacy and love, the new country becomes like a second homeland, the names of a foreign history become familiar to him.

He then experienced "Lenz im Herbst" or Spring in Autumn. As he explains in one of his prose meditations, he, born in October—the European autumn and the South American spring—having thought he would wither in exile, found instead an unexpected flowering.

Johan Luzian's acceptance of his new country was less resigned, more passionate. Born in Hamburg in 1903, he had to go into exile in 1936, after leading an active intellectual life in Germany as a theater actor, writer, and reader for a publishing house. The final point of his pilgrimage has been Chascomús, a small Argentine city located in the Province of Buenos Aires. In a pamphlet titled *Chascomús: Verse und Bilder* (1944, *Chascomús: Verses and Images*), Luzian immediately confronts the reader with the inevitable subject of exile: "We had to wander. . . ." It was an imposed destiny which brought him to the threshold of the pampas. But Luzian was able to adjust when he discovered the lake at Chascomús, where he stopped and put down roots: "But then there was the lake in the great green / silent curve of the flat land. . . ." The son of Hamburg, accustomed to having before him the great Elbe River, felt a certain familiarity with the water: "Waves, like old trusted words / beamed warmth and peace to me."

Another attraction of the new country was its democratic tradition. There, at Chascomús, a bloody battle had been waged the previous century against Juan Manuel de Rosas, the tyrant. It was this tragic conflict that inspired Esteban Echeverría's epic poem *Insurrección del Sud* (*Insurrection of the South*). The German poet, joining the history and the literature of the country of his exile, expressed agreement: "yet it is good to live in the shadow of those / who have once fallen for freedom's sake. . . ." He was also attracted to the new land because there he was able to plant the tree—a symbol perhaps of his life—of his own personal fulfillment: "we gave a tree life with our hands / and filled its roots with our love."

Luzian shares with fellow-exile Zech not only such arboresque motifs but also the theme of guilt, which he, however, occasionally intones in a more specifically political manner. In 1945 Luzian published *Tag des Gerichts, Gleichnisse und Balladen*, or Day of Judgment, Parables and Ballads. The primary intent of this book, it has been pointed out, lies in the area of "political poetry" that severely censures the political reality of Germany under Nazism. The book was written under the influence of the dramatic final historical moments of the Third Reich, which fill its verses with apocalyptic reminiscences. The exiles fled from the "Unheil" ("calamity") that spread to all parts and followed them everywhere; but the terrible moment of the destructive "Reiter des Todes" ("Rider of Death") finally arrived, and then those who had been persecuted became witnesses to the judgment.

But Luzian, like Zech, did not take up the pen only to accuse. His words are also an appeal in favor of the German homeland, in which not everything has been crime and barbarity. "I believe in the righteous three," Zech maintained (*Neue Welt*); and "Ten Righteous Men Alone . . ." is the title of one of Luzian's poems inspired in a Biblical account (*Tag des Gerichts*). Those ten righteous men would be enough to justify forgiveness for the country. And God can already find millions of victims in the concentration camps.

In 1952 Luzian published *Mondfahrt: Prosaverse* (*Journey to the Moon: Prose Verses*), a work that reveals a mature wisdom in its humor and in its maximum simplicity of expression. The preface, addressed to the "honorable reader," is a reflection on the destiny of the émigrés: they have become so many throughout the world that they constitute a "universal type" ("Welttypus"); they live like the "flowers of the air" found in South America, on air, light, moisture, and heat. "Our roots are in the air, in the air of humaneness." Nevertheless, Luzian does not lament his destiny as an exile. He is a man in whom the American spirit has become flesh. Against the powers and dogmas of the doctrinaires, he wants to protect his personal independence: "Do you want to bind yourself to one power, then give up your conscience!" He ascribes, thus, to that typical attitude that Jorge Luis Borges once characterized as "our poor individualism."

In spite of this intimate involvement with the country of his exile, the memory of his distant homeland, of its sky, its for-ests, and its soft light is not altogether forgotten. The last poem of *Mondfahrt*, titled "Return" ("Heimkehr"), is proof of this: "Upon a dream rainbow we come across the ocean. . . ."

The political intent in Luzian's poems is sometimes inspired in a deep religiousness, and, in this same vein, political reflections vested with an exhortatory tone can often be found in the poems of Paul Mayer (1889-1970). Exiled in Mexico between 1939 and 1955, he published a collection of verse titled *Exil* (1944). The love song of a young girl from Chipalcingo stirs in him the feeling of brotherhood: "All people—sisters, brothers"; the faithful gathered in a Mexican church are seen as messengers of a class struggle. The splendour of the sun in a cloudless sky, the richness of the flowering tropical vegetation, and a love full of joy form the vital framework for this profession of faith which does not conceal the gratitude felt toward the country of exile. Mayer's verses, then, can be said to serve as an introduction to the social theme in the poetry of the German exiles.

Social distress colors the poetry of Erich Arendt, the distinguished translator of Neruda, Alberti, and other modern masters of Spanish verse. The path of exile led this poet, born in 1903, to Colombian soil. He had previously been in Switzerland and had participated in the Spanish Civil War. He remained in Colombia eight years. The poetic expression of that stage of his life is found in the section called "Tag der bittren wilden Nesseln" ("The Day of the Bitter Wild Nettles") of *Aus fünf Jahrzehnten* (*From Five Decades*), a 1968 anthology of his poetry.

"Dürre" or Drought is the title of one of Arendt's poems in which the destructive power of nature is manifest most vividly; a vision of agony conjures expressions such as "the perishing waters," "the scream of herds in agony," and "skeletons of trees." Other compositions underscore, alter, and enrich the same intuition: the moon, a notable motif in this poet's work, is, as expressed in the poem titled "Transitory Day" ("Vergänglicher Tag"), a "death bell." And in a poem titled "The Lost Bay" ("Verlorene Bucht"), in a pounding rhythm that caught the attention of Volker Klotz, Arendt accumulates verses that evoke a landscape of total desolation: "From ashes the lifeless land / Sand, / a sea grey ashen land." This is how the despair of the exiled poet is projected to the Ibero-American soil; but it is also the same interpretation of the destructive or devouring nature found in a by now classic work of Colombian literature, *La vorágine* (*The Vortex*) by José Eustasio Rivera.

"With the heated scene, the tropics, the temperature of social misery rises," Volker Klotz observed and thus drew attention to another constant aspect of the poetry Arendt wrote in exile. A sky which has engulfed all the earth's consolation is the fitting backdrop for the appearance of a peon who, as one possessed, wields his machete above his head. The rice fields are not a sign of wealth or prosperity, but the reason for miserable existences such as Pedro Farrón's. "Ballade vom Hemd des Negers" ("The Ballad of the Shirt of the Black") is a moving story that shows the extent to which happiness is foreign to those who, like the protagonist, spend their days in work that only serves to extenuate them and to make other men rich: "He comes from the rice paddies, worn down, a shadow." Injustice, then, is as constant as the hostility of nature. And equivalent to the destructive force of the elements is the hatred that darkens the eyes of the Indians and blacks.

The persistent sad tone, the absence of joy—although not of love—are perhaps indirect ways of hiding a rarely expressed nostalgia. The poem titled "Ausfahrt" or "Departure" would seem to suggest something of this nostalgia in the eyes that contemplate "lurking, above the sea." But the dreams have died, and the sea no longer speaks of the homeland; its message is of an unfathomable primitive world that gives rise to mythical associations: "Now the waves beat harder: / waves of primeval time." The revolt of the oppressed culminates in a cry of Nietzschean rejection: "God died with the dolls / of childhood." Exile produces, thus, an anti-religious sentiment. Certain expressions allude to the weight of the Biblical curse. The poem titled "The Alien Herds" ("Die fremden Herden") contains these lines: "everywhere is / the unpromised land" and these: "Sweat / of the bone-tired blacks."

As Fritz Raddatz has pointed out, "night" is a key word in Arendt's poetry, as well it might be. It encompasses fully the expression of exile. From the attraction exerted by the darkness of the human skin, to the hatred provoked, in contrast, by daybreak, when light is like the yoke to which man is subjected, everything leads to the night, the mysterious center of this poetic world: "O rustling bride, the night!"

The social question also underlies, both in theme and approach, the *brasilianischer romanzero* that Ulrich Becher, born in 1910, wrote during his exile in South America. This Berliner, whose mother was Swiss, after finishing his studies and having begun his literary career writing prose and theatre pieces, went into exile in 1933. He first went to Switzerland and then to Brazil and America. During the 1940s, while in Brazil, Becher wrote a series of romances in which, with naturalistic detail, he gave an account of the picturesque and miserable life of the lower classes of society.

Attracted by this theme, the author intentionally focuses on reality from below. The objects he describes are characterized by elements of decadence or decomposition: "the moon steals away from Guanabara / like a piece of rotten orange peel." This procedure, applied rigorously, has an anti-illusionist effect. Instead of showing the beauties of the landscape, he focuses on repulsive details: "From the poorly lit tube of the Alfandega / plastered over with shiny patties / of the hundreds, of the hundreds, who spit out. . . ." And the terrible conditions, bordering on animalism, to which the inhabitants of the "morros," the hillsides, have been reduced, are not hidden from him either: "On the Morro of the Babylonians / the poor are sheltered in honeycombs." This exile wants to be an implacable witness; he takes advantage of his alertness as a foreigner to portray the environment and the characters with the greatest possible accuracy. The small children who inhabit this oppressively inferior world are the subject of some emotive moments. Agamemnon, the child who is attacked by hydrophobia and dies in the arms of his ignorant mother, is an example.

The nostalgia characteristic of exile, nevertheless, is present at given moments:

> . . . on the pier of homesickness, always
> contemplation would seize him and silent
> grief sprout for the lost home.

The pier stirs in the spirit the "bitter-sweet desire" which, for an instant, tears him from the reality he is intent on portraying.

The literary form of Spanish origin that Becher has selected reveals his purpose to assume fully the South American modality. The same can be said of the language he uses, as it is loaded with regional terms and rich in popular vocabulary. In his work the poetic language has been subjected to a perceptible

tension between its own German, European essence and the jumbled, exotic life of Brazil. (pp. 187-97)

It is not by accident that only a few German voices—Becher, Arendt, primarily—discover and lash out with clear awareness at the injustices they perceive. The Spanish poets . . . also forged verses for the political struggle or social analysis, but they vented their passion primarily during the years of the Civil War; they went into exile tired, parched, and perhaps disillusioned by the collective battles. That may explain why in exile they sought preferably the crystalline, quiet, solitary waters.

There can be no doubt that the poetry of exile, of Spanish and German poets alike, has a Biblical tone. This is obvious in some, such as Paul Zech, much more than in others. The echoes of Psalm 137, called the "Ballad of Exile," can unmistakably be heard. Sometimes it is the weeping that chokes the voices of poets such as Salinas and Moreno Villa, and sometimes it is the desolate abandonment under the emblematic poplars or willows, as evoked by Zech and imprecated by Alberti. Abraham's bargaining with Yahweh (Genesis 18:16-33) is repeated with conviction. Zech and Luzian appeal for hope and forgiveness in the name of the righteous—few or many, but real—in whom they find a foundation for redemption. . . . And Erich Arendt senses on his shoulders the weight of the Biblical curse, of having been expelled from paradise.

Various Latin American traditions also come to life in the poetry of these exiles. We can perceive in them the process of transformation that changed Europeans into Americans from the earliest days of the discovery and conquest of the New World. The Indian backdrop or typical intuitions of nature are a frequent feature of Zech's poetry; Luzian feels infected by the political fervor of the struggle against tyranny and by the spirit of individualism; . . . Arendt surrenders to the vertigo produced by the destructive voracity of the elemental powers. . . . And in several of these poets there is a repetition of the dazzling discovery, which Salinas savors with unequalled delight. Their poetry reveals how these Europeans start to become Latin Americans. (pp. 203-04)

> *Oscar Caeiro, "Profile of German and Spanish Exile Poets in Latin America," in* Latin America and the Literature of Exile: A Comparative View of the 20th-Century European Refugee Writers in the New World, *edited by Hans-Bernhard Moeller, Carl Winter Universitätsverlag, 1983, pp. 181-206.*

EGBERT KRISPYN

[*Krispyn is a Dutch-born American educator and critic. In the following essay, he discusses writings by German émigrés who did not return to Germany after World War II ended, positing a relationship between their literary objectives and their choice of permanent exile.*]

Most of the authors who were forced by the Nazis to flee their homeland returned to Germany in the late 'forties or early 'fifties. However, a number of them, representing different types of writers, perpetuated their exile voluntarily. They continued to write in German while living abroad, and their motives for doing so were diverse and complex. Nevertheless, there appears to have existed some relation between their choice of permanent exile and their literary-stylistic stance. This may be illustrated with reference to some exemplary cases.

Lion Feuchtwanger was one of those who remained in America, where he settled in 1941, until his death in December, 1958.

From the beginning of his writing career, his favorite literary vehicle was the historical novel, which by its very nature tends to treat subject matter with distance and objectivity. Feuchtwanger stressed this aspect of the genre by using a language modeled after the impersonal style of ancient chroniclers. How essential this narrative attitude was to him and his art becomes evident from his novel *Erfolg* (1930), one of the few works in which he does not deal with long-past events. In order to gain a "historical" perspective on personalities and political events in Bavaria from 1919 to 1923, which Feuchtwanger knew at first hand, he told the story as if from a point of time in the distant future. There appears to be an affinity between this urge for narrative remoteness and the state of exile which the author chose as a way of life. Apart from the obvious physical separation from the native soil which exile imposes, the problem of language is, in this context, of major importance. The isolation from the living mother tongue inevitably affects the exile's command of it, and especially for an author stagnation and loss of spontaneity in his artistic medium is an extremely serious matter. But Feuchtwanger interpreted this loss of linguistic vitality positively, because it stimulated more and more drastic stylization and thus contributed to the objectivity of expression he sought.

In Feuchtwanger's case there is a direct link between the choice of exile as a way of life and his nature as a writer of objective pseudo-chronicles. At the other end of the scale, among highly subjective lyric poets identifying totally with their creative cosmos, there can also be a profound connection between art and exile. Examples of this are Nelly Sachs and Else Lasker-Schüler, both of whom regarded themselves as representatives of the Jews in their suffering at the hands of the fascists. So their own flight and homelessness exemplified the fate of the persecuted people to which they devoted their poetry. Each in her own way, Nelly Sachs in a conceptual framework of gnostic speculation and Else Lasker-Schüler more subjectively intuitive, they manifested a fundamental affinity between a personal life of permanent exile and a literary oeuvre of lyric immediacy.

Yet another type of writer who voluntarily remained abroad after the end of the Nazi era is represented by the novelist Hermann Broch. In his trilogy *Die Schlafwandler* (1931/32) there is a successive shift of the scene of action from East to West, signifying the gradual emergence of a rational, "western" kind of man out of the mystically oriented "eastern" type. This symbolism is extended in the fascination of August Esch with America as the country of freedom and justice and the place where the future will happen. Broch's personal decision to perpetuate his American exile was consistent with the views expressed in his work, and indicates that in this instance, too, the unwillingness to return home after the end of the Nazi era was related to the mainsprings of the author's literary activity. Nevertheless it is difficult to draw generalized conclusions about the nature of exile as a way of life from the cases cited above. Too many personal and non-literary factors which elude the literary historian's grasp might have been involved in the choice of a permanent foreign domicile.

The basic issues on the creative level can therefore better be gauged by reference to a younger group of exiles who had not yet been launched on a literary career when they left their homeland. Growing up in a foreign environment, some of them were sufficiently rooted in their native language and culture to start writing in German—exile authors from the very beginning. Thus, for instance, Erich Fried, who has remained a German writer residing in England to this day. He provides a case in point which may illuminate one possible reason why a writer after more than thirty years continuous residence in another country may yet cling to his native language as his literary medium. Fried is extremely pessimistic with regard to the effectiveness of the word against the powers of evil, claiming that the poet cannot reveal his deeper insights to anyone. This explains, for instance, the apparent paradox that his poems protesting the Vietnam war are couched in the German language, which prevents them *a priori* from having a practical effect such as English texts might have by supporting pacifist tendencies in American public life. It may be assumed that in a sense this futility is intended as a demonstration of the impotence of the poetic word and spirit as such. The use of German in this context confirms that Fried considers himself as an exile—not so much from any specific country, as from society in general. This awareness of exile as an existential condition may well be the common denominator of all the various factors that prompt writers to opt for a life beyond their own linguistic realm.

Certain ontologic and metaphysical ramifications of the artist's essential outsider position can be traced in the cases of some writers who, like Fried, were exiled in their youth, but did not adopt German as their medium right from the start of their literary careers. Peter Weiss who, after numerous moves, settled in Sweden with his family, as a writer and film maker developed within the atmosphere and language of his new country. It was not until some years after the war, when he had lived in Sweden for almost a decade, that Weiss wrote his first work in German, *Der Vogelfreie*, which, however, was not published in the original version, but only in a Swedish translation. Another thirteen years passed before he, in 1960, made his debut as a German author with the micro-novel *Der Schatten des Körpers des Kutschers*. In the following years Weiss published his two predominantly autobiographical novels *Abschied von den Eltern* and *Fluchtpunkt*, which contain much information about the reasons for the reversion to his native tongue. It appears that due to his family background he never identified fully with the Germans, and used the language without attaching any nationalistic value to it. German to him was an instrument for obtaining knowledge and understanding without regard to boundaries, as he read translations of literary monuments from all major civilizations. But his exile radically changed the German language from a medium for the establishment of universal rapport into a manifestation of his total isolation. During the war German was the language of the enemy with whom no communication was possible, and which consequently confronted him with his inexorable fate as an exile.

After the defeat of the fascists, when international contacts became possible again, Weiss underwent a profound experience which drastically altered his relation to his native tongue again. Initially it was a sense of rebirth, in which all language became questionable to him, and which led to a feeling of absolute freedom. At first it overwhelmed him with an awareness of perplexity and vulnerability, but gradually he found his bearings and adopted German as his natural, personal means of expression, in which he could "give everything a name." The allusion, in this quoted remark from *Fluchtpunkt*, to the adamic act of nomenclature, may well point to the ultimate basis for the phenomenon of exile as a way of life.

Michael Hamburger who at age nine went to England with his parents, like Peter Weiss started writing in the language of his adopted country. Hamburger too, many years after the war, reverted back to German for some of his creative writing, and has commented on his position "between the languages" in terms that corroborate the essentially mystic nature of the decision to write in the native language while living permanently abroad. He asserts that the writer must always seek to find his way back to the first words and beyond, to that which was there before the words, and makes numerous other references to the ontologic aspect of poetic language. In this context it becomes clear that the state of permanent exile enables the writer to assign to his childhood language the status of a personal cypher for the *lingua adamica,* and thus provides him with an effective means for the symbolic evocation of the Lost Paradise. (pp. 58-60)

Egbert Krispyn, "Exile as a Way of Life," in Germanic Notes, *Vol. 3, No. 8, 1972, pp. 58-60.*

AUSTRIAN LITERATURE IN EXILE

HELMUT F. PFANNER

[*Pfanner is an Austrian-born American educator and critic specializing in German exile literature. In the following excerpt, he discusses exiled Austrian writers as a group differentiated from German exiles by distinctively Austrian concerns, dialect, and nationalist sentiments.*]

A large percentage (about one-third) of the German-language writers who fled the Third Reich were Austrians by virtue of either birth or their acquired citizenship. That many of them also felt distinctly Austrian rather than German, Czech, or Hungarian (based on the multi-national constitution of the old Austro-Hungarian Monarchy) has been reflected in their writings. They saw themselves as a part of that cultural tradition which the area along the Danube and centered in Vienna acquired during the past few centuries and which in 1918 was restricted to the present-day boundaries of this country that calls itself *Österreich.* Although the writers in question wrote almost exclusively in German, and Hitler had made Austria a part of the German Reich in 1938, they did not consider themselves Germans any more than a modern American author would consider himself an Englishman or a Chilean author would call himself a Spaniard. To be sure, the Austrian exile writers acknowledged the fact that they shared the language of their German colleagues who were also their companions in fate, but they did not believe that speaking the same language entailed the need for their identifying themselves in any political or even cultural sense with the German Reich. In their writings they expressed a very noticeable preference for Austrian subject matters, and their literary language contained certain linguistic features which are not found in the works of the German writers. These distinguishing marks of Austrian exile literature reflect various degrees of the writers' adherence to a social and cultural tradition which had been seriously disturbed and interrupted in the country from which they had fled as the result of Hitler's *Anschluß.*

All over the world, Austrian exiles liked to refer to themselves as "das österreichische Exil," thus clearly separating themselves politically and culturally from the Germans. But also from the perspective of the German refugees the Austrian exiles were seen as members of an independent country. Although both the German and the Austrian exiles shared the common goal of the defeat of the Nazis, neither the Germans nor the

Austrians thought of the other country when they made plans for the political reconstruction of their homelands after the war. Thus, while their compatriots at home were forced to serve the one National Socialist German State, the representatives of *das andere Deutschland* and of *das andere Österreich* expressed their national allegiance to two separate countries. This does not negate the widespread existence of pro-German sentiments among most Austrians, including members of all political parties with the exception of the Communists and the Monarchists, during the Second Republic. As historians have shown, these feelings changed quickly as a result of the *Anschluß,* and whatever pro-German sentiments may have been left among some exiles after 1938, they were blown away by the Moscow Declaration of 1943, in which the future independence of Austria was reconfirmed by the Allies. This political act enhanced the national consciousness of the Austrian exiles in all parts of the world, and some of them even took credit for having influenced the Allies' decision.

In order to continue to uphold their national identity and to preserve their socio-historical heritage the Austrian exile writers formed groups in all countries in which German-language exiles lived during the Third Reich, notably France, England, and the United States. They wanted, for themselves as well as for the foreign public, to uphold the concept of Austria as a separate political and cultural entity and to give moral support to the Allies' efforts in liberating their occupied homeland. In 1938 "La Ligue de l'Autriche Vivante" was founded in Paris, counting among its members the novelists Franz Werfel and Joseph Roth, the musicologist and writer of prose fiction Paul Stefan, and the political journalist Ludwig Ullman. When the French Army was defeated in 1940, the Austrian "Ligue" was dispersed and its former members were forced to flee the European continent; most of them went to England and to various countries in North and South America. In London and in other English cities Austrian exiles formed or joined such organizations as the "Austrian Centre" and the "Free Austrian Movement." There were well-known writers among them such as Erich Fried, Robert Neumann, Hermynia zur Mühlen, Ernst Sommer, Fritz Brainin, and Hilde Spiel. The weekly expatriate journal *Zeitspiegel,* published in London by and for the use of the Austrian authors, served them as a vehicle for expressing a strong national consciousness. In New York too the Austrian writers rallied behind their own national exile groups and periodicals. The two monthly journals *Austro-American Tribune* and *Austrian Labor Information* expressed the interests of the Austrian exiles as much as *Aufbau* and the *Neue Volkszeitung* reflected the particular cause of the exiled Germans. Serving the same purpose for Austrian exiles living in Latin America, *Austria Libre* was published with two simultaneous editions in Mexico City and in Montevideo. Among the separate theater groups which the Austrian exiles used to preserve and to build up their national consciousness the "Laterndl" and the "Blue Danube" must be mentioned in London as well as Ernst Lothar's "Austrian Theater" and Erich Juhn's and Oskar Teller's cabaret "Die Arche" in New York.

Austrian subject matter dominates heavily in all of the periodical and the book publications by German-language exile writers from Austria after 1938. The previously mentioned journals contain numerous articles on the political and social conditions in Austria during and after World War II. The country's cultural tradition was expounded in many literary portraits of Austrian figures in such realms as music, film, art, and literature. Emphasizing their cultural heritage seemed an important task to the Austrian exiles in their fight against the

Nazis, especially since Hitler had made it one of his stated goals to subject everything within his reach to German influence. (pp. 82-5)

In the autobiographical novel *Auf und ab* by Fritz Heydenau the hero, who lives in New York and falls in love with an American girl, eventually marrying her, can never free himself from his emotional ties to his homeland. When he passes a few produce stands on Manhattan's Second Avenue, they conjure in him a vision of the Vienna *Naschmarkt,* the largest fruit and vegetable market of his native city. From then on that part of the city means "Austria" to him, and he uses an Austrian coffee shop in New York as the emotional substitute for his homeland.

In a poem by Friedrich Bergammer entitled "Madison Avenue" a black boy sings a few lines from a Viennese song outside the exile persona's place of work in New York and thus awakens a chain reaction of nostalgic memories which confirm his belief that Austria still exists: "Er weiß nicht, wenn er eine Botschaft bringt, / der wie ein Engel für den Zweifler singt" ["He doesn't know, when he brings a message, / that he is singing like an angel for a doubter"].

Sometimes even music in its more abstract form served to stimulate some of the Austrian exiles' inner realization of their homeland. In her book of autobiographical stories and episodes set in New York City Adrienne Thomas relates how she once came upon a group of Viennese exile musicians who performed Schubert's quintet "The Trout" in a Manhattan basement apartment. Playing without an audience, they apparently were oblivious of their present location and felt themselves transposed into an Austrian mountain scenery.

The mental and emotional transference of their empirical surroundings by means of which the exiles tried to keep in contact with their physically remote homeland was perhaps best expressed by Richard Beer-Hofmann. Before his emigration from Austria Beer-Hofmann had stated that the only place where he could ever live or write was Vienna; he was reminded of this when he lived as an exile in New York City and somebody raised the question of whether he did not feel uprooted: "Wozu brauche ich denn Wurzeln," he asked, "ich hab' ja Flügel?" ["What do I need roots for when I have wings?"]

Another exile in New York, who often used his poetic "wings" for an inner flight to his Austrian homeland was Ernst Waldinger. As the title of one of his poetry collections indicates, his lyrical imagination constantly oscillated between the landscape on the American river Hudson, representing the location of his exile, and the Austrian Danube, signifying his birthplace. Sometimes in Waldinger's vision the autobiographical persona is carried from one continent to the other by an abrupt transition in the middle of a poem as, for example, in the sonnet "Der Piaristenplatz in der Josefstadt," in which the final triplet reveals the preceding description of a Viennese square as a mere illusion. . . . It was also Waldinger who found the sharpest line of separation between the German writer on the one side and the Austrian author expressing himself in German on the other. In another of his many exile sonnets the poet vowed: "Ich bin ein Sohn der deutschen Sprache nur. / Ich bin kein Deutscher, wohl ist mir darum" ["I am just a son of the German language. / I am not a German, which is a good thing as far as I'm concerned."]

The use of the German language as a means of literary expression was, of course, not an asset to the Austrian writers in exile, who had become largely dependent upon a limited reading audience in German and the slim chances of having their works translated into other languages. A world at war with Germany did not want to hear or read the enemy's language. Some Austrian and German writers actually felt ashamed that they shared the same language with the Nazi rulers, but it was less from a feeling of shame than from a sense of national pride that the Austrian exiles frequently pointed to the vernacular differences between their own use of German and that which was spoken by German exiles and the people in the Reich itself. In a poem entitled "Wienerisch" Ernst Waldinger proudly described his native dialect, that of Ottakring, Vienna's Sixteenth District, as:

> Leicht nasal und weich wie ein Kalfakter
> Unter allen deutschen Dialekten,
> Süffig, doch gefährlich, gleich den Sekten
> Unter Weinen, ohne den Charakter
> Preußisch-schnarrender Kommandotöne,
> Sehr melodisch, offen für das Schöne.

In the final stanza of this poem the author says that his characteristic brand of Viennese gave him a special Austrian accent in English, thus making his English sound altogether different from that of the German exiles. It was also very important to the poet to point to the difference between the Austrian and the Prussian intonation in the use of the same language. His evaluation of the two German dialects expresses the typical patriotic feelings of many Austrian exiles.

Traces of the Austrian-German idiom and pronunciation can be found in practically all the works of Austrian exile literature. For example, the typical omission of the conjugational "e" in the first person singular present-tense verb form is encountered throughout Grete Hartwig-Manschinger's poem "Ein Mann hat Heimweh," which contains the two lines: "Wenn ich Heimweh hab', bild' ich mir ein, / daß mein Coca-Cola ein Glas Wein" ["When I am homesick I imagine / that my Coca-Cola is a glass of wine"]. The slightly monophthongized Viennese pronunciation of the German diphthongs made it possible for Manschinger to rhyme the words "Café" and "Kai" in the same poem: "Ist der 'Hector' nicht ein Ringcafé / Und die East Side der Franz-Josefs-Kai?" ["Isn't the 'Hector' a 'Ring' café / And the East Side the Franz-Josef wharf?"]

It is even questionable whether the average German can understand all the vocabulary used by the Austrian exile writers. Otto Fürth wrote a poem in New York on the occasion of a reunion of former students who had all attended the same famous high school in Vienna. Reminiscing about their teachers and the humanistic education which they had received from them and which still united them after many years of separation, the poet also mentions the lunch which the boys would eat in the school yard:

> Die grauen Mauern, alten Pflastersteine,
> Wo man um zehn die Schinkensemmel aß
> (Auch Bosniaken und Salamibrote),
> Minutenlang an die Gefahr vergaß,
> Die oben in den Klassenräumen drohte.

> ["The gray walls, old cobblestones,
> Where you ate ham on a roll at ten
> (Also rye rolls, and salami on bread),
> And for a few minutes forgot the danger
> That threatened up in the classrooms."]

The noun compound *Schinkensemmel* consisting of *Schinken* (ham) and *Semmel* (a hard roll) may be familiar to some Germans living close to the Austrian border although *Brötchen* is much more commonly used in Germany for the same item.

However, what are *Bosniaken,* a word for which a German dictionary will at the most give the meaning as being synonymous to *Bosnier,* the people of Bosnia, a part of Yugoslavia? Austrians use the same word for a small rye bread in the form of an elongated hard roll, a favorite among many Viennese school children.

The special flavor of German as it is spoken in Austria transcends the linguistic elements of pronunciation and vocabulary, but one can still sense it in the pithy remark with which the brilliant Viennese essayist and writer of short stories Anton Kuh commented upon his anticipated exile in the United States: "Oh, das ist doch nicht so schlecht. Schnorrer braucht man überall." ["Oh, it's not so bad. Spongers are needed everywhere."] Though Kuh kept his inner tie to his Austrian homeland throughout his exile period, his untimely death in New York in 1941 prevented his return to Austria after the war.

In whatever form their patriotic consciousness was expressed by the Austrian exile writers during the seven years in which Hitler tried to eliminate Austria from the world's political map there is no doubt that their national loyalty also made it more difficult for them to find the road to professional success and social assimilation in their host countries. The correspondence of Oskar Jellinek, to mention but one example, is filled with lamentation over his inability to find the right outlet in America for his poetic raw material, which he considered to be deeply imbedded in the Austrian tradition. He clearly saw the cause of his literary ineffectiveness in exile in his inability to step outside the sphere of his cultural heritage, which he considered to be primarily Austrian, although he also lists German, Moravian, and Jewish elements as additional influences. Like Jellinek, who died in Los Angeles in 1943 as a lonely man and almost forgotten writer, many other Austrian exile intellectuals spent the war years in America waiting only for the day when they would be able to return to their homeland; or, if they did not return once the road was again open, they continued to live in the Western Hemisphere or in other parts of the world with their thoughts and inner feelings directed towards their old home.

Relatively few exile writers returned to Austria after the war. The works of those who did, together with those of many who did not, served the function of bridging the political and cultural gap between the First and the Second Republic in the slow but continuous growth of the Austrian national consciousness. Today Austrian literature can thrive again in its native surroundings, and new writers are supplying the German-language book market with widely recognized works of a distinctly Austrian character. Whatever credit is due to these younger writers for having contributed to the creation of the strongly emerging national identity of the Austrians after World War II, one should not forget that the specifically Austrian tradition in literature underwent a crucial test of survival during the years of the *Anschluß.* The fact that it did not succumb was at least in part due to the efforts of the exiles who not only maintained the idea of Austria as an independent country, but also the idea of a separate Austrian literature with its own national character. (pp. 85-9)

Helmut F. Pfanner, "Was There an Austrian Literature in Exile?" in Modern Austrian Literature, *Vol. 17, Nos. 3 & 4, 1984, pp. 81-91.*

GERMAN PUBLISHING IN THE UNITED STATES

ROBERT E. CAZDEN

[*Cazden is an American educator and critic. In the following excerpt, he examines the major German publishing companies in the United States and the aims and ideals for which German publishing was undertaken.*]

Of the many émigrés who became part of the general American book trade, some were totally unconcerned with German-language publishing. This was true of Dagobert Runes, founder of the Philosophical Library, and of Kurt Enoch, a key figure in the expansion of the American paperback industry. There were, on the other hand, a number of American publishing houses founded by German émigrés which were involved to some extent in the production of Free German books. . . . [Three firms deserve] mention. Each one—Pantheon Books, the Frederick Ungar Publishing Company, and the Schocken Publishing Company—has earned a special niche in both American and German publishing history.

Kurt Wolff and Pantheon Books. It is neither possible nor necessary to list all the achievements of this redoubtable German publisher since such accounts are readily available. The Kurt Wolff Verlag was the leading avant garde publishing house of the 1920s, the magnet that attracted so many young writers of promise (including Kafka, Werfel, Georg Trakl, and Max Brod) and particularly many members of that heterogeneous company of authors and artists now lumped together under the rubric "Expressionist." Abandoning Germany in 1931, Wolff spent most of the following decade in southern France, involved in various publishing enterprises.

In 1941 Wolff made his way to the United States where, at the age of fifty-five, he created for himself another career, that of an American trade publisher. Pantheon Books in a very short while became one of the most respected of American imprints and by the end of World War II could boast a yearly output of from 100 to 300 titles. That Wolff's perspective was European rather than German explains his share in establishing French Pantheon Books in 1942, a French-language affiliate that, under the direction of Jacques Schiffrin (originator of the Éditions de la Pléiade), published original editions of Charles Péguy, Vercors, André Gide, and Albert Camus. In Wolff's own words:

> There was only sense in [publishing books in French] during and directly after the war, that is during those years in which no French books came to the United States from France. Gide, for example, sent us manuscripts from Tunis, which we brought out in French since he was not able to send them to France and have them published.

Only two books entirely in German were published under the Pantheon imprint: the anthology *Tausend Jahre deutscher Dichtung* (1949) edited by Curt von Faber du Faur, and the first German edition of Hermann Broch, *Der Tod des Vergil* (1945). A bilingual selection of poems by Stefan George was published by Wolff in 1943; the introduction by Ernst Morwitz, a member of that closely knit group of devotees who helped create the George legend, gave the collection added lustre. Kurt Wolff is not to be considered an émigré publisher in any strict sense but rather, as Salzmann puts it, in the tradition of Bernard Quaritch and Bernhard Tauchnitz, "he opted for world literature whether his field of action was Germany or America."

Frederick Ungar Publishing Company. A publisher whose career proceeded along quite different lines was Friedrich Ungar of Vienna, founder of the Phaidon Verlag in 1922 and director of the Saturn Verlag from 1926 to 1938. Forced to leave his native Austria in 1938, Ungar transferred his business activities temporarily to Switzerland. In 1940 he decided to proceed to America, and by October of that year he could already announce the launching of the Frederick Ungar Publishing Company featuring illustrated educational books and inexpensive text editions for which the former Saturn Verlag was noted. These became Ungar's stock in trade for a number of years.

The actual publishing record of the firm is very inaccessible; corroborative details have not been forthcoming from the present management. The *Publisher's Trade List Annual* for 1946—Ungar's only entry prior to the 1950s—lists by title only a handful of educational volumes, most of them aimed at the immigrant audience. Reviews and advertisements in the German-language press and lists of Ungar publications that appeared on book jackets or in trade and specialized bibliographies have had to suffice as sources of information. Even so, the remarkable total of 110 German-language titles has been identified. Most were reprints of German poetry and fiction. Few of the literary reprints available for inspection carried a license from the U.S. Alien Property Custodian, though the large amount of paper utilized during a period of strict rationing suggests some kind of official sanction.

The seventy-two volumes of German literature reprinted by Ungar are a landmark in the history of Free German publishing in America. Included in this figure are fourteen volumes of Rainer Maria Rilke, which makes him, next to Thomas Mann, the most frequently reprinted German writer in the United States during the emigration. Most of these titles are not recorded in the standard Rilke bibliography compiled by Walter Ritzer in 1951, nor are all listed in the more recent (1966) catalog of the Richard von Mises Rilke collection. Although in the strict sense . . . Ungar was not a publisher of émigré literature, his achievement cannot be underrated. He provided numerous inexpensive volumes of German literature, reference books, and textbooks at a time when they were obtainable nowhere else.

Schocken Books. The Schocken Books imprint was formally registered in New York City in October of 1946, but the history of the original Schocken Verlag goes back to 1932. In that crucial year the German-Jewish businessman, art collector, and philanthropist Salman Schocken gave his name to a publishing house dedicated to the preservation of Jewish culture in Germany. Under the calculated permissiveness of the new German government the firm continued its precarious existence until the disasters of 1939. At that time a new Schocken Verlag was set up in Jerusalem. The New York house, headed by Theodore Schocken, one of the sons, was to be completely independent of the parent concern.

The importance of Schocken Books for German literature is secured by its being the only authorized publisher of the works of perhaps the most influential of all twentieth-century German writers, Franz Kafka. Seven volumes of the *Gesammelte Schriften* (and the English translations as well) were published in New York from 1947 to 1952. Kafka's great impact upon American writers of the postwar period may be traced back to these events.

The Aurora Verlag. . . . [Due] space must be given to an undertaking with an ideological orientation and unique form of organization that made it the most widely known émigré imprint to come from the United States. The Aurora Verlag of New York can trace its pedigree back to the Germany of Kaiser Wilhelm, where, in the autumn of 1915, a brash new periodical appeared on the literary horizon. *Neue Jugend* was its name, founded and edited by the young Wieland Herzfelde, newly returned from the Western Front. Herzfelde came into conflict from the outset with the German censors because of his radical leanings. After a number of tortuous maneuvers culminating in the official closure of his publishing house—the very first issue of *Neue Jugend* was numbered Heft 7 and began with page 123 to give the impression of an officially sanctioned periodical—Herzfelde regrouped his forces in 1917 under a new name, Malik Verlag. The firm's artistic director was Herzfelde's brother (one of the original group of German Dadaists) who for reasons of conscience anglicized his name to John Heartfield. Heartfield's reputation rests primarily upon a highly ingenious application of the technique of photomontage to the graphic arts, in particular to book jackets and posters.

A host of radical writers and artists were associated with the Malik Verlag throughout the entire Weimar era, a fact which has led many commentators to label it a Communist front, but it never was officially controlled by the party. One of Herzfelde's most celebrated co-workers was the artist Georg Grosz, some of whose famous print collections were published by the Malik Verlag. Radical literature of other lands, especially modern Soviet literature, were staples of the Malik list as the names of Upton Sinclair, John Reed, Mayakovsky, and Gorki would indicate. The future partners in the Aurora venture—Graf, Brecht, and Weiskopf—were also published by Malik. An adjunct to the Verlag was the Malik Buchhandlung, meeting-place for Berlin's Communist intelligentsia (so too Herzfelde operated the Seven Seas Bookshop in New York). Immediately following the events of 1933, the Malik Verlag was moved to Prague, although for legal reasons it was thought expedient for the firm to be registered in London. While most of the books published between 1933 and 1939 were printed in Czechoslovakia they still carried a London imprint, as did the last Malik title to appear in Europe—Brecht's *Svendborger Gedichte* (1939), which was actually printed in Denmark. Toward the end of 1939, Herzfelde found a more permanent asylum in the United States.

One of Herzfelde's first undertakings in America was the compilation (with the assistance of the German Writers Association in New York) of the December, 1939, issue of the literary journal *Direction* (Darien, Conn.) devoted in its entirety to "Exiled German Writers." With contributions by such eminent refugees as Oskar Maria Graf, Ferdinand Bruckner, Bertolt Brecht, Ernst Bloch (the philosopher), Klaus Mann et al., and with a cover montage furnished by brother John then in England, the issue, as Herzfelde acknowledged, "brought together for the first time those of us alone in a strange land and gave us reason to think ahead to additional joint efforts." The rejuvenation of the old firm was first attempted in 1942 as the result of a series of successful lectures and exhibitions sponsored by a group of émigré writers and artists that called itself Die Tribüne, Forum für freie deutsche Kultur. Herzfelde presented his plan in a widely distributed form letter from which the following details are taken:

> The unexpectedly successful reception of these [lectures] has convinced us that it is possible at this time to expand and intensify the cultural struggle against National Socialism through the formation of a German publishing house. We want to call it: Die Tribüne, Gemeinschaftsverlag für freie deutsche Liter-

atur. The concern would be a nonprofit undertaking carried on under the prescribed legal regulations. Capital will be raised through the sale of 1,000 shares of stock—at ten dollars each. We expect that many friends of our plan will sign for more than one share. In addition, we want to organize the patrons who have attended our affairs—we have the addresses of more than 2,000—into a Leser-Gemeinschaft ["Readers' Circle"] in order to simplify the chores of production and distribution. I will assume responsibility for the publishing end; the selection of manuscripts, however, I will not undertake alone but in consultation with colleagues in the area, such as [Berthold] Viertel, Graf, Bruckner, [Friedrich] Alexan. My work and that of my colleagues will be unsalaried.

On the first thousand copies of each publication no royalties will be paid—therefore the author will receive 30 free copies. Ten percent of all additional copies sold will go for royalties. At the present time we don't foresee publishing any books, but a *Schriftenreihe*—each small volume will be either 32 or 64 pages long. We want to inaugurate the series with a volume—*Freiheitsstimmen der Völker*. It will contain not documents of individual authors, but the declarations of people who represent such freedom movements, e.g. the *Bill of Rights, Declaration of the Rights of Man*, and similar items. This publication will set the tone of our undertaking.

The project so described never materialized and Herzfelde was forced to wait three more years before he could once more play the role of publisher.

After a year of preparation, the reincarnated Malik Verlag was presented to the American public. The new firm, known as Aurora Verlag, was organized on a cooperative basis by Herzfelde and ten of the leading exiled German poets and writers in America. Much of the financial backing was supplied by Mary S. Rosenberg whose "financial idealism" in this matter was praised by Kesten in the *Aufbau*. Aurora's program was greeted with great enthusiasm in the German-language press, with approbation in the American press, and with a certain coolness by hard-nosed anti-Communists. It appeared to many exiles as the first breath of fresh air, a long delayed expression of German intellectual vitality. Hermann Kesten found prototypes of the Aurora cooperative experiment in the old *Nouvelle Revue Française* and Insel Verlag. He agreed with Herzfelde in pointing to the shameful contradiction that, in wealthy America—a land that possessed the largest German-speaking population outside Germany, Austria, and Switzerland—no Free German book publisher had hitherto existed. The *Austro-American Tribune* of February, 1945, was equally forthright:

> It is astonishing that only today a publishing house for Free German books has been formed. There have been enough German manuscripts and readers of German books in North and South America during recent years. An isolated German book was published here and there, but this is truly a German publisher with a program.

A grand total of twelve titles graced the Aurora list during the years of its American tenancy, but at the same time the firm supplied posterity with a number of tantalizing bibliographical ghosts such as: Hermann Broch, *Die Buecherverbrennung;* Georg Grosz, *Unter der gleichen Sonne;* and John Heartfield, *Faschistenspiegel*. These were announced but never published. The span of Aurora books reached from Brecht's *Furcht und Elend des Dritten Reichs* and Ernst Bloch's *Freiheit und Ord-*

nung to fiction and drama by such stalwarts as Feuchtwanger, Graf, and Bruckner. All Aurora books appeared in editions of 2000 or more, relatively high figures for German books in the United States. The inexpensive volumes were put together with little pretense or show, and all carried the distinctive Aurora signet (made up of the letters D and T) designed by Herzfelde in 1942 for the stillborn Tribüne publishing program. This well-publicized undertaking ended abruptly in 1947 when Herzfelde, Brecht, and Bloch made their way back to Europe—to the Soviet sector of Germany. Here the last chapter of the Malik odyssey was unfolded; by 1948 the returned exiles were ensconced in occupied Berlin affiliated with the Russian-dominated Aufbau Verlag and publishing under the name of Aurora Buecherei. (pp. 101-06)

A discussion of the aims and ideals that inspired exile publishing might seem redundant at this point; nevertheless it is both possible and prudent to develop this topic in a systematic way. After briefly restating the basic needs which were filled by the publication that went on in the various and widely scattered exile enclaves, several special publishing problems are examined in more detail: books to aid in the Americanization of the new immigrant, books for prisoners of war, and books for postwar Germany.

To Maintain the Identity of the German Emigration. From 1933 to the outbreak of the European conflict, and to a lesser degree thereafter, the self-imposed mission of the Free German publisher was to solidify the anti-Nazi front. To this end both German and the languages of the host nations were utilized. Hermann Rauschning's *Die Konservative Revolution* (1941), in both German and English editions, is a good example of the political and polemical literature of this period. To scavenge among the flood of English-language books of this nature is outside the scope of the present study, but the total would be impressive. During the near isolation of wartime America, emphasis shifted to the presentation and reappraisal of the cultural and political heritage of the "other Germany," the land of Heine, Rilke, and Mann—the community of spirit in which the exiles understandably enrolled themselves. Contributing to this end were the reprints and new editions of classic and modern masters; among these publications were the Heine edition reissued by Mary S. Rosenberg, the numerous volumes of Rilke, the Pantheon collection of Stefan George, and the bilingual Hölderlin anthology brought out under the New Directions imprint. The preservation of self-identify was also the most pressing need of the various subgroups within the emigration, whether they were Austrians, Jews, Socialists, or Communists. This was most efficiently done through the medium of the newspaper which served the dual purpose of preserving group unity and facilitating intragroup communication.

To Maintain the Identity of the Individual. For the creative individual, the need to communicate was paramount. Scholars and scientists, not to mention journalists, were impelled to learn English or to have their contributions translated. The poet or novelist, on the other hand, desirous of writing in his native tongue, was faced by the economic facts of émigré life. Those without international reputations had to be content with the transitory medium of newsprint or to publish on their own. Several "Good Samaritans" did attempt to assist younger or relatively unknown authors—publishers such as Barthold Fles, Peter Fisher, and the Writers Service Center of Friderike Zweig. The dedication of Otto Kallir to Richard Beer-Hofmann, who hardly enjoyed an American reputation, was of the greatest importance in the propagation of that author's work both in

Alfred Döblin. By permission of Ullstein Bilderdienst.

German and English. But it was indeed blind fortune that favored the venerable Austrian-Jewish dramatist but neglected Heinrich Mann, Alfred Döblin, and Albrecht Schaeffer.

The Free German publisher played no really significant role in the Americanization of the new immigrants. . . . A few books were indeed aimed at the immigrant audience, in all about ten volumes. As examples we may cite: Robert M. W. Kempner, *Rechte und Pflichten der feindlichen Ausländer* (1942); B. Grossmann, *Taschenbuch über die Vereinigten Staaten für Einwanderer und Ausländer* (1947); and Bruno Russ, *A.B.C. für U.S.A.* (1939). One series that held out much promise, Schoenhof's *Amerika-Bücherei,* unfortunately suffered an untimely demise. In 1945, the Cambridge firm published the first volume of this popular-priced series, *Thomas Jefferson, Auswahl aus seiner Schriften,* hoping to make "American political thinking of stature and value . . . a part of the culture of the German-speaking immigrant." Selections from the writings of Thomas Paine and Abraham Lincoln were also announced but never forthcoming. (pp. 119-21)

During World War II in the neighborhood of 400,000 German prisoners were interned in the United States. American authorities, in contrast with their British allies, exhibited a certain diffidence toward the problem of reeducation (or de-Nazification as this was rather negatively termed). A lack of any positive United States program was the spur for lengthy discussions in the émigré press during the winter of 1944. The initial flurry of excitement was caused by reports from some of the camps of Nazi *Fememorde,* the assassination of anti-Nazi prisoners. It also irked the *Neue Volks-Zeitung* that one

Nazi camp leader wrote the United States Commandant demanding the removal of that newspaper from the camp library and canteen. Adding to the irritation of many émigrés was the lack of interest shown by American authorities in utilizing the talents of German exiles in the reeducation program. The British made more extensive use of qualified exiles in this sensitive area, a fact well known in the United States.

Belated though it was, government action did follow, and a large-scale program of cultural and political education was begun. Some eighty German-language newspapers were printed and distributed in the many camps that dotted the American countryside. As courses of instruction were developed, more and more German-language publications were sought by camp officials. This turn of events generated an enthusiastic response from Free German publishers and book dealers in both the Americas. From Chile the *Deutsche Blätter* solicited gift subscriptions for prisoners of war, while its editors, in an open letter "An die Deutschen Kriegsgefangenen in Nordamerika," attempted to build a certain community of feeling between prisoner and émigré:

> Different fates have led you and us to America, but the cause is the same—National Socialism. . . . Will we come to understand one another, we as Germans in America whether refugees or prisoners? That is the question that demands an answer at this, the most tragic moment in our history.

In the United States, Wieland Herzfelde related the program of the newly founded Aurora Verlag to the prisoner of war problem by emphasizing that:

> With the arrival in this country of hundreds of thousands of German prisoners of war . . . the demand for German books has suddenly risen to an unprecedented height without being met up to now by an adequate increase in the supply of good German books; that is, of books free from any vestige of Nazism. . . . In order to cope, to a modest extent, with the task arising from this situation, a number of writers, from Austria, Germany and Czechoslovakia now living in this country have banded together in a new publishing venture, Aurora Verlag.

The same report added that one of the first Aurora books was to be the anthology *Morgenroete*—"a reader for German prisoners of war." Although announced in 1945, publication was inexplicably delayed for two years—too late, of course, for its original purpose.

Gottfried Bermann-Fischer was the most diligent of his peers in the preparation of reading material for the POW camps. A special series of twenty-four paperbound volumes, *Neue Welt,* was printed with government approval for exclusive sale to prisoners at only twenty-five cents each. The twenty-four titles were selected from a list of forty by a committee of prisoners (a political move on the part of camp officials) and published in editions of 50,000 each. These books were the prototypes of the pioneer paperback series in post-war Germany, the Fischer-Bücherei. Not resting on these laurels alone, Bermann-Fischer was inspired to hold a competition for the best novel written by a prisoner of war. Perhaps it was a matter of tactful public relations but none of the contest notices in *Der Ruf* (the national POW literary journal) mentioned the name of the émigré publisher. The winning entry, Walter Kolbenhoff's *Von unserem Fleisch und Blut,* was published in Stockholm by Bermann-Fischer on his return to Europe in 1947.

Other Free German books, new and secondhand, were supplied by dealers such as Friedrich Krause and Wieland Herzfelde (Seven Seas Bookshop). Krause claimed to have been supplying POW camps with literature as far back as December, 1943. The Communist publicist F. C. Weiskopf jauntily commented on the prisoner of war trade for readers of *Freies Deutschland* (Mexico City):

> Some days ago I was browsing in a [New York City] book store and the mail just brought orders from the war prisoners camp. What does a camp librarian order? This one (one of the none-too-numerous rare birds) did not want too bad books on his list. Bertolt Brecht: *Private Life of the Master Race;* Agnes Smedley: *Battle Hymn of China;* Paul Merker: *Deutschland Sein oder Nichtsein;* Ernst Sommer: *Revolte der Heiligen;* Ludwig Renn: *Adel im Untergang;* Freiligrath; Herweigh [sic], Heine, Whitman and Wilkie.

The government did attempt to screen all books that were distributed to the camps though the resulting regulations were somewhat involved: new books could be sent directly from publisher to camp; older and used books first had to be scrutinized by the camp commandant; books published before 1930 outside the United States had to be sent to the official censor, POW Department, General Post Office, New York. Apparently the camps varied in their acceptance of Communist-sponsored literature. On one occasion the *German American* boasted that an unnamed camp official had ordered 121 copies of its publication *Erziehung vor Stalingrad,* an eye-witness report by the German Communist poet Erich Weinert. It was more usual to find the paper accusing the camps of discrimination against progressive, anti-Fascist literature.

The editors of the *German American* were publicly outraged when in 1944 the paper's application to be circulated in the POW camps was turned down because, and here they quoted from the offending letter, "The Office of Censorship expresses the feeling that the extreme anti-Nazi views expressed in your publication might be more misunderstood than helpful to German prisoners in this country and that it might tend to encourage political dissension within the camp." As of March, 1945, according to Albert Norden, the situation remained largely unchanged:

> Until recently German-language newspapers with subversive content, like the *Neue Volks-Zeitung,* circulated unhindered in the camps, while real anti-Fascists publications were forbidden. I saw in a camp in Trinidad, Colorado, a newspaper for sale under the name of *Der Spiegel* which was completely permeated with the perverted spirit of Nazism. . . . The ban against anti-Fascist books and papers that still is in effect in many camps should be lifted.

In Janus-like fashion Free German publishers faced an expanding market on two fronts: in the United States, the German prisoners of war; in Europe, a defeated Germany starved for intellectual nourishment. The émigrés hopefully prepared to satisfy both demands. The first Aurora catalog issued in 1945 contained the following unambiguous statement of purpose, "The founders of the publishing house foresaw that after the collapse of the Hitler regime Germany and Austria would be afflicted with intellectual as well as material famine and they wanted, true to the great humanistic tradition of German literature, to share in the cultural rebuilding." This utterance pointed in a quite different direction from the statements released to the American press which . . . emphasized the re-education of German prisoners of war. Aurora books did enjoy wide circulation in Europe, but only after Herzfelde had shifted his base of operations to Berlin.

Book dealers too were not hesitant to advertise under the banner of "books for Germany." Ernst Willard with his German Book Club had counted on the long dormancy of the German book trade and proved himself a poor prophet. Far and away the most industrious publisher of German books for Europe was the Bermann-Fischer Verlag, which until 1946 was still directed from New York. While the *Neue Welt* series was printed in the United States, books intended for the continental market were printed in Stockholm. In 1944, Bermann-Fischer declared that "the much discussed problem of the . . . re-education of the German people is essentially a publishing problem." Extending his remarks on that topic in an interview granted to *Publishers' Weekly,* he outlined the future plans of his firm. They were to include the preparation of German editions of important American books—e.g., Wendell Willkie's *One World*—and the issuing of textbooks to be ready for immediate use in liberated Germany. This latter goal was immediately qualified by the statement: "As no one can today prophesy what the educational plans for Germany will be and by whom directed, these books will not be manufactured until they are approved through the official channels."

The textbooks problem was an irritant to many German refugee intellectuals. Fritz Karsen, a former German educator, led the ensuing public debate by taking the position that at least a share in the preparation of new texts should be allotted to qualified émigrés. In this emotionally charged atmosphere, Bermann-Fischer named Professor Karsen to direct a group of émigré scholars and teachers who were authorized to prepare several series of history textbooks and German-language readers for both elementary and secondary schools.

The immediate efforts of the American occupation authorities to provide suitable textbooks were deemed most unsatisfactory by émigré critics; Ludwig Marcuse, for one, sharply castigated the use of outdated and "dangerous" books, actually reprints of texts originally written during the 1920s. The circumstances that led to the adoption of these pre-Nazi texts are described by Marshall Knappen, chief of the Religious Section and deputy chief of the Education Section of the American Military Government:

> The next possibility was the adoption of various texts then actually in the course of preparation for this very purpose by German refugees. Examination of sample manuscripts from these sources showed that excellent work was being done on them. Nevertheless, since reports of the project had already been published, the authorship could not be concealed, and these books would inevitably be open to the same objection as the forced use of refugees as teachers would be. If on later examination local German authorities should decide to use such texts, obviously we would be only too glad to approve these decisions. But at the time it was believed impractical to gamble that practically all local administrators would so approve these texts. Because German feeling against textbooks by foreigners was believed to be even stronger than it was against those by refugees, a similar objection applied to the suggestion that existing or specially prepared American or English texts should be translated. The difficulties involved in wartime printing forbade us the luxury of reproducing refugee or foreign texts unless they could be generally used.

> It was therefore concluded that the least of the evils confronting us was the reproduction of the best available texts from the Weimar period.

The American Military Government was aware of the shortcomings of these texts but felt that their use was an emergency measure to be endured until the Germans themselves could take on the job. In 1949 R. H. Samuel and R. Hinton Thomas caustically commented: "In the British and American Zones the writing of new textbooks is left almost entirely to German textbook committees, which so far have functioned extremely slowly." This policy was not one to appeal to the émigrés who in effect were barred from having their own textbooks used in German schools. Of Bermann-Fischer's planned series of texts, only two could be traced in licensed German editions—both appearing in 1947.

Under the direction of the Publication Division of the Office of War Information (OWI), an attempt was made to supply current American books to European readers as rapidly as possible. The program was threefold: to publish paperbound translations of American books in various languages; to export American trade books to Europe (the OWI acting either as purchaser or purchasing agent); and to stimulate European publishers to issue informative books about America. The twenty German-language translations which bore the Overseas Editions, Inc. imprint were issued in quantities of 50,000 to 60,000 per title. All Overseas Editions, including books in languages other than German, were printed in New York and added up to a grand total of some 3,500,000 copies. Another series of translations with the Éditions Transatlantique imprint, amounting to about 500,000 copies, was manufactured in London. Most of the German volumes were probably prepared by such émigré writers as Hermann Kesten, translator of Stephen Vincent Benét's *America,* though not all can be properly attributed. In the opinion of Maurice Davie, the émigré writer's "outstanding contribution was in translating into German the American books sent to Europe by the Council on Books under OWI." There was another side to the matter, and émigré publishers did not feel well served by events, their ambitious plans having been wrecked on the shoals of a pragmatic American occupation policy. However, this failure should not overshadow the real and substantial achievement of the Free German publisher in America. (pp. 121-26)

> *Robert E. Cazden, in his* German Exile Literature in America, 1933-1950: A History of the Free German Press and Book Trade, *American Library Association, 1970, 250 p.*

ADDITIONAL BIBLIOGRAPHY

Bance, A. F., ed. *Weimar Germany: Writers and Politics.* Edinburgh: Scottish Academic Press, 1982, 183 p.
  Thirteen essays on works of German writers written during the years of the Weimar Republic. Many of the writers discussed later became exiles.

Bentwich, Norman. *The Rescue and Achievement of Refugee Scholars: The Story of Displaced Scholars and Scientists, 1933-1952.* The Hague: Martinus Nijhoff, 1953, 107 p.
  Historical account of the emigration of German intellectuals from the Third Reich and their reception by the Allied nations.

Boeschenstein, H. *The German Novel, 1939-1944.* Toronto: University of Toronto Press, 1949, 189 p.
  Discusses novels written in Germany during World War II.

Boyers, Robert, ed. *The Legacy of the German Refugee Intellectuals.* New York: Schocken Books, 1972, 306 p.
  Reprint of the Fall 1969-Winter 1970 issue of *Salmagundi* magazine, which was devoted to studies of German refugee intellectuals. The volume contains several essays devoted to individual German exile writers.

Breitencamp, Edward C. *The U.S. Information Control Division and Its Effect on German Publishers and Writers, 1945-1949.* Grand Forks, N.D.: Privately printed, 1953, 100 p.
  Discusses American policies concerning the flow of information in occupied Germany after World War II. The book includes a section listing forty-six exiled writers with a succinct biography of each, and states that the United States Information Control Division promoted the writings of many exiled writers.

Broerman, Bruce M. *The German Historical Novel in Exile after 1933: Calliope contra Clio.* University Park and London: Pennsylvania State University Press, 1986, 128 p.
  Analyzes novels written in exile by Wolfgang Cordan, Bruno Frank, Robert Neumann, Edgar Maass, Lion Feuchtwanger, Heinrich Mann, Alfred Döblin, Joseph Roth, Thomas Mann, and Hermann Broch.

Closs, August, ed. "German Literature in Exile and Inner Emigration." In *Twentieth-Century German Literature,* edited by August Closs, Vol. 4, pp. 36-9. New York: Barnes & Noble, 1969.
  Lists several exiled writers and classifies five literary groups within and without Germany: exiles, Nazis, traditional nationalists, resistance fighters, and writers remaining in Germany who resist generalization.

Edinger, Lewis J. *German Exile Politics: The Social Democratic Executive Committee in the Nazi Era.* Berkeley and Los Angeles: University of California Press, 1956, 329 p.
  History of political opposition to Nazi Germany by disenfranchised Socialist and Communist political organizations.

Fermi, Laura. *Illustrious Immigrants: The Intellectual Migration from Europe, 1930-41.* Chicago and London: University of Chicago Press, 1968, 440 p.
  Historical discussion of the migration of European intellectuals to the United States and critical evaluation of scholars in the various arts and sciences, including literature.

Fleming, Donald, and Bailyn, Bernard, eds. *The Intellectual Migration: Europe and America, 1930-1960.* Cambridge, Mass.: The Belknap Press of Harvard University Press, 1969, 748 p.
  Collection of fourteen essays examining exiled scholars in the arts and sciences.

Fraser, James H. "German Partisan and Exile Publishing: Wieland Herzfelde and the Malik-Verlag." *Libri* 17, No. 3 (1967): 170-74.
  Discusses the Malik-Verlag, one of the most important German exile publishing companies.

Graf, Oskar Maria. "German Writers in America." *The New Republic* LXXXXVIII, No. 1273 (26 April 1939): 344-46.
  Discusses exiled German dramatists, novelists, philosophers, and critics, and singles out young writers in exile for special commendation.

Hirshler, Eric E., ed. *Jews from Germany in the United States.* New York: Farrar, Strauss, and Cudahy, 1955, 182 p.
  Collection of six essays on the history of German-Jewish immigration to the United States as well as the religious and cultural influence exerted by the immigrants on American life.

Jackman, Jarrell C., and Borden, Carla M., eds. *The Muses Flee Hitler: Cultural Transfer and Adaptation, 1930-1945.* Washington, D.C.: Smithsonian Institution Press, 1983, 347 p.
  Collection of nineteen essays discussing the movement of German intellectuals to the United States; the interaction of European culture, art, and science with the American academic and artistic milieu; and the adaptation of exiles to other parts of the world.

Kamla, Thomas A. *Confrontation with Exile: Studies in the German Novel.* Bern: Herbert Lang; Frankfurt am Main: Peter Lang, 1975, 188 p.
> Individual studies of sixteen novels written by German exiles that take the exile experience as their subject.

Kater, Michael. "Anti-Fascist Intellectuals in the Third Reich." *Canadian Journal of History* XVI, No. 2 (August 1981): 263-77.
> Discusses writers of the "internal emigration" who remained in Germany but resisted the Nazi regime.

Klieneberger, H. R. *The Christian Writers of the Inner Emigration.* The Hague and Paris: Mouton, 1968, 218 p.
> Discusses six writers who remained in Germany but "produced some of their best work as a protest, from a Christian and humanitarian standpoint, against the immoralities of Nazism."

Krispyn, Egbert. *Anti-Nazi Writers in Exile.* Athens: University of Georgia Press, 1978, 200 p.
> Historical study concentrating on difficulties faced by exiled writers.

Lengyel, Emil. "German Émigré Literature." *Books Abroad* 12, No. 1 (Winter 1938): 5-8.
> Discusses the effects of exile on the works of exiled German writers.

Lewis, Ward B. "Message from America: The Verse of Walt Whitman as Interpreted by German Authors in Exile." *German Life and Letters* 29, No. 2 (January 1976): 215-27.
> Discusses German admiration for Whitman as a proponent of democracy and mythologizer of America.

Liepmann, Heinz. "German Authors Who Write in Exile." *The New York Times Book Review* (25 October 1936): 8, 24.
> Early discussion of German exile writers as a group.

Mann, Erika, and Mann, Klaus. "The World of Books." In their *Escape to Life,* pp. 282-307. Boston: Houghton Mifflin Co., 1939.
> Personal account of exiled writers including Vicki Baum, Ernst Toller, Bruno Frank, Walter Hasenclever, Ferdinand Bruckner, Friedrich Wolf, Martin Gumpert, Heinz Liepmann, and Emil Ludwig.

Mann, Klaus. "Report on German Writers." *The Saturday Review of Literature* XVI, No. 12 (17 July 1937): 18.
> Reviews of Bruno Frank's *Der Reisepass,* Rene Schickele's *Die Flaschenpost,* Alfred Döblin's *Die Fahrt ins Land ohne Tod,* Joseph Roth's *Das falsche Gewicht,* Karl Tschuppik's *Ein Sohn aus gutem Hause,* and notices of the periodical *Mass und Wert,* a six-volume collection of the works of Franz Kafka, and Lion Feuchtwanger's "Moskau, 1937."

Moeller, Hans-Bernhard, ed. *Latin America and the Literature of Exile: A Comparative View of the 20th-Century European Refugee Writers in the New World.* Heidelberg: Carl Winter Universitätsverlag, 1983, 473 p.
> Eighteen essays devoted to German and Spanish Civil War exiles who settled in Latin America. The essays focus on the history of exile in Latin America, special problems faced by the exiles, the various genres of literature produced by exiles and native Latin Americans, differing regions of settlement, and individual authors.

Peyre, Henri. "The Study of Literature." In *The Cultural Migration: The European Scholar in America,* by Franz L. Neumann, Henri Peyre, Erwin Panofsky, Wolfgang Kohler, and Paul Tillich, pp. 27-81. Philadelphia: University of Pennsylvania Press, 1953.
> Discusses American culture from the viewpoint of an exiled European writer.

Pfanner, Helmut F. *Exile in New York: German and Austrian Writers after 1933.* Detroit: Wayne State University Press, 1983, 252 p.
> Historical account examining the experience of exiled writers who settled in New York.

Pike, David. "Stalin and the Intellectuals." *Internationales Archiv für Sozialgeschichte der deutschen Literatur* 10 (1985): 225-44.
> Examines the failure of German exiles to recognize and oppose the totalitarianism of Soviet leader Joseph Stalin.

Reinhold, Ernest. "German Exile Literature: Problems and Proposals." *Western Canadian Studies in Modern Languages and Literature* 2 (1970): 75-87.
> Discusses the events that caused exiles to flee Germany and Austria, defines the scope of German exile literature, appraises trends in scholarship devoted to exile literature, and suggests future directions of research.

Rose, William. "German Literary Exiles in England." *German Life and Letters* (April 1948): 175-85.
> Recollections of the author's meetings with several exiles, including Stefan Hock, Alfred Kerr, Leonhard Frank, Franz Werfel, Carl Zuckmeyer, Stefan Zweig, and Robert Neumann.

Spalek, John M. "Literature in Exile: The Comparative Approach." In *Deutsches Exildrama und Exiltheater,* edited by Wolfgang Elfe, James Hardin, and Gunther Holst, pp. 14-26. Bern: Peter Lang, 1977.
> Compares German exile literature with exile literature in general.

Stern, Guy. "Exile Literature: Sub-Division or Misnomer?" *Colloquia Germanica* 5, Nos. 1 and 2 (1971): 167-78.
> Argues for the recognition of exiled German writers as a loose but identifiable group, based on the shared experience of persecution and separation from their native land.

Strelka, Joseph P.; Bell, Robert F.; and Dobson, Eugene. *Protest—Form—Tradition: Essays on German Exile Literature.* University: University of Alabama Press, 1979, 144 p.
> Collection of nine essays demonstrating various critical approaches to German exile literature, by critics including Joseph P. Strelka, Manfred Durzak, and Egbert Krispyn.

Modern Supernatural Fiction

INTRODUCTION

While belief in the supernatural served as the basis for the mythologies of early civilizations, and afterward remained an enduring aspect of world folklore, it was not until the nineteenth century that a substantial body of works evolved that focused upon the otherworldly as a source of horror. Yet, by the early decades of the twentieth century a number of observers were already proclaiming the demise of supernatural fiction as a vital literary form. "The ghost story is dead," wrote Stephen Leacock in 1919, and this judgment has received the support of critics up to the present time. The historical evidence that made this pronouncement possible, and perhaps inevitable, is the conspicuous flourishing of supernatural literature that took place throughout the Victorian and Edwardian eras, particularly in England and America. This period has been called the golden age of supernatural fiction and is often the focus of critical studies of the genre. What critics find distinguishes the work of supernatural authors of this period is a level of artistry that crystallized diverse motifs from legend and folklore—such as the evil witch and the avenging spirit—into a means of expressing a sense of spectral fear. The factors that contributed to the rise of a modern literature of supernatural horror are a matter of varied speculation, as is the matter of its decline. But if supernatural literature did not in fact expire sometime in the 1920s or 1930s, it nevertheless ceased to be the assemblage of strikingly gifted writers who contributed to its golden age.

The immediate precursor of nineteenth-century supernatural horror fiction was the Gothic novel, which is commonly recognized to have begun its existence with Horace Walpole's *Castle of Otranto* (1764) and to have survived well into the following century. However, although Gothic novelists often included supernatural incidents in their works, they also pursued other concerns, particularly those related to eighteenth-century novels of morals and manners, which precluded the single-minded focus and inventiveness of their successors in portraying weird and ghostly phenomena. It thus remained for such early nineteenth-century authors as Edgar Allan Poe and Joseph Sheridan LeFanu to found a literature that, toward the end of the century, became a well-defined genre with exponents among both popular and serious authors. Although a few commentators have maintained that a literalistic belief in the supernatural has always been, and will always be, a prerequisite for the creation and enjoyment of horror tales, most critics propose special reasons to explain the relatively recent phenomenon of supernatural fiction as a literary form. Among these reasons, one is most often given: the nineteenth century was an age of scientific and technological advancement that had distanced itself from many of the superstitions of the past; as a consequence, it was precisely these superstitions, exiled from the progressive consciousness of the day, that emerged in works of literature. A corollary to this theory states that because earlier societies assumed the supernatural as part of the cosmic order, its manifestations could not inflict that peculiar dread known to modern humanity. This explanation has been most prominently articulated by Sigmund Freud in his essay "Das Un-

heimlich" ("The Uncanny"), and is based on the assumption that beneath the surface of civilized skepticism survive all the irrational fears of humanity's past. Thus, a common storyline in horror fiction involves an unbelieving protagonist to whom it is proven—with unpleasant consequences—that some aspect of the supernatural is true. A contrasting theory suggests that it was actually the development of science and technology, particularly as displayed in the scientific research of psychic phenomena and in such inventions as the electric light, that allayed superstitious fears and led to a decline in both the production and appreciation of stories devoted to them. This theory perhaps best accounts for the tendency among twentieth-century fiction writers to favor psychological and scientific horrors over those that have their roots in the archaic and essentially pastoral lore based on the existence of ghosts.

A central issue in the study of supernatural fiction is the apparent contradiction of deriving pleasure from the experience of horror. While other types of literature, especially popular genres such as westerns and mysteries, owe a measure of their interest to situations of menace, the literature of supernatural horror is structured entirely to disturb its readers to the extent that they may feel personally threatened, if only temporarily, by the implications of an eerie narrative. In an attempt to account for this paradoxical attraction, many critics have attributed a homeopathic purpose to fictional terrors, concluding that indulgence in such controlled fears acts as an innoculation or antidote for those less easily managed and observing that the popularity of horror fiction increases during times of social instability. Other critics regard an enthusiasm for horror fiction, especially in its more gruesome forms, as symptomatic of sadomasochistic impulses. In opposition to this view of a bestial and perverse readership, supernatural fiction has also been associated with emotions of a religious nature which have their source in the mystical awe of the unknown that may be inspired by an imaginary confrontation with unearthly forces. Alternatively, tales of terror are often considered simply a form of amusement much like such recreational diversions as carnival rides and water skiing.

Despite all contentions that supernatural fiction suffered a decline in the early decades of the twentieth century, this literary genre has continued to flourish and grow in popularity, assisted by television and movie adaptations and imitations. Although some might contend that it has radically changed in quality and substance, becoming merely a source of income for hack writers who exploit the more sensationalistic aspects of the form, horror fiction has always been allied to the lower types of commercial literature, from the "shilling shockers" of the Gothic period to the mass-market "pageturners" of the present day. Even those authors who are recognized as the most profound and artistic practitioners of literary supernaturalism, such as Edgar Allan Poe and H. P. Lovecraft, are often criticized as hopelessly vulgar and categorized far below the level of serious artists. At the same time, the highest examples of the supernatural genre have endured for the same reason as the more accepted classics of literature—their power to express through the medium of language some significant aspect of human experience. In the perception of many readers and critics, the works of such authors as Arthur Machen, Algernon

Blackwood, and Walter de la Mare do not "transcend" the essential traits of supernatural fiction but rather bring them to perfection. As Lovecraft stated in his study *Supernatural Horror in Literature:* "The oldest and strongest emotion of mankind is fear, and the oldest and strongest kind of fear is fear of the unknown. These facts few psychologists will dispute, and their admitted truth must establish for all time the genuineness and dignity of the weirdly horrible tale as a literary form."

THE EVOLUTION AND VARIETIES OF SUPERNATURAL FICTION

PHILIP VAN DOREN STERN

[*Stern was an American novelist, critic, and nonfiction writer. In the following excerpt, he traces the development of supernatural literature from its beginnings in antiquity to its maturity during the late nineteenth and early twentieth centuries.*]

The Egyptians, the Greeks, and the Romans all had their ghost tales; so too did the Chinese and the Arabs; savage tribes all over the world weave them into the structure of their lives, accepting them not as fiction but as fact. But the simple and naïve stories of primitive peoples, hair-raising in concept as they sometimes are, nevertheless seem poor things to us. They have little suspense and no atmosphere; they are merely bald, unvarnished reports of encounters with the supernatural beings that people an animistic universe. Apparently it is easy to make the uncritical savage shudder; believing in the actual existence of malignant forces, he trembles at their very mention.

Nor are the early tales of ghosts and hauntings that form a part of Greek and Roman literature much more sophisticated. Pliny the Younger has recorded an account of a haunted house in Athens which is often quoted as an example of the ghost story in classical literature. It is a disappointing tale. The clanking chains and horrid groans of the specter may have served to frighten an audience which demanded neither subtlety nor narrative skill, but to us the brief story possesses interest only as a literary curiosity.

The Middle Ages, which are ridden with werewolves, vampires, incubuses, and warlocks, did no better in furthering the development of the supernatural tale. People who live with ghosts and demons demand no literary artistry to make them dread creatures whose existence they have never questioned. The skepticism of a later age was needed to force writers to become more skillful.

The Renaissance still took ghosts for granted, but growing enlightenment required that they become beings of a higher order, projections of the mind rather than the animistic spirits that satisfied a more primitive age. Shakespeare's ghosts seem psychologically sound even to the modern mind. The scene in which Macbeth watches the shape of the murdered Banquo usurp his seat at the banquet table is particularly modern, for the apparition remains unseen by the guests and is obviously intended to be only the figment of the guilty Macbeth's disordered imagination. Yet Shakespeare, for all his frequent use of the supernatural, did little to further the technique of the ghost story. That was left to lesser masters.

All the centuries before the eighteenth contributed only slightly to its development, but they did create a rich storehouse of legend for later writers to use. The weirdly beautiful primitive conceptions of earliest times, the strange and hideous lore of the Middle Ages, and the black records of witchcraft in the sixteenth and seventeenth centuries are sources from which much of our modern supernatural literature springs. But the ghost story had to undergo a great change before it could become an art. It had to abandon the anecdotal form and take advantage of every trick of narrative skill. As fiction itself improved, the ghost story improved with it. The lessons learned by writers who were developing the novel and inventing the short story were applied; atmosphere, intelligently handled plotting, and, above all, suspense were utilized to produce the ever-mounting tension on which the ghost story depends for its peculiar power.

Oddly enough, the perfection of this most unworldly kind of literature exactly parallels the rise of the industrial age. The Romantic movement which did so much to further it began in the middle of the eighteenth century when Watt and Arkwright were laying down the foundations of our machine civilization. It may even be that the Romantic tale of the supernatural came into being as a sort of reluctant farewell to days when faith rather than reason ruled the world. At any rate, it is to the Gothic romances of the late eighteenth century that the origins of the modern ghost story must be traced. Horace Walpole, M. G. Lewis, and Ann Radcliffe were the progenitors; in their hands the artless tale took on form and was developed beyond the anecdotal stage.

The present-day reader who attempts to explore the musty pages of the Gothic novels will probably wonder why they made such an appeal to their contemporaries, for they contain every artistic fault imaginable. They stretch coincidence until it cracks; they pile horror upon horror until the reader ceases to care what happens; and what passes for dialogue in them sounds more than slightly ridiculous to the modern ear.

Naturally, the earliest ones were the crudest, but improvement came fast, and in 1794, when Ann Radcliffe's *The Mysteries of Udolpho* was published, the art of suggestive narrative suspense was born. Eino Railo, in an exhaustive study of the more macabre elements of English Romanticism, says of her contribution:

> Mere outward suspense, which can be evoked, for instance, by spirited action, danger, flight, battles, etc., is obviously not adapted to tauten the reader's soul to a susceptibility to terror; for this end an additional factor is needed.

> The suspense evoked by Walpole's *The Castle of Otranto* is superficial . . . but *The Mysteries of Udolpho* reveals what this additional factor is. The author creates a great part of her suspense by gradually exciting the reader's curiosity to its highest pitch by enigmatical hints, half-sentences, inexplicable and weird phenomena, until he begins dimly to discern and to fear something, the nature of which is hidden from him, and to which he himself gives the form most terrifying to him. Suspense of the kind that leads up to a state of terror is thus evoked by suggestion; in other words, the reader's imagination is to be excited into seeing in events, words, and hints, more than they need actually convey, and if possible, into working independently, imagining, suspecting, and fearing, as though outside of the book, in spiritual worlds of its own. If the author succeeds in providing a denouement in which the duly prepared soul of the reader can be held without the neutralizing effect of awakening doubt and sanity so completely that in-

tellectual control ceases, the literary experiment, which had as its aim the creation of terror, has succeeded in this part of its aim.

The greatest hindrance to success lies in brain-control, in the unflagging suspicion of the reader; this first must be eliminated and prevented from creating an inauspicious state of mind. The only effectual weapon for this purpose is suggestion. Action can be either natural or unnatural, credible or incredible; success does not depend upon such factors. This is decided solely by the author's power of transferring the reader, by means of suggestion, into the world in which the action takes place, into an atmosphere where even the most incredible events seem credible. [*The Haunted Castle, A Study of the Elements of English Romanticism*]

With the discovery of this essential element the tale of the supernatural moved forward rapidly. Conditions were ripe for it in the early nineteenth century. The age that produced Coleridge's *Ancient Mariner,* Mrs. Shelley's *Frankenstein,* and De Quincey's *Confessions of an English Opium-Eater* could be counted upon to take such stories to its heart. In England there appeared a master of the genre, Sheridan Le Fanu, who, like Melville, had to wait for another generation to give him the rank rightfully due him.

With Le Fanu, the ghost story became mature; there is nothing archaic about his tales; his dialogue at times may seem a trifle quaint and old-fashioned, but his psychology is as modern as Freud's. He knew how to play upon the reader's mind until it was hypnotized by his words. In his all-too-few short stories, terror became an art rather than a display of raw and bloody bones.

Almost contemporary with Le Fanu was Edgar Allan Poe, the strange American genius who, more than any other American writer, seems oddly born out of time and place. With Le Fanu and Poe the ghost story began the century-long era of its greatest development. After them came the great Victorians, some of whom dabbled with the supernatural, but it was lesser men who gave us our greatest tales. Dickens, Stevenson, Kipling, Hardy, Henry James, Conrad, and in France, De Maupassant, turned out occasional masterpieces of the supernatural but none of them is clearly identified with the genre. It remained for writers like Arthur Machen, Ambrose Bierce, Oliver Onions, Algernon Blackwood, Walter de la Mare, and Montague Rhodes James to make a speciality of the macabre. The thirteen years from 1898 to 1911 were the golden age of the ghost story. Fine stories were written before and since that time, but never has there been such a flood of them within so short a period.

Henry James' single and superlatively successful essay into the field, *The Turn of the Screw,* ushered in the brilliant era; M. R. James' first collection, entitled *Ghost Stories of an Antiquary,* came in 1904, to be followed by *More Ghost Stories* in 1911; Algernon Blackwood did nearly all his work between 1906 and 1910; Edith Wharton's *Tales of Men and Ghosts* was issued in 1910; Oliver Onions' *Widdershins* in 1911, which also saw the publication of F. Marion Crawford's *Wandering Ghosts.* During these flush years Kipling, Machen, and De la Mare were active, and it was then that the many volumes of that great treasure house of ancient folklore, Sir James Frazer's *The Golden Bough,* were being given to the world.

It is not easy to understand why this brief period at the turn of the century was so rich. Perhaps one clue lies in the fact that it marked the beginning of science's dominance of the world. It was then that the automobile began to replace the horse; man first learned to fly; and he found out how to talk through space and look through solid substance. Before such miracles, ancient ways of thinking went down. A fierce, new technological civilization then in the throes of birth was to bring horrors of its own upon mankind. Skepticism and disillusionment followed in the wake of wars and violent upheavals. Like the beginners of the Romantic movement, the men who were writing the supernatural literature of the early years of the century probably did not know that they were singing the swan song of an earlier way of life.

Since 1911 the ghost story has languished; a few occasional fine examples have appeared, but the impulse to write them has apparently weakened. Yet there has been no diminishing of the demand for imaginative literature. The popular success of stories like Lawrence Watkin's "On Borrowed Time" and Stephen Vincent Benét's "The Devil and Daniel Webster" indicates a continuing interest in the supernatural; the sensational rise of the mystery story shows that people are still engrossed with the problems raised by death in its more violent forms, and even such Sunday-supplement features as Tarzan and Superman are evidence that man's eternal craving for more than mortal power is still a vital theme.

But as for ghost stories themselves, the present outlook is dark. No commercial market exists for good ones, and a debased product is lowering the whole genre in public esteem. In America no so-called "respectable" magazine of large circulation will print a ghost story. This discourages the literary writer and causes him to abandon the field to hacks who grind out wild and fantastic tales for the pulps. The very subject has become cheapened and vulgarized; in a country where ghost stories are inevitably associated with the most lurid kind of writing and with the trashiest sort of motion pictures, one can hardly expect a serious author to devote himself to them.

This is truly regrettable, for the ghost story, in the hands of an artist, can and has become genuine literature. It is an exceedingly difficult and delicate form to master, requiring a distinguished style, deftness in handling atmospheric effects, a wide background in psychology and anthropology, a mature attitude toward life, and, above all, a narrative ability that few authors possess. And it is a dangerous form to tackle—an inept word or phrase, a shade of emphasis wrongly applied, or the clumsy handling of its gossamerlike structure will quickly turn a tale of terror into a gross parody that arouses only smiles of derision. To make a reader accept things which his sense of reason bids him reject is not easy; only a really skillful writer can sustain illusion and maintain the spell to the end. It is not surprising that out of the thousands of such tales that have been written only a handful of first-rate stories survive, and they have been kept alive by their literary quality. As in other forms of art, the years ruthlessly sift out all inferior efforts.

Examined critically, ghost stories seem simple enough in structure. Most of them follow a pattern that is almost as rigid as that of a sonnet. The setting is established with proper atmospheric embellishments, the main characters are presented, and then there are likely to be hints of the ghostly visitation to come. After that, events lead up swiftly to the time when the apparition—or whatever it is—makes its presence known. The success or failure of the entire story depends on the effect of this climactic moment upon the reader. A superlatively well-told tale acting upon a sensitive audience can result in greater emotional heightening than that produced by almost any other kind of literature. There is an actual physical response—the celebrated *frisson d'horreur* is no imaginary thing, as anyone who has experienced it will testify. The nervous system reacts as if it were being subjected to an electric shock. The short hairs at the base of the neck rise "withershins," and a definite shudder runs down the spine.

It stands to reason that a form of literature which can have such tremendous effect upon its readers must possess extraordinary power. Divorced from reality, dealing not with human beings and things natural to them, but with half-suggested, insubstantial creatures spun out of thought, the ghost story is in a class by itself. Other kinds of writing benefit from the many warm, rich human emotions they arouse, but the ghost story stakes everything on one cold, stark emotion—fear.

The fear it creates may be accompanied by a curious sort of wild beauty or panic awe, but fear is the *raison d'être* of the ghost story. If it succeeds in making its readers' skin prickle, it has accomplished its purpose; if it fails to do so, it has failed completely. There are no halfway measures, and all attempts to vary the simple theme or to mitigate its full power are unworthy of serious consideration. The humorous ghost story is no ghost story at all, and tales with rational explanations are sheer frauds.

A ghost story must be about the supernatural or it is not worth the telling. Nothing is more infuriating than the deceptive account that starts out like the real thing and then lets the reader down when the author suddenly drops the mask and cries: "Boo! It's all right—I was only joking." No one wants to be made a fool of. Sheets and lath and phosphorescent paint may serve to frighten children, but adults demand stronger stuff. They would rather believe that the phantom which made them shudder came from the very depths of hell than from someone's box of manufactured tricks.

However, a genuine belief in the supernatural is not needed for the enjoyment of the ghost story. There is a large enough residue of the primitive sense of wonder in most of us to give us a taste for inexplicable mystery. Grudgingly or willingly, depending upon our degree of skepticism, we grant—or are tricked into granting—the necessary supernatural premise, and then it is up to the author to carry on from there. But after granting this premise the reader should not be asked to fling all vestiges of common sense away. The story must have some foundation in reality, or it will seem so absurd that no one will care what happens in it. The skillfully told tale of fantasy should make only one departure from solid fact, as H. G. Wells has explained:

> Anyone can invent human beings inside out or worlds like dumbbells or a gravitation that repels. The thing that makes such imaginations interesting is their translation into commonplace terms and a rigid exclusion of other marvels from the story. Then it becomes human. "How would you feel and what might not happen to you?" is the typical question, if for instance pigs could fly and one came rocketing over a hedge at you. How would you feel and what might not happen to you if suddenly you were changed into an ass and couldn't tell anyone about it? Or if you became invisible? But no one would think twice about the answer if hedges and houses also began to fly, or if people changed into lions, tigers, cats, and dogs left and right, or if everyone could vanish anyhow. Nothing remains interesting where anything may happen.
>
> For the writer of fantastic stories to help the reader to play the game properly, he must help him in every possible unobtrusive way to *domesticate* the impos-

sible hypothesis. He must trick him into an unwary concession to some plausible assumption and get on with his story while the illusion holds. [From the preface to *Seven Famous Novels* by H. G. Wells]

Just as too much unreality spoils the ghost story, so will too little make it difficult to accept. The author must strike a medium between unrestrained fancy and sobering fact. He cannot make his ghost too solidly substantial or his readers will refuse to credit it. They have at least a vague concept of what a ghost should be, and it is better to let their concept remain vague. The unreal gains nothing from being made more concrete; ghosts are most convincing when they cannot be examined too closely—illusion vanishes when they can be touched or felt. You cannot analyze the mournfulness of a hoot-owl's cry or reduce to formula a moonbeam's magic. Ghosts have their own dimension, and they pine and fade away when they are brought into ours.

Imagination is needed for the writing of supernatural tales and also for the enjoying of them. The reader who is deaf to the sad, sweet tinkling of the dulcimer in "Kubla Khan" or who is unmoved by the glory of a phrase like "Charmed magic casements opening on the foam of perilous seas in faery lands forlorn" is not likely to have much use for a literature that depends upon suggestion and association for its effect. It comes from a realm where the subjective must rule unchallenged; it is closely akin to poetry, it belongs to the metaphysical, it is allied to aesthetics, and its products cannot be measured in inches or pounds, but only in terms of themselves and in comparison with one another. (pp. 4-15)

The provinces we have staked out in the dark reaches of the nether mind are inhabited not only by ghosts; horror dwells there also; and its dread region abuts upon the nearer bourns of an empty blackness where reason itself totters and is engulfed. But horror and fear, although of the same family and often mistaken for each other, are not identical. Unlike fear, which can be of long duration, horror is necessarily climactic in effect. The mind can stand only so much, then its protecting agencies quickly come to the rescue and benumb the nerves. Thus it will be seen that horror transcends fear and is even more powerful.

The word, of course, has been used much too loosely. There is no horror, for instance, about a corpse, no matter how unpleasant it may look. Nothing substantial can be truly horrible; it may, by some odd quirk of association, inspire horror, but horror itself can be found only within ourselves. It is an emotion that is rooted in the imagination rather than in anything in the external world.

True horror, fortunately, is a rare experience for most of us. We may be frightened, terrified, or even awestruck upon occasion, but a man may easily live out his whole life even in these extraordinarily troubled times and never come face to face with horror in his waking moments. In dreams, however, it is not uncommonly to be met with, and in them it can be encountered in full force. In real life the critical mind acts as a censor, so that even the most dreadful experiences are mitigated by ever-present reason which whispers reassuringly, "This can't be true," or "Perhaps it isn't so bad as it appears." But in dreams we have no such protection. In them we have to stand naked before unbearable horror, and if, panic-stricken, we seek to escape, we find ourselves pursued to the very brink of consciousness by a thing that would drive us mad if we were to confront it in the daylight.

Nightmares are the most horrible ordeals the human mind has to undergo, for it has no barrier to set up against them. The horror found in supernatural literature is closer to that experienced in dreams than to anything encountered in our waking life. In the ghost story, horror is induced by the dread apparition which comes to haunt the defenseless characters and causes the reader to shudder in sympathy with them. (pp. 15-16)

Ghost stories are fairy tales for grownups; in reading them we relive our childhood experiences—the fears they arouse are the echoes of fears we felt when we were very young, the suspense they create is the same heart-thumping agony we went through when we waited anxiously to hear what would happen to Little Red Riding Hood. They bring back to mind comparable moments encountered in other forms of imaginative literature— in legends, in myth, in poetry. We think again of Roland dying at Roncesvalles, sounding too late the horn he had disdained to use; we hear the mournful cry "Great Pan is dead!" roll out over the waters to be heard by lonely mariners on the night a bright star burned over Bethlehem; we see the roisterers around the candlelit table in the Mermaid Tavern where the souls of poets dead and gone still drink to their immortal muse. Memory-plagued and image-haunted, our brains are the real refuges of all the ghosts that ever walked the earth.

The impressions made in our earliest years lie deepest, and they shape the very structure of our being. Man never outlives the child that is within him. In our dreams we revisit the long-vanished places associated with our youth. Why search for haunted houses? They are to be found inside each one of us, and at night we creep into them to wander through their shadowy halls. He who says he never saw a ghost has never had a dream or probed his own soul. (pp. 21-2)

> *Philip Van Doren Stern, in an introduction to* The Midnight Reader: Great Stories of Haunting and Horror, *edited by Philip Van Doren Stern, Henry Holt and Company, 1942, pp. 1-22.*

JACK SULLIVAN

[*Sullivan is an American educator and critic specializing in English supernatural fiction, particularly the development and major authors of ghost stories of the late Victorian and Edwardian periods. In the following essay, he surveys supernatural fiction of the late nineteenth and early twentieth centuries, focusing on the works of English and American authors.*]

In the introduction to his famous 1942 collection of ghost stories [see excerpt above], editor and literary critic Philip Van Doren Stern declared the late nineteenth and early twentieth centuries to be the "golden age" of the genre. Although the statement may at first seem hyperbolic, one has only to begin recalling names from the period—Kipling, Machen, Henry James, M. R. James, Wharton, Bierce, de Maupassant—to recognize its essential accuracy, at least as an aesthetic proposition. An unprecedented eruption of first-rate ghostly tales began in 1872 with Le Fanu's *In a Glass Darkly* and continued unabated through World War I. The genre has enjoyed other high points in terms of popularity and quantity of tales produced, but never has it enjoyed such a happy coincidence of quantity and quality.

For it is precisely the literary quality of fiction from this period that is its most immediately striking feature. It is a particular kind of quality, a distinctly modern dexterity and unity that originated to a large extent in the work of Edgar Allan Poe and Sheridan Le Fanu, the first short story writers in English

to work out carefully planned aesthetic strategies of horror. They were also among the first to write modern short stories. Their habitual strict attention to unity of mood and economy of means is a quality we take for granted in short fiction today, but it was virtually unknown to their more didactically inclined contemporaries. The creation of mood for its own sake and the sustaining of that mood without moralistic or occultist interruptions was their specialty, one they cultivated in relative isolation.

In a sense, Le Fanu was more revolutionary than Poe, for he began the process of dismantling the Gothic props and placing the supernatural tale in everyday settings. His stories, especially those in *In a Glass Darkly,* have surprisingly quiet surfaces and ominous undertones; they rely on genuinely *ghostly* scenes, many of them unapologetically supernatural, rather than melodramatic ones. Thematically, they represent the first serious attempt to abandon the Gothic villain who gets his just deserts in favor of the innocent victim who is mysteriously or randomly persecuted by demons who refuse to be exorcised. Le Fanu's early and obsessive preoccupation with helplessness in a malign universe becomes the major theme of later horror fiction and of much mainstream fiction as well. Indeed, the dark, apocalyptic quality of early modern horror fiction is absolutely contiguous with a spirit of restlessness and malaise that some historians, citing the works of Freud, Huysmans, Schoenberg, and others, view as an emotional key to the age and as a premonition of World War I.

Stephen Spender, T. S. Eliot, and many others have written eloquently about the atmosphere of trauma that darkened this period and manifested itself in increasingly bizarre and subjective modes of expression. This was a transitional age characterized by convulsive social changes, ugly repercussions from an unpopular war, economic instability, a sneering cynicism about government and the established order, and a fascination with counter-cultures and occult societies. Since this is the cataclysmic climate in which the tale of terror seems to flourish, it is perhaps no accident that the Vietnam and Watergate periods also witnessed a spectacular revival of the genre.

Le Fanu and other early masters were able to communicate this terror most tellingly in the short tale, and it is fascinating how closely and consistently connected are the developments of modern supernatural fiction and modern short fiction. A remarkable number of early modern writers who pioneered the short story as a major form had, like Le Fanu, a penchant for the weird and the horrific. Hardy, Kipling, de Maupassant, Conrad, Stevenson, Turgenev, and others produced some of their finest work in the genre. To understand why the birth of the modern supernatural tale and the modern short story are so intermeshed, one need only think about the intent of modern supernatural horror. There are more supernatural stories with unity of mood than other kinds of early stories precisely because mood is fundamental to the genre. H. P. Lovecraft, one of the most astute critics of horror, wrote in *Supernatural Horror in Literature* [see excerpt below] that "atmosphere is the all-important thing," more important, for example, than plot. In some of the more original stories of Machen and Blackwood, amazingly little happens, just as little happens in the mainstream short stories of Anton Chekhov and James Joyce; tiny attenuations and crescendos of emotion provide the drama and terror.

There is, thus, a powerful emphasis on psychology in the supernatural fiction of this period, an emphasis characteristic of mainstream fiction as well. Poe and Le Fanu are again impressively forward-looking in this respect; their careful blending of hallucinatory psychosis and supernatural malevolence, so that the distinction between the two is ominously effaced, has a striking counterpart in the work of de Maupassant, Henry James, Bierce, and others. In James's *The Turn of the Screw* and *The Jolly Corner* (1908), what happens is not as significant as how a character perceives it happening—an emphasis that by no means denies the possibility of a supernatural interpretation. The drama of the story lies in the registering of the effect of the horrific happening on the mind—as in Poe's "The Black Cat" and Le Fanu's "Green Tea"—rather than the happening itself. Taken to an extreme, as it is in the work of James, Wharton, and de Maupassant, the *mind* becomes the locale of the tale, rather than England, America, or France.

This is perhaps the crucial explanation for the curiously international quality of much of the best horror fiction from this period. Turgenev's stories do not seem single-mindedly "Russian" (even though a Russian setting and sensibility are unobtrusively and tellingly present) any more than Le Fanu's genuine masterpieces ("Carmilla," "Green Tea") are "Irish." Rendering the nuances of terror on the mind of the victim—a recognizable, vulnerable mind with which the reader can identify—is what is important, much more so than an anthropologically accurate disquisition on the particular region, culture, or legend from which the horror springs. Even writers who specialized in myth and legend, such as E. L. White and F. Marion Crawford, were careful to relegate that specialty to the background and focus on the psychology of fear. E. F. Bleiler is right to maintain in his introduction to Le Fanu's *Best Ghost Stories* (1964) that Le Fanu's weakest work is his most parochically Irish, and we could make the same point about later writers. To cite the most obvious example, nothing is more irritating or more certain to compromise the mood of terror than a story heavily peppered with dialect. One approaches whole pages of Stevenson, Quiller-Couch, and even M. R. James (not to mention Van Helsing's diatribes in *Dracula*) with a feeling of dread that has nothing to do with the supernatural.

The issue of psychology in these tales is put into admirable perspective by M. R. James in the introduction to his anthology, *Ghosts and Marvels* (1927): "It is not amiss sometimes to leave a loophole for a natural explanation, but I would say, let the loophole be so narrow as not to be quite practicable." The "loophole" usually involves the possibility that the victim of an ostensibly demonic persecution was either mad or temporarily deluded. Since James has an abiding interest in the supernatural per se in his fiction, his loophole is extremely narrow. For other writers, it is much wider, sometimes to the point of making a *supernatural* reading "not quite practicable." By the end of a given tale, we usually know which reading the author wants us to adopt, but not always. De Maupassant, Henry James, Turgenev, and Charlotte Perkins Gilman (in her single and singular masterpiece, "The Yellow Wall Paper") lead us into a modern world of nightmarish ambiguity, which is not resolved by the ending of the story.

Thus, psychology does not comprise a separate category of tale but a preoccupation that spreads into all the weird fiction of this period. Henry James's statement in "The Art of Fiction" on the importance of the narrative point of view reflected a concern with psychological realism in the very form of fiction from which few major writers dissented. At the same time, a few artists, such as James, Wharton, Stevenson, de Maupassant, and Bierce, had a special, almost single-minded interest

Portrait of Algernon Blackwood. From Best Ghost Stories of Algernon Blackwood. *Dover Publications, 1973. Reprinted by permission of Dover Publications, Inc.*

in psychological nuance, and it is possible to categorize them as "psychological" writers, even though the supernatural appears frequently in their work. The *cante cruel* writers, with their spectacularly morbid interest in the extremities of mental and physical suffering, also fit into this category. Still, the classification is at best a tricky one. Even the most unambiguously demonic works have fascinating, sometimes central psychological aspects, as Leonard Wolf has shown in his self-consciously cute but perceptive book, *A Dream of Dracula* (1972); Stoker's *Dracula* lends itself almost irresistibly to a Freudian reading.

A classification more clear and distinct is the "cosmic" or "visionary" tendency in supernatural horror. This emphasis on visionary experience both in plot and narrative attitude marks the work of Algernon Blackwood, Arthur Machen, W. B. Yeats, Grant Allen, Elliot O'Donnell, William Hope Hodgson, Charles Willing Beale, Mrs. Campbell Praed, Oliver Onions, and R. W. Chambers; it also appears fairly frequently in the work of Stoker, M. P. Shiel, Sir Arthur Conan Doyle, Jonas Lie, William Clark Russell, G. S. Viereck, and many others.

By definition, all supernatural horror involves the occult and the mystical to some extent. In the cosmic tale, however, rarefied otherworldly visions are presented as part of an antimaterialist ideology that indicts Victorian scientism and technology and presents mystical experience as an alternative to the grayness and mechanized tedium of modern life. An aesthetically treacherous didactic strain mars much of this fiction, but in the masterpieces of cosmic horror, such as Blackwood's "The Willows" and Machen's "The White People," the creative strain is happily stronger. Unfortunately, this period is filled with oppressively preachy "true believer" works, most of them long occult novels, and most of them mercifully obscure. The most charitable thing we might say is that the average occult novel had little sense of terror or wonder. As Lovecraft points out in *Supernatural Horror in Literature,* the "trade jargon of modern occultism" has ruined many a tale.

Nevertheless, the flowering of occult and "psychical" societies, such as the Order of the Golden Dawn and the Society for Psychic Research, provided a favorable milieu for supernatural fiction. Machen, Yeats, Blackwood, O'Donnell, Blavatsky, and many others were members of such groups. For the real artists, the cosmologies of Rosicrucianism and other exotic belief systems provided a backdrop of imagery and incidents; for hacks and polemicists, it provided a ready-made jargon, a substitute for good writing. It should be added that most of the superior occult mythologies—those with a powerful literary resonance—were invented: Arthur Machen may have been a member of the Order of the Golden Dawn, but his Great God Pan mythos was a product of his own imagination.

Stylistically, the more mystically inclined writers favored lyricism and expansiveness. There is a seriousness of tone, an implied connectedness to apocalyptic forces and secrets, that is worlds removed from the urbanity of M. R. James or the acid humor of Ambrose Bierce, even though they both deal with occult themes. Renouncing the detached irony so characteristic of modern fiction, writers like Blackwood and William Hope Hodgson attempted to infuse their language with an intensity consistent with their concepts. It is a risky strategy, one that sometimes results in ponderousness and overwriting. When it works, however, it delivers an enormously sensual and poetic glimpse of other worlds and other modes of perception.

The cosmic vision in this fiction is complex, for it often fuses ecstasy and horror. There is a curious ambivalence in these stories; the characters want desperately to rid themselves of the routine and mechanization of their daily lives, but the weird and enticing otherworlds they escape to are usually self-destructive or unendurably frightening. Some, like E. F. Benson's archetypal "Man Who Went Too Far," never make it back and die hideous deaths. Others, like the narrator of Blackwood's "May Day Eve," desperately negotiate a re-entry into the same modern world that previously looked so grubby and dull.

Another major tendency in the fiction of this period, more modest in its intent and more straightforward in its thematic thrust, is the antiquarian school of M. R. James. The James school represents a liberation from Gothic melodrama and Victorian allegory in its most insistent and entertaining form. In an October 1923 interview for the *Morning Post,* James took a swipe at the hyperbole of the Gothic writers, the "vagueness" of Poe, and the "trivial and melodramatic" effects of Lord Lytton and his Victorian contemporaries. In his introduction to *Madame Crowl's Ghost* (1923), his pioneering collection of Le Fanu tales, he stated that Le Fanu was the only Victorian worth imitating. And in the introduction to his own *Ghost Stories of an Antiquary* he insisted that the sole purpose of his ghostly tales was to make his readers feel "pleasantly uncomfortable."

The aesthetic strategy of the James school is summed up in the introduction to *Madame Crowl's Ghost* with typically Jamesian lucidity:

> Let us, then, be introduced to the actors in a placid way; let us see them going about their ordinary business, undisturbed by forebodings, pleased with their surroundings; and into this calm environment let the ominous thing put out its head, unobtrusively at first, and then more insistently, until it holds the stage.

For the most part, James is true to his Le Fanu-inspired principles: the openings are low-keyed and full of "ordinary business" (as much as antiquarian pursuits can be called "ordinary"); the characters are stolid or cheerful rather than hysterical or neurotic; the invading presence sneaks gradually into the shadows of the story; and the horror that finally holds the stage is usually an "ominous thing" indeed. James's style, like Le Fanu's, is leisurely and careful, but it is also much more economical and urbane. The same qualities, with delightful variations, characterize James's disciples in the period, such as E. G. Swain and Sir Arthur Gray, as well as such later writers as Eleanor Scott, Frederick Cowles, and E. H. Meyerstein. Some (Swain and Gray, for example) were conscious imitators of James and worked contentedly in his shadow; others, particularly later artists like Wakefield and Hartley, had antiquarian styles and themes, but were much too individual and idiosyncratic to be conveniently placed in a "school."

One trait all the antiquarian writers shared was erudition. A major medieval scholar and church historian, James filled his tales with allusions to history, architecture, and all manner of antiquarian minutiae. His characters are learned collectors whose collections get them into trouble, and James is careful to make the demons that pounce on them seem chillingly authentic through the use of exact (although often invented) names and scholarly references. This antiquarianism only superficially resembles the antiquarianism in Poe, where collectors' exotica are linked with dramatically deranged psyches such as Roderick Usher's. The characters of James and his followers are at least sane enough to know that their ghosts are real, especially since the apparitions are often seen by more than one of them.

Nevertheless, if antiquarian characters do not, like Poe's, hallucinate their demons, or do not, like Chambers's and Machen's, chase after them, they do set themselves up for disaster. Related to the narrative detachment of the James school is a half-hidden *Wasteland* ambience, a sense of cultivated boredom and ennui, which has its roots in the 1890s "decadence" languors of Wilde's *The Picture of Dorian Gray* and Yeats's early weird fiction (a movement prefigured with exacting prescience by Poe). The haunted antiquaries in these tales surround themselves with rarified paraphernalia from the past (books, dollhouses, even ancient whistles) seemingly because they cannot connect with the present. For them, the modern world scarcely exists. The endless process of collecting gives these Edwardian reactionaries an illusory sense of order and stability—illusory because it is exactly this process that unleashes the horror. Because the characters are people of leisure, this gentlemanly horror fiction represents a sophisticated version of the old warning that idleness is the devil's workshop.

Again, it should be noted that neither antiquarian nor cosmic tales are entirely separate from the psychological ones. The psychology of the interaction between viewer and apparition was something most of the better writers were careful to depict. Also, it should be emphasized that "antiquarian" and "cosmic" refer to imaginative tendencies, not rigid categories. The wit, subtlety, and compression of the one and the mysticism, intensity, and otherworldliness of the other represent a basic emotional and stylistic division, but many writers, especially the more richly creative and complex, stubbornly resist codification. H. G. Wells, Arthur Conan Doyle, and the Bensons, to name only a few, have a fluidity of temperament and imagination that moves them sometimes in one direction, sometimes in another. Because of the occult interests of the time, the visionary group is the larger. Indeed, the antiquarian school is limited mainly to British writers, although its voice and sensibility are approximated in the work of Wharton, E. L. White, and others. It should be added that the most conservative writers, such as E. Nesbit, Mrs. Molesworth, and Sir Arthur Quiller-Couch, spin out a combination of terror and fairy-tale enchantment in such a charmingly old-fashioned storytelling manner that they seem to belong in none of these "modern" categories, but in a longed-for past.

Some devotees of the genre may object to the lack of a separate "Christian" category, but close examination reveals that Christianity makes a strangely feeble and fragmentary impression in the quality horror fiction of this period. Christian motifs do appear in works such as Stoker's *Dracula,* Machen's *The Great God Pan,* E. F. Benson's "Negotium Perambulans," and R. H. Benson's "The Watcher," but their basic movement is usually toward a vision more pagan or animistic than Christian. Despite Russell Kirk's assertion (in the Afterword to *The Surly Sullen Bell,* 1962) that ghost stories are Christian allegories, Lovecraft was surely right to maintain that orthodoxy of any stripe, Christian or occult, tends to have a deadening effect on the genre. Indeed, the weaker Christian stories of R. H. Benson, Charlotte Riddell, Oliver Onions (in his post-*Widdershins* phase), and Kirk himself fail precisely because they are hemmed in by orthodox allegory.

The reader can hardly fail to notice the heavy emphasis in this chapter on short stories and novelettes. As Poe and others have noted, a convincing mood of terror is much easier to sustain in a short tale than in a full-length novel. Since the major enterprise of this period *was* to create and sustain new worlds of terror—with a concomitant renunciation of heavy-handed allegory, sentimental love interest, needless subplots, irrelevant ratiocination, and other devices of earlier horror fiction—it is no accident that the major genre writers tended to edit out extraneous matter and produce shorter works. A large number of short stories from this period are peerless masterpieces, and it would be false to pretend that the novels, taken as a group, constitute a comparable achievement.

Nevertheless, several impressive supernatural horror novels were produced, often by the same writers who specialized in short stories. Considered solely on the basis of its power as a horror novel, Stoker's *Dracula* is perhaps the most spectacularly successful, as well as the most influential and popular. It has a singularly terrifying and poetic opening, a magisterial supernatural villain, and consistently vivid imagery. It also, unfortunately, falls apart near the end, as do most long horror novels.

Lovecraft makes the rather charitable point that a flawed supernatural narrative should be savored for its "isolated sections" of genuine horror "no matter how prosaically it is later dragged down." By that criterion, a number of novels in this period pass muster, including Hodgson's *The House on the Borderland,* and *The Night Land,* Beale's *The Ghost of Guir House,* Crawford's *The Witch of Prague,* Buchan's *Witch Wood,* O'Donnell's *The Sorcery Club,* Ewer's *Alraune,* Lee's *A Phantom Lover,* Marsh's *The Beetle,* Phillpott's *A Deal with the Devil,* Riddell's *The Uninhabited House,* and Viereck's *The House of the Vampire.* These novels have melodramatic or sentimental lapses that detract from their atmosphere, but they also have memorable moments of dread and wonder. Many

novels of the period, such as Robert Hichen's *The Dweller on the Threshold* and Marie Corelli's *The Problem of a Wicked Soul* are so saturated in fashionable spiritualist rhetoric that they do not qualify as horror fiction. Even the novels of Algernon Blackwood, as E. F. Bleiler points out in his introduction to Blackwood's *Best Ghost Stories* (1973), fall into the category of "mystical" rather than horror fiction.

The supernatural novelette, however, was one of the great forms of the period. Some of its most innovative pioneers were also pioneers of horror fiction. Beginning with Le Fanu's "Carmilla" and "Green Tea," the Victorian and early modern periods saw the publication of such enduring masterworks as Stevenson's "The Strange Case of Dr. Jekyll and Mr. Hyde," Conrad's *Heart of Darkness,* James's "The Turn of the Screw," Machen's "The White People," Onions's "The Beckoning Fair One," Turgenev's "Clara Militch," and Housman's *The Were-Wolf.* The novelette offered an ideal compromise, a way of painting on a wider canvas of horror than was possible in a short story without risking the hazards of a full-length novel. It is small wonder that it was a favored form.

It should be emphasized that most of the major works from this period, no matter what their length or category, have a basic theme: inexplicable presences and forces exist, both supernatural and psychological, that are aggressively hostile to humanity and can break into our world to create chaos and tragedy. The fundamental darkness of this fiction needs to be asserted to counteract the erroneous claim, perpetrated in numerous anthology introductions, that the horror story is not really horrible and does not really mean business, but instead is a form of allegory about the triumph of good over evil—or at worst a roundabout means of implying the existence of good by showing us evil. The reality is that the early modern masters, beginning with Le Fanu, present ominous visions of the universe in which good conspicuously does *not* triumph and is often absent altogether. The most powerful and ambitiously serious stories by writers such as Machen, Bierce, Hardy, Lie, and Hodgson portray panicked, often pathetic characters who are hounded and cruelly destroyed by forces they often never understand. As much as Kafka's Joseph K., they are persecuted for no clear reason. Nor do the representatives of science or religion (frequently an uneasy and unconvincing melding of the two) offer much relief. In Turgenev's archetypal "Father Alexyei's Story," one of the great Le Fanuesque pursuit tales from the period, a young man studying for the priesthood is persecuted to death by a jeering demon who has the power, among other things, to make him spit out the Eucharist and grind it underfoot when he attempts to take Communion. Not a shred of evidence exists to indicate that the young man has done anything to deserve such a fate. Indeed, he is a devout, earnest, orthodox believer who continually prays for, and does not get, God's help. It scarcely matters whether the demon is supernatural or psychological or whether, as is likely, Turgenev meant the reader to have either option: the sense of vulnerability in a threatening world is the same. When the despairing father, who never recovers from his son's tragedy, breaks down in tears and asks, "How have I deserved such wrath from the Lord?" the reader can only echo him—how indeed?

This is not to suggest that all the writers in the period have a vision as severe as Turgenev's (nor are all of Turgenev's horror tales this unremittingly horrible), but the most seriously intended works surely move in this direction. The tendency is apparent even in Blackwood, the most optimistic and upbeat writer of the period. Although his characters generally survive their horrific ordeals (in itself an unusually positive turn of affairs, given the tragic endings of most stories by Blackwood's contemporaries), they find themselves plunged back into an everyday reality they have already renounced as being profoundly cold and alienating. Neither the ghostly nor the empirical world is presented as a hospitable place.

Because the darkness in this fiction is difficult to sustain for very long, it generally erupts in a more disturbing and uncompromising way in short stories than in novels. The short stories of Bram Stoker, for example, tend to be bleaker than *Dracula,* which at least has a happy ending. Indeed, some of the darkest writers, such as Bierce (and earlier, Poe) did not write novels at all.

What makes the darkness bearable, indeed richly pleasurable, is the artfulness of this fiction—its subtle atmosphere, haunting imagery, and tragi-comic sense of humor. The literary quality of an astonishing amount of this fiction continues to go unrecognized by even the more savvy commentators.

In the December 5, 1980, issue of the *Times Literary Supplement,* A. N. Wilson exemplifies a dismally typical attitude when he writes: "We do not judge whether a horror film or ghost story is 'good' by the same standards by which we judge a real work of literature. All that matters here is whether we have been frightened." As anyone who has read even a smattering of James, Wharton, Onions, or any number of other first-rate writers can attest, this pronouncement presents a false dichotomy. Certainly in the horror fiction of the late nineteenth and early twentieth centuries, "whether we have been frightened" is entirely a function of whether the story is well written and imaginatively conceived. The stories that do not frighten are invariably those with no style and no vision. The best of these fascinating and powerful works reach beyond the boundaries of horror and Gothic fandom to all readers who enjoy and value beautifully crafted fiction. (pp. 221-30)

> *Jack Sullivan, "Psychological, Antiquarian, and Cosmic Horror: 1871-1919," in* Horror Literature: A Core Collection and Reference Guide, *edited by Marshall B. Tymn, R. R. Bowker Company, 1981, pp. 221-75.*

G. R. THOMPSON

[*Thompson is an American educator and critic who has written extensively on Gothic fiction, particularly the works of Edgar Allan Poe. In the following excerpt, he disputes the conclusions of Pamela Search, Julia Briggs, and Jack Sullivan regarding the origins of the modern psychological ghost story. Whereas these critics trace this type of supernatural tale to Walter de la Mare, E. T. A. Hoffmann, and Joseph Sheridan Le Fanu respectively, Thompson argues that its true source may be found in Washington Irving's "The Adventure of the German Student" (1824) and concludes with a discussion of the nature and development of American supernatural literature.*]

In the introduction to her well-known anthology *The Supernatural in the English Short Story* Pamela Search attempts to categorize the types and modes of supernatural agency in the tale of terror, the ghost story, and the Gothic tale. While she tries to keep her distinctions clear, she ends up blurring Gothic, horror, ghostly, and supernatural tales into one. Perhaps this loose classification is adequate for her purposes (and perhaps instinctively right), but along the way she makes a discovery. The "horror tale had its heyday in the earlier years" of the twentieth century, she writes; but "since then another kind of

weird fiction has come into its own—the psychological ghost story." What she means by psychological ghost story, however, is not a tale in which apparently supernatural events turn out to be the misperceptions of a nervous narrator or distraught character. As Search defines it, the psychological ghost story is "the *inconclusive* tale of the supernatural," exemplified by the tales of Walter De La Mare. In fact, she implies that De La Mare invented the type.

In stories like his, a *possible* supernatural agency is balanced off against a *possible* psychological "explanation," with more or less ambiguous results. We are unsure whether the events narrated are real or misperceived; we are not concerned, however, with psychological misperception in itself but with the inconclusive character of the story. This kind of tale, Search claims, is more effective than the old-fashioned ghost story because "when the horror is left undefined it becomes all the more real to us in our imagination, and the inconclusive ending of the tale leaves us with our doubts and fears unresolved, and therefore more terrible."

Now everyone knows that Henry James, not Walter De La Mare, invented the psychological ghost story. Search knows the conventional wisdom on the history of the type too. Therefore she defends her claim by suggesting that although in *The Turn of the Screw* (1898) James anticipated the technique, he did not combine "the supernatural with the psychological" nearly "so compellingly as De La Mare." At this point, Search's opinion about the quality of James's effects as compared with De La Mare's may be called into question, but we might not challenge her historical accuracy regarding the ghost story proper—even if the names of Bierce, Poe, Hawthorne, and Irving come momentarily to mind. But then we are brought up short by her comment that "there have been stories of this type ever since Le Fanu wrote his famous *Green Tea.*"

Joseph Sheridan Le Fanu (1814-73) may have been the greatest British ghost-story writer of the nineteenth century, but "Green Tea" is only vaguely about a "ghost" and it came late in his career (1869). "Green Tea" tells the story of a mild-mannered and morally upright minister, Mr. Jennings, who is bedevilled by a sinister monkey with glowing red eyes. Information is filtered through the papers of one Dr. Hesselius, who has "treated" Jennings for his apparently hallucinatory demon: the monkey is visible to no one but Jennings. At times it even sits on his Bible during sermons, so that he seems to his hearers nervous and distracted, frequently breaking off in the middle of a text. Jennings tries various means of warding off the demon, and it disappears from time to time, but always returns. Jennings finally consults Hesselius, who has treated many weird cases. Hesselius concludes after Jenning's suicide that a chemical reaction, the result of recurrent overdoses of strong green tea, must have opened up some "inner eye" in the man's mind. A rift in the tissue or interface between an occult world and the ordinary, everyday world allowed Jennings a glimpse of an alien realm of being. On the other hand, we are reminded, Jennings had a family history of suicidal mania. "Green Tea," Julia Briggs observes in her recent study *Night Visitors: The Rise and Fall of the English Ghost Story,* is "poised, somewhat mystifyingly, between these two explanations."

"Green Tea" is the focal point of another new study of the ghost story as well. Jack Sullivan, in *Elegant Nightmares: The English Ghost Story from Le Fanu to Blackwood,* devotes to the tale a chapter entitled "The Archetypal Ghost Story." Even if we grant for the sake of argument that "Green Tea" actually is an inconclusive story about a "ghost," it is still puzzling to discover that this new type is the archetype. What happened to the prototypes, where ghosts were either actual supernatural presences or were satisfactorily explained away? And how is it that the archetype is the new "variant" or a "development"? Sullivan writes that in 1839 "a new kind" of "ghost appeared in English fiction," with the publication of Le Fanu's "Schalken the Painter," a macabre tale about a demonic or ghostly lover who claims a living bride and transforms her into a ghost. The technique of narration, Sullivan claims, was "revolutionary"; there is a double point of view involving the perspective of the victimized young girl's befuddled uncle and that of her horrified fiancé. The plot moves toward a dream sequence, where a coffin is transformed into a Victorian four-poster. "Schalken the Painter" is, according to Sullivan, the "promising start" of a development in ghostly fiction that culminates thirty years later in "Green Tea," which represents the new ghost story in "its most uncompromising form."

Sullivan seems to sense that he is on shaky ground in his claims for Le Fanu, for he is quick to disqualify Edgar Allan Poe as a ghost-story writer. He observes that 1839 was not only the publication date of "Schalken the Painter," but also of Poe's "The Fall of the House of Usher." But in Le Fanu the ghost seems simultaneously "to emerge from within as well as invade from without." His concern with "Usher" implies that something similar happens in Poe. But Poe's story, he says, is an "exercise in cosmic paranoia rather than a tale of the supernatural." Sullivan has a point, but the same might be said of Le Fanu's "Green Tea," if it is to be read as the inconclusive tale he claims it is. Sullivan attempts to cover himself on another point as well: "As the less than reliable narrator of a horror tale, Hesselius is part of a tradition which begins with Poe's narrator in 'The Tale-Tale Heart' and culminates in the governess's account in *The Turn of the Screw*," but the "narrative problems are more complex than those in Poe." One wonders in what ways Poe's narrators before 1843—those of "MS. Found in a Bottle" (1833), "Berenice" (1835), "Morella" (1835), "Ligeia" (1838), and "William Wilson" (1839)—are so clearly reliable, or in what ways the double point of view of "Usher" is less complex than the editorial siftings of "Green Tea."

Sullivan, like most critics of the ghost story, admits that he uses the phrase "ghost story" as a "catch-all term." But since all the stories he deals with are, he says, "apparitional, in one sense or another . . . 'ghost story' is as good a term as any." If so, how then are the apparitions of Poe's tales "of a different order" from Le Fanu's in "Green Tea"? Although "horror story" is "not quite as all-inclusive" a term, Sullivan writes, "most English tales fall into the class of *both* ghost and horror story, so that the terms are almost interchangeable." He observes that "Lovecraft's 'supernatural horror' neatly fuses both terms," *ghost* suggesting the supernatural realm and *horror* apparently suggesting "physical mayhem and revulsion." Such comment echoes standard thumbnail definitions of one effect of the Gothic. Is the Gothic, then, different from the ghost story only in its wider applicability to fear-driven narrative, so that the ghost story is limited in its effect to an "apparition"? Sullivan tells us that there "is little to be gained . . . by attempting to determine precisely" what the limits are between "ghost and horror tales." This allows him to denigrate the Gothic tradition and claim as a novelty in the ghost story something that has already reached an apogee in the American Gothic tale as practiced by Irving, Hawthorne, and Poe.

In his eagerness to separate the ghost story from the Gothic, Sullivan claims that "the modern ghostly tale is as much a reaction against the Gothic as an outgrowth of it," for Gothic ghosts were largely "decorative," lacking the "more actively loathesome, menacing quality of modern ghosts." Part of this menacing quality comes from the centrally inconclusive nature of the Le Fanu "archetype." Sullivan attacks "theory-obsessed critics" who would read such a work as "Green Tea" as Freudian or Christian allegory and thus miss the teasing, elusive, enigmatic quality of the tale. As the archetypal ghost story, he says, "Green Tea" is representative of a fundamentally disordered universe, incapable of rational codification. This point, Sullivan claims, is not noted by other writers on the ghost story. If so, it must be the result of their inattention to the basic modes of the Gothic tale, for the disordered universe of the Gothic is the matrix from which the ghost story issues in its various forms.

Although it is conventional to divide the Gothic romance into two types—the supernatural and the explained supernatural—actually four modes may be usefully distinguished. Historical Gothic is ontologically undifferentiated. The presence of an occasional demon or ghost is not necessarily significant for either the ontology *or* the epistemology of a text. In supernatural Gothic, the occult is in fact a central assumption. In the explained Gothic, the final assumption is that the supernatural does not, finally, interpenetrate the everyday world: all seemingly occult phenomena are the result of misinformation or misperception. But in ambiguous Gothic, it is the *tension* between the supernatural and the everyday that generates dread. Briggs does a somewhat better job than Sullivan in setting forth the development of the psychological ghost story within the Gothic tradition. Although she too sees "Green Tea" as a prime example, she traces the inconclusive tale back to the German writer, Hoffmann, a contemporary of Irving: "If any one writer can be credited with the invention of this twist it is E. T. A. Hoffmann," who, she observes, had greater impact on French and American writers than on any English writer. She mentions "The Golden Flower-Pot" (1814, rev. 1819) and "A New Year's Eve Adventure" (1814-16), neither of which is strictly a ghost story, though supernatural realms do intrude on the everyday world. But she does not mention Hoffmann's predecessors in the inconclusive supernatural, notably Ludwig Tieck and J.A.K. Musaeus, who enjoyed a certain vogue in both Britain and America. Nor does she speak of Hoffmann's contemporaries, like Clemens Brentano, "Bonaventura," Achim von Arnim, Jean Paul Friedrich Richter, and other explorers of the supernatural and psychic realms in fiction. Similarly, she fails to mention key French writers, like Théophile Gautier and Prosper Mérimée, who were early concerned with the wavering line between the supernatural and the natural. She does acknowledge a later nineteenth-century writer, Maupassant, noting that "The Horla" (1887), a tale about an invisible creature haunting a possibly deranged narrator, antedates *The Turn of the Screw*. Other important omissions include major American writers: Brown, Irving, Hawthorne. Presumably this is because there are so few out-and-out ghost stories among the Americans, though the British examples cited are frequently not strict ghost stories either.

Like Sullivan, Briggs does deal with Poe, who, she says, "created the prototypes of a number of variations on the psychological ghost story." Why Poe is singled out as having written more ghost stories than Irving or Hawthorne is unclear; certainly those of his tales that could be said to deal with ghosts per se are as few as those of the other two American writers. Nevertheless, she identifies three prototypes of Poe's psychological ghost tales: one is the description of grotesque events in such a way as to throw doubt on the narrator's sanity; a second is the dramatization of the narrator's urge to self-destruction; a third is the indication of a particular form of mental disturbance, such as the schizophrenia of William Wilson. The only other historical commentary she offers is the observation that the psychological ghost story uses the Radcliffe method of rational explanation of seeming marvels, but with "a more open-ended effect." Apparently, then, the originator of the psychological ghost story in English is Poe, about whom Sullivan is so concerned. But I would like to press the matter back a generation further, to Washington Irving, a writer who was not only deeply influenced by German romantic fiction, but who also did in fact write *ghost* stories. (pp. 13-18)

[Irving's "Adventure of the German Student"] is equidistantly poised between psychological explanation and the demonic. (p. 27)

Young Wolfgang, a German student in Paris during the Reign of Terror, is initially presented as someone whose imagination has been "diseased" by his studies in "spiritual essences." He becomes obsessed by the idea that "there was an evil influence hanging over him," an "evil genius or spirit seeking to ensnare him and ensure his perdition." This characterization is background to a recurrent dream of a woman's face that "haunts" him both in sleeping and waking moments. This "shadow of a dream" becomes "one of those fixed ideas which haunt the minds of melancholy men, and are at times mistaken for madness." Thus contradictory suggestions are set up: he is mad and he is not. One stormy night he crosses the square where public executions are held and in the flashing lightning sees the guillotine. At the foot of the steps of the scaffold, revealed in a "succession of vivid flashes of lightning," is a "female figure, dressed in black," sitting on one of the steps, leaning forward. She looks up and in "the bright glare of the lightning" reveals to Wolfgang "the very face which had haunted him in his dreams," pale and disconsolate, though beautiful. He takes her to his apartment, where, after some soothing conversation, he suddenly asks her to pledge herself to him. He says to her:

> "I pledge myself to you for ever."
>
> "For ever?" said the stranger, solemnly.
>
> "For ever!" repeated Wolfgang.
>
> The stranger clasped the hand extended to her: "Then I am yours," murmured she.

Having spent the next morning looking for more spacious apartments, he returns to find her lying dead on the bed. When the police arrive, they inform him that "she was guillotined yesterday." Wolfgang undoes a black collar around her neck, and "the head rolled on the floor!" At this point the reader is confronted with two possibilities: either Wolfgang is mad and has hallucinated the experience, or he has spent the night with a ghost. On the surface, the tale seems to be in the explained mode, and critics have generally read it that way: the mad young German has carried away a corpse and made love to it. But the introductory characterization presents opposing possibilities, each equally viable. Somehow, though his imagination is diseased, he is not mad. His own response does not resolve either possibility. He returns to the obsession mentioned in the second paragraph of the tale: "The fiend! the fiend has gained possession of me!... I am lost for ever." The narrator then remarks: "He was possessed with the frightful belief that an evil spirit had reanimated the dead body to ensnare him." This observation neither confirms nor denies the actuality of

supernatural manifestation. Certainly, if she were in fact a ghost, Wolfgang's pledge "for ever" insures his damnation, and her response, "I am yours," also means "you are mine." Traditionally, a demonic pact drives one insane. From the moment of the pact—whatever the actuality of subsequent events—Wolfgang is damned. His "madness," whether at the scaffold or at the end, may be the sign of the pact. The story is poised, like Le Fanu's "Green Tea" thirty-five years later, between these two possibilities for a final ambiguous twist. (pp. 27-9)

The "Adventure of the German Student" is perhaps the earliest well-crafted example in English of the inconclusive psychological ghost story.... (p. 31)

From the foregoing discussion it is clear that British-oriented studies of the ghost story make a historical error in attributing the origin of the inconclusive psychological ghost story to Le Fanu's "Green Tea" or "Schalken the Painter," or to Richard Barham's "Henry Harris." The experimental fiction and drama of German Romanticists at the end of the eighteenth century antedate such techniques, and the American psychological ghost story precedes British examples by a generation or more. It is, however, apparently accurate to claim that the ambiguous mode of the Gothic, with its intricate manipulations of frames, its metafictional implications of point of view, its intrusions of humor, and its general polyphony of tone, was not much in evidence in Britain until after the publication of Le Fanu's later tales. *Wuthering Heights* (1848) perhaps presents a special case, but the major exception would seem to be James Hogg's *Private Memoirs and Confessions of a Justified Sinner* (1824), along with a handful of his tales about dream-selves. In America, however, the ambiguous mode is dominant. The early American ghost story is one manifestation of the Gothic impulse of American dark Romanticism. After Irving, the ambiguous Gothic tale reaches an apex with Hawthorne and Poe, who tend to work within the larger Gothic tradition rather than focusing on the ghost story. A reader searching for straight ghost stories in the writings of Hawthorne and Poe will in fact turn up fewer than a dozen that might qualify.

In part, this unghostly aspect of the development of American Romantic fiction may be explained by our major writers' immersion in the philosophical complexities of the Romantic movement. The conventional observation on the supposed preponderance of explained Gothicism in American Romantic fiction results from a partial misreading of such stories as Irving's "German Student." Such a reading posits the influence of the Radcliffe method of explained Gothic, without much substantiation of Radcliffe's appeal to the American mind or influence on American writers other than Charles Brockden Brown; it is related to the general proposition that a pragmatic American materialism is a national characteristic. While suggestive, the assertion is finally simplistic. For one thing, such a view ignores not only the ecclesiastical history of America, but also the later influence of Scottish Common Sense School philosophy and of British empiricism, as represented by Hume and Berkeley, whose philosophical inquiries seemed to cast doubt on the existence of materiality.

Just as for European writers, for Americans the human mind becomes the key element in the matter-spirit dilemma. Their speculation is marked by a recurrent apprehension that all matter may be a mental construct, just as all dreams of the spiritual world may be a delusion. Americans become obsessed with the subject-object dialectic in Kant, who is reinterpreted by German writers like Fichte, interpreted again by Coleridge, and once more reinterpreted by Carlyle—not to mention the numerous lesser translations and explications of German philosophy by Frederic Henry Hedge and other Americans. The transcendentalist writers in America—especially the later Emerson and Thoreau, but also even Whitman—grapple with the same matter-spirit-mind paradox as do the dark Romanticists, though the point of view is diametrically opposite. There is hardly any such thing as a simple American materialism discoverable in the Romantic era, and the philosophy of mind derived from Germany and Britain has a major influence on the form of American Gothic fiction.

Although a complete history of the Gothic tradition in America requires a meticulous survey of stories by minor popular writers, it seems safe to say of the major American writers that the ambiguous tale reaches another high point later in the century simultaneously with renewed interest in the ghost story as a genre. That the psychological ghost story, as defined here, does not reflect the concerns merely of the last half of the nineteenth century but those of the first half as well is a point especially pertinent to American fiction. The continuum between the earlier nineteenth century and the later as suggested by the related subgenres of the Gothic tradition deserves further examination, both for developmens in literary form and for the implications for the *Zeitgeist* of a century. The century between the beginnings of Romantic fiction and the outpouring of fantastic and occult fiction in the 1880s and 90s through the 1920s suggests a continuity of aesthetic and philosophical concerns for the writer in America.

I would suggest that the development of the major modes of Gothic tale-telling by the American Romantics leads directly to the inconclusive psychological ghost story associated with later nineteenth-century writers like Bierce, Howells, and James. Their ghost stories represent the continuation of the ontological and epistemological themes of the Gothic strand of American Romanticism. If one wanted to argue for a break in a continuous line of development, I should hazard, tentatively, the suggestion that it occurs not so much in the later nineteenth century as in the obsessively "realist" fiction of the first half of the twentieth, where the Gothic seems separate from the "mainstream" in a way that it is not in the nineteenth. For even southern "Gothic" writers, like Faulkner, Welty, or O'Connor, seems to have less connection with the ghost-story writers of the popular magazines, or with writers of "weird" tales like Lovecraft, than did their predecessors two generations earlier. The later nineteenth-century writers, I would argue, continue an unbroken line. Irving, Poe, and Hawthorne are the direct ancestors of Howell's formulation of the "vague shapes of the borderland between experience and illusion" in *Shapes that Haunt the Dusk* (1907), of James's deliberate ambiguity in "The Jolly Corner" (1908), "The Friends of the Friends" (1896), and *The Turn of the Screw* (1898), of Bierce's mystification in "The Damned Thing" (1893), "The Eyes of the Panther" (1891), and especially "The Death of Halpin Frayser" (1893).

In British writing of the second half of the century, we find an exaggerated interest and belief in psychic experience transcending normal perception and cognition, and a concomitant renewed belief in scientific verifiability of an occult realm. But in America, in tension with the persisting Romanticism generated by the transcendental movement, and in the midst of the popularity of spiritualism, writers associated with the rise of realism inherit the legacy of an unresolved dilemma from the Romantic age. Perplexity persists about the fusion

(or even relation) of material and spiritual worlds, of essence and perception. To see the development of the "supernatural" tale in nineteenth-century America divorced from its Romantic naturalist context (especially from the paradoxical materialist-spiritualist doctrines of transcendentalism) is to do violence to the historical record and distort our understanding of both the history of genres and the interconnection between world view and aesthetics in historical eras. For the mental apprehension of the body-spirit fusion persists as a problematic construct shaping by acceptance or denial—or by an indeterminancy in between—the world view of major nineteenth-century American writers. As a sub-genre of the Gothic tale of the "supernatural," the form of the development of the ghost story in America reveals the intellectual crises of an entire century. (pp. 31-4)

G. R. Thompson, "Washington Irving and the American Ghost Story," in The Haunted Dusk: American Supernatural Fiction, 1820-1920, *Howard Kerr, John W. Crowley, and Charles L. Crow, eds., The University of Georgia Press, 1983, pp. 11-36.*

ELIZABETH BOWEN

[*Bowen was an Anglo-Irish fiction writer and critic. Often compared with the fiction of Virginia Woolf, her novels and short stories display a similar stylistic control and subtle insight in the portrayal of human relationships. Bowen is also noted for her series of supernatural stories set in London during World War II. In the following excerpt, she contrasts ghost stories of the 1950s with their counterparts of the Victorian and Edwardian periods.*]

Do ghosts, in their nature, change with the times? As a theme, they are timeless; as institutions, they have a sort of stability—of however macabre a kind. Ghosts, we hope, may be always with us—that is to say, never too far out of the reach of fancy. On the whole, it would seem, they adapt themselves well, perhaps better than we do, to changing world conditions—they enlarge their domain, shift their hold on our nerves and, dispossessed of one habitat, set up house in another. The universal battiness of our century looks like providing them with a propitious climate—hitherto confined to antique manors, castles, graveyards, crossroads, yew walks, cloisters, cliff-edges, moors or city backwaters, they may now roam at will. They do well in flats, and are villa-dwellers. They know how to curdle electric light, chill off heating, or de-condition air. Long ago, they captured railway trains and installed themselves in liners' luxury cabins; now telephones, motors, planes and radio wavelengths offer them self-expression. The advance of psychology has gone their way; the guilt-complex is their especial friend.

Ghosts have grown up. Far behind lie their clanking and moaning days; they have laid aside their original bag of tricks—bleeding hands, luminous skulls and so on. Their manifestations are, like their personalities, oblique and subtle, perfectly calculated to get the modern person under the skin. They abjure the over-fantastic and the grotesque, operating, instead, through series of happenings whose horror lies in their being just, *just* out of the true. Ghosts exploit the horror latent behind reality: for this reason, they prefer prosaic scenes—to-day's haunted room has a rosy wallpaper. Half-tones of daylight, the livid hush before thunderstorms, glass-clear dusk or hallucinatory sunsets suit them better than out-and-out pitch-dark night. Worst of all, contemporary ghosts are credible.

Why ghosts remain so popular may be wondered. "*I heard a ghost story, the other day*" still is a way of commanding almost all conversation. Ghosts draw us together: one might leave it at that. Can there be something tonic about pure, active fear in these times of passive, confused oppression? It is nice to *choose* to be frightened, when one need not be. Or it may be that, deadened by information, we are glad of these awful, intent and nameless beings as to whom no information is to be had. Our irrational, darker selves demand familiars. But then, *are* ghosts irrational? It more and more appears that they work to plan—that, remorselessly, icily, they keep an end in view. What irks them? How are they to be placated? In former days, Christian burial of ill-used remains, the evening-up of an ancient score or putting right of a wrong used to settle the matter; now it is not so simple. Ghosts seem harder to please than we are; it is as though they haunted for haunting's sake— much as we re-live, brood and smoulder over our pasts.

Why ghosts should be so ubiquitous is another matter. Tradition connects them with scenes of violence—are we now to take it that any and every place is, has been or may be a scene of violence? Our interpretation of violence is wider than once it was; we are aware that the blow physically struck is but one means by which man injures man, that cruelty may be worst in its mental part, that the emotions have their own scale of torment, that the most deep-going outrages may be psychological. We fear that which hath power to hurt the soul. Inflictions and endurances, exactions, injustices, infidelities— do not these wreak their havoc, burn in their histories, leave their mark? *Who* knows what has gone on, anywhere? May not obsessions stay in the air which knew them, as a corpse stays nailed down under a floor? (pp. vii-viii)

[Ghostliness] has a poetic element. There must be, and must be conveyed, a sense of the *strange*—unearthly expectation and apprehension can only be rendered in fairly fine terms. Fear has its own aesthetic—as Le Fanu, Henry James, Montagu James and Walter de la Mare have repeatedly shown—and also, its own propriety. A story dealing in fear ought, ideally, to be kept at a certain pitch. And that austere other world, the world of the ghost, should inspire, when it impacts on our own, not so much revulsion or shock as a sort of awe.

Fiction is the ideal pacing-ground for the ghost—"apparitions," when they occur in real life, are apt to seem to lack meaning, or lack wholeness. About a ghost one longs to be told *more*—and of that, research often falls short: that, the imagination must supply. Yet ghost stories are not easy to write—least easy now, for they involve more than they did. . . . In our seeing of ghosts each of us has exposed our susceptibilities, which are partly personal, partly those of our time. We are twentieth-century haunters of the haunted. The subject, at any rate, goes far back. (pp. ix-x)

> *Elizabeth Bowen, in an introduction to* The Second Ghost Book, *edited by Lady Cynthia Asquith, J. Barrie, 1952, pp. vii-x.*

PAUL THEROUX

[*Theroux is an American fiction writer, critic, and travel writer who, since 1963, has lived outside the United States, first traveling to Africa with the Peace Corps and later settling in England. In the following excerpt, Theroux views the tradition of Christmas ghost stories in England as having its origin in the gloomy cast of English Decembers and in a residue of paganism in the "English character."*]

The tradition in England of ghost stories at Christmas is much older than Dickens. "It is evident enough that no one who writes now can use the Pagan deities and mythology," Dr. Johnson said in 1780. "The only machinery, therefore, seems that of ministering spirits, the ghosts of the departed, witches and fairies." Although Dickens is the most celebrated exponent of the machinery of ministering spirits at Christmas, of ghostly epiphany, there was no better practitioner of the English ghost story than Montague Rhodes James. His stories are more eerie than Dickens's, dustier than L. P. Hartley's, less harshly suburban than Elizabeth Bowen's, and though lacking the narrative gracility of his namesake Henry's, are much scarier for their persuasive antiquarian detail.

People die horribly in M. R. James's stories; their bones are found in marshy woods, finely spun with cobwebs or in ghoulish coitus—two skeletons embracing; their hearts are knifed out and diabolically used; they are murdered and burnt and visited by dark creatures from the distant past. Perhaps this is not so odd. M. R. James was himself an antiquary, a translator of the New Testatment Apocrypha, passionately interested in paleography and for many years Provost of Eton, where he had any number of pupils and colleagues to sit at his feet. The lovable and learned old bachelor is a natural teller of ghost stories. But the curious thing is that, nearly always, M. R. James used Christmas as the occasion for frightening his devotees with these strange tales. Indeed, he called the most hairraising of them his "Christmas productions."

The fireside, the indoor life which winter demands, the somberness and good cheer which combine to become something like hysteria—these matter. As does the dark, the penetrating blackness that makes the English December a month almost without daylight, filling the afternoon with a clammy graveyard gloom—everyone hurrying through the wet streets with his head down, and homeward-bound schoolchildren looking whitefaced and lost. In the countryside, the trees drip like leaking wounds in the darkness, and owls squeeze out hoots from where they creepily roost; in the city, the housefronts stare through the trachoma of torn curtains across deserted parks, and moisture blackens every brick with a look of decay, giving the oncesolid city some of the atmosphere of a hugely haunted ruin. It is the perfect weather, the perfect setting, for ghost stories,

M. R. James.

and it does not seem unusual to me that it has produced so many in England.

But why such stories as "Oh, Whistle, and I'll Come to You, My Lad"—or, for that matter, the one that begins with the ghost of Jacob Marley—at *Christmas*? I think, to understand this, one has to understand the English dislike of piety and church ceremony, the distrust of Catholic liturgy and the low esteem in which most English hold Catholicism. I say "dislike" and "distrust," but uneasiness is its true source, and I should say that in the English character is a kind of protesting residue of paganism. It is not very assertive, but you often see its horns and laurels in certain stories of Saki. If the December gloom is the right setting, then Christmas is the obvious occasion for an irruption of this paganism. It is a revolt against sanctimony—Christ pulls one way, pagan skepticism the other, and the result is frequently a blend of the pious and the supernatural, a species of half-belief that is persuasive because it is frightening: fear is the oldest excuse for reverence. And so the Christmas catharsis of the ghost story, that half-belief made into fiction, God in the shape of a bogeyman with a face of crumpled linen, making his annual visitation to an imperfect world. And because Christmas celebrates birth, we are nagged by its opposite, that things end; the ghost story celebrates the experience of death. In Dickens, the hero is usually given a reprieve; in M. R. James, he gets the chop. But Christmas is the only holiday that is specifically associated with a fictional genre, and though the English have contrived a characteristic way of expressing it, the tradition has a shadowy charm, and it is, ultimately, easy to see why it has caught on in other places. (pp. 1, 15)

> *Paul Theroux, "Christmas Ghosts," in* The New York Times Book Review, *December 23, 1979, pp. 1, 15.*

WILLIAM SCOTT HOME

[*In the following excerpt, Home traces changing views of horror among supernatural fiction writers, focusing on the work of H. P. Lovecraft and his successors.*]

"Life," H. P. Lovecraft wrote in his Commonplace Book, "is more horrible than death."

Death, with its threat of damnation, was horrible enough for the generations of fabulists which preceded him. Motley monsters in the mode of vampire, werewolf or Frankenstein's golem horrified in direct proportion to their ability to maim and kill. In ghost stories, such as Poe's repossession tales ("Ligeia," "Morella") the horror of death appears to lie in the possibility that it may not be complete. Differential death is now a scientific verity, within limits, but more acutely expressed to our minds in the materialistic mode of the Heald-Lovecraft "Out of the Eons," HPL's "The Thing on the Doorstep," or even Crowley's "Testament of Magdalen Blair," where the vision of unsuccoured roving vaporously beyond the grave inspires little fear. It represents rather a repulsion against life—a doubt as to whether its divers torments have an end.

Even Maturin's Melmoth and Poe's Man of the Crowd, the twin geniuses of all crime, appear to hurry through their lives in dread of the fruits of death. In whatever spot the Man of the Crowd's conscience awaited, it could have treated him no more kindly than William Wilson's did him.

To those who dealt with them, these creatures represented no violation of the natural order, but rather fitted into it as they knew it; in every case creatures and phantoms were themselves caged by certain laws of behaviour and dimension, knowledge of which gave men power over them, thereby freeing us from their terror. It is the rare tale in which hero/heroine does not emerge triumphant even if scathed, affirming life.

Poe's lifetime was not over before the horror tale underwent the next development. The massive cosmic forces buried deeply in the tedious novels of Edward Bulwer-Lytton were perhaps the first prefigurings of entities to come, evoking awe (as Scarborough has pointed out [see Additional Bibliography]) more than fear—had it not been that by the time they were encountered most readers were only capable of exhaustion. Still there is no suggestion that the massive shadow on the crater of Vesuvius or the vague cloudy malignity dogging unsuccessful conjurors can be ordered around or prevented from working damage upon those mortals who accidentally encounter them. The conceptual world of man is ruptured.

By the late 1880's this vein was further developed with genius simultaneously by Arthur Machen, who invoked these elemental presences under the name of Classical deities, and Chambers, who, picking a few names out of some unremarkable Bierce tales, evoked the first horror-city, where the shadows of men's thoughts lengthen at evening, the maddening book, the irresistible King who in fact wears no mask; against whose ebony glare no mind can do other than wither. That much of the inspiration of the first concepts is due to the introduction to the West of garbled versions of Indic myth presented by the Great Alluring Fat Lady Out Yonder, Mme. Blatavsky, whose influence on weird writing is constantly either under- or overestimated, is shown by the fact that both Machen and Blackwood were for a time disciples of Theosophy. Such altogether nonhuman colossi broke through shortly afterward in Blackwood's classic *The Willows* and in Hodgson (*House on the Borderland, Night Land,* "The Hog"); but where intrusions in Machen were countered with occult knowledge, or failing that, suicide ("Great God Pan," "White People"), in Blackwood and Hodgson escape, if occurring at all, was happenstance. There is no suggestion of a malign side of the universe here; the totality is one in which the human viewpoint is inconsequential. The beings in question were not preoccupied with men, but crushed them as men crush blades of grass. They fit no conceptual framework, but could overpower it in an instant; the order supposed to inhere in the cosmos did not exist. Then the many who became Darwin, Frazer, Planck, Jung, Freud, Einstein, and even the Great Fat Lady, had dismantled the old universe and nobody could put it back together again.

Poe was conscious that mankind violated the dictum that all matter tends to simplicity and disorder, but remade him worthy of his matrix. The horror of these innovators, by contrast, lay precisely in the discovery that one was *not* mad, that the recognisable and identifiable personality is awake within an unidentifiable environment. The threat of mutilation here is to the soul, the human-consciousness, rather than the body; death itself may be a gamble—would it lead to any relief or merely open a better-focused eye on the horrors?—but a life of horror-consciousness is beyond bearing.

The pablum of the Existentialists to the contrary, death is not what makes life absurd but what prevents its being absurd. Inability to accept it is as serious a defect as blindness to human mercy, justice or the existence of evil. Stories whose impacts depend upon physical threats to their characters, with a surfeit of perspiring narrators, chimerical monsters, mumbled prayers, sorcerers with varying degrees of animosity toward rosy cheeks, have become hackneyed—the joke everything turns into with age.

In the midst of his evolutionary process H. P. Lovecraft at the age of fifteen awoke to a sense of horror—of his own body. In "The Beast in the Cave" he is stricken with fear of a strange creature, dead before even seen, which is covered with hair. *At one time,* he stresses, it had been a man. The accretion of animal hair apparently ended its humanity. This adolescent essay was his first exercise in the evolutionary horror which became the dominant theme in his work. "If we knew what we are," he wrote, "we would do what Arthur Jermyn did—," though most of us know and none of us do it; even now, when we have seen a degeneration of *H. sap.* into monsters which make his Martenses almost comical by contrast and perhaps harbour a suspicion that a worldwide pyre might be the best treatment for the human genetic condition. It was real to Lovecraft who, even if he may not have foreseen it, would have accepted it.

Such degeneration was only occasionally immediate ("The Rats in the Walls"), more usually gradual, naturally evolutionary ("Arthur Jermyn," "The Lurking Fear," "The Horror at Red Hook"). The snarling, cannibalistic beast-self lurked even in those whose ape-ancestors were more than a few generations remote, making HPL's occasional grant of mantic armaments against the siege of external entities to his protagonists a cynical concession in view of the time-bombs ticking in their very flesh.

This horror of our origins is not without foundation. We laugh at apes because they are the closest kin we need not feel ashamed of laughing at; but if those bloodstained phylophagous Australopithecines (Machen's little people) survived, would it be funny? The most human of all animals—insightful, communicative, warfaring, xenophobic, cannibalistic, perverted—in fact, are rats, who inspire few of us with fraternal confidence.

It is easy to find horror in the animal nature of man—consciousness pulsing inside the bestial body, risen out of the slime and darkness: the darkness lingers on our bodies and the slime on our minds—bred of murder ever more facile and more augmented—haphazard and loveless breeding—cannibalism—plagues—carrion-scavenging, clawing and stamping, pushing and grubbing, dancing around split skulls and ripping out beating hearts in an ecstasy of freedom and blood-glut before awesome fires; is that strange alien glow trapped somewhere in the cerebrum's soft jelly, jostled by the smouldering gristle of the medulla, not a parasite, an intruder, a discarnate Monboddonian mind? Has it ever done other than shrink from those excesses which are the normalities of the beast? There was no reason for the animal man to disdain interbreeding with other beasts, such breeding being, after all, a purely animal function. There is nothing abnormal in Lovecraft's sexual prudery, which was carefully imposed in his time and place, but the epithet "hybrid" in his writings expresses not origin but his personal nausea of the spawning beast, applied so often toward the many ethnic groups which disgusted him (*in loco* mankind in general). In fact, infusion of nonhuman genes simply hastened the process he was sure would occur anyway.

Leonard Cline's unusual and disturbing novel, *The Dark Chamber,* which HPL praises highly, expressed the identical theme. The horror is innate in the biology of the characters; they "hover," Cline wrote, "in a haze of horror" in the course of life, the search for hereditary impressions necessarily leads to madness and death in the aeonian struggle of fang and claw.

The confinement of consciousness within the object of horror was stroke of genius which makes Lovecraft the third refraction-point of weird writing (after Poe and Machen-Blackwood-Hodgson). We may be free of horrors lurking in the future, but not of those crystallised in the past; from the prison of one's own genes there is no escape. The horror of the human mind netted in strange shapes ("The Shadow Out of Time," "The Outsider") is one with its persistence in decaying bodies ("The Thing on the Doorstep," "Cool Air"); in the caste society which shaped HPL's thinking there was not even freedom from the behaviour of recent ancestors ("Shadow Over Innsmouth," "The Festival," "The Case of Charles Dexter Ward"). Consequently, contra Freud and his gleeful school, Lovecraft says not that the monsters are within us—which renders them as horrible as the liver or larynx—but that we are within the monsters.

As Colin Wilson has pointed out, the writing of fantasy in whatever form is essentially an assertion of freedom. The ultimate freedom is the power to create, or to transmute nature in accordance with one's will (that Crowley was such a lousy weird writer merely shows that those who can do, and those who can't, write); its opposite is the ultimate confinement, the complete lack of power/freedom, such as death; such is the consequence of life's being an accident or joke, the body merely a pawn or cog in some vast scheme under some other control, manipulated for sport, gain or no reason at all. Thus Solzhenitsyn's *First Circle* is a horror story; Angel Asturias' *El Senor Presidente* is a horror story; and John Fowles' *The Magus* is a horror story; and the quality of their horror is not strained. For most people, these suitably sublimated representations of the monstrosity of being man not only suffice but are eminently preferable.

The Great Old Ones, Lovecraft said, created earth life as a joke or accident, but they seem not to have embodied the forces of destiny which would destroy it. This marriage of his basic horror theme to Blavatskian entities is simply an extension of the primal motive the monstrous, slobbering, mindless creatures dominating the universe—creating life (breeding) as a sport—quiescent under the evolution of human intelligence, apparently by the chance coincidence of a galactic timelock, but waiting to break loose again and return man to grunting, rending flesh. That such homicidal jellies managed or even cared to construct massive Riemannian cities can't be explained in human terms, but suggests titan purposes to their apparent chaos, perhaps requiring that human bodies be reduced to gibbering meat to provide the lubricant for some cosmic slide. Still, the history accumulated throughout these later tales (as summarised by Leiber) shows again the futility of existence, as culture after civilisation after race time and again are ground to dust by the cosmic wheel—the ultimate horror of pointlessness so overwhelming to us that even the Marxists reject it.

The truism that we do not know ourselves is today a platitude. While our cerebrums disport in the wildest visions, the cerebellum and medulla stay behind to operate the body, pumping the heart, squeezing the lungs, zapping tone to the muscles. The animal self is more dutiful, and more chained, than the human. Suppose it should decide to throw the man-mind out of its body? The brain has been shown to accommodate up to 4 personalities without stretching. Cancer is merely a case of amoeboid fission on the body's part by which the derivative organism very simply eats its parent alive. Rebellion of the body has afforded significant classics of weird writing (White's "Lukundoo," Whitehead's "Passing of a God" and influenced Ray Bradbury's more effective early stories ("Skeleton," "Fever Dream.")

Fear of both life and death in all its forms is of necessity more extreme and agonizing in the non-religious in their lack of either the conceptually real prospect of an alternative, or any superhuman reinforcement against the flesh-dwarfing forces of opposition. Necessarily, such impact is dulled for the reader who is otherwise disposed as it is heightened for he who is not. The power of HPL's writing depends from the fact that he seems really to have experienced these irruptions in their nakedness—the spate of often random words, the "Gods!", the hysterical metaphors ("after vigintillions of years") exactly as would have transpired had he been writing from fact. Whether this was designed and conscious or was the actual outburst of emotional involvement, we cannot say. Either way, it sets an enormous challenge to any successor, for with nothing more than the defective equipment of man, the self-excusing ape, can any mind face the ever more mysterious and more incomprehensible universe?

The more intensely scientific achievement preempts speculative writing, the more pressure is applied to such writers to find new channels to challenge the human drive. With moon landings, Mars probes, cell and gene manipulation, immaculate conceptions, memory transfers, maintenance of excised brains and remoulded personalities, claims of life in meteorites and revived from the aeons *all* accomplished facts, new facets must be turned on the human globe. Magic can be seen now as being not apart from logic, but its result; nor is it generally appreciated on what a close scientific basis many alchemists worked or the fact that their goals—transmutation of the elements, life prolongation and imitation, universal annihilation of matter—are long since attained. Free exercise of the will by which conformable changes can be made in the environment without other instrumentation now seems less fantastic.

The task of the weird writer since HPL has been not only to find other foci of horror buried in us and cast them in a means suitable for rendering them directly impressible upon the reader's mind—as Tennessee Williams puts it, to convey the sense of the awfulness of life more compactly than life does—but to deal with the fact that the contemporary reader already has the entire background of the field of weird writing and recognizes readily all the symbols, the personal pantheons exposed by Jung and Freud, and by contrast to his predecessors, he can be alerted to events by only sparsely scattered signposts. Occult dramas such as Schiel's wonderful *Vaila* and *Phorfor,* Poe's truest children, suggest a mode. Character development has become more important; fear and revulsion must now be expressed by minor traits rather than by a tiresome repetition of the invariable adjectives.

There will be no room again for monstrous beings which conform to a cosmic system in which human beings wield as much control as they do. Chance escape remains the mainstay (artistically achieved in W. F. Harvey's little-known but excellent "Midnight House") and need be no serious handicap; one brainless, ultramicroscopic virus can incapacitate a genius many worlds its own size. Eternal recurrence, the horror which drove Nietzsche mad, has had little reflection in weird fiction, though very interestingly in Chambers; Hodgsens' "One By One" reveals that both halves of the dualistic universe may wear deceitful masks and opens speculations on the finding of dia-

bolic tricks in sincerely good lives. The evolutionary horror has by no means been exhausted of possibilities; and the themes of *A Voyage to Arcturus* and *The Wizard of Earthsea* suggest beginnings rather than summations.

Bradbury, Matheson, Sturgeon and others have written competent and readable tales, but follow no system and contribute little to the development of the genre. Nor have many contributions come from other cultures. Lovecraft's racist nonsense aside, his observation that the Latin temperament possesses "knowing hardness preclusive of sheer panic fright" may not explain his popularity in France, nor the popularity of his imitators there; but it explains their poverty of ability, if not why the prolific (Germanic) Fleming Jean Ray is the worst of them all.

The works of Borges will undoubtedly be a guide to new aspects of philosophical horror (as Charles Williams showed that theology was a fertile subject); the takeover of our own familiar world described in "Tion, Uqbar, Orbis Tertius" is a masterpiece of suggestive subtlety, and there are twins to it throughout his work; and though the publications of other Latins—Cortazar, Angel Asturias, Garcia Marquez—reveal to Americans the consistent note of symbolic fantasy characteristic of Latin American writing, their regular fantasists (Dabove Ocampo, Bioy Casares, etc.) deal with rather minute spiritual transformations.

In an age when everyday horrors of extreme types have become commonplace, it requires supreme ability for the most Lovecraftian thinker to present us with that dark mirror in a guise sufficiently novel to shock us into such awareness that we see ourselves face to face, ourselves to know. (pp. 32-4)

*William Scott Home, "The Horror Theme after HPL,"
in HPL, 1972, pp. 32-4.*

THE "DECLINE" OF THE GHOST STORY

OLIVIA HOWARD DUNBAR

[In the following essay, Dunbar observes the eclipse of traditional ghost stories but perceives an emergence of modern forms of supernatural fiction.]

For approximately a generation, the ghost has been missing from fiction; after a disappearance so sudden and of such far-reaching implications that it is a matter of some amazement that those who profess to concern themselves with the phenomena of imaginative literature should have paid so little attention to it. It is a commonplace that ever since literature began, as well as considerably before that interesting period, what we call "the supernatural" has been a staple material of the tellers of tales. As there has always been a literature of love, so there has always been a literature of fear; and until the development of the present narrow and timorous popular taste, one had perhaps as strong an appeal as the other. Ghosts in their most literal acceptation—not as the more or less impersonal shades we have sometimes indifferently pictured them—have always been held an essential complement of tangible everyday life, inextricably bound up with religion, with love for the dead, with hunger for the unknown, with many of the most intimate and profound emotions; and their literary use has seemed, to the greater public, not only no less, but even more "realistic," than the modern exploitation of the commonplace.

Twenty-five years ago, even, the reader of magazine fiction was still able to shudder to his heart's content. Spectres glided with the precision of long-established custom through the pages of the more conventional compendiums of light literature. The familiar paraphernalia of supernatural incident,—draughty chambers, tempestuous nights, blood-stains, wan-faced women,—were still in constant and elaborate requisition. And while there was a discreet dribbling of phantoms from week to week or from month to month, a magnificent convocation of the spectral tribe occurred annually. That is to say, a curious association of ideas connected the maximum of ghostly prevalence with Christmas, the season of popular rejoicing; and by way of making sure of these dismal but doubtless salutary companions, it was customary, as Mr. Anstey once remarked, "to commission a band of ingenious littérateurs to turn out batches of ready-made spectres for the Christmas annuals." The business of chilling the popular spine was taken with due seriousness and was all the more effectually brought about in that the "magazine ghost," as this source of popular refreshment was termed, was as stereotyped and conventional as the old-fashioned novel-heroine. Its looks, manner, haunts, companions, and alleged errands were those long since laid down by tradition; it evinced no sensational modern unexpectedness.

But suddenly, and it must surely have seemed mysteriously, the magazine ghost vanished; nor were its eerie footprints traced. Whether by a concerted action of magazine editors, or by a swift and complete paralysis of the contributors' imaginations, or by a profound alteration of popular sentiment, or by the operation of a principle presently to be suggested, the literature of the supernatural ceased to be produced. Can this have happened without protest, without comment, even? The subject is rich in its possibilities of speculation. For if the acceptance and enjoyment of ghost-lore imply a childish quality of mind, as one sometimes hears superior persons assert, then our rejection of them would argue that we are the wisest generation that ever lived. If, again, the reading or writing of such tales demand a freshness of imagination that in our little day has become desiccated, then our plight is pitiable indeed.

There is at hand, of course, an easy but superficial explanation to the effect that a prevalence of ghost-stories must depend upon a stout popular belief in ghosts; and that having lost the one, we must forego the other. The slightest reflection shows that this position is untenable. Not believe in ghosts? We believe in them with all our hearts. Never before, since spectral feet first crossed a man-made threshold, have ghosts been so squarely, openly, and enthusiastically believed in, so assiduously cultivated, as now. We have raised ghost-lore to the dusty dignity of a science. The invocation of the spirits of the dead, far from having its former suggestion of vulgar mystery, is one of the most reputable of practices, which men of learning carry on publicly, with stenographers conveniently at hand. There even flourishes a "Haunted House Committee," appointed and maintained by the foremost society for the promotion of ghosts, and this for the express purpose of encouraging the presence of the shyer and less aggressive spectres in what seem their appropriate habitations,—of making them, as it were, feel at home. We believe in ghosts as sincerely as we believe in the very poor; and in similar fashion we endeavor to live among them, establish a cordial understanding, and write about them in our notebooks. Nor do we believe in them the less because, when on our learned behavior, we may refer to them as "phantasmogenetic agencies." Not believe in ghosts? They are our fetish. Let it never be imagined that ghost-stories have suffered decline because of our indifference to their subject-matter, "material" though our age is commonly held to be. By our very zest in their pursuit, we have possibly proved the reverse of Scott's mistaken theory that to see ghosts it is only necessary to believe in them,—to wish to see. Much truer is the proposition that the seer of ghosts commonly does not premeditate his vision; that spectres manifest themselves by preference to "unimaginative people in perfect health."

No small share of the fascination exerted by the ancient and outgrown ghost of fiction was due to its invariable and satisfactory conformity to type. However frequent its intrusion, or however familiar, it was never suffered to deviate from its character, so deeply rooted in human consciousness, as a source of dread. It was the function of the ghost to be consistently unpleasant, and that function was relentlessly fulfilled. No one personal characteristic of the ghost as we know it in song or story or as we learn from the unimpeachable testimony of our friends' friends, can explain its unequalled power to arouse the emotion of fear. Distasteful as is the ghostly habit of reducing its unfleshly essence to a threadlike, infinitely ductile filament—like a bit of transsubstantial chewing-gum—in order sneakily to penetrate keyholes; disturbing as is its fashion of upsetting our gravely accepted "laws of nature"; intolerable as is its lack of vocal organs (for phantoms, with few exceptions, cannot or will not speak);—neither one nor all of these undesirable characteristics can completely solve the interesting riddle of its fear-compelling power. And it is undoubtedly almost as remarkable that having for centuries, in and out of fiction, maintained this consistent and extremely prevalent personality, the ghost should have dropped out of literature altogether. Now, how can this have been?

To go as far back as the early English folktales and ballads, when the wherefore of phantoms was even better understood than now, and when fiction more essentially took its origin from life, ghost-tales gained their grim effectiveness from the accuracy with which they reflected popular belief. The audiences of that simple day had not attained a sufficient refinement of imagination to delight in vague, casual, incoherent spectres; every ghost had a name and date. What is more important is that there was no ghost that had not a reason for being. The ingenious notion that the spirits of the dead return from an allegedly peaceful Elysium simply to make themselves disagreeable, by way of easing their minds, had not yet suggested itself. On the contrary, the animistic trend of popular thought, which of course greatly favored the appearance of ghosts in general, assigned them likewise adequate and intelligible motives, among the chief of which were: to reveal treasure, to reunite happy lovers, to avenge a crime, and to serve as "a primitive telegraphic service for the conveyance of bad news." Ghosts were therefore not only the recognizable shades of the familiarly known dead; they were sinister symbols of crime, remorse, vengeance. If you shuddered at sight of them, it was for a better reason than weak nerves. Horror was not piled on horror, in early ghost-tales, merely to satisfy the artist's own sense of cumulative effect. Each detail had a powerful conventional significance, and the consequent power to arouse a strong primitive emotion. This system not only lent an artistic strength and symmetry to the early literature; it was intensely satisfactory to the Anglo-Saxon mind.

But inevitably, when the motives and the language of literature became more complex, the *rationale* of ghost-lore became affected. Phantoms began to lose their original force, fell into the habit of haunting from motives relatively unworthy. Evidences multiplied of their degeneration into a morbid and meddlesome tribe, with a sadly diminished sense of the fitting and the picturesque. Their visits were even concerned with the payment of debts, of strictly mortal contraction; and they lamentably lost caste by exhibiting themselves as the victims, rather than as the scourge, of conscience. A ghost has been known to go to the trouble of haunting a house for the mere purpose of ensuring the payment of a shilling,—an episode that might well permanently compromise the dignity of the entire spectral tribe. Likewise when they acquired the intrusive habit of giving evidence in trials, the original and forceful idea that ghosts were agents of retribution became seriously coarsened. Legally, the fact that the outcome of many an actual trial has hinged on ghostly testimony is of extraordinary interest. So far as imaginative terror-literature is concerned, however, the introduction of this matter serves as a mixed and weakened motive, only.

During the later years of the ghost's popularity in literature, it will readily be seen that the greater number of the earliest ghost-motives were outgrown. It is some time, for instance, since the motive of recovering buried treasure through supernatural aid has been able to "carry," the custom of burying treasure having itself somewhat tamely died out. Far more incongruous, even, came to seem the supernatural reunion of lovers, as in the familiar case where the posthumous suitor reappears to bear his still living sweetheart back to the grave with him. Ghosts that are to be understood as the projections of the spirit at the moment of death have always been popular, it is true, but this motive is not in itself strong or picturesque enough to serve as the backbone of a corporate section of imaginative literature.

In short, the only ghost-motive that retained its strength, plausibility, and appeal to the Anglo-Saxon mind was the retribution-motive,—the idea that the ghost's function was to recall, expiate, or avenge a crime. This was impressive; it was terrifying; it had moral and religious significance; it was not subtle; it was susceptible of indefinitely repeated adjustment to time and place. It was the perfect, perhaps the only perfect, ghost-motive for English literature. So valorous is the Anglo-Saxon temper that it scorns or is ashamed to tremble at mere empty shadow-tales. It demands not only to be impressed; there must be an adequate basis for the impression. The clue to the whole matter is that the ghost must not be a wanton and irresponsible power. It must be a moral agent.

Unfortunately, the realization of this simple truth has never been complete. Only subconsciously has the public known what it wanted. As for the tellers of tales, they seem, in those latter days of the ghost's literary existence, to have remained in criminal ignorance of the vital principle of their business. The decay of the ghost in fiction occurred, not through any loss of human interest in the spectral world, but through an indolent misapprehension, on the part of the story-tellers, of the real character of the ghost as we Anglo-Saxons have conceived it. Thus it came about that the ghost, previous to its subsidence, was, as Mr. Lang truly observed, "a purposeless creature. He appears, nobody knows why; he has no message to deliver, no secret crime to conceal, no appointment to keep, no treasure to disclose, no commissions to be executed, and, as an almost invariable rule, he does not speak, even if you speak to him." And he adds that inquirers have therefore concluded that the ghost, generically, is "not all there,"—a dreary result of scep-

ticism, indeed! At the same time, what direct and utilitarian folk could put up with a confirmedly inconsequent ghost, even for the creepy fascination of shuddering at his phantom footfall? And could there be, on the whole, a more perfect example of the operation of natural selection in art than that, the ghost of fiction becoming unmoral, superficial, and flabby, it was its pitilessly appropriate penalty to be dropped and apparently forgotten?

A small group of kindred volumes, which have appeared during the past year or so, now for the first time indicate that a perception of the true nature of the literary ghost is returning to the absent-minded craft. Stevenson had, it is true, an admirable perception of the terror-inspiring, and he did not make the mistake of being vague; but his was not the temperament that produces the perfect ghost-story. Mr. Henry James, in that masterpiece, "The Turn of the Screw," has shown that he can convey a sense of mystery and terror more skilfully than any of his contemporaries; but his work is probably too esoteric to stand as typical, and it remains true that the pattern ghost-tale must be writ large and obvious. If, as now appears, a half-dozen of the ablest writers of the day are realizing this, there is hope for the renaissance of the literary ghost. It has already been proved that the problem of its readjustment to our literature is not insuperable,—that the chambers of our untenanted imaginations stand ready and waiting to be haunted by wraiths that our logic can approve. There may indeed develop with time a regenerated ghost-literature well worth acquaintance; for, as an essayist of other times has somewhat grandiloquently observed, "Our inborn proneness to a love of the marvellous and unimaginable, which has originated in our imperfect acquaintance with the laws of nature and our own being, does not appear to suffer diminution as education and culture advance; for it is found to coexist with the highest intellectual development and the most refined critical temper." (pp. 377-80)

> *Olivia Howard Dunbar, "The Decay of the Ghost in Fiction," in* The Dial, *Vol. 38, No. 455, June 1, 1905, pp. 377-80.*

LAFCADIO HEARN

[*Hearn was an American fiction writer and critic. Often devoting his short stories and novellas to supernatural subjects, he is best known for his retellings of Japanese ghost stories. As a critic, Hearn ignored the moralistic conventions of Victorian criticism and emphasized the emotional effects of art rather than its social and ethical functions. In the following excerpt from an essay that originally appeared in Hearn's* Interpretations of Literature, *Vol. II (1915), he observes the modern vitality of supernatural fiction, discusses its origins and function, and examines the relationship between dreams and supernatural stories.*]

It would be a mistake to suppose that the stories of the supernatural have had their day in fine literature. On the contrary, wherever fine literature is being produced, either in poetry or in prose, you will find the supernatural element very much alive. Scientific knowledge has not at all diminished the pleasure of mankind in this field of imagination, though it may have considerably changed the methods of treatment. The success of writers today like Maeterlinck is chiefly explained by their skill in the treatment of the ghostly, and of subjects related to supernatural fear. But without citing other living writers, let me observe that there is scarcely any really great author in European literature, old or new, who has not distinguished himself in the treatment of the supernatural. In English literature, I believe there is no exception—even from the time of

Front cover of the American edition of Arthur Machen's 1894 book.

the Anglo-Saxon poets to Shakespeare, and from Shakespeare to our own day. And this introduces us to the consideration of a general and remarkable fact, a fact that I do not remember to have seen in any books, but which is of very great philosophical importance; there is something ghostly in all great art, whether of literature, music, sculpture, or architecture.

But now let me speak to you about this word "ghostly"; it is a much bigger word, perhaps, than some of you imagine. The old English had no other word for "spiritual" or "supernatural"—which two terms . . . are not English but Latin. Everything that religion today calls divine, holy, miraculous, was sufficiently explained for the old Anglo-Saxons by the term ghostly. They spoke of a man's ghost, instead of speaking of his spirit or soul; and everything relating to religious knowledge they called ghostly. In the modern formula of the Catholic confession, which has remained almost unchanged for nearly two thousand years, you will find that the priest is always called a "ghostly" father—which means that his business is to take care of the ghosts or souls of men as a father does. In addressing the priest, the penitent really calls him "Father of my ghost." You will see, therefore, that a very large meaning really attaches to the adjective. It means everything relating to the supernatural. It means to the Christian even God himself, for the Giver of Life is always called in English the Holy Ghost.

Accepting the evolutional philosophy, which teaches that the modern idea of God as held by western nations is really but a development from the primitive belief in a shadow-soul, the term ghost in its reference to the Supreme Being certainly could not be found fault with. On the contrary, there is a weirdness about his use of the word which adds greatly to its solemnity. But whatever belief we have, or have not, as regards religious creeds, one thing that modern science has done for us, is to prove beyond all question that everything which we used to consider material and solid is essentially ghostly, as is any ghost. If we do no believe in old-fashioned stories and theories about ghosts, we are nevertheless obliged to recognize today that we are ghosts of ourselves—and utterly incomprehensible. The mystery of the universe is now weighing upon us, becoming heavier and heavier, more and more awful, as our knowledge expands, and it is especially a ghostly mystery. All great art reminds us in some way of this universal riddle; that is why I say that all great art has something ghostly in it.

It touches something within us which relates to infinity. When you read a very great thought, when you see a wonderful picture or statue or building, and when you hear certain kinds of music, you feel a thrill in the heart and mind much like the thrill which in all times men felt when they thought they saw a ghost or a god. Only the modern thrill is incomparably larger and longer and deeper. And this is why, in spite of all knowledge, the world still finds pleasure in the literature of the supernatural, and will continue to find pleasure in it for hundreds of years to come. The ghostly represents always some shadow of truth, and no amount of disbelief in what used to be called ghosts can ever diminish human interest in what relates to that truth.

So you will see that the subject is not altogether trifling. Certainly it is of very great moment in relation to great literature. The poet or the story-teller who cannot give the reader a little ghostly pleasure at times never can be either a really great writer or a great thinker. I have already said that I know of no exception to this rule in the whole of English literature. Take, for instance, Macaulay, the most practical, hard-headed, logical writer of the century, the last man in whom you would expect to find the least trace of superstition. Had you read only certain of his essays, you would scarcely think him capable of touching the chords of the supernatural. But he has done this in a masterly way in several of the "Lays of Ancient Rome"—for example, in speaking of the apparition of the Twin Brethren at the battle of Lake Regillus, and of Tarquin haunted by the phantom of his victim Lucretia. Both of these passages give the ghostly thrill in a strong way; and there is a fainter thrill of the same sort to be experienced from the reading of parts of the "Prophecy of Capys." It is because Macaulay had this power, though using it sparingly, that his work is so great. If he had not been able to write these lines of poetry which I referred to, he could not even have made his history of England the living history that it is. A man who has no ghostly feeling cannot make anything alive, not even a page of history or a page of oratory. To touch men's souls, you must know all that those souls can be made to feel by words; and to know that, you must yourself have a "ghost" in you that can be touched in the same way.

Now leaving the theoretical for the practical part of the theme, let us turn to the subject of the relation between ghosts and dreams. (pp. 130-34)

Whether you believe in ghosts or not, all the artistic elements of ghostly literature exist in your dreams, and form a veritable treasury of literary material for the man that knows how to use them.

All the great effects obtained by poets and story writers, and even by religious teachers, in the treatment of supernatural fear or mystery, have been obtained, directly or indirectly, through dreams. Study any great ghost story in any literature, and you will find that no matter how surprising or unfamiliar the incidents seem, a little patient examination will prove to you that every one of them has occurred, at different times, in different combinations, in dreams of your own. They give you a thrill. But why? Because they remind you of experiences, imaginative or emotional, which you had forgotten. There can be no exception to this rule—absolutely none. . . . ["The Haunters and Haunted" by Bulwer Lytton is] the best ghost story in the English language. The reason why it is the best story of this kind is simply because it represents with astonishing faithfulness the experiences of nightmare. The terror of all great stories of the supernatural is really the terror of nightmare, projected into waking consciousness. And the beauty or tenderness of other ghost stories or fairy-stories, or even of certain famous and delightful religious legends, is the tenderness and beauty of dreams of a happier kind, dreams inspired by love or hope or regret. But in all cases where the supernatural is well treated in literature, dream experience is the source of the treatment. (pp. 135-36)

Bulwer Lytton's story of the haunted house illustrates the rule. Let us now consider especially the literary value of nightmare. Nightmare, the most awful form of dream, is also one of the most peculiar. It has probably furnished all the important elements of religious and supernatural terror which are to be found in really great literature. It is a mysterious thing in itself; and scientific psychology has not yet been able to explain many facts in regard to it. We can take the phenomena of nightmare separately, one by one, and show their curious relation to various kinds of superstitious fear and supernatural belief.

The first remarkable fact in nightmare is the beginning of it. It begins with a kind of suspicion, usually. You feel afraid without knowing why. Then you have the impression that something is acting upon you from a distance—something like fascination, yet not exactly fascination, for there may be no visible fascinator. But feeling uneasy, you wish to escape, to get away from the influence that is making you afraid. Then you find it is not easy to escape. You move with great difficulty. Presently the difficulty increases—you cannot move at all. You want to cry out, and you cannot; you have lost your voice. You are actually in a state of trance—seeing, hearing, feeling, but unable to move or speak. This is the beginning. It forms one of the most terrible emotions from which a man can suffer. If it continued more than a certain length of time, the mere fear might kill. Nightmare does sometimes kill, in cases where the health has been very much affected by other causes.

Of course we have nothing in ordinary waking life of such experience—the feeling of being deprived of will and held fast from a great distance by some viewless power. This is the real experience of magnetism, mesmerism; and it is the origin of certain horrible beliefs of the Middle Ages in regard to magical power. Suppose we call it supernatural mesmerism, for want of a better word. It is not true mesmerism, because in real hypnotic conditions, the patient does not feel or think or act mentally according to his own personality; he acts by the will of another. In nightmare the will is only suspended, and the personal consciousness remains; this is what makes the horror of it. So we shall call the first stage supernatural mesmerism, only with the above qualification. Now let us see how Bulwer Lytton uses this experience in his story.

A man is sitting in a chair, with a lamp on the table beside him, and is reading Macaulay's essays, when he suddenly becomes uneasy. A shadow falls upon the page. He rises, and tries to call; but he cannot raise his voice above a whisper. He tries to move; and he cannot stir hand or foot. The spell is already upon him. This is the first part of nightmare.

The second stage of the phenomenon, which sometimes mingles with the first stage, is the experience of terrible and unnatural appearances. There is always a darkening of the visible, sometimes a disappearance or dimming of the light. In Bulwer Lytton's story there is a fire burning in the room, and a very bright lamp. Gradually both lamp and fire become dimmer and dimmer; at last all light completely vanishes, and the room becomes absolutely dark, except for spectral and unnatural luminosities that begin to make their appearance. This also is a very good study of dream experience. The third stage of nightmare, the final struggle, is chiefly characterized by impossible occurrences, which bring to the dreamer the extreme form of horror, while convincing him of his own impotence. For example, you try to fire a pistol or to use a steel weapon. If a pistol, the bullet will not project itself more than a few inches from the muzzle; then it drops down limply, and there is no report. If a sword or dagger, the blade becomes soft, like cotton or paper. Terrible appearances, monstrous or unnatural figures, reach out hands to touch; if human figures, they will grow to the ceiling, and bend themselves fantastically as they approach. There is one more stage, which is not often reached—the climax of the horror. That is when you are caught or touched. The touch in nightmare is a very peculiar sensation, almost like an electric shock, but unnaturally prolonged. It is not pain, but something worse than pain, an experience never felt in waking hours.

The third and fourth stages have been artistically mixed together by Bulwer Lytton. The phantom towers from floor to ceiling, vague and threatening; the man attempts to use a weapon, and at the same time receives a touch or shock that renders him absolutely powerless. He describes the feeling as resembling the sensation of some ghostly electricity. The study is exactly true to dream-experience. I need not here mention this story further, since from this point a great many other elements enter into it which, though not altogether foreign to our subject, do not illustrate that subject so well as some of the stories of Poe. Poe has given us other peculiar details of nightmare-experience, such as horrible sounds. Often we hear in such dreams terrible muffled noises, as of steps coming. This you will find very well studied in the story called "The Fall of the House of Usher." Again in these dreams inanimate objects either become alive, or suggest to us, by their motion, the hiding of some horrible life behind them—curtains, for example, doors left half open, alcoves imperfectly closed. Poe has studied these in "Eleonora" and in some other sketches.

Dreams of the terrible have beyond question had a good deal to do with the inspiration both of religious and of superstitious literature. The returning of the dead, visions of heavenly or infernal beings,—these, when well described, are almost always exact reproductions of dream-experience. (pp. 138-42)

Lafcadio Hearn, "The Value of the Supernatural in Fiction," in his Talks to Writers, *edited by John Erskine, Dodd, Mead and Company, 1920, pp. 130-49.*

STEPHEN LEACOCK

[*A respected Canadian professor of economics, Leacock is best known as one of the leading humorists of the first half of the twentieth century. In the following excerpt, he laments what he views as the decline of ghost stories in the twentieth century and advances reasons for their popularity during the Victorian era.*]

It is a nice question whether Christmas, in the good old sense of the term, is not passing away from us. One associates it somehow with the epoch of stage-coaches, of gabled inns and hospitable country homes with the flames roaring in the open fireplaces. To appreciate a Christmas gathering one must have fought one's way to it on horseback through ten miles of driving snow, or ridden in an ancient closed coach wheel-deep in melting slush. To arrive off a suburban trolley, punctual to the minute, won't do. Somehow the magic is out of it. (p. 257)

Can one wonder, then, that the older "literature of Christmas" is passing away? And most of all, the good old Christmas ghost story, parent of a thousand terrors. How well one recalls its awful apparatus—its "figures" and its "apparitions," the "hollow voice" in which they spoke and the way in which, as the culminating terror, the figure "disappeared through the wall!" A humble trick it seems in these days to eyes that have watched Charlie Chaplin run up the side of a ten-story building and disappear into the sky.

Yet the people of the Victorian age, when ghost stories were ghost stories, loved nothing better than to get round a blazing fire as the night grew late and listen to a tale of "apparitions" and "figures" till even the stoutest of them took up his tallow candle to go to bed in a fit of the shudders, or, more dreadful and more delicious still, to read the awful tale in bed itself and by the uncertain light of the taper. (pp. 257-58)

I have before me as I write a little, forgotten volume published in 1852, and labeled the *Night Side of Nature* by Catherine Crowe. A whole generation has shivered over its pages, blown out its bedside candle, and buried its head under the clothes in fear. Miss Crowe—or no, she must have been *Mrs.* Crowe; such a woman would have been snapped up like Scheherezade—spares her readers no horror. She won't even label her characters by their names in ordinary Christian fashion. Here, for instance, is a dreadful tale concerning "the uncle of a Greek gentleman, Mr. M——, traveling in Magnesia." I confess that the very name is too much for me. I admit that I'd hate to be away off in the heart of "Magnesia" with a Greek called M——. This story (I dare not read it, the beginning is enough) is in a chapter headed "Troubled Spirits." What do you know about that? And here is another chapter called "Haunted Houses," and a still more terrible looking one headed "Miscellaneous Phenomena." No man I think can be blamed for admitting that he lives in deadly fear of miscellaneous phenomena. We all do.

And now why is it that the ghost story should have passed away, or rather, why did it flourish just at the time when it did? Here, I think, is the reason. The ghost story flourished best at that period (the middle of the nineteenth century) because at that period people had lost the belief in ghosts, at least as a serious, everyday part of their creed. The wonderful revelations of natural science were hurrying the thinking world in a cheap and vainglorious materialism: an apparition was dismissed as a mere "phosphorescence"—a vastly different thing; a noise behind a wainscot was a rat; a "sense of melancholy foreboding" was a stomach-ache. Everything was known and labeled and assigned to its true place in the universe—except

perhaps two or three awkward little problems which were bunched together as the "unknowable" and shoved into a corner.

In such a world there was no room for ghosts. Hence a ghost story was not a *true* story. It was a wild reversion of the imagination to the forgotten terrors of the past. In earlier days, in the middle ages, let us say, this was not so. A ghost story was a *true* story. It might be very terrible, yet it was after all merely a statement of terrible fact, not a wild terror of the imagination. If a man related that an evil spirit had appeared to him in the night, he meant exactly what he said. It was a plain statement of a distressing fact. It was just as if a man said nowadays that his tailor had turned up at his house in the day—the same sort of thing. It was a bothersome thing and might mean a lot of trouble to come, but there was nothing in the relation of it that involved the wide-eyed terror of the nineteenth century. The materialist, in his horrors of the night, paid the penalty of his vainglory by day.

And now the scene has changed again. The ghosts have all come back. They are buzzing round us all the time. Oliver Lodge and Conan Doyle have seen bunches of them. They think nothing of them. It appears that one can talk to them by telepathy, or by table-rapping, or with a ouija board or in a dozen ways: and then when one does, their poor minds are so enfeebled from living behind the wainscot that one can feel nothing but pity for their simple talk. One respects them in a way; they are a religious lot: they like to talk of how bright and beautiful it is behind the wainscot, but in point of intellect they are—there is only one word for it—"mutts."

As to a ghost story as an engine of terror under such circumstances, the mere idea becomes ludicrous. The modern guest in the East Wing would come calmly down to breakfast and say as he took his porridge—"There was an apparition in my room last night," in the same way that he would have spoken if there had been a bat in it. "Oh, I do hope it didn't disturb you?" says the hostess at the coffee pot. "Oh, not at all, I chased it out with a tennis racket." "Poor things," murmurs the lady, "but we don't like to get rid of them altogether. Teddy and Winifred are making a little collection of notes about them and their father's going to send it to the Psychical Research. But I do dislike the children sitting up at night in the ruined tower in the wood. It's so damp for them. Two lumps?"

So the ghost story is dead. Let it rest in peace—if it can. (pp. 260-61)

Stephen Leacock, "The Passing of the Christmas Ghost Story," in The Bookman *New York, Vol. L, Nos. 3 & 4, November & December, 1919, pp. 257-61.*

JULIA BRIGGS

[*Briggs is an English critic. In the following excerpt from her* Night Visitors: The Rise and Fall of the English Ghost Story *(1977), Briggs discusses the popularity of the ghost story in the late nineteenth and early twentieth centuries and explains why she considers the form to have declined in the years following its "golden age."*]

M. R. James in his preface to the anthology *Ghosts and Marvels* (ed. V. H. Collins, 1924) admitted that "the ghost story is at best only a particular sort of short story, and is subject to the same broad rules as the whole mass of them." He is right in the obvious sense that many important features—atmosphere, economy, well-managed climax, final twist—are common to both. At the same time the ghost story itself can be regarded as a special paradigm, involving suspense and the unknown, within the short story classification. In this wider sense many nineteenth-century authors wrote stories which display similar formal characteristics, yet contain no overtly supernatural elements. With the increasing taste for naturalism, the short story and the ghost story began to diverge and in the former fantasy became increasingly inward, a development partly anticipated by those ghost stories which have a psychological explanation. Traditionally the form has affinities with mystery and detective stories and, more recently, science fiction, yet while these first cousins have maintained a certain vitality in the mid-twentieth century, the ghost story now seems to look back over its own shoulder. It has become a vehicle for nostalgia, a formulaic exercise content merely to recreate a Dickensian or Monty Jamesian atmosphere. It no longer has any capacity for growth or adaption.

The end of the nineteenth century represents the high-water mark of the form. Between 1850 and 1930 or so it achieved enormous popularity and was patronized not merely by hack journalists but by many of the major writers of the day. Its remarkable success was closely connected with the growth of a reading public who consumed fictional periodicals avidly, magazines such as *Blackwoods,* the *Cornhill, Tinsley's, House-hold Words, All the Year Round, Temple Bar, St James's, Belgravia* and the *Strand,* to name only a few. These provided entertainment, eating up material as rapidly as radio and television do today and, like them, catering through different house styles for different social groups and tastes. The predominantly middle-class audiences enjoyed romance and pictures of high life, but also liked to read of familiar settings transformed by a sudden eruption of crime, violence or the supernatural. Ghosts, like detectives, commonly operated in middle-class homes. Several of the periodicals were intended for reading aloud to the whole family, which might consist of the young and old of both sexes, so that contributions were necessarily limited in their exploration of intimate adult relations and a dramatic narrative was generally preferred. Ghost stories were especially suitable for they provided short self-contained episodes which could be printed beside the full-length serials running from issue to issue. The elements of fear and suspense gave them a central momentum that was well designed for this purpose. Although in the 1830s and '40s long supernatural tales sometimes provided serials for the popular press, the taste for short ghost stories was encouraged by Dickens in his editorial role, first in special Christmas editions and later more regularly, so that by the end of the century a fearful tale every few issues was more or less *de riguer.*

While the great majority of work thus produced was mediocre, a number of more talented writers began to explore the ghost story's possibilities as a serious literary form. The continuing demand, an interesting phenomenon in itself, will not entirely explain what drew them to it. Many authors, good and bad alike, were dependent on periodical publication for their livelihood, or at the least for reaching a wide audience. Henry James, who was financially comparatively independent, found a certain artistic pleasure in squaring popular taste with his own highly demanding literary ideals in *The Turn of the Screw,* which he described as a "shameless little pot-boiler" in a letter to H. G. Wells. Although most stories were written to fill pages of forgotten periodicals by forgotten writers, the form nevertheless commanded sufficient respect for several major authors to achieve real distinction within it, while some lesser figures produced fine and memorable contributions. This suggests that it somehow managed to incorporate feelings of rel-

evance, even importance to the age, feelings which could not find expression so directly or satisfactorily to either writer or reader in other modes. Before speculating as to what these might have been, it is helpful to consider some of the general characteristics of the genre, several of which were closely linked to the feelings it evoked.

Invented ghost stories differ from first-hand accounts in that they share with all fiction an artificially imposed pattern. They have some point to them, whereas only too often genuine experiences and ghostly apparitions in life have no discoverable meaning or application. It was precisely on the grounds of prosaicness and pointlessness that the investigations of psychic research societies were rejected by most writers as unsuitable material for fiction, especially as there was something inherently materialistic in the quantitative and mensurative approaches of the psychic researchers to questions that are and always will be shrouded in the ultimate mystery of death itself.

This consequential patterning of the ghost story normally implies that there must be a reason (if not a strictly logical one) for supernatural events. If a ghost walks, it is because its owner has not been buried with due ceremony, because he has to atone for some great sin, or perhaps to warn, or provide information concealed during life—the existence of a second will or buried treasure, for instance. The dead seldom return merely to reassure fond relatives that they are not lost but gone before, or to dictate their latest symphony. Thus the behaviour of the traditional ghost resembles that of a restless sleeper whose bed is uncomfortable or who is troubled by guilt or an unfulfilled obligation. There is similarly an illogical logic in those "spirits created for vengeance" who usually seize on secret criminals, on hapless magicians who dabble with powers beyond their control, or on the fool who sells his soul to the Devil for some misconceived advantage.

Such notions of consequence and causality are part of most witchcraft systems in many different societies. Belief in the power and effectiveness of magic and spirits is very extensive and very old. Their inherent logic is totally false judged from a modern and strictly materialistic standpoint, and since the seventeenth century, Western European society has been gradually disengaging itself from these beliefs, substituting laws of causality that are subject to clearer proof. Nevertheless, though they have dwindled to the inferior status of superstitions, the older concepts have not entirely lost their power because most people occasionally think and react like savages; primitive magical laws still govern the outlook and beliefs of children, and are often reinstated in dreams, neurosis and madness. Reason has not yet succeeded in exorcizing those monsters that come forth in sleep; perhaps it never will. Freud's explanation for the power of ghost stories to affect us is that in them, the old logic of witchcraft and the spirit world reasserts itself: "We appear to attribute an 'uncanny' quality to impressions that seek to confirm the omnipotence of thought and the animistic mode of thinking in general, after we have reached a stage at which, in our *judgement,* we have abandoned such beliefs" (*Totem and Taboo, 1913,* trans. James Strachey, 1950).

Freud's account is not merely persuasive—it also explains the great popularity of the ghost story at the height of the nineteenth century. If, as he implies, the form depends upon the existence of a tension between an outmoded, but not entirely abandoned belief and a enlightened scepticism, such tension was notably present in the last century, when the material and spiritual conceptions of life were locked in a continuous conflict which no intellectual could entirely avoid. Questions of faith and doubt were considered of paramount importance where there was leisure for thought at all. The ghost story was well-suited to express ambivalent reactions, the sense of loss and gain, for it seemed at the outset to invite the reader's modern cynicism, only to vanquish it with a reassertion of older and more spiritual values. Even amidst its superficial terrors it might thus provide subtle reassurances.

Like a number of other nineteenth-century art forms the ghost story set about deliberately reviving the system of magical interaction between man and his universe that now belonged to a past increasingly identified with the Middle Ages. The conviction with which authors wrote of traditional beliefs was often related to their knowledge or intuitive understanding of that lost animistic world picture. It is striking how many of the most successful grew up in remote areas where folklore and oral tradition still flourished—Walter Scott and Sheridan Le Fanu are obvious examples. At their best, writers from such a background could combine a magical vision with an appreciation of more rational attitudes to the supernatural in their work. The importance of a clash between the prosaic and cynical modern world and evidences of long-forgotten forces acting within it had not escaped Scott's observant eye: "the person who professes himself most incredulous on the subject of marvellous stories, often ends his remarks by indulging the company with some well-attested anecdote, which it is difficult or impossible to account for on the narrator's own principle of absolute scepticism" (from the introduction to "My Aunt Margaret's Mirror," *The Keepsake*, 1828).

The narrator's scepticism may act as a disarming anticipation of that of his audience. If he himself voices their objections or reservations, then they may be more willing to accept his testimony without question. In fact a background of general scepticism or disbelief is one of the factors that distinguishes the ghost story of the last two centuries from earlier examples, encouraging writers to concentrate on creating an effect of verisimilitude in order to convince their readers of the reality of the world into which the unbelievable intrudes. There is an obvious contrast between the easy acceptance of the supernatural in primitive literature and the modern ghost story writer's careful exploitation of realism to lend conviction to his work. Freud comments in his essay on "The Uncanny" on the fact that fairy stories use supernatural elements without bringing them into direct confrontation with the ordinary world at all, thus avoiding the fear and tension characteristic of the ghost story:

> The situation is altered as soon as the writer pretends to move in the world of common reality. In this case he accepts all the conditions operating to produce uncanny feelings in real life; and everything that would have an uncanny effect in reality has it in his story. But in this case, too, he can increase his effect and multiply it far beyond what could happen in reality, by bringing about events which could never or very rarely happen in fact. He takes advantage, as it were, of our supposedly surmounted superstitiousness; he deceives us into thinking that he is giving us the sober truth, and then after all oversteps the bounds of possibility. We react to his inventions as we should have reacted to real experience.
>
> (*Collected Papers*, 1925)

Approaching the realism of the ghost story from a very different point of view, as part of his theory of modes, the critic Northrop Frye has distinguished between the ready acceptance of ghosts in "romance" and "high mimetic" and their appearance in "low mimetic," as he designates the mode of naturalistic fiction: "In low mimetic, ghosts have been, ever since Defoe, almost entirely confined to a separate category of 'ghost stories'" (*Anatomy of Criticism: Four Essays*, 1957). By seeing them as essentially belonging to the "low mimetic" mode Frye has rightly emphasized realism and the importance of a convincing portrayal of everyday life. The exceptions may be thought to prove the rule: Poe's more fantastic and dreamlike episodes, or the artistic fairy tales of Wilde are scarcely ghost stories at all, but much nearer to the mode of "romance." By failing to establish a familiar world they risk forfeiting our sense of fear.

There are two main ways in which the ghost story writer may evoke the recognizable world, and these can be used separately or in conjunction. He may either re-create the common fictive world of ordinary—usually middle-class—life, or he may use a strange and intimidating setting, which is nevertheless naturalistically described. This might be an out-of-the-way place, a landscape in which man is a helpless alien, where wide spaces, looming mountains or lowering trees convey a sense of menace; or it may be another period, an era long past, with the more animistic view of life this entails. Familiar surroundings create an illusion of security, while unfamiliar scenes can suggest the immanence or proximity of spiritual powers. A tension between the known and the unknown, security and exposure, the familiar and the strange, scepticism and credulity, must always be maintained.

The combination of modern scepticism with a nostalgia for an older, more supernatural system of beliefs provides the foundation of the ghost story, and this nostalgia can be seen as inherently romantic, even providing a possible definition of romanticism. It remains a central theme in Victorian literature, and a late romantic such as Thomas Hardy indicates within his poetry, deeply haunted as it is, some of the possible significances of the ghost, as a figure of the lost past, of what might have been, or of that greatest of all nineteenth-century spectres, the empty universe. Hardy incisively realized what lesser writers were only dimly aware of, because he saw it so vividly enacted across the Dorset landscape—the loss of an older, more stable and locally integrated life, with its magical ways of thinking and feeling.

Technical progress and modern urban life had displaced the older continuities, cutting the individual off from his past, both communal and personal, from the magical perceptions of childhood, from Wordsworthian glimpses of supernatural forces within nature. This in turn created a new and wholly terrifying vision. From Coleridge onwards, many of the great nineteenth-century writers were to be ghost seers, haunted by the ultimate horror of being "bare-shouldered creatures" falling through an incomprehensible universe of infinite emptiness, or by the ghosts of their own failure to be at one with themselves or their surroundings, both physical and intellectual. Out of an alienation, to which the decay of supernatural beliefs contributed, there emerged the figure of the double, neither the self nor another, a powerful symbol of unresolved inner conflict.

The certainties of an older faith had not after all been entirely replaced by the compensating certainties of science. Dreams of the advancement of learning were vexed to nightmare when new researches indicated vast unknown tracts, far outstretching the little areas of charted knowledge. Progress in medicine and the ability to prevent or cope with epidemics lagged far behind industrial techniques and the accompanying growth of conurbations that largely caused them. Then as today there was a strong sense that man's new power was an enemy as well as a friend, that the science of understanding man—body, and more importantly, mind—had fallen far behind the development of mechanical skills. Moreover science was beginning to reveal a picture of nature disturbingly, irreconcilably different from that of a benevolent goddess, a great mother whose children were "Fostered alike by beauty and by fear."

Lamarckian and Darwinian theories conceived nature as functioning on a principle of progressive conflict out of which man, the acme, ultimately evolved. But as a descendant of the beasts, he had a bestial inheritance within him which he must learn to sublimate and restrain. The lower instincts could be graphically represented in terms of such mutations as fauns and satyrs. As in Lear's tormented vision, "Down from the waist they are all Centaurs." The tendency to dress bestiality and sexual abandonment in the comparative decency of classical metaphor is characteristic of the later nineteenth century. Laughing Ceres and fruitful Pomona had given place as representatives of an ordered nature to goatfoot Pan, god of irrational panic, whose horns and hooves revealed his true satanic identity. Some writers inferred a connection between the strict system of sexual ethics with its constant emphasis on self-transcendence, and the evolutionary theory according to which man, the highest form of life, had gradually transcended the other animals.

Arthur Machen's lurid stories, written in the 1880s and '90s, combine the figure of Pan as an evil force, accidentally reached through the abuse of science, with "unspeakable" sexual orgies (described in terms of satyrs and fauns) and also with a moral and physical reversion, through a curious distortion of the evolutionary process, back to "the aboriginal slime." The sense of an unstable victory over the lower self is also present in the way that the upright Dr Jekyll gradually comes to revert involuntarily to the bent-over, hairy and libidinous Hyde, repressed for so long that at first he appeared small and starved. Many other supernatural figures such as the vampire or, more obviously, the werewolf symbolize a regression to the natural bestiality lurking within, and ignored at one's psychic peril. The unknown forces in man, forces that, like the new concept of nature, appeared dangerous and alien, were profoundly frightening.

The sense of the natural as somehow bestial was, like the ghost story itself, simultaneously traditional and modern. It had many affinities with the Calvinist or Puritan sense of innate bodily sinfulness, yet current evolutionary theories gave it a new relevance, connecting it with a widespread condemnation of sexual licence as a reversion to the animal nature. Alternative solutions to this increasingly divisive view of the self and the universe had already been sketched out before the end of the century. Meredith had perhaps anticipated Machen in his poem "The Woods of Westermain" where the vision of an appalling bacchanal results from a lack of self-knowledge or adequate psychic integration. Danger from within will continue to threaten if we do not learn to examine the darker places of the soul, while retaining the ideals appropriate to the lighter side:

> You must love the light so well
> That no darkness will seem fell.
> Love it so you could accost
> Fellowly a livid ghost.

Another reaction that goes well beyond Meredith's semi-classical, semi-modern doctrine of self-knowledge can be found in the neo-romanticism of D. H. Lawrence, for whom nature and the instinctive sexual life were once more sanctified. Early

in the next century the goat-foot god was reinstated and unlicensed orgy, associated by Machen with the powers of evil, now became a sacred mystery, the source of all that was most vital and creative in man. This change of attitude to intuitive response and the physical life of man is reflected in the supernatural fantasies of E. M. Forster and Algernon Blackwood which were often dramatized in terms of Pan, centaurs, dryads and the like. Now seen as positive and beneficent forces, these figures are part of a developing dialogue as to the true nature of man.

While many twentieth-century writers have been anxious to establish the fertility of the darker places of the soul, for the nineteenth century the release of the animal nature within, the night side, under mesmerism or in dreams, through drugs, delirium or madness, merely provided further fearful evidence of its ability to destroy rational and ordered life. Corresponding powers of exorcism lay only in priests or, increasingly, with doctors. The psychic doctor who could successfully "minister to a mind diseased" assumes a new importance for sufferers. In Le Fanu's "Green Tea" (1869) the inadequacy of the Church, now largely deprived of its magical powers, to cope with insubstantial "spectral illusions" is brought out by making the victim of them a clergyman himself, forced to resort to medical advice. Yet although doctors were commonly associated with scientific confidence in man's power over his environment, they themselves were far from infallible. Jekyll is a physician who patently fails to heal himself. In creating psychic doctors capable of releasing the ego from the terrifying grip of the incomprehensible, insubordinate id, the late nineteenth-century ghost story anticipated the advent of Freud, whose psychotherapy aimed at reducing the night side to mangeable proportions, and breaking up the potentially destructive doubleness of Victorian man.

But the mystery of the mind within, the unrecognizable face of the rejected and hidden Hyde, remains an obsession of that age, and one which the fantasy of the ghost story is particularly well-suited to express. The philosophical problem of whether apparently supernatural phenomena have any independent existence or are created in the human imagination, with all its implications for a "living" universe, or a totally subjective human vision are implicit in the question most basic to the ghost story, "Was it real or imaginary?" Interestingly enough, Le Fanu (in "Green Tea" and elsewhere), and later the philosopher William James, Henry's brother, both attempted to reach some sort of compromise on this issue. James wrote:

> Whether supernormal powers of cognition in certain persons may occur, is a matter to be decided by evidence. If they can occur, it may be that there might be a chink . . . if there were real demons they might possess only hysterics. Thus each side may see a portion of the truth.
> (Lecture to the Lowell Institute, Boston, 1896)

Closely linked with and arising out of more general questions about man's spiritual condition, and his often subversive inner life, is the problem of evil, and whether it is conceived as a force within man or all about him. The nature of evil in the universe has always been a central concern of literature, pagan and Christian alike, and since so many modern ghost stories are particularly concerned with malevolent spirits, they inevitably tend to gravitate towards the subject. "Green Tea," for example, treats the question with integrity and imagination, though ultimately the problem of the innocent clergyman's appalling haunting is left unsolved, and both Freudian and Swedenborgian explanations remain viable. A number of weaker or more melodramatic stories such as Machen's are raised above their actual level of achievement by the interest and weight of the question.

The ghost story appealed to serious writers largely because it invited a concern with the profoundest issues; the relationship between life and death, the body and the soul, man and his universe and the philosophical conditions of that universe, the nature of evil. Like other forms of fantasy—myths, legends or fairy tales—it could be made to embody symbolically hopes and fears too deep and too important to be expressed more directly. That fact that authors often disclaimed any serious intention—M. R. James declared that he only wanted to "give pleasure of a certain sort"—may paradoxically support this view. The revealing nature of fantastic and imaginative writing has encouraged its exponents to cover their tracks, either by self-deprecation or other forms of retraction. The assertion of the author's detachment from his work may reasonably arouse the suspicion that he is less detached than he supposes.

The depth of the issues touched on for a time guaranteed their authors' commitment, and when this failed, the stories began to fail too. After the trauma of the First World War and Freud's compelling expositions of the inner life, inhibitions seemed to develop and the majority of ghost stories written in the 1920s demonstrate fine structure, wit, elegance—everything, that is, except the writer's serious involvement with his subject. When it degenerated to an exercise in skill and invention, the decadence of the form had set in.

Although from the twenties it slipped into a decline from which it has never recovered, it did not, and indeed has not, lost all popularity, as today's numerous paperback anthologies indicate. Horror stories and ghost stories, often heavily dependent on their more powerful predecessors, continue to be written, though they have largely been replaced by science fiction as the central expression of the predicament of modern man. Yet the latter, even at its height, never attracted writers as diverse or as important. Essentially the history of the ghost story lies in its appeal not so much for the reader as for the writer, as the decline in standards rather than in popularity would suggest. (pp. 13-23)

For an age to which scientific advances had brought improving material circumstances and increasing spiritual discomfort, the ghost story set up counter-suggestions that provided reassurance, beneath its more obvious terrors: undermining the apparent predictability of the material world, it gave comforting proof that there *was* something beyond. Man was not, as he had come to fear, alone in a universe infinitely older, larger, wilder and less anthropocentric than he had previously supposed. (p. 24)

> *Julia Briggs, in an introduction to her* Night Visitors: The Rise and Fall of the English Ghost Story, *Faber, 1977, pp. 11-24.*

L. T. C. ROLT

[*Rolt was an English author of nonfiction works which were often concerned with the history of technology, particularly developments in the field of transportation. This interest is also displayed in his* Sleep No More (1948), *a collection of ghost stories in which railway and canal transportation provide the background or basis for supernatural incidents. In the following excerpt, Rolt disagrees with critics who speak of the decline of the ghost story and examines the works of prominent practitioners of the form in the nineteenth and twentieth centuries.*]

They could not appreciate light who had never known darkness, and so the brightness of the star that shone over the stable in Bethlehem was traditionally enhanced each Christmas season by the black contrast of fireside tales about what Mrs. Crowe called the "Night Side of Nature." When the winter wind boomed in the chimney, generations of storytellers would, like Mamillius, do their best to fright the company, invoking not merely sprites and goblins but the Prince of Darkness himself or his more fearful myrmidons: hell hounds and werwolves, demons of hideous aspect, witches and warlocks, and damned souls breaking from their unquiet graves.

Most of us can no longer appreciate the superstitious terrors which the mere mention of such creatures was once sufficient to arouse. They have become mere turnip ghosts whose element the flick of a switch will disperse. Nevertheless, the past dies hard. Notwithstanding electric light and every other form of scientific exorcism the ghost story held its own. Until recently no Christmas annual or Christmas number of a magazine was considered complete without a ghost story. It is only within the last decade or so that this venerable branch of the storyteller's art seems to have fallen into neglect.

Some literary critics account for the eclipse of the ghost story by maintaining that no amount of subtlety can any longer avail against the materialism and cynicism of the present time, in other words that it is an exhausted form doomed to extinction in a world of science fiction. Before jumping to the hasty assumption that the last fictional ghost has been laid, it were better to study a little more closely the history of the art and the works of its past masters.

Supernatural phenomena are only the raw material of the ghost story writer. They provide him with ideas, no more. The idea is only his starting point; his own imagination must supply the atmosphere of mounting suspense and the significant and usually malign influence of the supernatural upon the natural which seldom or never exists in fact but which gives the fictional ghost story its shape and plot. The oldest and simplest of these fictional embroideries is that of the man who spends a night in a haunted chamber. Sometimes he does so wittingly for a wager or out of sheer bravado and sometimes he is the victim of a cruel experiment or hoax on the part of his host, but in either event the result is the same. If his hair turns white overnight he has had a fortunate escape; death mysterious or self-inflicted or gibbering lunacy are usually his portion. In antiquity and perennial virility the victim of the haunted chamber shares the honours with the numerous rash speculators who, singularly failing to profit from the horrid example of their famous predecessor Doctor Faustus, persistently sign contracts with the Arch Fiend or one of his cohorts.

Simple basic plots such as these which stem directly from oral tradition, together with every grisly legend and superstition that memory had perpetuated were all raked up in the eighteenth century and flung into the melting pot of the Gothic novel, *The Castle of Otranto* and its successors. Like the witches in *Macbeth*, Horace Walpole and his imitators concocted a rare stew for their cauldron, but it is not one that we can stomach today. In its extreme form it was as crammed full with horrors both natural and supernatural as the most lurid of medieval "Last Judgments," and, like the latter, it is capable of inspiring no more than morbid curiosity today. For the Gothic writers simply did not know when to stop. They subjected their audience to such an unrelieved surfeit that they defeated their own object.

Nevertheless, the Gothic novel is true ancestor of the modern ghost story, for out of that phantasmagoria there emerged two of the first great masters of the supernatural art, Edgar Allan Poe and Joseph Sheridan Le Fanu. The former's *Tales of Mystery and Imagination* is justly famous as a classic of the art, displaying a sombre imaginative power infinitely superior to any of his predecessors. Yet Poe stands for the most part still very much in the Gothic tradition and is reluctant to discard its paraphernalia. So it is that stories such as "Ligeia" or the celebrated "Fall of the House of Usher," though they do not provoke irreverent laughter, have become for us period pieces, albeit magnificent ones, which no longer haunt our minds as their author intended they should, and as any successful ghost story must do. With the better stories of Sheridan Le Fanu it is quite otherwise. Although his work is unaccountably less widely acclaimed than Poe's, he is, when at the top of his bent—for his work is uneven in quality—a much greater master than Poe. The stage of his stories, too, is apt to be cluttered with tombstones, mouldering ruins, mantling ivy and such-like conventional Gothic properties over which the modern reader is apt to stumble. Nor is he a writer of remarkable inventive power or originality where his plots are concerned. They are for the most part old, conventional and simple, while more than once he repeats what is virtually the same story, changing only the setting and the names of the characters. And yet, despite all this, Le Fanu's stories linger uncomfortably in the back of the mind where Poe's are forgotten. The secret of this success and the basis of his claim to be the father of the modern ghost story is to be found in the infinitely guileful brilliance with which he conjures up his apparitions. This is a technique entirely his own to which all subsequent practitioners are indebted. If, for instance, we were to meet that foul dog in "Squire Toby's Will" we might at first suppose that there was nothing abnormal about it. So thought Charles Marston when the dog first appeared, for Le Fanu was the first to realize that the most grotesque and hideous monster ever conceived cannot be so frightening as the sudden revelation that the normal and familiar is not, after all, what it seems. From the moment when the dog is seen fawning and writhing in obscene ecstasy upon the tomb of old Squire Toby, its white body extended to a length quite disproportionate, it becomes a creature most horrible, the mere clattering of its claws in the nocturnal corridors of Gylingden Hall more disturbing in its import than the baying of all the hell-hounds of legend put together.

In the opinion of this reader, "Squire Toby's Will" is the best of Le Fanu's stories, but this is a matter of personal taste, for others are hardly less successful. No matter how old and stale the plot may be it is revivified by brilliant treatment. Thus "A Strange Event in the Life of Schalken the Painter" is no more than a variation upon the Faustean theme, yet where legions of Mephistophelian bargainers are forgotten, Le Fanu's infernal visitor has an unpleasant way of reappearing before the mind's eye. Minheer Wilken Vanderhausen of Rotterdam is not distinguished as a species by a cloven foot or a smell of brimstone. As in the case of the dog, we at first accept as natural the strange visitor to the studio of Gerard Douw and so become horrified when certain subtle peculiarities are remarked: the dark skin; the unblinking eyes in which the whites are visible all round the iris; and a stillness in repose so profound that no motion even of breathing can be detected.

The same may be said of the creatures that lurk in the pages of that brilliantly titled collection *In a Glass Darkly*. The concentrated malevolence of the little monkey-like being which ultimately drove the wretched parson of "Green Tea" to take

his own life and the menacing face of "The Familiar" which hounded the unfortunate Captain Barton to an equally melancholy end are both, it seems, disturbingly enhanced by the mere fact of their diminutive size. And surely no vampire, no, not even the eminent Count Dracula himself, has ever surpassed Le Fanu's "Carmilla." Here again, what makes this *revenant* so peculiarly dreadful is the perfection of its human disguise. Almost until the fearful end the semblance of the beautiful Carmilla continues to deceive and only we, the readers, are permitted to infer the horrid truth from her morning languors and from her growing passion for her host's ward, an unnatural lust of whose awful consummation we become so vividly aware that we long to cry a warning to the innocent victim, caught like a fly in the web of her seductions.

These three stories from *In a Glass Darkly* have only one fault. Each is presented as though it had been extracted from the case book of a pseudo-scientific investigator named Doctor Hesselius. This serious mistake has been perpetuated by other writers since Le Fanu, who have perhaps been influenced by detective story technique. To the latter the character of the investigator is as important as the Prince of Denmark in *Hamlet*, but in the ghost story he is an unwanted extra, attempting, as he must do, to rationalize and explain an occurrence which, if it is to make its full impact upon the reader, should remain as irrational and as inexplicable as a nightmare. Even the frequently employed technique of telling the ghost story at second hand must to some extent insulate the reader from the shock, knowing as he does that the narrator himself is not involved in the events which he describes. Hence, with rare exceptions, the most effective ghost stories are told in direct narrative. To

Joseph Sheridan Le Fanu.

cut these stories of Le Fanu's out of the frame in which Doctor Hesselius presents them would be a simple operation from which they would benefit immeasurably. One reason why "Squire Toby's Will" excels is that it is told directly; here no calm, detached voice is raised to allay our fears and distract them from that beastly dog.

A most fervent admirer of Le Fanu's work and one who did more than anyone else to rescue it from unmerited obscurity was that most widely celebrated of all the masters of the ghost story, Montague Rhodes James. James not only hailed Le Fanu as the first of the masters but freely acknowledged his own debt to him. Certainly the stories of M. R. James represents a logical development of Le Fanu's technique. In the creation of memory-haunting visitants and in devising unpleasant experiences for his luckless human characters, James's power of invention is unsurpassed. Moreover, no other writer in this field has ever maintained so consistent a standard. Not one of his stories fails in its effect, and connoisseurs rarely agree when asked to name his best work. A considerable factor in his success was the academic *milieu* in which practically all his characters have their being. It was not only one in which he moved himself and with which he was therefore thoroughly familiar, it was also perfectly suited to the display of his particular powers, distilling as it did an atmosphere which made his singular inventions all too easily credible. James's bookish, candlelit world, peopled exclusively by elderly Fellows of the Society of Antiquaries, Dons and Prebendaries who inhabit tall Queen Anne or Georgian rectories in the wilds of East Anglia, or enjoy the cloistered seclusion of quadrangle or Cathedral close, this world of his is, when we come to think of it, simply an ingenious variant of that Gothic gloom in which earlier and simpler writers wallowed. The difference is that whereas their characters lived in the ruins, so to speak, James's elderly and eminently respectable scholars visit them in the spirit of archaeological inquiry. When they do so they invariably pay a high price for their curiosity. The technique, though immensely effective and capable of many ingenious twists and variations, is basically extremely simple. It could be labelled, somewhat irreverently, the Aladdin's Lamp method. Murmur aloud the Latin inscription, study too closely the picture or the ancient book; blow that curious whistle, lay your hand upon the head of the carved figure or seek the treasure of Abbot Thomas, and you will presently find yourself in highly undesirable company. It is disconcerting to find a thin, hairy hand appearing on the desk beside your book when you are reading, or to confront a crumpled linen face in your hotel bedroom where there should only be an unoccupied bed. It is not pleasant when what you took to be a leather sack suddenly slumps forward and puts arms about your neck.

If James has a fault it is that he betrays, in some not easily definable way, a kind of impish glee, a malicious delight in his ability to frighten his readers. With infinite relish he sets about the task of freezing our blood and performs it most efficiently, but we are aware that his own blood has never cooled and that he does not believe a word of what he writes. If he is to carry his readers with him and achieve the highest pinnacle of success the writer of ghost stories must create the impression, whether it be true or false, that he himself believes that the events which he is describing *could* happen. If he does not do so he cannot hope to suspend his readers' disbelief.

The ghost stories of M. R. James are highly ingenious variations upon a theme, and their key and tone colour remains the same. To change the metaphor, the basic ingredients are seldom varied and all the skill lies in the way they are mixed and seasoned. James never essayed any entirely fresh recipe for horror comparable with, to quote a classic example, *The Turn of the Screw*. The literary fame of Henry James is, of course, far more widely based, yet this single brilliant achievement entitles him to a place among the masters of the ghost story. The horrible idea of childish innocence deliberately corrupted and debauched by a power of supernatural evil has since been exploited by other writers and seldom fails to produce the desired effect upon the reader, but never has it been developed with such skill and subtlety as in the original. When the antiquary in an M. R. James story suffers for his insatiable curiosity or acquisitiveness we may say to ourselves 'serve you right,' but there is something quite different and peculiarly dreadful about the notion of a small child becoming a victim of the dark powers.

Arthur Machen and Algernon Blackwood are much more uneven writers than M. R. James. Blackwood, particularly, can fail abysmally, and he sometimes introduces a tiresome successor to Le Fanu's Doctor Hesselius, improbably named John Silence. Yet when he is at the top of his form, Blackwood is incomparable, and if I were asked to name the most terrifying ghost story ever written my answer would be "The Wendigo." The strength of both Machen and Blackwood is the weakness of M. R. James; they succeed in convincing their readers that they believe their own stories. So effectually do they manage this that wisps of the sinister necromantic fog which pervades their stories seem to hang about the writers themselves. While we should, we feel, welcome as reassuring the person of M. R. James if we met him as we walked along a high banked lane on a dark night, we might well experience a qualm upon encountering the cloaked, white-haired Machen or the cadaverous figure of Algernon Blackwood.

The background and technique of their most successful stories is totally different from those of M. R. James. It is a paradox that whereas James, the hearty member of the trio, performs most of his conjurations indoors, Machen and Blackwood are predominantly outdoor men; they have to do with elemental things, and the particular brand of horror in which they excel is that of the worm in the bud, the terror or the rottenness that can lurk under nature's mask of beauty. Upon one side the fruit can present the smooth ripe bloom of perfection, while upon the other it is already black, corrupt and crawling with loathsome creatures. With splendid skill and sensibility they shock us with the contrast between this picture and that, pointing the ancient, enigmatic contradiction between the exquisite sweetness of the music of the Pan pipes and the pitiless, pagan cruelty of those hairy flanks and cloven feet.

Space does not permit us to consider other stars in the ghostly firmament such as E. F. Benson, H. R. Wakefield and Oliver Onions. These three, like Blackwood and Machen, are not always successful, and yet, with "The Room in the Tower," "Look Up There" and "The Beckoning Fair One," respectively, each has earned his place among the masters.

But where are the practising masters of today? That the most recent collection of original ghost stories to appear up to the time of writing received wider critical notice than previous ventures in this field is encouraging, but the quality of the book was not. With one possible exception the masters are not here. Well-known writers who should know better fall into every pitfall which can so easily entrap whoever would succeed in this minor but most subtle and sinister art. Some commit sins quite unforgivable and deadly; wax facetious or, as a writer of whodunits trails red herring clues, trick out their theme with supernatural *non sequitors* the effect of which is to mystify and perplex but not to terrify. That every hint of the sinister or abnormal must be strictly relevant to the central idea is a canon of the art which cannot be flouted. But the commonest fault of these modern stories is that they are too short. The very short ghost story is rarely successful. If it is to convince the reader, the process whereby the abnormal gradually intrudes and imposes itself upon the normal cannot be hurried, and hence an attempt to apply the fashionable technique of streamlining is disastrous. It means that the story begins on a note of unreality or of tension instead of first lulling the reader into a false sense of security.

One reviewer of this recent book maintained that the ghost story had no future because the number of possible plots was limited, that they had been worn out by over-use and were not in any case applicable or convincing in this materialistic atomic age. That the basic plots available are limited I agree, but that they are stale or inapplicable to the present day I most stoutly deny. On the contrary, never was a world so full of sinister possibilities awaiting exploitation. It is not without significance that the most successful story in the collection just referred to should be the one which is set most firmly in the present time. This is Michael Asquith's "The Uninvited Face." Here the theme is as old as the hills—it is the same as that of Le Fanu's "Green Tea"—but the treatment, with the victim an atomic physicist, and the clever introduction of surrealism, is as modern as the hour.

Yes, the ghost story has a future still, of that I am convinced. Scientist and materialist have not succeeded in banishing the Night Side of Nature. For Christian men the devil still walks abroad and has merely changed his disguise. (pp. 105-12)

L. T. C. Rolt, "The Passing of the Ghost Story," in
The Saturday Book, *Vol. 16, 1956, pp. 105-12.*

SUPERNATURAL FICTION AS A LITERARY GENRE

EDMUND WILSON

[*Wilson, considered America's foremost man of letters in the twentieth century, wrote widely on cultural, historical, and literary matters. He is often credited with bringing an international perspective to American letters through his widely read discussions of European literature. Wilson was allied to no critical school; however, several dominant concerns serve as guiding motifs throughout his work. He invariably examined the social and historical implications of a work of literature, particularly literature's significance as "an attempt to give meaning to our experience" and its value for the improvement of humanity. Although he was not a moralist, his criticism displays a deep concern with moral values. Another constant was his discussion of a work of literature as a revelation of its author's personality. In Axel's* Castle (1931), *a seminal study of literary symbolism, Wilson wrote: "The real elements, of course, of any work of fiction are the elements of the author's personality: his imagination embodies in the images of characters, situations and scenes the fundamental conflicts of his nature." Related to this is Wilson's theory, formulated in* The Wound and the Bow (1941), *that artistic ability is a compensation for a psychological wound; thus, a literary work can only be fully understood if one undertakes an emotional profile of its author. Wilson utilized this approach in many essays, and it is the most-often attacked element of his thought. However, though Wilson examined the historical and psychological impli-*

cations of a work of literature, he rarely did so at the expense of a discussion of its literary qualities. Perhaps Wilson's greatest contributions to American literature were his tireless promotion of writers of the 1920s, 1930s, and 1940s, and his essays introducing the best of modern literature to the general reader. In the following review of several anthologies of supernatural fiction that appeared in the 1940s, Wilson speculates on the reason for the popularity of the stories in these volumes, many of which he finds inferior to the less popular and more artistic achievements in the genre.]

There has lately been a sudden revival of the appetite for tales of horror. First, Pocket Books published *The Pocket Mystery Reader* and *The Pocket Book of Mystery Stories.* Then came *Tales of Terror,* with an introduction by Boris Karloff; *Creeps by Night,* with an introduction by Dashiell Hammett; and *Best Ghost Stories of M. R. James* (all three brought out by World). Finally, Random House has produced a prodigious anthology called *Great Tales of Terror and the Supernatural,* edited by Herbert A. Wise and Phyllis Fraser.

One had supposed that the ghost story itself was already an obsolete form; that it had been killed by the electric light. It was only during the ages of candlelight that the race of ghosts really flourished, though they survived through the era of gas. A candle can always burn low and be blown out by a gust of air, and it is a certain amount of trouble to relight it, as is also the case with a gas-jet. But if you can reach out and press a button and flood every corner of the room, leaving the specter quite naked in his vapor, or if you can transfix him out of doors with a flashlight, his opportunities for haunting are limited. It is true that one of the most famous of ghost stories, Defoe's "Apparition of Mrs. Veal," takes place in the afternoon; that it is a part of the effectiveness of *The Turn of the Screw* that its phantoms appear outdoors in broad daylight as well as indoors at night; and that that eeriest of all ghost stories supposed to be true, the anonymous book called *An Adventure,* purports to give the experiences of two English ladies visiting Versailles in the afternoon; but these are all in the nature of tours de force on the part of the apparitions or the authors. The common run of ghost needed darkness. It will be noticed in all these anthologies that most of the writers belong by training to the last decades of the nineteenth century, even though a few of their stories have been written in the first years of this.

What is the reason, then—in these days when a lonely country house is likely to be equipped with electric light, radio and telephone—for our returning to these antiquated tales? There are, I believe, two reasons: first, the longing for mystic experience which seems always to manifest itself in periods of social confusion, when political progress is blocked: as soon as we feel that our own world has failed us, we try to find evidence for another world; second, the instinct to inoculate ourselves against panic at the real horrors loose on the earth—Gestapo and G.P.U., tank attacks and airplane bombings, houses rigged with booby-traps—by injections of imaginary horror, which soothe us with the momentary illusion that the forces of madness and murder may be tamed and compelled to provide us with a mere dramatic entertainment. We even try to make them cozy and droll, as in *Arsenic and Old Lace,* which could hardly have become popular or even been produced on the stage at any other period of our history. This craving for homeopathic horror first began to appear some years ago in the movies—with the Frankenstein monsters, the werewolves, the vampires and the insane sadistic scientists, of whom such a varied assortment are now to be seen along West Forty-second Street; and recently, in such films as *The Uninvited,* the pictures, too, have been reaching back to pull toward us the phantom fringe which has been exploited by these anthologies.

The best of these volumes is the new Random House one, because it is the most comprehensive (though the book itself has the fault of so many American omnibuses and anthologies of being too cumbersome to handle comfortably in bed, the only place where one is likely to read ghost stories), and not unintelligently edited. The two collections in the Pocket Book series, both edited by Miss Lee Wright, are, however, quite well selected, and have the merit of costing only a quarter each. And yet one cannot read a large number of pieces in any of these compilations without feeling rather let down. The editors are always building up their authors: "Certain of these stories, like 'Lost Hearts' and 'The Ash-Tree,'" says the foreword to the *Best Ghost Stories of M. R. James*, ". . . should, we think, be skipped altogether by the squeamish and faint of heart"; a story by Robert Hichens is "unsurpassed for its subtle unfolding of a particularly loathsome horror"; and "Caterpillars," by E. F. Benson, is "brilliantly told, and without doubt . . . one of the most horrifying stories in this collection." Now, I find it very hard to imagine that any of these particular tales could scare anybody over ten. Two of them simply play on the gooseflesh that is stimulated in certain people by the idea of caterpillars or spiders, and demon caterpillars and demon spiders very easily seem absurd. Other stories much esteemed by these anthologists, such as the one mentioned above, by Robert Hichens—"How Love Came to Professor Guildea"—or Helen R. Hull's "Clay-Shuttered Doors," have promising macabre ideas—a great scientist who has cut himself off from all human relationships but is driven to desperation by an invisible imbecile who loves him; the wife of an ambitious New Yorker, who regalvanizes her decaying body and goes on playing her social role several months after she has been killed in a motor accident—but they are trashily or weakly done and do not realize their full possibilities. In either case, the authors content themselves with suggesting unpleasant sensations. They fail to lay hold on the terrors that lie deep in the human psyche and that cause man to fear himself.

These collections, of course, aim primarily at popular entertainment; they do not pretend to a literary standard. But I should like to suggest that an anthology of considerable interest and power could be compiled by assembling horror stories by really first-rate modern writers, in which they have achieved their effects not merely by attempting to transpose into terms of contemporary life the old fairy-tales of goblins and phantoms but by probing psychological caverns where the constraints of that life itself have engendered disquieting obsessions.

I should start off with Hawthorne and Poe, who are represented in these collections, but I should include, also, Melville and Gogol, who are not. The first really great short stories of horror came in the early or middle nineteenth century, when the school of Gothic romance had achieved some sophistication and was adopting the methods of realism. All four of these authors wrote stories that were at the same time tales of horror and psychological or moral fables. They were not interested in spooks for their own sake; they knew that their demons were symbols, and they knew what they were doing with these symbols. We read the tales of Poe in our childhood, when all that we are likely to get out of them is shudders, yet these stories are also poems that express the most intense emotions. "The Fall of the House of Usher" is not merely an ordinary ghost story: the house—see the opening paragraph—is an image for a human personality, and its fate—see the fissure that runs through

the wall—is the fate of a disrupted mind. And as for Gogol, he probably remains the very greatest master in this genre. I should put in at least "Viy" and "The Nose"—the former, a vampire story, one of the most terrific things of its kind ever written, and the latter, though it purports to be comic, almost equally a tale of horror, for it is charged with the disguised lurking meaning of a fear that has taken shape as a nightmare. I should include, also, "Bartleby the Scrivener" of Melville, which oddly resembles Gogol in this vein of the somber-grotesque, as well as "Benito Cereno," a more plausible yet still nightmarish affair, which ought to be matched farther on by Conrad's *Heart of Darkness*.

In the latter part of the century, however, the period to which Conrad belongs, these fables tend to become impure. There was by that time much more pressure on the artist to report the material and social facts of the nineteenth-century world, and it seems difficult to combine symbolism with the inventories of naturalistic fiction or the discussion of public affairs. You have Stevenson, Kipling, Henry James. In Stevenson's case alone, this pressure did not inhibit his fancy, for he rarely wrote anything but fairy-tales, but he has much less intensity and substance than Conrad or Kipling or James. Nevertheless, though I might do without Jekyll and Hyde, I think I should have to have "Olalla" and "Thrawn Janet" (it is queer that a writer so popular in his time should be represented in none of these collections). But with Kipling you run into the cramping effects of a technical and practical period. I should include a couple of stories of Kipling's—say, "At the End of the Passage" and "Mrs. Bathurst"—as examples of borderline cases of the genuinely imaginative story which is nevertheless not first-rate. In such an early tale of Kipling's as "At the End of the Passage" or "The Phantom Rickshaw," he is trying to write a mere vulgar ghost story, but something else that is authentic gets in. If we have carefully studied Kipling, we can recognize in the horrors of these tales—the blinded phantom, the wronged woman—obsessions that recur in his work and to which we can find the key in his life. But a story of this kind should convey its effect without our having to track down its symbols. We need nothing but the story itself to tell us that the author of "Viy" has put all the combined fascination and fear with which he was inspired by women into the vigil of the young student in the little wooden church beside the coffin of the farmer's daughter. When Kipling sets out later on to work up a more complex technique and attempts several layers of meaning, he gives us a piece like "Mrs. Bathurst"—the pursuit by a wronged woman, again—in which, however, the main character's sense of guilt is tied up through the symbol of the woman with his duty to the British Empire in connection with the Boer War, and he introduces a political element which seems clumsy and out of place in a ghost story and somehow gives Mrs. Bathurst a slight tinge of the newspaper cartoon. Henry James, a more serious writer, produced a strange special case in "The Turn of the Screw." He asserted that he, too, had aimed merely at a conventional ghost story intended for a more knowing audience than that susceptible to the ordinary kind; but readers familiar with his work and conscious of his preoccupations have tended to see in the tale something more: the governess is not really, as she tells us, defending the children in her charge against the influence of malevolent spirits, she is frightening them herself with the projections of her own repressed emotions. There are, however, points in the story which are difficult to explain on this theory, and it is probable that James, like Kipling, was unconscious of having raised something more frightening than the ghosts he had contemplated. At any rate, I should put in "The Turn of the Screw," and also "The Jolly Corner," which seems to me James's other best ghost story. In this latter case, the author is of course quite conscious of what he is doing, but there is here, as in "Mrs. Bathurst," an element rather difficult to assimilate (though Henry James does make us accept it) in the issue between England and the United States, a social and historical problem, which provides the moral of the fable.

During this period there were some very good ghost stories done by popular writers of distinction like Conan Doyle and W. W. Jacobs, but, capital fairy-tales though "The Monkey's Paw" and "Playing with Fire" are, I should not admit them to my ideal collection. Nor should I—on the basis of the specimens I have read—include anything from a different school, which grew up in the late years of the century and which was stimulated perhaps by the encroachments of the spread of the new methods of lighting on the old-fashioned kind of ghost. This school, which is represented abundantly in the Random House collection, derives, I take it, from Arthur Machen, and features, instead of resurrected bodies and insubstantial phantoms, a demonology of ancient cults driven underground by Christianity but persisting into our own day, and exploits the identification of the Devil with the pagan god Pan. Machen's story on this theme called "The Great God Pan" (in the Random House collection) seems to me to sum up in a fatal way everything that was most "ham" in the aesthetic satanism of the *fin de siècle*. M. R. James, a great favorite of these anthologists, played countless variations on this theme and had some really fiendish flashes of fancy, but he never took any trouble to make his stories seem even halfway plausible, so his hobgoblins are always verging on parody.

A better writer is Algernon Blackwood, who belongs to this same general group and has an even greater reputation than M. R. James. He, too, tends to lean on anti-human creatures that embody the forces of nature, but he is interesting for another reason: you can see in him very clearly the shift from a belief in evil spirits as things that come to plague us from outside to a consciousness of terrors inside us that merely take possession of our minds. But where Kipling or Henry James knew how to dramatize these terrors in solid images that command our credence, Blackwood, beginning as a rule with a locale which he has actually observed and which he more or less convincingly describes, invariably transposes the story, from the moment when the supernatural element appears, onto a plane of melting, gliding nightmare where nothing seems really to be taking place. Now, a story of this kind, to impress us, must *never* seem to be a dream. The tales of Poe, for all the wildness of their fantasy, are as circumstantial as Swift or Defoe; when Gogol retells a Ukrainian legend, he so stiffens its texture with authentic detail that we seem to hear the voices of the peasants and smell the countryside.

I should, therefore, decline to pass Algernon Blackwood, but I should certainly admit Walter de la Mare, who sometimes errs in the direction of the too dreamlike but makes up for it through poetic imagination. His story called "Seaton's Aunt" comes close to being a masterpiece in this genre, and I should include also "Out of the Deep," which is equally good in conception though not quite so good in execution. (The first of these has been included in *The Pocket Book of Mystery Stories* and the second in the Random House anthology.) De la Mare, a great admirer of Poe, has done work that is quite his own in this field of supernatural fiction; it is in my opinion superior to his verse. His stories at their best are poetic, psychologically subtle and creepy to a high degree.

And, finally, I should include Franz Kafka, also absent from any of these collections. Stories like *The Metamorphosis* and "Blumfeld, an Elderly Bachelor" are among the best things of their kind. The first of these unpleasant pieces deals with a young travelling salesman who suddenly wakes up on morning to find that he has turned into an enormous roach, to the horror of his parents, with whom he lives and who have been counting on him to pay off their debts; the second tells of an office worker, a selfish and bureaucratic upper clerk, who is haunted by two little bouncing balls that represent his niggardly consciousness of two children that help him in his office. The stories that Kafka has written on these two unconventional subjects are at the same time satires on the bourgeoisie and visions of moral horror; narratives that are logical and compel our attention, and fantasies that generate more shudders than the whole of Algernon Blackwood and M. R. James combined. A master can make it seem more horrible to be pursued by two little balls than by the spirit of a malignant Knight Templar, and more natural to turn into a cockroach than to be bitten by a diabolic spider. Kafka, who was writing these stories at the time of the last World War, had brought back the tale of terror to the true vein of Gogol and Poe. In his realm of imagination no social or political problems intrude in such a way as to spoil the show. The modern bourgeoisie and the Central European bureaucracy have turned into the enchanted denizens of a world in which, prosaic though it is, we can find no firm foothold in reality and in which we can never even be certain whether souls are being saved or damned. As an artist in this field of horror, Kafka is among the greatest. Living in the era of Freud, he went straight for the morbidities of the psyche with none of the puppetry of specters and devils that earlier writers still carried with them. Whether his making out of these subjects at that time of day the Hoffmannesque fantasies that he did make, and whether the rapt admiration for them in *our* time represents a retrogression or a progress in the development of modern literature in general, I shall not attempt to decide. (pp. 172-81)

Edmund Wilson, "A Treatise on Tales of Horror," in his Classics and Commercials: A Literary Chronicle of the Forties, *Farrar, Straus and Giroux, Inc., 1950, pp. 172-81.*

RUSSELL KIRK

[*An American historian, political theorist, novelist, journalist, and lecturer, Kirk is one of America's most eminent conservative intellectuals. His works have provided a major impetus to the conservative revival that has developed since the 1950s. The Conservative Mind (1953), one of Kirk's early books, describes conservatism as a living body of ideas "struggling toward ascendancy in the United States"; in it the author traces the roots and canons of modern conservative thought to such important predecessors as Edmund Burke, John Adams, and Alexis de Tocqueville. In the following excerpt, Kirk argues that, in order to be convincing, supernatural fiction requires a grounding in theological tradition.*]

Most modern men having ceased to recognize their own souls, the spectral tale is out of fashion, especially in America. As Manning said, all differences of opinion at bottom are theological; and this fact has its bearing upon literary tastes. Because—even though they may be churchgoers—the majority of Americans do not really hunger after personal imortality, they cannot shiver at someone else's fictitious spirit.

Perhaps the cardinal error of the Enlightenment was the notion that dissolving old faiths, creeds, and loyalties would lead to a universal sweet rationalism. But deprive the common man of St. Salvator, and he will seek, at best, St. Science—even though he understands Darwin, say, no better than he understood Augustine. Credulity springs eternal, merely changing its garments from age to age. So if one takes away from man a belief in ghosts, it does not follow that thereafter he will concern himself wholly with Bright Reality; more probably, his fancy will seek some new field—possibly a worse realm.

Thus stories of the supernatural have been supplanted by "science-fiction." Though the talent of H. G. Wells did in that *genre* nearly everything worth undertaking, a flood of "scientific" and "futuristic" fantasies continues to deluge America. With few exceptions, these writings are banal and meaningless. My present point, however, is simply that many people today have a faith in "life in other planets" as burning and genuine as belief in a literal Heaven and a literal Hell was among twelfth-century folk, say—but upon authority far inferior. It is amusing to see physicists like Dr. Harlow Shapley, having abandoned all hope for this world (which obdurately refuses to become Utopia), declare enthusiastically that there *are* people away out yonder, for they have not one shred of scientific evidence. Having demolished, to their own satisfaction, the whole edifice of religious learning, abruptly and unconsciously they experience the need for belief in *something* not mundane; and so, defying their own inductive and mechanistic premises, they take up the cause of Martians and Jovians. As for angels and devils, let alone bogles—why, hell, such notions are superstitious!

But if the stubborn fact remains that although not one well-reputed person claims to have seen the men in the flying saucers, a great many well-reputed persons, over centuries, have claimed to have seen ghosts; or, more strictly speaking, to have perceived certain "psychic phenomena." From Pliny onward, the literature of our civilization is full of such relations. Scholars have analyzed soberly these appearances, from Father Noel Taillepied's *Treatise on Ghosts* (1588) to Father Herbert Thurston's *Ghosts and Poltergeists* (1955). *The Journal of the Society for Psychical Research* has examined painstakingly, for decades, the data of psychic manifestations. Eminent people so different in character as the Wesleys and Lord Castlereagh have been confronted by terrifying apparitions. (pp. 231-33)

At the end of his serious book *Apparitions,* Professor G.N.M. Tyrrell remarks, "Psychical research has certainly not drawn a blank. It has, on the contrary, discovered something so big that people sheer away from it in a reaction of fear." This is true; and possibly some day these mystifying events will be properly examined in a scientific spirit, classified, and somehow fitted into the natural sciences—though I doubt it. At present, such phenomena submit to neither rhyme nor reason: the revenant seems unpredictable and purposeless, and the poltergeist behaves like a feeble-minded child. Thus it is that the True Narration of ghostly happenings almost never attains to the condition of true literature. To guess at any significance in these manifestations, we still have to resort to literary art— that is, to fiction. And art, after all, is man's nature.

Because this limbo has no defined boundaries and interiorly remains *terra incognita,* the imaginative writer's fancy can wander there unburdened by the dreary impedimenta of twentieth-century naturalism. For symbol and allegory, the shadow-world is a far better realm than the hard, false "realism" of science fiction. A return to the ghostly and the Gothick might be one rewarding means of escape from the exhausted lassitude and inhumanity of the typical novel or short story of the Sixties.

Unlike the True Narration, the fictional ghostly tale can possess plot, theme, and purpose. It can piece together in some pattern the hints which seem thrown out by this or that vision or haunting or case of second-sight. It can touch keenly upon the old reality of evil—and upon injustice and retribution. It can reveal aspects of human conduct and longing to which the positivistic psychologist has blinded himself. And it still can be a first-rate yarn. (pp. 235-36)

Mr. Gerald Heard once said to me that the good ghost story must have for its base some clear premise as to the character of human existence—some theological assumption. A notable example of such a story is Heard's own best piece of fiction, which is believe to be the most impressive supernatural tale of recent years: "The Chapel of Ease," a long short story of a mystical Anglo-Catholic parson who prays for the tormented souls of gallows crows, their bones laid beneath his ancient and half-derelict chapel. Rising in the pews, their ghosts hate the man who struggles to save them; and in the end the pain of the contest is too much for the priest, and he dies. All this is told with a chilly power peculiar to a writer himself a mystic and a poet.

George Macdonald and his disciple C. S. Lewis employ the ghostly and supernatural means in letters for a moral and theological end; and from them the rising generation of authors ought to learn that naturalism is not the only road to higher reality. Indeed, for the writer who struggles to express moral truth, "realism" has become in our time a dead-end street; it fully deserves now the definition in Ambrose Bierce's *Devil's Dictionary:* "The art of depicting nature as it is seen by toads. The charm suffusing a landscape painted by a mole, or a story written by a measuring-worm."

Amid nineteenth-century meliorism, Emerson never could credit the reality of evil. But a good many twentieth-century writers are unable to credit the reality of anything except evil. Now it can be said of the better ghostly tale that it is underlain by a sound concept of the character of evil. Defying nature, the necromancer conjures up what ought not to rise again this side of Judgment Day. But these dark powers do not rule the universe; they are in rebellion against natural order; and by bell, book, and candle, literally or symbolically, we can push them down under. This truth runs through the priest's ghost stories in R. H. Benson's *The Light Invisible;* also it is implied in some of the eerie narrations of W. B. Yeats' *Mythologies.*

I venture to suggest that the more orthodox is a writer's theology, the more convincing, as symbols and allegories, his uncanny tales will be. One of the most unnerving of all spooky stories is Algernon Blackwood's "The Damned," which takes place in an ugly modern house where the cellars seem to be full of souls in torment, doled out little drops of water by the medium-housekeeper. But in its concluding pages—and this is true of too many of Blackwood's creations—the power of the story is much diminished when the reader is informed that, after all, the cellars aren't really Hell: it is merely that people who formerly lived in the house *believed* in Hell and so invested the place with an unpleasant aura. Because the Christian tradition, with its complex of symbol, allegory, and right reason, genuinely penetrates to spiritual depths and spiritual heights, the modern supernatural story which isolates itself from this authority drifts aimlessly down Styx.

Though Freudianism retains great popular influence today, as an intellectual force it is nearly spent; and Freud's naïve understanding of human nature must make way for older and greater insights. For Freudians and positivists, only the "natural" exists. The philosophical and ideological currents of a period necessarily affecting its imaginative literature, the supernatural in fiction has been somewhat ridiculous much of this century. But as the rising generation regains the awareness that "nature" is something more than mere fleshly sensation, and that something lies both above and below human nature—that reality, when all's said, is hierarchical—then authors may venture once more to employ myth and symbol, to resort to allegories of the divine and the diabolical as lawful literary instruments. And in this revival the ghostly tale may have its part. *Tenebrae* ineluctably form part of the nature of things.

But enough; I am turning into a ghostly comforter. I do not ask the artist in the fantastic to turn didactic moralist; and I trust that he will not fall into the error that the shapes under the hill are symbols *merely*. For the sake of his art, the author of ghostly narrations ought never to enjoy freedom from fear. As that formidable moralist Samuel Johnson lived in dread of real eternal torment—not mere "mental anguish"—so the "invisible prince," Sheridan Le Fanu, archetype of ghost-story writers, is believed to have died literally of fright. He knew that his creations were not his creations merely, but glimpses of the abyss. (pp. 237-40)

> *Russell Kirk, "A Cautionary Note on the Ghostly Tale," in his* The Surly Sullen Bell, *Fleet Publishing Corporation, 1962, pp. 231-40.*

WALTER DE LA MARE

[*An English poet, novelist, short story writer, dramatist, and critic, de la Mare is considered one of modern literature's chief exemplars of the romantic imagination. His complete works form a sustained treatment of romantic themes: dreams, death, rare states of mind and emotion, fantasy worlds of childhood, and the pursuit of the transcendent. Best remembered as a poet and writer of children's verse, de la Mare is also recognized for his novel* Memoirs of a Midget *(1921), a study of the social and spiritual outsider, a concern central to his work. In the following excerpt, de la Mare illuminates the purpose and effect of the ghost story by comparing it with the detective story.*]

Detective stories and ghost stories . . . have a good deal in common, and the differences between them are peculiarly interesting. It is unlikely, too, to be a mere coincidence that, apart from a few scattered specimens of either kind of a date prior to Dickens and Edgar Allan Poe—that double-minded man of genius who was responsible both for "The Fall of the House of Usher" and "The Murders in the Rue Morgue"—the two *genres* began to flourish pretty much at the same time. Sheridan le Fanu's *Uncle Silas* and Wilkie Collins's *Moonstone* were published within five years of one another. And neither novelist has been outrivalled in his own most characteristic vein.

Moreover did not the author of *The Confessions of an English Opium-Eater* decant "Murder as One of the Fine Arts?" Devotees, too, of either order of story may delight—and not for entirely different reasons—in both. For my part, if by a stroke of good fortune the evening postman brought me two books, each of them a masterpiece in either kind, I should read the ghost story first, but perhaps a little more rapidly than usual, in order to get busy with the crime.

In both kinds of story a hunt is up. While reading them, that is, we are in fevered chase of what for some little time is to incite, evade and elude us; in the one a criminal, in the other what may be called the ghostly. As soon, however—and may the eventuality be deferred as long as possible!—as soon as we are sure of the criminal, as soon as he is securely within the nets of the law, or has escaped them for ever, our interest alike in spider, fly and web is apt rapidly to wane. *Finis* usually leaves us a little cold. And the tale fades quickly out of mind. Never so with a fine ghost story. That leaves us—as it should leave us.

In the detective story, again, we are beckoned on by a series of hints, clues, intimations, false or true in scent—selected by our Auguste Dupin, Sherlock Holmes, Dr. Thorndyke, Father Brown or another—which in passing we either attempt to weave together—or (as is usual with the indolent) are content merely to watch being woven together on our behalf. We go through this process possibly in a slightly excited but not necessarily in a rapt state of mind. Such "reactions" as horror, disgust, compassion may occur, but none of these is essential, simply because our author is providing us with a feast for the wits rather than for the emotions. The most scientific our specimen the less it is likely to bother about our sympathies. Little more than the rational powers are involved, the faculty that pieces a puzzle together. Not usually much imagination, still more rarely any profound stirring of the waters or fine æsthetic sensibility. We intently watch our Sherlock Holmes; we may respect, admire, marvel at, trust him. We don't often *become* him. He may even—and as a matter of fact, he does—win from us a sort of devotion. If, however, he remains aloof, aloof he may remain. The "case" will not suffer.

In the ghost story, on the other hand, the hints and clues, the decoy notes, stir and arouse states of feelings. They are the furtive fingerings of the breeze, and we the harp-strings. It proceeds towards it *dénouement*, and that may be soft as the whisper of the south wind, by evoking in us a series of unusual sensations and of rarified conditions of mind. Here also terror, horror, disgust, compassion, even reassurance or resignation, may be our final reward. But from its first page onwards, by means of subtle and cumulative innuendoes, every master-word a talisman, we must be laid under such a spell as will induce us to realize that we are in the presence and under the influence of something as far beyond normal sensibilities as it is beyond human control. Apprehension even of the skeletal hand of the Law is coarse by comparison.

Our detective, again, is chiefly intent on giving us the essential *facts* of the case, however artfully he may arrange and disguise them, and however rich his narrative may be in those priceless little sidelights on earthly life and human nature that may be incidental to it. In respect indeed to this harvest of sidelights we might even prefer his case to be a genuine case, since in all that most closely concerns human life no detective story is comparable to a carefully edited Trial, a trial reported *verbatim* and even *ad nauseam;* and this even though in the trial the villain of the piece is already in the dock and the issue never in doubt.

Facts as mere facts, on the other hand, are not the quarry of the ghost story. We must be made to believe in it. At its best it gives us imaginative truth. As with all fine fiction its illusion is its soverign charm. To be informed in a brief epilogue that such a story is even so much as *founded* on fact is nothing but a shattering anti-climax. "Atmosphere," then, is all important. As regards characters, setting, scene, circumstances, in both kinds of story they are of course in service to one main object, the story itself. But in the one kind—apart from the bizarre addition of the crime—they can be entirely commonplace; as indeed when Dr. Watson is master of the ceremonies they usually are. In the other kind they must never remain so. They must somehow be sicklied over with the pale cast of the phantasmal.

Then again, any story founded on a crime, and complete with its corpse (and few good detective stories are innocent of this fatal encumbrance), transports us into a region of the sinister and the dangerous which to the sensitive or conscience-ridden even the knock of a policeman at the door, or a glimpse of the gilded blindfold figure of Justice stooping her head over the cupola of the New Bailey, at once faintly hints at. The equivalent of this feat in the ghost story is the gradual conviction that this workaday actuality of ours—with its bricks, its streets, its woods, its hills, its waters—may have queer and, possibly, terrifying holes in it. And just as the criminal, until at least he stands revealed, is something of a ghost, fugitive and not as yet definitely embodied, so the ghost in some degree resembles the criminal. He is anomalous. He skulks or sighs outside the safe and the secure. Like the criminal, he is something we might be; but not, please God, as yet.

And even if in the ghost story we are given the evidence by which we may, if we so please, explain its ghost away, that evidence must not at any rate convince us that there was never *anything* to explain. Our interest, too, in the criminal as such has a good deal in common with our interest in the ghost as such. Both species are not only alien to the common run of things, but any close concern with either is to some minds morbid. And though this morbid is nothing but a scarecrow of a word, which, like a candle in a hollow turnip, need alarm only the ignorant, there it is. Yet the talk that kept Tennyson and Jowett up latest was talk about criminals. The talk that apparently never failed to engross Henry James was talk about the latest murder case. If minds so dissimilar as these were morbid—we must look elsewhere for the healthy. And if the Press is the looking-glass of Everyman, we shan't have to look a long way.

It is a strange fact, none the less, if this peculiar *penchant* be taken into account, that the murderer—even though he be the most infamous of his kind—is by no means necessarily an "interesting" human being. Even at his own trial, though he may be the most engrossed and is certainly the most closely observed, he is probably also the least "interested" creature in the court. One word from him, and that, we might assume, continually on the tip of his tongue, and this portentous panorama of justice, with all its conflicting tongues and rumours around him, would melt, dissolve and leave not a wrack behind. The murderer that pleads guilty, in short, is unlikely to become a popular character. Indeed it was a doleful hour for the sensationalist when Hare and his dreadful spouse became King's Evidence.

As for the host, though there *are* interesting ghosts in fiction . . . they are exceptional. In general, and Dr. James for one would prefer it so, they are very much the reverse of engaging. And whether they are engaging or not, actually to re-embody the usual kind of phantasm confronted in a ghost story, would be the worst possible service one could do for him—so far, that is, as making more interesting company of him is concerned.

So also with the murderer in the current detective story, which tends to be less and less concerned with psychology. He is "interesting" only, or chiefly, because he *is* a murderer, not because he is this particular specimen of a man. By a process

of self-delusion we may of course *make* him interesting, by taking him to be in himself what we ourselves might be in *our*selves if we ourselves had murder on our souls. Similarly, our ghost is "interesting" not because he was once a man, but merely because, whatever kind of man he once was, he is now reduced to a ghost, which is by no means the same process, according to authority, as that of a soul made secure in its freedom from the body.

These are only the bare bones of the matter, for the more interesting *per se* both murderers and ghosts are made to appear, so much the more interesting on this account will be the stories about them. Mrs. Florence Barclay, the author of *The Rosary,* is said to have returned thanks to Heaven that she had never admitted to the hospitality of her fiction any character whom she would not have welcomed to the Vicarage and to afternoon tea. That being so, we may be tempted to look a little askance perhaps at one or two of the characters that do make their appearance in her novels. Any such prejudice at any rate was a severe handicap to her ever becoming an expert in either kind of story now in mind.

Other authors have been less squeamish, but even to them a choice in far less respectable guests was open. And if it were merely a question of interest, one would rather perhaps share "tea and scandal" with Dr. Crippen, or with Charles Lamb's friend, Wainewright, "kind, lighthearted Wainewright," or even with his namesake (without the e) Henry, in much "a humane and kind-hearted man," or with Charles Peace—who, apart from other activities was an expert on mime, the fiddle and circumstantial evidence—than with, say, Seddon, Mrs. Manning or the atrocious Burke. And even Burke—when in the dock he heard the foreman of the Jury announce their verdict regarding the guilt of his fellow-pannel, Helen McDougal—"Not Proven"—turned to her, it is said, with a genuine smile of pleasure on his face: "Nelly," said he, "you are out of the scrape," and calmly awaited the pronouncement of his own doom." Apart from Dr. Crippen—who by all accounts was a friendly soul, and at the dreadful crisis of his life courageous—all these men were dangerous human beings. None the less, the first little group had the pleasanter brains.

Brains in ghosts are less material. Miss Jessel, for example, is likely, I fancy, to have been a more interesting companion in real life for qualities both of head and heart—so at least those glimpses of her on the other side of the pond watching the little girl with her toy boat, and in the nursery, weeping in the light of the window, seem to suggest—that Peter Quint can ever have been; though, alive, neither of them possibly would have held us spell-bound. But as ghost, Peter Quint is immeasurably the more deadly and impressive figure. If indeed the writer of ghost stories can invest his ghost with powers of the mind and imagination transcending not merely those of most of us, but his own when he was incarnate, then that writer's fiction will certainly not be the less valuable or impressive. Nor are we likely to resent meeting a murderer in fiction innocent of all suffocating hatred, darkness, meanness and stagnant horror, but guilty of murder for all that.

The company of Macbeth is, if anything even more enthralling after the murder of Duncan than it was before the crime. He is himself a haunted man with the first words he utters, "So fair and foul a day I have not seen . . ." And though Banquo's talk in Act II, Scene I, individualises him more clearly than any other passage, he hardly comes vividly alive or positively engrossing, at any rate in the same degree as Macbeth himself, until he is dead—yet walks again. In the supper scene, even though he be but a phantasm of his murderer's mind, he lives in very deed, and with the most curious luminousness—as of an unearthly coloured flame; like that, as I have read somewhere, which softly hovers over molten gold.

And last, from a technical point of view, the current detective story *need* only be decently written—concise, coherent, lucid, straightforward. One purple patch in the first chapter, but no flowers by request. In scenes so violent, in company so unendearing, in a style so terse, if not occasionally bald, we are not likely to be shocked by a split infinitive or a suspended relative—of either kind. It can even easily survive considerable quantities of American slang. So, but far less easily, *might* the ghost story. "Madam Crowl's Ghost" is, indeed, immensely enriched by the dialect of the child who tells the tale:

> It was a fine moonlight night, and I eat the apples, lookin' out o' the shay winda.... It is a shame for gentlemen to frighten a poor foolish child like I was.... There was two on 'em on the top o' the coach beside me. And they began to question me after nightfall.... "Ho, then," says one of them, "you'll not be long there!"

But this enrichment comes about not so much because her narrative is in dialect, as because it so tellingly conveys her country simplicity and naivety as compared with the bedizened, wicked, astute old woman, at odds with the evil one, God's Ape. "Lawk! But her nose was crooked and thin, and half the whites o' her eyes was open." The fine ghost story on the other hand must be far more than decently, it should be excellently written—every word, every cadence, every metaphor apt to the matter in hand. Here the finer shades make a supreme difference; not merely the dot over the *i* but where it's put. How else is all that is meant by atmosphere to be conveyed?

In what different aspects, too—relative to its powers, its intelligence, its methods, its intent and so on—may the spectral present itself!—the taciturn, evasive, famished guest in "Keeping His Promise," the visitor from over the Atlantic in "Afterward," the romantic "Fair One" in Mr. Oliver Onions' story, and the corrosive field in "Green Tea"—as compact of energy as the star which secretes itself in the company of the radiant Sirius.

And the objects around them—from the hard, bright moon in the heavens to the glittering scrap of glass bottle at the roadside, from the clock tattling on the chimney-piece to the squatting chairs—should seem as it were to condense their specific qualities under this influence. Enthusiasts from the C.I.D., contrariwise, hardly augment the human or spiritual significance of the objects they fix their stoat-like glance on. They make of them "exhibits," dingied or poisoned by the company they have been in. But when ghosts are about, objects become symbols. They too, like revenants themselves, waver in being, between two worlds.

There are few little feats indeed so subtle in operation as that of lulling and exciting the reader into the state of mind and fantasy essential in such a story. What wonder if a consummate specimen is a singularly rare achievement—since not merely the least verbal blunder, but even a momentary lapse from the requisite delicacy may be fatal to its effect?... So delicate indeed is this poise that it might perhaps have been an advantage to *The Turn of the Screw* as a story if the author of it had kept its origin dark. That a sort of refuse, of foreign matter, clings about the roots of any little green shoot from the actual that may flourish at last in full bloom in the imagination—a refuse that must at all costs be allowed no entry there—is emphasised

by Henry James himself. He would listen for a few sentences like a child, like that one of three in "The Ancient Mariner," to any such story in real life. Then, an expostulatory hand would be raised, a deaf ear turned. Oh, the just enough and how much it is! The little more and what worlds away! (pp. 18-27)

A critic . . . of *The Turn of the Screw* once suggested that its author neither intended to give us nor has actually given us a tittle of evidence that there were any ghosts in the house called Bly at all; that he merely introduces us, intimately enough, to an hysterical governess in love with her refractory charges' uncle and the slave of a disease fancy. . . . But while it is true that any experience of a similar nature in actuality can be as neatly dismissed—and morning coffee, toast and eggs and bacon are a wonderful antidote against the night-side of nature—one may speculate if in the centuries gone by the organism that first began to experience the effects of the rudiments of an eye sought its remedy in a privy dose of vervain or valerian. Or did it begin to boast itself of being "psychic," or claim the acquisition of a fifth sense?

"Well, gentlemen" says Fr. Girdlestone [in R. H. Benson's "Father Girdlestone's Tale"] to his fellow-ecclesiastics in the upstairs sala in Rome:

> "Well, gentlemen, I was aware during those seconds . . . that I had, as it were, stepped through the crust of the world of sense and even of intellectual thought. What I perceived of a person watching me was not of this plane at all. It was not one who in any sense had a human existence, who had ever had one, or ever would. It did not in the least resemble therefore an apparition of the dead."

Nowhere in the course of his story, it may be noted, does Fr. Girdlestone confide in us where or when he had seen any apparition of the dead which he asserts this person did not resemble. But the phrase brings to mind the words that Wycliffe put into the mouth of the mother of Samson, when she tells her husband how she has seen the messenger of God: "His look was like the look of an angel." So too: "And it came to pass when Joshua was by Jericho that he lifted up his eyes and looked and behold there stood a man over against him with his sword drawn in his hand." What lurks in these words, when read in their context, that so profoundly affects the mind; and in the same fashion as do certain salient moments in our everyday life when what is around us appears to become so strangely less like—what it usually seems to be like? (pp. 30-1)

> *Walter de la Mare, in an introduction to* They Walk Again: An Anthology of Ghost Stories, *edited by Colin de la Mare, E. P. Dutton & Co., Inc., 1942, pp. 9-32.*

THE TECHNIQUE OF THE GHOST STORY

PETER PENZOLDT

[*In the following excerpt, Penzoldt analyzes the structure of modern ghost stories.*]

Chekhov held that a story should have neither a beginning nor an end: but he reminded authors that if they have on page one described a gun hanging on the wall, sooner or later that gun must go off. On the other hand, Mr. Ellery Sedgewick has compared the short story with a horse-race. To him the start and the finish appear to be the most important things about it. Although diametrically opposed, both descriptions are true: they simply apply to the works of two different schools. The first school consists of those writers who have kept close to the naturalistic tradition, and, deliberately neglecting the rules of composition, based their work solely on a close and matter-of-fact study of life. The second school, whose views are more in the English tradition, holds that structure is the essential of any work of art. Though the different techniques favoured by these schools are often combined in the short story, a rough division of all short stories may be made, according to the predominating technique. But the ghost story, although it is usually in the English tradition, cannot be fitted into either of these divisions. Its structure is peculiar to itself, and must be treated as a separate genre.

Let us examine more closely why a ghost story with neither beginning nor end is impossible, and why the beginning in this particular genre is not likely to have the same importance as the end. In his fine collection of ghost stories Alexander Laing gives the following short paragraph entitled "Climax for a Ghost Story":

> "How *eerie*!" said the girl advancing cautiously. "And what a heavy door!" She touched it as she spoke and it suddenly swung to with a click.
>
> "Good Lord!" said the man, "I don't believe there's a handle inside. Why, you've locked us both in!"
>
> "Not both of us. Only one of us," said the girl, and before his eyes she passed straight through the door and vanished.

This might be simply the climax of a modern ghost story. But among primitive people, fishermen or peasants in a lonely mountain valley, or perhaps children, where ghost stories are still what they used to be, tales told by the fireside on a dreary winter evening, they are usually no longer than this paragraph. Wherever ghost stories are still accepted as truth, they contain nothing but the account of the apparition. For the listeners that is all that matters. They actually believe what they are told and are entranced, however short the story may be. For the educated reader it is different: he does not believe; he has to be convinced, and put into the right mood by a cleverly created atmosphere. Step by step the author leads him away from his everyday life into the realm of pure fantasy. When the spook finally appears, the reader must have wandered so far in imagination that he becomes a prey to those fears which reason would at once dispel. The climax in a ghost story is obviously the appearance of the spectre. It is evident, therefore, that the ghost story in its original form consists of nothing but the single climax. The modern literary ghost story also has a single climax, but this climax is preceded by the long exposition which is necessary to build up the atmosphere. Thus the structure of the ideal ghost story may be visualised as an ascending line leading up to the climax. There is no reason why there should be anything after the climax, except perhaps some explanations.

Now let us consider Chekhov's definition again. If the climax is the most important part if not the whole of the ghost story, and if its place is naturally at the end, a ghost story without an end cannot be imagined. Sedgewick's definition would be equally false. The beginning is only part of the exposition, a preparation for the climax at the end. Manifestly it would be absurd to give beginning and end the same importance. Thus it is the position and exceptional importance of the climax that chiefly distinguish the ghost story from the other types of short story.

As the climax consists of that manifestation of the supernatural on which the whole story centres, it may be expected to coincide with the denouement. Yet this is not always the case. Many stories, especially the longer ones, contain a number of apparitions. In such cases the author usually seeks to make the last appearance of the spectre the climax of the story. Either the recognition of the supernatural agency as such is postponed until then or "It" finally commits some deed of violence. The preceding manifestations cannot therefore be considered as a second, third and fourth climax; they must rather be looked on as forming part of the exposition and as being nothing but a preparation for the finale. We find this type of story throughout the [nineteenth and twentieth centuries]. Bram Stoker in "The Judge's House" uses it, as well as William Fryar Harvey several decades later. Harvey's "The Beast with Five Fingers" may afford a good example:

Shortly before his death, a certain Adrian Borlsover develops the power of automatic writing. Some being takes possession of his hand, and begins to communicate with his nephew Eustace. Thus the story opens with a manifestation of the supernatural. With his legacy from Adrian Borlsover, the nephew receives a small box containing a queer animal. It is the "beast with five fingers," his uncle's embalmed hand, animated by an evil spirit. The monster escapes and begins to haunt the house. One apparition follows another, until finally the hand is caught by Borlsover, nailed to a board, and shut up in the safe. Up to this point the suspense does not vary in intensity from apparition to apparition; no one event is sufficiently predominant to be called a climax. Tension and atmosphere neither increase nor decrease. This is because, until Borlsover tortures it, the "beast with five fingers" is nothing but an aimless presence. Its existence, not its action, is alarming. The reader would be amused rather than frightened by blinds pulled up or lights switched off for no reason at all, unless he knew that a mummified hand was doing the mischief. But from the moment that some burglars let the beast escape from the safe, it has a purpose, vengeance, and the tension of the story steadily tightens. As expected it finishes with Borlsover's death. Before the final catastrophe, we have a description of the victim's hopeless flight, his nervous breakdown and the last letter announcing his death, written by the embalmed hand. The story ends when the victim, thinking himself safe with his friend in a locked room, realises that "The Thing" can get in through the chimney.

> Saunders was standing with his glass half raised. "It can get in," he said hoarsely; "It can get in! We've forgotten. There's the fireplace in my bedroom. It will come down the chimney."
>
> "Quick!" said Eustace, as he rushed into the other room; "We haven't a minute to lose. What can we do? Light the fire, Saunders. Give me a match, quick!"
>
> "They must all be in the other room. I'll get them."
>
> "Hurry, man, for goodness' sake! Look in the bookcase! Look in the bathroom! Here, come and stand here; I'll look."
>
> "Be quick!" shouted Saunders. "I can hear something!"
>
> "Then plug a sheet from your bed up the chimney. No, here's a match." He had found one at last that had slipped into a crack in the floor.
>
> "Is the fire laid? Good, but it may not burn. I know—the oil from that old reading-lamp and this cotton wool. Now the match, quick! Pull the sheet away, you fool! We don't want it now."

There was a great roar from the grate as the flames shot up. Saunders had been a fraction of a second too late with the sheet. The oil had fallen on to it. It, too, was burning.

"The whole place will be on fire!" cried Eustace, as he tried to beat out the flames with a blanket. "It's no good! I can't manage it. You must open the door, Saunders, and get help."

Saunders ran to the door and fumbled with the bolts. The key was stiff in the lock.

"Hurry!" shouted Eustace; "the whole place is ablaze!"

The key turned in the lock at last. For half a second Saunders stopped to look back. Afterwards he could never be quite sure as to what he had seen, but at the time he thought that something black and charred was creeping slowly, very slowly, from the masses of flames towards Eustace Borlsover. For a moment he thought of returning to his friend, but the noise and the smell of the burning sent him running down the passage crying, "Fire! Fire!" He rushed to the telephone to summon help, and then back to the bathroom—he should have thought of that before—for water. As he burst open the bedroom door there came a scream of terror which ended suddenly and then the sound of a heavy fall.

The modern reader of ghost stories is naturally a sceptic, and a considerable amount of atmosphere has to be created in order to get him into the right mood. Yet atmosphere alone, however cleverly it may be built up, is rarely sufficient. Our reasonable age wishes to be convinced as well as bewitched. That does not mean that the author induces us to reason logically. A certain pseudo-logic, accepting the supernatural, is used instead. For example, in Alexander Woollcott's "Full Fathom Five" the ghost of a sailor appears, leaving behind him traces of water and a piece of seaweed. The story would inevitably miss its full effect unless we knew that the sailor was drowned after having been chased from home by a cruel father, and that the seaweed he left behind was of the special kind that only grows on corpses. These details, which form a sort of explanation that makes the story plausible, and therefore all the more horrible, are an integral part of the climax. When such devices as these are used, it becomes difficult to place the climax at the end.

This brings us to the question of the "double climax." I have to introduce this term, in order to distinguish this particular type of tale from those stories which show a succession of two, three or more climaxes. The use of more than one climax in a short story tends to diminish rather than augment its effect. It is as if one climax destroyed the other. The exposition and the atmosphere built up are a preparation for the climax. Each climax has its own particular features, and to these the exposition has to be exactly adapted. Thus if the same exposition has to serve for two climaxes, a discordance is unavoidable. Also, the first climax usually dispels the atmosphere built up in the exposition, and there is nothing left for the second climax. The reader comes upon it unprepared; he is no longer in the right mood, and so becomes wearied, and thinks the whole story ridiculous and absurd. Now the double climax has none of these disadvantages. It does not consist of two apparitions, but of one, followed by the necessary explanation. Only the knowledge of what is behind a manifestation conveys the full horror of it. "So that is why it walked at night!" "That's why the ghost killed the person who had wronged him in his lifetime." Everything becomes clear, and for that all the more

horrible. The reader is no longer able to "laugh it off" as something absurd. The eternal question—Is there a supernatural world with laws of its own, or are phantoms no more than pure hallucination?—is posed once more. The more suddenly the explanation is given, the more dramatic is the effect it produces. It should shock the reader. One could speak of a flashlight technique. Understanding should burst upon him as the daylight floods into a room when the shutters are flung back. If the truth dawns slowly the effect of surprise is lost. This is why many modern authors prefer to use only a few words. An object, for example a globe containing human ashes, discovered in a haunted maze ["Mr. Humphreys' Inheritance," M. R. James], may be sufficient to make the reader understand that some evil ancestor buried there did the haunting. In the classical tale there is usually a skeleton discovered behind the wainscot, and some explanation is added of how it got there. The most striking effect is obtained, if the explanation, or the object which forms the explanation, has in itself a supernatural, or at least an uncanny, character. For this reason most writers find it best to avoid too much precision in what they choose to reveal. An explanation that appeals to reason would destroy the reader's momentary belief in the supernatural.

One of the best examples of the double climax is certainly "The Treasure of Abbot Thomas" [by M. R. James]. An English gentleman manages to decipher a cryptogram concerning a treasure hidden centuries ago in the well of a German monastery. There are some allusions to a guardian watching the gold. The Englishman undertakes to lift out the treasure, and climbs down into the well, while his servant holds the rope. He finds the marked stone, mentioned in the cryptogram, removes it, and tries to pull out the bags from the cavity behind. Instead of them, he gets hold of a horrible slimy monster. With great difficulty, he escapes, and a friend of his replaces the stone in broad daylight. This is how the story ends:—

"I dare say it was, Gregory; but, thank goodness, that is over. Have you by the way, anything to tell me about your visit to that dreadful place?"

"Very little," was the answer. "Brown and I managed easily enough to get the slab into its place, and he fixed it very firmly with the irons and wedges you had desired him to get, and we contrived to smear the surface with mud so that it looks just like the rest of the wall. One thing I did notice in the carving on the well-head, which I think must have escaped you. It was a horrid grotesque shape—perhaps more like a toad than anything else, and there was a label by it inscribed with the two words Depositum custodi. ('Keep that which is committed to thee.')"

The carved figure on the well-head, and the mysterious Latin sentence, are comment enough. They hint to what must have happened down in the well, explain a little, but leave plenty to the reader's imagination. What makes this ending so perfect is that the apparition is explained by something which also bears the seal of the supernatural.

Many stories with a well-placed climax are followed by a short paragraph which does not really belong to the rest of the story. It tells us what people thought later about the events related, or how some of the main characters continued to be affected by what they had experienced. Such an *Ausklang*, as the Germans call it, has nothing to do with the double climax, and rather spoils the unity of the story. In his collection, Alexander Laing simply leaves out the *Ausklang* of "The Beast with Five Fingers." Personally I can only approve the judgment of this eminent anthologist. (pp. 15-20)

[In] a majority of ghost stories the double-climax technique is probably employed because it represents a more elaborate form and yields more possibilities for surprise and *coups de théâtre*. Yet it should also be kept in mind that it is easier to place an explanation at the end of a story than to write the exposition in such a manner that a simple climax is the perfect denouement.

The beginnings of ghost stories can be divided into three clearly separated groups:—

> A. Those in which the very first sentences hint directly at the climax.

> B. Those which immediately start working up an atmosphere, by the description of a gloomy landscape, an eerie old mansion, and so on.

> C. Those which open like any other short story, by referring to no supernatural element at all.

In their psychological effect, A and B are very closely related. They are more common in the nineteenth-century writers, but are also found in later stories.

A. The direct allusion to the climax is used in what is perhaps the first true ghost story written in English. This is how Daniel Defoe's "Mrs. Veal" begins:—

> This thing is so rare in all its circumstances, and on so good authority, that my reading and conversation has not given me anything like it. It is fit to gratify the most ingenious and serious inquirer. Mrs. Bargrave is the person to whom Mrs. Veal appeared after her death.

In the nineteenth century, Bulwer Lytton, Sheridan Le Fanu, Frederick Marryat, and other early ghost-story writers, showed a preference for this particular type of beginning. Here is an example from Bulwer Lytton's best-known story. "The Haunted and the Haunters":

> A friend of mine who is a man of letters and a philosopher, said to me one day, as if between jest and earnest—"Fancy! since we last met, I have discovered a haunted house in the midst of London."

> "Really haunted?—and by what—ghosts?"

There are, of course, more recent examples, although they are fewer in number. Modern authors are usually more delicate and less direct in their allusions. They are more careful to avoid revealing too much, and so reducing the tension. W. F. Harvey, for example, begins his story "Sambo" with the sentence "One thing is certain, Arthur should never have sent Janey the Doll," thus implying that there is some horror connected with the doll, but providing the reader with no further clue.

The reason why most modern authors have abandoned this type of opening is probably that it destroys the effect of surprise which is so necessary to the climax. Besides, it is difficult to maintain a suspense which is created by the very first words instead of being built up gradually. In many cases, the author allows it to drop after the beginning, and then resumes the usual increasing tension.

B. The most common opening is nothing more than a first step in the creation of the atmosphere. I quote here from "Squire Toby's Will," by Sheridan Le Fanu, but early ghost-story writers have by no means the monopoly of this type of beginning:

> Many persons accustomed to travel the old York and London road, in the days of stage-coaches, will remember passing, in the afternoon, say, of an autumn day, in their journey to the capital, about three miles south of the town of Applebury, and a mile and a half before you reach the old Angel Inn, a large black-and-white house, as those old-fashiond cage-work habitations are termed, dilapidated and weather-stained, with broad lattice windows glimmering all over in the evening sun with little diamond panes, and thrown into relief by a dense background of ancient elms. A wide avenue, now overgrown like a churchyard with grass and weeds, and flanked by double rows of the same dark trees, old and gigantic, with here and there a gap in their solemn files, and sometimes a fallen tree lying across on the avenue, leads up to the hall-door.

There are numerous possibilities besides the description of gloomy places. The introduction of a sense of foreboding, the feeling of being watched by inanimate objects, or a discussion of the supernatural by the characters in the story, are most of the most common devices. Here again later authors have had the most original ideas. For example, M. R. James begins his story "The Treasure of Abbott Thomas" with a full page and a half of Latin, thus cleverly putting to use the mysterious atmosphere which always surrounds old parchments and the sound of a dead language.

C. A story that is begun in a casual manner has the great advantage of keeping up the suspense until the climax is reached. The less we expect the intervention of the supernatural, the more impressive its sudden appearance will be. M. R. James was especially fond of this kind of beginning. This is how "The Haunted Doll's House" begins:

> "I suppose you get stuff of that kind through your hands pretty often?" said Mr. Dillet, as he pointed with his stick to an object which shall be described when the time comes: and when he said it, he lied in his throat, and knew that he lied. Not once in twenty years—perhaps not once in a life-time—could Mr. Chittenden, skilled as he was in ferreting out the forgotten treasures of half a dozen counties, expect to handle such a specimen. It was collectors' palaver, and Mr. Chittenden recognized it as such.

> "Stuff of that kind, Mr. Dillet! It's a museum piece, that is."

> "Well, I suppose there are museums that'll take anything."

Most recent authors choose to begin their stories in this fashion, but it is important to point out that this sort of opening was used as early as Walter Scott's "Tapestried Chamber" (1827) and Dickens's *Christmas Books*.

My analysis of the climax, and position of the climax, has been based on the fact that the exposition is nothing but a preparation for the climax. Therefore in a methodical study of the exposition we must talk what kind of exposition a particular climax requires. This leads us to the more general question, namely—what have all climaxes of ghost stories in common? The most obvious characteristic they seem to share is that none of them is believed. Can we, the children of a scientific age, give any credence to apparitions and psychical invasions? Yet the fact is that we can and do. We are dealing with stories, not with scientific dissertations, and if, as stories, they have the ring of truth, we will believe them as stories, implicitly. Now it is the exposition that makes the tale appear likely. In short, it makes a story out of what would else have remained the simple narrative of an event so fantastic that we would never have given it the slightest credence. In the exposition more than anywhere else, the artist appears, he challenges and defeats reality in the name of poetry, he becomes a demiurge and a magician. "I have the literary courage to face unbelief," writes Fitz-James O'Brien at the beginning of one of his finest stories; and long before him, Coleridge, discussing the *Lyrical Ballads,* said: "It was agreed that my endeavours should be directed to persons and characters supernatural, or at least romantic; yet so as to transfer from our inward nature a human interest and a semblance of truth sufficient to procure for these shadows of imagination that willing suspension of disbelief for the moment, which constitutes poetic faith."

It is our task to examine what artifice can be employed to induce the reader to accept the supernatural, and willingly suspend his disbelief. Most writers try to achieve a certain gradation, by hinting, first vaguely, and then more and more directly, at the climax. For example, in a typical ghost story there is first some occurrence that indicates the presence of a ghost, then the spectre appears but is not recognised as such; finally the presence of the supernatural can no longer be denied, and the story reaches its climax. Just as the position of the climax, and the different types of introduction, have hardly changed in the last hundred years, so this particular technique has varied little since Edgar Allan Poe created the prototype in "Ligeia" (1838) and "The Fall of the House of Usher" (1839).

Like all types of short stories, the ghost story had to struggle hard during the last century to find its proper form. In the early nineteenth century, when it was still a new form of art, some features of the novel on the one hand and the essay on the other can be clearly distinguished in it. In the eighteenth century it was usual to insert something resembling brief short stories either in a collection of essays or in the essay itself. Often these "short stories" were only narratives of events; sometimes they represented real fiction. Usually they taught a moral lesson. The work of Leigh Hunt contains some very good examples of this kind of essay writing. Some of the early ghost-story writers simply turned this process round, and adorned their stories with what are really short essays on metaphysics or science. Poe, in "The Gold Bug" (1843), "The Imp of the Perverse" (1845), "The Facts in the Case of M. Valdemar" (1845) and "A Mesmeric Revelation" (1845), proceeded in this manner. We find the same type of essay in Bulwer Lytton's "The Haunted and the Haunters" and Joseph Sheridan Le Fanu's "Green Tea" (1869). All are, of course, early writers. Their idea, apparently, was to give more probability to their stories by expounding some scientific or philosophical theory which they believed to be convincing. By discussing the supernatural as such, they managed to induce in the reader that peculiar state of half-belief which often results from a mere conversation on the subject. Later authors abandoned this technique; probably because they thought that it interrupted the narrative, destroyed the unity of the story, and tired the reader, who was more easily convinced by events clearly narrated than by theories he was likely to disbelieve.

In their length, the construction of their plots, and the sort of descriptions employed, the earlier ghost stories show the influence of the novel. Development of character, and the onward movement of time, have always been, and perhaps always will be, the pulse and nerve of the novel. They necessarily appear in any piece of prose fiction of a certain length. If a short story grows past a certain length, it is liable to become a short novel. Of course, any sort of development makes a more elaborate plot necessary, and such a plot, unless it be the plot of a play, requires more than a single climax. Conversely, only devel-

opment makes a series of independent climaxes possible; for then each of them appears in new circumstances, and is thus automatically preceded by a new exposition. Dickens, for example, avoided the danger which repeated climaxes usually involve by writing his *Christmas Books* as short novels with a clear development of character. Arthur Machen used a quite different technique to deal with the same difficulty. Development is totally absent from most of his stories. They are neither short novels nor real short stories, but are composed of a number of chapters, each of which could be considered as an independent short story, with its own exposition and climax. They are merely held together by a *Rahmenerzählung* ["framing narrative"]. Dickens has found no imitators of his method of handling his climaxes; Machen has only one: H. P. Lovecraft.

The early ghost stories also remind us of the novel in the length of their descriptions. Victorian writers loved long descriptions, and their public demanded them. If, to-day, we hear of a south-sea island, we are able to picture it at once. A short-story writer who chooses such scenery for his action need not waste words in describing the sand, the palms, and so on, for films, magazines, the radio and travelling, as modern means permit it, have given us a sufficient idea of what such places are like. This is the case with almost every imaginable setting. The scenery appropriate to the ghost story is no exception. There have been dozens of movies on the subject. In most countries there are numbers of horror and ghost stories read or acted on the radio, while comics endeavour to give us a clear picture of Frankenstein's and other monsters' secret lives. But the Victorian reader had to imagine every detail himself, and accordingly the author had to assist him. The result was the typically Victorian style of description. Even to-day this does not surprise us in a novel of two hundred thousand words, but in a short story of ten pages three pages of detailed description are now too much, and above all in a ghost story, where action is most important and cannot be constantly interrupted. This may explain why the earlier authors, with only a few exceptions, gradually disappear from anthologies. Another reason may be that their over-description of the events takes all terror from the supernatural.

In conclusion, it is worth noting that the exposition is that part of the story that literature adds to the primitive, orally-told tale. If the climax is not too absurd, and if the structure of the story is such that suspense is kept up until the end, the exposition makes all the difference between a good and a bad story. It reveals the author's personal art. . . . It is difficult to generalise, for there are scarcely any two authors who treat the exposition in the same way. . . . Nevertheless, it seems possible to discern the outline of a historical development: long descriptions and pseudo-scientific explanations appear in the short story while it still retains some of the characteristics of the novel and the essay. Towards the end of the nineteenth century when the short story becomes more and more an independent genre, these features disappear and action becomes all-important.

Thus the exposition of the ghost story has developed in much the same way as the exposition of the short story; but in all other respects the ghost story has a history of its own. (pp. 20-5)

Peter Penzoldt, in his The Supernatural in Fiction, *P. Nevill, 1952, 271 p.*

M. R. JAMES

[*James is considered the creator and foremost craftsman of the modern ghost story. Strongly influenced by the ghost stories of*

Joseph Sheridan Le Fanu, he avoided the atmospheric Gothicism of his predecessor's work and instead employed a simple narrative style designed to heighten the terrifying effect of his tales. In the following essay, which was originally published in 1931, James explains his interest in the ghost story and examines the qualities that distinguish its most successful examples.]

What first interested me in ghosts? This I can tell you quite definitely. In my childhood I chanced to see a toy Punch and Judy set, with figures cut out in cardboard. One of these was The Ghost. It was a tall figure habited in white with an unnaturally long and narrow head, also surrounded with white, and a dismal visage.

Upon this my conceptions of a ghost were based, and for years it permeated my dreams.

Other questions—why I like ghost stories, or what are the best, or why they are the best, or a recipe for writing such things—I have never found it easy to be so positive about. Clearly, however, the public likes them. The recrudescence of ghost stories in recent years is notable: it corresponds, of course, with the vogue of the detective tale.

The ghost story can be supremely excellent in its kind, or it may be deplorable. Like other things, it may err by excess or defect. Bram Stoker's *Dracula* is a book with very good ideas in it, but—to be vulgar—the butter is spread far too thick. Excess is the fault here: to give an example of erring by defect is difficult, because the stories that err in that way leave no impression on the memory.

I am speaking of the literary ghost story here. The story that claims to be "veridical" (in the language of the Society of Psychical Research) is a very different affair. It will probably be quite brief, and will conform to some one of several familiar types. This is but reasonable, for, if there be ghosts—as I am quite prepared to believe—the true ghost story need do no more than illustrate their normal habits (if normal is the right word), and may be as mild as milk.

The literary ghost, on the other hand, has to justify his existence by some startling demonstration, or, short of that, must be furnished with a background that will throw him into full relief and make him the central feature.

Since the things which the ghost can effectively do are very limited in number, ranging about death and madness and the discovery of secrets, the setting seems to me all-important, since in it there is the greatest opportunity for variety.

It is upon this and upon the first glimmer of the appearance of the supernatural that pains must be lavished. But we need not, we should not, use all the colours in the box. In the infancy of the art we needed the haunted castle on a beetling rock to put us in the right frame: the tendency is not yet extinct, for I have but just read a story with a mysterious mansion on a desolate height in Cornwall and a gentleman practising the worst sort of magic. How often, too, have ruinous old houses been described or shown to me as fit scenes for stories!

"Can't you imagine some ole monk or friar wandering about this long gallery?" No, I can't.

I know Harrison Ainsworth could: *The Lancashire Witches* teems with Cistercians and what he calls votaresses in mouldering vestments, who glide about passages to very little purpose. But these fail to impress. Not that I have not a soft corner in my heart for *The Lancashire Witches,* which—ridiculous as much of it is—has distinct merits as a story.

It cannot be said too often that the more remote in time the ghost is the harder it is to make him effective, always supposing him to be the ghost of a dead person. Elementals and suchlike do not come under this rule.

Roughly speaking, the ghost should be a contemporary of the seer. Such was the elder Hamlet and such Jacob Marley. The latter I cite with confidence and in despite of critics, for, whatever may be urged against some parts of *A Christmas Carol,* it is, I hold, undeniable that the introduction, the advent, of Jacob Marley is tremendously effective.

And be it observed that the setting in both these classic examples is contemporary and even ordinary. The ramparts of the Kronborg and the chambers of Ebenezer Scrooge were, to those who frequented them, features of every-day life.

But there are exceptions to every rule. An ancient haunting can be made terrible and can be invested with actuality, but it will tax your best endeavours to forge the links between past and present in a satisfying way. And in any case there must be ordinary level-headed modern persons—Horatios—on the scene, such as the detective needs his Watson or his Hastings to play the part of the lay observer.

Setting or environment, then, is to me a principal point, and the more readily appreciable the setting is to the ordinary reader the better. The other essential is that our ghost should make himself felt by gradual stirrings diffusing an atmosphere of uneasiness before the final flash or stab of horror.

Must there be horror? you ask. I think so. There are but two really good ghost stories I know in the language wherein the elements of beauty and pity dominate terror. They are Lanoe Falconer's "Cecilia de Noel" and Mrs Oliphant's "The Open Door." In both there are moments of horror; but in both we end by saying with Hamlet: "Alas, poor ghost!" Perhaps my limit of two stories is overstrict; but that these two are by very much the best of their kind I do not doubt.

On the whole, then, I say you must have horror and also malevolence. Not less necessary, however, is reticence. There is a series of books I have read, I think American in origin, called *Not at Night* (and with other like titles), which sin glaringly against this law. They have no other aim than that of Mr Wardle's Fat Boy.

Of course, all writers of ghost stories do desire to make their readers' flesh creep; but these are shameless in their attempts. They are unbelievably crude and sudden, and they wallow in corruption. And if there is a theme that ought to be kept out of the ghost story, it is that of the charnel house. That and sex, wherein I do not say that these *Not a Night* books deal, but certainly other recent writers do, and in so doing spoil the whole business.

To return from the faults of ghost stories to their excellence. Who, do I think, has best realized their possibilities? I have no hesitation in saying that it is Joseph Sheridan Le Fanu. In the volume called *In a Glass Darkly* are four stories of paramount excellence, "Green Tea," "The Familiar," "Mr Justice Harbottle," and "Carmilla." All of these conform to my requirements: the settings are quite different, but all *seen* by the writer; the approaches of the supernatural nicely graduated; the climax adequate. Le Fanu was a scholar and poet, and these tales show him as such. It is true that he died as long ago as 1873, but there is wonderfully little that is obsolete in his manner.

Of living writers I have some hesitation in speaking, but on any list that I was forced to compile the names of E. F. Benson, Blackwood, Burrage, De la Mare and Wakefield would find a place.

But, although the subject has its fascinations, I see no use in being pontifical about it. These stories are meant to please and amuse us. If they do so, well; but, if not, let us relegate them to the top shelf and say no more about it. (pp. 349-52)

> *M. R. James, ''Ghosts—Treat Them Gently!'' in his* Casting the Runes and Other Ghost Stories, *edited by Michael Cox, Oxford University Press, Oxford, 1987, pp. 349-52.*

EDITH WHARTON

[*Wharton is best known as a novelist of manners whose fiction exposed the cruel excesses of aristocratic society at the turn of the century. Her subject matter, tone, and style have been compared with those of Henry James, her friend and mentor. Many critics also note Wharton's affinities with Jane Austen and George Eliot, who shared her concern for the constricted status of women in modern society. In the following excerpt from the preface to a collection of her ghost stories, Wharton discusses the sensibility required on the reader's part to appreciate the supernatural in literature and examines the qualities that constitute excellence in a ghost story.*]

''Do you believe in ghosts?'' is the pointless question often addressed by those who are incapable of feeling ghostly influences to—I will not say the *ghost-seer,* always a rare bird, but—the *ghost-feeler,* the person sensible of invisible currents of being in certain places and at certain hours.

The celebrated reply (I forget whose): ''No, I don't believe in ghosts, but I'm afraid of them,'' is much more than the cheap paradox it seems to many. To ''believe,'' in that sense, is a conscious act of the intellect, and it is in the warm darkness of the prenatal fluid far below our conscious reason that the faculty dwells with which we apprehend the ghosts we may not be endowed with the gift of seeing. This was oddly demonstrated the other day by the volume of ghost stories collected from the papers of the late Lord Halifax by his son. The test of the value of each tale lay, to the collector's mind, not in the least in its intrinsic interest, but in the fact that someone or other had been willing to vouch for the authenticity of the anecdote. No matter how dull, unoriginal and unimportant the tale—if someone had convinced the late Lord Halifax that it was ''true,'' that it ''had really happened,'' in it went; and can it be only by accident that the one story in this large collection which is even faintly striking and memorable is the one with an apologetic footnote to the effect that the editor had not been able to trace it to its source?

Sources, as a matter of fact, are not what one needs in judging a ghost story. The good ones bring with them the internal proof of their ghostliness; and no other evidence is needed. But since first I dabbled in the creating of ghost stories, I have made the depressing discovery that the faculty required for their enjoyment has become almost atrophied in modern man. No one ever expected a Latin to understand a ghost, or shiver over it; to do that, one must still have in one's ears the hoarse music of the northern Urwald or the churning of dark seas on the outermost shores. But when I first began to read, and then to write, ghost stories, I was conscious of a common medium between myself and my readers, of their meeting me halfway among the primeval shadows, and filling in the gaps in my narrative with sensations and divinations akin to my own.

I had curious evidence of the change when, two or three years ago, one of [my ghost stories] . . . made its first curtsy in an American magazine. I believe most purveyors of fiction will agree with me that the readers who pour out on the author of the published book such floods of interrogatory ink pay little heed to the isolated tale in a magazine. The request to the author to reveal as many particulars as possible of his private life to his eager readers is seldom addressed to him till the scattered products of his pen have been collected in a volume. But when ''Pomegranate Seed'' . . . first appeared in a magazine, I was bombarded by a host of inquirers anxious, in the first place, to know the meaning of the story's title (in the dark ages of my childhood an acquaintance with classical fairy lore was as much a part of our stock of knowledge as Grimm and Andersen), and secondly, to be told *how a ghost could write a letter, or put it into a letterbox.* These problems caused sleepless nights to many correspondents whose names seemed to indicate that they were recent arrivals from unhaunted lands. Need I say there was never a Welsh or a Scottish signature among them? But in a few years more perhaps there may be; for, deep within us as the ghost instinct lurks, I seem to see it being gradually atrophied by those two world-wide enemies of the imagination, the wireless and the cinema. To a generation for whom everything which used to nourish the imagination because it had to be won by an effort, and then slowly assimilated, is now served up cooked, seasoned and chopped into little bits, the creative faculty (for reading should be a creative act as well as writing) is rapidly withering, together with the power of sustained attention; and the world which used to be so *grand à la clarté des lampes* is diminishing in inverse ratio to the new means of spanning it; so that the more we add to its surface the smaller it becomes.

All this is very depressing to the ghost-story purveyor and his publisher; but in spite of adverse influences and the conflicting attractions of the gangster, the introvert and the habitual drunkard, the ghost may hold his own a little longer in the hands of the experienced chronicler. What is most to be feared is that these seers should fail; for frailer than the ghost is the wand of his evoker, and more easily to be broken in the hard grind of modern speeding-up. Ghosts, to make themselves manifest, require two conditions abhorrent to the modern mind: silence and continuity. Mr. Osbert Sitwell informed us the other day that ghosts went out when electricity came in; but surely this is to misapprehend the nature of the ghostly. What drives ghosts away is not the aspidistra or the electric cooker; I can imagine them more wistfully haunting a mean house in a dull street than the battlemented castle with its boring stage properties. What the ghost really needs is not echoing passages and hidden doors behind tapestry, but only continuity and silence. For where a ghost has once appeared it seems to hanker to appear again; and it obviously prefers the silent hours, when at last the wireless has ceased to jazz. These hours, prophetically called ''small,'' are in fact continually growing smaller; and even if a few diviners keep their wands, the ghost may after all succumb first to the impossibility of finding standing room in a roaring and discontinuous universe.

It would be tempting to dwell on what we shall lose when the wraith and the fetch are no more with us; but my purpose here is rather to celebrate those who have made them visible to us. For the ghost should never be allowed to forget that his only chance of survival is in the tales of those who have encountered him, whether actually or imaginatively—and perhaps preferably the latter. It is luckier for a ghost to be vividly imagined than dully "experienced"; and nobody knows better than a ghost how hard it is to put him or her into words shadowy yet transparent enough. (pp. 1-3)

[The] more one thinks the question over, the more one perceives the impossibility of defining the effect of the supernatural. The Bostonian gentleman of the old school who said that his wife always made it a moral issue whether the mutton should be roast or boiled, summed up very happily the relation of Boston to the universe; but the "moral issue" question must not be allowed to enter into the estimating of a ghost story. It must depend for its effect solely on what one might call its thermometrical quality; if it sends a cold shiver down one's spine, it has done its job and done it well. But there is no fixed rule as to the means of producing this shiver, and many a tale that makes others turn cold leaves me at my normal temperature. The doctor who said there were no diseases but only patients would probably agree that there are no ghosts, but only tellers of ghost stories, since what provides a shudder for one leaves another peacefully tepid. Therefore one ought, I am persuaded, simply to tell one's ghostly adventures in the most unadorned language, and "leave the rest to Nature," as the New York alderman said when, many years ago, it was proposed to import "a couple of gondolas" for the lake in the Central Park.

The only suggestion I can make is that the teller of supernatural tales should be well frightened in the telling; for if he is, he may perhaps communicate to his readers the sense of that strange something undreamt of in the philosophy of Horatio. (p. 4)

Edith Wharton, in a preface to her The Ghost Stories of Edith Wharton, *Charles Scribner's Sons, 1973, pp. 1-4.*

L. P. HARTLEY

[*Author of the acclaimed novel trilogy* Eustace and Hilda *(1944-47), Hartley was an English novelist and short story writer whose fiction is unified by the theme of the search for individuality and meaning in the post-Christian era. In his examination of moral dilemmas he is often compared to Nathaniel Hawthorne, while his effective use of symbolism and close attention to craft and plot unity evoke frequent comparisons to the works of Henry James. Hartley's works also include numerous supernatural stories, most prominently the classic tale of "The Travelling Grave." In the following excerpt, Hartley ruminates on the problems of writing an effective ghost story and contrasts traditional and modern examples of the form.*]

[There] are endless difficulties in the path of the ghost-story writer. If not the highest, it is certainly the most exacting form of literary art, and perhaps the only one in which there is almost no intermediate step between success and failure. Either it comes off or it is a flop.

Ghost writers need a prepared atmosphere. I find it difficult even to write about them, here in the bright sunshine of an Italian morning. The natural and the visual impose themselves too much. To write a ghost story one has to tamper with one or the other, or with both. The self-sufficiency of the Italian scene, the impact of Latin human nature, so direct in its approach, delight the traveller from the North: they stimulate and fortify him, giving him from outside some spiritual vitamin which in his own country he can supply—if he can supply it

at all—only from within. Even the most impassioned devotee of the ghost story would admit that the taste for it is slightly abnormal, a survival, perhaps, from adolescence, a disease of deficiency suffered by those whose lives and imaginations do not react satisfactorily to normal experience and require an extra thrill. Detective-story writers give this thrill by exploiting the resources of the *possible;* however improbable the happenings in a detective story, they can and must be explained in terms that satisfy the reason. But in a ghost story, where natural laws are dispensed with, the whole point is that the happenings cannot be so explained. A ghost story that is capable of a rational explanation is as much an anomaly as a detective story that isn't. The one is in revolt against a materialistic conception of the universe, whereas the other depends on it.

The ghost-story writer's task is the more difficult, for not only must he create a world in which reason doesn't hold sway, but he must invent laws for it. Chaos is not enough. Even ghosts must have rules and obey them. In the past they had certain traditional activities; they could squeak and gibber, for instance; they could clank chains. They were generally local, confined to one spot. Now their liberties have been greatly extended; they can go anywhere, they can manifest themselves in scores of ways. Like women and other depressed classes, they have emancipated themselves from their disabilities, and besides being able to do a great many things that human beings can't do, they can now do a great many things that human beings can do. Immaterial as they are or should be, they have been able to avail themselves of the benefits of our materialistic civilisation.

Has this freedom made the ghost-story writer's task any easier? In a way yes, for it has given him a greater variety of plot and treatment. But in another way no, for a stylised ghost is much easier to handle, so to speak, than one whose limitations are uncertain. If he can only squeak or clank a chain, we know where we are with him. If he can only appear as a smell or a current of cold air, we also know. Simple as these effects are, if they are recognised much can be done with them. But if the ghost can be so like an ordinary human being that we can scarcely tell the difference, what is that difference to be? Where is the line to be drawn?

Banquo's ghost could occupy a chair and spoil the dinner-party, but Shakespeare does not let him eat or drink. I can't quote an instance, but I shouldn't be surprised to come across a modern ghost who could to both. Democracy has been extended to the spirit world. Fair shares for all! Why shouldn't a ghost eat or drink, as well as you and me? It isn't right that he shouldn't be allowed to! Yes, but a stop must be put somewhere to the spectre's material progress, or he will simply be—one of ourselves, and that he mustn't be. There must come a point, and it must strike the reader with a shock of surprise and horror, a tingling of the spine, at which we realise that he is *not* one of us.

That point is the crux of the ghost story, so it seems to me, the point at which it succeeds or fails; and the wider the choice of supernatural manifestations, the more difficult to find one which will carry conviction—for if a ghost can do this and this and this, why should he be debarred from doing *that?* What right has the author to deny him this small liberty? He has been arbitrary, we shall say, quite arbitrary, as well as unfair; not only our sense of justice but our æsthetic sense will be offended. Whereas in earlier days, when ghosts were so grossly underprivileged, when they had almost none of the advantages of materialism, the author's task was easier. The question, If a ghost *can't* do this, or this, or this, why should he be able to do *that*? is much easier to answer convincingly than the other.

But I am not so reactionary as to wish to take away the ghost's hardly-won privileges. If they have increased the difficulty of writing a ghost story, they have made the triumph of writing a good one all the greater. It will depend on the writer's imagination whether he can get away with it, whether he can convince his reader, for instance, that a ghost can make a telephone call but cannot speak on the wireless, whether, in fact, he can draw up a code of rules for ghosts which we—and they—will recognise. (pp. vii-ix)

> L. P. Hartley, in an introduction to The Third Ghost
> Book, *edited by Lady Cynthia Asquith, Pan Books
> Ltd., 1957, pp. vii-ix.*

CLARK ASHTON SMITH

[*Smith was an American author of horror and fantastic fiction
noted for its lush and intricate prose style (reflecting his work as
a poet influenced by the nineteenth-century Decadents), and for
its narrative perspectives that both reject and transcend the normal course of human affairs. His expertise was in writing inter-
planetary or alternate-world fantasies, which allowed for the
unrestrained, and invariably nightmarish, use of his artistic imagination. In the following essay, Smith presents an analysis of
atmosphere in supernatural fiction, using passages from stories
by Ambrose Bierce and Edgar Allan Poe as examples.*]

The term *atmosphere,* in application to fiction, is often used in a somewhat vague or restricted sense. I believe that it can be most profitably defined as the collective impression created by the entire mass of descriptive, directly evocative details in any given story (what is sometimes known as "local color") together with all that is adumbrated, suggested or connoted through or behind these details. It can be divided roughly into two elements: the *kinetic* and the *potential;* the former comprising all the effects of overt surface imagery, and the latter all the implications, hints, undertones, shadows, nuances, and the verbal associations, and various effects of rhythm, onomatopoeia and phonetic pattern which form a more consistent and essential feature of good prose-writing than is commonly realized. Many people would apply the word *atmosphere* only to the elements defind here-above as potential; but I prefer the broader definition; since, after all, the most intangible atmospheric effects depend more or less upon the kinetic ones and are often difficult to dissociate wholly from them through analysis. An attempt to achieve purely potential writing might result, I suspect, in something not altogether dissimilar to the effusions of Gertrude Stein! Or, at least, it would lead to an obscurity such as was practiced by the French Symbolist poet, Mallarmé, who is said to have revised his poems with an eye to the elimination of kinetic statement whenever possible.

A few examples of the use of atmospheric elements, taken from the work of recognized masters, should prove more illuminative than any amount of generalization. Take, for instance, this paragraph from Ambrose Bierce's tale, "The Death of Halpin Frayser," one of the most overwhelmingly terrific horror tales ever written:

> He thought that he was walking along a dusty road
> that showed white in the gathering darkness of the
> summer night. *Whence and whither it led, and why
> he traveled it,* he did not know, though all seemed
> simple and natural, as is the way in dreams; for in
> the Land Beyond the Bed surprises cease from trou-

bling and the Judgement is at rest. Soon he came to the parting of the ways; leading from the highway was a road less traveled, *having the appearance, indeed, of having been long abandoned, because, he thought, it led to something evil;* yet he turned into it without hesitation, *impelled by some mysterious necessity.*

Note here the *potential* value of the italicized clauses. The element of dream-mystery is heightened by the unknown reason for traveling the road, by the "something evil" which has no form or name, and the unparticularized necessity for taking the abandoned way. The ambiguity, the lack of precise definition, stimulate the reader's imagination and evoke shadowy meanings beyond the actual words.

In the paragraph immediately following this, the potential elements are even more predominant:

> As he pressed forward he became conscious that *his
> way was haunted by malevolent existences, invisible,
> and whom he could not definitely figure to his mind.
> From among the trees on either side he caught broken
> whispers in a strange tongue which yet he partly
> understood. They seemed to him fragmentary utter-
> ances of a montrous conspiracy against his body and
> his soul.*

Here, through the generalized character of malevolence imputed to things unseen and half-heard, images of almost illimitable spectral menace are conjured up. It should not be in-

Ambrose Bierce. Culver Pictures, Inc.

ferred, however, that precise statements and sharply outlined images are necessarily lacking in potential quality. On the contrary, they may possess implications no less frightful or mysterious than the wildly distorted shadow cast by some monster seen in glaring light. To illustrate this point, let me quote again from "The Death of Halpin Frayser":

> A shallow pool in the guttered depression of an old wheel rut, as from a recent rain, met his eye with a crimson gleam. He stooped and plunged his hands into it. It stained his fingers; it was blood. Blood, he then observed, was about him everywhere. The weeds growing rankly by the roadside showed it in blots and splashes on their big broad leaves. Patches of dry dust between the wheelways were pitted and spattered as with a red rain. Defiling the trunks of the trees were broad maculations of crimson, and blood dripped like dew from their foliage.

This, it would seem, is a prime example of kinetic atmospheric description, owing its power to a visual definitude and exactness rarely equaled. Consider a moment, however, and you will realize the added potential element which lies in the unexplained mystery of the bloody dew, and the abnormally strange position of many of the sanguine maculations. Things infinitely more dreadful and more horrible than the blood itself are somehow intimated.

In much of Poe's best work, the atmospheric elements are so subtly blended, unified and pervasive as to make analysis rather difficult. Something beyond and above the mere words and images seems to well from the entire fabric of the work, like the "pestilent and mystic vapor" which, to the narrator's fancy, appeared to emanate from the melancholy House of Usher and its inexplicably dismal surroundings. The profuse but always significant details evoke dimly heard echoes and remote correspondences. Suggestion is less easily separable from statement, and becomes a vague dark irridescence communicated from word to word, from sentence to sentence, from paragraph to page, like the play of lurid gleams along somber jewels cunningly chosen and set. To this suggestive element the rhythms, cadences and phonetic sequences of the prose contribute materially but more or less indeterminably. As an illustration of well-nigh perfect atmospheric writing, embodying the qualities I have indicated, I quote from "The Fall of the House of Usher" the description of the room in which Roderick Usher receives his guest:

> The room in which I found myself was very large and lofty. The windows were long, narrow and pointed, and at so vast a distance from the black oaken floor as to be altogether inaccessible from within. Feeble gleams of encrimsoned light made their way through the trellised panes, and served to render sufficiently distinct the more prominent objects around; the eyes, however, struggled in vain to reach the remoter angles of the chamber, or the recesses of the vaulted and fretted ceiling. Dark draperies hung upon the walls. *The general furniture was profuse, comfortless, antique and tattered.* Many books and musical instruments lay scattered about, but failed to lend any vitality to the scene. I felt I breathed an atmosphere of sorrow. *An air of stern, deep and irredeemable gloom hung over and pervaded all.*

Note here the carefully built impression of spaciousness combined with gloom and confinement, of lifeless and uncomforting luxury. Through the choice and emphasis of material details, an air of spiritual oppression is created, and the idea of a mysterious and monstrous unity between the building and

its hypochondriacal owner is cautiously foreshadowed. I have italicized two sentences in which I seem to find a very subtle congruity between the actual sound of the words and their sense. In the first, the frequent repetition of the consonants r, s, f, and t somehow emphasizes the image of "profuse" furniture; and the sharp dentals and sibilants add to the impression of things time-eaten and "comfortless." In the last sentence, the repeated letters, n, r, d, l, m, and v, are all of a heavy or deep-sounding character, giving, with the long, close and sonorous vowels, a hollow and funeral clang that echoes the meaning. Here, too, the very movement of the sentence is like the dropping of a pall.

From certain of Poe's tales and prose-poems, such as "The Masque of the Red Death," "Silence" and "Shadow," one can select even more obvious and overt effects of atmospheric color supplemented by sound and rhythm. For illustration, I shall quote a single sentence from the prose-poem, "Silence," and leave its analysis to the reader: "And overhead, with a rustling and loud noise, the grey clouds rush westwardly forever, until they roll, a cataract, over the fiery wall of the horizon."

From such instances as these, it will be seen how large a portion of the atmospheric elements in writing can sometimes be contributed by the mere sound of words apart from their meaning. The values implied are vaguely akin to those of music; and it should be obvious that really fine prose cannot be written without an ear for pitch, tone, movement and cadence. (pp. 51-4)

Clark Ashton Smith, "Atmosphere in Weird Fiction," in his Planets and Dimensions: Collected Essays of Clark Ashton Smith, *edited by Charles K. Wolfe, The Mirage Press, 1973, pp. 51-4.*

THE NATURE AND APPEAL OF SUPERNATURAL FICTION

H. P. LOVECRAFT

[Lovecraft is considered one of the foremost modern authors of supernatural horror fiction. Strongly influenced by Edgar Allan Poe, Lord Dunsany, and early science fiction writers, he developed a type of horror tale that combined occult motifs, modern science, and the regional folklore of his native New England to produce the personal mythology on which he based much of his work. As is evident from his own fiction, Lovecraft was well versed in the history of Gothic writing, and his Supernatural Horror in Literature *(1927) is one of the earliest and most comprehensive studies of this genre. From its opening statement—"the oldest and strongest emotion of mankind is fear"—to its concluding question—"who shall declare the dark theme a handicap?"—Lovecraft examines the literature of supernatural horror as an "essential branch of human expression." Discussing both major and minor works, from the myths of antiquity to pulp adventures of the modern era, his study provides a rationale for the functions of and motivations behind supernatural horror. He argues that the most successful specimens of the form inspire in the reader a sense of liberation, along with horrific revulsion, through fictional violations of the laws of the natural world. In the following excerpt, Lovecraft articulates his precepts for supernatural horror fiction, characterizes the supernatural literature of his time, and speculates on the future of the horror tale.]*

The oldest and strongest emotion of mankind is fear, and the oldest and strongest kind of fear is fear of the unknown. These facts few psychologists will dispute, and their admitted truth must establish for all time the genuineness and dignity of the weirdly horrible tale as a literary form. Against it are discharged all the shafts of a materialistic sophistication which clings to frequently felt emotions and external events, and of a naively inspired idealism which deprecates the aesthetic motive and calls for a didactic literature to "uplift" the reader toward a suitable degree of smirking optimism. But in spite of all this opposition the weird tale has survived, developed, and attained remarkable heights of perfection; founded as it is on a profound and elementary principle whose appeal, if not always universal, must necessarily be poignant and permanent to minds of the requisite sensitiveness.

The appeal of the spectrally macabre is generally narrow because it demands from the reader a certain degree of imagination and a capacity for detachment from everyday life. Relatively few are free enough from the spell of the daily routine to respond to rappings from outside, and tales of ordinary feelings and events, or of common sentimental distortions of such feelings and events, will always take first place in the taste of the majority; rightly, perhaps, since of course these ordinary matters make up the greater part of human experience. But the sensitive are always with us, and sometimes a curious streak of fancy invades an obscure corner of the very hardest head; so that no amount of rationalisation, reform, or Freudian analysis can quite annul the thrill of the chimney-corner whisper or the lonely wood. There is here involved psychological pattern or tradition as real and as deeply grounded in mental experience as any other pattern or tradition of mankind; coeval with the religious feeling and closely related to many aspects of it, and too much a part of our innermost biological heritage to lose keen potency over a very important, though not numerically great, minority of our species.

Man's first instincts and emotions formed his response to the environment in which he found himself. Definite feelings based on pleasure and pain grew up around the phenomena whose causes and effects he understood, whilst around those which he did not understand—and the universe teemed with them in the early days—were naturally woven such personifications, marvelous interpretations, and sensations of awe and fear as would be hit upon by a race having few and simple ideas and limited experience. The unknown, being likewise the unpredictable, became for our primitive forefathers a terrible and omnipotent source of boons and calamities visited upon mankind for cryptic and wholly extraterrestrial reasons, and thus clearly belonging to spheres of existence whereof we know nothing and wherein we have no part. The phenomenon of dreaming likewise helped to build up the notion of an unreal or spiritual world; and in general, all the conditions of savage dawn-life so strongly conducted toward a feeling of the supernatural, that we need not wonder at the thoroughness with which man's very hereditary essence has become saturated with religion and superstition. That saturation must, as a matter of plain scientific fact, be regarded as virtually permanent so far as the subconscious mind and inner instincts are concerned; for though the area of the unknown has been steadily contracting for thousands of years, an infinite reservoir of mystery still engulfs most of the outer cosmos, whilst a vast residuum of powerful inherited associations clings round all the objects and processes that were once mysterious, however well they may now be explained. And more than this, there is an actual physiological fixation of the old instincts in our nervous tissue, which would make them obscurely operative even were the conscious mind to be purged of all sources of wonder.

H. P. Lovecraft.

Because we remember pain and the menace of death more vividly than pleasure, and because our feelings toward the beneficent aspects of the unknown have from the first been captured and formalised by conventional religious rituals, it has fallen to the lot of the darker and more maleficent side of cosmic mystery to figure chiefly in our popular supernatural folklore. This tendency, too, is naturally enhanced by the fact that uncertainty and danger are always closely allied; thus making any kind of an unknown world a world of peril and evil possibilities. When to this sense of fear and evil the inevitable fascination of wonder and curiosity is superadded, there is born a composite body of keen emotion and imaginative provocation whose vitality must of necessity endure as long as the human race itself. Children will always be afraid of the dark, and men with minds sensitive to hereditary impulse will always tremble at the thought of the hidden and fathomless worlds of strange life which may pulsate in the gulfs beyond the stars, or press hideously upon our own globe in unholy dimensions which only the dead and the moonstruck can glimpse.

With this foundation, no one need wonder at the existence of a literature of cosmic fear. It has always existed, and always will exist; and no better evidence of its tenacious vigour can be cited than the impulse which now and then drives writers of totally opposite leanings to try their hands at it in isolated tales, as if to discharge from their minds certain phantasmal shapes which would otherwise haunt them. Thus Dickens wrote several eerie narratives; Browning, the hideous poem *Childe*

Roland; Henry James, *The Turn of the Screw;* Dr. Holmes, the subtle novel *Elsie Venner;* F. Marion Crawford, "The Upper Berth" and a number of other examples; Mrs. Charlotte Perkins Gilman, social worker, "The Yellow Wall Paper"; whilst the humorist, W. W. Jacobs, produced that able melodramatic bit called "The Monkey's Paw."

This type of fear-literature must not be confounded with a type externally similar but psychologically widely different; the literature of mere physical fear and the mundanely gruesome. Such writing, to be sure, has its place, as has the conventional or even whimsical or humorous ghost story where formalism or the author's knowing wink removes the true sense of the morbidly unnatural; but these things are not the literature of cosmic fear in its purest sense. The true weird tale has something more than secret murder, bloody tones, or a sheeted form clanking chains according to rule. A certain atmosphere of breathless and unexplainable dread of outer, unknown forces must be present; and there must be a hint, expressed with a seriousness and portentousness becoming its subject, of that most terrible conception of the human brain—a malign and particular suspension or defeat of those fixed laws of Nature which are our only safeguard against the assaults of chaos and the daemons of unplumbed space.

Naturally we cannot expect all weird tales to conform absolutely to any theoretical model. Creative minds are uneven, and the best of fabrics have their dull spots. Moreover, much of the choicest weird work is unconscious; appearing in memorable fragments scattered through materials whose massed effect may be of a very different cast. Atmosphere is the all-important thing, for the final criterion of authenticity is not the dovetailing of a plot but the creation of a given sensation. We may say, as a general thing, that a weird story whose intent is to teach or produce a social effect, or one in which the horrors are finally explained away by natural means, is not a genuine tale of cosmic fear; but it remains a fact that such narratives often possess, in isolated sections, atmospheric touches which fulfill every condition of true supernatural horror-literature. Therefore we must judge a weird tale not by the author's intent, or by the mere mechanics of the plot; but by the emotional level which it attains at its least mundane point. If the proper sensations are excited, such a "high spot" must be admitted on its own merits as weird literature, no matter how prosaically it is later dragged down. The one test of the really weird is simply this—whether or not there be excited in the reader a profound sense of dread, and of contact with unknown spheres and powers; a subtle attitude of awed listening, as if for the beating of black wings or the scratching of ouside shapes and entities on the known universe's utmost rim. And of course, the more completely and unifiedly a story conveys this atmosphere, the better it is as a work of art in the given medium. (pp. 12-16)

The best horror-tales of today, profiting by the long evolution of the type, possess a naturalness, convincingness, artistic smoothness, and skilful intensity of appeal quite beyond comparison with anything in the Gothic work of a century or more ago. Technique, craftsmanship, experience, and psychological knowledge have advanced tremendously with the passing years, so that much of the older work seems naive and artificial; redeemed, when redeemed at all, only by a genius which conquers heavy limitations. The tone of jaunty and inflated romance, full of false motivation and investing every conceivable event with a counterfeit significance and carelessly inclusive glamour, is now confined to lighter and more whimsical phases

of supernatural writing. Serious weird stories are either made realistically intense by close consistency and perfect fidelity to Nature except in the one supernatural direction which the author allows himself, or else cast altogether in the realm of phantasy, with atmosphere cunningly adapted to the visualisation of a delicately exotic world of unreality beyond space and time, in which almost anything may happen if it but happen in true accord with certain types of imagination and illusion normal to the sensitive human brain. This, at least, is the dominant tendency; though of course many great contemporary writers slip occasionally into some of the flashy postures of immature romanticism, or into bits of the equally empty and absurd jargon of pseudo-scientific "occultism," now at one of its periodic high tides. (pp. 87-8)

For those who relish speculation regarding the future, the tale of supernatural horror provides an interesting field. Combated by a mounting wave or plodding realism, cynical flippancy, and sophisticated disillusionment, it is yet encouraged by a parallel tide of growing mysticism, as developed both through the fatigued reaction of "occultists" and religious fundamentalists against materialistic discovery and through the stimulation of wonder and fancy by such enlarged vistas and broken barriers as modern science has given us with its intra-atomic chemistry, advancing astrophysics, doctrines of relativity, and probings into biology and human thought. At the present moment the favouring forces would appear to have somewhat of an advantage; since there is unquestionably more cordiality shown toward weird writings than when, thirty years ago, the best of Arthur Machen's work fell on the stony ground of the smart and cocksure 'nineties. Ambrose Bierce, almost unknown in his own time, has now reached something like general recognition.

Startling mutations, however, are not to be looked for in either direction. In any case an approximate balance of tendencies will continue to exist; and while we may justly expect a further subtilisation of technique, we have no reason to think that the general position of the spectral in literature will be altered. It is a narrow though essential branch of human expression, and will chiefly appeal as always to a limited audience with keen special sensibilities. Whatever universal masterpiece of tomorrow may be wrought from phantasm or terror will owe its acceptance rather to a supreme workmanship than to a sympathetic theme. Yet who shall declare the dark theme a positive handicap? Radiant with beauty, the Cup of the Ptolemies was carven of onyx. (pp. 105-06)

> *H. P. Lovecraft, in his* Supernatural Horror in Literature, *1945. Reprint by Dover Publications, Inc., 1973, 106 p.*

S. L. VARNADO

[Varnado is an American educator and critic. In the following excerpt, he discusses supernatural fiction in light of theologian Rudolph Otto's concept of the "numinous" and examines works by Arthur Machen, Algernon Blackwood, and H. P. Lovecraft as they relate to this concept.]

Everyone who has given the matter some consideration is aware of a great and overriding division in our mental lives. The two parts of this division have received a variety of names through the years without losing their identity. Generally speaking, these parts may be called *reason* and *intuition;* but a large and confusing array of synonyms has attached itself to each part. Modern psychology since Freud refers to them as the "conscious'' and the ''unconscious'' parts of the mind. In the nineteenth century the terms *understanding* and *imagination* were preferred. The medieval Scholastics knew these distinctions; there is an echo of them in Anselm's formula *fides quarens intellectum*. Some other terms for reason would be *thought, knowledge, logic,* and *science;* for intuition we might substitute *faith, mysticism, instinct, heart,* and *feeling.*

Although the terminology surrounding these two forms of cognition is at times obscure, the reality underlying them is not. The term *reason* obviously refers to that portion of our mental life about which we can form clear concepts and explicit judgments. The term *intuition,* on the other hand, suggests an immediate cognitive knowlege, the grounds of which cannot be made conceptual. Emerson called the latter ''instinct'' and ''spontaneity.'' It is Newman's ''illative sense,'' Augustine's ''illumination''; and it resonates in Pascal's epigram, ''The heart has its reasons which the reason knows nothing of.''

It is with this second category of mental experience—intuition—that the work of Rudolf Otto (1860-1937) is concerned. In his years as a professor of theology at Marburg University, Otto's studies of Luther, Kant, and Schleiermacher turned his interest toward what we would today term the ''psychology of religious experience.'' The subject has been illuminated since Otto's time by the work of Henri Bergson, Mircea Eliade, and others; but when Otto began his studies it was virtual terra incognita.

Otto set out to explore the essence of the religious impulse as it appeared in mankind's emotional life and feelings. Since the area he was concerned with is to some extent independent of concepts, Otto called it ''the non-rational.'' In his classic *The Idea of the Holy* he says: ''This book, recognizing the profound import of the non-rational for metaphysic, makes a serious attempt to analyze all the more exactly the feeling which remains where the concept fails.''

Searching for a term by which to characterize the nonrational aspect of religion, Otto began with the category of the holy *(das heilige)*. Holiness, he observes, is a category of interpretation ''peculiar to the sphere of religion.'' The holy includes ethical and rational concepts but also contains a specific element, or ''moment,'' which sets it aside from the purely intellectual. This ineffable, or nonrational, element in the holy ''eludes apprehension in terms of concepts.''

In order to describe this ineffable element in the holy—this ''unnamed Something''—Otto was forced to invent a new term, to

> find a word to stand for this element in isolation, this ''extra'' in the meaning of ''holy'' above and beyond the meaning of goodness. For this purpose I adopt a word coined from the latin *numen. Omen* has given us ''ominous,'' and there is no reason why from *numen* we should not similarly form a word ''numinous.'' I shall speak, then, of a unique ''numinous'' category of value and of a definitely ''numinous'' state of mind, which is always found wherever the category is applied. This mental state is perfectly *sui generis* and irreducible to any other; and therefore, like every absolutely primary and elementary datum, while it admits of being discussed, it cannot be strictly defined.

Because the numinous cannot be fully described by concepts, Otto suggests that the reader ''direct his mind to a moment of deeply felt religious experience, as little as possible qualified by other forms of consciousness.'' The feeling-state that results

consists of a number of distinct yet harmonious elements (or ''moments,'' as Otto prefers) which can be expressed by means of an ideogram—a symbolic phrase that, by analogy, suggests the numinous experience. For this purpose he chooses the Latin phrase *mysterium tremendum et fascinans,* ''a frightening yet fascinating mystery.''

In attempting to analyze the numinous emotion by means of this ideogram, Otto starts with the qualifying adjective ''tremendum.'' *Tremor* is the Latin word for ''fear,'' but Otto uses this merely 'natural'' fear to suggest ''a quite specific kind of emotional response, wholly distinct from that of being afraid.'' It is, in fact, more akin to dread or awe, and such words as the German *Scheu* (dread) and *grasslich* (grisly) or the English *uncanny* come closest to expressing its meaning. Physical reactions to this moment of numinous consciousness are as ''unnatural'' as the emotion itself. Otto mentions such phrases as ''my blood ran icy cold,'' and ''my flesh crept,'' adding, ''anyone who is capable of more precise introspection must recognize that the distinction between such a 'dread' and natural fear is not simply one of degree and intensity. The awe or 'dread' *may* indeed be so overwhelmingly great that it seems to penetrate to the very marrow, making the man's hair bristle and his limbs quake. But it may also steal upon him almost unobserved. . . .'' In contrast, merely natural fear may contain nothing of the numinous emotion. ''I may be beyond all measure afraid and terrified without there being even a trace of the feeling of uncanniness in my emotion.''

The distinction between ''natural'' emotion and numinous emotion is crucial to understanding Otto's theory. A passage from C. S. Lewis's *The Problem of Pain* offers a clear explanation of the distinction:

> Those who have not met this term [the *numinous*] may be introduced to it by the following device. Suppose you were told that there was a tiger in the next room: you would know that you were in danger and would probably feel fear. But if you were told ''There is a ghost in the next room,'' and believed it, you would feel, indeed, what is often called fear, but of a different kind. It would not be based on the knowledge of danger, for no one is primarily afraid of what a ghost may do to him, but of the mere fact that it is a ghost. It is ''uncanny'' rather than dangerous, and the special kind of fear it excites may be called Dread. With the Uncanny one has reached the fringes of the Numinous. Now suppose that you were told simply ''There is a mighty spirit in the room'' and believed it. Your feelings would then be even less like the mere fear of danger: but the disturbance would be profound. You would feel wonder and a certain shrinking—a sense of inadequacy to cope with such a visitant and of prostration before it. . . . This feeling may be described as awe, and the object which excites it is the Numinous.

In addition to the note of awe emphasized by Lewis, Otto distinguishes two other unique feeling-states suggested by the Latin word *tremendum.* The first he calls *majestas:* a sense of might, power, or ''absolute overpoweringness.'' The subject perceiving this numinous emotion experiences a sense of ''creature consciousness,'' of being ''dust and ashes,'' and of sheer self-depreciation. The feeling is especially strong in certain forms of mysticism and by analogy is related to the sense of religious humility.

A third element called forth by the *tremendum* is the ''energy'' or ''urgency'' of the numinous. The feeling is associated symbolically with expressions of God's vitality, passion, emotional temper, will, force, impetus. This feeling finds expression in the biblical concept of the "wrath" of God. Otto associates it as well with Fichte's *Absolute* and with Schopenhauer's *Will*. Goethe calls it the "daemonic." It is, Otto contended, at the root of all "voluntaristic" mysticism in which God is perceived as a "consuming fire." The sense of urgency—the daemonic—is strong among primitive religions but does not die out in more advanced ones.

These three affective states—awe, majesty, and overpoweringness—are suggested by the adjective *tremendum* which, in turn, qualifies the substantive *mysterium*. Otto describes the *mysterium* as the form of the numinous experience. "Conceptually," he says, "*mysterium* denotes merely that which is hidden and esoteric, that which is beyond conception or understanding, extraordinary and unfamiliar. The term does not define the object more positively in its qualitative character. But though what is enunciated in the word is negative, what is meant is something absolutely and intensely positive. This pure positive we can experience in feelings."

The feeling evoked by the *mysterium* can best be described by the word *stupor*. "It signifies blank wonder, astonishment that strikes us dumb, amazement absolute." The feeling is associated with the theological term *the wholly other (alienum)*, "that which is quite beyond the sphere of the usual, the intelligible, and the familiar." It is associated on the purely natural plane with objects that are puzzling, astounding, or surprising. As is the case with purely natural fear, however, the emotion quickly passes over into something qualitatively different from mere natural bewilderment.

To clarify his meaning Otto analyzes the "fear of ghosts." The real attraction of a ghost, he says, "consists in this, that of itself and in an uncommon degree it entices the imagination, awakening strong interest and curiosity: it is the weird thing itself that allures the fancy. . . . [It] is a thing which 'doesn't really exist at all', the 'wholly other', something which has no place in our scheme of reality."

These several "moments" (*mysterium tremendum)* now combine with a third moment, one which Otto designates by the word *fascinans*. *Fascinans* is at the opposite pole from the daunting aspect of *numinous*. It is the attracting or fascinating side of the numinous, "a bliss which embraces all those blessings that are indicated or suggested in positive fashion by any 'doctrine of salvation', and it quickens all of them through and through; but these do not exhaust it. Rather, by its all pervading, penetrating glow it makes of these very blessings more than the intellect can conceive in them or affirm of them." The combination of feelings evoked by these seemingly opposite states of numinous consciousness results in a strange "harmony of contrasts":

> These two qualities, the daunting and the fascinating, now combine in a strange harmony of contrasts, and the resultant dual character of the numinous consciousness . . . is at once the strangest and most noteworthy phenomenon in the whole history of religion. The daemonic-divine object may appear to the mind an object of horror and dread, but at the same time it is no less something that allures with a potent charm, and the creature, who trembles before it, utterly cowed and cast down, has always at the same time the impulse to turn to it, nay even to make it somehow his own. The "mystery" is for him not merely something to be wondered at but something that entrances him; and beside that in it which bewilders and confounds, he feels a something that

captivates and transports him with a strange ravishment, rising often enough to the pitch of dizzy intoxication; it is the Dionysiac-element in the numen.

This, in essence, is Otto's conception of the numinous. To grasp it fully, however, it is necessary to understand what he means in calling it an a priori concept. "The facts of the numinous consciousness point therefore . . . to a hidden substantive source, from which the religious ideas and feelings are formed, which lies in the mind independently of sense experience." This does not mean, however, that the numinous is a mere subjective feeling. Quite the opposite is true. The very nature of the numinous experience is such that it cannot be perceived unless the subject feels that there is indeed something objective before which he is a creature. To clarify the point, Otto cites William James's *The Varieties of Religious Experience*:

> It is as if there were in the human consciousness a sense of reality, a feeling of objective presence, a perception of what we may call "something there" more deep and more general than any of the special and particular "senses" by which the current psychology supposes existent realities to be originally revealed.

The importance of this sense of objectivity in the numinous cannot be overstressed, especially in considering its literary and artistic applications. The writer of numinous literature can produce the proper effects only if he or she convinces the reader, at least transiently, that the numinous reality exists independently of the self. In this sense, the writer's task is more demanding than that of the writer of fantasy, who is in no way constrained to make the reader believe in the imaginative object, whether a giant, dragon, or magic carpet.

The numinous, then, can be summed up as an affective state in which the percipient—through feelings of awe, mystery, and fascination—becomes aware of an objective spiritual presence. Otto would argue that the feeling is universal, that it exists in both primitive and more highly developed religions.

Throughout *The Idea of the Holy*, Otto emphasizes his contention that the numinous is not identical with the fully developed category of the holy. The concept of holiness must of necessity include theological and moral elements. The numinous may, in fact, exist in a form detached from the category of The Holy. . . . [It] may even take on the aspect of what Otto calls "the negative numinous," in which the daemonic element is emphasized. Thus it seems clear that the experience may further the analysis of literary and artistic works not generally conceived of as religious. (pp. 8-15)

[During the early years of the twentieth century] only a few first-rate writers devoted themselves exclusively to numinous themes. Among these the most original, and in many ways most interesting, was Arthur Machen (1863-1947), a Welsh writer of occult tales whose work enjoyed a considerable vogue in the years around the turn of the century. The son of a clergyman, Machen was born at Caerlon, Wales, the site of an early Roman military establishment in Britain. As a boy h. wandered the hills and woods of this picturesque region, absorbing the traditions of King Arthur, the Romans, and the elves and fairies—the "Little People," as he later called them. After an irregular education he went to London an entered journalism. In the 1890s he began a series of occult tales that made him famous.

Like Eliot, Yeats, and Joyce, Machen was interested in mythological themes. Like them, he created his "private" myth, one combining the gods of Greece and Rome with the legends of the "little people" of his native Welsh hills. But the little people of Machen's stories are in no wise the charming creatures of later folklore; they are a malign race, akin to pagan nature gods, who have "gone underground" in order to perpetuate their existence despite the impact of modern civilization. Most of the tales show these dark, shadowy creatures emerging in modern Wales, a region Machen depicts with authenticity and charm.

The unique, numinous quality of Machen's work derives from this juxtaposition of rational and nonrational elements: the normal unsuspecting life of the modern town and the countryside infiltrated by the uncanny "powers" of the past. The plots and characters of the tales frequently are bizarre and sometimes unhealthy. Machen was a close friend of A. E. Waite, a well-known occultist of the time. He was also a member of the notorious Order of the Golden Dawn, the occultist society to which Yeats belonged. Through such channels Machen rediscovered the ancient feeling for magic and the preternatural. With the exception of Matthew Lewis, no writer of Gothic fiction seems closer than Machen to the feeling-state Rudolf Otto describes as the "negative numinous." Despite this disturbing, all-too-real portrayal of the occult, Machen's work is infused with a subtle poetic quality that redeems its unsavory elements.

Machen's best-known work is *The Great God Pan*, a novelette typical of his work, both for its poetic power and for its incredible plot and occasionally horrifying details. The horrific

Arthur Machen. Photograph by E. O. Hoppe.

incidents in the story, which might seem mere bad taste in another context, are deliberate with Machen and are used to produce the sense of "daemonic dread (c.f. the horror of Pan)" that Otto speaks of when describing the sense of fear (the *tremendum*) in numinous feeling:

> It is this feeling which, emerging in the mind of primeval man, forms the starting-point for the entire religious development in history. "Daemons" and "gods" alike spring from this root, and all the products of "mythological apperception."

The underlying sense of horror in the narrative is built on a pseudo-scientific premise somewhat reminiscent of *Frankenstein*. A Welsh physician, Dr. Raymond, has discovered an operation on the brain ("a slight lesion in the grey matter") that will produce a "lifting of the veil" from human consciousness. As a result of the operation, its victim—a young Welsh girl—enters a twilight zone of human consciousness in which she meets and mingles with the powers of antiquity, notably the great god Pan. As in *Frankenstein*, this basically incredible situation is worked up with surprising touches of poetry, touches that evoke a feeling of primitive wonder on the part of the reader. "'You may think all this strange nonsense,' the physician remarks to a friend. 'It may be strange, but it is true, and the ancients knew what lifting the veil means. They called it seeing the god Pan.'"

As a result of the young girl's meeting with Pan, the god conceives an avatar—a beautiful but amoral woman named Helen Vaughan. In the remainder of the tale this demigoddess is shown spreading a web of evil over the quiet Welsh countryside and later in London, where she corrupts a series of lovers who are driven to suicide. Many of the subsequent incidents are bizarre, grotesque, and appalling (Edwardian readers thought them "shocking"); but Machen's unfailing instinct for the daemonic shapes this variegated material into something like organic unity. In one instance, a London artist named Meyrick, who has fallen victim to Helen Vaughan's "charms," leaves behind a collection of drawings which are later discovered by his friend, Villiers.

> Villiers turned page after page, absorbed, in spite of himself, in the frightful Walpurgis Night of evil, strange monstrous evil, that the dead artist had set forth in hard black and white. The figures of Fauns and Satyrs and Ægipans danced before his eyes, the darkness of the thicket, the dance on the mountain-top, the scenes by lonely shores, in green vineyards, by rocks and desert places, passed before him: a world before which the human soul seemed to shrink back and shudder.

The incantatory quality of these passages, which has influenced later writers, arises from the strain of "daemonism" Otto notes as the first perception of the numinous in primitive religions. Machen seems particularly adept at assembling the notes of this antique feeling. As the passage suggests, the satyrs, fauns, Ægipans, darkness of the thicket, and loneliness of desert places add up to that "shudder" ancient man felt when confronted by the mystery of the gods.

In addition to the daemonic, Machen excels in depicting "horror," a quality Otto found in primitive notions of *clean* and *unclean,* which result later in the numinous sense of the sacred and the profane. In the conclusion of *The Great God Pan,* Helen Vaughan's suicide results in the following loathsome transformation, which is witnessed and later recounted by a London physician, Dr. Robert Matheson:

I saw the form waver from sex to sex, dividing itself from itself, and then again reunited. Then I saw the body descend to the beasts from whence it ascended, and that which was on the heights go down to the depths, even to the abyss of all being.

I watched, and at last I saw nothing but a substance as jelly. Then the ladder was ascended again . . . for one instant I saw a Form, shaped in dimness before me, which I will not further describe. But the symbol of this form may be seen in ancient sculptures, and in paintings which survived beneath the lava, too foul to be spoken of.

A comment from Otto's *Idea of the Holy* may help explain such curious and appalling elements in Machen's work:

Between this [feeling of disgust] and the feeling of the "horrible" there is a very close analogy; and from this it becomes apparent, in accordance with the law of reciprocal attraction between analogous feelings and emotions, how the "natural" unclean or impure is bound to pass over into, and develop in, the sphere of the numinous.

Such prereligious factors appear constantly in Machen's work, giving it a unique sense of the numinous. His strange and disturbing harmonies, though somewhat esoteric, have gained him a secure place in the annals of supernatural fiction.

A writer of equal power and artistry in the period under discussion is Algernon Blackwood (1869-1951). Blackwood, a British author who emigrated to Canada early in his life, is the acknowledged master of supernatural tales of nature and the out-of-doors. The settings of his stories, rendered with unsurpassed authenticity, include lonely stretches of Canadian wilderness, desolate marshes of the upper Danube, and remote islands off the coast of northern Europe. Though not mythic in the sense of Machen's tales, many of these stories suggest a related feeling-state, namely, the sense of haunted presence that primitive man must have associated with sacred groves, mountains, streams, and other impressive natural objects.

The central impulse of Blackwood's stories clearly is related to what Otto describes as the feeling of "haunted places." "There is none of us," Otto says, "who has any living capacity for emotion but must have known at some time or at some place what it is to feel really 'Uncanny,' to have a feeling of 'eeriness.'" This feeling rises spontaneously in the mind and sometimes attaches itself to no particular object or being but rather to the surroundings.

If in this implicit form it is summed up in a phrase, this will be merely some such exclamation as "How uncanny!" or "How eerie this place." If the feeling becomes explicit it generally takes a negative form: "It is not quite right here. . . ." The English "This place is haunted" shows a transition to a positive form of expression.

Such obscure feelings may on occasion become explicit recognition of a transcendent Something, "a real operative entity of a numinous kind, which later, as the development proceeds, assumes concrete form as a 'numen loci,' a daemon, an 'ell,' a 'Baal,' or the like." The German expression *Es spukt hier* (literally, "it haunts here") is an offshoot of this same primary emotion. We can, Otto says, recapture the numinous sense of these words as they apply to "aweful," "holy," or numen-possessed places.

These remarks shed light on Blackwood's unique ability to recapture the emotion Otto describes. In Blackwood's best stories it is the numinous landscape or background that dominates; the human actors, perhaps to the bewilderment of certain readers, fill a subsidiary role.

A good example of this peculiar power is seen in Blackwood's best-known story, "The Willows." In the opening passages, the unidentified narrator—probably a young Englishman—and his morose Swedish companion proceed on a canoe trip into the upper reaches of the Danube, where, amid a lonely, remote marshland they come upon a small island entirely covered by willow trees. They make camp, prepare a meal, and carry out other ordinary tasks; but as night falls, an odd and seemingly alien emotion is aroused in the narrator by the willow-covered island.

Great revelations of nature, of course, never fail to impress in one way or another, and I was no stranger to moods of the kind. Mountains overawe and oceans terrify, while the mystery of great forest exercises a spell peculiarly its own. But all these, at one point or another, somewhere link on intimately with human life and human experience. They stir comprehensible, even if alarming, emotions. They tend on the whole to exalt.

With this multitude of willows, however, it was something far different, I felt. Some essence emanated from them that besieged the heart. A sense of awe awakened, true, but of awe touched somewhere by a vague terror.

Here, Blackwood explicitly differentiates the sublime from the numinous (in accordance with what Otto called the "association of feelings"). He locates this force, or power, in the landscape itself. The feeling aroused is similar to those mysterious emanations of sacred groves in Roman religion, for example, the "talking trees" of the *Aeneid*. Herbert Jennings Rose, an authority on ancient Roman religion, says of this feeling:

The Romans . . . believed in a supernatural power or influence which they called *numen*. . . . Until the time of Augustus it [was] never used to mean any personal or individual god. . . . Even inanimate things, if there is something holy or uncanny about them, may have, or even be, *numen*.

As the tale continues, this perception becomes explicit in the narrator's mind:

The psychology of places for some imaginations at least, is very vivid; for the wanderer, especially, camps have their "note" whether of welcome or rejection. . . . And the note of this willow-camp now became unmistakably plain to me: we were interlopers, trespassers; we were not welcomed. The sense of unfamiliarity grew upon me as I stood there watching.

The next day, the feeling of threat from the island and the willows is focused on a series of magical events. The narrator sees—or thinks he sees—enormous shapes moving within the branches of the trees, and each morning the willows appear to have moved closer to the tent. The canoe and its paddle are mysteriously damaged, effectively trapping the two men on the island. In addition, they discover strange patterns in the sand around their tent: basin-shaped indentations that vary in depth and size from that of a teacup to a large bowl.

These accumulating notes of the nonrational induce a feeling of hysteria in the Swede, who mutters vaguely of "forces" surrounding them, producing disorder and destruction. The narrator attempts to rationalize these growing fears, but eventually he too succumbs to them. The island and surrounding area, he concludes, have become the focal point for powers or influences that have "leaked through" from some dimension "beyond." The frontiers of this unknown world impinge on our world in the area of the camp; and the uncanny phenomena the two men have witnessed are evidence that the powers of this unknown dimension are groping about searching for them. It becomes clear, in fact, that they are to be the sacrificial victims of these powers.

In the frightening conclusion of the story, the two are "saved" by the appearance of the body of a peasant who drowned during the storm and whose body washed up on the island, thus providing a vicarious sacrifice. At dawn the two companions find his body in the sand with "Their mark. . . . Their awful mark!" upon it:

> just as the body swung round to the current the face and the exposed chest turned full towards us, and showed plainly how the skin and flesh were indented with small hollows, beautifully formed, and exactly similar in shape and kind to the sandfunnels that we had found all over the island.

The work of Machen and Blackwood added new, distinct notes to the numinous tale, the first by means of a "mythological" dimension and the second by infusing the genre with a sense of "haunted place." A third writer of the period, one who benefited from the work of both men, was H. P. Lovecraft (1890-1937). Lovecraft, who has become something of a cult figure for modern devotees of supernatural fiction, makes an interesting case study of numinous literature, since he was a self-proclaimed scientific materialist. Although he denied the reality of the supernatural, he used his impressive literary powers to depict it, thus demonstrating that Otto's concept cuts across numerous philosophical lines of thought.

Lovecraft was born and spent most of his life in Providence, Rhode Island. (pp. 115-23)

Most of Lovecraft's tales and novelettes are set in New England, a region he knew intimately and one he depicts with a realism surprising in such a reclusive figure. Various representative New England types, drawn with a charm reminiscent of Hawthorne, populate the stories. Like Faulkner's Yoknapatawpha series, Lovecraft's tales are related to one another by fictional towns and institutions—Dunwich, Innsmouth, Kingsport, Miskatonic University—which correspond to real places.

The ability to create a literary world of his own led Lovecraft to concoct a numinous mythology which came to be known as the "Cthulhu mythos." (p. 124)

Lovecraft attaches [bizarre names] to the gods of his pantheon: Azathoth, the blind idiot god; Yog-Sothoth, the "all-in-one and one-in-all"; Great Cthulhu, dweller in hidden R'lyeh; Shub-Niggurath, and so on. The entire "mythic concept," which is a source of intense interest to the fan of Lovecraft writing, may seem somewhat artificial to the casual reader; but, given Lovecraft's impressive prose rhythms, erudition, and convincing realism, this mythic concept seems to work, at least in his best tales. A unique vision of numinous reality emerges, a world of weird colors and shapes, but one that is anchored firmly in the ordinary world.

The pattern of most of Lovecraft's tales differs from that of [Henry James, Bram Stoker, Blackwood, and others. Whereas these writers begin] with a carefully constructed background of rational events from which the nonrational emerges, Love-

craft's method is to plunge immediately into his material, combining fantastic hints of the occult with pedestrian details. The opening passage of one of his best stories, "The Colour Out of Space," provides a good example of this technique:

> West of Arkham the hills rise wild, and there are valleys with deep woods that no axe has ever cut. There are dark narrow glens where the trees slope fantastically, and where thin brooklets trickle without ever having caught the glint of sunlight. On the gentler slopes there are farms, ancient and rocky, with squat, moss-coated cottages brooding eternally over old New England secrets in the lee of great ledges; but these are all vacant now. . . .
>
> The old folks have gone away, and foreigners do not like to live there. . . . The place is not good for imagination, and does not bring restful dreams at night.

Passages such as this, which reveal Lovecraft's admirable qualities as a prose stylist, are not hard to find in his work. His unfailing sense of rhythm, the exact yet poetic vocabulary, the clear-cut imagery, and especially the fantastic reach of his imagination entitle him to high rank in this regard. In addition, a wide and precise antiquarian knowledge of New England pervades Lovecraft's work. The architecture, history, and customs of his native region provide a realistic background for the nonrational atmosphere that broods over the tales. This element in his work has attracted numerous imitators, making the New England milieu a kind of stalking ground for modern Gothic writers.

As with other works of the supernatural, Lovecraft's stories show only minimal interest in character, motivation, and psychology. Lovecraft was a great admirer of eighteenth-century literature; in keeping with its norms, he sought to create *representative* types rather than strongly individualistic characters. He was a master of the art of representation, however, capable of summoning up type characters with swift, authentic touches. Indeed, his tales contain an impressive array of characters drawn from all segments of New England society: reclusive scholars, strange old mountain people from the hills of western Massachusetts, sea captains and sailors, professors from Miskatonic University, shy old spinsters living on their memories of the past, artists and writers, business people, physicians, and a considerable sampling of immigrants from Italy and the Orient.

This New England milieu, with its traditions and legends and faint effluvia of decadence, forms a fitting accompaniment to the supernatural machinery of Lovecraft's myth of elder gods and monsters. He once explained the theory behind this "cosmic myth" as follows:

> The "punch" of a truly weird tale is simply some violation or transcending of fixed cosmic law—an imaginative escape from palling reality—since phenomena rather than persons are the logical "heroes." Horrors should be original—the use of common myths and legends being a weakening influence.

Lovecraft may have derived his idea of phenomena as hero from Blackwood; there can be little doubt that the cosmic myth was suggested by Machen's work. Unlike either writer, though, Lovecraft shows a lack of reserve in depicting his frightful monsters and slimy creatures from outer space. The horrors are heaped up; the reader "sups full on horror." Moreover, the passages describing these numinous entities are worked up in a vocabulary of the outré. The following examples should suffice to make the point.

From *At the Mountain of Madness,* one reads of "that fetid, unglimpsed mountain of slime-spewing protoplasm whose race had conquered the abyss and sent land pioneers to re-carve and squirm through the burrows of the hills." In "The Call of Cthulhu," the monster is described as bursting forth "like smoke from its eon-long imprisonment, visibly darkening the sun as it slunk away into the shrunken and gibbous sky on flapping membranous wings."

There is a naïve quality about these descriptions, occasionally reminiscent of the naïveté of the older Gothic novels, especially *The Castle of Otranto;* yet it is probably deliberate and, surprisingly enough, it often works. Perhaps the key to Lovecraft's power lies in his ability to arouse what Carl Jung might have called numinous archetypes of the collective unconscious.

In his wide-ranging investigations Jung found recurring images of demons and monsters in the dreams and fantasies of his patients. These images, in turn, often corresponded with those he discovered in the religions and mythologies of primitive peoples. The correspondence between such archetypes was not, he thought, accidental; they were, in fact, transformed impressions of often-repeated experiences, and they were often numinous. "For when an archetype appears in a dream, in a fantasy, or in life," he wrote, "it always brings with it a certain influence or power by virtue of which it either exercises a numinous or a fascinating effect, or impels to action."

Unlike Freud, who interpreted such material as sublimated sexuality, Jung accorded it an important place in man's spiritual life: "We should never identify ourselves with reason," he says; "for man is not and never will be a creature of reason alone, a fact to be noted by all pedantic culture-mongers. The irrational cannot be and must not be extirpated." This, though overstating the matter slightly, may help explain the urgency of Lovecraft's nonrational visions and the fascination they hold for certain readers; for the gods of the "Cthulhu mythology" and the Jungian archetypes are both born of the impulse Otto called the *mysterium tremendum et fascinans.* (pp. 124-28)

S. L. Varnado, "The Numinous" and "The Modern Period," in his Haunted Presence: The Numinous in Gothic Fiction, *The University of Alabama Press, 1987, pp. 8-19, 115-29.*

VIRGINIA WOOLF

[*Woolf is one of the most prominent literary figures of twentieth-century English literature. Like her contemporary James Joyce, with whom she is often compared, Woolf is remembered as one of the most innovative of the stream of consciousness novelists. Concerned primarily with depicting the life of the mind, she revolted against traditional narrative techniques and developed her own highly individualized style. Woolf's works, noted for their subjective explorations of characters' inner lives and their delicate poetic quality, have had a lasting effect on the art of the novel. A discerning and influential critic and essayist as well as a novelist, Woolf began writing reviews for the* Times Literary Supplement *at an early age. Her critical essays, which cover almost the entire range of English literature, contain some of her finest prose and are praised for their insight. Along with Lytton Strachey, Roger Fry, Clive Bell, and others, Woolf and her husband Leonard formed the literary coterie known as the "Bloomsbury Group." In the following essay, originally published in 1918, Woolf analyzes the purpose and experience of reading supernatural fiction, focusing on Walter Scott's "Wandering Willie's Tale" (1824) and Henry James's* The Turn of the Screw (1898) *as examples of the supernatural and the psychological ghost story.*]

When Miss Scarborough [in her study *The Supernatural in Modern English Fiction*] describes the results of her inquiries into the supernatural in fiction as "suggestive rather than exhaustive" we have only to add that in any discussion of the supernatural suggestion is perhaps more useful than an attempt at science. To mass together all sorts of cases of the supernatural in literature without much more system or theory than the indication of dates supplies leaves the reader free where freedom has a special value. Perhaps some psychological law lies hidden beneath the hundreds of stories about ghosts and abnormal states of mind (for stories about abnormal states of mind are included with those that are strictly supernatural) which are referred to in her pages; but in our twilight state it is better to guess than to assert, to feel than to classify our feelings. So much evidence of the delight which human nature takes in stories of the supernatural will inevitably lead one to ask what this interest implies both in the writer and in the reader.

In the first place, how are we to account for the strange human craving for the pleasure of feeling afraid which is so much involved in our love of ghost stories? It is pleasant to be afraid when we are conscious that we are in no kind of danger, and it is even more pleasant to be assured of the mind's capacity to penetrate those barriers which for twenty-three hours out of the twenty-four remain impassable. Crude fear, with its anticipation of physical pain or of terrifying uproar, is an undignified and demoralizing sensation, while the mastery of fear only produces a respectable mask of courage, which is of no great interest to ourselves, although it may impose upon others. But the fear which we get from reading ghost stories of the supernatural is a refined and spiritualized essence of fear. It is a fear which we can examine and play with. Far from despising ourselves for being frightened by a ghost story we are proud of this proof of sensibility, and perhaps unconsciously welcome the chance for the licit gratification of certain instincts which we are wont to treat as outlaws. It is worth noticing that the craving for the supernatural in literature coincided in the eighteenth century with a period of rationalism in thought, as if the effect of damming the human instincts at one point causes them to overflow at another. Such instincts were certaintly at full flood when the writings of Mrs. Radcliffe were their chosen channel. Her ghosts and ruins have long suffered the fate which so swiftly waits upon any exaggeration of the supernatural and substitutes our ridicule for our awe. But although we are quick to throw away imaginative symbols which have served our turn, the desire persists. Mrs. Radcliffe may vanish, but the craving for the supernatural survives. Some element of the supernatural is so constant in poetry that one has come to look upon it as part of the normal fabric of the art; but in poetry, being etherealized, it scarcely provokes any emotion so gross as fear. Nobody was ever afraid to walk down a dark passage after reading *The Ancient Mariner,* but rather inclined to venture out to meet whatever ghosts might deign to visit him. Probably some degree of reality is necessary in order to produce fear; and reality is best conveyed by prose. Certainly one of the finest ghost stories, "Wandering Willie's Tales" in *Redgauntlet,* gains immensely from the homely truth of the setting, to which the use of the Scotch dialect contributes. The hero is a real man, the country is as solid as can be; and suddenly in the midst of the green and grey landscape opens up the crimson transparency of Redgauntlet Castle with the dead sinners at their feasting.

The superb genius of Scott here achieves a triumph which should keep this story immortal however the fashion in the supernatural may change. Steenie Steenson is himself so real and his belief in the phantoms is so vivid that we draw our fear through our perception of his fear, the story itself being of a kind that has ceased to frighten us. In fact, the vision of the dead carousing would now be treated in a humorous, romantic or perhaps patriotic spirit, but scarcely with any hope of making our flesh creep. To do that the author must change his direction; he must seek to terrify us not by the ghosts of the dead, but by those ghosts which are living within ourselves. The great increase of the psychical ghost story in late years . . . testifies to the fact that our sense of our own ghostliness has much quickened. A rational age is succeeded by one which seeks the supernatural in the soul of man, and the development of psychical research offers a basis of disputed fact for this desire to feed upon. Henry James, indeed, was of opinion before writing *The Turn of the Screw* that "the good, the really effective and heart-shaking ghost stories (roughly so to term them) appeared all to have been told. . . . The new type, indeed, the mere modern 'psychical case,' washed clean of all queerness as by exposure to a flowing laboratory tap, . . . the new type clearly promised little." Since *The Turn of the Screw*, however, and no doubt largely owing to that masterpiece, the new type has justified its existence by rousing, if not "the dear old sacred terror," still a very effective modern representatitve. If you wish to guess what our ancestors felt when they read *The Mysteries of Udolpho* you cannot do better than read *The Turn of the Screw*.

Experiment proves that the new fear resembles the old in producing physical sensations as of erect hair, dilated pupils, rigid muscles, and an intensified perception of sound and movement. But what is it that we are afraid of? We are not afraid of ruins, or moonlight, or ghosts. Indeed, we should be relieved to find that Quint and Miss Jessel are ghosts, but they have neither the substance nor the independent existence of ghosts. The odious creatures are much closer to us than ghosts have ever been. The governess is not so much frightened of them as of the sudden extension of her own field of perception, which in this case widens to reveal to her the presence all about her of an unmentionable evil. The appearance of the figures is an illustration, not in itself specially alarming, of a state of mind which is profoundly mysterious and terrifying. It is a state of mind; even the external objects are made to testify to their subjection. The oncoming of the state is preceded not by the storms and howlings of the old romances, but by an absolute hush and lapse of nature which we feel to represent the ominous trance of her own mind. "The rooks stopped cawing in the golden sky, and the friendly evening hour lost for the unspeakable minute all its voice." The horror of the story comes from the force with which it makes us realize the power that our minds possess for such excursions into the darkness; when certain lights sink or certain barriers are lowered, the ghosts of the mind, untracked desires, indistinct intimations, are seen to be a large company.

In the hands of such masters as Scott and Henry James the supernatural is so wrought in with the natural that fear is kept from a dangerous exaggeration into simple disgust or disbelief verging upon ridicule. Mr. Kipling's stories "The Mark of the Beast" and "The Return of Imray" are powerful enough to repel one by their horror, but they are too violent to appeal to our sense of wonder. For it would be a mistake to suppose that supernatural fiction always seeks to produce fear, or that the best ghost stories are those which most accurately and medically described abnormal states of mind. On the contrary, a vast amount of fiction both in prose and in verse now assures us that the world to which we shut our eyes is far more friendly and inviting, more beautiful by day and more holy by night, than the world which we persist in thinking the real world. The country is peopled with nymphs and dryads, and Pan, far from being dead, is at his pranks in all the villages of England. Much of this mythology is used not for its own sake, but for purposes of satire and allegory; but there exists a group of writers who have the sense of the unseen without such alloy. Such a sense may bring visions of fairies or phantoms, or it may lead to a quickened perception of the relations existing between men and plants, or houses and their inhabitants, or any one of those innumerable alliances which somehow or other we spin between ourselves and other objects in our passage. (pp. 293-96)

> Virginia Woolf, "The Supernatural in Fiction," in her Collected Essays, Vol. I, Harcourt Brace Jovanovich, Inc., 1967, pp. 293-96.

DRAKE DOUGLAS

[In the following excerpt, Douglas considers reasons for the enduring appeal of supernatural horror fiction.]

In a recent anthology of horror tales, Donald Wollheim made much of the fact that the world has changed. Horror—and here we speak of actual belief in the creatures of horror, rather than the mere enjoyment of them through books and films—thrives on the unknown, on darkness, aloneness, fear and ignorance. Our world has made tremendous strides in the past half-century, and most of these ingredients necessary for the belief in horror have been abolished. Science has answered most of our questions concerning the unknown horrors of the past, has clearly pointed out the impossibility of various superstitions being anything more than just superstitions, and has made it quite clear that under no circumstances can a man become a wolf, or a bat, or a creeping shred of smoky mist. The world today is neither dark (save, perhaps, in a political sense) nor lonely (at least in the sense of being physically alone). One cannot imagine a man-made monster or a werewolf creating a panic in the garish world of Times Square; more than likely he would be looked upon as a further interesting example of the native product. Dracula would simply not stir up much of a commotion in the bloodsucking centers of Wall Street or Madison Avenue. These creatures belong to the dimly lit, foggy back alleys of Victorian London. The invention of the electric and neon light would seem to have been sufficient to place these monsters permanently in their graves.

Aloneness, too, has changed in recent years. With automobiles, buses, subways, it is no longer necessary to walk down dark, unlighted streets. When the son of Dr. Frankenstein returned to his ancestral home, he traveled by train in a coach as gloomy and inhospitable as the terrain through which he passed; today he might make the same journey in a comfortable, well-lighted club car. Jonathan Harker on his fatal real-estate venture to Castle Dracula journeyed through dark and fearsome forests and mountain passes in an uncomfortable, horse-drawn carriage; today he might travel quickly by air. No matter where you might wish to travel today, you can journey in well-lighted comfort, with sometimes an excess of companionship. A woman walking down a dark street today peers anxiously behind her not through fear of vampires, but of the rapist or mugger. No one walks through a cemetery at midnight any longer, unless in obedience to some Halloween daredeviltry.

Ruined, deserted castles are not difficult to find in our world, but the further we move from the trappings of monarchy, the less interested are we inclined to be in these essentials of horror. To a modern American, who has never lived under the tyranny of a robber baron, and has never seen the towers and battlements of a castle glowering down upon his home, the past does not have as strong and possessive a hold. A ruined castle is of interest because of its association with great wealth and romance, and if the average tourist thinks of such a place in terms of history, he concentrates on the glamour of kings and queens, beautiful princesses and handsome princes, rather than on the oppression and brutality often visited upon the people in the village below. Even the castle of an actual historic vampire like the infamous Gilles de Rais, or a monster like the Marquis de Sade, becomes, to the tourist mind, something colorful and exciting.

We must, too, take into consideration the population explosion of the past century or more. Tales of witchcraft and vampirism were extremely believable in a Europe so much more sparsely populated than it is today. In, for instance, the fifteenth century, villages in Central Europe were isolated communities with little contact with an outside world which was unknown and terrifying. In the comparatively deserted forest-land surrounding such a village, anything might happen.

Why, then, this fascination for a world that no longer exists, this desire to be frightened by creatures whom we know lived only in the imagination of man? Why, in the latter portion of the ultra-scientific twentieth century, does civilized man still cling, like the most superstitious peasant and ignorant savage, to his tales of vampirism, lycanthropy and monster-making? Why has horror not gone the way of other outmoded fashions? Perhaps the anwer—without involving ourselves in pathological and psychological meandering—lies in the mind of man itself, springing from mankind's hereditary fear of the dark.

Most of man's religions stress evil as something darkly sinister, festering in and arising from black shadow. From earliest childhood we have learned of the evil powers of darkness that forever wait to drag us from the path of moral righteousness; Satan is refered to as the Black Prince, the Prince of Darkness. Light is Good, dark is Evil. So has it been since our earliest ancestors huddled in fear before the fire that held back the strange, unknown darkness that lay beyond the entrance to the cave. Such racial memories die hard. Have we, as a people, ever really forgotten our fear of the dark? Throughout our long and tortuous history, we have peopled the black shadows with vague, monstrous forms. Most children are born with this inherited fear that makes a night light essential in many homes. They know there is nothing standing in the dark corner of the bedroom, they realize there is no reason to hesitate before entering that dark room, but that twinge of fear, the touch of coldness at the base of the spine, remains.

Why, then, do we permit ourselves to revel in literature and films that play on this ancient fear, that help us to people the darkness with the strange and terrifying creatures that, in our early years, caused us to lie trembling in our beds with blankets pulled over our ears? Perhaps we are striking back at our own childhood, subconsciously proving to ourselves that we know those early fears to be groundless and can now turn to them for a source of amusement.

Perhaps Georges Lefebvre had part of the answer when he wrote of another time: "Melancholy and tears, despair and horror . . . reflection on ancient ruins . . . shook the boredom

of ordered life" [*The French Revolution, From Its Origin to 1793*].

Imagination is one of the most cherished attributes of the human mind, and it is just this attribute which, in our day and age, appears most in danger of extinction. Science has answered just about all our questions concerning life and the world about us. Perhaps it has answered too many questions, left us with too little food for our starving imagination to work upon. An overly mechanized world, in which we know the whys and wherefores of all that we do and all that happens to us, can be a rather colorless world in which to live, one in which the fancied worlds of our imagination become doubly valuable to us.

Much tradition and superstition have fallen under the impact of science, but cold, reasonable logic has in no way dimmed the lustrous appeal of horror, perhaps because we never really did believe it, anyway. We do not need to be told that it is impossible for a man to turn into a wolf; we've known that all along. Science smugly informs us that Dracula could not have lived on for hundreds of years, feasting on human blood; well, we never really believed he did, anyway. We are inclined to agree with the scientist that there is no such thing as a curse issuing from the violated tomb of a long-dead pharaoh, but it makes exciting, imaginative reading.

There may well be, of course, in the still little-understood labyrinths of the human mind, deeper and more ominous reasons for horror's continued fascination. Horror is a world of violence—emotional as well as physical—and even to the most civilized of minds, violence has an inescapable (if somewhat guilty) appeal. This compulsion to violence is part of our emotional composition, and the time in which we live, violent though it may be, gives the individual little opportunity for expression. We all occasionally feel the desire to strike out against supposed personal wrongs, and it is only our civilized nature that prevents us from the violent expression of this psychological urge. In the battle between the Frankenstein monster and a humanity which refused him the understanding he craves, we can find this expression of our own innate hostilities, for there are few of us who do not, at some time or another in our lives, feel we are not properly understood or appreciated. Perhaps, in some small way, the imaginative, often violent, world of horror provides us with a psychological safety value, a mental expression of the hostilities and the urge to violence which we must subdue within ourselves.

The world of horror is also one of death and the grave, and this, too, may provide a psychological basis for its continued popularity. Sigmund Freud and his followers speak often of the strange death wish which lies concealed in us all. There is a frightening, inescapable fascination about the grave and the insoluble mystery that follows the end of life. From the time of our birth, every moment brings us closer to death. It was Voltaire who possessed a clock which, with the chiming of each hour, intoned the solemn words: "One hour nearer the grave." Death is always with us—inescapable, inexplicable. It is the one aspect of life which can not be dismissed, which comes to us all, and there may for all of us be times—times unsuspected—when our minds reach out for the rest, the peace, the mystery of the grave. Perhaps the true fascination of Dracula is not his age-old conquest of death, but the ultimate victory of the specter which comes for us all.

All this may illustrate the reasons for the existence of this particular form of literature, but is there not something more,

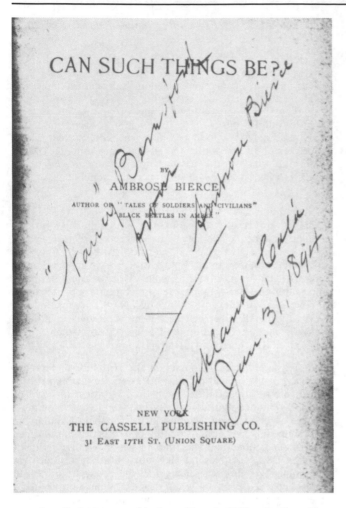

Inscribed title page of Ambrose Bierce's 1893 collection of supernatural and Civil War stories.

some explanation for the sudden, unusual popularity of horror today? To answer this, we need only look at the times in which we live.

Our age has been replete with its own horrors; perhaps we are attempting to forget the terrors of the atomic era by returning to older, somehow more comfortable horrors of the past. It seems peculiar to speak of the literature of horror as "escapist" fare, but, then, perhaps it depends on what it is we wish to escape from.

There is, too, fear of the future. We are no sooner accustomed to the various threats of the Atomic Age when we have the terrible possibilities of the Space Age thrust upon us. Since the days of H. G. Wells, and before, we have read stories of the monstrous figures and forms of life that may be encountered in other worlds. Wells gave us invading Martians of octopoidal form, Wyndham gave us walking plants, Heinlein gave us slugs that attached themselves to the nerve centers of man. For a time the horrors of science fiction quite eclipsed those of vampirism.

But the time when contact may be made with these beings from another world (if they exist, of course) is now coming rather uncomfortably close. We are reaching a point where we would rather not be constantly reminded of the dangers and terrors that may await us once we have been released from the binding

gravity of our own world. The monsters of ancient superstition are somewhat easier to understand than the plant people of Venus; at least we know they do not really exist, while Venus has yet to convince us of her harmlessness. Science-fiction monsters will no doubt always retain their own particular appeal, but they have already given way to the tried and true vampire. Our own monsters at least preserve the semblance of human form. Rather the horrors we know, than those we know not of. They come from a world that cannot be touched by progress, science or reasoning—the limitless, frightening but secure world of the imagination. (pp. 9-14)

> *Drake Douglas, in an introduction to his* Horror! *1966. Reprint by Collier Books, 1969, pp. 1-14.*

FERNANDO SAVATER

[In the following excerpt, Savater considers the paradoxical pleasures of supernatural fiction.]

Strictly speaking, the horror story is THE TALE par excellence, the prototypical story that we expect to hear when we sit with ears wide open at someone's feet, looking into the flickering firelight; it is the story that, by definition, deserves to be told. We are dealing here with a genre which eschews declamation or fulsome recitation, preferring to slide along in a whisper. This reveals its relationship to the primordial essence of the story, an expressive and fundamentally nocturnal mode, as inappropriate to high-sounding language as to pedantry. Both love and this sort of tale are framed in silence and whispered murmurings. Once the voice has been lowered, in the expectant near-silence filled only with the strange creakings of things that are not quite asleep, how can we resist the temptation to conjure up the ghosts that never leave us, to blaspheme (very much under our breath) against reason and its order, to summon up the elemental panic which our hard-working day or our fear of madness causes us to conceal until nightfall? Just for a moment we suspend the healthy hypocrisy that certifies us as sensible and enterprising citizens of countries buttressed by the progress of science and again see ourselves as we really are: inhabitants of the improbable, residents of nothingness, protagonists of a nightmare so devastating and forlorn that the only way we can preserve our sanity is to try to forget our wretched state insofar as we can. The dead whom we had incontinently thrust out of our sight before they began to frighten us come out of their tombs and show us their repulsive living putrefaction, refusing that quiet disappearance to which we consign them with frightened solicitude; they return conscious of the worm that gnaws them, as Blake said. Faced with this ominous return of the spectral, the good people, those the world's progress depends on—healthy minds, livers in excellent working condition—retreat toward sanity, gasping for fresh air, sun, and butterflies. But there is no lack of frantic creatures, viciously conscious of their own shudders, who once they have experienced the lash of the hair-raising sensation cannot get along without it and return incessantly to the authors who can best offer it to them. Among these twilight beings, gentle reader, I have the misfortune to be included.

The disproportionateness and violence of this pursuit does not fail to arouse astonishment among those who do not suffer from it, and who frequently turn to us and say, like the sirens in the second part of *Faust:* "Why do you dally / with this fabled horror?"

It is not easy to give a clear-cut answer to this question; the only thing one can do is to take refuge in that foolish dictum that there's no accounting for tastes, though the truth is that people scarcely do anything but try to account for them. The most usual method of dealing with the subject consists in referring to the well-stocked arsenal of psychoanalytical solutions, whose authority, in the perilous jungle of fear, seems indisputable. According to the doctrine of Vienna, the source of our terrors is to be found in the guilt feelings hidden in the very depths of our psyche, the result of those early sexual conflicts which sweetened the faraway years of our childhood. Childish transgressions and impossible desires, with the consequent fear of mutilating punishment, have stamped our flesh with their mark of anxiety. The fear that goes back to the law transgressed before we were even able to formulate it besieges our dreams, converting them into nightmares. Some persons, particularly obsessed by that unforgettable sin which they cannot remember, experience a certain joy—sadistic or masochistic? there must be a little of everything, for when the time comes to enjoy things we don't want to give up a single thrill—in seeing our most secret shudders literally represented; the invisible attacks that terrorize our souls are objectified and resolved on an imaginary level. The monsters who wander through the darkness of which we consist at last consent to take on a face and form; though their actions may be frightening, at least the fact that they are throwing off their anonymity is something of a relief. Man learns to adore what tears at him for long enough; we live so long with the specter that bears our name that in the end we become quite fond of him. To give a certain bulk and coloration to the anguish that gnaws at us frees us from it in a certain sense by projecting it outward; but, more than anything else, it allows us to see it, that is, admire it. How can we not deeply respect, and even take pride in, that abominable shadow which is the only great thing that was in us!

This theory of the fascination that seems to be part of what frightens us may sound exceedingly paradoxical, all the more since it is essential to repeat that even admired anguish emphatically does not cease to be anguish. But after all, the paradox contained in the psychoanalytical doctrine about dreams is no less of a paradox, despite all of Ernest Jones' rationalizing efforts. Even if we admit the compensatory and lenitive nature of dreams, whose purpose in large part is to maintain the state of sleep itself through the imaginary realization of desires that have gone unfulfilled during wakefulness, how can we explain the operation of nightmares, which sometimes prolong sleep as much as the happiest of dreams, but whose disagreeable and frightening traits appear to harmonize so little with the general doctrine about the role of our nighttime fantasies? The only way to make both positions agree is, I think, this: it must be admitted that to see and suffer through the complete story of our panic is one of the desires that disturb us, and the nightmare satisfies it with terible generosity. Between sheets dripping with sweat and twisted by our convulsive movements, we experience a pleasure for which we pay a price so high that we cannot even recall it later as pleasure, once we are awake. But the bed, that damp and tumbled bed which seems to have undergone a storm of frantic love, gives us the lie.

I shall leave the psychoanalytical language to those who really know how to use it; that is, to those who still think in a more or less openly declared way that the problem is one of cure, or, more modestly, of correct diagnosis. I write from the viewpoint of nonknowledge, from never having learned that language, and above all from resistance to the idea of being cured—my problem is that I can't manage to get sufficiently worse, through lack of courage—and out of the almost-joyous con-

fusion of the symptoms. First of all, we must emphasize the direct relationship of horror tales with death; the problem is death, its inevitability, its gloomy pomps, and, perhaps, its remedies. The subject of death leads us immediately to . . . the supernatural character of the horror stories dealt with in it. Real fright, that fright which is always, either implicitly or explicitly, the fear of death, can have no other basis than the supernatural. Those who do not believe in the supernatural never tremble—stones, for instance, and some social insects. Among the higher animals it is not easy to find cases of such placidity. One need not understand the supernatural in the sense of the transcendent, the spiritual (?), or the magical, although it can eventually be expanded to those and other areas by extension. The supernatural is, simply, what is inadmissible from the viewpoint of necessity, what is unjustifiable by any form of legality, the spontaneity which, instead of joining the productive norm that reason establishes, violates itself like unreason. Death is, we are told, the absolutely necessary thing, the paradigm itself of the unavoidable. We, the future dead men, see it, however, as something shocking, like the flouting of all norms, like an awful or perverse function of the arbitrary. If we could regard death as something really necessary, as fully natural, nothing about it would strike us as terrifying—neither its presence nor the corruption that comes with it nor any of its symptoms. Everybody who has tried to purge us of the evils of death has recommended it as something natural and necessary (Spinoza, Hegel, common sense, science) or nonexistent (Epicurus and the Christians agree about this, for different reasons). The first excuse is negated by our intuition, the second by evidence. Death is not in the future but here and now, incessantly. Nothing is more false than to think it absent as long as we are here and to say that when it comes we will no longer be there to receive it. Death is not compatible with my present self but is its necessary foundation. But its necessity, its naturalness, which constitute precisely death's strength and what we most fear about it, are the aspects of death which frighten us most; that is what we cannot get used to. We pretend to a certain resigned acceptance, a hypocritical familiarity, but the procession of horror goes on inside us and peeps through the slightest chink in our rationalist armor. Fundamentally, what we like about the horror tale is the possibility of openly considering as supernatural that death to whose naturalness we are forced to give lip service daily.

But to admit that death is supernatural is to begin to cherish the forbidden hope of escaping from it. The unthinkable comes to the aid of the impossible. The proceedings that aspire to save us from annihilation pass through the most unbearable agonies. The general theory that underlies all these antideath aims is the one summed up in the verses of the German poet, which tell us that precisely where the danger lies in wait, there also grows what will free us from it, or, more simply, the well-known Latin tag *simil similibus curantur* ["like cures like"]. To shake off the shadow of death requires going down to death itself, entering the dreadful redoubt where it holds sway. "Death's lurking-place is worse than death itself," Seneca tells us. But there the funereal materials are found with which some will try to build a precarious immortality—the coffin filled with the vampire's native Balkan earth, the fragments of cadavers that compose the tormented body of the Promethean creature, the beams of moonlight that will perform the miracle of the werewolf, the terrifying mesmerism that keeps M. Valdemar's body from inevitable decomposition.

All naturalness lost, its false aspect as an obvious thing abandoned at last, death recovers its mantle of freezing mist or its disconsolate nocturnal howls; it joins hands with crime and the accursed but also with magic, with the incantation that brings bodies to life and the pact with the devil, which confers an ignominious vitality. The naturalistic concept of death tries to attenuate its presence, with methods that range from euphemistic expressions when speaking of it to the makeup applied to dead bodies (though this, on the other hand, is certainly an undeniable sign that it is not so easy to become accustomed to death's sway). The supernaturalism of terror, however, exacerbates death's presence to the point of intolerability, tears away the veils that hide its repellent nakedness, and emphasizes its gloomy charms as much as possible. This establishes a conflict between concealments and revelations. Instead of the neat funereal elimination of the mortal remains, which disappear in a trice, there is the spine-chilling account of confinement and asphyxiation whispered by the dead man, conscious of his entombment. Instead of the discreetly displayed photograph of the departed taken one day on the beach, and the gradual fading of his name from family conversations, there is a howling apparition of his ghost or the stink of putrefaction and disturbed earth that accompanies the revenant's footsteps. Instead of the sensible "Let's not think about it," imposed by common sense with regard to death, there is the morbid obsession of the necromantic, the nighttime frequenter of cemeteries, the dissector, or the man desperately in love with a dead woman's bloodless beauty. Instead of that sense of relief that goes along with realization of the inevitable, there is the mania for digging up, for putting together again, for resuscitating, for sending messages from the beyond, characteristic of all those people in tales of terror who cannot accept death. "Bad taste" is contrasted with good, with the ability to cover up death's ravages which defines the civilization based on it. The invisible world makes its claim, comes out in the open, makes us pay for hiding it with a noisy accentuation of its most alarming traits. Death loses all its distance from us and appears as it really is: lord and master, center of the world, the black smell of all existence, the necessary reference point of every action, every glance. But this unveiling of death works against it; death's undisguised appearance damages it. From its arrogance and stereotypes a new hope of life arises, an overwhelming fury that shakes and raises the dead man, extracting another, more lasting kind of vitality from what ought to have been permanent extinction. Cemeteries are filled with activity by night, ruins are again peopled with despairing inhabitants, new and unimaginable species grow in foul-smelling woods and swamps. Though in the end death succeeds in imposing its equilibrium, and dust returns to dust, the power of the absolutely necessary has been exposed for a moment to an intolerable exception; the suspicion slips in that an indomitable will can trick death, seeking its weapons in the slime of corruption itself.

There is more. Actually stating the horrible is subversive, within the bounds of a normality guaranteed by resignation to the deplorable—at least on the level of appearances. The tone itself of the horrifying story contains an attempt to refute death rather than expressing a morbid rejoicing in its triumph, as the superficial observer sometimes believes. It is indifference, however feigned and disguised as "maturity," which issues the death certificate, not the howl of terror. To grow accustomed to an evil means collaborating with it, no matter how many scientific reasons are brought forward for the need to be respectful of it. The tale of terror is based on proclaiming that the stroke of death's claws on reality is something we can never really get used to. But what ferocious changes take place in those who rebel against necessity! How high a price they pay

for their subversive daring! Pale vampires with long fangs, ragged specters with cold curved claws, Lovecraft's abominable tentacular creatures, soulless puppets put together with cadavers, livid virgins who return to consummate their impossible love, sorcerers who become more and more like the demons they keep in their laboratory flasks. They are the unhappy heirs of the Foremost Rebel, the tatters of flesh that the spirit leaves caught on the barbed wire of reality when it tries to escape. Impaled, burned, exorcised, scalded with dreaded holy water, they, the protagonists of the horror story, are undoubtedly the true heroes of terrifying tales, and not those vapid, holier-than-thou creatures who prevail over them at the end of the story. Their name is Legion—the legion of the wounded in the greatest of wars of independence, of the revolution against death. Despite their inevitable final defeat, their mere attempt already constitutes a victory. The reader's feelings toward them are delicately ambiguous, resembling a terrorized recognition, a sort of frightened sympathy. On the one hand our peace of mind, our order, and our sanity demand that they be destroyed, that the menace they represent be smashed; but on the other hand we inevitably identify with their desires, and in our heart of hearts discover that their desperate howls are our secret hymn. They are the greatest danger that awaits us but also one of our best possibilities. Maybe we do not share their decision to seek arms against death in death itself, which presupposes, after all, a certain inverted recognition of its necessity and a new and hopeless justification of the inexorable; but in any case their struggle brings them closer to us, or at least brings them closer to the least submissive part of us. Despite our horror, their exploits are the ones that interest us and not the exploits of those who finish them off or escape from their clutches. What attracts us to them is an open secret, which can be expressed in these terms: we are of the same stock as ghosts.

Are we not, perchance, as supernatural as they, no matter how hard we try to bring ourselves down to the level of a "naturalness" which every one of our actions, not to mention our thoughts, denies with the innermost strength of conviction? The abominable strangeness of monsters' bodies duplicates the alarmed astonishment we feel about our own. We too have tentacles and fetid excretions and undergo changes we cannot control, and are gradually becoming something that is totally alien to us and that will end by terrifying us. They have hastened the process, that is all; they have felt an impatience to go right to the end, to try to go further still, to try to use degradation to their advantage. We recognize ourselves in their busy quiverings, in that insatiable soul which perverts life by trying to intensify it, in that fundamental, unmixed solitude of the inescapably different. If I'm pushed a little I will even say that monsters offer us the reverse of saintliness, owing no less to the sacred simply because it is black. The ghosts of horror stories are the blessed ones of that mad god who appeared to Lovecraft, howling in the darkness; his blood-curdling hagiography is both disconsolate and unconsoling, but it wounds us in our most vulnerable spot.

I have made a direct connection between the tale of terror and the supernatural; someone will be sure to remind me of the statement by Jacques Bergier, who makes Lovecraft "the inventor of the materialist terror tale." I think that I have made sufficiently clear what I understand by *supernatural* to be able to state that if *materialist* means something like "what is determined by necessary physical laws," the French critic's judgment is totally erroneous. Lovecraft's stories, like those of Machen, Chambers, and Hope Hodgson, are just as supernatural—in the sense I mentioned before—as any classical nineteenth-century ghost story, though it is true that they moved the challenge to necessity out of the space in which their predecessors had placed it. Before, the elements that sustained the inexorable were of a Christian and religious kind and served as a framework for the excursions of specters and vampires, still debtors to the devil and enemies of the Cross. Later, necessity assumed a scientific face, and the rebellion against it began to present itself as extravagances of archaeology, physics, or medicine, but this was true quite a long time before Lovecraft. It is true of Mary Wollstonecraft Shelley's famous novel and of "The Facts in the Case of M. Valdemar." What has changed has been the concept of the natural, which before was subject to the designs of providence and today is subject to those of science. Terror tales continue to appeal to the supernatural, whether this be the diabolical aspects of the Christian faith or the points at which scientific knowledge encounters a terrifying limit that breaks down its concept of normality.

In this regard, it is curious to point out the large part played by a certain type of neopaganism in the works of Machen, Blackwood, and Lovecraft. The term *paganism* must be taken in its most literal sense, for in most cases it is a question of forbidden cults that survive in forgotten villages, remote from urban, industrial civilization. In the devil-worship of the classical warlocks and vampires, or Lewis' accursed monk, pulsed the irrepressible presence of the much-persecuted Manichean dualism, Christianity's old twin brother. In Lovecraft's beings of the Old Order, or in Blackwood's elemental spirits, the outlawed pluralities of polytheism reclaim their rights. Monotheism, both the Christian kind and the science-oriented kind, continues to place terror in that difference and diversity which are opposed to it and looks with horror on the distinct return of the unforeseeable in the realm of the inevitably foreseeable, the return of the most terrifyingly remote past, which comes to disturb the dogma of progress with its poisoned emanations. The root of the panic lies in the fact that great Pan is not dead.

To sit down next to the fireplace and start to read a perfect story by Montague Rhodes James, or to squeeze into the subway as you read in snatches the magical lines of the wonderful Jean Ray—tombs yawn, ghosts emerge, and suspicious heaps of rags crawl along the sidewalk after us, or Number 13 of any street can be Maupertuis. The die is cast. We are victims of the oldest vice that literature has propagated—the desire for horrifying tales. Both good taste and every literary precept forbid us; psychiatry places us among the obsessive neurotics or mental defectives and recommends cold showers; the advocate of educational and politically conscious literature deplores the puerility of our escape mechanism. But we take no notice of anyone but Sade, only Sade, when he whispers in our ears, "Extinguish your soul, try to turn everything that alarms your heart into enjoyment." (pp. 149-58)

> *Fernando Savater, "What It Means to Tremble," in his* Childhood Regained: The Art of the Storyteller, *translated by Frances M. López-Morillas, Columbia University Press, 1982, pp. 147-58.*

ADDITIONAL BIBLIOGRAPHY

Ashley, Mike. *Who's Who in Horror and Fantasy Fiction*. New York: Taplinger Publishing Co., 1977, 244 p.
Seminal reference work which includes appendices listing major supernatural stories, contents of important anthologies of super-natural fiction, relevant magazines, and literary awards in the field.

Barclay, Glen St. John. *Anatomy of Horror: The Masters of Occult Fiction*. New York: St. Martin's Press, 1978, 144 p.
Contains essays on the works of Sheridan Le Fanu, Bram Stoker, H. Rider Haggard, H. P. Lovecraft, Charles Williams, William Peter Blatty, and Dennis Wheatley. The critic includes an introductory essay on "The Lure of the Occult."

Blackwood, Algernon. "Introduction to the 1938 Edition." In *Best Ghost Stories of Algernon Blackwood*, edited by E. F. Bleiler, pp. xii-xvii. New York: Dover Publications, 1973.
Blackwood's reflections on the incidents and motives that led to the writing of his supernatural stories. Blackwood observes: "The true 'other-worldly' story should issue from that core of superstition which lies in every mother's son of us, and we are still close enough to primitive days with their terror of the dark for Reason to abdicate without too violent resistance."

Bleiler, Everett F. *The Guide to Supernatural Fiction*. Kent: The Kent State University Press, 1983, 723 p.
Subtitled a "full description of 1,775 books from 1750 to 1960, including ghost stories, weird fiction, stories of supernatural horror, fantasy, Gothic novels, occult fiction, and similar literature." Author, title, and motif indexes are included.

——, ed. *Supernatural Fiction Writers*. 2 Vols. New York: Charles Scribner's Sons, 1985, 1169 p.
Includes sections with essays discussing the lives and works of English and American supernatural writers of the late nineteenth and early twentieth centuries. The authors range from such obscure or marginal figures as Arthur Quiller-Couch and Barry Pain to such major authors in the genre as H. P. Lovecraft, Arthur Machen, and Algernon Blackwood.

Butts, Mary. "Ghosties and Ghoulies: Uses of the Supernatural in English Fiction: Parts I-IV." *The Bookman* LXXXIII, Nos. 496-98 (January 1933; February 1933; March 1933): 386-89, 433-35, 493-94; and LXXXIV, No. 499 (April 1933): 12-14.
Survey of modern supernatural authors considering their works against a background of religion and myth.

Carroll, Nöel. "The Nature of Horror." *The Journal of Aesthetics and Art Criticism* XLVI, No. 1 (Fall 1987): 51-9.
Attempts to establish the precise emotions and sensations experienced as a result of reading horror fiction or viewing a horror film, concluding that these experiences are composed of disgust and fear which arise when confronting something impure.

Conklin, Groff, and Conklin, Lucy. Introduction to *The Supernatural Reader*, edited by Groff Conklin and Lucy Conklin, pp. 11-18. New York: J. B. Lippincott Co., 1953.
Discusses the enduring fascination of supernatural literature.

Crawford, Gary William. "The Modern Masters, 1920-1980." In *Horror Literature: A Core Collection and Reference Guide*, edited by Marshall B. Tymn, pp. 276-369. New York: R. R. Bowker Co., 1981.
Essay on the developments in English and American supernatural fiction after the First World War, followed by a descriptive bibliography of works published during this period.

Daniels, Les. *Living in Fear: A History of Horror in the Mass Media*. New York: Charles Scribner's Sons, 1975, 248 p.
Critical history of horror fiction and film. Chapter five focuses on several supernatural writers of the late nineteenth and early twentieth centuries, including Arthur Machen and Algernon Blackwood, who were associated with the English occult society the Order of the Golden Dawn. Daniels concludes with a discussion of other figures and trends in English supernatural literature of this time.

Davenport, Basil. "The Devil Is Not Dead." *The Saturday Review of Literature* XIII, No. 16 (15 February 1936): 3-4, 18, 20.
Meditation on the sources of fear in supernatural literature.

Derleth, August. "The Imaginative Story: The Horror Story" and "The Ghost Story." In his *Writing Fiction,* pp. 96-119. Boston: The Writer Publishers, 1946.
> Discusses examples of horror and ghost stories for the benefit of aspiring writers.

Ellis, Stewart Marsh. "The Ghost Story and Its Exponents." In his *Mainly Victorian,* pp. 322-31. 1925. Reprint. Freeport, N. Y.: Books for Libraries Press, 1969.
> Draws distinctions between Gothic fiction and ghost stories, and discusses the works of several modern supernatural authors, focusing on May Sinclair's *Uncanny Stories.*

Evans, C. S. "The Lure of the Occult." *The Bookman* LVII, No. 339 (December 1919): 110-12.
> Contrasts the literary ghost story with fiction intended to propagate occult systems of belief, praising the masterpieces of the former and deprecating the latter.

Frank, Frederick S. *Guide to the Gothic: Annotated Bibliography of Criticism.* Metuchen, N. J.: The Scarecrow Press, 1984, 421 p.
> Divided into two main sections based on author nationality and "special subject areas," the latter division encompassing such topics as "Victorian Gothic," "Gothicism and Science Fiction," "Manifestations of the Gothic in Popular Culture," and "Demonological Roots of the Gothic."

Gosse, Edmund. "The Abuse of the Supernatural in Fiction." *The Bookman* VI, No. 4 (December 1897): 297-300.
> Objects to rampant and inept use of the "supernatural" in novels of the day, using this term to subsume stories of science fiction (H. G. Wells's *The Invisible Man,* which Gosse praises as a successful "supernatural" narrative) and satirical fantasy (George Du Maurier's *The Martian*).

Kerr, Howard; Crowley, John W.; and Crow, Charles L., eds. *The Haunted Dusk: American Supernatural Fiction, 1820-1920.* Athens: The University of Georgia Press, 1983, 236 p.
> Collection of essays on the supernatural fiction of such authors as Washington Irving (see G. R. Thompson excerpt in entry above), Edgar Allan Poe, Henry James, W. D. Howells, Mark Twain, Jack London, and Fitz-James O'Brien.

Messent, Peter B., ed. *Literature of the Occult: A Collection of Critical Essays.* Englewood Cliffs, N. J.: Prentice-Hall, 1981, 188 p.
> Essays relating to major themes and figures in the field of supernatural literature, including "The Occult in Later Victorian Literature," by John R. Reed, "Green Tea: The Archetypal Ghost Story" by Jack Sullivan, "*Dracula:* The Gnostic Quest and Victorian Wasteland" by Mark M. Hennelly, Jr., and "H. P. Lovecraft and an American Literary Tradition," by Philip A. Shreffler.

Punter, David. *The Literature of Terror: A History of Gothic Fictions from 1765 to the Present Day.* London: Longman, 1980, 449 p.
> Chapters nine through twelve focus on such late nineteenth- and early twentieth-century authors as Bram Stoker, Ambrose Bierce, Robert W. Chambers, H. P. Lovecraft, Henry James, Walter de la Mare, Algernon Blackwood, Arthur Machen, and M. R. James. Punter's approach to supernatural literature is often psychoanalytic.

Sandoe, James. "Dagger of the Mind." *Poetry* 68, No. 111 (June 1946): 146-63.
> Briefly considers the supernatural as a source of horror in fiction, then focuses on "psychological thrillers," including detective and spy novels, as works which delineate "the horror of man's inhumanity to man."

Scarborough, Dorothy. "Modern Ghosts." In her *The Supernatural in Modern English Fiction,* pp. 81-129. 1917. Reprint. New York: Octagon Books, 1967.
> Compares ghosts in modern fiction with those in Gothic novels.

Search, Pamela. Introduction to *The Supernatural in the English Short Story,* edited by Pamela Search, pp. 7-20. London: Bernard Hanison, 1959.
> Discusses the most prominent authors of English supernatural fiction and examines various aspects of the genre, including horror tales, the psychological ghost story, and types of supernatural manifestations.

Sheridan, Daniel. "Later Victorian Ghost Stories: The Literature of Belief." *Gothic* 2, No. 2 (December 1980): 33-9.
> Contrasts two types of later Victorian ghost stories—those which are resolved by a natural explanation and those which have a supernatural solution—in order to illuminate Victorian attitudes toward skepticism and belief.

Sholl, Anna McClure. "Goose Flesh in Literature." *Catholic World* (December 1939): 306-11.
> Surveys the development of the ghost story from Daniel Defoe to such modern writers as Arthur Machen and Algernon Blackwood.

Sullivan, Jack. *Elegant Nightmares: The English Ghost Story from Le Fanu to Blackwood.* Athens: Ohio University Press, 1978.
> Insightful study of major and minor English ghost story writers. Sullivan views the works of these authors as expressing a vision of a menacing and disordered universe.

——. Introduction to *Lost Souls: A Collection of English Ghost Stories,* edited by Jack Sullivan, pp. 1-12. Athens: Ohio University Press, 1983.
> Discusses the supernatural tales of Edgar Allan Poe and Joseph Sheridan Le Fanu as the prototypes for the modern short story in English, contending that the techniques and themes of nineteenth- and twentieth-century supernatural writers typify those of modern fiction in general.

——, ed. *The Penguin Encyclopedia of Horror and the Supernatural.* New York: Viking Penguin, 1986, 482 p.
> Entries on major and minor figures in the field of supernatural horror, including authors, film directors, artists, and composers, as well as essays on such subjects as "Ghosts," "Horror and Science Fiction," "Urban and Pastoral Horror," and "The Sublime."

Summers, Montague. Introduction to *The Supernatural Omnibus,* edited by Montague Summers, pp. 7-37. 1931. Reprint. Middlesex, Eng.: Penguin Books, 1976.
> Detailed, authoritative history of supernatural literature. Summers contends that an author of supernatural fiction must be a sincere believer in the supernatural in order to produce convincing stories.

Visiak. E. H. "The Significance of Horror-Fiction." *The Nineteenth Century* CXX, No. DCCXIII (July 1936): 103-11.
> Examines various literary expressions of horror through their depictions of physical phenomena which indicate the insubstantiality of the material world and suggest the existence of a supernatural realm.

Williams, Blanche Colton. "Representative Ghosts." *The Bookman* XLV, No. 6 (August 1917): 599-605.
> Classifies ghost stories into several types and analyzes them for narrative structure and effect.

Wolf, Leonard. Introduction to *Wolf's Complete Book of Terror,* edited by Leonard Wolf, pp. xiii-xvi. New York: Clarkson N. Potter Publishers, 1979.
> Offers various reasons for reading horror fiction and provides a taxonomy of "terror literature" which distinguishes between internal and external terrors, material and supernatural terrors, and "wet" and "dry" terrors. Wolf observes that "terror tales do more than elaborate panic for the delectation of their readers. Terror writing validates our continually lingering suspicion that there are mistakes in the Creation; that God swept chaos under the rug at the end of that famous Sixth Day. In fear literature the vast troop of un-creatures—all those mixed-up beasts: part lion and part woman; part wolf and part man; part eagle and part serpent—are still nearby, gnawing away at unalterable Law."

The New York Intellectuals and *Partisan Review*

INTRODUCTION

The New York Intellectuals were a loosely knit, highly influential coterie of writers, political theorists, and literary and social critics gathered in New York City between the late 1930s and the late 1950s. United primarily by their discontent with the unbridled capitalism of the American economic system, members of the group sought to effect positive change through their creative and expository writings and through their journal *Partisan Review,* in which they championed leftist political ideologies and literary Modernism. Collectively these gifted authors constituted a significant force in American society, while the independent writings of such members as Saul Bellow, Lionel Trilling, Bernard Malamud, Irving Howe, Hannah Arendt, and Sidney Hook are among the most important literary and political works of twentieth-century America.

The events that shaped the political ideology of the New York Intellectuals began early in the 1930s. As idealistic young college students during the Great Depression, the original members of the group became convinced that capitalism had proved unworkable and that communism provided a suitable alternative; living and working in New York City, they participated to varying degrees in communist organizations. However, as the decade progressed, they became disillusioned with Soviet Communism under the totalitarian rule of Joseph Stalin, and with the American Communist Party, which retained its allegiance to the Soviet Union. By 1937, those individuals who initially formed the core of the group—Lionel Abel, James Burnham, Elliot Cohen, F. W. Dupee, Paul Goodman, Clement Greenberg, Sidney Hook, Mary McCarthy, Dwight Macdonald, William Phillips, Philip Rahv, Harold Rosenberg, Meyer Schapiro, Delmore Schwartz, Diana Trilling, and Lionel Trilling—were describing themselves as anti-Stalinist Marxists, and at the end of that year, Rahv and Phillips, who had been associated with *Partisan Review* in an earlier, Communist avatar, revived the defunct organ as a forum for the group's work and ideas.

Although the New York Intellectuals were concerned with the social evils of capitalism and the exploration of Marxist alternatives, the majority were writers or critics by profession, and their primary goal in publishing *Partisan Review* was, in the words of Phillips and Rahv, "to bring a rapprochement between the radical tradition on one hand and the tradition of modern literature on the other." While most American leftists considered proletarian art the most appropriate correlative to Marxism, the New York Intellectuals found proletarian art to be philosophically vapid and aesthetically trite, and instead advocated Modernism as a vital, liberating force. Sanford Pinsker has noted that the New York Intellectuals "thought of [themselves] as carrying the banner for European standards of political thought and literary experimentation against the forces of middle-brow philistinism," and, as a result, erudite discussions of the works of James Joyce, Thomas Mann, Franz Kafka, and Marcel Proust appeared in *Partisan Review* alongside analyses of the failures of capitalism.

Their criticism of Stalin and rejection of proletarian art distanced the New York Intellectuals from other American Marxists, but it was their involvement with exiled Bolshevik leader Leon Trotsky that marked their definitive break with the traditional Left. During the Moscow Trials of the mid-1930s, Trotsky had been tried in absentia and convicted of high crimes against the Soviet Union. Although an independent international commission led by the eminent philosopher John Dewey found him innocent of all charges, American Communists continued to anathematize him as an enemy of the Bolshevik Revolution. However, the New York Intellectuals greatly admired Trotsky's writings, pronouncing him "the only major Marxist leader who had written authentic literary criticism," and they continued to print his essays, manifestos, and letters in *Partisan Review*. The group was thus labeled "Trotskyite" by Stalinists, although their adherence to Trotsky's political beliefs was extremely limited. The ideological differences between the *Partisan* circle and the Stalinists led to bitter disputes and recriminations, often given vent in the pages of *Partisan Review* and the Stalinist *New Masses*.

Shortly after the revival of *Partisan Review,* the New York Intellectuals faced the first of many challenges to their always precarious ideological unity in the form of Adolf Hitler's Third Reich. As opponents of totalitarianism in any form, the New York Intellectuals were among the first Americans to denounce Hitler and his imperialistic aims, yet as strong opponents of the American capitalist system, they saw no reason to endorse an American military response which would require further sacrifices from the working classes and which would, if successful, greatly enhance the power of an established capitalist state. However, as the situation in Europe worsened, many New York Intellectuals became convinced that the United States must involve itself, and a vigorous controversy within the group ensued. One notable result of this division was the resignation of Dwight Macdonald, an opponent of the war, from the editorial board of *Partisan Review* in 1943. In his letter of resignation Macdonald charged that the *Partisan Review* editors, specifically Phillips and Rahv, had abandoned their Marxist principles, a charge that Phillips and Rahv hotly denied in a subsequent editorial.

Nevertheless, the political configuration and degree of committment within the *Partisan* circle had altered significantly during the early 1940s: Sidney Hook, the group's only professional political theorist, had begun to view Marxism as a hopelessly utopian ideal, the result of "a desperate quest for a quick and all-inclusive faith that will save us from the trouble of thinking about difficult problems," while, according to James Burkhart Gilbert, Phillips and Rahv "tended more and more to separate literature from politics" and to concern themselves with the former. Many members of the group followed Hook's lead, adopting a pragmatic, liberal approach to social and political issues, and endorsing evolution rather than revolution. At the same time, a second generation had joined the New York Intellectuals, including both students of the first generation and avid admirers of *Partisan Review,* and the political diversity of this contingent further attenuated the Marxist resolve of the group as a whole. Moreover, the majority of these second-generation New York Intellectuals were primarily concerned with literary issues, and the contributions of Bellow,

Malamud, Howe, Norman Mailer, Alfred Kazin, and Leslie Fiedler, and others gradually transformed *Partisan Review* into one of the most highly esteemed American literary journals.

During the 1950s, political considerations reemerged as a primary source of concern for the New York Intellectuals. Despite their support for American policies during the second World War, the majority still viewed themselves as opponents of the American capitalist government. Yet, as Howe has written, "given the growth of Russian power after the war and the real possibility of a Communist take-over in Europe, the intellectuals . . . had to reconsider their political responses. An old-style Marxist declaration of rectitude, a plague repeated on both your houses? Or the difficult position of making foreign policy proposals for the United States, while maintaining criticism of its social order, so as to block totalitarian expansion without resort to war." The New York Intellectuals, with few exceptions, chose the latter course, having recognized the danger posed by Stalin's regime more than a decade earlier. Unlike many other liberals, they also agreed with the contention of Senator Joseph McCarthy and political conservatives that American Communists and Communist sympathizers posed an equally serious threat; but, as political dissidents, former Communists, and strong proponents of free speech, they opposed McCarthy's blanket condemnations. Formulation of a policy of liberal anti-Communism dominated the political thought of the New York Intellectuals throughout the first half of the 1950s; in their last strong demonstration of political unity, they spoke out against the excesses of McCarthyism while continuing to echo the thesis of Sidney Hook's *Heresy, Yes—Conspiracy, No:* "communism . . . is the greatest menace to human freedom in the world today."

Historians agree that while many of the New York Intellectuals continue to play a significant role in American society, they no longer constitute a unified group. During the late 1950s and 1960s, Bellow, Malamud, and Mailer achieved independent success as novelists, while Kazin, Howe, Lionel Trilling, and Fiedler established themselves as leading literary critics. Others assumed positions of influence within the American government—Arthur Schlesinger Jr. as a member of President John F. Kennedy's staff, Irving Kristol as an intellectual consultant for the Nixon administration, and Nathan Glazer as an architect of the policies implemented by President Ronald Reagan. Moreover, with the gradual easing of cold-war tensions, differences that had existed within the group from the beginning became major sources of conflict. Having adopted an anti-Communist posture only in response to a perceived threat and not as part of an overall conservative philosophy, several of the New York Intellectuals, including Macdonald, Rosenberg, and McCarthy, returned to their radical leftist stance, while a number continued to adhere to a more moderate democratic socialism. The most often-discussed group, however, completely abandoned their opposition to capitalism and ultimately became the architects of neoconservatism. Many commentators have offered explanations for this development. Several note that the majority of the New York Intellectuals embraced Marxism in response to feelings of despair and alienation, due in part to their Jewish-immigrant background, and that after achieving personal and professional success, they came to accept and even support the capitalist status quo. Another interpretation is offered by Alan Wald, who locates the source of their neoconservatism in their failure to visualize a workable Marxist alternative to Stalinism. Still others view the neoconservatives' position as a logical response to twentieth-century developments, noting the economic failures of communism,

the totalitarian threat posed by the Soviet Union, and the apparent triumph of capitalism. Nevertheless, while the deradicalization of the New York Intellectuals dominates contemporary analyses, Alexander Bloom has pointed out that "neoconservatism is not what has happened to the New York Intellectual world; it is what has become of some of its members."

The contributions of the New York Intellectuals to American society remain an important legacy. A large number of their independent writings are ranked among the most renowned works of literature, history, and criticism written in the twentieth century, including Bellow's *Herzog* (1964) and *Humboldt's Gift* (1975), Kazin's *On Native Grounds* (1942), Hook's *Towards the Understanding of Karl Marx* (1933), Hannah Arendt's *Origins of Totalitarianism* (1951), and Lionel Trilling's many volumes of literary criticism. In their cultural observations, the New York Intellectuals often identified and described significant developments in Western culture and so, in the opinion of many, remedied the provincialism of American letters. Adopting exceedingly high standards in the evaluation of literature, and championing the so-called "difficult" modern works, they also contributed to the elevation of literary discourse in American journals. In a 1968 essay on the New York Intellectuals, Howe defined their primary achievement as the creation of "a new, and for this country almost exotic, style of work": cosmopolitan, erudite, and frequently contentious. In the political sphere, the early Marxist writings of the New York Intellectuals formed one of the central currents of American dissent, while the later works of those members now defined as neoconservatives have played a critical role in the formulation of contemporary public policy. Cultural historians conclude that as a result of these various contributions, the New York Intellectuals for nearly three decades represented the core of the American intelligentsia, acting as both the voice and conscience of the nation.

DEVELOPMENT AND MAJOR FIGURES

S. A. LONGSTAFF

[*In the following essay, Longstaff discusses the ideological development of the New York Intellectuals as exemplified by the changing editorial stance of* Partisan Review.]

What are we to make of the persistent influence of the "family" of writers known as the *New York intellectuals?* . . .

In 1974, almost four decades after the New York intellectuals first started forming into a cultural-political tendency, a book entitled *The American Intellectual Elite* appeared which purported to identify the seventy "most prestigious" American intellectuals of the Vietnam period. The author [Charles Kadushin], a sociologist, had tackled his subjects by means of an elaborate sampling plan and standardized interviews and questionnaires—a research strategy unlikely to win the cooperation of the more "literary" of his subjects. But however problematic these procedures, the book's roster of elite intellectuals contains few surprises. The New York writers are well represented. At the top, along with such "outsiders" as Noam Chomsky and John Kenneth Galbraith and such "friends" as Robert Silvers and Edmund Wilson, are [Lionel] Trilling, Dwight Macdonald, Mary McCarthy, Irving Howe, Daniel Bell, Norman Mailer, and Susan Sontag—all members in good standing of the New York family.

Amidst vast changes in U.S. cultural-political life, this group endured; and in that endurance lies a remarkable record of literary and editorial achievement, commitments abandoned or subtly recast, and—above all—ceaseless position-taking and intramural wrangling that no one interested in American high culture could ignore. To focus on the New York writers' fate and achievement is thus to touch the intellectual nerve of not one but several ages, from the thirties to the seventies. It is also to shed light on the defensive mentality of such family publications as *Commentary* and the *Public Interest*, magazines which in recent years have displayed much resourcefulness in their efforts to shift the intellectual center of gravity in the U.S. in a rightward direction. Herewith, then, an interpretive sketch of the New York family from its "Stalinist" provenience to the neoconservatism of the present day.

Partisan Review was originally a product of the feverish hopes for social transformation that took hold of American literature during the Depression. It was launched in 1934 under the auspices of the John Reed Club of New York, which meant it had the blessing and financial help of the Communist party. *PR* was intended as the organ of the budding proletarian literary movement—a magazine of criticism, stories and poetry to run in tandem with the more political and Moscow-oriented *New Masses*, then in its heyday. But this arrangement proved unworkable almost from the start. Proletarian literature turned out to be a losing strategy which the party was happy to abandon after 1935 in favour of the literary latitudinarianism of the Popular Front. *Partisan Review*'s founding editors, two young critics from New York, William Phillips and Philip Rahv, had always been slightly uncomfortable with a *Tendenz* aesthetic; the shift in favour of liberal tolerance and patriotism in the arts now made them thoroughly disenchanted with the party's approach to culture, which, as Rahv once remarked, was interested in authors rather than books. Still, no open break with the *New Masses* was made at this point. The two editors struggled to keep their magazine afloat, signalling their differences with the party's cultural assumptions in a number of ways yet always stopping short of outright apostasy. But it was tough going, financially and otherwise, and after a few makeshift arrangements they gave up, folding the magazine in the fall of 1936.

Then in the winter of 1936-37 the second round of the Moscow Trials burst upon New York, playing hob with left-wing sentiments and loyalties. Emboldened by this fresh impulse to opposition, Rahv and Phillips now joined forces with Dwight Macdonald, F. W. Dupee, George L. K. Morris, and Mary McCarthy and began to think of reviving their magazine, this time in opposition to the party and its cultural orbit. For a time their plans were kept dark. But in June 1937, the League of American Writers convened its second Writers' Conference in New York. This party-run event, which like all League activities after 1936 aimed at marshalling the support of big-name writers behind the war in Spain and other Popular Front causes, provided an irresistible chance to strike opposition colours. This is what the conspirators now did (albeit reluctantly on the part of Rahv and Phillips), choosing a session chaired by Granville Hicks, the party's most popular critic, to scorn the party's literary enthusiasms and flaunt their admiration for Trotsky. Nothing of course could have been more provocative, and the whoop-de-do that surrounded the *PR* group at the conference assured the most abusive of welcomes when plans for their

magazine matured in the fall. "A Literary Snake Sheds his Skin for Trotsky" was the way Mike Gold greeted the magazine's formal announcement, in a column he did for the *Daily Worker* even before the first number appeared.

The 1937 Writers' Conference can thus be taken as the inauguration of the second *Partisan Review,* its baptism by fire. The very intensity of the invective lavished on the editors the moment their apostasy was known bespoke the magazine's future importance even as it reflected the crumbling fortunes of the Communist literary movement. A boycott was attempted. Some writers who thought of contributing to the new *PR* (William Carlos Williams for one) allowed themselves to be bullied into line. But from the start the editors could count on the sympathy of established figures like James T. Farrell and Edmund Wilson (even then the dean of American literary journalists). And soon James Burnham, Sidney Hook, Harold Rosenberg, Lionel Trilling, and an unknown poetic *Wunderkind* by the name of Delmore Schwartz were contributing regularly.

The first two years of the second *Partisan Review* were a time of feverish excitement for the writers who now gathered around the magazine. It was the twilight of the thirties. All the frightful tendencies of the interwar period were coming to a head. Still, it was a time when they could act in the world with a flamelike purity of intention. Fearful of their isolation, hungry for some sort of public resonance, they yet exulted in their holy conspiracy on behalf of the twentieth-century masters of the avant-garde and against what they saw as the forces of patriotism and power worship being inflicted on their country's advanced culture. They had, in short, the strength of their innocence, or as some were later to put it, the strength of their illusions. At all events, their magazine prospered, especially after the shock of the Hitler-Stalin pact in August 1939, which sunk the standing of Communism and the Soviet Union in the eyes of most American intellectuals.

But the war followed hard on, bringing some painful choices. In keeping with their Marxism or independent radicalism, now chiefly expressed in terms of a vague admiration for Trotsky, the editors' first inclination was to see the war as primarily a struggle between rival forms of capitalism. For all its evils, Nazism objectively speaking was simply a rationalization of bourgeois rule under conditions of extreme economic dislocation; and for America to enter the war would be to invite domestic fascism and the collapse of the workers' movement— or so the argument went. But as the German onslaught gathered momentum in the Spring of 1940 and the United States became increasingly involved in the fray, the editors found it difficult to hew to this line. Macdonald, still an active Trotskyist, never wavered, but Phillips and Rahv did. (Dupee and McCarthy were no longer involved, and Morris, as always, kept pretty much in the background.) The upshot was an editorial struggle, at first muted, then openly acknowledged, and finally culminating in Macdonald's resignation in 1943 when he moved off to start his own magazine, *Politics.* Though unwilling to speak in patriotic accents, Phillips and Rahv had quietly come to the realization that the war was their war. With Macdonald's departure they could relax the posture of left-wing opposition and concentrate on those cultural issues bearing on the fate of the avant-garde that war and totalitarianism had brought to the fore.

This proved a prescient strategy. A new intellectual generation was coming of age, one that still felt drawn to the oppositional postures of the thirties but had been personally unhinged by the war. Hence its eagerness to trade in Marx for Freud and, above all, its hunger for the least word about the giants of literary modernism, whose luminous, solitary heroism was far more compelling at this time than *littérateurs* acting in history like Malraux or Trotsky could be. For this wartime generation (whose predicament is depicted in Saul Bellow's first novel, *Dangling Man*) *Partisan Review* served as mentor and moral authority. The magazine eased its readers' accommodation to America's new centrality in world affairs even while distancing them from anything that smacked of homegrown innocence and patriotism. In opposition to the finger pointing and cultural nationalism of such writers as Van Wyck Brooks, Archibald MacLeish, and Bernard DeVoto, *PR* made cults of James and Kafka while printing the stern critical strictures of T. S. Eliot; and generally it responded to the wave of literary patriotism it confronted by being resolutely highbrow and "European." Even its undertone of sympathy for the Allied cause, some expression of which could hardly be avoided, was filtered largely through the lens of British experience, especially by George Orwell, whose "London Letter" appeared regularly in *PR* during the war years.

It was on the whole a most unlikely and difficult editorial balancing act, one whose success in retrospect seems based on Phillips and Rahv hitting on just the right mixture of insight into their country's future power and cultural importance and obfuscation of how much the magazine's previous commitments had been shifted or actually compromised. But no less significant in this success were the initiatives taken to overcome the magazine's isolation. During the war, Rahv and Phillips looked in several directions for cultural allies. And found them: in Allen Tate and other Southern apostles of the New Criticism who had started *Kenyon Review* in 1940; in the group that gathered around Cyril Connolly's *Horizon* in England; in the network of social democrats of Menshevik and Bundist ancestry that had become attached to David Dubinsky's ILGWU and Sol Levitas's *New Leader;* and—most improbably—in the Uptown, anti-Zionist American Jewish Committee, which on the initiative of Elliot Cohen was to launch *Commentary* in 1945. On these and other, less important, centers *PR* worked its influence, even while assimilating something of their varied interests to its own expansive outlook. In the process the magazine, together with Dwight Macdonald's *Politics,* was able to nourish a distinct second generation, writers and editors of exceptional promise like Daniel Bell, Alfred Kazin, Leslie Fiedler, Saul Bellow, William Barrett, Elizabeth Hardwick, Irving Howe, Irving Kristol, and Isaac Rosenfeld; while its established figures—Trilling, Rahv, Macdonald, Sidney Hook, Delmore Schwartz, and Mary McCarthy—became much better known. Increasingly this band of "outsiders," whose marginality to both their Jewish and American origins was being turned inside out at this time, were able to order the debates that preoccupied intellectual America during the forties—their sway extending slowly while the war was on, spectacularly once it had ended and normal contacts with Europe could be resumed. And by the end of the decade they had succeeded in imposing not only their preoccupations but their characteristically ebullient modes of assertion and debate on the rest of the U.S. literary world.

All this happened under the impetus of the Cold War. The United States, busy consolidating its leadership of the Western block, was rapidly becoming more dependent on its intellectuals (including its literary highbrows), hence more indulgent of their claims to an exalted status and public support. The Cold War years also witnessed America's assumption of cultural paramountcy in the West, an ascendancy in art and ideas commensurate with her military and economic preponderance. These developments catapulted *Partisan Review* into international prominence. As the most "European" of literary groupings in America, it answered the need for a force that could overcome a lingering U.S. reputation for cultural backwardness. There was also the tremendous moral prestige it enjoyed from its early and passionate "anti-Stalinism," which had the added weight of coming from within the Marxist camp. And, finally, there was its unrivalled sensitivity to the links between high culture and politics. All these factors now fitted it in the eyes of many (including some strategic figures in the U.S. foreign-policy establishment) for a leading part in the cultural Cold War. The opportunities that opened up for those connected with the magazine were thus as dazzling as they were unexpected. From a small and isolated circle in the culturally peripheral America of the thirties, this group was transfigured into the intellectual arbiters of the age that dawned after World War II.

Recognition and a certain type of acceptance came, as it were, overnight. Suddenly foundations and government agencies were eager to extend their patronage, while universities now began hiring literary types whose only qualification was that they wrote authoritatively, if often unfastidiously, about subjects that defied easy compartmentalization. A rapprochement was taking place between intellect and power. And however much acceptance sat uneasily on their shoulders, the *PR* writers were leading the way. Yet, paradoxically, throughout this period of their ascendancy, *Partisan Review* remained every bit a little magazine, its judgments and enthusiasms unremittingly highbrow, its monies garnered haphazardly from "angels," its circulation never much over 10,000. It paid its contributors next to nothing, its more or less full-time assistant editors only 1,500 dollars a year. All of which was entirely in keeping with the avant-gardism so strenuously and confidently advanced in its pages. Nor did its littleness prevent the magazine from nurturing a large and loosely connected "family" of writers of varying ages and interests, many of whom against all their own expectations were fated to make brilliant careers in the fifties and sixties. As the organized center of this expanding circle, *Partisan Review* registered its concerns, spoke up for its accomplishments, regulated entry and standing within its orbit, saw to the recruitment and training of its newest voices, provided its members with a passport to outside centers of power and creativity, and generally served as an emblem of their collective standing in the wider world.

It was their experience of the debacle of the thirties that continued to give the *PR* writers their special stamp during this period. All but the very youngest members of the group had been implicated in the blighted hopes and organized disingenuousness of the intellectual radicalism of that day (even if only by virtue of their opposition to it). And long after Communism ceased to be a force in American intellectual life, it continued to excite their deepest concern. In this there were seeds of a sorry chapter to come; but also some important advantages like the sensitivity to social context and historical movement that distinguished their criticism from that of other American champions of the avant-garde, most notably the New Critics.

In any case, the *PR* writers' postwar anti-Communism ("anti-Stalinism" in their term) was far from being simply a matter of lost certainties and sour memories. Like most Western intellectuals, they were knocked off balance by the East-West polarization that followed the war and fearful lest some or all of Western Europe be swept into the Soviet orbit. Their anti-Communism was also complicated by something more affirmative: a growing attachment to America itself. This attachment gave rise to a feeling that, for all its raw innocence (or perhaps because of it), the United States now embodied the highest possibilities of Western life. This, baldly speaking, was a vertiginously novel way for secular Jewish intellectuals to feel; and it led to the corollary that there had been something pathetically misguided, if not deeply and self-denyingly dishonest, about the characteristic postures of rejection and dissent that had marked their outlook during the thirties and early forties.

These themes were played up with increasing boldness in the decade after 1945, especially in *Commentary* and *The New Leader*. *Partisan Review*, with its different constituency, was naturally more sensitive to the abundant ironies that stuck to such notions. But by 1952 even *PR* was ready to express its attachment to its country in unambiguous terms. The occasion was a famous symposium entitled "Our Country and Our Culture." Of the twenty-four participants (many of them ranking among *PR*'s closest collaborators) only three—Irving Howe, Norman Mailer, and the outsider, C. Wright Mills—really resisted the assumptions of the symposium. The rest, with varying reservations and warnings about complacency, were inclined to agree with the editors that American intellectuals were indeed more accepting of their country and that on the whole this was a good thing. Power, they felt, now comported itself with more maturity; the needs of writers and artists were better understood. This altered climate made America's past tutelage to Europe in cultural matters, which had been a touchstone of the magazine's outlook throughout the thirties and most of the forties, no longer necessary. Even more important, it made any posture of literary antinomianism or exacerbated alienation inappropriate.

With its overriding unity of tone and observation and its outspoken expression of views that had been forming for a decade or more, "Our Country and Our Culture" was something of a high-water mark in the *PR* community's cohesiveness and élan. But even then, in 1952, seeds of division were present. And the magazine was never again to enjoy such an unruffled confidence nor stand so high in the intellectual community at large. The most immediate and visible breach was made by Irving Howe. Taking pointed aim at both Lionel Trilling and *Commentary*, Howe used *Partisan Review*'s pages in the first number of 1954 to issue a personal brief against the rapprochement between mind and power that was taking place and the intellectual timidity and conformity that he felt marked the age. The same animus also went into a magazine, *Dissent*, which provided a forum to other *PR* dissidents (notably Harold Rosenberg and Paul Goodman) and which Howe was instrumental in getting under way.

But the misgivings gathering force in the early and middle fifties touched more people than Howe could reach or *Dissent*, with its political rather than cultural emphasis, could rally. They had to do with the climate generated by the country's concern with loyalty and security—in a word, with *McCarthyism*. Not that *PR* ever printed a word that could be construed as endorsing McCarthy. In fact, countless offhand references to the Wisconsin senator's bullying and buffoonery appeared in its pages. But there was no sustained discussion of the threat to liberty and civilized values that the senator and his legions posed. And for a growing number of the magazine's erstwhile admirers, and some, too, in its inner circle, such avoidance was deeply troubling.

This sense of disquiet was nevertheless slow in forming, and when it did break out it was less *Partisan Review* that stood in the line of fire and more the American Committee for Cultural Freedom. The ACCF was the American branch of the Congress for Cultural Freedom, an organization of Western and some Third World intellectuals that had ostensibly been set up in 1950 to combat Communism in the realm of international culture. Like *Partisan Review*, to which indeed it was closely linked, the ACCF was hostile to the liberalism expressed in magazines like the *Nation* or Kingsley Martin's *New Statesman* or put into practice by Robert Hutchins in his capacity as head of the Fund for the Republic. It was this sort of liberalism's allegedly shallow grasp of Communism that provoked ACCF contempt, its tendency to make allowance for lying and ruthlessness on the left, and above all its moral incapacity to face up to the intellectual corruption of the thirties said to be epitomized by figures like Alger Hiss and Owen Latimore. This much, in any case, everyone in the *PR* camp could agree to. But the ACCF, or at least the element led by Sidney Hook that dominated its executive committee and ran its day-to-day operations, insisted on something more. It said that any shifting of the spotlight away from the sins logical and necessary to the Communist enemy and its liberal apologists was in itself dangerous—and sometimes Communist inspired. McCarthyism, in this view, was a nuisance, or an embarrassment, or an excrescence on what was still a sound system of protection for civil liberties. It was even, according to a vocal right-wing faction in the ACCF led by James Burnham, a useful and commendable force for exposing the Communist menace. But whatever McCarthyism was in the ACCF view, it was not *the* major threat to cultural and political freedom in the United States, the dangers to which were in any case being puffed out of all proportion. Those who said so, it insisted, were innocently, or not so innocently, weakening American prestige abroad and playing into the hands of the Communists.

As the ACCF carried these views into the court of educated public opinion, as it mounted attack upon attack on the beleagured victims of the Congressional Committees and the FBI while at the same time giving the impression that McCarthy was of secondary importance, there was a stir of embarrassment within its own ranks. Some who had been happy to join when the ACCF had been organized in 1950 now drifted away. Others, who quickly earned the label of *anti-anti-Communists*, tried to oppose the ACCF leadership from within without much success. A group headed by Mary McCarthy thought of starting a magazine that would put an anti-ACCF viewpoint into the field. The project came to nought. Finally Senator McCarthy—by this time desperate for anything to keep his name in the headlines—fastened on some ex-Communists employed by the Voice of America in connection with its Eastern-European theatre. Through such figures as Bertram Wolfe and James Rorty, among others, the Voice of America had close ties with the ACCF; and the ACCF leadership also felt the Voice was doing an effective job beaming anti-Soviet propaganda into the satellite countries, which now made McCarthy's reckless charge into something more than a nuisance or embarrassment. And with the senator now stumbling toward his inglorious denouement, the ACCF lashed out against him, actually citing him by name this time where before it had declined to do so, and in the process ridding itself of its right-wing, pro-McCarthy faction.

There were to be more shocks, more defections from the ACCF ranks, and more recriminations between the anti-anti-Communists and those around *Partisan Review* who backed the

ACCF leadership. By the time of the Voice of America debacle, however, the damage had been done. The ACCF record during this period is open to different interpretations. (It is still a matter of bitter controversy.) But what cannot be gainsaid is that its handling of the McCarthy question divided the *PR* writers and diminished their magazine. The split, in fact, touched the editors themselves, with Phillips supporting the ACCF leadership, Rahv doing all he could to distance the magazine from its excesses. But Rahv's efforts were not enough. Many who had once genuflected before *Partisan Review*'s reputation for moral incisiveness, now found in its hemming and hawing over the period's multiple threats to civil liberties something particularly askew—or worse, shabby and inhumane. The magazine was never to recover its old authority.

From 1952 to 1955, *Partisan Review* thus suffered from its connection with the ACCF, even as its Olympian dismissal of the Beats a few years later convinced many observers that years of touting James and Eliot had made it hostile to the freshest impulses of American writing. Murmurs of "Establishment" could now be heard. But if the magazine began to decline as a force in American culture in the second half of the fifties, it was due almost as much to the changing market for advanced or "difficult" literature as to any drift to the right, or political callousness, or misreading of the *Zeitgeist*. By the mid-fifties, if not before, the educated public had well nigh surrendered to the authority of the avant-garde, to the extent at any rate of accepting the mythology surrounding the early twentieth-century heroes of modernism (Proust, Yeats, Joyce, Mann, Kafka, Eliot, etc.) whom *PR* and its cultural allies had made it their business to promote. "Scholarship," which up to the forties had been loath to admit any living writer as a topic of research, let alone as an entry in the curriculum, was now willing to make a place for "criticism" in the country's leading English departments. Likewise magazines that catered to the metropolitan upper-middle class, such as the *New Yorker* or the *Atlantic,* were softening their traditional hostility toward avant-garde writing. Under the circumstances, Rahv and Phillips could hardly expect to monopolize the best efforts of writers they had discovered and nourished in less receptive times.

But if the magazine itself lost influence—and it is important to stress the loss was gradual—most of the writers associated with it did not. Nor, in spite of the strains of the McCarthy years, did their sense of community dissolve. Political differences continued to rankle. They were indeed to burst out anew with the rupture of intellectual temper that came in the sixties. But with the Cold War losing its urgency and the ACCF more or less going out of business after 1956, many within the *PR* family who had been at odds with each other had their sense of community rekindled by a cultural current few had anticipated.

This was the ascendancy of "Jewishness" in American letters, which was to have such a fateful significance, not only for American Jews and American society as a whole, but (as some would argue at any rate) for Jews everywhere. The *breakthrough,* to use the most apt of the several terms applied to this rise to literary prominence, partook of many aspects of a movement, with various literary idols pulled down (Hemingway especially), reputations fought for, honours captured, and critical categories invented. But we get a better sense of its impact if we see it as the crystallization of a mood. The mood was one in which certain themes associated with Jewish existence—wandering and homelessness, urban fluidity and chaos; the playful intermixing of the vulgar and the sublime, the streetwise and the erudite—became the very idiom by which America's literary culture spoke to itself and the world. (Auden's oft-repeated remark about Kafka—"It was fit and proper that Kafka should have been a Jew, for the Jews have for a long time been placed in the position in which we are all now to be, of having no home"—suggests something of the receptivity to such terms.) *Partisan Review,* to be sure, had had a great deal to do with preparing the way for this mood, especially inasmuch as there had always been something about its roughhouse polemical style and even its cultural preoccupations that reflected the Jewish backgrounds of the greater part of its editors and writers. But this secular Jewish dimension, as it were, had pretty much gone unacknowledged, especially by the first generation of *Partisan* writers. It was only in the fifties that it was brought to explicit statement.

Two publishing events touched off the change: the appearance of Bellow's *Adventures of Augie March* in 1953 and of a collection edited by Irving Howe and Eliezer Greenberg entitled *A Treasury of Yiddish Stories* in 1955. In the forties *PR*'s chief imaginative writers—Rosenfeld, Schwartz, McCarthy, and Bellow himself—had cultivated a special, inbred appeal and won modest acclaim by observing the canons of the well-made modernist novel. *Augie March,* however, was something else: a freewheeling, lyrical, untidy evocation of urban-immigrant life that convinced many observers that in Bellow a writer had finally emerged who could do full justice to the social fluidity of the postwar era. Casting aside a concern with the isolated, introspective, alienated self that had cramped his early work, Bellow now celebrated the openness and exuberance of American life—which made his book a sort of fictional analogue of the statements that appeared in the "Our Country and Our Culture" symposium a year before. But what impressed most

Saul Bellow. © Jerry Bauer.

people—what made *Augie March* the single most important event and Bellow the exemplary figure of the breakthrough—was less the book's message and more its success in rendering American experience through the sensibilities of a larky Jewish *schlemiel* and by means of a virtuoso intermixture of Yiddishisms, American slang, and elevated literary English.

Augie March was not only a critical but a popular success, the first novel drenched in Jewish life to impress both the critics and the reading public; and it established Bellow as unofficial laureate of American letters. It was also, though no one saw it at the time, a premonition of Bellow's later, formal break with his modernist upbringing, a turning away from literary *angst* and alienation that in due course a number of other members of the *Partisan* fraternity were also to make. *A Treasury of Yiddish Stories* in a very different way was a move in the same direction inasmuch as it offered a literature rich in sweetness and human affirmation as an antidote to the nihilism and experimental imperatives of modernist writing. Howe's idea was to make contact with the immigrant world he had known in his childhood. But editing and introducing the *Treasury* was far from being simply an exercise in nostalgia. By invoking names like T. S. Eliot and Bertold Brecht (not to mention a host of others out of the pantheon of world literature) in his attempts to place such Yiddish masters as Sholom Aleichem, Mendele, and Peretz, Howe was attempting a novel conjuncture: not simply the rescue of a minor literature and its assimilation into the cultural mainstream, but nothing less than the reconciliation of two alternative worlds of assumption about Jewish life in the Diaspora. In the past these worlds had been at ferocious odds with each other. Now, Howe was signalling—as in a different way Bellow was too—an emotional truce was possible. There was no longer any need for Jewish secularists to divorce their intellectual interests from the promptings of their ethnic-religious backgrounds.

Publication of the *Treasury* touched off a vogue in Yiddish literature that has lasted to this day, and it also launched the curious, not to say phenomenal, career of Isaac Bashevis Singer as an American writer. Howe and his collaborator had been assisted in the venture by Kazin, Rosenfeld, and Bellow, who presumably were acting on the same impulses. In any event, the collection's success was further proof (if any were needed) of the sway the *PR* writers continued to exercise over literary taste in America.

They were less sectarian now, were these men and women of the thirties; and, notwithstanding the Jewish vogue (which never did cause much of a stir in the founding generation), less inwardly absorbed in literature. The Age of Criticism was passing and with it some of the solemn enthusiasm for writers like Kierkegaard and Dostoevsky, whose bleak acceptance of human evil had helped literary people adjust themselves to the mood of intellectual powerlessness that had set in after World War II. Under the circumstances the Village-Bohemian round of bars and parties and endless talk began to pale. Academic jobs that might have been scorned in the years immediately after the war and of course would not have been offered before it—jobs with careers attached to them—now were accepted. They were accepted gratefully or grudgingly, as the case may be, often out of a sense of exhaustion or even disgust with the literary life. But they were accepted all the same.

All this, to be sure, may be put down to age. A writer rarely hopes so extravagantly or dares as much at forty as at thirty or twenty-five. But it also reflected *the age*, or *the culture*, as the *PR* writers themselves might put it. The culture not only

had careers, comfort, and fame to offer. It also wanted distinguished intellectuals to provide some tone to public functions at home and abroad, and it expected them to take their place among the representatives of the various interests and constituencies that make up the country's official and unofficial elite. This was a reflection of the new maturity of power that some observers, most notably Lionel Trilling, had glimpsed even back during McCarthy's heyday. (As events were to show, however, this maturity had its sinister aspect which Trilling and some others identified with *PR* were unprepared to contemplate.) But it took the advent of the Kennedy administration to make it official. Saul Bellow as Jackie Kennedy's guest at a White House reception for André Malraux! Or Norman Podhoretz airing his views on the urban crisis over lunch with the President himself! This was heady recognition indeed—and so unexpected after the semi-official philistinism of the Eisenhower years. And yet who on reflection could fail to see this recognition as something ordained in the logic of developments that had come about since the war?

In the fifties and early sixties the *PR* writers thus entered upon a serene Indian summer of influence and acclaim. Now widely known, even to some extent outside intellectual circles, they naturally drew the criticism and generated the resentment that established power tends to draw and generate. Yet with the exception of the stir caused by Kerouac, Ginsberg, and the Beats generally, what opposition there was had neither formed into a coherent attitude nor taken on intellectual weight. Perhaps the most indicative sign of the group's standing during this period was the grudging respect paid by old adversaries like the *Nation* and the *New Statesman*—as if the rancorous disagreements of the McCarthy period could be easily forgotten. *Partisan Review* itself, as we have seen, was less vital and important than it used to be. But doing their best writing now not so much for Phillips and Rahv as for publications launched from within *PR*'s orbit (*Commentary, Encounter, Dissent,* and, starting in 1963, the *New York Review of Books*), this group continued to order the debates and broadly set the tone of their country's literary culture.

Vietnam changed everything, dividing and embittering the New York family as completely as it altered the temper of intellectual life in the larger society. It is doubtful whether there has ever been such a rupture in moral feeling in the United States as the one precipitated by the sudden visibility of military and political failure in the winter of 1964-65.

The break was the more painful and bewildering for its being so sudden. Not that premonitory flashes were lacking. The campaign for nuclear disarmament, which prospered with the relaxation of Cold War feelings in the late fifties; the Port Huron inaugural of the American New Left in 1962; the drift of the Civil Rights movement away from gradualism; and (most upsetting of all) the upheaval at Berkeley in the fall of 1964: these developments certainly ruffled the surface of the intellectual calm that prevailed during the first half of the sixties. Yet, Berkeley aside, none of the reflections provoked by them gave evidence of any widespread pessimism or sense that the forces of democratic enlightenment were in retreat. A sanguine outlook persisted. It was sustained at first by the promise and vaunted style of the Kennedy administration and, after the assassination, got buoyed up once again by the extraordinary popularity of President Johnson's civil rights initiatives and other domestic reforms and the electoral rout of Senator Goldwater in November 1964.

Then late in the spring of 1965, after several months of agitation in the universities over the massive troop build-up in Vietnam, and in the immediate wake of the U.S. intervention in the Dominican Republic, Robert Lowell made public a letter he had written refusing an invitation to read his poetry at a White House Festival of the Arts sponsored by the President and Mrs Johnson: "Although I am very enthusiastic about most of your domestic legislation and intentions [it read in part], I nevertheless can only follow our present foreign policy with the greatest dismay and distrust. . . . We are in danger of imperceptibly becoming an explosive and suddenly chauvinistic nation, and we may even be drifting on our way to the last nuclear ruin." To many, the Festival seemed a crude if characteristically Johnsonian gesture aimed at placating intellectual criticism and perhaps capturing some of the highbrow aura enjoyed by the previous administration. Hence the stir over Lowell's refusal, especially when news of it appeared on the front page of the *New York Times* and led in the weeks following to extensive journalistic coverage of the moral unease that the Festival had brought to the surface. Lowell's letter took many thoughtful Americans by surprise, even as its personal directness focused the mood forming against the war. Rarely, as one observer put it, has a writer's expression of concern over his government's conduct had such an immediate public resonance.

Lowell's gesture had been conceived within the small circle running the *New York Review of Books,* which now became a bellwether of dissent on the war. When the *Review* had first appeared in February 1963, its sole aim had been to meet the need for a comprehensive reviewing organ—an American *TLS* was what its organizers actually had in mind. Under the circumstances names were important and the *Review* had drawn heavily on the family, as well as on literary London, in getting underway. ("*Partisan Review* on newsprint" was one of its early tags.) And it had done so without worrying overmuch about anyone's political outlook. Which explains why names like Daniel Bell, Nathan Glazer, and Lewis Coser (though not Sidney Hook or Leslie Fiedler) were almost as likely to appear in the *Review*'s pages during the early years as, say, Paul Goodman or Philip Rahv.

Launching the *New York Review of Books* can thus be taken as one more instance of the *PR* family's collective preeminence. In a certain sense it was the last such instance. Lowell's gesture not only signalled a change in the *Review*'s tone and interests, it also revealed differences of feeling and commitment that proved to be unbridgeable. The same can also be said about a decision made by the *Review*'s inner circle around the same time to open its pages to I. F. Stone, the veteran Washington journalist. Stone's "Stalinist" background during the thirties and the forties had long made his name anathema in family circles, and his appearance in the *Review* shocked and angered many, especially when he was given a leading role in the paper's bitter assault on the war.

Hence the breakup and dispersal of the New York fraternity. The intellectual antinomianism that gathered hurricane force in the second half of the sixties left many old *PR* reputations severely battered, especially after it was revealed, in 1966 and 1967, that the ACCF's parent organization, the Congress for Cultural Freedom, had been partly funded by the CIA. The upshot was a spate of intramural accusations and recriminations and the emergence of two camps. Defensive about the past and deeply affronted by the new mood, which seemed to them a reckless dismissal of the very idea of intellect, many *PR* figures now gravitated toward *Commentary* where editor Norman Pod-

horetz's earlier questioning of Cold War assumptions now gave way to a feeling that an intellectual counterforce was needed to stand up to the rampant "anti-Americanism" on the left. This grouping also found an ally in Daniel Bell and Irving Kristol's new publication, a pointedly non-literary magazine called the *Public Interest,* which they launched in 1966; and it received unstinting, if not entirely uncritical, support from Irving Howe and others around *Dissent.* Howe's leadership and example proved especially important, as it turned out— and not simply because of his extraordinary energy and polemical skills. Unlike many in the *Commentary* faction, Howe and his colleagues had not been taken in by the Congress for Cultural Freedom.

Toward the end of the sixties some of the writers who gathered around *Commentary* shook the habits of a lifetime and started thinking of themselves as conservatives, especially as conventional liberal opinion, while usually avoiding programmatic agreement with the New Left, more and more gave itself over to an emotional rapport with it. Perhaps, too, the increasing number of contacts with Washington and other seats of direct influence on social policy enjoyed by some of the writers around *Commentary* and the *Public Interest* had something to do with this rightward shift. In any case, all in this camp refused to be remorseful about their anti-Communist activities during the fifties, the CIA's part in sponsoring some of them notwithstanding. Most important, all put the highest priority on defending what they felt was defensible about their country— about its foreign policy as well as its domestic arrangements— against the vehement spirit of rejection then surfacing in practically every intellectual quarter. In marked contrast were the activities of those *PR* writers who moved left with the *New York Review.* This faction generally took hope in the political and intellectual energies unleashed during the sixties, even as they despaired over the war and what they felt the war revealed about America's sclerotic institutions and its technocratic bent for human destruction. Some of the older adherents—Macdonald, Rahv, McCarthy, Dupee—now came full circle back to the radicalism of their early careers. All contributed—some very effectively—to the swelling chorus that drove President Johnson from the White House in 1968.

The acrimony that broke out at this time between *Commentary* and the *New York Review* was of course crossed by many concerns unrelated or only dimly related to the war and the New Left: most notably, long-smouldering misgivings about modernism and, indeed, about literature itself as a way of equipping the educated mind to deal with the world; and also about the situation of Israel and American Jewry. How one felt about these and other matters had a bearing, often a decisive bearing, on which camp one was drawn to. But at the deepest level it was what one thought about America that mattered: how one made sense of its promise and fulfillment, its recklessness and irrationalities. More explicitly than ever before, the war had turned how U.S. writers felt about their country into the pivot of their intellectual identities.

Unwilling or unable to respond to the new mood, some *PR* veterans retired to the sidelines; death and the disablement of advancing years also took their toll. Of those who remained active as literary journalists after 1966, an overwhelming majority found it necessary to choose one camp or the other. In the accusations and recriminations that now filled the intellectual airwaves, many charges bearing on conduct during the McCarthy era were blared forth once again; and there is a sense in which the rancorous disputation of the mid-sixties involved a rekindling of animosities that had previously divided anti-anti-Communists from ACCF partisans. But to focus on the tenuous roots of this quarrel would be to miss its main significance. The *New York Review*'s turn to the left and *Commentary* and the *Public Interest*'s equally decisive contribution to the new intellectual conservatism that was emerging in response to the antinomianism of the sixties was an ending, not a continuation. For all the shifting and contradictory postures and intramural differences that had complicated its sense of mission over the years, the *PR* family had survived magnificently into the sixties with its basic feelings about intellect and politics intact. Now its working mythology no longer served. The cohesiveness of three decades had disintegrated.

Since the breakup of the *PR* community in 1966-67, there has been a dispersal of cultural authority in the United States. No single magazine or circle of writers now has the capacity to define issues and make reputations that *Partisan Review* once did. And if *Commentary* and the *New York Review* remain important publications (indeed, in some respects, more important than ever) this is largely due to the success each has had in corralling new writers and catering to constituencies not hitherto reached by literary journalism. And yet one can't quite leave it at that. Even today, in the mid-seventies, some of the magazine's original circle, like Hook, McCarthy, and Rosenberg, are still being heard from; while many members of the second generation—writers like Bell, Howe, Kristol, Kazin, Hardwick, and Bellow, who started out in the late thirties or the forties and have had long productive careers—continue to work away in full harness. And for that matter *Partisan Review* itself still enjoys a curious, flickering life as an academic quarterly, with William Phillips there at the helm, a living monument to a half-forgotten age.

But it is in the third generation, the generation of the fifties—of Podhoretz, Epstein, Sontag, Kramer, Marcus, and Roth—that the *PR* legacy is now most apparent. It lives in the ardency of their concern for issues in which politics and culture intersect and the gifts they bring to publications like *Commentary* and the *New York Review*. In this sense, though the United States is far more culturally polycentric than it was twenty-five or twenty or even ten years ago, the influence of *Partisan Review* is far from having ebbed completely away. (pp. 556-72)

S. A. Longstaff, "The New York Family," in Queen's Quarterly, *Vol. 83, No. 4, Winter, 1976, pp. 556-73.*

NORMAN PODHORETZ

[*In the mid-1950s Podhoretz established a reputation for literary criticism that incorporated a leftwing political orientation. As editor of* Commentary *since 1960, he shifted the focus of that periodical from current Jewish issues to a broader concern with many aspects of American culture. His early criticism, gathered in* Doings and Undoings: The Fifties and After in American Writing *(1964), displays his tendency to relate external social and political issues to the literary work in question. In two autobiographical works,* Making It *(1968) and* Breaking Ranks: A Political Memoir *(1979), Podhoretz chronicles his gradual change in political orientation from leftwing radicalism toward conservatism. In recent years Podhoretz has completely abandoned his leftist position to become a leading neoconservative political essayist. His recent books include the controversial* The Present Danger: Do We Have the Will to Reverse the Decline of American Power? *(1980) and* Why We Were in Vietnam *(1982). In the following excerpt from* Making It, *Podhoretz summarizes the literary and political opinions of the New York Intellectuals, dividing the members into three distinct generations.*]

About ten years after I first set an eager foot into it, the New York literary world began to acquire a recognizable identity in the (more or less) popular mind and even to be spoken of as an Establishment, which no doubt it would have been had it still been in existence. By the mid-1960's, however, it had all but completely disintegrated, its cohesiveness destroyed in the third generation (mine) by the inexorable processes of acculturation. To that extent it resembles many other Jewish families in America, and indeed, anyone who wishes to understand that world would do well to pick up Murray Kempton's clue and to think of it as a Jewish family. Neither the rival idea of a clique nor the posthumous idea of an Establishment can convey so accurately the true flavor of how it operated or can account for its characteristic qualities, its strengths and its weaknesses.

Of course the metaphor of a Jewish family runs into certain difficulties of its own, for several core members (Dwight Macdonald, Mary McCarthy, F. W. Dupee, William Barrett, Elizabeth Hardwick, John Thompson, James Baldwin, and the late Richard Chase) and a few kissing cousins (Robert Lowell, Ralph Ellison, John Berryman, Kempton himself, Michael Harrington, Robert Gorham Davis, the late James Agee, and the late William Troy) were not Jewish at all. Nevertheless, the term "Jewish" can be allowed to stand by clear majority rule and by various peculiarities of temper I shall try to describe; and the term "family" by the fact that these were people who by virtue of their tastes, ideas, and general concerns found themselves stuck with one another against the rest of the world whether they liked it or not (and most did not), preoccupied with one another to the point of obsession, and intense in their attachments and hostilities as only a family is capable of being.

The designation "literary world," on the other hand, is more misleading, for only a very few core members (Saul Bellow, the late Delmore Schwartz, perhaps the late Isaac Rosenfeld, perhaps James Baldwin, and perhaps Mary McCarthy) were known primarily as poets or novelists; and although most of the others were always much interested in literature and habitually wrote about it, at least seven (Meyer Schapiro, Harold Rosenberg, Dwight Macdonald, Paul Goodman, Clement Greenberg, the late Robert Warshow, and David Bazelon) mainly wrote about painting or films or social problems, and at least six more (Sidney Hook, the late Elliot Cohen, Hannah Arendt, Daniel Bell, Nathan Glazer, and Irving Kristol) could hardly be said to have had literary interests at all. A more embracing, if more confusing, term than "literary," then, might be "intellectual," for Jewish or not, literary or not, everyone who ever belonged to the family was unquestionably an intellectual in a very distinct tradition and of a very passionate kind.

At the point when it adopted me and I embraced it for my own, the family spanned two generations, separated by a period of ten to fifteen years; and those few of us who were to make up the third and last generation were separated from the second by a roughly equivalent gap in age. The Founding Fathers, born around 1905, included a few (Philip Rahv and Meyer Schapiro) who had been brought over to America from Russia or Lithuania as children and who continued to speak with noticeably foreign accents all their lives. Most of the other members of the founding generation, however (Trilling, Hook, Rosenberg, Goodman, Greenberg, and Lionel Abel), were born in New York of immigrant Jewish parents from Eastern Europe, or at least raised in New York. Of the rest, Macdonald came from a prosperous (Protestant) Brooklyn family and was educated at Exeter and Yale, and Dupee, of midwestern Protestant background, also went to Yale where he and Macdonald were classmates and close friends.

With the exception of Hook, who wanted to be a philosopher, Schapiro, who probably wanted to be a scholar, and Greenberg, who probably wanted to be a painter, they all as young men had literary ambitions and dabbled, some of them even giftedly, in poetry and fiction. Only Goodman, however, was to make any kind of real stir in the thirties with anything but criticism of one variety or another. Criticism was the mode they all excelled in, all of them being not only marvelously intelligent and learned (in some cases in a style one associates with autodidacts of a particularly maniacal type), but also madly in love with ideas, and (Trilling and Dupee excepted this time) by nature pugnaciously polemical in argument. Insofar as they were formed by native American influences of the immediate past, it was by the Greenwich Village rebels of the teens and twenties, the battlers against philistinism, commercialism, and bourgeois values—writers like Edmund Wilson and Van Wyck Brooks, and the "red-ink boys," as Mencken called them, around the old *Masses,* John Reed, Max Eastman, and Floyd Dell—and also by the expatriate novelists and poets of the period like Pound, Eliot, Hemingway, Anderson, and Dos Passos.

But this particular American ethos was perhaps the least important element of the tradition which they were later to make their own. To describe it in the most general way, that tradition grew out of an effort to forge an alliance between avant-gardism (which is to say, the movement of formal experimentation) in the arts, and radicalism (specifically, Marxist revolutionary socialism) in politics. Probably all the members of the founding generation had been socialists (unless Goodman sprang a communitarian anarchist from the cradle) as well as "modernists" in the twenties, and several of them became Communists while— and this was the unusual twist—remaining modernists in the early thirties. *Partisan Review,* which was of course to be the main family magazine, began publication in 1934 as the organ of the John Reed Clubs, a Communist Party youth group, and then broke about two years later not over politics as such but over literature—Phillips and Rahv, out of the good modernist belief in the autonomy of art, refusing to countenance bureaucratic dictation of their literary tastes and refusing to accept the Stalinist dogma that experimental poets of politically conservative bent like T. S. Eliot were to be attacked as decadent while tenth-rate proletarian novelists like Jack Conroy were to be promoted as great. When Phillips and Rahv, with the help of Macdonald and Dupee (and later Greenberg), resumed publication of the magazine in 1936, it was with the same modernist sympathies and the same belief in the autonomy of art but with a changed political orientation. Still preaching revolutionary socialism, of a vaguely Trotskyite brand, *Partisan Review* was now violently anti-Stalinist, and would continue to be long after the revolutionary socialism had gone the usual way of youthful revolutionary ardors.

This combination of a commitment to left-wing anti-Stalinism and a commitment to avant-gardism became the distinguishing family trait. To be sure, one or two writers in America outside the family (the name of Edmund Wilson comes to mind) were similarly marked off, but not many more than one or two. The great majority of American literary people in the thirties were Stalinist in their political sympathies as well as "middlebrow" in their literary tastes (that is, uneasy with or downright hostile to the modernist movement and much happier with the naturalistic tradition as represented most powerfully at that moment by Theodore Dreiser). Stalinism, of course, did not necessarily entail middlebrowism, for there were some "highbrows" (that is, friends of modernism), like Malcolm Cowley and Kenneth

Burke, who were with the Stalinists (Burke even making use of his acrobatic ingenuity to write a defense of the Moscow Trials); nor, as the examples of Eastman and James T. Farrell indicate, did anti-Stalinism always consort with a friendliness toward modernism. Finally, there were the Southerners like John Crowe Ransom, Allen Tate, and Robert Penn Warren who had their own distinguishing family trait: like Eliot and Yeats and Joyce themselves, they were modernists and at the same time avowed political conservatives.

It was because the political-literary position they held was so unusual that the Founding Fathers, in the highly charged polemical atmosphere of the thirties when friendships and marriages were made and broken on the basis of political views alone, got stuck with one another like a family against the rest of the world. But there was more to it than the word "position" suggests, for out of that position developed an intellectual style which for a long while was almost unique to *Partisan Review,* and which eventually came of its own force to be identified in the eyes of many with the quality of intellectuality itself.

The elements were these: out of the experience of the break with Stalinism, independence of mind—meaning a mind dictated to by nothing but its own sense of reality, and highly skeptical, even suspicious, of other senses of reality; out of the schooling in Marxism, a tendency to view all phenomena, including the arts, in their historical and social context; *but,* out of the schooling in modernism, a simultaneous belief in the irreducible status and freedom of a work of art; out of the schooling in modernism too, a passionate interest in the great masters of that movement and a contemptuous distaste for their "middlebrow" enemies and for the "philistine" critical rhetoric typically employed by such; out of the feeling of beleaguered isolation shared with the masters of the modernist movement themselves, elitism—the conviction that *others* were not worth taking into consideration except to attack, and need not be addressed in one's writing; out of that feeling as well, a sense of hopelessness as to the fate of American culture at large and the correlative conviction that integrity and standards were only possible among "us." The style, then, was characteristically hypercritical, learned, allusive; it took its bearings not from any American tradition of letters (as, for example, Wilson's at least partly did) but from heavier modes of critical discourse which could be traced to France or Germany or Russia.

And, indeed, it was mainly on Europe that the family had its eyes. There were so many people there who would in the coming years be revealed as relatives—Orwell, Koestler, Spender, Merleau-Ponty, Silone, and a dozen others—and so few outside the family proper in America itself. The terms in which the family discussed things, the language it spoke, was a language that seemed to make more sense to European than to American ears; the books which were the family's touchstones and the issues it considered relevant all had greater currency in Europe than in America; and the ideas and tastes to which the family was attached constituted an ambience suggesting Paris rather more than it did New York (New York, appropriately enough, was the *New Yorker* crowd at the Algonquin Round Table, with one foot on Broadway and another on the best-seller lists). Thus, when the family spoke of itself or was spoken of as "alienated," the reference might be to any number of things, but the deepest thing of all was this: *They did not feel that they belonged to America or that America belonged to them.*

Here we have the final element which distinguished their intellectual style from all others then current, giving it a tone of disinterestedness—as of a man who has nothing to gain and nothing to lose—in relation to social, political, and even cultural problems, and rooting it in considerations not of the practical or the viable but of the despairingly moral. (pp. 109-17)

But if not to America, then to what did the family think it belonged? Not, certainly, to the Jewish people. They, of course, were universal men. As good Marxists, they regarded Zionism as yet another form of bourgeois nationalism, they considered the "Jewish question" a minor aspect of the crisis in capitalism, and they looked forward with great equanimity to the disappearance under socialism of the Jews as a distinct people, seeing no point in their survival.

So little point did the family see in Jewish survival that the threat being posed even at that moment by Hitler to the actual physical survival of Jewish men, women, and children did not, to judge by the files of *Partisan Review,* seem a matter of urgent concern. Clement Greenberg showed himself superlatively well qualified for the article on Jewish self-hatred he was to write a decade later in *Commentary* by arguing now, in 1940 (echoing Trotsky, also a Jew), that World War II—the war against *Hitler*—did not merit "our" support; Macdonald, who at least had the excuse of not being Jewish, agreed with Greenberg in crying a plague on both warring houses, resigned from *Partisan Review,* and went on to found his own magazine, *Politics.* There his Trotskyism cheerfully gave way to anarchism and pacifism, a shift which for a time brought him into alliance with Goodman, who, like Rosenberg, had earlier broken with the family for reasons that were partly personal and partly political (Goodman as an anarchist found their Marxism uncongenial—also "they wouldn't print my pieces"—and Rosenberg found it shallow). Phillips and Rahv, with the blunt good sense that always saved both of them from the more egregious potentialities for political stupidity inherent in the radical position, made a hash of the anti-war argument, and Greenberg too resigned (though continuing as a contributor), leaving *Partisan Review* completely in their control. Among the other casualties of World War II would be their revolutionary socialism.

To compensate for the weakening of the family in consequence of these defections and schismatic happenings, the second generation was by now heaving into view. It was truly a second generation in that the Founding Fathers had exerted a formative influence upon its members, helping to shape their ideas, their tastes, their prose, and in general their conception of the nature of true intellectuality and of the intellectual life itself. In the case of the older or more precocious members of the second generation—Mary McCarthy (who possibly even belongs among the first), Delmore Schwartz, William Barrett, Saul Bellow, Isaac Rosenfeld, Richard Chase, and Alfred Kazin—it was perhaps not so much a question of having been formed by the first as of having discovered in themselves a natural affinity with the family style. This may also have been the case to a lesser degree with those members of the second generation who came into visibility a little later, toward the end of the war and right after it: Leslie Fiedler, Irving Howe, Elizabeth Hardwick, Daniel Bell, James Baldwin, David Bazelon, Robert Warshow, Nathan Glazer, and Irving Kristol (the last three, of course, all joining the editorial staff of *Commentary,* which, founded in 1945, was to become along with *Partisan Review* the other main second-generation center). Politically, all were anti-Stalinist, many of them not via a prior period of Stalinism but through Trotskyism or democratic socialism, and those who were literary were strongly committed to modernism (which,

with Schwartz and Barrett, who joined Phillips and Rahv on the staff of *Partisan Review,* amounted almost to a religion).

Still, as might be expected, important differences showed up between the two generations. The second, for example, was much less Marxist in its thinking than the first, though equally given to the seeing of things in historical and social context, and far more Freudian, though equally disinclined to make explicit use of psychoanalytic concepts in critical discourse. The second generation also wrote, or at any rate published, much more fiction and poetry than the first, though everyone in the second wrote literary or social criticism as well. And finally, while the second generation was even more attached to the idea of its own alienation than the first, in reality it felt somewhat more at home in America than the first, just as those who were Jewish tended to be more comfortable with that fact than their elders had been.

Marxism, the creation of a baptized German Jew, issues the command: "Transcend yourself and join in the universal struggle to bring about the self-transcendence of all men!" Psychoanalysis, the creation of an acculturated German Jew who never underwent baptism, demands by contrast: "Accept yourself for what you are and make use of it!" It is accordingly no accident, as disciples of both schools of thought once liked to say, that Jews have been among the most eager listeners to these calls, many of them responding first to one and then to the other at different periods of their lives. Thus it was with the second generation: from Marx to Freud, from self-transcendence to self-acceptance. Schwartz, Bellow, Rosenfeld, Kazin, Fiedler, and Howe—products every one of Yiddish-speaking households—all proclaimed their Jewishness, took relish in it, wrote stories, poems, and articles about it; and so, at the same time, did several members of the first generation, like Rosenberg and Goodman, begin to do. Of course more was involved here than the influence of Freud: Hitler's altogether irrefutable demonstration of the inescapability of Jewishness was no doubt an even more important factor in the emergence of this new attitude.

As with Jewishness, so with Americanness. But here the case is more complicated. Both Schwartz and Rosenfeld (whom Schwartz once jokingly called "the Jewish Franz Kafka") said in a 1944 symposium that Jewishness was not only a joy to them but a valuable asset in that it rendered them doubly alienated from American society. Yet nothing could have been clearer about those two extravagantly endowed young men, neither of whom the gods would ever allow to grow old—one from New York and the other from Chicago, and each in his own ebullient way embodying all the nervous energy, the quick brilliance, and the boisterousness of spirit of the American big city itself—than the easy relation they had to the national culture, both "high" and "low": Hawthorne as well as Hollywood, the New England transcendentalists as well as the New York Giants. And much the same could be said of the whole second generation. The problem of how to reconcile the man in him who loved Hollywood westerns and the man who loved Henry James became the leading theme of Warshow's work, and less explicitly of Bellow's and Fiedler's; it was not a problem which had interested the first generation, and it would never become a problem for them either.

When Rahv, of the first generation, wrote about American literature—and he did so with originality and depth in several seminal essays—it was with the eye of the learned outsider. When the twenty-five-year-old Kazin, of the second generation, turned his amazingly precocious attention on the same subject in *On Native Grounds,* it was with the aggressive conviction that this literature was *his.* The story, in fact, is told of Kazin's extreme irritation with another member of the family (second-generation) who once teased him about a phrase he had used in a piece on Parkman's *Oregon Trail* in *Partisan Review:* "*Our* forests, Alfred?"—which suggests that not everyone of the second generation, not even Kazin himself, had so assured a feeling of at-homeness in America. The nuances of individual feeling aside, however, a tendency to adopt a more benign attitude toward American society certainly was discernible within the family, first generation as well as second, throughout the postwar years.

Thus *Partisan Review,* which since the late forties had been in what was to prove the greatest period of its glorious history, published a symposium in 1951 astonishingly entitled "Our Country and Our Culture," the pronoun by itself being as telling as anything the participants had to say. And indeed why *not* "our" this time? They had, as Mary McCarthy later said, just gone through a war and discovered that they had, whatever ideology might dictate, a personal stake in the victory of America. Besides, the depression was over, the war was over, there was more money around, there were teaching jobs and grants and fellowships to be had, and the big publishers were at last becoming aware of the family's existence (whereas before only a very few had been: Rosenfeld's first collection of stories, to take only one example of many, had to go begging to a tiny and unknown firm in Minneapolis).

Then too, of course, there was politics. As anti-Stalinists who could no longer entertain the hope, if they ever really had, that a true socialist revolution was in the offing, the family was naturally driven to support America as the main defense against the Soviet threat. But if in what was just then beginning to be called the cold war they were all on the side of America, they held differing views of what being on the side of America entailed. Because America was better than Russia, did that mean that America was good, and if so, how good? Because Stalinism was an international menace, did that mean that it was also a domestic threat—greater, say, than McCarthyism? As the 1950's wore on, as Eisenhower followed Truman, as the Oppenheimer case followed the Hiss case, as McCarthy followed McCarran, and as Khrushchev followed Stalin, these two questions were to become a major source of trouble to the family, leading to bitter personal disputes, shifting hostile alliances, and a general weakening of ties.

Hints of all this trouble had already begun to appear by the time I arrived on the scene in 1953, but the crisis was still a long way off. Meanwhile, the main element in the intellectual atmosphere of those years—years which were later to be lumped vulgarly and indiscriminately with the latter part of the decade as the dull fifties—was an exhilaration at the sudden and overwhelming appearance of new possibilities, in life as in consciousness. There was a world out there which no one, it seemed, had bothered to look at before, and everyone, happily shedding his Marxist blinkers, went rushing out to look. At what? Why, at America, of course—"America the Beautiful," as Mary McCarthy called it, by no means altogether ironically, in an article in *Commentary.* (pp. 118-25)

Norman Podhoretz, "The Family Tree," in his Making It, Random House, 1967, pp. 109-36.

THE INFLUENCE OF JUDAISM

RUTH R. WISSE

[*Wisse is a Rumanian-born Canadian critic who has translated numerous works of Hebrew and Yiddish literature into English. In the following excerpt from an essay in which she discusses works by Thomas Bender (see Additional Bibliography), Russell Jacoby, Alexander Bloom, Alan Wald, and Mark Schechner (see excerpts below), Wisse examines the importance of Judaism in the commitment of the New York Intellectuals to Marxism and Modernism, and in their ultimate abandonment of both.*]

By now, most educated Americans know something of the New York intellectuals and their achievement. When William Phillips and Philip Rahv (born William Litvinsky and Ivan Greenbaum) revived the defunct *Partisan Review* (born Communist) in December 1937 as an independent Marxist periodical, they attracted a distinguished circle of contributors who turned the magazine into an exciting intellectual forum. Sidney Hook, Lionel Trilling, Diana Trilling, F. W. Dupee, Mary McCarthy, Meyer Schapiro, Harold Rosenberg, Dwight Macdonald, Clement Greenberg, Lionel Abel, and James T. Farrell were among its original featured writers. Younger by some ten to fifteen years, Saul Bellow, Isaac Rosenfeld, William Barrett, Irving Howe, Elizabeth Hardwick, Delmore Schwartz, Alfred Kazin, Leslie Fiedler, Richard Chase, and Robert Warshow broke into its pages soon after. A "third generation" included Hilton Kramer, Steven Marcus, Susan Sontag, and Norman Podhoretz, the last named of whom was later to characterize the movement as a "Family" of founding fathers and competitive offspring [see excerpt above]. Unlike the Bloomsbury social set in England that finally narrowed around Virginia Woolf, or the court that Jean-Paul Sartre gathered in Paris around *Les Temps Modernes,* this large, fluid American circle had no dominant personality or even, finally, one single magazine at its center, but kept expanding outward, regenerating itself time and again through newer journals like *Commentary* (which was founded in 1945 and featured such writers as Irving Kristol, Nathan Glazer, Daniel Bell, and Paul Goodman) and, much later, in the 60's, the *New York Review of Books* (whose American contributors were mainly drawn from the *Partisan Review* and *Commentary* stables). It became perhaps the largest community of intellectuals in modern times.

This community of the New York intellectuals, most of whom were the children of Jewish immigrant families, changed for all time the atmosphere of American letters. Coming of age between the 1920's and 1940's, they still, as individuals, faced active discrimination in the formal institutions of American higher learning and in the attitudes of the intellectual elite. If, in the 1890's, William Dean Howells had shown a rare hospitality to immigrants when he promoted the translation of Morris Rosenfeld's Yiddish poetry into English and later encouraged the English fiction of Abraham Cahan, much more typical of American men of letters was the fear, expressed most memorably by Henry James, that Anglo-American culture would be fatally contaminated by the incursion of "foreign" elements.

Up until the 1930's Jewish intellectual life in New York had flourished in Yiddish, in a half-dozen daily newspapers, tens of journals and miscellanies, a network of theaters and cafés. Three generations of American Yiddish writers and poets had turned New York into a world center of Jewish creativity. But the same intellectual pressure that had fueled this rise of Yiddish culture in the immigrant community also determined the children's rapid accommodation to English. Parents who wished the best for their children encouraged their passage from home. The public schools, however insensitive some may have been to the feelings of the Yiddish-speaking child, quickly taught him English and thereby held out to him possibilities of advancement and education that he could never duplicate in his immigrant world.

It was to be expected that the young immigrant intellectuals, suspended at first between a home to which they no longer belonged and a society in which they did not yet feel themselves at home, should have expressed a sense of estrangement and alienation. Characterizing the "Family" as a whole in the period that he came to know it, Norman Podhoretz wrote in *Making It* (1967) that "They did not feel they belonged to America or that America belonged to them" [see excerpt above]. Consider, however, the Americanness of this emotion. One can hardly imagine Franz Kafka, Max Brod, Hugo Bergmann, or any other member of that precocious circle of Jewish intellectuals in Prague earlier in the century complaining that he did not feel he "belonged" to Czechoslovakia, or Czechoslovakia to him. The force of Podhoretz's observation derives from the very American expectation that these intellectuals *should* have felt at home in their country, that some anticipated attachment was missing. And in fact by the time *Making It* appeared, the mutual attachment had formed. The New York intellectuals were the first "immigrant" group to be fully absorbed into American literary culture, enlarging the idea of America as it encompassed them.

Although its most famous figure is a novelist, Saul Bellow, not even his fiction, rooted as it is in ideas, challenges the dominant image of the group as a community of *thinkers*. Delmore Schwartz aspired most of all to be a great poet and also came to be well-known for his short stories, yet the philosopher William Barrett has reminded us that Schwartz too was trained in philosophy and "retained from his immersion in it an amazing intuition about ideas." Thus while the phrase New York intellectuals may require some geographic qualification, since some prominent members (including Bellow) hailed from the Midwestern metropolis of Chicago, the choice of the term intellectuals is entirely accurate. These were not, primarily, academic scholars, applying disciplined method to the investigation of a given body of material; nor, though many at least at first were Marxists, were they *orthodox* Marxists, answerable to historically determined laws. They were a literate street gang, using whatever tactics they had at hand in defense of their shifting territory. Ideas were animate—at least as real as the people who held them, to judge from the emphasis in most of their memoirs on intellectual debate rather than on the usual kinds of personal gossip. Ideas were their sport, profession, passion. A tribute to their achievement could well be entitled *The Opening of the American Mind*.

It therefore comes as something of a shock to discover that a major tendency of the books that have lately appeared about the New York intellectuals is to downplay their ideas in favor of other factors. The New York intellectuals believed that their ideas could affect the course of human events. The academics who now write about them with varying degrees of detachment treat them as a curious sociological episode, or as failed revolutionaries, or at any rate as something other than the cultural and political vanguard they set out to be. To be sure, the authors of these books are scholars, and an inevitable prissiness sets in when academics go about analyzing living subjects. In the case of such brilliant subjects, there is also a predictable falling-

off in intellectual quality and style. But I am referring to something more insidious—a revisionism that exploits the opportunity afforded by scholarship to reduce its subject, to render it harmless, or to falsify its nature. (pp. 28-9)

[One] is left wondering: why, if they are not interested in the ideas of the New York intellectuals, and they seem no less eager to attack than to defend them, are today's authors attracted to them in the first place?

The answer is to be sought, I think, in the central notion of the intellectual that was championed by the *Partisan Review* writers in the late 1930's and that still beckons to the generation of scholars that came of age in the 1960's. As formulated by the editors of the magazine in their opening statement, it was a notion of "unequivocal independence." And here, rather than in any of the false or side issues discussed by their academic chroniclers and critics, lies the true problem raised by the New York intellectuals.

Independence from what? In the context of the time, independence from the Communist party, to which the magazine had originally been attached, and also from Stalinist dogmas that exerted an authority beyond the political organization Stalin had set in place. While continuing to acknowledge the importance of Marxism as a political standard, and as one of the two criteria—the other was modernism—informing its opposition to bourgeois society, *Partisan Review* was henceforth to place its editorial accent "chiefly on culture and its broader social determinants."

The original editorial statement . . . presented an embattled group of dissenters ranged against the totalitarian trend in the Communist movement that could "no longer be combatted from within." The justification for their rhetoric of heroic resistance derived from the simple fact that by the 1930's the Soviet Union had already established a worldwide apparatus to ensure an eventual global domination. But note: it was not to any *political* reality (such as a state) that the group mounted its active opposition, but rather to an ideology that had limited their freedom of expression and creativity. In real terms, *their* polity, the state in which *they* lived, allowed them to put out any magazine they liked, and even placed no restrictions on the development of modernism (except in the area of obscenity).

Thus, though it undoubtedly required courage to make a public disavowal of Stalinism in the intellectual climate of the time, the liberty the *Partisan Review* writers championed was a liberty they already enjoyed. To twist the famous phrase of Lionel Trilling, they stood at a *bloodless* crossroads of literature and politics, declaring their independence not only from a system to which they were not subject, but also and at the same time their disaffection from its political alternative, the system that granted them freedom.

Although *Partisan Review*'s declaration of independence did not mention Jews, for those of the New York intellectuals who were themselves Jewish (and they were the majority by far) it justified the same kind of disengagement from the idea (and, later, the reality) of a Jewish polity, and on the same "heroic" grounds. This might seem peculiar. As Jews, most of the New York intellectuals had been the targets of active discrimination, limiting their access to the best American universities and their prospects of employment. As Jews, too, they inherited the history of persecution that had brought their parents to America. The dramatic rise of anti-Semitism between the world wars should have sharpened their sense of injury and danger. To be a Jew was to be on the side of the persecuted.

But even less than opposition to Stalinism required (as it seemed to them) enlistment in the cause of democracy did opposition to anti-Semitism appear to require enlistment in the cause of the Jews. And as in the former case, so too in the latter, Marxism provided the most obvious grounds for keeping one's distance. Marxists in pursuit of a classless international order expected the Jews to lead the process of national self-dissolution because they lacked a country of their own. Unlike, say, the Italians, whose socialism was an expression of their patriotism, the Jews, having delayed their *risorgimento* from the 19th to the 20th century, were to eliminate the phase of national consolidation by dissolving their national identity. The end-product of this divestiture was to be the "non-Jewish Jew," the perfectly deracinated, perfectly cosmopolitan creature.

As for non-Marxist forms of cosmopolitanism (of the kind championed, for instance, by . . . Randolph Bourne), these also restricted the engagement by Jews in Jewish matters. Cosmopolitan Jews might sponsor magazines for the preservation of Jewish writing, or scholarship for a deeper understanding of Jewish history and culture, but not committees to save imperiled Jewish communities overseas.

In short, Zionism and other forms of Jewish political mobilization were opposed by both the hard and the soft American Left, even when they did not require an outright rejection of Jewish particularism altogether. Nathan Glazer has recently observed that among those Jews who were involved in the creation and sustaining of *Partisan Review*, Marxist affiliation did not seem to demand the sort of denial of their Jewishness that was common in Europe. Because social or political acceptance in America did not depend on conversion to Christianity, American Jewish intellectuals did not feel compelled to renounce their Jewishness—or, what may be more to the point, to affirm it strongly. Some of them even thought they were universalizing the best of Judaism by freeing its ethical kernel from the husk of the Law, much as the early Christians had sought to do—though this was not an analogy they applied to themselves. But whatever the motive and circumstance, the fact remains that even today, when, as Glazer notes, everywhere except in the universities "Marxism and all its variants are in ruins, if one views them in serious intellectual terms," questions of Zionism and Judaism still seem out of place in the pages of *Partisan Review*.

Admissible, then, as an item of ethnic identification, Jewishness was forbidden any further claims. Orthodox Marxism denied the existence of a separate Jewish question; but resistance to orthodox Marxism did not imply political or communal allegiances of another order. Applying the model of heroic defiance to all forms of commitment, even to democratic and fraternal obligations that had been conceived as guarantors of freedom, the independent radicals held themselves aloof from political accountability. To this day some Jewish intellectuals cannot distinguish between the totalitarian conformism that was demanded by the Comintern and the voluntary submission to communal priorities of a functioning Jew.

If anti-Communism was one axis of independence from both totalitarian dictates and democratic or fraternal responsibilities, modernism was the other. Modernism was the arena in which the anti-social instincts, the philosophic pessimism, the disintegrating forces that bourgeois democracy feared and tried to stave off could be admitted and given play. A serious student of modern art and culture had to be prepared to follow this vision wherever it might lead, and it certainly led beyond the bounds of his Jewish home. However distant he might other-wise feel from T. S. Eliot and Ezra Pound and the other apostles of modernism, the American Jewish intellectual shared their contempt for the bourgeoisie, and for his own brand of it, the parochial Jewish community.

One such characteristic judgment can be found in the contribution by Lionel Trilling to the "Under Forty" symposium on "American Literature and the Younger Generation of American Jews" that appeared in the *Contemporary Jewish Record* in 1944. In response to a series of questions on the Jewish writer's attitudes to his Jewishness, Trilling remarked that he could not discover anything in his professional intellectual life which could be specifically traced back to his Jewish birth and rearing—and that the Jewish community could give no sustenance to the American artist or intellectual who was born a Jew. These sentiments gained persuasiveness from the fact that their author described himself as a knowledgeable Jew, raised in an Orthodox home, familiar with "Jewish cultural movements," and qualified to speak as an insider. Moreover, he declared it a point of honor not to deny or escape being Jewish, and he also acknowledged that in declaring this he was not saying very much: "Surely it is at once clear how minimal such a position is—how much it hangs upon only a resistance (and even only a passive one) to the stupidity and brutality which make the Jewish situation so bad as it is."

Yet far from tendering this minimalist position apologetically, Trilling made it the springboard of an attack on what he took to be its opposite, the contrived literature of Jewish self-realization of which Ludwig Lewisohn was then the best-known exponent. Lewisohn, whose Jewishness (unlike Trilling's) had remained an impediment to employment in a university, and who in the 1930's became an outspoken Zionist and critic of assimilation, had written a novel suggesting that intermarriage was a sick response to the Jewish situation, and that a healthier alternative lay in Jewish self-acceptance. Trilling must have known that Lewisohn was but a mediocre writer even before he turned to Jewish themes, yet he used this poor book as the occasion for a wider offensive against affirmative Jewishness:

> This was a literature which attacked the sin of "escaping" the Jewish heritage; its effect, it seems to me, was to make easier the sin of "adjustment" on a wholly neurotic basis. It fostered a willingness to accept exclusion and even to intensify it, a willingness to be provincial and parochial. It is in part accountable for the fact that the Jewish social group on its middle and wealthy levels—that is, where there is enough leisure to allow a conscious consideration of social and spiritual problems—is now one of the most self-indulgent and self-admiring groups it is possible to imagine.

One hears the echo of Karl Marx himself in Trilling's identification of the Jew with the smug bourgeois—and perhaps one hears too the strains of Trilling's analyst, for whom an "adjustment" to Judaism may have seemed more neurotic than separation from it.

Trilling's was in any case only the most literate of a number of similar contributions to this symposium. Alfred Kazin, impatient with the dreary middle-class chauvinism he encountered in Zionist clubs, wrote: "I never found chauvinism any more attractive in Jews than in anyone else . . . or lack of imagination and sympathy, or foolish pride that Uzbeks have in those who are only Uzbeks." Clement Greenberg spoke of the suffocating middle-class behavior of American Jews: "No people on earth are more correct, more staid, more provincial, more commonplace, more inexperienced. . . ." Delmore Schwartz and Isaac

Rosenfeld did not dwell so heavily on the defects of the smug Jewish middle class but instead described their own alienation from it in terms that echoed the sentiments of many an American writer decrying native provincialism and the leveling influence of mass culture.

So great was the distance these Jews felt between themselves and their community that they voiced no sense of special responsibility toward the fate of their fellow Jews in Hitler's Europe. In 1944—1944!—they expressed their sorrow at the massacre then going on, and nothing more. (Commenting on American Jewish writers a year later, the Yiddish critic Shmuel Niger bitterly observed, "We suffer not only from Jews who are too coarse, but also from Jews who are too sensitive.")

Was there some other American model of Jewish self-realization Trilling could have found, aside from the writings of Ludwig Lewisohn with their supposed "willingness to be provincial and parochial"? The answer is yes. He could have troubled to inspect, for example, a magazine like the *Jewish Frontier,* sponsored by the League for Labor Palestine, whose writers balanced Trilling's own brand of opposition to the "middle class" with a sense of Jewish urgency. "Parochial" may describe the concentration of these writers on the Jewish crisis, but not what such concentration demanded of them. Monitoring the news from London and Berlin, Warsaw and Moscow, Jerusalem and Washington, *Jewish Frontier* was the first American publication to report on the systematic murder of the Jews. The effort to rescue refugees and to establish a Jewish state in Palestine required of these Labor Zionists, and also of many middle-class Jews organized in B'nai B'rith and Hadassah, a fine attentiveness to complex geopolitical realities. In fact, an attachment to the Jewish fate, as those intellectuals knew who assumed it, was not overly limiting, but on the contrary much too taxing, too extending. The century's history, after all, was being written on Jewish flesh.

As a young man, Lionel Trilling had written in his notebook, "Being a Jew is like walking in the wind or swimming: you are touched at all points and conscious everywhere." Such a Jew could easily be engulfed once the wind and water began to rise. Rather than exposing themselves to the storm, the New York intellectuals (including Trilling himself) spent the 1940's as a Jewish *arrière-garde,* sheltered by the conviction that they were serving a higher purpose. Only decades later did some of them suddenly discover the Jewish state, which had meanwhile transformed world politics and culture.

"Unequivocal independence" turns out to have been an ideal of unencumbered boyhood. The Jewish intellectuals prided themselves on being good sons—they did not deny their Jewish origins—and in their writings they accorded the world of their childhood at least as much warmth as it had offered them; but no reciprocal sustenance. One should keep in mind, in fairness, that their ambivalence toward Judaism was probably also inherited from parents who were prepared to wear out the old-country traditions until they became quite threadbare, while consecrating their children to something "better." Discouraged in different ways by both their parents and the country that had not yet learned to trust them, they made a virtue of the filial role. It is just this mixture of forced and voluntary alienation that appeals to today's new generation of university academics, eager for reasons of their own to keep alive the heroic image of the non-Jewish Jew and the anti-American American.

Sooner or later, however, youthful independence is expected to give way to maturity, sons are expected to become fathers in their turn. For the Jewish intellectuals this proved to be a very slow process.

In the sphere of culture and the arts, maturity came sooner than in the sphere of politics. The Jewish intellectuals joked about their use of the first-person plural pronoun when writing about America. But the query, *our* forests, Alfred?, intended to mock Kazin's presumption of proprietorship in his interpretation of American literature in *On Native Grounds,* had a serious side to it as well. They all had to perform an audacious act of appropriation, to take a kind of responsibility for American culture, and to do so without necessarily relinquishing their identity as Jews. In scholarship, possession of American and English culture could be acquired through knowledge and authority. But in the creation of works of imaginative literature, a deeper self-disclosure was required, for without the release of the Jew in himself, a writer simply could not free his own voice.

Once again, Lionel Trilling's contribution to the "Under Forty" symposium is an instructive historical source. "I know of writers who have used their Jewish experiences as the subject of excellent work," he wrote, but "I know of no writer in English who has added a micromillimeter to his stature by 'realizing his Jewishness,' although I know of some who have curtailed their promise by trying to heighten their Jewish consciousness."

Forcing the imagination is indisputably hard on literature, and few programmatic novels of any sort ever transcend the scaffolding of their intentions. But it was characteristic of Trilling, and of the 1940's, that he should have seen only this side of the problem, while the fiction he himself wrote betrayed the opposite weakness: if no writer could add to his stature by artificially "realizing his Jewishness," a writer could certainly diminish his stature by deliberately refusing to realize it.

Trilling's only novel, *The Middle of the Journey,* is a nearly-great work of fiction. There is no better introduction to the moral and political crisis that overtook young progressive idealists in the late 1930's than this resonant story of John Laskell, a young man who recuperates from the sudden death of his fiancée and his own near-fatal illness by convalescing at the rural home of friends. These friends, the Crooms, are ineducable fellow-travelers, unable to face human limitations whether these take the form of simple mortality or the fact of human wickedness. They cannot bear to hear about Laskell's brush with death; they mistake their unprincipled, selfish handy-man for a noble savage; they deny the testimony of Gifford Maxim, a character modeled on the real-life figure of Whittaker Chambers, who is trying to quit his career as a Communist agent without being killed. In the course of the narrative Trilling brilliantly exposes the intellectual, moral, and political failures of liberals like the Crooms who destroy the good they claim to uphold.

But there is something dead in Trilling's rendering of his protagonist John Laskell that keeps the book this side of greatness. Laskell, identified by almost all critics with the author's perspective, has no past, and none of the social substantiality that Trilling as a critic so appreciated in other writers. Yet it seems clear not only from Trilling's biography but from the context of the book and the problem it addresses that Laskell should have been a Jew—"touched at all points and conscious everywhere." Whatever Trilling's artistic reasons for making Laskell a man without a culture, he did thereby "curtail the promise" of his book.

Indeed, something similar could be said of the early fiction of Saul Bellow and Bernard Malamud. But both Bellow and Malamud later overcame this problem. The artistic distance between Bellow's *Dangling Man* and his *Herzog,* and between Malamud's *The Natural* and his *The Magic Barrel,* suggests in these cases too that "Jewish consciousness" had to be fully liberated from cosmopolitan parochialism (if that term be allowed) before the American Jewish writer could produce an American classic.

Trilling might more accurately have observed that the literary imagination could not be forced in *either* direction, and that Jewish writers would seize the cultural initiative only when Jews themselves began to feel at home in America: literature may be autonomous in setting its own goals, but it can never be independent of its social and cultural sources. And there is an irony here, for the very embourgeoisement that the young (as opposed to the older) Trilling and his fellows professed to find so repugnant was what made it possible for them to detach themselves without strain from the world of their parents and to join without guilt the literary chorus of anti-Babbittry and anti-Main Street. Their accelerating distaste for the Jewish community from which they had emerged was only the other side of that same process of acculturation, and every bit as parochial as the ethnocentricity they were attacking. As the Jewish bourgeoisie tried to keep up with the Joneses, so they were trying to keep up with the (T. S.) Eliots, and both began to succeed at exactly the same time.

In the political sphere, the assumption of mature responsibility was a more complicated undertaking, requiring as it did not only the cultivation of a voice of one's own, but a felt concern for the larger political good. And here, too, "parochial" self-realization was required, first, because no one can be trusted to benefit mankind who is not prepared to protect his small part of it, and, second, because American democracy encouraged the practice of enlightened self-interest as a legitimate ground of public service. On this score, it must be said that perhaps the majority of the New York intellectuals have never completed the transformation from sons into fathers. The story of those who did may one day be counted the truly remarkable achievement of the New York intellectuals as a whole.

The ones I am speaking of did not relinquish the Marxist club in order to go on smashing idols, . . . but in order to smash the Marxist club itself, and with it the idol of the intellectual as righteous avenger or haloed outcast. I do not have in mind Philip Rahv, who in the late 60's came to believe that the old radicalism could live again in the New Left, or Rahv's firm opponents in that belief, whose own brand of nostalgic socialism has nevertheless allowed them to maintain to this day their posture of marginality. Rather I refer to those who have come to be called neoconservatives, and are called that name for the simple reason that they offer no apology for their defense of their country's freedoms and laws, or for their desire to conserve family, religion, and a predominantly market economy.

Irving Kristol says that the neoconservatives' approach to the world is more "rabbinic" than "prophetic," a distinction that explains a good deal about the antagonism they arouse. Any number of modern Jewish intellectuals had found it possible to identify with the biblical Prophets as fellow outsiders, individualists, poets, voices of conscience, and above all, scourges of the rotten rich. But Jewish civilization has survived through the ages thanks to the rabbis, who had, among their other distinctions, weeded out the few reliable Prophets from the many more false ones against whom they maintained a constant vigilance. Intellectuals themselves in their devotion to texts and ideas, the rabbis were also teachers, guides, indispensable links in a chain between past and future, servants of the community. In taking for his intellectual model the rabbi rather than the prophet, Kristol challenges the reign of the radical and the iconoclast, if not the entire "adversary culture" (Trilling's phrase) that has dominated modern intellectual life.

Though opponents of neoconservatism accuse it of hard-heartedness, or selfish conceit, it seems rather to have been born of political penance. The discipline of much neoconservative thought is rooted in self-examination on the part of those who lived long enough to see the consequences of their youthful enthusiasms. The "two cheers" for capitalism offered by Kristol and other former radicals seems to correspond to two major failures of their erstwhile Marxism.

For one thing, as Sidney Hook writes in his recent autobiography, *Out of Step,* "We were so convinced that capitalism was doomed that we ignored its resources of recovery"; once the rhetoric was stripped away, capitalism showed itself better equipped than socialism to provide for the greatest economic good of the greatest number, because it responded more vigorously to the actual requirements of people, and because the resultant economic growth strengthened democratic institutions.

For another thing, the intellectuals had conveniently disregarded the will-to-power concealed in socialist prescription, as it is concealed in all systems that do not openly accredit competition. Socialist intellectuals do not often admit that one of their great incentives for supporting state control of the source of supply and the regulation of the market is the power that accrues to them when businessmen are bridled. If we were to look for mean motives, of the kind intellectuals are quick to find in others, we would put them under suspicion for their insistence that the realm of ideas alone remain beyond the control of government, while other forms of ambition are to be forever chained. Neoconservatives, having lost their faith in intellectual infallibility, tend to be correspondingly more respectful of other areas of initiative.

And what, finally, of the Jews? One of the greatest moral and intellectual failures of the New York intellectuals was their disregard of the Jewish fate, both before and during World War II and in the decades that followed. Curiously, though many other sectors of the American community—including the press, various levels of government, and Jewish organizations—have come under indictment in recent years for their apathy in the face of evil, if not for their passive complicity in it, no such accusations have been leveled against the group of whom the most might have been expected and from whom so little was forthcoming. The myth of "unequivocal independence," or what amounts to the same thing, unequivocal irresponsibility, is apparently still so firmly attached to the intellectuals that no one sees fit to judge them by the same standards that are applied to their fellow citizens.

The intellectuals themselves have been uncharacteristically shy in reappraising this part of their past, but we need not take their silence completely at face value. Consider the strange case of Philip Rahv: although no one continued to insist so long or so stridently on his Marxism, or to demonstrate a greater lack of apparent interest in the disposition of the Jews, upon his death in 1973 Rahv left his money to the state of Israel. In trying to account for this strange leavetaking, William Barrett has recalled a glum conversation the two men had many years earlier about the lack of conviction of Americans. "I wish I were in Israel,'' Barrett recalls Rahv saying with yearning, ''at least people there believe in something.'' Barrett sees the posthumous bequest as an expression both of Rahv's pessimism over his own world and his dream of something better, elsewhere. Because by the time of his death no Communist land could be imagined as that better place, Israel was invoked as a lone last refuge of political idealism.

If Barrett is right, however, Rahv's quixotic testament was no less a mistake than his old indifference to the fate of the Jews. There were indeed those who hoped, however belatedly, that a socialist Israel would somehow replace their lost ideal of a socialist Russia or a socialist America; they were bound to be disappointed once again. Israel is not that place; no place is. And anyway, they had misdiagnosed the problem: bourgeois society was never so flawed as was their dream of a new kind of human being who could transcend it.

Other Jewish intellectuals have seemed to draw sounder conclusions. Saul Bellow's *To Jerusalem and Back* (1976) is not a romantic's hankering for a higher Israel but an intellectual's attempt to destroy the ideas that seek to destroy the Jewish state. Similarly, the neoconservatives' passion for the defense of the free world, which they refer to without irony as the free world, and which emphatically includes the state of Israel, seeks to repair former sins of omission by themselves and others. Pitched now against their own youthful pieties, these former radicals introduce into the world of ideas a rare sense of political responsibility. No one reading the *Partisan Review* manifesto of 1937 could have foreseen so remarkable a transformation. (pp. 33-8)

> *Ruth R. Wisse, ''The New York (Jewish) Intellectuals,'' in* Commentary, *Vol. 84, No. 5, November, 1987, pp. 28-38.*

MARK SHECHNER

[*In the following excerpt, Shechner focuses on the importance of Jewish heritage in the postwar deradicalization of certain New York Intellectuals.*]

To consider the fate of those writers and intellectuals who started out in the thirties is to examine those paradigms of experience and belief that gave order to their lives and a collective identity to their generation: their initial embrace of radical ideas and progressive movements and their eventual disillusionment with both during the years roughly between 1936 and 1945, that is, between the first of the show trials in Moscow and the end of the Second World War. We recall such repentent ex-communists, fellow travellers, Trotskyists, and free-lance revolutionists as James Burnham, Irving Kristol, Will Herberg, Granville Hicks, Sidney Hook, Whittaker Chambers, Max Eastman, Max Shachtman, and John Dos Passos, whose headlong flights from revolutionism to reaction exemplified the panic and instability of those years. So common was the experience that it would appear, in retrospect, to be the defining feature of the era's moral history and a living dramatization of Ignazio Silone's prophecy that the final struggle would be between the communists and the ex-communists. By the early 1950s, the class of '39, acting out rituals of atonement for sins both real and imagined, had assumed spokesmanship for the spirit of postwar deconversion that went by the name of Moral Realism or Crisis Theology or Realpolitik or Pluralism or Pragmatism or the End of Ideology. As we are yet reminded by the passions that can still be aroused by talk of the Hiss or Rosenberg trials or by the charges that continued

to be traded even into the early 1980s by such veterans of the cultural Cold War as Lillian Hellman, Mary McCarthy, and Diana Trilling, there remain pockets of the intellectual life in America where one's moral credit is still computed from the year, even the month, in which one resigned from the Communist party or walked out of the John Reed Club or League of American Writers or let it be known in the right places that one would no longer turn somersaults for the Soviet Union.

Viewed from far enough away, this experience seems entirely unified, and many of the survivors continue to speak of it as *the* experience of *the* thirties or of *our* generation, as though it were a great collective saga with its own oral tradition— who said what to whom the day Zinoviev confessed—its own stations of the cross, and its own secularized myths of death and resurrection. But as we draw close to individual lives, the appearance of uniformity dissolves. The syndrome of pure and simple reaction was not the universal experience, which rarely traced a flawless arc from Union Square to the American Enterprise Institute. Not all postwar sentiment among retreating radicals Kristolized on the right, and not everyone who had once sworn solidarity with striking miners in Harlan County or subscribed to the Comintern's policy of united front from below or waged bitter factional wars over whether the Soviet Union should be regarded as a degenerate worker's state or a bureaucratic collectivist one later signed up for duty with the *Reader's Digest* or pled the case of the free world and its free markets in the pages of *Time, Life, Fortune, National Review, Reporter, Freeman, The Public Interest, Encounter* or *Commentary*.

More definitive of the prewar Left's fate than its eventual anticommunism was its decomposition. A comprehensive history of the great disillusionment would highlight just how complex and eccentric post-Marxist careers could be. It would point out that residuum of anarcho-pacifists who wrote for Dwight Macdonald's *Politics* in the 1940s and never did get around to supporting America's war effort. It would note the stubborn holdouts for solidarity with the Soviet Union who went underground on command in the 1950s and needed the invasion of Hungary and Krushchev's de-Stalinization speech in 1956 to drive home to them the bitter truth. It would feature Edmund Wilson, who passed through Marxism like a night train through the Finland Station on his way to becoming a Yankee curmudgeon. It would take account of the art critics Harold Rosenberg, Meyer Schapiro, and Clement Greenberg, who found more to sustain them in Klee, Michelangelo, Duchamp, or de Kooning than in the pronouncements of their generation's leading spokesmen. It would highlight the religious converts who genuflected to Earl Browder one day and Fulton Sheen the next. And it would give special attention . . . to the outpatients of culture who amended their enthusiasm for social progress by embracing Alienation or Psychoanalysis or Gestalt Psychology or Orgonomy or the Tragic Sense of Life or The Will in Repose or whatever promising schemes for interior revitalization could be shored up against their ruins.

The retreat from radical allegiances fractured the intellectual life of a generation. In the first two postwar decades, no single issue or point of view could command the center of thought as the failures of capitalism had in the 1930s or the Vietnam War would in the 1960s. Even the momentous political trials of Alger Hiss in 1949 and Julius and Ethel Rosenberg in 1950 and 1951 rallied intellectuals into postures of combat only by stirring up their nostalgia for seeing Shelley plain and giving them momentary respite from the ambiguities of post-Marxist politics. Such a complication took place not because the postwar era marked the end of ideology; only Marxism gave signs of being depleted. What it lacked was the ruling idea and sense of common pursuit to give definition to its conflicts. Not even anticommunism, which served as a halfway house for the disenchanted, was ever a comprehensive world view, let alone a sufficient basis for a national politics. It never had a cogent program, save containment abroad and purification at home, and except for purposes of slander and self-advancement, it gave no more guidance to presidents than it did to municipal mayors, since little that matters in the routine operation of electoral politics or government at any level obeys its crude polarities. What are the respective communist and anti-communist (and anti-anticommunist) views on street sanitation, neighborhood redevelopment, nuclear power, sex education in the schools, the death penalty, the Federal Reserve Board, tax reform, nuclear power, water pollution, affirmative action, free trade and protectionism, the Islamic revolution, the PLO? (In Buffalo, where the politics are fiercely patriotic, communism takes a back seat to abortion, crime, utility rates, unemployment, and snow removal as the great bête noire at election time.) That prominent anticommunists these days have strong views on such issues has nothing to do with anticommunism as such. Anticommunism developed in America as a theology without doctrines, a faith without articles, giving it a pragmatic adaptability that positive ideologies invariably lack. That is why a resourceful opportunist like Richard Nixon could rise to power on public fears of domestic subversion and ideological contamination and, once in power, strike Metternichian deals with the Soviet Union, citing for domestic consumption the opportunities for American business, and open relations with China, citing the need for allies against the Soviet menace. Even for intellectuals, who esteem ideologies as sticks with which to beat one another, left anti-Stalinism, which became liberal anticommunism after the war, was a conundrum shot through with compromise, and no one could be surprised at how easily these anticommunists were outflanked and thrown into disarray in the 1950s by the more self-assured and resolutely anti-intellectual assaults upon communism spearheaded by HUAC, Senator Joseph McCarthy, and the campaign of big business to roll back the New Deal. When the liberal anticommunists regained their balance in the 1960s in time to make serious bids for power, it was not strictly as anticommunists at all but as antimodernists and gladiators of culture, taking up arms against the cultural threat they defined as the "adversary culture" or sometimes the "new class" which they, with their special treason-seeking radar, were uniquely equipped to detect.

But if anticommunism as a world view did not provide post-Marxist intellectuals with a secure base of operations, it was, for two decades, the soil in which social thought invariably took root. "The Cold War," as Alan Trachtenberg has reminded us, "was an inescapable fact of life, implicated as much in the spectacular development of technologies of warfare and of communication and transportation as in the unprecedented concentration of power in government agencies, especially those concerned with military affairs and with espionage. . . . The picture of a world divided between 'us,' 'free' and democratic, and 'them,' totalitarian and 'godless,' seemed unshakable, as was the corollary of a need for military strength, preparedness, vigilance." What has to be remembered about the Cold War mind is its apocalyptic pessimism, the conviction that Armageddon is just around the corner, if it hasn't happened already, not with a bang but a whimper. While the United States escaped from World War II virtually unscathed and with

unprecedented power and responsibility on the world scene, the immediate postwar years had brought home sharply the burden of that power in a series of shocks that undercut our élan and turned it into doubt, suspicion, and no small degree of self-laceration. The closing of the Soviet noose around Eastern Europe (to be blamed on Yalta), the fall of China to communism (to be blamed on the State Department), the Russian explosion of an atomic bomb in 1949 (to be blamed on espionage), and the palpable threats to Western interests in Greece, Berlin, and Korea brought the welcome news that not only would our celebration be brief but that our triumph might well have been an apparition, a dream of victory from which we had just awakened to the truth of defeat. Though Americans were no strangers to international power politics before the war, they experienced for the first time the exposure of world leadership and the vulnerability of being the bull's-eye on someone else's coordinates.

The American response to these traumas took two distinct forms that were linked historically but not, it seems, inevitably. One was the garrison state. Unlike the earlier postwar era, America did not demobilize; rather it retooled for the next struggle, putting the American economy on a permanent wartime footing. In diplomatic terms, the new reality took shape behind the Truman Doctrine, which elevated containment into the cardinal principle of American diplomacy, and the NATO and SEATO alliances, which formalized and armed the borders of the "free world." But for the first time in American history, diplomatic warfare took on a distinct ideological coloring, as the potential for ideas as weapons finally sank in and intellectuals in unprecedented numbers were recruited to oversee the new arsenal that was being geared up to meet the ideological challenge of communism. That Jews—to return to our subject—should have figured prominently in this mobilization should surprise no one. (pp. 31-6)

In reviewing the literary record of the first postwar decades, we would automatically single out for special consideration the converts to the inner life, because the artistic by-products of their conversions were particularly rich: much of what was vital in American writing after the war came down in the fertile precipitate of ideas and attitudes released into their thought by the chemistry of socialism on the wane. Yet I call them converts to the inner life advisedly, since such emphasis upon private experience as one finds in the early fiction of Bellow, Rosenfeld, Schwartz, Malamud, and the Normal Mailer of *Barbary Shore* and *The Deer Park* is richly interfused with social consciousness. Turn inward these writers most certainly did; though unlike the symbolists and modernists whom they looked to for lessons in how to charm the unconscious into speech, they did not lock themselves up in Axel's castle. Not for them the oozy synesthesia of *La Nausée* or the Freudian psychodramatics of *Ulysses*. They were unmoved by dissolving perspectives and infinite regresses. They proved to be the most circumspect of modernists. While cheering the rebellious imperatives of the alienated self and adopting the techniques of symbolism and myth that were the formal counterparts of their mood of recoil, they also paid careful attention to the world they anathematized. We can scarcely mistake Bernard Malamud's grocery stores or Saul Bellow's rooming houses or the Brownsville streets of Alfred Kazin's memoirs for the indeterminate or parodic worlds of vanguard fiction. These writers had buckled on the reality principle as securely as one buckles on a seat belt.

In such writing, the harsh world of conditions, exploited with dogmatic fervor by novelists of an earlier decade, is not forsaken for the lush foliage of the dark interior—the flowers of evil—but given an extra degree of resonance. Reality is spiritualized without being dematerialized. It shimmers and becomes, at times, almost intolerably vivid. Such writers pioneered a realism beyond Marx, though not, it seems, beyond Dostoevsky, for even as they flirted with depths beyond what reason alone could countenance, cheering Dostoevsky's underground man and his insistence that two plus two *could* make five if one willed it, they clung fast to a realism that was too deeply rooted to be overthrown by merely literary passions. The postwar Jewish writers favored the self-consciousness of Kafka or Joyce to that of Rimbaud, a self-consciousness haunted by history, not overwrought nerves, whose interior life contained both a social dimension and a political agenda. Saul Bellow's *Dangling Man* and *The Victim*, books so pointedly Russian and dismal, are early instances of a world view that treats the inner life as a theater of *social* drama. Norman Mailer's *Barbary Shore*, with its imaginary rooming houses with real Trotskyists in them, could have been that generation's signature book had it dealt more skillfully with its materials.

The lessons that socialism had taught the Jewish writers about the material foundations of reality, which they absorbed in copious drafts even as they grew skeptical about Marxist calls for a workers' international and socialist appeals for nationalization of productive capital, were appended to the lessons of their own working-class upbringing. They made much of the thick coils of environment and the power of circumstances. Socialism taught them little that childhood poverty had not taught better, that one did not always have choices. Without the shields of money or caste or old boychik connections to defend them against the harsher realities of life, they grew up with a profound respect for the power of property and institutions and a finely tuned receptivity to the weight and solidity of the circumstances in which life is carried on. They never forgot what the Depression taught them: that the irreducible key to life in America was money, and that there was no shame in joining the struggle and battling your way to the top. "What made Sammy run," observes Irving Howe, "was partly that his father and his father's father had been bound hand and foot." The Jewish writers' fathers had fled from pogroms in Galicia and service to the czar in Russia to wind up in America behind a cart or a counter or a table piled high with piecework. They had exchanged the ghettoes of racial oppression for those of economic necessity. It was a step upward of a sort, though in the early years you had to be a skilled opportunist or a Hegelian (from such misery as this must come the synthesis) to see the lower East Side as a marked improvement in your worldly position. The Jewish writers grew up with the economics of scarcity, the only economics they knew: their first paychecks as writers, in some instances, would come from the WPA's Federal Writers' Project in the late 1930s. The world was very much with them, or against them as the case may be, and the ethic of achievement in which they were steeped as thoroughly as their grandfathers were steeped in Talmud and Torah left no room for aristocratic sighs of *contemptus mundi*. How could they reject the modern world when they had scarcely been uptown to catch a glimpse of it? The world to be savored in all its particularity and strangeness was all the more precious for being available to them largely through books, which served as their port of entry into the exotic realms of American manners and morals.

These sons of peddlers and garment workers found a haven in the library, where the great world, as a vast panorama of books, poured out its secrets to them, and they learned to cherish the intricacy of its manners, the strangeness of its rites, the elegance of its decor. As Alfred Kazin recalls,

> For almost five years I had worked toward the book [*On Native Grounds*] in the great open reading room, 315, of the New York Public Library, often in great all-day bouts of reading that began when the place opened at nine in the morning and that ended only at ten at night. . . . Year after year I seemed to have nothing more delightful to do than sit much of the day and many an evening at one of those great golden tables acquainting myself with every side of my subject. Whenever I was free to read, the great Library seemed free to receive me.

There it was, in the grand chambers of the public library, amid the chronicles of a world that was hidden from them in fact but revealed to them in spirit, that these Jews discovered life outside the ghetto to be as rich in customs and folkways, in taste and order, as the one within. There a young Alfred Kazin learned to write as confidently of the gilded parlors and panelled boardrooms he had never seen as he would *only later* of the Brownsville streets on which he still lived. Philip Rahv would discover, in the Jackson Square Public Library (which F. W. Dupee referred to as "Rahv's alma mater"), an affinity with Henry James that would prove more durable than his fading passion for Karl Marx, while Lionel Trilling would discover, in Columbia's Low Library, a mind as intricate and subtle, solid and "Hebraic," as his own: Matthew Arnold. Culture was their romance.

The spirit that animated their writing, fiction and criticism alike, was the spirit of total surrender to canonical texts, as the library replaced the synagogue, Western history displaced biblical lore, and the novel came to do service for the Torah. The word is overdrawn, as if it were holy writ. "There was something about the vibrating empty rooms early in the morning," says Kazin of the Public Library, "light falling through the great tall windows, the sun burning the smooth tops of the golden tables as if they had been freshly painted—that made me restless with the need to grab up every book, press into every single mind right there on the open shelves." Is this library not a temple? Has Kazin not been at prayer? Not for such young men as this the affected languors of the well-bred or the despairs of the sated. Busy as they were absorbing whatever these books could tell them about history and culture, they gave themselves no time to become a lost generation. Lamenting the modern wasteland was strictly a pastime for Ivy League alumni.

How much of this secular transcendence is a residue of the God-intoxicated Hasidism of their grandparents, exalting the splendor of this earth as the handiwork of divinity, is difficult to say, for there are lines of force in this writing that are difficult to trace with any assurance and which the writers themselves may hardly be conscious of. The best one can claim with any assurance is that the Hasidic spirit seems to insinuate itself into the writing of Bellow, Rosenfeld, Kazin, and Fiedler, though it commonly admits indebtedness to Whitman and Emerson rather than the Bal Shem Tov. Bellow's Moses Herzog, in a phrase borrowed from the French philosopher Jean Wahl, speaks of "transcendence downward" as his personal aesthetic, and it was an aesthetic that captured many of Bellow's contemporaries who, bereft of all traditional forms of spirituality, could not leave the spirit alone and brought it into the home as a household god. Even Lionel Trilling, that patriot of evanescence and apprentice to Arnold, Freud, and Hegel, acknowledged in two of his most influential essays in *The Liberal*

Imagination that class and money were basic to the novel. "[The novel] tells us about the look and feel of things, how things are done and what things are worth and what they cost. . . . Every situation in Dostoevski, no matter how spiritual, starts with a point of social pride and a certain number of rubles." To be sure, Trilling was characterizing the novel in its great nineteenth-century incarnation and not the fiction of his contemporaries, which had less of a taste for class, institutions, and the bric-a-brac of traditional cultures. It was the nineteenth-century novel, with its thickness of social texture and density of moral implication, that Trilling found congenial to his own brand of moral intelligence, in no small measure because the great social drama of the novel, the drama of class conflict and class mobility, bore directly upon the social drama of his generation of Jews: the movement from one social class and cultural milieu to another.

Yet at the very moment Trilling was promulgating such views, to speak of money, class, and social pride was already passé in an atmosphere dominated by the asocial methodologies of the New Criticism. Not only did that smack of the shopworn litanies of the 1930s, but it hearkened back to outmoded patterns of social conflict, like the combat between a prosperous and self-satisfied bourgeois class and the restive young artists who rebel against it in the name of higher values: truth, art, the life of the senses, the uncreated conscience of their race. Not only had middle-class authority over the terms of culture been fatally undermined by a half-century of modernist assault, but the educated portions of the middle class had even gone over the rebellion and come out from behind their masks of power and privilege to recite in unison the last word in alienation: *we are all ill*. Yet it is precisely the *backward* note in Trilling's criticism, his consistent allusion to the material solidity of a life founded upon tradition and property, that is his trademark, as it is that of his generation of Jewish intellectuals. Having imported the corrosive spirits of Kafka, Dostoevsky, Freud, and Marx into American letters, the New York intellectuals maintained an untimely interest in social forms and values that were being undercut by the very writers they championed. Their sense of conflict and revolt belonged to the nineteenth century as did their image of the whole life. It might be said of the Jewish writers that they established their credentials as moderns by grounding themselves firmly in the last century—in Tolstoy, Chekhov, Arnold, Mill, Twain, Melville—heeding the example, in this as in so much else, of their Yankee paterfamilias, Edmund Wilson. "It was as though he came into being with the steam engine," recalled Mary McCarthy of Philip Rahv. "For him, literature began with Dostoevsky and stopped with Joyce, Proust, and Eliot; politics began with Marx and Engels and stopped with Lenin. He was not interested in Shakespeare, the classics, Greek city states; and he despised most contemporary writing and contemporary political groups. . . .

In our age of Beckett, Borges, Burroughs, Robbe-Grillet, Nabokov, and the fifty-seven varieties of French critical theory that sanctify the more splendid alienations and boost the "decentered universe" . . . as our birthright, the New York intellectuals by and large are not to be found among the advance men for future shock or the metaphysicians of the void. They constitute an intelligentsia as opposed to an avant-garde, upholding the name of reason in public life above all. "When the intelligentsia turns its attention, or renders homage, to a work of art," observes Renato Poggioli, "it almost always functions in terms of ideological adhesion, that is to say, it attaches itself to content." Or, as Saul Bellow has complained,

a bit disingenuously one feels, "Art in the twentieth century is more greatly appreciated if it is directly translatable into intellectual interests, if it stimulates ideas, if it lends itself to discourse. Because intellectuals do not like to suspend themselves in works of the imagination. They prefer to talk." Largely averse to formalism in all its aspects, the Jewish writers in America, none more persistently than Bellow himself, have continued to devote themselves to reason, reality, and discourse, and to produce a fiction and a criticism that brood over questions of social ambition, social justice, moral judgment, sexual conflict, duty, and guilt, as though the avant-garde had not dismissed them as ephemeral or indeterminate or, worst of all, irredeemably bourgeois. Where among any of the *Partisan Review* critics, for all their youthful campaigns for rebellion and modernism, does one find a taste for the Romantic rebel described by Rimbaud as *"le grand malade, le grand criminel, le grand maudit, et le suprême savant"* ["the great invalid, the great criminal, the great accursed, and the supreme savant"]? They refused to let go of this world and persisted in wrestling with it because, ineluctably, it was there.

The 1940s did produce one notable exception to this rule, though one that confirms the Weltanschauung shared by the rest: Delmore Schwartz, the only poet to penetrate the *Partisan Review* inner circle and the one writer of that generation in whom the waters of modernism ran clear. Unlike the others, he had no tolerance for the drag and friction of daily living, for what E. M. Forster once called "the world of telegrams and anger," though in the end he suffered more telegrams and anger than any of them. He had no politics to speak of, no

Delmore Schwartz, whose troubled life served as the inspiration for Bellow's novel Humboldt's Gift. © *Rollie McKenna.*

inherited cultural baggage he would not gladly jettison, and little more than a midsummer night's dream of history. His imagination lacked the specific gravity of experience and locale, and his romance of origins, no less strong than that of his contemporaries, lacked the grit and vitality of a Yiddish past and ghetto childhood; it was entirely a family romance in the Freudian sense, looking no farther back than his own lamentable birth or, as in his famous story, "In Dreams Begin Responsibilities," the dark hour of his parents' courtship. Having thrown over the ballast of all that was solid and circumscribed, he sought to ground himself in poetry alone, which turned out to be a little like touching down on a cloud. He wrote endless epic poems and verse tragedies about himself, their manner as conspicuously Miltonic as their matter was conspicuously neurotic. He even kept a journal in blank verse, as if to remind himself that nothing less than *Paradise Lost* was the model of his own tragic passage through this veil of tears. In the end, his only anchor was the guilt that bore him down entirely, drawing him to the profession of poetry as to a priesthood of the guilty, but giving him neither doctrine nor experience on which to train his agony. He had nothing of Baudelaire's contempt or Joris-Karl Huysmans's voluptuary metaphysics or Proust's genius for reverie or Eliot's scholarship or Joyce's love and hate of Ireland. He declared himself daily for Beauty and Art, but never knew quite how to conjure up either except to invoke Pegasus, broadcast his misery, and wait for the reviewers to anoint him troubadour of misery.

> I am to my own heart merely a serf
> And follow humbly as it glides with autos
> And come attentive when it is too sick,
> In the bad cold of sorrow much too weak,
> To drink some coffee, light a cigarette
> And think of summer beaches, blue and gay.
> I climb the sides of buildings just to get
> Merely a gob of gum, all that is left
> Of its infatuation of last year.
> Being the servant of incredible assumption,
> Being to my own heart merely a serf.

"A poet shouldn't be that unhappy," Auden said of him, but, then, misery was his very charter as a poet, his precise and sole claim to the calling.

A photo of Schwartz in James Atlas's biography shows him in his twenty-fifth year standing by a table piled high with his notebooks, his collected works, one would guess. One hand is draped with studied languor over a small stack of books—presumably *Oedipus, Hamlet,* and *Werther*—the other holds up a plaster bust of Homer for his dreamy contemplation. The young Narcissus is lost in thought: the tragic sense of life is upon him, and his eyes do not meet Homer's blind gaze except perhaps in infinity where, for all we know, blind gazes, like parallel lines, intersect. On the facing page is a photograph whose tortured narcissism is blunter: Delmore staring intently into a mirror at an afflicted Delmore, "the furtive / Fugitive, looking backward . . . his / Ghost in the mirror, his shameful eyes, his mouth diseased." Only the muse of tragedy can give rise to such trouble, for nothing less than the Fall of Man can be the cause of it. As a poet, Schwartz went in for essentials. Impatient with the given rhythm of things, he short-circuited the normal processes of crime and punishment and got right to the guilt without troubling with the sin. His fondness for the iconography of Christ on Calvary reflected his own secularized version of original sin; his guilt, so far as can be learned from his poetry, attached itself to nothing he had actually done. It was too pure, too bound up with the flagging energies of

the universe itself, the entropy of the stars, to be reduced to specific crimes.

Schwartz was, the point bears emphasizing, born into an affluent though profoundly unhappy family, and was therefore a generation up on the other *Partisan Review* intellectuals in being middle class and miserable and free to abandon himself to mere neurosis. A haut-bourgeois aristocrat of the spirit, he did not rise by luck and pluck from the ghetto like the rest of them; he had the misfortune of falling from a higher place—Washington Heights to be exact—which, when the poetic fever was upon him, he mistook for paradise. He shared the birthright of the *poète maudit* of every age, a cosseted but turbulent childhood that could be blamed for his ills and abjured daily with fanfare and tears. He had a world to lose and apprenticed himself accordingly to the great Christian practitioners of *contemptus mundi:* Rimbaud, Baudelaire, Proust, Pound, and especially Eliot. He even entertained wishes, common to poets of his day, of becoming a Catholic. Lacking the leaded keel of a traditional culture, he adopted poetry as a surrogate culture that gave sanction to his misery, his narcissism, his guilt, his love of vast and airy things.

> For poetry is like light, and it is light.
> It shines over all, like the blue sky, with the same blue justice.
> For poetry is the sunlight of consciousness:
> It is also the soil of the fruits of knowledge in the orchards of
>   being:
> *It shows us the pleasures of the city.*
> *It lights up the structures of reality.*
> *It is a cause of knowledge and laughter:*
> *It sharpens the whistles of the witty:*
> *It is like morning and the flutes of morning, chanting and*
>   *enchanted.*
> *It is the birth and rebirth of the first morning forever.*

In view of such an ardent nostalgia for heaven, we may wonder what Alfred Kazin had in mind in declaring that "In Dreams Begin Responsibilities," in which a twenty-one-year-old Schwartz implores his parents in a dream not to marry because the result will be monstrous, "was the greatest fable I was ever to read of 'our experience.'" Their experience? On the face of it, Schwartz's aspiration was to be all that his generation on the whole was not: transcendent, world-historical, an apostolic successor to Homer, Shakespeare, and Goethe. The disparity between his ambition and his achievement tells us something about the limits beyond which a Jewish intellectual of his generation could not venture. He strikes us now as more the admonitory example than the prophet, a reminder of what the void holds in store for those who launch themselves toward the firmament without inertial guidance systems to hold their point in the churning gravitational fields of the psyche. It may be overstating a point to insist that Schwartz's fate might have been less tragic and his poetry more durable had he been more Jewish, but it may not be wide of the mark to think that he suffered from a personal culture too thin to stand up against the vertigo that vision alone can release in the romantic ego that would rather play Hamlet or Byron than find moral examples closer to home. Schwartz immersed himself in poetry, in sharp contrast to the others of his generation—Bellow, Rahv, Fiedler, Trilling, Kazin—who took their cues from the novel, which offered them the balance and skepticism, the grain of salt, that poetry can ill afford, and which, in its realism, its "manners," its attention to social conflict, social aspiration, social mobility, and social snobbery, could be reconciled with the tatters of Jewishness remaining in them and even be made to stand for them.

I don't wish to give the impression that a purely aesthetic tension between realism and modernism or bourgeois and bohemian tastes has been the driving force of the Jewish imagination in America. That would be putting the aesthetics before the history, the taste before the circumstances, and in treating of Jewish writers, even those most committed to *L'art pour l'art,* one begins with the circumstantial. Behind the formal tensions in the writing of Jews is the demiurge of history and the twin demons of the Jewish imagination throughout its years of exile: past and future, the one called Torah or tradition or Yiskor or "remembering thee O Zion," the other, "when the Messiah comes" or "next year in Jerusalem." What Jewish book of importance, from the Bible to *The Interpretation of Dreams,* has not been a quarrel between memory and desire, between melancholy recollection and prophetic longing, between Mr. Sammler's prison and Mr. Sammler's planet?

From this dual venture of breaking free of the Jewish past while standing firm against the full impact of modern life has emerged a sensibility divided against itself, at once conservative in its nostalgia and radical in its disconnection from nearly every remnant of Jewish history save its most tragic moments. Yet, despite their detachment from Jewish history, the Jewish intellectuals remained, in their relation to Jewish life at large, something less than aliens. They were subsidized rebels, taking flight from their culture with its tacit blessing for the dormitories of parentally approved alienation, where the naked lunch looked gratefully like a tongue sandwich and every path out of Bohemia was a turnpike to *Commentary.* They did not make a clean break with their social base. They uprooted themselves from the middle class only to return to it for moral reinforcement and even inspiration—sometimes just for lunch. The revolts they affected in their youths came to seem, later on, bar mitzvahs, demonstrations that, contrary to Thomas Wolfe, you *could* go home again. You had to. Your lotkes were getting cold. There was little besides the passion for writing and an instinct for rebellion to bind them to the young men of 1919, who returned from the Great War to New York, "to the homeland of the uprooted," as Malcolm Cowley called it in *Exile's Return,* "where everyone you met came from another town and tried to forget it; where nobody seemed to have parents, or a past more distant than last night's swell party, or a future beyond the swell party this evening and the disillusioned book he would write tomorrow." Trilling, Mailer, Kazin, Howe, among others, didn't migrate halfway across America to find Greenwich Village or Columbia; they just got on the bus or the IRT. Leslie Fiedler took the Holland Tunnel from Newark; Allen Ginsberg, a decade later, hitchhiked in from Paterson. Even Bellow and Rosenfeld, who came from a Chicago neighborhood that was little more than Williamsburg writ small, uprooted themselves in the spirit of homecoming. The small towns they forsook in their pursuit of the great world were a far cry from Winesburg, Ohio; the shtetl of Brooklyn was itself something of an international enclave with its own restless and exploratory spirit, its own candy store cosmopolitanism. William Barrett recalls his astonishment in the thirties to find, in visiting the homes of his Jewish schoolmates, "that they could bring into the midst of their family, and as noisily as they liked, their own radical ideas on the intellectual themes of the classroom." The rich vein of sentimentality one finds in some of Bellow's heroes, which the wife of one nastily dismisses as his *nostalgie de la boue,* is more than an indulgence of memory; it is a living bridge of family ties and street corner connections that keeps him mindful of his origins, no matter how high he may rise.

In an autobiographical sketch written in 1946, Irving Howe recalls the painful attendance of the young intellectual, himself, at a family Seder at which he self-consciously keeps watch on himself, "he whose head may have been buzzing a few hours back with Kafka or Existentialism or the theory of permanent revolution or Chagall's technique, and he wonders: where does he fit in now?" In 1946, Howe's point would have been the deep chasm that had opened up between the young rebel's adopted values and the dwindling ceremonial life of the Jewish people, which troubles him with recollections of warmth and ease he no longer can share. "The words of the prayer, which he does not understand, and the melodies of the chants, which touch some subterranean sources of kinship, stir in him a feeling of continuity that conflicts with his rejection of the ceremony." But from another point of view, one informed by the knowledge of Howe's subsequent career as the celebrant and historian of Yiddish culture, the striking fact is not that the young man is a stranger at the Seder but *that he is there anyway* and that his very being is saturated in the ceremonies from which he feels alien.

Howe, whose voracious studies of modernism, communism, American fiction, and Yiddish culture typify the ambition, restlessness, and fractured sensibility of the second-generation intellectual, has coined the phrase "tradition as discontinuity" to characterize the heritage of the American Jew, whose fundamental experience of the historical life of his people is the loss of it. True enough, and yet, if one takes a long enough view of these discontinuities they begin to look like traditions. That the agitated young apprentice to Kafka and Trotsky should mature into the anthologist of Aleichem and Peretz should not surprise us; it is perfectly natural. "The longest way round," James Joyce has his Leopold Bloom observe, "is the shortest way home," and Joyce, we recall, gave a lifetime of exile from Ireland to recreate the history and moral geography of his people.

The cycle of exile and return, rebellion and reconciliation that marks the lives of contemporary Jewish intellectuals gives us a double perspective on such books as Kazin's lyrical memoirs, *A Walker in the City, Starting Out in the Thirties,* and *New York Jew,* Howe's own refulgent history of the immigrant generation, *World of Our Fathers,* and those portions of Bellow's *Herzog* or Doctorow's *Ragtime* that throw such rainbows of love on the lower East Side or Montreal's Napoleon Street. On the one hand we see them as instances of the past honored as it only can be by men who are cut off from its customs and values: freshened up and put on display as exhibit and myth. Delancey Street or Napoleon Street or Rockaway Avenue now constitute a romance of the irretrievable, as colorful and mysterious in their gritty way as Easter Island or Macchu Picchu. But here is an alienation crossed by longing: these exhibitions of conspicuous nostalgia are fashioned out of love. This is how, one begins to think, culture renews itself, through the exiles' return, and it may not be too far-fetched to suggest that a culture's surest guarantee of staying power is the vitality and success of its rebels.

The Jewish intellectuals who ventured forth into America did not return empty-handed from the other world, but brought back with them souvenirs of travel, among whom was the wife, the shikse, who put the stamp of authenticity upon their dreams of the American heartland. They are also returned with new histories, new interpretations of *their* past which, on the face of them, had bearing upon historical Judaism. It is a striking feature of their generation's labors that the Jewish intellectuals' most thoroughgoing efforts to be reconciled with the past were not their aureate memoirs of Williamsburg or scholarly reconstruction of Jewish socialism or theater but their devoted investigations *of other people's traditions,* traditions at once more progressive than Ashkenazic Judaism and, in their own right, grounded in history and bound up in elaborate codes of manners and morals. Lionel Trilling steeped himself in Matthew Arnold, E. M. Forster, John Stuart Mill, and the tenets of English liberal humanism; Philip Rahv improvised a concordat between Dostoevsky and Henry James; Alfred Kazin compiled the annals of American realism; Leslie Fiedler discovered the mythos of homosexuality and miscegenation at the heart of the American novel; Irving Howe, after his eclectic fashion, apprenticed himself in turn to Karl Marx, Leon Trotsky, Sherwood Anderson, William Faulkner, and Thomas Hardy, all the while reading Sholom Aleichem on the sly. Allen Ginsberg became America's only Buddhist to look, sound, and behave exactly like a Hasidic rebbe. Here is no Torah, no Talmud, no recitation of the *shema,* but the next best thing for a Jew in the labors of casting off the shackles of the rabbinic tradition but anxious not to become too up-to-date all at once: the guidance of highly moralized literatures and instruction in principles of conduct from cultures with more experience than his own in bootstrap morality.

Lionel Trilling's example is telling here. Trilling had no nostalgia for his Jewish origins and went so far as to announce that efforts made by Jewish-American writers of his generation to reclaim their roots were of no avail to their writing. Though he had begun publishing in 1925 in Elliot Cohen and Henry Hurwitz's *Menorah Journal,* the monthly publication of the Menorah Society, whose broad purpose was to form a nonsectarian, humanist, and progressive Jewish consciousness in America, he readily deserted that enterprise and its efforts at cosmopolitan Jewishness in 1930 for the riptides of the intellectual mainstream, which meant largely the *Nation* and the *New Republic,* but included a brief and gingerly debut as a leftist in V. F. Calverton's *Modern Quarterly/Modern Monthly.* In 1944, reflecting on the depth and import of his Jewishness, he refused to waste any sentiment on his youthful torments over his Jewish identity, with which the better part of his *Menorah Journal* stories and essays were concerned, or to recognize any redeeming grace in the parochialism of organized Jewish life. "As the Jewish community now exists," he observed, "it can give no sustenance to the American artist or intellectual who is born a Jew. And so far as I am aware, it has not done so in the past. I know of writers who have used their Jewish experience as the subject of excellent work: I know of no writer in English who has added a micromillimeter to his stature by 'realizing his Jewishness,' although I know of some who have curtailed their promise by trying to heighten their Jewish consciousness." Subsequently, he declined Elliot Cohen's invitation to join the editorial board of *Commentary* when it was being formed.

Trilling's break with the Jewish past, then, was more thoroughgoing and irreversible than that of other Jewish intellectuals. He was no self-conscious rebel like Irving Howe, taking flight from his father's world in youth only to bow to its authority—now become its charm—in middle age. Nor was he an accomplished funambulist like Alfred Kazin, making an original synthesis out of Winesburg and Williamsburg by draping his American dreams in folds of Baltic melancholy. Trilling resisted the appeal of cultural blends and combinations and shunned the exotic possibilities of the hyphenated identity. He was a refiner, whose sensibility was established upon disso-

ciation, upon cutting away parts of the self and suppressing the past. Jewishness was transformed and heightened, refined practically out of existence. Old associations were kept at bay, the unconscious squelched, "authenticity" taken to task, and a curriculum of reading taken on as a surrogate identity. The simulated English bearing was not just a literary taste or professorial affectation; it was an identity.

The strain of anglophilia that was particularly intense in Trilling was latent in the very schooling of his generation; in more attenuated form it left its mark on Kazin, Bellow, and Schwartz, and became particularly visible in the hundreds of Jewish academics who flocked into "English" after the war and quickly became leading authorities on Shakespeare, Joyce, *Paradise Lost,* and *The Faerie Queene.* And yet, though the gap between British and traditional Jewish culture would seem to be vast, there are points of moral contact that make the transfer of loyalties relatively convenient. It is not difficult for a Jew who has been indoctrinated at home in habits of responsibility, prudence, thrift, study, achievement, and other moral austerities of the "Protestant ethic" to lend sympathy to a literature so saturated with a concern for individual conduct as the British, and especially the Victorian, with its stress on faith, discipline, stoic forbearance and self-improvement—all that is implied by stiffening the upper lip and biting the bullet. It was the appeal of one culture grounded upon ethical precept for another.

Trilling's anglophilia was wholly consistent with his rabbinism, its fulfillment rather than its contradiction, and he became more the Jew by becoming more the Victorian. The catalyst for this daring gambit was Matthew Arnold, Trilling's guide to the nineteenth century and his ideal Hebraist, his master in strictness of conscience. Like Arnold, he extrapolated from life to art, from society to fiction, preferring in art as in life all that was problematic, thick, and morally ambiguous. Like the rabbis, he distrusted art, a distrust especially marked in his suspicion of modernism. Trilling's brand of anglophilia, one suspects, was a back door Judaism after all, with the novel its Torah and criticism its commentary. (pp. 44-57)

Mark Shechner, "The Aftermath of Socialism," in his After the Revolution: Studies in the Contemporary Jewish American Imagination, *Indiana University Press, 1987, pp. 32-57.*

PARTISAN REVIEW

G.A.M. JANSSENS

[*In the following excerpt, Janssens provides a detailed history of* Partisan Review, *discussing the journal's contributors, detractors, editorial policies, and ideological evolution.*]

Partisan Review was first published by the John Reed Club of New York in early 1934 as a "Bi-Monthly of Revolutionary Literature." Its opening editorial was somewhat ambiguous. Like most of its militant Marxist contemporaries it would "combat not only the decadent culture of the exploiting classes but also the debilitating liberalism which at times seeps into our writers through the pressure of class-alien forces." But it would not forget to keep its own house in order: "We shall resist every attempt to cripple our literature by narrow-minded, sectarian theories and practices." *Partisan Review* would publish the best creative work of the members of the John Reed

Club as well as of non-members who shared its "literary aims." The first volume was full of the simplistic party rhetoric of most Marxist little magazines. A writer's political convictions were often more closely examined than his literary abilities. For instance, a review, in the first issue, of Archibald MacLeish's *Poems 1924-1933* began ominously: "We know what Archibald MacLeish thinks about Marxism," and the second issue stated that T. S. Eliot's "gods are the caricatures and monsters of fascism." The first issue also featured a discussion of four Marxist little magazines, *Left Front, The Anvil, Blast,* and *Dynamo,* "which prove—despite the sneers and sarcasm of the literary liberals—the growing vitality of revolutionary writing in America." In the fourth issue, Ramon Fernandez, who three years earlier in *The Symposium* had attacked Marxism as a dangerous evil, penitently confessed how "I Came Near Being a Fascist." But a number of contributions, notably those by one of its editors, Philip Rahv, had an air of independent inquiry which was indicative of a growing revolt against party strictness. This new note did not go unnoticed. One influential Marxist critic, Granville Hicks, rebuked the magazine publicly for printing the work of "well-established writers" who did not belong to the John Reed Club, instead of encouraging "the less mature members."

In its second year the magazine waned. Although it continued as a bi-monthly it only published four issues, the last two of which were reduced from ninety-six to sixty-four pages. In its third year it merged with another Marxist magazine, *The Anvil.* The first issue of *Partisan Review and Anvil* appeared in February 1936. The editors described it as a monthly which, "though continuing the traditions of its predecessors," would be "broader in scope and, we believe, more mature." It was certainly more

William Phillips. © Lütfi Özkök.

critical of the Communist Party line. The fifth monthly issue announced a summer recess during July and August; the editors intended to take advantage of this interval in order to work out "a program of enlarging the magazine and broadening its appeal," and they announced that the September number would contain "several pieces of unusual interest." But the September number never appeared. The last issue of 1936 came out in October. It was entitled *Partisan Review* with in small letters underneath "Combined with the *Anvil.*" It was the last number of the merger magazine.

It was not till December 1937 that the first number of the reconstructed *Partisan Review* appeared. Its editors were three Yale friends—F. W. Dupee ("who had been literary editor of the *New Masses* just long enough to see through its pretensions"), Dwight Macdonald ("who, having but lately discovered the socialist cause, was ready to devote to it his abundant energies and capacities"), and George L. K. Morris ("a modern painter who was able to undertake the financing of the venture")—and William Phillips and Philip Rahv, who had been on the editorial board of the earlier *Partisan Review.* Its contributors, apart from the editors, included Delmore Schwartz, J. T. Farrell, Arthur Mizener, Edmund Wilson, Pablo Picasso, Lionel Abel, James Agee, Mary McCarthy, Sidney Hook, William Troy, and Lionel Trilling. The editors succeeded in making it "a 'strong' issue, for obvious tactical reasons." The opening editorial was a declaration of independence. The editors retained their faith in revolutionary socialism; they still believed that any magazine that "aspires to a place in the vanguard of literature today, will be revolutionary in tendency"; but they were also convinced that any such magazine would be "unequivocally independent. . . . Indeed we think that the cause of revolutionary literature is best served by a policy of no commitments to any political party." Their critical independence was exemplified by their resolution to work within the tradition of the literary magazines of the 1920's which the more orthodox Marxists had dismissed as decadent expressions of a bourgeois culture: "As our readers know, the tradition of aestheticism has given way to a literature which, for its origin and final justification, looks beyond itself and deep into the historic process. But the forms of literary editorship, at once exacting and adventurous, which characterized the magazines of the aesthetic revolt, were of definite cultural value; and these forms *Partisan Review* will wish to adapt to the literature of the new period." The editorial accent would fall "chiefly on culture and its broader social determinants" instead of on party politics, and it would keep an open mind in its judgment of literature. "Conformity to a given social ideology or to a prescribed attitude or technique, will not be asked of our writers. On the contrary, our pages will be open to any tendency which is relevant to literature in our time."

Partisan Review appeared as a "Literary Monthly" till September 1938. After that it continued as "A Quarterly of Literature and Marxism" till the autumn of 1939. From 1940 to the end of 1943 it appeared bi-monthly and converted into a quarterly again in 1944. In 1941 Frederick Dupee left *Partisan Review* and Clement Greenberg joined the editorial board. Greenberg, Macdonald, and Morris left in 1943 leaving only William Phillips and Philip Rahv with one new editor, Delmore Schwartz, in charge.

The December 1937 editorial, which announced the break with the Communist Party, had clearly stated that literary contributions would be judged on purely literary merits; the magazine would keep its politics and its literature separate. The theory and practice of this policy would attract considerable criticism. An editor of *The Hudson Review,* for instance, thought that, as a magazine, "P. R. has only rarely managed to resolve its dual nature, part political, part literary" [William Arrowsmith; see Additional Bibliography]. The Autumn 1938 issue, which marks *Partisan Review*'s first appearance as "A Quarterly of Literature and Marxism," contains an eloquent editorial statement in the form of a letter to Malcolm Cowley. In *The New Republic* of 19 October [see Additional Bibliography], Cowley had attacked *Partisan Review* as "factional," "anti-Soviet," and as a perpetrator of "literary crimes." His main charge had been that in contrast to its alleged editorial policy, *Partisan Review* used its literature for political ends. The editors answered that Cowley had mistaken their renunciation of the Communist Party for devotion to "an above-the-battle kind of pure Literature, such as the *Dial* once stood for. . . . But we have never aspired to stand for Pure Literature." They felt that the contemporary writer must concern himself with politics "if his work is to have any deep meaning for our time." In the course of their refutation of Cowley's article, the editors declared themselves to be against Stalinism which had "ceased to be a revolutionary tendency," and in fact was "rapidly turning into the opposite." They considered the influence of the Communist Party "a major threat to both literature and revolution in our time." Against Cowley's charge of low literary standards, they adduced the flattering notices of their *Review* in "such non-political and exclusively literary magazines" as *Poetry, New Directions,* and *The Criterion.* In the following issue, the editors reiterated emphatically that the artist or intellectual could not remain indifferent to the political developments of his time. In their obituary on the death of *The Criterion* they maintained that in later years *The Criterion*'s influence had not been constructive because Eliot had cultivated "abstraction from worldly issues. . . . But to English intellectuals the plea for aloofness came as a dry wind to the drought-stricken. Detachment? They were already perishing of it!"

In the summer of 1939 *Partisan Review* published a statement of the League for Cultural Freedom and Socialism. As all the editors were among the undersigned, this statement had a direct bearing on the political and cultural position of their magazine. It was addressed "to all artists and writers who are concerned about the present drift of the United States to reaction and war." Reaction was threatening not only in Germany, in Italy, and in Russia—"where nationalism and personal dictatorship are replacing the revolutionary ideals of freedom and democracy"—but also in the United States:

> Increasingly, experimentation is discouraged in the creative arts; a premium is put upon the conventional and the academic. The social sciences are witnessing the revival of various forms of obscurantism, the rise of an intolerant orthodoxy. Educators are being intimidated through loyalty oaths. Government censorship cripples W.P.A. theatre, art, and literary projects. Terrorism is exercised by the Catholic Church over such cultural enterprises as the movies. Covert sabotage hinders the publication of work by independent and revolutionary writers. And in heresy hunting bodies like the Dies Committee, many of these tendencies find official and concentrated expression.

The statement noted a general weakening of the radical positions which the intellectuals had conquered after 1929. The Communist Party could no longer sustain them; indeed the most active forces of reaction were "the so-called cultural organizations" which the Party controlled. But the failure of the Party must not lead intellectuals to abandon "the ideals of revolutionary socialism." Intellectual freedom must be insisted upon and all theories and practices must be rejected which "tend to make culture the creature of politics, even revolutionary politics. We demand COMPLETE FREEDOM FOR ART AND SCIENCE. NO DICTATION BY PARTY OR GOVERNMENT."

During the next few years *Partisan Review* kept a vigilant watch for further signs of reaction. The decline of Marxism and the revolutionary cause was a frequent subject of debate. Another frequently discussed problem was America's attitude to the war in Europe. Generally speaking, *Partisan Review* moved from a militantly revolutionary and anti-war position to the recognition that the chances of revolution were lower than before and that American participation in the war was inevitable. This gradual editorial shift was deplored by Dwight Macdonald who in 1943 left the magazine "in high political dudgeon."

In the summer of 1940 Philip Rahv wrote *Partisan Review*'s contribution to the debate of "What is Living and What Is Dead" in Marxism. Rahv drew attention to the disaster of communist movements everywhere, and to the fact that "everywhere, including in the Soviet Union, it is not the social revolution but the counter-revolution which has triumphed." It was true that events had confirmed the Marxist analysis of bourgeois economy and imperialist wars, but they had failed to confirm the Marxist prognosis of a proletarian revolution once the objective conditions for such a revolution had ripened: "and objective conditions, considered on an international scale, have not only been ripe but at times rotten-ripe." Marxist doctrine had optimistically assumed that as capitalism decayed the revolutionary awareness of the working class would increase. But there was no workers' movement of any size or influence which was "carrying forward the revolutionary tradition" and which could be seriously counted on "to utilize the opportunities for action that will no doubt arise in the near future."

Rahv tried to steer a middle course between the revisionists, who were now "in the pink of condition, thriving as they do on routs and defeats"—and the diehards, who mistook "their doctrinal inflexibility for scientific rectitude." Rahv was more interested in the practice than in the theory of Marxism. His emphasis on historical experience and on experimental verification as a rationale for political action profoundly influenced *Partisan Review.* It gave the magazine the necessary flexibility to adapt its ideological position to the rapid changes of its political environment. But it never jeopardized its intellectual independence. In 1941, Dwight Macdonald could justly claim that, "in its three years of existence, the present *Partisan Review* has steadfastly opposed all forms of totalitarian oppression, both red and black." In the spring of 1942 the editors once more demonstrated their intellectual alertness by establishing a new department, "Dangerous Thoughts," which would have the function of "a 'listening post' to give publicity to the more significant instances of suppression of free thought from month to month."

But although the editors were in agreement about the necessity of independent inquiry and freedom of thought, they differed on the issues of revolutionary socialism and American participation in the war. Their disagreements were brought into the open when Philip Rahv challenged the "Ten Propositions on the War" published in the summer of 1941 by Dwight Macdonald and Clement Greenberg, who had once more defended the ideals of revolutionary socialism and of non-participation in the war. These Propositions, Rahv thought, had put his fellow-editors "into a snug sectarian hole." He could not adopt their position because he regarded it "as morally absolutist and as politically representative of a kind of academic revolutionism which we should have learned to discard long ago." Greenberg and Macdonald had been completely impervious to the "shattering surprises of the past two years" and were still advocating the "same old orthodox recommendations. Again we read that the social revolution is around the corner and that imperialism is tottering on the edge of the abyss, and again we fail to recognize the world as we know it." Again Rahv's main argument was that the programme put forward by Greenberg and Macdonald was unrealistic, a Utopian vision completely out of touch with actual political developments. Hitler's swift conquests had changed the political picture entirely; his military defeat had become "the indispensable pre-condition of any progressive action in the future." This defeat could only be brought about by "the combined might of the Anglo-American imperialism and Stalin's Red Army." The orthodox Marxists had hoped that the different capitalist camps would exhaust each other and then they would take over. But events had turned out otherwise. All indications were against the possibility of a successful revolutionary movement in America or in England. Rahv was not arguing against a revolutionary policy as such but practical conditions made such a policy illusory. The assertions of Greenberg and Macdonald wholly ignored "the element of time, which is the one element one can least afford to overlook in political calculations." Rahv believed not only in the necessity of American participation in the war, but also in an ultimate Anglo-American victory: "There is every reason to believe that once America is fully drawn into the struggle its offensive power will astound the world."

The extent of the editorial disagreements necessitated a "Statement by the Editors" on the actual entrance of the United States into the war. As *Partisan Review,* "while primarily a cultural magazine," had always been "concerned with politics," a question of its future editorial policy naturally arose:

> For some time, as recent issues of the magazine have made clear, the editors have disagreed on major political questions. The complexity of the world situation, indeed, is reflected in the fact that no two editors hold the same position on all major issues. The actual outbreak of hostilities has not altered this line up. It is clear, therefore, that *Partisan Review* can have no editorial line on the war. Its editors will continue to express themselves on the issue as individuals.

But they remained unanimous about the necessity of the "fullest freedom of expression on political matters." In subsequent issues this freedom was mainly exercised by Dwight Macdonald. There was, for instance, his vehement refutation of James Burnham's argument in *The Managerial Revolution.* Burnham had been a fellow-Trotskyist of Macdonald and his sudden abandonment of doctrinaire Marxism, which he had first embraced in the pages of *The Symposium,* had amazed many of his revolutionary friends.

But Macdonald's revolutionary zeal was decreasingly relevant to the trend of *Partisan Review.* The contents pages of the first issues of 1943 stated once more explicitly that the articles published in the magazine, "whether written by editors or contributors, represent the point of view of the individual author, and not necessarily of the editors." None of the other literary reviews had thought such editorial caution necessary, except *The Symposium.* This is symbolic of a distinct resemblance between *Partisan Review* and *The Symposium,* especially if we take into account that they were not edited simultaneously. Firstly, these two magazines had more regular contributors in common with each other than with any of the other literary reviews. We may mention Dwight Macdonald, William Phillips, Philip Rahv, and Frederick Dupee—in other words, all of the important editors of *Partisan Review* prior to 1943—Lionel Trilling, William Troy, Harold Rosenberg, and James Burnham. Secondly, both *The Symposium* and *Partisan Review* were New York magazines and both took an active interest in Marxism. As *The Symposium* had first appeared before the leftist political agitation due to the depression had gained momentum, its turn to Marxism came late in its career. It was, of course, largely instigated by James Burnham, and it appears no coincidence that Burnham was a valued contributor to the early *Partisan Review* (in later years, Julian Symons thought he had been an editor), and that Philip Wheelwright contributed regularly to *The Kenyon Review* in a vein very much in accord with Ransom's editorial policy. Indeed, the different interests of the two editors of *The Symposium* point to the two major traditions of the literary review in the 'Thirties and after: we find the radical and secular trend of James Burnham again in *Partisan Review,* and the aesthetic and religious trend of Philip Wheelwright in *The Kenyon Review.* Another way of saying the same thing is that *The Symposium* published work of a number of characteristic contributors both to *Partisan Review* and to *The Criterion.*

The internal dissent among the editors of *Partisan Review* was resolved in the summer of 1943 when Dwight Macdonald tendered his resignation. As it had been an editorial habit to publish the more significant letters to the editors in a special section of the magazine—a habit which added liveliness to its pages and which gave the editors ample scope to clarify their positions—Macdonald's letter was printed in the July-August issue of 1943. Macdonald felt that the divergence between his own opinions and those of the other editors could no longer be bridged: "This divergence is partly cultural: I feel *Partisan Review* has become rather academic, and favor a more informal, disrespectable and chance-taking magazine, with a broader and less exclusively 'literary' approach." But the divergence was mainly political. The value of *Partisan Review,* according to Macdonald, had been its "Marxian socialist cultural" direction. This had distinguished it "from other literary organs like *Southern Review* and *Kenyon Review,*" and had accounted for much of its intellectual success. But the interest in Marxism had been reduced to "a minority of one," and since Pearl Harbor, the editors had tended to discourage all political discussion. The remaining editors answered that they naturally regretted Macdonald's resignation but regretted even more that Macdonald had "allowed himself to be carried away by political passions." They maintained that he had left because he had failed to transform *Partisan Review* into a "political magazine with literary trimmings." *Partisan Review,* "which from its very inception has been edited mainly by literary men," never wanted to put itself forward as a substitute for a political movement.

Macdonald's resignation forced the editors once more to clarify their views concerning the selection of the political and the literary subject-matter of their magazine: "We could never agree to 'subordinate' art and literature to political interests. It is precisely this sort of disagreement which led, in 1937, to our break with the Stalinists. . . . Macdonald speaks of the magazine's 'intellectual success'; but he shows his bias in ascribing it largely to the Marxist slant rather than to the specific modulation achieved in combining socialist ideas with a varied literary and critical content. This will continue to be the policy of the magazine.'' The reconciliation of the political and the literary contents of their magazine had always been an awkward problem for the editors. About two years before Macdonald's resignation, Julian Symons has suggested to them that ''a statement of editorial attitude, with regard to the relation between your political views and the creative work you publish, would be useful.'' *Partisan Review* had then just published Eliot's *East Coker*. The editors retorted that Symons's question had ''always been a hard one'' for them to answer, but that they had ''always felt that literary values must come first in judging literature.''

As the political situation worsened, these literary values became more and more prominent. When Macdonald resigned one of the reasons certainly was, as the editors wrote, that his political interests tended to eliminate his literary interests, but it was equally true, as Macdonald maintained, that *Partisan Review* was becoming increasingly literary and less political. In this connection it is significant that Macdonald's successor was a purely literary man, Delmore Schwartz, who had been one of the most regular and esteemed young contributors to *The Southern Review*, but who had also, in 1938, won the prize of $100 which *Partisan Review* had offered in a contest for the best short story.

Partisan Review's campaign for literary independence had started in 1937 with its break with the Communist Party, which also meant a break with other Marxist little magazines. It differed from non-Marxist little magazines in its emphasis upon ''ideas and intellectual attitudes.'' Its new ideological independence and the contemporary literary and political situation naturally led to a closer identification with its fellow literary quarterlies. The first issue of the reconstructed *Partisan Review* in 1937 contained contributions by Delmore Schwartz, Wallace Stevens and Arthur Mizener, and its first quarterly issue (Winter 1939) featured R. P. Blackmur's review of ''Nine Poets.'' The group book review which was carried on in the next few issues by such critics as Philip Rahv, Randall Jarrell and David Daiches, may well have been inspired by the example of *The Southern Review*. Philip Rahv for one was greatly impressed by *Southern Review*'s performance: ''I think the recent numbers of your Review have been excellent,'' he wrote to Robert Penn Warren in 1939; ''Its varied and bountiful content and the freedom and independence of its general approach make it all the more valuable at a time when almost all the intellectual organs have lost all sense of their real function.''

In the autumn of 1940 the editors intended to underline their political independence and, perhaps also, their waning revolutionary optimism, by publishing *Partisan Review* under a new name, *The Forties*, beginning with the first issue of 1941. ''We are making this change because the old name, pertinent when the magazine first appeared in 1934, has more recently led to many misunderstandings of the magazine's purpose and character.'' But the reactions of their readers were so unfavorable—somebody suggested, as an alternative name, *The American Criterion*—that the editors decided to continue as *Partisan Review*. Most of its readers, however, sympathized with its gradual turn to literary matters. This was illustrated by the results of the questionnaire which the *Review* sent out to its subscribers in early 1941; nine out of ten wanted more articles, and again nine out of ten of these wanted more articles on writers and writing; the number of those who wanted more political articles was considerably smaller.

We have noted previously that *Partisan Review*, like its fellow quarterlies, took a very sombre view of the contemporary literary situation. Indeed, in their retrospect of the first ten years of the magazine, the editors Phillips and Rahv prided themselves on their percipience in this matter:

> Long before the popular critics acknowledged the slump in contemporary writing, we repeatedly noted in editorial articles, that, compared with the high level achieved in the twenties, the literature of the thirties and forties has shown a decline in originality, integrity, and creative power. Hence it seemed to us that in this period a magazine dedicated solely to experiment and innovation could not but turn into a futile undertaking, as the paucity of material on which such a magazine must subsist would eventually compel it to adopt meretricious standards, permitting the souvenirs of past experimentation to be passed off as the vital discoveries of the present.

Perhaps the most famous indictment of the literary situation by an editor of *Partisan Review* appeared in the *Kenyon Review* in 1939: Philip Rahv's ''Paleface and Redskin.'' Rahv's discussion of the ''split personality'' of American literature, exemplified in the persons and the works of Henry James and Walt Whitman, will be familiar. ''At present,'' Rahv wrote, ''the redskins are in command of the literary situation, and seldom has the literary life in America been as intellectually impoverished as it is today.''

The literary reviews were undoubtedly representatives of the waning paleface tradition. Their fight was against the lowbrow writer and critic and their hold on the reading public. But whereas Rahv had written an indictment in terms of a theory of American literature, *Partisan Review*, like its fellow quarterlies, chose for its specific adversaries Van Wyck Brooks and Archibald MacLeish and, later on, Bernard DeVoto. In late 1941 Dwight Macdonald led off with an attack on Van Wyck Brooks's lecture ''Primary Literature and Coterie Literature.'' Brooks had built his argument around an antithesis between ''primary'' and ''secondary'' writers. The former was ''a great man writing,'' ''one who bespeaks the collective life of the people'' by celebrating ''the great themes . . . by virtue of which the race has risen—courage, justice, mercy, honor, love.'' The work of the ''secondary,'' or ''coterie'' writer only reached ''a mere handful of readers.'' His work had brilliant ''form'' but lacked ''content.'' He was ''a mere artificer or master of words,'' who perversely celebrated the ''death-drive'' instead of the ''life-drive.'' Brooks's examples of primary writers included Tolstoi, Milton, Dostoievsky, Goethe, Whitman, and Whittier. His secondary writers included Joyce, Proust, Valéry, Pound, Eliot, James, Rimbaud, and Hemingway. Among his ''secondary'' critics were Eliot, Richards, Winters, Pound, Tate, and Ransom, in contrast to such ''primary'' critics as Arnold, Taine, and Sainte-Beuve.

Macdonald called Brooks's lecture ''the boldest statement to date of that cultural counter-revolution opened by Archibald MacLeish's attack on the 'irresponsibles'.'' Unlike his literary contemporaries, he saw Brooks's and MacLeish's positions as manifestations of political decline. Indeed, he mentioned Brooks's lecture in one breath with James Burnham's *The Managerial Revolution*. Brooks, according to Macdonald, had no use for modern writers because they exposed the weaknesses and absurdities of a dying bourgeois culture. But he had to admit that, for all his boldness, Brooks nowhere dared to ''assert that bourgeois society in this century is in a flourishing condition. He simply *assumes* this crucial point—or, more accurately, doesn't seem aware it *is* crucial, and that writers can be expected to exhibit his 'primary' virtues only in a 'primary' historical period." According to Macdonald, Brooks's values and methods were "the specific cultural values of Stalinism and the specific methods of the Moscow Trials." Brooks was representative of the drift of totalitarianism which after the Hitler-Stalin pact had deserted Stalinism to support the official government line. His was the "*official* approach to culture" which had for its aim "the protection of a historically reactionary form of society against the free inquiry and criticism of the intelligentsia." He had become the "leading mouthpiece for totalitarian cultural values."

Macdonald's article served as an opening for a much wider debate. It was sent to some twenty writers with a request for comments on it. Seven writers reacted to this request, among them Allen Tate, the future editor of *The Sewanee Review,* and John Crowe Ransom, the editor of *The Kenyon Review.* If the editors of *The Southern Review* were invited to comment, they failed to do so. It was of course at this time—late 1941—that they were planning their own editorial on MacLeish and Brooks which never appeared. But the trend of their editorial policy and their earlier attack on the position of Howard Mumford Jones permit one to surmise that their reactions would have been very similar to Tate's. Tate was as radical as Macdonald in his rejection of the "Brooks-MacLeish Thesis," but on cultural rather than on political grounds:

> Mr. Macdonald seems to feel that the great writers of our time were consciously exposing the evils of capitalism; yet I believe that the most we can say, if we are not going to succumb to special pleading, is that they have written out of a vision of life in our time, or out of a vision of the evils of life which are common to all times; and it is this tragic view which Mr. Brooks cannot understand, because he holds the moralistic and didactic view which can be extended, as he has extended it, into the nationalist and patriotic view.

Brooks had always seen literature as chiefly a symptom, but Tate had "an uneasy suspicion" that Macdonald was defending the moderns as symptoms also. He wondered whether they would not become unnecessary after "the triumph of Mr. Macdonald's socialism."

Ransom's reception of Macdonald's article illustrates how in *The Kenyon Review* the Brooks-MacLeish affair was to some extent overshadowed by other priorities, particularly the attack on science. Ransom accepted "a good deal of the substance" of Brooks's generalization as Macdonald had reported it. He too felt that the moderns were not "primary" or "great" writers: "Our literature with its brilliance is less creative and positive than other literatures have been." But he did argue "in defense of the greatness of a few moderns, such as James, Yeats, and Proust." He did not explain the direction of contemporary fiction and poetry in cultural or political terms but in terms of the rise of science:

> I find myself more and more imagining that the epochal thing that has happened to us is a sudden crisis of language and expression. For the first time in human history we have pure science, which is pure prose, and that means that we have pushed language to the point where it is the perfect instrument for science. The esthetic and imaginative elements of language that used to clutter it—the figures of speech for example—have been spotted and thrown out. The consequence is that literature, with its imaginative order of knowing, is homeless. It has to make up its

own occasions, and it becomes factitious and technical in a degree that was never known before.

The lowbrow attitude to literature and the growing literary nationalism remained frequent topics of the editorial interest in *Partisan Review.* Their increasing prestige was deplored by William Phillips in early 1944. The "rediscovery of America" had become "practically an occupational disease not only of popular writers and reviewers but also of people who once had at least one foot in the movements of literary revolt." This literary nationalism had been accompanied by "a wave of anti-intellectualism" which threatened to wipe out the remaining traces of earlier experimentation and of the former radical spirit. But what was "perhaps even more remarkable" was the absence of a new generation of writers with a common direction. The publication of Bernard DeVoto's *The Literary Fallacy* only confirmed the editors' gloomy predictions. Philip Rahv called the book "as vicious and mindless a tract as any so far produced by those who have set themselves the task of subverting the critical spirit of modern art and thought."

The preceding remarks will go to show that the literary reviews were unanimous in their condemnation of the activist anti-intellectualism and literary nationalism of the early 'Forties, but *Partisan Review* differed greatly from its contemporaries in the explanations it offered and in the remedies it proposed. This was due to its secular, rationalistic, positivistic attitude towards the contemporary world. Although it was highly critical of specific abuses, it tried to expose them without rejecting the world in which they occurred. It opposed the numerous contemporary myths which had been propagated to throw light on the complexity of the modern scene and often also to obstruct the development of its most characteristic traits. It was probably this secular, positivistic quality of *Partisan Review* which led John Palmer, the editor of *The Sewanee Review,* to describe it, in a letter to T. S. Eliot in 1946, as "morally suspect." Palmer remembered the great disappointment of the editors of *The Southern Review*—he himself had been managing editor at the time—when Eliot's *Four Quartets* began to appear in *Partisan Review.* "Perhaps this will appear as nothing else than underhand remarks about a rival publication: but I do regard the *Partisan Review* as morally suspect, and I worried over what explanations there might be for your choice of it for so very important an occasion."

Partisan Review's attitude was most clearly formulated in a series of essays entitled "The New Failure of Nerve" which was started in early 1943. The title of this series had been derived from Gilbert Murray's *Four Stages of Greek Religion.* Murray had characterized the period from 300 B.C. to the first century of the Christian era as marked by "a failure of nerve." This failure of nerve had exhibited itself in "a rise of asceticism, of mysticism, in a sense, of pessimism; a loss of self-confidence, of hope in this life and of faith in normal human efforts; a despair of patient inquiry, a cry for infallible revelation: an indifference to the welfare of the state, a conversion of the soul to God." Surveying the cultural tendencies of the early 'Forties, Sidney Hook, whose essay opened the new series, noticed many signs pointing to a new failure of nerve in Western civilization. Although its manifestations were more complex and sophisticated and characteristic of a secular culture, at bottom they betrayed "the same flight from responsibility, both on the plane of action and on the plane of belief, that drove the ancient world into the shelters of pagan and Christian supernaturalism." Liberalism, not as a nineteenth-century economic doctrine, but as an intellectual temper, as "faith in intelligence, as a tradition of the free market in the world of ideas'' was everywhere on the defensive. Hook noticed signs of intellectual panic in almost all fields of ''theoretical life,'' but there was a primary attitude underlying them all. It exhibited itself as ''a loss of confidence in scientific method, and in varied quests for a 'knowledge' and 'truth' which, although they give us information about the world, are uniquely different from those won by the process of scientific inquiry.'' These truths were often regarded as superior to truths of science and common sense, but Hook considered them ''gateways to intellectual and moral irresponsibility.''

Hook's essay was accompanied in the same issue by contributions of John Dewey and Ernest Nagel which were in essential agreement with Hook's defence of scientific methods against the increasing ''obscurantism.'' I. A. Richards, who was asked to comment on these three essays in a later issue, tried to steer a middle course. He felt that representatives of both sides in this ''old intellectual war'' were more interested in warfare itself than in ultimate solutions. ''They belong already to one party or the other, their reading serves to stiffen their necks, inflame their hearts and anneal their colours.'' Neither party would admit to any doubt. But Richards wondered ''whether the thinker, if we separate him from the polemist, does not need both the language of religion and the language of science.'' Richards did not expect, however, that his intermediary solution would be acceptable, and the continuing polemics between the two opposing camps in *Partisan Review* and in *The Kenyon Review* proved that his mediation was indeed as illusory as he himself considered it. (pp. 287-307)

> G. A. M. Janssens, *"The Forties and After,"* in his
> The American Literary Review: A Critical History
> 1920-1950, *Mouton, 1968, pp. 248-314.*

PARTISAN REVIEW

[*The following editorial statement appeared in the first issue of the revived* Partisan Review *in 1937. Although the editorial board of the journal was at that time composed of William Phillips, Philip Rahv, Mary McCarthy, Dwight Macdonald, George L. K. Morris, and F. W. Dupee, the statement was crafted primarily by Phillips and Rahv.*]

As our readers know, the tradition of aestheticism has given way to a literature which, for its origin and final justification, looks beyond itself and deep into the historic process. But the forms of literary editorship, at once exacting and adventurous, which characterized the magazines of the aesthetic revolt, were of definite cultural value; and these forms *Partisan Review* will wish to adapt to the literature of the new period.

Any magazine, we believe, that aspires to a place in the vanguard of literature today, will be revolutionary in tendency; but we are also convinced that any such magazine will be unequivocally independent. *Partisan Review* is aware of its responsibility to the revolutionary movement in general, but we disclaim obligation to any of its organized political expressions. Indeed we think that the cause of revolutionary literature is best served by a policy of no commitments to any political party. Thus our underscoring of the factor of independence is based, not primarily on our differences with any one group, but on the conviction that literature in our period should be free of all factional dependence.

There is already a tendency in America for the more conscious social writers to identify themselves with a single organization, the Communist Party; with the result that they grow automatic in their political responses but increasingly less responsible in

an artistic sense. And the Party literary critics, equipped with the zeal of vigilantes, begin to consolidate into aggressive political-literary amalgams as many tendencies as possible and to outlaw all dissenting opinion. This projection on the cultural field of factionalism in politics makes for literary cleavages which, in most instances, have little to do with literary issues, and which are more and more provocative of a ruinous bitterness among writers. Formerly associated with the Communist Party, *Partisan Review* strove from the first against its drive to equate the interests of literature with those of factional politics. Our reappearance on an independent basis signifies our conviction that the totalitarian trend is inherent in that movement and that it can no longer be combatted from within.

But many other tendencies exist in American letters, and these, we think, are turning from the senseless disciplines of the official Left to shape a new movement. The old movement will continue and, to judge by present indications, it will be reënforced more and more by academicians from the universities, by yesterday's celebrities and today's philistines. Armed to the teeth with slogans of revolutionary prudence, its official critics will revive the petty-bourgeois tradition of gentility, and with each new tragedy on the historic level they will call the louder for a literature of good cheer. Weak in genuine literary authority but equipped with all the economic and publicity powers of an authentic cultural bureaucracy, the old regime will seek to isolate the new by performing upon it the easy surgery of political falsification. Because the writers of the new grouping aspire to independence in politics as well as in art, they will be identified with fascism, sometimes directly, sometimes through the convenient medium of ''Trotskyism.'' Every effort, in short, will be made to *excommunicate* the new generation, so that their writing and their politics may be regarded as making up a kind of diabolic totality; which would render unnecessary any sort of rational discussion of the merits of either.

Do we exaggerate? On the contrary, our prediction as to the line the old regime will take is based on the first maneuvers of a campaign which has already begun. *Already*, before it has appeared, *Partisan Review* has been subjected to a series of attacks in the Communist Party press; already, with no regard for fact—without, indeed, any relevant facts to go by—they have attributed gratuitous political designs to *Partisan Review* in an effort to confuse the primarily literary issue between us.

But *Partisan Review* aspires to represent a new and dissident generation in American letters; it will not be dislodged from its independent position by any political campaign against it. And without ignoring the importance of the official movement as a sign of the times we shall know how to estimate its authority in literature. But we shall also distinguish, wherever possible, between the tendencies of this faction itself and the work of writers associated with it. For our editorial accent falls chiefly on culture and its broader social determinants. Conformity to a given social ideology or to a prescribed attitude or technique, will not be asked of our writers. On the contrary, our pages will be open to any tendency which is relevant to literature in our time. Marxism in culture, we think, is first of all an instrument of analysis and evaluation; and if, in the last instance, it prevails over other disciplines, it does so through the medium of democratic controversy. Such is the medium that *Partisan Review* will want to provide in its pages.

> *"Editorial Statement," in* Partisan Review, *Vol. IV,
> No. 1, December 1937, p. 3.*

PHILIP RAHV AND WILLIAM PHILLIPS

[*In the following excerpt from their epilogue to the 1946* Partisan Reader *anthology, the editors of* Partisan Review *explain the magazine's editorial philosophy.*]

We like to think that through the years *Partisan Review* has been something more than a periodical anthology of the best available writing. From the very first number, the magazine has lived the life of its times. The note it struck has been peculiarly its own, that of combining intellectual disinterestedness with engagement in the cultural and social issues of the period; and while it has been essentially partisan to radical values, it has at the same time always been on the side of literary standards. Its interest has been at once literary and political because from the beginning, in its persistent no less than in its changing attitudes, it has sought to express the appeal of both these orders of modern experience.

For the history of *Partisan Review* has been typically modern, typically of a piece with the intellectual experience of our time. Conceived in the fall of 1933 and born in February, 1934, the magazine emerged from the womb of the depression crying for a proletarian literature and a socialist America. The early thirties, it will be recalled, were years of radical fervor, and many intellectuals, inspired by the promise of the classless Utopia, were converted to Marxism in theory and to the Communist Party in practice. A number of younger writers—not a few of whom mistook their revolutionary zeal for literary talent—felt it was their duty to lead the way, and throughout the country they banded together in John Reed Clubs with the aim of applying organizational methods to the enlistment of the arts in the service of the revolution. Naturally, the next step was to start new left magazines, and the editors of this volume, together with a few other members of the local chapter, decided that the John Reed Club of New York must set the pace with a publication of its own.

The one remaining problem was to raise the necessary funds. The Communist Party, despite its close supervision of all such "cultural" activities, was not disposed to finance any of them. We obtained the money by staging a public lecture by John Strachey on Literature and Dialectical Materialism (subsequently published in book-form by Covici-Friede). Strachey, widely heralded as an urbane exponent of Marxist ideas, had just arrived in this country, and a large and enthusiastic audience gathered to hear him. The profits of that lecture were sufficient to cover the costs of not more than two issues. We did not think beyond that, for in the flush of our newfledged faith we took it for granted that once launched the magazine would somehow manage to overcome all financial obstacles.

The first issue, published in February, 1934, contained several "proletarian" stories of the type popular in that period, a chapter from James T. Farrell's *Studs Lonigan,* and two sketches by Grace Lumpkin; the poetry was full of revolutionary pathos, promises of salvation and threats to the ruling class; and in the critical section we featured attacks on Archibald MacLeish (for his *Frescoes for Mr. Rockefeller's City*) and on Henry Hazlitt's conservative reading of literary history. The entire issue was aggressively social-minded, in accordance with the values of the radical movement at the time; nevertheless, from a literary point of view, it represented an effort to put forward the best writing then produced by the Left. In the editorial statement opening the issue we dedicated ourselves to revolutionary aesthetics, Marxist thinking, and good will toward the Soviet Union: all of which on the surface apparently represented the typical Communist position. Yet in a few months we had initiated a basic criticism of the party-line notions by which the "literary movement," as it was called, was then dominated; and from then on our differences with the Party grew until the breaking-point was reached some years later. (It should be made clear that when we speak of such differences we are referring only to ourselves, that is, to the present writers. For while *Partisan Review* was officially the organ of the John Reed Club, the actual editing as well as money-raising was done mostly by ourselves, and thus the magazine necessarily reflected our own interpretation of the Marxist approach to literature. The rest of the editorial roster, constantly changing and dwindling in number, was chiefly made up of writers rewarded for political loyalty or paid off for their literary prestige by an honorary appointment to our editorial board. By the summer of 1936, however, some time after the change in Communist policy dictated a dissolution of the John Reed Clubs, *Partisan Review* had only one editor besides ourselves.)

Our differences with the Party may be said to have originated in a protest against the official idea of art as an instrument of political propaganda. Also, orthodoxy as a way of thought being repellent to us, we could not support the Communist attempt to set up a monopoly of radical ideas. We were far more responsive to Marxism as a method of analysis than to organizational pressures and maneuvers. Nor could we go along with our "comrades" of the *New Masses* and other Communist publications in their practice of ignoring the difference between good and bad writing in order to judge it primarily on grounds of political expediency, namely, whether or not its political content coincided with the current specifications of the party line. From the standpoint of the commissars of culture, whose real interest lay in the manipulation of intellectual opinion so as to reflect the most credit on Soviet and Comintern policies, we had committed the unforgivable sin of taking seriously the idea of infusing literary life with a revolutionary spirit.

In its Stalinist period the editorial program of the magazine was thus directed on the one hand against reactionary ideas and on the other against the literal-minded pieties, distortions, and sectarianism of the movement with which we were officially associated. It can in all fairness be claimed, we think, that *Partisan Review* was the only Marxist literary periodical of the thirties which resisted the debasements of writing and the rejection of the creative tradition then hailed in many quarters as "progressive" achievements. We published writers like Silone, Farrell, and Dos Passos at the time when they were regarded with suspicion in party circles; and at all times we encouraged the carrying over of the modern sensibility into the expression of leftist themes.

But in that early period our criticism of the party line was confined to its cultural operations. On the whole, despite our growing skepticism, we tended to believe in the political integrity of the Communist movement. Gradually, however, we came to the realization that the intellectual vulgarities we had decried had their source in the corruption and totalitarian essence of Stalinism itself. The last barriers of our faith were overthrown by the revelations of the Moscow trials, in the validity of which we could not believe for one moment; and soon we were convinced that this movement, afflicted with an incurable disease, was perverting intellectual life as it had perverted the libertarian ideals of the socialist tradition. It became clear to us, as it had by this time to a number of other writers, too, that Stalinism was not the agent but the enemy of democratic socialism. Now bent on secession, we planned to turn the magazine into an organ of independent radicalism as well as of serious and experimental writing in general. But the shock of our disillusionment made us lose heart politically; and the slackness of our mood, coupled with the financial predicament of the magazine, forced us to suspend publication. That was in the fall of 1936. *Partisan Review* did not appear again till the end of 1937, when it came out under new auspices, with a thoroughly renovated editorial staff and policy, prepared to make a go of it on its own. Freedom from organizational ties and commitments was more than sufficient compensation for being deprived of the sense of security bred in belonging to a movement such as the one we now renounced—a movement of far-reaching influence and power which knew so well how to maintain the illusion of dissidence and revolutionary idealism within the easy comforts and satisfactions of conformity.

Thus during the initial period of the magazine's existence its editors learned a wonderfully concrete lesson as to what the relations between Communism and the intellectuals came to in reality. Still, it would not do to say that our present appraisal of that period is wholly negative. For in a sense it is not without certain nostalgic memories that we now think of those early days, when in our militant innocence we set out to preach our illusions to the world at large. We have not forgotten that back in the early thirties we lived through a moment of high confidence and inspiration, a moment perhaps never to be recovered in our lifetime, when many intellectuals, enraptured by the mythology of triumphant socialism in Russia, experienced an emotion of historic depth such as Wordsworth's generation must have felt in the first years of the French Revolution:

> But Europe at that time was thrilled with joy,
> France standing on the top of golden hours,
> And human nature seeming born again.

Put Russia in place of Wordsworth's France, add America to his Europe, and you can conceive of the buoyant mood that impelled us to seek enlightenment and our share of social responsibility in the sphere of Soviet Communism.

Bereft of these consolations, and prepared to accept a more individual type of social and literary responsibility, we brought out *Partisan Review* again in 1937. Besides ourselves, the new editorial staff of *Partisan Review* included F. W. Dupee, who had been literary editor of the *New Masses* just long enough to see through its pretensions, Dwight Macdonald, who, having but lately discovered the socialist cause, was ready to devote to it his abundant energies and capacities, Mary McCarthy, who brought a lively talent to the magazine, and George L. K. Morris, a modern painter who was able to undertake the financing of the venture. On the whole we made up a varied and argumentative group, bound together, however, by common values and aims.

How shall we describe our editorial emphasis, which was at times high-pitched, at times subtle and even seemingly contradictory? We conceived of ourselves as truly radical in the Marxist sense. While the old *Partisan Review*, subject to the strict division of labor imposed by its party mentors, did not directly engage in political discussions but asserted its bias through literary means, we now selected the literary content of the magazine on a broader and more integral basis—integral, that is, to the medium of writing—while publishing at the same time articles on central political subjects. Our own politics at the time might be summed up as a kind of independent and critical Marxism: independent of all party organizations and programs, and critical insofar as we were inclined to re-examine the entire course of socialism in order to understand its present plight. It goes without saying that we were intransigently anti-Stalinist; and though in some quarters—where people took their cue from the Stalinists—we were quickly stamped as Trotskyite, the truth is that of all the editors only Dwight Macdonald was a member of that party, and he but for a short time. Our editorial position could then be said to have been Trotskyite only in the sense that we mainly agreed with Trotsky's criticism of the Soviet regime and that we admired him as a great exponent of the Marxist doctrine. Beyond that we were not willing to accept many of the specific theories and practices of the Trotskyites, while they, on their part, greeted the first issue of our new publication with a diatribe that demonstrated nothing more than their affinity with the Stalinists—at least so far as their attitude toward the intellectuals was concerned.

But our principal interest, editorially, was in bringing about a rapprochement between the radical tradition on the one hand and the tradition of modern literature on the other—a rapprochement that virtually all left-wing magazines had in the past done their utmost to prevent. It was our idea that this could not be accomplished by converting one tradition to the other, for the result of that could hardly be anything more than a false show of unity. It seemed to us that a reconciliation could be effected only by so modulating the expression of both traditions as to convey a sense at once of the tension between them and of their relevance to each other within the common framework of our civilization. At this point we might add that not infrequently we have been asked to explain the ostensible lack of continuity between the social views stated in *Partisan Review* and some of its purely literary pieces. To this we have replied that there is no necessary contradiction in the attempt to maintain within one context an interest both in imaginative expression and in political ideas. The problem of the relation between literature and politics is not to be approached abstractly; there are no iron-clad laws regulating this relation; and any attempt to reduce it either to an aesthetic or to a sociological formula is doomed to scholasticism. It is a problem which, as editors, we could meet only from issue to issue as it were, depending on the political situation and on the literary state of mind at any given time. Actually, it is the extreme one-sidedness of modern intellectuality which makes it seem odd that an essay on Henry James or W. B. Yeats should appear side by side with an analysis, say, of the socio-economic theories of Rosa Luxemburg or of Stalin as an historical personality. It is precisely from this union of sensibility with a radical temper that *Partisan Review* has derived its tone and quality. In the realm of action priorities may be inescapable, but in the realm of thought it is not always necessary to submit to them. This much, however, can be said: That the specific emphasis of the magazine has not been without influence among its literary contributors, in that it has led some of them to modify their previous attitudes of superiority or indifference to political issues; and in the same way some of the readers of the magazine who were first drawn to it on political grounds have been led to realize that the claims of the imagination cannot be subordinated to the utilitarian demands of the political mind.

Of course the story of the magazine is only partly told by dwelling on its particular modulation of literature and politics. One side of *Partisan Review* patently belongs to the tradition of the "little magazine" in America, in the sense that one of its chief functions has been to print the kind of writing which, because of qualities that do not satisfy the requirements at the moment both of the popular and the staid, cannot find its way either into the commercial or the academic periodicals. In another sense, however, *Partisan Review* stands somewhat out-side the "little magazine" tradition. Historically the "little magazine" has been an enterprise in publishing experimental writing, whereas *Partisan Review* has been quite as much a magazine of general ideas as of experiment in the arts. The products of experiment have fallen off considerably in recent years, and modernism, for the most part, has become more a matter of striking an attitude than of genuine achievement in the development of language and form. Whatever may be true of the other arts, this has certainly been the case in literature; and in *Partisan Review* we have tried to steer clear of the artiness and snobbery characteristic of the sectarian avant-garde, which, in its aspiration to be up-to-date at all costs, indiscriminately adores Evelyn Waugh one year and Henry Miller the next. Long before the popular critics acknowledged the slump in contemporary writing, we repeatedly noted in editorial articles that, compared with the high level achieved in the twenties, the literature of the thirties and forties has shown a decline in originality, integrity, and creative power. Hence it seemed to us that in this period a magazine dedicated solely to experiment and innovation could not but turn into a futile undertaking, as the paucity of material on which such a magazine must subsist would eventually compel it to adopt meretricious standards, permitting the souvenirs of past experimentation to be passed off as the vital discoveries of the present.

In point of creative work—let us admit it here and now—*Partisan Review* has been unable to equal the record of some of the little magazines which flourished in the more fertile period that closed with the twenties. We did not have the good fortune of coming across such essentially "*new*" writing as *Ulysses* and *The Waste Land*, or the more significant early fiction of such modern American authors as Anderson, Hemingway, and Faulkner; and the fact is that none of the contemporary journals can boast of such large satisfactions. If we have published poets like Eliot, Stevens, and Marianne Moore, it has been after their merit was generally recognized. Naturally, we have attempted to locate and bring forward the younger talents, and a considerable number of them have expressed themselves to the top of their bent in the pages of *Partisan Review*. At the same time we have been aware that the energy of writing finds its outlet these days not only in "new" creative work but also in the fresh approaches that have lately been made to the literature of the past and in the forays and divagations of critical thought.

The next turning-point in the existence of the magazine was reached in the summer of 1943, when Dwight Macdonald resigned from the editorial staff. (In the meantime—to keep the record straight—Mary McCarthy, F. W. Dupee, and George L. K. Morris left the magazine for reasons involving no personal or editorial differences; Clement Greenberg, now art critic of *The Nation*, was on the staff from January, 1941, to the winter of 1943, when he entered the army .) The differences that arose between Macdonald and ourselves were largely traceable to the crisis within the radical movement that was precipitated by the war. The dilemma of the Left showed itself in a widespread disillusionment and a return to positions at once more popular and more conservative; while among those who remained within the Marxist fold there was a further breach, some urging a reappraisal of the Marxist system, and others reasserting their attachment to it. In our group, Macdonald generally upheld the more orthodox views, particularly on the war issue, though we also disagreed on other counts, such as the question of the nature of fascism, which we tended to define in terms more consistent with the Marxist approach. Moreover,

Macdonald's primary interest in political journalism conflicted with our conception of the intellectual purposes of the magazine, which, we felt, should not be forced into a set political pattern, especially since that pattern was now in itself open to question. After an exchange of letters in the pages of *Partisan Review*, Macdonald left to found a new organ, *Politics*, in which he has been able to set his own course.

At the same time that Macdonald resigned, Delmore Schwartz joined our staff, and it is now about two and a half years that the three of us have been responsible for the editorial direction of the magazine. In this most recent period our effort has been to sustain the radical and secular orientation of *Partisan Review*. Thus in the last years we have steadily opposed such regressive trends as the neo-Americanism of Brooks, DeVoto, and a host of lesser patriots, the growing identification of the liberals with the ideology and power-drives of Stalinism, and the tendency to abandon objective modes of analysis in favor of religiosity, metaphysical generalities, and testimonials of moral rectitude. In this way, the general premises and perspectives of the magazine have been affirmed; but in the selection of literary material as well as in our critical approach to writing we have necessarily been guided by a recognition of the ambiguities and contradictions inherent in creative effort. Hence we have published religious poets like Eliot, Auden, and Robert Lowell—as well as many other writers whose beliefs we do not share—on the ground that the value of a work of art cannot be reduced to its pattern of ideas.

So much for the intellectual history of *Partisan Review*. But the story of the magazine would be incomplete without a word about its more prosaic side—its sheer problem of survival. A magazine that does not command the resources either of a profit-making project or of an endowed one nevertheless has all the responsibilities and the overhead of any practical enterprise. Only by the most rigid economy have we been able to keep the magazine going, thus enabling us to escape the fate of our predecessors in the field of the "little magazine," whose lavish expenditures eventually ran them aground. Paying only two dollars a page for contributions, we have survived because of the sustained interest both of our regular contributors and our readers, who now number six thousand—a relatively large circulation, by the way, for a publication such as ours. The fact is that there is a basic and insidious division in American culture between the highbrow and the lowbrow, which is reflected in the fabulous prosperity of virtually all lowbrow periodicals, and in the chronic poverty of the highbrow ones. If some of the latter have been able to keep going, it has largely been by turning themselves into harmless academic miscellanies—which appears to be the only proper basis for eliciting the financial support of foundations, universities, and other philanthropic bodies pledged to assist cultural projects. (pp. 679-87)

      William Phillips and Philip Rahv, "In Retrospect: Ten Years of 'Partisan Review'," in The Partisan Reader: Ten Years of Partisan Review 1934-1944, an Anthology, *edited by William Phillips and Philip Rahv, The Dial Press, 1946, pp. 679-88.*

FREDERICK CREWS

[*An American psychoanalytic critic, Crews is best known for his mordant satire of the art of literary criticism,* The Pooh Perplex *(1963). He has also written studies of the works of E. M. Forster, Henry James, and Nathaniel Hawthorne. In the following excerpt, Crews discusses the editorial policies of* Partisan Review *under the direction of Phillips and Rahv, focusing in particular on Rahv's central role in formulating those policies.*]

"Little magazines" are, for the most part, the mayflies of the literary world. Launched on implausibly idealistic manifestoes, briefly sustained by charity and overwork, and imperiled by an ever-worsening ratio of creditors to subscribers, they soon complete their scarcely noticed flights and sink away, to be replaced by swarms of others. Ephemerality is the little magazine's generic fate; by promptly dying it gives proof that it remained loyal to its first program. Conversely, when such a journal survives for decades and effects a change in the whole temper of cultural debate, we may be sure that a metamorphosis has occurred. In outward respects—format, financing, even the number of paying readers—the magazine may still be technically "little," but its editors will have shown a quite untypical gift for retreating from untenable positions, anticipating new currents of opinion, and harmonizing interests that would seem on their face to be incompatible.

This rule applies nowhere more strikingly than to *Partisan Review,* the longest-lived and most influential of all our magazines that began by being "little." At its inception in 1934 it was not much more than a strident house organ of the Communist party and one of its literary brigades, the John Reed Club of New York City. The numerous members of its editorial board were to all appearances obedient Stalinists who would promote the official line of proletarianism—or, a little later, the relative latitudinarianism of the Popular Front. But by 1936 the most active of those editors, William Phillips and Philip Rahv, had learned all they would ever need to know about the nature of the Soviet dictatorship and the folly of allowing ideologues to enforce critical judgments. They ceased publication; the mayfly seemed to have fallen on schedule.

In fact, however, Rahv and Phillips were busy gathering collaborators, most of whom were recent converts to anti-Stalinism like themselves. In 1937, with the help of F. W. Dupee, Dwight Macdonald, Mary McCarthy, and George L. K. Morris, they reconstituted the magazine, now advocating at once a purer radicalism than the Party's and devotion to the highest critical standards irrespective of ideology. Before long *Partisan Review* had attracted contributions not only by such survivors of leftist militancy as Sidney Hook, Meyer Schapiro, Lionel and Diana Trilling, Isaac Rosenfeld, Delmore Schwartz, Clement Greenberg, Irving Howe, Lionel Abel, and Harold Rosenberg, but also by figures as eminent and diverse as Malraux, Ortega, Silone, Eliot, Auden, and Dylan Thomas.

No one could deny that the new *Partisan Review* was a success, even though no one could explain how neo-Marxist political commentary was to be reconciled with "The Dry Salvages" and highbrow discussion of the modern masters. Not even Trotsky, the idol of the hour for intellectuals who wished to regard themselves as having moved to Stalin's left and not his right, could make room for James, Proust, and Gide on the revolutionist's bedtable. But Phillips's and Rahv's eclectic policy was psychologically appropriate both for themselves and for their generation of former Communists. After years of monotonous proletarianizing, bright leftists were aching to do critical justice to complex and resistant texts—but they were not ready to admit that there is nothing especially radical about such activity. They gravitated to *Partisan* as the one journal in which they could bid good riddance to the Thirties without seeming to do so.

Partisan also became the vehicle for another and closely related adaptation. In the Forties and Fifties, the period of its greatest sway, the magazine was among other things a forum for debate about making one's peace with America. Nearly all of its older mainstays had believed at one time that fascism was a logical development of capitalism and that any war joined by the United States would shift the country definitively into its totalitarian phase. But no prior dogmas could prevent well-informed Jewish intellectuals from grasping the special character of Hitlerism. In the pages of *Partisan* and in hairsplitting private encounters, they inched their way from pacifism toward lukewarm support of the war—a process that was capped by the pacifist Dwight Macdonald's resignation in protest from the editorial staff in 1943. Less than a decade later, in a famous symposium canvassing the most prominent members of the *Partisan* circle, all but a few of twenty-four respondents concurred with Phillips's and Rahv's proposal that America had indeed become "Our Country and Our Culture."

Such a rapprochement with the patriots amounted to a conspicuous and at times mortifying compromise of the *Partisan* writers' vanguard identity. It should be noted, however, that they had never constituted an avant-garde in the usual sense of the term. Politically, they had been drifting ambiguously toward the liberalism they professed to despise. Culturally, they welcomed association with such established and unradical personages as Eliot, Stevens, Tate, and Ransom. The poetry and fiction they wrote themselves were hardly experimental. And as judges of contemporary literature they shunned extremes, saving their approval for manifestly dignified ironists like the early Lowell and the early Bellow. For a supposed little magazine, *Partisan* was concerned to an unusual degree with previously established literary values such as complexity, moral seriousness, and a sense of the past.

In retrospect it seems evident that after about 1940, the radicalism of the *Partisan* writers was largely a matter of style. Their progress, at least until they became polarized by McCarthyism, was a fairly steady movement toward the American center; but they camouflaged that movement by drawing around themselves every available form of disciplined pessimism, from psychoanalysis and existentialism to the arid, elusive visions of Kafka and Eliot. As Alfred Kazin has said of them, "They would never feel that they had compromised, for they believed in alienation, and would forever try to outdo conventional opinion even when they agreed with it." In this manner assimilation retained much more of the urgency and energy of revolt.

In a society still rife with anti-Semitism and suspicion of radicals, however, the early *Partisan* critics were by no means assured of a friendly audience. As Lionel Trilling could attest from bitter experience, university departments of English not only had a narrow gentlemanly idea of "the tradition," but also a gentleman's agreement about blood qualifications for discussing that tradition. The championing of modernism in *Partisan* can be understood in part as a turning of the table on the professors. Of course the *Partisan* writers were sincere in their taste for the thorny moderns. Yet we cannot fail to notice that by placing extremity and alienation at the very heart of modern experience, they were in effect supplanting one tradition with another—one that they were already better prepared to gloss than were the salaried connoisseurs of Keats and Browning.

In view of their standing as outsiders on probation, however, it is not surprising that the *Partisan* critics preferred their pessimism well diluted with cultural decorum. Writers like Céline and Henry Miller, irreverent beyond all civility, were not celebrated in *Partisan;* the ideal figures would be those who already had a foothold on respectability and who emanated more, not less, portentous allusiveness than the favorites of the academy. When a *Partisan* critic set out to analyze such a model modern, the journal's usual tone of iconoclasm was apt to give way to a strangely incautious awe.

Thus Delmore Schwartz, a co-editor at the time, ingenuously entitled a 1945 essay "T. S. Eliot as the International Hero." Schwartz doesn't ask us to regard Eliot as a hero; he reminds us why we already do. The reason is that Eliot happens to be the quintessential modern cosmopolite, belonging to all and therefore none of the world's capitals, haunted by war and decay, and attuned to the defining feature of modernity, namely impotence. "We ought to remember," wrote Schwartz, "that the difficulty of making love . . . is not the beginning but the consequence of the whole character of modern life." Modern man is like Gerontion:

> He lives in a rented house, he is unable to make love,
> and he knows that history has many cunning, decep-
> tive, and empty corridors. The nature of the house,
> of love and of history are interdependent aspects of
> modern life.

Such remarks, absurd in their literal content, tell us something about the anxieties and mannerisms to which *Partisan* writers could be susceptible. To treat "Gerontion" as an accurate picture of "our" condition was both to play one's role as a bearer of grim tidings and to take social shelter beneath Eliot's none too capacious umbrella. Readers were not reminded that Schwartz's nondenominational mournfulness over "modern man" differed notably from Eliot's exclusivism. Not a word about Hakagawa bowing among the Titians, or, more significantly, about the "Jew" squatting on Gerontion's window sill. To be fully critical about such details would have been to strike too personal and querulous a note—and before an audience not devoid of prejudices like Eliot's. It was more prudent to write in universal terms, to ascribe prophetic souls to the gloomier modernists, and in so far as possible to overlook their often reactionary views.

The need to appropriate alienation, whether or not one still felt alienated oneself, also exacted a price in the *Partisan* critics' ability to consider ideas on their merits, apart from their usefulness in conferring adversary status. This holds even for the mildest, subtlest, and most peripheral member of the circle, Lionel Trilling. He called Freud and Nietzsche to the witness stand to vouch for our imperiled condition, but he could not afford to cross-examine them about the cogency of their propositions; they were, after all, his spiritual guardians against such paddlers of the mainstream as Van Wyck Brooks and the *Times Book Review*'s vox populi, J. Donald Adams. Trilling needed little coaxing in order to rehearse the terrible antinomies of modern existence and the stern tasks allegedly confronting "us." It seemed that liberalism, meaning the bureaucratic progressivism to which he was in fact quite reconciled, had to be fertilized by imagination; imagination had to be sobered by an unspecified political concern; the ego was not master in its own house; and modern literature was at once our finest possession and a seedbed of libidinous and nihilistic anarchy. The recompense for living with such difficult knowledge, such conflicting imperatives, was of course an awareness that the philistines of the mass culture weren't up to doing so.

In the Fifties and Sixties, when the social climate had become less invidious and the *Partisan* writers had gained the recognition they deserved as our first and only intelligentsia, they could afford to begin dissociating themselves from what Bel-

low's Herzog called "the commonplaces of the Wasteland outlook, the cheap mental stimulants of Alienation, the cant and rant of pipsqueaks about Inauthenticity and Forlornness." Yet even then their bias toward modernism remained strong, for only the great moderns stood between them and a more threatening wasteland, the culturally chaotic one inhabited by trolls like Ginsberg and Kerouac. By the Sixties some *Partisan* graduates were looking back to the modernist classics with an almost professorial nostalgia, as the last serious writing our demotic Western world was likely to produce.

That may look like an oddly patrician stance for one time champions of proletarianism to assume. In truth, however, the seeming paradox of combining more or less left-wing sociopolitical commentary with lofty aesthetic discourse had never been much of a paradox at all. Behind both kinds of enterprise lay the same animus against the bland middle class, and more especially against "nativism"—the distinctly WASPish idea that American civilization is culturally rich in just those respects where it most sharply diverges from European precedent. What united Marx and Proust, Nietzsche and Joyce, Freud and Camus was their equidistance from Iowa. The lapsed Marxists surrounding *Partisan* disputed many points with one another, but they all seemed to agree, as did the writers they most admired, that literary value was not a matter for the people to decide.

Yet if *Partisan* was held together by elitism, as a magazine of debate it was also significantly open to interaction with outsiders. The "we" so frequently invoked in its pages was meant to designate, not the immediate clique in favor with the editors, but all readers willing to acknowledge the modern crisis of values and the necessity of lodging belief elsewhere than in the Soviet Union on the one hand and warmed-over Christianity on the other. That was a numerous group, and *Partisan* helped to make it more so. Phillips and Rahv were always more concerned to publish intelligent speculative discourse than to promote modernism or any other fashionable cause.

Nevertheless, we are far enough removed from the Forties and Fifties to perceive that for a long while there was not only a recognizable *Partisan* style—wide-ranging, cutting, self-assured—but also a *Partisan* world view. It was a complex of attitudes and positions derived in part from the debacle of the American left, in part from the concurrence of separatist and assimilationist impulses within the so-called New York family, and in part from the personality of Philip Rahv, by all accounts the ruling figure at *Partisan* during its most influential period.

Rahv, indeed, was in most respects the quintessential *Partisan* contributor. He was anti-nativist and pro-modernist; he distrusted the academy and its weakness for "idealistic" spiritual transports; he felt permanently betrayed by Stalin; he endorsed psychoanalysis as a body of truths too upsetting for optimists and literary professors to comprehend; he craved disputation and was ever watchful for new trends that would bear denouncing; and he treated well-known authors and problems as if no one had discussed them before, or never adequately. Most importantly, he tried in his own criticism to do what he and Phillips as editors were doing only by juxtaposition, namely to bring together sociopolitical consciousness and sensitivity to great literature. In making that effort, Rahv epitomized the magazine's project of freeing analytic intelligence from party-mindedness without stripping it completely of radical purpose.

Before the *Partisan* critics broke with Stalinism they had been practitioners of revolutionary subordination: books were weapons in the class war, and the chief function of criticism was to identify which side was served by a given work. Once that phase was over, the question became how far to go in the direction of sheer aestheticism. Should one now praise *The Golden Bowl* as fervently as one had recently been praising *The Lower Depths?* Were an author's ideas and attitudes nothing more than a *donnée* after all, incidental to the produced sensations that really mattered? What, if anything, could an ex-Stalinist say about literature that wasn't already being said by the suave and ingenious New Critics?

Rahv's answer was that ideas and attitudes counted as much as before, but no longer in the same way. An author lacking a sense of history or an awareness of the social issues of his time was still to be faulted—not, however, because of his deviation from Marx and Engels but because his imagination was incomplete. The critic's task was first to submit himself to that imagination without making fixed ideological demands of it, but then, rather than lose himself in some contrived ecstasy, to draw back and ask what dimensions of the world were being ignored or distorted. Thus, for example, Rahv, who did much to revive interest in Henry James and wrote perceptively about him, eventually decided that James was too narrow, for he took his society for granted and "made a metaphysic of private relations, giving the impression that they are immune to the pressures of the public and historical world." Other critics might challenge Rahv's judgment, but all could recognize that he was writing from a thoroughly considered position. It was a kind of shadow Marxism, whereby one could still value mimesis and social compassion without insisting on determinism or dogmatizing about "structure" and "superstructure" or issuing veiled threats in the name of history.

The most important literary value for Rahv, however, was more Shakespearean than Marxian: a tolerance for contradiction, a capacity to grant full imaginative reality to people not of one's own party. He found that value supremely exemplified in Tolstoy and Dostoevsky, two writers whose more particular opinions he largely rejected. And he found it undeveloped in D. H. Lawrence, who tended to pit his "mouthpiece" characters against contemptible adversaries, and utterly lacking in the later work of Norman Mailer, whose vacuous superhero Rojack rapes and murders his way through a world that exists only as a field of megalomaniac desire. If Rahv was huffy about such cases, it was because he had learned from the major developments of his age that unmediated will and a failure to credit one's opponents with humanity are defects that can entail appalling mass criminality.

It would seem, then, that Rahv had survived the Thirties with a rare combination of concrete historical awareness and individual morality, the best fruits of both Marxism and conservatism. To be sure, that fact did not make him a great critic. His ideas were mostly derivative, his range of literary interests was restricted to the novel from Gogol onward, and he was too much given to humorless scorn, righteously condemning tendencies he had managed to avoid himself. Yet he was also capable of sustained and generous appreciation; witness five completed chapters of his projected book on Dostoevsky . . . . Those chapters show a fine subtlety and empathy, interrupted only by the occasional squeaking of his hobbyhorse: settling scores with the Soviet Union. By reading selectively . . .— combining, say, the pieces on Tolstoy, Kafka, and Dostoevsky with such influential essays as "The Cult of Experience in American Writing," "The Dark Lady of Salem," "The Heiress of All the Ages," and "Religion and the Intellectuals"—

one can come away with the impression of a mind whose irritability and unforgivingness were more than overbalanced by possession of a coherent yet flexible outlook, neither as prescriptive as the ideologues' nor as indeterminate as the aesthetes'.

A rather different picture of Rahv emerges, however, when we attend to his strictly political writings . . . . (pp. 3-4, 6)

Rahv was implacably and persuasively contemptuous of Stalin's show trials, of the conformist atmosphere in postwar America, and of the zeal of penitents like Whittaker Chambers, who could pass so readily from Stalin to Jesus because they had been unworldly absolutists all along. Yet when considered together, the political writings make us conscious of a persistent and damaging evasion. More than anyone else in his circle, Rahv showed himself incapable of understanding that values as well as tactics were entailed in the general backing-off from revolutionary activism.

Even in the most superficial terms, Rahv's politics were inconsistent. In his own view he had changed direction only once, when he repudiated Stalin as a traitor to Marx. Thereafter he considered himself an independent Marxist or, as he sometimes said, a democratic socialist. Little was heard of this Marxism in the Forties and Fifties, however; in that period Rahv conveniently simplified things by referring to himself and *Partisan* as "anti-Communist." He and Phillips, for example, wrote in 1953 that their "ideal reader" would be someone "concerned with the structure and fate of modern society, in particular with the precise nature and menace of Communism." But in 1967, emboldened by the newer collegiate radicalism, Rahv defiantly told *Commentary* that he had never broken with "communism, in its doctrinal formulations by Marx *or even by Lenin*" (emphasis added). He professed himself scandalized that official America still rejected "not the Stalinist aspect of communism but communism as such, authoritarian or not."

One might say that the unclarity here could be resolved merely by attending to the difference between capital and lower-case *c*"s. Rahv was a communist, not a Communist. Fair enough— but apart from disapproving of mass murder and slave-labor camps, what difference in principle was involved? Was Lenin a nonauthoritarian, a communist with a small *c?* And hadn't Marx himself accepted the necessity of concerted violence against those who stand to lose by the revolution? To ascribe Soviet terror entirely to Stalin was to indulge in an inverse cult of personality, a flight from essential issues.

Toward the end of his life, sizing up the imprudent radicals of the Vietnam era, Rahv began to sound like a born-again Leninist of the familiar type. In "What and Where Is the New Left?" he declared that "violent assaults on the class-enemy" are inadvisable "if undertaken prematurely, . . . before the challengers of the status quo can count on at least an even chance of victory in an armed struggle with the police." With avuncular sagacity he pointed to the need for "a guiding organization—one need not be afraid of naming it a centralized and disciplined party," practically and ideologically alert "so as not to miss its historical opportunity. . . ." Rahv neglected to say how such a party, once its "armed struggle" was over, would wither away in favor of a nonauthoritarian democracy. A lifetime of political argument and observation had failed to teach him that repression flows naturally from defining others as "the class-enemy."

If we ask why Rahv was so obtuse on this point, I think the answer must be sought in an irrational appeal that Marxism makes to people of a certain prickly, combative, and power-hungry disposition. Where others need friends, they need class-enemies. Lacing such hateful antagonists, they would no longer be able to connect their will to domination with an ultimately benign historical drama, guided by transpersonal forces. In a word, they would be just plain bullies. By retaining faith, however inactively, in what he called "the principles of classic Marxism, its knowledge and foresight," Rahv succeeded in mistaking his native Manichaeism for revolutionary vigilance. But he paid a price in squandered bile, not just against the capitalists (for in fact he had little to say about them) but more especially against everyone who struck him as following an incorrect line: Stalinists and professional anti-Stalinists, pacifists and patriots, McCarthyites and fellow travelers, ideologues and idealizers. Dissociation on all sides was his one strategy for retaining a sense of mission.

Like other Americans who rejected Stalin only because he was a counter-revolutionary, Rahv never admitted the extent of his debt to liberal capitalism. As an editor, he stood behind the shield of the First Amendment. As a judge of literature, he upheld a magnanimity of vision that could never flourish in a state founded on the victory of one former underclass. And as both editor and critic, he took for granted a readership of people who would believe that values can be absorbed from unorthodox books, and who would be free to change their minds and indeed their lives if they agreed with his own independent reasonings. The contemporary world offered no basis for imagining that such readers would be available under a Marxist dispensation.

The irony of Rahv's political nondevelopment is that, unlike the sophists who warned against "repressive tolerance," he actually did appreciate guaranteed liberties. After World War II he had to admit that America had thus far "sustained that freedom of expression and experiment without which the survival of the intelligence is inconceivable in a modern society." Meanwhile the record of entrenched Marxism in the management of culture was unambiguous. But for Rahv to embrace the liberal institutions that protect "freedom of expression and experiment" would have been to jeopardize his adversary identity; he could no more do that than Trilling could question Freud's gratuitously tragic ideas about civilization, or than Schwartz could reject Eliot on the grounds of his anti-Semitism. It was easier to keep hoping that history would one day give birth to a true realm of freedom as described by Marx, in which one would not have to thank the class-enemy for revocable favors.

Fortunately, the shallowness of Rahv's political thought had little effect on his best literary criticism. We can now understand, however, why nearly all of that criticism was written in the Forties, when he and others were under maximum pressure to show that they could reach a nonsectarian audience. The Rahv we see in earlier and later periods reveals a sensibility dissociated between revolutionary impulses and a belief in cultural hierarchy.

Toward the end of his life that dissociation became painful; the New Left had reignited his wrath against the ruling class, but it had also quickly dissolved into a "counterculture" utterly alien to his temperament. Meanwhile, under new leadership, *Partisan* had turned its back on the great moderns and was flirting with pornography, rock music, and the newest of liberties, freedom from interpretation. Fulminating against

"swinging reviewers" and "our contemporary porno-aesthetes," Rahv sounded just like the academic traditionalists he had always disprized. Was there no way to restore cultural norms and simultaneously continue to struggle against the system? *Modern Occasions* was founded, and soon foundered, on that dim prospect.

Some cultural conservatives have argued that promoters of literary nihilism such as they claim the early *Partisan* critics were have only themselves to blame for the anarchy they now oppose. Trilling himself, appalled by the mood of the Sixties, is known to have spoken ruefully of "modernism in the streets." Such remorse, however, betrays a teacher's illusion that mostly unread books are more determinative of mass conduct than are wars and baby booms. In any case, the tasteful kind of modernism favored by *Partisan* was always less likely to lead to Molotov cocktails than to dry martinis. It would be especially far-fetched to accuse Philip Rahv of having incited the new anti-authoritarianism, for unlike some of his contributors, he had never equated modernity with the overthrow of moral restraint. As for his political militancy, it slumbered for three decades before being briefly aroused *by* the New Left.

Rahv's program of political and literary seriousness was exactly the same in 1970 as it had been in 1940, but everything else had changed. In the early years he and his friends were sufficiently close to their leftist past for their devotion to literature to be seen as a courageous break with the party line, a more high-minded radicalism. Again, modernism was still a tradition to conjure with, not a staple of every curriculum. Above all, *Partisan* was just beginning its spectacularly successful work of propagating its cultural position. As the word from New York radiated outward, the adversary fever which had been so essential to the magazine's self-image necessarily subsided. Then the veterans of the Forties found themselves inhabiting a larger world, full of prosperity, compromise, and chatter about the authors they had once claimed as their own. Rahv and his associates had helped to shape a new literary establishment, more democratic and sophisticated than its predecessor. In doing so, they phased themselves irreversibly out of business as spokesmen for an alien vision. (pp. 8, 10)

Frederick Crews, "The Partisan," *in* The New York Review of Books, *Vol. 25, No. 18, November 23, 1978, pp. 3-4, 6, 8, 10.*

LESLIE FIEDLER

[*Fiedler is a controversial and provocative American critic. While he has also written novels and short stories, his personal philosophy and insights are thought to be most effectively expressed in his literary criticism. Emphasizing the psychological, sociological, and ethical context of works, Fiedler often views literature as the mirror of a society's consciousness. Similarly, he believes that the conventions and values of a society are powerful determinants of the direction taken by its authors' works. The most notable instance of Fiedler's critical stance is his reading of American literature, and therefore American society, as an infantile flight from "adult heterosexual love." This idea is developed in his most important work,* Love and Death in the American Novel *(1960), along with the theory that American literature is essentially an extension of the Gothic novel. Although Fiedler has been criticized for what are considered eccentric pronouncements on literature, he is also highly valued for his adventuresome and eclectic approach which complements the predominantly academic tenor of contemporary criticism. In the following essay, which was written in 1956, Fiedler discusses the nature of* Partisan Review *and the journal's role in American culture.*]

I cannot write about the *Partisan Review* objectively and coolly. In dealing with it, I have the sense of beginning my own autobiography, or, more precisely, of treating that part of my life which is typical rather than peculiar: my life as an urban American Jew, who came of age intellectually during the Depression: who discovered Europe for the imagination before America: who was influenced by Marxist ideas, Communist and Trotskyist; who wanted desperately to feel that the struggle for a revolutionary politics and the highest literary standards was a single struggle (but who had more and more trouble believing it as the years went on); whose political certainty unraveled during the second World War . . . I forget after a while whether I am writing about myself and my friends or about the magazine we used to fight for and argue over in 1937 and '38 and '39. I do not mean we *liked* it, then—far from it! Every issue seemed to us to fail some large, abstract notion of *Partisan Review*-ness, some ideal, it now seems clear to me, of ourselves. No sooner was *Partisan* a year old than this year's level seemed to us a vast falling off from the year before. The point is, of course, that what is merely typical of oneself is bound to appear comic, embarrassing, depressing and a bore; and yet—I remember K., now the author of two novels, one of whose first ambitious pieces of fiction was a parody of a *Partisan Review* story we all mailed off together as a huge joke, but who, ten years later, was publishing regularly in *PR*. I remember my own sense of being misrepresented when I, in turn, began to appear in its pages; and my special horror when, after only three contributions, I was mentioned in two separate attacks on *Partisan* as representative of its intellectual vices.

By now I have come a long way from the pattern of my past: a Professor of English Literature, improbably asked for letters of recommendation by aspiring students; a father of six children, who lives over five hundred miles from the nearest big city and is surrounded by those who, if they know *Partisan* at all, have picked it up in a university library rather than off the "literature table" of a deviationist Marxist sect. Yet I have accepted my fate with all its contradictions: I stand somehow for *PR* and *PR* for me; I do not like it, but I cannot deny it. I know that even my feeling of being misrepresented is typical, as is my lack of love for the magazine. It is not a publication one loves; only its enemies are passionate. Nor does *PR* love its own children; I am aware that at the very moment I am losing a good academic job because I have appeared too often on its pages (and am therefore obviously "negative" as well as Jewish), *PR* is preparing to blast me publicly for believing in God. This strikes me as reasonably just as well as amusing— as amusing almost as the letter I had not long ago from a writer who is perhaps the best of the younger American novelists. "As for *PR*," he writes, "you know I never took that dodo for a phoenix. . . ." We both remember, of course, that it was *Partisan* which almost alone published him in the days when he was fighting to establish his reputation; but his comment is also just and a joke and part of the history of the magazine.

The real riddle of *Partisan Review* has always seemed to me the question of how the mouthpiece of so small and special a group as I have been defining (I should be much more surprised to discover that I am a "typical American" than that I am a typical *Partisan* writer) has managed to become the best-known serious magazine in America, and certainly, of all American magazines with intellectual ambitions, the one most read in Europe. That these are facts, I think there can be no doubt; at least, they are invariably mentioned with horror in anti-*Partisan* tirades. For better or for worse, *PR* has come to symbolize highbrow literature in America, and to suffer the twin indig-nities of the highbrow in our world: to be despised without understanding, and to be taken up by the culturally fashionable in equal ignorance.

Two examples, picked at random out of many, may serve to make the point. In a recent article, a certain reputable professor of American Literature sought to make clear his contempt for the politics of Mark Twain by writing, "We know this type well: the liberal who is not the tough realist. . . . You will find him vending his misanthropy in the *Partisan Review*." The reputable professor feels free to assume that there will be no doubt among academic readers about the meaning of his allusion. But the symbol is effective in Hollywood as well as at Princeton or Harvard. A couple of years ago, I paid a brief visit to an acquaintance who had been translated from an editorship in a publishing house to the position of a movie producer; and I found him in the midst of the appropriate splendor: white rugs on the floor, ponies for each of his children—and in the middle of a large, free-form cocktail table—a single copy of *PR*—to show, I suppose, that he was not yet lost to intellectual respectability.

Not only the purveyors of culture, however, high and low, accept this equation of *Partisan* and highbrow; it holds water for people who have never even seen the periodical, perhaps have never known one of its readers in their lives. It is, as a matter of fact, by no means easy to meet such readers. In its nearly twenty years of history, *PR* has never claimed more than ten thousand subscribers, and probably has considerably fewer at the present moment; and yet it is referred to in such mass-circulation journals as *Life* and *Time* with perfect confidence that it will stir the proper responses in their vast audience. Most of its subscribers have, to be sure, clustered about the two great cities of New York and Chicago (44%, according to a poll taken one year by the editors); and New York, at least, has been traditionally the taste-making center of the nation.

Besides, the split among the various kinds of art in America and their appropriate audiences into low, middle, and high has surrendered the creation, consumption, and judgment of serious literature into the hands of the very few. It is against those few that *Partisan*'s five to ten thousand faithful must be measured, and not against the 160,000,000 of the latest census figures. In that relatively restricted group, the thirties were marked by a turning away from the hinterland of America to Europe in a search for literary materials and examples. In that constant turning from East to West to East which characterizes our culture, the vanes pointed East once more; and no one seemed better suited for mediating between Europe and America than the kind of second generation Jew who in America's big cities was trying to find his own identity in the pages of *transition* and Karl Marx's *Capital*. Certainly, the Jews were the only immigrant group that had brought with it a considerable Old World culture to which it clung, refusing to cast it into the melting pot with the same abandon with which southern European or Scandinavian peasants were willing to toss away their few scraps of European spiritual goods.

It was the sons of the original Jewish immigrants, disabused of the legend of a Golden America by the Great Depression and attracted toward the Communist Party, who formed the core of the John Reed Club of New York which first sponsored the *Partisan Review*. In a handful of American cities, such "cultural" organizations, controlled by the Communists and called after native American radicals like John Reed or Jack London, flourished in the late thirties—as part of a strategy aimed at capturing the prestige of the "intellectuals" for the cause of the Soviet Union. It is important to remember that *PR* was born of such a marriage of Greenwich Village and Marxism—or more properly, from the attempt to woo the disaffected, rootless American, who wandered into New York in search of cultural freedom, from Bohemianism to Radicalism.

Partisan Review in its present form, however, begins with a declaration of independence from the orthodox Communists who ordained its beginnings. Its emergence as an independent journal is one symptom among many of the growing uneasiness of a certain segment of American writers, whom the Depression and the Spanish Civil War had persuaded into a temporary alliance with the Communist Party. From 1937 on (the new *PR* appeared first in the fall of that year), the Communists in America lost more and more of their respectable, intellectual fellow-travelers—indeed, almost deliberately jettisoned them for movie stars, script writers, and authors of detective stories as the Popular Front reached its peak of development. Into the cultural vacuum thus created, moved the *Partisan Review*. It was for many a transition from "revolutionary art" back to old-style "aestheticism" or forward to middle-class accommodation (though of this they were not then aware): for others merely the way into a lonelier and lonelier non-conformism.

From the Communists, the new periodical inherited, first of all, a name (at one point later on, when no one was any longer clear exactly what they were "partisan" *for*—there was an unsuccessful attempt to change that name); second, two editors: Philip Rahv and William Phillips, who alone have remained with the publication through countless editorial shifts, thus giving the magazine what continuing character it has; and third, a certain kind of bad manners, traditional in the Marxist movement. There is a polemical vigor and toughness about *PR* which has survived almost all its causes; occasionally that toughness hardens into a pose, but it is always a safeguard against stuffiness and gentility. Born into a dispute (thirty days after its inception, its editors were already labeled by their old comrades "slanderers of the working class . . . turncoats . . . agents provocateurs . . . strikebreakers!" and they were returning abuse for abuse), it has continued to ignore the rules of gentlemanly debate. Often when its collaborators have no one else to attack, they gouge and kick each other like marines stirred up to fight among themselves, just to keep their hands in. Though its founding fathers tend more and more to show their old scars rather than risk getting new ones, they have remained old soapboxers, which for me, at least, seems preferable to the young academicians or genteel undergraduate admirers of Wyndham Lewis who are found, for example, in *The Hudson Review*. Of all American magazines of discussion, only *Partisan* can be said never to talk to itself; to a few, yes, or to a crowd expected in advance to be hostile—but that is something else again.

There were two motives which impelled the editors of the new *PR* to break from the domination of the Communist Party: first, a desire for cultural autonomy, a feeling that orthodox Stalinism was hedging literature about with the "zeal of vigilantes"; and second, political disagreements of a Trotskyist hue with the official Communist line. Both led to long-term difficulties that have helped determine the nature of the magazine. From their second motive, the editors of *PR* (though most of them did not in fact ever become official Trotskyites) inherited a minor but troublesome vice: an obsessive anti-Stalinism and a myopic concern with sectarian Marxist politics, that, especially in the earlier years, hedged the magazine about with a technical jargon and the sort of parochial fervor which baffles and bores an outsider. After a while, even the insiders, who were not of

the sternest, began to wilt at the prospect of yet another scholastic debate on the nature of the Soviet State.

From the first motive, *PR* inherited a whole Chinese nest of interlocking questions, which they have never solved theoretically but which their whole career has been an attempt to answer in practice. If one really believes (as *PR* declared in an early manifesto) that "the tradition of aestheticism" is dead or ought to be and that literature finds its "final justification" in the "historic process," how can one avoid setting political standards for art and eventually harrying the artist precisely as the Communists have done? This is an especially acute problem if one's approach to the "historic process" is revolutionary or even liberal; for it is a baffling fact of our time that many contemporary artists of the first rank are politically reactionary, as in the cases of Yeats, Eliot, Pound, Lawrence, etc. Does one print the work of such misguided writers for the sake of some presumed independent aesthetic value? And how can such values exist if works of art are really rooted in history?

The *de facto* answer of *PR* has been to print Allen Tate, T. S. Eliot, and other artists whose politics it abhors. For a while, indeed, it was the chief American outlet for Eliot, not only his poetry but even an occasional essay on social matters; and as time went on, certain old standbys like James T. Farrell seemed actually to be pushed aside in favor of defter though less "revolutionary" authors, especially those enjoying critical acclaim. What lay behind such a strategy? Unkind critics accused *PR* of institutionalizing schizophrenia; unkinder ones insisted that its editors were shamelessly pursuing "big names."

The truth is, I think, that *PR* has been obsessed with the notion of a two-fold *avant-garde,* political and artistic, both segments regarded as a threat by middle-class philistines. Since the magazine actually came into being at the end of a period rather than a beginning, at the moment when experimentalism in art was being consolidated and academicized all over the world, the concept that serious art is, *per se,* as revolutionary as Marxism has been difficult to maintain. It has been somewhat easier to foster that illusion in respect to painting by espousing the newer versions of abstractionism, or in music, with a spirited apology for the twelve-tone row, than to sustain it in defense of these newer writers, who (aside from such "standards" as Eliot) have been the actual official favorites of *PR:* Malraux, Silone, Koestler, Sartre, Moravia, or George Orwell, to whom *Partisan* once awarded a one thousand dollar literary prize. Ideologically, these writers may represent progressive trends; but technically, they are not very interesting, ranging from glib traditionalism to simple ineptness; and in Orwell's case actually being on record against "advanced" art. Just as *PR* comes into existence at the instant of the liquidation of revolutionary politics as a force in American intellectual life, so it presides (quite unconsciously at first) over the liquidation of experimentalism in art. This has irked various defenders of post-World War I "new literature," ranging from Parker Tyler to Paul Goodman to Harold Rosenberg, men who began as collaborators of the magazine but have one by one withdrawn from its pages. Rosenberg has written a valedictory attack on what *Partisan* has become, dubbing its present writers a "herd of independent minds" and treating them as enemies of serious art.

Despite the fact that *PR*'s notions of an *avant-garde* reach nostalgically back to the very twenties whose values it betrays, those notions have helped develop one of its most valuable features: a series of acute exposés of certain highly regarded writers who pander to the timid, cheery bourgeois mind, which, even after fifty years, persists in the belief that the aging pur-veyors of the ''new literature'' (even Eliot!) somehow subvert morality and patriotism. The second World War brought to America a peculiarly violent recrudescence of this attitude; philistine apologists like Archibald MacLeish cried out that the antiwar, antisentimental nature of our literature in the twenties and thirties had left us powerless in the forties to combat Fas-cism, while Van Wyck Brooks was insisting that the ''sec-ondary'' literature of Joyce or Proust or Eliot had all along been an offense to the human spirit.

Dwight Macdonald in an essay called *Kulturbolschewismus* and M. D. Zabel in *The Poet on Capitol Hill* demonstrated with wit and passion how such arguments, proposed in the name of American democracy, actually represent totalitarian impulses, paralleling the attacks on the arts of Germany and Russia. In the atmosphere of controversy and self-congratulation which surrounded these two pieces, the editors were able to defend their previous principles of selection against the charges of contradictoriness by declaring, ''It is coming to be something of a revolutionary act simply to print serious creative writing.'' When the culture-sensors ten years later closed in on Ezra Pound, who had been awarded a coveted literary prize, *Par-tisan*'s editors, troubled by his anti-Semitism, were no longer so certain where their hearts lay; but in 1941 they were cou-rageous and unequivocal.

Our entry into the war followed hard on these polemics, bring-ing a crisis in the history of *Partisan Review*. The editors found themselves not only confused but not even sharing a common confusion about the attitude to take toward our participation in the fight against Hitler. Dwight Macdonald, who had played a leading editorial role in the years just before Pearl Harbor and was still maintaining the traditional revolutionary position (the defeat of Hitler could only be forwarded by a redoubled struggle for socialism in the United States), left the board of editors; and with his going the magazine came to take political stands on specific issues less and less often. McCarthyism for a little while stirred it to specific political discussion and forced the resignation of the most right-wing of its long-time asso-ciates, James Burnham; but in general *PR* tended more and more to invest its post-Marxian zeal in considering broadly defined problems of American culture. The clash of High Brow and Low Brow has gradually usurped the place of Class War in its working mythology.

The editors have moved since variously toward skepticism, New Dealism and non-Marxian socialism; and though occa-sionally a cry is raised in its columns against the ''Age of Conformism,'' most of its collaborators have been able to imagine no formulation of their plight which transcends the dilemma of adapting to current American life or sighing for the good old revolutionary days. Yet despite all changes, *PR* has re-mained in tone and tactics different from other American mag-azines of its category: the only periodical in our intellectual community for which politics in the European sense (something beyond choosing between Democrats and Republicans on set occasions) has ever existed. That old political passion survives in two forms: in the conviction that art is rooted in society, however one understands that society, and must be discussed in terms of those roots; and in a stubborn secularism which has outlived the revolutionary beliefs which once sustained it. From Edmund Wilson to Lionel Trilling, the most characteristic critical voice of *PR* has attempted to assert the sociological thesis against an evergrowing tendency toward intrinsic or ''pure'' textual criticism, and has sought to defend it against its pro-

fanation by the Stalinist or liberaloid theory that art must em-body ''progressive'' ideas.

Occasionally in reading *Partisan* these days one has the sense of a weary but gallant voice crying, ''Rosinante to the road again,'' as the editors print the replies to their latest question-naire on the Return to Religion. When they reconsider their other long-time favorite problem: the Relation of the Intellec-tual to American Culture, they cannot help being aware of how far they have come since, say, Dreiser's offhand dismissal of official ''Americanism'' in the earliest of their symposia. But when it is a matter of ''the retreat to faith,'' the old forces rally round and the majority opinion, naturalist and ''scien-tific,'' rings out loud and clear, as if nothing had happened in twenty years—and we were all rebels still—with no income tax returns to trouble us.

In 1950, a symposium on ''Religion and the Intellectuals'' took up where an earlier discussion labeled ''The New Failure of Nerve'' had left off seven years before; but whereas in the earlier forum, part at least of *Partisan*'s fervor was directed against doctrinaire Marxism, this time the Marxist issue was left far out on the periphery. The finish of the first Symposium had found Professor Sidney Hook (who is almost the official spokesman for *PR* in these matters) closed in argument with an orthodox Socialist; the close of the second found the same Professor Hook grappling with a slippery Christian apologist, Ernest van den Haag. Hook has always struck me as a brilliant though cruel polemicist and a courageous man, but his views on religion are vitiated by the fact that he can, apparently, never really credit the fact that anyone actually believes in God. His attitude in this regard is like that of an uninitiated small boy toward sex: he has heard of it, and he pretends to give credence to its reality, but that papa and mama really *do* it is unthinkable!

It remains further to be said that its origin in the Village-Marxist atmosphere of New York has influenced *PR* in two other significant ways: leaving it peculiarly ''European'' and reso-lutely anti-''academic.'' Its European flavor is partly a matter of the taste of its editors; its favorite literary ancestors are Dostoevsky and Tolstoi; its favorite moderns, Malraux, Koest-ler, Silone, Kafka, Musil, Sartre, Moravia, etc; and translations of their works will frequently be the only imaginative literature in a given issue. Even more characteristic, perhaps, are those communications from European cultural centers, which lend much of its peculiar tone to *PR:* the Paris letters of H. J. Kaplan and Nicola Chiaramonte, as well as the Italian letters of the latter and the London letters by Koestler and Orwell (attempts to institute similar regular communications from American cen-ters away from New York have always stuttered out to nothing) have kept *Partisan*'s readers in touch not only with the literary and political news but with the very gossip of Europe—a nar-row and sometimes *chic* Europe, to be sure, but a real one. The *PR* reader has, by virtue of these letters, always felt a good deal closer to Paris than to, say, Missoula, Montana; and though there is something a little absurd about this, there is also something valuable. *PR* has kept open a dialogue between our writers and certain writers on the continent; and it alone has been able to do this because it alone among our periodicals has been interested in and articulate about those ''general ideas,'' with which the continental mind engages so passionately but which most Americans notoriously ignore in favor of docu-mented facts or textual analysis. The most famous of these general ideas is the somewhat ambiguous one of ''alienation'': a concept which joins together the Marxist beginnings of *PR* with its early leanings toward depth psychology and its later interest in existentialism.

The belief in the "alienation" of the writer and intellectual from the community in a time of decaying values has seemed to certain of its critics to obsess the *Partisan Review*, and to lend a characteristic note of melancholy to its fiction and poetry as well as to its more ideological pieces. Protests have rung out from the beginning against the mixture of self-pity and bravado implicit in this view of the writer at odds with his world; and just lately, for instance, the editor of a provincial little magazine has described it as an "attitude which seems to come from reading *The Golden Bowl* on the B.M.T. subway." In one sense, such a view is indeed a peculiarity, almost a disease of the social group out of which *Partisan* comes: a development of the special sense of loneliness of the city-dweller, the Jew, the Marxist in an un-Marxist America—and especially of the left-wing Communist cut off even from the comforting sense of solidarity with the Soviet Union and "right-minded" liberalism. On the other hand, it is the traditional European view of the artist in America from Baudelaire on Poe to D. H. Lawrence on the classic American authors; and as mass culture advances throughout the Western world, it comes to describe the plight of the artist everywhere. It is true enough that "alienation" has sometimes been celebrated by *PR*, rather than explored; but on the other hand, its writers have done more than any others I know to describe the situation of a minority high culture in a mass society committed to the majoritarian principle.

In its earliest manifesto, *PR* declared its defiance of all "academicians from the University"; and it has continued its rather harried financial existence via "angels" and begging letters—but always without the sponsorship of any educational institution. This has been especially difficult in America, where the intellectual and his pursuits are granted full recognition and status only when they are associated with "higher education" and the universities have stood almost alone in subsidizing serious magazines. Even the Rockefeller Foundation, which in recent years has given support of one kind or another to such ventures, has invested only in periodicals whose respectability was already insured by an institutional connection, *Kenyon Review, Sewanee Review*, etc. *Partisan* has accordingly remained quite different in tone from those magazines that have defined themselves against the tendencies of old-line literary scholarship and whose *raison d'être* has been the struggle to reform the teaching of literature in the college classroom. *PR*'s ideological center has never become (no matter how many professors it lists among its contributors) the argument between the "New Critics" and the "Old Scholars," that is, a debate about pedagogy. It arises rather from that strange mingling of malicious gossip and disinterested argument about ideas that characterizes a social evening in New York. What the café is for Europe, such parties are for America—and it is out of them that *Partisan* has drawn its reigning concerns and its tone.

There are certain obvious limitations implicit in originating in so tight and isolated a world; obviously, personalities will play too large a part in any magazine nurtured by that milieu. Marriages and divorces, the falling out with an old mistress or the acquiring of a new one may end by influencing a political manifesto or the review of a new novel. Even the fiction of *PR* tends inevitably toward the *roman à clef*, its contributors feeding on each other like a mutual benefit association of cannibals. And the final absurdity (which I am not inventing but reporting) is the *PR* writer who produces a novel pillorying another *PR* writer (thinly disguised) for having in a previous book portrayed too bitterly still another *PR* contributor.

Moreover, the editors, to whom the literary cocktail party has been not only a source of images and ideas but also a university, end up without the protection of a traditionally acquired education—and are helplessly jostled by fad and fashion in a frantic drive to keep up with the latest thing. A critic of *PR* writing in 1949 could quite justly observe that up until that time, the magazine had never printed any full-scale article on a literary figure who flourished earlier than the latter half of the nineteenth century. This is, I think, an inevitable consequence of the scrappy, disordered, and largely contemporary culture out of which *PR* is improvised; it is a big price to pay for avoiding the curse of "academicism."

Yet certain qualifications must be made to these more general charges. On the one hand, *Partisan* has always included among its key contributors such generally cultured men as Edmund Wilson; and on the other hand, the American universities have undergone a revolutionary change since 1937 so that the sort of writer who once would have free-lanced out of some big city Bohemia ends up at Iowa State or North Carolina College for Women; and consequently, there has been an inevitable rapprochement between *PR* and what it likes to call "the academy." Not only have professors become its contributors, but its contributors have become professors. The last few years have seen an odd sort of united front between *PR* and *Kenyon Review*, the best of the academic-New Critical quarterlies, whose editor, John Crowe Ransom, not only writes for *Partisan* but has enlisted two of its editors, Rahv himself and Delmore Schwartz, to serve with him in the "School of Letters," a Rockefeller sponsored set-up which grants an M.A. in literature.

Besides, there has always been a loose, hard-to-define but nonetheless real connection between *PR* and Columbia University, which, trapped in the midst of New York City and fed by the subways, manages to be in certain important respects the least academic of academies. Since the death of the old Village and the institutionalization of the American writer, Columbia has come more and more to serve as a kind of intellectual center for the city and consequently for the New York-oriented throughout the nation. *Partisan Review* represents, in the light of this, one more colonizing attempt on the part of a university which has also made its influence felt decisively in such ventures as Readers' Subscription (the high-brow book club of the United States), and Anchor Books, whose distribution of serious, large format books in paper binding has revolutionized American publishing. Among the editors of *Partisan Review*, there have always been professors from Columbia like F. W. Dupee and Lionel Trilling; and in the list of *PR*'s regular contributors still others play a large part, including Meyer Shapiro, whose shadowy but enormous reputation among New York intellectuals as a polymath and whose formative influence on many of those intellectuals cannot be assessed in terms of his relatively limited publication. Lionel Trilling is, of course, the most interesting and influential of the group; much of his criticism has appeared in *PR*, as well as the two short stories which made him a reputation as a fictionist; yet he manages to preserve a remarkable aura of respectability not granted any of his colleagues. Those who condemn all else about the magazine, specifically exempt him from the general blame; yet he is in most ways not untypical: Jewish, a New Yorker who refuses to leave that city, an exploiter of the themes of anguish and alienation, a naturalist searching for tragedy. But in him the ordinarily annoying pose is mitigated by a soft-spoken style which is modesty itself—and combined with the stance of a nineteenth-century English gentleman-dissenter to produce a version of the *PR* writer as a belated Matthew Arnold.

Whereas Trilling embodies and modifies, in a secondary way, the *PR* spirit, another Columbia figure has presided over the very definition of that spirit: the figure of the eminent philosopher John Dewey, who himself wrote occasionally for *PR*, but whose influence has made itself felt even more effectively through his disciples, Ernest Nagel and Sidney Hook. As a matter of fact, it is the Naturalism of the Columbia school that has outlasted the collapse of its Marxism and that shores up the secularist tough-mindedness of *Partisan Review*. *PR* was, as one might expect, attracted for a while to the French version of Existentialism. Its atheism, its attempt to find a non-Marxian basis for the revolutionary attitude, its early defiance of Stalinism—all these seemed especially sympathetic to the *Partisan Review* mind. William Barrett, a former professor of philosophy, who finally filled the editorial vacuum left by the resignation of Dwight Macdonald, led the enthusiastic acclaim of Sartre, who threatened for a while to stand permanently in the niche left empty for *PR* by the fall of Karl Marx. But there was something too hasty and *willed* about this allegiance, which has in the last couple of years been struggling vainly to survive the personal encounter of *PR*'s editor with the representatives of Sartrean philosophy. No, Existentialism was for *PR* only an adventure, an affair; their true love has waited patiently for them at home: the spirit of John Dewey. In an unexpected way this alienated, Europe-oriented periodical comes to rest with the most "American" of philosophical systems: the same Deweyan pragmatism which, on another front, has nurtured the progressive educationist. It is a final irony.

What then shall I say at last of *Partisan* and the piece of myself which it represents? After scanning nearly twenty years' worth of it all at once, I feel bound to report that I have felt it to be frequently pontifical and boring, occasionally ritualistic in its repetition of a few sacred themes, generally depressing in the sense it gives of the narrowing down and drying up of political adventurousness and aesthetic experimentalism. I have found its symposia heavy-handed and its culture spotty. I have been appalled by its genuflecting to big names, amused by its occasional compensatory indulgences in the grayest sort of Germanic scholarship, exasperated by its over-adulation of Silone; and at one point I found myself muttering that if I came across the name of Kafka or Jean-Paul Sartre once more I would burn the whole damned pile of back issues. I have been provoked by the number of its contributors, who, having no apparent love for literature, deal with it like a subject they have drawn at random out of a hat; and I have turned away in disgust from certain young operators who by learning to say "milieu" and "situation" have imposed themselves on the editors.

Yet I cannot despise a magazine which has never been afraid of ideas or paralyzed by worries about "good taste"; which has served as a bridge between Europe and America, the free lance and the university; which above all has printed, often before anyone else, such writers of fiction as Saul Bellow, Mary McCarthy, Lionel Trilling, and Delmore Schwartz, such poets as Randall Jarrell, Robert Lowell, and John Berryman, such critics as Edmund Wilson and Lionel Trilling. It is a strange enough bird, the *Partisan Review,* a scraggier, shabbier, more raucous phoenix than we might have hoped for, and one not above crying out its own name at the top of its voice; but it is our only real contender for the title. Blasted into ashes

by its enemies, mourned prematurely by its friends, despaired of by its own editors—it yet somehow survives; and that is, after all, the point. (pp. 41-55)

Leslie Fiedler, "'Partisan Review': Phoenix or Dodo?" in his The Collected Essays of Leslie Fiedler, Vol. II, *Stein and Day, 1971, pp. 41-55.*

LITERARY PHILOSOPHY AND PRACTICE

ALEXANDER BLOOM

[*An American scholar and historian, Bloom is the author of* Prodigal Sons, *a full-length historical study of the New York Intellectuals in which he attributes the group's marked rightward political shift to the increased success of its members. In the following excerpt from that work, Bloom examines the basis for the New York Intellectuals' rejection of proletarian literature in favor of literary Modernism.*]

A decade after their revival of *Partisan Review*, Rahv and Phillips recalled their initial aim for the "new" journal. They hoped "to bring about a rapprochement between the radical tradition on the one hand and the tradition of modern literature on the other." They sought something new. Virtually all left-wing magazines had in the past done their utmost to prevent the rapprochement. The proletarian-literature movement tried to convert one tradition to the other, leading "to a false show of unity," the editors maintained. Instead,

> it seemed to us that a reconciliation could be effected only by so modulating the expression of both traditions as to convey a sense at once of the tension between them and of their relevance to each other within the common framework of civilization.

In place of the old "falsity," the *PR* critics aimed to establish a new harmony. The "modulation" they sought would maintain a radical base, without adversely affecting the literature or banishing important writers because of conservative political tendencies. The definition of radical activity came into question, as did the requirements for revolutionary literature. Rahv and Phillips found themselves "frankly skeptical of the old imperatives." To them, novels and poems, were "rarely weapons in the class struggle." Instead, a new, intermediary position seemed necessary, one between the apolitical independence of the twenties writers and the programmatic hard line which Rahv and Phillips saw in proletarian literature. Radicalism remained vitally important, as did good literature. Marxism might be a guide for action and for literature, but whether literature itself could be a guide for action was a different matter. This emerged as "one of the problems that *Partisan Review* [was] dedicated to explore."

The *PR* critics found that though literature did not create labor strikes, it still might change consciousness. "Our program is the program of Marxism," they declared in their first editorial. Along with this, however, they found it perfectly legitimate to reawaken their interest in modernist heroes of their younger days. In the next few years they explored both of these areas and tried to "modulate" between the analysis of the Marxists and the insights of the modernist writers. The attempt to bring modernism into the revolutionary fold raised the question of the relation between the avant-garde and society. Modernism had begun as an artistic revolt, as the efforts by various artists to break free from the constraints they felt had been imposed by traditional literary forms. In a recent review of the history and nature of modernism, the English critics Malcom Bradbury and James McFarlane described modernism as a "movement towards sophistication, technical display, internal self-scepticism," with parallel technical features appearing in various artistic movements, "anti-representationalism in painting, atonalism in music, *vers libre* in poetry, stream-of-consciousness narrative in the novel." In the late 1930s the *PR* critics attempted to bring that spirit of liberation into the world of revolutionary politics. This appeared particularly appropriate, given the second set of modernist attributes which Bradbury and McFarlane noted: "Experimentation does not simply suggest the presence of sophistication . . . it also suggests bleakness, darkness, alienation, disintegration. . . . The crisis is a crisis of culture; it often involves an unhappy view of history— so that the Modernist writer is not simply the artist set free, but the artist under specific, apparently historical strain." Amid radical politics, economic, dislocation, and highbrow literary tastes, a more politicized modernism might provide the best frame through which to analyze society and its art.

The concept of identifying and understanding the interrelated roles of radical politics and literary modernism proved attractive to other members of the emerging *PR* community. Linel Trilling, uncomfortable with proletarian literature, agreed with this less overtly political style. "We learn not to expect a political, certainly not an immediately political, effect from a work of art," Trilling wrote in *PR*, "and in removing from art the burden of messianic responsibility which it never discharged and cannot discharge, we may leave it free to do whatever it actually can do." Writers as well as literature would be freed. No longer conscience-bound to write for the masses, Trilling felt he could now write for the intellectual class.

The achievement of literature's fullest potential—the discovery of what literature "actually can do"—required something new, the critics believed. "A decade of fellow-travelling and revolutionary manipulation has drained American writing of so much of its energy," Rahv maintained. And the chief culprit of this deprivation was, obviously, the proletarian-literature movement. "Ostensibly a literature of the working class, it was really nothing more than a cultural publicity-agency for the Stalin mob in this country." Because so many influential critics remained with the "mob," the first task was its discrediting.

The *PR* critics castigated proletarian literature along two main lines. They held the proletarian writers and critics who unswervingly praised the movement responsible for the sorry state of American letters. Rahv mocked the presentations of Joseph Freeman and Malcom Cowley at the American Writers' Congress of 1937. Freeman had hailed the literary revival as equal to that of 1912 to 1916, while Cowley spoke of the richness of the radical literary movement. Whereas only a few years earlier Rahv had hailed the outpouring of radical literature, now he said this "renaissance" was "manufactured . . . an imaginary crop of masterpieces." "Actually, of course," he wrote, "literature in America has seldom been so stagnant as it is at present."

In addition to their fabrication of masterpieces, Phillips found the literary styles of American radicals contributing to the sad condition of American writing. Socialist realism, he claimed, was "really a throwback to the 'slice-of-life' formula of popular fiction—a method that could not possibly carry the weight of new sensibility and a new consciousness." This defect lowered both the quality of literary works and literary tastes. The

constant praise for "conventional, mediocre, and culturally backward authors" reduced general literary standards, Rahv argued. "Even intelligent readers appear unable to discriminate between genuine literary art and that which is patently commercial and popular in character."

The other major difficulty with proletarian literature derived from the treatment of the writers themselves and the role assigned to literature in the Stalinist movement. Writers were being asked to ally themselves not with the working class but with the Communist party disguised as the working class. Rahv saw this as a contract with "all the specific stipulations . . . left to be written in." The humbling of writers within the party structure revealed more than an unfortunate instance of the subjugation of art to politics. It also provided a microcosmic example of the tactics which marked Stalinist behavior everywhere, "a miniature version of the powers which in Russia had resulted in the replacement of the dictatorship of the proletariat by the dictatorship of the Communist Party."

Rahv and Phillips felt it insufficient to admit that they had merely been wrong about radical literature, that their high hopes had been dashed on the tensions between political goals and cultural standards. Instead, they chose to portray themselves as the defenders of the duped and abused artists, as men interested in quality literature *and* radical politics fending off both the philistine and the dictatorial notions of the Stalinists. Once this position was articulated, however, their own claims to the carrying of the radical literary mantle became much more secure. By dispensing with proletarian literature as it existed, they hoped to clear the decks for their own formulations about the proper approach for radical literature.

They had not, as we have seen, abandoned their beliefs in radicalism or their interest in Marx. They did seek, however, a redefinition of the role of Marxist criticism and the entire Marxist perspective in literature. "The truth of the matter," wrote Phillips, "is that Marx was not a literary critic, and no amount of textual research can convert him into one. Nor was Engels . . . so far as I know, they were silent on those questions of literature which occupy western criticism." What Phillips did find in Marx and Engels regarding literature, he believed directly contradicted the notions of the proletarian-literature camp: "At no time did Marx and Engels either state or imply that art is but a class weapon, nor did they sponsor a proletarian art to educate the workers in the theory and tactics of communism." Phillips discovered instead that both Marx and Engels saw literature as qualitatively different from other elements in the political process—in fact, wrote Phillips, quoting Marx, "certain periods of highest development of art stand in no direct connection with the general development of society, nor with the material basis and the skeleton structure of its organization." He cited examples from Engels which reaffirmed this position and freed the poet of any obligation to furnish the reader with ready-made historical solutions for the future. Phillips concluded that "many of the statements . . . read like direct polemics against the kind of 'Marxist criticism' advocated by Michael Gold and Granville Hicks."

Phillips's interpretation of a proper Marxist position of the relation between literature and politics allowed the *PR* critics to pursue their own critical arguments while believing their Marxism still valid. In view of this new Marxism, the restrictions which were implicit in the brand of criticism offered by Granville Hicks at the American Writers' Congress could be loosened. Marxism, Phillips found, was "not a closed system, nor a formula for declaring that all ideas inspired by other ways of thinking are false." That had been the problem with the proletarian critics. Marxism was a *"method,"* and it proved more fruitful "to speak of *Marxist criticisms* in the plural, or of *ventures in Marxist criticism."* For Marxism to maintain any validity in literary pursuits, it would surely have to operate in a less structured and more open atmosphere, one in which critics would assume a new role and escape the reins which had been placed on their potential in the movement for proletarian literature.

The function of critics showed another central failure of proletarian literature. Radical critics had been the "pawns" of the Stalinists, Rahv held. The potential for the revitalization of literature had been stifled, and this resulted in a general decline of American art and writing. Phillips offered a contrast: "The major impulses of European art can be traced in practically every instance to the existence of an active intelligentsia." Since the Renaissance, Phillips believed, the immediate sources of art had been this intelligentsia, which made up "a distinct occupational grouping in society."

The outstanding failure of American national culture was precisely "the inability of our native intelligentsia to achieve a detached and self-sufficient group existence." At no time was this more evident than during the Stalinist-dominated days of proletarian literature. Rather than denigrating critics and other intellectuals and placing them in servile roles, Phillips, Rahv, and other *PR* critics called the critical role essential. The American environment, however, militated against this development, Phillips found. American intellectuals evidenced an "ambivalent psyche, torn between the urge toward some degree of autonomy and an equally strong tendency to self-effacement." The Stalinists exploited this second tendency. In an effort to become part of a popular movement, critics had willingly sacrificed their rightful role. They wrote "publicity" for Stalinist hacks, rather than the criticism which would improve literary standards. Phillips called for a reversal of form, a reaction against the "natural inclination to merge with the popular mind." Only through the active leadership of intellectuals could the complexities of modern life be explained. Thus, intellectuals ought not to submerge themselves in political and cultural movements but to lead them from above. "Modern art with its highly complicated techniques, its plaintive egotism, its messianic desperation, could not," Phillips concluded, "have come into being except through the formation of the intelligentsia of a distinct group culture, thriving on its very anxiety of being an elite."

The editors perceived this elite as standing not outside of radicalism but in the vanguard of radical literature. The critics at *Partisan Review* continued to hold out the hope of a revolutionary impact for creativity, only now in a much less politicized sense. In the summer of 1939 *Partisan Review* published a call from the League for Cultural Freedom and Socialism, an anti-Popular Front coalition. Many of the signers were members of the intellectual community around *PR,* including all the editors. The position of the league was not only that Russian, German, and Italian culture was dominated by totalitarians but also that in America the cultural gains of recent decades were being sacrificed. "In the name of 'spurious' anti-fascist unity, numerous intellectuals are deserting their hard-won critical independence. . . . In the name of a 'democratic front' against tyranny abroad they put up with increasing tyranny at home." To counter these forces and this worrisome trend, the signers claimed "to unite to defend their independence."

> The defense of intellectual freedom requires, moreover, that we reject all theories and practices which

tend to make culture the creature of politics, even revolutionary politics. We demand COMPLETE FREEDOM FOR ART AND SCIENCE. NO DICTUM BY PARTY OR GOVERNMENT. Culture not only does not seek orders but by its very nature cannot tolerate them. Truly intellectual creation is incompatible with the spirit of conformity; and if art and science are to be true to the revolution, they must first be true to themselves.

The best that could be done—the radical thing to do—was thus "to infuse literary life with a revolutionary spirit," as Rahv and Phillips would later claim to have accomplished. In the process, they found that all the modernist and avant-garde writers, neglected or attacked during the days of proletarian literature, could be brought back into the fold. Thus, the requirements for revolutionary denotation could now be significantly broadened, and writers without a direct political philosophy or even with a conservative one could be viewed as revolutionary, in the new sense. Phillip Rahv discovered the revolutionary spirit in Henry Miller, whom he identified as "the artist as desperado" and the "biographer of the hobo-intellectual and the poet of those people at the bottom of society."

Even so conservative a figure as Dostoevsky took on revolutionary characteristics. *The Possessed* provided contemporary society with a "pre-Marxist" picture of revolution, Rahv argued, Stalinism a "post-Marxist" view. In the character Verkhovensky and his philosophy of Nechayevism could be seen an early equivalent of Stalinism. "Verkhovensky's attempt to overthrow the Czar without the active intervention of the masses is equivalent to Stalin's attempt to build socialism in Russia in isolation from the fate of the international working-class." Despite the enormous questions raised by this interpretation, Rahv continued to proclaim Dostoevsky's revolutionary importance and insight. Admitting that he "labored to give his genius a religious sanctification" and "that his philosophical and political views . . . ran counter to progressive thought," Rahv nonetheless found that Dostoevsky

> discovered inversions and dissociations in human feeling and consciousness which to this day literature but imperfectly assimilated. Reactionary in its abstract content, in its aspect as a system of ideas, his art is radical in sensibility and subversive in performance.

Artistic sensibility could be radical and subversive, Rahv claimed without further definition, and all the heroes of the modernist movement—Joyce, Eliot, Pound, Kafka—could be put into this revolutionary corps. Thus, the favorites of the critics' youths, the writers whom the twenties exiles had favored and the thirties radicals dismissed, could be called men of literature and of radical insight. In fact, it was discovered that they possessed previously unnoticed radical sensibilities.

Having witnessed the failures of radical literature within the social-realist movement, the *PR* critics now focused on the avant-garde as the truly revolutionary force. Dwight Macdonald, in his review of Soviet cinema, held that its decline was a result of the replacement of avant-garde artists with Stalinist bureaucrats. This paralleled the replacement of the Old Bolsheviks; "whole advanced political theories clashed with a backward society." Similarly, Soviets with progressive notions in art found themselves "opposed by conventional, even reactionary artists."

Macdonald's articles on Soviet cinema prompted the response of an artistically minded clerk in the New York customshouse.

Clement Greenberg had held a variety of jobs since his graduation from Syracuse in 1930, none using his artistic training or interests. Born in the Bronx, of an immigrant family, he "spoke Yiddish as soon as [he] did English." His father, a small shopkeeper and then a manufacturer of metal goods, provided the family with a comfortable, if not prosperous, existence. Graduating from college as the Depression struck, Greenberg spent the next two and a half years at home, where he independently studied German, Italian, French, and Latin. Married and divorced in the mid-thirties, he finally secured regular employment with the Civil Service Commission in 1936. In 1937 he moved to a position in the Appraiser's Division of the Customs Service. Like Melville and Hawthorne before him, he used his spare time to write, including a letter to *Partisan Review*. Macdonald thought the letter worthy of a fuller presentation and arranged to meet Greenberg for lunch. The letter became Greenberg's first contribution to *PR*, "Avant-Garde and Kitsch," published in 1939. The luncheon meeting and the expansion of the letter into an article prompted Macdonald to joke that he had "invented Clement Greenberg."

"Avant-Garde and Kitsch" was significant not just because it launched the career of one of America's important art critics. Greenberg's argument added to Rahv's notion about the radical impact of modern culture. Going beyond Rahv's identification of writers with radical "sensibilities," Greenberg offered a schematic guide for an understanding of which art forms actually aided radicalism and which impeded it. "The true and most important function of the avant-garde was not to 'experiment,'" as might traditionally be thought, "but to find a path along which it would be possible to keep culture *moving* in the midst of ideological confusion and violence." While the avant-garde propelled society, "kitsch"—middlebrow culture, movies, comic books, Tin Pan Alley, Coca-Cola, Luce publications, and rayon stockings—helped perpetuate the capitalist system of class interests. Furthermore, kitsch could be dominated by dictators, whereas the avant-garde could not. Proletarian literature—middle-brow and dominated by a variety of dictators—fell into the category of kitsch, in Greenberg's view. True avant-garde art and literature, by contrast, was "too innocent" and "too difficult to inject [with] effective propaganda." Kitsch was "more pliable to this end."

Avant-garde culture did possess one essential attribute which kitsch did not, one which became very important for radicals. Kitsch proved incompatible with true socialism. Only when socialism had been instituted could a true, meaningful global culture be achieved, Greenberg argued, and only the avant-garde could bring about this development. Offering a bit of circuitous logic, Greenberg made two assumptions—only the avant-garde moved society along and only when society had moved to socialism would culture fully flourish—and then used each to justify the other. Like Rahv's equation of Verkhovensky and Stalin, it required the acceptance of the authors' propositions as truths.

These various propositions and assumptions combined to form a literary and artistic position, one which defined the roles of literature and of critics. Discovering the radical sensibilities of the modernist writers, it restored them to places of importance. Their belief that the avant-garde was the force which propelled culture and society toward socialism justified the radical writers' abandonment of proletarian literature and their renewed focus on modern literature. An interpretation of Marxist criticism, counter to the *PR* critics' notions of what Stalinists believed, similarly pointed to the radical truth of revolutionary modernism. Finally, artistic and critical independence emerged as a cardinal principle. Only when a writer was able to wander off in his own direction—to follow his own muse—could his contribution achieve full meaning for society at large. Thus, the process by which a writer came to speak for and to society was reversed. Misguided proletarian novelists had consciously set out to speak to a preconceived mass audience. The modern writer had to feel his way toward his rightful audience. Lionel Trilling summarized this position in the introduction to a collection from the first decade of *Partisan Review*:

> The writer who defines his audience by its limitations is indulging in the unforgivable arrogance. The writer must define his audience by its abilities, by its perfections as far as he is gifted to conceive them. He does well, if he cannot see his right audience, within immediate reach of his voice, to direct his words to his spiritual ancestors or posterity, or even, if need be, to his coterie. The writer serves his daemon and his subject. And the democracy that does not know that the daemon and the subject must be served is not, in any ideal sense of the word, a democracy at all.

In Trilling's analysis we can see the changed literary position which the *Partisan* critics advanced. At the same time that Trilling saw the potential of a large audience for writers, he also justified the necessity of restricting an audience. Rather than seeking a mass audience by striving for the lowest denominator, the writer should aspire to the audience's highest qualities, its "perfections." If this was not immediately apparent, then a limitation of audience rather than literary quality should follow. "Spiritual ancestors," such as the modernist writers, or a "coterie," such as the *Partisan* crowd, should

Alfred Kazin. © Nancy Crampton.

become the focus. Ultimately, the larger audience and democracy, itself, would be best served. At the same time, all proscriptions which had been placed on the artist during the days of proletarian literature were removed; yet, the potential benefits remained.

In revolutionary modernism the New York Intellectuals argued a theory of literature and of culture which satisfied their intellectual demands while allowing them to believe they had not sacrificed their radicalism. They justified the notion of a coterie, even if only as a temporary grouping awaiting a true mass audience. Finally, revolutionary modernism would produce better literary achievements as well as a better balance between intellectual endeavors and radical politics. "In view of what has happened," Philip Rahv concluded, "is it not clear that the older tradition [of artistic independence] was a thousand times more 'progressive'—if that is to be our criterion—was infinitely more disinterested, infinitely more sensitive to the actual conditions of human existence, than the shallow political writing of our latter days?" Proletarian literature was inferior *and* significantly less radical. Turning the tables on his old allies, Rahv accused them of the very shortcomings they had once attributed to the modernists. "Whether we choose Soviet novels by orthodox authors," he observed,

> or recent "militant" works by the Frenchmen Aragon and Malraux; or the revolutionary prose and verse of American writers like . . . Michael Gold, Clifford Odets, John Howard Lawson, [and] Albert Maltz . . . in none of them shall we find an imagination or sensibility which is not of a piece with some variety . . . of the bourgeois creative mode.

Thus, in revolutionary modernism, in the belief that through avant-garde culture and literary insight subversive activities could accompany literature of high standards, the *PR* writers found a position which was more congenial to their own notions of literary radicalism than was proletarian literature. The hesitations and ambivalence which had prompted their abandonment of proletarian literature were gone and the basic priorities of art and politics set straight. Furthermore, they could apply the old radical criticism of progressive and social-realist writers—that they were acting within a bourgeois frame—to their former radical associates.

Revolutionary modernism offered the *Partisan* writers and others a version of literary criticism which criticized proletarian writing without abandoning the radical ground. In addition, the critics rescued and promoted the names of leading modernist writers and established a base from which to proclaim their position. Most important, this newly articulated philosophy promoted the role of the intellectual as well as that of the artist. Perhaps as much as anything else, this was the key element which drew the young New York Intellectuals to the *Partisan* position. The literary critics of the community's second generation would begin from the position carved out by the elders in the late 1930s. The creation of new radical criticism had been the ostensible reason for a "new" *PR*. Revolutionary modernism and the promotion of the avant-garde became the first perceptible position with which the reborn magazine became identified. From the outset, it characterized the philosophy of the critics who wrote for the journal and became a pillar of New York Intellectual thinking. (pp. 84-93)

> *Alexander Bloom, "The 'Partisan' Mind: Cultural Turns," in his* Prodigal Sons: The New York Intellectuals & Their World, *Oxford University Press, 1986, pp. 84-97.*

GRANT WEBSTER

[*Webster is an American critic and the author of* The Republic of Letters *(1979), a study of American literary criticism since the Second World War. In the following excerpt from that work, he analyzes the New York Intellectuals' critical philosophy in terms of Renato Poggioli's theory of the avant-garde.*]

The only way one can begin to talk sensibly about literary criticism in New York City is to make one's way through *Making It* and other accounts by interested parties to a more basic intellectual reality. The point is not to criticize Norman Podhoretz's book, which has suffered enough, but to point to its essential inaccuracy as literary history, quite apart from its merits as confession or exposé.

The first problem is one of focus, which is closely related to Podhoretz's attempt to categorize the New York Intellectuals as a Jewish family [see excerpt above]. A minor error is his assumption that there are three "generations" of intellectuals, which leads Podhoretz into a mania of genealogical categorization reminiscent of Vance Packard's *The Status Seekers* or *Esquire*'s July 1963 charts of the "red-hot center" of literary life. All the criticisms Harold Rosenberg made in 1958 of Podhoretz's attempt to distinguish his mature, family-oriented generation from the older, alienated, ex-Red Marxists still apply. Rosenberg says: "When I first encountered this 'Marxist' generation in the mid 'thirties it already had its present character; it was, in its own terms, 'responsible' and 'mature' and opposed to personal radicalism and Bohemian life. . . . Today's younger generation of intellectuals consists of the late arrivals to the generation that made its appearance as American 'Marxists' and which has lived its entire life with Marxism." Socially, as ex-Marxists, and as defenders of a single tradition of modern literature, the group which Podhoretz describes has a single character, is a single entity, whatever one may think it is.

The more important misconception is Podhoretz's attempt to categorize the New York Intellectuals as a Jewish family. Other writers echo Podhoretz's claim. In a symposium on "New York and the National Culture," Irving Howe says: "These things are hard to measure objectively. Still, do we not all feel in our bones that for good and/or bad something of the moral fervor, the polemical fury, the passion for idea and ideology that prevailed among the New York writers had its roots in secular and no doubt pre-secular Jewish life?" In his account "The New York Intellectuals" [see excerpt below], Howe says: "I am working on the premise that in background and style there was something decidedly Jewish about the intellectuals who began to cohere as a group around the *Partisan Review* in the late 30's—and one of the things that was 'decidedly Jewish' was that most were of Jewish birth!"

One very important difficulty that neither of these writers mentions is that Jews differ culturally; this fact is important here because (as E. Digby Baltzell shows in *The Protestant Establishment*) the lives, values, and careers of German, Russian, and other Jews vary enormously, as does American reaction to them. Podhoretz himself brings up a second difficulty of his hypothesis:

> Of course the metaphor of a Jewish family runs into certain difficulties of its own, for several core members (Dwight Macdonald, Mary McCarthy, F. W. Dupee, William Barrett, Elizabeth Hardwick, John Thompson, James Baldwin, and the late Richard Chase) and a few kissing cousins (Robert Lowell, Ralph Ellison, John Berryman, Kempton himself,

Michael Harrington, the late James Agee, and the late William Troy) were not Jewish at all. Nevertheless, the term Jewish can be allowed to stand by clear majority rule and by various peculiarities of temper I shall try to describe.

Considered genetically, then, the New York Intellectuals are only partly or questionably Jewish, but considered formally, there is nothing identifiably "Jewish" about their work at all, no "peculiarity of temper" which can be related to their existence as Jews, as opposed to their existence as New Yorkers, or educated men, or journalists, or political beings.

Podhoretz nowhere isolates what he considers to be the formal qualities of Jewish writing, but he does mention that because of "the feeling that a book is something special, belonging to a different class of phenomena from articles or lectures," the family's "characteristic form has been the short piece": "Like the Talmudic scholars who were surely numbered among their forefathers, they not only regard books as holy objects but, haunted by what was perhaps the most ferociously tyrannical tradition of scholarship the world has ever seen, they seem to believe that one must have mastered everything before one is entitled to the temerity of saying anything on paper." It is unclear here whether Podhoretz is distinguishing between Talmudic books and intellectual articles, in which case the Intellectuals would not be "Jewish" in their essays; or whether, as seems more likely, he is paying a false historical compliment to the Intellectuals' standard of scholarship. In either case, as its history from Addison to Eliot demonstrates, the critical essay is not proved to be a "Jewish" form, nor is New Testament or Formalist explication "Jewish."

Alfred Kazin tries to isolate as the formal quality of Jewish writing its concern with a particular theme: "Just as it was Southern writers, with their knowledge of defeat and their instinctive irony, who in the 40's spoke to the chastened American mind, so it is Jewish writers who now [1966] represent to many Americans the unreality of their prosperity and the anxiety of their condition." However it may apply to fiction, "Jewishness" is irrelevant to criticism, irrelevant to the "key book on Matthew Arnold and to the definitive biographies of Henry Adams, Henry James, James Joyce" which Kazin rightly cites as monuments of scholarship by Jews.

Another claim for a parallel between Jewishness and the Intellectuals' criticism is made by Isaac Rosenfeld in 1944: "But the position of Jewish writers—artists and intellectuals in general—is not entirely an unfortunate one. For the most part the young Jewish writers of today are the children of immigrants, and as such—not completely integrated in society and yet not wholly foreign to it—they enjoy a critical advantage over the life that surrounds them. They are bound to observe much that is hidden to the more accustomed native eyes. The insight available to most Jewish writers is a natural result of their position in American life and culture. Jews are marginal men." But since non-Jews also are immigrants here, and since the exclusion of Jews from parts of Anglo-Saxon society is forced on them, while the alienation of the intellectual from all bourgeois society is voluntary, marginality is not uniquely Jewish, and again the parallel seems forced.

It is more likely that the actual state of affairs for these critics is somewhat like that described by Lionel Trilling, who says that although "it is never possible for a Jew of my generation to 'escape' his Jewish origin," nevertheless "I cannot discover anything in my professional intellectual life which I can specifically trace back to my Jewish birth and rearing. I do not

think of myself as a 'Jewish writer.' I do not have it in mind to serve by my writing any Jewish purpose. I should resent it if a critic of my work were to discover in it either faults or virtues which he called Jewish." For Podhoretz and Howe, then, the "Jewish" Intellectual is a product of definition; all the people one wishes to call "Intellectuals" are Jewish or "Jewish by proxy," while the people one does not wish to call Intellectuals are excluded whether or not they are Jewish. Furthermore (as Howe points out) the model of all these "Jewish" Intellectuals is Edmund Wilson, whose voice (as Podhoretz points out) "has always been the voice of the old Anglo-Saxon America." One must conclude that the attempt to categorize the accomplishment of the New York Intellectuals as "Jewish" is mistaken.

What we do have in the Intellectuals, as one (and only one) part of New York literary culture, is a group of men and women whose intellectual life is defined in terms of a dialectic or tension between social reality and avant-garde tastes. On the one hand they acknowledge the reality of society, defined in quasi-Marxian terms as the struggle of classes, the importance of economic motives, the existence of institutions, and (as Trilling defined the reality of Dreiser): "material reality, hard, resistant, unformed, impenetrable, and unpleasant." In this half of their concern, the Intellectuals are essentially bourgeois and realistic in a way which is fully supportive of their own economic interests and the interests of the capitalist state. The literary half of their intellectual life, however, is defined by the idea of the avant-garde, which as Renato Poggioli has shown in his *The Theory of the Avant-Garde*, is marked by its antagonism toward bourgeois culture, its compulsive desire to make cultural fashion, and its defense of the avant-garde, "modernist" tradition in literature and art. Hence, the Intellectuals are essentially cultural middlemen, and the group's charter involves a dialectic or tension between these two forces as they have developed during the last forty years.... (pp. 209-12)

This charter is understandable only "genetically," in terms of a historical trauma which marked the Intellectuals for life. In brief, these Intellectuals come of age in Marxist circles in the New York of the thirties and define themselves intellectually in relation to the futuristic and radical politics of that time. As Irving Howe puts it, "The Movement was my home and passion, the Movement as it ranged through the various left-wing anti-Communist groups." However, this political ardor was soon destroyed by the inescapably totalitarian events in Russia, chiefly the Moscow trials from 1936 to 1938, when Stalin killed hundreds of thousands of his countrymen, and by the Nazi-Soviet pact of 1939, which wedded Marxism with the Fascist persecutor of the Jews. The result was the death of Marxism in Intellectual circles in America for thirty years. The important result of this shift for literary criticism is the displacement of what was originally a political radicalism onto literature, which can be seen clearly in the change that takes place in the *Partisan Review* from 1936 to 1937. All the revolutionary expectations of the Intellectuals' early years are sublimated into a defense of "modernist" literature, and their geographical Utopia becomes Bohemia, not Russia. one may characterize the Intellectual in this early period in terms of Edmund Wilson's books, as a person en route from the *Finland Station* to *Axel's Castle*. For literary purposes, then, the Intellectuals' movement into the literary avant-garde in about 1937, rather than their earlier flirtation with Marxism, marks their significant alienation from bourgeois America, and the opposition of bourgeois liberalism to new alienated and aristocratic avant-garde values creates a tension which marks the Intellectuals' thinking during the period of their greatest achievement and influence, from 1939 to 1952. In this period they establish the literary authority of their group with the publication of Rahv's *Image and Idea* (1949), Chase's *Herman Melville* (1949), *Quest for Myth* (1949), and *Emily Dickinson* (1951), Trilling's *The Liberal Imagination* (1950), Howe's *Sherwood Anderson* (1951), and Dupee's *Henry James* (1951).

In their prime, the Intellectuals are defined by their allegiance to *both* bourgeois society *and* the avant-garde. Their ideal charter is the tension Trilling found in F. Scott Fitzgerald: "As much as to anything else in Fitzgerald, we respond to the delicate tension he maintained between his idea of personal free will and his idea of circumstance: we respond to that moral and intellectual energy. 'The test of a first rate intelligence,' he said, 'is the ability to hold two opposed ideas in the mind, at the same time, and still retain the ability to function'." As Trilling said even more clearly of himself: "I think that literature in its relation to life is polemical." This idea of dialectic or tension between society and the imagination serves the Intellectuals as both the ideal form of the mind and their conception of the "modernist" tradition in literature. As Irving Howe says, the modern writer "presents dilemmas; he cannot and soon does not wish to resolve them; he offers his *struggle* with them as the substance of his testimony; and whatever unity his work possesses, often not very much, comes from the emotional rhythm, the thrust toward completion, of that struggle." More directly important for our purposes, the tension between society and the mind serves the Intellectuals as the standard of value of their literary criticism. As Alfred Kazin says: "Conflicts remain at the heart of every achieved work of literature. They are resolved without being diminished, and in such a way that we gratefully re-experience the conflict."

The Intellectuals whose work is marked by this dialectic between social reality and literary imagination include Edmund Wilson, Lionel Trilling, Diana Trilling, Harold Rosenberg, Dwight Macdonald, F. W. Dupee, Philip Rahv, Clement Greenberg, Elizabeth Hardwick, Mary McCarthy, William Phillips, Delmore Schwartz, Richard Chase, Alfred Kazin, the early Leslie Fiedler, Robert Warshow, Isaac Rosenfeld, Irving Howe, Steven Marcus, and Norman Podhoretz. One artistic value they defend is that of *Axel's Castle,* that is, that avant-garde modernism which becomes fashionable in the twenties and is associated with Picasso, Nietzsche, Stravinsky, Freud, Valery, Eliot, Dostoevsky, Kafka, Mann, Stendahl, Proust, Lawrence, Henry James, James Joyce, Yeats, Gide, and Rilke. In their realistic and bourgeois selves they join the American intelligentsia in discussing "proletarian realism" in the thirties, and after World War II they show some interest in political novelists like Silone, Malraux, and Moravia; they also support Jewish writers of the forties and fifties, particularly Saul Bellow, Bernard Malamud, and Philip Roth. Throughout, their main effort is to reinterpret American literature and culture in terms of their dialectic. They have centered their publishing in the *New York Times Book Review*, in *Commentary, The New Republic, The Nation,* and other leftist, anti-Communist, partly political magazines, and most importantly, in the *Partisan Review*. (pp. 212-16)

If the prototypical act of the Intellectual is his flight from his bourgeois home to enlist in the avant-garde, then a systematic study of the nature of the avant-garde ought to illuminate the careers and literary values of the New York Intellectuals. Such a study, Renato Poggioli's *The Theory of the Avant-Garde,* maintains that the "avant-garde" is a modern phenomenon which began in France in about 1870, when "art began to contemplate itself from a historical viewpoint." Avant-garde movements are characterized by a compulsive *activism, antagonism* to bourgeois culture and solidarity within the avant-garde sect, *nihilism,* and *agonism,* a tension and a struggle that will allow art to triumph in the future. According to Poggioli, the avant-garde is an outgrowth of Romanticism, sometimes marked by decadence, and is stylistically pluralistic, subject to changes in fashion, eventual decay, and replacement by a new avant-garde.

Though the Intellectuals have seen themselves as part of the avant-garde for years, and discourse at length on the subject, their discussion is unsatisfactory because they do not have as clear and systematic an understanding of the concept as Poggioli provides, and because they are not self-aware enough to apply the concept to their own careers, particularly in the matter of their own obsolescence as avant-gardists. The four ways in which the concept of the avant-garde illuminates the Intellectuals' careers are: (1) their antagonism toward the general culture, their consequent alienation, and the solidarity this builds within their groups; (2) the avant-garde nature of the literary tradition they defend; (3) the fashionable nature of their cultural concerns; and (4) their move from an avant-garde Bohemia to the intelligentsia and their consequent retirement as avant-gardists.

When the Intellectuals' history begins in 1937 with the founding of the "new" *Partisan Review,* New York Intellectuals put themselves in the classic avant-garde position of *antagonism* toward the bourgeois culture on literary grounds. Lionel Trilling describes the antibourgeois character of their literary tradition: "The author of *The Magic Mountain* once said that all his work could be understood as an effort to free himself from the middle class, and this, of course, will serve to describe the chief intention of all modern literature." And in 1972 Norman Podhoretz echoes the same view, saying: "My belief is that Intellectuals have a spiritual role to play not based on any systematic ideological preconception. Their role is to be critical of the culture. . . . I'm saying something similar to Trilling in *The Liberal Imagination.* I consider it much the job of the intellectual periodical to play the adversary role of that community. That is what I try to do." The important thing about the New York writers' antagonism toward the bourgeoisie is that it is absolutely typical of avant-garde movements everywhere. What is to them hard-thought-out and individual decision-making appears to others to be simply a set of conventional responses. This typicality is seen clearly in the specific points on which they choose to oppose the general bourgeois culture: their opposition to the professoriate and to the mass media.

The antiacademic bias of the Intellectuals sometimes seems a mere rhetorical warming-up, a flourish of swords, but the insult to the sterile professor and to hidebound scholarship remains a favorite trope. In the forties and fifties the *Partisan Review* runs a feature called "Report from the Academy," in which the insensitivity of professors and the deadening effect of hard study are regularly pointed out. For example, Professor Richard Chase of Columbia begins a discussion of A. O. Lovejoy and the "history of ideals" by saying that "the chief purpose of the departments of literature in American graduate schools is to teach prospective teachers how to avoid discussing literature." Similarly, Professor Newton Arvin of Smith discusses professors as part of a capitalist "managerial revolution," describing them as follows: "None of the definitive characters [*sic*—characteristics?] are missing: the veneration of quantity, the lust of the tangible, the mental ingenuousness, the passion for organizational machinery, the instinct for the immediate and the solidly visible, and (to put it negatively) the contempt for ideas, the hatred of literature and the arts, the fear of criticism, and (singular as it sounds) the distrust of learning itself. Philistinism, obscurantism, anti-intellectualism—these are as truly the stamps of the successful academician as of the successful entrepreneur." One sees here an avant-garde attack on the whole academic enterprise which is clearly distinguishable from proposals for the reform of graduate study like the chapter in Wellek and Warren's *Theory of Literature* (1949 edition only) entitled "The Study of Literature in the Graduate School." (pp. 225-27)

The second typically antagonistic position the Intellectuals take is opposition to "mass culture," which begins in about 1940, perhaps as a reaction to their previous espousal of proletarian literature. The Intellectuals' reaction against mass culture should be carefully distinguished from such sympathetic examinations of popular culture as George Orwell's "Boys' Weeklies" (1939), Robert Warshow's movie reviews for the *Partisan Review,* and many later studies. The purpose of the Intellectuals' opposition is to put down mass culture as inferior to the elite modernist art with which they identify; theirs is a polemical position, not an analytical one. Their view is explained clearly by Clement Greenberg in "Avant-Garde and Kitsch," where he shows how the birth of the avant-garde coincides with the rise of social revolutionary thought and democratic and industrial society, how the avant-gardists use their concept of the bourgeois to define what they are not, and how they "emigrate from the markets of capitalism" to find an absolute (nonobjective) art and a pure poetry, the usual subjects of which are the disciplines and processes of art itself. The tradition the Intellectuals defend is thus in large part negatively defined as "nonkitsch," and the danger to it is not that it is unknown, but that it will become more popular and hence, ipso facto, vulgarized. Dwight Macdonald, the Intellectual who has written most about mass culture, posits that a "Midcult" does this and he notes that "the special threat of Midcult is that it exploits the discoveries of the avant-garde." Ironically, some of Macdonald's best writing is on the movies. Before he became an Intellectual he wrote a series on Hollywood directors for *Symposium* (March-June 1933), and since rejoining the midculture he has reviewed movies for *Esquire;* his movie criticism is collected in *Dwight Macdonald on Movies* (1969). Robert Warshow avoided this stereotyped opposition to the movies in his *The Immediate Experience* (1964), but in general the Intellectuals' attitude is one of haughty disdain. As Philip Rahv says in 1952, "But if under present conditions we cannot stop the ruthless expansion of mass-culture, the least we can do is keep apart and refuse its favors." The Intellectuals' consistent snobbishness about mass culture is particularly ironic because it is largely the importance of New York City as a center of mass culture, of the publishing, television, and magazine worlds, and as home of the *New York Times,* which gives importance to their views as *New York* Intellectuals, as opposed to San Francisco or Cambridge or Ann Arbor Intellectuals.

This sense of personal antagonism toward the majority culture is expressed in the lives of the Intellectuals as a state of *alienation,* "the feeling of uselessness and isolation of a person who realizes that he is now totally estranged from a society which has lost its sense of the human condition and its own historical mission." Lionel Trilling isolates as a cause of this

feeling the Intellectuals' divorce from family life. Speaking of his own past, he says: "It is the fact that the intellectuals of the Twenties and Thirties were likely to assume that there was an irreconcilable contradiction between babies and the good life. . . . Intellectual men thought of [children] as 'biological traps,' being quite certain that they must lead to compromise with, or capitulation to, the forces of convention." And elsewhere, in re Orwell, he says: "The prototypical act of the modern intellectual is his abstracting himself from the life of the family." This psychological alienation is given the support of a doctrinaire dogma in the thirties by the Intellectuals' allegiance to Marxism, which cuts them off from this capitalist society while promising them fulfillment in the future, and by their self-identification as Jews, which combines the outcast and the Chosen People in a similar fashion. Kazin's memory of the times seems to combine Marxism and Jewishness:

> It seemed to me that we were specially interesting because we were among the dispossessed of history; I saw us as the downtrodden, the lonely, the needy, in a way that fitted my faith in a total redemption. There are times in history when a group feels that it is at the center of events. Poor as we were, anxious, lonely, it seemed to me obvious that everywhere, even in Hitler Germany, to be outside of society and to be Jewish was to be at the heart of things. History was preparing, in its Jewish victims and through them, some tremendous deliverance and revelation.

As Marxists of the thirties turn into well-paid liberals of the fifties, however, the Intellectuals' alienation becomes not so much a matter of being cast out of society as the fantasy of a loss of identity through the operation of a totalitarian society like that portrayed by Kafka, or by Orwell in *1984.* In "The Orgamerican Phantasy," Harold Rosenberg traces in such sociological fictions of the fifties as Reisman's *The Lonely Crowd,* Whyte's *The Organizational Man,* or Spectorsky's *The Exurbanites* the theme of "the post-radical critic [who] suffers also a nostalgia for himself as an independent individual. Rosenberg dismisses the reality of this alienation as being related not to totalitarian tendencies in the society but to the Intellectuals' move to the intelligentsia: "The fear-augury that the Orgman will become everyone in a quiet, unopposable totalitarianism is not a conclusion based on social analysis but a projection of the fate they [the Intellectuals] have chosen for themselves." The feeling of alienation is described by Podhoretz as "simply the feeling that this was not *my* country. . . . I was a citizen, and a highly interested one, of a small community in New York which lived by its own laws and had as little commerce as it could manage with a hostile surrounding environment. As an intellectual I was as ghettoized as my ancestors in Eastern Europe had been as Jews." Perhaps the best-known summary of the alienation of the Intellectuals in the fifties is Irving Howe's "This Age of Conformity," which combines the stock themes of the avant-garde: attacks on the traditionalism of professors, the debasing effect of mass culture, the pressure to conform exerted by institutions, and regret for the lost alienation and independence of the avant-garde.

The concomitant of antagonism and alienation, the permanent condition of the avant-garde, is "solidarity *within* a society in the restricted sense of that word—that is to say, solidarity within the community of rebels and libertarians." This group identity is expressed by Intellectuals in their constant use of "we" to refer to their own opinions, which culminates in Trilling's essay "Our Hawthorne." The origin of the Intellectuals' unique use of "we" may lie in their radical past; Malcolm Cowley reminisces of writers in the thirties that "all the new proletarian writers seemed to gather strength by thinking in terms of 'we,' not 'I', and by merging themselves first with other workers in the arts—provided they were true proletarians under thirty—then with an audience of workers drawn from all the trades and professions; then finally with the entire working class.'' Harold Rosenberg's remarks on Robert Warshow support and expand this interpretation: ''Warshow's entire approach is an 'us' approach, that is to say, a mass-culture approach—though his 'us' is not the masses but the small mass of the intellectuals.'' Rosenberg's charge is essentially that the Intellectuals are expressing the values of their group, their common experience, and that they are ''reluctant to face the mass-culture consequences of their historical self-definition.''

The tendency to inflate one's private and fallible opinions into general truths which this ''we'' leads to is expressed with pride by Leslie Fiedler in the preface to his *End to Innocence:* ''I have, as a matter of fact, been pleased to discover how often I have managed to tell what still seems to me the truth about my world and myself as a liberal, intellectual, writer, American, and Jew. I do not mind, as some people apparently do, thinking of myself in such categorical terms; being representative of a class, a generation, a certain temper seems not at all a threat to my individuality. . . . I like to think of myself as registering through my particular sensibility the plight of a whole group.'' The question is not, as Fiedler suggests, the threat to his individuality, but the justness of his claim to speak for multitudes when in fact he may be speaking for only two or three cronies. Irving Howe reveals the compulsive nature of this habit in a footnote to his ''The New York Intellectuals'': ''Is it 'they' or 'we'? To speak of the New York Intellectuals as 'they' might seem coy or disloyal; to speak of 'we' self-assertive or cozy. Well, let it be 'they,' with the proviso that I do not thereby wish, even if I could, to exclude myself from judgment.'' But twenty-three pages later he slips back into the spurious group-identity of ''our intellectual life'' and says: ''In place of the avant-garde we [sic] now had the *style of fashion.*'' The latest reincarnation of this durable pronoun is found in Howe's account of *his* immigrant Jewish ancestors in New York City, *The World of Our Fathers.* The compulsion to speak for a group rather than as a private individual only reinforces that Lionel Trilling says in 1942: ''The intellectuals, the 'freest' of men, consciously the most liberated from class, is actually the most class-marked and class-bound of all men.'' It seems to be literally impossible for individual Intellectuals to think of themselves as anything but extensions of a group, or to avoid inflating what are essentially personal opinions, or the opinions of a gaggle of twenty or thirty friends, into the representative statements of an age, generation, or some other impressive but fictitious entity. As a group, then, the Intellectuals are avant-gardist, and their preoccupation with mass culture, their antiacademic stance, and their sense of the alienation of their critical community can be understood as the consequences of their original choice of the idea of the avant-garde as the basic concept of their critical charter.

The most influential aspect of the Intellectuals' embrace of the avant-garde is the metamorphosis of the idea of Marxist revolution which they had held in the thirties into the idea of literary revolution carried on by modernist writers. This shift is made easy because ''avant-garde'' itself has both political and cultural connotations. It is a political term in that it comes from a military context (the lead troops are the avant-garde) which is extended to mean being in the lead of a revolutionary movement, on the barricades, in the vanguard of history. The term is thus easily applied to the new artist who also sees

himself as creating a new cultural Utopia. Ironically, in 1940 the Intellectuals were really part of the critical *derrière-garde,* defending what artists had created and critics like Edmund Wilson and R. P. Blackmur had criticized in the twenties. Further irony is provided by the fact that the avant-garde artists the Intellectuals defend—Yeats and Eliot, Pound and Joyce, Lawrence and Gide—are political conservatives, as Lionel Trilling notes. The originality of their charter, then, lies in the combination of an avant-gardism drawn from leftist revolutionary political expectations but kept exclusively in the area of literary imagination, and liberal ideas also drawn from leftist ideology but transformed in accordance with the bourgeois aspirations of the charter's adherents. Maintaining such a charter is tricky since it involves suppression of the fact that as a liberal, one is also a bourgeois, for by definition an avant-gardist opposes the bourgeois. These are the two ideas the Intellectuals manage to hold in tension, and they function splendidly for a time to develop a normal criticism and a new critical tradition.

Having set themselves apart as a literary class alienated from the vulgar public and from learned professors, much as doctrinaire New Critics isolate themselves with the poem by using the ''intentional'' and ''affective'' fallacies, the Intellectuals simultaneously develop their own tradition, which becomes a new kind of aesthetic orthodoxy in which one must believe in order to be an Intellectual. The primary characteristic of this orthodoxy distinguishes it sharply from Formalism: it is about the novel, not poetry. As Norman Podhoretz says: ''I do not go to literature for the salvation of my soul, but only to enlarge or refine my understanding, and I do not expect it to redeem the age, but only to help the age become less chaotic and confused. The novel—let me restrict myself to that, since it is the literary form with which I have been most closely connected . . . plays a unique, and uniquely valuable, part in the life of our age.'' This strategy of reducing literature to the novelistic genre is typical; Phillips, Sontag, Podhoretz, Rahv, Kazin (except for his Blake essay), Dupee, Rosenfeld, and Macdonald, among others, have not written (or at least have not collected) a word about the poets of this or any other time, with the exception of a couple of reviews praising Robert Lowell and attacking the ''beats.'' The objection is that they reach conclusions about literature which are presented as universal, but are really generic.

Philip Rahv, echoing in part Irving Howe's ''This Age of Conformity,'' carries this tendency into literary theory in ''Criticism and the Criticism of Fiction,'' where he belittles Formalist critics of novels for being too much influenced by the techniques drawn from the criticism of poetry. The three particular points Rahv refers to are (1) ''the current obsession with the search for symbols, allegories, and mythic patterns in the novel,'' as exemplified by R. W. Stallman's reading of Stephen Crane; (2) the identification of ''style as the 'essential activity' of imaginative prose,'' as exemplified by John Crowe Ransom's essay ''The Understanding of Fiction''; and (3) technicism, ''the attempt to reduce the complex structure and content of the novel to its sum of techniques,'' as in Mark Schorer's ''Technique as Discovery.''

Another characteristic of the Intellectuals' tradition is that they omit any consideration of English literature before 1800 and refer to the continent of Europe for their literary authority. The Intellectuals have written nothing about Chaucer or Shakespeare, much less Webster, Dryden, Fielding, Sterne, or Dr. Johnson, and they deal with romantic and modern English literature only as it can be seen as part of the modernist dialectic. To Podhoretz, English literature seems "in the nature of an entailed national inheritance carefully fenced around . . . against trespassers from outside the family." The Intellectuals' literary criticism is thus in large part a criticism of translations, written in English for English-speaking readers but often referring to another cultural reality expressed in another language. As Howe admits: "No American critic—especially if like myself, he reads Paz through the roughened lens of translation—can engage such a writer without severe risks of misapprehension." This fact, added to their antipoetic bias, may account for the Intellectuals' lack of interest in literary style. As Malcolm Cowley has said, "Language is the specifically human gift and the cohesive force that holds each tribe and nation together," and a great limitation of the Intellectuals is that their heart and their tongue belong to separate cultures.

As the Intellectuals establish their own literary tradition in the forties, they make some attempt to continue their former interest in the "proletarian literature" of the thirties by praising novels written on political subjects or in a naturalistic style—for example, Henry James's *The Bostonians* or the novels of Malraux, Silone, Orwell, and Moravia. The fashion is seen at its narrowest in the subgenre of the ex-Marxist novel (Koestler's *Darkness at Noon* or Trilling's *Middle of the Journey*), where former party members and fellow travelers ruminate on the meaning of it all, Irving Howe is the only Intellectual who applies this political interest to literary criticism to any great extent. In *Politics and the Novel* he defines a political novel as "the kind in which the *idea* of society . . . has penetrated the consciousness of the characters in all of its profoundly problematic aspects, so that there is to be observed in their behavior, and they are themselves often aware of, some coherent political loyalty or ideological identification. They now think in terms of supporting or opposing society as such; they rally to one or another embattled segment of society; and they do so in the name of, and under prompting from, an ideology." Howe finds the tension of a political novel in the struggle between the abstract nature of ideology and the specific nature of human behavior and says that this type of novel must be judged by the amplitude of its moral vision, like any other novel. Though he has returned to naturalists like Hardy and Gissing, even Howe no longer writes about political literature, perhaps because, as Rahv says in 1952, "the rout of the left-wing movement has depoliticized literature."

A third characteristic of the Intellectuals' tradition is that goodness equals modernism, and the Intellectual critics are fairly well agreed on the qualities of good modern literature and the authors who embody them. The key ideas are "complexity," "difficulty," and "conflict." Thus Philip Rahv, speaking of James, says: "In modern literature, which bristles with anxieties and ideas of isolation, it is above all the creativity, the depth and quality of the contradictions that a writer unites within himself, that gives us the truest measure of his achievement. And this is not primarily a matter of the solutions, if any, provided by the writer . . . but of his force and integrity in reproducing these contradictions as felt experience." In the forties, Lionel Trilling usually speaks of literature in the context of what it can do for the liberal political mind, and one can infer from such statements what he sees as the value in literature: "The job of criticism would seem to be, then, to recall liberalism to its first essential imagination of variousness and possibility, which implies the awareness of complexity and difficulty. . . . Literature is the human activity that takes the fullest and most precise account of variousness, possibility, complexity, and difficulty."

Irving Howe undertakes the most extensive recent discussion of what the Intellectuals mean by modernism in "The Idea of the Modern," where he describes the avant-garde movement which Poggioli sees more accurately and fully. Howe also defines modernism briefly in this 1961 book, *Thomas Hardy:*

> *Jude the Obscure* is Hardy's most distinctly "modern" work, for it rests upon a cluster of assumptions central to modernist literature: that in our time men wishing to be more than dumb clods must live in permanent doubt and intellectual crisis; that for such men, to whom traditional beliefs are no longer available, life has become inherently problematic; that in the course of their years they must face even more than the usual allotment of loneliness and anguish; that in their cerebral overdevelopment they run the danger of losing those primary appetites for life which keep the human race going; and that courage, if it is to be found at all, consists in a readiness to accept pain while refusing the comforts of certainty.

Looking back on Trilling and the others in 1957, Norman Podhoretz observes: "They all set out to show that liberalism was guilty of a failure to take a sufficiently complicated view of reality. Complexity became a key word in the discourse of the period. . . . revisionism came out for the more subtle, skeptical temper with its inhibiting awareness of human limitations and its 'tragic sense of life'. . . . the critique of liberalism added up to a defense of wisdom as opposed to rational speculation, to a defense of the qualities of *maturity* against the values of youth."

Of the authors the Intellectuals do like—those who constitute their "tradition"—all write after 1800, most are novelists, and most are continental. According to Irving Howe, the Intellectuals "helped bring back the old world to a country that in part had fled from it. . . . The theme of return figured significantly in their work—in the dissemination of Russian moods and styles, the explication and advocacy of modernist masters like Kafka, the popularization of Marxist ideas, the insistence that in our time literature can only be international." Marshall Berman also opines that "New York Intellectuals are basically nineteenth century Russian intellectuals, right?. . . They felt that politics, art, everything that might be going on posed some immediate and desperate moral problem. And this sense of life as being desperately problematical and therefore how to live as a moral person evoked endless anguish."

Though nineteenth-century Russian or Russian-Jewish intellectualism has not been studied as, much less demonstrated to be, a source of American literary criticism, it is clear that the New York Intellectuals' origins and interests are neither scholarly nor derived from English traditions; rather, the Intellectuals seem to select their literary favorites not so much for their specifically literary qualities, not on a formal basis, but for their usefulness in illustrating ideological points, in showing "the condition of modern man." Thus Rahv is more interested in Dostoevsky than anyone else, partly because he is an immigrant from Russia, but mostly because Dostoevsky illuminates for him the nihilism of the intellectual betrayed by his movement. Kafka, who is very fashionable in the forties, similarly illuminates the alienation of the Intellectuals and modern man as they are faced with bureaucracy and mass society. Thomas Mann is interesting as a Humanist in exile, an intellectual dispossessed by Hitler. Henry James—everybody's favorite—is the very model of complexity and poised "withdrawal." Edmund Wilson remarks that "a novelist whose typical hero invariably decides not to act, who remains merely an intelligent onlooker, appeals for obvious reasons to a period when many intellectuals, formerly romantic egoists or partisans of the political Left, have been resigning themselves to the role of observer or passive participant in activities which cannot command their whole allegiance. The stock of Henry James has gone up in the same market as that of Kafka.'' The real importance of the Europeans to the Intellectuals is as a standard of value, in the literal sense of a flag to rally 'round. Thus F. W. Dupee says in a review of *On Native Grounds:* ''To the critic in fact [alienation] may even apply in a double sense. With Europe's better developed culture as a standard, he sometimes feels estranged not only from America at large but from much of its literature.'' (pp. 228-35)

According to Poggioli, the third attribute of the avant-garde is that it follows the ''cult of fashion'': ''Avant-garde art, because at times its own creation is no more valid or enduring than a fashion, cannot but submit to the influence of fashion.'' For the Intellectuals, fashion is operative chiefly in the area of general cultural ideas, since their literary opinions are consistently modernist. The best way to illustrate the course of the Intellectuals' allegiance to fashion is to recall the various *Partisan Review* symposia and discussions in which the editors solicited opinions from people they considered knowledgeable on topics of current importance. The point of returning to these symposia is to note both their fashionable nature and the compulsion with which the Intellectuals create new issues. It is a fact that basic issues do not change as often as the Intellectuals' interests. Moreover, many basic issues like the atom bomb, the Pentagon, the automobile, the population explosion, or the energy crisis, are not discussed by the Intellectuals at all. Thus, for the avant-garde Intellectual, as for the avant-garde artist, the only error is to be out-of-date; ''the only irremediable and absolute aesthetic error is a traditional artistic creation, an art that imitates and repeats itself.'' One notes, too, that the Intellectuals never confront any issue in a practical way, or propose solutions to any of the problems, but simply halt the discussion when they get bored. The only result of the Intellectuals' social theorizing is that he makes up his mind. A ''*very* high member of the Kennedy administration'' illuminates this point in his reaction to Podhoretz: ''I [Podhoretz] asked him whether he disagreed with what I was saying. 'No, no,' he answered, 'what you're saying is all very well, but what should we do about it?' Do? I was not accustomed to thinking in such terms, I was accustomed to making critical analyses whose point was to understand a problem as fully as possible, not to affect or manipulate it.''

The fourth stage in the history of the Intellectuals, which is most important because it is least understood, is the collapse of their dialectic in the fifties as they leave their journalistic Bohemia to ''make it,'' usually in secure positions in universities, and their ''modernist'' tradition is replaced by new avant-garde movements. Norman Podhoretz, among others, misunderstands the Intellectuals' changing situation: ''What the *Partisan Review* symposium [''Art, Culture, and Conservatism,'' (Summer 1972)] seems to represent is an effort by some of these apologists to fight back by casting the critics of the new sensibility and the counter-culture in the role of the old bourgeois antagonists of an embattled avant-garde. This is so absurd a scenario that only such wildly imaginative apologists as Leslie Fiedler and Suan Sontag might have lent it a touch of plausibility. But they are absent here, and the lesser talents on whom the editors are forced to rely simply do not measure up to the job.''

In order to understand the decline and fall of the Intellectuals as avant-gardists, one must apply Poggioli's distinction between two types of avant-garde publics:

> One is the group made up of those for whom the valid fashion, in poetry, painting, sculpture, architecture, or theater, is the fashion of one single movement, or of a few movements forming a single series; for them any manifestation alien to that movement, or that series, is not avant-garde art, or is not art at all. The other is the group formed by those individuals who consider the fashions of the various avant-gardes as a whole;. . . they accept every variation of modernims with the same unidfferentiated and immoderate enthusiasm, without exception or reservation.

In these terms, the Intellectuals obviously belong to the former group, which identifies exclusively with the avant-garde ''modernism'' of the twenties. Thus, since about 1955 they have applied their habits of thought and used their modernist tradition to judge a reality and a literature which have changed dramatically since their charter was first formed. It is not that the Intellectuals have left the avant-garde, but that a new avant-garde has arisen and left them behind, mired in the literary fashion of what is now a past age. The essential tension of the Intellectuals since about 1955 has not been, as it was earlier, a tension between reality and mind, between liberal politics and avant-garde literature, but a tension between their desire to remain the avant-garde and their reluctance to give up the tradition of their youth. As Irving Howe notes: ''*Partisan Review* betrays a hopeless clash between its editors' capacity to apply serious [i.e., liberal, modernist] standards and their yearnings to embrace the moment.''

In part, the cause of the Intellectuals' metamorphosis into a *derrière-garde* is simply the action of time, but looked at in socioeconomic terms they cease to be avant-gardist because they have become part of the ''intelligentsia,'' the group which includes all professionals, ''not only the man of letters and the artist, teacher, scholar, the scientist and man of the cloth, the journalist and social worker, but also the engineer and technician, the lawyer and doctor, the veterinarian and midwife, the accountant and surveyor.'' This move is basically a fulfillment of their earlier bourgeois aspirations, and as they move from being marginal journalists to the status of professors and Kennedy intellectuals their economic alienation is cured with a vengeance. By moving to the universities they become cultural functionaries, bureaucrats of the mind, a trend which culminates in the values of *Making It.* After surveying the accomplishments of the Intellectuals in the thirties and forties, Mary McCarthy notes: ''Meanwhile, like most American writers, professors, and editors, we were getting richer. And less revolutionary. Not just because we had more money, but because we are getting older, and because, according to our analysis, it was not a 'revolutionary situation.'''

The dating of the Intellectuals' shift to the intelligentsia is not, of course, exact, since it involves the careers of many individual men, but it seems to take place between 1948 and 1953. Philip Rahv speaks of it as a *fait accompli* in 1952, in the *Partisan Review* symposium ''Our Country and Our Culture.'' It takes twenty years for their new status as conservatives to sink in, however; not until the 1972 symposium ''Our Country and Our Culture.'' It takes twenty years for their new status as conservatives to sink in, however; not until the 1972 symposium ''The New Cultural Conservatism'' is it officially noted that Intellectuals have ''a noticeable reluctance to receive new works, new writers, new forms,'' and that their conservatism "inflates established figures, and celebrates old values, old works, old institutions as though they can never be changed or added to or replaced." This conservatism is basically a projection of the Intellectuals' own worries onto the culture, in the manner of their earlier symposia "Failure of Nerve" (1943) or "Religion" (1952). In the 1972 symposium, Morris Dickstein analyzes the new conservatism correctly as "a noisy campaign by a few well-situated editors and critics to reverse the cultural direction of the Sixties . . . in short, backlash." (pp. 237-40)

The Intellectuals' loss of their avant-garde position and the solidification of the tradition of their own group into orthodoxy lead them to reject any cultural reality beyond modernism (except for their concern with their own status as newly powerful Intellectuals). In the forties they totally ignore New Directions writers like Henry Miller, John Hawkes, Kenneth Rexroth, Edward Dahlberg, Gertrude Stein, or William Carlos Williams. In their writing they do not confront the destruction of Europe in World War II and the central fact of the atomic bomb, which makes total destruction of the world possible. William Barrett observes that although Philip Rahv accepted for publication in the *Partisan Review* a piece by Anatole Broyard entitled "The Hipsters," "Broyard represented to him another generation and new things with which he didn't want to cope. His mind was turned backward, rehearsing the sacred canon of the Great Moderns. The other pole of his conservatism was his Marxism."

In a literary context the Intellectuals say little about the Existentialism of Beckett and Sartre or the Theatre of the Absurd, which arose in reaction to the destruction of old values. According to Lionel Trilling: "There is no possible way of responding to Belsen and Buchenwald. The activity of mind fails before the incommunicability of man's suffering." Unlike George Steiner or Hannah Arendt, the Intellectuals do not even attempt to come to terms with the new escalation of man's inhumanity to man, though they try to confront Arendt's book on Eichmann. With the exception of Richard Poirier, they ignore or see through the "Marxist" categories of their youth, the rise of the Beatles and rock-and-roll, the "beat" generation and the angry young men, the new interest in drugs and slums and pollution, Che Guevara and the black revolution, women's lib and the occult. Richard Kostelanetz has assembled a telling list of the sins of omission of Irving Howe, and the list applies *a fortiori* to the other Intellectuals, who have almost abandoned social and political speculation:

> The frame of political concern expressed in *The Radical Papers* encompasses . . . a number of problems of obvious relevance. However, *The Radical Papers,* as well as Howe's *Steady Work,* conspicuously neglect to confront in any significant way such important dimensions of contemporary social and political existence as the impact and potential of automation and other new technologies, the restructuring of the content of education, . . . the power and influence of all electronic media of communication, the individual's role and ethical responsibility in a bureaucracy, . . . the rapidly increasing rate of population expansion (and the question of eugenics), the administration of a guaranteed annual income, . . . the general awareness of the increasing gap of generational difference, the depletion of natural resources, the pollution of the environment, etc., etc. The point of this list is that the Marxian frame that apparently encases Howe and his fellow dissenters perceives primarily the modern guises of nineteenth century

problems, only to neglect the predicaments and possibilities that have developed since Marx's day.

(pp. 244-45)

Looked at in Poggioli's terms, what has happened is that the agonistic and nihilistic strains in avant-garde thinking which were subordinated by the modernists' activism, experimentalism, and antagonism toward bourgeois culture have been reborn in the sixties as a new avant-garde movement so strange to the New York Intellectuals that they are unable to recognize it as avant-garde at all. The problem for most of the Intellectuals is thus not only awareness of the death of their avant-garde but self-awareness, the realization that this death applies to them. Lionel Trilling says in 1948: "Surely the great work of our time is the restoration and the reconstitution of the will." Irving Howe laments in 1949: "Where, all the while, is the opposition, the rebellious and exuberant *avantgarde?* Nowhere in sight, for it no longer exists." And in 1957, in his long article "The Fate of the Avant-Garde," Richard Chase pronounces more analytically: "There is no service in attacking the avant-garde critics . . . [for] their specifically polemical task of the last forty years has expired with the success of the movements they championed. They have not yet clearly formulated what their duties in this interim period are. Meanwhile, they suffer from the well-known maladies of the avant-gardist, especially on the ebb-tide of his influence: sterility, academicism, willful and excessive intellectuality."

That this particular avant-garde movement should be past history is no particular tragedy for most of its members, who have done their bit to defend their tradition and have gone forward into successful academic careers. The only ones who still insist on playing the old adversary role are Macdonald, Irving Howe, and Norman Podhoretz. Macdonald and Howe are given to issuing "unto the breach once more" statements rallying their friends to the good old cause. In his "Masscult and Midcult," Macdonald concludes: "But if we are ever to have more than [accidental culture] it will be because our new public for High Culture becomes conscious of itself and begins to show some *esprit de corps,* insisting on higher standards and setting itself off—joyously, implacably—from most of its fellow citizens." Howe ends "The New York Intellectuals" with the plea: "Yet, precisely at this moment of dispersion, might not some of the New York writers achieve renewed strength if they were to struggle once again for whatever has been salvaged from these last few decades? For the values of liberalism, for the politics of a democratic radicalism, for the norms of rationality and intelligence, for the standards of literary seriousness, for the life of the mind as a humane dedication." For God, for Irving, and St. George! Howe is quite right in affirming that freedom is essential to the avant-garde Intellectual, but he is less aware that in gaining tenure he has lost his own avant-garde position.

One must then conclude of the Intellectuals that their careeers as critics are best understood as parts in an avant-garde play; they have played, and played well for the most part, roles in a drama that is now concluded. The conventional nature of their activity, in later years especially, is revealed by a remark of Podhoretz's: "It is simply that a public existed when she [Susan Sontag] arrived on the scene which was searching for a new Dark Lady [to replace Mary McCarthy], and she was so obviously right that a spontaneous decision was made on all sides to cast her for the role—exactly as I in my time had been chosen for a role I seemed practically born to play." Now the drama is ended. "This *is* the inevitable, inexorable destiny of each movement: to rise up against the newly outstripped fashion of an old avant-garde and to die when a new fashion, movement, or avant-garde appears." The difficulty is that the actors are still around. The problem, as Poggioli notes, is one of succession: the avant-garde is dead; long live the avant-garde! (pp. 250-51)

Grant Webster, "The Essential Dialectic: Reality versus Imagination," in his The Republic of Letters: A History of Postwar American Literary Opinion, The Johns Hopkins University Press, 1979, pp. 209-51.

ALAN M. WALD

[*In the following excerpt from his study* The New York Intellectuals: The Rise and Decline of the Anti-Stalinist Left from the 1930s to the 1980s *(1987), Wald examines social and political themes in fiction by members of the group.*]

Virtually all of the imaginative writing by the New York intellectuals is unambiguously political in its intent, a point sometimes missed by cultural historians. Some suggest that the New York intellectuals disdained the Communist Party's "proletarian" literature movement because of their desire to depoliticize art or else ingenuously accept at face value the many declamations of the New York intellectuals against the evils of ideology. Lionel Trilling states forthrightly in the 1975 introduction to his *The Middle of the Journey* that the book was largely intended as a political intervention: "From my first conception of it, my story was committed to history—it was to draw out some of the moral and intellectual implications of the powerful attraction to Communism felt by a considerable part of the American intellectual class during the Thirties and Forties."

In addition, during the 1930s and after, several of the New York intellectuals claimed that imaginative literature might play a special role in exploring and validating political ideology. For example, in his influential 1939 essay, "Proletarian Literature: A Political Autopsy," Philip Rahv argued as follows:

> There are certain forms of demagogy, however, which a medium as palpable as faction—unless it degenerates to the level of pulp propaganda—excludes by its very nature. Thus the media of art, if only by that fact alone, prove their superior humanity to the media of politics. The kind of casuistry which may easily pass for truth within the pseudo-context of a political speech or editorial, will be exposed in all its emptiness once it is injected into the real context of a living experience, such as the art of fiction strives to represent. The novel is the pre-eminent example of an experiential art; and to falsify the experiential terms in which it rationalizes itself is infinitely more difficult than to falsify abstract reasoning. Whereas politics summarizes social experience, the novel subjects it to empiric analysis.

Rahv's argument—that the demands of representation are such that it is more difficult for authentic art to falsify life than it is for strictly "ideological" discourse to do so—appears to be a sophisticated Marxist literary formulation. Rahv alludes to Henry James as a genuine artist who achieves critical distance from propaganda by following the "law of art," which requires that ideas developed in imaginative literature of the first rank be vivified through the convincing recreation of human experience. This view of the literary medium is an early example of a similar view expressed by Lionel Trilling in his more well-known statement in *The Liberal Imagination* (1950) that "literature is the human activity that takes the fullest and most precise account of variousness, possibility, complexity, and difficulty." (pp. 227-28)

Lionel Trilling in 1957. © Rollie McKenna.

In *New York Jew* (1978) Alfred Kazin insightfully described Lionel Trilling as "the most successful leader of deradicalization" in the postwar era. A good deal can be learned about Trilling's ideological and artistic evolution during the 1940s by examining two of his short stories that preceded *The Middle of the Journey,* although, in another context, these same stories might be analyzed for other themes and issues. "Of This Time, Of That Place," which appeared in the same issue of the *Partisan Review* as Sidney Hook's "The New Failure of Nerve," introduces what became for Trilling and most of his fellow writers a standard motif: the vicissitudes of a middle-aged person undergoing a profound change in values. The story concerns the unexpected decision of Joseph Howe, a former modernist poet turned English professor, to inform Dwight College's superficial and naive dean about the psychological problems of his most brilliant student, Ferdinand Tertan, even though Howe knows this will result in Tertan's dismissal from the college and his probable institutionalization. At the story's end, Howe, his arms linked with the dean en route to an academic procession, finds himself connected, by the dean's other arm, to a dishonest, opportunist student named Blackburn. Although Howe symbolically withdraws his arm, he had already decided to participate in the ceremony. Significantly, he has just been promoted to full professor and guaranteed a permanent position at the college.

The pivotal events in the story occur when, after concluding that Tertan has characteristics that conventional society would consider to be marks of "madness," Howe at first resolves that he will *not* bring Tertan to the attention of the administration and have him removed from school. Thus it is very much to his surprise that Howe finds himself, at the very next moment, requesting to see the dean in order to *report* Tertan: "[I]t would always be a landmark in his life that, at the very moment when he was rejecting the official way, he had been, without will or intention, so gladly drawn to it." What can one conclude but that the story is a testament of acceptance of the once-abhorred society by the former rebel Joseph Howe? Morally, he has doubts about the "official way"; emotionally, he is relieved after he submits to the pressure to "do the right thing."

The importance of Howe's promotion, as well as his tenuous relation to Dwight College, seems to link the story to Diana Trilling's 1977 memoir of her husband, "Lionel Trilling, a Jew at Columbia," in which she describes his difficulties in achieving a secure academic post during the depression. In 1932 Trilling was appointed as an English instructor at Columbia, the same position held by Howe at Dwight College before he betrayed Tertan. However, Trilling nearly lost his position because of prejudice against him "as a Freudian, a Marxist, and a Jew." Finally, after Trilling published his doctoral dissertation on Matthew Arnold, Columbia President Nicholas Murray Butler decided in 1939 to promote him to assistant professor "under his summer powers." Soon Trilling found that he had become substantially deradicalized.

If the anxieties surrounding Lionel's promotion as depicted by Diana Trilling in her 1977 memoir were in fact worked into "Of This Time, Of That Place," which was published two years after the events she describes, it is interesting to note that the prejudice directed against Trilling as a Jewish Freudian Marxist has been displaced by the prejudice Howe encounters because of his former connections with modernist poetry and his potential connection with the "mad" Tertan.

En route to a faculty dinner party, Howe discovers an article in a literary journal by an establishment critic denouncing his two books of poetry as mad, self-intoxicated, and irresponsible—words that might well describe Tertan. Later, Howe has an argument with his student Blackburn who, angry about the grade Howe had given him, threatens to tell the dean about the unfavorable article. Although Howe dramatically rebukes Blackburn for the threat, he later gives him a higher grade than he deserved, enabling Blackburn to receive the dean's praise for being the first member of his class to secure a job after graduation. Blackburn had also threatened to tell the dean that Howe had recommended the unstable Tertan for the college literary society, but by this time Howe had already betrayed Tertan.

The ideological thrust of the story advocates accepting the "official way" despite its imperfections. But Tertan so deftly understood the art of fiction that the reader is permitted to apprehend all the limitations and contradictions of such an acceptance while at the same time appreciating its attractiveness for the protagonist. From the beginning we learn that Howe has tired of the social and cultural rebellion of his youth: "At twenty-six, Joseph Howe had discovered that he was neither so well off nor so bohemian as he had once thought." We observe how he becomes increasingly comfortable in the dull college environment, enjoying parties at faculty homes and even the silly ritual of cap-and-gown cermonies. Finally, a young woman, Hilda Aiken, begins to fall in love with Howe, and a conventional courtship seems imminent.

Trilling does nothing to make either the academic environment or the "official way" more interesting and attractive than they would be in real life; he clearly demonstrates that it is Howe

himself who has changed and who is in the process of succumbing to the dull bourgeois world he once scorned. Even more impressive is the dignity that Trilling manages to assign to Tertan. In the closing scene the "mad" student stands apart from the others in the academic procession, but when Tertan merely glances at Howe standing arm-in-arm with the dean and with Blackburn, Howe feels so guilty that he drops the dean's arm.

Although secondary characters like Blackburn, the dean, and even Tertan are not fleshed out, they effectively embody the ambiguous forces acting upon Howe. Blackburn incarnates the real "insanity" of corruption and dishonesty that the "official way" gives free rein to in our society, and the dean functions as the well-meaning but obtuse arbiter who permits this sad state of affairs to exist. Tertan, however, is scarcely a personification of "madness," for Trilling imparts virtually nothing about the nature of his alleged illness and its causes. Instead, Tertan seems to be an incarnation of the true modernist hero of Howe's earlier period—passionately devoted to mind and truth, unqualifiedly hostile to a mundane, materialistic, sham world run by narrowly "scientific" principles, and expressing himself through a style of writing that is difficult and "disordered." Tertan's final comment is a scornful remark about "instruments of precision" in apparent reference to the camera Hilda is using to capture Howe's likeness. Trilling stated in a subsequent commentary that the "instruments of precision" may also have been intended to suggest Tertan's ironic judgment on the values of the society that had judged him abnormal.

There is no "casuistry" in the story, no "abstract reasoning" about which Rahv was so concerned; the ambivalent world of Joseph Howe is vivified through his behavior and his progressive accommodation to the "official way." But the story is highly ideological nonetheless. Most striking is Trilling's semiconscious account of how the alienation of the nonconformist can serve to foster capitulation, a condition that the nonconformist accepts with resignation and implication urges the reader to accept. Alienation in this context is not meant in the Marxist sense but in the manner in which it was discussed by the New York intellectuals in the 1940s: the painful, but purportedly salutary, sense of inevitably being compelled to remain apart, especially as experienced by the ex-radical and the secular Jew.

In "Of This Time, Of That Place," Howe is uncomfortable at every turn, never more than half committed to any alternative, always standing with one foot outside of a situation. As a modernist he had been alienated from the dominant culture, but he was alienated as well from his very stance of alienation. In accommodating to the "official way," he still recognizes that it is corruption, and he is even able to objectify his own behavior—to watch his own strange actions as if disembodied. And yet, in practice, he cooperates: his alienation yields an unexpected capitulation even though, from the pragmatic point of view, it produces a skepticism of abstract ideas and an immersion in concrete experience. Trilling regards this surprising outcome in a half-bemused, half-tragic manner. In his artistic practice, if not in his conscious theorizing, a part of Trilling may have indeed recognized that experience is "ideology's homeland" and thus a likely route to co-optation.

In contrast to this self-reflexive toying with his anti-ideological ideology, Trilling's 1946 story, "The Other Margaret," reveals an increasing blindness to his own ideological transgressions, one that works to the detriment of his artistic capacities. The story looses a highly loaded assault on the radical analysis of and solution to race and class oppression: indeed, one might even call it the first anti-affirmative action short story. There are two Maragrets in "The Other Margaret." One is the thirteen-year-old daughter of Stephen Elwin, a publisher of scientific magazines: the other is the family's black maid.

Maragaret the maid is hostile to her well-off employers, showing her resentment by "accidentally" breaking expensive things around the house. Margaret the daughter is under the influence of a "progressive" schoolteacher, Miss Hoxie. Thus the daughter protests that the maid Margaret cannot be blamed for what she does; as a black person she carries the burden of her race and class. In addition to constantly repeating that "society" is responsible for all bad behavior, the daughter Margaret also argues that blacks who are loyal, reliable, and courteous, like a former maid, Millie, have a "slave psychology."

However, by the end of the story the daughter is exposed as a hypocrite who really, deep in her heart, does not accept her teacher's radical ideology; when the maid finally breaks something that the daughter truly values, a clay lamb that she had made as a gift for her mother, she bursts into tears and denounces the maid as having done it intentionally and thus being personally responsible.

But neither Margaret forms the center of consciousness in the story. Once more, the protagonist is an adult approaching middle age who suddenly has undergone a change. The change in Stephen Elwin's attitude is described in a scene on a bus as he is returning home after purchasing a painting of a king by Rouault. He witnesses a nasty old conductor trick a little rich boy into missing his bus. The reader is told that Stephen's habit of mind is such that he would normally feel compassion for the conductor, a poor working man who had never had the advantages of the rich boy: "But now, strangely, although the habit was in force, it did not check his anger. It was bewildering that he should feel anger at a poor ignorant man, a working man. It was the first time in his life that he had ever felt so."

Leaving aside the unlikely possibility that the middle-aged Elwin had never before felt anger toward a worker, it is important to recognize that the basis of his change in consciousness is bound up in his recollection, at several points, of Hazlitt's famous sentence, "No young man believes he shall ever die." Just before the final conflict with the maid Margaret, this revelation comes to him as a flash of light: "It seemed to him— not suddenly, for it had been advancing in his mind for some hours now—that in the aspect of his knowledge of death, all men were equal in their responsibility. . . . Exemption was not given by age or youth, or sex, or color, or condition of life."

Trilling's decision to present this banality as the portentous revelation of the story is an aesthetic and intellectual catastrophe. In what way can the observation that all are fated to die negate or even challenge the fact that different races and classes face substantially different kinds of obstacles in their struggle to survive or the fact that individual behavior cannot be fully assessed outside of its social context? What makes the inevitability of death a guide to conduct of any sort?

Trilling takes this non sequitur even further in the closing pages when Elwin concludes that his daughter for purely selfish reasons has needed to believe that society rather than individuals is responsible for bad behavior so that she herself would not have to feel guilty if she someday found herself committing an immoral act! Thus the story not only provides a partly Freudian critique of a political position, but it is also connected to Gerard Manley Hopkins's poem "Spring and Fall (To a

Young Child)." The poem begins, "Margaret are you grieving / Over Goldengrove unleaving," and ends, "It is the blight man was born for, / It is Margaret you mourn for."

Trilling attempts to modulate the absurdity of this abstract position by having Elwin protest that what he really needs to communicate to his daughter is a "double truth," one that recognizes both social and individual responsibility for human behavior. But, for unexplained reasons, he lacks the ability to do this. This and other failings suggest that an atypical instance of rigidity on the part of Trilling has overwhelmed the method of his art so that, in spite of his caveat about "double truth," any reader who holds a more materialist view of the nature of social oppression is left dissatisfied. Why didn't Trilling at least attempt to suggest some of the concrete reasons for the maid Margaret's unruly behavior? Why are we denied all insight into the consciousness of the working class and of black characters, while every attempt is made to reveal the thoughts and feelings of the middle-class Elwins?

Finally, why is the "radical" point of view reduced to the repetition of simple phrases such as "we can't blame her" and "she's not responsible," and why is the only defender of this perspective a thirteen-year-old who bursts into tears after her clay lamb is broken? Is this a fair statement of the radical position? Is Trilling justified in claiming that the radical view is so devoid of complexity?

One possibility is that "The Other Margaret" may be partially intended as a response to Richard Wright's *Native Son* (1940), about a black youth who is tried and executed for two murders. The very title of Wright's book underscores the notion that the killer, Bigger Thomas, is a product of society, but a close reading of the text shows that Wright, a Communist Party member of the time, intentionally avoided the temptation to make Bigger into a mere victim of circumstance. There are two murders in the book. The first, of Mary Dalton, is accidental. Bigger inadvertently suffocates her when he fears he might be caught violating white society's taboo of being found in a white women's bedroom in the middle of the night. The second, involving Bessie Mears, is a cold-blooded homicide committed in the hope of facilitating his flight from the police. Mr. Max, Bigger's Communist-supplied lawyer, does not plead for Bigger's freedom in the speech to the judge; he argues instead for a life sentence. Thus the most famous radical work of fiction of the time, whatever its weaknesses, certainly does not take the simplistic view of responsibility and oppression attributed to the daughter Margaret and her propagandistic schoolteacher, Miss Hoxie.

In 1946, James T. Farrell, who was still attempting to retain his revolutionary Marxist political position, published a brief comment on "The Other Margaret" in the *New International,* theoretical organ of the Workers Party, to which Farrell had recently switched allegiance after a dispute with the Socialist Workers Party. He praised the story's execution as "adroit" but charged Trilling with "tendentiousness" in his choice of characters and events and for the unfair ways in which Trilling presented the contending philosophies. Farrell concludes: "Thus, while we can recognize the skill with which this story is written, and while we can concede it the merit of producing a certain cultivated milieu of our time, we should realize that it is cleverly organized to present a reactionary moral view with insidious pervasiveness. I use the word reactionary here because Trilling's story establishes a conclusion concerning freedom and responsibility at the expense of those who most need to be free, and on the basis of citing relatively trivial incidents."

Shortly afterward, Irving Howe, then a young leader of the Workers Party, made his debut in the *Partisan Review* by attacking Farrell's analysis: "[T]he story is not a thesis or an argument; it is, however imperfectly executed, a work of art. It is therefore concerned with and dipped in emotional ambiguity; it pictures a situation of conflict between ideas about race, class, and morality and deeply-imbued folk attitudes. Had it been Trilling's purpose to advance a thesis on morality, he would have written an essay. His purpose was rather to dramatize a situation." Farrell may have misread a few minor aspects of the story, but Howe's protest augurs better as a defense of "Of This Time, Of That Place" than of "The Other Margaret."

From the beginning of the narrative, Stephen Elwin has been in search of wisdom. Wisdom and naiveté are continually counterposed throughout the story. Elwin purchases the portrait of the king by Rouault precisely because it suggests wisdom: "One could feel of him [the king] . . . that he had passed beyond ordinary matters of personality and was worthy of the crown he was wearing." Neither a young soldier nor the daughter Margaret is able to appreciate the portrait and consequently they are shown to be naive.

The daughter Margaret is also shown to be foolish through her association with innocence as connoted by the clay lamb. "Why, darling," cries her mother when she spies the gift, "it looks just like you!" A further episode reveals the daughter's naiveté: after self-righteously refusing to believe her mother's story about an underpaid worker who made an anti-Semitic remark, Margaret discredits herself by inadvertently making an anti-Semitic gesture.

Elwin, on the other hand, is continually the epitome of wisdom. It is he, after all, who purchases the portrait of the king. Moreover, after initially feeling that he behaved foolishly in becoming angry at the conductor on the bus going home, he has a revelation: "It then occurred to him to think that perhaps he had felt his anger not in despite of wisdom but because of it." Finally, after his major confrontation with his daughter, we are told that he had "defeated his daughter" and that the daughter's continued defense of the maid Margaret was "stupid and obstinate."

Where, then, is the ambiguity that Howe sees in "The Other Margaret"? Perhaps it lies only in the inability of Elwin to articulate his "double truth" at the end of the story. It certainly does not reside in the interaction between the two positions presented. But the implication is clear that with time and experience Elwin will have the courage to overcome his timorousness and act appropriately, that is, according to his new philosophy of death as an equalizer. Farrell's use of the term "reactionary" may have been too extreme, but Howe clearly failed to see the ominous implications of Trilling's assault on the "progressive" political position in light of the *zeitgeist* of the postwar period. He also missed the implications of Trilling's charge, via Elwin (there can be no doubt that the author and his character coincide in this instance), that the radical teacher had "corrupted" her student. The purge of left-wing teachers from the New York City school system had already begun, and a national witch-hunt of leftists in colleges and universities would soon follow. One might possibly argue that there are other more complicated elements in the story (for example, Lucy, the mother, seems to share an oversimplified version of Stephen Elwin's position), but one must conclude that the seven types of ambiguity depicted are mere window dressing for what is unambiguously a blatant assault on the left.

Howe seems to echo Rahv in his differentiation between a story (experience) and an argument (ideology); his view also seems to dovetail with Trilling's own praise of authentic literature as taking the "most precise account of variousness, possibility, complexity, and difficulty." But "The Other Margaret" *is* more an argumentative thesis than an ambiguous dramatization,which would be drenched in ideology anyway. It foreshadows the contention of Trilling's later book, *The Liberal Imagination,* that certain kinds of liberal and radical intellectuals (represented here not only by Miss Hoxie and her thirteen-year-old dupe, but by Elwin himself before his change in consciousness) easily fall prey to oversimplified social theory because of emotional rather than valid intellectual reasons. Many of the artistic problems of the story derive from Trilling's having gone too far in oversimplifying the oversimplification that he wants to refute. He was too zealous in honing his assault. Both Farrell and Howe were correct in pointing out that Trilling's skills of depiction in "The Other Margaret" are still considerable, and of course the story depicts much more than the political issues on which I have focused. But there is definite evidence that Trilling employed character and action in "The Other Margaret" that was based on political bias and polemical intent of a kind not found in "Of This Time, Of That Place."

Trilling's stories dramatize a recurring theme in the World War II fiction produced by the New York intellectuals during the 1940s: a change in consciousness away from the ideologies of Marxism and radical modernism on the part of a central character with a left-wing or bohemian past. Several longer works published about the same time contain striking structural similarities: Edmund Wilson's *Memoirs of Hecate County* (1946), Trilling's *The Middle of the Journey* (1947), and Mary McCarthy's *The Oasis* (1949) all create imaginary semirural environments where the main characters, temporarily absent from or commuting to New York City, are confronted with a clash of carefully selected viewpoints. This structural motif allows these writers unusual freedom in dramatizing various arguments, but it also suggests that both the problems and solutions presented in fiction are often far removed from the life experiences of ordinary Americans—the working class, racial minorities, the urban masses.

The texts are at least partially conscious of this phenomenon; this is also suggested by the fact that the terrain on which the leading characters have their revelation or "real experience" is itself somehow illusory, a rural idyll divorced from the social reality of struggle in the urban centers. Oddly enough, then, the "experience" in which the characters are educated is false and simplified. This confirms the contention of Eagleton and others that there is a high degree of half-conscious self-reflexivity in literary texts themselves. In other words, the narrative structures of the works of fiction manifest an inherent criticism of the works' own premises, which is that by immersing oneself in "experience" one can evade the deceptions and temptations of ideology. This would be an example of what Eagleton considers an "authentic art that can distance and critically reveal the very ideology being produced by the literary text."

All three works include elements of the roman à clef, which suggests their insular character as well as the possibility that they might serve some sort of therapeutic function. Trilling acknowledged that his character Gifford Maxim is derived from his college classmate Whittaker Chambers; McCarthy is unmistakably clear in her portraits of her close associates Philip Rahv (as Will Taub) and Dwight Macdonald (as MacDougal MacDermott); Edmund Wilson's recently published notebooks reveal the autobiographical basis of his book, and the critic Sherman Paul has persuasively argued that Wilson's Sy Banks is based on Paul Rosenfeld and that the Milholland brothers express the views of Van Wyck Brooks and Archibald MacLeish during World War II.

Finally, each book not only describes but *advocates* an "end of ideology"—a theme that surfaced in literature at least ten years before it was articulated by the sociologists Daniel Bell and Seymour Martin Lipset. In each instance, ideology is rejected primarily because of its inherent tendency to oversimplify. The common primary target in each book is the fallacy inherent in employing radical social theory, especially class analysis, as a means of changing society. (pp. 231-40)

Of all the novels and stories of the 1940s that express an ostensible rebellion against ideology in the name of experience, only *The Middle of the Journey* presents a hero and final perspective suggesting that its author might play a leading role in directing intellectuals of subsequent decades. This contrasts with Saul Bellow's *Dangling Man* (1944), Isaac Rosenfeld's *Passage from Home* (1946), and Eleanor Clark's *The Bitter Box* (1946), each written by an individual formerly associated with the anti-Stalinist left. All depict a kind of disillusionment with either radicalism or modernist/bohemian rebellion as the result of an immersion in experience; their protagonists, however, tend to be either younger or older than those of Wilson, McCarthy, and Trilling, and these novels are set in an urban locale. (pp. 245-46)

Although Bellow was considerably influenced intellectually by the anti-Stalinist left, surprisingly little of his Trotskyist experience worked its way into his fiction or memoirs. . . . [Some] of his college writing had political themes, and his second contribution to the *Partisan Review*, "The Mexican General," depicts the assassination of Trotsky from the point of view of Mexican police officials involved in the aftermath. There are passing references to Trotskyism in other short stories as well as in *The Adventures of Augie March* (1953), which may derive its main character in part from Abraham Liebick, a gifted young Trotskyist from Chicago's Marshall High School who was killed while serving in the Navy's Medical Corps in the Pacific. *Dangling Man* (1944) is about a restless young intellectual who joined the Communist Party in 1932 but broke away at the start of World War II, which approximates Bellow's relationship with the Trotskyists. While waiting to be drafted, the young man's disillusionment extends from radicalism to his circle of bohemian friends. At the end of the novel he has become skeptical of all the former values that he had acquired during his political and cultural rebellion. With bitter irony he submits to the experience of the majority of his generation by celebrating his last day as a civilian: "I am no longer to be held accountable for myself; I am grateful for that. I am in other hands, relieved of self-determination, freedom cancelled. Hurray for regular hours! And for the supervision of the spirit! Long live regimentation!"

Rosenfeld wrote only one story, "The Party," reflective of his experiences in the Trotskyist movement. It is told through the eyes of someone different from himself, a full-time functionary who works in the party's printshop and draws cartoons for the party paper. The story presumably depicts the decline of the Workers Party during the mid-1940s, when he was no longer a member. In it Rosenfeld describes the peculiar men-

tality of a devout but self-abnegating member loyal to the forms of the movement—the rituals of party interventions and social affairs, the veneration of "old guard" leaders and the dynamics of faction struggle—even as its political content is lost. In this sense the story is simply a variation on the "end-of-ideology" motif. Rosenfeld's ideologues are brutally satirized because they remain impervious to experience. *Passage from Home* has a more complex development, because, unlike "The Party," a change occurs in the outlook of the main character. Here Rosenfeld traces the awakening consciousness of fifteen-year-old Bernard Miller who leaves his father to live with his nonconformist aunt. Returning to his father at the end, Bernard's immersion in experience has taught him that the bohemian alternative to the alienation of conventional life is illusory, and he becomes resigned to his outsider status. Thus experience teaches that alienation is the permanent condition of humanity. (pp. 247-48)

Clark's *The Bitter Box* (1946) traces the disillusionment with the Communist Party of a rather unimpressive bank clerk, John Temple, who in personal frustration one day quits his cloistered job to immerse himself in the experience of political activism. Although he achieves moral, social, and even spiritual comfort by devoting himself to party affairs, the underlying horror of his experience is revealed when he learns the fate of his friend Brand, who was "liquidated" because he knew too much about the party's underground activities. In this connection, Herbert Solow's relationship to Whittaker Chambers provided important background for Clark's novel, just as it did for *The Middle of the Journey*. Strangely, the novel is not directly political, even though it reflects in many other ways the anti-Stalinist experiences of the 1930s: the factional struggle between Brand's party and the opposition group (People's Will), whose leader is assassinated, suggests the Stalinist-Trotskyist conflict; the political turns and sudden changes in Brand's party's line suggest the "Third Period," Popular Front, and Hitler-Stalin Pact convolutions of the Communist Party; the party's newspaper, the *Word*, echoes the *Worker* (albeit with a religious twist), and the literary magazine *Everybody's* suggests the *New Masses*. But, as in Rosenfeld's "The Party," Clark creates as a center of consciousness a rather narrow mind subjected primarily to pressures and motivations other than those stemming from political theory.

Until 1945 James T. Farrell was a dependable ally of the Socialist Workers Party. Except for Meyer Schapiro, Clement Greenberg, and Dwight Macdonald, he was virtually alone among the anti-Stalinist intellectuals in adhering to a revolutionary internationalist point of view during World War II. From 1941 to 1945 he served as chairman of the Civil Rights Defense Committee, which had been formed to defend the Trotskyist trade union militants in Minneapolis Teamster Local 544 and leaders of the SWP. These union militants and party leaders had been prosecuted as the first victims of the Smith "Gag" Act, which made it unlawful to advocate the overthrow of the U.S. government or to belong to any group advocating such an overthrow.

Farrell wrote and published fiction steadily during these years, arguing that there is an interdependency between the advancement of culture and the struggle for human liberation, although Farrell's fiction differed from that of John Dos Passos, who wrote explicitly political novels. Some of Farrell's work, such as his antifascist novelette *Tommy Gallagher's Crusade* (1939), dramatized important political issues, but his *Studs Lonigan* trilogy demonstrated that he was primarily a novelist of human character. Farrell was acutely sensitive to the psychological costs of living in a class society, and his conceptions of individual consciousness and social destiny were infused with a materialist outlook. This is most evident not only in the *Studs Lonigan* trilogy, but also in Farrell's second series, the O'Neill-O'Flaherty pentalogy: *A World I Never Made* (1936), *No Star Is Lost* (1938), *Father and Son* (1940), *My Days of Anger* (1943), and *The Face of Time* (1953). Although the pentalogy centers around the life of Danny O'Neill, Farrell preferred that the five books be called the "O'Neill-O'Flaherty series" because the main characters are derived from both families. Both the *Studs Lonigan* trilogy and also the O'Neill-O'Flaherty series, conceived about the same time and thematically interconnected, provide an exposé of the false consciousness created by the institutions of capitalist society. A third series, the Bernard Carr trilogy—consisting of *Bernard Clare* (1946), *The Road Between* (1949), and *Yet Other Waters* (1952)—evolved somewhat later but was still linked to the revolutionary Marxist period in Farrell's literary development.

The O'Neill-O'Flaherty series, comprising a sprawling 2,500 pages, suffers by comparison with the *Studs Lonigan* trilogy because its five units, read separately, lack cogency. Yet their cumulative effect is more potent and complex, and Danny O'Neill is a wholly unique creation. Studs Lonigan's humanity is only dimly perceived behind the warped values absorbed from his environment; his notions of evil, engendered by Father Gilhooley's sermons, are haunting and amorphous, and his daydreams of a better life, associated with his would-be childhood sweetheart, Lucy Scanlan, are vague and romantic. In contrast, Danny O'Neill, an autobiographical persona, is much more intelligent, thoughtful, and sensitive than Studs, and he moves, despite setbacks, unrelentingly toward victory over his environment. As Danny escapes the predestined roles prepared for him by his family and subculture, the skillful precision with which Farrell probes the processes of human consciousness demonstrates a literary debt to Joyce and Proust.

Using stream of consciousness and associational techniques, Farrell roots the emotional development of Danny in a childhood trauma when his parents, Jim and Liz O'Neill, turn him over to the care of his widowed grandmother, Mary O'Flaherty. Danny's mind and personality are thereafter subtly shaped by his interaction with the two families, one middle class and the other working class. The respective class differences in attitude and outlook are acutely dramatized by two of the central male characters: Danny's uncle, Al O'Flaherty, a shoe salesman, and Danny's father, Jim, a teamster. Al O'Flaherty worships conventionalized notions of education and culture, while Jim fears that Al will turn Danny into a soft "dude."

Chronologically, the pentalogy begins with *The Face of Time*, published last in 1953, which follows Danny's emergence into consciousness at the very time his grandfather, Tom O'Flaherty, is dying. It concludes with Danny's college years in *My Days of Anger* (1943), which emphasizes his renunciation of religion, his initial encounters with philosophy and modern literature, and his first eager steps as a writer. Of the five novels, only *A World I Never Made* achieved popular success, and this may have been partly due to a well-publicized trial in which Farrell was accused, and acquitted, of including obscenity in the novel. But the O'Neill-O'Flaherty series never attained the stature of the *Studs Lonigan* trilogy because it lacks the dramatic focus afforded by Studs Lonigan's violent eruption into young manhood followed by ill health and death. What is superior about the O'Neill-O'Flaherty series is its relentless

detailing of the generational conflicts among big-city Irish-American families whose members are depicted in all of their intermediate stages of acculturation and economic advancement. Moreover, the series enjoys a distinct position: it is perhaps the definitive examination of the social basis of the emergent consciousness of an artist in the process of rebelling against the shackles of his lower-middle-class cultural heritage in order to redefine his own personality and objectives in Marxist terms.

Critics harshly accused Farrell of lacking a sophisticated literary technique, but Farrell never made excessive claims about his writing style. He stated that he wrote primarily from his unconscious, achieving characterization by intensely identifying with each of his fictional creations as he imaginatively recreated a world seen through their eyes. Although he admired the consummate craftsmanship of Henry James and James Joyce, he endeavored to achieve a "clear path" to his unconscious. Part of what Farrell meant was that he relied on his own imaginative resources in attempting to create the "body image" of each of his main characters. The notion of the "body image"— meaning the total sense of oneself, including the visceral—was assimilated by Farrell at the outset of his career from the Freudian psychiatrist Paul Schilder. Farrell saw a correlation between the work of Schilder and the views of William James, George Herbert Mead, and John Dewey, which argued that human character is a social product. This approach to fiction required an intimate knowledge of the thoughts, emotions, and social circumstances of one's characters; and this is part of the reason why the bulk, although not the entirety, of Farrell's work centers around the experiences of his family and acquaintances in familiar Chicago and New York environments. Even in those works in which an autobiographical persona, usually Danny O'Neill or Eddie Ryan, is not the main character, he sometimes appears in a cameo role as if to facilitate the process of empathizing with the other characters. (pp. 248-51)

Although there has been a steady revival of interest since 1975 in Farrell's life and writing, his greatest impact was and probably will always be linked to his multifaceted role as a radical novelist and activist during the Great Depression and World War II years. An indication of renewed interest in him came at the time of the publication of his fiftieth book, *The Dunne Family* (1976). In celebration of this literary milestone, a "Salute to James T. Farrell" was held at the St. Regis Hotel in New York City. Norman Mailer, one of several prominent novelists who addressed the gathering, stated that Farrell's works had modified the sensibility of many writers of his generation and that Farrell's relentlessness in pursuing his literary goals in spite of all adversity should be a model for others to follow. A second indication of a minor Farrell revival came on 7, 14, and 21 March 1979, when the National Broadcasting Company presented *Studs Lonigan* as a television miniseries that was seen by millions of viewers. Shortly afterward he received the Emerson-Thoreau award from the American Academy of Arts and Sciences.

But the brief spurt of interest in Farrell during the four years prior to his death will probably not alter his literary stature significantly. Three aspects of his work have been debated at length. While he was praised in the 1930s for his powers of observation and his bold use of American speech, he was accused early on of masquerading documentaries as novels and charged with being insufficiently selective in the experiences he depicted. In the 1940s some critics began to argue that he was a prisoner of the moribund school of naturalism; others claimed that he was a repetitious writer, clumsy, and devoid of grace and style.

The issue of Farrell's selectivity is a central one. Opinions range from that of Ann Douglas, who wrote in a eulogy that "Farrell's work constitutes the last important experiment to date in American literature with what can be viewed as deliberately unedited material," to that of Diana Trilling, who said that "the truth is that Farrell is a meticulous craftsman, choosing both incident and language with care and skill." Trilling's assessment is more accurate, but the corollary is that the care and skill of selection must be guided by a clear and compelling vision that establishes priorities in the relationships revealed. During the first phase of Farrell's development, when he was animated by a Marxist anger at the manner in which class relations impeded human development, his vision was vividly sustained and focused on precise objectives. However, in the years leading up to "A Universe of Time," Farrell's anger dissipated into stoicism: a new vision had to be developed that made demands for which his technique was not always fully prepared.

The claim that Farrell was a simple environmental determinist or a prisoner of the putatively dated school of naturalism has largely been discredited. Farrell himself criticized the limitations of the naturalist perspective as early as his 1936 *A Note on Literary Criticism:* at that time he linked naturalism to mechanical materialism and accused it of fostering an expansive rather than an intensive approach to art. In 1964 Edgar Branch, Farrell's most reliable critic, published a convincing essay, "Freedom and Determinism in James T. Farrell's Fiction." Branch demonstrated that Farrell's "functional conception of the self" in his fiction was one that exhibited "a full pattern of human conduct . . . that accommodates freedom." Branch's conclusion that Farrell is a "critical realist" seems apt.

Farrell's greatest weakness as a writer was that he failed to develop either sufficient consciousness about or a sophisticated theory of the uses of language in writing fiction beyond admirable but rather simple notions that language must serve the end of accurately recreating character and environment. There is no doubt that his heavy reliance on personal experience made Farrell's work appear redundant to many critics. In short, his prose failed to communicate to many readers the true diversity of the experiences he aspired to depict.

A famous man by the time he was thirty, Farrell's three decades from the mid-1940s to the mid-1970s witnessed a reversal of fortune; his survival as a writer became an ordeal. Hounded by censors in 1948 when Philadelphia police attempted to stop the sales of *Studs Lonigan,* sneered at by a herd of literary detractors, and harassed by publishers who did not find his books sufficiently marketable, he persisted in a curmudgeonly sort of rebellion and drifted into near obscurity. In the 1950s friends urged him to settle down to a teaching post, but he refused. Unwilling to let monetary considerations influence his writing and inhospitable to new cultural trends, he persisted in using his art idiosyncratically to tell the truth as he saw it. At one point he was evicted from his apartment for nonpayment of rent, and on another occasion financial desperation forced him to sell the movie rights to *Studs Lonigan* for a pittance. But he only became stronger in his belief that he must resist commercial forces. In 1961, at what was probably the nadir of his career, he publicly declared, "I began writing in my own way and I shall go on doing it. This is my first and last word on the subject."

Future biographers will have to probe the psychological causes and artistic consequences of such single-minded determination, but Farrell himself justified his defiant pursuit of his own literary objectives in terms of social value. Quoting from Tolstoy's *What Is Art?* (1897-98), he explained that the purpose of his writing technique is to "infect [the reader] with feeling" so as to awaken the reader's mind to the social forces at work in shaping one's life. "The most important thing that a person can do is teach," wrote Farrell at the outset of an essay, "The Value of Literature in Modern Society." Farrell's ability to sustain a loyal readership in spite of decades of aggressive assault by critics suggests that his endeavor to transform his personal experiences into art resounded in the emotions and intellects of a significant audience. (pp. 261-63)

> Alan M. Wald, "The New York Intellectuals in Fiction," in his The New York Intellectuals: The Rise and Decline of the Anti-Stalinist Left from the 1930s to the 1980s, *The University of North Carolina Press, 1987, pp. 226-63.*

POLITICAL PHILOSOPHY

TERRY A. COONEY

[*In the following excerpt, Cooney considers apparent contradictions in the political ideology of the New York Intellectuals as logical stages in their intellectual maturation.*]

Between the early 1930s and the end of the 1940s, a majority of the New York Intellectuals made the political trek from self-conscious radicalism to Cold War liberalism. The early positions—whether Communist, Trotskyist, or other—shared a faith in socialism and a harsh critique of capitalist society; the positions of the fifties had in common a sharp hostility to the Soviet Union and (in general and with qualifications) a positive attitude toward the United States of America. The shift was not a matter of sudden conversion but of gradual migration. Few in the *Partisan Review* circle fit the image of the transformed radical who became in the fifties a raging conservative or a professional ex-Communist. Many, in fact, demonstrated a considerable consistency in values and intellectual loyalties even as their attitudes toward American society underwent an apparent transformation. To stress this continuity is not to deny the political shift, but to suggest a context within which it can be better understood.

Some explanations would place the course taken by the New York Intellectuals within a very general pattern. Youth is idealistic and subject to fits of rebellion, a familiar argument holds, while age brings a greater acceptance of the world. Exile leads logically to return, rebellion to later acceptance. Such an explanation is not without its appeal, but the temptation to embrace this established model must be held at bay. The notion that rebellion is cured by age robs radicalism of its power and significance; an assumption that exile precedes integration saps the meaning from exclusion and isolation. In their very generality, moreover, such ideas fail to say much about specific historical situations or particular people; the pattern invites assertion: it does not encourage investigation.

Two other general explanations for the political shift in the *Partisan Review* camp point toward more substantial encounters with a distinct historical experience. One would underscore

Sidney Hook delivering a speech at a 1949 anticommunist rally. UPI/Bettmann Newsphotos.

the importance of national and international events, making shifts in political perspective a reasoned response to a changing world. The other would emphasize the acquisition of property and status, asserting that a capitalist America became increasingly attractive to writers on the make. Both of these explanations are too narrow in themselves, but each may reasonably contribute to a more complex account.

Between 1930 and 1945 young intellectuals were forced to confront a series of events that pushed and tugged at their ideas and values from several directions. The depression threatened frustration for a whole generation of young people trying to begin adult careers. Personal experience made it easy to believe that capitalism in general had failed, that the economic collapse represented the unraveling of a whole system. Those with a literary bent, already steeped in a critique of commercialism and business civilization, were particularly prone to adopt the language of radicalism to carry that critique to a new level and to celebrate the downfall of Babbittry. Individual and social ambitions, attraction to the explanatory power of Marxism, a humane response to the depression's effects, sensitivity to questions of prejudice and discrimination, and the values associated with literary sophistication all seemed to push young intellectuals toward the adoption of a radical political posture in the 1930s.

The rise of National Socialism in Germany pressed intellectuals to come to terms with a horrific politics and an ever more ominous series of events. At first fascism served only to strengthen the appeal of the left; yet Hitler stirred up sensitivities among the New York Intellectuals that ultimately contributed to the disintegration of their radicalism. Nazism helped create a heightened awareness at the first *Partisan Review* of attitudes, ideas, and values that the editors saw as regressive. The increasing use of terms associated with fascism to develop a critique of the Communist Party marked Phillips's and Rahv's pathway toward an anti-Stalinist position. Moreover, fascism drew attention to the dangers of a highly centralized and dictatorial government, to the dark possibilities of mass parties and movements, to the repressions of a closed system, in ways that could not ultimately flatter Stalin and the Soviet Union. Indeed, the regimes of Hitler and Stalin gradually came to be joined in the concept of totalitarianism. In moving toward greater acceptance of existing political arrangements in the United States, the New York Intellectuals were in part recognizing their own government's importance in resisting both Hitler and Stalin.

When *Partisan Review* turned against the Communist Party in 1937, it did not abandon radical politics but took up an independent radical position leaning heavily toward Trotsky—a position regarded at the time as a break to the left. Yet the example of the Soviet Union continued to weigh heavily on all radical thought, and for most of the New York Intellectuals the road to the left led back eventually toward the center. The Soviet example posed a number of difficult questions that many found it enervating even to consider. Was Soviet communism a natural and logical outcome of Marxism? Did the socialist vision necessarily point toward a "totalitarian" state? Did Stalinism make belief in the original promise of the Russian Revolution impossible? Were all ideological commitments dangerous? The *Partisan Review* intellectuals for the most part answered these questions in the negative before 1945, and some continued to do so thereafter, but the need to answer them at all revealed a radicalism on the defensive, drained of its positive energies. Interest in socialism simply began to "wither away," according to William Phillips, and gradually it came to be assumed "that the verdict of history was in—against socialism."

Partisan Review's hostility toward the Communist Party grew out of a cumulative experience. If the break in 1937 was not quite the example of fierce courage and pure principle that the legend upholds, it was an act that did require a considerable amount of nerve and one that was rooted in a solid allegiance to intellectual and cultural values. The Communist Party did indeed try to repress its opponents; it did make its cultural policies the tail on a political dog that changed directions regularly; it did demand that the actions of the Soviet Union be weighed on a different scale from those of other nations, if they were weighed at all. The *Partisan Review* intellectuals confronted the implications of the Moscow Trials and the Popular Front at a time when most writers on the left did not; they upheld the belief that critical thought must be directed toward all systems and ideas, even if their practice was imperfect. One need not defend the later tendency among many New York Intellectuals to press the anti-Stalinist campaign when Communist-baiting had become something of a national sport in order to believe that the migration away from Stalinism and toward greater acceptance of America was a reasonable and intellectually consistent response to domestic and international events.

It is possible, then, to explain *Partisan Review*'s course as a series of reactions to the momentous historical developments of its formative period. In considering the magazine within this context, arguments implying that its editors and supporters were more intelligent and virtuous at one time than another fall flat. The assumption that during their radical years the New York Intellectuals were truants or callow youths who came to their senses only when they got an early start on the Cold War carries no more weight than the belief that they were courageous and insightful radicals in the thirties who lost all integrity and judgment when they discovered substantial merit in the American system. An explanation from events suggests that it made about an equal amount of sense for the *Partisan Review* writers to embrace radicalism and to let it go, regardless of later feelings about those decisions. A similar conclusion might be reached after looking at the case for the influence of prosperity and status.

The argument that the New York Intellectuals turned away from radicalism when they began to prosper in the forties may carry a good deal of credibility. Who, after all, would deny the power of self-interest? And who would argue that prosperity and growing recognition are true friends of radicalism? The United States after 1940 was a country on its way toward a long economic boom. Although this future was not always obvious along the way, and although writers and intellectuals experienced no sudden rush to wealth, economic recovery and expansion opened up an ever wider set of opportunities that brought benefits trickling into the lives of most. The gains were hardly overwhelming by the standards that would be established in coming years, but then it did not take much to give someone who had been on the Federal Writers' Project a sense of greater well-being.

Money was seldom the direct measure of this growing success. Although Philip Rahv had married a woman of means in 1940, he was clearly delighted to be paid $125 a month to write a column for the *American Mercury* in 1943. Rahv had nothing against money, yet he probably treasured the recognition and the sense of an expanding cultural purview even more. The New York Intellectuals were beginning to be acknowledged for their work and employed to continue it. Academic jobs opened up for some in the forties: F. W. Dupee went permanently into university teaching; Delmore Schwartz did so fitfully; others, including William Phillips, had their hopes. Novels, stories, and poems appeared from many to whom the *Partisan Review* circle could lay some claim: Delmore Schwartz, Saul Bellow, Mary McCarthy, Elizabeth Hardwick, Isaac Rosenfeld, Paul Goodman, Harold Rosenberg, and even Lionel Trilling. Trilling was rapidly becoming a leading critic, and Alfred Kazin had made an impressive start with *On Native Grounds*. The New York Intellectuals during the forties were clearly beginning to benefit from the network they had created around *Partisan Review* as individual accomplishments and the successes of the magazine fed each other in a process that pushed ahead the whole group's reputation.

As a general proposition, then, it might be only reasonable to suggest that a trend toward increasing opportunity, recognition, and reward made it considerably easier for the New York Intellectuals to find something good about American society. Yet any attempt to tie this improving status to specific stages in the drift away from radicalism quickly runs into trouble. Such explanations also flounder when they imply a moral failing. If a responsiveness to economic pressures, an alertness to professional opportunities, and a pattern of changing political views add up to a moral failing, then such a failing existed at the time the New York group took up radical politics as much as at the time their radicalism weakened.

Either an explanation from events or an explanation from self-interest can tell only part of the story behind *Partisan Review*'s changing attitude toward American society. Both explanations assume too narrow a range of human motivation, and neither gives sufficient attention to particular ideas and values. For the *Partisan Review* circle, the conception of themselves as intellectuals mattered a great deal. Ideas were important to them. If they were sometimes subject to intellectual fads, if they felt the breezes of international politics and tasted the first fruits of a ripening success, they did not cast aside their basic values in a headlong rush toward the attractions of the moment. The more significant changes in attitude that did occur had to be justified, at least to themselves, in terms consistent with on-going commitments and loyalties. This was true for the break with the Communist Party in 1937, and it was true for the increasing receptiveness toward America in the 1940s.

The nature of *Partisan Review*'s early critique of American culture deserves another look. Harsh words were directed toward what the United States presently was, not toward its inherent potential. Even before 1937, Phillips and Rahv had found reason for optimism in American conditions; and despite a sincere radicalism, many of *Partisan Review*'s complaints rested on values and goals that were not inherently radical. American culture was attacked in the 1930s because it was parochial, because it carried a strong strain of nativism, because it seemed limited by a rural mentality, because it was hostile to ideas; in short, because it did not measure up at all well by cosmopolitan standards. The vision of an integrated society welcoming diversity and encouraging a sophisticated art was the goal embodied in the idea of synthesis, and it provided an effective critical platform. But there was, from the start, plenty of room short of that goal for the image of a parochial American society to change. When in the early 1940s America began to look better to the New York Intellectuals, it was not simply because their viewpoint was changing but because the national culture was changing as well.

Daniel Aaron has written that "The Jewish intellectual's disenchantment with the Soviets . . . happened to coincide with a small but perceptible lessening of discriminatory practices and the opening of opportunities in letters, the arts, and education." Just at the time the *Partisan Review* intellectuals were losing any solid base in a radical movement, in other words, American society was moving slowly toward that tolerance of ethnic diversity which was basic to cosmopolitanism. Few could have anticipated the scope of the changes that would come. The decline in discrimination began at a time when anti-Semitism was highly visible in its most virulent forms, and the widespread collapse of that prejudice in the post-war period was, as John Higham has noted, "totally unforeseen by the social science of the 1940s and 1950s." Yet Higham has pointed out as well that anti-Semitic agitation from the late thirties on was "more than counter-balanced by the rise of the broadest, most powerful movement for ethnic democracy in American history." Jewish intellectuals were a part of this movement, and they knew they were not alone in opposing discrimination. No one would have claimed that a full acceptance of diversity had arrived, but cosmopolitan values did seem to be gaining strength in American culture.

The changing ethos in many universities required the New York Intellectuals to modify one of the favorite negative presumptions of the literary radical tradition—the prejudice against the academic. The "academic" had generally been associated with writing that was by definition dry and dull, that failed to engage the vital ideas of the present, and that was unbearably conservative either by intent or through lack of imagination. In the first *Partisan Review,* Phillips and Rahv had spoken of academic writing as "not so much a quality of style as a content marginal to important literary problems: a pedantic treatment of minor ideas with the emphasis placed on 'data' rather than on analysis." Moreover, the academy had seemed a bastion of genteel parochialism.

Change came to academia in the 1940s for many reasons. A generation of immigrant children was coming to full intellectual maturity. World War II played havoc with the normal enrollments, courses, and student bodies at many universities. In the postwar period veterans' benefits and other forces fed a major expansion of higher education, opening up jobs for a wider range of faculty in an increasing number of specialties. As many of the New York Intellectuals began to gravitate toward the universities, they not only helped to change the academic environment by their presence but also learned through direct contact that all was not as bleak as it had seemed. Irving Howe later remarked that the group had "discovered that scholarship could have a value and dignity of its own, and that if there were professors—good lord, plenty of them!—as small-minded and arid as we had supposed, others really cared about ideas and possessed a quiet learning that made our own absorption in the contemporary seem provincial." As the universities came to seem more diverse and enlightened, the idea that American culture was dominated by a parochial tradition had to give way at the very least to a more complex view. There was room in America, it seemed, for intellectual sophistication and variety. How else could the New York Intellectuals explain their own growing success, or that of *Partisan Review?*

American society also gained credibility simply by surviving depression and war roughly intact. That was not what radical doctrine had predicted. Capitalism was supposed to die in the depression; governments were expected to fall; a capitalist democracy could not fight a war against fascism without becoming fascist itself. As such predictions fell flat, radicalism seemed increasingly tired, unable to generate a significant body of work in either literature or social thought. Even those who continued to call themselves radicals found it hard to deny that American society had demonstrated an unexpected vitality.

The increased consciousness of civil liberties brought about by Hitler and Stalin did much to alter *Partisan Review*'s negative judgment of American conditions. True socialism, as the New York Intellectuals understood it, promised an invigoration of intellectual life, an opening up of culture to a larger audience, and the free circulation of ideas. Stalinism had demonstrated how thoroughly this vision could be corrupted and how easily cultural life could be restricted in the name of radicalism. Hitler, meanwhile, had brought under attack some of the most basic values of modern thought and demonstrated the consequences that a denial of civil liberties might have, especially for Jews. Having assumed from the start the desirability and the prevalence of civil liberties and rational public discussion, the New York Intellectuals were forced by the late 1930s to conclude that such things were hardly secure. The same American society that had seemed a corrupting environment for intellectual life in the early thirties was beginning to look like the best the world had to offer a decade later. Despite a marked sensitivity around *Partisan Review* to restrictions on speech or political opinion during World War II, what seemed most impressive over time was that the United States went through the war with liberties largely preserved.

Philip Rahv observed after the war that "in America we are in an especially favorable position" to oppose the antics of reactionaries, "since the American concept of nationality is built on political rather than on ethnic or religious foundations." Like Randolph Bourne, Rahv apparently believed that cultural and political loyalties could be separated, and he wished to emphasize the virtues of a concept of nationality "political to the core." In the American case, this seemed a guarantee of diversity. The sense of a provincial, nativist cultural tradition suffocating intellectual life had been substantially modified in Rahv's view.

Behind Rahv's cautiously positive evaluation of the American scene lay a whole set of changing conditions that made not only the national setting but also the immediate cultural prospects more attractive to the New York Intellectuals. some of these changes were difficult to measure or define in precise terms, but they were nevertheless clearly felt. Irving Howe has recalled, for instance, that during the forties there was "a change of style and tone in the life of the New York middle class. . . . Culture was coming into fashion as a sign of a more comfortable and refined mode of living." The New York Intellectuals told themselves as well that the prestige of business had been dealt a serious (not crippling) blow by the depression, allowing a greater variety of influences to have some impact. Echoes of a notion that cultural power would accompany American political power after the war also surfaced occasionally in *Partisan Review,* providing additional, if vague, reason for optimism about the future of intellectuals in America.

The New York Intellectuals were themselves making a respectable contribution to a longterm shift in the cultural climate. Under way since the late nineteenth century, the gradual American growth from provincialism toward equivalency with European cultures reached fruition in the 1940s. William Phillips recognized the trend shortly after the birth of *Partisan Review* when he acknowledged the "cosmopolitanization" of American culture achieved in the 1920s. Rahv and Phillips sought to continue the process when they urged "Europeanization" in the mid-1930s. *Partisan Review* promoted in particular the ideas of Marx and Freud, the works of modern literature, an interest in European politics, and a consciousness of postwar movements, including existentialism. The New York Intellectuals helped to create an awareness of European ideas in America just as they brought American intellectual life to the attention of Europeans.

Even as the *Partisan Review* circle was doing its bit to make American culture more cosmopolitan, major forces were at work toward the same end. Thanks primarily to Hitler, a remarkable flood of scientists, artists, musicians, philosophers, writers, and political theorists crossed the Atlantic to enrich the life of the new world. H. Stuart Hughes has called this migration "the most important cultural event—or series of events—of the second quarter of the twentieth century"; it produced a "shift in intellectual weight that made the former pattern of deference toward the Old World no longer necessary or appropriate." Two-thirds of the intellectual migrants were Jewish. The United States was serving as a haven for a European intellectual elite, and in the process American culture was gaining that equivalency with Europe that had long been a dream. The New York Intellectuals were far from insensitive to such changes.

Indeed, the increasing intellectual prominence of America was concentrated and even exaggerated for many members of the *Partisan Review* circle by the transformations in their immediate environment. Generally preoccupied with New York and convinced that the city represented the American cultural future, they gave singular attention to New York's status in national and world affairs. Already a city of international significance, New York grew in stature in the 1940s both because of domestic trends and because of the influx of intellectual immigrants. Yet what changed New York's *international* position most dramatically was the crippling of European centers by the war. New York seemed to shine more brightly as the lights of its rivals were obscured.

In commentaries on the fate of European culture, Paris received special attention. Paris was "the 'eye' of modern European civilization," the editorial column of *Partisan Review* noted in 1939. Central to developments in politics as well as in the arts for more than a century, Paris was "the expression of the best integrated culture of modern times," a culture now under serious threat. A year and half later, Paris had indeed fallen to fascism. Harold Rosenberg gave vivid expression to the sense of intellectual loss in the opening sentence of his obituary essay: "The laboratory of the twentieth century has been shut down." The culture of Paris had been international, and Rosenberg proclaimed its contribution in emphatically cosmopolitan terms: "Because Paris was the opposite of the national in art, the art of every nation increased through Paris. No folk lost its integrity there; on the contrary, its artists, renewed by this magnanimous milieu, discovered in the depths of themselves what was most alive in the communities from which they had come." Paris had seemed to embody the intellectual and cultural values most precious to the New York Intellectuals, and its loss added to the feeling at the dawn of the forties that the best traditions of Western civilization were under siege.

But was there not a ray of hope? Might not another city play the role in the future that Paris had played in the past? Rosenberg was cautious in declaring at the end of his essay, "No one can predict which city or nation will be the center of this new phase"; yet the effect of this statement was to focus attention exactly on the question of what new center of cultural and political ideas might arise. Rosenberg's analysis seemed to offer clues. Paris had risen "not because of its affirmative genius alone, but perhaps, on the contrary, through its passivity, which allowed it to be possessed by the searchers of every nation." (In what country was there a city relatively free of an oppressive national tradition and possessed by peoples of many lands?) Again, Rosenberg insisted that an international center could not rise "by its own genius alone" but only as a result of "currents flowing throughout the world." (And where were such powerful currents depositing migratory intellectuals in the 1940s?) Rosenberg spoke directly only once. From the anti-Stalinist viewpoint, the response of the "Paris Left" to the events of the late 1930s had demonstrated an abandonment of intellectual principles. It was in another country that the best traditions of modern intellectual life had been upheld: "during the Moscow Trials we learned with surprise and alarm that it was here, in America! that the greatest opposition to the criminal burlesque was being voiced." Rosenberg's analysis seemed to suggest on each of these points that Paris might well be replaced as the leading center of intellectual life in the West by his own New York—New York, which had long been open to the people of many nations and subject to their influence; New York, which was a magnet for Europe's intellectual refugees; New York, which had led the opposition to the Moscow Trials.

The New York Intellectuals' "surprise" that France should fail the intellectual tests of the thirties and that America should

pass them suggested a repetition in the *Partisan Review* circle of what was becoming a familiar pattern. Writers of the twenties, in going to Europe, had often discovered America. So too, the New York Intellectuals, in their attentiveness to European cultural developments, found that America measured up surprisingly well. At a personal level, contact with European intellectuals who came to New York tended not only to boost the confidence of the *Partisan Review* circle but also to remind its members, through differences of manners and tastes, of just how American they were. When after the war some of the younger New York Intellectuals began to go to Europe for extended visits, testimony on the surprising discovery in oneself of a strong American identity, sparking a new interest in American culture, became a common form.

In trying to explain the development of a more positive attitude toward American society and culture among the New York Intellectuals, then, movements occurring on two fronts must be kept in mind. Many intellectuals were shifting around in their views of the American environment; the environment was also changing and moving in a direction that made it more attractive to the *Partisan Review* circle. The two processes were intertwined and mutually reinforcing. Sharply conscious of "the sudden emergence of America as the repository of Western culture in a world overrun by Fascism," the New York Intellectuals harkened well to the appeal of what Alfred Kazin called in 1942 "the pride of helping to breed a new cosmopolitan culture."

By no means all of the New York Intellectuals rushed to embrace America in the 1940s, but many were increasingly ready to see the United States as the chief defender of the cultural traditions they treasured and as the strongest proponent of those civil liberties on which freedom of thought must rest. New York—their city—had become the center of American culture, and it seemed for a moment to be just possibly the next great center of Western civilization. This did not mean that the old literary radical dream of a sophisticated and well-integrated culture had come to pass, but it did mean that the dream was passing. The growing belief that American culture had gained equivalency in the contemporary world with the cultures of Europe, and the evidence that a cosmopolitan society was now emerging, took much of the edge off a vigorous tradition of cultural complaint.

The conditions of the 1940s that had given New York its special prominence proved in time to be a passing thing. European cities recovered from the world and re-established their cultural importance, though none could claim the dominance of an earlier Paris. Within the United States institutions of learning and the arts flourished in a number of cities, bringing about a decentralization of high culture over a period of two or three decades. The New York Intellectuals themselves were a part of this process. Though many clung to familiar turf, others heeded the call of universities and migrated North and West. The national and international forces that had helped to create the New York of the forties later worked to diminish that city's supremacy.

As the patterns growing out of World War II gradually broke down the physical unity of the New York Intellectuals, the political and cultural issues of the postwar period led to division of another kind. Continuing agreement on opposition to Stalinism and the Soviet Union meant less and less once those attitudes had become the norm. The New York camp found itself more and more divided over just how eagerly Cold War policies should be embraced, over just how far the critique of liberalism should go, and especially over just how much of a threat domestic communism posed. These later divisions make the early to middle forties a time in between. The New York Intellectuals were carrying on a balancing act in these years. Still very much attached to ideas and values brought with them out of the thirties, they were nevertheless aware of new possibilities. Having been in their own eyes an embattled minority, they were on their way to becoming in the eyes of others an "establishment." It was a time when tensions and ambiguities in the outlook of the New York Intellectuals ripened within forms both old and new.

The need to balance ideas and loyalties that were not in natural harmony had been evident from the first. The young *Partisan Review* intellectuals sought to combine within some broader vision a commitment to a sophisticated literature and an interest in radical politics; a loyalty to rational, scientific thought and a belief in the powers of artistic insight; a sense of themselves as Jews (in the majority of cases) and an identity as Americans. Though the balancing of such ideas went on with varying degrees of success, claims of synthesis achieved did not dominate their thought so much as consciousness of the oppositions in art and experience. This was true of the mature criticism of the New York Intellectuals as much as it was true of their youth, and it applied whether the discussion was of doubling or the dialectic, of repression or negation. In the forties, as new wine began to mingle with old among the New York Intellectuals, some of the vessels designed to balance the ferment of ideas proved supple and equal to the task; others began to split at the seams.

One of the most successful devices for the containment of opposing ideas was the concept of alienation. The idea offered sweeping explanatory powers: alienation provided a general theory purporting to deal with great chunks of modern experience, and at the same time it invited application to the details of individual existence. In the New York camp, it furnished an umbrella under which discussion from either a Marxist or a Freudian perspective might take place, probably blurring the lines between them and allowing some to migrate more easily from one to the other. Both society and art could be discussed in the language of alienation, preserving the belief that politics and literature could be dealt with from a unified perspective. Discussions of alienation might be hard-headed and rationalistic in tone, or they might involve a rather romantic treatment of the loneliness of the modern artist. Alienation allowed New York writers to indulge both the penchant for finding world-historical significance in their own experience and the taste for abstract theoretical debate. The concept of alienation seemed to provide the New York Intellectuals with both power and flexibility in ideas, the combination they had consistently sought.

That was not the end of it. With its claim that existing institutions had not earned the intellectual's support—indeed, had pushed him away—the idea of alienation provided a ready justification for standing apart. The writer could declare himself alienated from America, from Jewish culture, from the war, or from radical politics with equal facility, using the concept as selectively as he wished. Yet the whole idea suggested not some simple escape but a conscious effort to come to grips with problems of both politics and culture. To call oneself "alienated" was to suggest a heightened awareness, to imply a sophisticated analysis of one's social and intellectual position that was the first step toward solving the problems that had created alienation. The alienated were thus superior to the well-adjusted; they could even be an intellectual elite

and a cultural avant-garde. By the 1940s, for the most part, the New York Intellectuals had given up the notion that the moment for radical synthesis was at hand; but through the concept of alienation, they continued not just to condemn the inadequacies of established society but to make the implicit claim that the future belonged to them.

Alienation, as the idea was used by the New York Intellectuals, was not the same thing as true isolation from society or total rejection of it. The alienated could live neither with existing culture nor without it. This relationship of awkward dependency lay at the root of Isaac Rosenfeld's lovely paradoxes: the outsider was sometimes the "perfect insider," and alienation from society could function "as a condition of entrance into society." Like the claims of writers in the 1920s that they were a lost generation, the declarations by the New York Intellectuals that they were alienated represented both a serious idea and a conscious pose. The language of alienation allowed the New York Intellectuals to have it both ways: they could continue to think of themselves as outsiders and radicals even as they began to experience intellectual, political, and economic integration into American society. It was not at all clear in the 1940s whether this integrating process would continue; the concept of alienation helped the New York Intellectuals maintain a certain distance in a period of flux and kept their options open.

Even in the heyday of alienation, what remained basic to many of the New York Intellectuals' judgments were those cosmopolitan values that had also stood behind their Marxism in the thirties. (The writer was alienated in part because the society fell short of the cosmopolitan community that would make him feel at home.) This cosmopolitan perspective continued to give the New York Intellectuals some sense of common values and some of their critical bite. Yet the years of hot and cold war revealed limitations as well as strengths—weaknesses in the cosmopolitan viewpoint itself and in the New York Intellectuals' ability to abide by its tenets.

Tension between principle and practice emerged, for example, over matters of intellectual and political tolerance. Cosmopolitanism assumed a context within which a free exchange of ideas was the norm; and *Partisan Review* had generally defended the principles of openness and diversity, first within the Communist Party and later against the repressive tendencies of both fascism and Stalinism. Even as the editors of *Partisan Review* split over the proper attitude to take toward World War II, they were able to agree that the magazine's main task must be "to preserve cultural values against all types of pressure and coercion," which meant a defense of "the fullest freedom of expression on political matters."

Yet there was a contrary pattern as well. In their actual political commitments and in their stance toward opponents of varying stripes, the New York Intellectuals often revealed an outlook not so much pluralistic as Manichean. They seemed happiest when presenting political issues as a struggle between the forces of light and the forces of darkness. Before 1937 *Partisan Review* divided the world primarily between radicalism and reaction. In the late 1930s, the forces of light dwindled to the limited circle of the anti-Stalinist left. During the war—or afterward for some—the United States became the chief defender of political good, and evil was increasingly embodied in a Janus-faced totalitarianism looking to both right and left. The emphatic, emotionally charged, often moralistic positions that the New York Intellectuals established, and the tendency to identify their own views with fundamental intellectual in-

Hannah Arendt in 1954. AP/Wide World Photos.

tegrity, worked against the commitment to openness and free thought proclaimed in their public statements and implicit in their attachment to cosmopolitan values.

The multiple pressures of the early 1940s pushed to the fore a growing contradiction in the way the New York Intellectuals saw themselves. The pages of *Partisan Review* tended to convey an image of rebel intellectuals defending a minority position and upholding the best traditions of radicalism. In 1942 the editors launched a column called "Dangerous Thoughts" with the presumption that an open intellectual forum would, in itself, help to sustain "democratic civilization" and threaten repressive power. In 1944 Philip Rahv put the magazine on the side of "cultural bolshevism" and reminded readers of its opposition to the "world-wide campaign . . . against all cultural forms of dissidence and experiment." The New York Intellectuals continued in the 1940s to see themselves as dissenters and to emphasize the importance of a wide latitude for ideas. Yet this same group had begun to convey a different message based on a different self-perception. Unrelenting in their opposition to the Communist Party and its liberal sympathizers, the New York Intellectuals moved in the 1940s toward ever fiercer condemnation. Angered by the news of Trotsky's death in 1940, William Phillips wrote that "some kind of moral and intellectual pogrom should be started against the Stalinists." Philip Rahv suggested in mid-war that a particular opponent was "really getting out of bounds and should be stepped on." Sidney Hook called in 1945 for *Partisan Review* to "meet the challenge of Stalinist totalitarianism head-on and plan for concentrated fire in each issue on some phase or other of the theme." None of these remarks clearly called for repressive measures, and all might be individually explained as

demands for a kind of vigorous intellectual attack not incompatible with the notion of full and free expression; yet such comments reflected a desire not simply to refute opponents but to discipline and subdue them that had little to do with cosmopolitan tolerance.

The language of pogroms and concentrated fire did not suggest activities to be undertaken by a dissident minority but the campaigns of a group with considerable intellectual power. Even as they cultivated the image of radical dissenters, some in the *Partisan Review* circle were beginning to feel their oats and to enjoy the fact that in their relations with the Stalinist intellectuals, they were now on top. The tensions between a pluralistic and a dualistic view of politics, between a belief in tolerance and a desire to push political opponents beyond the pale, and between the image of themselves as a rebellious minority and the willingness to speak like cultural and political enforcers testified to the difficulties the New York Intellectuals met in trying to maintain a coherent intellectual position against the corroding effects of their own illiberal impulses. Values consistent with cosmopolitanism remained dominant in the war years, but evidence was already appearing that the language of diversity, free expression, and tolerance might all too easily survive while the spirit behind it decayed. When the defense of an open society began to grow for some into a rationale for repression, cosmopolitan values were being perverted, not fulfilled.

The New York Intellectuals fell short of their own ideal in another sphere as well. Secure in the worldiness and breadth of their own urban perspective, members of the *Partisan Review* circle remained largely insensitive to the possibility that they were nourishing a parochialism of their own. Quick to condemn the narrowness of other American viewpoints, they refused to credit the evidence that New York for all its varied life was a province with its own limitations. Attacks on *Partisan Review* and its supporters—whether launched by midwestern radicals in the thirties or rival literary critics in the forties—were often exaggerated and unfair, but they were usually rooted in a legitimate resentment of the New Yorkers' assumption that they held a monopoly on intellectual sophistication. If the attitude of the New York Intellectuals mellowed with time and their own dispersion, the feelings expressed all too vigorously by Philip Rahv in the early 1940s never quite went away:

> If you lived in Chicago for a while you'd realize the importance of PR: it's like an island of culture in an ocean of barbarism. In New York our friends no less than we tend to take the magazine too much for granted; once, however, you step out of the charmed circle it comes to you as a revelation that this little magazine is in fact the only decent organ of American writing today. (And don't tell me about the *Kenyon Review* and the *Southern Review*!)

This extravagant assertion had little in common with a spirit of cultural openness and receptivity.

It was not merely that on this occasion or that one the New York Intellectuals failed to show respect for ideas and traditions running counter to their own. It was not simply that they sometimes fell short of the cosmopolitan ideal. Rather, they had a blind spot, a deep-seated prejudice, built into their very notion of cosmpolitanism. And in this case the problem was not theirs alone but part of a whole inheritance. The assumption that rural America and its traditions were hostile to intelligence, rationality, and sophistication had become a critical commonplace by the nineteen twenties, just in time for the older New York Intellectuals to imbibe it with their first long draught of literary ale. In the thirties, the sense of a great gulf between the urban and the rural intensified within the *Partisan Review* camp: the rural was now associated with nativism, anti-Semitism, nationalism, and fascism as well as with anti-intellectualism and provincialism; the urban was associated antithetically with ethnic and cultural tolerance, with internationalism, and with advanced ideas. New York as the largest city, the most open and diverse, was presumed to be the most distant from rural norms. The New York Intellectuals simply *began* with the assumption that the rural—with which they associated much of American tradition and most of the territory beyond New York—had little to contribute to a cosmopolitan culture.

Such a view closed the minds of the *Partisan Review* circle on too many questions and cut off that searching inquiry and rich borrowing of ideas that should have been a cosmopolitan strength. The New York Intellectuals, for example, could never get past their negative assumptions about the native radical tradition in order to see it clearly; because it was rural, it simply must be narrow and reactionary. It was no accident that members of the New York group later associated McCarthyism with populism in the expectation that each would discredit the other. Populism meant rural anti-intellectualism and nativist prejudice to *Partisan Review* from the beginning, and those things were what many feared in McCarthyism. Though they might disagree emphatically over the need for a domestic security campaign in the early 1950s, few of the New York Intellectuals were immune to the pleasures of distinguishing between their own sophisticated anti-communism and the crude rural variety of McCarthy and his kind. Defining the issues in this way reaffirmed standing cultural assumptions. At the same time, it provided a convenient shelter within which a good many intellectuals could avoid reconsideration of their own attacks on "totalitarian liberals" and the like. By interpreting cultural and political issues through the urban-rural lens, writers could even mask assertions of superiority and expressions of anti-democratic sentiments as the judgments of an objective expertise. Invidious distinctions between urban and rural were so familiar to a wide intellectual audience that few questioned them or challenged their implications.

If there were failures to fulfill the ideals of tolerance, openness, and full inquiry, there was also a weakness at the heart of cosmopolitan theory. The notion of a cosmopolitan culture assumed that it would be continually enriched by contributions from people of different national and ethnic traditions. When Randolph Bourne was writing about trans-nationalism and when *Partisan Review* was getting under way in the thirties, there seemed little reason to doubt the existence or the strength of multiple cultures within the United States. In the years following World War II, however, after two or three decades with immigration much reduced and assimilation proceeding apace, the question could be asked of those taking a cosmopolitan position: what will preserve the ongoing vitality of those particularistic cultures on which cosmopolitanism draws? The New York Intellectuals were vulnerable on this point when it came to discussions of Jewish identiy in the 1940s. The position defined by Bourne had tried to stake out a territory between assimilation and cultural pluralism; yet in the absence of strong ethnic enclaves, a cosmopolitan position would rapidly become the equivalent of an assimilationist stance, leading toward that drabness and lack of variety that Bourne abhorred. It gradually became apparent in the potwar period that, as an understanding of the place of ethnicity, the cosmopolitanism of the New York

Intellectuals could remain viable only if a good many people rejected it.

For all that can be said about the limitations of the New York Intellectual brand of cosmopolitanism—whether those limitations were inherent in the perspective itself or products of an imperfect application of it—the ideas that came out of the *Partisan Review* circle formed one of the richer patterns in American culture during the late 1930s and the 1940s. There was a spirit of serious intellectual aspiration around the magazine that refused to be stifled, and there was serious accomplishment. If the editors and their associates sometimes fell short of their own ideals, they also managed to embody those ideals and to give them life in one campaign after another. The values of cosmopolitanism were generous ones, and ones to which the *Partisan Review* intellectuals clung with more than cutomary consistency and integrity. In their finer moments, they stood as an American presence speaking out against narrowness, confinement, dogma, and fraud. And it was especially at such moments that they gave substance and meaning to the fundamental impulses of the cosmopolitan vision. (pp. 251-69)

> Terry A. Cooney, "A Tolerable Place to Live," in his The Rise of the New York Intellectuals: "Partisan Review" and Its Circle, *The University of Wisconsin Press, 1986, pp. 251-69.*

RUSSELL JACOBY

[*Jacoby is an American historian and the author of several studies of twentieth-century Western thought. In the following excerpt from one such study,* The Last Intellectuals, *he views the conservatism of many New York Intellectuals as a manifestation of the acceptance of intellectuals as a distinct class in American society.*]

The [New York Intellectuals] receive, and deserve, attention for several reasons. As the last public intellectuals they loom large in the cultural firmament. They have viewed from outside, as their successors could not, the professionalization of cultural life; and perhaps because of their origins as free-lance authors, their writings often shine. They write to be read. Many continue to play active roles in letters and politics. They have presided over the intellectual scene for decades.

Moreover, they largely defined a cultural politics that not only has survived relatively intact but in the recent period has dominated American letters. It is often forgotten that the "neoconservatism" of the 1980s is a restatement, frequently by the same figures, of the conservatism of the 1950s. "By now the 'new conservatism' is an old story." This statement—made [by Richard Chase] three decades ago—indicates the conservative continuity through the entire postwar period. To be sure this conservatism was, and to some degree is, "liberal"; its architects were generally former radicals with lingering commitments to reform. Moreover, pure conservatism never acquired deep roots in the United States—a point Trilling made in his *The Liberal Imagination.* Nevertheless, this liberal conservatism has structured American culture since the war.

The success and presence of fifties intellectuals through the eighties is not simply due to their genius. After ebbing in the 1960s, some realities of the 1950s, especially a cold war ethos and anticommunism, revived and sparked interest in the original cultural script and cast. It is also due to something else. Few younger intellectuals have arisen to challenge the old guard. The visibility of last generation intellectuals reflects the absence of new public thinkers. With little to measure it against, the work of fifties intellectuals may appear more impressive than it actually was or is. A study that is unsparing toward young intellectuals must be equally unsentimental about the elders.

Even a cursory survey of these elders reveals that they were not a random collection of intellectuals. Rather, in the 1950s New Yorkers and Jews commanded the cultural heights, and often defined the terms and scope of debate. Any study of recent American intellectuals must assess the New York and Jewish contributions. Typically these studies emphasize the immigrant roots, Marxism, brilliance, and versatility of the New York intellectuals. Yet a fresh scrutiny partially revises conventional wisdom. The talent and vigor of the New York and Jewish intellectuals cannot be challenged. In retrospect, however, their radicalism seems shaky, and their accomplishments not small, but smaller than supposed. (pp. 76-8)

In plotting cultural life often the less original thinkers register most faithfully the zeitgeist. In his evolution and politics, Norman Podhoretz exemplifies the trajectory of New York Jewish intellectuals. Like the others, he was first of all a publicist—a journalist, a book reviewer, and an essayist who wrote well and easily. He established a voice and a presence. From the back cover of his first book, *Doings and Undoings,* the young Podhoretz stares out, tie loosened, eyes squinting, cigarette dangling—someone to be reckoned with. He is described as "the most brilliant young critic of our day."

From the first, as well, he spelled out a conservatism that he only once lost sight of. In 1957 a twenty-seven-year-old Podhoretz touted the mature life against revolution and bohemia. "On the whole," he proclaimed, postwar America offered "a reasonably decent environment for the intellectual." This situation required a new intellectual garb since "the old style of 'alienation,' represented by commitment to the ideal of Revolution and an apartment in Greenwich Village" smacked of the 1930s. The 1950s called for a "new style of 'maturity,'" that assumed "the real adventure of existence was to be found not in radical politics or in Bohemia but in the 'moral life' of the individual . . . in a world of adults."

For Podhoretz "the trick" was to "stop carping at life like a petulant adolescent" and get "down to the business of adult living as quickly as possible." This was not "conformity" but the realization that "the finest and deepest possibilities" of life could be found "*within* 'bourgeois' society."

Twenty-five years later, after a short detour opposing bougeois society, or at least the war in Vietnam (a fact he no longer remembers), Podhoretz repeats his old wisdom. In almost the same words from decades earlier—although somewhat more hysterically—he advises his son in an afterword to his memoir *Breaking Ranks* that radicalism constitutes "a refusal . . . to assume responsibility . . . in a world of adults." It is a "contemptuous repudiation of everything American and middle-class." Of course, Podhoretz has learned some things in the intervening years. He warns his son of a "spiritual plague," coursing through the nation's bloodstream, which attacks "the vital organs of the entire species, preventing men from fathering children and women from mothering them." To be adult, he tells his son, is to be a father. "There can be no abdication of responsibility more fundamental than the refusal of a man to become, and to be, a father, or the refusal of a woman to become, and be, a mother."

Podhoretz personifies the continuity of a conservatism—or a new conservatism or a liberal conservatism—through the post-war decades. Of course, he does not represent all New York Jewish intellectuals, but he is hardly an isolated or rare case. Yet according to standard interpretations, Jews as political radicals are "over-represented" in cultural and social life; an impoverished immigrant people with a vast pride and love of culture, they naturally rebelled against discrimination and injustice.

"The Jewish contribution to the Left in the United States during the twentieth century," begins a book on Jewish radicalism, "ranks the highest of any immigrant or ethnic group. . . . American Jewry has provided socialist organizations and movements with a disproportionate number—sometimes approaching or surpassing a majority—of their leaders, activists, and supporters." Another study demonstrates that Jewish predominance continued into the New Left, especially in its early stages: Jews, 3 percent of the United States population, constituted a majority of the New Left's membership and its leaders.

This seems true enough. Yet the familiarity with this proposition undermines a dispassionate evaluation of its validity for New York intellectuals. An overview of many New York and non-New York careers suggests not a flat refutation but a critical revision. "In 1972 alone," states a study of American conservatism, "[Nathan] Glazer, Sidney Hook, Lewis Feuer and Seymour Martin Lipset appeared in [the conservative] *National Review*. What did these men have in common? None had been previously known as a conservative. All were Jewish. Three (Glazer, Feuer, and Lipset) had been at Berkeley (birthplace of the student revolution) early in the 1960s. . . . Perhaps most interesting was the fact that all had at one time been 'radical.'"

If Jewish intellectuals gravitated toward radicalism in large numbers, they also hastily beat a retreat. By the 1950s not simply Glazer, Hook, Feuer, and Lipset but Irving Kristol, Lionel Trilling, Daniel Bell, Leslie Fiedler, and scores of others traded in their red pasts for blue chip careers. In contrast non-Jewish (and usually non-New York) intellectuals seemed more willing or able to retain radicalism throughout their careers.

Generalizations of this type are vulnerable to a series of convincing objections. It would be easy to list non-Jews who rapidly abandoned their radicalism. Moreover, all intellectuals responded to the dominant political and social realities: not ethnic peculiarities but historical events drove intellectuals from the earlier ramparts. Irving Howe underlines the disillusionment with communism, the impact of McCarthyism, and the prosperity of the postwar period—plus simple aging—to explain the growing conservatism of Jewish intellectuals. This cannot be denied.

Nevertheless, the chart of the larger currents should not neglect the smaller eddies, which are critical precisely because they sustain a sometimes rare species, the American radical; and these eddies seem tinted by ethnic or religious hues. Again, this is a delicate and elusive matter, which, of course, is no reason to avoid it.

The long view suggests not how many, but, compared to the non-Jews, how few Jewish intellectuals remained radicals and dissenters. This could almost be seen in pairs of kindred Jewish and non-Jewish intellectuals: Lionel Trilling (1905-75) and Dwight Macdonald (1906-82); Daniel Bell (1919-) and C. Wright Mills (1916-62); Norman Podhoretz (1930-) and Michael Harrington (1928-). Other non-Jews could be added: Edmund Wilson, Gore Vidal, Paul Sweezy, John Kenneth Galbraith, Christopher Lasch. But the list of Jewish public intellectuals who remained devoted to a radical vision seems shorter.

Scenes from the 1960s: Lewis Feuer, a professor at Berkeley and once a New York socialist, glimpses the end of civilization in the Berkeley campus protest. He describes the student movement as a magnet for "the morally corrupt," those advocating "a melange of narcotics, sexual perversion, collegiate Castroism." Feuer never recovers from the fright. On the other coast three students, one carrying a can of beer, are applauded after berating a faculty meeting at New York University. A scandalized Sidney Hook, once a Marxist, calls the event "the most shocking experiences in my life." Meanwhile, uptown Dwight Macdonald wanders around Columbia University and concludes that the student disturbances are a justifiable response to an intolerable situation. He and his wife befriend many student radicals.

Is this typical, the New York Jewish intellectual denouncing youthful radicalism while the non-Jewish counterpart offers sympathy? Is it possible that Jewish intellectuals visited radicalism, while more non-Jewish intellectuals stayed the winter? Is it possible that a solid American background provided more sustenance for the long haul than the immigrant past common to many of the Jews?

Estrangement from a Christian civilization, runs the usual argument, edged Jews into reformism or revolution. Yet this argument can be reversed, or at least recast: personal alienation does not engender a hardy radicalism. The angst that expresses the pain of separation also craves union—or its substitute, recognition and acceptance. The social critique founded solely on alienation also founders on it.

The economic realities of Jewish and immigrant life go far in explaining a vulnerability to conventional success, money and recognition. Those who worked too hard with their hands wanted their children to do better with their heads. "I entered C.C.N.Y. [College of the City of New York] in 1936," recalls Irving Howe. "It was understood that a Jewish boy like me would go to college. How could it be otherwise when the central credo of the immigrant world was 'my son should not work in a shop'? That was the beginning and the end of all desire and wisdom." Moreover, for Jewish intellectuals to complete college or secure academic posts was especially sweet; compared to the Christians, it often marked firsts for their families.

No dense Freudian theory is necessary to explain that economic deprivation and cultural estrangement often led to an identification, and overidentification, with the dominant culture. Jewish intellectuals from Yiddish-speaking families—Trilling, Fiedler, Howe, Kazin—often fell in love with American and English literature. The phenomenon is familiar, but its relevance for American intellectuals has not been noticed. The "foreigner"—the Jewish intellectual—embraced his new cultural home, sometimes dispatching critical acumen for recognition and approval. The native son, lacking a similar estrangement, kept a distance, often turning to foreign sources. While Trilling drenched himself in American and English literature, Wilson studied Russian. Sidney Hook stuck to John Dewey, while C. Wright Mills wandered into the thicket of German neo-Marxism.

Is it possible that solid American backgrounds allowed—obviously did not compel—a distancing that sustained radicalism for the long haul? That the anxiety of illegitimacy, or persecution, did not haunt the all-American intellectuals? That their sometimes more monied or aristocratic background gave them better footing? Did more principles and less angst infuse the radicalism of non-Jewish intellectuals? Did the radicalism steeped in anxiety slide into conservatism, while the Texan, Puritan, or Scottish identities of Mills or Wilson or Vidal or Galbraith gave rise to a bony radicalism more resistant to economic and social blandishments?

Trilling and Mills exemplify the contrasts between Jewish and non-Jewish intellectuals. Trilling typifies the successful and moderate Jewish professor with a radical past; Mills, the American rebel suspicious of compromise and adjustment. Trilling's Yiddish-speaking parents (his father was a tailor and an unsuccessful furrier) encouraged his studies; it was assumed that he would attend college, and like other Jewish intellectuals, he commenced a lifelong commitment to English literature. His talent and devotion paid off: Trilling, who entered Columbia University as an undergraduate, was the first Jew tenured in its English department.

Everything about Trilling, from his name to his demeanor, implied a successful adjustment to Anglo-American culture. As his wife later wrote, "in appearance and name" Trilling made a "good gamble" for an English department looking for its first Jew. "Had his name been that of his maternal grandfather, Israel Cohen, it is highly questionable whether the offer would have been made." As a polished and judicious commentator on humanism and literature, Trilling earned an endowed chair, showers of awards, honorary titles, national recognition. For intellectuals caught between a leftist, often ethnic, past and cold-war prosperity, Trilling struck the right tone; he contributed to "reconciling a depoliticized intelligentsia to itself and the social status quo."

For some of his old acquaintances, on the other hand, Trilling had gone too far; Alfred Kazin recoiled from his "exquisite sense of accommodation," his nerveless abstract prose, his penchant for words like "scarcely," "modulation," "our educated classes." "For Trilling I would always be 'too Jewish,' too full of my lower-class experiences. He would always defend himself from the things he had left behind."

The differences with Mills are instructive. Mills also came from a modest economic background: his father was an insurance salesman in Waco, Texas; his mother, a housewife. Nothing else tallies with Trilling. Mills did not seek an academic career, nor was he encouraged as a scholar; he enrolled in Texas Agricultural and Mechanical College to become an engineer. When he transferred to the University of Texas, he stumbled upon philosophy and sociology. Until his last years he retained doubts about an academic life, distrusting professional conventions, which he frequently flouted. While he obviously prized his Columbia University position, unlike Trilling, he did not settle happily into it; his colleagues found him abrasive and strident.

For an immigrant family, a university career—status, salary, and security—signified unalloyed advance. Herein lies a critical difference between an American and an immigrant experience. Mills recalled a family past—his grandparents—of independent ranchers. Whether this was fact or fiction hardly matters, for it shaped a vision of self and world: life as an employee in an office—university, government, or publishing—did not measure up no matter the title, money, or respect. The same could be said of other venerable intellectual radicals, such as Wilson or Vidal or Galbraith; they looked back to families of independent farmers, statesmen, or rebels that seemed to provide a secure base for a radical life. This is captured in the title of Galbraith's memoir of his Scottish-Canadian past, *Made to Last.*

In his autobiography, Kenneth Rexroth, poet and lifelong bohemian, pondered the role of genealogy in casting a peculiar American rebel. He believed his own past provided "a kind of family epic in which I thought, and still think of myself, as called to play a role." An ancestory of "Schwenkfelders, Mennonites, German revolutionaries of '48, Abolitionists, suffragists, squaws and Indian traders, octoroons and itinerant horse dealers, farmers in broad hats, full beards and frogged coats, hard-drinking small-town speculators" engendered a personality resistant to conformity.

Rexroth did not think that his past was atypical. "Most American families that go back to the early nineteenth century, and certainly those whose traditions go back to the settlement of the country, have a sense of social and cultural rather than nationalist responsibility. The sense that the country is really theirs, really belongs to them, produces radical critics, rebels, reformers, eccentrics."

Wilson and Vidal have aired kindred thoughts. Gore Vidal once noted that he shared with Wilson a "sense" of America and roots in a Puritan tradition. Wilson recollected in *Upstate* that even after a thirty-five-year absence, he felt he belonged in the town of his youth, his parents, his grandparents. Everyone knew him or the family; everyone was related; several houses belonged to family connections. "Our position was so unquestioned in this little corner of Lewis County [New York] that I have never ceased to derive from it a certain conviction of superiority." As a "member of a half-obsolete minority" of Americans, it was for Wilson just a short step to solidarity with even "more old-fashioned Americans," the New York State Indians, the Iroquois, in the battle with developers. (pp. 85-93)

To believe that Mills or Wilson or Rexroth or Vidal, and others, found resources for a rebellion in their all-American family pasts is perhaps to succumb to myths they themselves invented. Yet these myths enabled them to resist the lure of success, so tempting to more desperate immigrants. Trilling's pleasure that the rich respect professors and Podhoretz's glee that he has "made it" have to be set against Mills's ode to failure as certifying integrity. "Veblen's virtue is not alienation; it is failure.... There is no failure in American academic history quite so great as Veblen's." For Mills, these are words of praise.

Several qualifications to this discussion must be introduced. The shift of Jewish intellectuals to the right has frequently been noted. Yet it is easy to overstate this migration; it is also easy to confuse the visible public intellectuals with the larger, more submerged, and perhaps more stable, radical Jewish community of social workers, lawyers, editors, teachers, unionists, and political activists. The new conservatism may be confined to the more public intellectuals. And even within this select grouping, of course, some Jewish intellectuals continue to place themselves on the left. In this category belong people associated with *Dissent,* like Irving Howe, or *The Nation,* like Norman Birnbaum; and there are others. Nevertheless, this does not dispense with the issue. While "some" is imprecise, it appears that more Jewish intellectuals now, especially in comparison to the past, identify with conservatism.

The short or shrinking list of Jewish radical intellectuals includes a disproportionate number from one sector of the political spectrum: anarchism. Perhaps this is also true of the non-Jewish radicals. The pink thread of the Wobblies and Veblen runs through the cloth of American dissenters.

Of the Jewish radicals, Paul Goodman, Noam Chomsky, Murray Bookchin, and to some degree Isaac Rosenfeld represent versions of anarchism. The peculiar resiliency of anarchists, of course, is not mysterious. To the extent that they are anarchists, they distrust large institutions, the state, the university, and its functionaries. They are less vulnerable to the corruptions of title and salary because their resistance is moral, almost instinctual. (pp. 95-7)

Some years ago Daniel Bell observed that memoirs of the New Left and the beats flood the world, but aside from several older novels (by Tess Slesinger and Mary McCarthy) and a single memoir (Podhoretz's *Making It* [see excerpt above]), little has appeared by New York intellectuals. "There are almost no memoirs, no biographical accounts, no reflections." For Bell the autobiographical dearth explains the emphatic contribution of New York intellectuals, which includes himself, to American culture. Ashamed of their immigrant and drab origins, the New Yorkers turned to culture with a vengence. They did not want to discuss their family pasts; they wanted to discuss ideas. "The very nature of their limited backgrounds indicates what really animated and drove them was a hunger for culture."

Bell's remarks were off the mark—and not only because of unfortunate timing. Bell announced the absence of New York memoirs in 1976, on the dawn of an outpouring: Irving Howe, William Phillips, Lionel Abel, William Barrett, and Sidney Hook offered their reminiscences [see Additional Bibliography]. Bell also managed to forget that two volumes of the best memoir of the lot, Alfred Kazin's *Walker in the City* and *Coming Out in the Thirties,* had appeared some time earlier (his third volume, *New York Jew,* was published in 1978); and that Podhoretz's *Making It* was partially patterned on Mailer's 1959 *Advertisements for Myself.*

It is true that New York intellectuals established a high profile in American culture, often overshadowing non-New Yorkers; and this is due in part to the reasons that Bell—and many before him, including Veblen—outlined. Jews became intellectuals for the same reasons they became shopkeepers: they were not automatically excluded, and they commanded the prerequisities, wits and gumption.

Yet familiarity imbues this argument with more truth than it may contain; the superiority of New York Jewish intellectuals is assumed, not established. In discussions of the 1950s, for instance, there is much talk of Trilling or Rahv or Podhoretz and little of William H. Whyte, Kenneth Burke, or John Kenneth Galbraith. This is reasonable, even just, if is believed that the New Yorkers made themselves into premier intellectuals while the others were something else: popularizers or commentators. But this is questionable.

By quality alone, it is simply not possible to sharply distinguish the oeuvre of New York intellectuals from that of non-New Yorkers. Essay by essay, book by book, the collective work of New York intellectuals is neither so brilliant nor so scintillating that all else pales. It is almost more feasible to reverse the common opinion: the significant books of the fifties were authored by non-New Yorkers. The books by C. Wright Mills or Jane Jacobs or Rachel Carson possessed an energy and originality that the New Yorkers' books rarely matched.

If this is true, then New York intellectuals receive the lion's share of attention less by reason of genius than by sociological luck: their New York location and their personal and physical proximity to the publishing industry. In addition, their tireless monitoring of themselves lays the groundwork for further studies (and myths). For those padding cultural histories with reports on what writer X said to editor Y at Z's party, the New York scene is a motherlode. It would be more difficult to fluff up a study of Norman O. Brown or Kenneth Burke, around whom there were no circles and little gossip.

Cultural attention and intrinsic merit rarely tally, but even within the rarified universe of Freud studies, New Yorkers tend to edge out non-New Yorkers; for instance, the writings of Lionel Trilling and Norman O. Brown on Freud belong to approximately the same period. For concentrated intellectual probing Brown's *Life Against Death* may have no match in American studies of psychoanalysis; compared to this book Trilling's Freud writings are casual and familiar.

Trilling, however, wrote a partially autobiographical novel, offered several essays about himself and his milieu, and, as a New York intellectual, figures in a number of memoirs. His collected works are published replete with a reminiscence by his wife, Diana Trilling. Some books on Trilling have appeared, and more are in the offing. Brown, on the other hand, was never part of the New York scene; *Life Against Death* is appreciated, indeed treasured, but its author is rarely written about. For American cultural history he hardly exists *not* because of a minimal contribution but because of a minimal impact on New York circles.

To characterize the complex world of New York intellectuals is, of course, exceedingly difficult. Yet automatic deference to its unparalleled brilliance and heady intellectualism should be resisted. A cool appraisal of New York intellectuals reverses Bell's judgment; they are best—most convincing, articulate, observant—when they are discussing their own lives, but the compelling theoretical works by New York intellectuals are in very short supply. Bell got it exactly wrong: precisely because of their immigrant past and fragile situation, New York intellectuals specialize in the self; theirs is the home of psychoanalysis, the personal essay, the memoir, the letter to the editor. In style and subject matter their writings are generally highly subjective. Of course, this is not a failing. An intensely personal voice permeates their most brilliant writings, for instance Kazin's work—including, obviously, his autobiography.

Even the most philosophical of the New York intellectuals failed to produce an imposing theoretical oeuvre. If Trilling was the New Yorkers' consummate literary critic, their "professor of English who could really think, whose writing . . . moved to the movement of ideas," Sidney Hook was their philosopher. Bell dedicated *The End of Ideology* to Hook: "I owe most . . . to Sidney Hook . . . one of the great teachers of the generation." Irving Kristol also designated Hook as the "great teacher" of their group. Others concurred; Dwight Macdonald, William Phillips, William Barrett, Nathan Glazer, even Howe and Kazin, all praised Hook as the philosophic genius of the group. "Sidney Hook is America's Number One Marxist!" proclaimed Macdonald. By virtue of his productivity, theoretical acumen, and feistiness, Hook would seem to deserve all accolades.

Hook's early work justified these appreciations. His *Towards the Understanding of Karl Marx* (1933) and *From Hegel to Marx* (1936) brought originality, breadth, and European thought to an American Marxism dulled by dogma and provincialism. These books, which sought to give a John Dewey twist to Marxism, have rightly been called "absolutely the best" American books on Marxism of the thirties.

Yet Hook's later works sadly lack the force and excitement of these books. Herein lies an old tale: as a Marxist sympathizer he wrote thoughtful and philosophical books; as a sworn enemy of Marxism, he fell into a philosophical rut, endlessly recasting the same positions. Of course, it is daunting to summarize the oeuvre of an individual who lists more than twenty books to his credit. Yet the numbers are more intimidating than the contents. Hook's books are almost exclusively anthologies he edited or compilations of his own essays that had appeared in diverse periodicals. Essays and lectures compose books like *Reason, Social Myths and Democracy* (1940); *Academic Freedom and Academic Anarchy* (1970); *Revolution, Reform and Social Justice* (1975); *Philosophy and Public Policy* (1980), *Marxism and Beyond* (1983). Books with titles indicating coherent philosophical efforts, such as *The Quest for Being* (1961) or *Pragmatism and the Tragic Sense of Life* (1974) are filled with lectures, forum contributions, and magazine pieces. For instance, *The Quest for Being,* which is typical, contains two lectures, several essays from *Festschrifts* and philosophy journals, two contributions from *Commentary,* five from *Partisan Review,* and an exchange of letters.

There is nothing wrong with assembling lectures and essays; but in repeating the same arguments and points they do not elaborate a philosophical position. And repeat they do: reading Hook in 1985 is very much like reading him in 1975, 1965, 1955, 1945, and almost 1935. No book by Hook is complete without a reiteration of the threat to democracy from communism and its supporters. Even books that might seem distant from his usual concerns, for instance, *Philosophy and Public Police* and *Pragmatism and the Tragic Sense of Life,* are filled with familiar Hook essays ("Law and Anarchy," "Are There Limits to Freedom of Expression?"). His *Education and the Taming of Power* (1974), a classic Hook grab bag of essays, including one from the mid-1930s, is dedicated "To those who have suffered without yielding in the cause of scholarship and academic freedom at home and abroad at the hands of political tyrants, cowardly administrators, colleagues and student mobs." In his most recent book, Hook is still quoting from an American communist newspaper of 1937 as proof that communist professors "violated the norms of academic freedom and integrity."

Like other New York intellectuals, Hook is primarily a political essayist. Since the 1930s he has written almost no sustained book; he is a philosopher who has contributed almost nothing to philosophy. His complete bibliography suggests he delighted in letters to the editor, rejoinders, and replies to rejoinders; their subject is usually the communist threat and someone's misunderstanding of it. Even the editor of the Hook *Festschrift,* which gushes with praise, calls him a master of "*applied* intelligence," meaning he wrote little philosophy.

The problem is not the essay form, which hardly precludes philosophy, but what Hook did with it, which was very little. Unlike the essays of other New York intellectuals, Hook's lack elegance. They seem hurried, written by an angry author, and they do not improve when collected together. Chapter one of *Education and the Taming of Power* begins this way: "The time for plain speaking about American education in our day is long past due. A hoax is being perpetrated on the American public in the name of educational 'reform,' 'innovation,' and 'freedom.'" Chapter two opens with "There is great deal of nonsense talked about philosophy of education." Hook is more a stump orator than a philosopher.

Hook recently pondered why in the renaissance of Marxist scholarship, his own work is not cited. More than a score of books "in which I have discussed some aspects of Marxism," he complained, go unmentioned in a new "dictionary" of Marxism. The reason may be that for decades Hook has contributed nothing to Marxist scholarship. Long ago he ceased to grapple with Marxism or philosophy. Hook is an essayist, polemicist, raconteur. He specializes in politico-cultural stances, but since his Deweyian expositions of Marx in the mid-1930s, he has not produced an original and coherent philosophical work.

If Hook is ignored by current Marxist scholars, an "extra" theoretical reason plays a role: leftists feel little affection for a philosopher who has worked nights to establish the grounds to exclude subversives, communists, and student radicals from universities. Hook's publications relentlessly raise the alarm that leftists, communists, radicals, and what he calls "ritualist liberals" endanger freedom. He is slower to register any other threats, although the blinkered vision is exactly what he holds against the left.

The only time that Hook raised the issue of Nazi anti-Semitism in the prewar period was to score points against communism. "Let us remember," he wrote in 1938, "that it was from Stalin that Hitler learned the art of uprooting and wiping out whole groups and classes of innocent citizens. We cannot with good conscience protest against Hitler's treatment of the Jews and remain silent about the six million . . . who fill the concentration camps in Russia." In his study of New York intellectuals, Alexander Bloom comments that "so entrenched was he [Hook] in the anti-Stalinist campaigns that he could not discuss" on its own terms the Nazi war against the Jews.

Until recently arguments about "intellectuals" took their cue from the Dreyfus Affair of the 1890s. The artists, writers, and teachers, including Emile Zola, who challenged the state's prosecution of Dreyfus became known as the "intellectuals." For the anti-Dreyfusards they were a new and objectionable group. As one anti-Dreyfusard wrote,

> The interference of this novelist [Zola] in a matter of military justice seems to me no less impertinent than, let us say, the intervention of a police captain in a problem of syntax or versification. . . . As for this petition that is being circulated among the *Intellectuals!* the mere fact that one has recently created this word *Intellectuals* to designate, as though they were an aristocracy, individuals who live in laboratories and libraries, proclaims one of the most ridiculous eccentricities of our time.

Moreover, the Russian term "intelligentsia," which dates to the 1860s, gradually passed into English or at least rubbed off on "intellectuals," darkening its oppositional hues. The intelligentsia, which prepared the way for the Russian Revolution, was almost exclusively defined by "its alienation from and hostility towards the state."

This history colored subsequent discussions. Some thinkers wanted to overcome this past; others to reclaim it. When H. Stuart Hughes looked into the future of intellectuals, he also looked to their past in the 1890s. (Perhaps his most important book surveyed intellectuals at the turn of the century.) Nevertheless, the 1950s and 1960s bleached out much of the original pigments. Discussions about intellectuals do not cease, but the terms change. Where once there was talk of intellectuals as critics and bohemians, now there is talk of intellectuals as a

sociological class. The shift in idiom illuminates the shift in lives.

The old questions seem less urgent, since they had been answered not by agreements or conclusive arguments but by events. As with the controversy about suburbia, "progress" is marked less by resolution than neglect; heated issues slip out of sight bcause they reflect a past no longer encroaching upon the present. In the 1980s few are asking about the future of independent or bohemian intellectuals. This is settled: there is no future. Instead, commentators and scholars ask if intellectuals constitute a "new class."

Of course, there is still no agreement, but the reformulation of the question registers the restructured lives. Intellectuals live less as independent writers or poets and more as professional groups, interest coalitions, perhaps classes. For some, like Alvin Gouldner, the "new class" of intellectuals and technicians constitutes "the most progressive force in modern society." Irving Kristol disagrees; the new class is an "ambitious and frustrated class." An editor of *The Wall Street Journal* has discovered—or hallucinated—that "many of the great fortunes built from business empires have now been captured by intellectuals, and are now being used . . . to attack business and advance the New Class."

To Daniel Bell "new class" is a "muddled" category. Instead, he proposes to classify intellectuals by their institutional attachments, which he numbers at five: business, government, university, medical, and military. Bell's list indicates the distance traveled. The sociological idiom of class and institutions supplants talk of independent intellectuals, who survive as curiosities.

Today intellectuals travel with curricula vitae and business cards; they subsist by virtue of institutional backing. The standard first or second question among academics is not "who?" but "where?" meaning with which institution someone is affiliated; it makes a difference. In 1964 Lewis Coser called Edmund Wilson a "monument" from a "half-forgotten past." Twenty years later that past is fully forgotten. To put it sharply: in the 1950s, the future of unaffiliated intellectuals engendered discussion; in the 1980s, the future of an intellectual class. The substitution of class for intellectuals encapsulates the change. (pp. 100-09)

> *Russell Jacoby, "New York, Jewish, and Other Intellectuals," in his* The Last Intellectuals: American Culture in the Age of Academe, *Basic Books, Inc., Publishers, 1987, pp. 72-111.*

ACHIEVEMENT AND SIGNIFICANCE

IRVING HOWE

[*A longtime editor of the leftist magazine* Dissent *and a regular contributor to the* New Republic, *Howe is one of America's most highly respected literary critics and social historians. He has been a socialist since the 1930s, and his criticism is frequently informed by a liberal social viewpoint. Howe is widely praised for what F. R. Dulles has termed his "knowledgeable understanding, critical acumen and forthright candor." Howe has written: "My work has fallen into two fields: social history and literary criticism. I have tried to strike a balance between the social and the literary; to fructify one with the other; yet not to confuse one with the other. Though I believe in the social approach to literature, it seems to me peculiarly open to misuse; it requires particular delicacy and care.'' In the following excerpt, Howe discusses the New York Intellectuals' contribution to American thought and culture during the 1930s and the subsequent dissolution of their ideological unity.*]

The New York intellectuals are perhaps the only group America has ever had that could be described as an *intelligentsia*. This term comes awkwardly to our lips, and for good reason: it suggests, as Martin Malia, a historian of Russian culture, writes, ''more than intellectuals in the ordinary sense. Whether merely 'critical-thinking' or actively oppositional, their name indicates that [in Russia] they thought of themselves as the embodied 'intelligence' . . . or 'consciousness' of the nation. They clearly felt an exceptional sense of apartness from the society in which they lived.''

Malia's phrase about ''consciousness of the nation'' seems special to the problems of the Russian intellectuals under czarism, but the rest of his description fits the New York intellectuals rather well: the stress upon ''critical thinking,'' the stance of active opposition, the sense of apartness. Or, perhaps more accurately, it is a description which fits the past of the New York intellectuals. And just as the Russian ''intelligentsia'' was marked by a strongly Westernizing outlook, a wish to bring Russian culture out of its provincial limits and into a close relationship with the culture of Western Europe, so the New York intellectuals have played a role in the internationalization of American culture, serving as a liaison between American readers and Russian politics, French ideas, European writing. (p. 212)

The social roots of the New York writers are not hard to trace. With a few delightful exceptions—a tendril from Yale, a vine from Seattle—they stem from the world of the immigrant Jews, either workers or petty bourgeois. They come at a moment in the development of immigrant Jewish culture when there is a strong drive not only to break out of the ghetto but also to leave behind the bonds of Jewishness entirely. Earlier generations had known such feelings, and through many works of fiction, especially those by Henry Roth, Michael Gold, and Daniel Fuchs, one can return to the classic pattern of a fierce attachment to the provincialism of origins as it becomes entangled with a fierce eagerness to plunge into the Gentile world of success, manners, freedom. As early as the 1890's this pattern had already come into view, and with diminishing intensity it has continued to control Jewish life deep into the twentieth century; perhaps its last significant expression comes in Philip Roth's stories, where the sense of Jewish tradition is feeble but the urge to escape its suburban ruins extremely strong.

The New York intellectuals were the first group of Jewish writers to come out of the immigrant milieu who did not define themselves through a relationship, nostalgic or hostile, to memories of Jewishness. They were the first generation of Jewish writers for whom the recall of an immigrant childhood does not seem to have been completely overwhelming. (Is that perhaps one reason few of them tried to write fiction?) That this severance from Jewish roots and immigrant sources would later come to seem a little suspect, is another matter. All I wish to stress here is that, precisely at the point in the thirties when the New York intellectuals began to form themselves into a loose cultural-political tendency, Jewishness as idea and sentiment played no significant role in their expectations—apart, to be sure, from a bitter awareness that no matter what their political or cultural desires, the sheer fact of their recent emer-

gence had still to be regarded, and not least of all by themselves, as an event within Jewish American life. (pp. 214-16)

The Jewish immigrant world branded upon its sons and daughters marks of separateness even while encouraging them to dreams of universalism. This subculture may have been formed to preserve ethnic continuity, but it was the kind of continuity that would reach its triumph in self-disintegration. It taught its children both to conquer the Gentile world and to be conquered by it, both to leave an intellectual impress and to accept the dominant social norms. By the twenties and thirties the values dominating Jewish immigrant life were mostly secular, radical, and universalist, and if these were often conveyed though a parochial vocabulary, they nonetheless carried some remnants of European culture. Even as they were moving out of a constricted immigrant milieu, the New York intellectuals were being prepared by it for the tasks they would set themselves during the thirties. They were being prepared for the intellectual vocation as one of assertiveness, speculation, and free-wheeling; for the strategic maneuvers of a vanguard, at this point almost a vanguard in the abstract, with no ranks following in the rear; and for the union of politics and culture, with the politics radical and the culture cosmopolitan. What made this goal all the more attractive was that the best living American critic, Edmund Wilson, had triumphantly reached it; he was the author of both *The Triple Thinkers* and *To the Finland Station;* he served as a model for emulation, and he gave this view of the intellectual life a special authority in that he seemed to come out of the mainstream of American life.

That the literary avant-guarde and the political left were not really comfortable partners would become clear with the passage of time; in Europe it already had. But during the years the New York intellectuals began to appear as writers and critics worthy of some attention, there was a feeling in the air that a union of *the advanced*—critical consciousness and political conscience—could be forged.

Throughout the thirties the New York intellectuals believed, somewhat naïvely, that this union was not only a desirable possibility but also a tie both natural and appropriate. Except, however, for the Surrealists in Paris, and it is not clear how seriously this instance should be taken, the paths of political radicalism and cultural modernism have seldom met. To use [Renato] Poggioli's terms, the New York writers were more an ''intelligentsia'' than an ''intellectual elite,'' and more inclined to an amorphous ''proletarianizing'' than to an austere partisanship for modernism.

The history of the West in the last century offers many instances in which Jewish intellectuals played an important role in the development of political radicalism; but almost always this occurred when there were sizable movements, with the intellectuals serving as spokesmen, propagandists, and functionaries of a party. In New York, by contrast, the intellectuals had no choice but to begin with a dissociation from the only significant radical movement in this country, the Communist Party. What for European writers like Koestler, Silone, and Malraux would be the end of the road was here a beginning. In a fairly short time, the New York writers found that the meeting of political and cultural ideas which had stirred them to excitement could also leave them stranded and distressed. Radicalism, in both its daily practice and ethical biases, proved inhospitable to certain aspects of modernism—and not always, I now think, mistakenly. Literary modernism often had a way of cavalierly dismissing the world of daily existence, a world that remained intensely absorbing to the New York writers.

Literary modernism could sometimes align itself with reactionary movements, a fact that was intensely embarrassing and required either torturous explanations or complex dissociations. The New York writers discovered, as well, that their relationship to modernism as a purely literary phenomenon was less auuthoritative and more ambiguous than they had wished to feel. The great battles for Joyce and Eliot and Proust had been fought in the twenties and mostly won; and now, while clashes with entrenched philistinism might still take place, they were mostly skirmishes or mopping-up operations (as in the polemics against the transfigured Van Wyck Brooks). The New York writers came at the end of the modernist experience, just as they came at what may yet have to be judged the end of the radical experience, and as they certainly came at the end of the immigrant Jewish experience. One shorthand way of describing their situation, a cause of both their feverish brilliance and their recurrent instability, is to say that *they came late*.

During the thirties and forties their radicalism was anxious, problematic, and beginning to decay at the very moment it was adopted. They had no choice: the crisis of socialism was worldwide, profound, with no end in sight, and the only way to avoid that crisis was to bury oneself, as a few did, in the left-wing sects. Some of the New York writers had gone through the "political school" of Stalinism, a training in coarseness from which not all recovered; some had even spent a short time in the organizational coils of the Communist Party. By 1936, when the anti-Stalinist *Partisan Review* was conceived, the central figures of that moment—Philip Rahv, William Phillips, Sidney Hook—had shed whatever sympathies they once felt for Stalinism, but the hope that they could find another ideological system, some cleansed version of Marxism associated perhaps with Trotsky or Luxemburg, was doomed to failure. Some gravitated for a year or two toward the Trotskyist group, but apart from admiration for Trotsky's personal qualities and dialectical prowess, they found little satisfaction there; no version of orthodox Marxism could retain a hold on intellectuals who had gone through the trauma of abandoning the Leninist *Weltanschauung* and had experienced the depth to which the politics of this century, most notably the rise of totalitarianism, called into question the once-sacred Marxist categories. From now on, the comforts of system would have to be relinquished.

Though sometimes brilliant in expression and often a stimulus to the kind of cultural speculation at which they excelled, the radicalism of the New York intellectuals during the thirties was not a deeply grounded experience. It lacked roots in a popular movement which might bring intellectuals into relationship with the complexities of power and stringencies of organization. From a doctrine it became a style, and from a style a memory. It was symptomatic that the *Marxist Quarterly,* started in 1937 by a spectrum of left intellectuals and probably the most distinguished Marxist journal ever published in this country, could survive no more than a year. The differences among its founders, some like James Burnham holding to a revolutionary Marxist line and others like Sidney Hook and Lewis Corey moving toward versions of liberalism and social democracy, proved too severe for collaboration. And even the radicalism of the *Partisan Review* editors and writers during its vivid early years—how deeply did it cut, except as a tool enabling them to break away from Marxism? Which of those writers and readers who now look back nostalgically have troubled to examine the early files of this important magazine and read—with embarrassment? amusement? pleasure?—the political essays it printed?

Yet if the radicalism of the New York intellectuals seems to have been without much political foundation or ideological strength, it certainly played an important role in their own development. For the New York writers, and even, I suspect, those among them who would later turn sour on the whole idea of radicalism (including the few who in the mid-sixties would try to erase the memory of having turned sour), the thirties represented a time of intensity and fervor, a reality or illusion of engagement, a youth tensed with conviction and assurance: so that even Dwight Macdonald, who at each point in his life has made a specialty out of mocking his previous beliefs, could not help displaying tender feelings upon remembering his years, God help us, as a "revolutionist." The radicalism of the thirties gave the New York intellectuals their distinctive style: a flair for polemic, a taste for the grand generalization, an impatience with what they regarded (often parochially) as parochial scholarship, an internationalist perspective, and a tacit belief in the unity—even if a unity beyond immediate reach—of intellectual work.

By comparison with competing schools of thought, the radicalism of the anti-Stalinist left, as it was then being advanced in *Partisan Review*, seemed cogent, fertile, alive: it could stir good minds to argument, it could gain the attention of writers abroad, it seemed to offer a combination of system and independence. With time the anti-Stalinist intellectuals came to enjoy advantages somewhat like those which have enabled old radicals to flourish in the trade unions: they could talk faster than anyone else, they knew their way around better, they were quicker on their feet. Brief and superficial as their engagement with Marxism may have been, it gave the intellectuals the

Irving Howe. © copyright 1988 by Layle Silbert.

advantage of dialectic, sometimes dialectic as it lapsed into mere double-talk.

Yet in fairness I should add that this radicalism did achieve something of substantial value in the history of American culture. It helped destroy—once and for all, I would have said until recently—Stalinism as a force in our intellectual life, and with Stalinism those varieties of Populist sentimentality which the Communist movement of the late thirties exploited with notable skill. If certain sorts of manipulative soft-headedness have been all but banished from serious American writing, and the kinds of rhetoric once associated with Archibald MacLeish and Van Wyck Brooks cast into permanent disrepute, at least some credit for this ought to go to the New York writers.

It has recently become fashionable, especially in the pages of the *New York Review of Books,* to sneer at the achievement of anti-Stalinism by muttering darkly about "the Cold War." But we ought to have enough respect for the past to avoid telescoping several decades. The major battle against Stalinism as a force within intellectual life, and in truth a powerful force, occurred before anyone heard of the Cold War; it occurred in the late thirties and early forties. In our own moment we see "the old crap," as Marx once called it, rise to the surface with unnerving ease; there is something dizzying in an encounter with Stalin's theory of "social Fascism," particularly when it comes from the lips of young people who may not even be quite sure when Stalin lived. Still, I think there will not and probably cannot be repeated in our intellectual life the ghastly large-scale infatuation with a totalitarian regime which disgraced the thirties. Some achievements, a very few, seem beyond destruction.

A little credit is therefore due. Whatever judgments one may have about Sidney Hook's later political writings, and mine have been very critical, it is a matter of decency to recall the liberating role he played in the thirties as spokesman for a democratic radicalism and a fierce opponent of all the rationalizations for totalitarianism a good many intellectuals allowed themselves. One reason people have recently felt free to look down their noses at "anti-Communism" as if it were a mass voodoo infecting everyone from far right to democratic left, is precisely the toughness with which the New York intellectuals fought against Stalinism. Neither they nor anybody else could re-establish socialism as a viable politics in the United States; but for a time they did help to salvage the honor of the socialist idea—which meant primarily to place it in the sharpest opposition to all totalitarian states and systems. What many intellectuals now say they take for granted, had first to be won through bitter and exhausting struggle.

I should not like to give the impression that Stalinism was the beginning and end of whatever was detestable in American intellectual life during the thirties. Like the decades to come, perhaps like all decades, this was a "low dishonest" time. No one who grew up in, or lived through, these years should wish for a replay of their ideological melodramas. Nostalgia for the thirties is a sentiment possible only to the very young or the very old, those who have not known and those who no longer remember. Whatever distinction can be assigned to the New York intellectuals during those years lies mainly in their persistence as a small minority, in their readiness to defend unpopular positions against apologists for the Moscow trials and the vigilantism of Popular Front culture. Some historians, with the selectivity of retrospect, have recently begun to place the New York intellectuals at the center of cultural life in the thirties—but this is both a comic misapprehension and a soiling

honor. On the contrary; their best hours were spent on the margin, in opposition.

Later, in the forties and fifties, most of the New York intellectuals would abandon the effort to find a renewed basis for a socialist politics—to their serious discredit, I believe. Some would vulgarize anti-Stalinism into a politics barely distinguishable from reaction. Yet for almost all New York intellectuals the radical years proved a decisive moment in their lives. And for a very few, the decisive moment.

I have been speaking here as if the New York intellectuals were mainly political people, but in reality this was true for only a few of them, writers like Hook, Macdonald, and perhaps Rahv. Most were literary men or journalists with no experience in any political movement; they had come to radical politics through the pressures of conscience and a flair for the dramatic; and even in later years, when they abandoned any direct political involvement, they would in some sense remain "political." They would maintain an alertness toward the public event. They would respond with eagerness to historical changes, even if these promised renewed favor for the very ideas they had largely discarded. They would continue to structure their cultural responses through a sharp, perhaps excessively sharp, kind of categorization, in itself a sign that political styles and habits persisted. But for the most part, the contributions of the New York intellectuals were not to political thought. Given the brief span of time during which they fancied themselves agents of a renewed Marxism, there was little they could have done. Sidney Hook wrote one or two excellent books on the sources of Marxism, Harold Rosenberg one or two penetrating essays on the dramatics of Marxism; and not much more. The real contribution of the New York writers was toward creating a new, and for this country almost exotic, style of work. They thought of themselves as cultural radicals even after they had begun to wonder whether there was much point in remaining political radicals. But what could this mean? Cultural radicalism was a notion extremely hard to define and perhaps impossible to defend, as Richard Chase would discover in the late fifties when against the main drift of New York opinion he put forward the idea of a radicalism without immediate political ends but oriented toward criticism of a meretricious culture. What Chase did not live long enough to see was that his idea, much derided at the time, would lend itself a decade later to caricature through success.

Chase was seriously trying to preserve a major impetus of New York intellectual life: the exploration and defense of literary modernism. He failed to see, however, that this was a task largely fulfilled and, in any case, taking on a far more ambiguous and less militant character in the fifties than it would have had twenty or thirty years earlier. The New York writers had done useful work in behalf of modernist literature. Without fully realizing it, they were continuing a cultural movement that had begun in th United States during the mid-nineteenth century: the return to Europe, not as provincials knocking humbly at the doors of the great, but as equals in an enterprise which by its very nature had to be international. We see this at work in Howells's reception of Ibsen and Tolstoy; in Van Wyck Brooks's use of European models to assault the timidities of American literature; in the responsiveness of *The Little Review* and *The Dial* to European experiments and, somewhat paradoxically, in the later fixation of the New Critics, despite an ideology of cultural provincialism, on modernist writing from abroad.

The New York critics, and most notably *Partisan Review*, helped complete this process of internationalizing American culture (also, by the way, Americanizing international culture). They gave a touch of glamour to that style which the Russians and Poles now call "cosmopolitan." *Partisan Review* was the first journal in which it was not merely respectable but a matter of pride to print one of Eliot's *Four Quartets* side by side with Marxist criticism. And not only did the magazine break down the polar rigidities of the hard-line Marxists and the hard-line nativists; it also sanctioned the idea, perhaps the most powerful cultural idea of the last half-century, that there existed an all but incomparable generation of modern masters, some of them still alive, who in this terrible age represented the highest possibilities of the human imagination. On a more restricted scale, *Partisan Review* helped win attention and respect for a generation of European writers—Silone, Orwell, Malraux, Koestler, Serge—who were not quite of the first rank as novelists but had suffered the failure of socialism.

If the *Partisan* critics came too late for a direct encounter with new work from the modern masters, they did serve the valuable end of placing that work in a cultural context more vital and urgent than could be provided by any other school of American criticism. For many young people up to and through World War II, the *Partisan* critics helped to mold a new sensibility, a mixture of rootless radicalism and a desanctified admiration for writers like Joyce, Eliot, and Kafka. I can recall that even in my orthodox Marxist phase I felt that the central literary expression of the time was a now half-forgotten poem by a St. Louis writer called "The Waste Land."

In truth, however, the New York critics were then performing no more than an auxiliary service. They were following upon the work of earlier, more fortunate critics. And even in the task of cultural consolidation, which soon had the unhappy result of overconsolidating the modern masters in the academy, the New York critics found important allies among their occasional opponents in the New Criticism. As it turned out, the commitment to literary modernism proved insufficient either as a binding literary purpose or as a theme that might inform the writings of the New York critics. By now modernism was entering its period of decline; the old excitements had paled and the old achievements been registered. Modernism had become successful; it was no longer a literature of opposition, and thereby had begun that metamorphosis signifying its ultimate death. The problem was no longer to fight for modernism; the problem was now to consider why the fight had so easily ended in triumph. And as time went on, modernism surfaced an increasing portion of its limitations and ambiguities, so that among some critics earlier passions of advocacy gave way to increasing anxieties of judgment. Yet the moment had certainly not come when a cool and objective reconsideration could be undertaken of works that had formed the sensibility of our time. The New York critics, like many others, were trapped in a dilemma from which no escape could be found, but which lent itself to brilliant improvisation: it was too late for unobstructed enthusiasm, it was too soon for unobstructed valuation, and meanwhile the literary work that was being published, though sometimes distinguished, was composed in the heavy shadows of the modernists. At almost every point this work betrayed the marks of *having come after*.

Except for Harold Rosenberg, who would make "the tradition of the new" a signature of his criticism, the New York writers slowly began to release those sentiments of uneasiness they had been harboring about the modernist poets and novelists.

One instance was the notorious Pound case, in which literary and moral values, if not jammed into a head-on collision, were certainly entangled beyond easy separation. Essays on writers like D. H. Lawrence—what to make of his call for "blood consciousness," what one's true response might be to his notions of the leader cult—began to appear. A recent book by John Harrison, *The Reactionaries*, which contains a full-scale attack on the politics of several modernist writers, is mostly a compilation of views that had been gathering force over the last few decades. And then, as modernism stumbled into its late period, those recent years in which its early energies have evidently reached a point of exhaustion, the New York critics became still more discomfited. There was a notable essay several years ago by Lionel Trilling in which he acknowledged mixed feelings toward the modernist writers he had long praised and taught. There was a cutting attack by Philip Rahv on Jean Genet, that perverse genius in whose fiction the compositional resources of modernism seem all but severed from its moral— one might even say, its human—interests.

For the New York intellectuals in the thirties and forties there was still another focus of interest, never quite as strong as radical politics or literary modernism but seeming, for a brief time, to promise a valuable new line of discussion. In the essays of writers like Clement Greenberg and Dwight Macdonald, more or less influenced by the German neo-Marxist school of Adorno-Horkheimer, there were beginnings at a theory of "mass culture," that mass-produced pseudo-art characteristic of industrialized urban society, together with its paralyzed audiences, its inaccessible sources, its parasitic relation to high culture. More insight than system and more intuition than knowledge, this slender body of work was nevertheless a contribution to the study of that hazy area where culture and society meet. It was attacked by writers like Edward Shils as being haughtily elitist, on the ground that it assumed a condescension to the tastes and experiences of the masses. It was attacked by writers like Harold Rosenberg, who charged that only people taking a surreptitious pleasure in dipping their noses into trash would study the "content" (he had no objection to sociological investigations) of mass culture. Even at its most penetrating, the criticism of mass culture was beset by uncertainty and improvisation; perhaps all necessary for a beginning.

Then, almost as if by common decision, the whole subject was dropped. For years hardly a word could be found in the advanced journals about what a little earlier had been called a crucial problem of the modern era. One reason was that the theory advanced by Greenberg and Macdonald turned out to be static: it could be stated but apparently not developed. It suffered from weaknesses parallel to those of Hannah Arendt's theory of totalitarianism: by positing a *cul de sac*, a virtual end of days, for twentieth-century man and his culture, it proposed a suffocating relationship between high or minority culture and the ever-multiplying mass culture. From this relationship there seemed neither relief nor escape, and if one accepted this view, nothing remained but to refine the theory and keep adding grisly instances.

In the absence of more complex speculations, there was little point in continuing to write about mass culture. Besides, hostility toward the commercial pseudo-arts was hard to maintain with unyielding intensity, mostly because it was hard to remain all that *interested* in them—only in Macdonald's essays did both hostility and interest survive intact. Some felt that the whole matter had been inflated and that writers should stick to their business, which was literature, and intellectuals to theirs, which was ideas. Others felt that the movies and TV were beginning to show more ingenuity and resourcefulness than the severe notions advanced by Greenberg and Macdonald allowed for, though no one could have anticipated that glorious infatuation with trash which Marshall McLuhan would make acceptable. And still others felt that the multiplication of insights, even if pleasing as an exercise, failed to yield significant results: a critic who contributes a nuance to Dostoevsky criticism is working within a structured tradition, while one who throws off a clever observation about Little Orphan Annie is simply showing that he can do what he has done.

There was another and more political reason for the collapse of mass culture criticism. One incentive toward this kind of writing was the feeling that industrial society had reached a point of affluent stasis where major upheavals could now be registered much more vividly in culture than in economics. While aware of the dangers of reductionism here, I think the criticism of mass culture did serve, as some of *its* critics charged, conveniently to replace the criticism of bourgeois society. If you couldn't stir the proletariat to action, you could denounce Madison Avenue in comfort. Once, however, it began to be felt among intellectuals in the fifties that there was no longer so overwhelming a need for political criticism, and once it began to seem in the sixties that there were new openings for political criticism, the appetite for cultural surrogates became less keen.

Greenberg now said little more about mass culture; Macdonald made no serious effort to extend his theory or test it against new events; and in recent years, younger writers have seemed to feel that the whole approach of these men was heavy and humorless. Susan Sontag has proposed a cheerfully eclectic view which undercuts just about everything written from the Greenberg-Macdonald position. Now everyone is to do "his thing," high, middle, or low; the old puritan habit of interpretation and judgment, so inimical to sensuousness, gives way to a programmed receptivity; and we are enlightened by lengthy studies of the ethos of the Beatles.

By the end of World War II, the New York writers had reached a point of severe intellectual crisis, though as frequently happens at such moments, they themselves often felt they were entering a phase of enlarged influence and power. Perhaps indeed there was a relation between inner crisis and external influence. Everything that had kept them going—the idea of socialism, the advocacy of literary modernism, the assault on mass culture, a special brand of literary criticism—was judged to be irrelevant to the postwar years. But as a group, just at the time their internal disintegration had seriously begun, the New York writers could be readily identified. The leading critics were Rahv, Phillips, Trilling, Rosenberg, Abel, and Kazin. The main political theorist was Hook. Writers of poetry and fiction related to the New York milieu were Delmore Schwartz, Saul Bellow, Paul Goodman, and Isaac Rosenfeld. And the recognized scholar, and also inspiring moral force, was Meyer Schapiro.

A sharp turn occurs, or is completed, soon after World War II. The intellectuals now go racing or stumbling from idea to idea, notion to notion, hope to hope, fashion to fashion. This instability often derives from a genuine eagerness to capture all that seems new—or threatening—in experience, sometimes from a mere desire to capture a bitch goddess whose first name is Novelty. The abandonment of ideology can be liberating: a number of talents, thrown back on their own resources, begin to grow. The surrender of "commitment" can be damaging:

some writers find themselves rattling about in a gray and chilly freedom. The culture opens up, with both temptation and generosity, and together with intellectual anxieties there are public rewards, often deserved. A period of dispersion; extreme oscillations in thought; and a turn in politics toward an increasingly conservative kind of liberalism—reflective, subtle, acquiescent.

The postwar years were marked by a sustained discussion of the new political and intellectual problems raised by the totalitarian state. Nothing in received political systems, neither Marxist nor liberal, adequately prepared one for the frightful mixture of terror and ideology, the capacity to sweep along the plebeian masses and organize a warfare state, and above all the readiness to destroy entire peoples, which characterized totalitarianism. Still less was anyone prepared—who had heeded the warning voices of the Russian socialist Martov or the English liberal Russell?—for the transformation of the revolutionary Bolshevik state, either through a "necessary" degeneration or an internal counterrevolution, into one of the major totalitarian powers. Marxist theories of Fascism—the "last stage" of capitalism, with the economy statified to organize a permanent war machine and mass terror employed to put down rebellious workers—came to seem, if not entirely mistaken, then certainly insufficient. The quasi- or pseudo-Leninist notion that "bourgeois democracy" was merely a veiled form of capitalist domination, no different in principle from its open dictatorship, proved to be a moral and political disaster. The assumption that socialism was an ordained "next step," or that nationalization of industry constituted a sufficient basis for working-class rule, was as great a disaster. No wonder intellectual certainties were shattered and these years marked by frenetic improvisation! At every point, with the growth of Communist power in Europe and with the manufacture of the Bomb at home, apocalypse seemed the face of tomorrow.

So much foolishness has been written about the New York intellectuals and their anti-Communism, either by those who have signed a separate peace with the authoritarian idea or those who lack the courage to defend what *is* defensible in their own past, that I want here to be both blunt and unyielding.

Given the enormous growth of Russian power after the war and the real possibility of a Communist take-over in Europe, the intellectuals—and not they alone—had to reconsider their political responses. An old-style Marxist declaration of rectitude, a plague repeated on both their houses? Or the difficult position of making foreign policy proposals for the United States, while maintaining criticism of its social order, so as to block totalitarian expansion without resort to war? Most intellectuals decided they had to choose the second course, and they were right.

Like anticapitalism, anti-Communism was a tricky politics, all too open to easy distortion. Like anticapitalism, anti-Communism could be put to the service of ideological racketeering and reaction. Just as ideologues of the fanatic right insisted that by some ineluctable logic anticapitalism led to a Stalinist terror, so ideologues of the authoritarian left, commandeering the same logic, declared that anti-Communism led to the politics of Dulles and Rusk. There is, of course, no "anticapitalism" or "anti-Communism" in the abstract; these take on political flesh only when linked with a larger body of programs and values, so that it becomes clear what *kind* of "anticapitalism" or "anti-Communism" we are dealing with. It is absurd, and indeed disreputable, for intellectuals in the sixties to write as if there were a unified "anti-Communism" which can be used to enclose the view of everyone from William Buckley to Michael Harrington.

There were difficulties. A position could be worked out for conditional support of the West when it defended Berlin or introduced the Marshall Plan or provided economic help to underdeveloped countries; but in the course of daily politics, in the effort to influence the foreign policy of what remained a capitalist power, intellectuals could lose their independence and slip into vulgarities of analysis and speech.

Painful choices had to be faced. When the Hungarian revolution broke out in 1956, most intellectuals sympathized strongly with the rebels, yet feared that active intervention by the West might provoke a world war. For a rational and humane mind, anti-Communism could not be the sole motive, it could be only one of several, in political behavior and policy; and even those intellectuals who had by now swung a considerable distance to the right did not advocate military intervention in Hungary. There was simply no way out—as, more recently, there was none in Czechoslovakia.

It became clear, furthermore, that United States military intervention in underdeveloped countries could help local reactionaries in the short run, and the Communists in the long run. These difficulties were inherent in postwar politics, and they ruled out—though for that very reason, also made tempting—a simplistic moralism. These difficulties were also exacerbated by the spread among intellectuals of a crude anti-Communism, often ready to justify whatever the United States might do at home and abroad. For a hard-line group within the American Committee for Cultural Freedom, all that seemed to matter in any strongly felt way was a sour hatred of the Stalinists, historically justifiable but more and more a political liability even in the fight against Stalinism. The dangers in such a politics now seem all too obvious, but I should note, for whatever we may mean by the record, that in the early fifties they were already being pointed out by a mostly unheeded minority of intellectuals around *Dissent*. Yet, with all these qualifications registered, the criticism to be launched against the New York intellectuals in the postwar years is not that they were strongly anti-Communist but, rather, that many of them, through disorientation or insensibility, allowed their anti-Communism to become something cheap and illiberal.

Nor is the main point of *moral* criticism that the intellectuals abandoned socialism. We have no reason to suppose that the declaration of a socialist opinion induces a greater humaneness than does acquiescence in liberalism. It could be argued (I would) that in the ease with which ideas of socialism were now brushed aside there was something shabby. It was undignified, at the very least, for people who had made so much of their Marxist credentials now to put to rest so impatiently the radicalism of their youth. Still, it might be said by some of the New York writers that reality itself had forced them to conclude socialism was no longer viable or had become irrelevant to the American scene, and that while this conclusion might be open to political argument, it was not to moral attack.

Let us grant that for a moment. What cannot be granted is that the shift in ideologies required or warranted the surrender of critical independence which was prevalent during the fifties. In the trauma—or relief—of ideological ricochet, all too many intellectuals joined the American celebration. It was possible, to cite but one of many instances, for Mary McCarthy to write: "Class barriers disappear or tend to become porous [in the U.S.]; the factory worker is an economic aristocrat in com-parison with the middle-class clerk. . . . *The America . . . of vast inequalities and dramatic contrasts is rapidly ceasing to exist*" (emphasis added). Because the New York writers all but surrendered their critical perspective on American society—*that* is why they were open to attack.

It was the growth of McCarthyism which brought most sharply into question the role of the intellectuals. Here, presumably, all men of good will could agree; here the interests of the intellectuals were beyond dispute and directly at stake. The record is not glorious. In New York circles it was often said that Bertrand Russell exaggerated wildly in describing the United States as "subject to a reign of terror" and that Simone de Beauvoir retailed Stalinist clichés in her reportage from America. Yet it should not be forgotten that, if not "a reign of terror," McCarthyism was frightful and disgusting, and that a number of Communists and fellow-travelers, not always carefully specified, suffered serious harm.

A magazine like *Partisan Review*, was, of course, opposed to McCarthy's campaign, but it failed to take the lead on the issue of freedom which might once again have imbued the intellectuals with fighting spirit. Unlike some of its New York counterparts, it did print sharp attacks on the drift toward conservativism, and it did not try to minimize the badness of the situation in the name of anti-Communism. But the magazine failed to speak out with enough force and persistence, or to break past the hedgings of those intellectuals who led the American Committee for Cultural Freedom.

Commentary, under Elliot Cohen's editorship, was still more inclined to minimize the threat of McCarthyism. In September 1952, at the very moment McCarthy became a central issue in the Presidential campaign, Cohen could write: "McCarthy remains in the popular mind an unreliable, second-string blowhard; his only support as a great national figure is from the fascinated fears of the intelligentsia"—a mode of argument all too close to that of the anti-anti-Communists who kept repeating that Communism was a serious problem only in the minds of anti-Communists.

In the American Committee for Cultural Freedom the increasingly conformist and conservative impulses of the New York intellectuals, or at least of a good number of them, found formal expression, I quote at length from Michael Harrington in a 1955 issue of *Dissent*, first because it says precisely what needs to be said and second because it has the value of contemporary evidence:

> In practice the ACCF has fallen behind Sidney Hook's views on civil liberties. Without implying any "conspiracy" theory of history . . . one may safely say that it is Hook who has molded the decisive ACCF policies. His *Heresy Yes, Conspiracy No* articles were widely circulated by the Committee, which meant that in effect it endorsed his systematic, explicit efforts to minimize the threat to civil liberties and to attack those European intellectuals who, whatever their own political or intellectual deficiencies, took a dim view of American developments. Under the guidance of Hook and the leadership of Irving Kristol, who supported Hook's general outlook, the American Committee cast its weight not so much in defense of those civil liberties which were steadily being nibbled away, but rather against those few remaining fellow-travelers who tried to exploit the civil-liberties issue.
>
> At times this had an almost comic aspect. When Irving Kristol was executive secretary of the ACCF,

one learned to expect from him silence on those issues that were agitating the whole intellectual and academic world, and enraged communiqués on the outrages performed by people like Arthur Miller and Bertrand Russell in exaggerating the dangers to civil liberties in the U.S.

Inevitably this led to more serious problems. In an article by Kristol, which first appeared in *Commentary* and was later circulated under the ACCF imprimatur, one could read such astonishing and appalling statements as "there is one thing the American people know about Senator McCarthy; he, like them, is unequivocally anti-Communist. About the spokesmen for American liberalism, they feel they know no such thing. And with some justification." This in the name of defending cultural freedom!

Harrington then proceeded to list several instances in which the ACCF had "acted within the United States in defense of freedom." But

> these activities do not absorb the main attention or interest of the Committee; its leadership is too jaded, too imbued with the sourness of indiscriminate anti-Stalinism to give itself to an active struggle against the dominant trend of contemporary intellectual life in America. What it *really* cares about is a struggle against fellow-travelers and "neutralists"—that is, against many European intellectuals. . . .
>
> One of the crippling assumptions of the Committee has been that it would not intervene in cases where Stalinists or accused Stalinists were involved. It has rested this position on the academic argument . . . that Stalinists, being enemies of democracy, have no "right" to democratic privileges. . . . But the actual problem is not the metaphysical one of whether enemies of democracy (as the Stalinists clearly are) have a "right" to democratic privileges. What matters is that the drive against cultural freedom and civil liberties takes on the guise of anti-Stalinism.

Years later came the revelations that the Congress for Cultural Freedom, which had its headquarters in Paris and with which the American Committee was for a time affiliated, had received secret funds from the CIA. Some of the people, it turned out, with whom one had sincerely disagreed were not free men at all; they were known accomplices of an intelligence service. What a sad denouement! And yet not the heart of the matter, as the malicious *Ramparts* journalists have tried to make out. Most of the intellectuals who belonged to the ACCF seem not to have had any knowledge of the CIA connection—on this, as on anything else, I would completely accept the word of Dwight Macdonald. It is also true, however, that these intellectuals seem not to have inquired very closely into the Congress's sources of support. That a few, deceiving their closest associates, established connections with the CIA was not nearly so important, however, as that a majority within the Committee acquiesced in a politics of acquiescence. We Americans have a strong taste for conspiracy theories, supposing that if you scratch a trouble you'll find a villain. But history is far more complicated; and squalid as the CIA tie was, it should not be used to smear honest people who had nothing to do with secret services even as they remain open to criticism for what they did say and do.

At the same time, the retrospective defenses offered by some New York intellectuals strike me as decidedly lame. Meetings and magazines sponsored by the Congress, Daniel Bell has said, kept their intellectual freedom and contained criticism of U.S. policy—true but hardly to the point, since the issue at stake is not the opinions the Congress tolerated but the larger problem of good faith in intellectual life. The leadership of the Congress did not give its own supporters the opportunity to choose whether they wished to belong to a CIA-financed group. Another defense, this one offered by Sidney Hook, is that private backing was hard to find during the years it was essential to publish journals like *Preuves* and *Encounter* in Europe. Simply as a matter of fact, I do not believe this. For the Congress to have raised its funds openly, from nongovernmental sources, would have meant discomfort, scrounging, penny-pinching: all the irksome things editors of little magazines have always had to do. By the postwar years, however, leading figures of both the Congress and the Committee no longer thought or behaved in that tradition.

Dwight Macdonald did. His magazine *Politics* was the one significant effort during the late forties to return to radicalism. Enlivened by Macdonald's ingratiating personality and his table-hopping mind, *Politics* brought together sophisticated muckraking with torturous revaluations of Marxist ideology. Macdonald could not long keep in balance the competing interests which finally tore apart his magazine: lively commentary on current affairs and unavoidable if depressing retrospects on the failure of the left. As always with Macdonald, honesty won out (one almost adds, alas) and the "inside" political discussion reached its climax with his essay "The Root Is Man," in which he arrived at a kind of anarcho-pacificism based on an absolutist morality. This essay was in many ways the most poignant and authentic expression of the plight of those few intellectuals—Nicola Chiaromonte, Paul Goodman, Macdonald—who wished to dissociate themselves from the postwar turn to *Realpolitik* but could not find ways of transforming sentiments of rectitude and visions of utopia into a workable politics. It was also a perfect leftist rationale for a kind of internal emigration of spirit and mind, with some odd shadings of similarity to the Salinger cult of the late fifties.

The overwhelming intellectual drift, however, was toward the right. Arthur Schlesinger, Jr., with moony glances at Kierkegaard, wrote essays in which he maintained that American society had all but taken care of its economic problems and could now concentrate on raising its cultural level. The "end of ideology" became a favorite shield for intellectuals in retreat, though it was never entirely clear whether this phrase meant the end of "our" ideology (partly true) or that all ideologies were soon to disintegrate (not true) or that the time had come to abandon the nostalgia for ideology (at least debatable). And in the mid-fifties, as if to codify things, there appeared in *Partisan Review* a symposium, "Our Country and Our Culture," in which all but three or four of the thirty participants clearly moved away from their earlier radical views. The *rapprochement* with "America the Beautiful," as Mary McCarthy now called it in a tone not wholly ironic, seemed almost complete.

In these years there also began that series of gyrations in opinion, interest, and outlook—so frenetic, so unserious—which would mark our intellectual life. In place of the avant-garde idea we now had the *style of fashion*, though to suggest a mere replacement may be too simple, since as Poggioli remarks, fashion has often shadowed the avant-garde as a kind of dandified double. Some intellectuals turned to a weekend of religion, some to a semester of existentialism, some to a holiday of Jewishness without faith or knowledge, some to a season of genteel conservatism. Leslie Fiedler, no doubt by design, seemed to go through more of such episodes than anyone else:

even his admirers could not always be certain whether he was *davenning* or doing a rain dance.

These twists and turns were lively, and they could all seem harmless if only one could learn to look upon intellectual life as a variety of play, like *potsie* or *king of the hill*. What struck one as troubling, however, was not this or that fashion (tomorrow morning would bring another), but the dynamic of fashion itself, the ruthlessness with which, to remain in fashion, fashion had to keep devouring itself.

It would be unfair to give the impression that the fifteen years after the war were without significant growth or achievement among the New York writers. The attempt of recent New Left ideologues to present the forties and fifties as if they were no more than a time of intellectual sterility and reaction is an oversimplification. Together with the turn toward conservative acquiescence, there were serious and valuable achievements. Hannah Arendt's book on totalitarianism may now seem open to many criticisms, but it certainly must rank as a major piece of work which, at the very least, made impossible—I mean, implausible—those theories of totalitarianism which, before and after she wrote, tended to reduce Fascism and Stalinism to a matter of class rule or economic interest. Daniel Bell's writing contributed to the rightward turn of these years, but some of it, such as his excellent little book *Work and Its Discontents*, constitutes a permanent contribution, and one that is valuable for radicals too. The stress upon complexity of thought which characterized intellectual life during these years could be used as a rationale for conservatism, and perhaps even arose from the turn toward conservatism; but in truth, the lapsed radicalism of earlier years *had* proved to be simplistic, the world of late capitalism *was* perplexing, and for serious people complexity *is* a positive value. Even the few intellectuals who resisted the dominant temper of the fifties underwent during these years significant changes in their political outlooks and styles of thought: e.g., those around *Dissent* who cut whatever ties of sentiment still held them to the Bolshevik tradition and made the indissoluble connection between democracy and socialism a crux of their thought. Much that happened during these years is to be deplored and dismissed, but not all was waste; the increasing sophistication and complication of mind was a genuine gain, and it would be absurd, at this late date, to forgo it.

In literary criticism there were equivalent achievements. The very instability that might make a shambles out of political thought could have the effect of magnifying the powers required for criticism. Floundering in life and uncertainty in thought could make for an increased responsiveness to art. In the criticism of men like Trilling, Rahv, Stuart Chase, and F. W. Dupee there was now a more authoritative relation to the literary text and a richer awareness of the cultural past than was likely to be found in their earlier work. And a useful tension was also set up between the New York critics, whose instinctive response to literature was through a social-moral contextualism, and the New Critics, whose formalism may have been too rigid yet proved of great value to those who opposed it.

Meanwhile, the world seemed to be opening up, with all its charms, seductions, and falsities. In the thirties the life of the New York writers had been confined: the little magazine as island, the radical sect as cave. Partly they were recapitulating the pattern of immigrant Jewish experience: an ingathering of the flock in order to break out into the world and taste the Gentile fruits of status and success. Once it became clear that waiting for the revolution might turn out to be steady work

and that the United States would neither veer to Fascism nor sink into depression, the intellectuals had little choice but to live within (which didn't necessarily mean, become partisans of) the existing society.

There was money to be had from publishers, no great amounts, but more than in the past. There were jobs in the universities, even for those without degrees. Some writers began to discover that publishing a story in *The New Yorker* or *Esquire* was not a sure ticket to Satan; others to see that the academy, while perhaps less exciting than the Village, wasn't invariably a graveyard for intellect and might even provide the only harbor in which serious people could do their own writing and perform honorable work. This dispersion involved losses, but usually there was nothing sinister about it—unless one clung, past an appropriate age, to the fantasy of being a momentarily unemployed "professional revolutionist." Writers ought to know something about the world; they ought to test their notions against the reality of the country in which they live. Worldly involvements would, of course, bring risks, and one of these was power, really a very trifling kind of power, but still enough to raise the fear of corruption. That power corrupts everyone knows by now, but we ought also to recognize that powerlessness, if not corrupting, can be damaging—as in the case of Paul Goodman, a courageous writer who stuck to his anarchist beliefs through years in which he was mocked and all but excluded from the New York journals, yet who could also come to seem, in his very rectitude, an example of asphyxiating righteousness.

What brought about these changes? Partly ideological adaptation, a feeling that capitalist society was here to stay and there wasn't much point in maintaining a radical position or posture. Partly the sly workings of prosperity. But also a loosening of the society itself, the start of that process which only now is in full swing—I mean the remarkable absorptiveness of modern society, its readiness to abandon traditional precepts for a moment of excitement, its growing permissiveness toward social criticism, perhaps out of indifference, or security, or even tolerance.

In the sixties well-placed young professors and radical students would denounce the "success," sometimes the "sellout," of the New York writers. Their attitude reminds one a little of George Orwell's remark about wartime France: only a Pétain could afford the luxury of asceticism, ordinary people had to live by the necessities of materialism. But really, when you come to think of it, what did this "success" of the intellectuals amount to? A decent or a good job, a chance to earn extra money by working hard, and in the case of a few, like Trilling and Kazin, some fame beyond New York—rewards most European intellectuals would take for granted, so paltry would they seem. For the New York writers who lived through the thirties expecting never to have a job at all, a regular pay check might be remarkable; but in the American scale of things it was very modest indeed. And what the "leftist" prigs of the sixties, sons of psychiatrists and manufacturers, failed to understand—or perhaps understood only too well—was that the "success" with which they kept scaring themselves was simply one of the possibilities of adult life, a possibility, like failure, heavy with moral risks and disappointment. Could they imagine that they, too, might have to face the common lot? I mean the whole business: debts, overwork, varicose veins, alimony, drinking, quarrels, hemorrhoids, depletion, the recognition that one might prove not to be another T. S. Eliot, but also some good things, some lessons learned, some "rags of time" salvaged and precious.

Here and there you could find petty greed or huckstering, now and again a drop into opportunism; but to make much of this would be foolish. Common clay, the New York writers had their share of common ambition. What drove them, and sometimes drove them crazy, was not, however, the quest for money, nor even a chance to "mix" with White House residents; it was finally, when all the trivia of existence were brushed aside, a gnawing ambition to write something, even three pages, that might live.

The intellectuals should have regarded their entry into the outer world as utterly commonplace, at least if they kept faith with the warning of Stendhal and Balzac that one must always hold a portion of the self forever beyond the world's reach. Few of the New York intellectuals made much money on books and articles. Few reached audiences beyond the little magazines. Few approached any centers of power, and precisely the buzz of gossip attending the one or two sometimes invited to a party beyond the well-surveyed limits of the West Side showed how confined their life still was. What seems most remarkable in retrospect is the innocence behind the assumption, sometimes held by the New York writers themselves with a nervous mixture of guilt and glee, that whatever recognition they won was cause for either preening or embarrassment. For all their gloss of sophistication, they had not really moved very far into the world. The immigrant milk was still on their lips.

In their published work during these years, the New York intellectuals developed a characteristic style of exposition and polemic. With some admiration and a bit of irony, let us call it the style of brilliance. The kind of essay they wrote was likely to be wide-ranging in reference, melding notions about literature and politics, sometimes announcing itself as a study of a writer or literary group but usually taut with a pressure to "go beyond" its subject, toward some encompassing moral or social observation. It is a kind of writing highly self-conscious in mode, with an unashamed vibration of bravura and display. Nervous, strewn with knotty or flashy phrases, impatient with transitions and other concessions to dullness, willfully calling attention to itself as a form or at least an outcry, fond of rapid twists, taking pleasure in dispute, dialectic, dazzle—such, at its best or most noticeable, was the essay cultivated by the New York writers. Until recently its strategy of exposition was likely to be impersonal (the writer did not speak much as an "I") but its tone and bearing were likely to be intensely personal (the audience was to be made aware that the aim of the piece was not judiciousness but rather a strong impress of attitude, a blow of novelty, a wrenching of accepted opinion, sometimes a mere indulgence of vanity).

In most of these essays there was a sense of *tournament*, the writer as gymnast with one eye on other rings, or as skilled infighter juggling knives of dialectic. Polemics were harsh, often rude. And audiences nurtured, or spoiled, on this kind of performance, learned not to form settled judgments about a dispute until all sides had registered their blows: surprise was always a possible reward.

This style may have brought new life to the American essay, but in contemporary audiences it often evoked a strong distaste and even fear. "Ordinary" readers could be left with the fretful sense that they were not "in," the beauties of polemic racing past their sluggish eye. Old-line academics, quite as if they had just crawled out of *The Dunciad*, enjoyed dismissing the New York critics as "unsound." And for some younger souls, the cliffs of dialectic seemed too steep. Seymour Krim has left a poignant account of his disablement before "the overcerebral, Europeanish, sterilely citified, pretentiously alienated" New York intellectuals. Resentful at the fate which drove them to compare themselves with "the overcerebral, etc., etc.," Krim writes that he and his friends "were often tortured and unappeasably bitter about being the offspring of this unhappily unique-ingrown-screwed-up breed." Similar complaints could be heard from other writers and would-be writers who felt that New York intellectualism threatened their vital powers.

At its best the style of brilliance reflected a certain view of the intellectual life: free-lance dash, peacock strut, daring hypothesis, knockabout synthesis. For better or worse it was radically different from the accepted modes of scholarly publishing and middle-brow journalism. It celebrated the idea of the intellectual as antispecialist, or as a writer whose speciality was the lack of a speciality: the writer as dilettante-connoisseur, *Luftmensch* of the mind, roamer among theories. But it was a style which also lent itself with peculiar ease to a stifling mimicry and decadence. Sometimes it seemed—no doubt mistakenly—as if any sophomore, indeed any parrot, could learn to write one of those scintillating *Partisan* reviews, so thoroughly could manner consume matter. In the fifties the cult of brilliance became a sign that writers were offering not their work or ideas but their persona as content; and this was but a step or two away from the exhibitionism of the sixties. Brilliance could become a sign of intellect unmoored: the less assurance, the more pyrotechnics. In making this judgment I ought to register the view that serious writers may prove to be brilliant and take pleasure in the proving, but insofar as they are serious, their overriding aim must be absolute lucidity.

If to the minor genre of the essay the New York writers made a major contribution, to the major genres of fiction and poetry they made only a minor contribution. As a literary group and no more than a literary group, they will seem less important than, say, the new critics, who did set in motion a whole school of poetry. A few poets—John Berryman, Robert Lowell, Randall Jarrell, perhaps Stanley Kunitz—have been influenced by the New York intellectuals, though in ways hard to specify and hardly comprising a major pressure on their work: all were finished writers by the time they brushed against the New York milieu. For one or two poets, the influence of New York meant becoming aware of the cultural pathos resident in the idea of the Jew (not always distinguished from the idea of Delmore Schwartz). But the main literary contribution of the New York milieu has been to legitimate a subject and tone we must uneasily call American Jewish writing. The fiction of urban malaise, second-generation complaint, Talmudic dazzle, woeful alienation, and dialectical irony, all found its earliest expression in the pages of *Commentary* and *Partisan Review*—fiction in which the Jewish world is not merely regained in memory as a point of beginnings, an archetypal Lower East Side of spirit and place, but is also treated as a portentous metaphor of man's homelessness and wandering.

Such distinguished short fictions as Bellow's *Seize the Day*, Schwartz's "In Dreams Begin Responsibility," Mailer's "The Man Who Studied Yoga," and Malamud's "The Magic Barrel" seem likely to survive the cultural moment in which they were written. And even if one concludes that these and similar pieces are not enough to warrant speaking of a major literary group, they certainly form a notable addition—a new tone, a new sensibility—to American writing. In time, these writers may be regarded as the last "regional" group in American literature, parallel to recent Southern writers in both sophistication of craft and a thematic dissociation from the values of

American society. Nor is it important that during the last few decades both of these literary tendencies, the Southern and the Jewish, have been overvalued. The distance of but a few years has already made it clear that except for Faulkner Southern writing consists of a scatter of talented minor poets and novelists; and in a decade or so a similar judgment may be commonly accepted about most of the Jewish writers—though in regard to Bellow and Mailer settled opinions are still risky.

What is clear from both Southern and Jewish writing is that in a society increasingly disturbed about its lack of self-definition, the recall of regional and traditional details can be intensely absorbing in its own right, as well as suggestive of larger themes transcending the region. (For the Jewish writers New York was not merely a place, it was a symbol, a burden, a stamp of history.) Yet the writers of neither school have thus far managed to move from their particular milieu to a grasp of the entire culture; the very strengths of their localism define their limitations; and especially is this true for the Jewish writers, in whose behalf critics have recently overreached themselves. The effort to transform a Jewishness without religious or ethnic content into an emblem of universal dismay can easily lapse into sentimentality.

Whatever the hopeful future of individual writers, the "school" of American Jewish writing is by now in an advanced state of decomposition: how else explain the attention it has lately enjoyed? Or the appearance of a generation of younger Jewish writers who, without authentic experience or memory to draw upon, manufacture fantasies about the lives of their grandfathers? Or the popularity of Isaac Bashevis Singer who, coming to the American literary scene precisely at the moment when writers composing in English had begun to exhaust the Jewish subject, could, by dazzling contrast, extend it endlessly backward in time and deeper in historical imagination?

Just as there appear today young Jewish intellectuals who no longer know what it is that as Jews they do not know, so in fiction the fading immigrant world offers a thinner and thinner yield to writers of fiction. It no longer presses on memory, people can now *choose* whether to care about it. We are almost at the end of a historic experience, and it now seems unlikely that there will have arisen in New York a literary school comparable to the best this country has had. Insofar as the New York intellectual atmosphere has affected writers like Schwartz, Rosenfeld, Bellow, Malamud, Mailer, Goodman, and Roth (some of these would hotly deny that it has), it seems to have been too brittle, too contentious, too insecure for major creative work. What cannot yet be estimated is the extent to which the styles and values of the New York world may have left a mark on the work of American writers who never came directly under its influence or have been staunchly hostile to all of its ways. (pp. 216-44)

> *Irving Howe, "The New York Intellectuals," in his* Decline of the New, *Harcourt Brace Jovanovich, 1970, pp. 211-65.*

ADDITIONAL BIBLIOGRAPHY

Aaron, Daniel. "The Case of the *Partisan Review*." In his *Writers on the Left*, pp. 297-303. New York: Harcourt, Brace, and World, 1961.
> Discusses the political and editorial stance of *Partisan Review* prior to its 1937 revival by Rahv and Phillips.

Abel, Lionel. *The Intellectual Follies*. New York: W. W. Norton, 1984, 304 p.
> Reminiscences of Abel's affiliation with the New York Intellectuals.

Arrowsmith, William. "*Partisan Review* and American Writing." *Hudson Review* 1, No. 4 (Winter 1949): 526-36.
> Contends that "the editors of the *Partisan Review* have done American writing a serious disservice" by focusing only on recondite, nihilistic literature.

Atlas, James. "The Changing World of the New York Intellectuals." *New York Times Magazine* (25 August 1985) 22 ff.
> Discusses the history and current status of the New York Intellectuals.

Barrett, William. *The Truants: Adventures among the Intellectuals*. Garden City, N. Y.: Anchor Press/Doubleday, 1982, 270 p.
> Memoirs. Barrett was an associate editor of *Partisan Review* and provides firsthand accounts of significant events.

Bell, Daniel. "The 'Intelligentsia' in American Society." In *Tomorrow's American*, edited by Samuel Sandmel, pp. 22-46. New York: Oxford University Press, 1977.
> Discusses the New York Intellectuals as an example of a cohesive intellectual elite in American society.

Bender, Thomas. *New York Intellect*. New York: Knopf, 1987, 422 p.
> Historical study of intellectual life in New York City from 1750 to the early twentieth century, making frequent references to the New York Intellectuals.

Cowley, Malcolm. "*Partisan Review*." *The New Republic* LXXXXVI, No. 1245 (19 October 1938): 311-12.
> Argues that polemics have been allowed to supplant the literary aims of *Partisan Review*.

Decter, Midge. "Socialism and Its Irresponsibilities: The Case of Irving Howe." *Commentary* 74, No. 6 (December 1982): 25-32.
> Reviews Howe's autobiography, *A Margin of Hope* (see entry below), which Decter pronounces "an oddly enclosed and unmoving piece of work."

Dickstein, Morris. "Up from Alienation: The Case of the New York Intellectuals." *Revue Française d'Etudes Americaines*, No. 16 (February 1983): 45-54.
> Examines the cultural and political factors that influenced the New York Intellectuals.

Epstein, Joseph. "Polonius Remembers the *Partisan Review*." *Sewanee Review* XCII, No. 4 (Fall 1984): 604-17.
> Negative review of William Phillips's memoirs (see entry below), charging that Phillips's "reigning tone is that of a modern-day prose Polonius specializing in the higher sententiousness."

Fiedler, Leslie A. *Being Busted*. New York: Stein and Day, 1969, 255 p.
> Reminiscences. Fiedler states in his preface: "This is, despite its autobiographical form, a book not about me . . . so much as one about social and cultural change between 1933 . . . and 1967. . . . Its true subject is the endless war, sometimes cold, sometimes hot, between the dissenter and his imperfect society."

Gilbert, James Burkhart. *Writers and Partisans: A History of Literary Radicalism in America*. New York: John Wiley and Sons, 1968, 303 p.
> Thorough examination of the activities of leftist writers from the turn of the century to the postwar period.

Hart, Jeffrey. "The New York Intellectuals and the Socialist Legacy." *National Review* XXXIX, No. 17 (11 September 1987): 58-63.
> Discusses the history of the New York Intellectuals, disputing the claim that the conservatism of several members represents a betrayal of their former ideological positions.

Hollinger, David A. "Ethnic Diversity, Cosmopolitanism and the Emergence of the American Liberal Intelligentsia." *American Quarterly* XXVII, No. 2 (May 1975): 133-51.

Examines the historical factors that contributed to the increasing conservatism of American intellectuals during the mid-twentieth century.

Hook, Sidney. *Out of Step: An Unquiet Life in the 20th Century.* New York: Harper and Row, 1987, 628 p.
Autobiography. Hook discusses his involvement with the New York Intellectuals at length, but deemphasizes his role as an influential member of the group.

Howe, Irving. *A Margin of Hope: An Intellectual Autobiography.* San Diego: Harcourt, Brace, Jovanovich, 1982, 352 p.
Provides extensive discussions and critiques of the varying ideological positions of the New York Intellectuals.

Kazin, Alfred. *Starting Out in the Thirties.* Boston: Little, Brown, and Company, 1962, 166 p.
Reminiscences of Kazin's Marxist period and his early involvement with *Partisan Review.*

———. *New York Jew.* New York: Alfred A. Knopf, 1978, 307 p.
Volume Three of Kazin's memoirs, covering the period from World War II to the late 1960s. Includes many reminiscences of New York Intellectuals.

Kostelanetz, Richard. "The New York Literary Mob." In his *The End of Intelligent Writing,* pp. 39-59. New York: Sheed and Ward, 1973.
Views the political and literary conservatism of the New York Intellectuals as a negative influence in the contemporary publishing industry.

Kramer, Hilton. "*Partisan Review:* Down the Memory Hole." *New Criterion* 2, No. 1 (September 1983): 1-10.
Examines the political history of *Partisan Review,* arguing that the account presented in William Phillips's memoirs (see entry below) is distorted by misguided liberalism and personal bitterness.

———. "The Importance of Sidney Hook." *Commentary* 84, No. 2 (August 1987): 17-24.
Review of Hook's autobiography, *Out of Step.* Kramer supports Hook's criticisms of various other New York Intellectuals.

Kristol, Irving and Howe, Irving. "The New York Intellectuals." *Commentary* 47, No. 1 (January 1969): 12-16.
Two-part essay in which Kristol defends himself against the charge of apostasy he finds inherent in Howe's earlier "New York Intellectuals" essay (excerpted above), while Howe reiterates the charge.

Lasch, Christopher. *The Agony of the American Left.* New York: Alfred A. Knopf, 1969, 212 p.
History of the American Left in the twentieth century which frequently refers to the activities of the New York Intellectuals.

Lowell, Robert. "The New York Intellectual." In his *Notebook, 1967-68,* p. 112. New York: Farrar, Straus, and Giroux, 1969.
Poem written in response to Irving Howe's 1968 essay (excerpted above).

O'Neill, William. *A Better World: The Great Schism—Stalinism and the American Intellectuals.* New York: Simon and Schuster, 1982, 497 p.
Contrasts the largely negative responses of the New York Intellectuals to the increasing totalitarianism of Joseph Stalin's regime with the reactions of leftist intellectuals more sympathetic to the Soviet Union.

Pells, Richard H. *The Liberal Mind in a Conservative Age.* New York: Harper and Row, 1985, 468 p.
Study of "the way certain American writers in the 1940s and 1950s interpreted and tried to cope with the major events of their time," including discussions of a large number of New York Intellectuals.

Phillips, William. "On *Partisan Review.*" *Triquarterly* (Fall 1978): 130-41.
Discusses the history of *Partisan Review.*

———. *A Partisan View: Five Decades of Literary Life.* New York: Stein and Day, 1983, 312 p.
Memoirs. Phillips states that he felt compelled by the distorted accounts of William Barrett, Norman Podhoretz, and others to publish his own recollections of the New York Intellectuals.

Roskolenko, Harry. *When I Was Last on Cherry Street.* New York: Stein and Day, 1965, 248 p.
Provides numerous personal impressions of the New York Intellectuals.

Schrecker, Ellen W. "Born to Trot." *The Nation* 245, No. 3 (1-8 August 1987): 94-6.
Favorable review of Alan Wald's study *The New York Intellectuals* in which Schrecker focuses on the group's abandonment of Marxism.

Shechner, Mark. "New York Intellectuals." *Salmagundi,* Nos. 76-77 (Fall 1987-Winter 1988): 204-17.
Review of *The New York Intellectuals* in which Shechner notes that the story of the group's quarrels and rise to power contains much humor.

Westbrook, Robert. "Stream of Contentiousness." *The Nation* 244, No. 21 (30 May 1987): 726-30.
Discusses Sidney Hook's *Out of Step* (see entry above), pointing out inconsistencies in Hook's account of his moral and political development.

Nigerian Literature in the Twentieth Century

INTRODUCTION

Two distinct literary traditions exist in Nigeria: the oral tradition, which is made up of folktales, proverbs, and legends, and the written tradition, which began in the mid-1940s and includes novels, drama, and poetry. Oral literature in Nigeria has been passed on in the indigenous languages of that country, the most prevalent of which are Igbo (or Ibo), Yoruba, and Hausa. Most examples of this native literature, which is explicitly moralistic and intertwined with tribal religion, concern such subjects as ancestor worship and loyalty to the tribe. Written literature in Nigeria began to proliferate after World War II in the form of cheaply printed fiction and nonfiction that retained the moralistic character of oral literature but often championed Western attitudes toward romance, marriage, and material possessions. In the late 1950s and 1960s, Nigerian writers began to publish novels, plays, and collections of short stories and poetry. These works, which often incorporate elements of the earlier oral tradition, collectively comprise a literature that is both modern and traditionally African.

The part of Western Africa now known as Nigeria existed for centuries as the homeland of diverse and for the most part isolated peoples. This region was first explored by Portuguese navigators in the second half of the fifteenth century, and was evangelized by Christian missionaries in the middle nineteenth century. Between the 1860s and the 1890s the separate areas of Western Africa were ceded by various tribal groups to the British Empire, which retained control of them until 1960. During this period of British colonialism, English was imposed on Nigeria as its national language. Because of the diversity of languages and dialects in Nigeria, English remains a national common language, as well as the language in which most Nigerian literature is written, as works in indigenous languages are able to reach only a provincial audience. Although many critics and writers find that English has developed in accordance with Western experience, and is thus unsuited for the expression of African life, Nigerian writers have attempted to reflect native languages and traditions in their English-language works. For example, Amos Tutuola, who wrote the first internationally recognized Nigerian novel, *The Palm-Wine Drinkard,* used a narrative framework based on Western literary models in order to translate Yoruba legends into English. This method of cultural transmission was developed further in the plays of Wole Soyinka, which integrate Nigerian mythology and customs with the conventions of Western realistic drama. The novels of Chinua Achebe, especially *Things Fall Apart, No Longer At Ease,* and *Arrow of God,* replicate Igbo speech patterns in English and dramatize the conflict between traditional African and modern European mores, ideals, and beliefs.

In 1960 Britain granted independence to Nigeria, and in 1963 the tribal regions were united into a single republic. Three years later, army officers from the Igbo tribe overthrew the civil government and instituted a military regime. This government was itself overthrown six months later by a Hausa contingent of the military, and Igbos, persecuted by members of other tribes, began returning to their traditional homeland in eastern Nigeria. In 1967 this region declared itself the in-dependent Republic of Biafra, precipitating a civil war that lasted until 1970, when Biafra, its people starving, surrendered. During and after the war, the output of Nigerian writing decreased and the works that were published offered a more cynical view of modern life than the writings of previous years. The country remained under a military dictatorship until 1979, when civilian rule was reestablished; four years later, this government was overthrown in another military coup. Since that event, social and political unrest has continued to trouble Nigeria.

Much of Nigerian literature displays a strong political cast, ranging from anticolonial and socialist polemics to expressions of pessimism about the possibility of constructive political change. Social awareness is also a pronounced aspect of Nigerian writing, with the prime concern of the majority of writers being the betterment of Nigerian society. Although nationalistic and often anti-Western in its implications, Nigerian writing has gained widespread international recognition and interest as a rich and significant body of literature.

SURVEYS OF NIGERIAN LITERATURE IN ENGLISH AND NIGERIAN LANGUAGES

D. S. IZEVBAYE

[*In the following excerpt, Izevbaye surveys Nigerian prose, drama, and poetry written in English.*]

What is most often emphasized about the role of a colonial language like English is its ability to promote communication between separate peoples and reduce what Joseph Jones has described in *Terranglia* as "an incessant Babel of clamorous nationalisms." Nationalism is of course a legitimate political means of discovering one's personality, as it is a means of giving literary expression to one's identity. This identity need not find expression only in local vernaculars. In a multilingual society a foreign language has an initial advantage over the vernaculars since it is not merely a medium for international communication but also a means of achieving cohesion within the nation. In a similar manner a common language like English can help to develop the national character of a literature. In spite of being part of an international community, writers from a country which shares in the common wealth of the English language can retain their national individuality because of the nature of their relationship to the language. The attempt to describe the local landscape in a foreign tongue will itself create a sufficient need for modifying the language. But the more important pressures from the living vernaculars will affect the use of a second language either by causing linguistic interferences in the work of the less sophisticated writers or by providing a source of linguistic experiments for the more sophisticated ones. Thus English provides a basis for a national literature by creating a meeting point for the country's cultural diversity. Because this diversity finds expression in a multiplicity of local languages it appears at first to be a mixed blessing. This is implied in "Were I to Choose," a 1957 poem by Gabriel Okara. At thirty-one, the poet takes stock of his world and sees in his growth from childhood to adulthood not a growth in understanding through a common language but the confusion of Babel:

> And now the close of one
> and thirty turns, the world
> of bones is Babel, and
> the different tongues within
> are flames the head
> continually burning.

Okara's expression of frustration either here or in his better known 1959 poem, "Piano and Drums," is not a typical reaction. But it dramatizes the need for a common national language by using an image which anticipates that of Joseph Jones, and which finds its closest parallel in an identical image used for a different purpose by another poet, J. P. Clark. Clark sees English as a means of taking "a positive step back from Babel's house of many tongues."

But the advantage of English does not lie merely in its ability to perform this unifying function, for it is an historical accident that gave it this advantage over any of the local vernaculars that could have performed the function as effectively. Its second function has been to gain for Nigerian literature a much wider audience than is available to the older vernacular literatures in, for example, Hausa and Yoruba. Fagunwa's *Ogboju Ode Ninu Igbo Irunmale,* the earliest work by the first important Yoruba fiction writer, was published in 1938, and *Gandoki,* a Hausa tale by Bello Kagara, was published in 1934. The earliest works in English to be known to the outside world are Tutuola's *The Palm-Wine Drinkard,* published in 1952, and Achebe's *Things Fall Apart,* published in 1958. Although both came about two decades after the vernacular works, they have received much greater attention because they were written in English. Such attention from an audience whose taste has been influenced by its familiarity with the tradition of English literature has had the effect of emphasizing the indebtedness to English literature more than anything else, especially since some of these debts are explicit enough.

Many of the literary devices and forms are familiar enough even when they do not derive directly from a particular English writer or school. This is true of the novel, a form stimulated by contact with Europe. With the occasional exception of a novel like Okara's *The Voice* (1964) which is closer to the allegory or morality tale than to realistic fiction, many Nigerian novels operate within the well-tried convention of developing an ordinary story chronologically and telling it in the third person. But even the experiments can be related to contemporary practice elsewhere. Achebe's *A Man of the People* (1966) has a more sophisticated technique than *Things Fall Apart,* being an ironic first-person story of how a young man is forced to operate double moral standards in the tough political environment in which he finds himself. In *The Interpreters* (1965), Wole Soyinka tells the story of a group of characters in search of identity in a corrupt and changing society. The technique of using rapid, sometimes baffling, time shifts to reveal the influence of past events on the present action of characters belongs to a tradition that has developed under the influence of Joyce and Faulkner. The method of blending two incidents from the past and the present by making one fade into the other at a point of association derives from the use of montage in cinematography.

Apart from such general experiments within a well-known tradition, there are explicit instances of borrowing from specific works. The best known of these are the phrases from Yeats and Eliot which Achebe uses for the titles of his first two novels. Such features make the literature at first seem an extension of the literary province of English, although the English influence is only one of at least two factors that have influenced the literature. The second factor, the background of vernacular cultures, has helped to give Nigerian literature its character, and can provide a touchstone for understanding and identifying the peculiar characteristics of the literature. A common feature is the reference to products of modern technology in a setting of ancestral Nigerian cultures where traditions die hard. The combination is sometimes an uneasy one, but it often shows not a rejection, but a struggle to understand and assimilate some of the foreign items. The expression of this struggle accounts for the experimental approach to English by Nigerian writers, and may be seen in phrases like Achebe's "iron horse" for bicycle and Nkem Nwankwo's "landboat" for motor car. The composure with which Amos Tutuola offers us the cultural mixture in *The Palm-Wine Drinkard* is matched only by the resourcefulness of his hero who sees magic and technology as equally acceptable means of getting out of trouble, and therefore employs them indiscriminately. At a threat from beasts in a spirit-infested jungle, he takes over control of the situation by commanding:

> I told my wife to jump on my back with our loads, at the same time, I commanded my juju.... So I became a big bird like an aeroplane and flew away with my wife, I flew for 5 hours before I came down, after I had left the dangerous area.

Achebe's description of the problems and the possibilities in the use of English by an African writer makes allowance for Tutuola, whose solution he does not accept in principle:

> Those who can do the work of extending the frontiers of English so as to accommodate African thought-patterns must do it through their mastery of English and not out of innocence. Of course, there is the obvious exception of Amos Tutuola. But even there it is possible that he has said something unique and interesting in a way that is not susceptible to further development.

In spite of their differences both writers experiment in a manner which suggests a confident acceptance of English. It is a confidence that assumes the relevance of the local vernaculars. This assumption expresses itself in various literary styles, and can be seen working consciously or spontaneously in the work of various writers. It exists as an enactment of a people's way of life and modes of thought in the novels of Achebe where the style is itself a demonstration of the Ibo saying that "proverbs are the palm-oil with which words are eaten." An important part of Achebe's achievement is the way in which he successfully creates a feeling of authenticity in the speech and thought of his characters by a sufficiently accurate transcription of the modes of expression of a non-English people. Without tampering with the normal patterns of English as Tutuola does, he convincingly creates the awareness that English is merely the telegraphic line across which the vernacular speech is being simultaneously transmitted and translated to the reader. The exuberance and sheer verbal joy of Soyinka's writings similarly has its source in the vernacular; for the Yoruba, like many other Nigerian groups, delight in making sense out of mere sound. The influence of the vernacular can be seen at its most conscious and most extreme in *The Voice,* a novel in which

Gabriel Okara tries to handle English not just as a new language, but almost as an extension of his own vernacular.

Apart from the more obvious influence of English literature, there are two important antecedents to the literature. First, there is the oral tradition of folktales, folksongs and traditional festivals. The oral tradition is an importanat background to the literature because it is the first experience of literature for most Nigerians. Although the oral form of transmitting literature exists in all cultures it is more alive and more strongly felt in a country like Nigeria than in countries with longer histories of literacy. It is therefore more often treated by writers as the primary, though not necessarily more accessible, literary tradition. The other, but not so influential, antecedent to the literature in English is the vernacular literature. Each of the two vernacular examples referred to earlier is within a tradition of creative writing dating back to early in the century. The oral tradition is antecedent to both the English and vernacular traditions, while the written vernacular traditions are antecedent to the English, as is now becoming evident in the use being made of Yoruba material.

The presence of the oral tradition is best felt in Tutuola's *The Palm-Wine Drinkard*, a work that is often treated as the missing link of Nigerian literature. This work, like the five others which have followed it so far, belongs a little outside the normal experience of written fiction. The medium is alien to the matter and manner. Each of the romances repeats the same basic story—a human venture into the fearful world of ghosts, spirits and Deads. Because of the ink and paper medium the stories come in a more extended form. There is therefore a repetition in the use of certain types of incident, and this has produced the mythical pattern which Gerald Moore first analysed ten years later [in *Seven African Writers*]. Within this extended pattern which developed as a result of the more leisurely control afforded by writing, Tutuola exhibits the typical qualities of the traditional teller of tales, the most obvious of which is the raconteur's freedom to innovate as he goes on. The elusive "allegorical" manner comes from a tradition of personification in which the characters in a tale, be they animal, vegetable or mineral, are seen as having a soul or essence, and are therefore given a corresponding proper name. Similarly, Tutuola's synthesis of traditional Yoruba and modern scientific ideas belongs to the vernacular tradition, for it is part of that tradition to be innovative by assimilating all new elements in order to reflect the changing nature of the society. This is what has happened to the Yoruba myths of Sango and Ogun. Developing originally from an age when real technological power was only a dream, the myths of Sango, god of thunder and lightning, and Ogun, god of iron and war, have now become the very real myths of electricity and metal technology.

Even more typical of such a tradition is Tutuola's cosmography. In his map of the universe the boundary between fact and fantasy, if it exists at all, is very tenuous:

> I could not blame the lady for following the Skull as a complete gentleman to his house at all. Because if I were a lady, no doubt I would follow him to wherever he would go, and still as I was a man I would jealous him more than that, because if this gentleman went to the battle field, surely, enemy would not kill him or capture him and if bombers saw him in a town which was to be bombed, they would not throw bombs on his presence, and if they did throw it, the bomb itself would not explode until this gentleman would leave that town, because of his beauty.

The triumph of beauty over scientific power is a magical triumph. As there are no limits to magic, there is no boundary between living and dead, between Man and Spirit. If there is, it is merely slightly physical, being no more than that which separates town and bush in Tutuola's works, or Town Dwellers and Forest Dwellers in Soyinka's play, *A Dance of the Forests* (1962). The adventurous may cross into either realm. The view of the world which occurs in these two works is valid socially as well as artistically, and occurs in works from different areas of Nigeria. It is used in a novel like Elechi Amadi's *The Concubine* (1966), a story about an attractive and good-natured but unfortunate woman, who the villagers insist is the wife of a sea god.

While the growth of a Nigerian literature is being strongly influenced by the combination of these three traditions in various degrees, the literary tradition is also developing, mainly in response to social changes. Social change is a common theme in Nigerian fiction, and writers are often concerned with the relationship between the city and the rural areas. Cyprian Ekwensi brings to the Nigerian novel his Ibo sympathy for rural life; from his urban upbringing he brings a reporter's gift for evoking city life. *Jagua Nana* (1961), his most successful novel so far, is an impressive chronicle of Nigerian city life. It is concerned with the fortunes of a Lagos prostitute. But apart from being an effective character study of a prostitute, Ekwensi's portrayal of Jagua becomes an appropriate opportunity for a fairly comprehensive picture of the city. Because Jagua's "profession" enables her to move at all social levels we get a picture of what "Lagos life" is like at the British Council meetings where young men improve their minds, or at night clubs where young women sell their loves to swell their purses. The story also takes the reader into the den of thugs, and Ekwensi develops it to include the search for leisure by politicians, rich traders and lonely executives. The social realism of the novel is enriched by the almost literally transcribed pidgin speech of the characters, for pidgin belongs to urban Nigeria.

Like most Nigerian novels, *Jagua Nana* is not as experimental in form as *The Interpreters*. Although it has a similarly functional disorder in its ordering of incidents, it is not the same kind of novel and one does not expect the artistry and the power of organization which one often finds in Soyinka. But its episodic form and journalistic style are appropriate for its theme. The closest that it gets to a symmetry of form is in its use of the contrast between the city and rural areas, a common contrast in the Nigerian novel. Jagua's return home in this novel is not so much an invitation to the virtues of pastoral life, as a device for emphasizing the sterility of city life in spite of its seductiveness. The savagery of the city merely drives Jagua to the outskirts of the city, not out of it. It takes the death of her father and her brother's insistence to make her leave it. The temporary fertility with which the author consoles his heroine, and the oddly self-conscious treatment of sex in the last chapter of the book, together suggest that the rejection of the city is the author's rather than the character's.

It is not only among novels about urban life that the picaresque novel is found. It is appropriate for the purely comic purpose of Nkem Nwankwo's *Danda* (1964), a novel which derives its humour from its irreverence for all established values, whether these are traditional or recent. The loose form enables the author to make the best of his hero's nonconformity. The hero's irreverence, which provides the comedy, is possibly the product of a society experiencing great change, for it also fortifies the comedy of Soyinka the satirist, who charges head down at all establishments, especially where these provide a refuge for the unworthy and the hypocritical. A typical *Danda* incident is that of the boorish relation from the backwoods enjoying the good fortune of his better educated "brother" from the city. As the herdsman in his dirty clothes climbs into the shiny car of his kinsman, he appeals to a maxim that is traditionally accepted but is wholly irrelevant in the present situation as far as the kinsman is concerned: "What belongs to one belongs to one's kindred."

It is a slightly similar inadequacy of ancestral wisdom that gives Achebe's work its sometimes wry humour. In *Things Fall Apart* the men of Umuofia hear news of men with white skins and no toes, but they treat it with levity, dismissing it with flippant allusions to lepers. It is no laughing matter when the white man turns up with his guns. Such inadequacy is present when the men tie the "iron horse" of a murdered white man to a tree to prevent it from running away to call other white men. The incident is not really comic because its uncomfortable humour rests on our knowledge that the villagers' action is not completely foolish. Since it arises from ignorance rather than naïvety, it does not permit us to feel superior to the victims of this self-betrayal. The more serious purpose in Achebe's novels often reins in the comedy.

It is the awareness of the historical significance of local events which dictates the form of the village novels of Achebe. The form is not merely episodic, but is made sufficiently loose and flexible to incorporate the details of social life. That is why Achebe can evoke a society whose complexity and self-sufficiency are realized within two hundred pages. Achebe's works are an important interpretation of his people's history. Just as Ekwensi is concerned with survival at the urban level, so is Achebe concerned with survival at the historical level. His first three novels are studies in defeat. The two so-called village novels examine in turn the inadequacy of unyielding strength and then of a fine intelligence stubbornly applied, in coping with the problems of social change. Both novels show the inevitability of change and consequently the necessity for adaptation.

In *Things Fall Apart,* Okonkwo's strength of will is shown to be an extreme reaction to his experience of a weak father. The author shows his disapproval of such inflexible strength by making it operate against socially approved codes, as when Okonkwo beats his wife during the Week of Peace, or his killing of his ward. Ezeulu, the hero of *Arrow of God* (1964), is defeated for a similar inflexibility of will. From the start he is shown to possess the fine perception that is necessary for survival in his kind of situation. His intelligence is at its finest when he proposes to enroll his children in the white man's school, a mode of adaptation which the author evidently approves of:

> The world is changing. I do not like it. But I am like the bird Eneke-nti-oba. When his friends asked him why he was always on the wing he replied: "Men of today have learnt to shoot without missing and so I have learnt to fly without perching." I want one of my sons to join these people and be my eye there. If there is nothing in it you will come back . . . My spirit tells me that those who do not befriend the white man today will be saying *had we known* tomorrow.

Ezeulu is ruined because either he is unable to sustain this perception or he refuses to let it guide his actions. His deter-

mination to avenge his wronged god blinds him to the established adaptive processes of his society. The people of Umuaro can cite "numerous examples of customs that had been changed in the past when they began to work hardship on the people." Ezeulu's hubris is his refusal to eat the new yam in spite of these precedents.

In spite of the heroic tone and the elegiac mood, these novels are not nostalgic. The elegiac mood comes from the author's original intention to show that the African past "with all its imperfections was not one long night of savagery," and is artistically necessary for creating a society that will become familiar without footnotes or explanatory asides within the text. If the tragic mood indicates an affirmation of the validity of the past, the movement of the plot indicates an acceptance of the present as it is. At the end of both novels the fate of the hero is played in counterpoint against the general social adjustment which takes place. In *Things Fall Apart* the sympathy is weighted in favour of the hero because of the patent cowardice of the crowd.

> The men of Umuofia were merged into the mute backcloth of trees and giant creepers, waiting. . . . Okonkwo's matchet descended twice and the man's head lay beside his uniformed body.

> The waiting backcloth jumped into tumultous life and the meeting stopped. Okonkwo stood looking at the dead man. He knew that Umuofia would not go to war.

And, yet, in spite of this faint-heartedness, the inexorable character of the people's experience shows that there is wisdom in their action. The guide to behaviour is provided, ironically, in the proverb of Eneke the bird who, when asked why he was always on the wing replied: "Men have learnt to shoot without missing their mark and I have learnt to fly without 'perching' on a twig." True foolishness is exposed when a particular interpretation turns the meaning of this proverb against the interpreter. This is clear even if we need to look for the relevance of the use of Yeats's phrase for the title of the novel. Yeat's theory of historical change in "The Second Coming" does not stop with the mere statement that things fall apart, but also implies that because all important social and historical change is drastic and tragic, it is necessary to adapt or be destroyed. No one knows better than the people of Umuaro in *Arrow of God* that "these are not the times we used to know and we must meet them as they come or be rolled in the dust."

As a novelist, Achebe is not, however, obsessed with adaptation at all costs. In the village novels the historical processes which made adaptation a condition for survival also destroyed the heroic last stand for tradition and prepared the ground for the moral decline of the present. This is the link between Achebe's novels of the past and the two novels about contemporary life. The anti-heroes of his urban novels are willing to roll in moral dirt if it will enable them to survive. In his examination of this other side of the coin of survival, he does not give artistic approval to the kind of adaptation which demands not only a renunciation of idealism but also of social morality. It is partly because of the ability to move comfortably in the corrupt society that Odili survives in *A Man of the People.* And even though Odili is not as deeply involved in filth as other characters, Obi the hero of *No Longer at Ease* is really a finer, if feebler, man in spite of his dirtier hands. Achebe's emphasis on the necessity for constant personal adjustments to changes in social situations as well as the need for a sustaining moral code is also strongly felt in the post civil war stories. It is responsible for the buoyant spirits of "Civil Peace," and the redeeming act of sacrifice by Gladys in "Girls at War."

In contrast to Achebe we do not find a moral position giving direction to Soyinka's plot in *The Interpreters*. Its more exploratory form is dictated by the need to dramatize the psychological problems of a group of individuals who are kept together mainly by their common reaction against a corrupt society in which actions and events seem meaningless. The characters are constantly seeking to create meaningful patterns by piecing together fragments of their experience both from the past and in the present. The problem is explored in an appropriately episodic manner. Certain recurrent motifs provide a meaningful link between episodes, just as the images of bridge and water indicate the search for continuity and meaningful relationships. Water is in fact a complex, often ambiguous symbol, sometimes representing both continuity and flux, and sometimes being used in association with sex to show how one of the key characters is repeatedly seduced and made too impotent to move from a disabled position to a more active and meaningful life.

If the formal characteristics of the Nigerian novel, a literary genre that has developed mainly under European influence, have been influenced to an important extent by the need to portray the problems of the Nigerian society, Nigerian drama is able to draw nourishment from roots that extend even more deeply. West of the Niger there has been a steady development of dramatic performance, so that it is now usual to link the dramatic activities in town halls and university theatres with church plays and the traditional rituals and festivals which are still performed today. The frequency of song and dance which make the works of Hubert Ogunde and Duro Ladipo "operatic" has been adapted by Soyinka in *Kongi's Harvest*.

The Euopean influence is still strongly felt, of course, especially in the continued use of the "picture-frame." But playwrights are conscious of the need for a creative breakaway from the constricting limits of the proscenium arch, and of the advantages of a courtyard performance. The call for such theatrical freedom had been made by Soyinka as early as 1963. Within dramatic texts, European influences range from the deliberate Shakespearean echoes of J. P. Clark's *The Masquerade* (1964), an adaptation of a folktale, to the transplantation of the Greek theme of Oedipus on African soil in Ola Rotimi's *The Gods Are Not to Blame* (1971). The fact that dramatists writing their first plays are more strongly attracted by the possibilities of tending such foreign material on local soil when there is an existing tradition of popular drama suggests, not just the vitality and prestige of Greek plays, but the fact that the home soil is congenial to such themes and may give them growth. The pathetic involvement of the human and the divine is natural to Clark's *Song of a Goat* in spite of the Greek suggestion of its title. The problem is not with the literary resonances but with the development of a theme whose power to communicate its dramatic idea is largely restricted to the immediate cultural environment from which it is evolved. Later Clark turns to the more substantial qualities of the local environment for the material of *The Raft* and adapts a local saga for *Ozidi*.

If Clark takes his cue directly from oral sources after a brief flirtation with European drama, Ola Rotimi turns to the use of historical material in the tradition of the popular drama. History as a source of dramatic themes was popularized by Duro Ladipo and taken up by Ola Rotimi who has now written two historical plays after his Greek adaptation. *Kurunmi* (1972), the first of

these plays, is a swiftly-paced tragedy based on a historical reconstruction of nineteenth-century Yoruba wars. This type of material has had an ambiguous value for Nigerian drama. While it provides an opportunity for evoking the heroism and glories that must have existed in a country's history, it also carries the temptation of exaggerating the heroism and failing to qualify the rhetoric used to justify carnage.

Soyinka wrote *A Dance of the Forests* to commemorate Nigeria's independence. The play shows how a playwright may interpret traditional material and contemporary political events for his own artistic purpose. Forest Head, Soyinka's version of *Olu igbo*, the Yoruba supreme forest god, takes the opportunity of a tribal celebration to expose the presence of envious murder, murderous incompetence and murderous passion within the human community. He leads the central characters on a spiritual journey deep into the forest in order to make men discover their own regeneration through a series of confrontations which would uncover hidden guilt. Probably the most striking thing about the play is the cynicism underlying the playwright's adaptations of traditional gods and religious institutions. Forest Head, traditionally a god that can be appealed to as giver of health or wealth, is made a limited, almost ineffectual god, because he is unable to change the course of events which he himself originally ordained for mankind by fixing a neutral pattern of cause and consequence. The best he can do is to help men see the dangers in the vicious option they have chosen:

> My secret is my eternal burden—to pierce the encrustations of soul-deadening habit, and bare the mirror of original nakedness—knowing full well, it is all futility. Yet I must do this alone, and no more, since to intervene is to be guilty of contradiction, and yet to remain altogether unfelt is to make my long-rumoured ineffectuality complete; hoping that when I have tortured awareness from their souls, that perhaps, only perhaps, is new beginnings.

These words help to bring out the Town Dwellers' blindness. They place soothsayers and dirgemen at the centre of their communication with gods, relying on the mere power of the Word and on the efficacy of sacrifice to alter events which are the consequences of their own original sins. But though an individual may occasionally interfere with the vicious pattern by a humane act, as the artist unconsciously does in the play, the odds against mankind are really too strong, because the active principle of evil among the gods will insist on interfering with human affairs. This is the function of Eshuoro in the play. *Oro* is the traditional cult of justice through retribution. Soyinka, however, sees retribution as another aspect of vengeance, as he combines *Eshu*, the spirit of mischief, with *Oro*, the punitive principle. The new creature, Eshuoro, is meant to represent the unpredictable and wayward aspect of retribution which continues the malignant cycle by seeking links with wronged human beings.

The play has not proved a producer's favourite because the meaning—a complex combination of the political theme with the more personal theme of individual regeneration—is locked up in the use of traditional gods and the symbolism of acrobatic dances, and it does not have the clarity and friskiness of an earlier play like *The Lion and the Jewel*.

Soyinka blends traditional material more easily into two later plays, *The Road* (1965) and *Kongi's Harvest* (1967). The latter play draws on traditional festivals with the singing and dancing, and uses the harvest idea as a central image for its political comment. The play is topical, being a satire on contemporary dictatorship.

But it is rescued from excessive topicality by the element of myth which Soyinka employs in his criticism. The monster yam which is harvested during Kongi's reign is Soyinka's way of showing that one man's tyranny over others is a crime against the earth. The yam is described as being "Like a giant wrestler with legs / And forearms missing." The "wrestler" yam represents mother earth's protest at the tyrant who has wrestled and thrown her other sons. *The Road* is less topical, although as in all Soyinka's major writings the artist casts a satiric eye at specific national problems. The "road" refers literally to the country's death-traps, incompetently maintained and recklessly used at great risk to life and limb. But it very quickly becomes mythical, as with most images in Soyinka. It is simultaneously the hungry god whom we encounter in his poem "Death in the Dawn" and the Professor's path to the meaning of death. The presence of thugs and politician suggests the political road to destruction. Again in Soyinka, the spiritual or religious meanings become more important than the political ones.

In a recent play, *Madmen and Specialists* (1972), written about the time of the Nigerian civil war, a humane attitude can be glimpsed beneath the enveloping cynicism. Old Man in the play says "a part of me identifies with every human being." *Madmen and Specialists* is the drama of a doctor who loses his medical vocation in the wars. As usual, Soyinka examines the spiritual significance of a political action. When Dr. Bero, the specialist, tells his sister how he sat down to a communion of human flesh his description of the dehumanizing experience of war becomes a definition of the driving force behind warmongering:

> Afterwards I said why not? What is one flesh from another? So I tried it again, just to be sure of myself. It was the first step to power you understand. Power in its purest sense. The end of inhibitions. The conquest of the weakness of your too human flesh with all its sentiments. So again, all to myself I said Amen to his grace.

The grace that was said before this "meal" shows how impossible it has been for man to resist the temptation to war. The historian in *A Dance of the Forests* found war the only consistency in human history. The grace pronounced by Dr. Bero's father translates this view of war into a religious statement. We still have Soyinka's playfulness, but the usual exuberance has been disciplined to produce the grim utility of the "grace": "As Was the Beginning, As is, Now, As Ever shall be . . . world without. . . . " The playwright perverts the usual meaning by merely applying a new punctuation and elevating a mere adverb, "as," into the substantive divinity, "As." Even the elision of the final "end" has the effect of suggesting that the god "As" will eventually do without the world.

This sheer delight in wit is reminiscent of Elizabethan practice. In the following example, it almost erases the mood of gloom which has been created in our minds, except that the playwright manages a political denunciation even while tossing his puns around:

> you splint in the arrow of arrogance,
> the dog in dogma, tick of a heretic,
> the tick in politics, the mock of democracy,
> the mar of marxism, a tic of the fanatic. . . .

Such punning is in the vernacular tradition in which the syllabic sounds of names and titles are manipulated to yield a desired meaning for the purpose of praise or blame. In this passage Soyinka suits his sounds to his meaning, and the passage is as earnest as it is playful.

Writers who can rely on a background of such a vernacular tradition would naturally carry over its literary practices into their poetry. The *double entendre*, a device found in proverbs and riddles, can be particularly effective for political mockery because usually the sexual innuendo reinforces the more direct political mockery. Thus in "Cuba Confrontation," one of Clark's lighter poems, the sudden shift from the lizard exemplar to the far-fetched simile of the courtesan is meant to point out that the braggart male can turn out to be a woman after all:

> With my hammer head
> I'll smash up the earth,
> Said
> The lizard:
> And up reared
> The aroused crown,
> And then down
> The blow
> Came—like a courtesan's head,
> Deep in her pillow.

The conceit can also be used for a serious purpose without any humorous effect, as in the title of Soyinka's second collection of poems, *A Shuttle in the Crypt* (1972). This refers to the incarceration of creative energy, for the shuttle is a "unique species of the caged animal, a restless bolt of energy, a trapped weaver-bird yet charged in repose with unspoken forms and designs." Soyinka's poetic art does not, however, derive from the oral tradition. The sources of his techniques are mainly *literary,* and except for "Idanre" where he adapts a few Yoruba incantations for his Ogun epic, the poetry remains largely individual in form. What Soyinka adapts from the vernacular tradition is the religious system rather than the literary technique. This provides him with a useful parallel for his synoptic view of history. In "Idanre" he adapts the Ifa divination technique in which an understanding of contemporary problems is arrived at by interpreting the problems of a mythical, usually non-human protagonist. "Idanre" is a re-telling of the Yoruba myth of Ogun, god of war, in order to predict the bloody climax of the Nigerian experience. The hero of the poem is a god who becomes drunk and gets out of control when invited to a feast.

In contrast, J. P. Clark and the late Christopher Okigbo, two of the other major Nigerian poets, have shown greater interest in utilizing the literary properites of Nigerian oral poetry, as distinct from the use of landscape, religious systems and images from their environment. Whereas Soyinka's work has remained mainly consistent in style almost from the first, the works of Okigbo and Clark have increasingly shown an experimental interest in the devices of the oral tradition. This increasing interest may best be described as a homecoming for both poets, since both began by using English poets as models until they found their feet and later attempted to develop certain verse techniques found in vernacular poetry.

Okigbo began his experiment with traditional poetic forms by emphasizing that instrumental music and the performing arts of singing and dancing are important to his poetry. Not only are his poems mainly "songs," "laments" and "dances," they are also dedicated to instruments for artistic performance like flutes, drums and masks. Although the models for the early poems were Pound and Eliot, some of the later poems have the structure of traditional Nigerian poetry. "Lament of the Masks," a poem dedicated to W. B. Yeats, adopts the structure and phrasing of Yoruba praise poetry.

Okigbo's borrowing of phrases from other writers recalls *The Waste Land*. But this same quality makes his verse akin to older poetic forms which are similar in their use of fixed formulas. The made-up phrase is common property, and the originality depends on each poet's use of well-known phrases, as poets used epithets in epics and kennings in Old English poetry. The structure of Okigbo's poems also has this ancient quality. Each poem is a sequence which can be lengthened, shortened, or re-arranged by the poet. The formal range of such poetry is limited. Each new poem is often a structural repetition of an earlier poem and the poet's career is an almost unending spiral of a single thematic development.

The repetitive structure is organic to Okigbo's theme, that of spiritual rebirth. Because the group of sequences called *Labyrinths* deals mainly with the exploration of a personal experience, it deals almost exclusively with a central protagonist and uses obscurity as a deliberate device to keep the poems personal. But in a sequence called "Distances" the poet ends his artistic and spiritual quest to enter a public career as a mantic poet.

Although J. P. Clark is a very different kind of poet from Okigbo, his career may also be mapped very roughly as a movement from the use of European models towards a creative adaptation of the devices of vernacular poetry, as well as a progress from personal experience to a poetic involvement in the political crisis which hit the country as from the mid-sixties. The poems in *A Reed in the Tide* (1964) bear the stamp of poets like Hopkins and Dylan Thomas whose work Clark obviously admired. Some of the best-known lines in the volume come from an early poem, "Night Rain," where the poet tells how

> like some fish
> Doped out of the deep
> I have bobbed up bellywise
> From stream of sleep
> And no cocks crow.

However, the strongest impression on the poems is not the shadow of poets like Hopkins and Thomas but the poet's eye for the Nigerian landscape. Moreover, Clark attempts, even under the constricting influence of other poets, to make the lines of his poems follow the development of his subject. It is, however, in a later volume, *Casualties* (1970), that the poet breaks completely free from the formal restrictions of his early work to experiment with a more prosaic freedom of expression. In this latter volume it is tempting to see the later Yeats displacing Hopkins and Thomas as the poet's idol, in his search for the bare, hard expression. But even a slight familiarity with the true models for this volume would direct one to folksong and folktale as the groundwork for the poems.

Casualties, like Okigbo's last poems and Soyinka's "Idanre," has the Nigerian crisis as its main subject, because no serious poet can ignore the important issues of his time. So for the first time, all the major Nigerian writers are united in writing about a common subject. This is significant for the development of Nigerian literature. A national literature requires more than local images, landscapes and belief systems for the formation of a character that is distinct from that of neighbouring countries with similar vernacular cultures, a common historical

association with colonizing Europe, and a common European lingua franca.

The presence of English in Nigeria has done more than provide an opportunity for communication with a wider world. It has offered a new medium for literary expression and the challenge of a new imaginative activity in which the experiences of various cultures may find a common channel. Molly Mahood once drew attention to the signs of a dramatic renaissance in Africa. There is also an opportunity for a kind of renaissance in the other literary forms. A renaissance is after all an awakening of creative energies caused by the turbulence at a confluence of cultures. (pp. 136-53)

> *D. S. Izevbaye, "Nigeria," in* Literatures of the World
> in English, *edited by Bruce King, Routledge & Kegan*
> *Paul, 1974, pp. 136-53.*

ERNEST N. EMENYONU

[*In the following excerpt, Emenyonu discusses literature published in the Igbo language, most prominently the novel* Omenuku *by Pita Nwana.*]

The first Igbo to publish fiction in Igbo was Pita Nwana. His novel *Omenuko* was published in 1933 after it had won an all-Africa literary contest in indigenous African languages organized by the International Institute of African Languages and Culture. It is a biographical novel based on actual events in the life of the hero, Omenuko, whose home was a favourite spot for students and tourists in Eastern Nigeria in the fifties. The novel has been reprinted several times in various Igbo orthographies and is still a classic in Igbo literature. The first edition was in the Protestant orthography, but it was soon afterwards issued in the other orthographies and this accounts for its general acceptance and wide readership. It is today the most widely read novel in the Igbo language.

For generations Igbo children have begun their reading with *Omenuko*, and children who do not have the opportunity to go to school could still read *Omenuko* at home or at adult education centres. Omenuko's "sayings" have become part of the Igbo speech pattern which the young adult is expected to acquire. Very little is known of the author of *Omenuko*. He has published no further books. He seems, therefore, to have been the reporter of the pioneer generation of Igbo literature and not its creative genius.

Omenuko is set in Okigwi, one of the densely populated areas in Imo State. The action takes place in the rural communities, around busy market places, where commercial activities go side by side with serious matters, such as settling disputes and planning community projects. The market is more than a meeting place for local affairs. People drink palm wine, pour libations, as haggling and bargaining go on over their agricultural products. Families live within walled compounds where the head of the family supervises his immediate and extended families from his *obi*.

Loyalty to the family often gives way to a larger cause— allegiance to the village, which in turn gives way to the clan. Villagers are joined to each other by a tight pattern of intersecting paths which converge at major markets where the entire clan meets to consider affairs of primary concern to all the clan's people. Forests separate one clan from the other, constituting not just physical boundaries, but also symbolic cultural and economic boundaries. Justice at the clan level rests with the elders, who are believed to perform the will of the ancestors.

This setting is relevant to the action in the novel and helps to bring out the conflict in which the hero is trapped. It is characteristic of the people, knit together as they are by natural and human factors, to stick together, see things as a group, and act as a group. To exist is to live with the group. Ostracism, whether voluntary or compulsory, is as a result of an individual alienating himself from the group or consciously going against the tenets of communal life. The theme of the novel, offence and expiation, emerges from this communal attitude to life.

The novel is set in the last few decades of the nineteenth century, but the most important actions take place in the first two decades of the twentieth century. Omenuko is said finally to have returned to his hometown (at the end of the novel) in ''1918 towards the end of the tenth month.'' The final episodes in the novel happened in the 1930s when Omenuko is portrayed in his retirement as growing prosperous despite the depression of 1929 and the economic reversals of the years that followed it. This setting forms a background for two distinct generations. Before 1900 government and political control in the areas now occupied by the Igbo, were in the hands of the Igbo.

> The affairs of the village are decided by a general assembly in which men and women can participate. However, effective control is in the hands of the elders, members of an age set whose turn it is to govern the village at a particular period in their age-grade cycle.

This is the era covered by the first few chapters of the novel. The change in the Igbo political system came in the first decade of this century when the British Colonial Administration took complete control of Igbo land. According to Victor Uchendu,

> The direct administration had two important features: It based the Colonial Administration of Igbo land on all-purpose native courts, which were established by the Native Courts Proclamation (1900) and derived their revenue from indirect taxation. Following the Proclamation, Igbo land was arbitrarily carved into Native Court Areas, formed by grouping sovereign political units. Each Court Area constituted a native court system, an all-purpose administrative machinery. The British district commissioner was the president of the court: other personnel included warrant chiefs, the court clerk, and the court messengers.

This is the era covered in the later part of the book where references are made to warrant chiefs, paramount chiefs, white men, the court and the prisons—all of which were features of the new British administration. The novel, therefore, covers two periods which are close in time but wide apart in the events that characterized them. A large part of the novel, then, illustrates a point of transition from one age to the other. The hero, Omenuko, moves from one age to the other and through his actions and attitudes the author reflects something of the particular society of the time. In the period covered in the early stages of the book, there was a kind of autonomy in Igbo behaviour. Individuals were free to act as they chose as long as they did not break popular village sanctions or mores. If they did, they were not in danger of the white man's retribution (his presence was hardly felt) but the judgement of the elders in their local villages.

This explains why Omenuko was able to sell his neighbours' sons into slavery and escape justice simply by going outside the jurisdiction of his community elders. But by the time of the later part of book everybody was accountable to the courts of law and the white man. Ezuma refers to this in the later part of the book (Chapter 8 which describes the ransoming of those Omenuko sold into slavery) when he says,

> Remember too, these are the days of the white man. If these children express a desire to be returned to their homes, we would have to let them go, that is, if we refuse to liberate them now. If care is not taken, we might even be in trouble then and they could still go home as they wish, without our having to be paid any money for that.

This awareness of the changing times and the point of transition highlighted in the novel is evident also in some of the contrasts in the behaviour of the characters. Many people had taken to the new Christian religion, which was one of the organs of the imperialist régime, more so when Christianity was advertised as holding the key to the white man's ''knowledge'' and good jobs. But there were still many people who remained loyal to the old religion. They would not give up the rituals which honour the dead, nor would they cease to pour libations to the ancestors, and make obligatory sacrifices to placate angered deities, and restore distorted harmony in nature.

The novel covers part of the period in Igbo history with which Chinua Achebe is concerned in *Things Fall Apart* and implies also some of the tensions between adherents of the old religion and the Christian converts, but the author of *Omenuko* avoids a confrontation between the two religions. There are tensions within the society about the changes that are coming over it, but the two forces never clash, and cross-cultural conflicts are kept to a minimum. Generally the people of Omenuko's age accept the *Pax Britannica* unquestioningly. The white man appears to have all the answers and his word is law. However there are some people who would at some times be so disgusted with the white man that they would repudiate him to his face. For example, when the District Commissioner tended to place Omenuko's Warrant chieftaincy above the interests and welfare of his community, the people defied the white man's authority. When he threatened them about breaking the law by attacking Omenuko and his people, they replied that they were ready for the consequences.

> We will be prepared to listen to the law, only when we have killed Omenuko. If you want to execute all of us because of a stranger who came into our midst, we would prefer to die, rather than allow our eyes to see our ears. The District Commissioner was shocked at all these utterances . . . without their being afraid of the law or the power of authority.

But in spite of all this, Nwana manages to prevent a head-on collision between the Igbo and the British such as occurs in *Things Fall Apart*.

The author of *Omenuko* is able to confine the falling apart of things to his hero alone, although he is sufficiently ambivalent, if not critical, about some of the traditions and general attitudes of his society.

In Pita Nwana's novel *Omenuko*, the hero from whom the novel takes its title openly commits a criminal act against his society. A merchant by profession, when the novel opens he has lost all his goods on his way to the market following the collapse of a rickety bridge. With amazing rapidity, Omenuko sells most of his companions (neighbours' sons and relatives who were apprenticed to him), into slavery for the sake of his own economic survival. He refuses to take responsibility for this—an outrage towards his fellow men, an abomination to the gods of the land, but in particular, the earth and sky gods. Obstinate and very strong-willed, Omenuko waits too long before coming to terms with his people. Because of the enormity of his crime and his recalcitrant behaviour, Omenuko is required to offer a sacrifice of atonement in the highest terms ever prescribed by the chief priests of the two angered deities. In the process, he learns self-discipline and comes to appreciate the true values of his society, its concept of right and wrong, and what constitutes true success and failure. For instance, after he has offered the sacrifice of reunion, Omenuko confesses to his brothers, ''I am happier and more at ease now than I have ever been since the day I fled from our town. If death comes to me now, I shall not be afraid.''

Omenuko is intelligent and resourceful, but he is also cunning and capricious. He has an overpowering tendency to use to personal advantage anyone who comes his way. The first instance of this, the selling of his apprentices to make up for his lost goods, is the source of all the conflicts in the novel. But after this first act, Omenuko's subsequent reactions show a series of progressions in evil and selfish aggrandisement. He is intelligent and crafty enough to recognize the limits of his ability. He would be fighting a losing battle from the start if he tried to fight his people alone. So Omenuko uses his brothers to provide the moral support necessary in his fight with his people. When he initially solicits the support of his brothers, they respond with serious reproach.

> His brothers told him that it [the selling of his apprentices] is a thing unheard of and can never please the ear that hears it . . . They blamed him for his rash act, because it is an event which can never be forgotten in life. They wondered how he could summon up courage to sell the children of his fellow men merely because his goods fell into a river. ''Was it the fault of your fellow men that you lost your goods?''

But Omenuko is able to coerce them into submission with a threat to their own existence. He threatens suicide and asks them to prepare to fend for themselves in life. He knows full well the effect of this on his helpless young brothers. Thus, they not only forgive him, but acquiesce in his plans to go into exile as a group. Omenuko realizes the weak points in his brothers and fully capitalizes on them. He knows that they will offer little or no resistance if they realize how seriously any action of his could affect all of their individual destinies. Thus he puts forward well-calculated ideas in his speech:

> My ancestors and God [notice that he invokes both the ancestral deity and the Christian God] on high have put me in a condition of life worse than death. I must die. You must therefore prepare, each of you, to fend for himself. I am ready to die.

This successfully disarms them, but he further ensures their continued support when he threatens to kill ''all the chiefs and parents of the young men'' whom he had sold into slavery. Since he planned to ''die with them,'' his brothers are quick to recognize that he would be leaving them a legacy of irreconcilable enmity with their community. They would be the ones to suffer when he was no more. According to them, the situation would be 'what our ancestors describe as a legacy that passes from generation to generation! Our children will have to suffer for it and our children's children likewise will suffer for it.' Omenuko had made the suffering local, and his brothers had been personally touched; and as they switched their sentiments, the author removed them from their role of impartial commentators and chorus, to that of active participators and accomplices. They could no longer be the rationale that governed Omenuko's decisions, because they had themselves become one with Omenuko. As part of Omenuko, they

no longer asked, ''Is that not enough, must you but contemplate a crime worse than you had already committed?'' They merely did things and ran errands for his interests.

But they had lost something else of greater significance. They were no longer in a position to mediate between Omenuko and the people, nor could they ascertain the wishes of the deities on his behalf. It was an office which Igwe had to be called in to fulfil later in the story. Assured of his brothers' support, Omenuko becomes bold enough to challenge his townspeople more successfully, balancing his conflicts and estrangement in the town with the privileges of his brothers' firm support and co-operation. It was this togetherness that solidified their decision to flee the town. Although it would seem here that the original theme of alienation of the individual from his community has been broadened into alienation of a family unit from society at large, the author does manage to keep the focus of the action on Omenuko as a character. On the night of their flight, his younger brother Nwabueze is dispatched to go down the major road to see whether he could hear any sounds or observe anyone coming from the place towards which they proposed to escape. It is significant that Nwabueze never heard any sound except the ranting of a lunatic, one who had lost his senses. The cries of the lunatic were shattering to the peace and quietness of the night, in the same way that the turmoil inside Omenuko was affecting the peace of mind of his family and the immediate world around him. Omenuko was himself like a lunatic. In common with Ibe Ofo, the lunatic, he had been chained (symbolically, but no less significantly) and confined to a cell. Ibe Ofo suffered physical pain and responded with cacophonous groanings; Omenuko suffered emotionally but he bore his torturing grief in silence. He owes this to his self-confident nature and his evident ability to take care of himself whatever happens.

When they had left the town behind them, rain fell in torrents and there were clashes of thunder. The heavens and the natural elements seemed to have broken out in turmoil and rebellion. So the entire universe was uneasy, and this is a symbol of the fact that harmony, the natural harmony, had been upset by the hero's cruel actions. This is the crux of the action of the novel. There is much in the novel to suggest that there is a general feeling among Omenuko's peers and contemporaries that he has upset the balance of nature through his own actions and their ramifications both internal and external. Omenuko's overweening ambition to rise above his humble beginnings seems to have produced an extreme reaction in his character: he always puts profit above humaneness. Profit becomes his guide in most of his major actions in the novel; humaneness becomes a consideration only later when he can afford it. Consequently, he is always on top of things, scheming and grasping, the cool man and the easy-talking operator. Few of the people he meets recognize him truly for what he is, not even the white District Commissioner (who is as gullible as Omenuko's brothers and friends), but each is sceptical in some ways about his motives and intentions. Chief Ike hints at this when he equivocates about facing Omenuko in a public trial.

> Sir, Omenuko is a great orator. Perhaps he would use this to my disadvantage when he comes here. He may falsely deny me and still appear to be saying the truth before your eyes.

Indeed, Omenuko knows what to say and when to say it to disarm an opponent in any situation. He knows too when to create a situation of fear in the minds of the people and then take full advantage of the situation he has created and manipulated, as he does over the Mgborogwu chieftaincy while in exile. These elements, destructive yet ingenious, make Omenuko an effective character.

He is a grasping, smooth, cool operator, making fortunes even in the face of disaster. He is wholly wound up in himself, generous to a fault when he can afford it, grasping when necessary, cruel and inhuman when his own fate is in the balance. The non-Igbo reader may find it hard to sympathize with Omenuko and even more difficult to admire him as a character. But, ironically, among the Igbo, Omenuko is generally admired. He probably evokes the same reactions as the tortoise, the trickster in Igbo folktales. People may not enjoy the tricks the tortoise plays on other animals, but they can still laugh with him at his victims, and might even admire his cunning and ingenuity while the innocent suffer. The average Igbo is probably least likely to find fault with Omenuko's economic motives, much as he may disagree with all his methods.

It is significant that in his exile at Mgborogwu, it is these same factors—an overweening ambition and his grasping and indifferent nature—that bring him into conflict with his hosts. By Igbo custom, when Omenuko fled his hometown, he could have sought refuge among the kinsmen of his mother's maiden family. Instead, he fled to Mgborogwu, where he was without patrilineage (*umunna*) and therefore without citizenship either in the world of men or in the domain of his ancestors. The people seized upon this when they rose against him for seeking to hold the highest office in their land. They protested to the white District Commissioner, "We can never allow this to happen in this our own land, that one who is after all, a stranger should be our head and chief executive." Omenuko views every opposing action from his hosts as due to their jealousy over his increasing prosperity. Therefore he asks the District Commissioner to exonerate him, but punish his opponents severely. Nevertheless, Omenuko is unable to produce any strong case to prove that he is entitled to any rights of citizenship in Mgborogwu. The District Commissioner seems to have taken a simplistic view in this matter of citizenship for he only sees the threat to Omenuko's life and advises him to return to his original homeland to avoid being assassinated by his angry hosts.

For Omenuko, it is an episode that clearly goes beyond the rivalry over a vacant chieftaincy. It brings home to him the full implications of his sin against his people and his escapist method of severing connections with his heritage rather than face the consequences of his rash conduct. This action, which leads to Omenuko's eventual return to his native land, is very important because it provides the plot with a neat resolution. It provides for the novel its circular structure as it shows a point of return from exile. (This has become a common characteristic of many later Igbo novels. Cf. Achebe's *Things Fall Apart*, Ekwensi's *Jagua Nana*, Agunwa's *More Than Once*, etc.) It is consistent with the author's view in the preface of the novel that "no matter how successful a man may be in a foreign land, he cannot fail to realize eventually that indeed there is no place like home." The bridge episode is an important landmark in the novel for it marks the point of Omenuko's departure from the right path of life. From then onwards, he wanders aimlessly like the prodigal son, pruning here and piling there to make a living but never really achieving full harmony in his existence until he returns at the end of the novel to that point from which he deviated several years before. The circular structure of the novel thus lends justification to Austin Shelton's remarks that,

> The African writer sees social change in part as change from cultural wholeness to fragmentation and disorientation of the individual, who can regain "wholeness" of self and proper orientation to behaviour as well as obtain the deserved rewards only through his maintenance of traditions or a return to the traditionally sanctioned behavior.

Omenuko tries various devices to prevent his "return." He tries exaggerated acts of charity, as well as other diplomatic manoeuvres, but to no avail. They only serve as a temporary bridge to reconciliation and continued tolerance of the offender by the offended hosts. Omenuko then realizes more than ever that his original sin against his people has left indelible scars and though he may be tolerated wherever he goes, he will never win full acceptance anywhere but among his own people. This moral evolution in the hero prepares the way for the final and most important action in the novel. Omenuko is later to inform his relatives and household in exile,

> I am not a citizen of Mgborogwu and I have also been rejected by my original homeland . . . The primary thing I should do now, is to seek a reconciliation with both human beings and gods whom I have greatly offended and sinned against, and re-establish links with them.

Thus, Omenuko, true to his character, shows his sense of insecurity and disillusionment only when it is desparately necessary to do so. So long as his exile did not seriously threaten his ambition to be wealthy and prosperous, Omenuko could tolerate it. There were times when he considered it lucky that he had reason to flee his town, as "Whenever he thought about his past and reflected upon his present position [as Chief], he thanked God and his brothers that he stayed alive." But, as at home, Omenuko places material concerns above human life and interests in his place of exile. He is able to grow rich on the Mgborogwu people, but has little regard for them. He feels no compunction in plotting their destruction, and at one point, wages a full-scale war against them to satisfy his selfish designs. No human life is worth preserving whenever Omenuko's egocentricism is challenged. He virtually seized the Mgborogwu throne at the death of the ruling king, and when the people press charges against him he completely outwits them, so that instead of being stripped of the chieftaincy, Omenuko wins for himself a separate kingdom.

The bringing of Omenuko back into harmony with man and the gods is accomplished through a ritual sacrifice, in the process of which a close friend of Omenuko, Igwe, acts as an intermediary between Omenuko and his family on the one hand, and the people and their deities on the other. This sacrifice is very important because of its role in the novel. It is not the ordinary Igbo traditional sacrifice where an offender makes an offering and pours libation and expects the goodwill of the gods. Instead, Omenuko is tantalized to the utmost before the Chief Priests make known to him the wishes of the gods. When he asks to be told how he can atone for his past sins, the priest of the earth-goddess at first refuses to discuss the matter with Igwe, Omenuko's emissary, and consents to do so only when he has the advantage of Omenuko. The priest of the sky-god similarly refuses to discuss the matter but in addition, is scornful of Omenuko—

> Your Omenuko who wants to make peace with angered deities, can he go through the rituals doing everything that would be asked of him? Go and ask Omenuko, the sheep that wants to grow horns, how stable his neck is.

This sacrifice also offers the reader another ample opportunity to examine the character of Omenuko himself, and his relationship to religious ritual, to the priests, to the chiefs, to his cousins, and to everyone he meets. The author analyses sin and forgiveness within Omenuko, and projects a kind of Islamic atmosphere in the later part of the novel. He portrays in his hero a Moslem air of acceptance—an unquestioning acceptance of one's fate, which seems to explain some of Omenuko's reactions to life and its hard knocks. Consequently, he tackles the rituals of the sacrifice in his characteristically carefree manner, doing what the priests expect of him, saying the correct things, ransoming the men just as easily and good-naturedly as he once sold them into bondage.

Now, as in the other major actions in the novel, Omenuko is able to dominate at the same time that he is asking for favour, and equally attempts to move fate at the same time that he seems to seek expiation of his sins. Early in the novel when he lost his goods in the river, although he agonized and moaned his fate, he was at the same time plotting his way beyond the tragedy. When he accepted the fact that he would have to surrender the Mgborogwu chieftaincy to its rightful prince, Obiefula, he nonetheless went behind the scenes to procure (almost by swindling) a new crown for himself, outwitting the District Commissioner, at the same time that he appeared to be a humble servant who only carried out orders faithfully. He goes home when he can well afford it, having secured his material future abroad. He swiftly placates the gods as a way of putting them (and their menaces) out of the way, and also as a way of putting his past life decisively behind him.

He had gone the full cycle, exploiting gods as easily as he exploited the white man and the local people. This fact may explain his voluntary retirement at the end of the novel. He has lived a full life with a chequered history which provokes many ethical considerations. The fact that Omenuko, the hero of the book, was still alive at the time the book was in circulation helped to make its impact even stronger.

People visited Omenuko and heard the story of the novel confirmed by his own lips. This is perhaps why he became a kind of household word among the Igbo people. Everyone who read or heard about the book and its story knew for sure that there was a living Omenuko somewhere in Igbo land.

The concentration on the hero allows Nwana to explore fully the fate of the alienated individual in a situation where identification with the group seems the only way to keep alive. The Christian religion was known to welcome apostates of the old religion as well as outcasts who were taboo in the Igbo culture. This trespassing is what spells disaster for the Igbo communities in Chinua Achebe's *Things Fall Apart* and *Arrow of God*, which like Nwana's are novels of Igbo tradition. But Omenuko does not embrace the alternatives which the new religion offers. When he commits an abomination against the traditional gods, he could seek refuge in the Christian camp, as Okonkwo's son does in *Things Fall Apart*, and Oduche in *Arrow of God*. But Omenuko does not. Instead he goes into voluntary exile, where he lives his own life, often remaining courteous to his natal home. He testifies to this when he appears before his people several years later to pledge loyalty to the laws of the land and seek reconciliation. He informs them that

> although I was in another land, and even as chief there, I was still observing the laws and customs of my homeland. There are no laws of our land which I do not remember.

The author clearly presents the fate of the hero as being a result of his personality and individual shortcomings. (pp. 33-47)

The strong influence of *Omenuko* on later Igbo writers is most apparent in a much later novel published in Igbo in 1963 as *Ije Odumodu Jere (Odumodu's Travels)*. The novel is set in the later part of the nineteenth century. The hero, Odumodu, is born in a poor family but works his way to the top by dint of hard labour. His adventures carry him into foreign lands (Europe, North America, Cuba) where he is antagonized by many of his hosts. He survives and eventually returns to his original home a wealthy man and immediately sets about to modernize his community.

Like Omenuko, Odumodu is involved in a succession conflict (to a foreign throne) and the timely intervention of an outsider saves him from assassination. Omenuko loses his goods when he and his companions fall into a river. Odumodu also loses his possessions in a shipwreck in which he is the sole survivor. There is a very close similarity in tone and content between *Odumodu's Travels*, chapter ten, and chapter four of *Omenuko*. The dying king of Finda wills his throne to Odumodu, a foreigner, in the same way that Chief Mgborogwu bequeaths his throne to Omenuko, an alien and a fugitive from justice. In both cases, the people conspire to work against the dead kings' wishes. The heir apparent of Finda tries to have Odumodu assassinated while in Mgborogwu, the chiefs rise in rebellion against Omenuko and make attempts on his life. Odumodu flees from Finda and goes to Mimba from where he finally escapes to his hometown, Ahaba, where he is received with great celebration and festivities. He settles down, builds modern houses, and is appointed chief of his people. In the same way, Omenuko flees from Mgborogwu to Ikpa Oyi from where he finally flees to his hometown in Okigwi. He settles down, builds modern houses, declines to be the chief of his people, but accepts the honorary position of peacemaker and "overseer." Thus both novels describe a departure and a return.

But *Odumodu's Travels* may also have been influenced by other sources. The preoccupation with European history and wars, the author's knowledge of navigation and oceanography, and the sensitive reactions to life in Europe and the theme of the slave trade, parallel such treatments in *Equiano's Travels* [an autobiography by an Igbo who was sold into slavery]. Odumodu was nearly as versatile as Equiano. He was a teacher, a carpenter, a cook, a sailor, an administrator, a counsellor and a preacher. *Odumodu's Travels*, too, has many things in common with Daniel Defoe's *Robinson Crusoe* and Jonathan Swift's *Gulliver's Travels*. The account of the shipwreck of Odumodu and his subsequent captivity by a gang of dwarfish creatures "who crawled in and out of holes," reads like an account of Gulliver's experiences with the Lilliputians.

Perhaps the strongest influence on *Odumodu's Travels* is that of Christian missionaries. Apart from verbatim quotations which the author makes from the missionary *Primer* (1927), there are more pervasive influences in plot and characterization. The hero is caught between two worlds. He tries to be Igbo but is caught up in Western ways. The author strives to build his theme into a race issue but succeeds only in making a case for his hero as a Christian. He succeeds in showing some differences in behaviour which result from belonging to another culture. He does not succeed in portraying the deep-rooted racial conflicts that he seems to be striving so hard to reveal. However hard he tries to stress his hero's blackness, the question of race remains only on the surface of the novel. The narrative dangles between moving in the direction of racial prejudice, and a conflict in codes of values. Bell-Gam settles for the more manageable theme. Odumodu triumphs over the oppressive white race not because he is black, but mostly because he is a Christian who practices the teachings of the Bible as well as the Christian doctrines. The opposition of the citizens of Finda to his marriage with their princess does not deter Odumodu from working to improve for the people of Finda, their standards of living and methods of government, as well as their moral values. The author invests Odumodu with uncommon qualities of humility and selfless service. He wants to devote his time to the service of his fellow human beings, and when Finda does not give him the chance, his missionary zeal to spread the word moves him to migrate to Mimba, where he builds schools, trains teachers, and instils in the masses an appreciation of the dignity of labour. He admonishes them with, "whoever is not ashamed to work with his hands will never die of starvation. No work is too mean or inferior for a man in need." The image that the author projects of his hero throughout the novel is one of a suffering but undeterred missionary. He is rejected by the very people he seeks to "save." He loses everything in his possession, including his wife and children, but Odumodu is neither discouraged nor dissuaded from his mission to "go forth and teach all nations." He advises all the people he meets and converts to "live your lives according to the ten commandments." One of the successes of the novel is that the author is able to dramatize for the white worlds of Finda and Mimba, some of the unpleasantness and irritations which missionaries may even unknowingly cause the people they have come to convert. The implication of this irony becomes apparent when one remembers that Odumodu is a black African Christian endeavouring to convert Europeans and teach them "the good life" in the nineteenth century, the era of European "civilizing mission" to Africa.

Unlike *Ije Odumodu Jere*, D. N. Achara's *Ala Bingo* shows a strong indebtedness to and influence of the Igbo oral narrative. *Ala Bingo* is a long moral fable. The background of the story is the world of slavery, and the imaginary feudal world of lords and serfs. The action takes place around Uzuakoli, Ozuitem, and Item, all familiar Igbo towns, but it moves away from the real world to the supernatural world. The narrative is told in two parts. Most of the action in the first part takes place in the real world while the second part is set in the supernatural world. The theme—"civility costs nothing but buys everything"—is consistent throughout, but while the first part of the narrative focusses on the older generation of characters, the second part deals with the problems of the younger generation. The two parts are connected structurally because the second segment is a development of the first, and exists because an earlier dilemma had been resolved thereby making room for a new phase of social experience.

The first part, the discovery and wooing of a river maiden, shows three different situations which illustrate the major weaknesses in the character of the king. The king spies what appear to be human footprints near his river. He wants to know to whom these footprints belong, yet he cannot find out. Consequently, he seeks help from his servants. However, the only servant who can help him is the one the king refuses at first to see. Why? Because the servant is sick and the king will have to go to him to receive information rather than the servant coming to him. But because his curiosity concerning the footprints is so great and because his other servants cannot find out to whom the footprints belong, the king must relent. He must humble himself, disregarding appearances, and visit the sick servant. In the second situation, the king wants to meet the river maiden but does not know how. He goes to see the Lord of the East to ask about this, but he is arrogant and demands the Lord of the East to send a royal escort to receive him. The king has to be made humble again. The Lord of the East will not receive him until he apologizes. The king has been tested with a serf, and a Lord, and neither experience is effective in curing him of the excesses of his personality. The third situation shows his last chance and is the most severe of his tests. The king needs information on how to get hold of the river maiden and make her his wife. The only person who can give him the information is a leper and the king will have to go to him. It is only when the king has nowhere else to turn that he finally turns to the leper. The leper directs him to the Lord of the West who alone can solve his problem. And this time the king goes humbly as a man in need.

It is the king's obstinacy that brings about his humiliation before a leper, a taboo to all mankind. It is a kind of education to the king who is egotistic, pompous and intolerably arrogant, yet incurably simple-minded and naive. "Igbo echi eze" (the Igbo recognize no king) is a popular Igbo dictum and this story is a running commentary on this Igbo social attitude. The king in the story is blind for he fails to recognize from his high office the true meaning of greatness and the cordial relationship that should exist between a monarch and his subjects. The whole first segment of the book deals with the king learning to disregard outward appearances and to assume humility. The second part of the book is a test of the king's ability to apply the lessons he learned from self-knowledge to his royal functions. He must decide the successor to the throne between two sons of equal strength, and possibly twins. This is the dilemma he must resolve, but he has learned enough to know that "a king who is beset with a complex problem could consult his entire household, including his servants and serfs." Thus it is from his subjects that he gets the idea that since the two rival claimants are of equal physical strength, the final decision could be based on intelligence tests—exercises in the skill of solving riddles and interpreting proverbs. The sub-plot then focusses on the explanation of "why the first son succeeds his father" and thereby provides a useful commentary on the Igbo patrilineal system.

The king wisely chooses Ezi-Amuru (learning from experience) over Amachagburu (Pedantry is suicidal) because he is no longer blind, and has learned to search for inner meanings and deeper significances in every situation of life. Emmanuel Obiechina has pointed out that one major characteristic of Igbo oral narrative is that

> the offender is hardly ever left in a state of permanent disgrace and deprivation. He has to suffer and often suffer severely before he is rescued and restored, very much chastened and refined by his punishment.

Achara has kept very close to this tradition in his portrayal of the king in *Ala Bingo*. The book thus presents a theme pertinent to the life of its community reflecting in the process something of the culture from which the story comes. The king is made to suffer severely, but he is not left in a state of permanent disgrace and deprivation. He is refined instead by his punishment (several Igbo oral narratives portray this uncanny look at kingship). The riddles, proverbs and other oral performances interwoven with the story help to strengthen the plot, while also making the style of the narrative more vivid and accurate.

A sizeable number of other works in Igbo exist but few have any serious literary significance or *Omenuko*'s wide readership and popularity. It seems there is no longer much enthusiasm among the Igbo people for creating literature in their vernacular. Part of this . . . is because of the age-long controversy over an acceptable orthography. It was a problem for the early missionaries and today it is still unresolved. It has only been overshadowed by the fact that the present-day Igbo writers have generally come to see and accept English not only as the official language of Nigeria, but also as the language of Igbo literature. Mazi Chidozie Ogbalu, the founder of the Society for the Promotion of Igbo Language and Culture, has so far done more than any other single person in the field of Igbo language publications and in the revival of a general interest in Igbo language and culture. He has encouraged the use of Igbo in communication, instruction, official and non-official Igbo businesses. He encouraged his students at St. Augustine's Grammar School, Nkwerre, D.M.G.S., Onitsha, and elsewhere, to collect Igbo oral performances. He has often organized competitions in these areas and with the use of his own printing press and bookshop (Varsity, Onitsha) published and distributed many of the materials so collected. He was one of the first Igbo to engage seriously in the controversy over orthography. In 1952 he (with the late Mr. Daniel Chukudike Erinne) published a monograph entitled *An Investigation Into the Ibo Orthography* (Goodwill Press) and three years later, he published a manual *Teach Yourself the All-Accepted Igbo Orthography* (Varsity, 1955), designed to help the average Igbo to get acquainted with the orthography that was being advocated. Some of his other publications in Igbo are: *Igbo-English Dictionary* (1959), *Omenala Igbo* (1960), *Ilu Igbo* (1961), *Akuko Nigeria* (3rd ed. 1964), *Mbediogu* (n.d.), *Osua-Okowa* (n.d.), and *Dimkpa Taa Aku* (n.d.). His undaunted spirit bodes well for the revival and growth not just of Igbo, but of African vernacular literatures in general.

Pita Nwana's *Omenuko* was truly a work of art conceived by an Igbo for the Igbo about the Igbo. Its great success seems a good augury for the revival of vernacular literature among the Igbo. It immediately awakened in the Igbo a spontaneous love for reading. Many people inside and outside school read *Omenuko* for its wit, its volatile humour, and its insistent moral overtones. But, nothing ever came again from the pen of Pita Nwana despite the best-seller image of his first work. There are many people who would remember the novel possibly without remembering its author, and some would scarcely associate the novel with an author. It seemed to such readers like the book of wisdom sent from on high and to search for its author would be like searching for the author of the Bible. One reason for this is that while the novel was in circulation its hero, Omenuko, was still alive and therefore diverted, by his presence, all the attention from the author. (Little attention would have been paid to any of the authors of the Gospels of the New Testament, if Christ had been physically present at the time of publication.)

The ever stronger emphasis which came to be laid on the English language in schools a decade after the publication of *Omenuko,* did not help to prolong the life of *Omenuko* as an Igbo text. While the attention to English did not entirely obliterate the popularity of the novel, it became gradually apparent over the years that only an English translation would save it from obscurity. Newspapers in the English language were coming out in increasing numbers; religious tracts were also being issued in English; the radio was featuring greater numbers of broadcasts in the English language and local musicians had begun to render their songs as much in the English language as in Igbo. (Israel Njemanze, alias "Nwoba," one of the leading Igbo musicians at this time, composed songs

which featured English and Igbo lines within the same song. His most popular tune "Never make a lover with an Igbo lady" composed early in the forties, was rendered entirely in English except for Igbo refrains and ideophones.) The medium of instruction in schools was changing entirely to English after the first two years in the "Infant Classes," and English translations of the Bible were being sold side by side with the Igbo version. In the mid-forties even more revolutionary changes had taken place in the schools. The schools opened with songs in the English language (chosen from either *Sacred Songs and Solos, Hymns Ancient and Modern,* or *Hymnal Companion*). Prayers (from the *Book of Common Prayer*) were said in English and Headmasters addressed the pupils in English. Some schools reserved Wednesday morning for opening in Igbo, when prayers, songs and announcements were all in the Igbo language. There were schools where it was punishable to converse in the vernacular except at the approved periods—the breaks, after classes and the official period of Vernacular in the school timetable. A failure in the English Paper in any given examination meant a failure in the entire examination. Thus English was unanimously encouraged and cultivated to the detriment of the vernacular.

It is no wonder then that the Igbo writers in the later forties did not have much enthusiasm for following the example of Pita Nwana by creating literature in the indigenous language. Instead they began to write in English. Most of the new writers were young, often primary school leavers, who felt an urge to use the little English they had acquired at school in a creative way. What they wrote was published in cheap paperbacks of between ten and fifty-odd pages, produced locally. Their themes centred on the "new Culture" that was noticeable everywhere as the values of the West surged more forcefully than ever to replace the Igbo ways, encouraged in part by the tales of the Igbo ex-servicemen of the Second World War. Soon there emerged the era of pamphlet literature among the Igbo: The pamphlets, by their nature and content, had the same type of popular appeal and wide acceptance as did *Omenuko* a decade earlier. As more and more pamphlets reached the market the great enthusiasm for *Omenuko* gradually but steadily dwindled and another epoch—the era of transition—had begun in the course of modern Igbo literature. Nevertheless, Pita Nwana remains a formidable name in the historical development of modern Igbo literature. Today, *Omenuko* appeals more to students of Igbo language and culture and learners of Igbo language than the general Igbo reader like those who picked up the book some decades ago for pleasure and entertainment. (pp. 50-8)

Ernest N. Emenyonu, "Pioneer Igbo Writers," in his The Rise of the Igbo Novel, *Oxford University Press, Nigeria, 1978, pp. 33-59.*

ADEBOYE BABALOLA

[*Babalola is a Nigerian educator, dramatist, and critic. In the following excerpt, he surveys literature in the Efik and Hausa languages.*]

Efik is one of the many dialects spoken by the various ethnic groups that occupy the basin of the Cross River in Eastern Nigeria. The people, generally referred to as Efiks, Ibibios, Anangs and Ekois, number about 3,500,000. But Efik has gradually become the principal language of the area because for nearly two centuries now it has been the language of commerce and of the Christian religion from Ikom near the Cameroons border to Calabar at the mouth of the Calabar River.

On the arrival at Calabar of the Rev. Hope Masterton Waddell and Mr. Samuel Edgerley, a printer and catechist, on the 10th day of April, 1846, under the auspices of the Jamaica Mission of the Church of Scotland Mission, a well-planned study of the Efik language began. The first major publication in the language was the Holy Bible in Efik (1868).

With the commencement of the serious study of the Efik language by Christian missionaries and the encouragement they gave to the Efik people in order to get them to be able to read the Efik Bible, some authors started to write down the traditional fireside tales of Efik oral literature. They also wrote down the romantic poems and the tales of courage and trickery usually told at the meeting and parting of lovers, at community get-togethers on moonlit nights and on the way to the farm or to the spring. Here is a classic example of a verse from a love song written by E. N. Amaku in praise of a lover whose name begins with the letter "E."

> "E" mi—o—o,
> Mmaha nditi,
> Nti ndunke,
> Ndun idige k'ima.

This means:

> My Love "E"
> I don't like to remember
> If I do, I wouldn't like to be here
>   (without him/her).
> If I am here, it wouldn't be voluntarily.

In similar vein these authors wrote on a large number of secular topics. New ideas brought by contact with Europeans led to the coining of new words in Efik which enriched the Efik language and subsequently gave birth to Efik literature of the new age. Then emerged a nobler breed of writers, some of them very versatile in prose, poetry and drama—the Amakus, the Nkanas, the Elizabeth Asibons, the Edyans, to name a few. Their themes were no less varied and enchanting.

The most dignified prose writers are E. N. Amaku and E. E. Ijkana. In Mr. Amaku's greatest prose work, *Edikot Nwed Mbuk,* the author depicts Efik culture in all its variety. The principal animal characters in this six-volume series are Ekpe (Leopard), famous for his agility and bravery, and Ikut (Tortoise), notorious for his craftiness. From here the author proceeds to paint an exquisite picture of the grandeur of Etinyin Abasi (which literally means "Our Father God") and the splendour of his domain, including Esop Ndito Ison (the Court of the Elites or Aristocrats) and the exploits of Abasi Ekpenyon, an illustrious prince in that kingdom. After Amaku comes E. E. Nkana, whose name has become a household word among the Efik-speaking peoples because of his fascinating novel *Mutanda Oyom Namondo.* Here he makes the gods and goddesses of traditional belief come alive in the adventures of a king, Mutanda, who went in quest of his lost son, Namondo.

The most notable Efik poet is the versatile E. N. Amaku, whose name has already been mentioned above. Prominent among his poetic works are *Ufok Uto Iko Efik* and *Enem Inua Iko,* both of which are anthologies of Efik poems—some serious, others lighter; some secular, others religious; some plaintive, others romantic. In one of his best-known poems he eulogizes Idorenyin (Hope). Another worthy contributor to Efik poetry is Elizabeth Asibon, whose poems are broadcast daily from Calabar over the network of the Nigerian Broadcasting Corpora-

tion. Her most popular work is an epic poem composed in 1956 to commemorate the visit of Queen Elizabeth II to Calabar.

Written Efik drama dates back to the early days of Christian missions in Calabar when religious plays were written for special Church ceremonies. From these developed the production of secular plays, partly romantic and partly historical, for the entertainment of kings as well as the general public. Foremost among the playwrights is Ernest A. Edyan. His major plays are *Asibon Edem, Sidibe, Akpamon Idim* and *Bokit Ekon Mban. Asibon Edem* is generally acclaimed the most fascinating and the most dignified of Edyan's plays. This play is a tragedy depicting historical events in the political and social life of the great prince Asibon Edem of old Calabar. It portrays vividly various aspects of Efik life and culture ranging from the luxurious life of the princes in the royal court to the commoners' hard life on the plantations; from the influence of the diviners to the absolute authority of the "Ekpe" society. The play depicts how, in spite of the apparent harmonious blending of the plans of the deities with those of human beings, the gods can at will thwart a man's ambition to become a king even on the eve of the man's coronation.

What does the future hold in store for Efik literature? It appears that with the creation of the South-Eastern State of Nigeria additional emphasis is likely to be laid in the schools' curricula on the study of Efik, which now serves as the main vehicle of communication among the various ethnic groups of the State. This should lead to a rapid development of Efik literature through the exertions of budding writers who evidently abound among the new generation.

Although the Hausa people must have had the knowledge of writing before 1800, it was evidently put to use only by a close circle of Muslim leaders (who mostly wrote in Arabic and for religious purposes), and it was only at the start of the twentieth century that written Hausa literature came into being. The first Hausa novel to be published is in fact barely a generation old. Many of the modern works are clearly in the line of direct and immediate continuity from the older, oral Hausa and Arabic forms. Not only do some of these works give fresh renderings of old tales but also some modern Hausa novels draw upon certain characteristic elements of motif, setting and style in the older forms, and in poetry the influence of an earlier Arabic verse form is often very visible. Nevertheless, certain works, together with the birth of the drama, point to new trends and developments in the literary tradition.

To appreciate fully modern Hausa prose fiction one must first recognize the influence on it of Hausa folklore and Arabian tales. The world of Hausa folklore is prominently, though not exclusively, peopled with animals having human characteristics and tendencies. It is in fact a significant reflection of human society in which, however, seniority is determined not by age (as in real Hausa society) but in most cases by sheer physical size and strength. In such a world, therefore, the tiny creatures would be easily victimized but for the fact that their greater intelligence protects them and even turns the tables in their favour. This theme, the victory of brain over brawn, runs through most of the animal stories. Thus the spider, the hare and the jackal often exploit the stupidity of the hyena, or even the elephant, to their advantage. In other tales where human beings figure, certain other qualities, such as keen and upright moral conscience, become the weapon of the otherwise helpless. Another popular feature is the stereotyped figure of the ogre, the incredibly gigantic and strong man-eating monster who lives in the solitary wilds or in caves, hoarding wealth and keeping as maid or wife a young human beauty. Set against him is the figure of the human hero, whose additional weapons include courage, strength, a fatal sword or some supernatural charm. And in the spirit world proper, we come across all kinds of djinns and fairies, evil and good. The human hero fights his way, against them or with their help, always to victory. From a more political view, the figure of the Waziri, invariably wicked, cunning, disloyal and power-hungry, passes on unchanged.

Although published later than *Gandoki, Magana Jari Ce* is the first work that should be examined against this background, not only because the setting is clearly older but also because it demonstrates a direct affinity with indigenous Hausa folklore and with Arabian sources. Imam, in the three volumes of this magnificent work, imaginatively blends traditional narrative vigour with the charm of Arabian romance. The fountain of these tales is a parrot, not a beautiful princess as in *A Thousand-and-One Nights* which evidently is Imam's source of inspiration. Imam does not merely borrow certain tales from the Arabic work; he also borrows, and transmutes, the overall plot. The stories the parrot narrates vary widely in nature and appeal, but they all more or less point to some moral, and in the first volume serve to make Musa, the Emir's son, forget his intention to ride to the battleground to meet his mate. The affinity of *Magana Jari Ce* to folklore does not lie only in the tales narrated by the parrot, but also in the basic plot of the book

itself. The parrot at first is simply a common bird, useless except as a pet. But he soon turns out, owing to his infinite wisdom and perception, to be indispensable to the King not only privately but also officially. It is the parrot that tells of approaching enemy troops, and advises on how they can be surprised and routed, and discloses the plots made by the Waziri against the Emir, the Emir's only son, and the state. Against his superior knowledge the human beings appear as pathetic puppets under the benign shadow of a god-figure. This is essentially the theme in the animal stories; the supremacy of intellect and knowledge over other kinds of power. Some of the stories include only animals, others feature both animals and humans, while others have humans only. Humour, pathos and excitement flow through the tales. The basic setting seems to be an essentially pre-Islamic one, although some of the tales are clearly Islamic. In any case, it takes us back much earlier than most other works of the time.

A later work, Ingawa's *Iliya Dam Maikarfi* (1965), seems much more definitely to be Islamic in setting. Probably influenced by the earlier *Gandoki,* this epic is marked by a strong supernatural content. Iliya is born of a peasant couple who had for long been praying for a child. This opening illustrates a very popular theme in modern as well as traditional Hausa literature. People marry to beget so that in their old age there will be someone who will show them love and kindness and will also perpetuate their kind. Childlessness is the King's initial problem in *Magana Jari Ce* and recurs in many a later work. Often, in literature as in real life, it leads to quite ridiculous beliefs and practices which might otherwise never be contemplated.

Iliya, born to this couple after years of wedlock, falls ill at two years old and subsequently becomes paralysed in both arms and legs. One day after he has grown into manhood, alone in bed in the compound, Iliya suddenly receives and entertains as guests three men in Arab attire, each counting a rosary. They have come, we are told, to test and heal him; they are angels:

> Then one of them fetched water in a calabash, said a prayer, and handed it to Iliya, saying, "Wash your face and your body." Iliya received [it] with his healthy right hand, and washed all over. In the twinkling of an eye, lo, Iliya's body became right again, as if it wasn't his. His paralysed legs and arms all straightened up so much so that unless one knew beforehand, one would not say that Iliya had once been lame.

And when they have finished their ministration on him and infused him with superhuman strength, one of them warns him to continue to believe in God and serve him meticulously, and then reveals to him that he will be famed throughout the world and that he will be victorious over all except a certain human called Wargaji, whom he is therefore not to fight but to befriend. Iliya's mission, a rather obscure one, is to journey to Kib City without wasting any time on the way. "And as soon as they finished talking, Iliya sought those learned men but could not find them."

It is in the course of this journey that Iliya fights battle upon battle; he is victorious in each and on meeting Wargaji he befriends him. At last he accomplishes his mission, and as he has nothing else to do, he sits on a rock holding his sword, his horse standing behind him, and prays to Allah to transform him and his horse into stone. His prayer is answered and here ends the story—a rather unusual ending in that it appears to immortalize man although it is written in an Islamic vein. Is

Chinua Achebe. Courtesy of the author.

it perhaps the pre-Islamic pagan belief in legendary heroes rearing its head up against all odds? Or is it a possible pointer to future literary developments?

While *Iliya Dam Maikarfi* is pure legend, *Gandoki* blends history and legend. It is a narration by the hero of his experiences during the difficult period of European colonization of Northern Nigeria. In this thrilling novel, Bello essentially follows history which he uses as a sort of springboard to plunge from a war with the white man to wars with djinns and giants. Gandoki, the hero, is perhaps the greatest adventurer in modern Hausa fiction. His whole life centres upon an almost obsessive love for war. He will not hesitate to intervene anywhere where a battle is likely to occur; rather, he will go to any extent to invite trouble. When news reached him at Kwantagora that the English had captured Bida, he immediately went thither leaving his wife and son at home. Whenever any daring act is to be done, and men are slow to act, it is Gandoki who leads. When the colonial wars were almost over, he felt that he was getting rusty and was therefore ill at ease; so he set out together with his brave son, Garba, on a pilgrimage to Mecca, but the white men again scattered their caravan and foiled their aim. One day, after a fierce battle in which all but the two of them were killed, they fell asleep while resting in the wilds. They awoke to find themselves flown over to the spirit island of Sayalana in India. It turned out that the battalion they had fought previously belonged to the ruler of that island. It is from here that their tough, incredible experiences with the spirit world really begin.

As in *Iliya Dam Maikarfi*, the more contemporary world of *Gandoki* is strongly controlled by the supernatural. The great adventurer and his son are able to perform their military feats not only because they are strong and courageous, but also because they have armed themselves to the teeth with charms. Gandoki, for instance, has some charms and amulets that protect him from missiles or bullets or sharp edges and others that confer invisibility on the user and, above all, he possesses the how-on-earth-did-you-manage-to-escape charm. Here, as elsewhere, in modern Hausa literature, the reader is led to a willing suspension of disbelief.

While it stands out among other works in being firmly rooted in history, *Gandoki* is nevertheless somewhat typical of those works closely influenced by the older literary forms. Like the heroes of old, Gandoki survives incredibly narrow escapes fighting battles not only with ogres but also with djinns and white men. Through his sense of humour, his humanity and his narrative power, his account of his life, tough as it is, is redeemed from the uneasy vagueness overhanging the horizon of Iliya's world.

Dau Fataken Dare . . . and *Tauraruwar Hamada* are two interesting and similar stories of notorious but prosperous thieves. In the latter, Ahmed Daura satirizes current superstitions. M. Danye is charged with the formidable task of stealing "the Star of the Desert," the peerless beauty after whose name the novel is titled, and bringing her to the Emir of Langeri. He consults an astrologer before he sets out, but nevertheless he undergoes much suffering in enforced servitude and imprisonment. In the course of his varied adventures he is reformed and at the end becomes not only an immortal but also a king. Thus, while Iliya is simply eternalized by being transformed into rock, here M. Danye and his friend Dabo are immortalized, and, the reader is told, "Right now if you go to Damas you will find them. And the snake visits them every week." Thus the immortality theme is developed here.

While *Tauraruwar Hamada* is akin to *Iliya* and the other stories which may be said to constitute one phase of a tradition, it appears to point to a new trend such as satire of the contemporary habit of consulting so-called *mallams,* who claim to have the power to foretell the future. Instead of going back to a past rich in superstition and the supernatural, modern Hausa fiction is here beginning to look at and comment on contemporary realities. In a small way, therefore, *Tauraruwar Hamada* may be regarded as introducing new ideas which develop in the later novels and receive fuller treatment in drama and in later poetry.

Earlier Hausa poetry, on the other hand, belongs to a different phase. As might perhaps be expected, the early modern poetry is heavily didactic and religious, like early Islamic Arab poetry. Perhaps all of this poetry has been written by artists who are to a greater or lesser degree conversant with Arabic and Arabic verse form, for apart from the fact that quantity is a feature common to both languages, and also that Hausa poetry has followed Arabic in the bare stylistic arrangement of the verses, rhyme seems to be one clear area of direct influence and some poems show traces of Arabic verse metre.

Perhaps the longest religious poem is the ode *"Imfiraji"* of the blind ascetic Aliyu Namangi. In this poem, written in eight volumes, he devotes a substantial portion to the praise of the Prophet; moral and religious teaching; vivid descriptions of Heaven and Hell; the life of man from the moment of his conception in the womb to the hour of death; and a criticism of contemporary social evils.

The vast religious poetry of this phase includes works by Alhaji Muhammadu Givandu, Baba Maigyada and several later poets such as Muazu Hadeja. In Muazu Hadeja's anthology of poems (published by Gaskiya) there are five poems on religious and moral teachings. The other poems in the anthology are social rather than religious. All through the volume the reader is treated to the remarkable spontaneity of Muazu Hadeja's lyricism.

From the predominantly religious phase we pass on to the more social, in which the literary works are concerned with contemporary society and examine and diagnose the strengths and weaknesses of social habits and customs from a wider viewpoint than the religious. Some of this poetry also takes on a strong political twentieth-century outlook. From purely religious teaching modern Hausa poetry can be seen as gradually covering wider moral fields. Society is thereby often satirized and out of this some sort of political and nationalistic literature is somehow born. Thus a general condemnation of adultery from the Islamic viewpoint develops into a social, even sociological, study of the prostitute by, first, Hamisu Yadudu Funtuwa in "Uwar Mugu" (= lit. "mother of the evil one") and, later, by Muazu Hadeja.

The poetry of this phase is full of indignant attempts to rouse society from its slumber. Saadu Zungur and Muazu Hadeja in their political poems warn the Hausas that they must awake and catch up with the rest of Nigeria. Zungur condemns, as indignantly as Hadeja does, prostitution, mendicancy and other social evils.

In another poem Zungur celebrates the illustrious exploits of the Nigerian Army during the Second World War:

> O, How proud and happy we are, the
> Nigerians have made a name.
> To the troops of liberation and trust,
> O Lord, for the sake of the son of Amina,
> Give your lasting reward.

In yet another poem contemporary with this one, the poet warns against rumour-mongering during war. This preoccupation of literature with contemporary realities is also illustrated by the few works of drama published. In *Zamanin Nan Namu* and *Jatau Na Kyallu* Makarfi attacks the social life of the day. The former dwells on the evils resulting from lax and inattentive upbringing of children, especially daughters, and the latter shows up the vices of prostitution. Jatau, once a wealthy, respectable man with three wives, makes Kyallu, a notorious example of a prostitute, his fourth. He ends up by divorcing his other wives and losing all his property. Then Kyallu leaves him, a poor wretch who only then realizes how foolish he has been.

In *Mallam Inkun Tum*, Dogondaji cleverly caricatures the all too credulous dependence of the ignorant on *mallams;* and Tunau in *Wasan Marafa* takes us back to an earlier period when the value of Western education was still unknown. The theme of the play is the importance of personal hygiene as well as the usefulness of sending children to school.

While the literature of the first category generally draws upon older forms in style and even theme, that in the second tends to free itself from them. The late Sir Abubakar's *Shaihu Umar,* set in an older world of slavery and the slave trade, is essentially a work showing the new trend. An account of a man's hard life from childhood to middle age, *Shaihu Umar* is essentially realistic and devoid of the fantasy that fills and sometimes overflows novels from the earlier period. No ogres are present, the supernatural content is minimal, and there is no obvious moralization. It is a very taut and imaginative work which is marked by a serious awareness of human suffering and human goodness. Umar, the hero, is impressively portrayed. In the shifting patterns of suffering and joy, in the struggle with physical pain and keen sense of bereavement, this work is essentially a record and, in a deeply religious sense, an optimistic one, of man's struggle with the vicissitudes of his life.

Shaihu Umar is thus clearly a major development in the literary tradition of modern Hausa fiction. Its poetic counterparts are the politically prophetic poems by Zungur and Hadeja. Furthermore, the new trend in poetry is represented by Namangi's last-published religious poem *Kasbur Ragaibu,* as well as by the poems of Mudi Sipikin, and those of Abubakar Ladan, Akilu Aliyu, Baba Maigyada, Yusufu Kantu and Aliyu (a Zaria Emir). With regard to drama, the very fact of its birth is a result of the new promising development in Hausa literature. (pp. 55-63)

> Adeboye Babalola, "A Survey of Modern Literature in the Yoruba, Efik and Hausa Languages," in Introduction to Nigerian Literature, *edited by Bruce King, 1971. Reprint by Africana Publishing Corporation, 1972, pp. 50-63.*

ADEBOYE BABALOLA AND ALBERT S. GERARD

[*Gérard is a Belgian critic who has written extensively on African literature. In the following excerpt, Babalola and Gérard survey literature in the Yoruba language.*]

In the nonliterate African societies that received the cultural impact of Western civilization through Protestant, and especially British, missionary activity, the emergence and development of a creative written literature was a by-product of the need to make the word of the Christian God available to converts in their own mother tongue. Within the limitations of their linguistic competence, which was often far from negligible, the missionaries not only reduced the local language to writing but also taught their converts how to read and write it, printed translations of Biblical passages, made revisions of such European fiction as was suitable for edifying entertainment, and encouraged gifted converts to compose original hymns and moralizing fiction for school reading. It must be clearly understood, however, that this activity, which stimulated creative writing, did not bring oral composition to an abrupt end. Among the Yoruba, whose literature is our concern here, the various genres of spoken art remained and still are very much alive in farmsteads, villages, and towns. Still, the development of creative writing in Yoruba is particularly worth surveying as a good example of the historical pattern observable in most areas of the Black Continent that once formed part of the British Empire. (pp. 188-89)

The first Yoruba poet to achieve wide acclaim was J. Sobowale Sowande (1858-1936), writing under the pseudonym Sobo Arobiodu. His *Iwe Arofo Orin (Book of Carefully Composed Poetic Utterances),* in the Egba dialect of Yoruba, appeared in 1920. Sowande's poems were composed on the pattern of the traditional songs sung in Abeokuta at the festivals of Oro, the god of punishment, but since the author was a Christian, Oro is hardly mentioned. The poems center on the writer's experience of life and his observations on contemporary events and manners. Sowande published five further volumes in Abeokuta before he died.

Another Abeokuta pioneer was Kolawole Ajisafe (1877-1940), a prolific writer whose works include anthologies of original poems and prose discourses on the problems of human life. His earliest significant volume of poetry was *Aiye Akamara (Human Life Full of Pitfalls,* 1921), a meditation on life's vicissitudes. In 1934, he published *Gbadebo Alake (Gbadebo, King of Abeokuta),* a short verse biography of the then recently deceased king of Abeokuta, containing some outspoken criticism of his policies.

These works were inevitably impregnated with the new religious outlook, even though some authors, like Sowande, had made use of traditional poetic forms. The link between traditional beliefs and writing in the modern vein is to be found in *Iwe Kini Awon Akewi (First Book of Minstrels' Utterances),* an anthology compiled by Adetimkan Obasa (1878-1948) in 1927, and published by a society of well-to-do elderly citizens, Egbe Agba-O-Tan. In the preface, the editor stated that his labors on the book had started as far back as 1886 and that the originality to which he could lay claim practically ceased at assemblage, the contents being mostly traditional Yoruba sayings of the proverbial type embodying the ancestral wisdom of Yoruba society. Two further volumes were issued in 1934 and 1945. All three books were well received at the time of their publication, and from then on have been held in high esteem, especially for making Yoruba gnomic lore available in written, classified form. But in spite of the author's disclaimers, a few of the poems in his books were of his own composition. Particularly striking is the humorous poem entitled *Alaseju (Overdoer),* in which he pokes fun at various kinds of extremes in personal conduct. Several poems from Obasa's anthologies were translated into English by Adeboye Babalola and published in *African Affairs* in the early 1950s.

The early 1930s witnessed the emergence of original prose fiction in Yoruba with *Igbehin A Dun (tabi) Omo Orukan (The Sweet Shall Succeed the Bitter, or The Orphan,* 1931) by Akintunde Akintan (1890-1957), editor of the bilingual weekly

Eleti Ofe. It is a realistic and moralizing novelette about a Yoruba girl who started life unhappily as an orphan in the 1860s but subsequently married a king and enjoyed a happy family life. The Sunday-school morality, the "realistic" setting, and the facile optimism of the book are typical of much of the early fiction produced in African languages prior to World War II.

Legitimate prose fiction in Yoruba had its beginning in 1938, when Olorunfemi Fagunwa (1903-1963) produced *Ogboju Ode Ninu Igbo Irunmale (The Brave Hunter in the Forest of Embodied Spirits)*. In this frame story an elderly hunter recounts his adventures in the thick forest where he had undertaken an expedition on the orders of a king. In Yoruba folklore, the forest is the seat of supernatural forces and the abode of trolls, gnomes, ghosts, and sundry other uncanny beings. A number of those stories are genuine folk material, illustrating the fanciful creativeness of the Yoruba mind in its beliefs about spirits and witches and the weird incidents that can happen in the forest. At the same time, however, the novel deals with everyday problems in the traditional life and thought of the Yoruba: it extols courage and perseverance and condemns wickedness, cruelty, greed, and ingratitude; it describes the rivalries between co-wives in polygamous families; it illustrates parents' problems in choosing husbands for their daughters. Fagunwa tells the story in the manner of a Yoruba folktale narrator, introducing numerous didactic observations. But the influence of Christianity and of Bunyan is equally perceptible: the transcendent deity of the Yoruba, Olodumare, is identified with the Christian God; several Biblical figures intrude into the narrative, as well as such allegorical characters as Starvation, Peril, and Chaos.

Like all Yoruba works mentioned so far, Fagunwa's first novel was published locally. But it met with such considerable and deserved success that his later novels were brought out by Nelson's in Edinburgh. Most of them are developed on the same pattern: the story starts in real life when a visitor comes to the author's house. This visitor soon becomes a narrator whose story plunges into a forest world of supernatural beings while becoming a vehicle for the author's sermonizings. Each of Fagunwa's next three novels—*Igbo Olodumare (The Jungle of the Almighty*, 1949), the story of *Ireke Onibudo* (1950), and *Irinkerindo Ninu Igbo Elegbeje (Irinkerindo the Hunter in the Town of Igbo Elegbeje*, 1954)—is therefore both a quest story and a frame story, resembling the medieval chivalric romances of Western Europe, the structure of which enables the writer to avail himself fully of the world of fantasy created by the teeming imagination of Yoruba society.

Fagunwa's last novel, *Adiitu Olodumare* (1961), the story of a man whose name means "God's mystery-knot," is different from its predecessors in one important respect at least. Although the theme of perseverance in the face of adversity still plays a conspicuous role, the fantasy element is strongly reduced, and realistic depiction is increased, especially in connection with the courtship and marriage of Adiitu and Iyunade, both of whom are normal human beings. Another interesting point of divergence, reflecting perhaps the puritanical materialism of popular Victorian fiction, is that Adiitu's quest aims, at least in part, at the acquisition of wealth: his perseverance enables him to rise from extreme poverty to become the richest man in town.

It was Fagunwa's outstanding contribution that he made the more literate Yoruba fully aware of the value and originality of their traditional legacy. He showed how folktales could be legitimately and profitably used for narrative prose fiction in the Gutenberg era. While initiating one of the most remarkable trends in African indigenous literature, his example prompted other Yoruba authors to spread the imaginative lore of their society through the medium of English. Significant research has, indeed, already been devoted to this theme, particularly to the influence of Fagunwa's works upon Amos Tutuola (b. 1920) the first Nigerian writer to achieve worldwide fame in the early 1950s.

At the same time, however, the more down-to-earth, realistic trend launched by Akintunde Akintan was continued by Adekanmi Oyedele (1900-1957) in *Aiye Ree (What People Do!*, 1947), a story based on the traditional way of life of the Yoruba people before the coming of the Europeans. Only in the narrative do we find the Fagunwa touch—numerous didactic effusions, the stringing together of several isolated episodes, and so forth. The overriding theme of the tale is the certainty of predestined events in a person's life. After this promising beginning, Oyedele did not produce any other novel.

The realistic orientation was taken up almost ten years later by another writer of the same generation, Chief Isaac Oluwole Delano (b. 1904), who, like Fagunwa, has played a leading role in the cultural life of the Yoruba people. His first novel, *Aiye D'Aiye Oyinbo (Changing Times: The White Man Among Us*, 1955) is a historical novel ranging in time span from before the Europeans' arrival in Yorubaland right up to the contemporary era. The first-person narrator is a female, and the chief character is her husband, a village head, who experiences vicissitudes in the course of the superimposition of the British system of indirect rule on the traditional pattern of local government—a theme that was soon to be handled in English by Ibo novelist Chinua Achebe in *Things Fall Apart* (1958). Delano brilliantly adopted a narrative style fashioned on the characteristic mode of the Yoruba elders' delivery of their recollections. Consequently, the novel is rich in Yoruba proverbs and idioms, and the prose has a delightful measured tread.

As Delano devoted much of his time to promoting the study and the teaching of the Yoruba language, several years elapsed before he published his second novel, *L'Ojo Ojoun (In Days of Yore*, 1963). A historical novel constructed round the events which led to the passing of the Liquor Licence Ordinance in Lagos to control the consumption of strong drinks by the people of Yorubaland, it is both an adventure story and a pageant of Abeokuta and its farmlands at the start of the twentieth century. The central character is the narrator's father, a warrior turned farmer, who was converted from so-called "pagan" worship to Christianity and lived a long life as a leader of his rural community amid the changes brought by European civilization.

Thanks largely to Fagunwa and Delano, the printing of creative works in Yoruba increased perceptibly in the 1950s. Fagunwa's first tale had been printed by the CMS Bookshop in Lagos; his other works were published by Nelson's in Edinburgh. While other major British publishers, such as Longmans and the University of London Press, were becoming interested in the new market resulting from the growth of education, a few collections of short stories were privately printed locally. Besides, official help was also available in Nigeria. In 1953, the Western Region Literature Committee in Ibadan began issuing a number of short novellas. It was superseded in 1954 by the General Publications Department of the Ministry of Education, also in Ibadan. These official publishing ventures developed in close touch with Yoruba cultural societies such as Egbe Ijinle Yoruba, which contributed to the launching of *Olokun,* a journal for the promotion of modern Yoruba literature, in 1957.

But only one more member of the elder generation emerged as a result of the increase in Yoruba publications. This was Chief Joseph Folahan Odunjo (b. 1904), whose works were mostly for juvenile readers and have a strongly didactic turn. His first printed work, *Agbalowomeeri* (1958) was one of the earliest written dramas in Yoruba. The characterization is slight, but the play has a momentous plot dealing with a covetous headchief whose vices lead him to an untimely death in the forest of the spirits. *Akojopo Ewi Aladun (A Collection of Enjoyable Poems,* 1961) followed—an anthology of poems, mostly didactic, but having the traditional ring of Yoruba poetry with its lofty phrasing and carefully worked out pauses. In 1964, Odunjo produced two short novels, *Omo Oku Orun (The Deceased Woman's Daughter)* and *Kuye,* the story of a boy, each of which handles the edifying motif of the long ill-treated child who ultimately enjoys good fortune.

Throughout Black Africa, the progress of modern literature has been closely linked with educational developments, even though there may be such remarkable exceptions as Malagasy's J. J. Rabearivelo in French or Thomas Mofolo in Southern Sotho. But the example of A. C. Jordan in Xhosa, or of the French Negritude school, definitely shows that access to higher education proved conducive to a widening and a deepening of the writers' minds. While the elder generation of modern Yoruba writers were mostly school teachers essentially preoccupied with the need to provide prose fiction suitable for school reading, the many initiatives, official and otherwise, for the promotion of Yoruba writing that were taken in the decade following World War II led to the emergence in the mid-1950s of a number of younger writers who made a determined attempt at greater diversification, producing not only novels and novellas, but also poetry, plays, and adaptations of European masterpieces. Whether or not they were aware of the revaluation of African values that was taking place in French-speaking Africa under the aegis of Negritude, it is noteworthy that several sought inspiration, as their elders had done, in the native fund of folklore, myth, history, and legend. *Olorun Esan (God Takes Vengeance,* 1953) by Gabriel Ibitoye Ojo (1925-1962) is a verse rendering of a folk story illustrating the moral that "Everyone shall reap what he sows." *Ogun Kiriji (The Kiriji War)* by Olaiya Fagbamigbe (b. 1930) is a poetic account, based on oral sources, of an internecine war fought from 1880 to 1893. The Fagunwa vein of fantasy was further exploited by Ogunsina Ogundele (b. 1925) whose two novels so far— *Ibu Olokun (The Deeps where Olokun Reigns Supreme,* 1956) and *Ejigbede Lona Isalu Orun (Ejigbede on His Way to Heaven from Earth,* 1957)—deal with protagonists journeying from heaven to earth and back via the oceanic deeps, becoming involved in all sorts of fantastic situations. The same trend reappeared some ten years later, when D. J. Fatanmi (b. 1938) published *Korimale Ninu Igbo Adimula (Korimale in Adimula's Forest),* expressly dedicated to the memory of D. O. Fagunwa. Indeed, there is no mistaking the Fagunwa model in this romance: Korimale is a brave hunter who encounters numerous weird creatures in a mysterious forest; the story is replete with sermonizing advice, and the moral is clearly drawn at the end of the tale.

Folk traditions and oral history thus provided a vast fund of topics for the younger writers of the 1950s. But the stream of realistic depiction of present-day Yoruba society, beset by social, political, and ethical problems arising from the impact of a new materialistic and individualistic civilization upon ancestral culture did not run dry. It was soon joined by Femi Jeboda (b. 1933), whose full-length novel, *Olowolaiyemo*— which was not published until 1964—won first prize in a competition organized by the General Publications Section of the Ministry of Education at Ibadan to celebrate Nigeria's attainment of independence in 1960. The name of the title character means Mr. People-rally-only-round-the-well-to-do: his story is designed to portray the seamy side of city life in twentieth-century Yorubaland. This had been a major theme of vernacular prose fiction in South Africa, where the "Jim-goes-to-Jo'burg" motif has been featured repeatedly since the 1920s. Jeboda's novel provided a Yoruba expression for the realistic critique of modern urban mores which had been the central theme of the Ibo writer Cyprian Ekwensi in his English novels of the preceding decade. Also in 1964, Jeboda published a slight novelette written at an earlier date, *Afinju Adaba (Mr. Audacious Dove),* a moralizing picaresque story dealing with the adventures and misadventures of a mischievous character who goes from one escapade to another until he finally lands in prison.

Like their elders, most of these writers belonged to the schoolteacher class. In providing reading matter for schools, they sought to record the oral legacy and preserve its spirit, offering moral parables and admonitions, while at the same time turning the language into a suitable instrument for literary writing. But in the mid-1950s the need for a more sophisticated approach began to be felt by members of the younger generation who had received higher educational training.

In 1954, Adeboye Babalola (b. 1926), then a schoolmaster at Igbobi College, Lagos, published a Yoruba translation of *The Merchant of Venice.* Two years later came his *Pasan Sina (The Whip Descends on the Wrong Person,* 1958), which, together with Chief Odunjo's *Agbalowomeeri,* can be said to have laid the foundations for printed drama in Yoruba. This play in five acts focuses on a schoolboy who becomes a masquerader in order to flog his teacher, but unfortunately beats the wrong person in the execution of his plan. The farcical plot with its moralizing implications still exhibits the characteristics of school drama, but around it the author has woven a portrayal of the traditional Yoruba way of life enacting various customs. Babalola, who now teaches at the University of Lagos, has not given up creative writing, but he later turned to the scholarly study of oral poetry for his Ph.D. dissertation on the *ijala* traditional chants of Yoruba hunters.

Babalola's Shakespeare translation and both his and Chief Odunjo's plays are important stepping stones in the emergence of Yoruba drama out of its own prehistory. In Western Nigeria as elsewhere in Africa, "modern" theatrical activity, as distinct from traditional cult ceremonies and masquerades, had originated in the 1930s, chiefly in the form of Biblical plays; the scriptural texts were handled quite freely, and actors would often indulge in the ribald humor so characteristic of the mystery cycles of medieval Europe, while African-type music and songs played a considerable role. In the 1940s a teacher and choirmaster named Humbert Ogunde began to secularize this syncretic medium. He first turned it to purposes of popular entertainment, but in the 1950s, as local political life with its attendant ills was beginning to develop in Nigeria, the so-called folk opera also became an instrument for shrewd, humorous, and effective social criticism. As the first author-actor-producer of note, Ogunde was soon imitated by E. K. Ogunmola and others. Although the works of this group were exceedingly successful, few, if any, ever reached print. Publication was not achieved until Duro Ladipo, a musician who turned to dramatic composition, received a modicum of formal theatrical training at the Mbari clubs of Ibadan and Oshogbo. He decisively heightened the intellectual level of the Yoruba folk opera through his searching imaginative rendering and ethical reassessment of past history, usually as recorded in Samuel Johnson's *History of the Yoruba*.

Two trends, then, account for the organic growth of the folk opera. One is the native tradition of dramatic rituals, ceremonies and recitings, interspersed with song and dance, and leaving much room for improvisation. The other is the imported notion of school drama as a pedagogical instrument in the service of religious teaching. Odunjo's *Agbalowomeeri* signaled the emergence of school drama into print while the folk opera grew into an important segment of modern oral art. But the cross-fertilization process between native dramatic genius and alien, modern-type education entered a new phase in the mid-1950s. It is highly significant that Ogunmola successfully staged an operatic adaptation in Yoruba of Amos Tutuola's novel in English, *The Palm-Wine Drinkard*. The contribution of written knowledge to the growth of this new popular performing art has been tremendous. As a consequence, Samuel Johnson's *History of the Yoruba* is well on its way to becoming an African Holinshed, which such dramatists as Duro Ladipo and Obotunde Ijimere (b. 1930) assiduously scan for breathless stories of past wars and heroic sacrifices, which they turn into myths.

But while such talented men who were primarily interested in the theater as a performing art were turning increasingly to learning and literature, there was a correlative and converging tendency on the part of authors who were primarily "literary" writers to outgrow the somewhat childish, all too overtly sermonizing character of school drama, and to seek models and inspiration in the masterpieces of the western world. The most obvious source of inspiration was of course Shakespeare, some of whose works had been translated into several Bantu languages of South Africa, while a Swahili version of *Julius Caesar* was to be published in 1963 by Tanzania's President Julius Nyerere.

The impulse given by Babalola's translation of *The Merchant of Venice* came indirectly to strikingly original fruition in the mid-1960s when Olanipekun Esan, a classics scholar at the University of Ibadan, sought inspiration in Greek and Latin literature. Esan's plays include *Teledalase (The Creator's Will Must Prevail*, 1965), a verse tragedy based on Sophocles's *Oedipus; Esin Atiroja (The Tiptoeing War Horse*, 1966), a poetic version of the Trojan Horse story in Vergil's *Aeneid;* and *Orekelewa (Beauty Personified)*, a prose comedy based on Plautus's *Mercator*. These adaptations of Latin or Greek classics are *not* word-for-word translations, but original recasts in Yoruba mold, with African names for characters and places. A similar procedure of Africanization, designed to make classical and Western masterpieces less exotic and therefore more accessible to the African audience, was also adopted by Julius Nyerere in the revised edition of his *Juliasi Kaisari*.

Meanwhile, the increasing sophistication in modern Yoruba literature was becoming apparent with the versatile talent of Adebayo Faleti (b. 1935), whose chief contribution was to introduce into formal writing elements of the ironic humor so widespread in African societies (but which unfortunately, has seldom been permitted to break through the crust of pompous earnestness African writers all too often seem to think is nec-

essary to their dignity). Faleti's humor was already much in evidence in his early long narrative poems such as *Eda Ko L'Aropin (Never Underestimate Someone's Future Achievements*, 1956). It also permeated his brief novella *Ogun Awitele (A War Well-Publicized in Advance*, 1965), in which a hunter narrates the experience of his colleagues and himself in night encounters with armed thieves, men and women, who had given advance notice of their intention to loot the town. The comedy consists in the fantastic accounts of the proven efficacy of Yoruba medicinal and incantatory charms used by both the thieves and the night-watch hunters.

While his novella betrayed a new, mildly satirical, attitude toward traditional lore, Faleti's first play, *Nwon Ro Pe Were Ni (People Thought She Was a Mad Woman*, 1965), evinced a more serious approach and a deepening of the writer's inspiration: the comedy of playful banter between drummers and dancers as well as between palm-wine drinkers in a bar is woven into the tragedy of a well-known citizen who is condemned to ten years' imprisonment for plotting a human sacrifice for a secret cult in order to achieve perennial wealth. More recently, Faleti attempted full-scale novel writing with *Omo Olokunesin (Son of the Master of the Horse*, 1970), a historical novel set in the pre-nineteenth-century days of the Otu kingdom in Yorubaland. The story is told by three narrators, each of whom supplies a segment of the tale; then the threads are drawn together in the concluding section, recounted by the first narrator. The novel deals with the strategem successfully employed by bands of slaves in the tributary towns to achieve not only their own personal freedom but also political freedom for all the people that were subjected to the cruel rule of the Otu overlords.

The latest member of this promising generation to have emerged on the scene of Yoruba creative writing is Afolabi Olabimtan (b. 1932), a lecturer in Yoruba at the University of Lagos. His short play, *Oluwa L'O M'Ejo Da (Only God Can Judge a Person Correctly*, 1966) uses a closely knit plot centering on a murder to depict the shameful practices of various groups among the citizens of a town in Yorubaland. His realistic story of a lad nicknamed *Kekere Ekun (Leopard Cub*, 1967) focuses on a Christian character who married a second wife; but the main interest of the book resides in the overall portrayal of many aspects of present-day rural life, which appears to be dominated by the antinomy between the requirements of the Christian ethos—disseminated through the schools and through the strong corporate life of church congregations—and the undaunted persistence of traditional belief in medicinal charms, traditional institutions such as polygamy, and traditional rites such as the popular cult festivals. In *Aadota Arofo (Fifty Poems*, 1969), Olabimtan experimented, not altogether successfully, with Western poetic forms such as stanza schemes and rhymed couplets; but the genuine novelty of the work was an effort to introduce into Yoruba literary poetry the sort of critique of party politicking and of apelike imitation of Western mores that had earlier received expression not only in Nigerian novels and dramas written in English since the 1950s, but also in the Nigerian folk opera. It was perhaps the example of the latter which prompted Olabimtan to write his second play, *Olaore, Afotejoye (Chief Olaore, King by Treachery*, 1970), depicting how the good King Obalowo fell because of an error of judgment he had made. Though the work is presented as a historical tragedy, its many deliberate anachronisms call attention to contemporary situations, particularly to the antagonisms and treachery that had torn up the most important political party in Western Nigeria in the early 1960s. The contemporary creative writer in Yoruba has a relatively small audience of grown-ups because of the still high percentage of adult illiteracy and the continuing indifference of many educated Yoruba citizens to their mother tongue. Yet after a century of slow growth following the early hymns of the Otta converts in the mid-nineteenth century, Yoruba writers have managed, in the course of the last thirty years, to produce a fairly impressive and diversified body of creative writing, assimilating the alien genres of novel and drama, ranging in theme from the recording and adaptation of traditional lore through social criticism and the imaginative interpretation of history and myth. The future development of this literature depends on the determination of gifted writers to produce literary works in Yoruba in compliance with the dictates of their own genius, and not merely to meet the demands of the school market.

Yet, what we have surveyed here is only a small portion of the tremendous wealth of Yoruba literature, the major part of which is still oral. The influence of oral lore and the persistence of oral composition in modern days should not be underestimated. Considerable work is being done by Yoruba and other scholars on the tape-recording, transcription, analysis, and publication of oral material. But beyond that, it needs to be stressed that this invaluable legacy is a potent source of inspiration for modern writers. From Fagunwa to Ogundele, many fiction writers have delved into the inexhaustible fund of tales, legends, and myths produced by the fantastic imagination of Yoruba society, adapting their materials to the needs and requirements of this modern age, while at the same time trying to preserve their indigenous quality for a literate audience often prone to despise the fantasies of preliterate times.

But the contribution of Yoruba society to world literature extends beyond the limitations of its own language: the example of Fagunwa in using the native legacy prompted Amos Tutuola to resort to the same type of material. Written in recognizable, although highly idiosyncratic English, Tutuola's original romances have in turn called the attention of the literary world to the peculiarities of the Yoruba creative imagination. It is not impossible that the very success of Tutuola encouraged such a highly gifted and educated writer as Wole Soyinka (b. 1935) to use elements and patterns from Yoruba lore to construct his famous drama, *Dance of the Forests* (1960), which won him renown as the best African playwright in English. Wole Soyinka is a graduate of the University of Leeds. The trend he represents, Yoruba drama in English, was recently joined by Wale Ogunyemi (b. 1939), a professional actor who improved his craft in the extramural drama workshops organized by the University of Ibadan and later helped to organize the highly successful Theater Express Company in Lagos. Nor does Yoruba literature in English ignore the second main stream of inspiration which came to the fore in the realistic novels of I. O. Delano and Femi Jeboda. The psychological, social, and ethical problems raised by the acculturation of Yoruba society are central to the English novels of Timothy Mofolorunso Aluka (b. 1920).

Creative writing by Yoruba authors thus presents a vast spectrum of imaginative literature. From works in the oral tradition, it ranges through the folk opera (which rarely reaches printed form), to the prose, drama, and poetry written in Yoruba, and, beyond that, to the growing corpus of creative works written in English. But we need to take it a step further. Broad as this spectrum is, Yoruba literature exceeds even its limits, as illustrated by the work of Ola Balogun (b. 1945), a graduate of the universities of Dakar and Caen. His two plays, *Shango*

and *Le Roi-Elephant*, printed together in 1958, are based on semilegendary events which have come to have mythical significance for the Yoruba. But the literary importance of the works derives mainly from the fact that they establish Balogun as the only African author from the former British Empire who writes in French.

The diversity of these achievements gives Yoruba society a unique place in the larger picture of Nigerian, or even Black African, literature. Needless to say, there is no African ethnic group without its own legacy of oral literature: tales, praise poems, myths, epics, proverbs. That is the common denominator. Beyond that, it needs to be stressed that, where French and Portuguese influence was paramount, there was little effort to develop a modern literature in the African languages. But in the British Empire, the demands of missionary action often proved highly favorable to the promotion of literary writing in local tongues. Finally, in a number of areas, especially South Africa, West Africa, and, more recently, East Africa, an impressive amount of creative writing was printed in English. Such has been the case with Nigeria, which is now the most important producer of poetry, drama, and fiction in English in Black Africa.

But such developments were shaped differently among different ethnic groups. It is probably significant that the Ibo of Eastern Nigeria prefer to resort to English and have hardly produced any written literature in their own language, while the Muslim Hausa of Northern Nigeria have hardly produced any creative writing in English, remaining loyal both to their oral art and to the Islamic tradition of *ajami*—writing in their own language and in the Arabic script. Only the Yoruba—a nation of some 13 million within the Republic of Nigeria—have proved equally fertile in their own tongue and in the alien language introduced by the colonial conquest. (pp. 190-204)

Adeboye Babalola and Albert S. Gérard, "A Brief Survey of Creative Writing in Yoruba," in Review of National Literatures, *Vol. II, No. 2, Fall, 1971, pp. 188-205.*

EMMANUEL OBIECHINA

[*In the following excerpt, Obiechina discusses the Nigerian popular literature known as Onitsha Market literature.*]

Any literature whose appeal is to the masses must have at least three predictable characteristics: it must be simple in language and technique; it must be brief, and it must be cheap.

Simplicity and accessibility go together. The particular works should not make too great demand on the intellectual and emotional effort of the reader. The habit of long and sustained pouring over printed matter belongs to a small privileged minority prepared by education and practice. Books aimed at the vast majority of the people must be brief and able to communciate their interests instantly as minute rather than large doses of experience. Again, since the generality of people, (even in highly industrialized countries but more so in underdeveloped ones), live at an economic level at which they struggle incessantly to supply basic needs and conveniences, literature ranks a low priority with them and must be provided as cheaply as possible if they are to patronize it at all.

The Onitsha Market pamphlets comprise literature par excellence for the masses. They are literature about common people by some of their members for everyone's enjoyment—though its staunchest consumers remain the common people. Among the most devoted readers of the pamphlet literature must be listed grammar and elementary school boys and girls, lower-level office workers and journalists, primary school teachers, traders, mechanics, taxi-drivers, farmers and the new literates who attend adult education classes and evening schools. University graduates and people with post-grammar-school education tend to ignore this literature in favour of the more sophisticated novels, drama and poetry.

The pamphlet authors have themselves a fair idea of the kind of audience for which they produce and they sometimes define this audience in the prefaces and introductions accompanying their works. Thus, Cletus Nwosu, author of *Miss Cordelia in the Romance of Destiny,* says in the introducion to his book: "I have made the book as simple as possible so that an average boy can enjoy it without his dictionary by his side." A publisher's notice to Sigis Kamalu's *The Surprise Packet* states among other things:

"I have in my list of customers the best literary brains . . . well read and intelligent indigenous authors, journalists and professional writers. We have turned and are busy turning out volumes of sensational pamphlets on good morals. There is no school boy or student in the whole Federation who has not read pamphlets published by me." A Nigerian Union of Authors' certificate of suitability attached to H. O. Ogu's *How to Fall in Love With Girls* (A Drama) states simply that having gone through the manuscript, the Union "recommends its suitability for use in schools and colleges for dramatization purposes." Occasionally, some of the novelettes manifest a broad, catholic appeal which their authors take pains to emphasize in the introduction as in R. Okonkwo's *Never Trust All That Love You* in which the author writes: "This booklet . . . has been edited at the request of the publisher to meet the literary taste of several readers and all lovers of novels and stories."

The Onitsha Market pamphlets have a large audience. This is reflected in their sales figures. In a majority of cases, 3 to 4,000 copies are sold before a work goes out of print and is superseded; but the more popular of them sell several thousand copies. Thus, Ogali A. Ogali's play *Veronica My Daughter* has recorded a sale of 60,000 copies and *The Nigerian Bachelor's Guide* by A. O. Ude, of 40,000 copies. Most of the books are issued once or twice and then go out of print but the more popular ones, like the two mentioned above, are re-issued several times and thus reach the largest body of readers.

The pamphlets sell well because they cost so little. When they first appeared in the late nineteen-forties, they were sold for between 1/- and 1/6 a copy. Since then, the increased cost of production labour and newsprint have forced up prices to between 1/- and 3/6d. But even then, they still remain within reach of most of the readers.

This is of course not to underrate the hard-headed monetary calculation that goes into the pamphlet enterprise. As a matter of fact, the printing and publishing of the pamphlets have developed into a major industry centered on the Onitsha Market. Here, the publishers band themselves into a kind of guild with regulations and rules of conduct. They have common practices for commissioning works to would-be authors and they have evolved entrepreneural techniques for regulating the pamphlet business and making money out of it. Initial capital outlay for purchase of a printing press, employment of the services of editors, compositors, type-setters, and so on, all come into the calculation, and so the margin of profit which the printer-publishers expect from their undertaking. The low

cost of the pamphlets is, in the long run, part of the strategy for maximizing profit.

For the authors of the pamphlets consideration for monetary gain is of secondary importance only. Unlike the printer-publishers, the satisfaction of being seen in print is often adequate compensation to the pamphlet authors. Authorship is held by them in high esteem amounting almost to awe. Cletus Nwosu in a Preface to *Miss Cordelia in the Romance of Destiny* gives reasons why he has chosen to become an "author" as:

> (i) to write a book for the interest and amusement of all Nigerian students;
>
> (ii) for the purpose of dedicating it (the book) to his boyhood friend and companion—Lawrence Chikwendu, and
>
> (iii) to add his name to the list of Nigerian Authors.

The same reverential attitude to authorship is clearly shown in the first editorial opinion of the *Nigerian Authors Magazine* (1962), an organ set up by the popular authors to serve the interest of the pamphlet literature, which says: "'Author' is, in our own candid opinion, and in the opinion of those who matter in the literary field, a prouder title than 'king'."

In the face of the immense prestige attained by the pamphlet aspirant who has his story published, financial consideration becomes of little consequence. Most of the authors of the popular pamphlets would accept, especially for their maiden works, mere token payments of a few shillings for their manuscripts, though the better known ones do receive considerable sums. Publishers could, and do, exploit new authors' anxiety to be published to pay low prices but established authors insist on fair rewards, sometimes amounting to £10. 10s. for a manuscript.

Most of the pamphlet authors are, like the more sophisticated novelists and dramatists of West Africa, amateurs rather than professionals. They have some fulltime occupation from which they earn their living and merely take up writing as a pastime. A large number of the pamphlet authors are school teachers, local printing press owners and book-sellers but a considerable number of them are also journalists, railwaymen, traders, clerks, artisans, farmers and even grammar-school boys. The latter write under false names to escape detection by their school authorities and sometimes in their real names where they have the support and sympathy of their teachers.

The authors are often encouraged by their more educated friends and kinsmen, their writers' associations, their publishers and, if students, sometimes by their teachers. Such supporters of the authors express their enthusiasm by contributing more or less commendatory prefaces to the finished works. They sometimes include in the prefatory notes much biographical information about the authors as well as furnishing such details as how and why the authors came to be involved in pamphlet writing.

The relationship between the authors and the publishers of the Onitsha Market literature is an interesting one. Publishers either commission well-known writers or insert brief advertisements in published works inviting would-be authors to send in short stories and plays, sometimes with an accompanying promise of money payment. When a manuscript has been handed in by the author and paid for by the publisher, then the author's interest in it tends to come to an end. Thus it is not unusual for such a work to carry the name of the publisher, instead of its author's. That explains why several works occasionally appear under one man's name while some others appear under fanciful borrowed names like Speedy Eric, Strong Man of the Pen, Highbred Maxwell, Money-Hard and so on.

There is of course always a tacit understanding between author and publisher as to what the popular taste would dictate for each story of play. At all times, the interest of the popular audience is paramount and if the writer, whose creative compulsions might draw him somewhat out of the direct line of the popular taste, may not be immediately aware of this taste, the publisher, with his eye set on profit and the sales figures, cannot afford to ignore it. Thus it is not unusual for a publisher to give detailed specifications as to the content of a commissioned work as well as to insist that certain themes, attitudes and even forms of languge be played up as a means of arresting popular interest. This further explains why occasionally a title on the page of a book differs, by a very wide margin, from the actual content of the work. Whenever this happens, the publisher would be seen to have used his more superior hunch to divine what title is best suited to arrest popular attention, in spite of what actually is contained between the covers.

Popular propensities are also decisive in determining the format of the Onitsha Market Literature. Because its audience is composed largely of new literates who cannot grapple with large volumes, the popular authors have understandably chosen the pamphlet—a much briefer and more manageable form than say the novel—for conveying their peculiar experiences. The normal pamphlet has between ten and seventy pages. Its top-cover, as also sometimes its back-cover, carries beautiful photographs of film-stars or hand-drawn pictures illustrative of the titles. The attractive covers are meant to arrest attention and sometimes contain illustrative sketches and pictures which help to enliven their contents.

The scope of the pamphleteering literature is very wide. Some of the pamphlets appear in the Igbo vernacular while others are written in English. The English ones are much more accessible to the multi-lingual reading public of Nigeria. Some of the pamphlets are fiction while others deal with non-fictional subjects. Among the non-fictional are those which teach the technique of examinations and others which provide advice for young men and women on how to cope with the problems of modern life, advice ranging from how to fall in love to how to launder clothes. Some booklets record local history, collections of folk-tales, proverbs and anecdotes peculiar to Igboland. The fictional ones comprise novelettes (often wrongly labelled "novels" by the authors), dramas based on love and marriage incidents, or about prominent Africans. Others carry tales of adventure and wonder. By far the largest group of the fictional pamphlets concern love situations and marriage.

In the main, the content of the pamphlet literature reveals a pre-occupation of their authors with the problems of a changing society in which the growth of new cultural elements has stimulated new desires, new attitudes and new values. The pamphlet literature articulates these vast sweeping changes and attempts to provide some kind of guidance and direction to the masses of the people caught in the violence and confusion arising from the changes.

In the treatment of its major themes and interests, the Onitsha Pamphlet Literature retains its popular quality of simplicity and lightness. Even while dealing with what might appear the most serious subjects, its approach is hardly ever solemn. The desire to entertain and amuse is always paramount in the pamphlets. The typical pamphlet author paints his picture with a light comic brush. That is why the pamphlet scene is teeming with comic, ridiculous and grotesque characters and incidents. There are "bombast" characters like Bomber Billy in Ogali's *Veronica My Daughter*, "pidgin" characters like Chief Bombey in R. Okonkwo's *The Game of Love* and such deliberately created comic names as Ototofioko. These are there for their "laughs" effect. The same desire to amuse and entertain is responsible for the melodramatic treatment of many of the situations in the pamphlets, the sensationalizing of incidents and the reinforcing of descriptions with much titillating detail. It accounts for many of the fights and slap-stick knock-abouts, many of the broad jokes and vituperative name-calling and the use of expressions and sobriquets widely current at the Onitsha Market. The Onitsha Market Literature as its name implies partakes of the humour, the informality and the openness of life in Onitsha Market.

The Onitsha Market Literature is concerned with the business of living. It is literature about young men and women who are intensely alive and who, because they are so alive, have numerous problems arising out of the complexities of modern life. Most of those at whom the literature is directed have superficial contact with the modern way of life and are therefore in great need for guidance and help if they are to cope with life's complex problems.

There are in the first place the techniques of modern living which must be mastered. Then there are skills to be acquired and jobs to be held down. There is the problem of operating the modern economic machinery with its close association with the almighty cash. For those just emerging from peasant self-sufficiency the problem of adjustment to the new system looms very large in the horizon. It is both an economic problem and a moral one.

Literate education is the key that opens the door to success and the achievement of most of the desirable objectives of the young men and women in their aspiration to modernity. A number of the pamphlets, in response to a keenly felt need, are therefore directed towards helping the reader to acquire new knowledge

Gabriel Okara. Photograph by Isaac Uzuegba. Courtesy of Heinemann Educational Books Ltd.

to enable him to pass examinations and improve himself generally. There are numerous titles indicative of the educational interests of the pamphlets such as *How to Write Good English and Composition, How to Write Better Letters, Applications and Business Letters, How to Succeed in Life, How to Know Hausa, Ibo, Yoruba and English Languages, How to Know Proverbs and Many Things, How to Make Meetings, Pocket Encyclopaedia of Etiquette and Commonsense.* There are also numerous texts for primary schools and popular examination-made-easy booklets for every conceivable subject.

The educational interest is so seriously pursued by the pamphlet authors that within some of their works, they find space for some unrelated information which might enrich a reader's knowledge. These are inserted in the final pages, usually under the heading of *Things Worth Knowing.* For example, at the end of the pamphlet telling the story of Chief Awolowo's treason trial (the pamphlet is philosophically titled *The Bitterness of Politics and Awolowo's Last Trial* and written by Mazi Raphael Nwankwo) the publisher thoughtfully inserts the following information which has no bearing on the subject of the book but is calculated to inform the reader: "The world population was said to have reached 3,180,000,000 in mid—1963. This amounts to a gain of 185 million in only three years. Of this population, the Republic of China occupies almost one quarter." This is the kind of information provided by the United Nation's statistical publications which may not be available to most people. The pamphlet literature brings it to its numerous local readers.

The intention of the pamphleteers to spread education through their books is praiseworthy but the result has not always proved entirely happy for the educational system as a whole. Because the pamphlets provide ready-made knowledge, their readers go to them for "reach-me-down" answers which they readily use parrot-wise at examinations. The love for the acquisition of new knowledge is therefore almost negated by the tendency of writers and readers to give and receive education painlessly and the habit of thinking and writing in cliches grows with the spread of model answers and "knowledge-without-tears" booklets.

Another group of improving pamphlets does not concentrate on regaling the reader with knowledge but on reforming his morals and refining his attitudes in order to prepare him to face the social, economic, and emotional problems of the present day. These pamphlets embody open or implicit didactic intentions.

Didacticism is expressed in the pamphlet literature in many ways. Often, it is of the nature of warnings against the moral dangers and pitfalls of town life, and sometimes of giving the reader, in pseudophilosophic and sententious manner, a certain kind of insight into contemporary life. Sometimes the didacticism takes the form of cautionary tales embodying explicit and implicit lessons.

The didactic purpose is often stated in the authors' prefaces. This is one of the conventional practices in the pamphlet literature. A few typical examples alone need be mentioned here.

"There are three points that stand as key or a guide in the writer's mind," states Raphael Obiora in *Beauty is a Trouble* "first, to find out whether the story is educative, secondly, to see that it is entertaining, and third, to see that it is instructive." The young grammar-school boy, John Ngoh, writes in *Florence in the River of Temptation:* "My aim in composing this novel is to expose vice and praise virtue. To this end I hope my

readers will find in this novel an unforgettable lesson which will be their guide in times of difficulties." N. O. Madu writes in *Miss Rosy in the Romance of True Love:* "The case dealt with in this story is a valuable one, and readers will discover for themselves that the married life of today is often a force, a bargain or a vulgarity rather than a great spiritual enterprise. This book . . . will show how far true this statement is. What the expressions 'I love you' and 'My dear' carry after them or when they come from the lips of a woman, can be found under the cover of his book." Thomas Iguh warning the reader against obsession with love in *The Sorrow of Love* writes: "This novel is designed to serve as a lesson to some of our young boys and girls who feel that there is another heaven in the game of love." S. E. Eze says simply of his book, *How to Know a Good Friend,* "It contains important facts and gives good advice to men and women." G. O. Obiaga, a pharmacist, writes in the preface to his brother C. O. Obiaga's novelette, *Boys and Girls of Nowadays:* "The story is full of life, and it depicts the life of young men and women of Nigeria today. The moral drawn from it is educative, cautioning and forestalling all in one, and I hope all and sundry will read and enjoy this story and keep a copy of this interesting booklet."

Sometimes the language in which the moral purpose is stated is not as soberly prosaic as that employed by the above authors but can be extremely witty or even titillating as in Speedy Eric's *Mabel the Sweet Honey that Flowed Away.* "Her skin," the author writes, "would make your blood flow in the wrong direction. She was so sweet and sexy, knew how to romance. She married at sixteen. But she wanted more fun. Yet it ended at seventeen. And an end! So thrilling." The last remark applies to the story of course, not to Mabel's life which is obviously censured.

Some of the prefaces are quite amusing because they contain some clearly incongruous or downright absurd statements. An example is in R. Okonkwo's *Never Trust All That Love You* which announces that the author "is showing modern Nigerianization . . . (and the) . . . capacity of educating the illiterates, who through the means of reading the good novels written in good English language learn greatly." The implication that illiterates can read "the good novels" and that only they need instruction in the use of good English is of course ridiculous but it demonstrates once more the degree of the anxiety of the pamphlet authors to instruct and improve their audience. Illiteracy and the inability to communicate properly are recognized as terrible handicaps to anyone intending to make the best of contemporary life and its numerous opportunities.

If the writers' manifestoes read in part like tracts for the times, it is mainly because the times need tracts. The writers attempt to correct a lot that is wrong in contemporary society. They deal with the more immediate problems which confront the average young man and woman within the changing social situation, problems of how to make and keep money, of whether or not it is desirable to fall in love, of whether parents are justified in intervening to determine who should or should not marry their daughters and so on. (pp. 3-10)

The quest for the good life is most clearly illustrated in the pamphlet literature by those authors who deal with the problem of money and material wealth.

On the level at which the popular writers perceive modern life, money is a very desirable thing. They accept you cannot get very far without it. You need it to equip yourself with the modern necessaries of life such as household furniture, good clothes, decent meals, and the new prestige goods that would raise your standing in society. If you are on the lower wrungs of the economic ladder, you need money to purchase yourself a bicycle, a radio and to get yourself a wife. On the higher economic level, you would need a motor car, a radiogram, a house, money to provide sumptuous and lavish parties as befits your dignity and to buy gorgeous and costly clothes that would symbolize your social standing. Whether you are within the higher or lower income bracket, you need money to educate your children and the children of your close kins and generally to help your parents and the members of your extended family out of their numerous financial problems.

For the popular authors therefore it is of the greatest importance that a man must work and earn money. They are not at all concerned like the intellectual authors of West Africa as to whether the mere possession of money and material wealth is enough to ensure individual happiness. There is only one case in which the value represented by money is superseded by a higher value and that is in the matter of marriage. The popular authors generally agree that when the choice is between marriage based on love and a marriage based on money, the interest of love should supersede that of money. Apart from this case, which is at all events a special one, money and the values represented by it stand very high in the estimation of the popular authors. It is to them a necessary element in the individual's quest for self-fulfilment. The means of its acquisition must of course be scrupulously honest (there are many instances in the tales in which its illegal or immoral acquisition is shown to be the undoing of apparently successful men). But the ability to earn "good" money is often pictured as both a virtue and a means to individual happiness.

The writers therefore extol hard work and frugality (which they are careful to distinguish from miserliness and meanness). "When you are poor," writes Okenwa Olisa, one of the foremost of the didactic pamphlet authors, "be an industrious man. Don't sit idle. You cannot win raffle when you do not sign it, it is when you sign it you will watch what will be the result. That is, you will not become rich when you do not work, it is when you work that you will begin to watch what your labour will produce. To be rich is very hard, but some people do not know. Some people think it is a thing of chance. God cannot send you a parcel of food from heaven. He can only bless and protect you. Don't imitate (the rich) when you have no money. You know that a hungry man who does not take care will eat poison, as well as a poor man who imitates (the rich) will steal." (pp. 12-13)

The popular pamphleteers welcome the existence of opportunity in society which leaves the door open for the individual to get on. Their tales are full of instances of those who have started life from the most humble stations and pulled themselves up to lofty heights of economic success. In most of their novelettes, everybody has a recognized and named trade or a profession or attends school, with the purpose of preparing for a trade or a profession. Some of the chief heroes are those who go to work in the day and study for external certificates and degrees at night. They are allotted really virtuous roles in the tales. Protagonists generally prosper in their chosen occupations but their successes and triumphs soon become failures when they allow themselves to be diverted from their serious occupations. What the evidence of their own eyes and everyday experiences show to the popular writers is that in a ruthlessly competitive society that man is a failure (and therefore unhappy) who cannot exert himself or is foolish enough to throw away his hard-earned money.

The pamphlet writers therefore regard it as their duty to warn their readers through cautionary tales, exempla or anecdotes, against the evils through which individuals easily lose their money, especially in the urban areas. They single out three major sources of financial ruin to the unwary town-dweller going after flashy, money-grabbing women; addiction to the bottle; and "high life" or the tendency of an individual to live beyond his economic means. Thus, their pamphlets carry such cautionary titles as *Money Hard To Get But Easy to Spend, Why Boys Never Trust Money Monger Girls, Drunkards Believe Bar Is Heaven, Beware of Harlots and Many Friends, Beware of Women, Why Harlots Hate Married Men and Love Bachelors, Money Hard But Some Women Don't Know, Why Men Never Trust Women, Never Trust All That Love You, Be Careful: Salutation Is Not Love.*

The pamphlet writers employ different techniques for putting across their economic lessons. A writer might use one in the nature of a tract for the times in which he emphasizes the positives of a money-making working life as in the following extract from Okenwa Olisa's *Money Hard To Get But Easy To Spend:*

> He who seeks for money and wants to have it must not say that the rain is too much, he must work under it. He must not say that the sun is coming, he must work under it. He must sing his favourite song and work. He must not fear work. He must work hard. He must be obedient. He must be humble. He must be punctual to his work. He must endure insult, abuse. He must take trouble of many kinds. He must not play with his business. If a tradesman, he must be honest and sincere to his Customers. He must improve his handwork in order to attract customers. He must not charge too much. He must not play with his business, otherwise his business plays with him.

This tract is obviously directed to the small man and not the business executive or the high-level civil servant. It is a guide to the apprentice, the manual worker, the artisan, the shopkeeper and everyone within the lower income bracket. (These are the usual audience of the pamphlet literature). That is why there is such emphasis on obedience, humility, and honesty, sincerity and improvement of handwork in order to attract customers. The man in the executive position does not need these injunctions; rather, it is the apprentice, the self-employed tradesman, the trader and those in subordinate positions who need them.

It is not enough however to work hard and show a clear determination to earn. Money once earned must be prudently used or it would soon vanish away. The writers therefore sometimes list the main dangers to the proper husbanding of money. Here, for example, is Okenwa Olisa's list in *No Condition Is Permanent.* The section is titled "Another Advice to Men About Money."

> When you have money these misbehaviours could drive it out and you fall woefully: pride, recklessness, carelessness, highlife, excess happiness, chasing badly, drunkenness, wickedness, enviousness, unnecessary economicals, having confidence in everyone, deceit and fraud, pretence, claiming too know and superiority, forgetting God.

The presence of some items in this formidable list is somewhat surprising but there is no doubt that the author if called upon to do so could expatiate quite convincingly on why each "misbehaviour" could prevent an individual from saving his money or spending it in a desirable manner. The items which appear oddest here include "wickedness," "enviousness" and "forgetting God." However, anyone familiar with popular African beliefs will recognize the view usually held that a wicked or envious man never truly prospers. He may make his money by employing doubtful or immoral means but something soon happens to rob him of his ill-gotten lucre. A fire, thieves, costly litigation—any of these things could sweep away in the briefest possible moment all that the evil man has immorally built up. And a man who forgets God is likely, sooner or later, to do something unwise which will end in his losing his money. (pp. 15-17)

Marriage is a major theme in the Onitsha Market Literature. Next only to love, it engages the attention of a considerable number of the popular authors. In its treatment we see one of the areas of confict in contemporary Africa. The source of conflict often centres on the determination of parents (especially fathers) to have a dominant voice in deciding who should marry their daughters and the equally determined efforts of the daughters to resist what they regard as an intolerable interference in a matter which touches them intimately. The parents invoke the old family tradition whereby parents have a right to influence in a decisive manner their children's marriage while their children invoke the Western marriage tradition which allows the intending couples the final say in their marriage affair. Most of the authors, because they belong to the generation of the children rather than that of the parents, share the view of the children in the matter and use their medium to champion the cause of the former and damage that of the latter. The pamphlet field is so wide of course that it admits of a number of significant exceptions as we are going to see.

The theme provides one of the stereotyped plots of the popular pamphlets. Usually, there is the father, the villain of the piece, who is portrayed as an old-fashioned and capricious autocrat with some private, often ignoble, motive for wishing to marry his daughter to a particular suitor whom his daughter has very good reason to abhor. The old man may show decided partiality towards this suitor because he is an old friend of the family (as in Cletus Nwosu's *Miss Cordelia in the Romance of Destiny*), because he is rich and will pay a high bride price (as in Ogali's *Veronica My Daughter*, Highbred Maxwell's *Back to Happiness* and R. Okonkwo's *The Game of Love*), because he is both rich and an old friend (as in Okenwa Olisa's *Elizabeth My Lover*), or because he is a prominent politician whose glory would be expected to reflect on his wife's family (as in Olisa's *About Husband and Wife Who Hate Themselves*).

In full confrontation with the father are the lovers, the daughter and her chosen suitor. Between these adversaries of great determination stands the mother of the family torn between her loyalty to her husband and her maternal duty to help her distressed daughter. In the end, her gentle persuasion and appeal to human compassion often triumphs and she induces the father to give in to the views of the young people. After all, the father is fighting for his authority, a mere abstraction when compared with the tangible fact that the daughter is fighting for her whole future and happiness.

Sociologists of the African scene put forward numerous plausible explanations for the break-down of the old marriage code in Africa and the increasing assertion of young people of Western-oriented marriage customs. One does not however have to be a sociologist to see that the two dominant factors of European domination of Africa—the factors of Christianity and modern education—transform the lifeways and alter the attitudes of present-day Africans to the extent that a number of assumptions of the old tradition are stringently questioned or rejected. Marriage is one area of social life in which the impact of Europe is most strongly felt. The introduction of Western system of marriage laws as well as the inculcation of Christianity undermine the traditional system by providing an alternative to the old marriage code.

The young people's attitude to marriage in the popular pamphlets is not the least influenced by the type of literature studied by them at school. In many of the texts set for their examinations romantic attachment as a basis for marriage is rigorously promoted. Any grammar-school boy or girl who has read Shakespeare's *Romeo and Juliet, Twelfth Night* or *As You Like It,* Jane Austen's novels, Emily Bronte's *Wuthering Heights* and even Dickens's *David Copperfield* (these are among the popular set-books for the English literature course in West Africa) cannot but be acquainted with the central position of love and mutual attachment in the marriage system of the English people. These novels and plays and some of the poetry as well portray romantic love as an aspect of marriage either as a central theme or in a peripheral kind of way. Young people who are extremely impressionable and who use the experience they find in books to ratify their own aspirations to modernity, cannot but be influenced by the "romantic" notions contained in their literature texts. No doubt also, the great mass of romantic films which are widely displayed in the cinemas as well as such widely available magazines as *Woman's Own* and *True Romance* and such romance fiction as written by Marie Corelli and Bertha Clay which carry numerous stories dealing with romantic love and marriage, cannot but affect the attitudes of those whose vision of life is being determined by new and radical influences which they have come to associate with "the good life" and "progress." (pp. 21-2)

[By] the nineteen forties, the average young man and woman whose education had progressed beyond the primary level had acquired enough of the "romantic" notions about marriage through formal literary reading and reading of "romantic" books and magazines to begin to feel resentful of the old custom of parentally-organized marriage.

The daughters who suffer most when a marriage goes wrong are therefore the most unyielding in their refusal to respect the match-making authority of their families. They are often defiant and voice their reasons for flouting the views of their parents with clarity and conviction. Thus, Veronica (Ogali's *Veronica My Daughter*), a mere college girl, makes this pretty and impertinent speech before her father, rejecting his candidate and affirming her own choice of suitor:

> Papa, I must be candid now. I love Mike and I think nothing on earth can separate us. If you flog me, I must still love him. If you curse me, I must still love him. If you cut off my head, well, I must still love him in the world beyond. I know your opinion. You want me to marry that old illiterate man, Chief Bassey—No! the more I see him, the more I am offended. In fact, the mere sight of him is annoying: but the more I see Mike, the more I love him. I have decided to marry Mike and I assure you we are wedding in a few months time, that is a month after the examination. If you give your hand to it—all good. If you do not, I assure you nothing stops it.

Elizabeth in Olisa's *Elizabeth My Lover* appeals to her father thus: "Don't fight against nature. Nothing on earth stops my marriage with Mr. Ototofioko. If you like purchase ten more guns. Whether you like it or not I must follow Ototofioko today otherwise I die. I love Mr. Ototofioko deeply and cannot be happy without him.''

Occasionally, the tone of a girl's protest is indignant, truculent or downright abusive, as in Thomas Iguh's *Alice in the Romance of Love* in which Alice tells her father ''I'll paint you in the real colours that befit a slut and octopus, a menace and a double-faced man.''

It is not difficult to see that the authors' sympathy lies with the girls whose attitude is regarded as ''progressive'' because they stand for the concept of marriage as an affair between two young people ''in love'' and not with the fathers who, by insisting on their customary right to select their daughters' future husbands are regarded as ''reactionary,'' old-fashioned and a nuisance.

The authors show their support for the daughters and dislike for the fathers in a number of ways. One method is to make the fathers as unattractive as possible. They are not only depicted as arbitrary autocratic and small-minded, but they are further damned by being shown as illiterate. The daughters and their collaborating mothers are given the virtue of good education and made to speak immaculate Queen's English while the fathers speak the most atrocious ''pidgin.'' The preferred young suitors are given various qualities of excellence which these writers imply qualify them incontestably for the young girls' favour while their rivals (the men favoured by the fathers) are given such damnable qualities as make their aspiration appear both ridiculous and indecent. For example, in *Veronica My Daughter,* the favoured young suitor is not only an enterprising journalist and ''novelist'' but also a holder of the inter B.A. degree (very much highly regarded in the 1940s and 1950s) while Chief Bassey, his rival, is old, illiterate and vulgarly rich (notice how his idea of marriage is of something akin to an auction sale). Again, in Benjamin Chiazor's *Back to Happiness,* the favoured suitor is an honest hard-working student while his rival is a pretender to wealth and a thief. (pp. 23-5)

We must of course treat with suspicion some of the overgeneralized assumptions of the pamphlet authors on this matter of love and marriage relationship. They seem to repose too much confidence in the all-sustaining strength of love in marriage relationship. And this love is often built on no sounder basis than that the man involved is young, is ambitious, has attractive manners and is physically appealing. Marriage certainly needs stronger props than those qualities. It is rather immature and unrealistic to think of marriage almost entirely in terms of love without at the same time considering adequately the material means of sustaining the marital home. Prudence dictates that the material aspect of the married state should be given considerable weight. The economic problems of marriage cannot be sneered out of existence, nor can the fact that love itself is soon fatigued if it has to be sustained in an empty belly and under the emotional strain of a lack of the basic necessities of life.

In the matter of parental intervention, much can be said for and against it when it is viewed in all its stackness. But the matter becomes a non-problem if young people recognize that certain facts of life are more accessible to older people by the very fact of their having lived longer. There is an Igbo saying that what an old man sees sitting might elude a young man even when he climbs a tree. In the matter of determining suitability in marriage, perhaps age with its accumulation of experience might prove helpful to the inexperience of youth.

Young people need not therefore be too quick to discard the well-intentioned advice of their elders.

The traditional Igbo attitude to marriage is that given certain basic pre-conditions such as a good family background (including the fact that the parents are good, honest and decent people, that there is no hereditary disease or crime in the family and that the family is not fond of going to law), the adequacy of the material circumstances, the quality of strength, manliness, good sense and good breeding of the young suitor and the full support of the adult members of the families of the couple, there is no reason why the marriage between a man and a woman should not prove successful. A further consideration is that neither of the two people should have a physical revulsion for the other. Given all these conditions, the Igbo believe that a man and a woman could go into marriage and mutual accommodation and affection would grow thereafter with domestic intimacy. In other words, young people are encouraged to seek first the substantial things of marriage and ''romance'' will be added unto them, not the other way round as is constantly made out by the pamphlet authors. Older people who advise young intendant couples on the basis of the traditional norms cannot be at such total odds with the prudential and sensible among the young.

Often enough, older people complicate and confound the problems of younger people in the matter of marriage. Herein therefore is the real problem. Parents with marriageable daughters, especially if they are not so well off, tend to prefer suitors who are best able to pay them high bride wealth. The happiness of their daughters assumes a mere secondary consideration to their desire to make money. This tendency was very much accentuated in Eastern Nigeria in the years following the end of the Second World War when many of the returning ex-servicemen armed with their not inconsiderable war bonuses outbid all their rivals in their determination to collect the most beautiful women. Gone forever were the days when a man could obtain a wife by making a token payment of a few bags of cowrie shells, a few yams and livestock. With the introduction of modern economy based on a cash nexus, a man had to pay hard cash and pay it abundantly before he could hope to procure a wife for himself. The return of the soldiers made marriage a very costly exercise almost out of the reach of the not-very-well-to-do. School teachers, artisans, students, peasant farmers and even low-level white collar workers suddenly found themselves stripped of their girl-friends and fiancees. Unscrupulous parents did roaring business conferring their daughters on those who could afford to pay the highest prices. The position became scandalous as bridal wealth soared from under £50 before the war in many parts of Eastern Nigeria to anything above £100 after the war. In fact, in some towns in Onitsha and Owerri provinces, the bridal money for a girl who had had elementary education rose to £300.

Young men could hardly be expected to save up such large sums of money and since they were determined to get married, many found themselves in the clutches of wicked money-lenders. The Eastern Nigerian Government in the attempt to remove the hardship caused by high bride price, enacted a law in 1953 restricting bride price to £30. In spite of legislation, however, unscrupulous fathers found a way of circumventing the provision. They issued receipts for £30 to young men who might have paid anything up to £200 or more. A thriving ''black'' market went on and still goes on behind the scenes and a prospective husband might find his would-be father-in-law suddenly turning against him if he proves too insistent on his right to pay the "government" rather than the "proper" price. He may actually see a wealthy old man or a prosperous polygamist who is prepared to do the "right" thing snatch his girl away.

The pamphlet authors, because they belong to the low income group which suffers most from the avarice of the parents, glorify the girls who are strong enough to defy their mercenary parents and stand up for their rights and their young unwealthy lovers. When they hand out rough treatment to parents who attempt to marry their daughters against their will to wealthy suitors, these writers are dealing with a subject which, if it has not affected them personally, has probably affected many of their friends and some of their readers. They handle the theme with a crusading zeal against a much-hated social abuse.

The scope of the pamphlet literature, as we said earlier, is too wide for there to be absolute unanimity on any specific subject. In this matter of marriage, there are significant differences of opinion among some of the authors. In Momo Aroye's *Stella at a Beauty and Fashion Parade,* Stella, a much idealized heroine, is a "modern" girl who respects traditional values. She loves flowers and modern ballroom dancing and is fairly educated. And yet, she goes and marries a man chosen for her by her father and makes her family life a model for other young women to copy. In Nwosu's *Miss Cordelia in the Romance of Destiny,* Cordelia begins by rejecting a man chosen for her by her father and selecting her own young man. Just before the marriage takes place, the priestesses of the town prohibit it on the traditional ground that the couple are distantly related and so could not become husband and wife. In Ngoh's *Florence in the River of Temptation,* Florence actually tells her lover that even though she loves him and would very much wish to marry him, he must first write and obtain her father's consent. This the young man does and Florence's father proving reasonably agreeable, the marriage is happily celebrated.

In most of the pamphlets, young girls put love above every other consideration. But there are some exceptions. A girl may actually desert a young man to whom she is deeply attached for a more educated and a wealthier suitor who would provide her with greater economic security. This is the theme of Egemonye's *Broken Engagement.* Here, the perfidious young lady leaves her grammar school boy-friend and marries a U.K. trained lawyer who is also a Ph.D. degree holder. The author tries to soften the blow by declaring that, "In fact, she confessed that she loved that man and held him in honour as her Lord and husband but that her secret thoughts, were on Dammy" (the jilted young lover). There is no doubt however that this young lady who sacrifices love to status and economic security is regarded by the author as extremely perverse.

This last novelette reveals a surprising grasp of the complexity of human motives and actions. It shows that what is ideal may not always be attainable and that the best of aspirations may sometimes be completely thwarted by unforeseen circumstances. Such maturity in the handling of theme appears only intermittently in the pamphlet literature and shows when it does that not all the pamphlet authors are naive or innocent in their view of the contemporary life. (pp. 30-3)

The theme of love excites the Onitsha Market pamphleteers. The subject is seen by them in all its aspects—in its glorious and triumphant aspect, in its tragic aspect, in its comic aspect and even in its melodramatic aspect. From whatever aspect they see it, the subject fascinates them. They simply revel in it and write about it with feeling and a degree of seriousness which people display towards a newly discovered reality or a new experience. The subject is so popular that a large proportion of the creative pamphlets (perhaps up to a third of them) deal with it. The immense variety of ways in which the writers see the subject is reflected in such titles as *The Voice of Love, Public Opinion on Lovers, Love in the Real Sense. Salutation is not Love, Love is Infallible, The Sorrows of Love, The Bitterness of Love, The Miracles of Love, Tragic Love, Disaster in the Realm of Love, They Died in the Bloom of Love, The Price of Love, The Disappointed Lover, Love with Tears, The Game of Love, Romance in a Nutshell, Love is Immortal, Love at First, Hate at Last, The Sweetness and Kingdom of Love, The Temple of Love,* and so on and so forth.

Many of the young writers sing the praise of Love. It is simply an intoxicant which they drain with eagerness in order to give themselves a feeling of living in the present, of being 'modern' in outlook. They express extravagant, high-blown sentiments about love, often in verse or what passes for verse. Thus, a character wishing his girl-friend farewell in a lengthy doggerel describes his conception of love in the following words:

> Love is the precious jewel in our life.
> The Sweetest thing this earth has ever known.
> Found in a labourer's cottage, on a stool,
> Then in a palace, sitting on a throne.
>   (Highbred Maxwell: *Forget Me Not*)

The association of love with verse in the popular pamphlets owes everything to the study of English Literature by the authors, in which a large number of the poems deal with the theme of love. Thus, many of the young lovers in the Onitsha pamphlets are made to regard verse as the proper form for conveying their sentiments about love. In Adiele Madumere's *Make Friends,* for instance, two girls crossed in a love triangle compose lengthy sentimental poems telling the story of their unfortunate experience before actually taking their own lives, thus converting a potential tragedy to melodrama. The verses destroy the sense of reality of the situation.

It was the English poet Tennyson who describes the poet as

> Dowered with the hate of hate, the scorn of scorn,
> The love of love . . .

The popular authors, because they take their idea of love from poetry (often very poorly digested), tend to see it in terms of stock sentiments and express it in cliches. They are often, like the poets, in love with the idea of being in love. Thus, a grammar-school boy who is prevented from doing his prep work by his girl-friend justifies himself by making this exaggerated speech in praise of love:

> What is a Secondary School and what is an examination? What do I care for the future life since the present is heaven to me? I cannot imagine any other temporal thing a man can require in this life if he got a sweetheart. Wealth? Damn it. Education? Forget about it. I am better off than the richest American filmstar or the most famous university professor when I have my arms around you.

When later the voice of tradition intervens to break up this whirlwind love affair, because, unknown to themselves, the boy and the girl are cousins, the boy writes a rather disappointing letter to his girl accusing her of leading him astray. "Deceived by the thrills of your hungry kisses," he writes in retrospect, "I was unable to find out whether your love was actually a righteous one or whether it was merely an admiration of my boyish loveliness and sportsmanship." (Nwosu: *Miss Cordelia in the Romance of Destiny*).

There are many embarrassing cases in the love booklets like the one referred to above, which goes to show that the authors (and through them, their characters) have not assimilated the essence and full import of romantic love. The idea alone captivates their imagination, making them aspire to it with the single-mindedness with which they go after everything they regard as progressive and desirable. In the last-mentioned novelette also, a girl tells her friend who is somewhat late in catching the fancy: "I am surprised . . . that at this stage of your life you have not even heard of the word 'love.' No wonder you were often sullen and lonely." (pp. 37-8)

The popular authors have in a great majority of cases accepted romantic love and the Western values of marriage introduced through contact and inculcated through education and Christian missionary teaching. To the authors, romantic love and marriage are the channels through which present-day West Africans express and emphasize their individuality, their liberation from traditional constraint and the customary imposition of the older generation. The emergent values they espouse are entrenched in individual responsibility. The individual man or woman, they imply, has a right of free choice in love and marriage and should abide the consequences of such choice.

There are of course a number of serious questions which one must raise with regard to the pamphlet authors' projection of purely modernist values of love and marriage. First, have the Western concepts of love, courtship and marriage been fully and adequately understood and assimilted to the consciousness of people for whom they write? In the matter of romantic love, for example, is it not obvious that without the historical background of courtly love and chivalric romance, aspiration to it could only degenerate to mutual exploitation and giving of free rein to lust and license? Secondly, is it a wise policy for present-day Africans to throw over the board some of the values of their traditional culture which had sustained their people's attitudes to love, sex and marriage from time immemorial? Can those values be shown to be irrational and inadequate for sustaining a modern, progressive way of life? Which of the values, European or traditional-African, are capable of ensuring greater happiness for individuals, in the light of what we already know about present-day love and marriage experience?

These questions are quite pertinent because they seem to be lost sight of or deliberately ignored by most of the pamphlet authors. In the matter of romantic love, it seems never to occur to the authors that the insistence on pre-marital chastity by most, if not all, traditional West African societies could well be the answer to the problem of young girls who are ever so easily ruined and put in the "motherly condition" by the young men with whom they are "in love." It is not fully appreciated by the popular authors that by throwing off the inconvenient but protective authority of parents, young men and women have succeeded in exposing themselves to temptations at a time when, because of their limited experience of life, they are most vulnerable to these temptations.

Again, the popular authors tend to accept the exteriorities of Western romantic love and marriage while being only scantily sensitive to their underlying spirit. They know about the gestures, the holding of hands, the kiss, the passionate embrace, the grimaces, everything that attracts the one sex physically to the other. These are easily learnt from romantic fiction and from the cinema and television. But what about the tenderness, the constant struggle to be at one's best behaviour in the presence of one's lover, the desire to please and protect the loved one? These are not as easily accessible as the external expressions of love. And yet they are the proper stuff of romantic love as conceived in Europe.

In the historical memory of every European people, there is this image of a brave young knight kneeling solemnly, not before the altar of God, but before a beautiful, white-bossomed maiden, his mistress, in defence of whose honour he would attempt the impossible and hazard even his life. Today, several centuries after the event, the European male's attitude to the female sex continues to be conditioned by what is still left of it in the historic memory of the race. Every European male is a kind of a "knight," every European female, a kind of a "lady." The European "knight" gets up when the European "lady" enters a room, he vacates a seat for her and will immediately do something when it becomes clear that the European "lady" is in difficulty or in distress. Not all European males live up to the standard of course, but those who do not know that they are falling short. The attitude of reverence, devotion, worship and tenderness is carried into the area of romantic love. It gives love a semi-ritual significance and makes it the stepping stone to matrimony and integration.

In the African system, every male is also a "knight." He appreciates the admiration of the female sex but he will perform feats to earn the admiration of the whole people. His spring force is not the desire to earn the love of one woman but to be worthy of the affection and respect of the whole people. When he has achieved this, any woman will be proud to share in his glory, as his wife. Whereas the European "knight" having won the admiration of his "lady" goes to her for reward through love and marriage, the African "knight" is endowed with a "lady" by the community in recognition of his justification of his manhood. What he does with this "lady" thereafter remains of serious public concern. In other words, whereas the European man and woman seek integration and fusion of individualities in love and marriage, their African counterparts seek complementation. Whereas the European couple attempt to become one body and one flesh (to use a Christian image), the African couple remain collaborative individuals whose autonomy is attested to and constantly reinforced by the community of their fellows.

In the light of the differences in cultural conditioning, it is easy to see why in the pamphlet literature the attempt by individuals with their African background to express in European style their romantic love, falls far short of the ideal and appears somewhat ridiculous. The pamphlet authors' commitment to "modernity" in this matter of love needs serious reconsideration. (pp. 44-6)

Emmanuel Obiechina, in his Literature for the Masses: An Analytical Study of Popular Pamphleteering in Nigeria, *Nwankwo-Ifejika & Co. Publishers, 1971, 84 p.*

THE ENGLISH LANGUAGE AND AFRICAN LIFE

PETER YOUNG

[In the following excerpt, Young examines how Nigerian writers use words and speech patterns from indigenous languages in works written in English.]

Until quite recently—say 1966, the year after Soyinka's *The Interpreters,* and the year of Achebe's *A Man of the People*—

Amos Tutuola. From African Authors: A Companion to Black Writing, 1300-1973, Volume I, *by Donald E. Herdeck. Black Orpheus Press, 1973.*

the comparison of techniques has generally had to go outside the immediate bounds of African literature. Now African writers can be set one against the other, rather than against European literary reminiscence. The paradox of this shortening of the critical paradigms for African literature is that far from rendering criticism parochial it allows for the first time a fair degree of criticism on the literature's manifest terms and a consequently greater freedom from inhibition about "universal" critical value-judgments, which might in any case be expected to establish their own relativity.

An adequate criticism of African literature, like that of any other literature, presupposes the establishment and acceptance of a set of precritical criteria between writer and reader. The acceptance of these criteria in most literary circumstances is to be taken for granted by both writer and reader, and the creative element that singles out a good writer from a bad one, though in itself ultimately unanalysable, can none the less rely confidently for its effect on a fund of cultural and linguistic experience shared by reader and writer. This holds good for as long as a literature remains national and monolingual; the matter becomes more difficult, more demanding of effort in a large part of the readership, when a literature becomes in any true sense international and multilingual. (p. 24)

Any division between the influences of a language and the culture of which it is at the same time the vehicle and a part is never wholly satisfactory. When, to take a simpler type of example, an Ibo writer chooses to transfer into his use of English certain words for which there are no suitable translation equivalents in the language (such as names of foods, clothing and other culturally bound objects), he is not so much being influenced by his mother tongue as being compelled by simple denotational necessity. When, however, he tranfers such a word as *dibia,* for which none of the possible English translation equivalents will do (for example "priest," "doctor," or even the collocation "native doctor," which in its West African use is nearer than either of the other two), he is up against a more difficult problem. None of the possible British, or West African, English equivalents may carry the proper degree of solemnity or imply a sufficient sense of the respect in which the *dibia* is held. And yet he is unable by simple transference of the word into English to achieve the effect that prompted the decision with any but another Ibo reader. Attempts to surmount problems of this kind have had a profound effect on the stylistic freedom, and thus the "quality," of African writing in English, and I shall return to some discussion of it later. The point to be made at the moment is on a rather more general level and concerns the tendency general among critics to imply a separateness for the oral tradition as an influence in the African writer's work. Just as it is unsatisfactory to divorce a language from so intimate a part of it as the oral tradition, it is equally unsatisfactory to imply a division between the oral tradition and the total complex of culture that makes the writer the man he is, expecting or hoping to achieve certain effects upon his readers. A quickness to make such divisions is, I think, largely behind the readiness to dismiss cultural content as "local colour," whereas it is probably more often than not due to a breakdown in response and communication between the impatient European, who is frequently inclined to think of the *dibia* as a "witch-doctor" in any case, and, for instance, Achebe or Flora Nwapa, who are trying to convey what the *dibia* is to an Ibo. Once again, the problem must be dealt with by an appeal to the reader to make a larger precritical effort than he normally expects to make in his armchair. The caution is doubly important in that for many writers cultural content does remain at the level of "local colour." It is this that is an important difference between the "poorer" and the "better" writers, those who write out of a form of card-index experience and those who write out of the total cultural self. This division in the handling of cultural experience, which can be verified easily enough, reflects, perhaps even rests on, the historical background of modern African writing in English. (pp. 25-6)

At the risk of oversimplification, a convenient division can be proposed in the types of linguistic and cultural material the writer has to transfer into English; the non-deliberate, the involuntary drawing upon the immediate cultural and language environment; and the deliberate, or experimental, in which specific efforts are made to modify the medium. We cannot, of course, always be certain about the degree of deliberateness at any one time, though forms from the indigenous languages or English items peculiar to general usage in West Africa can be readily identified, such as the names of foods and clothing (garri, agbada, etc.), or recontextualization or compounding of elements already in the language (storey-building, mammy-wagon). Some degree of certainty, too, is possible in the determination of "mistakes" in the selection of an English translation equivalent or an item of vocabulary or grammatical feature unacceptable to the reader of bilingual balance. One can also be sure about the deliberateness of the use of proverbs by writers such as Achebe, or the reorganization of syntax as in the work of Okara. One knows that when a transferred item of vocabulary is attached to an explanatory tag (e.g. "*obi* or hut"), the explanation reveals a deliberate act of transfer aimed at at least part of the readership. It is a little more difficult to be certain of the degree of deliberateness involved in the effects of translation from the mother tongue resulting in forms not otherwise found in the use of English in West Africa or elsewhere, but some decision can be arrived at according to the degree of bilingual balance manifested by the writer, and frequently by his declared intentions in the matter. All these features, as well as others related to them at all levels of language (including "mistakes," as Tutuola's eulogists have revealed), perform stylistic functions of one kind or another which distinguish African writing from that of any other part of the English-speaking world. At present I am concerned most with those forms that are clearly deliberate—not because they are necessarily more stylistically relevant, but because they reveal more clearly the African writer's search for the solution to the problems of creative expression.

In much the same way there can be said to be a worth-while distinction between cultural material transferred for specifically literary reasons and cultural information at the level of "local colour."

At some point almost every African writer has been committed to explanation, if not to information for its own sake. The most obvious problem of cultural and linguistic transfer is, of course, the fact that transfer does not automatically assure intelligibility throughout the complex readership, not only that outside Africa but that outside the writer's own region. Though the inward direction of more recent writers away from non-African readership has had far-reaching effects, the problem of communication across cultural and linguistic barriers exists within Africa and, indeed, usually within African nations. In other words, the African writer has been forced to attend to the medium, not at the exclusively literary level in a community where a certain reliability of response on the part of the reader can be expected, but at the pre-literary level of adaptation and establishment of criteria previous to response and criticism.

In a well-known statement, Achebe reflects the attitude of most West African writers in his general confidence that "the English language will be able to carry the weight of [his] African experience," tempered by the knowledge that "it will have to be a new English, still in full communion with its ancestral home but altered to suit its new African surroundings." The significant word here is perhaps "altered," with its connotation of deliberation. Indeed, the problems of response to the medium have frequently given way to a concentration on its mechanisms.

Part of Achebe's attempt to fashion his language to "its new African surroundings" has depended on the form of adjustment to the communication of unfamiliar material, the parenthetical explanatory tag or "cushioning." The commonest form of cushioning is the most obvious ("*obi*, or hut"; "*chi*, or personal god"; "*nno*, or welcome") and though Achebe never loses control … the total effect is one of distraction for writer and reader, an inhibition of syntax and fluency, that is no small contribution to the frequently remarked "stilted" language of African novels. Achebe's particular gift is perhaps that he remains for the greater part of the time in sufficient control to avoid the stylistic tar-baby that so swiftly puts an end to the novels of Rattray and Nzekwu.

A more covert form of cushioning offers rather more encouraging results. This is the almost equally familiar resort to fashioning the immediate context of transferred material so that its meaning is made as clear as possible. Amadi, as well as Achebe, is a leading exponent of this device, and uses it freely in *The Concubine*: "the okwos tore the air, the drums vibrated under expert hands and the igele beat out the tempo meticulously." The passage clearly refers to musical instruments, though the cushioning is by implication from the context: the "okwo" might be a wind instrument, or possibly a relatively high-pitched, rapidly beaten percussion instrument such as the xylophone-like *ékwé*, and the "igele" is certainly a percussion instrument, of whose function in the orchestra we also gain an idea. This method is, however, only superficially more liberating since it demands not simply brief tags of explanation but large "areas" of immediate context to make it work. It is less obtrusive, but it still involves detail beyond the immediate requirements of expression.

The African writer walks a narrow path, and not all are as sure-footed as Achebe. Bernth Lindfors has pointed out the appropriateness of Achebe's transference into English of Ibo proverbs, varying from those of the rural setting of a novel such as *Arrow of God* to those of the urban *No Longer at Ease* and *A Man of the People*. Indeed, it is precisely this control, and the integration of the material and expression, that singles out Achebe as far more than a pioneer of technique. But even here the inhibition of method over motive makes itself felt. A careful comparison of proverb translations in Achebe's novels with their Ibo sources reveals a very high degree of closeness to the originals, notably in attempts to preserve syntactical equivalence as far as possible. The two examples that follow, set out for comparison with Igbo and word-for-word equivalents, are taken from *No Longer at Ease*.

> if you want to eat a toad you should look for a fat and juicy
>   one
> onye chōlụ ilī awò lìi ǹke mālụ àbùbà
> who want to-eat toad eat that-of having fatness

> the start of weeping is always hard
> mbido akwā nà-àfịa ārụ
> starting weeping (habitual) is-difficult (for the) body

The slightest breakdown in the writer's control of appropriateness, frequent in writers other than Achebe and, most of the time, Amadi, results in an isolation of the proverb in its surroundings that is potentially as restrictive as the most blatant cushioning. Achebe himself, in his Foreword to Whiteley's collection of traditional oral texts in the Oxford Library of African Literature, has mentioned the difficulty of translating Ibo proverbs and riddles *(inu)* because of the resulting isolation from the whole pattern of allusion and direct cultural reference in the African language. The translation of proverbs in a novel in English involves not only a transference from one language but also a transference from one medium to another, from a spoken to a written culture. In its source-language a proverb, or indeed a whole fable or myth, serves as the point of reference for a whole complex of inventive allusion. As soon as the proverb is written down in another language its flexibility is lost, and what has been a signpost becomes a monument. It is Achebe's recognition of the need to avoid this separation of a proverb from its environment in his careful maintenance of appropriateness that assures him of success. However, as a general route to literary liberation it is precarious, for whereas the "African vernacular" he has compounded for himself shows flexibility in his hands, it remains a solution to immediate artistic problems rather than a prognosis of a new African medium in English.

One sign of the limitations of the method is hinted at in the work of Achebe himself. In *Arrow of God,* the third of his novels and the last before his significant turning to satire in *A Man of the People* (1966), Achebe almost entirely discards the most obvious type of cushioning for the more covert type. This is in itself revealing. But, though *Arrow of God* is I think inferior in delicacy of craftsmanship to *Things Fall Apart* and the complementary irony of its sequel *No Longer at Ease,* Achebe achieves an integration of language and theme through means less exclusively concerned with the mechanisms of language. The effect is achieved even though this novel is the most deliberately didactic of the three, perhaps not least because in this final "hymn to the past," directed primarily at his own people, Achebe can revert from a dependence upon the mechanism to a shared intimacy of response. The tragedy of Ezeulu, high priest of Ulu, depends upon the nature of the deity himself and on the realization that he is created by men in the image of the organic spirit of the clan. The interplay of the theme of culture conflict and the break-up of the organic society with the spiritual decline and eventual madness of Ezeulu equals anything in *Things Fall Apart,* where the tragedy, not essentially different in the dependence on cultural values for effect, is more mannered. The subjection of the medium to a point of greater balance in *Arrow of God* makes a fine piece of craftsmanship into a powerful novel. (pp. 37-41)

The most concerted attempt to preserve the mother tongue through translation is Gabriel Okara's attempt in *The Voice* (1964) to transfer Ijo syntax and lexical rules into English. The closeness with which Okara does so can be determined by comparison with Ijo sources, and, as one would expect, he is unable to remain consistent in his method. But the failure does not lie in this inconsistency, which would not wholly invalidate the method, or even simply in "an annoying literary squint," but in a fundamental misconception about the nature of language—that anything as complex as total meaning can be conveyed by preservation of very few of its parts. Syntax alone is not the vehicle of meaning, nor are a language's rules of collocation. It has been remarked that Okara is a much better poet than novelist and that *The Voice* is most successful in short lyrical passages. Without wishing to beg the question of the incompatability of "the language of poetry" and "the language of prose," I think it quite possible that the fundamental weaknesses of meaning in *The Voice* are less apparent when subject to the firmer organization and control demanded by a verse-form. Indeed, there is a sense in which they are more acceptable, or at least accepted, there. However, the importance of Okara's work depends not on his success or failure but in the clearly conveyed realization that the artistic liberty of the African writer in English lies in the integration of expression and experience. By revealing one route to that end to be a cul-de-sac, *The Voice* remains a positive force in the development of the West African novel in English.

The same transitions can be followed equally closely in poetry and the drama. Examples of directly informational verse are numerous, and Adeboye Babalola's "The Trouble-Lover" provides an extreme example.

> He is fond of marrying wives of other men,
> And so he often finds himself in hell at home.
> For sometimes his stolen wives are past-mistresses
> In the art of domineering over husbands, of all kinds.
> For instance, he once married Shango's wife,

That is, the God of Thunder's spouse,
But in his house she made him ill at ease
By belching fire from her mouth whene'er she spoke.

A transitional form of the informational poem is that in which the description is enlivened into significance with a final bias of comment. Yetunde Esan's "Ololu—an Egungun" is of this type. After the description of the *egungun* and the awe he traditionally inspires, the two last stanzas turn to a nostalgic sense of tradition and change.

> I peeped out—a great crowd, all men,
> I looked again—what did I see:
> A tall thin man,
> In plain pyjamas,
> Barefooted, bareheaded, marks on his face.
>
> And suddenly I wished I were back
> In the good old days when Ololu was
> A semi-god,
> With seven skulls,
> Not—no one in particular.

For my part, I find this far more satisfactory as poetry than Babalola's poem, which may or may not be justified by its didacticism. But it remains at a wholly different level of experience than such poems as Soyinka's "Abiku" or the "Dance of the Half-Child," dependent on the Yoruba idea of the *ibeji,* which concluded the 1960 Nigerian Independence production of *A Dance of the Forests.* Both these poems are still essentially "transitional," and also illustrate the use of the complex concept of the Yoruba god Ogun, which provides a useful and convenient example of the development of the use of tradition in Soyinka's work as a whole.

Ogun is the Yoruba god of creation, of exploration, of war, of iron and everything associated with iron, from the axe of the carver to the modern motor-road, and his many characteristics and associations allow Soyinka the greatest freedom in literary interpretation. In *A Dance of the Forests* the immortality of Ogun is set against the mortality of Demoke, a carver, creative user of fire and metal, whom the god "will not forget." Demoke's mortal reflection of Ogun's aspect of creativity is brought out in Part One of the play in the discussion of the deaths by fire in the crashed lorries "Chimney of Ereko" and "Incinerator." The acid humour in the cynicism of the lorries' names becomes doubly significant when in the discussion of what kind of death one or other of his companions would prefer Demoke recoils from death by fire and chooses what to them seems a no less frightful end. The lorries and the road are Ogun's, but the offence against creativity is not. The contradiction might also appear to exist within the deity of Ogun himself as the god of war. But Demoke's mortal circumscription in his comprehension of Ogun's infinite nature, which he instinctively honours, creates a tension between the complementary parts of the whole work, the significance of myth, the wisdom of traditional Yoruba belief and the cynical contradictions of the modern age. The "topicality" of *A Dance of the Forests* is not simply in the "Gathering of the Tribes" in the Federation at Independence (the play was first performed as part of the celebrations), but in the universal topicality of the re-fusion of total African experience. Soyinka refers obliquely to this wider significance when in his preface to *Idanre* he describes the poem in the light of tragic events in Nigeria following October 1965 "as part of a pattern of awareness which began when [he] wrote *A Dance of the Forests.*" Indeed, the pattern is increasingly distinct in Soyinka's work until it finds its clearest resolution in *Idanre.*

In *The Road* (1960), as he remarks in his prefatory note for the producer, the *agemo* ("religious cult of flesh dissolution"), the festival of Ogun, and the symbolic expression of dance, are integrated by Soyinka in his exploration of the link between the mortal and the infinite.

> The dance is the movement of transition; it is used in the play as a visual suspension of death—in much the same way as Murano, the mute, is a dramatic embodiment of this suspension. He functions as an arrest of time, or death, since it was in his "agemo" phase that the lorry knocked him down. Agemo, the mere phase, includes the passage of transition from the human to the divine essence (as in the festival of Ogun in this play), as much as the part psychic, part intellectual grope of Professor towards the essence of death.

And in *The Interpreters* (1965), itself the expression of complex past and present, the pattern is elaborated. In sharp contrast to his earlier externalized humour at the expense of modified Christianity (and its obvious analogy with the Nigerian political scene) in *The Trials of Brother Jero* (1963), the religion of Lazarus, as opposed to the muddled eclecticism of his congregation, is vested with mystical significance, which together with the theme of corruption and death and Kola's ever-changing and expanding painting of the Yoruba Pantheon sets up an unusually strong network of internal relations. But it is in *Idanre,* in the disciplines and liberations of poetry, that Soyinka achieves the full effects of his range.

In *Idanre* the Yoruba myth of the Creation, and especially Ogun's part in it, is the structuring force. Ogun is felt everywhere in the poem, a force as hard and terrible as the veined rock that in Man's first rebellion against an inexorable "doom of repetition" Atunda rolled down to smash the god's "fearsome nature" from the primal deity.

> Light, more
> Than human frame can bear
> Set flanges to a god, control had slipped
> Immortal grasp.

In the following passage from the second section of the poem based on the postdiluvian phase of the creation myth, the awesomeness of the superhuman masculinity of the fashioning of the Earth after the first flood is set against the gentle Oya who adds grace to Ogun's hard power, and man moves closer to hope.

> Opalescent pythons oozed tar coils
> Hung from rafters thrashing loops of gelatine
> The world was choked in wet embrace
> Of serpent spawn, waiting Ajantala's rebel birth
> Monster child, wrestling pachyderms of myth,
>
> *And at the haven of a distant square*
> *Of light, hope's sliver from vile entombment*
> *She waited, caryatid at the door of sanctuary*
> *Her hands were groves of peace, Oya's forehead*
> *Dipped to pools and still hypnotic springs*
> *And now she is a dark sheath freed*
> *From Ogun's sword, her head of tapered plaits*
> *A casque of iron filigree, a strength*
> *Among sweet reeds and lemon bushes, palm*
> *And fragrances of rain*

Idanre is, in spite of everything, a poem of hope, of faith in the human spirit. Man can free himself from an apparently inevitable "doom of repetition" in the world's eternal cycle of evil and corruption. Atunda's first revolt against the implacable power of the godhead shows man has a chance to leave the cycle, for in the very act of rebellion he creates a point of bias, "a kink" as Soyinka calls it, from which evolution is possible. The "self-devouring snake" of eternal recurrence is by rebellion modified from hopelessness to hope. As Soyinka remarks in a note: "Even if the primal cycle were of good and innocence, the Atoọda [Atunda] of the world deserve praise for introducing the evolutionary "kink.""

> Evolution of the self-devouring snake to spatials
> New in symbol, banked loop of "Mobius Strip"
> And interlock of re-creative rings, one surface
> Yet full comb of angles, uni-plane, yet sensuous with
> Complexities of mind and motion.

The modern world, as complex and contradictory as the nature of Ogun himself, may offer some hope of deliverance from the re-enactment of historical inevitability in the vision of "Harvest," the earth's forgiveness, the transition from night to dawn and "resorption in His alloy essence."

It is not simply in the matter of intellectualism that in *Idanre* we have moved a long way from Babalola's "Ojo, the Trouble-Lover."

> He's frightful as the Iron god, for
> He sometimes runs about in the streets
> Holding high aggressively a glittering axe.

It is Soyinka, too, who among African writers has most liberated the English language from the more mechanistic preoccupations with style. He still uses the devices of cushioning, it is true, though his preference for glossaries and notes does something to avoid intrusion of information at the wrong moment. But above all, as with his use of the heritage of tradition, it is his reassertion of intuitive response to the linguistic environment as he finds it in all its complexity that assures him his success. It is this that makes his prefatory note on translation in *The Forest of a Thousand Daemons,* in which he asserts the "sense" over the "precise original," the most significant statement on the subject by an African writer to date, and that book as a whole the most successful attempt at continuous translation. The total linguistic environment is neither the mother tongue nor English. It is for him the leap from Yoruba, to English, to pidgin or to any number of shades of allusion and meaning between, the reflection of experience, whole as it is all these, or the best means at the best moment.

Soyinka's use of pidgin illustrates this freedom of multilingual balance in the joyous exploitation of the West African extension of diglossia. It is a technique he uses time and again: in the third scene of *Brother Jero*, when Chume's increasing excitement at conducting the service for the fleeing prophet is reflected in the transition from "Church English" to deeper and deeper pidgin; in *The Interpreters*, when Lazarus's controlled preaching is superbly contrasted with the imperfectly understood and reproduced church rhetoric of the verse feeder, or when Egbo frantically questions the night-club waiter about Simi's giving him the slip, in a beautifully handled mixture of English, pidgin and Yoruba. The following speech is one of several of the kind by Samson in *The Road*.

> A driver must have sensitive soles on his feet. Unlike his buttocks. His buttocks would be hard. Heavy-duty tyres. But not the feet you see. Because he does not walk so much, and he has to be able to judge the pressure on the pedals exactly right. I have such thick soles you see so I always revved the engine too much or too little. Then it was Fai! Fai! Fai! You think say I get petrol for waste? Take your foot commot for ancelerator! Small small! I say small small—you

tink say dis one na football game. Fai fai fai! You dey press brake—Gi-am!—as if na stud you wan' give centre back. I say do am soft soft! Fai fai fai! All a waste of time. Every time I started the lorry it went like a railway—gbaga gbaga—like clinic for hiccup. Other times it would shoot off like sputnik— fiiiiom! That was when I got it worst of all—Fai fai fai fai! You wey no fit walka na fly you wan' fly? Ah, sometimes I wonder why I didn't go deaf. *(He stands for a while, trying to remember.)*

This freedom of intuition over the scales of modern linguistic and cultural experience more than anything else sets Soyinka apart from his contemporaries. Significantly, too, his weaknesses as a writer can be ascribed to the same liberation of response where it lapses into an ensnaring verbal facility and mannered obscurities of expression, as it does occasionally in, for example, *The Interpreters,* or even *Idanre.* The balanced craftsmanship of the simpler plays such as *Brother Jero* or *The Lion and the Jewel* has an ease not possible in a play like *A Dance of the Forests,* which for all its apparent difficulty attempts a wider ranging through Soyinka's awareness. Nor is it inconsistent, though perhaps potentially misleading critically, to note his "debts" to modern English poetry, notably that of T. S. Eliot, for these are no less part of his total pattern of awareness.

Soyinka's response to language and experience as elemental rather than mechanical truths represents the most advanced point on the long route which, historically and in microcosm, the African writer has had to travel towards using the English language and the heritage of tradition as what they have become, parts of the total modern experience rather than modifiable, separate conceptions. As a whole his work realizes the transition from the pre-literary preoccupations imposed by historical circumstance and a shrinking modern world to the natural literary starting point of self-possession which the African writer has so long been denied.

The transition in the handling of the oral tradition and the cultural heritage, if not exactly similar to the transitions in the history of eighteenth- and nineteenth-century English Romanticism, shares with Romanticism a development from surface to depth. The purely descriptive nature poetry that existed side by side with or gave way to the nature poetry of moral comment such as Dyer's "Grongar Hill," or later extensions such as Cowper's "God made the country, man made the town" passage in *The Task,* was as far from the "soul of moral being" of *Tintern Abbey* as the two poems by Babalola and Yetunde Esan are from the novels of Achebe or from *Idanre.* The transition shares with romanticism, too, a profound faith in the wholeness of the human spirit and its place in the total scheme of things.

In language the progress has been similarly one of reintegration, following essentially pre-literary concern: the gradual assertion of painfully re-established response over induced attention to the means.

Christopher Okigbo expresses the triumph at the end of *Limits* ("Fragments out of the Deluge," IX and X) as he refers to the European intrusion.

> And the gods lie in state
> And the gods lie in state
> without the long-drum.
> And the gods lie unsung
> And the gods lie
> veiled only with mould,
> Behind the shrinehouse.

> Gods grow out,
> abandoned;
> And so do they . . .

Until at last:

> The Sunbird sings again
> From the LIMITS of the dream,
> The Sunbird sings again
> Where the caress does not reach,
>
> of Guernica,
> On whose canvas of blood,
> The newsprint-slits of his tongue
> cling to glue . . .

> *& the cancelling out is complete.*

The African writer's spiritual and creative independence figured in Okigbo's lines has not become a withdrawal by rejection, as many would have had it, but one of gradually, often painfully, re-established harmony in the total pattern of his awareness. Professor Jones has remarked that for African literature to be "universal" it must first be "truly local." Indeed, this self-containment essential to the survival of the creative African consciousness, avoiding the simplistic solution of isolation, is ultimately of universal importance. Writing of E. M. Forster, in spite of *A Passage to India* a novelist apparently remote from the concerns of modern African literature, K. W. Gransden implies the full meaning and promise of the African writer's achievement to the world at large.

> The good place must be small enough to be known by heart. This insistence on the local, the truly known, seems especially valuable in our age of 'internationalism' in which the values of the great world, designed to appeal to all by meaning nothing to anyone, are gradually replacing felt values derived from specific traditions.

From mere reminiscence and example for enlightened argument to protest and rejection, the African writer has worked out his relationship to the wider world. Over two centuries he has sought to realize the reassertion of "felt values" in the reconciliation of his own identity and literary integrity. Now, on his own terms, he offers it against "the values of the great world." It is a meaningful internationalism the West cannot afford to ignore. (pp. 42-50)

> *Peter Young, "Tradition, Language and the Reintegration of Identity in West African Literature in English," in* The Critical Evaluation of African Literature, *edited by Edgar Wright, Heinemann Educational Books Ltd., 1973, pp. 23-50.*

NANCY SCHMIDT

[*Schmidt is an American anthropologist specializing in African studies. In the following excerpt, she examines the influence of African oral tradition on modern Nigerian fiction.*]

Nigerian fiction in English has recently attracted considerable attention because of the rapid increase in works available outside Nigeria and the nuances of culture conflict which the fiction depicts. Most often Nigerian fiction is discussed as if it were derived wholly from the English literary tradition of which it is a part. However, the African oral tradition has had great, though not always obvious, influence on Nigerian fiction, even though the content of the fiction may bear little superficial resemblance to that of oral tradition. Critics frequently point out weaknesses in plot and character development in Nigerian fiction, without indicating that plot and characterizations in Nigerian fiction are very similar to those in West African oral literature.

Less than 20 of nearly 350 works of Nigerian fiction in English which have been examined deal with traditional characters in a traditional setting, and seven of these are by one author, Amos Tutuola. The Nigerian fiction which includes traditional characters and traditional settings consists of essentially well-known oral tales which are retold with modern elaborations, or personifications of animal characters. For example, many of the events in Tutuola's stories can be traced directly to Yoruba tales which have been recorded, or have been retold by other writers in both English and Yoruba, thereby indicating that they are a part of the contemporary oral literature. And all the major motifs in Tutuola's stories, like journeys to other worlds, magical transformations, difficult initiations, gaining wisdom through suffering, and so on, are common in West African oral literature, as well as in the oral literature of other parts of the world.

Each of Tutuola's book-length tales is based on a journey to another world from that in which the hero or heroine lives. As might be expected, Tutuola uses in his tales both familiar items from Yoruba oral literature, as well as local variations of Yoruba oral literature which have not previously been recorded. For example, he explains the presence of universal death as resulting from death having been captured in a net in the land of the dead and taken to an old man in the land of the living. When death is released from the net at the old man's door, it does not know where to go, and so has been running around the world ever since. Tutuola also personifies drum, song, and dance, which use their human capacities to save people from monstrous creatures and severe punishments. Despite the predominantly traditional orientation of Tutuola's stories, their content is marked by European influence that has been interwoven with the oral tradition to create his fantasies which are told in the "best Yoruba tradition." (pp. 26-8)

In actual plot structure there is a great similarity between the traditional fantasy tales of Tutuola and novels and chapbooks in English. In each of Tutuola's fantasies, one character travels widely and has many different adventures, and no minor character has any important role in influencing the development of the plot or in influencing the personality of the major character. In most of the novels (especially those written before 1965) and novelettes, one character experiences the clash of traditional and modern cultures in several different places and in a variety of ways, but no other character emerges as a distinct personality or markedly influences the development of the plot. Both Tutuola's stories and most novels and chapbooks lack extensive description of character, scene, or background to the narrative. Their unity, as in the cycles of West African oral tales, is achieved through the major character who is easily identifiable, even though not described, and experiences a series of actions or adventures in which he is central. Their unity does not derive from any particular logical connection of the many actions included in the plot, nor does it necessarily consist of a unified series of events which lead to a climax.

Likewise, Nigerian short stories resemble traditional West African tales, since they are rarely more than anecdotes, with a specified or implied moral, rather than the stories with a developed plot which are common in the English literary tradition. In the traditional tales, action centered on one person, as in the tale cycles, or on several persons or animals, none of whom was truly dominant. Similarly, in the short stories the

action either centers on one person (who often tells the story), or on the action of several persons, none of whom is truly dominant, even though one name may appear in the title of the story. Although some short stories lack the statement of a specific moral lesson at their conclusion, most have morals which are self-evident to any reader familiar with the setting of the story. Dialogue is frequently used in the stories and other kinds of fiction and sometimes it dominates short stories, but it is purely conversational and rarely reveals the motivations of the characters, or illuminates their personalities. Monologues or descriptions, in which characters examine themselves or reflect upon their lives are very rare in Nigerian fiction, except plays.

The emphasis on action and narrative and the relatively infrequent use of description in the fiction does not appear to be a result of lack of writing ability, for some clear verbal pictures have been written by authors trained at the university level and familiar with a wide range of English literature. For example, the sounds of the night are described:

> The world was silent, except for the shrill cry of insects, which was part of the night, and the sound of the wooden mortar and pestle as Nwayieke pounded her foo-foo.
>
> Nwayieke lived four compounds away, and she was notorious for her late cooking. Every woman in the neighbourhood knew the sound of Nwayieke's mortar and pestle. It was also part of the night.
>
> [Chinua Achebe, *Things Fall Apart*]

Or feelings may be tersely stated, as in the case of a man who has recently murdered a boy:

> Once he got up from bed and walked about his compound. He felt like a drunken giant walking with the limbs of a mosquito. Now and then a cold shiver descended on his head and spread down his body.
>
> [*Things Fall Apart*]

Since writing good narrative is not emphasized in the English educational system under which the Nigerian writers have been trained, and writers with all levels of education produce works with relatively great narrative emphasis compared to the development of scene and character, this extensive use of narrative has probably been influenced by the oral tradition with which all the writers have been familiar from childhood. Even those writers who use description write stories which are primarily narratives of the traditional type.

There is other evidence of the influence of forms of oral literature in Nigerian fiction, one of the most notable being the use of proverbs. The use of proverbs in fiction is not in itself a distinguishing feature, since proverbs are used in fiction throughout the world. However, traditional proverbs, universal proverbs, and Western wise sayings are used in nearly 80% of Nigerian fiction. Traditional proverbs alone can often be specifically identified in most novels and plays, where there is much dialogue in which they might occur. Although specific frequencies of the use of proverbs in other literature are not available for comparison, proverbs seem to be rarely characteristic of the whole body of a written literature, which makes the frequency of their occurrence in Nigerian fiction seem unusually high, especially since a large number of different authors from diverse backgrounds and with different amounts of formal education are involved.

Proverbs are an integral part of oral literature, as they are of West African life. They have also been used in English literature with varying frequency, depending on changes in the social environment. They have most often been used in ages of controversy and satirical criticism, and are frequently found in literature that characterizes the folk or appeals to the folk, when appeal to the fundamental emotions is made, *and during times of nationalistic and racial striving*. Therefore, frequent use of proverbs might be expected in Nigerian fiction, especially because of the controversial nature of the contemporary Nigerian value system which is developing through the incorporation of both traditional and modern elements, and because the social climate is one of nationalistic striving and the assertion of African capabilities. The West African oral tradition which used proverbs extensively in many contexts, in both pointed and indirect statements, contains much material which could be utilized in such social circumstances.

In Nigerian novels and plays in which proverbs are used in greatest concentration, they are most frequently used in village settings, in contexts which refer to criticism of culture change or conflicts of culture values, as well as in traditional ceremonies, greetings, and rites. Chinua Achebe, who makes extensive use of proverbs in his novels, often repeats the same proverbs in several different circumstances and in several different novels. For example, he uses the proverb "When an adult is in the house the she-goat is not left to bear its young on its tether" on four different occasions in [*Arrow of God*]: 1) to indicate that people's behavior was cowardly compared to that of their ancestors, 2) to indicate the shamefulness of village elders in allowing one of their clansmen to be killed without demanding retribution, 3) to explain to policemen why the man they are seeking got away, 4) to urge village leaders to stop the spread of fear before it reaches dangerous proportions. Achebe uses proverbs both to give information and to express the motives and thoughts of characters. When a man is deeply in debt and is unable to pay the premium on his car, he rationalizes his inability to pay in terms of the proverb:

> It is not right to ask a man with elephantiasis of the scrotum to take on smallpox as well, when thousands of other people have not had their share of small diseases.
>
> [Chinua Achebe, *No Longer at Ease*]

As in West African oral narrative, Achebe also uses a series of proverbs in immediate succession, when a character in a traditional setting is speaking or thinking seriously.

The playwright, Wole Soyinka, uses this same device, as when a man discusses the difficulty of being patient:

> The eye that looks downward will certainly see the nose. The hand that dips to the bottom of the pot will eat the biggest snail. The sky grows no grass but if the earth called her barren it will drink no more milk. The foot of the snake is not split in two like a man's or in hundreds like the centipede's, but if Agere could dance patiently like the snake, he will uncoil the chain that leads into the dead.
>
> [Wole Soyinka, *A Dance of the Forests*]

Soyinka also makes use of proverbs in a satirical manner, especially in his play about the meeting of traditional and modern cultures, *A Dance of the Forests*, which he wrote for Nigeria's independence celebrations. Drama, of course, lends itself particularly well to the use of proverbs in dialogue or in a series of questions. Proverbial references can also be based on tales, just as they are in oral literature. For example, a man answers his wife's questions in the following manner:

> They say when the rock hit the tortoise, he shrugged his shoulder and said, "I've always been cracked." When his wife met him, she asked, "When did you begin to clatter?"
>
> [*A Dance of the Forests*]

To anyone familiar with Yoruba tortoise tales, the origin of this comment is clear, despite its expression in modern idiom.

The same proverbs, both traditional and Western, may be used by different authors, indicating a wide range of applicability of the proverbs, as well as a tendency for the authors to think and express comparisons in terms of proverbs. For example, in the novel, *Blade Among the Boys,* Onuora Nzekwu uses the previously mentioned proverb about the tethered goat to explain why a boy is sent away to live with his grandmother, and Thomas Iguh uses it in a chapbook novelette, *The Disappointed Lover,* when a woman tries to persuade her daughter to tell the truth.

A proverb may also be used as the basis for a recurrent theme without being explicitly stated. For example, Cyprian Ekwensi states that the theme of *Beautiful Feathers* is the following proverb:

> However famous a man is outside, if he is not respected inside his own home, he is like a bird with beautiful feathers, wonderful on the outside, but ordinary within.

This idea is discussed on several occasions in the novel without the proverb being explicitly repeated, although it is clearly implied by the context. Without specifying the proverb, Achebe uses the same theme in *Things Fall Apart,* in a discussion of how a man is not truly a man regardless of his great prosperity if he cannot rule over his wife and children. To a reader familiar with West African oral literature and values, this discussion would probably bring the proverb to mind, and thereby enhance the meaning of the passage; whereas to a reader unfamiliar with the oral literature, the appropriate proverb would not be evoked and the passage might appear to be superfluous explanation, or would be understood only in terms of the literal meaning of the words. Likewise, generalized proverbs like, "The start of weeping is hard" [Achebe, *No Longer at Ease*], which are common in West African oral literature, will have more specific connotations for readers familiar with the oral literature.

A common topic of the chapbooks is the many difficulties caused by beautiful women, and the problems encountered as a result of having beautiful wives. A Yoruba proverb used in the chapbooks which would be known to Nigerian readers is, "He who marries a beauty marries trouble." Thus the use of traditional proverbial wisdom in modern settings can be a device for evoking associations with a common theme that may be applicable in both settings, and may enhance the meaning of the less familiar setting. Furthermore, it is not unlikely that when animals which are common in West African oral literature like the dog, chicken, hawk, lion, tortoise, ram, goat, monkey and elephant are used in describing persons or in making comparisons, which they commonly are in Nigerian fiction, their proverbial implications will be evoked for those familiar with oral literature. (Field research is essential for determining the kind and extent of such associations which Nigerian readers make.)

As indicated in the preceding examples, the extensive use of proverbs seems to be an important aspect of Nigerian fiction. Whether the proverbs can be recognized as traditional: "Let the hawk perch and the eagle shall perch. Whichever bird says to the other, 'Don't perch,' let its wings break,'' [Thomas Iguh, *Alice in the Romance of Love*] or are derived from Shakespeare, ''The evil that men do must continue to live after them,'' [Nkem Nwankwo, *Dando*] or are universal, ''He who waits will see what is in the grass,'' [Cyprian Ekwensi, *Burning Grass*] may be significant in determining the sources of inspiration and the originality of the individual authors. However, to the Nigerian reader, if proverbs or other elements of oral literature appear to be authentic in the context of the story or are meaningful to the readers as such, then for all practical purposes, they are folklore and serve similar functions in the fiction. Where conversation in proverbs seems natural, the tales told at the fireside by fictional characters are familiar, and the themes of incidents are those commonly portrayed in oral literature. Folklore of tradition is a coherent part of the fiction so far as the Nigerian reader is concerned.

Several novels which have contemporary settings incorporate traditional tales in the context of their plots. The tales are always told in village settings as a group is seated around a fire or by an old woman or a mother to a child. These are the same situations in which tales are really told, and in fiction they are used to illustrate a moral about some culture conflict which has occurred in the plot of the story.

Epigrammatic naming which is similar to the praise names of oral literature is frequently used in Nigerian fiction. It is used in traditional situations, as in a modern version of a Hausa tale where a town is called ''The Land Where Everyone Holds Himself In a State of Readiness,'' and its leader is ''The Sorrow in Your Heart Is Little'' [Cyprian Ekwensi, *An African Night's Entertainment*]. Derivatives of praise names are also used in the same situations in which they are used in contemporary Nigerian life, especially to name lorries and cars: ''The Chimney of Ereko,'' ''God My Saviour,'' ''Trust No Man,'' and ''God's Case No Appeal,'' for example. The frequent use of epigrammatic naming probably derives from the oral tradition, as it is uncommon in the English literary tradition.

Praise names are also applied to items of particular significance, like a double spring bed which is called ''Holy of Holies'' [Achebe, *No Longer at Ease*], or used to designate personal qualities of an individual, like a beautiful pious girl whose name is ''Comfort'' [C. N. Aririguzo, *Miss Comfort's Heart Cries for Tonny's Love*], or the wicked ''Mr. Monger,'' who forbids his daughter to marry [Okenwa Olisah, *About Husband and Wife Who Hate Themselves*]. Nicknaming is also common, especially in the chapbooks, to designate a person's qualities, as the proud girl who is dubbed ''Peahen of West Africa'' [Cletus Gibson Nwosu, *Miss Cordelia in the Romance of Destiny*], and the maker of love charms who is called ''Put Me Among Girls'' [Ogali A. Ogali, *Okeke the Magician*]. Praise names are commonly used for similar purposes in West African oral literature. They are a brief way of describing persons, places, and things, so that their frequent use in fiction which is largely narrative adds a descriptive dimension which would otherwise be lacking.

These examples and others which could be cited indicate that West African oral literature has had extensive influence on Nigerian fiction in English, despite its dominant concern with contemporary life. The primarily narrative nature of the fiction can be traced to the oral tradition, as can the use of proverbial references and praise names for description and the use of proverbs and tales for providing commentary on the actions of the characters. These aspects of African oral literature are important influences on the way in which Nigerian authors develop their stories and the way in which the fiction is understood by different segments of the Nigerian audience and by European audiences. (pp. 28-38)

Nancy Schmidt, ''Nigerian Fiction and the African Oral Tradition,'' in New African Literature and the Arts, Vol. 2, *edited by Joseph Okpaku, Thomas Y. Crowell Company, 1970, pp. 25-38.*

WOLE SOYINKA

[*A Nigerian dramatist, poet, novelist, autobiographer, and critic, Soyinka was the recipient of the 1986 Nobel Prize in literature, the first African to be so honored. While writing of the political and social conditions of modern Nigeria and using European dramatic forms, he infuses his material with indigenous myth, legend, and folklore to create a distinctly modern African synthesis. He is concerned with the problems of progress and tradition in a society violently changed by European colonialism, and in his later works explores the destruction of war and the corruption and tyranny of ''reformed'' governments. Opposed to the ''negritude'' movement in African literature, which advocated the elimination of all Western literary influences, Soyinka has remarked that a tiger need not proclaim its ''tigritude'' and that he prefers not to ignore the realities of African cultural development in an effort to retreat to a mythical ''pure'' Africa of the past. In the following essay, Soyinka criticizes African writers who blatantly imitate European literature as well as those who idealize traditional African life, arguing that the best African literature is the result of individual artistry drawing on the complex realities of modern Africa.*]

Only when the political creature who persistently emerged from the common back cloth of an imposed identity—primitivism—began to display evidence of will, of individuality, of localized social and historical causation, only then did the European observer begin seriously to accept the validity of a creative imagination for the African, outside folklore and ritual. Even so he still fights a rearguard action today. It has grown subtler. Accommodation is his new weapon, not dictation. The European critic, full of the burden of an alien tradition, appears to have brainwashed himself of existing standards. In some cases he has even undergone a deliberate mental retardation, a sort of: Takes a simpleton to understand a child.

In this, he has been confidently abetted by his subject, the African self-interpreter. He himself provides instances when European condescension is amply justified. Encountering Camara Laye's *Radiance of the King*, will the critic not say, Why has this man not stuck to the simple, straightforward narrative of his *Dark Child?* For presumably the Western critic knows his Kafka. The cultivated naïveté of *The Dark Child* charmed even the African reader. Even if it often grew precious, it carried an air of magic, of nostalgia, which worked through the transforming act of language. If the author was selective to the point of wish fulfillment, it was unimportant. That a reader could be so gracefully seduced into a village idyll is a tribute to the author.

But most intelligent readers like their Kafka straight, not geographically transposed. Even the character structure of Kafka's *Castle* has been most blatantly retained—Clarence for Mr. K.; Kafka's Barnabas the Messenger becomes the Beggar Intermediary: Arthur and Jeremiah, the unpredictable assistants, are turned into Nagoa and Noaga. We are not even spared the role of the landlord—or innkeeper—take your choice! It is truly amazing that foreign critics have contented themselves with merely dropping an occasional ''Kafkaesque''—a feeble sop to integrity—since they cannot altogether ignore the more obvious imitativeness of Camara Laye's technique. (I think we can tell when the line of mere "influence" has been crossed.) Even within the primeval pit of collective allegory-consciousness, it is self-delusive to imagine that the Progresses of these black and white pilgrims have sprung from independent creative stresses.

At the conference of African writers in Kampala, last June, it was readily observed that the irreverence, the impatience that marked the critical sessions was the most memorable aspect of the entire conference. This attitude was natural. In order to condemn the European critic for his present patronage, for—at the other end—his rigid sensibility, for his unavoidable exclusion from the African imagination, there was an obligation toward total rejection of all substandards, of pastiche and stereotype. The sessions were truly ruthless, often wrongheaded.

It was the same at an Afro-cultural conference in Europe not long ago, where a young French-speaking intellectual gathered all his intolerance into one sentence, "How can an African write like Kafka?" It was dishonest, he claimed. He pitted his sincerity against Camara Laye's. In the end, he conceded after much argument that Kafka was probably a South African black who escaped to Germany after the treason trials! As a principle therefore, his protest was untenable. It belongs in the same restrictive ideology of regional art. Forgetting that the African is one of the inspirations of modern European art today, the black or white Africanist turns his back on an abstract canvas, protesting that he came to view an exhibition of paintings by Africans. In many instances, this is justified; for the contemporary interpreters of African themes have not truly assimilated the new idioms. It is merely naïve to transpose the castle to the hut.

There are, in fact, two kinds of offerings directed at the moment to the European palate. One is for acceptance in the Western creative idiom. I have mentioned the example of *Radiance of the King*. There is William Conton's proper resolution in *The African* of a Durham-to-Jungle adventure by an outrageously imposed Christian forgiveness; and there are the new poets in Nigeria who regroup images of Ezra Pound around the oilbean and the nude spear. The prophets of negritude at least dared these and scorned them, substituting a forthright although strident reaffirmation of truly "African" values, but breeding only the second offering, the burnt offering, image of the charred skin on a defiant platter. It is futile now to knock negritude; it is far more useful to view it as a historical phenomenon and to preserve the few truly creative pieces that somehow emerged in spite of its philosophical straitjacket.

But it is not so easy to ignore the facile exploiters of the fallacy, since they, even more than the muscular emblem-bearers of negritude, have been welcomed most readily into the bosom of the foreign critic. In a special issue of the *Times Literary Supplement*, a critic, reviewing a novel by a Nigerian writer, Nzekwu, says: ". . . but he cannot help presenting the traditional Ibo religion and culture in the more attractive light. It is this that will be the main attraction to the European reader: the masquerades, the prayers, the charms and the tribal social structure are described from within and with a luminous comprehension." And, to substantiate his intercultural awareness? "He is also old-fashioned enough to tell a straight story with a moral. This is the kind of story his people like." Obviously, a book that has something both for the European and for the African reader cannot help but be successful! Even the fumbling first novel of this writer is described as "very successful,"

and with two other Nigerian novelists the writer makes, "an unbeatable Treble Choice."

A very long time ago the discerning African rejected the anthropological novel. Perhaps during the next twenty years his foreign counterpart will do the same. Since even now African writers work against a similar back cloth, it is on the level of interpretation that the individual artist, as in any other culture, must be judged. Overeffusiveness at obvious window dressing (loincloth only, preferably menstrual) has created a most unfortunate prejudice against truly imaginative writers like Amos Tutuola, and worse still dammed the man's true creative channels. Of all his novels, *The Palm-Wine Drinkard* remains the best, and the least impeachable. This book, apart from the work of D. O. Fagunwa who writes in Yoruba, is the earliest instance of the new Nigerian writer gathering multifarious experiences under, if you like, the two cultures and exploiting them in one extravagant, confident whole. A study of his material, his imagery reveals this. But of course Tutuola has little in common with his African, even his Nigerian counterparts. The African writer-intellectual chooses often to dramatize his dilemma and the hollowness of his anguish indicates only too clearly that he first of all created it. A society, an intrusion, an all too predictable conflict—this was the formula, compounded in near equal proportions. Some laughed, full of hysteria; others, full of the dignity of tragedy, invoked the entire catastrophe and died. From a distance, the cultural intruders felt themselves rebuked, sympathized with and praised.

This theme is not for Tutuola, but the legacy, the imaginative duality is. The deistic approach of the Yoruba is to absorb every new experience, departmentalize it and carry on with life. Thus *Sango* (Dispenser of Lightning) now chairmans the Electricity Corporation, *Ogun* (God of Iron) is the primal motor-mechanic. Those who consider the modern imagery of Amos Tutuola a sign of impurity represent the diminishing minority of the African primevalists. And even the more accommodating ones find only charm and quaintness in Tutuola's shotgun image-weddings. Unfortunately, in attempting to interpret his symbolism, little attention has been paid to his modern experience; after all Tutuola lives *now*, and he responds to change and phenomenon. Not, in fact, except for indefatigable American scholarship, that it serves any useful purpose to reduce a writer's symbols even to events of spiritual exploration (and I have read a thesis that turned three of Tutuola's Ghostesses into the three regions of Nigeria!), but it is a useful corrective to bear in mind the appreciative approach of a similar intuition—the poetic, that is.

". . . a brief, thronged, grisly, and bewitching story . . . nothing is too prodigious or too trivial to put down in this tall, devilish story." This was by Dylan Thomas. Here now is one of Tutuola's physical struggles with Nature at its most humanly thwarting: "But as we were going on and when it was time that we wanted to branch to our left, to continue the journey inside another bush as usual, we were unable to branch or to stop, or to go back, we were only moving in the road towards the town. We tried all our best to stop ourselves but all were in vain." Even if this did not come in the chapter, "On Our Way to the Unreturnable-Heaven's Town," the meaning would still, in the context, be obvious. But has Tutuola's inspiration in this instance come from folklore? It is likely. Or else from the Sunday sermon? Death or the Devil winds up the road behind the sinner and he cannot turn back. Again why not? Should it matter? A minutae essayist indignantly dismissed the Christian contribution of these two source materials and argued

Wole Soyinka. From African Authors: A Companion to Black Writing, 1300-1973, Volume I, *by Donald E. Herdeck. Black Orpheus Press, 1973.*

himself blind to a third immediate possibility. The escalator. In today's African's ever-growing back cloth of symbols, the escalator has a more vivid suggestiveness than the magical egg of plenty.

This is an important point, not in the immediate context of the Unreturnable-Heaven's Town, but in assessing how individual writers make their creative emergence from the true, not the wishful untainted back cloth. We are now attuned to the loss of Hamlet the histrionic. Hamlet of the grand gesture has been relegated for the Oedipal prince. But the sex preoccupations of Western culture should not be allowed to intrude to an extent detrimental to the enjoyment of what Amos Tutuola primarily is—a storyteller in the best Yoruba tradition, pushing the bounds of credibility higher and higher and sustaining it by sheer adroitness, by a juxtaposition of analogous experience from the familiar. It is typical that even the last war should spill onto *The Palm-Wine Drinkard.* The hyperbole of the bomb and the Complete Gentleman—"... and if bombers saw him in a town which was to be bombed, they would not throw bombs on his presence, and if they did throw it, the bomb itself would not explode until this gentleman would leave that town, because of his beauty"—is not a rupture in the even traditionalism of Amos Tutuola. It is only writers with less confidence who scrupulously avoid such foreign bodies in their vision of the

traditional back cloth. The result in Tutuola is a largeness that comes from an acceptance of life in all its manifestations; where other writers conceive of man's initiation only in terms of photographic rites, Tutuola goes through it as a major fact of a concurrent life cycle, as a progression from physical insufficiency, through the Quest into the very psyche of Nature. *The Palm-Wine Drinkard,* as with Fagunwa's *Ogboju Ode* and universal myth, is the epic of man's eternal restlessness, symbolized as always in a Search. Between the author's own exorcism and the evidence of his immediate environment, we may continue our own presumptuous search for meaning.

If however we elect to return, like Tutuola's hero, wise *only* from the stress of experience, it will not have been a totally valueless journey. For Tutuola involves us in a coordination of the spiritual and the physical, and this is the truth of his people's concept of life. The accessories of day-to-day existence only become drawn into this cosmic embrace; they do not invalidate it. Questioning at the end what Tutuola's reality is, we find only a tight web enmeshing the two levels of perception. In his other books, strain becomes evident, effect for the sake of effect; the involved storyteller has yielded to the temptations of the extraneously bizarre, a dictation of his early outsider admirers who thus diffused his unified sensibility. Tutuola is not a primitive writer. With this objection removed, it is possible that the audience for which Tutuola wrote primarily (not that he thought consciously at first of any audience) would come to recognize him for what his talents offer—the contemporary imagination in a story-telling tradition.

Chinua Achebe chose to bring out his back cloth in relief at the areas of tension. In a sense—not a pejorative one—he is a chronicler, content to follow creases and stress lines, not to impose his own rearrangement on them. That this can be a creative process is demonstrated by the inexorable fate that overtakes his hero, Okonkwo, in *Things Fall Apart.* The demand we make of an expressed way of life is, first and foremost, reality. The writer must impress an acceptance. Enactments of tribal peculiarities must emerge from characters in that society, not interfere with our recognition of basic humanity, not be just a concession to quaintness-mongers. Why, for instance, do we accept so easily and unreservedly the accident of the hero's exploded gun especially as a prelude to the final downfall of one of the village elite? Dissected coldly, events that are not part of the dramatic progression of character or other events are instantly suspect. But Achebe has established another pattern, a rhythm compounded not merely of motives but of understated mysteries—mysteries as much to the characters as to their remote observer—of physical influences on daily routine, of a man's personal *chi,* of initiations, of guilt and purifications whose ethics are not those of a court of law but of the forces of Nature cycle, of the living and the dead. It is a subtle process, and its first principle, faithfully observed by the author, is the philosophy of acceptance. Not blind, slavish acceptance but a positive faith, an acceptance of forces that begin where the physical leaves off.

And within this, a difference of delimitations. For instance, where does a man leave events to his *chi,* to the communal *chi,* and where does he pursue them in defiance of apparent futility? We can respect and be overpowered by the tragedy of the man who destroys himself asserting the latter, but we cannot be anything other than impatient, as for instance in *No Longer at Ease,* with a modern driftwood, manipulated by events and making never a show of resistance. It is imperceptive to allege, as has been done, that the superiority of *No Longer at Ease* is the familiar delusion of exotic backsplash. The escape formula of most African poets and writers is there admittedly, status quo, intrusion and conflict, but Chinua Achebe has added the remaining dimension, individual depth in a credible hero. In a personal confrontation with values and implicit assertiveness that go beyond those of the society—and here is the point, society is not even—Okonkwo's opposition is one that has in fact dictated his actions and his distinct personality in that society. Where the society says: "When a man blasphemes, what do we do? Do we go and stop his mouth? No. We put our fingers into our ears to stop us hearing." Okonkwo retorts: "If a man comes into my hut and defecates on the floor, what do I do? Do I shut my eyes? No! I take a stick and break his head." The apostate Nwoye (through Okonkwo's eyes now), the nine ancestral spirits who administer justice in the land, even the lackey-agents of the new order are figures of this book's *moment* and contribute in their separate pressures toward the destruction of the man who became separated from his good *chi*. There is no good and no evil, however, only concepts of continuity—what works for society and what does not. And this knowledge, this magic is achieved from within society itself. The author, understanding this, has excluded all private imposition. He preserved the same integrity in *No Longer at Ease*. He preserved also, ineffectually, the evocative style imposed upon the former book by its framework of nostalgia, of a remote perspective, and total absence—let it be stressed—of sentimentality. Achebe required a stronger, more ruthless approach to create any lasting impression for such an effete character as the hero of his second book. Society emerges rather uncertainly even where it is felt as a corrupting agent. Language lends nobility to the life and downfall of Okonkwo; the same language in *No Longer at Ease* merely rebukes the author, as if he has taken his main character too seriously. It is doubtful if Achebe's forte lies in the ability to spit occasionally, or to laugh from the belly when the situation demands it, but he must learn at least to be less prodigal with his stance of a lofty equipoise. For this has bred the greatest objection to his work, this feeling of unrelieved competence, of a lack of the active spark, inspiration.

Compassion is the twin brother of Mongo Beti's grand iconoclasm (or perhaps what we are looking for is a word that combines the two). *Mission to Kala*, bawdy, riotous, bursting on every page with sheer animal vitality, reads like that rare piece of studied artistry, an unpremeditated novel. In the literary effort to establish the African as, first before all else, a human being, Mongo Beti with this novel has leaped to the fore as the archpriest of the African's humanity. Mongo Beti takes the back cloth as he finds it, asserting simply that tradition is upheld not by one-dimensional innocents, but by cunning old codgers on chieftaincy stools, polygamous elders, watching hawklike the approach of young blood around their harem, by the eternal troublemaking females who plunge innocents, unaware, into memorable odysseys. Hospitality is not, as we are constantly romantically informed that it is, nearly so spontaneous. There is a mercenary edge, and this, alas, is not always traceable to that alien corrupt civilization!

Peter Abrahams, Alan Paton, Onuora Nzekwu, William Conton—like the poetasters of the cultural dilemma—one after another they fall down and fail at the altar of humanity because they have not written of the African from the dignity and authority of self-acceptance. Peter Abrahams (*Wild Conquest, A Wreath for Udomo*) is especially something of a marvel in this respect—his black characters do not appear to talk, they use dialogue; they do not argue, they hold disputations. As for

feeling, emotion, that is surely an invention of the English greens on Sunday. *Mine Boy* sustains its threat to be an exception until Abraham's stagy exploration of the black-white relationship reduces his characters to cardboard. Alan Paton's *Cry, the Beloved Country*, simply debases the gift of sympathy. Nzekwu shares with Conton the gift for fictitious heroes, waiting vainly for human metamorphosis at the magic application of a spurious denouement as dictated by "Literature as a Higher Art." And foreign critics conspire by suspending the meaning of tragedy. Writers like Chinua Achebe, Mongo Beti and lately the South African Alex la Guma are, however, making restoration to the human image of the African. Mongo Beti, unlike the others, has employed the medium of comedy, or as he himself puts it, "my first, perhaps my only love: the absurdity of life." It is a love that many Africans tend to spurn, for it flatly rejects inflation:

> Come and restore
> Again to us
> The dignity
> Of our ancestral past
> The charity of heart
> And benevolence of soul
> Regard for age . . .
> And readiness to use
> Our strength
> To animate the weak.

The lines of a Ghanaian poet. And pure fiction. The ancestral spirits surely enjoyed the irony, for only a few pages away in the same publication the following stage directions appear in a play, *The Council of Abura*, also by a Ghanaian. "A stalwart ruffian near-by readily obeys the command and strikes the poor blind face." New dimensions in ancestral animation.

Mongo Beti has made tradition a thoroughly viable proposition. His Kala is the entire sweep of our now familiar back cloth, interpreted faithfully through a most suspiciously exact vein of wonder and participation. He has translated the slight alienation of his hero into village terms, with no condescension, no stances; the magnificent candor of the hero, Jean-Marie Medza, stranger to Kala, creates a vigorous clarity in characters, a precision of edges that Chinua Achebe, with no such uninhibited agent to hand, achieved in neither of his books. Sex is restored to its natural proportions, not a startling discovery made by the European every publishing day, nor a neo-Africanist venture sung by the apostles of negritude and sanctified in shrines to puberty. Beti makes sex an unquestioned attitude; the result is that he demonstrates a truly idyllic love dignified by humor, by pathos, and crucial to the novel as a major factor in the development of a young, sensitive personality.

So, it can be done. Biblical ponderosities in the mouth of black dignity prove, in the end, as unreal as gutturals in the mouth of Hollywood fantasia. And the bald imitation of European *personal* idioms is simply so much schoolboy exercise. Only through the confidence of individual art, like the early Tutuola, through the hurtful realism of Alex la Guma, the sincerity of Chinua Achebe and the total defiant self-acceptance of Mongo Beti, can the African emerge as a creature of sensibilities. These are only a few examples. Idealization is a travesty of literary truth; worse still, it betrays only immature hankerings of the creative impulse. (pp. 387-96)

Wole Soyinka, "From a Common Back Cloth: A Reassessment of the African Literary Image," in The American Scholar, *Vol. 32, No. 3, Summer, 1963, pp. 387-96.*

CHINWEIZU, ONWUCHEKWA JEMIE, AND IHECHUKWU MADUBUIKE

[*Chinweizu is a Nigerian historian, poet, and critic whose interests include African nationalism and ecology; Jemie is a Nigerian poet and critic specializing in African oral literature. In the following excerpt, Chinweizu, Jemie, and Madubuike criticize Nigerian poetry for its reflection of European literary and religious influences.*]

[A] common failing among African critics is their habit of attempting to force African works into the procrustean beds of an alien aesthetic. This brand of criticism insists on applying Western paradigms or models to African works, predictably concluding that the African work fits the Western model and, by implication, is thereby worthy of recognition by "the world." This is the mentality of cultural inferiority which responds to the foreign cultural challenge with "proof": "We've modelled ourselves after you; we've met your standards. Please accept us!"

In their effort to subsume African works under the supposedly legitimizing categories of the Western aesthetic, similarities become translated into influences, even in cases where these similarities are cleary fortuitous. For instance, Anozie imputes the conflicts and supernatural events in Tutuola's *Palm Wine Drinkard* to Biblical influences, even though African folklore and mythology, to which Tutuola is, above all, faithful, is replete with such conflicts and events. Similarly, Charles Nnolim goes to great pains to demonstrate that Achebe's *Things Fall Apart* is an African epic, by which he presumably means an epic written by an African to European specifications. He claims that *Things Fall Apart* is "modelled on" *Beowulf,* and he proffers as proof that "as in *Beowulf* there lurk in *Things Fall Apart* certain persistent elements in Anglo-Saxon thinking like *Wyrd* (Fate)." We suppose that in Nnolim's thinking the Anglo-Saxons not only invented but also hold a world-wide copyright on the concept of Fate.

The truth of the matter is that his use of English apart, Tutuola's mythic imagination is completely within the Yoruba African tradition. For proof, read D. O. Fagunwa who depicts a similar world—but in Yoruba. And Achebe's *Things Fall Apart* was, as he himself has often said, a deliberate (and successful) effort to recreate a pre-Westernized African reality, using authentic Igbo characters, situations, values and religious concepts, and bending the English language to express Igbo proverbs and idioms. That it was written after *Beowulf* and shares some similarities with *Beowulf* does not mean that it was modelled on *Beowulf.* (That I am a man, and older than you are, does not mean I am your father). Nnolim's *post hoc propter hoc* fallacy perpetuates the colonial attitudes which seek to deny the originality of our traditions and to deprecate the fidelity of some of our artists, such as Tutuola and Achebe, to those traditions.

These attitudes must be traced to the failure of our learned critics to develop a contemporary African aesthetic. To develop a contemporary African aesthetic calls for a search into African oral and written traditions—an endeavor which our learned critics tend to disdain.

Artistic sensibility usually determines a writer's characteristic emotional and intellectual responses to literature. It determines what experiences he converts into literature, and how he treats them. It also sets up standards of valuation which determine what is valued, what is held in low esteeem, and what is ignored. An African poetics must be grounded in an African

sensibility, and the incontestably uncontaminated reservoir of African sensibility is the African oral tradition. It is from there, therefore, that we must extract the foundation elements of a modern African poetics.

Usually a poetics is an after-the-fact codification of exemplary devices and characteristics extracted from an already established and acclaimed body of masterpieces—the classics of a given culture. Some might say that there is at present not a sufficient body of contemporary African writing, and that much of the oral tradition has not been recorded and made available; and therefore we do not have as large a body of masterpieces as is desirable for that analysis that must precede the formulation of a poetics. This may be true. However, because contemporary African culture is embattled and, in addition, is patently being led astray by apers of alien traditions, African writers and critics can no longer postpone the investigation necessary for the formulation of a poetics. Otherwise the field will, before long, be pre-empted by an alien and deleterious one.

Therefore, African writers and critics should begin now the explorations that would guide further efforts to extract a poetics as more traditional and modern works become available. Given our circumstances, the formulation of a poetics, however tentative, must go hand in hand with the creation of works which help refine that poetics. (pp. 69-72)

Understandably, much of contemporary African poetry has so far been protest poetry. The other large category has been privatist and mystical poetry. A general survey compels us to ask: Where is the narrative tale? Where are the parables, fables, paradoxes, myths, legends and proverbs? Our forebears were minters of proverbs; we are their heirs, are we not? Where is the poetry of tenderness that conveys the tenderness and does not merely refer to it? Where are celebrations of laughter and joy? In spite of our oppressive reality we still laugh, do we not? Where is the poetry of wit, where is the humour? Where is the poetry that realizes these emotions and affects, the poetry that does not merely celebrate them in the abstract? Where is the choral poetry, or don't our women sing together as they circle their dances at naming ceremonies, puberty rites? Where are the love songs, the songs of courtship, wedding songs, farm songs of planting and harvesting, funeral dirges, hunting songs, drinking songs, the songs that celebrate absences, deaths and other varied aspects and transitions of a regular full life? Our forebears were entertainers; we are their heirs, are we not?

If we are serious about reconnecting our poetry with our past, and with our present for that matter, with life as we live it in our society, our poets must begin to include these themes and forms in their works. The present preponderance of poems of privatist mysticism and of protest (in particular, of grim-faced protest: *protest does not have to be grim-faced to be effective!*) should be cut down to healthy size. We are not against either. But we ask, in addition, that privatist poetry be made lucid and accessible, and that our protest voices should not be turned exclusively outward to Europe, to America, to audiences of white faces, to the supposedly exclusive foreign sources of our hurts, but should turn homewards, to an African audience, against African wrongs. Especially after the decade of the 1960's, there is plenty to protest in African life. Our poets should stop regarding themselves as primarily orphic messengers to the West.

The artist in the traditional African milieu spoke for and to his community. His imagery, themes, symbolisms and forms were all drawn from a communally accessible pool. He was heard. He made sense. But our "moderns"?. . . . When you cannot speak to your people there is a burning temptation either to speak to yourself (privatist mysticism), or to speak for them to outside ears (orphic messengers); to pose as ambassadors to foreigners, to pretend to be bearers of self-composed messages from your people to the rest of the world. The outsiders hear and understand you (perhaps), but your own people wonder what's going on, what the jabbering is all about.

The African writer or critic must confront this issue of what community he is writing for. Is he content to scribble exotic marginalia to the literatures of Europe? Is he content to write for an audience whose interest in his work is mostly exotic? Or is he more interested in writing for a community whose members, in reading his works can confront their own life experiences and find them illuminated? Who will quote him to their children in order to make their lives more intelligible to them? Let us point out that the immortality of a work—something most writers desire—depends on writing for a community for whose situation the work is resonant with meaning, a community which finds itself expressed in the work. Writing for an alien community which takes only exotic delight in your life is probably the surest route to unremembrance.

Let it also be noted that the demands of an artist's cultural community are the features against which he must sharpen his craft. It should therefore not surprise us that Africa's colonial and neocolonial writers, being overly devoted to their European and American audiences and mentors, trim their sails to the modernist squalls from the West. Simplicity of diction is therefore devalued, artificially difficult diction is esteemed, African themes that would make sense in an African cultural matrix are eschewed, leaving the thematic vacuum we pointed out above. The African writer and critic should understand that what makes a good work of art is in large measure defined by the central expectations and concerns of a given culture. They should therefore work from the standpoint of the African community, not the Euro-American, not that of some abstract "Civilization de l'Universel."

We would like to call an end to the debate over the use of Western languages by African writers. The use of these languages is a part of the problem of contemporary African culture. Ideally, African literature should be written in African languages. But the same historical circumstances that presently compel African nations to use Western languages as their official languages also compel African writers to write in them. Until those historical circumstances are changed—and we hope they change soon—it is pointless debating whether or not to use these Western languages in our literature.

A more immediate issue is how to write well in those languages. And we have argued all along that to write well in English today it is necessary to write clearly, using contemporary 20th century diction and idiom, so that anyone literate in the language can make literal sense out of every sentence or line that is written. It's so little to ask! Let the educated elite worry about the many layers of rich meaning that may be buried beneath that surface clarity. This is not to suggest that what is needed is a poetry of nursery rhymes; but even so, some of the great poetry of the world has the linguistic clarity and simplicity of nursery rhymes. Consider "Humpty Dumpty":

> Humpty Dumpty sat on a wall
> Humpty Dumpty had a great fall
> All the king's horses and all the king's men
> Couldn't put Humpty together again.

And Blake's "The Tiger":

> Tiger! Tiger! burning bright
> In the forests of the night,
> What immortal hand or eye
> Could frame thy fearful symmetry?

And Langston Hughes' "Harlem":

> What happens to a dream deferred?
>
> Does it dry up
> like a raisin in the sun?
> Or fester like a sore—
>
> And then run?
> Does it stink like rotten meat?
> Or crust and sugar over—
> like a syrupy sweet?
>
> Maybe it just sags
> like a heavy load.
>
> Or does it explode?

Any literate child can read and understand these poems; and at the same time, any industrious Ph.D. could, if he chooses, spend the rest of his life pondering their metaphysical profundities. By the way, that would be a less unhealthy endeavor, we think, than puzzling out obscure syntax. Similarly, one could spend a lifetime pondering the profundity of social dialectic embodied in the following lines translated from the traditional Yoruba poem, "New Yam":

> You put the yam to bed in the ground
> it will bring you money
> that will plant you on top of a beautiful woman

In short, anybody who can read what is popularly known as Onitsha Market literature, or Frank Aig-Imoukhuede's poem "One Wife for One Man," or the works of Amos Tutuola, or, to use non-Nigerian examples, Okot p'Bitek's *Song of Lawino* or Matei Markwei's "Life in Our Village," should be able to read whatever our other poets write in English. This simple literacy test should define the African writer's primary audience and community. Any African writer who insists on making the West his primary community on the grounds that he can thereby reach a larger audience, should be told that if he writes with clarity on matters of sufficient general concern to his educated African peers, chances are that most literate Africans will appreciate him, and he will have all the audience he needs. In addition, foreigners will also appreciate him (as they appreciate Tutuola), and rather than have less of each audience he will have more of each. Our artists may have something to learn from one of the greatest Chinese poets, Po Chu I, who wrote and rewrote his poems, correcting and simplifying his diction, till, when read, they were intelligible to the random peasant he met in his walks. But that takes humility. (pp. 73-6)

As we said before, it is from the oral tradition that we must extract the foundation elements of a modern African poetics. . . . The following is a summary of some of the aesthetic positions illustrated by [the oral tradition]. . . .

Language and Imagery: One of the most telling qualities of African oral literature (and one which we believe it shares with other oral traditions) is its economy of means. This may be seen in the density of meaning compressed into a line of proverb, and in the spare uncluttered style of our epics, folk tales and court chronicles: their control of their matter displays an almost ruthless exclusion of extraneous embellishments. The oral tradition, being auditory, places high value on lucidity, normal syntax, and precise and apt imagery. Language or imagery that is not vivid, precise, or apt compels the listener to puzzle it out, interrupts his attention, and makes him lose parts of the telling. We see no reason why these virtues of the oral tradition should be abandoned just because literature becomes written and visual. These qualities, which are mandatory in the auditory medium, should be insisted upon in the written. For even abundant leisure cannot be blamed if it gets impatient with unnecessary puzzles that keep it from the experience it wants to share. Also, whether or not they have precedents in our oral tradition, these qualities must be insisted upon out of sheer courtesy to the reader.

Structure and Logistics: Efficient structure and logistics is valued in the oral tradition, for it takes you through to the climax without tedious or unnecessary diversions. Contemporary poetics should make the same demand upon writers.

Poetic License: Where poetic license enriches the devices of the literary language, it is welcome. But it must not be misused. Where it leads to inconsistencies between imagery, tone and mood, it must be curbed. License is laudable when it leads to felicitous and mellifluous expression.

Other Considerations: While obscurity, sentimentality, cliches of expression and attitude, vague or unrealistic situations, incongruence of thought and feeling, and inadequacy of substance behind an emptily assertive tone can damn a work, what may make a work memorable includes the following: lyricism of speech, musicality of rhythm, mellifluousness (smooth and easy flow), emotional intensity and sweep of vision, evocative power, and concreteness of imagery and persona. As in folk tales, the personification of animals, deities and ghouls evokes them more vividly than an abstract presentation.

Equally important in making a work memorable, and in situating it within a tradition, are its fidelity to traditional forms and themes, the importance of whatever social issues it deals with, and, in the case of an embattled culture such as ours, how *engagée* it is, and what contribution it makes toward raising our consciousness. These considerations, we think, must be made part of any African poetics.

Our job as writers is to be articulate, and to present to our audiences the stresses and joys of our societies as they take place, not just in the private psychological transformations of individuals, but also in their public manifestations. We must capture and recreate the tone, flavor and texture of life in our society for those who read us. And if many have to do that in borrowed languages, that is not a fault to be interminably lamented, not a fault of the writer alone, but a symptom of the deeper decay within our culture. When the deep diseases of our culture are cured most writers will write in the indigenous languages. What we write in borrowed Western languages will still be African if it is addressed to Africans and if it captures the qualities of African life. It will be a species of African literature written in English or French or Portuguese, etc.

In conclusion, we would like to emphasize that whatever the language he writes in, a writer is a maker; let him make beautiful and effective things. And a maker needs technique; let him master it to good effect. And lest technique run away with him, let him have a clear purpose before him as he makes. If he would bore us, let him bore us; but he should not bore when he wants to delight or amuse. That would be unpardonable. (pp. 79-81)

> *Chinweizu, Onwuchekwa Jemie, and Ihechukwu Madubuike, "Towards the Decolonization of African*

Literature—Part II," in Okike, *No. 7, April, 1975, pp. 65-81.*

J. A. RAMSARAN

[*In the following essay, Ramsaran discusses the use of folklore and myth in early English-language Nigerian literature.*]

No aspect of the developing literature of West Africa is so much neglected as the folktale which is still a most vigorous form of expression in the cultural life of the people. Perhaps because of its very popularity and age-old association with a largely non-literate society the folktale tends to be forgotten or is deliberately by-passed by sophisticated writers and readers who equate modernity with excellence. But this particular *genre* of African literature has great artistic merit and conforms to very strict requirements of the art of the traditional story-teller.

It is an art impossible to reproduce perfectly in a foreign language as many collections of fables and tales by travellers, missionaries, anthropologists and others amply demonstrate. The failure of their translations is due largely to the fact that they seldom if ever try putting across the total effect of the originals with their integration of action, dialogue and song. The subtle suggestions of language operating together with archetypal themes which spring from the collective unconscious of a people are beyond the power of translation; but granted that there are yet certain universals of experience common to mankind as a whole, it is not impossible for one with the help of creative writing to get very near to identification with a race culture one has not inherited in its entirety like the individuals born within it.

The collection of the missionary remains a mere collection of dry bones of moral values catalogued and exhibited; the anthropologist's, *qua* anthropologist's, specimens of oral literature remain slices of life which one may take or leave as they suit one's purpose in contributing to one's understanding of life or achieving some degree of tolerance with the life of people seen as the section of a culture under a microsope. Neither of these categories of writers are by virtue of their vocation creative writers. And it needs both the techniques of creative writing and the intuitive genius of the imagination to transmute folktales from one medium into another—from the living breathing voice to the written word of the same language. How much more formidable is the task of the translator?

The student of literature gets little nearer, if at all, by a study of parallels in folklorist literature, or by collating and grouping tales as regards narrative form, themes, morals, etc. Only in so far as this activity contributes to an awareness of the total experience in which the tales have their genesis will it be justified in the final analysis as a fruitful form of literary activity. Short of actually belonging to a society or having shared in its experience from an early age, one can only hope to approximate to such a total experience through an intelligent understanding of the work of creative writers and artists who have entered completely into the life of the tale as a living organism drawing its sustenance and significance from the people whose imagination gave it birth.

African works of art in the museums of Europe and America remain mere "artefacts" because they are not drawing life from their natural surroundings: they are not being lived with, and are devitalized because they are denied the social function of a meaningful commerce with minds kindred to those of their original creators. It is the same with the folktale cut off from its context of everyday living. The resourcefulness of the tortoise and the astuteness of the spider as themes of West African folklore, when translated by missionaries and anthropologists for the benefit of non-Africans, are little more than a bald statement of certain characteristics of human nature anywhere in the world.

Very few folktales have as yet been given a written form in their original tongues by West Africans themselves. D. O. Fagunwa is perhaps unique in his sustained effort to give Yoruba tales their authentic rhythm in the Yoruba language; and the result achieved by him has been acclaimed by his compatriots, who read Yoruba, as eminently successful. It is because Fagunwa's tales flourish in their natural element with the spontaneity of lived experienced that his work is invariably preferred to that of Amos Tutuola whose voice acquires a stutter in English.

But since English is the common language of the majority of literate Nigerians, and since it is the medium of the growing literature of other West African countries with English-speaking associations, it is important to consider whether English as a literary medium is performing its function efficiently as regards the treatment of folktales as literature. It is in this connection that a just appreciation of Amos Tutuola's work throws light on the potentialities of the folktale in West African writing in English.

Tutuola's work has so far been either praised or blamed for the wrong reasons. It is not its "wonderful pidgin" nor its exotic quaintness that makes his work important in a consideration of West African literature. His writings preserve at least two essential qualities of the native folktale: its dramatic spirit and its identity as lived experience integrated into the whole of life as seen and felt by the writer. The conventions common to most folktale literature—repetition and refrain whether of spoken words and phrases or sung passages, transformations through charms and potions, crystallization of morals into proverbial and gnomic sayings—all these are only effective in Tutuola's writing in so far as they are subordinated to the working out of the drama in the context of the lives of the chief protagonists in his stories. And it is when, as so often happens, he is carried away by undue use of some particular aspect of the folktale technique that the equilibrium of the narrative is disturbed and the artistic tension of the story destroyed.

Close study of an episode where he comes near to achieving the necessary balance will show the skill of Tutuola when he is at his best. In *The Brave African Huntress* he incorporates into the chapter "I Became the Private Barber for the King of Ibembe Town," a folktale known for centuries, in one form or another, in many lands. It is reminiscent of Ovid's tale of King Midas's ass's ears (*Metamorphoses*, Bk.XI) and an Indian tale told about the Emperor Alexander. Tutuola's Nigerian king embarrassed by the discovery that his head has sprouted horns seeks the help of the African Huntress as his barber who is sworn to secrecy about the king's predicament; and the rest of the Nigerian tale is along the lines of the ancient tale. But it will be observed that this episode in Tutuola's book is deftly woven into the pattern of the African Huntress's career, and is in keeping with the general tenor of the book in which the incongruous of the fantastic and the commonplace are made credible in the twilight world of the African jungle.

In the Indian version of the tale, as in Ovid, what happens after the message of the music concerning the king's secret has been proclaimed to the world doesn't matter. Not so in Tutuola,

for the exposure of the secret leading to civil war between pro-horn and anti-horn factions in the kingdom of Ibembe provides the Huntress with the opportunity of escaping from the pro-horn faction who demanded her life.

Rhythm, repetition and proverb integrated into this episode make the Nigerian tale a satisfying experience for the foreign reader. Though I must confess that having heard the Indian tale as a child Tutuola's bugle does not seem to me to be adequate for the refrain—"The head of the king of Ibembe sprouts two horns." *The king of Ibembe* calls for a talking drum or two at least. In the Indian version the monstrous phenomenon of horns in a human head, the fear of exposure, the insidious whispering of the secret into the ground, and the resounding effect of the dramatic revelation are orchestrated into an enchanting concern of strings, woodwind, percussion and drum.

Another example of a well integrated episode based on a folktale is that of the ungrateful hunter in *Simbi and the Satyr of the Dark Jungle*. The treatment of this tale is more elaborate than the one in *The Brave African Huntress*. It has a more heightened quality of suspense and the drama builds up to a satisfying climax. It also has the further merit of complete integration with the theme of the book, wisdom through suffering—a suffering caused by the "beastly" ingratitude of man to man, and ironically relieved by animals humanised through man's kindness.

These two intances are by way of demonstrating how the folktale in Tutuola has preserved its dramatic quality along with relevance to the fortunes of the protagonists of the books in which the particular tale is incorporated. It is not like the specimen of some rare or exotic insect displayed in its inert form in a glass case; but can be seen in its living moving existence as a portion of the larger world with its constant play of light and shade. The reader foreign to the African world of Tutuola's stories, by such a treatment of the folktales, builds up an apperceptive mass of meaningful data, and as a result comes to accept the characters in their enviroment as a fact in his own imaginative experience.

Thus the African folktale helps to give life and form to Tutuola's fiction and in doing so preserves its own vitality. This is also true of its function in the first of Chinua Achebe's books, *Things Fall Apart,* which shows signs of becoming a West African classic. In this book, however, there is also occasionally a subtle use of folktale and myth where references to specific tales function with the effect of classical allusions in European literature. Such, for example, are Nwoye's recollection of the Earth and Sky myth and the Mosquito's Wooing of the Ear. Unfortunately, aiming at a non-Nigerian reading public Achebe has been forced to dilate upon such references which consequently lose their compression and native power to illumine and move on without dissipating the concentration of the reader. But where the leisurely ritual of story-telling falls properly into place the folktale and the novel as a whole come to life with a vividness that can hardly be surpassed:

> The world was silent except for the shrill cry of
> insects, which was part of the night, and the sound
> of wooden mortar and pestle as Nwayieke pounded
> foo-foo. . . . Every woman in the neighbourhood knew
> the sound of Nwayieke's mortar and pestle. It was
> part of the night. . . .
>
> Low voices, broken now and again by singing, reached
> Okonkwo from his wives' huts as each woman and
> her children told stories.

It is not impossible in such an atmosphere to believe that tortoises once flew! Which is the subject of the tale which follows the prelude quoted above.

It is quite conceivable that the Nigerian novel will gradually establish itself as a regional expression of human sensibility and experience; that this regional expression with its world of associations and allusions will grow increasingly familiar to readers everywhere. In this way the Nigerian novelist and his readers ouside West Africa will establish a rapport which is only in its initial stages at the present time. But the full establishment of such rapport will depend, in the first instance, upon the writer's faith in and complete acceptance of his own world. In other words, he must not hesitate among other things to use the riches of folklore and myth at his disposal which form a living part of the everyday experience of the community to which he belongs.

Tutuola and Fagunwa have shown how old tales are transformed in a new context, and Achebe's book has given some indication as to how successfully proverbs, tales and myths can be exploited to give authenticity and beauty to the West African novel. More recently J. P. Clark and Wole Soyinka have demonstrated how these very elements can give substance and sap to the growing Nigerian theatre. The former's *Song of a Goat* and the latter's *A Dance of the Forests* have moved a long way from Tutuola's raconteur literalism with its chance felicities, and Achebe's studied sedateness to a dynamic use of proverb and myth transmuted into poetry.

A close look at all these writers shows that the potentialities of African folklore and mythology as a vitalising force in West African literature are unlimited, whether used to form the basis of prose narrative, song and drama, or to charge them with the quickening power of allusions and symbols. (pp. 17-19)

> *J. A. Ramsaran, "African Twilight: Folktale and Myth in Nigerian Literature," in* Ibadan, *No. 15, March, 1963, pp. 17-19.*

OSSIE ONUORA ENEKWE

[*In the following excerpt, Enekwe contrasts traditional and modern Nigerian drama.*]

Traditional Nigerian theatre has received scant attention compared with the modern one that is European in impulse and ideology. The audience of this modern theatre is made up mostly of members of the Nigerian bureaucracy who have little interest in drama, but who attend plays for prestige or out of pity for the performers and students gradually being nurtured in European culture. The elitist character of this modern theatre is well articulated by Kalu Uka. Though conceding there are traditional elements that could be used by our modern dramatists, he argues that traditional drama does not exist. Moreover, he thinks it acceptable for the modern theatre to be preoccupied with a small elite audience that "may be a totally European or White one, needing new light or information about an African or an African country. . . ." Despite the fact that the elitist audience constitutes no more than one-percent of a potential Nigerian audience, and that the traditional groups have a large and eager following, it is the undernourished modern and elitist theatre that has attracted Western critics looking for something new (but familiar) on the "dark continent."

By adapting Nigerian novels or folk tales to the stage, some modern dramatists try to create an indigenous drama. But a play peopled by Nigerian characters in a Nigerian setting is not truly Nigerian unless its form derives from an experience that is meaningful to Nigerians. Nor is a play Nigerian if it expresses a foreign value that denies the cultural context of the play.

Our major modern dramatists—notably Wole Soyinka and J. P. Clark—have failed to create authentic Nigerian dramas despite their expressions of concern for the preservation of our indigenous culture. Although Soyinka has introduced song, dance, and other traditional elements into his plays, his dramaturgy remains rooted in the English stage where he served his apprenticeship. His rhapsodic flights, usually festooned with abstract Western ideas, are as incongruous as the syntax he often draws from Elizabethan and Jacobean dramas. Soyinka's plays are full of intellectual energy, but stultified by his inability to write clear and appropriate dialogue. Although his *The Lion and the Jewel* is set in a Yoruba village, its attitudes are European. In this otherwise lively play, Lakunle, a fatuous school teacher who apes the British, wants to marry Sidi, a village belle who is reluctant because Lakunle is too poor to pay the customary bride price. However, Lakunle thinks he can succeed by making speeches. His rival, Baroka, the village chief, is noted for his sexual powers and lures the unwilling Sidi to his bed by insinuating impotence, like Horner in *The Country Wife.*

Unfortunately, Soyinka's Sidi belongs more to England than to Nigeria. A Yoruba girl living in a Yoruba village could not be involved in such sexual intrigues. Besides, Soyinka makes her speak like a whoring Jacobean wench. Baroka has invited her to supper—as if this kind of thing happens in a Yoruba village—and Sidi hopes to see him "thwarted, to watch his longing / his twitching hand which this time cannot / Rush to loosen his trouser cords." She addresses Baroka's senior wife in a speech that is Jacobean in syntax, diction, and tone:

> . . . Oh such an idea
> Is running in my head. *Let me to the place* for
> This supper he promised me. Sadiku, what a way to
> mock the devil. I shall ask forgiveness
> For my hasty words . . . No need to change
> My answers and consent to be his bride—he might
> Suspect you've told me. But I shall *ask a month
> to think on it.* [my emphasis]

The plays of J. P. Clark are also adulterated by foreign elements, as several foreign critics have observed. After seeing *Song of a Goat* and *The Masquerade* during the Commonwealth Arts Festival in 1965, Harold Hobson commented:

> They are written in very inflated language, and in structure owe a great deal to classical Greek tragedy. This detracts from their value, for what we would like to see is something really expressive of Africa, not an African exercise on European models, however eminent. The small audience, many of them London Nigerians, though very friendly to the company, seemed to regard the dramatist's intensely tragic story as some sort of amiable joke.

I do not object to foreign influences; after all, no culture can grow without them. But I deplore a cultural contact that leads to the destruction of our culture, thereby inducing in our people a sense of rootlessness. We need a modern theater that has its roots in the Nigerian soil and can therefore absorb foreign elements without losing its own character. We must insist that the Nigerian culture be the medium within which synthesis of values occurs so that the indigenous culture does not become a mere shadow of the European culture. Nigerian dramatists must study the aesthetic habits of our own people so as to create a relevant and viable theatre.

Nigerian traditional theatre often combines stylization, symbolism, realism, and other techniques. The *Ikaki* play performed by the Ekine society among the Kalabari of Southern Nigeria, for example, is dominated by stylized rhythmic gesture that is dictated by the drum, while it also exhibits many realistic techniques. Like other plays of the Ekine, *Ikaki* has its peculiar "set of drums" that is so demanding that prospective performers begin training in childhood. In *Ikaki*, the natural environment provides a strong realistic contrast to the symbolic action. Ikaki, the main character, who is represented by a tortoise masquerade, is an embodiment of evil in Kalabari culture. He is accompanied by his two sons who are also represented as masquerades. One is Nimite Poku (Know All), the other Nimiaa Poku (Know Nothing)—a moronic character who, with his foolish mother, Aboita, foils the devious and cunning Ikaki. Nimiaa Poku's gambols and tumbles cause the family considerable annoyance. From the town square where the play begins, Ikaki leads his children to the river, with the spectators close behind them, where he searches in vain for a boat. Later he finds one at "the beach of the gods," where Ekine members who are both chorus and stage hands present Ikaki with a drum and help him and his children into a boat. From the beach, the audience observes:

> With Ikaki at the stern and Nimite Poku amidships, the boat quickly reaches deep water. But no sooner is it well out into the river than Nimiaa Poku plunges the crew into confusion. Paddling almost as briskly backward as the others are paddling forward, he brings the boat to a shuddering standstill. The onlookers, crowded at the water's edge, abuse him joyously. Realizing something is wrong, he takes remedial action by bailing with his basket. Unfortunately, he bails water from the river into the boat. The leakiness of the basket averts the worst; but a considerable amount of water comes aboard nonetheless, and the boat starts to look a little low in the water. Nimite Poku jumps angrily on his brother, and both fall into the bottom of the boat. The audience roars ecstatically. Then Ikaki intervenes to pull the two brothers apart and gives Nimiaa Poku a sharp cuff. Almost immediately, upset at having hurt his son, he starts to pet him.

After much trouble, they reach land and are rejoined by the Ekine members who escort them back to the town square where other scenes are performed. In one, Ekine members flirt with Aboita, Ikaki's wife; Ikaki, the devious character, is contradicted at every turn. This play shows, in the words of one critic, how "the disturbing real-life experience of plausible psychopaths is controlled, confined, and cut down to size."

Onuora Nzekwu's account of an Opobo carnival includes a description of *Mingi Oporobo*. A river monster of that name menaces the community and is killed by Kaligbo Ogbunjigbe, a brave fisherman. There is not effort to create illusion by using the river, but props, including a real canoe, paddles, a fishing net, and representations of the shrines of the god of fortune, are freely used. Whereas the fisherman is dressed realistically in a simple fisherman's attire, the monster and other fish are represented by masquerades with appropriate headpieces. *Mingi Oporobo*, like *Ikaki*, combines realism and stylization. Also, a clumsy character similar to Nimiaa Poku constantly impedes the action as Kaligbo goes in search of the river monster. As in the Asian theatre, dramatic illusion is not stressed, and the audience does not desire it.

The *Okumkpa* play, which is staged by the Afikpo, is much more localized than the preceding plays and shows a predilection for dealing with social problems. It comprises about eight sections or scenes, each of which is marked by a particular type of action. The scenes intermingle, although they are separated by a pause in the music, dancing, or acting. In the first section about one hundred masked and costumed men move through the village singing. Later, they take a central place in the village common and are surrounded by a large audience of the entire community. The stage is, simply, the ground halfway between the chorus and the senior male members of the audience, who are the main but of the satire and ridiculed by the performance, which deals exclusively with the life of the community. The leaders of the performance, who are equivalent to directors and producers, stand facing the elders. Behind them sit the musicians who keep a sense of movement in the play and accompany the dancers. The Ori (principal actors and dancers who also sing with the chorus) sit behind the musicians. At the beckoning of the leaders, the actors step out to perform, combining pantomime and dialogue. If the audience has a problem hearing what is being said, it calls for an explanation, and the leaders go 'round to explain the action, sometimes repeating phrases of songs. Between acts the audience shows appreciation by giving presents to the performers.

Humor is the essence of the performance. Unity is achieved by certain common themes—ridicule of elders, of the sexes, and of foolish persons—and by reappearance of the same foolish persons in different acts and songs. The following is a description of a short scene dealing with the predicament of Chief Isu, who was fined by the elders for becoming a Muslim:

> Since he now wishes to withdraw from the faith, he calls in the Afikpo seniors and objects to the fine. They insist that he pay the £5 and feed them in addition. His wife prepares the food, the elders eat it, and he pays the fine. His fellow elders divide the money amonst themselves at the gathering, as is the custom. The chief's wife begins to cry because they did not include her husband in the sharing, even though he is a member of the grade. She cannot understand why he got nothing. This skit ridicules the chief for becoming a Muslim for opportunisitc reasons, and his wife for thinking that he should have a share of the fine because he is a member of the group that fined him!

Typical of this play is the absence of myth, legend, or any type of fantasy. It is as if the whole community is X-rayed while entertained. Constant motion and the uninterrupted sound of singing, music, speech, the voices of the leaders, or a combination of these characterize the performance. Ottenberg points out that progression and return to the first section creates "a fine shifting pattern of color and movement, a contrast of darks and lights, or of beauty and ugliness. . . ."

Ottenberg's comment that it is a performance of skilled amateurs is important, for it draws attention to the non-commercial interest of the performers, which is typical of Igbo artists as well as many other African performers. I remember how New York audiences were surprised that the black South African actors, John Kani and Winston Ntshona, in the award-winning *Sizwe Banzi is Dead* and *The Island*, were not professionals. Kani and Ntshona are skillful amateurs as are the actors in the *Okumkpa* and in all the plays considered thus far. Although the performers are amateurs, they spend more time perfecting their art than might be expected of non-professionals.

The few plays that I have described suggest that the traditional theatre is communal, utilitarian, and pragmatic, without compromising its value as entertainment. Its communal nature is related to its social function as a stabilizing factor, as evidenced in *Ikaki* and *Okumkpa*. Since this theatre deals with the life of the community, the audience is spontaneously led to participate. Such theatre is doubly entertaining because it is not averse to relishing life while commenting on it. Moreover, its composite nature—integrating mask, music, song, dance, mime, poetry, and acting—appeals to all the senses at once.

In this theatre, scenery or background is not created spatially, for action is usually polychronic and cannot be restricted to a specific locale. Varied actions and themes co-exist, intermingle or clash, separate, without destroying the overall unity of the performance. The audience's attention is constantly broken and redirected.

Space is not defined by stage props and scenery, for the use of setting is pragmatic. Costumes in our traditional theatre may create aesthetic distance, but they also help define space for, together with other forms in the configuration, costumes create a total environment. All the elements have the effect of drawing the audience into an aesthetic experience that is at once cerebral, visceral, and charged with psychic energy. That is why music, dance, and other forms *seem* to be emphasized more than speech, since speech is just one of the constituents of our theatre.

In Igbo, the word "egwu" means dance, music, play, game, joke, fun, drama, and so forth. A composite idea of theatre requires that a dramatist acquire various artistic skills, since each of the art forms is not merely complementary, but integral. It is not surprising that the most successful troupes in the Nigerian theatre, traditional or modern, are those that have succeeded not simply in using other art forms, as Soyinka does, but in integrating all the elements, especially dialogue, music, and dance. Apart from Hubert Ogunde, Duro Ladipo, and others who operate in what is called the Yoruba Operatic theatre, and the plays of Rotimi and in the modern Nigerian theatre who have created works that have integrated speech, music, dance, and mime in the manner of traditional dramatists. Ola Rotimi in *The Gods are Not to Blame* has Africanized Sophocles' *Oedipus Rex* by revamping the plot, suiting it to the Nigerian audience, and introducing a great deal of singing, dancing, and communal discussion. However, he is still inhibited by his European-oriented notion of a formal stage. Meki Nzewi has succeeded in appealing to a large mixed audience by combining forms, but his immersion in European music has drawn him into absurd decisions; the leading lady of *The Lost Finger* sings and dances as if she were performing in a European opera. One of the merits of the Yoruba operatic theatre, and the plays of Rotimi and Nzewi, is that they are not bogged down by elaborate speeches, as are the plays of Soyinka and Clark. Furthermore, the plays of Rotimi and Nzewi can easily dispense with the proscenium arch, box set, or other formal scenery.

The enthusiasm of Nigerian audiences for the Yoruba Operatic theatre and the plays of Rotimi and Nzewi is evidence of the vitality of the indigenous form of drama. (pp. 62-6)

Ossie Onuora Enekwe, "Theatre in Nigeria: The Modern vs. the Traditional," in yale/theatre, Vol. 8, No. 1, Fall, 1976, pp. 62-6.

POLITICS AND THE NIGERIAN WRITER

JAMES BOOTH

[*Booth is an English educator and critic. In the following excerpt from his study* Writers and Politics in Nigeria, *he offers an account of Nigerian politics following independence from England in 1960 and the relationship between politics and literature in Nigeria.*]

[Problems] of neocolonial dependence and cultural confusion [are] faced by all independent black African states. Each country however presents a different version of these problems, modified by its own unique history, geography and demography. Indeed it may often seem to the despairing observer that all attempts, by politician or writer, to confront the essential problems of post-colonial society, are doomed to be thwarted by the messy accidents of particular times and places: ethnic jealousies, the arbitrary national boundaries left by colonialism, even purely personal rivalries between members of tiny governing elites. In the case of Nigeria all such particular problems seem to focus on its very status as a "nation," a role for which it seems less fitted than most other African states. Its constitution is, uniquely in Africa, a federal one. Since independence in 1960 both the nature and the number of the units making up the federation have changed several times. First there were three "regions," later increased to four, then (briefly) twenty-one "provinces," then twelve "states," and now there are nineteen states. The right balance of power between central federal authority and local administration has proved extremely difficult to find.

The immediate and urgent priority for any newly-formed nation is the establishment of a sense of national identity and of national unity. In the early years most African ex-colonies made at least some show of success, however dubious, in this difficult task. Zambia, Tanzania, Kenya, Ghana and Senegal all presented, in the period immediately following independence, a strong appearance of unity under a charismatic leader, a "father of the nation," who actively promoted a "national" ideology: Zambian (Christian) humanism, African socialism, the African Personality or Négritude. In Nigeria such a show of unified national consciousness (however flimsy) was scarcely possible. The various African socialisms for instance, with their stress on the (ever-extending) family, though most useful in nations such as Tanzania with few ethnic tensions, would be more likely to foster division in a nation so ethnically diverse as Nigeria. The obvious candidate in Nigeria for national leadership of the Kyerere-Kenyatta kind, Nnamdi Azikiwe, could clearly never achieve this status, because as an Easterner his motives were suspect in the eyes of Westerners and Northerners. Such suspicions as these have been a central element in Nigerian politics. It can be argued that the regional diversity of Nigeria confers certain advantages. Chief Obafemi Awolowo, former premier of the Western Region, felt that "the heterogeneous character of the peoples of Nigeria is in itself a potential check on the emergence of a totalitarian form of government." And this argument possesses a certain force. It is difficult to imagine a Bokassa or an Amin ever gaining control in a nation with so many large and powerful minorities. Nevertheless this ethnic and cultural diversity does also constitute the greatest barrier to national unity and thus to the formation of a national culture from which a truly "Nigerian" literature may arise.

The problem is inherent in the very concept of "Nigeria," that "arbitrary block" carved out of Africa by the British, and

Cyprian Ekwensi. Courtesy of Century Hutchinson Ltd.

including within its borders peoples with cultures, histories and languages as different from each other as those of Britain and China. Nigeria came into existence during the "Scramble for Africa" which followed the Berlin Conference of the imperial powers (1884-5). At first the North and South of the colonial "Protectorate" remained quite separate. And, as Ruth First remarks, when the two territories were brought nominally under one administration in 1914, "the only bond of political unity was the person of Lugard, the governor-general." Indeed, it was not until the setting up of the Legislative Assembly in 1946 that Northerners and Southerners actually sat together on any Nigerian consultative or governing body. Political power in the North, where communications are relatively good, has always tended to be centralised. As Michael Crowder remarks: "In the open savannah of the north, the organization of large political units was much easier than in the dense forests of the south." In the nineteenth century this power fell to the Islamic Fulani through a *jihad* or war of conversion, which imposed the feudal and aristocratic system known as the Hausa-Fulani emirates. A vivid and highly coloured impression of life in the North during the colonial period can be gained from the early novels of the Anglo-Irish writer Joyce Cary, who was in the Nigerian Political Service from 1913 until 1919. The action of his first published novel, *Aissa Saved* (1932), centres on the attempts of Bradgate, a harassed District Officer to restrain the aggressive fervour of a group of Christian converts who wage a holy war on their pagan neighbours, abetted by a naive British missionary couple. Bradgate's Moslem protegé, Ali, seems to be the best hope for the future with his enthusiasm for the sound British virtues of duty, uprightness and impartiality. But he is tortured to death by the Christians when he attempts to stand in their way. The Moslem rulers are portrayed as effete, crafty and corrupt. The climax of the novel is one of bloodshed and chaos, as the Christians resort to human sacrifice and meet the pagans in pitched battle. As a conscientious administrator

Cary endorses in this novel the official government policy in the North at that time: disapproval of disruptive missionary activity and co-operation with the Moslem emirs, even while recognizing their corruption. It is only such a policy, he implies, that can avert the kind of anarchy and violence which he portrays in the novel. Useful though it was however in preserving order under colonialism, this policy has had far-reaching consequences for modern Nigeria, by ensuring the educational and social backwardness of the North in comparison with the South. The effect of such attitudes on the part of the colonial administration was to isolate the North from many of the progressive influences which were transforming the South, and to preserve in power an autocratic and archaic ruling class.

In the South Christian missionary activity, and the Western education that went with it, met with great success, especially in the East. Thus a primary source of potential division in Nigeria has been an antagonism between North and South; the South more advanced, better educated, and Christian or traditional in religion, the North backward and Islamic. At independence the constitution bequeathed by Britain stipulated that representation in parliament should be on the basis of population. The North proving far more populous than the South (although the census was fiercely questioned) thus retained a built-in and indefinite political control of the Federation, a fact much resented in the South. Conversely the North has always suspected that the more dynamic, Westernised Southerners will seek to dominate it politically. National unity under these circumstances can only be a matter of compromises and balances of power. During the period of civilian rule which followed independence (1960-6) government depended on coalitions between the North and one or other of the main ethnic groups of the South, the Ibos of the East or the Yorubas of the West. The idea of a "national culture" in such a situation must seem a mere pipe-dream.

During the colonial period it never proved possible to govern the country effectively as a unit: each region presented its own particular problems. Lord Lugard's policy of "Indirect Rule" (adopted for reasons of economy) worked best in the North where a well-established political structure already existed. The emirs acted as tax-gatherers and agents for the colonial power in return for its support and a large degree of internal autonomy. In the West the system of "warrant chiefs," chosen from among the local traditional rulers, worked reasonably well since it could rely on an existing aristocracy of "obas" or chiefs, though one much less rigid and stable than that in the North. The strong and widespread Yoruba traditional religion resisted (and resists) Christianity more effectively than the more localised religions of the East, but it did not present any serious political threat to the colonial authorities. In the East however the traditional social organisation was quite different, as one can see from the historical novels of Ibo village life by Chinua Achebe. In *Things Fall Apart* and *Arrow of God,* we are introduced to a society where consensus seems as important as authority; a kind of communalist democracy tempered by patriarchy, where law and custom are a function of the whole community rather than an imposition from above. Such a politically decentralised society was quite unprepared for the imposition of "chiefs" by the central colonial authority. The action of *Arrow of God* concerns this moment in Nigerian history. The authorities choose a local priest of the god Ulu, who being the most respected man in the community is considered the most suitable candidate for the post of Warrant Chief. The result is a head-on clash between different concepts of society. The priest, Ezeulu, flatly refuses to accept personal temporal power of a kind disapproved of by his community. Indeed he considers the offer an insult to his true spiritual role:

> "Tell the white man that Ezeulu will not be any-
> body's chief, except Ulu."

The confrontation brings disaster on the village. Ezeulu, imprisoned for his "insolence," isolates himself within his pride and refuses when released to change the rate at which he eats the sacred yams. Since harvest cannot begin until these yams are consumed the livelihood of the people is threatened and they begin to question the wisdom of their priest. The colonialist's attempt to bring an orderly administration to this previously harmonious society thus causes chaos and demoralisation. A different, but common, result of the imposition of warrant chiefs was the exacerbation of local rivalries. The representatives of hitherto well-balanced factions would vie for the favour of the whites, with the unprecedented power it now conferred. Or, in the absence of traditional chiefs, unscrupulous and ruthless individuals would step into the gap. Better educated men from the coast would use their greater access to the whites to tyrannise over those further inland. And eventually the intense bitterness and resentment caused by such disruption of traditional habits and values forced the abandonment of this Indirect Rule policy in the Eastern Region. After the Aba riot of 1929 the Warrant Chiefs were withdrawn and direct rule reinstituted.

During the colonial period then the Ibos of the East, the Yorubas of the West and the Hausas of the North constituted quite separate social and political entities. This fact was recognised in the pre-Independence Nigerian constitutions. The Richards Constitution introduced in 1946 divided Nigeria into three "Regions" each with a separate "Deliberative Assembly." Above these was a unitary "Legislative Council." When this system was replaced in 1954 by the Macpherson Constitution, agitation in the Western Region for greater autonomy and devolution of power was directed as much against central control *as such,* as against the colonial regime, while the fears of the Northern rulers that early Independence would surrender domination to the South made them equally anxious for as much regional devolution as possible. After Independence the problems persist. Indeed they are potentially more intense now that the centre, the federal authority, is no longer controlled by the alien colonialist, but by fellow-Nigerians with their own (real or suspected) ethnic and regional biases. The political turmoil of Nigeria during the 1960s was mainly caused by the fears within each Region that one or both of its rivals would take control of the centre and use the central power to limit its freedom.

The situation is further complicated by the existence beside these three large ethnic groups of the minorities—sometimes very large and influential minorities. These are chiefly concentrated in three areas: the Mid-West, inhabited by Urhobos and Itsekiris, traditionally dominated by the Yorubas; the Delta region, inhabited by Ijaws, Ibibios and others, traditionally dominated by the Ibos; and finally the Middle Belt, inhabited by the Tivs, Kanuris and others, often non-Moslems, but dominated by the Moslems of the Hausa-Fulani North. In one respect these minorities are a great unifying force within the nation since they tend to favour a strong central government which will protect them from their more powerful neighbours. The existence of the minorities, however, constantly threatens to upset the balance of power between the majorities. In the period preceding Independence the East gave a great deal of

support to the idea of a fourth Region to be created in the Mid-West, since this would deprive their Western rivals of territory and influence. In response the West supported the Delta minorities in their desire for separate status in the Federation in a COR (Calabar, Ogoja and Rivers) state, to be carved out of the East. And both Southern Regions naturally supported the setting up of a new Middle Belt Region which would weaken the North. The alarming instability of such a complex power balance with its potential for endless new coalitions and shifts of allegiance, is obvious. In the period prior to Independence all these issues came to the surface as majorities and minorities manoeuvred for advantage. And Independence solved none of these radical constitutional problems. Indeed Chief Awolowo argued in his autobiography, published in the year of Independence (1960) that Britain's failure to act upon the findings of its Minorities Commission and create all three proposed new Regions at a stroke, condemned Nigeria to chronic instability.

One inevitable result of the regional diversity of Nigeria has been that literature in English has developed at different rates in different areas. Any "Nigerian" literature—any literature intended to have more than regional significance—must . . . be written in English (at least for the time being). Nor surprisingly therefore, in view of the degree of early missionary penetration and the level of educational development, all the writers of national significance to have emerged so far have been Southerners: Yorubas, Ibos or members of the Southern minorities. Moreover within the South itself cultural diversity is inevitably reflected in the literature which has appeared. There are of course some universal themes. The rejection of colonial distortions for instance is a theme which will appeal to all citizens of newly independent nations, whatever their local preoccupations. Achebe explores this theme through what he knows at first hand, which is specifically Ibo, but the wider application is nevertheless perfectly clear. This is not however the case to the same degree with the school of writers who followed Achebe in the 1960s in creating heart-warming pictures of Ibo village life. Much of their work lacks Achebe's sense of wider issues and they thus seem provincial. These novelists: Nkem Nwankwo, Flora Nwapa, and John Munonye (Elechi Amadi, an Ikwerre from the adjacent Delta region, could be added) could be said to constitute an 'Ibo domestic school' of writing. Their characteristic gentle humour and warm sense of communal solidarity seem peculiar to their region. The West too has its characteristic literary forms and styles. Drama rather than the novel seems a natural preference for several Yoruba writers, often with a ritualistic element derived from traditional religious festivals. Some of the plays of Soyinka, and those of Ola Rotimi and Duro Ladipo form a clear group of this kind. (John Pepper Clark, an Ijaw from the Delta region aligns himself in his plays with this Western group.) Again there is a distinction to be made between the writer who achieves a more universal level through his Yoruba material, as does Soyinka, and one whose appeal is primarily local, such as Rotimi. In itself there can be nothing wrong with cultural diversity. Any national literature is bound to have its roots in local and provincial particularities: witness Burns, Hardy and Lawrence in Britain. In Nigeria however, such distinct regional schools of writing uncomfortably emphasize the lack of the kind of cultural community which, despite diversity, does exist in Britain. More concretely they throw into prominence the lack of any comparable literature in English from the North. An observer seeking hard evidence of the existence of a "Nigerian" culture must conclude that there is as yet no such thing: only Ibo culture, Yoruba culture, Hausa culture, etc.

The political upheavals of 1966-7 demonstrate in all its complexity the interaction between the national problems of post-colonial dependence and corruption, and the specific local problems of tribalism and disunity. The leader of the *coup* of January 1966, the idealistic and puritanical Major Nzeogwu seems to have been motivated entirely by "Nigerian" motives. He was disgusted at the excesses of the ruling elite *as a class,* irrespective of ethnic considerations. He was a Nigerian first and an Ibo second. (As a Mid-West Ibo he belonged to a group which sometimes dissociates itself from the Ibos of the heartland.) His second name, Kaduna, refers to his place of birth in the North. He had lived much of his life in the North, spoke Hausa fluently and had many Hausa friends. His plan was to strike simultaneously at both regionalism and corruption by assassinating the rulers of all three major Regions. It is clear from the broadcast which he made on Radio Kaduna the day after the assassinations that he saw his actions entirely in the "Nigerian" context.

> Our enemies are the political profiteers, the swindlers, the men in the high and low places that seek bribes and demand ten per cent; those that seek to keep the country divided permanently so that they can remain in office as Ministers and VIPs of waste; the tribalists, the nepotists; those that made the country look big-for-nothing before the international circles; those that have corrupted our society and put the Nigerian political calendar back by their words and deeds . . . We promise that you will no more be ashamed to say that you are a Nigerian.

It was by a characteristically tragic irony that the *coup* led by Nzeogwu resulted in the worst outbreak of violent "tribalism" in recent Nigerian history. By accident and by the incompetence of his co-conspirators the task of assassination was thoroughly carried through only in the North, where Nzeogwu himself was in command. In the East the whole affair was botched: and in the West, although the Yoruba chauvinist and beneficiary of the shamelessly rigged 1965 election, Samuel Akintola, was killed, a crucial candidate for assassination, the Ibo, Major-General Aguyi-Ironsi, escaped. The result was that all the internal divisions of Nigeria were suddenly luridly highlighted in the eyes of the Northerners by what looked suspiciously like an Ibo-dominated plot aimed at taking control of the Federal government. This interpretation seemed confirmed when Ironsi persuaded his fellow-Ibo, Nzeogwu, to surrender power to him, and then in the following May proclaimed a new constitution abolishing the powerful Regions and setting up twenty-one "Provinces" which would clearly be easily dominated by the (Ibo-controlled) centre. In the abstract such a measure might seem an excellent method of undercutting regional rivalries. Indeed a similar system has now been adopted. But at this time of heightened suspicion it could only arouse antagonism.

At the same time Ironsi threw open all civil service posts throughout the nation to unrestricted competition on merit, a move which would clearly have flooded the civil service with dynamic and well-educated Southerners. To the cry "Araba," ("let us part") massacres of Ibos began in the North, Ironsi was assassinated and all the "Nigerian" aims of the coup were forgotten in ethnic conflict. The committed "Nigerian," Nzeogwu, compelled by events to participate in the "Biafran" secession, became an embittered man. Indeed a rumour has circulated that his death in action fighting for Biafra in 1969 was in fact due to a conspiracy on his own side caused by his continued open criticism of the secession.

Nzeogwu's failure and disappointment can be seen to follow the same pattern as that of all Nigerian intellectuals during the 1960s, as the crude simplifications of tribal chauvinism shattered their ideal of a new unified and independent Nigerian nation. As one would expect, the early writers, educated abroad away from local rivalries, and acutely aware of the world context, show an intense nationalistic idealism over Nigeria. The cosmopolitan Easterners are particularly enthusiastic. Chinua Achebe gently satirises his own youthful idealism in the naive poem "Nigeria" which the young protagonist of *No Longer At Ease* (1960) writes in London (in 1955).

> God bless our noble countrymen
> And women everywhere.
> Teach them to walk in unity
> To build our nation dear;
> Forgetting region, tribe or speech,
> But caring always each for each.

Beautiful Feathers (1963) by the Northern-born Ibo, Cyprian Ekwensi, has an even wider, international perspective. The action concerns the leader of the Nigerian "Movement for African and Malagasy Solidarity," who is an ardent pan-Africanist. Ekwensi dedicated the novel "To Léopold Sédar Senghor of Négritude Fame and Alhaji Sir Abubakar Tafawa Balewa, Patron, Society of Nigerian Authors" (and also of course a Northerner, a Moslem and Prime Minister of the Federation). To Nigerians with such wide perspectives as these the events of the summer of 1966 must have seemed a ghastly irrelevance to the essential problems of the new nation. But as massacres of Ibos increased and the exodus to the East from North and West began to create a *de facto* secession events forced Eastern intellectuals to an abandonment of "Nigeria" and support for the new "Biafra." A separate Ibo nation seemed at the time to offer the only hope for the future. This was a painful and difficult decision, made only when no other option seemed open, as can be seen from the letter by an unnamed Ibo quoted by Sunday Anozie, in which the decision of the poet Christopher Okigbo to volunteer for service in the Biafran army is discussed.

> After all it was a great shock, as you will yourself have experienced, in a short time to have to change political allegiance under the grim strains of the massacres and to feel that there was no hope or trust in the country that you had believed in all your life and that the only course was to create a new nation.

It is difficult to see what other view the Ibo intellectual could have taken at this time. The writers played their part in the war effort. In 1969 Achebe toured the United States with his fellow-Biafrans, Cyprian Ekwensi and the Ijaw poet, Gabriel Okara, in an attempt to gain support for Biafra. Okigbo was killed in action in August 1967.

Among intellectuals in the Western Region in the early 1960s a similar "Nigerian" idealism existed. No-one's contempt for prejudice and provincialism could be more robust than that of T. M. Aluko in his early novels, while Wole Soyinka goes so far as to record his wholehearted approval of the January *coup* and its aims.

> I could not, when the nature of the 15th January was finally digested, deny the rush of euphoria. I did and still wish that the revolt in the West had achieved victory as a people's uprising. Given a few more weeks this would have been realized.

Generally speaking however, the secession was not so great a trauma in the West as in the East, where the population felt that its very life was being threatened. Soyinka nevertheless refused to keep quiet and wait for the war to end, and attempted practical action. At the outbreak of the massacres he travelled to the North in an attempt to create a united front against violence among all intellectuals. The disappointments he met with are harrowingly described in *The Man Died* (1972). He felt that the only answer lay with a "Third Force" led by Victor Banjo, one of the original *coup*-plotters, a Yoruba ostensibly with the Biafran side. He began to advocate a UN ban on arms sales to either side in the conflict. Naturally enough his actions were interpreted by the Federal authorities as sedition and he was imprisoned for twenty-six months (1969-71). Soyinka's position was that the whole war was taking place on a false ground, it was an irrelevance to the nation's problems, and its outcome would be to embattle its rulers behind a mass of arms generated by the war and supplied by speculators and profiteers, individual and national, outside the country. Moreover it would accustom the people to the use of force in the solution of social and political problems.

> Militarist entrepreneurs and multiple dictatorships: this is bound to be the legacy of a war which is conducted on the present terms. The vacuum in the ethical base—for national boundary is neither an ethical nor an ideological base for any conflict—this vacuum will be filled by a new military ethic—coercion.

In Soyinka's view the war, instead of resolving the problems of ethnic rivalry and institutionalised corruption, intensifed both.

> The war means a consolidation of crime, an acceptance of the scale of values that created the conflict, indeed an allegiance and enshrinement of that scale of values because it is now intimately bound to the sense of national identity.

Despite the Federal victory the issue of unity still remains. And the process of national reconstruction has again involved attempts to solve this most intractable problem. In 1967 General Gowon had reduced Ironsi's twenty-one Provinces to twelve States. In the latest reorganisation under Lieutenant-General Obasanjo in 1976 the number has been increased to nineteen, in a division ironically similar to that of Ironsi. With the breaking up of the monolithic Regions it is hoped that a greater sense of national identity will emerge. Ethnic tensions still abound however. A tendency towards a localised micro-nationalism *within* the states has already been remarked. Professor S. Aluko describes what he calls "statism," a prejudice which ensures that all important posts within a state not under the control of the Federal Government are given only to natives of that state. The answer to such problems can only come with time; with the extension of Federal authority, with greater regional mobility and the improvement of education. An encouraging development here is the introduction in 1978 of a new, unified entry system for the universities, whereby a large proportion of students will be placed in universities outside their ethnic homeland. The difficulties at all levels are nevertheless great, and prospects for real national unity and a healthy national culture seem still uncertain. (pp. 21-34)

> James Booth, "Nigeria: Federation and National Culture," in his *Writers and Politics in Nigeria, Africana Publishing Company, 1981, pp. 21-34.*

JOHN F. POVEY

[*Educated in South Africa and the United States, Povey is an English critic who has written extensively on African authors. In the following excerpt, he examines the impact of Nigeria's civil war on the literature of that country.*]

It was not until ten years after the conclusion of World War I that a series of novels began to be published recording the shame and betrayal of that disaster. *All Quiet on the Western Front, Death of a Hero,* and *A Farewell to Arms* were among the works that defined the attitudes of a generation; after them few could believe in the heroics of war or tolerate what Ezra Pound called "the old lie," "*dolce et decorum est. . . .*" A decade of inward contemplation was required before the spiritual malaise engendered by this war and the discovery of the political betrayal perpetrated were understood to the full and could be articulated in all their compassion and anger. Perhaps things move faster now or perhaps there is less possibility of being surprised by the discovery that war is an atrocity, so there is no period of immobilizing shock. Our knowledge of history has shaped our attitudes concerning war's carnage and its hideous pointlessness. Many writers had already established the truth that the destruction wrought by war is not only material but social, and the rediscovery of this fact in subsequent wars begins to seem nothing more than the recognition of an old stock theme.

For Nigerian writers there seems to have been no need for a period of contemplation and absorption. Already after the Nigerian civil war the writers have begun to speak with that familiar but still poignant voice of bitter appraisal. In a way, this agonized tone is the more expected since the violence of internecine struggle is invariably the more devastating when it is fratricidal. In their latest works, major writers have distilled their themes from their experience of war, and there are new writers, too, finding that the sharpness of events has honed their incipient writing skills into efficient instruments to declare the personal and social disaster they encountered.

It is the Biafran side that is most regularly told. It was the successful Igbo novelists who did so much to establish Nigeria in its predominant position in the contemporary writing of Africa. Yet their expressions of concern are too humane to be entirely partisan. It is the horror of the war, as much as the defense of a faction, that sustains their recent work. It is the loss of faith after the idealism of willing sacrifice that motivates the scornful ironies that form their plots.

In a sense, the subject of secession can be anticipated in several pre-war books. The strangly prescient conclusion of Chinua Achebe's last novel, *Man of the People*, anticipates the first Nigerian army coup. Cyprian Ekwensi's last novel, *Iska*, describes at length the Hausa/Igbo riots that were a major trigger of the separationist decision. But since the war itself there have been several other important books. Some writers inevitably show in their own lives the personal change that accompanies social upheaval. It is said that Ekwensi, now living in Lagos, prefers to work on his series of children's adventure stories concerning Samankwe, an adventurous young primary school boy. Achebe has remarked several times in lectures given during his extended stay in this country that he wants to experiment now with poetry rather than begin his next long-awaited novel.

It is revealing that few books treat war as a military issue. The recorded anecdotes are of small tragedies and personal pains, sometimes raised to the point of becoming symbolic microcosms of the human situation. It is not the large scale movements of armies—no *War and Peace* here—but the disasters of personal cruelty, the suffering, looting, rape, and the contrasting moments of generosity and compassion.

The disaster was inevitably stronger on the Biafran side, not only because they lost, with all the attendant misery that defeat produced, but because the optimism of the longing for independence suffocated under greed and corruption. Achebe's bitter poem, "Air Raid," is the more devastating for being so apparently casual and detached in its ironic surface calm and black humor:

> It comes so quickly
> the bird of death
> from evil forests of Soviet technology
> A man crossing the road
> to greet a friend
> is much too slow.
> His friend cut in halves
> has other worries now
> than a friendly handshake
> at noon.

Perhaps this mood of resentment is most powerfully and dismally expressed in Chinua Achebe's short story, "Girls at War." He describes a situation at the distribution center where in front of starving crowds, army officers load their own cars with the food brought in by plane the previous night. The crowds make "ungracious remarks like 'War Can Continue' meaning the WCC!" It is a world where a man can buy something for five Nigerian shillings or fifty Biafran pounds, where a driver earns ten pounds a month in an economy where *gari* was selling in the market for "one pound per cigarette cup." Against this misery Achebe comments on the senior officers' girl friends with high-tinted wigs and shoes from Gabon. In this context, allied with the story of the moral disintegration of Gladys, the heroine, the title becomes scathingly ironic, as does his earlier title *Man of the People*. "You girls are really at war, aren't you?" The response is bold and cynical: "That is what you men want us to do." It is the overall disintegration of propriety and morality that enforces Achebe's despair, not because he has a naive belief that these things don't usually happen in war, but because this time it ought to have been different. The fervor once had a hard, clean edge. Now "too many girls were simply too easy these days. War sickness someone called it." The immoral women were only a part of a deeper disintegration; they were only "a mirror reflecting a society that had gone completely rotten and maggoty at the center."

Other writers reiterate the attitude, though the tones vary. In *The Combat*, Kole Omotoso's novel dedicated to Christopher Okigbo, the poet killed in battle, the war is on the margins of the events that motivate the book, and yet the remarks are applicable more widely in the historical context. From the other side he talks of the lorry drivers who "hid cutlasses and sometimes guns to protect themselves from army deserters who formed gangs and kept stolen money united in their pockets rather than fighting to keep Nigeria united." Isidore Okpewho attempts a kind of optimism in his novel, *The Last Duty*, for at least he argues that the true last duty is an obligation to suffering humanity as a whole and not merely to one side in a regrettable battle. But his thinly disguised fictional war between Federal Zomba and secessionist Simbia records largely bitter scenes of indiscipline and rape, and violence that spurts spasmodically even within the army itself. In continuing symbols he describes the aftermath of a soldier's execution by firing squad: "As grim faced soldiers untied their executed comrade from the stake a patrol of vultures hovered darkly beneath the pale canopy of the midday sky."

John Munonye's latest novel, *A Wreath for Maidens*, has perhaps most in common with the mood of the 1914-18 war novels and their consistent themes. He touches on the cruel way in which war exploits the optimism of the young, calling up those who should be protected rather than destroyed:

> "Thousands and thousands of boys are now getting depraved and brutalized in the camps, not to count those who die unburied in the battlefield each day. I often feel sick when I think about it."
>
> "What alternative do you suggest?" . . .
>
> "Except perhaps to conscript all those in our midst who led the country into its present troubles, and send them into the thick of it."

In this conclusion he is close to the attitudes of, say, Aldington or Siegfried Sassoon, who thought that the conniving politicians should also be responsible for fighting the war they created. Another common theme from earlier wars that is reiterated by Munonye is the arrogance and indifference of the officers safe in their base staff headquarters planning campaigns with only casualties as a probable result to be called defeat or victory. There is a Captain Okenna who

> at a time of utmost danger had ordered the company into the field of battle while he himself escaped with relations to the far rear. . . . He did not return when it was known that the survivors . . . had pushed the attackers back. His mission this time was to see for himself the amount of booty that had been captured. There were many cartons of beer. . . .

It is an old though no less discreditable story for its familiarity. Perhaps one recalls a play written in such a different context, Soyinka's *A Dance of the Forests*, which details the banal repetition of persistent human cruelty and greed across generations.

There is a dismal and ironic pairing to be found in two books, Elechi Amadi's *Sunset in Biafra* and Wole Soyinka's *The Man Died*. Each records episodes of imprisonment for unspecified crimes in conditions of haphazard and inconsistent cruelty. The similarity of the experience is striking—yet the jails and jailors were from opposite sides of the war. Amadi was in a peculiar situation. He had been a captain in the Nigerian army but had resigned. When the war came he was in Eastern Nigeria. He was doubly suspect not only because he had been an enemy soldier but because he came from the Rivers area and had supported the formation of a separate Rivers State. This was an anathema to the Biafrans who had incorporated these regions within their Igbo-controlled Biafran nation. On his arrest he was accused of training guerrillas for the Rivers State. The Biafran concern was understandable, yet as Amadi commented, many had wanted a separate state "for the same reason the Ibos want secession." His treatment in jail was the cruelty less of deliberate viciousness than of an inability to recognize the consequences of casual decisions for incarceration without any preparations or provisions. Yet his position always on the edge of execution allowed him to see the situation from a peculiarly middle ground. It was only much later after Federal troops had advanced that he rejoined these forces and attempted to reestablish efficient and honest administration in the captured territories. Most of all he conveys the sense of horror and irrational fear that permeated the region. The fear of the Federal troops was dominant. In the hospitals as the troops advanced, there were desperate attempts to flee: "Some who had disconnected their drip-feeds were trying to crawl to safety with bandages and plastic tubes trailing behind them—such was the strength of their belief in the ruthlessness of the Federal Forces.'' That this fear was not entirely unjustified is clear from passing remarks that ''the less scrupulous private soldiers exploited them. Molestation was rife and civilians appeared to have no rights at all.'' There was also a sadistic and neurotic second lieutenant who arrived bragging of the title, ''Terror of Bonny.'' Amadi comments, ''We all cheered with enthusiasm believing he had been a terror only to the rebels. We were grievously mistaken. Within a few days he had established a grim reign of terror. Private soldiers and civilians alike were beaten up, locked up, and shaved at the least excuse, sometimes for the sheer pleasure of it.''

Amadi at least had the comfort of believing that there was a sense of propriety and order in things and that local crimes could be attributed to individual malignancy or an accidental sloppiness of discipline unavoidable in time of war. No such luxurious belief in a merely temporary and intermittent lapse in the moral order was possible for Wole Soyinka. His book, *The Man Died,* is the most powerful study to come out of this Nigerian struggle, though perhaps one is only finding another way to reiterate that Soyinka is the one undeniable genius of African letters. In one sense the war is marginal to Soyinka's own disaster. He was arrested on some trumped-up charges of treason through collaboration with the enemy and was jailed and treated with that casual mixture of cold indifference, deliberate cruelty and sometimes transient compassion that is common situation in prison life. He was never able to find out the reason for his incarceration and in some ways Soyinka is writing another Kafka novel, but this time from real life. His story matches a depressingly long list of similar deplorable imprisonments from Koestler and Solzhenitsyn to the Robben Island imprisonment of Alex La Guma. It is a dismally familiar tale but the moment when it ceases to shock us is the moment when we too lose a substantial amount of our spiritual liberty. Soyinka asks us to respond without any of the convenient equivocations. ''Each individual will make only a simple act of choice—do I say yes to this or no.'' The nature of this choice is rendered the more profound in that it is identical with the response we should equally be required to make for Amadi, in the hands of the other side—enemy or ally as that might be. It is this double threat, the recognition that the abuse of power comes from both sides and even more widely, that makes the painful recognition that one fights not on political sides but along the lines drawn up along the inescapable validity of moral principle. These will not necessarily be color lines. Soyinka writes of his horror and resentment when he is put in chains: ''It was another black man [who] had given the order . . . that I was not a 'convict' in a chain gang in South Alabama or Johannesburg but in Lagos.'' This compounds the understandable bitterness of his suffering and the hardships imposed: ''These men are not merely evil, I thought. They are the mindlessness of evil made flesh.'' This is simultaneously true and yet becomes something deeper than the condemnation of a regime, for we know that it exists also on the other side of the fence.

In *The Combat,* Omotoso has one of his politicians generate a splendid malapropism. He shouts the old slogan, ''Workers of the world unite!'' The people sitting at the table took over from him and shouted, ''We have nothing to lose but our gains.'' Later the politician in a vigorous bid to gain arms supplies argues: ''As you know we cannot in this age of intercontinental ballistic missiles resort to the crude ways with which our ancestors settled their disputes, clubbing and clawing one another.'' And yet the net consequence of the recent novels indicates only too clearly that wars, no matter they are fought with clubs, guns or ballistic missiles, inevitably expose the crude ways of our ancestors, for they permit the exhibition of the bestiality of man, theoretically controlled by the civilized trappings of society. This is the evidence of the moral disaster that inevitably attends war, no matter the morality by which its political intentions and aims can be cloaked and justified.

Soyinka approaches that deepest of all theological truths: the inherent capacity for evil and cruelty that is eternally present in the hearts of many men. The awareness to be derived from these stories is that there are no victories in war, only the mutuality of defeat, a defeat not only for a nation but for the human spirit. (pp. 354-60)

> *John F. Povey, ''The Nigerian War: The Writer's Eye,'' in* Journal of African Studies, *Vol. 1, No. 3, Fall, 1974, pp. 354-60.*

D. S. IZEVBAYE

[*In the following excerpt, Izevbaye considers political themes in Nigerian poetry.*]

It is still with some uneasiness that one associates poetry with politics even though the association itself must have been as old as man's political awareness. Politics has always been a major concern of poetry whether as a theme or as an important conditioning factor. From the time of the classical Greek gift to the Trojans and of Shakespeare's attempt to gauge the pressure of a crown on a weak man's skull, to Wilfred Owen's death in the First World War and Christopher Okigbo's death in the Nigerian Civil War, the association has hardly been a congenial one. From the point of view of politics, the discord is a result of poetry's interference in unfamiliar territory. The classic statement of this objection was, of course, Plato's ban on certain categories of poets from his ideal republic. On the other hand, although there have been poet-politicians, political interference in poetic activity is equally resented by poets. The attempt to keep politics at respectable distance from poetry has been a rallying-point for poets of different nations. Thus one can say that more than twenty centuries after Plato, a modern State like the U.S.S.R. has still not succeeded in putting Plato's theory into practice. The contrary argument put forward by Wellek and Warren in the mid-forties, that ''in Soviet Russia, literature is, at least in theory, again becoming a communal art and the artist has again been integrated into society,'' must be seen against the background of Christopher Caudwell and the thirties in England, or as a statement of modern socialist goals. It has little immediate relevance, that is, for understanding contemporary situations and circumstances that are removed from this period or objective. If there is any temptation to see contemporary African literary art in terms of a harmonious union of writer and State, Soyinka's appraisal of that relationship should dispel the illusion:

> Independence in every instance has meant an emergency pooling of every mental resource. The writer must, for the moment at least (he persuades himself), postpone that unique reflection on experience and events which is what makes a writer, and constitute himself into a part of that machinery that will actually shape events. Let this impulse be clearly understood and valued for itself; the African writer found that he could not deny his society; he could, however, temporarily at least deny himself. He therefore took his place above the effects of the narrowness of vision which usually accompanies the impatience of new

nations, African, European or Asian. He, the special eye and ear, the special knowledge and response, lost even his re-creative consciousness which from time to time, left active and alert in his creative work, might have demanded a re-examination of his own position.

Lenrie Peters, the Gambian poet, shows a similar concern over the consequence of a poet's audience, because the interest of an audience is often extra-literary and, as a result:

> You can ruin your art
> Trying to please them
> Although you know you shouldn't.

He however acknowledges the comparative freedom of modern African writers from State interference although in spite of this political gain for art, the subordination of art to other claims is still very much in evidence:

> Yevtushenko disdains
> Stalin was a barrier to art
> You had to put him in
> Like pepper and salt
> And then play the part
> At least he was a hard nut
> To be cracked with a sledge-hammer
> Or simple disaster
>
> Here you write as you please . . .
>
> But the cold invisible hand
> Call him Stalin, Bureaucrat or tramp
> Rules the professions, politics, Religion
> As well as art, inside out.

> [Lenrie Peters, *Satellites*]

The objection to the association between poetry and politics is not often restricted to political interference in the creative act. On the other side of the coin is the danger that a poet who is interested in politics might be overwhelmed by his subject, an obvious reason behind the familiar question whether politics is a proper subject for poetry. The extent of this thematic problem is adequately measured in Gerald Moore's description of the recent political crisis in Nigeria as "the onset of events which seem almost to defeat the controlled utterance of art." Such a danger is real enough, but not beyond control; hence the current attitude that politics is as valid a subject of poetry as any other because, as Ezekiel Mphahlele puts it, "politics are a human activity." Some writers have gone further than that, even suggesting, like Wilfred Owen, that the mere suffering of war is itself intense enough to be poetic:

> Above all I am not concerned with Poetry
> My subject is War, and pity of War.
> The Poetry is in the pity.

Many African writers would concede that politics could provide the right degree of intensity for creative inspiration and poetic effect. Thus in a review of *Kongi's Harvest,* Dipoko the Cameroonian writer, argues that an artist who "is talented and works very hard, will achieve the consistent grandeur of the greatest works of art which have their source in committed passion." (pp. 143-46)

Although every individual has a right, by virtue of his membership of society, to participate in the operation of the political machinery, a clear distinction ought to be drawn between the various means of participation. A distinction ought to be made between a political poem or a satire on the one hand, and a political tract in the other. For example, Ifeanyi Menkiti's "Reflections" on the Civil War is a political tract pretending to be a political poem. It starts off with an ironical statement on the July *coup* and soon drifts into partisanship by offering the usual one-sided view of the Civil War as a religious war, thus ignoring all other issues basic to it:

> Operation Mecca,
> And Medina came earlier;
> Allah, the noble steed,
> Islam riding thee,
> Onward and southward
> to Lagos and Pitaua;
> the conquest uninterrupted to the sea.

This demonstrates the main problem of political poetry—control of material. The question it raises is: if poetry duplicates the role of other activities and does not do it more effectively, can it justify its existence? The problem with this poem is not its one-sided view. A poem on the same subject by a non-Nigerian who did not even visit the crisis scene shows where the problem lies. In Michael Thorpe's "For Christian, Alive or Dead," there is implied a similar partisanship in the distribution of sympathy along tribal lines and, worse still, distance from the actual event and a provocative generalization. But in spite of this and the banality of the couplet with which it closes, the poem includes an additional dimension which Menkiti's poem lacks. It avoids political analysis to focus on a question in which every man—and poets in particular—may claim expertise, i.e., compassion for suffering humanity:

FOR CHRISTIAN, ALIVE OR DEAD

> Time photographs of an African war
> Make "black heart" again seem no metaphor,
> Somewhere, an Ibo I know may be hiding—
> Or wallowing, bloated, in the turbid Niger:
> Had he lived, he meant to be a doctor
> And would have healed the wounds of every tribe
> But the surgery of history
> Assigned him a patient's anonymity;
> He might have been in that photograph,
> Hopeless-eyed, hands above head,
> Just before the crazed soldier with rifle
> Raised rolled his eye and shot him dead.
>
> "Internal" wars are magazine news
> And tribal cuts confound larger views:
> But those pictures are in black-and-white
> Which puts the matter in its proper light.

In what ways has the poet's response to the pressures of a political crisis affected his art? Menkiti's "Reflections" shows that political analysis is not in itself art—it is copying the method of the political analyst. And as Elimo Njau puts it, "Copying puts God to sleep." The solution adopted by most of the important Nigerian poets is to keep at a proper distance from poetry. That is, politics is still present, but it appears in disguise. The poet is aided in this by two major considerations. First, he constantly aims at universality, not topicality, for this is the only way he can ensure permanence for his art. Secondly, he is often constrained by respect for good taste, or censorship or libel laws; the last two are, however, the least important here, for why may not a poet tread the same path as the political scientist, and with the same degree of impunity?

The first factor seems to account for J. P. Clark's solution to the problem of political analysis and the human questions involved in poetry. In the political poems which appear in *A Reed in the Tide,* especially "His Excellency The Masquerader" and "The Leader," he seems to seek a breadth of relevance for humanity in general. That is why Gerald Moore's identification of the poems with Zik and Awo respectively is not really necessary. The specific items may be uncompromisingly regional, but the general import of the poems is a much more catholic one, for the poem reaches beyond the problems of the particular region with which it deals towards something that is more fundamental to mankind, as the following comparison will suggest:

HIS EXCELLENCY THE MASQUERADER
(Clark)

He serves
To ford between swamp and sand,
He serves!

The bridge stands,
All that stone and steel put together

It stands;

But bolts drop
And steel that should be blue
At close grip
  Shows brown . . .

And for such service, song more than

Water and sand;

In Ojoto
So they worship the masks,
Altho' in season—
The masks!
O take off the mask! And behind
What wind! What straw!

HIS EXCELLENCY
(Auden)

As it is, plenty;
As it's admitted
The children happy,

And the car, the car
That goes so far,

And the wife devoted
To this as it is,
To the work and the banks
Let his thinning hair
And his hauteur
Give thanks, give thanks . . .

Let him not cease to praise,
Then, his spacious days;
Yes, and the success
Let him bless, let him bless:
Let him see in this
The profit larger
And the sin venial
Lest he see as it is
The loss as major
And final, final.

The two poems are separated by thirty years and an ocean, the middle-class comforts of car and banking system in Auden's poem argues a different cultural background from that of the peasant vigour of Clark's raffia-covered dancer. But both poems dramatise the outward splendour masking an inner decay which is usually a sign of an impending revolution, be it Marxist or military. The specific details of place, period and person are not essential for an appreciation of such parables.

In his latest volume, *Casualties* [1970], a collection of poems on the Nigerian crisis, Clark seeks to separate political analysis from poetic sensibility by relegating political analysis to the footnotes. In effect, we have two books in one—a section on poetry and another on political explanation. The purpose of

John Pepper Clark. From African Authors: A Companion to Black Writing, 1300-1973, Volume I, *by Donald E. Herdeck. Black Orpheus Press, 1973.*

the second section seems to be mainly to put the record straight. The relationship between the two sections, or even the value of the juxtapositioning, is not very clear because an understanding of Clark's poetic method makes the poems much less obscure than some of his earlier poems.

Clark's method in most poems is that of the parable. It is basically the technique of the extended metaphor, or a process of simple substitution. That is, a simple correspondence is created between the participants in the parable and the actors of a real-life drama. This is different from the allegorical method because it generally avoids the tendency to personify abstractions. A good illustration of such a technique is Wonodi's lines in ''Lament of the Exiles'':

> I fear the harmattan dust,
> I fear the gradual wearing of the riverbanks.

Here, the harmattan dust suggests a Northern invasion of the South. It should be noted that although the method is described as ''simple'' the effect is complex and the symbol is perfectly apt. In Clark's ''The Reign of the Crocodile,'' crocodile is more than a mere metaphorical substitution—it is also an appropriate sobriquet because, according to Clark, ''Major-General Aguiyi-Ironsi was famous for his swagger-stick, a stuffed crocodile.'' The same aptness of symbol is present in Okigbo's thunder and elephant for army and powerful politician respectively. Similarly, Clark uses "desert" and "sea" in "The Burden in Boxes" to represent Northern and Southern Nigeria respectively, just as earlier in "His Excellency The Masquerader" he uses "swamp" and "sand" for the same purpose. This is a progression towards myth from the more realistic setting in an early poem like "Fulani Cattle" where the cattle route reflects the vegetation of the country. Thus, while Clark's poems are about the political crisis the test of their endurance must ultimately be their general independence of the notes, their intelligibility. The choice of natural life-forms converts political events into fables and this slight remove from the immediate event neutralizes the effect of the topicality of the events.

Soyinka's poems on the crisis avoid the use of fable and therefore seem to be based on greater literary realism. But the specific political events which the poems deal with are related to wider human issues. By focusing attention on man's sensual and gastronomic needs the poet heightens the hideous aspects of the game of death. That is the main point about the confrontation between the hedonist and the terror-stricken warrior in "Civilian and Soldier." In "Ikeja, Friday, Four O'clock" the wry punning reveals the degree to which human violence has perverted the course of things. The normal course of life is indicated by the plethora of images associated with feasting and lusting. The events in Ikeja begin with a feast of sorts, but instead of the usual loaves of bread it offers "loaves of lead" and blood for wine. The same method for suggesting perversion occurs in his *Poems from Prison* in which birds and flowers become euphemisms for planes and bombs thus suggesting that man's mimicry of nature has a monstrous and unnatural purpose.

Poems from Prison symbolise the degree to which Nigeria's major writers got physically and emotionally entangled in the crisis. The effect on their art must have been greater than can be indicated here because poetry is primarily a vehicle for the private vision while war is a public event. The novel is traditionally the form that is spacious and elastic enough to accommodate public crises and wars conveniently. Yet the reason why poetry had to get involved is implied in the title poem, "The Casualties":

> The Casualties are not only those who are dead;
> They are well out of it.
> The casualties are not only those who are wounded,
> Though they await burial by instalments . . .
> The casualties are not only those who started
> A fire and now cannot put it out. Thousands
> Are burning that have no say in the matter.

In short, the casualties include the stay-at-homes for, in spite of their merriment and private parties, these are

> All sagging as are
> The cases celebrated for *kwashiorkor*.

One of the effects which involvement has on the poetry is on poetic form. In Clark's poems there is a relaxing of the control on line length, especially in "The Casualties" and in "Seasons of Omens." The personal emotion seems to be so overwhelmed by the extent of the disaster that the poet needs a freer, Whitman-like form in order to cope with the need for cataloguing the various consequences of the war. Rhyme and stanza form seem to be abandoned, and repetition appears to be the only real source of control. The variety of items in the catalogue saves the formal repetition from monotony, and at the same time the repetitive form itself rescues the catalogue from its chaotic formlessness. The formal repetition also does service

when a jazzy, light-hearted tone is required to mask the mockery of dishonest intentions of hypocrisy, as in "What the Squirrel Said."

Soyinka, on the other hand, generally sticks to the more controlled stanza form. Nevertheless, the poem "For Fajuyi" seems to owe its concentrated effect and its rapid shift of metaphor to the poet's response to a situation that is as thoroughly rotten as that pictured in the novels of the mid-sixties. So that when one redeeming event occurs to hold out hope for humanity, the poetic expression comes in a rapid, concentrated flow as if from the fulness of a heart that has found one pearl of great price in a land of dross. Hence the situation is fertile ground for deification, and this is what, in fact, happens in the poem. The rapid shift of metaphor is an attempt to capture the many-sided qualities of the hero who is portrayed as having the glory and brevity of a flame, the true temper of steel, the irresistible action of a spring-lock, the miraculous growth of a mustard seed and the regenerative power of the sun. Thus he is

> (. . .) Flare too rare
> Too brief, chivalric steel
> Redeems us living, springs the lock of Time's denial
> Out from miser earth, thrust from dark, a mystery kernel
> Latent till the stress of storms
> Sudden soared a miracle of boughs
> Recreative temper as the sun's, diurnal.

However, the hope for man sparked off by the hero's action does not really destroy the poet's scepticism, for although the nobility is as diurnal as the sun's, the occurrence of such a noble act is seen as "a lonely feat" and the death of the hero leaves the field to the triumph of weeds which, for the poet, is the only constant.

In his emotional or physical involvement in the crisis, the Nigerian poet has still had time for his art but the poetry has had to be harnessed to the more important business of living. As a result, the poet has taken one great stride towards forging anew that absence of real discourse between the poet and his public described by Clark as the broken communication line which distinguishes the new, complex, and often masterly poetry of the sixties from the rather artless pioneer writing of the thirties and forties [see excerpt above]. Pioneer verse may not have been great poetry by any standard, but at least it retained an ideal link of understanding with its audience through the common goal of self-rule. One may ask whether in the circumstances of the sixties in Africa an attempt to achieve this ideal state of understanding between the poet and his audience might not represent a relaxation of the demands of art. Howbeit, the first approach towards recapturing this line of understanding in the sixties and early seventies is the poet's new concern with something that makes sense to both—politics—in addition to his earlier concern with traditional myths, religion and customs. He does not yet speak with a public voice, in spite of *Casualties*. But if Soyinka's epic, "Idanre," is not more accessible to the average reader than his earlier poems, the October 1966 poems are at least a starting-point for the more persevering reader. (pp. 160-67)

D. S. Izevbaye, "Politics in Nigerian Poetry," in Présence Africaine, No. 78, second quarterly, 1978, pp. 143-67.

NIGERIAN WRITERS AND SOCIETY

CHINUA ACHEBE

[*A Nigerian novelist, poet, and essayist, Achebe is one of the most prominent figures in African literature. His works are often concerned with traditional African values and the cultural changes resulting from European colonization. While there is a didactic urgency in Achebe's work due to his strong desire for the betterment of social and political conditions in Nigeria, he has been highly praised for the artistry and imagination of his writing. The following was originally delivered as a lecture to the Nigerian Library Association and is entitled "The Role of the Writer in a New Nation."*]

Although I have cast the title of this lecture in rather general terms, I hope you will permit me to talk specifically of the role of the writer in a new *African* nation—and even more specifically still—the role of the writer in the new Nigeria.

It is natural for a people at the hour of their rebirth to cast around for an illustrious ancestor. The first Negro African nation to win independence in recent times chose the name of the ancient kingdom of Ghana. Then Mali followed Ghana's example. Here in Nigeria, as you know, there was a suggestion to change the country's name to Songhai, the third of the great empires of the Sudan. Historians everywhere are rewriting the stories of the new nations—replacing the short, garbled, despised history with a more sympathetic account. All this is natural and necessary. It is necessary because we must begin to correct the prejudices which generations of detractors created about the Negro. We are all familiar with the kind of thing I mean. If these prejudices were expressed only by the unenlightened it might be said that with the spread of enlightenment they would disappear. But men of distinction have been known to lend support to them.

Thomas Jefferson, the great theoretician of American freedom believed—at least in his active years—that negroes had a lower grade of talent than whites.

The poet, Kipling, said something about black men being half-devil and half-child.

The famous humanitarian Albert Schweitzer sees no reason to doubt that he is the black man's brother; only he thinks of himself as the older or the "senior" brother.

One independent country in the African continent today is committed to the belief that the rule of white people is synonymous with civilization and the rule of black people is the negation of Christianity and civilization.

In a world bedevilled by these and much worse beliefs is it any wonder that black nations should attempt to demonstrate (sometimes with exaggerated aggressiveness) that they are as good as—and better than—their detractors?

This presents the African writer with a great challenge. It is inconceivable to me that a serious writer could stand aside from this debate, or be indifferent to this argument which calls his full humanity in question. For me, at any rate there is a clear duty to make a statement. This is my answer to those who say that a writer should be writing about contemporary issues—about politics in 1964, about city life, about the last *coup d'état*. Of course, these are all legitimate themes for the writer but as far as I am concerned the fundamental theme must first be disposed of. This theme—put quite simply—is that African peoples did not hear of culture for the first time from Europeans;

that their societies were not mindless but frequently had a philosophy of great depth and value and beauty, that they had poetry and, above all, they had dignity. It is this dignity that many African peoples all but lost in the colonial period, and it is this that they must now regain. The worst thing that can happen to any people is the loss of their dignity and self-respect. The writer's duty is to help them regain it by showing them in human terms what happened to them, what they lost. There is a saying in Ibo that a man who can't tell where the rain began to beat him cannot know where he dried his body. The writer can tell the people where the rain began to beat them. After all the novelist's duty is not to beat this morning's headline in topicality, it is to explore *in depth* the human condition. In Africa he cannot perform this task unless he has a proper sense of history.

Let me give one small example to illustrate what I mean by people losing faith in themselves. When I was a schoolboy it was unheard of to stage Nigerian dances at any of our celebrations. We were told and we believed that our dances were heathen. The Christian and proper thing was for the boys to drill with wooden swords and the girls to perform, of all things, May-pole dances. Beautiful clay bowls and pots were only seen in the homes of the heathen. We civilized Christians used cheap enamel-ware from Europe and Japan; instead of water-pots we carried kerosene tins. In fact, to say that a product was Ibo-made was to brand it with the utmost inferiority. When a people have reached this point in their loss of faith in themselves their detractors need do no more; they have made their point.

A writer who feels the need to right this wrong cannot escape the conclusion that the past needs to be recreated not only for the enlightenment of our detractors but even more for our own education. Because, as I said, the past with all its imperfections never lacked dignity.

The question is how does a writer recreate this past? Quite clearly there is a strong temptation to idealize it—to extol its good points and pretend that the bad never existed.

When I think of this I always think of light and glass. When white light hits glass one of two things can happen. Either you have an image which is faithful if somewhat unexciting or you have a glorious spectrum which though beautiful is really a distortion. Light from the past passes through a kind of glass to reach us. We can either look for the accurate but maybe unexciting image or we can look for the glorious technicolour.

This is where the writer's integrity comes in. Will he be strong enough to overcome the temptation to select only those facts that flatter him? If he succumbs he will have branded himself an untrustworthy witness. But it is not only his personal integrity as an artist which is involved. The credibility of the world he is attempting to recreate will be called to question and he will defeat his own purpose if he is suspected of glossing over inconvenient facts. We cannot pretend that our past was one long, technicolour idyll. We have to admit that like any other people's past ours had its good as well as its bad sides.

This is why, in spite of my great admiration for Camara Laye as a writer I must still say that I find "The Dark Child" a little too sweet. I admit that recollections of one's childhood tend naturally to be spread over with an aura of innocence and beauty; and I realize that Camara Laye wrote his book at a time when he was feeling particularly lonely and homesick in France. But I maintain that any serious African writer who wants to plead the cause of the past must not only be God's advocate; he must also do duty for the devil.

This is one of the things Wole Soyinka was saying in *A Dance of the Forests*. Those who want to resurrect an illustrious ancestor to grace their celebration may sometimes receive a great shock when the illustrious ancestor actually shows up. But, I think, it is still necessary that he should appear.

What I have said must not be understood to mean that I do not accept the present-day as a proper subject for the novelist. Far from it. My last but one novel is about the present-day and the next one will again come up to date. But what I do mean is that owing to the peculiar nature of our situation it would be futile to try and take off before we have repaired our foundations. We must first set the scene which is authentically African; then what follows will be meaningful and deep. This, I think, is what Aimé Césaire meant when he said that the short cut to the future is via the past.

I realize that some writers particularly from South Africa may object strongly to what I have said. They may say "we are not tribal any more; we live in cities; we are sophisticated. Why should we beat the drums of the old gods? This is precisely what Verwoerd wants us to do and we have no intention to oblige him."

Perhaps they are right to feel this way; I just don't know. It is for them to discover how best to explore the human condition in their part of the continent. I speak for myself and for this place and now. Sophistication is no substitute for a spiritual search for one's roots.

It is clear from what I have said so far that I believe the writer should be concerned with the question of human values. One of the most distressing ills which afflict new nations is a confusion of values. We sometimes make the mistake of talking about values as though they were fixed and eternal—the monopoly of Western civilization, and the so-called higher religions. Of course, values, are relative and in a constant state of flux.

Even within the Western civilization itself there is no unanimity, even within one country there are disagreements. Take the United States which is the most powerful country in the so-called Free World and whose constitution has inspired many a movement for equality and freedom. Does freedom there mean the same thing for everyone? For the late J. F. Kennedy and for the school children who shouted "we are free" when they heard of his assassination or their elders who celebrated with champagne? Now if there can be so much spiritual confusion in an almost homogenous culture how much more in an African country trying to build a modern state with tools fashioned in the tribe or clan? Some years ago—in 1958 or 59—there was an accident at a dance in a Nigerian city. Part of a wall collapsed and injured many people—some seriously. Incredible as it may sound some car-owners at that dance refused to use their cars to convey the injured to hospital. One man was reported as saying that his seat-covers would be ruined.

The African writer may ask himself: Why was such callousness possible? Is this an example of what some people have called the elemental cruelty of the Negro? I am afraid it's nothing so fanciful. It merely shows a man who has lost one set of values and has not yet acquired a new one—or rather has acquired a perverted set of values in which seat-covers come before a suffering human being. I make bold to say that such an incident could not have happened in a well-knit traditional African so-

ciety. Of course, it would have been quite permissible to treat a stranger and an enemy with such cruelty. But then you were not obliged in those days to live next door to an enemy—as you have to do today. In fact the whole concept of enemy and stranger has changed. So we need a new set of values—a new frame of reference, a new definition of stranger and enemy. The writer can help by exposing and dramatising the problem. But he can only do this successfully if he can go to the root of the matter. Any incompetent newspaper-man can report the incident of the seat-covers. But you need a writer to bring out the human tragedy, the crisis in the soul.

Take another example. Any one who has given any thought to our society must be concerned by the brazen materialism one sees all round. I have heard people blame it on Europe. That is utter rubbish. In fact the Nigerian society I know best—the Ibo Society has always been materialistic. This may sound strange because Ibo life had at the same time a strong spiritual dimension—controlled by gods, ancestors, personal spirits or *chi* and magic. The success of the culture was the balance between the two, the material and the spiritual. But let no one under-rate the material side. A man's position in society was usually determined by his wealth. All the four titles in my village were taken—not given—and each one had its price. But in those days wealth meant the strength of your arm. No one became rich by swindling the community or stealing government money. In fact a man who was guilty of theft immediately lost all his titles. Today we have kept the materialism and thrown away the spirituality which should keep it in check. Some of the chieftaincy titles and doctorate degrees we assume today would greatly shock our ancestors!

Let me mention just one more example of the crisis in our culture. Why is it that Nigerians are content with shoddy work? Put a man to sweep this room and in nine cases out of ten he will scamp through it leaving most of it unswept. Why? Because it is government work, and government is alien, a foreign body. When I was a boy, strangers from another part of Iboland were coming for the first time to our village during the planting season to work for the villagers for so much money and three meals per day. One day one of these strangers came to plant my mother's coco-yams. At the end of the day he received his pay, ate his last meal and left. About two or three weeks later the coco-yams began to sprout and the whole village saw what this man had done.

When he had got tired of planting he had simply dug a big hole in the ground and buried a whole basket of coco-yams there. Of course by the time his crime was discovered he had left the village and was not likely to come back. Now this sort of crime was only possible when societies that were once strangers to one another suddenly began to mix. Apply this on the national sphere and you will begin to understand our problems. The village code of conduct has been violated but a more embracing and a bigger one has not been found.

The writer in our society should be able to think of these things and bring them out in a form that is dramatic and memorable. Above all, he has a responsibility to avoid shoddiness in his own work. This is very important today when some publishers will issue any trash that comes out of Africa because Africa has become the fashion. In this situation there is a real danger that some writers may not be patient enough and disciplined enough to pursue excellence in their work.

This brings me to the linguistic question. In this discussion I am leaving out writers in the various Nigerian languages. It is not that I underrate their importance. But since I am considering the role of the writer in building a new nation I wish to concentrate on those who write for the *whole* nation whose audience cuts across tribe or clan. And these, for good or ill, are the writers in English.

For an African, writing in English is not without its serious set-backs. He often finds himself describing situations and modes of thought which have no direct equivalent in the English way of life. Caught in that situation he can do one of two things. He can try and contain what he wants to say within the limits of conventional English or he can try to push back those limits to accommodate his idea. The first method produces competent, uninspired and rather flat work. The second method can produce something new and valuable to the English language as well as to the material he is trying to put over. *But* it can also get out of hand. It can lead to simply *bad* English being accepted and defended as African or Nigerian. I submit that those who can do the work of extending the frontiers of English so as to accommodate African thought-patterns must do it through their mastery of English and not out of innocence. Of course, there is the obvious exception of Amos Tutuola. But even there it is possible that he has said something unique and interesting in a way that is not susceptible to further development. I think Gerald Moore in his *Seven African Writers* is probably right when he says of Tutuola that he stands at the end of a fascinating cul-de-sac. For the rest of us it is important first to learn the rules of English and afterwards break them if we wish. The good writers will know how to do this and the bad ones will be bad, anyway.

In closing, let me remind you of a theme that has been recurring in Sedar Senghor's thinking of late. He says that Africans must become producers of culture and not just its consumers.

African societies of the past, with all their imperfections, were not consumers but producers of culture. Any one who reads Fagg's recent book *Nigerian Images* will be struck by the wealth and quality of the art which our ancestors produced in the past. Some of this work played a decisive role in the history of modern art. The time has come once more for us, artists and writers of today, to take up the good work and by doing it well enrich not only our own lives but the life of the world. (pp. 157-60)

Chinua Achebe, "The Role of the Writer in a New Nation," in Nigeria Magazine, No. 81, June, 1964, pp. 157-60.

MABEL AIG-IMOKHUEDE

[In the following excerpt, Aig-Imokhuede reflects on the advantages and pitfalls of the West African writer.]

Being a West African Writer has this advantage—that most of the time one is treading on virgin ground. There is so much to be explored, there is such freshness and primeval virility about everything that the eyes of jaded Europeans are now turned towards Africa looking for adventure there—this time intellectual adventure.

One might say that this is a time for any writer to be living in Africa. He has so many opportunities, he can easily sell his stuff. True, he can easily sell his stuff—but in this one fact lies several pitfalls.

First—this European public who are going to buy his books—what do they want? Good writing? Yes, in theory. But in actual fact one discovers that looking for freshness in writing so easily degenerates into sensation-hunting. A badly written book may thus easily be accepted by the foreign public—just because it contains things not heard of before, ideas and happenings so strange that they can only come from a place where, they imagine, people are still close to Nature and basic human feelings are expressed in the most primitive way. About this sort of attitude I'm inclined to plead like Dennis Osadebay in his "Young Africa's Plea"

> Don't preserve my customs
> As some fine curios
> To suit some white historian's tastes—
> changing the last line to
> To suit some whiteman critic's taste

Again, the young West African writer is likely to be pampered, because he is like an only son of doting parents. He is still new. They have not grown used to the idea of him and so they make more of him than is warranted. He is therefore likely to become swollen headed and with very little to show for it. Thus, again, bad stuff is easily produced, the writer being self-satisfied and not bothering to improve. Third and fourth rate writers in the country of the blind then acquire the fame and standing of first rate writers in more enlightened countries.

Now, what is the fate of the young West African writer who does not want to pander to this popular idea of what he should write? Is he doomed to failure? I don't think so. Genius will rear its head anywhere, only it takes time, for posterity has always been a good judge of ability. I have always had the confidence that when the history of the literature of this country comes to be written, the pure will be sifted from the dross and preserved—and that is what really matters.

But coming back to the present—if the West African writer cannot hope for justice abroad because people think he must write about strange things—where should he look for his market? Home?

The situation in West Africa at the moment is such that a writer who writes in English hoping that his books will be read by his own people is a writer without a public. The great mass of the people is illiterate and of the literate a considerable number is literate only in their vernacular languages. From this has arisen an interesting situation—a situation in which the writer cannot reach the majority of his public because he has grown so far from them that he cannot be understood. What is the answer to this?

Some people think there should be more literature in the vernacular. But who is to write it? Is it the writer whose whole upbringing in the schools has been directed at perfecting his skill in the use of the English Language with detriment to knowledge of his own mother tongue? No, the present breed of writers cannot do it. Perhaps a future generation will.

There is one more problem facing the West African writer—a problem not of his own making, but which looms up menacingly in the path of his progress—and this is the touchiness of the public which he may have at home.

It is amazing sometimes the number of things we are touchy about in this country. Words uttered with quite innocent intentions rouse us to a frenzy. We see insults in innocent remarks and people, especially foreigners, have to mind their "p's and q's" when talking with us—

The cause of all this touchiness lies in our past history. But one is half-way to the cure when one has known the cause of an illness—and it should be so with us in this respect. The interesting thing about it all is that we do not lack a sense of humour—visitors to our country have always commented on our cheerful attitude and our readiness to laugh at every joke—but it would seem there are some jokes which are taboo and the unwary writer may so easily tread on our corns, and provoke a storm.

Now what are these things which are taboo? First, anything that savours of advertisement. A writer, we imagine, is a sort of ambassador, he must portray his country in glowing terms not write about the seamy side of life in his country or he is a traitor. But the writer who is worth his salt would disagree with this. For him "Beauty is Truth and Truth is Beauty," as the poet Keats says. What matters to him as an artist is not whether the picture is beautiful but that he should paint it with honest fidelity. And what the public does not realise is that a writer is not a political ambassador. If he contributes good material to world literature that surely is good advertisement. After all there are seamy sides to life in every country and it is only cowardice to hide from grim or unpleasant realities.

What else should the writer beware of? Irreverence? Because of their newness certain professions are looked upon with disproportionate reverence among us. I remember the outlook of shocked protest that greeted the writings of one of our gifted writers who "derided" the noble profession of law. I wondered what we would have done to Goldsmith who wrote about the village schoolmaster with such irreverence, or with the judge who wrote "Brothers-in-Law," or with Richard Gordon who laughed at doctors in his "doctor" series.

This attitude seems to preclude the writing of satire in Nigeria. I am looking forward to reading the first satirical work in this country and to watching people's reaction to it. I should be proud to shake its author's hand—not for the literary merits of his work but for his own courage in daring to laugh at "sacred" things. . . .

What then is the West African Writer to do in this equivocal situation? What I am going to suggest is not a cure but a palliative. He should write for the overseas markets meanwhile, but with the full determination not to pawn his soul. After all, writers everywhere have always had this problem—whether to pander to the tastes of their public and make huge sales or to write with conscience and be satisfied with the praise of a few. In our present circumstances we cannot afford to have a low standard in anything, least of all literature. Even in the world of nuclear weapons, literature still has a place. Let us hope then that the time will come in this country and other parts of West Africa, when literature will come into its own. (pp. 11-12)

Mabel Aig-Imokhuede, "On Being a West African Writer," in Ibadan, *No. 12, June, 1961, pp. 11-12.*

JOHN PEPPER CLARK

[*Clark is one of Nigeria's most highly regarded poets and dramatists, whose verse dramas have been compared to Greek tragedies for their mythic richness. His critical writings reveal a broad knowledge of both Western written literature and African oral literature. In the following excerpt, Clark discusses the relationship between Nigerian poets and their audience.*]

Nigeria possesses two traditions of poetry—poetry of the "oral tradition" which the various Nigerian peoples have always practised according to their own needs and conventions, and poetry of the "literate tradition," a product of the colonial experience that Nigerians have all suffered together. Of this latter, which is our concern here, there are again two separate traditions, one belonging to the generation that reached its prime in the thirties and forties, and the other to the present generation of poets now fully realizing itself. This is not just a distinction in time. Between the groups there exist definite differences, principally in the matter of performance and the public each enjoys. Indeed our primary objective here is to prove that in the development of poetry of the literate kind in Nigeria there ran at one time a direct line of communication between poet and public, a link that practically disappears between the later poets and the public, and is only now being studiously cultivated for reasons not completely literary. This is the kind of link that Sir Herbert Grierson in his inaugural lecture at Edinburgh more than half a century ago elaborated for English literature under the title *The Background of English Literature*.

The case as outlined then for English literature holds good today for Nigerian poetry written down in English. First, "the most ordinary speaker or penny-a-liner and the greatest poet are alike linked to their audience by certain media of which the first is the language they use. English journalist and English poet use the English language because they are writing for English-speaking people, though there may be all the difference in the world in the degree of precision and delicacy with which they use that language." Secondly, "the speaker and writer is connected with his audience by other links as well as that of a common language—by a body of common knowledge and feeling to which he may make direct or indirect allusion confident that he will be understood, and not only this, but more or less accurately aware of the effect which the allusion will produce. He knows roughly what his audience knows, and what are their prejudices. A people is made one, less by community of blood than by a common tradition." Thirdly, the Classical and Biblical "are the two most important vistas in the background of (English) literature until, at any rate, very recent days—literature and history to which a poet might refer with some confidence of being understood, and further, a certain feeling towards which of interest, respect, or reverence was a tie that connected him with his audience, a feeling on which he could count to give values to his picture." The fourth point is that for one reason or another, "these days are past. Long threatened and slowly modified, our traditional education has . . . rapidly disintegrated . . . Now if a poet wishes to give his work a literary background, if he is one of those whose inspiration is caught from books, whose imagination loves strange civilizations and scenery remote in time or space, then he writes necessarily for a limited audience, and to that extent he creates his own background from himself.

"But the more general result, the most characteristic tendency of recent poetry, has been to eliminate any conscious reference to a literary background altogether, to give poetry a setting not of literature and tradition but of nature and actuality."

That of course covers the whole long sweep of English literature from Chaucer to almost our own day. With the "moderns" Hopkins, Yeats, Eliot and Pound we come to a traumatic break in the line of communication that prevailed all along between poet and public in England. The course of Nigerian poetry written down in English, admittedly a very short one, shows a line of contact and break quite similar to that drawn above by Grierson. At one extreme end of the line is a poet like Chief Dennis Osadebay whose compeers are Dr Nnamdi Azikiwe, Mr A. K. Blankson, Mr Christopher Okejie and Chief Kola

Balogun, and at the other a poet like Mr Christopher Okigbo, with little or no communication between both poets.

But one or two modifications must be made in our adoption of the Grierson formula. It is not that the Bible and the Classics are necessarily the main vistas upon which earlier Nigerian poetry in English as distinct from the later poetry opens. Nor is it that when such vistas actually feature in one, are they for that reason absent in the other. Indeed, the evidence may very well be the reverse! What must be remembered is that during the first half of the development of Nigerian poetry in English there was a union of language and feeling between the poet and the public. In the latter half, probably as a result of changes in education and outlook, poets and people no longer seem to share that one language and viewpoint to life, either on the personal or national level.

Chief Dennis Osadebay's *Africa Sings* was published by the author himself in 1952. It is a collection of some hundred poems written "between 1930 and 1950, some in Nigeria, some at sea and others in England." All of them first appeared "in Nigerian, British and Indian papers and magazines, notably the *Nigerian Daily Times, Daily Service, Comet, Eastern Mail, West African Pilot, Empire,* and *Aryan.*"

A single vista informs these poems, that of one man's first awakening to a vision of himself and his environment. To use the poet's own words again: "The theme running throughout the book is the urge in the heart of the African to be free and the desire that African nations should take their rightful places in the world family of free nations. Africa sings, not only songs of love and joy, but also touching lamentations flowing from the soul of teeming millions, yearning, pleading, struggling, waiting." Accordingly, there abound in the collection laments, pleas, explanations, resolves and thanks by Young Africa, a prototype character that is the personification of all nationalist suffering and aspiration on the continent and beyond. Closely connected with this strain are the odes, making up more than a third of the volume, addressed to assorted subjects and persons. The roll-call ranges from workers, union leaders, priests and political leaders, including Hitler and Mussolini, to the poet's old school, his adopted towns, a Yaba doctor who cured him of a malarial attack, and to the River Niger, the Palm Tree, and his Raleigh Cycle. Obviously, these are subjects very close to the poet's consciousness, although others, especially the foreigner and expatriate overlord of that time, might not hold them dear:

> Don't preserve my customs
> As some fine curios
> To suit some white historian's tastes.
> There's nothing artificial
> That beats the natural way,
> In culture and ideals of life.

Allied to this new claim and pride for properties, old and indigenous to Africa, is the bold stake constantly made by the poet on the intellectual wealth of Europe:

> Let me play with the white man's ways,
> Let me work with the black man's brains,
> Let my affairs themselves sort out
> Then in sweet rebirth
> I'll rise a better man,
> Not ashamed to face the world.

Again and again he expresses the same resolve:

> On library doors
> I'll knock aloud and gain entrance,
> Of the strength
> Of nations past and present and will read.

> I'll brush the dust from ancient scrolls
> And drinking deep of the Pyrrhean stream,
> Will go forward and do and dare.

Besides this overall feeling of personal and national consciousness, the other property immediately noticeable in this poetry is the language. The stock of words, the syntactic constructions, the well-worn imagery are of the kind to reach at once the regular readership of the newspapers which first featured these poems. Then there are the inversions taken for obvious poetic effects, the sedulous rhymes, the recurrent epithets, the clichés and echoes, and the apostrophizing habits all of which evoke a ready response in an audience familiar with their popular proverbial lines taken from Pope, Gray and the hymn-makers Isaac Watts, William Cowper and the Wesley brothers.

The poet wants no material wealth, and echoing St Peter, announces boldly "not gold not silver do I crave." But he must win for himself the Golden Fleece of education, the one treasure that would make Young Africa the co-equal of Europe and free him of political and mental bondage:

> I do not crave for riches
> Nor worldly pomp and power;
> I ask for God's free air
> And shelter from the elements;
> Give me these rights of man;
> The right to think my Thoughts,
> The right to say my views,
> The right to stand erect.

These are sentiments spelling out a vision of life fully shared by poet and public alike in the Nigeria of Herbert Macaulay and Dr Nnamdi Azikiwe.

It may also be said that the poet at this point of the development of a written poetry in Nigeria was actually part and parcel of a people and generation only then taking their first firm grip on a foreign tongue that for better or worse had become for their countrymen the language of prestige, business, and education. He had therefore to master the language first, a difficult task for a junior customs officer just freshly matriculated, before working experiments with it. This is not to say that the later poets have had a shorter cut to learning English and writing poetry. Rather they may be said to have been born into a tradition of speech already accepted and aspired to by all. Therefore the atmosphere for learning would be less hostile and the tensions easier on the nerves. Furthermore, Nigerian poets of today have had a longer time to study in depth both language and medium, enjoying the additional benefit of a wider choice of practice and models. In this context, credit must be given Chief Dennis Osadebay who really is a pioneer poet celebrating the rising sun of his people. The realistic ring of voice he obtains in *Blackman Trouble* by a bold use of pidgin is therefore remarkable:

> I no get gun, I no get bomb,
> I no fit fight no more;
> You bring your cross and make me dumb
> My heart get plenty sore.
> You tell me close my eyes
> Your brother thief my land away.

Style and tone here sound much more convincing than Mr Frank Aig-Imoukhuede, almost twenty years after, achieves in the much admired *One Man One Wife.* Furthermore, Chief Osadebay well demonstrates here that pidgin, far from being confined to humorous writing, possesses the potential for registering a wide range of the human mind, pathos included.

The chain of instant communication, so strong between Chief Osadebay and his audience, breaks almost defiantly, in the hands of Mr Christopher Okigbo. With him feeling and language are no longer the common property of poet and public. "I don't read my poetry to non-poets!" he told a conference of writers at Kampala in 1962. But perhaps we should listen to him through his acknowledged master and model Ezra Pound. "If we never write anything save what is already understood," the master says in *Thrones*, "the field of understanding will never be extended. One demands the right, now and again, to write for a few people with special interests and whose curiosity reaches into greater detail."

> DUMB-BELLS outside the gates
> In hollow seascapes without memory, we carry
> Each of us an urn of native
> Earth, a double handful anciently gathered.
> And by salt mouths by yellow
> Sand banks sprinkled with memories spread
> To the nightairs our silence,
> Suffused in this fragrance of divers melodies:
> This is our swan song
> This is our senses' stillness:
> For we carry in our world that flourishes
> Our worlds that have failed . . .
> This is the sight of our spirits:
> For unseen shadows like long-fingered winds
> Pluck from our strings
> This shriek—the music of the firmament.

What kind of audience hears this music? For, to quote Ezra Pound once more, "Here, surely, is a refinement of language." Mr Okigbo himself in his earlier poem "Limits" acknowledges this limitation or complete lack of listeners, for there the poet is—

> Tongue-tied without name or audience,
> Making harmony among the branches.

Even in the later piece *Lament for a suite of long-drums and seven tusks* where Mr Okigbo consciously draws upon the Yoruba Oriki and the tradition of Ibo praise poetry, both ancient forms of art establishing immediate contact between artist and audience, there is the same apparent break in communication between poet and public. Like Palinurus, the lost leader he sings of, the poet here seems all "alone in a hot prison" keeping at best "the dead sea awake with nightsong." Consequently, when the drums beat out "on the orange yellow myth of the sands of exile,"

> Long-drums dis-
> Jointed, and with bleeding tendons
> Like tarantulas
> Emptied of their bitterest poisons

the effect upon the audience that should be participating in an urgent experience is:

> like a dead letter unanswered,
> Our rococo
> Choir of insects is null
> Cacophony
> And void as a debt summons served
> On a bankrupt—

although:

> the antiphony, still clamorous
> In tremolo,
> Like an afternoon, for shadows;
> And the winds
> the distant seven cannons invite us
> To a sonorous
> Ishthar's lament for Tammuz.

This is poetry that proceeds by a technique different from the early simple statements and sentiments of Chief Dennis Osadebay. Overall movement or logistics, as Mr Okigbo himself calls it, is gained here by the accumulated utterance, often separated by parenthesis and then woven together again by use of the old narrative "and," so that the phrasing sounds on the whole fragmentary, while the frequent repetitions, as if for breath, as well as the increasingly latinate and exotic words and names, make for a total effect that at best attains musicality and at worst prolixity.

Such language is not for sharing with the general public. Nor is the feeling that generates it; that too is very private. In the words of Grierson we may say of a poet like this that his "inspiration is caught from books." And his "imagination loves strange civilizations and scenery remote in time or space" to such an extent "he writes necessarily for a limited audience" since the poet "creates his own background from himself." As a matter of fact, Okigbo's *Lament for a suite of long-drums and seven tusks* recalls the Babylonian hymn *Lament of the Flutes for Tammuz*, sung at the secret rites of Adonis in Syria:

> At his vanishing away she lifts up a lament,
>   "Oh my child!!" at his vanishing away she lifts up a
>   lament;
> "My Damu!" at his vanishing away she lifts up a lament.
>   "My enchanter and priest!" at his vanishing away she lifts
>   up a lament,
> At the shining cedar, rooted in a spacious place,
>   In Eanna, above and below, she lifts up a lament.
> Like the lament that a house lifts up for its master, lifts she up
>   a lament,
>   Like the lament that a city lifts up for its lord, lifts she up a
>   lament,
> Her lament is the lament for a herb that grows not in the bed,
>   Her lament is the lament for the corn that grows not in the
>   ear,
> Her chamber is a possession that brings not forth a possession,
>   A weary woman, a weary child, forspent.
> Her lament is for a great river, where no willows grow,
>   Her lament is for a field, where corn and herbs grow not.
> Her lament is for a pool, where fishes grow not.
>   Her lament is for a thicket of reeds, where no reeds grow.
> Her lament is for woods, where tamarisks grow not.
>   Her lament is for a wilderness where no cypresses (?) grow.
> Her lament is for the depth of a garden of trees, where honey
>   and wine grow not.
> Her lament is for meadows, where no plants grow.
> Her lament is for a palace, where length of life grows not.

The distancing achieved here by Okigbo is of course relative, that is, the poem is obscure in inverse proportion with the ignorance of the reader vis-à-vis the poet. In other words, only the reader who posesses a field of reference corresponding in area to that evoked by this literary imagination will appreciate at once and fully the themes and allusions of this brand of poetry. But for many readers, this is asking a lot, and among the few who claim to understand and share with the poet his experience there is often disagreement. Mr O. R. Dathorne, for example, in a review of *Limits* in *Black Orpheus* Vol 1 No 15, pontificates: "*Silences*, which appeared in *Transition* 8 is the liturgy of the intending initiates who 'camp in a convent in the open' and *Limits*, exploring the penetralia of the unconscious state of non-being, narrates the progress towards nirvana"; while Mr Paul Theroux in his essay "Six Poets," reprinted in *Introduction to African Literature*, edited by Ulli Beier, is convinced that all Okigbo's poetry "can be considered from the point of view of all theologies, mythologies—each yields an interpretation." An omnipresent all-inclusive vista like this will of course include the subordinate ones of the Classics and the Bible which indeed are significant ones for Mr Okigbo.

Claims like these must emanate from true believers. Without being sceptical, it may safely be said that, seen against the performance and philosophy of Chief Dennis Osadebay, gone here are the public statements, the identification of personal problems with the struggles and aspirations of divers peoples just beginning then to recognize themselves as of a corporate body with one country, one destiny, one God. In this process Nigerian poetry has moved from the pages of daily newspapers, from the soapbox and platform of popular political meetings, held in cinema halls and the open market-place, to the private study of the individual and the exclusive confines of senior common-rooms.

In between these two extreme points and within the second segment of the national graph come Mr Okigbo's contemporaries like Mr Gabriel Okara and Mr Wole Soyinka, each in his own individual position. By our fourth rider, again in the words of Grierson, these poets in their performance and language "give poetry a setting not of literature and tradition but of nature and actuality." In so doing each carries a measure of communication, complete or partial, commensurate with the degree of validity successfully realized by him in the treatment of a particular subject. It is this concern for "nature and actuality" that provides the personal link between each and his audience, a much wider one than Mr Okigbo enjoys, if at the same time much narrower than Chief Osadebay's. The drums, pianos, changeling girl as well as storks and snows of Mr Okara are subjects directly recognizable to his audience. Similarly, the abiku, the accident-prone traveller and London "digs" hunter of Mr Soyinka, and I suppose my own night-sleeper, Agbor dancer, Fulani cattle, Ibadan and other evocations of that kind. These are natural concrete subjects realized for the reader in a personal memorable way by each poet in the unconscious hope of adding some fresh dimension to life.

Mr Okara, who of this group of poets occupies a position perhaps closest to Chief Osadebay's in the line of communication, provides in "One Night at Victoria Beach" probably the best evidence demonstrating the difference between earlier and later Nigerian poetry written in English:

> The wind comes rushing from the sea,
> the waves curling like mambas strike
> the sands and recoiling hiss in rage
> washing the Aladuras' feet pressing hard
> on the sand and with eyes fixed hard
> on what only hearts can see, they shouting
> pray, the Aladuras pray; and coming
> from booths behind, compelling highlife
> forces ears; and car lights startle pairs
> arm in arm passing washer-words back
> and forth like haggling sellers and buyers—

Now compare this with "Thoughts at the Victoria Beach: Lagos" by Chief Osadebay:

> The Waters stretched from the tropic shores
> And seemed to kiss the sunlit skies afar;
> The waves riding in Majesty,
> Glided to and fro like lords of the silvery bar.
> The off washed sands gave forth a smile
> To beautify the sphere and heaven extol;
> The noble palm and mangrove trees
> Stood with their heads aloft as the waters roll.

> Poor mortals—birds and beasts and men—
> Ran here and there in vain attempt to keep
> Their lives from the quenching winds of death,
> And sought in vain to solve the mysteries deep.

Both poems, though on the same subject, are worlds apart in language and attitude. The wind, waves, and sand of Mr Okara carry all the menace, urgency and movement of the snake; in the hands of Chief Osadebay they remain static, decorative motifs as those upon any painting from Nigeria's palm tree-and-lagoon school. In the composite scene of priests in prayer, a pub dinning with highlife music, a pair of lovers caught haggling like the fisherwomen on the beach, Mr Okara conjures up with a few strokes the changeless fair of human wishes. Here wares, precious and worthless, lie cheek by jowl, indistinguishable from one another. The serious and the comic are close neighbours, and in the claims and counter-claims of each for attention, there is no telling who is the central figure to the drama of life.

This human interest is hardly realized in concrete terms in the Osadebay poem. There, instead of an active drama of flux, we are fobbed off with a tableau of poor mortals running "to keep their lives from the quenching winds of death." And they stop at the same time to seek "in vain to solve the mysteries deep." Later, the poet says:

> My mind rummaged the Universe
> In search of why's and wherefores of life.

In that uncanny quest he discovers the Ruling Cause, the Universal Scheme as he had the Divine Origin, the Creative Principle, the Universal Source and the Universal Soul in the earlier poem "Awareness." These are big words and still bigger concepts. Together with the free use of capitals, an adjective to every noun and a regular resort to the devices of pathetic fallacy and elision, they represent the popular pastiche of an age when bombast was the best weapon in the armoury of the freedom fighter.

Bombast served on the one hand to prove Young Africa had become the equal, if not the better, of the Englishman at his own language, and on the other it served to confuse and befuddle the adulating mob. The woolly-thinking nationalist had only to fire off a string of -isms unknown to the masses and they went delirious with thunderous cheers for a hero who was a walking book. By the time of Mr Okara's entry into the field of poetry such gimmicks had quite exhausted themselves. Recluse or aristocrat, the poet no longer was of the people. Withdrawn into himself, his problems had become his own, his language one constantly geared to express issues personal to his own sensibility. The day of short circuit for both poet and public had set in.

With the later poets, the new dimension of achievement is perhaps not always realized sufficiently for the picture to be instantly visible to a large section of an already limited audience. My own "The Imprisonment of Obatala" provides a notorious example about which pupils and teachers alike are constantly writing in to the poet for exposition! And I dare say Mr Soyinka's new long poem "Idanre" will be regarded by many as carrying a similar if not stronger dose of constipation. Difficult though "The Imprisonment of Obatala" may be, it can be said without presumption that the poem demands no more of the reader than does Mr W. H. Auden's poem "Musée des Beaux Arts." Just as a knowledge of Greek mythology and of the painting by Brueghel is essential for anything like a full appreciation of the Auden poem, so is a knowledge of Yoruba mythology and of the painting by Susanne Wenger a considerable aid to an understanding of "The Imprisonment of Obatala." But obviously both Yoruba culture and Nigerian poet labour under a handicap beside Greek civilization and the maestro Auden. Add to this those two old disabilities first diagnosed by Dr I. A. Richards a quarter of a century ago and very rampant today among readers of poetry in Nigeria, by which I mean inhibition and a proneness to stock response, and the chances of the poet making the touchline are lame indeed.

To switch metaphors, it must be admitted that a culture curtain or culture gap does exist between poet and public, sometimes only partially so, particularly where the poet draws upon one individual subject or incident that can be programmed by way of brief notes, as in Mr Soyinka's "Abiku" and mine; at other times as in Mr Soyinka's "Idanre" where a poet is consciously exploiting a whole system of thought that is of occult nature, then the curtain or gap between the uninitiated public and the poet can be complete and prohibitive.

The average teacher of poetry in Nigeria, trained only in the appreciation of traditional English poetry, exhibits very strongly built-in reactions against modern Nigerian poetry, indeed against all modern poetry, and therefore cannot easily accommodate novelty. Possessed of reflexes conditioned as those of Pavlov's dog, he reacts readily to any item out of the double vistas of the Classics and the Bible that according to Grierson inform English poetry. But the slightest reference to the religion, history and oral traditions of his own peoples leaves him sniffling at once for explanations. With an audience of such listeners the break with the artist may be considered as complete. It is however not irreparable. For the public it is a matter of overcoming its own psychological and educational inertia; for the poet one for coming out of his often cryptic soul. (pp. 61-74)

> John Pepper Clark, "The Communication Line between Poet and Public," in his The Example of Shakespeare, *Northwestern University Press, 1970, pp. 61-75.*

CYPRIAN EKWENSI

[*Ekwensi is a Nigerian fiction writer whose works are among the most popular in African literature. Regarding his concept of African fiction, he has stated: "My own definition of African literature is literature based on African character and psychology. This means that the main theme may be anthropological, traditional, or modern, but the traits, temperaments, and reactions of the characters will be peculiarly African due to influence of tribe, culture, and history." In the following excerpt, Ekwensi discusses the writer's place in Nigerian society and the relationship of Nigerian literature to both world literature and African literature.*]

What useful need is served by Nigerian writing? To answer this we must go back to our own oral literature and think also of the folk-telling group under the trees in the moonlight. We must think of our musicians and ballad singers, our dramatists and carvers. For all literature is part of culture and literature can never usefully be isolated from culture as a whole.

In the days to which I refer, culture was part of life and not a fashionable pre-occupation. The carver carved for religious reasons, the folklorist told his tales to impart moral dictums to his listeners, and the musician lamented the passing of heroic warriors, or the death of some great ruler. Culture as a whole was integrated into normal living habits.

There is still a need, we find, for our own present-day society to absorb spiritual x-rays. Apparently these act like a kind of balm. But strive as we may, the days when the folklorist, the ballad singer and the carver were an integral part of life are gone. In those days one had no option but to be engulfed in the cultural stream. Now there is an option; one can choose to be outside it and still survive, even prosper. And so we have this product of the modern age: the Nigerian Writer.

Nigerian creative writers write in their own brand of English or in one of the many Nigerian languages. In a country whose strength lies in the diversity of its peoples and ideas it would be a pity if they should all write in just one language. Indeed, the writer in a Nigerian language reaches a far larger audience within the country than the writer in English whose main audience remains outside Nigeria. But to reach the world, there are only about five languages in which he can effectively do so. English and French are just two of them.

Some critics of Nigerian writing in English talk of losing the authentic African idiom, but one need only read novels written by West Indian writers—Samuel Selvon, Vidia Naipaul, Jan Carew, George Lamming—to see how pliable the language can be made to be and how the authentic "ring" of the original idiom still manages to come through and therefore differentiates African English from that written by say, an Oxford undergraduate.

In my many years of writing I found that the phrase "African Writing" as used by critics does not necessarily mean writing by Africans. There still lingers in certain minds the idea that unless the subject matter be ritual murder, circumcision or the racial situation, the novel is not "African." Nigerian Writers still have to face the problem of showing that ours is a harmonious and multi-racial society, stable and happy. The background may be different but a Nigerian novel can deal with such modern subjects as the project syncom and still be African.

My own definition of African writing is writing which reveals the psychology of the African. I use the term psychology very broadly to embrace reactions to situations and to the social order, religious beliefs, interpretation of moral codes, interrelationships within the family. These factors inter-acting, create the African character which gives its stamp to African writing. The subject matter is incidental.

African writing is unique. It can be written by no one else but the African. The writing intimately identifies itself with the people of Africa, their aspirations, failures, hopes, frustrations, their culture, history and soul. (pp. 217-18)

> Cyprian Ekwensi, "Problems of Nigerian Writers," in Nigeria Magazine, *No. 78, September, 1963, pp. 217-19.*

ADDITIONAL BIBLIOGRAPHY

Achebe, Chinua. *Morning Yet on Creation Day.* Garden City, N. Y.: Doubleday, 1975, 175 p.
    Collection of essays concerned with various aspects of Nigerian writing.

Adedeji, J(oel) A. "A Profile of Nigerian Theatre 1960-1970." *Nigeria Magazine,* Nos. 107-09 (December 1970-August 1971): 3-14.
    Traces the development of early English-language Nigerian drama.

———. "Oral Tradition and the Contemporary Theater in Nigeria." *Research in African Literatures* 2, No. 2 (Fall 1971): 134-49.
    Discusses how oral tradition is used in modern Nigerian drama.

———. "The Genesis of African Folkloric Literature." *Yale French Studies,* No. 53 (1976): 5-18.
    Examines African folklore and modern literature produced from it.

Anafulu, Joseph C. "Igbo Life and Art; Igbo Language & Literature: Selected Bibliographies." *The Conch* III, No. 2 (September 1971): 181-204.
    Lists works concerning the indigenous culture of the Igbo regions of Nigeria.

Babalola, (S.) Adeboye. *The Content and Form of Yoruba Ijala.* Oxford: Clarendon Press, 1966, 395 p.
    Discusses the Yoruba art of *Ijala,* or chanting to the god Ogun, and provides numerous examples of *Ijala* chants.

———. "The Role of Nigerian Languages and Literatures in Fostering National Cultural Identity." *Présence Africaine,* No. 94 (second quarterly 1975): 53-83.
    Argues that to encourage development of a national identity, Nigerian literature must be written in Nigerian languages.

Baldwin, Claudia. *Nigerian Literature: A Bibliography of Criticism, 1952-1976.* Boston: G. K. Hall & Co., 1980, 147 p.
    Lists criticism of Nigerian literature in general, criticism on specific authors, and anthologies of Nigerian literature.

Banham, Martin. "A Piece That We May Fairly Call Our Own." *Ibadan,* No. 12 (June 1961): 15-18.
    Discusses colonial influence on Nigerian writing and the emergence of a Nigerian national voice.

———. "The Beginnings of a Nigerian Literature in English." *Review of English Literature* 3, No. 2 (April 1962): 88-99.
    Examines the growing "culture emancipation" of Nigerian literature from that of England and Europe.

———. "Nigerian Dramatists in English and the Traditional Nigerian Theatre." In *Readings in Commonwealth Literature,* edited by William Walsh, pp. 135-41. Oxford: Clarendon Press, 1973.
    Surveys several modern Nigerian dramatic works and examines their relationship to traditional Nigerian theater.

Beier, Ulli. "Nigerian Literature." *Nigeria Magazine,* No. 66 (October 1966): 212-28.
    Survey of early English-language Nigerian literature.

Berrian, Albert H. "Aspects of the West African Novel." *CLA Journal* XIV, No. 1 (September 1970): 35-41.
    Discusses "nationalistic and counter-nationalistic sentiments" in African fiction.

Chinweizu, Onwuchekwa Jemie, and Ihechukwu Madubuike. "Towards the Decolonization of African Literature." *Okike,* No. 6 (December 1974): 11-27.
    First part of a two-part essay discussing European influences on African literature. In this part, which focuses on African poetry, the critics fault African poets for unaesthetic use of language, foreign and ambiguous imagery, and obscure meaning. (See entry for an excerpt of the second part, which focuses on European criticism of African writing.)

Chukwukere, B. I. "The Problem of Language in African Creative Writing." *African Literature Today,* No. 3 (1969): 15-26.
    Examines the achievements of African novelists writing in English and discusses specifically the writings of Cyprian Ekwensi and Chinua Achebe.

Collins, Harold R. "The Novel in Nigeria." In *Writers the Other Side of the Horizon: A Guide to Developing Literatures of the World,* edited by Priscilla Tyler, pp. 51-58. Champaign, Ill.: National Council of Teachers of English, 1964.
    Surveys the novels of Amos Tutuola, T. M. Aluko, Cyprian Ekwensi, Chinua Achebe, and Onuora Nzekwu.

Dathorne, O. R. "West African Novelists in English." In his *The Black Mind: A History of African Literature,* pp. 156-210. Minneapolis: University of Minnesota Press, 1974.

Surveys five major West African novelists and several newer novelists.

Drayton, Arthur D. "The Return to the Past in the Nigerian Novel." *Ibadan,* No. 10 (November 1960): 27-30.
    Discusses the various approaches to Nigerian history offered by early Nigerian novels.

Ebeogu, Afam. "The Poetry of Odia Ofeimum: An Example of Nigerian Avant-Garde Literature." *Okike,* No. 23 (February 1983): 81-94.
    Discusses the social protest poetry of Odia Ofeimum, comparing his work with that of other Nigerian avant-garde poets.

Egudu, R. N. "The Nigerian Literary Artist and His Society." *Ufahamu* IV, No. 1 (Spring 1973): 59-74.
    Examines the political and social content and implications of several works of Nigerian literature.

Galperina, Y. L. "Under the Sign of Ogun: The Young Writers of Nigeria, 1960-1965." *Africa in Soviet Studies* (1969): 162-83.
    Discusses political and social themes in Nigerian writing.

Hewitt, Julia Cuervo. "Yoruba Presence: From Nigerian Oral Literature to Contemporary Cuban Narrative." In *Voices from Under: Black Narrative in Latin America and the Caribbean,* edited by William Luis, pp. 65-85. Westport, Conn. and London: Greenwood Press, 1984.
    Discusses the retention of Yoruba oral narratives in the Americas and the appearance of important elements of these accounts in Cuban folklore.

Jones, Eldred. "Jungle Drums and Wailing Piano: West African Fiction and Poetry in English." *African Forum* 1, No. 4 (Spring 1966): 93-106.
    Examines the impact on West African literature of the increasing confrontation between the culture of Africa and those of other parts of the world.

King, Bruce, ed. *Introduction to Nigerian Literature.* New York: Africana Publishing Corporation, 1972, 216 p.
    Collection of fourteen essays on Nigerian oral and written literature.

Klima, Vladimir. *Modern Nigerian Literature.* Prague: Oriental Institute in Academia, 1969, 203 p.
    Surveys Nigerian long fiction and discusses issues, themes, and problems in Nigerian novels.

Laurence, Margaret. *Long Drums and Cannons: Nigerian Dramatists and Novelists.* New York and Washington: Frederick A. Praeger, 1969, 209 p.
    Examines the work of eleven prominent Nigerian writers.

Lindfors, Bernth. "African Vernacular Styles in Nigerian Fiction." *CLA Journal* IX, No. 3 (March 1966): 265-73.
    Surveys the vernacular styles developed by Chinua Achebe, Nkem Nwankwo, and Gabriel Okara.

———. *Folklore in Nigerian Literature.* New York: Africana Publishing Co., 1973, 178 p.
    Ten essays concerning the use of various aspects of oral tradition by Amos Tutuola, Chinua Achebe, Wole Soyinka, Cyprian Ekwensi, and other Nigerian writers.

———. "Achebe's Followers." *Revue de littérature comparée* 48, Nos. 3 and 4 (July-December 1974): 569-89.
    Discusses Nigerian writers influenced by Chinua Achebe's work.

———. *Early Nigerian Literature.* New York and London: Africana Publishing Co., 1982, 198 p.
    Examines the first literary efforts of several Nigerian writers and discusses early trends in popular Nigerian literature.

Moore, Gerald. "'Reintegration with the Lost Self': A Theme in Contemporary African Literature." *Revue de littérature comparée* 48, Nos. 3 and 4 (July-December 1974): 488-503.

Views several works of African literature as attempts by writers to reunite with, or establish some relationship with, the uncorrupted self they consider themselves to have been in childhood.

Nkosi, Lewis. "English-speaking West Africa: Synthesizing Past and Present." In *A Handbook of African Affairs*, edited by Helen Kitchen, pp. 285-95. New York: Frederick A. Praeger, 1964.
Discusses writers and attitudes toward literature in Nigeria and Ghana.

Nwachukinu-Agbada, J. O. J. "Content and Form in Nigerian Pidgin Poetry: The Pigdin Poetry of Aig-Imoukhuede and Mamman Vatsa." *Chelsea* 46 (1987): 91-105.
Discusses Nigerian poets who use pidgin English as an alternative to standard English in their work.

Obiechina, Emmanuel. *Culture, Tradition and Society in the West African Novel*. Cambridge: Cambridge University Press, 1975, 296 p.
Discusses the antecedents, appearance, and development of the novel in West Africa.

O'Flinn, J. P. "Towards a Sociology of the Nigerian Novel." *African Literature Today*, No. 7 (1975): 34-52.
Analyzes the reasons why novels began to be written in Nigeria and examines the effects of the Nigerian civil war on Nigerian novels.

Ogunba, Oyin. "Modern Drama in West Africa." In *Perspectives on African Literature*, edited by Christopher Heywood, pp. 81-105. New York: Africana Publishing Corporation, 1971.
Explores three categories of English-language drama written in West Africa: propagandistic drama, traditional drama, and satirical drama.

Ogungbesan, Kolawole. "Literature and Society in West Africa." *Africa Quarterly* XI, No. 3 (October-December 1971): 216-24.
Traces the development of West African written literatures in relation to the societies in which they are produced.

Okonkwo, Juliet I. "The Talented Woman in African Literature." *African Quarterly* XV, Nos. 1 and 2 (April-September 1975): 36-47.
Discusses protrayals of women in African literature that transcend mere "types."

Olatioye, Tayo. "Public Poetry of West Africa." *Ufahamu* VI, No. 1 (1975): 74-95.
Examines the relationship between politics and poetry in West Africa.

Omotoso, Kole. "The Missing Apex: A Search for the Audience." In *Publishing in Africa in the Seventies*, edited by Edwina Oluwasanmi, Eva McLean, and Hans Zell, pp. 251-61. Ile-Ife, Nigeria: University of Ife Press, 1975.
Discusses the lack of an African audience for African literature and proposes solutions to the problem.

———. "Politics, Propaganda, and Prostitution of Literature." *The Iowa Review* 7, Nos. 2 and 3 (Spring-Summer 1976): 238-45.
Contrasts the writings of the "first generation" of Nigerian writers, who published outside of Nigeria for a largely European and American audience, with those of a "new generation," who are publishing within Nigeria for a native audience.

Panter-Brick, S. K. "Fiction and Politics: The African Writer's Abdication." *The Journal of Commonwealth and Comparative Politics* XIII, No. 1 (March 1975): 79-86.
Traces the development of political disillusion and despair in African novels of the late 1960s and early 1970s.

Parry, John. "Nigerian Novelists." *Contemporary Review* 200 (July 1961): 377-81.
Surveys the novels of Amos Tutuola, Cyprian Ekwensi, and Chinua Achebe.

Povey, John (F.). "West African Drama in English." *Comparative Drama* 1, No. 1 (Spring 1967): 110-21.
Analyzes modern Nigerian drama as a continuation of indigenous African dramatic rituals.

———. "West African Poetry: Tradition and Change." *Africa Today* 15, No. 4 (August-September 1968): 5-7.
Discusses the conflict between past and present as exemplified by modern Nigerian poetry.

———. "The English Language of the Contemporary African Novel." *Critique* XI, No. 3 (1969): 79-96.
Considers various stylistic techniques developed by African writers to adapt the English language to African subject matter.

Priebe, Richard. "Escaping the Nightmare of History: The Development of a Mythic Consciousness in West African Literature." *Ariel* 4, No. 2 (April 1973): 55-67.
Analyzes the ways in which myth is used by various Nigerian writers.

Ravenscroft, Arthur. "An Introduction to West African Novels in English." *The Literature Criterion* X, No. 2 (Summer 1972): 38-56.
Surveys prominent West African novels written in English.

———. "Novels of Disillusion." In *Readings in Commonwealth Literature*, edited by William Walsh, pp. 186-205. Oxford: Clarendon Press, 1973.
Discusses several novels, including Chinua Achebe's *A Man of the People* and Wole Soyinka's *The Interpreters*, that express disillusion with the prospect of political change.

Roscoe, Adrian A. *Mother Is Gold: A Study in West African Literature*. Cambridge: Cambridge University Press, 1971, 273 p.
Discusses the origins of West African literature and examines West African poetry, prose, and drama, concluding that West African literature "reveals a steady advance towards literary independence."

Shelton, Austin J. "Behavior and Cultural Value in West African Stories: Literary Sources for the Study of Culture Contact." *Africa* XXXIV, No. 4 (October 1964): 353-59.
Analyzes the values promoted in four works by West African writers.

———. "The Articulation of Traditional and Modern in Igbo Literature." *The Conch* 1, No. 1 (March 1969): 30-52.
Surveys oral literature in the Igbo language as well as written literature in English by Igbo writers.

Soyinka, Wole. *Myth, Literature and the African World*. Cambridge: Cambridge University Press, 1976, 168 p.
Series of four lectures on literature and society given by Soyinka at Churchill College in Cambridge in 1973.

Taiwo, Oladele. "Nigerian Drama." In his *An Introduction to West African Literature*, pp. 68-83. Surrey, England: Nelson, 1967.
Discusses folk-opera, new drama, and the written play in the development of Nigerian drama.

———. "The Link between Tradition and Modern Experiences in the Nigerian Novel." *Studies in Black Literature* 5, No. 3 (Winter 1974): 11-16.
Discusses the attitudes toward African indigenous culture and relationships established between tradition and modern experience in the writings of Amos Tutuola, Tafawa Balewa, Chinua Achebe, Obi Egbuna, Nkem Nwankwo, and Gabriel Okara.

———. "The Use of Comedy in Nigerian Fiction." *The Literary Half-Yearly* XV, No. 2 (July 1974): 107-20.
Discusses developing forms of comedy in Nigerian literature as reactions to cultural and historical conditions during colonialism, independence, and civil war.

Tibble, Anne. "West Africa." In *African English Literature*, edited by Anne Tibble, 87-116. New York: October House, 1965.

Surveys the works of twenty West African poets, dramatists, and novelists.

"Writing in West Africa: A Chance to Adapt and to Experiment." *The Times Literary Supplement* (10 August 1962): 570-71.
Discusses Onitsha market literature, poetry in pidgin English and Krio, and other types of literature that "Africanize" the English language.

Tucker, Martin. "West Africa by Africans." In his *Africa in Modern Literature: A Survey of Contemporary Writing in English,* pp. 66-127. New York: Frederick Ungar Publishing Co., 1967.
Discusses the writings of Chinua Achebe, Cyprian Ekwensi, Onuora Nzekwu, Wole Soyinka, Thomas M. Aluko, Gabriel Okara, Christopher Okigbo, and William Conton.

Russian Symbolism

INTRODUCTION

Russian Symbolism was the dominant literary movement in Russia between 1900 and 1910. Inspired by the French literary movements of Symbolism and Decadence, which flourished during the 1880s and 1890s, the Russian Symbolists augmented the aesthetic and spiritual qualities of their counterparts in France with elements of Russian philosophy to produce the richest body of Russian literature since the "Golden Age" of the early nineteenth century. Like the French Symbolists, the Russian Symbolists were primarily concerned with the nature of a reality beyond the material world and sought to express the essence of that reality in their writings. Both groups rejected utilitarianism and formal conventions in literature in favor of highly personal artistic expression: their subjects commonly revolved around individual consciousness, while their style relied on symbol and suggestion to communicate meaning indirectly. The Russian Symbolists diverged from their French counterparts in their increasing emphasis on metaphysical concerns. Indeed, the Russian Symbolist movement is often considered to comprise two distinct "generations" of writers, with the first predominantly influenced by French Decadence, which is characterized by its morbid and perverse subject matter, and the second more strongly influenced by Russian and German philosophy and Orthodox Christianity. Critics note, however, that Russian Symbolism was a highly complex literary phenomenon and that the division into two generations is an extreme simplification of the development of Russian literature during this period.

Russian interest in French Symbolism first became evident in the early 1890s, when translations of works by Charles Baudelaire and other prominent poets associated with the French Symbolist movement began to appear in literary journals in Moscow and St. Petersburg. The beginning of the Russian movement is usually dated from 1892, when Dmitry Merezhkovsky delivered a series of lectures entitled "O prichinakh upadka i o novykh techeniyakh sovremmenoi russkoi literatury" ("On the Causes for the Decline and on New Currents in Contemporary Russian Literature"). Lamenting the dominance of "suffocating, deadly positivism" in contemporary literature, Merezhkovsky praised the works of the French Symbolists as a revitalizing force, commending in particular what he saw as "the three main elements of the new art: mystical contents, symbols, and a broadening of artistic sensitivity." During the next few years many previously unknown poets and fiction writers, including Konstantin Balmont, Zinaida Gippius, and Fyodor Sologub, began to publish works in the style of the French Decadents and Symbolists. Based on the concept that esoteric parallels exist between the material and spiritual worlds, and that insight into the latter can be attained by means of "symbols," this literature was created largely as an expression of transcendent vision. At the same time, it incorporated such qualities as perverse eroticism, morbidity, pessimism, occultism, and aggressive individualism, and was harshly criticized for its generally decadent spirit. In 1894 and 1895, Valery Bryusov, with a few friends, published three collections of their own poetry and translations of works by French and Belgian Symbolists under the title *Russki symvolisti* (*Russian Symbolists*). Writing under several pseudonyms to give the impression that Symbolism was a widespread movement in Russia, Bryusov created a scandal with his poetry (winning particular notoriety for his one-line poem "O cover your pale legs"), which was derided by critics for its sensual imagery and pretentiousness. Symbolist writing was also criticized as obscure, if not incomprehensible, due to its hermetic subjectivity and its technique of suggesting, rather than stating, subject matter. Widespread critical mockery, however, succeeded in focusing broad public attention on the new trend in Russian letters, attracting many new readers and imitators, and by the end of the decade Symbolism was established as an important artistic school under the unofficial leadership of Bryusov.

The turn of the century saw the emergence of the "second generation" of Russian Symbolists, the most prominent of whom were Vyacheslav Ivanov, Aleksandr Blok, and Andrey Bely. These writers repudiated the decadence of their predecessors, turning Symbolist technique instead to the exploration of metaphysical concerns in an attempt to synthesize art and religion. Propounding a view of the artist as visionary and possessor of higher knowledge, the second generation Symbolists utilized their works to herald the imminent end of Western civilization and the dawn of a new spiritual era. According to Renato Poggioli, their "emphatic claim that poetry and religion are one remains the most characteristic of all the original tenets of Russian Symbolism." By 1904, the aesthetic and spiritual ferment of Symbolism had inspired radical changes in both Russian literature and Russian intellectual life. The predominant utilitarianism of nineteenth-century Russian letters was succeeded by a Modernist sensibility, literary standards were elevated, and dozens of new writers were published. Between 1904 and 1909 Russian culture flourished, with the success of the Symbolist movement in literature paralleled by an aesthetic revival in the arts. Closely associated with the Symbolist writers were the artists of the Mir iskustva ("World of Art") group, who shared and furthered many of the Symbolists' artistic goals.

During this same period, however, the Symbolist movement itself became increasingly fragmented, as rival factions debated points of aesthetics and philosophy. These controversies reached a crisis in 1910, when writers who saw Symbolism as a purely aesthetic doctrine engaged in a virulent debate with those who espoused Symbolism as a religious worldview. These ideological differences, which proved irreconcilable, coincided with declining public interest in Symbolism. Although individual Symbolists continued to produce highly regarded works after 1910, the dominant position in Russian letters was assumed by writers of the avant-garde generation, such as the Acmeists and Futurists, who adopted the Symbolists' technical innovations while rejecting their mystical orientation.

Despite the relatively short duration of the Symbolist movement, the achievements of the period have exerted a profound influence on the development of Russian literature; as D. S. von Mohrenschildt wrote in 1938: "From the beginning of the century to the present day most of the best Russian prose and poetry, both Soviet and émigré, derives more or less directly from the Symbolist group." The most important accomplishments of individual Symbolists were in the genres of poetry, drama, and criticism, while the Symbolists' technical innovations, introspective concerns, and iconoclastic spirit initiated the Modernist revolution throughout the Russian arts. With the advent of an official literary school in Soviet Russia, Symbolism was proscribed as ideologically undesirable; as a result, the movement has received little scholarly attention and few editions of Symbolist works have been republished. Among Western critics, however, Russian Symbolism is viewed as both a significant movement in world literature and the richest period in twentieth-century Russian letters.

DOCTRINES AND MAJOR FIGURES

D. S. von MOHRENSCHILDT

[*A Russian-born American critic and historian, Mohrenschildt founded the* Russian Review *and served as that journal's editor from 1941 to 1974. In the following excerpt from an essay written in 1938, he relates the development of the Russian Symbolist movement and introduces its principal figures and artistic goals.*]

In Russia, as elsewhere in Europe, the Symbolist movement started as a reaction against the positivism and utilitarianism of the preceding epoch. The eighties and the early nineties were periods of pervading rationalistic thought. Dostoevski and Turgenev were dead. Tolstoi had withdrawn from literature to expound his dogmatic, rationalistic Christianity. The poetry of the so-called civic poets had sunk to the lowest possible level. It was the "autumnal" period of Russian literature.

The term *Symbolism* assumed by the Russian originators of the movement meant to them essentially what it meant to their French prototypes. It signified, first of all, that ordinary descriptive language failed to convey unique personal feelings and emotions; that these could be conveyed only suggestively through association of ideas and carefully constructed imagery. In the second place, it implied a transcendental world view, as expressed, for example, by Vladimir Soloviev, in the following lyric:

> Dear friend, do you not see
> That everything we see is but
> Reflections, shadows of that which is
> Invisible to our sight?
>
> Dear friend, do you not hear
> That life's reverberating noise
> Is but the altered echo of
> Transcendent harmonies?
>
> Dear friend, do you not sense
> That nothing in the world apart
> From this exists: that one heart speaks
> Mutely to another heart?

But in a deeper psychological sense Symbolism, in its origin, was a spontaneous revolt against all social and moral values. The leader of the new movement, Briusov, describes it in the following terms:

> The most valuable thing in the new art, is the eternal thirst, the anxious search. . . . The reign of positive science is passing. . . . We feel crowded, we are stifling, we can bear it no longer. We are oppressed by society's conventions; we are suffering from the conditional forms of morality, from the very conditions of knowledge, from all that is superimposed upon us.

It was a credo of nihilism, a complete denial of all values.

From the beginning Nietzsche and Dostoevski supplied the amoral and apolitical tone to the movement which later acquired a great variety of forms. But it was the group of French Symbolist and Parnassian poets which exercised in the nineties the greatest influence on the younger generation of Russian poets.

"We need a new tongue!" Rimbaud had cried in 1870, and in 1893 Briusov felt the impossibility of expressing in the language of Pushkin the sensibilities of the *fin de siècle*. The new poetry was to be a poetry of suggestive indefiniteness, of half-tones as opposed to the old poetry of full tones; its aim was "to hypnotize the reader and to invoke in him a certain mood." There were to be no distinctions between the perceptions of the different senses. "Les parfums, les couleurs, et les sons se répondent" ["perfumes, colors, and sounds correspond"] was learned from Baudelaire and Poe; the striving to approximate in poetry the effects of music, from Verlaine; the wilful obscurity and instrumentation of words, from Mallarmé.

Technically, classical Russian syllabism was abandoned. *Vers libre* and other verse forms and devices new to Russian prosody were introduced. But the most bizarre innovation was imagery: "windows of meaningless dreams," "the music of roses," "silken gardens," "violet hands on enamelled walls," and especially the line, "Oh, cover your pale feet!"—resulted in accusations of mystification or insanity. A hopeless pessimism

Portrait of Zinaida Gippius by L. Bakst, 1905. From Russian Literature Triquarterly, *No. 4, Fall, 1972. By permission of Ardis Publishers.*

pervaded the new poetry. Despair, boredom, and a "cosmic loneliness" were then the new poets' prevalent moods. Like most of their contemporaries in the West, they fled from the social and political life of their time and sought refuge in the unusual, the artificial, and the occult.

The new poetry was revolutionary for Russia. In form and content nothing could be further removed from it than the classicism of Pushkin, the Schilleresque romanticism of Lermontov, or the pallid didacticism of the "civic" poets. The cultivation of form for its own sake was an ideal foreign to Russian literature, and the consequent reaction of the new poets against the traditionally social and moral content of literature was more violent in Russia than elsewhere in Europe. Yet, while excessive pessimism, artificiality, and the striving for unusual effects were characteristic tendencies of contemporary European poetry, in Russia they represented a phase of adolescent rebellion and were not the expression of ripe age or lives as tragic as those of Baudelaire, Verlaine, and Rimbaud.

In the nineties, Briusov, Balmont, and Sologub were the three most original exponents of the new school. These three, particularly Briusov, fought the battle of Symbolism. In the next decade, with the outstanding talent of Blok and the amazing versatility of Bely, the battle was finally won, and the renaissance of Russian poetry was nearly accomplished.

Briusov was first to introduce and popularize the aesthetic ideals of Poe and Baudelaire. As one of the founders of the publishing house, Scorpion (1899), and the editor of the Symbolist's principal review, *Vesy (The Scales),* his influence on the younger generation of poets was paramount. But when Symbolism became generally accepted by the public and the critics, Briusov's place as leading theoretician of the movement was taken by Bely, for whom it remained to transform the Symbolist method into a complex metaphysical philosophy.

Briusov's own poetry fell short of the precepts he taught. His craftsmanship was always careful and often brilliant; but excessive erudition and lack of musical quality withheld it from the level of great poetry. At its best, it is gorgeous and majestic; at its worst, cold and rhetorical. His favorite themes were meditations on the history of civilizations, the mystical aspects of carnal love, and evocations of the life of modern industrial cities, similar to those of the Belgian poet, Verhaeren. Like his poetry, his prose is predominantly cold, erudite, academic. *The Fire Angel,* a semi-fantastic, historical novel of sixteenth century Germany, dealing with witchcraft trials and black magic, is a characteristic attempt to reproduce an historical epoch while at the same time endowing it with a general metaphysical significance.

Briusov was primarily an aesthetician. He had a sharp intelligence and a vast field of knowledge. His mystic and religious preoccupations were mostly ephemeral and academic, but his place in Russian literature as the initiator of an important literary movement is definitely assured. (pp. 1193-95)

Konstantin Balmont is a direct antithesis to Briusov. He was probably the least "intellectual" poet of the time, but he had a lyric gift of considerable spontaneity and power. His pantheistic outbursts of joy, his hymns, to the sun, fire and the planets, his exoticism, and above all his musicality and rhythmic inventions, expanded and enriched the poetic consciousness of the time. Balmont was all radiance, youth and exaltation—

> Like the sun ever youthful will we
> tenderly fondle flowers of flame.

His new message of daring and pagan joy found a quick response in the young generation:

> I would be bold, I would be daring
> And of the clustered grapes weave crowns. . .

were lines recited by thousands of his admirers.

Balmont's inspirations, like those of Briusov, were chiefly foreign: Wilde, Baudelaire, Verlaine, Shelley, and Whitman. The latter two he translated into Russian. Nietzsche's influence was also reflected in Balmont's amoralism and in his cult of "daring." His Symbolism was simple, non-metaphysical; the sun, the earth, fire, bright colors, and precious stones were his favorite images. Balmont's gift was purely lyric, and his best poems are found in the collection, *Let's Be as the Sun* (1903). (pp. 1195-96)

Intuitively to comprehend reality and to express it in symbols was to Sologub an inward necessity, not a literary theory. And we find in him a curious combination of extreme egotism and amoralism, with a transcendental world view entirely his own. He was probably the most essentially Russian among the decadents and the most decadent of the Russians. In all his poems, novels, stories, and fairy tales, dreams and reality coalesce. Sologub's poetry may be described as a circle, "a fiery circle," in the center of which is the "I." He had a sharp, burning sense of his ego, amounting to solipsism—"For in all and everything there is only I, and there is no one else, never was, and never will be."

The outward world to Sologub is madness, suffering, and cruelty; it has no meaning and no structure. The only escape is within one's self where one can find unity, calm, and beauty. In Sologub this idealism is wedded to a perverse sensuality and to something akin to satanism. God is identified with the creator of the earthly and evil world, Satan with the world of inward calm and beauty. Hence, his sarcasm and irony and perpetual references to sorcery, witches, and demons. Sologub's poetry is highly conscious and perfect in workmanship. He uses words in their secondary, not ordinary, sense, as symbols of his own Manichaean philosophy. Most of his poetry is quite untranslatable into English. In prose, Sologub's best known work in Russia and abroad is the semi-fantastic novel, *The Little Demon,* or in French, *Le démon mesquin.* It is both realistic and symbolical. Outwardly it is the life of a schoolmaster (Sologub was himself a schoolmaster) in a small provincial town who gradually becomes insane. The hero, Peredonov, is probably the most repulsive creation in all literature, and his name has entered the Russian language to express the acme of vulgarity, hypocrisy, and cruelty. Inwardly the novel is permeated with a lyric quality and the language is superb in its clarity and balance. When the critics, upon its appearance, identified the hero with the author, Sologub replied: "No, my dear friends, it is not I, it is you."

Sologub was closely associated with the second, metaphysical, stage of Russian Symbolism. There was little of the aesthete in him; he saw all art as symbolic, as "a window into eternity." Like all Russian Symbolists he remained non-political, an extreme individualist to the end. (pp. 1196-97)

Briusov, Balmont, and Sologub renovated Russian prosody and extended the range of poetic consciousness. But it was, as usual, the minor poets who best typified the atmosphere and sensibilities of the time. The life and work of a minor Symbolist, Alexander Dobroliubov, is an example, though perhaps extreme, of the Russian *fin de siècle.* This Russian prototype of Huysmans' Des Esseintes lived in a black coffin-shaped room, smoked hashish, and preached suicide to young school girls. Like Rimbaud, he soon abandoned literature altogether, joined a religious sect, and wandered on foot throughout Russia, in chains, clad as a simple peasant and living on alms. His collection of verse, entitled *Natura naturans—Natura naturata* met with ridicule, but Briusov recognized his talent and, after Dobroliubov's disappearance from literary circles, published a collected edition of his work. Dobroliubov's poetry and rhythmic prose evince a deeply mystic nature and a genuine lyric gift. He used, with considerable success, a variety of verse forms, especially *vers libre*, and experimented in writing symphonic compositions, with musical terms, such as *andante*, *scherzo* and *allegro*. (pp. 1197-98)

Closely associated with the tendencies exemplified by the early Symbolist poets was an aesthetic revival in the arts. The alliance of literature and the arts is best represented in Diaghilev's *Mir Iskustva (The World of Art)*. Although primarily devoted to art, this review (1898-1904) accepted contributions from the Symbolist poets and philosophers. An exceptionally brilliant group of artists contributed to *Mir Iskustva*: Benois, Bakst, Nouvel, Roerich, Sudeykin, Grabar, and others, over whom presided the guiding genius of its founder, Diaghilev. Reproductions of the best foreign and native painters and of original designs by contemporaries, exceptionally able art criticism and the high level of the prose and poetry—combined to make the magazine a unique cultural event. The aim of the review was to raise the standards of the artist, and to train the public to appreciate what was best in modern and ancient art.

No phase of art was left unaffected by the *Mir Iskustva* group of artists. Nikolai Roerich's mystical symbolism and Scythian researches; Benois' discovery of the Italian *barocco*, Bakst's orientalism, Sudeykin's colorful genre motifs—contributed later to the international success of the *Ballet russe*, and to the technical innovations of Tairov's and Meyerhold's productions. In literature the review awakened interest in mythology and folklore, both native and foreign. The best direct expression of Symbolism in painting was perhaps achieved by Roerich. No better illustrations than his symbolic paintings could have been provided for the poems of a Blok or a Soloviev.

Extreme individualism, combined with the cult of pure beauty, led to a complete emancipation of the artist from social duties and obligations. Nowhere in Europe has the abyss between the artist and society, with all that it implies, been so profound as in Russia at the end of the century. The poets of 1890-1900 despised all social and moral values, hated the mob, and needed no public. They sang of themselves and to themselves. Inevitably, like the majority of Western poets at the end of the century, they reached a psychological impasse and began to search for new values. Foreign culture, it was said, could not satisfy Russia, and the doctrine of art for art's sake was false; it was a snake biting its own tail. Literature and life must be reunited, and religion alone could accomplish this. The second phase of the Russian Symbolist movement combined the aestheticism of the preceding decade with powerful religious and mystical influences. It was a period of Messianism and of intense striving for a synthesis of art and religion.

Various influences produced this new orientation of Russian Symbolism. First came the Religious Philosophical Society founded by the Merezhkovskis in 1902. The meetings of this society attracted tremendous interest throughout Russia and were attended by all the most advanced representatives of the intellectual and artistic world. The Messianic rôle of Russia, Pan-Mongolism, the death of Western civilization, cosmic consciousness, and similar philosophical and metaphysical problems were the daily subjects of debates and discussions. Blok, Bely, Ivanov, and other Symbolist poets, as well as religious philosophers such as Rozanov and Berdyaev, were *habitués* of these meetings. Their effects upon literature were to divorce it even more completely from political and social actualities, and to make it in content predominantly esoteric and mystical.

Another source of inspiration for the second phase of Russian Symbolism was the personality and the teachings of Vladimir Soloviev (1853-1900), poet, mystic, theologian, one of the most original thinkers that Russia had produced. In the nineties Soloviev published a collection of poems which dealt with his mystical experiences. As a youth he had had several visions of Sophia, the Divine Wisdom, and later in his life he had a strange mystical communion with the Finnish lake Saima. These experiences he recorded in a series of lyrics, genuinely mystical throughout and characteristically interwoven with humorous irreverence. These lyrics exercised a powerful influence on subsequent Symbolist poets, especially on Blok and Bely.

To Soloviev more than to any other Symbolist the outward world was a *forêt de symboles* ["forest of symbols"]. Reality could be perceived neither by the senses nor by the intellect, but could only be revealed to us, and the poet for Soloviev was the sole possessor and revealer of reality. The poet's function could thus be expressed in the words of Rimbaud: "Le poète définirait la quantité d'inconnu s'éveillant en son temps, dans l'âme universelle" ["The poet should describe the unknown as it awakes in the universal soul during his time"].

We shall not go into Soloviev's gnostic philosophy and metaphysics, except for mentioning two of his ideas which held particular fascination for Russian Symbolists. One, an extension of the old Slavophile doctrine, was belief in the preordained superiority of the Russian nation and her special mission in bringing about a religious and cultural synthesis of the East and the West; the other, unrelated to the first, was a strangely concrete faith in the Antichrist, who also figured in Soloviev's work as a symbol of evil and the forerunner of universal destruction. The latter idea was accepted literally by Merezhkovski and was carried to absurdity by his public prophecies of the approaching end of the world. But to the greatest of the Symbolist poets, Blok, Soloviev's ideas served merely to reinforce his own intuitions of Russia's approaching catastrophe, which he foretold time and again with an uncanny foreknowledge. Another poet-philosopher, Ivanov, found in Soloviev the inspiration for his revolutionary philosophy, known as Mystical Anarchism, which preached revolt against all external conditions of life and complete emancipation of the spirit. During the early years of the revolution (1917-20) Soloviev again seems to have been the principal inspiration of another movement—the revolutionary Messianism of Ivanov-Razumniak, who welcomed Bolshevism as a purifying and destructive force, identifying it, at the same time, with Christianity.

The principal Symbolist organ of expression, the review *Vesy*, started in 1904 under the unofficial editorship of Briusov, was primarily an illustrated literary review with an excellent art department (Bakst, Roerich, Sudeykin, Bruneleschi), and its importance was to literature what Diaghilev's *Mir Iskustva* was to art. Throughout the review's existence (1904-1909) it published the bulk of the Symbolists' works and extensive foreign contributions by Verhaeren, René Ghil, Jean Moréas, Remy de Gourmont, and René Arcos. In outward appearance the review was more *decadent* than *Mir Iskustva*. Its title page was adorned with peacocks, and it abounded in Beardsleyesque illustrations.

An important feature of the review was its prose. It was predominantly involved and "ornamented," and in subject-matter tended toward the esoteric and occult. The new review was to be "a window into eternity." Its aim was to establish once for all that all art is fundamentally symbolic; that the ideal of art is not beauty, but religion, and that literature in Russia was, and always had been, "an outward expression of a living religious confession."

A characteristic article by Bely, "The Apocalypse of Russian Poetry," defines the new, apocalyptic rôle of Russian poetry. The Russian Symbolists, says Bely, are prophets; their function is to proclaim the end of the world's history and to gather the "faithful" for the coming universal struggle against Antichrist. The article is full of occult references to "The Beast," "The Eternal Spouse," "The Great Sinner"—the sources of which are Soloviev's utterances on the forthcoming Mongol conquest of Russia and the death of European civilization. Ellis, another abstruse theoretician of Russian Symbolism, considers the new movement the highest and most perfect manifestation of art. Symbolism, he believes, foreshadows a new form of human consciousness and a higher stage in the evolution of mankind.

The concept of a poet as a *Theurg*—a term devised by Soloviev to mean possessor of secret knowledge revealed to him alone—became prevalent in the years 1904-10. Literature as a whole was then identified with Symbolism, and the mission of the Russian Symbolists was to proclaim the death of Western civilization and the birth of a new era for mankind. *Vesy* became the principal purveyor of these views. But before the decade was over a reaction against the apocalyptic concept of Russian literature set in.

The greatest of the Symbolist poets was Alexander Blok (1880-1921). In his youth he was a disciple of Soloviev and one of the original members of Merezhkovski's Religious and Philosophical Society. His first collection of verse appeared in book form under the title *Verses about the Beautiful Lady* (1904). These poems record Blok's spiritual association with a person half real, half divine, who somewhat resembles Soloviev's Sophia and Dante's Beatrice. She is the object of Blok's ideal love. Like Soloviev's poems to Sophia, Blok's poems were drawn from mystic experiences and were based on dreams. The elusiveness and verbal melody of these lyrics is unsurpassed even by such masters of musical verse as Verlaine. Merezhkovski's group, particularly Bely, at once recognized in Blok a poet-prophet and awaited new mystic revelations. But the revelations never came.

Blok's ecstatic experiences which had produced these lyrics suddenly ceased. His next period was more earthly, midway between dream and reality. The Beautiful Lady became during this period the Stranger who appears in the famous poem by that name, seen now in a cheap café and only through the vapors of wine. The poem is hard in outline, condensed, and rich in rhythm and associations. Blok's poems of the middle period are rich and varied in content. They express his cosmic boredom, his religious resignation; some are realistic *genre* pictures, others bitterly ironic denunciations of his earlier mysticism and ideal love. All are marvels of concentration, balance, and vividness of presentation.

In an article published in 1910, and in a poem called "The Artist," Blok explains his process of creation. The first stage is a presentiment, a dream, a state of poetic trance; the second stage is when reason enters and drives out the dream; all that is left of it is embodied in concrete form—the poem is finished.

In Blok's poems, written from 1907 to 1916 and collected under the title of *Native Land*, Russia becomes the final object of his dreams. Here again is the Beautiful Lady, but now she is Russia. Through all these poems runs the prophecy of Russia's forthcoming suffering, purification, and ultimate glory. Again Blok is waiting for an Apocalypse, this time through blood and destruction.

The revolution of 1905 aroused in Blok a passing interest, but he was soon bored. Earthly politics were not his province. At the same time, his diary shows a tendency away from aesthetic and mystic idealism. He had tired of the empty verbosity of the Merezhkovski coterie. He wrote in 1907 to his mother:

> It is strange to contemplate a small group of Russian intelligentsia which, in the course of a decade, has been repeatedly changing a multitude of world views and which has split itself into some fifty hostile groups, while a vast nation has preserved its one monotonous and stubborn conception of God.

Despair is the central theme of Blok's poetry, and it was especially pronounced in the years preceding the revolution. He seems to have been constantly at war with himself, with his literary friends, and with the *bourgeois milieu,* of which he was a part and for whose spirit he had the utmost contempt. When the Bolshevik revolution came, Blok definitely welcomed it. "It seemed to him," his aunt records, "that the old world was really destroyed and that in its place there must appear something new and beautiful." To him the revolution meant the realization of his visions of apocalyptic glory for Russia. A reflection of this feeling is found in his greatest poem, *The Twelve,* written in January, 1918. The story is that of twelve red guardsmen patrolling in a blinding snowstorm the streets of revolutionary Petrograd, shooting and bullying the *bourgeoisie,* quarreling among themselves and shooting a girl by mistake. As they march onward into the raging blizzard, a hungry mongrel shambling at their heels, Christ appears at their head, leading them on. The symbolism of the poem is not difficult to understand, though there is considerable disagreement as to its interpretation. Quite inevitably Christ must stand for the salvation and glory of Russia, which Blok has prophesied for so many years. The blinding snowstorm represents the spirit of the destruction of all that men had once loved (the girl who was shot, the mangy dog, the priest, etc.). Salvation would come through purification of blood and suffering. The poem is a magnificent epic of the revolution. The music of the dissonances deliberately introduced, the variety of rhythms, precise and vivid imagery, the songs of the streets—produce effects of extraordinary vastness and beauty.

In the same month as *The Twelve* Blok wrote his last poem, "The Scythians," a powerful invective against the Western nations. After this poem he became silent. He seems to have lost faith in everything—in the Revolution, in Christ, in himself. He was tired and sick. Again, as in the case of the Beautiful Lady, his visions had betrayed him. Bolshevism was not the spiritual force that would renovate Russia, but was an extreme manifestation of Western materialism and complete mechanization of life. Gorki drew a terrible picture of the last days of Blok's life. His final utterances were a bitter denunciation of the intellect:

> The thing is that we have become too clever to believe in God and not strong enough to believe in ourselves. . . . The brain, the brain. . . . It is not an organ to be relied upon— it is monstrously developed. It is swelling like a goitre.

(pp. 1198-1203)

The extreme expression of Symbolist mentality is probably to be found in Andrey Bely (1880-1934). His whole life is a kaleidoscope of rapidly changing literary, philosophical, and metaphysical ideas and concepts. No one theorized so much about Symbolism or helped so much to make of it a metaphysical *Weltanschauung*. Although more complex and brilliant than Blok, he lacked the latter's emotional depth, and is regarded by some critics as a sort of metaphysical mountebank of Russian Symbolism. Like Blok, Bely makes his appearance in literature as an adept of Merezhkovski's group of mystics. He is anxiously awaiting with them the revelations of Sophia, the Feminine Hypostasis, which would transform the whole of life. Soloviev, Nietzsche, and later Steiner's Anthroposophy were Bely's principal influences throughout his life. Black magic, satanism and spiritism—everything esoteric and occult seems to have held irresistible fascination for him, especially in the early years of his literary career. But all these interests Bely takes in the spirit of a spoiled child receiving new toys; he plays with them for awhile, then discards them.

Bely's first, typically *fin de siècle* verse is indistinguishable from that of his contemporaries; but soon, under the influence of Soloviev's teachings, he embraced Symbolism as a general philosophy of life. His *Symphonies* (1902-1908), written in rhythmic prose, represent direct attempts to make literature approach to the conditions of music. They have several meanings and are written in a musically organized prose, with counterpoint and an elaborate system of movements, themes, and *leit-motifs*. Here, in addition to Poe and Verlaine, one discovers Maeterlinck, with his paraphernalia of swans, lotus, reeds, and canoes, Merezhkovski's prophesies about the end of the world, and above all Bely's own mystic exuberance and tomfoolery. The subject of the *Symphonies*, so far as can be discerned, is the great apocalyptic struggle between the good and the evil forces of the universe. The public and critics received the *Symphonies* with indignation and scorn, and for a time Bely replaced Briusov as the stock target for assaults on the new school.

In 1904 Bely revolted against Merezhkovski's Messianism, and in a series of poems ridiculed the latter's prophecies. All his former hopes and aspirations now ended in an insane asylum, as expressed, for example, in his poem, "Madman" (1904). In the following year, however, Bely, like so many other Symbolists, was carried away by the revolutionary movement, and for a while tried to reconcile it with Soloviev's mysticism. Failing in this, he temporarily became more sober and turned for inspiration to Russia. His poems, written between 1905-1908, are similar to those written during the same period by Blok. They are excellent *genre* poems dealing with hoboes, peasants, and various aspects of rustic life. In these Bely elaborates new rich rhymes, alliterations, assonances, and experiments with a variety of foreign and native verse forms. Some poems evince a sharp sense of humor, quite unusual in most Symbolists' poetry. But this period did not last very long. Beginning with the poem, "Despair" (1908), Bely lost his faith in Russia and the Russian people. Russia now is "all in a drunken mist." But his pessimism and despair have little in common with the tragic intensity of Blok. In Bely, even his most earnest poems are chiefly magnificent acrobatics in word and sound play. Simultaneously with his poetry, Bely wrote and published in *Vesy* and other contemporary reviews, his brilliant but fantastic critiques, interpreting Symbolism, and expounding his metaphysical views.

In 1909 Bely began to write a series of Symbolist novels, which are perhaps his greatest contributions to Russian literature. One of these novels, *St. Petersburg* (1913), can be regarded as typical of his ideology and prose style. *St. Petersburg* was written in the period when he was under the spell of Steiner's Anthroposophy—an occult science built on the assumption of exact parallelism between microcosm and macrocosm. This novel, like the rest of Bely's prose, has three different meanings: a philosophical-symbolical meaning, derived from a mixture of Soloviev's teachings and Steiner's Anthroposophy; a realistic, satirical meaning; and an obvious narrative one. Without a knowledge of Steiner the esoteric meaning escapes one. Nor is it essential, for the story itself is most absorbing. It centers about the bureaucrat, Ableukhov, and his revolutionary son. A terrorist revolutionary gives the son a bomb containing a clock-mechanism which is to explode within twenty-four hours and destroy his father. The suspense is excellently maintained by a detailed account of the twenty-four hours. In a general way, the son and the father are symbols of cosmic ideas. They represent the apocalyptic struggle of the East and the West, of Christ and Antichrist. Russia is the center of this vast, cosmic struggle, the outcome of which, Bely suggests, is as yet unknown, but will be revealed, "perhaps tomorrow, perhaps in five thousand years."

In *St. Petersburg,* as in his other prose works, Bely successfully combines penetrating realistic descriptions with his mystical symbolism. His strikingly original prose style has been variously termed "free-impressionistic" or "ornamented," and its best counterpart in the West is the style of James Joyce's *Ulysses.* The essential thing in Bely's style is its disjointed, rhythmic quality, its focusing of attention on sounds and association of words. At his best, as for example in the first part of *St. Petersburg,* he produces suggestive, vivid, and harmonious effects; at his worst, he degenerates into meaningless word-play, or worse still, hysteria. Nevertheless, ornamentation has had a vast effect on modern Russian prose style, and it is chiefly to Bely and several other Symbolists that the credit belongs for rendering it more varied and flexible.

Like Blok, Bely welcomed the Bolshevik revolution. In a series of poems, especially in the well-known and very mediocre poem, "Christ Is Risen" (1918), he identified Bolshevism with Christianity, more completely even than did Blok in *The Twelve.* Russia was now "the Messiah of the days to come." Purified through suffering, she was to discard obsolete Western civilization and give to the world a new Logos. During 1918-20, the terrible years of revolutionary slaughter and devastation, Bely became the center of the Messianic renaissance of Russia. He founded the *Volfila* (Free Philosophical Association) for the discussion of mystical metaphysics, he edited mystical miscellanies, lectured, taught poetry to the proletarian poets, and, with Gorki, became the most influential literary figure of the day. At the same time he began to reinterpret history in order to show that all civilizations had tended toward collectivism. In 1933, a year before his death, Bely published a volume of memoirs and recollections of the Symbolist group of 1900-1905. In this volume he depicted his former friends and colleagues as degenerates, and apparently tried to rehabilitate himself in the eyes of the Bolsheviks. In a brief foreword to this book, Kamenev has pointed out that the author, in spite of the many years of his association with the Communists, remains, as the memoirs clearly show, the most typical representative of the literary group he described—that group which, at the beginning of the century, anxiously awaited the fulfillment of Merezhkovski's prophecies concerning the end of the world.

The last major figure of Russian Symbolism to be discussed here, Vyacheslav Ivanov, poet-scholar, mystic and philosopher, exemplified the most harmonious blending of Western culture with Slavophile traditions. In the Western sense, Briusov and Ivanov were the most learned among the Symbolists. Unlike Briusov, Ivanov combined his great scholarship, particularly in the mystic religions of Greece, with a Christian mysticism, derived partly from Soloviev. The essential feature of his thought was a synthesis of Dionysus and Christ.

At the beginning of the century Ivanov's oddly archaic and rugged verse attracted the attention of the Symbolists. He joined their circles and was for a time under the influence of the Merezhkovskis. In 1905 he became a co-founder of an ephemeral revolutionary philosophy, known as Mystical Anarchism, which took as its motto Ivan Karamazov's words: "I accept God, but I do not accept His world." The creed was symptomatic of the intellectual hysteria of the time. It failed to attract a sufficient following and gradually disintegrated, but Ivanov in the meantime became the leader of the St. Petersburg Symbolists, while Briusov was their leader in Moscow.

From 1905 to 1911 Ivanov's apartment in St. Petersburg, known as "The Tower," became the central gathering place of the most advanced intellectuals of the day. New poets were read and criticized there, and metaphysical and mystical conversations lasted until early morning. All those who were privileged to attend their midnight gatherings describe them in their memoirs and letters as the outstanding intellectual experiences of their lives. The learning, poetic gift, and personal charm of the host made him the undisputed leader among the younger generation of Symbolists.

The period of "The Tower" coincided with Ivanov's best poetry, contained in the collection of *Cor Ardens*. His verse, very conscious and ornate, but rich in cadence and imagery, has been described as "Byzantine" and "Alexandrian." One of its features is Ivanov's fondness for substantives and passive verb forms, which, together with his elaborate imagery, often produced effects of magnificence and splendor. He greatly enriched the language through his use of archaisms, Greek idioms, and elaboration of new words. Ivanov's poetry is predominantly metaphysical and mystical. In conformity with his belief in a new mythological age, art in general (poetry in particular) was for him an expression of communal religious experience, and was to be judged by religious and mystical standards. His mysticism is thus non-individualistic like that of other contemporary Symbolists, but is wedded to a non-political group-sense. (pp. 1203-07)

An atmosphere of religious enthusiasm akin to that of early Christianity pervaded Russian literature during the first decade of the century. The lives and works of Blok, Bely, and Ivanov show clearly the evolution of Russian Symbolism from Western to native sources of inspiration. Symbolism, as interpreted and practiced by the second generation of Russian Symbolists, was no longer merely a method of creation, but a metaphysical world-view, representing the religious searchings and intuitions of the entire Russian people. The nihilism of the nineties, nourished chiefly by Western poets and philosophers, was replaced in the nineteen hundreds by a burning faith in a special mission preordained for Russia, and by an acute anxiety for her destiny. It was a faith inspired in part by national folklore and the early history of the country, partly by the works and personalities of Dostoevski and Soloviev.

The years 1904-10 were years of triumphant Symbolism. The Symbolists' ideals were at last accepted by the critics and public alike, and a host of new poets had arisen, who all started their careers as pupils of the older Symbolists. From the beginning of the century to the present day most of the best Russian prose and poetry, both Soviet and *émigré,* derives more or less directly from the Symbolist group. Symbolism had renovated the Russian language. Gone were the characteristic virtues of Pushkin's eighteenth-century style—precision, clarity, and the strictly logical use of words. The primary meaning of words was now largely subordinated to sound, and words acquired a new range of emotional values. A variety of new rhythms, rhyme-schemes, and verse forms became a permanent part of Russian prosody. Prose, too, underwent profound modifications. Through the use of popular colloquial language by Sologub, Bely, and other Symbolists, prose became immeasurably more flexible, less conventionally "literary," more rhythmic, and richer in emotional content. New effects were achieved in all branches of literature through a conscious blending of mystic idealism with ironic realism, of the real with the imaginary, of the grand with the prosaic, the best examples of which are found in the works of Blok, Bely, Sologub, or Remizov, who is perhaps the most original pupil of the Symbolist School. In addition to raising the standards of artistic workmanship, the Symbolists elevated the intellectual level of the society in which they lived to heights hitherto unknown to Russia. New cultural vistas were opened. In their thirst for universal knowledge, Briusov, Ivanov, Merezhkovski and religious philosophers, like Shestov and Berdyaev, exemplified the very spirit of the Italian Renaissance. No group of contemporary writers in Western Europe could be found to compare with the Russian Symbolists in learning and erudition of the most diversified kind. The Russian intelligentsia, through the Symbolists, became more European and at the same time more national.

Symbolism was not, of course, the only trend in Russian literature prior to the revolution. There were other literary groups, such as the Gorki-Andreev school of prose writers, the so-called civic poets, and the political writers of the Marxist school. But the aesthetes, mystics, and religious philosophers comprising the Symbolist group alone accomplished the remarkable renaissance in Russian art and literature.

The gradual disintegration of the Symbolist School begins with the discontinuance in 1909 of the review, *Vesy.* According to its editors, it was the triumph of their ideals that was the principal reason for the suspension of the review; its mission had been accomplished. Actually, however, ideological differences between its editors and a growing reaction of the intelligentsia against the mystical preoccupations of the Symbolists was the real cause for *Vesy's* suspension. New rival schools, as the Futurists and the Imagists, began to spring up. They attacked the Symbolists' idea of the mystical essence of poetry and refused to regard life as a forest of symbols. "We want to admire a rose," said the Imagists, "because it is beautiful, not because it is a symbol of mystical purity." The concept of the poet as seer and prophet was opposed now by the concept of him as an artisan and master of his craft.

Symbolism as an organized and self-conscious movement died in Russia shortly before the Communist revolution. It is one of the paradoxes of history that the Russian Symbolists, representing a society "refined beyond the point of civilization," rebelled against their own excessive culture and welcomed the Revolution. Some, as Blok and Bely, hoped that the Bolshevik revolution would destroy altogether the old *bourgeois* world and in its place would give rise to a new spiritual culture, more elemental and freer from the fetters of Western civilization. From the beginning of the century the Symbolists never ceased to prophesy the coming of a great catastrophe, which, after a period of wars and great suffering, would ultimately lead to a new, spiritually higher era for mankind. When the Bolshevik revolution came, the Symbolists quite inevitably saw in it the fulfillment of their prophecies. Aside from Balmont and the Merezhkovskis, all the principal Symbolists refused to leave Russia, although, naturally, they had nothing whatever in common with the aims and ideals of communism. The worst years of the civil war, terror, and destitution, were the period of Russia's purification through suffering, as symbolized in Blok's *The Twelve,* and prophesied two decades before by Soloviev—foreshadowed even earlier by Dostoevski. But as time went on, it became apparent that spiritual revival had not come. The realization that their prophecies were apparently false had different effects on each of the major Symbolists. Blok denounced the revolution; Sologub died prematurely, a broken man; Briusov entered the Communist Party; Bely and Ivanov, while doing lip service to Marx and Lenin, continued, for a time at least, to live in vague hopes of the millennium. Not one of the Symbolists became a true Marxist—not even Briusov. Most of them ceased to write or produced only inferior work. Although, technically, Symbolism is still a live influence in Russian contemporary literature, its metaphysics is long since gone. (pp. 1207-09)

> D. S. von Mohrenschildt, "The Russian Symbolist Movement," in PMLA, Vol. LIII, No. 4, December, 1938, pp. 1193-1209.

RENATO POGGIOLI

[*Poggioli was an Italian-born American critic and translator. Much of his critical writing is concerned with Russian literature, including* The Poets of Russia: 1890-1930 *(1960), which is considered one of the most important examinations of this literary era. In the following excerpt from that work, he examines the second generation of Russian Symbolists, discussing their poetic and philosophical views, the influence of Vladimir Solovyev on the development of Russian Symbolist philosophy, and the relationship of Russian Symbolism to Decadence, French Symbolism, and other literary movements.*]

Out of the midst of Russian culture as it had matured from the end of the nineteenth century, there appeared at the beginning of the twentieth three men who, after having developed in isolation and silence, proclaimed themselves the prophets of a new faith, the harbingers of a new truth. For their creed or message they took the old name of Symbolism, an abstract term which the poets of the preceding generation had used less frequently than the more concrete Symbolist or Symbolists, and which the new men understood in other ways than their elders had. Yet the very fact that these three new poets, and all those who joined them, called themselves by the same label seems to imply that, while aware of being the announcers of a new tiding, they still felt themselves to be the heirs of the poets who had immediately preceded them. This is why it fell not upon the poets of either generation, whom the contemporary observers distinguished merely as old and new Symbolists, but to later critics to differentiate them sharply enough to designate the newcomers as Symbolists, and their predecessors as Decadents. The new group assigned itself the task of reinterpreting Symbolism in terms both more national and more universal: its three leaders, who were Vjacheslav Ivanov, Andrej Belyj, and Aleksandr Blok, made the bold attempt to supply Russian Symbolism with that mystical intuition and metaphysical insight which, all their theoretical declarations notwithstanding,

Dmitry Merezhkovsky. The Bettmann Archive, Inc.

earlier Symbolists both Russian and Western, perhaps with the exception of Baudelaire, had conspicuously lacked.

These three men, who grew and ripened at first without knowing each other—Ivanov in Germany, Belyj in Moscow, Blok in Petersburg—drew their doctrines from many, varied sources. Ivanov, the oldest of the three, had learned some of his lessons from Nietzsche; but later, like his two younger colleagues, he turned to a nearer, and perhaps fresher, spring: to the theological speculations of a Russian thinker of the end of the century, Vladimir Solov'ev. Brjusov and his school had already shifted the attention of Russian poetry toward the recent French example, and, although in lesser measure, toward other modern European experiences, but these new Symbolists spread their nets deeper and farther and drew their inspiration also from the poets of nineteenth-century Germany, especially from such early Romantics as Novalis. Poetry was their main, but not exclusive, concern, precisely because they placed it at the center of all cultural activity and considered it not the handmaid, but the sister, of theology. This is why, through or beyond the ways of poetry, they turned to all sorts of religious experience, in its cultivated as well as in its uncultivated forms, showing sympathy, interest, or at least curiosity for the strange and wild beliefs of the Russian dissenters, as well as for the Neoplatonic tradition or medieval mysticism. From the heretical eschatology of both sectarians and mystics they developed a messianism or a millenarianism of their own, conceiving the hope, both fanatic and vague, that they would witness in their own lifetime a Second Coming, or a New Advent.

From all these complex and perplexing doctrines they wrung an oppressing and obsessive sense of the haunting presence of supernatural powers, either good or evil, even in the world of everyday reality; and they viewed poetry both as a passive, almost mediumistic instrument, registering the emanation or irradiation of that presence, and as an active spiritual force, liturgical and theurgical in essence, producing epiphanies and portents. For them, poetic inspiration could derive only from religious initiation and ecstatic vision; this is why they conceived of their group as if it were a monastic order or a mystical sect rather than a literary school. Since they came at the right time, when idealism and spiritualism were again becoming fashionable, when a large section of the Russian intelligentsia felt perplexed and bewildered longing not so much for a revival of the ancestral faith as for sentimental consolations and emotional thrills, they found an audience ready to listen to their siren voices and to be seduced by them. Their novelty surprised and impressed even those among their elders who could not change their ways and follow them or their new path; Brjusov himself greeted the new poets as "seers," although he considered them, to use the double title of one of his volumes of collected essays, as being both "near" to, and "distant" from, himself.

Brjusov would certainly have been unable to accept the creed of the new poets, whose gospel has often been summed up, by themselves and their critics, in the closing lines of Goethe's *Faust*.

> Alles Vergängliche
> ist nur ein Gleichniss;
> das Unzulängliche
> hier wird's Ereigniss;
> das Unbeschreibliche
> hier ist's getan;
> das Ewig-Weibliche
> zieht uns hinan.

> ["Transitory things are symbolical only. Here the inadequate finds its fulfillment. The not expressible is here made manifest. The eternal in woman is the gleam we follow."—Translated by Barker Fairley.]

It is indeed true that Ivanov, Belyj, and Blok started with the belief that even a passing phenomenon may be understood as a noumenon or as a highly significant symbol; that the unreal, or, as they would have said, the ideal, may become act or deed; that even the ineffable may find, especially in poetry, voice and speech; and, above all, that through the mediation and the contemplation of the principle of love, of the Eternal Feminine, man may ascend to high heaven from this low world. The last of these beliefs was, as a matter of fact, the cornerstone of their faith; yet they drew it not so much from Goethe as from other poetic and mystical precedents, the most immediate and influential of which were the visions and the fantasies of Vladimir Solov'ev, the only modern Russian whom, along with Dostoevskij, they considered their apostle and master.

The brief span of Vladimir Solov'ev's life occupied less than the whole of the second half of the nineteenth century, since he was born in 1853 and died in 1900. Thus he practically belonged to the same generation as Chekhov, although the latter, in thought as well as in deed, represented that generation far more typically than Solov'ev. While Chekhov lived in the present, as a man of his own time and a child of the earth, Solov'ev lived either in the past or in the future, as a surviving ghost or as an untimely prophet. His great merit, or, more simply, his natural task, which endeared him forever to the Symbolists, was that of denying the main cultural trends of his own positivistic and ideological age, and of standing almost alone for the very spiritual values which both the leaders and

the camp followers of Russian late-nineteenth-century thought had stood against. Even his adversaries were willing to recognize that Solov'ev was perhaps the first Russian thinker who was also a philosopher in the technical sense of the term, and that he had shaped a system as consistent and compact as any of the constructions of Western speculative thought. The Symbolists, however, did not admire and praise him for this, but rather for his extravagant mystical temper, for the transcendental digressions of his mind from the rational path. They paid tribute to him for having replaced nineteenth-century utilitarianism and materialism with a new idealism, not philosophical, but visionary and apocalyptic in temper. Solov'ev had indeed broken the tradition which had made philosophy the handmaid of politics and sociology, to make it again the handmaid of theology, although in a new and different sense. In so doing, Solov'ev had not only prepared the ground for Russian Symbolism, but had also laid the foundation for a school of religious thinkers which, like a new Platonic Academy, survived the downfall of Holy Russia and of the tsarist empire, by finding a new abode in the West and flourishing even in exile.

All of Solov'ev's disciples, whether avowed or not, followed his example in making the City of God the main object of their speculative concern. Like their master, and their Symbolist brethren, they refused, however, to believe that no reconciliation is possible between the City of God and the City of Man; and in the messianic spirit of the Russian tradition, a spirit which they shared with their godless adversaries, with all those who believed in the secular religions of either revolution or progress, they still held fast to the hope that an ideal or heavenly order would sooner or later rule even the world of man.... [Some] of them developed this hope into what they called "the religion of the Holy Ghost," which consisted in the apocalyptic expectation of the imminent advent of a third and final phase in human and sacred history: a phase to be ruled by the third person of the Trinity as the previous ones, the Biblical and the evangelical, had been ruled by the other two. This expectation was often tied to the old myth of Moscow as the Third Rome, to the belief that Russia was to become the last of the three kingdoms of the spirit. It may not be amiss to recall at this point that the first Russian who developed that myth, the early sixteenth-century cleric Filofej of Pskov, had derived the idea of the three Romes from the heterodox doctrines of an Italian mystic of the twelfth century, Joachim of Flora, who, like Solov'ev and his poetic disciples, had prophesied that the third person of the Trinity would sway the last age of the world in womanly form. All too many of Solov'ev's followers treated that incarnation as an allegory of Holy Russia, thus falling back on the Slavophile idealization of Orthodoxy, on a national messianism as narrow-minded as Dostoevskij's. When understood in this restricted sense, the religion of the Holy Ghost represented at least a partial deviation from the teachings of its master, who conceived the future mission of Russia in cosmopolitan terms, dreaming of the reunion of all Christian churches, and revealing outright Catholic sympathies just before his death. The only writer who was to follow, up to its final issue, the same path, was Vjacheslav Ivanov, whose ultimate conversion to the faith of Rome, determined as it was by the shattering impact of the Revolution and its aftermath, must still be viewed as the logical consequence of the dream of a really ecumenical church.

It was the same religious universalism, as well as a sane mistrust in the reactionary and nationalistic belief that the Russians were the only "god-bearing people" on earth, that had led

Solov'ev to write the poem significantly entitled *Ex Oriente Lux,* ending with the famous question whether the Russia of the future would conquer the West with the sword or with the cross, or, in the poet's words, whether she would represent the East of Xerxes or the East of Christ. If Solov'ev was perhaps still willing to give that question an answer of doubtful hope, Aleksandr Blok would later give instead the reply of despair, when in the revolutionary poem *The Scythians* he proclaimed that Red Russia, seeing that the West was unwilling to join hands with her, had no alternative but to ruin Western civilization by opening the gates defending Europe from Asiatic barbarism.

All the mystical and idealistic writers of the beginning of the century found in Solov'ev's writings not only their Gospel, but also their Apocalypse. Thus, for instance, the strange work he entitled *Three Conversations on War, Progress, and the End of World History* (1899-1900) is but a prophecy of the imminent coming of the Antichrist, which was to be literally accepted by Dmitrij Merezhkovskij, who based on that prophecy his own absurd philosophy of history. Others sought in Solov'ev's work a justification for their attempt to build a learned, syncretic religion, grounded on the hypothesis that Christianity had been foreshadowed in the faiths of many nations and ages, especially of Oriental antiquity. As for the Symbolists, particularly if they aspired to a prophetic role, like Vjacheslav Ivanov, they were mainly attracted by the two main utopias of Solov'ev's thought. The first of them, which took the name of "free theosophy," consisted in the belief that the mind could and should unify all fields of knowledge and establish a synthesis of science, philosophy, and theology. The other, which took the name of "free theocracy," was but a projection of the hope that human society could and should change into a mystical commonwealth, under the suzerainty of the Holy Ghost. Yet, even more than by Solov'ev's intellectual and moral utopias, the Symbolists were influenced by his mystical and erotic myths.

The most important of these myths is that of the corporality of the spirit, within which Solov'ev included such different notions as the Christian dogma of the double nature of Jesus, as "son of man" and "son of God"; the worship of His Mother; and the allegory of the Church as the bride, or the body, of Christ. It was within the framework of this myth that Solov'ev introduced his own version of the Dostoevskian antithesis between the "god-man" and the "man-god." It is not the person but the human race which will redeem again the world once redeemed by the sacrifice of the man-god. The advent of what Solov'ev called "god-mankind" was for him the Second Coming, or another incarnation of the Godhead; and it was on the expectation of this reincarnation, of this return of the dove of the spirit, that he based the chiliastic utopia of his own "free theocracy." In brief, Solov'ev founded both his evangelical and his apocalyptic beliefs on the cornerstone of the famous utterance in the Gospel of St. John: "and the Word was made flesh."

Solov'ev was not only the philosopher or the theologian of the Incarnation, but its mystic or seer. As such, he went beyond the letter and the spirit of that dogma and unfolded from it the hypothesis that the whole of creation is ruled by a single, all-embracing feminine principle. It was through that principle that Solov'ev introduced within the abstract scheme of his all-too-idealistic system of thought the intuition of the universal presence of the vital power of love, which generates life and conquers death. According to the spontaneous contradictions

of his thought, Solov'ev now would consider that power as pure nature, as the energetic matter which the Greeks named ὕλη; and now would spiritualize and personify it into a mystical and divine feminine being, to which he gave the Gnostic name of Sophia. Sophia was for him what the mystics of Neoplatonism would have called the World-Soul. Solov'ev sometimes treated her as if she were another incarnation of the Holy Ghost, or even a hypostasis of the Mother of God; and he raised her, in his own version of Marian worship, almost to the status of a fourth person of the Godhead. At any rate, Solov'ev built around the figure or person of Sophia a theogonic and cosmogonic conception, which was but another variant of his doctrine of the identity of Word and World, of his notion of the spirituality of matter and of the materiality of the spirit.

The cult of Sophia was bound to become the main motif of Solov'ev's poetry, and, after him, of Russian Symbolism. His poetry is but a constant invocation of her name or persistent evocation of her image. In his poems he depicts Sophia after the "woman clothed with sun" of the Book of Revelation, exalting her mystical presence in man's and life's nether world. The poet, who calls her the Eternal Friend, seems at times to believe that she is already on her way to bless mankind forever with her advent: "Know that now the Eternal Feminine here descends in a body incorruptible." Solov'ev celebrated Sophia not only in his lyrics, but also in his letters, as well as in other literary works, the most important of which is perhaps the narrative poem *Three Meetings* (1899). Here he reported the three apparitions of Sophia, as they had taken place within his own mystical experience, or rather, within the objective reality of his life. Solov'ev boasted of the same mystical precocity as Dante (who was nine years old when he had the first physical and spiritual revelation of his Beatrice), and claimed to have witnessed Sophia's earliest visitation when, still a child, he had recognized her image over the altar of a Moscow church. Her second appearance occurred, of all places, in the library of the British Museum; the third and last, in the Egyptian desert, near the Pyramids. Yet *Three Meetings* is not merely a transcription of three ecstatic visions or moments of grace; it is also a strange document of their very opposite, as well as of the nihilistic side of Solov'ev's enigmatic character. There and elsewhere Solov'ev revealed the tendency to put his own mystical insight to the acid test not only of a skeptical incredulity, but even of a blasphemous cynicism. In this, too, Solov'ev anticipated that sense of revulsion which Blok was later to feel for the object of his worship, and which led him to replace adoration with mockery, and idolatry with iconoclasm.

Solov'ev's poetry helped the Russian Symbolists not only to build the religion of their sect, but also to develop the poetics of their school. In this sense, its influence fully coincided with the literary theories of the foreign poets whom the earlier Russian Symbolists had taken as their own masters. Independently from them, and with great literalness and emphasis, Solov'ev had stated in verse the view that poetry is the highest of all instruments of vision. Poetry was for him both the vessel and the vehicle of that "prophetic dream" which he viewed as the only means "to discover eternal truth." Only such a dream could help man to reconcile into a new harmony all the contrasting aspects of reality, or, in the poet's words, "to marry the white lily to the crimson rose." Solov'ev held the revelations of poetry to be both possible and necessary precisely because he believed that our perceptions of the physical world, even if only as dim reflections in a dark mirror, foreshadow a higher spiritual reality which we could not reach merely by means of our senses or our thoughts. Dear Friend, asks Solov'ev rhetorically in one of his poems, don't you see that all which appears to us is but a shadow of what escapes our sight? Don't you know that the visible is but a ray of the invisible, that the wordless dialogue of two hearts is but an expression of the ineffable? It is evident that such a mystical and poetic doctrine implied the use of that vague device which many others, before and after him, defined by the term "symbol," even though Solov'ev hardly used that word.

The modern reader of Solov'ev's poetry fails to be deeply impressed by it, and may find all too obsessive the conventional Nordic background of his poems, perennially oppressed by the whiteness of their clouds, mists, and snowstorms; constantly haunted by the presence of too many phantoms or ghosts; all too feebly illuminated by the gemlike flicker of dying embers which give neither light nor heat. Yet the lover of Russian verse will recognize in them the anticipations of the elemental landscapes and of the ecstatic imagery which are such a great part of the poetry of the early Blok. Still, despite the varied manifestations of Solov'ev's influence, nothing was bound to affect the poets of Russian Symbolism as much as the enigmatic feminine being which had inhabited the wastelands of his imagination. The figure who Solov'ev had called the Eternal Friend would reappear in Blok's early work under the name of the Beautiful Lady. Blok, Belyj, and Ivanov would make her not only the subject of their poetry, but also the object of their worship. And it was more than a coincidence that the youngest of all the members of the new cenacle, who was to join hands with Blok and Belyj, forming with them another triad, was the nephew of the philosopher and his spiritual heir Sergej Solov'ev. The latter heeded more fully than the master or any other disciple the mystical call, and after having written a beautiful biography of his uncle and two charming books of poems, left forever the career of letters for the vocation of the priesthood.

It was not the first time in literary history, from the Provençal "courts of love" and Dante's *fedeli d'amore* ["followers of love"] to Novalis or to the Pre-Raphaelite Brotherhood, that poetry had turned into an apotheosis of womanhood, and that poets had acted as if they were the sacred servants of that cult. The poetry of erotic mysticism, which may be viewed as an offshoot of both Christian dogmas and Eastern heresies, whether understood allegorically or not, had always tended to shape itself into schools which were also sects. The reason for this may well be seen in those Gnostic or Manichaean doctrines and attitudes which in his book *L'Amour et l'Occident* Denis de Rougemont considers the original springs of the poetry of the troubadours, of the medieval romances, and of the modern mystique of passion and love. Still, among the poets of our time, none took the ritual of initiation and the liturgy of revelation so seriously as the founders of Russian Symbolism. They undertook their task with such single-minded devotion and simple-minded literalness that every one of them deserves being called a "knight-monk," to use the label which Blok was later to coin for their master Solov'ev. Yet the definition applies particularly well to Aleksandr Blok himself, who, in the naïveté of his youthful idealism, seemed to many also a reincarnation of the hero of a famous poem by Pushkin, the "poor knight" symbolizing that poverty and purity of spirit without which no quest after the Holy Grail can succeed. Dostoevskij had used Pushkin's "poor knight" as an emblem for the protagonist of *The Idiot,* the quixotic and Christ-like Prince Myshkin, and Blok resembled that character also, being like him endowed with a visionary gift while devoid of any power to redeem or to heal.

If Blok was the "seer" of the new faith, Belyj was the theologian who formulated its dogmas, and Sergej Solov'ev the priest who performed its rites. When Blok married Ljubov' Mendeleeva, whose first name means "love" (and who, as her surname indicates, was the daughter of the great Russian scientist who founded modern chemistry, the discoverer of the periodic law and the framer of the periodic table of the elements), Belyj interpreted that private event in symbolic and mythical terms, as the alliance of poetry with the religion of love and with the magic of science. Blok's friends read her patronymic, Dmitrievna, as if it meant daughter of Demetra, instead of daughter of Dmitrij, and they saw in this the token of another spiritual harmony, joining poetry with the earth spirit, and pledging a new cosmic order.

The early Russian Symbolists were attracted not only by religious and metaphysical hopes, but also by less unworldly promises. They really believed that the return of the dove of the spirit would announce the emergence of a new human world from the receding waters of history's deluge. Blok expressed this expectation by hailing the "dawns" (*Zori*) of a new era, all the mystical signs which seemed to forebode the ascent of a brighter sun, the coming of a day without clouds. Yet the "dawns" of Blok were bound to be as imaginary and deceitful as the far more modest and personal dreams haunting the imagination of some of Chekhov's characters, and which Chekhov himself had called "mirages." From their provincial isolation, Chekhov's "three sisters" dream simply of a richer existence for people like themselves, which could include the possibility of a journey to Moscow, or the certainty of a change for the better in the near future. But the three sisters realize that even such simple hopes will remain forever mere "mirages," and content themselves with thinking that "life will be better three hundred years from now."

The fanciful "dawns" of those three Symbolist spiritual brothers, as a matter of fact, showed themselves to be even far more human, sentimental, and private "mirages." One could even say that what the poets of Russian Symbolism took as dawns, as the announcement of daybreak, were instead, as they later realized, twilights, revealing the agony of a moribund hour. Yet at first Blok, Belyj, and Sergej Solov'ev mistook the sunset for the sunrise; at least for a while they deeply believed in their own apocalyptic and eschatological dreams, without ever doubting that the hoped-for palingenesis was at hand. Like early Christians, they expected to see the Kingdom of God in their lifetime. In the approaching descent upon earth of the feminine incarnation of the cosmic and divine order, they anticipated a radical renewal of Russian life, the conversion, or even the rebirth, of the Russian soul, the transformation of Russia into the Zion of a new world.

The political and religious reaction which followed in the wake of the "little revolution" of 1905, which was in its turn stirred by the defeat of tsarist Russia in the war with Japan, was destined, however, to shatter this dream. Blok, with his almost mediumistic sense of the invisible forces which were changing the world around him, had started losing his faith earlier, partly under the influence of personal and private factors, or, more simply, of his marriage to Ljubov' Mendeleeva, in whom he now saw a real woman, rather than the incarnation of the Eternal Feminine which his friends still insisted on seeing. For this reason, Sergej Solov'ev and Andrej Belyj had considered him a traitor, and yet Belyj was destined a few years later to follow his former friend on the path of despair and disbelief. Belyj was, however, the first of the two to try to bring back the religion of their youth, by replacing the spiritual worship of the heavenly Sophia with a more earthly and humble cult, which found its object in the feminine personification of an all-sinful and all-suffering mother—Russia. In this, naturally and spontaneously, Blok was to follow Belyj's lead; and, several years later, after the upheaval of 1917, both of them found for a while in the Revolution a resurrection of their old dreams.

Of the three masters of Russian Symbolism, Vjacheslav Ivanov was the only one who, while often changing attitude or outlook, succeeded in keeping faith, if not in the religion of Sophia at least in the Symbolist ideal. At the end of his life . . . he saved that ideal and all the hopes connected with it by a return to traditional religion and by a conversion to the Roman Church. Even before that return and that conversion, he had succeeded in preserving the bond between poetry and religion, precisely because he conceived of that bond in less literal and immediate terms than the other members of his sect. In brief, he saw in poetry not so much a mystical or speculative instrument, able to do religion's work by itself, as a special mirror reflecting religious experience in emblematic images and allegorical visions. Thus Russian Symbolism, in both theory and practice, survived only with Ivanov and went into exile with him. Even as an old *émigré* Ivanov cultivated the theoretical and artistic heritage of the school, integrating it with the metaphysical traditions of the past, thus acting as the only religious humanist of his sect.

Belyj too went abroad, where for a while he thought he had found anew the verities he sought. Yet what he brought back after his return to the land of the Soviets was but the ghost of Russian Symbolism: the poetic and literary ideal he tried to keep alive was a Symbolism of his own, interpreted, so to say, almost in surrealistic terms. As for Blok, who was destined to remain in his native land and to die all too young, he was the only one of the three who accepted with lucid despair the defeat of the dreams of his youth. He did so precisely because nature had endowed him with a higher prophetic vision and with greater poetic gifts. In his last years he heeded the lessons of reality and life, and turned his art from an instrument of revelation into a mirror of truth. Unlike Ivanov and Belyj, he refused to whiten the sepulcher, or to embalm the corpse, of Symbolism. The dark grace of his genius allowed him, almost against his will, to save from the ruins of his faith that poetry which he, like his brethren, had once placed on the single cornerstone of belief.

Despite Blok's final denial, the emphatic claim that poetry and religion are one remains the most characteristic of all the original tenets of Russian Symbolism. Yet Russian Symbolism, especially if we neglect or de-emphasize that claim, will in the long run appear to the cultural historian but a peculiar variant of the general European movement by the same name. The main difference between the Russian and other local brands of the same product is one of tradition and orientation, as is shown by the fact that the Russian Symbolists learned their craft not only from their immediate foreign predecessors, who were mainly French, but also from the poets of German Romanticism, as well as from their Russian disciples, who had kept the memory of German poetry alive during the whole of the nineteenth century, and who include such glorious names as Zhukovskij, Tjutchev, and Fet. It was from Romantic Germany that Solov'ev had drawn the images, as well as the ideas, of his own poetry, while Blok was bound to begin his career as a modern and original disciple of Zhukovskij. In this direct connection with the Romantic tradition Russian Symbolism

Unfinished portrait of Valery Bryusov by Mikhail Vrubel, 1905.

differed strongly from its French counterpart. Baudelaire and all his near and distant followers, from Mallarme to Valéry, accepted as valid the impatient reaction which took place in French poetry, from Gautier's "art for art's sake" school to the Parnassian movement, against Romantic poetry, which in France had sinned too much in the direction of impassioned eloquence and emotional subjectivism.

In this regard the modern poets of England and America seem to have adopted, unlike their Russian brethren, the antiromantic stand of their French predecessors. Their sense of hostility or aloofness toward the Romantic heritage was and still is chiefly due to a conception of poetry which is based on the premise of impersonality, and which requires the rejection of any kind of autobiographical pathos or subjective lyricism. The modern poets of Germany and Austria, who had learned their lessons from the same French masters, failed, however, to feel a similar compulsion, and considered themselves the continuers of the great German poets of the early nineteenth century, especially of Novalis and Hölderlin. What motivated this attitude was also the fact that German Romantic poetry, more intensely than the English and to a far higher degree than the French, had been full of anticipations of Symbolism; this is the reason why the modern poetic movement in Germany and Austria took the very apt name of *Neuromantik*. From this viewpoint, Blok, Ivanov, and Belyj are far nearer to George, Rilke, and Hofmannsthal than to any of the other groups of poets of the same time. It is perhaps for this reason that the literary historian Semen Vengerov labeled the whole of Russian Symbolism, broadly considered, and including all the Decadent and neo-idealistic trends which emerged at the end of the century a "neoromantic movement."

Despite this, Blok, Belyj, and Ivanov conceived of poetry in a way which diverged only in part from that of the leaders of French Symbolism, and of their followers in all other European countries. And, at least at first, they based that conception, even more consistently and persistently than their foreign masters or their fellow disciples from abroad, on a dualistic view of man's life and of God's universe. Following old religious and mystical notions, Poe and Baudelaire had distinguished between a higher and a lower world. Man, who lives "down here," cannot enter into communication with "up there" other than by way of "symbols." According to an established mystical view, what we call a "symbol" is the one device by which the human mind may not only express, but even discover, a relationship which it could not fathom by itself. Only "symbols" are supposed to bridge the gap which separates heaven and earth, the human and the divine, the temporal and the eternal, the material and the spiritual. By using a method made up in part of mystical foresight, and in part of Platonic "reminiscence," the poet is thus deemed able to link a series of symbols in a chain or a ladder, through which he and the reader may ascend, if only briefly, from the world of things to the world of ideas, thus reestablishing a precarious equilibrium, a fragmentary or temporary harmony, between the two conflicting spheres of human experience.

In mystical literature the "symbol" is called "correspondence." But, from a famous sonnet by Baudelaire where the latter term is used in a slightly different sense, "correspondence" has come to mean a particular device, expressing the connection existing between divers kinds of symbols. Whereas the symbol establishes a kind of vertical relationship between the lower and higher sphere, thus transcending the fundamental duality of the real and the ideal, the "correspondence" establishes a horizontal relationship and affirms the existence of a parallelism, symmetry, and even identity, between symbols belonging to different forms of expression. In brief, the "correspondence" presupposes a semantic analogy between different sense perceptions, as well as between different art media and linguistic techniques. In practice, the "correspondence" implies that there may be an equivalence in suggestion and meaning between a verbal symbol and a visual or musical one. This means not only that the human mind may reach the same revelation through a pattern of words as through a pattern of colors or a pattern of sounds, but also that each one of those patterns is translatable into any one of the other two. It is on the presupposition of such a double relationship, on the basis of what Baudelaire, following Swedenborg, called the "universal analogy," that the Symbolist poet endeavors to perform his set task, which, according to Blok's definition consists of trying "to catch, through snatches of words, the confused march of other worlds."

The French Symbolists, who followed in many ways the example set by the Parnassians, often paid more than lip service to the notion that poetry must be impersonal and objective, and that it can express as well as painting or sculpture a formal ideal primarily plastic in essence. This is what Baudelaire himself tried to do, especially when he attempted to reshape verbal symbols into a visual key, or to transfer a pictorial or sculptural work of art into a poem, replacing other artists' colors and lines with sounds and words of his own. Similar attempts were made by some minor modern Russian poets, but not by the greater and more genuine Symbolists. Thus, in an even more extreme form than its French counterpart, Russian Symbolism primarily represents, among the main trends of modern poetry, the one which aims at fashioning its own formal ideal after the pattern of the musical one.

That ideal had first been formulated in the West, and originally had not been limited to poetry alone, as Baudelaire demonstrated as a critic of painting when he analyzed the effects of Delacroix' art in musical terms; or as Walter Pater sensed when he stated that in the modern aesthetic situation all arts seemed to tend toward "the condition of music." Yet in the West itself that tendency or trend was bound to reach its climax in the art of verse. This is proved by the fact that the two most important attempts to define the new poetry as it developed in France were based more on the theory of music than on the practice of symbolism. Mallarmé once declared that the paramount intent of himself and his colleagues had been *de tout réprendre à la musique,* "to take everything back from music," and his great disciple Valéry was later to paraphrase and limit his master's statement by maintaining that the common aim of the French Symbolists had been *de réprendre à la musique leur bien,* "to reclaim from music their own," or to recover from the latter a native gift properly and originally belonging to poetry alone. If we compare these with similar attempts by the Russian Symbolists to define the doctrine of their school, we shall see that they too single out music as the poetic principle for excellence, but attribute to music a higher power and a larger domain than Mallarmé or Valéry ever did. Thus, for instance, Andrej Belyj claims in one breath the identity of poetry, music, and symbolism when he says: "Music ideally expresses symbols; the symbol is always musical." Yet, when read in the context of his theories, these words obviously imply the precedence of the musical sense over symbolic insight. As for Blok, his exaltation of what he called after Nietzsche "the spirit of music" entails the notion that the spirit itself is but music. For Blok the latter is not merely the root of poetry, but the source of all power and vision, as he suggested when he proclaimed, rephrasing the opening sentence of St. John's Gospel, that "in the beginning was music," rather than "the Word."

The very excess of their metaphysical claims prevents the literary historian or critic from using such pronouncements as reliable indications, if not of the aims the Russian Symbolists sought to achieve, at least of the directions toward which they tended to move. Their visionary outlook ruled their minds a posteriori as well as a priori, and determined even their evaluation of Russian Symbolism as a historical fact. In brief, we cannot take at its face value even their posthumous appraisal, because it often tends to assume, as in Blok's case, too negative a bias. Strangely enough, we may assess better the contributions of European Symbolism in general, and of Russian Symbolism in particular, by using as a starting point the belated post-mortem report which Paul Valéry wrote on French Symbolism itself.

That report took the form of a retrospective manifesto, which Valéry drafted in 1920 as a preface to a book by a fellow poet. Of particular interest to us is that in those pages Valéry singled out the attempt to recapture the "spirit of music" as the very mission of the school he had joined in his youth. After stating that the poetic principle of Symbolism was a musical one, Valéry treats all of its manifestations as corollaries of that postulate: "The obscurities and peculiarities Symbolism was so often blamed for . . . the syntactical disorder, the irregular rhythms, the oddities of vocabulary . . . , the constant imagery . . . , all this may be easily inferred, once the principle is acknowledged.'' Valéry was aware that the attempt had led to divergent, and even negative, aesthetic effects; after all, as he said of the poets of his own generation and tongue, ''some would cherish Wagner, others Schumann.'' Yet one should not forget that what Valéry had in mind in those pages were the intentions rather than the achievements of the Symbolist school: hence the unavoidable conclusion, at least on the part of the reader, that the view that poetry and symbol are, either potentially or actually, musical in essence, is hardly more than a metaphor, expressing an artistic ideal which was never to be realized in practice, and which individual poets would treat at most as either an exalted abstraction or a vague program. Yet that view is significant as the symptom of an aspiration which was both genuine and inborn, and the tendency so revealed is peculiar and important enough to be taken into account by the student endeavoring to understand the difference between modern Symbolism, or Symbolism with a capital S, and eternal symbolism, or symbolism with a small initial.

If modern Symbolism, of which Russian Symbolism is but an integral part, envisages its operations under the guise of a musical analogy, medieval symbology, which is perhaps the most typical manifestation of universal or recurring symbolism, views its own products in graphic, or better, emblematic, terms. The modern Symbolist poet may glimpse with his mind, or rather sense with his heart, a hidden truth or a higher reality; yet, being unable to contemplate that truth with clarity, and to express that reality in its fullness, he will be satisfied with merely suggesting it. But the medieval symbolist does not content himself with guesses or hints, and wishes to communicate as completely as possible, with the means at his disposal, his own mystical experience. Thus his aim is to visualize and represent: or, more precisely, to give the objective image of a reality which cannot be perceived through the senses. It has been said that modern Symbolism is dynamic, and medieval symbolism is static, by which is generally meant that the former is more interested in the psychological process of revelation, and the other, in its speculative results. At any rate, precisely because it is the reflection of a consistent and systematic world view, medieval symbolism is often able to tie its emblems together and to raise a series of emblems to the level of what the early painters of Christendom used to call a ''story.'' Modern Symbolist poets, however, use their symbols as if they were separate images, which they cannot relate to any pattern except that of their mood. This is another way to say that symbolism may at best reappear or survive in modern culture only as a paradox or as an exception, and that it will manifest itself only in rhapsodic fashion and fragmentary form.

Thus medieval culture was able to treat each symbol as a part of a whole, as a link in the chain which took the name and shape of allegory. Modern Symbolism has, however, fully divorced itself from allegory; and it has done so not as a matter of choice, as is generally believed, but as a matter of necessity. It is the sense of such a necessity, felt even by those who are not conscious of it, which motivates that antithesis between symbol and allegory of which the modern mind seems to be so inordinately fond. Separating the two, or opposing the one to the other, is an operation of dubious validity if we look at symbolism *sub specie aeternitatis;* yet it becomes justified from the standpoint of historical Symbolism. Allegory is, after all, incompatible with a poetry based on melos and pathos alone, or reduced only to the lyrical mode, which modern culture considers the whole of poetry, or at least its most perfect and absolute form. But allegory has no place in modern poetry for reasons more substantive than this. Allegory is both possible and necessary in those cultures where the poet shares with his community, or at least with a considerable body of the faithful, a set of solid and concrete beliefs, which he is able to express with the objectivity of contemplation, rather than with introspective lyricism. This is certainly not the case with modern poetry, and with modern Symbolism in particular. What makes the latter's position highly paradoxical is that modern Symbolism starts, at least ideally, from the presupposition of a bond between religion and poetry, although in practice it ends by preaching no other religion than that of poetry itself, thus replacing the deification of the Logos with the idolization of the Word.

Modern Symbolism derives that presupposition from Romantic idealism, rather than from the Christian tradition, which refuses to identify religion and poetry, since it submits the latter to the former, or even to philosophy, which it views in its turn as but the handmaid of theology. Yet, despite this, perhaps only in order to assign to poetry a lofty spiritual task, modern Symbolism accepts for a time, and only problematically and hypothetically, the philosophical foundations of Christian dualism, and treats poetry as if it were a kind of mystical ladder, bridging the gap between a lower reality and a higher one. It is according to a similar aesthetic mysticism, which was already part of the metaphysical speculation of Northern Romanticism, that Kierkegaard gave his suggestive definition of the poet as ''a spy of God.'' The formula is quite significant, since it seems to imply that the poet tries to discover the secrets of Heaven by stealth, and almost against God's will. What is even truer is that the modern poet looks at God from perspectives through which God cannot be seen. These perspectives, which the modern poet does not choose by himself, but simply accepts as imposed by the historical condition or cultural situation of which, whether willingly or unwillingly, he is a part, are those of either a monistic idealism or an equally monistic materialism, or even that skeptical or scientific pluralism which is perhaps the dominant trait of modern culture. All these tendencies have deprived modern man of the sense of the sacred, have reduced the divine to a daydream or a wishful thought. Symbolism started as the poetry of an illusion, rather than of a hope; one could say that no Symbolist poet ever tried to become a ''seer,'' but was at best, and only intermittently, a ''spy of God.''

The idealism and the spiritualism of the early French Symbolists were essentially negative in character; they were primarily an outright denial of that positivism and materialism which from the middle of the nineteenth century on had become the salient traits of the culture of the West. Yet one could extend to the whole of European Symbolism, with slight qualifications and reservations, what Valéry rightly said of all the poets who, like him, had learned their lesson from the direct example of Mallarmé; ''A young and rather stern generation rejected the scientific dogma, which tended to be no longer fashionable, without adopting the religious dogma, which was not yet so.'' It was precisely because they had appeared on the literary horizon a little later, that so many of the Symbolists who wrote in other languages than French felt far more attracted than their French predecessors by those religious or mystical creeds which in the meantime had become fashionable again. Yet even in their case we can hardly speak of a return to established dogmas or traditional beliefs.

If in view of this consideration we classify all the major poets of European Symbolism into different groups according to the quality and substance of their faith, we shall see that all of them fall into the following categories. The first one is that of the non-believers, of those who refuse the ideas of both religion and God, and fail to see in the cosmos any other order than a mental or poetic harmony of their own, which they often project on frivolous and even profane objects. This category is an important one, since it includes such outstanding representatives as the highest-ranking poet of French Symbolism, Stéphane Mallarmé, as well as some of his most skillful disciples in France and abroad, from Paul Valéry to Wallace Stevens. The second category is made of those who waver continuously between doubt and faith, or who base their poetry not so much on faith as on doubt. Some of them, like Baudelaire, seem to believe more in disorder than in order, in sin than in redemption, and are often of the Devil's party, whether they know it or not. Others, like T. S. Eliot, are far more effective as critics of the City of Man than as upholders of the City of God; the real theme of their verse is the denial of present-day reality rather than the affirmation of a higher and permanent realm of being. The third category is formed by all those poets, so well represented by Rilke and George in Germany and by Yeats in the English-speaking world, who have built the edifice of their poetry on the shaky foundations of arbitrary creeds and personal beliefs. Some of them, like Yeats, who is perhaps the greatest of this band, have tended to replace Christian dogmas with non-Christian myths; and all these poets, as well as the poets belonging to the other groups, have replaced parables with fairy tales, and public allegory with private symbolism.

One could say that while none of the leaders of Russian Symbolism finds a place within the first of these categories, all of them rightly and naturally belong to either the second or the third, or even better, to both of them at once, according to the varying tendencies of their temperament, or to changing phases of their career. Generally they fit better within the second category qua poets, from the viewpoint of their concrete achievements, as [can] be easily shown in their individual profiles and through the analysis of their work; while they fit better within the third qua prophets, from the viewpoint of their abstract attitudes or self-conscious poses. Thus, for instance, Belyj was, of the three leaders of Russian Symbolism, the one who, in a sense, chose a solution similar to Yeats', clinging, as a means of keeping his faith, to the arbitrary beliefs of strange and occult sects. Blok leaned toward the solution of Rilke, which was to make poetry not only out of faith but out of anguish as well. Ivanov took the same path as Stefan George and acted always as if he were a high priest of poetry, in whom the religious habit could survive even the loss of faith in God. Yet, precisely because of the rigid consistency of his creed, if not the absolute constancy of his devotion, the last of these figures may be considered the most systematic theorist of the three; and this may well justify the attempt to summarize the poetics of Russian Symbolism through the particular perspective of his views.

From beginning to end Vjacheslav Ivanov insisted on the tie between Symbolism and mysticism, and saw the cornerstone of the new poetry in man's faith that a divine order rules equally the physical and the spiritual world. It was from this postulate that he drew as a corollary the tenet that "the poetic image is a microcosm reflecting the macrocosm." Ivanov's outlook implied that art is, or should be, related to religion, to a religion which he, however, understood more as theurgy than as theology: "A genuine symbolic art attains the religious sphere,

insofar as religion itself is primarily an act, the act of perceiving the tie between the sense of life and all that exists." It was this conception that led the early Ivanov to understate the differences, and to overemphasize the similarities, between the modern or historical variant of Symbolism and its archetypal forms: "Symbolism seems to be within the new poetry but a reminiscence of the holy language of the ancient sages, who had given to the words of common speech a special, secret meaning, which was known to them alone, thanks to their knowledge of the connections between the sphere of the sacred and the experience of the senses."

It was on this supposed dependence of the new poetry from that eternal symbolism after which the religious spirit of humankind seemed to be constantly yearning, that Ivanov based his claim of the independence of Russian Symbolism from its French counterpart: "The study of the work produced by our Symbolist school will show how superficial was the Western influence on us; how little we thought out what we borrowed and imitated; how those borrowings and imitations were in the long run unproductive; finally, how much deeper are the roots reattaching to its native soil what in our poetry is genuine and vital." And it is quite significant that Ivanov saw the most distinctive quality of the school or movement of which he was a leading member in the very fact that "Russian Symbolism could not be, and did not want to be, merely art."

All the poets of the second generation of Russian Symbolism, who were the only Symbolists in the proper sense of the term, fully agreed with this view, differing in this from the poets of the older generation, who here are called Decadents. Thus Valerij Brjusov, the most influential and representative of the latter, was the one who most consistently claimed that Symbolism was primarily, and even exclusively, art. As late as 1910, at the time of the controversy raised in the review *Apollo* by the poets of a third generation who condemned at once Decadents and Symbolists, Brjusov defined Symbolism purely and simply as an "artistic method," the discovery of which had been the particular merit of the poets of the two older generations, all of whom were of "the so-called Symbolistic school." Brjusov felt, however, that that method was neither particular nor exclusive, but inclusive and general: he saw in it not *an* artistic method, but *the* artistic method par excellence, which found its distinction not within, but outside, itself: "It is this method that spells the difference between art and that rational knowledge of the universe which is characteristic of science, as well as between art and that endeavor to penetrate the occult by irrational means which is characteristic of mysticism. Art is autonomous: it has its own method and mission."

Brjusov's proud belief in the autonomy of art implied a recognition of its limits, and the relative moderation of his views becomes more apparent when they are compared with Ivanov's ambitious claim that the whole of the life of the spirit is the poet's province. It is such a claim which marks the difference that separates not only Ivanov's generation from Brjusov's, but, more generally, Russian from French Symbolism. Even Poe, Baudelaire, and Rimbaud had asserted their belief that poetry should become an instrument of universal revelation only in tentative or hypothetical terms. Later on, speaking in retrospect, and bringing to their logical conclusion not only his ideas, but also those of his master Mallarmé, Valéry found a paradoxical merit in the fact that, at least within French Symbolism, philosophy, and even ethics, tended to shun poetic creation and "to dwell only among the reflections preceding the actual works." How skeptical this statement sounds when contrasted with Ivanov's oracular utterance that "the function of Symbolism is to express the parallelism of the phenomenal and the noumenal!" And it is on the strength of such philosophical pretensions and metaphysical ambitions that Ivanov was finally led to affirm not only the independence, but even the superiority, of Russian Symbolism, in regard to its French counterpart: "What Mallarmé wanted was simply that our thought, after completing its circle, would redescend to the very point the poet had prescribed it should stop. For us Symbolism is instead an energy which frees itself from the boundaries of the given world, launching the soul on the motion of a spiral shooting upward."

Despite this evident allusion to the Mallarmean image of poetry as a hyperbola, Ivanov here seems to fail to realize that even the poetic ideal of his own generation was a curve fatally bound to return to the plane of the earth. Only experience could teach him later to recognize this harsh truth. The very range of his vision allowed him to understand better than his fellow poets that "crisis" of Russian Symbolism, which was so widely discussed in the years between 1905 and the war. Ivanov succeeded in doing so because he was able to view it as the reflection of a broader and older crisis, that of modern Symbolism itself. Ivanov stated his views in this regard in an essay which he wrote in 1907 under the title of "Art and Symbolism." In that essay Ivanov acknowledged that the modern artist is paradoxically led to Symbolism by his own extreme subjectivity:

> The artist pushes so far the isolation of his own intimate experience and independent creation that ultimately he severs himself from the crowd, and tragically realizes the reciprocal incommunicability of the souls, each one of which remains enclosed within the shell of its own solitude. The language of things, circumscribed by separate concepts, must be replaced by allusive references, by a suggestive and fluid imagery: and this is what we mean by the ancient term "symbol." This is how subjective symbolism is created, and its aim is to mediate between lonely spirits.

It would be difficult to express better the limits of modern Symbolism, as well as the singularity of its task; and Ivanov is here fully aware of how much it differs, in scope as well as in function, from medieval or eternal symbolism. Yet, almost against his better judgment, he persisted in believing that a reconciliation of the two is not only possible, but even imminent:

> Besides and beyond this newfangled Symbolism, and at first, as in Baudelaire's case, in improper combination with it, another and older kind of symbolism may arise. Its norm, through Novalis and Goethe, brings us back to the great anagogic poetry of Dante and of his predecessors, or to a symbology which has nothing to do with subjective idealism, being exclusively intent on revealing within the objects it represents their full ontological significance and the seal of their value. Here, and only here, the word "symbol" reacquires its genuine meaning, and suggests a contemplation of reality through the perspective of its connection or analogy with a higher or truer reality. This type of objective representation implies an ascent *a realibus ad realiora* ["from one reality to a higher reality"].

The passage, however, concludes with the implied acknowledgement that a return to objective symbolism would involve a reversal of the cultural foundations of the modern world, and a revaluation of all its values: "Such a view of Symbolism is an outright denial of the analytical and relativistic principle of our modern, critical culture, while subjective symbolism is but a reaffirmation of that culture."

Precisely because of this the attempt to restore objective symbolism within a modern cultural framework could not succeed. Ivanov himself had described elsewhere the symbol as "the cryptogram of the ineffable": an ideal definition of its traditional function, which was to convey an ecstatic or mystical vision that normal human language could not express. Any mystical vision is a transcendental, even if temporary, victory of the soul over the self. Only through that victory may the personal soul momentarily attain the divine, or join with the world soul. As for what we call ecstasy, it is but the liberation of the spirit from the bonds which chain it to either the psyche or the mind, or to both. Only by means of symbols may the mystic or spiritual seer be able to communicate a unique and universal experience to his fellow men. But at best the modern spirit treats symbols as hieroglyphics, which, far from revealing the ineffable, suggest merely the occult; or, at worst, only vaguely and obscurely hint at the poet's private being and inner world. Goethe once said that "in a true symbol the particular represents the universal, not as a dream or shadow, but as the living and instantaneous revelation of the unfathomable." If this definition is right, then we must acknowledge that modern

Portrait of Konstantin Balmont by V. A. Serov, 1905. From Russian Literature Triquarterly, *No. 4, Fall, 1972. By permission of Ardis Publishers.*

poetry has produced symbols which represent the particular alone, and as dream and shadow at that.

In brief, modern Symbolism leads to one of two blind alleys, intellectualism or irrationalism. The second alternative is the more frequent. By being made a vessel of the irrational, the symbol turns into a microcosm reflecting another microcosm, thus becoming something not too different from what Freud means by that very word: a symptom of spiritual trouble and psychic disorder, the distorted mirror of the artist's neurosis, of the poet's narcissism. Belyj unintentionally avowed as much in a passage where he praised modern Symbolism as the attempt to express "the deepest layer of our consciousness" by means of images which are symbols insofar as they suggest the "inner perceptions" of that consciousness. Such a statement tends to imply, beyond the terms used and the meaning intended, that symbols are but spontaneous or even automatic expressions of that unconscious which is the scientific object of "depth psychology."

Symbolism so understood ends by becoming unwillingly a kind of glorified expressionism. If this is true, how slight its achievements look when compared with the pretensions of its practitioners! For instance Valerij Brjusov, the great master of Russian Decadence, or of the earliest stage of Russian Symbolism, went so far as to affirm, in his famous essay "Key of Mysteries," which he wrote for *The Scales* in 1904, that Symbolism was the culminating phase in the process of development of modern art, a process which he described as a progressive liberation from the chains of intellectualism. "The history of the new art is above all the history of its deliverance. Romanticism, Realism, and Symbolism are but three stages in the artist's struggle for freedom." As for Belyj, he went even further, maintaining that Symbolism was not simply the culmination of a gradual evolution, but a synthesis of all previous traditions, not only of Romanticism and Realism, but of Classicism as well: "Symbolism is at once Classicism, Romanticism, and Realism: it is Realism insofar as it reflects reality; it is Romanticism insofar as it is a vision corrected by experience; it is Classicism for unifying form and content."

Of all these sweeping generalizations the only one still acceptable is the one which relates Symbolism to Romanticism, since the former was obviously the latter's offspring. As for the preposterous assertion that Symbolism includes even Classicism itself, it may be easily rejected on the grounds of the principle which T. S. Eliot stated in his essay on Baudelaire, that "a poet in a romantic age cannot be a 'classical' poet except in tendency." Notwithstanding all claims to the contrary, this principle is valid for the whole tradition of modern poetry, from Baudelaire to Eliot himself, and applies even more fully to the Russian poets of Belyj's generation, who, unlike their French masters and English colleagues, failed to take seriously the ideal which Eliot was to express in such a definitive way in "Tradition and the Individual Talent": "Poetry is not a turning loose of emotion, but an escape from emotion; it is not the expression of personality, but an escape from personality." It was because of their refusal to make their own, at least up to a point, the Parnassian tenets of the impersonality of art and of the artist's *impassibilité*, that the Russian Symbolists, along with their German brethren, deserved and welcomed that neoromantic label which all their other Western peers refused to accept.

It is from a special viewpoint that one must consider Belyj's affirmation that Symbolism allied itself with even the most obvious of its literary opposites, at least in historical terms.

That opposite was Realism, then still alive as a parallel line of aesthetic development, as well as a noble precedent, and the supreme tradition of Russian literature. The Russian Symbolists had to take a stand toward that tradition, through which the Russian genius had already manifested itself; and their stand, at least in generalities and principles, could not be but a negative one. Any attempt to reconcile these two opposites was bound to end in disaster, or with the bloodless victory of the stronger of the two. Blok was the only one who understood that the duality of those two outlooks could not be resolved; that chaining the two together would bring about the destruction of the weaker link. Yet he not only faced the challenge and accepted his own defeat, but acknowledged that defeat as both natural and just.

Being the least critically minded of the poets of his nation and time, disdainfully indifferent to literary problems as such, Blok saw that duality not as conflict between Symbolism and Realism, but as the duel between imagination and truth. First he doubted, and then denied, the ultimate validity of the artistic and religious creeds of his generation when confronted with the prose of life, with man's daily existence in a profane world. It was in his letters and diaries, rather than in his essays, that he confided his misgivings about the poetic sect which had made him one of its patron saints: "Symbolism, the 'correspondences,' the 'moments,' all these things are childish trifles." It was there that he repudiated mysticism not only as an error, but also as a moral flaw: "We need reality. Nothing in the world is more awful than mysticism." By reality Blok meant a deep ethical experience, a keen understanding of both outer and inner truth: "We must show our fellow men our true, said, human face, not the mask of a literary school which does not exist."

That literary school did, however, effectively exist, even though it had ultimately to come to terms with the cultural reality of which it was historically a part. It was the naturalistic temper of modern culture which led that school to sever the bonds which, at least ideally, still seemed to tie it to medieval symbolism. By doing so the new poetry ended by denying its very doctrine of the word. Medieval symbolism had been an offshoot of what the historians of philosophy designate as medieval realism, which is the very opposite of modern philosophical Realism. Medieval realism maintained that words are not vain sounds, but the proper names of things, which in their turn are but earthly reflections of eternal and absolute archetypes. In brief, each word was thought to be the objective, although shadowy, symbol of a metaphysical idea. Modern Realism claims instead that art must mirror things as things, as objects which are enclosed within a purely physical space, and which we perceive only through our senses. Literary realism uses words just as visual and plastic realism uses colors and volumes: as external stimuli which reproduce in our minds the material image of things. In brief, even in the most abstract forms, modern art tends toward sensory illusions, which are highly subjective in character, and which differ only in degree from what the Symbolist poet calls "symbols."

There is no need to challenge the validity of the term symbol as it is being used in connection with modern poetry, precisely because it may mean nothing and everything, as Valéry remarked in a passage full of insight: "In vain did those who watched these experiments, and even those who put them into practice, attack the poor word itself. It means only what one wants it to; if someone fastens his hopes upon it, he will find them there!" The task of the historian of literature, and of the critic of poetry, is to point out that the modern poet uses words as symbols not in the religious sense, as metaphysical visions or mystical emblems, but in the semantic sense, as verbal icons. Potebnja, a Russian philologist and literary theorist of the late nineteenth century, had already put this principle in a nutshell by stating that "a symbol is a mere metaphor," and nothing more.

Thus for a modern poet the noun "rose" stands for either *a* rose or his own mood. If such a verbal sign acts within the structure of the poem as a "guidepost word," to employ a formula of which the Russian Symbolists were very fond, it is precisely because that sign points, through or beyond the objects, to the subject, or to the poet's self. But for the medieval poet a rose is *the* rose, while being at the same time the allegory of love, whether sacred or profane. This means that for the medieval symbolist the thing is the vessel of the idea, and the idea the substance of the thing. Hence the belief that the spirit may be understood through the letter, and the letter through the spirit. Thus the obscurity of the letter is but a veil, which both conceals and reveals. It was Carlyle who attributed to the symbol the double requisite of "concealment" and "revelation." The mystical tradition claims that the symbol, although occult to the uninitiated eye, is evident to the initiated one. The modern Symbolist seems, however, to conceive the symbol as a chiaroscuro, as an interplay, even within the poet's mind, of darkness and light. Thus, instead of becoming the custodian of a mystery, he simply remains the watchman of the Sphinx, of its enigmas and riddles.

Such was the paradoxical outcome of the central doctrine of Symbolism, from which that movement took its name and flag. No less paradoxical was the outcome of the other of its main theories, which is perhaps more crucial than the first: the one according to which music is the ideal condition of all art. As we already know, the Russian Symbolists took that principle both more seriously and more broadly than their French masters and Western colleagues, and did not hesitate to extend it to the whole domain of the spirit, beyond the realms of words and forms. Thus Andrej Belyj held that music is not only "the substratum of poetry," but also the power which helps man to realize that "the visible world is but a veil over an abyss." In such a definition the idea of music is changed from a literary metaphor or an aesthetic analogy into a philosophical myth. There is no need to recall that Belyj drew the very image of the veil over the abyss from a famous Tjutchev poem to realize that the myth is a catastrophic one, that music is for Belyj not an echo of the harmony of the spheres but the prophetic din of that "last cataclysm" which will destroy creation itself. For Blok music was the voice of chaos, suddenly breaking loose in the natural and the social world: the wild song of the elements, or of the masses in revolt. It was such a worship of the "spirit of music," no less than the belief that "the world" is "idea and representation," that ultimately led the Russian Symbolists to follow the path already taken by their beloved Schopenhauer, and to end their vain search with the surrender of their hopes to a sort of cosmic nihilism.

At least consciously, the surrender was never total, and allowed temporary restorations of the faith lost through despair and disbelief. Even Blok, at such a late date as 1910, when he was left with few illusions, reasserted against the enemies of Symbolism the claim of his youth, and maintained that the poet is "the lonely keeper of a mysterious treasure, although there are around him others who know of the treasure.... Hence, we, the few knowing ones, are the Symbolists...." In reality the Symbolists did not know the treasure, but merely knew *of* it; or rather, dreamed of its existence all too vividly, and never found it when they sought it. One could even say that while some good Symbolist poetry was written in the illusion that the Holy Grail was within reach, far better poetry was written out of the fear that the quest would fail, or even the realization that it led to a dead end. There is no doubt that the Symbolist attitude bore better fruit when dealing with the psychic states which precede or follow the ecstatic trance, rather than with the mystical experience itself. The moods which the poets of Symbolism expressed most successfully were expectation and hope, especially when mixed with hesitation and doubt, or disenchantment and loss of faith, with the attendant falling back of the soul from what Mallarmé called *azur* to what he named *ici-bas* ["down here"]. Thus the main muses of Symbolism were the muse of escape, which led the poet to seek refuge, in the title of one of Baudelaire's poems, "anywhere out of the world"; and the muse of failure and despair, which brought him back to an unholy earth and to an all-too-human world. In either case Symbolist poetry turned into a forward- or backward-looking yearning for an impossible Symbolism.

Truly enough, many of the noblest monuments of that poetry were erected on other pedestals than these. Some of the poets chose as their ground either a relative acceptance or an outright denial of the inner dialectics of Symbolism. In their awareness that the modern mind was unable to solve the conflict between the ideal and the real, or to transcend the ego as well as the world, a few poets, for instance Yeats, made great poetry out of the dialogue or debate of the soul with the self. Others, like Mallarmé and Valéry, renounced the view of poetry as experience of the infinite, and reduced it to an exacting and yet futile exercise within the finite world of form. Exceptional as they were, even these eccentric solutions tend to prove that all the highest achievements of Symbolism were attained in a state of tension within its own system of belief: in a kind of antagonistic reaction against its very creed. Thus Symbolism ended in a symbolism of negation, in an allegory of failure, in a chant of nothingness.

It was such nihilism that led so many Symbolist poets to an escape into the aesthetic cult. One could extend to the whole of modern Symbolism, as well as to its Russian variant, the conclusion which Valéry drew for the French school: "In the profound and scrupulous worship of the arts as a whole, it thought it had found an unequivocal discipline or even a truth. A sort of religion was very nearly established." Also in Russia that sort of religion had already been established in the climate of Decadence, and this may help to see how closely the Russian Symbolists of the second generation were connected with their predecessors. There is no doubt that from a broad historical viewpoint Decadence and Symbolism must be considered as different branches of the same tree. It is equally evident that they share many outstanding traits, besides their common leaning toward aestheticism, toward the self-adoration of the poet and the idolatry of art. Here it may suffice to cite, as a single example, the tendency on the part of the genuine Symbolists to yield no less supinely than their Decadent brethren to the temptations of the demonic and the seductions of Satanism, to the superstitious worship of the blind and dark forces of the underworld.

Yet, despite this, one must never forget that the relationship between the two is a dialectical one. This is so true that no less a Marxist than Lev Trotskij refused to throw together these two variants of modern literature under the single label of bourgeois Decadence, or Decadent Bohemia, as the critics of the Left usually do. Trotskij differentiated between the two trends by means of distinctions which others had already made before him, such as those separating the younger from the older generation and the "mystics" from the "aesthetes." This is what Trotskij had to say in a penetrating page of his book *Literature and Revolution:*

> The Decadent school, which preceded Symbolism, sought the solution of all artistic problems in the personal experiences of sex, death, and the like, or rather, in nothing else but sex and death. . . . Hence . . . the need to find a higher sanction to individual demands, feelings, and moods, thus enriching and elevating them. Symbolism . . . seemed to the intelligentsia to be an artistic bridge toward mysticism. In this concrete, sociological meaning . . . , Symbolism was not merely a method of artistic technique, but an escape for the intelligentsia from reality, its means to build a new world. . . .

Despite his distaste for both schools, at least here even Trotskij betrays or displays a relative preference for Symbolism. Thus he follows the general rule according to which all such parallels work without exception to the disadvantage of Decadence and the profit of Symbolism. So, for instance, such an early observer as Volynskij contrasted the two tendencies so as to imply that Symbolism was mainly positive and Decadence mainly negative in character. While defining Decadence as the temptation to yield to that "wicked, devilish beauty" which attracts the soul from below, Volynskij defined Symbolism as the lofty attempt to mediate between the human world of appearances and the divine world of the occult. Later a critic who was at once a socialist and a mystic, Ivanov-Razumnik, brought that invidious comparison to the extreme point when he stated, paraphrasing Horace, that Decadents *fiunt* or "are made," while Symbolists *nascuntur* or "are born." Although willing to admit that the soil of Decadence was poetically less fertile than that of Symbolism, the impartial literary historian must reject the partisan claim that the two movements were unrelated in tendency, opposed in direction, and incommensurate in artistic value. In reality Decadence and Symbolism were but different faces of the same coin, or parallel variants of the same historical situation. As a matter of fact, if asked to designate that situation by a single term rather than with both, one should choose Decadence, which, albeit less attractive, is certainly the more inclusive, and perhaps also the more honest, of the two. One might even maintain, reversing Ivanov-Razumnik's statement, that all the Russian and Western poets of that age were born Decadents, although many of them made themselves into Symbolists (one could even claim that not a few of the latter reverted to Decadence, at least in part). Certainly this view, if accepted, would disentangle the web of the whole problem, and solve all terminological confusion, with a simple rule: that there were Decadents who were not Symbolists, but that there was no Symbolist who was not a Decadent as well.

It was the outlook of Decadence that fashioned even the social and political attitudes of the Russian Symbolists, as it fashioned those of their Western peers. True enough, among the latter all too many refused to take any political stand, flaunting their scornful indifference to any social issue or civic concern; or, when willing to take sides, they chose all too often to ally themselves with the parties of the extreme Right, while most of their Russian brethren joined those of the extreme Left. Although differing in stand, all such attitudes stemmed from the same root: the modern artist's radical dislike for that bourgeois society within which he lives, on the claim, half true and half false, that he is no part of it. It matters little whether his protest leads him to withdraw from the political arena, or to embrace either one of the two ideologies of subversion, the reactionary or the revolutionary. If the Russian Symbolists showed a marked preference for the latter alternative, it was because they were affected even more than their Western brethren by that sense of doom which is the core of the Decadent spirit. They felt the morbid attraction of the impending disaster and tried to change even the dark forebodings of their personal ruin into the radiant hope that the catastrophe would bring about a new society and a new world.

Symbolist art and poetry tended always toward a tone of "high seriousness," although the Decadent spirit all too often infected them with that gloom which was its most fashionable mood. Being far more naïve and less skeptical than their Western colleagues, easily swayed by the seduction of hope as well as the temptation of despair, the Russian Symbolists denied themselves the opportunity to release their minds from the hold of perplexity through the practice of irony and jest. Modern art as a whole neglects the lowly but effective purgation of laughter and ignores the therapeutic virtues of comic relief. Decadents and Symbolists were particularly devoid of a sense of humor; yet even French Symbolism indulged in the bitter banter of a Tristan Corbière or in those sophisticated drolleries to which Jules Laforgue gave the name of *fumisteries*. The almost fanatic frenzy of their inspiration led the Russian Symbolists to vent their spleen in blasphemy and sacrilege rather than mockery and farce.

It was the ultimate degradation of their ideal that made the Russian Symbolists deeply aware of what they called the "crisis," or even the "breakdown," of Symbolism. Yet, at least outside of Russia, many refused to hold such a pessimistic view. Thus for instance Valéry never saw a failure in the fact that Mallarmé, who had started to write poetry as a means for "the orphic explanation of the earth," had closed his career by avowing that not even the "throw of dice" of thought and art could abolish chance and its whims. Valéry admitted that Symbolism could be either a "spiritual illusion" or an ideal truth, but a truth which was, as he said, "a frontier of the world," on which man could not settle for long. He also acknowledged that "the overenlightened zeal" of the Symbolist outlook might have "resulted in an inhuman state," yet he never felt that such a state had been unproductive, even if it bore other fruits than the ones dreamed of.

The tree of theory is gray, but the tree of life is of another color, although it may well not be green. Even Baudelaire, who once affirmed that "prosodies and poetics proceed from the very structure of the spiritual being," could mock without fear of contradiction his beloved Poe for pretending to have written "The Raven" after a pre-established plan. As Baudelaire said on that occasion, poetics is one thing and poetry is another, and the second is never written after the pattern laid down by the first. This truth fits particularly well the case of Symbolism. Yet, despite all appearances to the contrary, the poetics of Symbolism was in its own way as influential as the poetry itself. There is no doubt that we must see in that poetics the root of all those literary and artistic movements which appeared later, with the avowed intention of destroying the shrines and denying the sacraments of Symbolism. What Surrealism tried to achieve, for instance, was merely to replace the daydreams of the soul with the nightmares of the psyche, thus acting as an inverted Symbolism. Like the Decadents, and like the heretics and renegades of Symbolism, the Surrealists sought refuge in a reality darker and lower than what one might call the realism of daylight, which, despite the label of their choice, they replaced, as Ortega y Gasset was the first to remark, with a kind of "infrarealism." In painting, the heritage of Symbolism is to be seen not only in post-Impressionism, as is generally believed, but also in Cubism and abstract art, which on the one hand act as visual and plastic equivalents of "pure poetry," and on the other, develop to extremes the iconoclastic tendencies of later Symbolism. Futurism is in its turn but an agonized attempt to transcend both Decadence and Symbolism, to project the present into the future, to replace the divine order with a man-made and machinelike world.

In the light of history Symbolism must then be considered not a heresy or a fallacy, but rather a paradox. The paradox lies in the fact that it paved the ground for the advance-guard while trying to restore the dream of a poetry belonging to another time as well as to another world. This is the reason why the Symbolist attitude remains even now, although under different names and forms, a standard aesthetic attitude, one of the main constants of Western poetry and art. Using as apt formulae the titles of two books in which the English scholar and critic C. M. Bowra assessed the contributions of the last two generations of European poets, one could say that even "the creative experiment" of the post- and anti-Symbolists is but one of the many variables of "the heritage of Symbolism." It matters little that Symbolism failed both as a spiritual quest and as a literary method; or that this sect or school carried the seeds of perdition within itself. What really matters is that despite all this it was a highly seminal movement. In the long run its nemesis turned into a catharsis: it is true that its sancta sanctorum changed into a Pandora's box, but it is equally true that the latter became in its turn a horn of plenty, full of rich and novel fruits.

Notwithstanding the claims to the contrary made by many of its Western representatives, Symbolism was both the offspring and the heir of Romanticism; and no less than Romanticism it succeeded in affecting the future development of Western verse, of which, directly or indirectly, it became the supreme and almost the single norm. From this viewpoint Symbolism has been performing for contemporary poetry a task similar to that which Petrarchism and Platonism fulfilled for the lyrical poetry of the Renaissance, with the difference that the lyrical poets of the Renaissance treated Petrarchism and Platonism as formal or abstract ideals, so removed from life that they could never enter into conflict with it. It is its own conflict with life which finally destroyed the Symbolist movement as a going concern. Yet, precisely because no other vital movement has arisen to take its place, Western poetry is still haunted by its ghost. Through the unique but eloquent example of Boris Pasternak that ghost may well haunt even the poetry of today's Russia, despite the powerful exorcisms by which Soviet culture has tried to conjure away the phantoms still left abroad by the vanished idealism of the past. (pp. 116-52)

> *Renato Poggioli, "Symbolism," in his* The Poets of Russia: 1890-1930, *Cambridge, Mass.: Harvard University Press, 1960, pp. 116-52.*

P. GUREV

[*Gurev was a Russian Marxist critic. In the following excerpt from an essay originally published in 1914, he discusses literary and sociological influences on Russian Symbolist poetry, examines its principal themes, techniques, and philosophical bases, and assesses its artistic and spiritual value.*]

When Russian symbolism first made its appearance in the early 1890s under the name "decadence," it was completely out of harmony with the prevailing mood in literature and criticism. The total lack of public-spiritedness of its adherents, their declaration of the principles of pure art, carried to the limit—the limit in versification and style—all of this was so out of step with the prevailing atmosphere in the literary world that the decadents were looked upon as charlatans, the followers of some sort of eccentric fad which could not last long. People explained the appearance of the decadents as a blind imitation of French decadence, without admitting even the thought that, possibly, the conditions for the appearance of a similar tendency had ripened in Russian society. A hail of jibes descended on decadents; disconcerted critics and readers dismissed the very possibility of a serious attitude toward such poetry. The extremism and pranks of its practitioners concealed the essence of decadence from everyone and long deprived it of serious attention on the part of critics and society. Decadence, it was decided, was a soap bubble destined to be shortlived. But Russian criticism was wrong in denying a future to decadence: the past two decades of Russian poetry have indisputably proceeded under the banner of the decadents, whose acknowledged leaders were Konstantin Balmont, Valery Bryusov, and Fyodor Sologub, followed by Vyacheslav Ivanov, Alexander Blok, and Andrey Bely.

Likewise there was nothing abrupt or unexpected in the appearance of symbolist poetry, as it might have appeared earlier. Setting aside extremism in expression and verse, and directing our attention to the ideas and moods of symbolist poetry, we see that the major motifs of symbolist poetry had already been established and even elaborated in the work of Dostoevsky, as well as in the poetry of Fet, Tyutchev, and Vladimir Solovyov, and that it is only because of the general public's unfamiliarity with these poets and its incomprehension of Dostoevsky's profundity that the decadents seemed to be opening a new world. The entire cycle of moods and ideas of Russian symbolism is contained in the poetry of Fet, Tyutchev, and Solovyov, as well as in the novels of Dostoevsky. The symbolist poets continued their tradition, merely taking the poetry of symbols out from the rural byways of literature onto its "highway." Let us first note the influence of Dostoevsky.

First of all, symbolist poetry is related to the fiction of Dostoevsky by the fact that the City has left its indelible and peculiar impression on them both. The hopeless isolation of Dostoevsky's heroes, their wild fantasies, their warped psychology, their boundless exaltation of their "I," their profound degradation in an abyss of sin and voluptuousness—which does not destroy their craving for heavenly purity—the union in one heart of the ideal of Sodom and the ideal of the Madonna: all of this found an echo in the verses of Balmont, Bryusov, and Sologub. Parallel to the apologia of the hero who can in conscience allow himself a crime (Raskolnikov) and to the Karamazovian "everything is permitted," we can set Balmont's line: "The laws are not for me, since I am a genius!" Both in Dostoevsky and in the decadents one must note a morbid love of evil, of torments, of moral anguish, in which Dostoevsky's heroes find a peculiar voluptuousness. Even the "revolt" of Ivan Karamazov, his non-acceptance of the world, is echoed in certain lines by Balmont, particularly "The world must be entirely justified in order for it to be possible to live." The work of Dostoevsky was not understood by critics and society in all of its psychological and philosophical depth. Not having understood Dostoevsky, they also could not understand the decadents, who to a significant degree were his spiritual offspring. And although some critics (for example, Skabichevsky) noted at the time the important circumstance that Dostoevsky was the first major artist of the city, they did not further investigate this profoundly important peculiarity of his work. Not having elucidated the social foundations of Dostoevsky's work, they forfeited an understanding of decadence as well.

From Fet the symbolists inherited one of his central motifs, the aspiration to break loose from the fetters of coarse reality, from the "blue dungeon." The influence of Fet particularly detectable in Balmont's verses of his first period; the two poets are similar both in their withdrawal into a region of azure dream and in their airiness, elusiveness of color, and transparency of outline. In *Notes on Fet,* Strakhov depicts Fet's muse in this manner: "But whether the world is a phantom or reality—isn't it all really the same? It is importunate, it embraces us on all sides, it will not give us peace and draws us to itself, sometimes caressing and lulling but more often tormenting us. Where is there salvation, where is there sanctuary? In song, answered Fet to himself, and he was right: those songs which he sang all his life were his actual salvation, his liberation from the world." The poetry of Fet particularly evinced the aforementioned duality of existence, which was taken up by the symbolists. Fet allowed man the possibility of looking into that "secret crucible in which the prototypes seethe." Such glimpses were provided by inspiration and in ecstasy. The ideas of "contact with other worlds" and of the transparency of this world were expressed in Fet's notable lyric, which begins his *Evening Lights.* We cite it in its entirety, as it also expresses the philosophical essence of symbolist poetry:

I am exhausted by life, by the perfidy of hope,
When I yield my heart to them in battle,
And day and night I close my eyes
And somehow strangely at times I recover my vision.

The gloom of everyday life is still darker,
As after a bright autumnal flash of lightning,
And alone in the sky, like a friendly call,
There shine the golden eyelashes of the stars.
And so transparent is the endlessness of the fires,
And so accessible the whole abyss of ether,
That I look straight out of time into eternity
And your flame I recognize, sun of the world.

And motionless on the fiery roses
The live altar of the universe burns,
In its smoke, as in creative visions,
All force trembles, and all eternity appears in a dream.

And everything which rushes along the abysses of ether,
Each light, corporeal and incorporeal,—
That is only your reflection, o sun of the world,
Only a dream, a passing dream.

And in the universal flow of these dreams
Like smoke I arise and involuntarily melt away,
And in this recovery of sight and in the forgetting
It is easy for me to live and not painful to breathe.
                    [Translation by Richard Gustafson]

A poet with such a perception of the world could not obtain wide renown during the heyday of civic motifs in literature and poetry. Fet had, both in life and after death—until most recently—an insignificant circle of readers.

In another early poet, Tyutchev, we find the same basic motifs that were subsequently elaborated by the symbolist poets, the

same consciousness of the duality of existence and "contact with other worlds":

O my prophetic soul,
O heart filled with disquiet,
How you flutter on the threshold,
As it were, of two realities.

Another poem contains a proud summons to the solitude which is inescapable because we are powerless to reveal our soul to another person.

How will the heart express itself?
How will another understand you?
Will he understand what it is that you live by?
A thought that is spoken is a falsehood;
By stirring up the springs you will cloud them:
Drink of them and be silent.

Love of evil, which is strewn invincibly everywhere, recognition as the world's essence of something irrational, acknowledgement of the "chaos" which "stirs" behind the visible forms of the real—these are the fundamental motifs of Tyutchev's poetry, and this is what makes Tyutchev a great symbolist. "Tyutchev stands as a great master and progenitor of the poetry of allusions" (Bryusov, *The Far and the Near*). At the same time as Baudelaire (and even earlier than he), yet completely independently from him, Tyutchev was concerned with the same themes as the French poet.

Vladimir Solovyov is a poet-philosopher. The small volume of his lyrics is closely and vitally related to his philosophy. Solovyov's mysticism and his cult of Beauty as a superterrestrial essence powerfully influenced the work of two symbolist poets, Blok and Bely. All of Solovyov's poetry is a passionate surge toward "unearthly shores," a surge having for him all the palpability of the real. His profound mysticism and religiosity were peculiarities of Solovyov's psychological make-up, which left a particular imprint on his whole life and activity. The penetration into the beyond and the intuition of it were, according to Solovyov, the only suitable subject for "pure lyricism." In Solovyov's works, poetry of worldly, earth-bound sensations is almost completely non-existent; these, in his opinion, stand outside true poetry. Despite the originality of his philosophy, as reflected in his lyrics, Solovyov is similar to Tyutchev and Fet in his postulation of "other worlds" and "unearthly shores." (pp. 101-04)

These forerunners of symbolism in Russia point to the fact that the emergence of symbolist poetry was not an unexpected occurrence—and here we observe that same continuity of literary trends which is a phenomenon common to the entire history of literature. To deny the influence of French symbolism or that of the poetry of Edgar Allan Poe is certainly impossible, but it is also necessary to note that Balmont was influenced not only by Baudelaire and Poe but also by Fet, while Bryusov fell under the influence equally of Verlaine and Verhaeren and of Tytuchev's poetry, and Blok and Bely were shaped to an immeasurably greater extent by Solovyov than by Western European symbolism.

But these precursors of Russian symbolism were isolated phenomena against the backdrop of Russian literature. They clearly acknowledged their estrangement from the general trend and sensed the "unseasonableness" of their work. They stood in the shade, enjoying fame only among a small circle of readers, and did not create schools around themselves, nor did they attempt theoretically to substantiate the principles of their creative work. In short, during their lifetimes they did not set a trend in literature. Symbolism as a trend arose only in the 1890s when Balmont and Bryusov came forth with their verses—when they, together with Merezhkovsky, proclaimed a new "credo," a kind of "aesthetic manifesto." The question quite naturally arises, why did symbolist poetry, which heretofore had been a hidden, unnoticed, and, as it were, an underground current in Russian literature, turn into a broad and noisy current, beginning with the 1890s? It is obvious that this poetry, previously almost unknown to the broad circles of Russian society in the verses of Tyutchev and Fet, had found its reader; obviously, in certain strata of this society a psychological dislocation had occurred, and the interests, ideas, and moods of the symbolists became congenial to these strata. The burgeoning of symbolist poetry's influence can be explained only by profound, gradually swelling changes in the socio-economic sphere, viz. a rapid development of urban life and the rise of the Russian bourgeoisie, hence, of the bourgeois intelligentsia, and of the intelligentsia in general, uniting within itself segments of various social classes. These factors created both the readership with whom symbolist poetry had an affinity and the poets who cast in sharper relief the motifs already noted in the poetry of Tyutchev, Fet, and Solovyov. . . . In comparing Russian symbolist poetry with Western European (mainly French) poetry, it is necessary to observe that in Russian symbolism the motifs of decadence and decline do not so exclusively and wholly predominate; Russian symbolism is healthier than Western European symbolism. If we take the work of Balmont and Bryusov as a whole, without spurning or overlooking a single lyric, then amidst the motifs of decline and renunciation of life we encounter creative impulses, love of life, and a radiant acceptance of life. In Russian symbolist poetry there are "flowers of evil," but there are also Balmontian hymns to the Sun; there is the refined, intimate mysticism of Maeterlinck, but there is also a Pushkinian clarity and love for the earth. One need merely recall such lines of Bryusov's as:

> The years go by. But I am ready,
> Like a boy, to breathe
> My love with the inevitable power of fiery verse.
> As before, I childishly believe
> In the joy and truth of changing dreams.
>
> I only dreamed the past;
> Life's solution is ahead;
> The soul still wants to search,
> The heart quivers in the chest.

                                            (pp. 105-06)

But one should not overestimate these features of symbolist poetry either. Later we shall see that though there is indeed a wholeness in the symbolists' work, it is unquestionably the wholeness of "decay." Our symbolist poets frequently strive to overcome the decadent within themselves, but without success or hope of success. Yet, if the words of Georges Rodenbach, "Art is a means of forgetting life," can fully be applied to the work of the French symbolists, with respect to Russian symbolism they can be accepted only with some reservation. The healthier atmosphere of Russian symbolism suggests the thought that it was created by social conditions not quite corresponding to those in Western Europe.

The characterization of symbolist poetry as exclusively urban raises no doubts whatsoever. The countryside stands completely outside this poetry. True, in it one frequently encounters non-urban scenery and descriptions of nature, but to the symbolists nature is merely a pretext for purely lyrical and mystical utterances. The city has left its heavy mark on their poetry. But in precisely the same way as with nature, the life and struggle of the proletariat have remained utterly foreign to symbolist poetry. It originated in the bourgeois strata of society, and the entire cycle of its ideas and moods does not overstep the bounds established by its bourgeois origin. . . . If the non-aristocratic intellectuals of the 1860s and 1870s characteristically aspired to tie their fate to the peasantry, the bourgeois intellectuals—for whom the way to the *muzhik* ["peasant"] was psychologically closed, while their own class, the bourgeoisie, displayed the flabbiness and weakness of a dying order—had but one way out: to bury themselves in the realm of purely personal experiences and cultivate those feelings, moods, and ideas which develop in an environment of solitude and estrangement. Whereas the non-aristocratic intellectual characteristically aspired to merge with the life of the people, to dissolve in the sea of the populace, it is characteristic of the bourgeois intellectual to escape into himself and only there find that world in which it is possible to live. "I closed my eyes, and the world was inside me." Reality offers no interest; it cannot capture and fill the soul with its content, for everything in it is worthless, empty, and ugly. "I hate mankind and run swiftly from it; my only fatherland is my desert soul" (Balmont). "I do not see our reality, I do not know our age, I hate my native land, I love the ideal of man" (Bryusov). . . .

The theme of solitude is the fundamental motif of symbolist poetry. In all the experiences of the symbolist poets, we encounter, either directly or in reflected form, the fact of their estrangement not only from the life of groups, but also from the life of another individual, even their beloved. Solitude is by turns extolled as the delight and happiness of life—it alone remains to the man not wishing to mingle with the crowd—and cursed: he strains to break out of it, seeks salvation among people, in love for a woman, but in vain. He remains alone and alienated from all. A complex internal process begins in his soul—the adaptation of the whole psychological apparatus to the basic fact of solitude. In the novels of Dostoevsky we more than once encounter a depiction of the rebirth which is undergone by a solitary man who has escaped into himself. One need only recall Raskolnikov, Kirillov *(The Possessed)*, and the hero of the tale "White Nights." All the forces of his soul recede deep into the individual; his surroundings interest him less and less, and he separates himself from life, as it were, with a translucent screen through which everything seems to him less real, phantomlike. The real world loses something in palpability and weight, and reality comes to resemble a dream; but, in exchange, the images engendered by the soul acquire the brilliance and force of actuality. Dostoevsky demonstrates how such a solitary man is susceptible to all that is fantastic and wild, how it is easy for him, no longer feeling the fetters of life, to come to the most terrifying conclusions and to believe in their incontrovertibility. Thought does not come into conflict with life, is not regulated by it, and roams unchecked, feeling itself omnipotent. This loss of the sensation of the real to a greater or lesser degree pervades all of symbolist poetry. The unreality and illusoriness of human life is the main content of the work of several of its representatives. Sologub can serve as an outstanding example; for him, all of life is the fruit of his "I." He carries through his negation of life, his acknowledgement of it as an illusion, more consistently than all the rest.

> There is no way of life nor are there any customs,
> there is only an eternal mystery being acted out.
> There are no plots or intrigues, and all beginnings
> have been long since begun and all denouements long
> since foretold. . . . What are all the words and dia-
> logues?—A single, eternal dialogue with the ques-

tioner answering himself and thirsting for an answer. And what are the themes? Only love, only death. There are no different people, only one ''I'' in the whole universe, willing, acting, suffering . . . and saving itself from the savagery of a terrifying and hideous life in the embrace of the eternal consoler— Death.

(Sologub)

In endless variations, reality is depicted now as a dream, indistinct and mysterious, now as a nightmare, terrible and wild, or gray and soiled. The boundary between dream and reality is effaced; the symbolist poets often dwell in some sort of novel, half-illusory, fantastic world, where fantasy and life are strangely and whimsically intertwined. Here is a lyric of Bryusov's which vividly depicts such a state:

> Each day and night I have roamed
>   in the country of my dreams;
> Like a sick moth, I have hung
>   on the stalks of flowers.
> Like a star on high, I have shined
>   and lay on a wave;
> This world of my dreams I have kissed
>   in a half-sleep.
> Now I roam all day, I roam
>   Like an invalid;
> All day, like a star on high,
>   I am apart from people.
> And in all that surrounds,
>   in the light and in the dark,
> There is only dream, only dreams
>   without end appear.

Such a perception of life through the translucent shroud of dream and reverie lends a nuance of etherealness and incorporeality to the symbolists' pictures of nature; rather than pictures of reality these are diffuse dreams, vague reveries.

Left to themselves, the symbolists know only their own ''I'': this is the alpha and omega of their existence. The entire sphere of their sensations and moods is limited by the bounds of their ''I''; for them it is difficult, nigh only impossible, to reconstruct the spiritual life of another person, since they do not like people at all and are not interested in them. Even when love for a woman is concerned they are infinitely more fascinated and carried away by their subjective experiences and the nuances of their feelings than by the soul of the beloved. Despite the fact that the symbolists devote much attention to love, they have rendered almost no clear female images. All the forms and nuances of love—from tender, half-childish infatuation to nearly bestial passion—have been described by these poets, but in all of these descriptions we see only their ''I''; the images of the beloved women are indistinct, indefinite, and frequently lacking altogether.

But it would be a mistake to think that their work displays a striking enthusiasm for the individual, that they are preachers and apostles of individualism. This one cannot say. Their individualism loses a significant degree of its value because their personality is deprived of wholeness and unity: it is dissolved in the passing moment. Individualism is the proclamation of a powerful, whole, and harmonious personality; but a personality cannot become such if every instant swallows it whole and each moment is regarded as equivalent to any other. The individualism of the symbolists lacks energy. An individualism pervaded by a contemplative attitude toward everything inevitably leads to the idea of the equivalence of all moments and denies the necessity of sacrificing one moment for the sake of another. With the symbolist poets, the center of the per-

sonality vanishes and its disintegration draws near. The aspiration to engrave one's soul in the given moment is quite characteristic of the symbolists. ''I put only the transitory into verse,'' says Balmont. There are such verses of his as:

> We are thrown into a fantastic world
> By some powerful hand.
> For a funeral meal? A battle? A feast?
> I do not know. I am always another.
> I am confused with every passing minute.
> I live only in betrayal.
> Not in vain am I incarnated here.
> And while awake—I sleep.
>
> We always change—
> Today ''no,'' tomorrow ''yes''—
> Today me, tomorrow you.
> All in the name of beauty.

In his early articles, which were supposed to constitute the *credo* of the new school, Bryusov even attempted to make the ''moment'' the cornerstone of its creative work. ''And it is not man who is the measure of things, but the moment,'' he pronounced, amending the celebrated dictum of Protagoras. Of course, such assertions cannot be taken entirely seriously— this is impossible psychologically—but the tendency to subdivide the personality pervades the symbolists' work to a considerable extent. In their theories and in certain poems individualism is carried to the absurd, to the point where the personality disintegrates. It is for this reason that these poets cannot be regarded as Nietzschean, although Nietzschean motifs are not uncommon in their verse. Nietzsche considers man as something which must be transcended; each man is but a bridge to the Superman. The ideal that Nietzsche thus places before man imparts strength and integrity to his individualism. Here we find not only the subordination of one moment to another, but the subordination of a whole life to a high ideal. Nothing like this is possible where the ''moment'' reigns over the personality and where an ideal of the personality is out of the question.

The declaration of the supremacy of the moment is the limit beyond which it is impossible to go, beyond which non-existence begins; here individualism abolishes itself. The dominion of the ''moment'' is the most graphic and significant expression of decadence. In reality, of course, it could not be expressed in poetry—this would have brought about the death of poetry as well. Such a harsh formulation of the subdivision of the personality as in fact exists in the symbolists' poetry was obviously intended by them as a challenge to realism and to tendentious art, which advanced the demand that art be subordinated to a particular idea. One senses a lone personality alienated from society throughout the work of the symbolists. Such a personality always has a propensity for purely aesthetic experiences, which by their very nature *are ineffectual yet fully accessible* even if the personality has totally withdrawn from life and people. The cult of pure beauty, art for art's sake— these principles lie at the very basis of symbolist poetry.

Of the ''eternal'' triad of Good, Truth, and Beauty, the symbolist poets recognized only Beauty. They are indifferent to good and are sooner prepared to extol evil, since it has more of that poisonous, delicate beauty which entices the broken soul. Paeans to Evil are far from rare in the work of the symbolists:

> I am happy there is suffering on earth;
> I weave it into a fabulous pattern,
> And I make dreams out of others' fears.

Deceit, madness, disgrace,
Senseless horror—these are sweet to see.
Dust and litter I twist into an ornate tempest.

—Balmont

(pp. 106-10)

The symbolist poets are amoral and profoundly indifferent to the grief and joy of other people. This significantly narrows the scope of their creativity; they are psychologically unable to respond to everything, being solely preoccupied with their "I"—here they achieve genuine virtuosity in the description of all the subtleties of their own experiences. But their "I" is not an inexhaustible source, and symbolist poetry has, not without foundation, been reproached for the poverty of its content. Life in all of its manifestations is not reflected in the symbolists' work, and this makes symbolist poetry a poetry for the few.

The symbolist poets do not seek truth, because for them it has already been found: it is that which exists inside them, and inside them reign "moments"—today "yes," tomorrow "no." Truth and good are nothing special; they are closely bound up with mankind and they become fully tangible only through participation in human life, struggle, efforts, and downfalls. Outside of this context, truth and good are merely pale and bloodless concepts, utterly foreign and therefore unnecessary.

The spiritual order of the symbolist poets has been shattered once and for all. They are hopelessly bereft of inner harmony, and utterly lack simplicity and clarity. In complete accord with this is the fact that we never encounter laughter, humor, or irony in their work. It seems that these votaries of the beautiful never smile, so it is hard to believe in their sincerity when they extol the joy of life or the happiness of love. Everything bearing the stamp of sociability and interpersonal relations is alien to them. Laughter—that radiant god—appears only among people, in the crowd, amidst friends; by its very nature laughter is social and inaccessible to those solitaires who have withdrawn into themselves and renounced life. In the symbolist poets' most joyous hymns one senses a psychological breakdown, for instance in the hymns and invocations of Balmont. There is none of that redeeming clarity and radiance of spirit which infects us with love for life more strongly than the most multicolored and magnificent rhetoric. Behind the symbolists' invocations and hymns, insofar as these are to be found in their poetry, one senses the painful process of a struggle undergone with their own estrangement from life; although the struggle has ended in a sort of victory, the victor is left maimed forever. Not love for life but an impotent striving to fall in love with it—this is what one finds in their most radiant works.

Everything which is not their "I" touches the symbolist poets but little. This explains the exclusively lyrical character of their poetry. It is the lyricism of a modern, devastated soul, the poetry of a solitary heart. Even if they undertake to write an epic, they prefer to select subjects from long-past eras; they withdraw, in Bryusov's expression, "into mysterious, bygone ages." Here there is greater scope for fantasy, here they are free in their quest after beauty; they are uninterested in the past destinies of humanity—its battles, victories, and defeats—but hope to find here glimmers of unusual beauty as yet unexperienced and unknown. They are drawn either by a thirst for novel aesthetic experiences, a craving which, in a person deprived of all other life, can take on extraordinary proportions and intensity. It is possible to create the beauty of the past even while remaining in one's "ivory tower"; for this, it is unnecessary to go among people. It is easier and far less disquieting to reproduce, from books and monuments, antiquity, the middle ages, and the era of minuets and powdered wigs than to plunge into actuality, where one inevitably will collide with living people and their sufferings, struggles, victories, and defeats. Not for nothing did Bryusov write at one point: "I do not see our reality, I do not know our age." This is quite true with respect to symbolist poetry as a whole.

But the more decisively the symbolists cut their ties with truth and good, the more strongly they bind themselves to beauty: it is as if their spiritual energy, liberated from the power of good and truth, is entirely spent in the quest and contemplation of beauty. Indeed, what remains for the bankrupt, solitary soul? Only the cult of beauty. In the symbolists' hymns to beauty, their idolization of it as a sort of superhuman, superterrestrial essence, their poignant impulses toward this absolute which they themselves have created, one can feel how irrevocably and hopelessly they have withdrawn from life and from living relations with people. On the other hand, it is clear that beauty is their only refuge, that it alone enables them to endure a life deprived—for them—of any other content.

I know only the whims of my dream,
All I give for the creation of joy
And of the sumptuous inventions of beauty.

—Balmont

Sundered from the communal life of people, they cling with all the strain of desperation to that which is left them. In their worship of beauty they are capable of such monstrous assertions as, for example, we find in the French symbolist Mallarmé: "The world exists to provide material for beautiful books." Bryusov expresses the same thought in the lines: "Perhaps everything in life is but a medium/For vivid and melodious verse."

The quest after beauty—this is the driving spirit of symbolist poetry. But how to the symbolists understand beauty? There are two distinctive elements in their conception of it: above all, the absolute character of beauty, beauty conceived metaphysically. For them beauty is an absolute concealed within the objects and phenomena of life and bearing the stamp of the beyond. As an absolute, beauty never lends itself to full elucidation, and this imparts a tragic character to the symbolists' quest after beauty. They are not averse to applying to themselves Baudelaire's verse about "the sphinx Beauty, against whose stone breast poets bruise themselves."

We find a similar notion of beauty in Fet, Vladimir Solovyov, and also in Dostoyevsky, in the utterances of his heroes (Prince Myshkin: "Beauty will save the world"). Connected with this absolute conception of beauty is the symbolist poets' exaltation of beauty above all else; in their work beauty truly is located "beyond good and evil." They view it as absolute and emancipated from good and truth. It would be possible to cite many corroborating examples; even Merezhkovsky, that failure as a symbolist poet, has exclaimed:

We break all laws
And cross all barriers
For our new art.

In Bryusov and Balmont one frequently encounters a readiness to extol everything in view of the equivalence of everything from the perspective of beauty.

I strangely loved the haze of contradictions,
And greedily did seek fatal intrigues.
All dreams are sweet, all speech is dear,
To all the gods I dedicate my verse.

Bryusov

I only know the whims of dream,
And I'd yield all to happily erect
The beauty of sumptuous inventions.

. . . .

The whitest flowers grow from slime.
Blood's the reddest flower on the scaffold
And death a lovely theme for painting.

Balmont
(pp. 111-13)

The often one-sided aspiration to find beauty everywhere sometimes leads the symbolist poets to a complete poverty of inner content. A great many of their lyrics are bereft of all meaning, and a serious attitude to them is unthinkable. They frequently lose all sense of proportion and in their urge to transform the world aesthetically they incline to empty mannerism. It turns out that it is not possible to put *every* "transient moment" into verse. Carried away by the purely external beauty of the verse, by the richness of the rhyme, by the music of consonances, the symbolist poets repeatedly destroy the harmony of content and form, most often in the sense that their content is much poorer than the form in which it is invested; this gives many of their verses the character of beautiful trinkets. Richness of form—this, it seems, is the generally acknowledged merit of symbolist poetry. The symbolist poets not only further developed the old forms of Russian versification, they also created much that was new in this area. Perfecting the old and creating the new, they acted in full accord with the content of their poetry; the new content required the perfection of old forms and the creation of new ones. The exceptionally lyrical character of their poetry, its extreme subjectivism, demanded a greater variety of forms to reproduce the slightest nuances of a refined soul; the poetry of vague moods and sensations required a greater musicality of verse. A certain abstractness and elusiveness of words were necessary because the symbolist poets were attempting to convey the feeling of their own "contact with other worlds," their insight into "that world where prototypes seethe," for which purpose a clear-cut and highly colored language was unsuitable.

The variety of meters and the wealth of rhythms are striking—one need only leaf through the lyrics of Balmont and Bryusov. Almost every one of their poems is written in its own meter. The symbolists were the first among the Russian poets to pay particular attention to the correspondence of the meter and the form of poetry to its content. Frequently a single poem is written in several meters because of a change in content or a shift in emotional coloration. As an example of the successful switching of meters in a single lyric, one may point to Bryusov's "Temptation."

Poetry may approximate to painting, to sculpture, or to music. The predominance in his poetry of one of these elements should not be accidental in the case of a real artist. Poetry approximates to painting in the work of the so-called landscape poets; for example, the French Parnassians or the Russian poet Bunin: here distinctness of contour and vividness of color are important. In such poems there is little lyricism; in any case, the picture, the image—and not the striving to pour out one's soul—comes first. In contrast, the richer the emotional content of poetry, the more natural it is that it approach music—the ideal art of the emotions. Among the Russian symbolists one encounters in profusion verse painting and verse music—more of the latter, on account of the lyricism of this poetry. Landscapes without lyrical coloration are almost non-existent in their work. As an example of a poem where music is clearly

felt and painting is almost completely absent—so indistinct and uncolored is it—one can cite Balmont's poem "Chords":

In the beauty of melody,
As on a still, mirror-like surface,
I discovered the outlines of dreams
Untold by anyone before me,
Pining and confined
Like plants under blocks of ice.

I gave them the power to delight,
I gave beauty to their birth,
I shattered the ringing blocks of ice;
And, like soundless hymns,
Luxuriant lotuses breathe
Above the expanse of the mirror-like water.

And in the soundless melody,
On this new mirror-like surface,
Their live round dance generates a new world,
Not yet fully revealed.
But linked to the known world
In the depth of reflecting waters.

The musicality of the verse is achieved by means of the meter, rhythm and abundance of open vowel sounds. The symbolist poets often successfully use alliteration, internal rhyme, and other similar devices. (pp. 114-15)

The numerous new word formations of symbolist poetry, many of which have already obtained citizenship, are directly connected with the fact that symbolist poetry aspires to "contact with other worlds." Symbolist poetry has been succinctly defined as the poetry of allusions. Reality is important for its apertures into another, concealed world—thus think the symbolists. A difficult task arises: to communicate their insights, their sensations of this other world, which, of course, they do

Cover by N. Feofilakrov for Vesy, *No. 7, 1906.*

not see, do not hear, but only vaguely feel. Hence the symbolists' complaints about the poverty of human language. Even Tyutchev had raised the question: "How can the heart express itself, how can another understand you?" and came to the hopeless conclusion that "a thought expressed is a lie." The matter seemed hopeless to Fet as well, who exclaimed, "O, if only it were possible to express oneself without words!" In order to create an "allusion" to something unearthly, a language of nuances and a certain abstractness is necessary, since this "something" is completely abstract. Thus, a distinct, definite, and highly colored language was inadequate for the symbolists. Hence, for example, arises the need for so-called "Balmontisms"—i.e., words ending in *—ness (—ost')*, e.g., *mirrorlikeness (zerkal'nost')*, *verblessness (bezglagol'nost')*, *caressingness (laskatel'nost')*, and so on.

Suffice it to compare the old poetical expression "the mirror of the waters" and the new "mirrorlikeness of the waters." Indisputably, the first image is more concrete and, so to speak, more earthy than the latter, and this springs from the fact that the ending *—ness (—ost')* is the ending of words which express abstract concepts. The Russian symbolists were the first to undertake a detailed study of Russian verse; one need only mention the scrupulous investigation of the iamb as used by Russian poets in Bely's book *Symbolism*. If we believe in the coming flowering of Russian poetry—when it will return again to externally youthful life and scoop up as much as it can hold of life's inexhaustible wealth—then all of these perfected and novel modes of expression will be grasped and still further developed by it. In this alone, symbolist poetry is a major epoch in the history of Russian verse.

Symbolist poetry is closely allied to metaphysical, mystical, and religious strivings. No other trend in poetry is so firmly and necessarily bound to philosophy. Such a solid bond exists neither in realism nor in romanticism, although it is quite possible for a realist artist to be a metaphysician in the sphere of philosophy or a religious seeker. Such, for example, was Tolstoy, but he was not prevented from being a realist by his fascination with Schopenhauer, Buddhism, or Christianity. He was a realist by disposition and no metaphysical systems could compel him seriously to doubt the realness of human life. But we cannot imagine the opposite: that a symbolist poet could be an adherent of positivism and the enemy of mysticism, religiosity, and metaphysics. This is quite understandable because symbolist poetry is based on pure metaphysics, on the assumption of the existence of two worlds; without "contact with other worlds" there can be no symbolist poetry. For the realist artist this world is too vivid and alive, it troubles and attracts him too much for there to arise in him the need to peer into "the secret crucible in which the prototypes seethe" (Fet). The realist is vitally bound to life and to people; the idea of the illusoriness of this world psychologically cannot arise in his consciousness. Only the weakening of this vital bond creates the basis for the emergence of the idea of the world's unreality and of the possibility of another, more real word. Two different attitudes come into play here: the realist senses all the reality of life; to the symbolist life seems illusory—there are less durable ties between him and life. We can quite agree with Balmont, who in his collection *Mountain Heights* says: "The realists are caught, as in breakers, in concrete life, beyond which they see nothing; the symbolists, estranged from actual reality, see in it only their dream, they look at life—out of a window. . . . The one is still enslaved by matter, the other has escaped into the sphere of ideality." One can agree with this, with the reservation that the realists see nothing

beyond real life, because beyond it there *is* nothing. It is characteristic that all the most prominent Russian symbolists have also operated as the theorists of a new poetry. There even exists the opinion that they have operated and continue to operate more as theorists than as poets. "Among the leaders of Russian symbolism there are more theoreticians of what is new in the literary movement than creators. They display infinitely greater awareness that a new word is needed than strength to say this new word" (Gornfeld, *Books and People*). In any case, they theorize zealously. And it is here—their creative work aside—that it becomes clear how firmly they have bound their creativity up with metaphysics, mysticism, and religion. This is not peculiar to Russian symbolism; it was so with Edgar Allan Poe and the French symbolists. Let us examine how the symbolists define poetry. One of the fathers of symbolism, Poe, says: "The origins of poetry lie in the cravings for a more insane beauty than that which the Earth can give us." Baudelaire, in his noted poem, "Correspondences," regards all of nature as an array of symbols speaking to us of the world beyond. The Russian symbolists speak even more clearly, defining works of symbolism on the basis of the metaphysical systems of the philosophy of Kant and various others. According to the Russian symbolist poet and theoretician Vyacheslav Ivanov, the chief mark of symbolist art is the "consciously expressed parallelism of the phenomenal and the noumenal; the harmoniously discovered consonance of that which art depicts as external reality *(realia)* and that which it discerns in the external to be an internal, higher reality *(realiora)*." The slogan of symbolism is *"a realibus ad realiora,"* i.e., a summons from the real to something still more real which alone expresses the essence of all that exists (V. Ivanov, *Among the Stars*). Andrey Bely proceeds from neo-Kantianism in raising the edifice of symbolism (Bely, *Symbolism*). Ellis asserts that the basis of symbolist art is Schopenhauer's philosophy of contemplation (Ellis, *The Russian Symbolists*).

In exactly the same way almost all of the symbolist poets are involved in religious quests. And again, this is a phenomenon common to symbolist poetry everywhere. The mother country of symbolism, France, is full of such examples: Baudelaire, Verlaine—who was accorded the honor of having his later poems printed in the journals of the Catholic church—Huysmans, who ultimately became a Trappist monk. One might also note the quiet emotion aroused in Georges Rodenbach by Catholic old Bruges. And we have seen how earnestly the poets of the new school participated in the recent phase of "God-seeking" in Russia.

Almost all of the symbolist poets also lay claim to mysticism and see in mystical insight the highest form of knowledge (Bryusov). But certain writers, evidently considering themselves mystics *par excellence*, deny that the decadents have the capability for mystical experiences and find theirs to be refined, yet purely empirical. This is how Berdyaev looks on the Russian decadents (*Russian Thought*, 1907). He recognizes as mystics only Tyutchev and Vladimir Solovyov. This is not so important in our view, the mysticism of Berdyaev, Tyutchev, and Solovyov being nothing other than refined, yet purely empirical experiences; but it is characteristic of the confusion of concepts which is connected with mysticism. What is important is that the symbolists feel a need for experiences of this kind; what is important is their aspiration to peer "from time into eternity."

Be that as it may, symbolism aspires to be an integral *Weltanschauung*, not limiting itself to the sphere of purely artistic problems, and one cannot deny the consistency and wholeness of this world view. Metaphysics and symbolism can provide a logically complete world outlook, the *theoretical* basis of which is the bifurcation of reality (the phenomenal world and the noumenal world) and the *practical*, the escape from reality into the sphere of Dream. Such a world view certainly cannot be regarded merely as the affair of this or that poet or philosopher; it becomes the common world outlook—of course, in different variations and with different nuances—of the cultural representatives of definite social classes, the ideology of the declining bourgeoisie. We see that everywhere symbolism as a literary trend has brought to the fore first-class artists of the word; parallel to this we observe a ubiquitous inclination toward the realm of metaphysics and religious inquiry. Obviously, to this tendency toward symbolism and metaphysics corresponds a general psychological change in certain classes. We have already noted the psychological basis of both symbolism and metaphysics—escape from collective life into the realm of purely individual experiences, profound and protracted inner solitude, and absence of living ties with the life, work, and struggle of the collective.

The symbolist poet, as a psychological type, is to a certain extent an extraordinary phenomenon in the history of mankind. Of course, from the midst of social groups doomed to extinction as well as from the midst of déclassé elements, there have always emerged poets and writers who have evolved similar themes and forms related to symbolism; but their experiences and feelings have heretofore lacked such acuteness and tension. Modern life is full of such lacerating discordances and is notable for such a furious rate of development that all experiences naturally are exacerbated. All of this has affected symbolist poetry as well. The close union of symbolism and metaphysics points to the profound crisis in the consciousness of the bourgeois cultural representatives and transcenders: what we behold is their capitulation in the face of life.

What, then, are the conclusions to be drawn?

Symbolist poetry has two fundamental insufficiencies. The first is its narrow scope: a vast side of life remains completely outside this poetry. The symbolist poets have little love for life and know it but little. They dwell outside life, and the rays of their poetry illuminate only the tiny world of their own "I."...

In their work there is precious little of "life." Can one say, perhaps, that their "I" is so completely reflected in their work and that this "I" is so rich that the symbolist's ignorance of life and indifference to it is thereby completely redeemed? Yes, their "I" and that alone is present in their work, but, knowing their attitude toward life, one may guess in advance that it cannot offer any particular riches. Of what sort is the content of their "I"? Solitude, its joys and torments; love for woman; nature, permeated by their lyricism; a vague but ardent aspiration to escape into a realm of dream and forget real life. The symbolist poets demonstrate by their own example how the human "I" narrows in proportion as its vital ties with life and with people are cut. Even love ceases to be a relationship between two beings; even the beloved woman is for the symbolists but a shadow, but a means to experience a series of instants of their own "I." It is no wonder that after all of the content that his "I" is psychologically capable of has been drained, after experiencing a love which does not give happiness, finding itself in a state of indifference to life, the symbolist poet's soul pours forth hopeless and gloomy sounds:

> A great disgust for others and myself
> Grows powerfully within and rules my fate.
> I'd love but can't; not seeking, there's nothing to expect,

> And all my dreams are false, and all desires—lies.
> Should truth reveal or not reveal itself to us,
> Should I succeed to live to ripe old age,
> Should you, of whom I always think, show me your love,
> Should I go off and wander or fail to live another day—
> It's all the same, it's all the same, if I go on at all,
> I've looked at life so long and sized it up.
> I give myself to fate, just like a fallen leaf,
> There's just disgust for others and myself.

> —Bryusov

Herein lies the second major inadequacy of this poetry. The point is not that the symbolist poets are antisocial and apolitical, although indifference to the enormous social problems of our times cannot be counted as a virtue either. The important thing is that the path to experiences to which the symbolists beckon us in a fatal way grows even narrower and ultimately leads to a "great contempt both for people and oneself"—indeed, leads to the complete extinction of the human soul.

What, then, are the merits of this poetry? On what is its right to immortality based, and does it have such a right? Unquestionably it does and, unquestionably its best exponents have created much that is "eternal."

Russian symbolist poetry has its own cycle of ideas and feelings, its own content and its own style, first elaborated by the symbolist poets themselves. Consequently, we have before us a complete literary movement, which serves to express the ideology of certain social classes in a particular phase of their historical development. As such an ideology, symbolism has every right to our attention. Symbolism should also attract public interest because it is a general, European trend in poetry, and as such marks a characteristic and noteworthy evolution in the socio-economic relations of all the states having a European culture.

Symbolism, therefore, has all those rights to attention which belong to any genuine art expressing the ideology of a particular class.

But when the discussion turns to merit of symbolist poetry, this can only be understood to mean the value of symbolism for the future culture of mankind, for the culture of the proletariat. Symbolism, as the poetry of the alienated man, is, of course, the diametrical opposite of future poetry, which will be thoroughly social and human. The poetry of weariness and renunciation of life can have nothing in common with the poetry of life and struggle. It is hard to imagine that the ideas and moods of symbolist poetry could have a place in the poetry of the future. But its achievements in the area of form and style, carried out in an original way, must be incorporated into any poetry of the future no matter what form it takes. From the example of Verhaeren, we see what can be done by a poet of the popular masses and of social struggle who does not scorn all the achievements of symbolist poetry. In his work, Verhaeren provides us with a prototype of the future poetry of the masses, profound and all-embracing in content, expressive and vigorous in form. The poet of the future cannot be less sonorous than Balmont or less vigorous than Bryusov. While working out the forms of his works, he must pass through the school of symbolist poetry. Only under these conditions will the poetry of the future be able to master all the wealth of subject matter which history is preparing for it. (pp. 116-20)

P. Gurev, "Summing Up Russian Symbolist Poetry," in The Noise of Change: Russian Literature and the Critics (1891-1917), *edited and translated by Stanley Rabinowitz, Ardis, 1986, pp. 101-21.*

THEORIES OF SYMBOLISM

D. MEREZHKOVSKY

[*Merezhkovsky's 1893 essay* On the Reasons for the Decline, and the New Currents, in Contemporary Russian Literature, *excerpted below, is often considered the manifesto of the Russian Symbolist movement. Assessing the late nineteenth century as a time of conflict between materialism and idealism, he applauds the ascendance of symbolic art and discusses its nature.*]

In the epoch of naive theology and dogmatic metaphysics the area of the *Unknowable* was constantly confused with the area of the *Unknown*. People did not know how to demarcate them and did not understand the full depth and hopelessness of their ignorance. A mystical feeling intruded on the boundaries of exact empirical investigations and destroyed them. On the other hand, the coarse materialism of dogmatic forms subjugated religious feeling.

The newest theory of cognition has erected the indestructible dam, which had for ages divided terra firma, accessible to people, from the limitless and dark ocean that lies beyond the limits of our own cognition. And the waves of this ocean can no longer penetrate into inhabited land, into the area of exact science. The fundament, the first granite blocks of a cyclopic building—the great theory of cognition of the XIX century, was laid by Kant. Since then work on it has gone on uninterrupted, the dam rises higher and higher.

Never before has the boundary between science and faith been so sharp and inexorable, never before have people's eyes experienced such an unbearable contrast of darkness and light. In the meantime, while the firm soil of science on this side of phenomena is flooded with bright light, the area that lies on the other side of the dam, "the depths of holy ignorance," in Carlyle's expression, the night where we all came from and to which we must inevitably return, is more impenetrable than at any time before. In the past, metaphysics threw its brilliant and misty cover on it. The primal legend lit this abyss a little with its dim but consoling light.

Now the last dogmatic cover has been torn away forever, the last mystical ray has gone out. And now contemporary people stand defenseless—face to face with the indescribable darkness, on the boundary between dark and light, and nothing protects their hearts any longer from the terrible cold that blows from the abyss.

No matter where we go, no matter how we try to hide behind the dam of scientific criticism, we feel with our whole essence the proximity of the secret, the proximity of the ocean. There are no boundaries! We are free and alone!. . . It is not possible to compare any subjugated mysticism of past ages with this horror. Never before have people felt with their hearts the necessity of believing and understood with their reason the impossibility of believing. The most characteristic feature of XIX century mystical aspiration is contained in this ailing, insoluble dissonance, this tragic contradiction, in the unheard-of intellectual freedom, in the audacity of negating.

Our time must be defined by two opposing features—it is a time of extreme *materialism* and, at the same time, of the most passionate *idealistic* outbursts of spirit. We are present at a great, significant struggle of two views of life, two diametri-cally opposed world views. The last claims of religious feeling are colliding with the last conclusions of empirical knowledge.

The intellectual struggle that filled the XIX century could not help being reflected in contemporary literature.

The prevailing opinion of the crowd has been realistic until now. Artistic materialism corresponds to scientific and moral materialism. The vulgar side of negation, the absence of a higher idealistic culture, the civilized barbarism amid the grandiose discoveries of technology—all of this put its particular stamp on the relationship of the contemporary crowd to art.

Recently, E. Zola spoke the following very characteristic words about France's young poets, the so-called *Symbolists,* to Monsieur Huret—a newspaper interviewer, who wrote the book *L'enquête sur l'évolution littéraire en France*. I will quote these words in the original, lest I weaken them in a translation:

> Mais que vient-on offrir pour nous remplacer? Pour faire contrepoids à l'immense labeur positiviste de ces cinquante dernières années, on nous montre une vague étiquette "symboliste," recouvrant quelque vers de pacotille. Pour clore l'étonnante fin de ce siècle énorme, pour formuler cette angoisse universelle du doute, cet ébranlement des esprits assoiffés de certitude, voici le ramage obscur, voici les quatre sous de vers de mirliton de quelques assidus de brasserie . . . En s'attardant à des bêtises, à des niaiseries pareilles, à ce moment si grave de l'évolution des idées, ils me font l'effet tous ces *jeunes* gens, qui ont tous de trente à quarante ans, de coquilles de noisettes qui le chute du Niagara.

> ["But what can they offer to replace us? As a counterbalance to the immense positivist labor of the past fifty years they show us a vague 'Symbolist' label that stands for shoddy verse. As a conclusion to the marvelous end of this vast century, as a formulation of this universal anguish of doubt, this disturbance of minds that are eager to know something certain, there is instead obscure prattle, cheap doggerel, composed by beer hall regulars. . . . At such an important moment in the evolution of ideas, all these *young* men who are in their thirties and forties, lingering over trifles and similar foolishness, remind me of nutshells dancing on Niagara Falls."—Translation by Ronald E. Peterson]

The author of *Rougon-Macquart* has a right to exult. It seems that none of the past works of genius has enjoyed a material success, or had a halo of thunderous acclaim in the newspapers, like that of the positivistic novel. Journalists recount with reverence and envy how high a pyramid could be made of the yellow tomes of *Nana* and *Pot-Bouille*. Zola's last novel has been translated with astounding zeal five or six times into Russian, and even the greatest works of world literature have not been translated in a similar manner into our language. The same inquisitive Huret searched out the chief poet-Symbolist, Paul Verlaine, in his favorite cheap cafe on the Boulevard Saint-Michel. Before the reporter stood a man no longer young, crumpled by life with a sensual "face of a fawn," with a dreamy and tender gaze, and a huge, bald skull. Paul Verlaine is poor. Not without the pride characteristic of "the insulted and humiliated," he names as his only mother "l'assistance publique"—welfare. Of course, this person is far from the Academic chairs next to P. Loti that Zola dreams of so ardently and jealously.

Nevertheless, the author of *Débâcle*, as a true Parisian, is too carried away with contemporary life, noise, and the vanity of the literary moment.

It is an unforgivable error to think that artistic idealism is some recent discovery of Paris fashion. It is a return to the ancient, eternal, never-dying.

That is why these young rebels should be frightening for Zola. It's no business of mine that one of the two is a beggar, who has spent half his life in prisons and hospitals, and that the other is a ruler of literature, if not today, then tomorrow, a member of the *Académie?* Is it my business that one has a pyramid of yellow volumes and the Symbolists have ''quatre sous de vers de mirliton?'' Well, four lyrical verses can be more beautiful and truthful than a whole series of grandiose novels. The strength of these dreamers is in their *revolt.*

In essence, the whole generation of the end of the XIX century bears some type of revolt in its soul against suffocating, deadly positivism, which lies like a stone on our hearts. It's quite possible that they will perish, that they will not succeed in doing anything. But others will come, nevertheless, and continue their work because their work is *vital.*

''Let people be called to account soon, and with great craving for the pure and noble, which has been completely banished at this time.'' That is what the author of *Faust* predicted sixty years ago, and now we notice that his words are beginning to come true. ''And what is reality all by itself? Its true depiction, which can give us a more precise knowledge about certain things, can bring us pleasure; but actually the higher utility that is in us is contained in the ideal that emanates from the heart of the poet.'' Then Goethe formulated this thought even more strongly: ''the most immeasurable and inaccessible (to the mind) the given poetic work is, the more beautiful it is.'' It wouldn't hurt Zola to recall that these words do not belong to capricious Symbolists, pitiful nutshells dancing on Niagara Falls, but to the greatest poet and naturalist of the XIX century.

The same Goethe said that a poetic work should be *symbolic.* What is a symbol?

In the Acropolis above the architrave of the Parthenon some traces of a still extant bas relief depict a most common and evidently insignificant scene: nude, well-built youths are leading young horses and taming them calmly and joyfully with muscular arms. All of this executed with great realism, if you want, even with naturalism, with a knowledge of the human body and of nature. But there is, after all, hardly more naturalism in Egyptian frescoes. And they affect the viewer, however, completely differently. You look at them as you would a curious ethnographic document, as you would a page of a contemporary experimental novel. Something completely different draws you to the bas relief of the Parthenon. You sense in it a breath of *ideal* human culture, a *symbol* of the free Hellenic spirit. A human tames a beast. This is not simply a scene from everyday life, there is in addition a whole revelation of the divine side of our spirit. That is why there is such ineradicable greatness, such calm and wholeness of life in the deformed piece of marble, above which millenia have flown by. A similar symbolism penetrates all the creations of Greek art. Isn't Euripedes' Alcestis, dying to save her husband, a symbol of maternal compassion, that inspires the love of a man and a woman? Isn't Sophocles' Antigone a symbol of the religious-maidenly beauty of female characters that is reflected in medieval Madonnas?

Ibsen's *Doll's House* has a characteristic detail: during a very significant dialogue between two characters a servant comes in and brings a lamp. The tone of the conversation in the well-lit room suddenly changes. It is a trait worthy of a physiologist

and naturalist. The shift from physical darkness to light influences our inner world. An artistic *symbol* is hidden under a realistic detail. It's hard to say why, but you will not quickly forget this significant correspondence between the altered conversation and the lamp that lights the misty twilight.

Symbols should naturally and unintentionally pour from the depths of reality. If the author contrives them artificially, in order to express some idea, he turns them into dead allegories that evoke nothing but revulsion, which everything that is dead does. The last minutes of Madame Bovary's agony, accompanied by a banal ditty about love that is sung by an organ grinder, the scene of insanity in the first rays of the rising sun after the tragic night in *Ghosts,* were written with more merciless, psychological *naturalism,* with greater penetration into reality, than the boldest human documents of the positivistic novel. But with Ibsen and Flaubert, besides a current of thoughts expressed with words, you involuntarily feel another, deeper current.

''Any thought that is uttered is a lie.'' In poetry, what is unsaid and twinkles through the beauty of a symbol acts more strongly on the heart than what is expressed by words. Symbolism makes the very style, the very artistic substance, more inspired and transparent, something that shines all the way through, like the thin walls of an alabaster amphora in which a flame is burning.

Characters can be symbols. Sancho Panza and Faust, Don Quixote and Hamlet, Don Juan and Falstaff are, according to Goethe's expression, *Schwankende Gestalten.*

Dreams that haunt mankind are sometimes repeated from century to century and accompany it from generation to generation. It is impossible to convey the idea of these *symbolic characters* with any words, for the words only define, delimit a thought, and symbols express the limitless side of thought.

We cannot, at the same time, content ourselves with the crude photographic exactness of experimental snapshots. We demand and foresee new, still undiscovered worlds of sensitivity according to the hints of Flaubert, Maupassant, Turgenev and Ibsen. This craving for the unexperienced, this pursuit of nuances, of the dark subconscious in our sensibility, is a characteristic feature of the approaching ideal poetry. Baudelaire and Edgar Allan Poe have already said that the beautiful should *astonish* us a little, should seem unexpected and rare. French critics, more or less successfully, called this feature— *impressionism.*

Those are the three main elements of the new art: *mystical contents, symbols,* and a broadening of artistic sensitivity. . . . (pp. 17-21)

D. Merezhkovsky, ''On the Reasons for the Decline, and the New Currents, in Contemporary Russian Literature,'' in The Russian Symbolists: An Anthology of Critical and Theoretical Writings, *edited and translated by Ronald E. Peterson, Ardis, 1986, pp. 17-21.*

JAMES WEST

[*West is the author of* Russian Symbolism: A Study of Vyacheslav Ivanov and the Russian Symbolist Aesthetic *(1970). In the following excerpt from that work, he presents and analyzes thirteen varying definitions of ''symbolism'' by its most prominent practitioners.*]

The following passages all contain either a definition of "symbolism" (and in one case of "the symbol"), or a characterization of "good art" which, in its context, is equivalent to a definition of symbolism. Chronologically, they span the Russian symbolist movement from its comparatively early stages to its aftermath.

The first three statements are by Valeriy Bryusov, and date from the 1890s.

I The symbolist tries to arouse in the reader by the melody of his verse a particular mood which would help him to apprehend the general meaning—and this is all.

II In symbolism poetry has for the first time attained its essential form, and has begun to act upon the soul by means that are proper to it. Symbolism is poetry's realization of itself, the conclusion of all its questing, a radiant crown to the history of literature, whose rays are projected into eternity.

III The creative artist has one aim: to express his own mood, and to express it fully. General comprehensibility or accessibility is impossible to achieve, for the simple reason that people are different from one another.

The fourth definition is from *The Battle for Idealism*, a collection of essays by Volynsky (A. L. Flekser), published in 1900.

IV What is symbolism? Symbolism is the fusion of the phenomenal and the divine worlds in artistic representation. From this definition there emerge clearly the two principles necessary for symbolist art. Like any art, symbolism is directed towards the simple and plainly visible events of life, . . . towards natural phenomena and the phenomena of the human spirit. . . . The very concept of the *phenomenon*—the finest poetic achievement of contemporary philosophy—has a logical meaning only in the idealist view of the world, in which the visible and the invisible, the finite and the infinite, the sensibly real and the mystical are fused in an indissoluble unity, as the inalienable signs of two interconnected worlds. Not for one moment does symbolism exceed the legitimate bounds of art. In the light of its ideas and concepts, it sees phenomena and represents only phenomena. This fundamental characteristic of symbolist art indicates to us the proper rôle of the writer's mystic state of mind in the creation of his poetic scenes and images. But art should never become either an act of worship or an abstract philosophy.

Bal'mont offered the following definition in a lecture to a Russian audience in Paris, given in 1900.

V How may we define symbolism more accurately? It is poetry in which two contents are mingled, not forcibly but organically: abstraction masked and beauty made manifest,—they combine as easily and as naturally as the water of a river is harmoniously blended with the sunlight on a summer morning. However, whatever hidden meaning a particular symbolist work may have, its concrete content is always complete in its own right; in symbolist poetry it has an independent life, rich in overtones.

The next four passages are all by Andrey Bely, and were published between 1906 and 1911, in the period during which the symbolist movement reached its height in Russia and began to decline.

VI A symbol is the integument of a Platonic idea. Ideas, which differ in their degree of intensity, enable us to see these successive degrees as a progressive circumscription of the single world idea. The concept of the world idea arises inescapably if we allow, with Vladimir Solov'yov, the existence of generic and specific ideas [a footnote here refers the reader to Solov'yov's *Lectures on Godmanhood*]. . . . The world idea, according to Solov'yov, can be equated with the World Spirit. We may regard the process of liberation and revelation of the World Spirit as an ascent from the original specific idea to the generic. This process—the process of objectivation of the Idea—suggests itself to us as a succession of ascending degrees. A ladder is formed stretching from earth to heaven, from the visible to the essential.

VII The essence of art is an absolute principle which reveals itself through the particular aesthetic form. The meaning of art is a process of revelation whose purpose is dictated by this principle: it is possible to discern a purpose behind the formal relationship in creative art; and further—to link this purposefulness with more general principles. It must be remembered that if the question is formulated in this way, the resulting deepening of the implications of aesthetics means that art is inevitably made subject to more general norms; there is revealed in aesthetics a supra-aesthetic criterion; art at this point becomes not so much art (τέχνη) as a creative revelation and transformation of the forms of life.

VIII Art is the symbolization of values in images drawn from reality.

IX The symbolist art of the last decades, as far as form is concerned, does not depart essentially from the methods employed by art throughout the ages. . . . Symbolist art, from the point of view of the ideas it contains, is for us in most cases not new . . . the novelty of so-called symbolism lies in its overwhelming abundance of the antique.

"Ellis" (L. L. Kobylinsky) was perhaps the most naïvely dogmatic theorist of the Russian symbolist movement. He contributed regularly to *Vesy*. In 1908 Ellis composed a tirade against the "symbolist theatre," in which he defined symbolism thus:

X The essence of symbolism is the ability to capture the subtlest overtones of things, without distorting their real appearance, the ability to understand . . . the persistent "regards familiers" of any thing in the great temple of Nature.

The essence of symbolism lies in *correspondences* [sic], the innumerable elusive *correspondences*, which can scarcely, and in any event only partially be embodied, and which never coincide exactly with the world of appearances. The only means of conveying them has always been and will always be the lyrical poet's "confuses paroles," whose most essential property, it must be acknowledged, is their inaccessibility to the average man, preoccupied with life's anxieties, their aristocratic exclusivity and their absolute unsuitability for any kind of social experiment. It is no accident that the outstanding symbolist poets of our age have been bad dramatists, and the greatest of them have not been dramatists at all.

In 1911 the magazine *Apollon,* which became the vehicle for a campaign to restore order and clarity to symbolist art, published an article by Innokentiy Annensky, originally written in

1903 as a draft introduction to his first volume of poetry. It was entitled *What Is Poetry?* and included the following passage:

> XI   Instead of the tedious hyperbole which in the poetry of the past was used conventionally to convey complex and often invented emotions, the new poetry seeks exact symbols for feelings, i.e. for the real substratum of life, and for moods, i.e. for that form of spiritual life which more than anything else establishes a bond between people, entering with equal justification into the psychology of the crowd and of the individual.

In January 1914 a public discussion was held in St Petersburg on the problems of contemporary literature. The participants included Ivanov, Chulkov, and Anichkov; and Fyodor Sologub, who worked his contribution into an article published the following year in *Russkaya mysl'*. Here are several of the generalizations put forward in this article:

> XII   Art is more than a mirror held up to the accidents of life.... The soul of man always thirsts for live action, and live creativity, it longs to create within itself a world analogous to the outside, objective world, but constructed independently. The vital life of the human mind consists not only in observing objects and bestowing upon them expressive names, but in the constant endeavour to grasp the vital links between them, and to locate the whole of the phenomenal world on a single plan of universal life. Objects appear to our consciousness not individually, but in their overall relatedness to each other. As our awareness of the relations between things grows in complexity, the whole content of the world around us is reduced to the smallest possible number of general principles, and each object is perceived in relation to the highest generalization that can be thought of. Thus all objects become nothing more than intelligible signs of certain all-embracing relationships.... Life itself no longer seems a succession of more or less diverting episodes and appears to the consciousness as part of a world process directed by the Only Will.
>
> [The art of our day] is religious, because it involves tragic acts of willing. Tragedy is always religious, and there is only one will. Also, the art of our day is religious because it is symbolic, and symbolism always gives us a sense of the general interrelatedness of things; it refers all phenomena to a single general principle and like religion, endeavours to penetrate to the meaning of life.
>
> The poet is again becoming a priest and a prophet, and in the temple where he performs his rites art should become a dome, it must become a vast shining dome over life.
>
> ... The art of our day in covering life with this magnificent dome, even though it is built not for life but for the purposes of art alone, none the less asserts life as a creative process. It asserts only that life which strives to be creative, and rejects that life which stagnates in the fetters of the prosaic.

G. Chulkov's *Vindication of Symbolism* appeared in his book *Our Fellow-Travellers*, published in Moscow in 1922. He sums up his account of symbolism:

> XIII   Thus, symbolism is one of the means at the disposal of art, whose sense and significance lie in the cognition and celebration of reality, sometimes internal, sometimes external to the creative individual.

> ... On the aesthetic plane, the criterion of symbolism is the moment of correspondence between the thing represented and the general, the whole, the infinite which is revealed behind the thing.

The most obvious feature common to all these statements is, predictably, a preoccupation with what lies behind the external appearance of things. A concern for the values beneath the surface is present in the self-evident assertions of Bryusov and Annensky that the artist should capture and convey moods and feelings (I, III, XI). Both, however, make it quite plain that they are calling for something altogether more far-reaching than simply "impressionism." For Bal'mont, impressionism was to be distinguished from symbolism by its subjectiveness and fragmentariness: "... the impressionist is an artist who speaks a language of allusions to subjective experience, and by his fragmentary indications recreates in others an impression of what he is able to view as a whole." Bryusov in particular states (in passage I) what Bal'mont here implies for the case of the symbolist: that the mood aroused by the symbolist's "impressionistic" technique is a stepping-stone to the understanding of an objective "whole," a comprehensive meaning underlying experience.

The majority of the statements we are considering make a more explicit reference to a hidden meaning in the objects represented in a work of art. At its weakest, this is the "subtlest overtones of things" (X) which according to Ellis (who takes his cue from Baudelaire's *Correspondances*) the symbolist art-

Portrait of Andrey Bely by L. Bakst, 1905. From Russian Literature Triquarterly, *No. 4, Fall, 1972. By permission of Ardis Publishers.*

ist should capture. Chulkov's "the general, the whole, the infinite which is revealed behind the thing" is only slightly less vague (XIII). For Bely, it is the purpose of art to reveal "an absolute principle" (VII), for Sologub—"the highest generalization that can be thought of" (XII).

Sologub, however, stresses the relation between the object and the underlying principle: ". . . each object is perceived in relation to the highest generalization. . . ." The whole paragraph, with its insistence that art is a process by which the phenomenal world is related to a single principle, is virtually a paraphrase of Vladimir Solov'yov. Bely's process of purposeful revelation (VII) is kindred; indeed, Bely, Volynsky, and Bal'mont, as well as Sologub, all stress that the secret revealed by art is the bridge between the real and the divine or "supernatural" world, between "the visible and the invisible, the finite and the infinite" (Volynsky, IV). Bal'mont sees in symbolist poetry "two contents mingled . . . organically" (V): his "beauty made manifest," and his image of sunlight blending with water, echo Solov'yov's *Beauty in Nature;* Bely (VI) openly expounds Solov'yov's teaching and describes symbolism as "a ladder stretching from earth to heaven."

Amidst the general agreement that art reveals a truth of a higher order behind the phenomenal world, there are several warnings that the representation of reality is still fundamental to art, even if the artist has a higher end in view. Volynsky emphasizes that "symbolism is directed towards the simple and plainly visible events of life," as well as towards "the phenomena of the human spirit," and that "it sees phenomena and represents only phenomena" (IV); Bal'mont issues a reminder that the "concrete content" of a symbolist work of art is always "complete." Bely makes the point in its most essential form: "Art is the symbolization of values in images of reality" (VIII). These warnings to some extent represent a plea for truth to life, but there are signs that, at least for some symbolists, the object of their attention was not "real life" in the conventional sense. Bely calls for "a new attitude to reality" (IX) and speaks of art as "a *creative* revelation and *transformation* of the forms of life" (VII). This recalls strongly Solov'yov's vision of art as a force transfiguring reality as does Sologub's view of life as "part of a world process directed by the Only Will" (XII). When Chulkov discerns the meaning of art in "cognition and celebration of reality" (XIII), he is employing the terminology coined by Ivanov in the same situation (he uses Ivanov's word "oznamenovanie"). But the reality which Chulkov knows and celebrates is "sometimes internal, sometimes external to the creating individual," suggesting the idea of an autonomous "reality of the imagination." Sologub speaks explicitly of "a world analogous to the outside, objective world, but constructed independently" by the artist within himself (XII), and further declares that art is an edifice "built not for life but for the purposes of art alone," though it "asserts life as a creative process." Even in these brief statements there is evidence of a strong tension between, on the one hand, a principle of objectivity in which the idea of truth to reality is compounded with Solov'yov's notion of the subservience of art to a higher, objective truth residing *outside* man and the phenomenal world, and, on the other hand, recognition of the autonomy of the artistic imagination and the world it "creates."

In addition, the question of the function of art, and the value for man of the revelation it can bring of the true order of things, is raised in the passages under consideration in strongly conflicting terms. For Annensky, art is an activity which "more than anything else establishes a bond between people" (XI).

This is strongly reminiscent of Ivanov's contention that true art is a form of "communal action" in which the barriers that isolate the individual are broken down. Ivanov regarded art in this respect as a religious activity, and gave paramount importance to the tragic theatre, both for the common involvement of the spectators implicit in this art form, and for its significance as a development from Dionysian religious rites. Sologub speaks explicitly of "a world analogous to the outside, objective world, but constructed independently" by the artist himself (XII), and further declares that art is an edifice "built not for life but for the purposes of art alone," though it "asserts life as a creative process." Even in these brief statements there is evidence of a strong tension between, on the one hand, a principle of objectivity in which the idea of truth to reality is compounded with Solovyov's notion of the subservience of art to a higher, objective truth residing *outside* man and the phenomenal world, and, on the other hand, recognition of the autonomy of the artistic imagination and the world it "creates."

In addition, the question of the function of art, and the value for man of the revelation it can bring of the true order of things, is raised in the passages under consideration in strongly conflicting terms. For Annensky, art is an activity which "more than anything else establishes a bond between people" (XI). This is strongly reminiscent of Ivanov's contention that true art is a form of "communal action" in which the barriers that isolate the individual are broken down. Ivanov regarded art in this respect as a religious activity, and gave paramount importance to the tragic theatre, both for the common involvement of the spectators implicit in this art form, and for its significance as a development from Dionysian religious rites. Sologub's definition of symbolist art likewise suggests that the task of revealing "the relations between things" is a common endeavour, and that symbolist art is an activity at least analogous to religion (XII). For Volynsky art is a religious activity to the extent that its aim is "the fusion of the phenomenal and divine worlds," but he is careful to stress that it should never "exceed the legitimate bounds of art" or "become either an act of worship or an abstract philosophy" (IV). Bryusov, on the other hand, dissents from the common assumption that art unites people; one would assume from passage III that he saw creative art as accessible only to those who in some respect resemble the artist. The issue here is that of "the poet and the crowd" which so vexed Ivanov; and what in Bryusov was probably only a preoccupied aloofness may be seen carried to its logical conclusion in "Ellis" for whom the "most essential property" of (symbolist) poetic speech is its "aristocratic exclusivity and . . . absolute unsuitability for any kind of social experiment," to the extent that the notion of symbolist theatre is abhorrent to him. (pp. 108-15)

[It] should by now be plain that . . . the narrow question of the relation of art to reality in the symbolist aesthetic can only be examined in the light of the form which the symbolists *wished* this relationship to take, and of the not necessarily artistic expectations which they called upon art to fulfil. From the foregoing sample alone, we must assume that these expectations were high and often had only a tenuous connection with strictly aesthetic questions—if, indeed, they did not precede all aesthetic questions. Sologub looked to art for a revelation of nothing less than "the meaning of life" (XII). Bely, it will be remembered, concluded that art is "subject to more general norms" (VII), and indeed, in Vladimir Solov'yov's aesthetic, which was Bely's inspiration at this point, art subserves the higher spiritual and social organization of mankind. Chulkov was speaking for the majority of symbolists when he declared that "the question of the aims of art is indissolubly linked with that of the meaning of life." (p. 116)

James West, in his Russian Symbolism: A Study of Vyacheslav Ivanov and the Russian Symbolist Aesthetic, *Methuen & Co. Ltd., 1970, 250 p.*

FRENCH SYMBOLISM AND RUSSIAN SYMBOLISM

EVELYN BRISTOL

[*In the following excerpt, Bristol compares the Russian Symbolists' literary and philosophical concerns and poetic techniques with those of their French counterparts.*]

A major difference between French Symbolism and the Russian school of the same name is that the French poets aimed at verbal suggestiveness or musicality, whereas the Russians emphasized the notion of religious discovery, or truth. French Symbolism began to emerge during the waning years of a well-developed Romantic movement and was in part a reaction against high rhetoric. Verlaine wrote in his "Art poétique," "Prends l'éloquence et tords-lui son cou!" ["Take eloquence and wring its neck!"] Whereas the Romantics had valued the intensity of feeling, the new goal was rather a subtlety of emotions. In Russia the Symbolists were separated from Romanticism by a period of ascendant Realism, whose notion of a utilitarian literature they most specifically opposed. Russian Symbolists were unfatigued by Romanticism, and had every reason to reach backwards to that movement in their search for weapons against Realism. Russian Symbolism had therefore a more old-fashioned appearance than French Symbolism; it was more philosophical and religious. Nevertheless, Russian Symbolism also had an affinity with the school of Realism which it nominally rejected; for both reflected the moral quest characteristic of Russian literature; both sought ideals of their own devising.

The major French writers, from Baudelaire through Mallarmé, became increasingly elusive in their manner of expression. They addressed themselves to mysteries, or spheres of meaning, which they posited beyond words. Baudelaire's famous poem "Correspondances," derived from Swedenborg's philosophy, placed the relationship between heavenly and earthly beyond expressibility; his synaesthetic perceptions in the same poem created a similar verbal impasse among earthly phenomena: "Les parfums, les couleurs et les sons se répondent" ["Perfumes, colors, and sounds correspond"]. In "Élévation" the object of his inspired comprehension was a new sign of the transcendental: "Le language des fleurs et des choses muettes!" ["Language of flowers and mute things!"] Even more indicative for future literary methods were the tropes which facilitate his reticences about his own feelings. In "Spleen" (J'ai plus de souvenirs que si j'avais mille ans ["I have more memories than if I were a thousand years old"]) his self-deprecation is rendered effective by the simile of a dresser stuffed with old mementos, which is in turn a graveyard; his non-utterances at last become those of a sphinx, and one who sings only when touched by the rays of the setting sun. Verlaine was unconcerned with mysteries of a religious nature, but did much to create a taste for the elusive within the consciousness. His most tantalizing subject, and most imitated, was a melancholia whose cause is nameless. His lines "C'est bein la pire peine / De ne savoir pourquoi" ["That is truly the worst pain / To not know why"] all but suggest that the direst

pain is the most delicious. He originated the concept of landscapes of the soul, so named in "Claire de lune," where ecstasies are the rising water of the fountains. Sounds also replaced emotions. His opening lines "Les sanglots longs / Des Violons / De l'automne" ["The slow sobbing / of violins / of autumn"] characterize not autumn, but the perception of it. "De la musique avant tout chose" ["Music before everything"] (from "Art poétique") was not only the most widely accepted slogan of the Symbolist movement, it evoked precisely that impulse to the form of the song without words that so suited the age. Mallarmé's inaccessibility results from his pointing so consistently to meanings beyond the capacities of words. His poems suggest that silence itself is a mystic presence, always containing more meanings than expression. In the poem "Sainte" the archetype of perfection is the silent music of a graphically depicted saint. Mallarmé's burdened imagery does not erase the notion that the consciousness is the real object of depiction; in "Autre Éventail" the fan's dream of flight can only be the poet's. Yet in a mystical way the mind may achieve the ideal. The Neo-Platonic perfection of the implicit ("la faute idéale de roses") beside which experience is but an empty grape skin, is the subject of "L'Aprés-midi d'un faune." Mallarmé's opinion that art emanates from *L'Idée* is contained in the lecture "La Musique et les lettres." Precisely Mallarmé, who was prone as a poet to silence, became the object of the Symbolists' especial esteem and was the *maître* of their *cénacle* ["coterie"].

Russian Symbolism did not become increasingly suggestive; it became increasingly explicit about the necessity of mystical striving in everyday life. The Russians paid relatively less attention to verbal practices, landscapes of the soul, or music, and more to the soul's goodness, measured by its capacity for attainment. The Romantic resignation of Zhukovsky and the disillusionment of Lermontov were modified by a new sense of spiritual urgency. Konstantin Bal'mont represents the movement as a whole in his progression from the passivity of the 1890s to the ecstasies of the early years of the new century. Beginning with *Pod severnym nebom* (1894), he portrayed a langorous, but unavailing desire innate in both mankind and nature to rise to an unidentified ideal state. But after 1900 attainment is his keynote; nature is a pantheistic whole in which the poet's individuality is not lost but enhanced by cosmic identifications; the title "Budem kak solntse" (1901) epitomizes his confidence. Fedor Sologub and Zinaida Gippius exemplified a decadence that was born of a despairing idealsim.... Neither Sologub nor Gippius became optimistic after 1900, and the change had caused Bal'mont to adopt a Nietzschean position "beyond good and evil." Sologub and Gippius did not wish, in the totality of their œuvres, to shock, but to create a feeling of compassion for the earthbound.

Briusov's avowed position as an observer sets him apart within the Russian movement; he was not by vocation a seeker of metaphysical truths, which he, in fact, discounted. Instead, he made a cult of art itself, a dedication which became apparent in the section "Blizkim" of *Tertia vigilia* (1900), where he extolls the artists of the ages. In "Ia" (1899) he himself lives only for words. Later, in "Poetu" (1907) he exhorts the artist to bring his life as sacrifice to dispassionate witnessing. Briusov's aestheticism suggests an influence from the French Symbolists, but he did not learn their hints, their reticence, and he lacked their form of mysticism—their sense of a meaning beyond words. His worship of art was a wider kind of Neo-Romanticism; he further resembles the earlier Romantics in that his poetry asks for pity for him as a martyr to art, if not to metaphysics. In the poem "Votvet" (1902) his inspiration is compared to a toiling ox.

The second wave of Russian Symbolists, who entered literature after 1900, initially most resembled the English Romantic poets and German thinkers because of their faith in a goodness and harmony innate in nature. Viacheslav Ivanov symbolized this divine essence variously by nature scenes, or by evoking the Eternal Feminine, Christ, and Dionysis. . . . In his joy he proclaims mysteries rather than suggesting the elusive. He differs from the Romantics in that, being familiar with several European currents, he has a feeling for the relativity of symbols. But his sublimity and his grandeur pall, and we miss intimacy, where there might be nuances. The prankishness of Andrei Belyi in *Zoloto v lazure* (1904), together with his childish, folklore imagery, make convincing his faith in a transcendental ideal; his mood is infectiously sanguine. Nearly the exclusive subject of Aleksandr Blok in *Ante lucem* and *Stikhi o prekrasnoi dame* (1905) was his impatience to find signs of a divine feminine essence in landscapes and cityscapes; he would not rest without a miracle. The sense of personal tragedy which informs the metaphysical disillusionment of Belyi and Blok after 1905 is a further sign of their singular preoccupation. . . . The inevitability of failures in attainment was their new subject, but not the inexpressibility of some things. Moreover, their melancholias and self-lacerations illustrate, as had the spleen of the first wave, the Russian perception of decadence as a fall from grace.

From this difference in emphasis between the French and the Russian schools, that the French were attentive to the evocative and the Russians to metaphysics, others flow. The lyric hero, sometimes glorified in European Romanticism, was lowered by the French Symbolists, but not among the Russians. In the poems of Baudelaire, the figure tends to become an everyman; he recedes from view in the best of Verlaine, and is often totally absent in Mallarmé. Romantic exultations and despairs became in the poems of Baudelaire the property of the average reader, whom he addressed in a prefacing poem to *Les Fleurs du Mal* as "mon semblable,—mon frère!" ["my double,— my brother!"] His persona is no superman but a citizen of Paris; the worst of his vices, and ours, is *Ennui*:

"Il en est un plus laid, plus méchant, plus immonde!"

["There is one more hideous evil, and unclean!"]

The emotions of Verlaine's persona tend to be commonplace; they are the previously unexplored trivia and vagaries of existence, the calm attainment, and disturbances which are accessible to all—nostalgia, married happiness, absences, religious quandaries. His settings are the familiar surroundings of cultivated consciousness, with literary and artistic allusions, Parisian scenes, gardens, or the not too distant countryside. His objects are often mundane. He combined the malaise of Baudelaire with the modesty of vision inaugurated by Théophile Gautier, Baudelaire's master. Mallarmé's terse way of speaking was even more novel, and the narrators of his separate poems barely seem to coalesce into one persona. His joys and sorrows appear to derive from literature, and he often views himself without solemnity:

"La chair est triste, hélas! et j'ai lu tous les livres."

["The flesh is sad, alas! and I have read all the books."]
(from "Brise marine")

Visible are the slimmest sketches of interiors and landscapes, and intimacy with the narrator is restricted to knowing his habits

of mind, especially his equivocating, but not his biography. Significantly, these French poets did not claim in their verse any superior susceptibility to the aesthetic and none considered his creative capacity a gift or lesson to humanity.

The lyrical ego of the Russian Symbolists was in every case more prominent, as with the Western Romantics; and sometimes enhanced by Nietzschean self-affirmation or by the cloak of the poet-priest creating a liturgical art. In any case, the Russians tended to create dramas out of their changing attitudes toward the universe, a grand subject. Bal'mont's elan after 1900 derives from pantheism together with self-assertiveness. . . . His participation in the world's evil betrays Nietzsche's influence. All the poets of the first wave flaunt this sin of pride. Sologub posed as more evil and guilty than others; he rehearsed his escapist daydreams, his dedication to Satan, his insanity and unnamed sins, and thus set himself apart from society, by whom he elsewhere felt belittled and ridiculed. Gippius held herself above the herd by her demands for a love in Christ. But she knew too well that she detested the commonplace; she was a Romantic and could not stand mediocrity; thus her own love was empty and invalid. She was tempted by pride as Verlaine was by the Flesh. Briusov intended to shock society with his previously forbidden subjects, such as the indulgence of sexual passion and the contemplation of torture; he hints at lunacies kin to Sologub's. His subsequent preoccupation with the leaders of world history and with mythical figures, as in "Akhilles u altaria," argues an admiration for naked power. Audaciousness itself finally suggests itself as his true subject. In "Ia" rejection of any ideological commitment outside art freed him from the academy and society alike. Finally, Briusov's martyrdom is perhaps more convincing than the other Symbolists' in that his dedication to art brought no recorded warmth or rewards to himself.

The poets of the second wave, without being tempted by pride, were poets more susceptible to the doctrine of poet as priest or as the recipient of divine intuition. In Ivanov's verse art is the path to the divine, not only for the poet, but for his people, whose voice he is. In the poem "Vospominanie" art embodies the collective memory of eternal beauty. In his articles, especially in "Poet i chern'," the poet is portrayed as aspiring, at his best, to mythmaking. Therefore his own attempts to fathom the divine essence within substance are at once personal, and democratic.

The youngest, Belyi and Blok, were perhaps the most individualistic in that they made the most coherent dramas of their mystical searches. When Belyi in *Zoloto v lazure* invites us to join him in a return to youth to share idealistic hopes, or to childhood for the sense of the uncanny in folk and fairy tale stories, he is relatively self-effacing and entertaining. But in his disillusionment after 1905 he began to castigate himself for this show of naivete as though it had been complacency. He thinks of himself as lunatic or dead. . . . He gains in strength; yet his is another instance of a Russian Symbolist who draws attention to self-lacerations that exclude the remainder of mankind—as Baudelaire did not. Blok's aspirations and disillusionment were yet more explicit. He shaped his œuvre into a "legend of the poet" as in the Romantic era, as though a Byron or Pushkin. His early search for mystical communion with Saint Sophia was, indeed, exclusive, but humble and without disdain for others. In the period of his infatuation with the Stranger, he still manages to convince us that he has not lost sight of perfection, and he punishes himself because he has lowered his idol. His dedication to country follows as though it had been a penance imposed by his idealism. In "Na pole Kulikovom" (1908) he exclaims: "O Rus'moia! Zhena moia!" ["Oh, my Russia! My wife!"] In all, the Russians were not given to acknowledgments of the universality of their emotions and capacities; they stressed their separateness from humanity, as had the Romantics.

In France Symbolist imagery was an introduction to realism, a descent from Romantic poetry, which had pictured nature in its grander aspects, past civilizations, exotic lands, and cosmic spaces. None of the symbolists relinquished Romantic imagery entirely, but Baudelaire modified the Romantic tendency to darkness, not of the starry night, but of rain, autumn, and the deprivation of light, he added a closeness and decline, rot. . . . He also introduced in "Tableux parisiens" the slum and squalor, with old, shriveled, and helpless people, like his women in "Les Petites vieilles"; they are shown not as unusual sights, but as the regrettably commonplace. Verlaine thought of himself as working in the school of Baudelaire, and he made even more memorable the dismal watery and autumnal scenes; they match his outstanding theme: a melancholia without specific cause, a sinking without motivation. But his range is greater. With Verlaine the difference between the Symbolists and the Parnassians becomes apparent. The Symbolists brought not the past, but the present, in domestic and in urban scenes. Verlaine's imagery can be associated with developments in graphic art, even beyond his connection with Watteau. In *La Bonne chanson* he pictured his wife with impressionistic brightness and vagueness. Mallarmé's imagery is similarly familiar, although often allusive. He discarded the autumnal rains for azure and white, even when melancholy, as in "L'Azur," which begins "De l'éternel azure la sereine ironie" ["From the eternal azure the serene irony"] and whose subject is the absence of the ideal. He often describes the play of clear light and mists. Most important, his imagery changes rapidly, as in a kaleidescope; it evokes, perhaps illuminates, but does not present. Both "Hérodiade" and "L'après-midi d'un faune," with nymphs and faun, are more erudite than exotic.

In Russia Symbolist imagery is strikingly more varied; it appears to derive from the several currents of nineteenth century poetry, including European Romanticism, French Symbolism, and sometimes Parnassianism. Nature is common among the Russians, sometimes in the dismal guise of the early French Symbolists, sometimes with the grandeur seen since Byron. Bal'mont used the watery nature of the French Symbolists in the nineties, then he changed to exotic scenes, including northern and Mediterranean Europe, and India, to signal his change of mood. He brought the bright colors of the dawn and sunset, and occasionally fire. Gippius remained narrow in range, and nearly allegorical; her dust and rain seem quite of a piece with Baudelaire's and Verlaine's sad landscapes, but hers symbolize her own or the world's lack of love, boredom, and depression. Sologub's landscapes picture realistically the low-lying nature of Russia, but elsewhere he returned to Romanticism to bring astral spaces and the figures of magic and fairy tales, such as imps, queens, and witches. Briusov eschewed nature imagery and preferred the signs of civilization, past or present; the inevitability of evil and corruption was one of his principal themes. He differentiated between the imagery of closed spaces, impotent melancholia, and psychological aberration on the one hand, and the grand scenes of great figures on the other. His vivid depictions of Greek myths and historical scenes in widely flung geographical areas stem from Victor Hugo and from the Parnassians. He was a literary scout, essaying genres. He popularized the urban scenes with distressing details that had been a part of Symbolism since Baudelaire.

The variety and colorfulness of Symbolist imagery after 1900 was owing in part to a "dawn" mentality which seemed to call for an awakened imagination. Yet the resulting scenes were, for a time, essentially Romantic. Ivanov perceived the divine essence in the heavens and oceans, in abysses above and below (as had Merezhkovskii). His exotic settings included the Alpine mountains, the Mediterranean, and others. Belyi created in *Zoloto v lazure,* especially for his sunsets, the palette of a myriad pastel colors that became associated generally with Russian Symbolism. . . . His nature scenes erupt in creatures of fantasy and folklore such as his giants and centaurs. Blok was seldom a poet of nature; the fogs, or stars, or sunsets of his initial search for the Beautiful Lady belong to softly colored cityscapes. After 1905 the imagery of Belyi and Blok became more modern. Belyi appears in the guise of a clown, but we see realistically the suburbs and countryside where other vulgar human stories take place. Next he pictures the murky Russian steppes with trains and taverns, a corrupted wilderness. When Blok's idealism became tainted, he turned at once to the city at night, with taverns and crowds. After that his imagery refreshingly portrays the allusive content of a modern mind, the Igor Tale for Russia, Verlaine's masquerades from *Fêtes galantes,* the *commedia del'arte,* Don Juan, the southern scenes of his Italian journey, his own rooms, Russia's snowstorms, a plausible mixture of reality and allusions. It might be said of Russian Symbolist imagery in general that a breadth of cultural experience was harnassed for some rather narrow and specific aesthetic and religious views.

A philosophical tendency of the Symbolist movement was the discarding or modification of Christianity in favor of some form of Neo-Platonism. Dualisms such as heaven and earth, and good and evil, tended to give way to monistic systems, the divinity then being hidden within substance. Thus Baudelaire's avowed Swedenborgism, which introduced the notions of correspondences and synaesthesia. Baudelaire's soaring to spiritual elevation and his dedication to Satan (in "Les litanies de Satan") were mere symbols of religious inclinations. Verlaine's Catholicism was secure; he addressed God and he lapsed into self-destructive indulgences. What he contributed to the dissolution of the Christian system was an extraordinary moral lassitude. He acknowledges God, good and evil, but is indifferent. Verlaine was a genuine leader. This impulse to obviate guilt appears to have been one of the deeper currents of Symbolism. Mallarmé espoused Neo-Platonism, citing the example of Schopenhauer. The problem of good and evil dissolves in his monistic system, taking with it innocence and guilt. In "L'après-midi d'un faune" the world of contingency, suggested only mythically, is like a veil, beyond which the perfect world of Ideas casts its spell even on the faun.

The Russians were more securely tied to Dostoevskian questions of evil and guilt, but there were as many philosophical systems among them as individuals. Russian Romanticism had left no coherent doctrinal legacy, and the Symbolists themselves created the first period of well-developed metaphysical concerns. The first wave of Russians was obsessed with evil, which they regarded as an essential part of the world order or of human nature, but imposed on us by fate. They protested against, and sometimes partook of, that evil. Bal'mont in his first, pessimistic period posited an impersonal divine essence in nature, from which he was cast out. In his second, pantheistic period, his identification with nature's vitality opened for him the right to be evil as well as good. For the first wave, evil remained to be explored in order to get at truth; Baudelaire had been in a similar position. Sologub's poetry shows him, throughout, obsessed and angered by the irresponsibility of the heavens in causing suffering. If he pictured a gnostic dualism, then it was the gods who separated mankind, and him especially, from the still and distant perfect harmony. When, after 1900, he opposed to this dualism a Schopenhauerian vision of the universe as an eternal, amoral process, forever creating and destroying, then evil was inevitable. Gippius not only doubted it to be in the power of mediocre humans to rise to a perfect love, but she was moved to pity the devil, being certain herself that evil was imposed on all. . . . Briusov resembled Sologub in assuming the world to be more evil than good, and appeared to join it as a protest, disdaining guilt. His worship of art as the creation of value was not pure in atmosphere like Mallarmé's; but included the notion of making art out of evil, as in "K portretu K.I. Bal'monta" (1899). The whole first wave as though remained on a philosophical plane with Byronism, they were not saved by monism if they espoused it.

The optimism of the second wave resulted precisely from their attempt to see the world as a monistic system without evil. Ivanov alone succeeded. Almost his sole subject was the varieties of affirmation. His Parnassian visions of antiquity, his evocations of Christ and of Sophia, and his panoramic abysses are presented as multiple perceptions of the single divine principle which is before us and within us. Belyi hoped that his Sophian, innate harmony would effect a kind of utopian salvation by becoming manifest in the world; Blok sought personal attainment. When their expectations collapsed, their monistic vision of the universe remained intact, and what they regretted was their own presumption. Blok's apparent blasphemies, as in the exclamation, "In vino veritas" ["In wine is truth"] of "Neznakomka" (1906), are self-punishments. He then espoused a divine Russia that would destroy his own culture.

Symbolists often perceived a hiatus between art and religion, whereas Romantics, who tended to equate goodness, truth and beauty, usually did not. Symbolists had learned to express their spleen, for example, in verse. Baudelaire exclaimed in "Hymne à la Beauté," "De Satan ou de Dieu, qu'importe?" ["From Satan or from God, what does it matter?"] He considered hashish dreams to be a pernicious substitute for the *gout de l'infini* ["taste for the infinite"]. Verlaine's call for music in his "Art poétique" bespeaks an indifference to the divine. He considered the divine only one of the subjects of art, not its alter ego. Mallarmé's Neo-Platonism made pure ideas the object of all the arts, but he did not state whether their perfection was meant to include goodness and even morality. The French considered their calling as artists was a service to beauty, not morality.

Beauty was treated as a stepchild in the Russian Symbolist movement, and sometimes held suspect, or equated illogically, even by its devotees, with Decadence, or moral decline and lassitude. This curiously un-Romantic view of beauty may have survived from the era of Russian Realism. A cardinal premise of the Russian Symbolist school was that intuition brings knowledge (truth), not necessarily beauty. In fact, sensual refinement was seldom portrayed by the Russian Symbolists. For Bal'mont, art was at first a path to the ideal; but it became in his second period the quality of audacity, as in "Sin miedo" where the poet is exhorted to be like a dagger. For Sologub inspiration was the entrance to a higher spiritual state, whose attainments must be relinquished on return to reality. Briusov

extolled artists in *Tertia vigilia*, but in "Ia" he treated his own devotion to art as though it must run counter at least to conventional notions of the good. Indeed, Russian critics regarded the first generation of Symbolists, regardless of what they said in their verse, as poets without morals.

The tragedy of the younger members of the second wave was that they came to realize that their art did not yield religious truths, that art and religion are separate. Blok wrote in "K Muze" (1912), "Zla, dobra li?—Ty vsia—ne otsiuda" ["Are you cruel or are you kind? You are not of this world"]—a close parallel to the sentiments of Baudelaire in "Hymne à la Beauté."

In sum, the French were on the track of suggestiveness, the psychology of everyman, music, and beauty, with or without morality. But the Russians, still clinging to the religious faith of Romanticism, or perhaps the didacticism of Realism, clung to goodness, with or without beauty. If Decadent, they accepted the label evil. The Russians thus reached backwards to find in European Romanticism support for the identification of truth and goodness (an impulse which Hegelianism had presumed during Realism). They adopted some innovations of Symbolism, but they did not react against Romanticism, they gave it, too, a belated life in Russia. (pp. 69-78)

> *Evelyn Bristol, "From Romanticism to Symbolism in France and Russia," in* American Contributions to the Ninth International Congress of Slavists: Literature, Poetics, History, Vol. II, *edited by Paul Debreczeny, Slavica, 1983, pp. 69-79.*

GEORGETTE DONCHIN

[*Donchin is the author of* The Influence of French Symbolism on Russian Poetry *(1958). In the following excerpt from that work, she analyzes characteristic themes in Russian Symbolist poetry, tracing the influence of the French Symbolists, particularly Charles Baudelaire, on the subject matter.*]

The Russian symbolists would have been the first to deny the presence of any themes in their work—so convinced were they of the utter vagueness and almost incorporeal quality of their poetry. But this *mot d'ordre* ["watchword"] of symbolist aesthetics expressed itself mainly in their manner of writing—perhaps because manner meant more to the symbolists than content—and exerted a comparatively minor influence on the subject-matter. There are undoubtedly a number of themes characteristic of symbolist poetry: some are a direct sequel of symbolist aesthetics, some are traditional themes of all poetry treated in a new manner, and finally others are a reflection of the new modern age. They all have however a distinctive tinge which assigns them to one specific school of poetry, and links various writers into one related group. Symbolist poetry displays a certain common attitude or point of view towards the subject-matter, and this allows us to proceed to a classification of "symbolist themes," which is to some extent necessarily artificial.

One of the constantly recurring themes in the early symbolist poetry was a feeling of pessimism and acute *malaise*. At first it was accepted passively, with a deep awareness of one's impotence and helplessness. Already Minskij considered that *taedium vitae* was as unavoidable "as a swirling dust when winds meet. . . ." Merežkovskij pondered over the possibility that decadence was historically inevitable, a natural end of Russian literature. His poetry was pervaded by a specific fatigue, by a feeling of metaphysical ennui and indifference, and he compared his generation to rootless flowers. His early poems are one constant variation on the oppressive boredom of life and his own weariness and lassitude. . . . Likewise, Zinaida Hippius feels that there is no issue from her hopeless grief. . . . [She] almost seems proudly to parade her helplessness before the world. One suspects a certain pose in this attitude which emerges time and again in her poetry (viz. especially *Belaja odežda*). Zinaida Hippius has been often called a typical product of the *fin de siècle*, and in her early poetry she appears as tired, refined and fading as the St. Petersburg decadents whom she herself thus characterised. . . . The generations of the 1880's and 1890's were deeply aware of the fact that they lived in a transient, chaotic period, that they belonged to a dying world, but stood at the same time on the threshold of a new one. Dissatisfaction and deep pessimism, fear of both the present and the future, and in some cases a faint hope, itself tinged with a strange disquiet, pervaded all the poets of the turn of the century. They seemed to have suddenly lost the ground from under their feet, and were terrified by the sudden appearance of a vacuum. They were prepared to fill it with anything, almost at any price. . . . Marxist criticism ascribes literary decadence to political and social conditions in Russia. Undoubtedly, the literary *malaise* of the Russian poets was to some extent provoked by the conditions in which they lived. But, after all, the *fin de siècle* atmosphere held sway throughout Europe, and cannot be viewed only in relation to Russia. At the same time, the almost complete detachment of Russian symbolist poetry from social and political affairs makes one wonder to what extent this poetry could have been influenced by such factors. These take on a deeper meaning if related to the general climate of the age—an age of transition, of chaos, of spiritual unrest and political disturbance, of new social patterns. It must be also stressed that Russian symbolism—especially in its early stages—was an essentially literary movement, and literary influences played a rather important part in its formation. Thus the modernist poet inherited much from the romantics; in a way, and especially in his "negative phase," he was the spiritual child of the Russian "superfluous man," and at the same time he was also impressed by the *ennui baudelairien* which reigned supreme in almost the entire new Western literature, and which Baudelaire himself perhaps defined best in a letter to his Mother: ". . . Ce que je sens, c'est un immense découragement, une sensation d'isolement insupportable, une peur perpétuelle d'un malheur vague, une défiance complète de mes forces, une absence totale de désirs. . . . Je me demande sans cesse: A quoi bon ceci? A quoi bon cela? C'est là le véritable esprit de spleen. . . ." ["What I feel is great discouragement, a sense of unbearable isolation, a perpetual fear of some vague calamity, a complete lack of confidence in my powers, a total absence of desires. . . . I am constantly asking myself: What good is this? What good is that? This is the true spirit of spleen. . . ."] Romanticism had extracted much interest from the analysis of ennui. But Baudelaire extended the field to such an extent as to make it almost his own. He experienced *taedium vitae* in a variety of forms, and went through all the vagaries of boredom. The similarity of moods is striking. The early Russian decadent poetry seems to provide an illustration of this Baudelairean attitude. Like Baudelaire, the Russian poets see everywhere merely *le spectacle ennuyeux de l'immortel péché* ["the tedious spectacle of immortal sin"]. But soon the Russian modernists add a slightly different interpretation to this quasi-romantic spleen, and shift imperceptibly from "decadence" to "symbolism." They are no longer petrified by a total absence of desires; and like Baudelaire again (viz. *Moesta et errabunda*) they try to escape

from their spleen into space and time, whether travelling or evoking memories or simply longing for another world, another mode of life—however undefined, however illusive. . . . Most of them are just waiting, expecting, hoping, and dare not express or define their hopes. How much of it was really sincere and how much literary pose, is difficult to assess at present. Belyj noted that his fellow poets were particularly fond of seeing themselves as prophets of a new dawn, as harbingers of a new spring, as superior men who sensed that humanity was on the threshold of a new cultural era. Bal'mont saw them as people who thought and felt at the turn of two periods— one finished, another not yet begun. "They see that the twilight has come to an end, but the dawn is still hidden somewhere behind the horizon of the decadents." Enriched by different influences and various new interests, such as religion, mysticism, and even occultism, the trend gains in intensity and creates a real surge—not of true mysticism, as many Russian critics would like to have it, but of mystical mood, background, atmosphere. There are several testimonies to the existence of a highly charged atmosphere at that time. This was not mysticism, but an indefinable mood of foreboding, a climate of expectation of a miraculous and undecipherable mystery. . . . [Their] wish to plunge into the unknown was obviously a desire for escape. Actually, almost the entire range of subjects in symbolist poetry can be correlated to the one theme of escapism. The importance attributed to art assumes a new significance if one considers, as the symbolists did, that art is the best means to forget life, for it allows the poet to live in a passive way and frees him from the duty of active participation in life. Escapism forces the modernists to prefer dreams to reality. Just as imaginative experience is preferred to life, the world of artificial inventions is preferred to reality and, at the same time, while the world is being transformed into a playhouse and man into an actor, the deepest emotions become simply theatrical subjects. Shunning life, the modernists move away from people, into solitude and death.

The theme of loneliness haunted all Russian symbolists, the older and the younger generation alike. In a way solitude was connected with poets' egoism. Already Minskij claimed that he was so made that he could love only his own self. . . . Time and again he stresses, almost proudly, that he does not love anybody, that people are as alien to him as he is to them, that he is heedless of others and does not share his joys with anyone. The same theme constantly recurs in Minskij's *Xolodnye slova* and *Gorod smerti*. (pp. 120-27)

Zinaida Hippius, who echoed her husband when she claimed that the decadents face a miserable death in their solitude and should unite with people in the name of God, described her own poems as the product of a lonely mind and hence unnecessary to anyone else. She admitted that she herself could not live with people . . . and that solitude had a great fascination for her. . . . Merežkovskij despaired about the utter loneliness of the decadents who went into the terrible "underground" of Dostoevskij; he thought this too great a price for receiving the freedom of art. He tendentiously expressed the hope that the decadents would soon embrace those from whom they were estranged, and cited Aleksandr Dobroljubov who left everything to go among the people. . . . But in spite of Merežkovskij's preaching, in his own life he never cared for other people, and disregarded them completely. . . . [His] attitude is strikingly reminiscent of that of Baudelaire, who developed with unequalled vehemence the romantic cliché of the poet's fate, misunderstood and victimised in an indifferent society. His sense of aloofness often developed into a strong dislike for his *prochain* ["neighbor"], a dislike which was connected at the same time with his pride and his dandy's horror of altruism or pity. Baudelaire's work supports his frank admission to his Mother: "J'ai une haine sauvage contre tous les hommes . . ." ["I have a savage hate of all men . . . "]. This theme of aloofness and solitude was taken up by all the Russian symbolists.

In spite of his later optimism and somewhat artificial though exuberant paganism, Bal'mont too passed through all the stages of fashionable loneliness and despair. Together with Brjusov he considered himself isolated on his poetic path, alone in the wilderness . . . , but in contrast to Merežkovskij and Zinaida Hippius he did not seem to complain so much of his isolation; he rather proudly announced it to the world. This again is linked with his strongly felt and expressed egoism. Ehrenburg once jokingly said of Bal'mont that no other poet ever spent so much time on the deck of a boat or at the window of a train, and saw nothing during his travels but his own soul. This self-preoccupation was characteristic of all the symbolists poets, but was perhaps especially conspicuous in Konevskoj, Bal'mont, and Sologub. To a great extent this was no doubt responsible for their withdrawal into themselves and for the realisation that, in the depths of their soul, they were barred from the outside world and therefore unavoidably lonely. On the other hand, it may be argued that the symbolist withdrawal into the ego was the consequence of their wish for escape, an escape from the world, from life, and from people. All these moods were closely interwoven, and it is difficult to establish their precedence. But the rather proud display of isolation in the case of Bal'mont . . . seems to support, even more strongly than in the case of Zinaida Hippius, the theory that the feeling of loneliness pervading symbolist poetry perhaps owed more to a consciously reproduced literary attitude than to a deep and sincere feeling of *fin de siècle*. Was not the withdrawal of poets within an Ivory Tower a common literary attitude typical already of the romantics? (pp. 127-30)

All the shades of the feeling of loneliness are represented in Brjusov. . . . A critic once said of Brjusov that his feeling of estrangement from life was in a certain measure the cause of his duality, for he could not merge with life from within and was capable only of observing it from without. This may be true of all the symbolists, if one considers their essential inability to be passive observers of life. In spite of attempts to the contrary, Brjusov remained till the end an individualist content only with his own company. . . . In 1924 he still entitled a cycle of his poems: "Alone with oneself" (in *Mea*).

Among the symbolist poets who truly seemed to enjoy their solitude was Sologub. He was happy to evade reality and seek refuge in a fantastic world of his own imagination. Loneliness was not terrible for him, for his ego was in everything and everything was in his ego. Life among people was a burden to him. . . . There rarely was a writer more concerned with himself. All his poetry is merely an illustration of his subjective views on the world and life. Rejection of life and love of solitude and imaginary world were not incidental additions to Sologub's work—they were the very basis of his whole philosophy.

The second generation of symbolists seems to have suffered more intensely from the feeling of isolation. Blok's tragedy might have been a tragedy of solitude. He considered union with people as the only means to overcome isolation. But this was theory. In reality he hated people. He hated in particular the intelligentsia, yet could not help belonging to it. This duality runs through both his work and life. Ivanov-Razumnik claimed

that Blok was unable to withstand the loneliness of spirit and therefore sought salvation in mysticism.

Belyj was equally aware of his "cosmic" isolation. At a certain moment he seemed to accept it, but most of his early poems show that he struggled hard against the "icy deserts" of "cosmic loneliness." Yet even in his expectancy of a better unknown, Belyj still feels that he is alone. . . . Belyj's estrangement from life has been compared to that of Gogol'. In particular, Gul' drew an interesting parallel between the two. Belyj followed Gogol' into a dead world, into a terrible panopticon where people were only wax dummies and life a profound nightmare. The poet enlivened his dead atmosphere, his waxwork people only by his orchestration of sounds. It is true that in many respects Gogol' and Belyj were bound by a certain spiritual kinship, but as far as alienation from life was concerned, Belyj followed the general symbolist trend rather than Gogol'.

There is no doubt that a feeling of isolation pervaded all the intellectuals at the turn of the century; the early symbolists often sought escape in death, in negation of all positive values, in amorality, despondency, pessimism; later, unable to find help in their respective abysses, they turned towards "higher" spheres, towards neo-Christianity, toward mysticism. There is no doubt that they received their first incentive from Poe, Baudelaire, Ibsen, Nietzsche. That this stimulus was to be singularly powerful in Russia can be seen at once—by the striking similarity of themes. The isolation of all the symbolists in their creative process and in the whole construction of their poetic thoughts, as well as their complete irrelevance to everything connected with life, has been noted by many contemporary Russian critics. In particular Aničkov said that the whole group of new poets could be called "a school of lonely poets," and he drew attention to the fact that ". . . it is precisely thanks to their artistic loneliness that our poets enter the international school of the so-called young ones, the school of Vielé-Griffin, de Régnier, Verhaeren, Dehmel, Przybyszewski, etc. . . ."

The pessimistic attitude of the symbolists towards life was bound to result in an intensified preoccupation with death. The theme of death is perennial to all poetry, but after Baudelaire a new conception of it pervaded modern poetry. Death was no more opposed to life, and the haunting fear of death gave way to a conception of death as a welcome means of escape. The romantics, feeling that the universe was too narrow for them, had called for the infinite (*l'infini*). Baudelaire, seeing in this world merely banality and boredom, sought the unknown, death, in order to find "something new." A mystical attitude to death characterises all the French symbolists, especially Villiers de l'Isle Adam, Huysmans, and Rodenbach. For Maeterlinck, death is no more an inexorable frontier, an eternal source of anxiety and despair. The hero of many of Maeterlinck's plays, it is intangible and occult, always present, in everything invisible, in all the silences. For all the poets who shun the feverish activity of life, death is now the beatific peace for which they yearn, and thus gradually the modernists come to substitute death for life. It was Baudelaire who was mainly responsible for the complete revival of the cult of death. Professor Mansell Jones argues that Baudelaire was not a poet of death. And yet the French poet was obsessed by just that idea. He devoted to it the final section of *Les fleurs du mal*, and though the cycle is composed only of five sonnets, they belong to the best of Baudelaire. Moreover, the theme of death finds its way into all his poems, and in his *Petits poèmes en prose* he explicitly states that *tout est néant, excepté la mort* ["all is nothing, save death"], that death is *le seul vrai but de la détestable vie (Le tir et le cimetière*) ["the only true objective of detestable life (the gunshot and the graveyard)"]. Baudelaire's mysticism of death is very complex and its background is formed both by Catholic and medieval tradition, both by cheap macabre romanticism and nihilism. French traditional criticism greatly stresses Baudelaire's obsession with death: "L'idée unique de Baudelaire est l'idée de la mort; le sentiment unique de Baudelaire est le sentiment de la mort. Il y pense partout et toujours, il la voit partout, il la désire toujours. . ." [Gustave Lanson, *Histoire de la litterature français*]. Baudelaire's despondency is closely linked with his mysticism of death, but he is not really a necrological poet though his poetry is full of necrological emphasis. He undoubtedly bequeathed something of his attitude to the early Russian symbolists who, at the same time, also adopted his philosophy of death as a means of escape. For Baudelaire, as for so many of his followers, to die was to escape "anywhere out of the world," to travel towards the unknown, presumably conceived as a new life (cf. *Le voyage*).

The new attitude to death is reflected in the entire Russian symbolist poetry. One of the first, Zinaida Hippius welcomes death. . . . (pp. 131-35)

A great number of necrophil poems can also be found in Brjusov. His second volume of verse is already significant in this respect. Like other modernists, the young Brjusov seeks relief in death. . . . (p. 136)

Sologub's treatment of the theme of death is more complex. He traversed a wide range of feelings about death. At first, death seemed terrible to him, then he saw it as equivalent to life. But soon Sologub came to consider death a deliverer. . . . Sologub perceived beauty, truth and freedom in death. All his heroes, including his favourites—children, dream about a pleasant and comforting death. This trend of thought can already be traced in his first volume of verse. Expressing originally a quiet sadness about the sense of life, he searches for the truth which he feels must be hidden somewhere. Later he is overcome by a cold despair. Finding no answer in life, he seeks it in death. Sologub is brought to do so by sheer passivity. . . . [The] thought of death is based solely on a feeling of weakness and impotence. It develops into a despair which throughout Sologub's work accompanies his fear of life and his attempts to discover its meaning. Life for Sologub is terrible, he is compelled to reject it. It is synonymous with philistinism [and] pettiness . . . ; it is therefore useless to look at life for the meaning of humanity. And Sologub tries to satisfy his need for escape successively in the creation of fantastic worlds, in a cult of beauty, in loneliness, in "blessed irrationality" (*blažennoe bezumie*), and more frequently looks for salvation in death. In his early days—like Maeterlinck in his first plays—Sologub can only express fear of the inevitability of death, and all his thoughts are controlled by this fear mingled with despair. . . . But then Sologub discovers that life and not death is something to be afraid of, and after this volte-face he becomes the most expressive chanter of death among all the Russian symbolists. . . . Belyj once wrote that Sologub spoke about death as a lover, but that it was difficult to call him a demonist, for there was a silent sadness in his peace with death. And yet Sologub's attitude to death is closely connected with his satanism and demonism, his apotheosis of evil, sadism, and morbidity. These themes are not limited to him, they run throughout most of the works of the other symbolists.

Just as in the France of the late 1880's, in Russian too there intervenes between the early modernism and the later brand of mysticism a rather strange and peculiar state of mind—a kind

Portrait of Aleksandr Blok by K. Somov, 1907.

of satisfaction in depravity, a mystical love of evil. As far as Russian symbolist poetry is concerned, this state of mind was strongly fed by Baudelaire. Baudelaire was considered the first decadent poet, for no one before him had celebrated "ces détraquements du cœur et des sens, cette obscure sensualité cruelle, sadique, cette curiosité pour l'anormal, cette hantise du macabre, toute cette perversion que Baudelaire nous découvre en ces poèmes vibrants et rapides qui mêlent 'l'écume du plaisir aux larmes des tourments'" ["these breakdowns of the heart and senses, this obscure and cruel sensuality, this curiosity in the abnormal, this obsession with the macabre, all this perversion that Baudelaire reveals to us in his swift and vibrant poems which blend 'the dregs of pleasure with the tears of torment'" (Paul Fort and Louis Mandin, *Histoire de la poésie française depuis 1850*)]. The apotheosis of evil and perversion is perhaps stronger in Sologub than in any other Russian writer. Again this may be a literary pose, an acknowledgment of the prevailing fashion, but with Sologub it is however so constant as to become second nature. If benevolent death is the positive pole of Sologub's world, hatred of everything sunny and vital is his negative pole. Most of his poems end with murder, suicide, or madness. . . . The persistence of the themes of death and sin is quite remarkable in Sologub; he is at the same time a sadist, a *déseperé*, and a mystic. His sadism is quite outspoken. The only passion which is sweet to him is one which is united with cruelty. For him, pain is a redemption for bliss. Passion itself leads to freedom; the way to liberate oneself lies in the pleasures of passion and perversity. Naturally, all the hostile critics exploited this trait of the poet to the hilt. Vojtolovskij . . . claimed that his thirst for flagellation and torment was an outcome of his desire to imitate Dostoevskij. Others considered the Marquis de Sade the ''progenitor of all our small and great Sologubs.'' Sadistic scenes in Sologub's work have been listed, and he was accused of importing into Russian literature ''poisonous seeds from Western Europe,'' of originating pornography in Russia.

In spite of obvious exaggerations, there is a grain of truth in all these statements. Sologub was undoubtedly familiar with the works of Huysmans, as well as with those of Saâr Péladan and other French satanists of the mid-1880's. Huysmans's mysticism and erotomania were not alien to the Russian poet. But there is no need to go as far back as the original teachings of the Marquis de Sade. All Sologub's perversions can be found in Baudelaire and in the symbolist misconception of Nietzsche's immorality. Eroticism was no more than a *sujet à la mode* [''fashionable subject'']. Zinaida Hippius tried to put things into their proper perspective when she told her French readers that the erotic tendency in symbolism was nothing new and could be explained in part by social circumstances, the censorship stifling all expressions of individuality and allowing only a certain liberty of *mœurs*. Kuzmin's erotomania and that of Ivanov, under the cover of Hellenism, was no more than *enfantillage* and *barbarie* [''childishness'' and ''coarseness'']. Yet even Zinaida Hippius had to admit that Sologub and Brjusov were more serious in their eroticism. On the other hand, the erotic trend might have been a relic of naturalism and the only form of it acceptable to the modernists.

Echoes of Western glorification of Evil in all its forms, from demonism to sexual vice, can be found in almost all the Russian symbolists. Zinaida Hippius describes evil in a bored, *blasé* manner. . . . Dobroljubov is a typical demonist in the peak period of his literary decadence (1859-1897). Bal'mont pays his tribute to foreign trends and sings of sin and crime and perversion. A French critic once said of him that he wanted to be passionate like Byron, diabolic like Baudelaire, tender like Verlaine, and lugubrious like Poe. Motifs of evil are found in the young Blok, whose *Neznakomka* is in a way the incarnation of evil, ''a devilish mixture of several worlds, especially blue and violet.'' Blok's demonic notes occur particularly in *Snežnaja maska, Prekrasnaja dama,* and *Rasput'ja.* The idea of sacrifice and redemption through evil runs throughout the correspondence of Blok and Belyj. But next to Sologub, it was Brjusov who expressed most persistently the strange fascination of evil for all the symbolists. . . . Amoralism in Brjusov is usually connected with pronounced eroticism. The range of evils analysed by Baudelaire is equally narrow: for all his fascination with human vices, these are predominantly, though not exclusively, sexual. Brjusov's indebtedness to Baudelaire in this respect is apparent from his earliest poems. The first sadistic tones appear in *Pro domo suo* (1894), *Vestalis Virgo* (1895), *O matuška, gde ty.* A certain Baudelairean reminiscence—details of the beloved's corpse—can be found in two poems of 1895: *I snova* and *Purpur blednejuščix gub.* The manner of the latter is almost typically Verlainean. Some details from *Fantom* (1894-5) are also reminiscent of Baudelaire, especially the image of the swollen corpse of the woman. The erotic themes which started in *Chefs d'œuvre,* subsided in *Me eum esse,* but revived anew after 1900. *Pytka* (1902) illustrates a typically Baudelairean sadistic theme: love is compared to torture, to the agony on the cross. The more excruciating the

pain, the greater the lovers' delight. . . . In a similar vein are many poems from *Iz ada izvedënnye* and the whole section *Mgnovenija.* Typical are the scenes of the lovers chained together in a hold (*V trjume*), or entombed in a crypt (*V sklepe*), or embracing on the wheel in a torture chamber (*V zastenke*). . . . Like Baudelaire, Brjusov also revelled in all the coarsest and most naturalistic details of passion. His interest in the physiological side of love is almost copied from Baudelaire. . . . Passion is represented as a self-inflicted suffering in many poems from *Stephanos,* especially in the cycle *Pravda večnaja kumirov.* The masochistic character of love reappears in *Vse napevy* (1909). Brjusov's delight in suffering connected with love is apparent even in some of his post-revolutionary poems.

Purely Baudelairean also is Brjusov's constant inclination to interrupt his ecstasy in order to know the sensation of bitterness hidden beyond it. The background to this attitude is provided by a certain masochism, by a conception of beauty as essentially sad or even tragic, and an awareness that there is beauty in evil and evil in beauty. Brjusov shared with Baudelaire the view that sensual pleasure is in the very knowledge of evil and that the extraction of beauty from evil provides an almost aesthetic pleasure derived from overcoming the difficulty of the task. Baudelaire's proud exclamation:

> Tu m'as donné ta boue et j'en ai fait de l'or. . . .
>
> [''You gave me your filth and from it I made gold. . . .'']

found an echo among the Russian modernists. Thus Bal'mont too pretended to find a certain mystery even in the ugliest aspects of life. . . . In a slightly narrower sense, especially in his attitude to love and women, Brjusov closely followed Baudelaire. . . . Baudelaire's view of woman as a poisonous evil (viz. *Le vampire*) is taken over by Brjusov who reaches the same conclusion. . . . Not only the theme as such is to be found in Brjusov; his insistence on certain details is also strikingly similar to those used by Baudelaire. Baudelaire's famous comparison of lovers to corpses:

> Comme au long d'un cadavre un cadavre étendu. . .
>
> [''As corpse stretches out beside corpse. . . '']

reappears in a dozen variations in Brjusov's poems. . . . Brjusov seems to have taken over from Baudelaire the most superficial and the most debatable audacities of the French poet: namely his affectation for the macabre, his taste for mystification, and his conception of love both as a source of ecstasy and an object of execration (viz. especially *Le flacon* and *Une charogne*). This ''scandalising'' side of *Les fleurs du mal* has tended to obsess Baudelaire's followers both in France and in Russia. Was it as a consequence of his spleen or as an introvert affirmation of the artist's power to subdue nature and life, that Baudelaire developed such a taste for the artificial, for the macabre, the exotic, for everything that was abnormal? His magnification of the ''contra-natural'' may well have been a result of his hatred of instinct, a hatred of theological origin; or of his cult for sterile beauty, a cult of an aesthetic order which impelled him constantly to pursue the artificial; or even of his *goût de l'infini* [''taste for infinity''] which made him avoid at all cost the usual limitations of men. Whatever the case, and even if this aspect of his poetry is today relegated to a secondary position, Baudelaire moulded an entire mode of thought and feeling among the younger generation. It was precisely his morbidity that Verlaine and the symbolists admired so much. The Russians, like so many of their contemporaries in France, thought that Baudelaire had come to teach depravity as a form of aestheticism, or sadism as a way of life. A fantastic over-insistence on the perversity of Baudelaire has prevailed until recent times. Certainly there was some sensationalism and cheap satanism bequeathed by the tradition of melodrama and the *roman noir* ["horror novel"]; demonism and morbidity had been fashionable in the times of Baudelaire. But though this fashion had been partly inherited from the romantics and might have been merely an artificial device of the time, the young symbolist poets in France as well as in Russia regarded it as an attitude denoting a daring innovation, a reflection of *their* times, the last word in modernism, a necessary component of their intensity of feeling. Brjusov's poetry, more than anybody else's in Russia, is permeated by this "Baudelairean" climate. He was said—like Baudelaire—to have experienced all the poisons of his time, and to have reflected "like a true mirror, the spirit of the time and the sickness of his country."

The taste for the unusual and the artificial expressed itself not only in morbidity and perverted eroticism. The attitude of the symbolist poets to nature illustrates well their predilection for artificiality which, partly, was no more than the outcome of their aestheticism. As early as 1892, in a sonnet imitated from Rimbaud, Brjusov proclaimed his break with nature and set as his ideal an artificial beauty. . . . Brjusov openly acknowledged the French influence in this particular aspect of his philosophy: "I read at that time Baudelaire and Verlaine. I imagined that I held in contempt [everything] young and natural, that paint was more beautiful to me than the bloom of youth, that naive love was ridiculous, that I wanted all the refined evinces of artificiality.". . . In his poetry Brjusov lived up to his theories. At first, in *Russkie simvolisty* the theme of nature still occurs, but has almost disappeared with *Chefs d'œuvre*. In the rare cases where nature is depicted, it is treated in an impressionist manner. Fet had already used impressionist psychologisation of nature. Verlaine however goes further and turns nature into emotion, and the lyrical subject into *une machine à sensation* ["a mechanism of feeling"]. Though influenced at first by Fet to some extent, Brjusov rather follows Verlaine in his treatment of nature. Thus many early poems are almost typically Verlainean, especially *Zvëzdy zakryli resnicy*, where nature is dissolved in emotion, and *Mračnoj pavilikoj*, where nature almost becomes a rationalist allegory. In the subjective manner of Verlaine are also the early poems *Glaza* (1898), *K bol'šoj medvedice* (1898), *Duxi zemli* (1898), and partly *Paporotnik* (1900), which is reminiscent of Tjutčev too. Not only does Brjusov forsake nature; he also transforms it and, like Baudelaire, tries to create his own artificial nature independent of reality, a kind of *paradis artificiels*. His manner here is undoubtedly influenced by Mallarmé, and poems like *Prolog* (*Gasnut rozovye kraski*—1892), *Ten' nesozdannyx sozdanij* (1894), *Zolotistye fei* (1892) achieve such a degree of vagueness that even impressionism would seem substantial by comparison. Contempt of real nature is also characteristic of Brjusov's second volume of verse. His later poems are equally remote from nature as it exists. For instance *Orxidei i mimozy* describes a fantastic artificial world, while the whole cycle *U morja* (from *Tret'ja straža*) is composed of poems which may be termed a cerebral creation and not a description of nature.

Sologub also considers nature as the world of his imagination and, though he transforms it according to his fancy, his artificiality is not quite the same as that of Brjusov. He is not indifferent to nature. His claim that nature is merely a product of his imagination . . . is rather connected with his extraordinary egocentricity. But at the same time it is, as in Baudelaire

and in Brjusov, one of the most hyperbolic affirmations of art's absolute autonomy. For what attracts Sologub to the artificial is the affirmation of the omnipotence of the poet, who is capable of commanding nature and life to bow to his whims. Thus Sologub proudly claims to have created nature all by himself. . . . Yet his imaginary nature is not all artificiality. Sologub presents it merely in his own manner, depriving it of everything showy, strong, decorative. His colours are subdued, almost lifeless, dull and greyish. He hates the sun, and his nature is always nocturnal, damp and muddy, moon-lit. If it is true that Sologub was the only modernist to apprehend and like nature, it must be said that he liked it in a peculiar and morbid way. This was his tribute to modernism and decadence.

Artifice appears in one guise or another in all the Russian symbolists. Minskij may have started with a somewhat pantheistic attitude to nature but he soon admitted his shame at having been moved by it. . . . Konevskoy sought in nature only mystery and a promise of *l'au delà* ["the beyond"], and though his attitude to nature was mainly pantheistic—he has been called the most healthy and joyful poet of Russian literature after Puškin—he also loved a certain artificiality. . . . Bal'mont went through a wild pantheistic period which, in a way, also signified a distortion of nature and a tribute to paganism. At a certain time nature was for him a "white country," icy deserts, snow, and he was passionately opposed to the sun which he called "a mourning torch" (*traurnyj fakel*). Later, under the influence of Baudelaire and Poe, white gave way to burning red, to evil flowers, abysses and perversity, abnormal heroes, chimeras, hunchbacks, corpses, putrid odours, etc. His frantic search for new impressions . . . leads him to discover and admire morbid beauty, morbid nature, and morbid passion. . . . Then again he sings real hymns to the sun, the wind, the sea, the fire, the moon, and the rain. He seeks common ground with the elements, feel in them a strong, vital force enhancing his individualism. He almost becomes the poet of the sun. After *Budem, kak solnce* Bal'mont turns to a milder nature, and perhaps for the first time sees it as it is. But all the successive phases of Bal'mont were only exercises in traversing the widest possible range of experiences and attitudes. Whatever the force of his self-persuasion and self-conviction, Bal'mont was anything but sincere, and Brjusov's words addressed to him throw a revealing light on both of them:

> . . . Ya v tebe lublu
> Chto ves ty lozh.
>
> ["What I love about you
> Is that you are all lies."]

For *iskusstvo lži*, the art of lying and artifice, was one of the highest achievements in the eyes of all modernists.

Artificiality is also apparent in the numerous "puppet" themes chosen by the symbolists, especially by the younger generation. Both Belyj and Blok discovered early that life was something other than it appeared to be, that people behaved and indeed were like cardboard dolls. This theme is especially noticeable in Belyj's first three books and in Blok's plays. Sologub had already concluded from his fear of reality that life was merely a play:

> Vsya zhizn—igra. . .
>
> ["Life—is a game. . ."]

and the comparison of man to puppet was one of his favourite devices (especially in *Melkij bes*).

The distortion of reality also expressed itself in a certain amount of exoticism in which the symbolists indulged. Brjusov's exotic poems appeared mostly in *Chefs d'œuvre*. Because of them he was often compared to the Parnassians, but Brjusov protested and never acknowledged this influence. In 1900 he wrote to Gor'kij: "In [Hérédia] . . . everything is depicted from aside, while in my [work] there is everywhere my 'ego'!" In 1907 he publicly declared: "Jamais je n'ai été Parnassien, jamais je ne le serai et maintes fois dans mes articles je combattis l'ésthétique parnassienne!"

Indeed, Brjusov and the other symbolists disregarded almost completely the *couleur locale* ["local color"] and the *couleur du temps* ["color of the time"] which were so treasured by the Parnassians. Historical exactitude was suspect in their eyes, and they leaned towards vagueness, often using legendary heroes merely as mouthpieces of their own feelings. Exoticism was for them mainly yet another expression of their intense dislike of ordinary life, yet another means of escape. Their fascination with medieval themes, partly inherited from the romantics, can be traced to the same origin. . . . It seems that Vengerova had been quite wrong when she tried to convince the French readers of the *Mercure de France* that Russian symbolism was so original as to owe nothing to its French predecessors: "Tout autre est le symbolisme russe. . . . Le symbolisme russe ne cherche guère à créer un monde de beauté imaginaire qui serait une protestation contre la réalité. La fantastique d'Edgar Poe, la recherche des sensations artifiielles, du rare de Baudelaire, lui sont étrangers—ou presque étrangers. Le symbolisme russe est fortement lié à la réalité—il en est sorti. Ses regards sont attachés à la vie. . . ." ["Russian Symbolism is entirely different. . . . It does not seek to create a world of imaginary beauty that would be a protest against reality. The fantasy of Edgar Poe, the quest for artificial sensations, the exoticism of Baudelaire are foreign to it—or almost foreign. Russian Symbolism is strongly tied to reality—it proceeds from there. Its gaze is fixed on life. . . ."] Nothing could be more inaccurate. Artificial in its early stages, Russian symbolism sought to create an imaginary world of its own throughout its existence. This imaginary world was essentially escapist and, as such, a protest against reality. Symbolism was rooted in reality in one sense perhaps—but this was not the sense implied by Vengerova, besides which it applies both to Russian and French symbolism, and thus destroys her argument—namely, that the symbolist poets' mystical yearning for other worlds ended paradoxically by making them attach more value to the sensations and appearances which constituted their daily life. In this respect, the symbolist "desire for transcendental orders of experience is no denial of the here and now." But the increased awareness of reality in the symbolists is still connected with artificiality, for they saw reality through a haze of imagination more than *à travers un tempérament*. The great importance of imaginative experience in symbolist poetry should not be underestimated.

The first attempt to supersede appearances in order to relate the multiple phenomena of life to the mysterious forces which propel it and transform it, was made by Verhaeren. His was the first real effort to get rid of the decadent heritage of symbolism, to exorcise inner demons—complexes and obsessions—by projecting them outside himself, to sublimate the first tendencies of symbolism, to pass from subjective symbolism to a symbolism which, if not objective, at least was *objectivé*. And thus the theme of the city has become one of the themes of symbolist poetry.

At the same time, decadence was closely linked with urban culture, and the appearance of urban motives in Russian symbolist poetry owes much not only to Verhaeren but also to Baudelaire.

Baudelaire was the first critic to establish the theory of the *Beauté moderne*. As early as 1859 he deplored the absence of a genre which he wished to name *le paysage des grandes villes* ["landscape of the big city"], namely " . . . la collection des grandeurs et des beautés qui résultent d'une puissante agglomeration d'hommes et de monuments, le charme profond et compliqué d'une capitale âgée et vieillie dans les gloires et les tribulations de la vie" ["The collection of grandeurs and beauties that results from a mighty assemblage of men and monuments, the profound and complex charm of an old capital aged in the glories and tribulations of life"]. He attempted to provide this *paysage des grandes villes* in his *Tableaux parisiens,* and thus proved also "the first poet to face modern life and to insist that it had not only a beauty but a heroism of its own. . . ." But as Professor Mansell Jones rightly remarks, it is evident that Baudelaire looked for that beauty mainly in the mind of his generation, in the temperament of a peculiar modern type. Gautier called Baudelaire's poems *une peinture des dépravations et des perversités modernes* ["a picture of modern depravities and perversities"]. Baudelaire's attraction to the town can be explained partly by the suitable background it provided to the Baudelairean dandy and to the type of vices the poet was most interested in; it reflected and partly provoked the poet's spleen, and provided him with a wealth of human material. Laforgue said of Baudelaire that he was the first to speak of Paris *en damné quotidien de la capitale*. . . . On the other hand, the city, with its artificial structures in stone, satisfied Baudelaire's theoretical hatred of nature. Confronted with the tumultuous spectacle of modern life, Baudelaire admitted in theory the whole of modern civilisation as potential *matière d'art* ["subject matter"] but concentrated in practice upon the tragedy of a peculiar type of modern temperament which he shared with many of the artists of his time, but which was by no means universal.

Verhaeren's conception of beauty was much more universal. He strove to give it an ever larger sense in order to cover all the manifestations of the artistic thought of the world. And though Baudelaire undoubtedly influenced one facet of Verhaeren's urban poetry (especially in his early phase)—his fascination with depravity, with the ugly, tragic, vicious and sinister aspects of modernity, his sombre portrayal of the monstrous modern city—the Belgian poet gave a new and larger sense to this type of poetry. More objective than Baudelaire, and faced with newer developments in urban culture, Verhaeren ceased to use the city as a background for decadence and used it as a background for the study of human progress, for the adoration of energy in all its contemporary manifestations. By 1902 he had broadened his vision and exalted the powers of human life and progress, formulating a rather vague but optimistic social ideal (cf. *Les forces tumultueuses*). Verhaeren's impact on the development of urban poetry in Russia was to be decisive.

Among the Russian symbolists no one was so constantly concerned with urban culture as Brjusov. He introduced the urban motif into his earliest poems and throughout his life was concerned with the town, whether seen through Baudelairean eyes, or through Verhaeren's prism.

Some critics however considered Bal'mont the forerunner of urban literature in Russia. Thus Čukovskij saw in Bal'mont's poetry the essence of modernity, and claimed that impressionism was connected with town life. The modern poet does not describe what he sees, but what he thinks he sees—says Čukovskij—he replaces all serious feeling by the lie of the passing impression, by the importance attributed to the instant. Living in towns, modern poets are illusionists by necessity. And so the superficiality of feeling, the speedily alternating imagery, the constant change, the chaos, the importance of the external, the replacement of the beautiful by the pretty—all these traits belong to the whole urban poetry, and especially to Bal'mont who was its first representative. Čukovskij's judgement is somewhat naive, though impressionism may be connected to some extent with the accelerated pulse of modern life as exemplified in the modern city. We may safely discard however his contention that Bal'mont was the first typical urban poet in Russia. Brjusov did not agree with this description of Bal'mont. In a postscript to his letter to Čukovskij of 4 February 1907, he wrote: "On the contrary, I do not agree at all with your characterisation of Bal'mont. In no sense whatever do I consider him a poet of urban culture. He is a romantic. He is a stranger among us. He is a poet of the past and only by accident is he among us. . . ." Nevertheless, Bal'mont did pay some tribute to urbanism when it had become a theme approved by all the symbolists. But he had been much more conservative than Brjusov, having begun his literary career by chanting old themes; and though he presented nature in a decorative and artificial manner, he nevertheless dwelled on it throughout his work. Zinaida Hippius and Sologub who were organically linked with urban culture, rarely introduced urban motifs in their poetry. Blok's urban themes appear only after 1905. And thus there seems to be little doubt that Brjusov was the first to introduce urban poetry in Russia.

D. Maksimov, Brjusov's best biographer, considered that the poet's particular place in Russsian symbolism was due to two factors: to his link with French decadence, and to the urban character of his work. Nekrasov's tradition counted for almost nothing in the urban influences on Brjusov. And though one cannot speak of specifically urban themes in the earliest poems of Brjusov, the setting in these enables one to discern two fundamental subjects—love and the town, in contrast to the traditional nineteenth century themes of love and nature. This early change of position is undoubtedly due to the French symbolists, to some extent perhaps to Verlaine, but chiefly to Baudelaire. One of Brjusov's earliest urban poems, *Mertvecy osveščennye gazom* (1894-95), is a typical echo of the French decadent manner. Like Baudelaire, Brjusov presents all his erotic poems against the background of urban culture. Themes devoted to the town are much more frequent between 1898 and 1899. The first urban cycle entitled *Gorod* (later changed to *V stenax*) is included in *Tertia vigilia*. Brjusov's treatment of the town in this cycle is in Verlaine's manner—impressionist and serving merely as a general "musical" background. Occasionally even in later poems Brjusov's attitude to the city seems to owe more to Verlaine than to Verhaeren. Against this "musical" background, the descriptions of human types connected with the city appear almost realistic.

A more profound approach to urban motifs starts with Brjusov's admiration for Verhaeren—an admiration which originated in 1899 and grew steadily with the years. In *Tertia vigilia* one can already discern a certain note and imagery reminiscent of Verhaeren. But the impact of the Belgian poet gains in strength after 1900, and his influence proves extremely important in Brjusov's mature work. Brjusov adopts the manner and *genre* of Verhaeren: he develops the *genre* of traditional lyrics, and follows Verhaeren's example in creating specific lyrico-de-

scriptive poems and prophetic monologues. Such are many of Brjusov's 1900-1905 poems which can be characterised as having an objective content and a philosophic and social interpretation; some of them are written in *vers libre*. Thus, after his first contact with Verhaeren, Brjusov leaves behind him the city drawn in the soft, lyrical and impressionist tones of Verlaine, which was preponderant in *Tertia vigilia*. Verhaeren taught Brjusov to discard such a superficial view of the town, and to see it from within, in all its social and cultural complexity. Under the influence of Baudelaire, the terrible and frightening face of the great city had already appeared in *Chefs d'œuvre*, but it was only later that Brjusov became fully aware of its significance.

Like Verhaeren who dreamt all his life of writing an epic of human destiny situated in the city of the future, Brjusov also conceived the idea of a city to come. In his interpretation he again followed the Belgian poet whose faith in the future set him apart from most French symbolists. Thus Brjusov reflects in his poems the beauty of the new city, its grandeur, its dynamism, its growing vitality. Such an interpretation of urban themes was entirely *terra incognita* in Russian poetry of the 1900's. Mirskij claimed that Brjusov's urban poems were based primarily on the poet's cult for everything great and powerful, that grandeur in all its forms was the main theme of Brjusov's poetry. . . .

Brjusov was always aware of the new thematic range that Verhaeren had opened before him. He realised that the Belgian poet brought into poetry all the aspects of contemporary life and reflected its movement by picturing contemporary cities and factories and the social struggle. He had a deep respect for Verhaeren's search for new forms in poetry, designed to correspond to the introduction of the new subject matter. Like Verhaeren, Brjusov understood that the present epoch contained potentially all the developments of the future, and he called upon the poets "to study closely their times" (*vsmatrivat' sja v sovremennost'*). . . . Thus Verhaeren detached Brjusov from the narrow path of purely individualist experiences, and impelled him towards the universal and the all-human. But in a sense his influence on the Russian poet was limited. Vacillating between Baudelaire's pessimism and Verhaeren's faith, Brjusov did not always show a preference for the latter. His failure to translate successfully some of Verhaeren's poems throws an interesting light on Brjusov's psychology. On the whole his translations are masterly, but there are instances when the Belgian poet fails to inspire Brjusov. Thus his rendering of the symbolic blacksmith's dream of a socialist future (*Le forgeron*) falls quite flat: it is pale and almost sentimental. . . . All the subjective elements of the poem are missing in Brjusov's translation; the rhythm and the sweeping movement of the original are lost. This may be simply due to Brjusov's technical shortcomings. It is interesting to note however that Brjusov himself considered *Kuznec* to be a very faithful translation. His adaptations from Verhaeren reveal much better the affinity between the two poets. It is significant also that in his choice of Verhaeren's poems Brjusov omitted all those in which the Belgian poet figures as philosopher and thinker and expresses his mystical positivism. Brjusov is at his best in such poems as *Ženščina na perekrestke, Mor, London, Čisla, Mjatež, Svin'i, Ne znaju gde;* these satisfied even Vološin who demanded from translators of poetry "an organic capacity for a miracle." Vološin maintained however that on the whole Brjusov's translations from Verhaeren were merely an expression of gratitude and respect for a poet who had been perhaps the greatest poetic revelation to Brjusov. The real Verhaeren in Russian is not to be found in Brjusov's translations—says Vološin—but in some of Brjusov's original poems which best embody the spirit of the Belgian poet; and the critic names in particular *Kon' bled* and *Slava tolpe*.

Slava tolpe is indeed the best illustration of Brjusov's profound affinity with Verhaeren. The poem is unmistakably inspired by *La révolte (Les villes tentaculaires):* it has the same rhythm, the same colour tonality, the same force in the description of the mob.... Yet Černov's remark that *Slava tolpe* ought to have appeared in a volume of translations from Verhaeren and not in *Puti i pereput'ja* is not substantiated. The poem is not a paraphrase of *La révolte;* it succeeds in bearing the characteristic stamp of the Russian poet, though the model is just as characteristic of Verhaeren. Brjusov does not simply borrow from Verhaeren the image of the surging crowd and the objective passages relating to the streets soaked in the insurgents' blood. The movement of the city in revolt is similar in both cases, but Verhaeren concentrates on the rebellious crowd, while Brjusov introduces a note of modernity which is entirely absent from the French poem. He is not only interested in the crowd as such, but in the street with its offices buildings and its string of carriages and its prostitutes.... Brjusov is on the whole much more pessimistic than Verhaeren. What seems to be his own vision of the city of the future lacks the peaceful and clear notes of the Belgian poet. The image that rises before his eyes is dark and frightening and presages the decadence of a whole civilisation.... Brjusov often takes up a Baudelairean motif and develops it into a Verhaerenesque sociological prophecy. He tends however towards a Baudelairean mood. There is also a Baudelairean background of debauchery and vice in *Gorodu*, though the whole poem is clearly indebted to Verhaeren: Verhaeren saw the city as an octopus extending its grasping tentacles, sucking the life blood of humanity—Brjusov envisaged it as a dragon raising a poisoned knife over its own head.

What Verhaeren really did for Brjusov was to widen considerably his subject-matter range. He showed him that there were no themes unsuitable to poetry, that philosophical and sociological motifs could be treated by a poet. In this lay his main influence on Brjusov. When, on the threshold of the twentieth century, Brjusov suddenly discovered Verhaeren, his urban themes and his sense of a new pulse of life instantly appealed to the young Russian poet. The climate which surrounded the two poets and the age in which they lived could explain to a great extent their spiritual kinship. They were both attuned to receive the meanings of their own times. Earlier than anyone else in Russia, Brjusov senses the advent of a new sensibility with its demand for a variation of the existing poetic language. This revolution of sensibility which was taking place all over the world had already been understood by Verhaeren; which is why, when Brjusov came into contact with the older poet, recognition was instantaneous. It is in this light that Vološin's words have to be considered: "Brjusov was born to become a poet of the city, and Verhaeren was for him a revelation pointing the horizons of those paths along which he himself advanced." With Verhaeren's example before him, Brjusov was the first Russian poet to incorporate within the bounds of poetry themes which had hitherto been considered utterly untranslatable into the language of poetic beauty.

Brjusov—the real predecessor of urban poetry in Russia—must also be credited with some formative influence on Blok—the poet of the city. Blok repeatedly acknowledged the elder poet as one of his masters: he certainly learned from him much of the art of writing poetry. But as an aesthetician or as a personality, Brjusov seems to have had little impact on Blok. Sophie Bonneau tends to minimise Brjusov's influence on Blok: she limits it to a purely literary influence of texts, and confines it in place to *Urbi et orbi* (1903) and to the poem *Kon' bled* (1903-4), and in time—to the year 1904. This allegedly purely textual influence led however to the appearance of urban motifs in Blok's poetry and to an indirect reinterpretation of both Baudelaire's and Verhaeren's urban themes.

By the end of 1903, the theme of the city begins to appear in Blok's poems. At first there are scarcely a realistic descriptions: the town is mainly phantasmagoric, elusive, deceitful; the concrete details are lost in a maze of chimeric illusions. Strange and fantastic, the city is "a terrible world" inhabited by "small black people" and "drunken red dwarfs." Blok follows Dostoevskij in his constant intersection of two planes—the real and the imaginary.

The publication of Brjusov's *Urbi et orbi* strongly impressed Blok. In a letter to Belyj he declared that its contents were a series of unparalleled revelations, almost a work of genius. The sequel to this admiration was Blok's cycle of poems *Gorod*, which owes its whole theme to *Urbi et orbi*. The first poem of this cycle, *Poslednij den'*, bears a marked resemblance to Brjusov's *Kon' bled*, which in its turn is so close to the spirit of Verhaeren. But while Brjusov's street seethes with life and swarms with the crowd, Blok's street is quieter and in a way more spiritualised.

Blok's direct contact with the poetry of Verhaeren may perhaps account for his short-lived spell of social enthusiasm and compassion for the miserable people of Russia (cf. *Fabrika*). There are also many Verhaerenesque images throughout Blok's 1903-4 poems (for instance *Eja pribytie*).

Blok's second volume of verse—*Nečajannaja radost'* (1904-1906)—marks a transitional period in the poet's work. The social phase is forgotten, the "decadent spirit" is in the ascendant. Life in the city is confined to restaurants, cabarets, *cafés chantants* with gipsy music; the streets seem to live only at night, under electric lights. The lights of the great city provide the background to themes of passion and despair, joy and suffering, struggle and ruin, fate and death. This is the period of *Kometa, Snežnaja maska, Faina*, the period of *Neznakomka* in which the image of the unknown woman is taken from Brjusov's *Proxožej* and in which the wine is a true Baudelairean *paradis artificiel*. It is obviously to this period that Kogan refers when he unexpectedly declares: "It is impossible to imagine Blok in Lausanne or in the country. One can imagine him only on the boulevards of Paris or in the restaurants of St. Petersburg."

By the use of real and supra-real planes, by the spiritualisation of everyday sordidness, Blok turns the city into one of his greatest mystical *décors*. On the plane of reality, his city—like that of Brjusov and Baudelaire—is closely associated with vice and evil and an all-pervading feeling of profound solitude. And again as in Brjusov and Baudelaire, the city of Blok is merely the scene of the poet's hopeless grief, his personal abyss, the disquieting narrow street on his way towards escape.... Only after 1906 does Blok turn towards a more concrete presentation of reality. But his main achievement is to have almost effaced the division between life and mirage, and to have endowed every day life with mystical meaning.

The study of the French impact on the choice of themes in Russian symbolist poetry points to the name of Baudelaire more frequently than to any other. While Mallarmé did not exert any tangible influence on the content of poetry—his achievement lay in revolutionising the manner of presenting literary problems—Baudelaire inaugurated modern poetry and enriched its field. Baudelaire's direct influence on the Russians was certainly great. But one should not forget the extent of his indirect impact as well. By the time Baudelaire influenced the Russians, French poetry had undergone a considerable transformation: "Il est une façon de sentir avant Baudelaire et une façon de sentir après lui" ["It is a way of perceiving before Baudelaire and a way of perceiving after him"], wrote André Suarès. Almost everything that the Russian modernists drew from French symbolism may be traced back to Baudelaire, for "toute la littérature actuelle est baudelairienne. . . . [Elle l'est] par la technique interne et spirtuelle, par le sens du mystère, par le souci d'écouter ce que disent les choses, par le désir de correspondre âme à âme avec l'obscure pensée répandue dans la nuit de l'univers" ["all of present-day literature is Baudelairian. . . . (It is such) by virtue of the inward and spiritual technique, the sense of mystery, the concern with listening to what things are saying, the desire to correspond soul to soul with the obscure thought dispersed into the night of the universe"].

Having engendered some of the greatest modern French poets, Baudelaire also determined many of the moods which shaped the new sensibility of the Russian poets at the turn of the century. (pp. 136-63)

Georgette Donchin, "Themes in Symbolist Poetry," in her The Influence of French Symbolism on Russian Poetry, *Mouton & Co., 1958, pp. 120-63.*

THEMES IN RUSSIAN SYMBOLIST POETRY

EVELYN BRISTOL

[*In the following excerpt, Bristol examines the juxtaposition of idealistic and decadent elements in the works of the most prominent Russian Symbolist poets.*]

Statements of doctrine by Symbolists both in France and in Russia indicate that the literary movement was based on a form of philosophical idealism, often Neo-Platonism. But its theoreticians were silent about the decadent themes which appear in Symbolist poetry. Symbolists liked to represent themselves as attuned to the ineffable—or if mystics, to the divine—but their works reveal an inclination to philosophical pessimism and other forms of melancholia. Indeed, a tension between belief and cynicism can be noted in their works which resembles, and sometimes overlaps with, a juxtaposition of good and evil. Among the French, Charles Baudelaire called the opening section of *Les fleurs du mal* (1857) "Spleen et Idéal." Paul Verlaine dedicated his collections of verse alternately to Christian ideals of purity, as in *Sagesse* (1881), and to self-indulgent bohemianism, as in *Parallélement* (1889). Stéphane Mallarmé's satyr in "L'Après-midi d'un faune" (1876) is the emblematic representative of amorality brought to glimpse the world of Platonic Ideas. And Joris-Karl Huysmans's arch-decadent hero, des Esseintes, exhausted himself in sensual delights before being brought near to Catholic conversion.

The idealistic, or mystical, aspect of the movement, which was its rallying point and banner, received its programmatic assertion by Baudelaire in his 1859 article on Théophile Gautier, in which he wrote, "C'est cet admirable, cet immortel instinct du Beau qui nous fait considérer la Terre et ses spectacles comme un aperçu, comme une correspondance du Ciel" ["It is this admirable, this immortal instinct for Beauty that makes us consider the World and its spectacles as a glimpse, as a correspondence of Heaven"]. His avowed debt to Swedenborg, whose doctrine prescribed correspondences between the heavenly and earthly spheres, gave rise to the overwhelming importance that Symbolists attached to the metaphor, and consequently to the symbol. A more definitely monistic form of idealism derived from the thinking of Schelling, Fichte, Hegel, and especially Schopenhauer, all of whom posited an essential spirit in a unified cosmos. Another, extremely productive, current of idealism was inaugurated by Verlaine in his famous opening line, "De la musique avant toute chose" ["Music before everything else"]. Whatever "music" meant to Verlaine, to Mallarmé and the Russian Symbolists it denoted a nonverbal spiritual progression which could be suggested by the use of words as an artistic medium. Verlaine's dictum also expressed the general preference of idealists for the incorporeal arts of hearing over those of sight. Mallarmé candidly adopted Schopenhauer's Neo-Platonism and considered "la notion pure" to be the aim of poetry. In writing of the dance he used the indicative word "idée."

But decadence, which was not considered necessary from an ideological point of view and was not promulgated, has to be understood from its examples. It arose, in part, from the Romantic literature of ruins, graves, and autumnal imagery. But when it was allied with Symbolism, it applied more directly to the alienated hero and thus included an edge of cynicism and pique. An ancestor of the decadent figure may have been the amoral *Lui* of Diderot's *Le Neveu de Rameau* (1762). Amorality was later joined by arrogance and ennui in the fashionable type of the London dandy derived from Byron's characters, especially Childe Harold. In general, the decadent hero can be said to have embodied a reversal of expected values regarding morality and health. In his religion he was a Satanist and blasphemer. He preferred his melancholia to happiness and could not rise above ennui to vigor. He was drawn to death rather than to life, and he cherished his insanity. He sought sensual refinement rather than spiritual elevation. And he disdained the mob. In four poems called "Spleen," Baudelaire provided powerfully suggestive models for decadence. He described a crippling boredom that is punctuated by remorse and a sense of homelessness. In imagery and mood he often had recourse to death. He also initiated the subsequently familiar scenery of fogs and rain. Furthermore, in the poem "Les litanies de Satan," he was the first to show a possible functional role of decadence in relationship to idealism: his demon is the adoptive father of those whom God has deprived of paradise. Throughout the Symbolist movement decadence was made to appear as the cry of the frustrated and doubting idealist. In the essays in *Les Paradis artificiels* (1869), Baudelaire indicated that a true aspiration to the infinite can, with drugs, be replaced by a false sense of attainment. Verlaine's early poetry provided the pattern for a gentler and more nostalgic melancholia which is typified by his opening line, "Il pleure dans mon coeur" ["There is weeping in my heart"]. But in his mature poetry, Verlaine's bouts of blasphemy, eroticism, and degradation are always sensed as lapses from Christian virtue and the hope for salvation. In general, the decadent was prone to elevate his own ennui to cosmic proportions, and then to describe the universe in terms that coincided with Schopenhauer's. As Schopenhauer did not ascribe any moral purpose to his constantly evolving spirit, in his system the world is meaningless. It is probably impossible to estimate the magnitude of Schopenhauer's direct influence, as opposed to a confluence with his tendencies. It is obvious, however, that the hopefully idealistic current of Symbolism was accompanied, from the incipience of the movement, by decadence, which sometimes acted as a foil to idealism.

In Russian literature, decadence became popular earlier than idealism, although the initiates of the inner circles were either dedicated to an idealistic revival, as was the case in St. Petersburg, or at least aware of the centrality of idealistic premises to Symbolism, as were its younger adherents in Moscow. The document now considered to be the initial polemic of the Russian movement. Dmitrii Merezhkovskii's essay, *O prichinakh upadka i o novykh techeniiakh sovremennoi russkoi literatury* (1893), called for a new literary mode that would both reflect the new idealism and be spiritually uplifting as well. And some of the coterie around Merezhkovskii in St. Petersburg showed more concern for the philosophical renaissance than for the literary one. But in the 1890s the public was won over by Russian poetry that was remarkably imitative of Baudelaire and Verlaine, and whose practitioners were primarily Konstantin Bal'mont in *Pod severnym nebom* (1894), *V bezbrezhnosti* (1895), and *Tishina* (1898) and Fedor Sologub in his first two books. Valerii Briusov was still maturing as a poet, and Zinaida Gippius was as yet not as well known. All exhibited melancholias, frustrations, and a spiritual impotence in their verse, particularly Bal'mont and Sologub, who depicted a character who is enervated, wilting, and neurasthenic. . . . [Poems] by Bal'mont show this lassitude also afflicting mankind at large, and throughout his three books nature itself is shown drooping and sorrowing. A resigned desire for death is displayed in some poems in his first two books, and in *Tishina*, in the section ''Akkordy,'' we find an alternate decadent impulse, a paroxysm of splenetic revolt, which has a demonic character.

In Sologub's first book, his melancholia appears mysterious because it is unmotivated. In his second book, he seems to have degenerated into a life of fruitless daydreams that are filled with pain, and from there he descends to quietism, that is, an indifferent resignation to death, a sentiment expressed in the incantatory poem ''Rastsvetaite, rastsvetaiushchie.'' He also offers confessions of unspecified sins, guilty obsessions, or even insanity.

Briusov began as a more audacious poet. In *Chefs d'oeuvre* (1895), he flaunted his eroticism, which was sometimes programmatically painful or destructive. He evoked exotic scenes that were both florid and primitive, set, for example, in Africa or the Easter Islands. He dwelt not only on sins, but on physical torture, vulgarities, and ugliness. In his second book, *Me eum esse* (1897), his treatment of these themes is more intimate, and therefore pervaded by guilt and shame. He also added the option of death to his list of subjects, especially in the section ''Veian'e smerti.''

Nevertheless, all three decadent poets included in these books published in the 1890s poems of an idealistic, religious, or moralistic cast. Because Russian literary criticism has exhibited a puristic tendency to distinguish between idealistic and decadent poets, the doctrinal idealism of the so-called decadents, Bal'mont, Briusov, Sologub, and Gippius, has often been underestimated. Thus, in all three of his books, Bal'mont showed aspirations to the ineffable, and in the poem ''Zachem'' he complained that mankind is given a soul but denied spiritual attainment. He often wrote of weak things, himself, or nature, that strive upward to light, or life, or the elevated, and sink

again into sadness and murkiness. In the section ''Snezhnye tsvety'' of *Tishina*, he rose to the experience of miracles and an identification with the eternal. . . . Throughout Briusov's *Me eum esse*, an awareness of innocence and purity sharply contrasts with the surrounding depictions of cruelty and corruption. The book opens with a section dedicated to a distant ideal symbolized by the stars, and the penultimate section, ''Zavershenie,'' is dedicated to the mystic capacity, to art, presentiments, and mysteries. If decadence is not explained here by the failure of mystical aspirations, it is plain that the contrast between the two directions was used structurally by Briusov, and that each tendency heightens the other.

During the first several years of the new century, a general spirit of metaphysical optimism replaced the uncertainties characteristic of the 1890s. Not only did there appear a new wave of mystics, but ameliorating changes took place in the work of the decadents as well. Bal'mont executed a well-known change from passivity to self-assertion. In *Goriashchie zdaniia* (1900), he abandoned his neuraesthenia and alienation to become a passionate participant in life in its natural and divine aspects. The section, ''Antifony,'' is a celebration of the idealistic view, in that he praised artistic creation, entertained visionary utopias, explored the solipsistic outlook, and identified with the springtime. In the sections ''I da i net'' and ''Indiiskie travy,'' he became a pantheist and coursed upward to blend with the multiplicity of phenomena and with divinity. In *Budem kak solntse* (1903), he dwelt on his interchangeability with natural phenomena, which is the putative origin of his verse. This is the sense of the poem ''Ia izyskannost' russkoi meditel'noi rechi.''

In his new collection, *Sobranie stikhov* (1904), Sologub began to balance his pessimism and his optimism. The result was the dichotomous view of the universe for which he was to be labeled Manichean. Now he too entertained visions of perfection, of utopias, of ideal beauty. In *Book 3* of his verse he sought the absolute and anticipated attainment in death, he imagined a paradise on a distant planet, Oile, and he experienced ecstasies in nature. In *Book 4* he encompassed the world in his solipsism, imagining himself as both the world's first cause and its multiplicity.

With the appearance of Zinaida Gippius's first book of poetry it was apparent that she, like Verlaine, was a Christian writer. Never a spiritually sanguine author, Gippius's poetry is pervaded by a spiritual hunger. She aspired to a unique, absolute love that would encompass both Christ and an earthly companion. (pp. 269-73)

In his new books, *Tertia vigilia* (1900) and *Urbi et orbi* (1903), Briusov found, like Mallarm'aae, a sacred goal in art. Thus *Tertia vigilia* includes not only the usual section of spiritual aspirations, ''Milaia pravda,'' but also one in praise of creative individuals, ''Blizkim.'' In *Urbi et orbi*, an essential thought—that artists can create spiritual and cultural values out of the crude and earthly material at hand, even of evil—reaches its culmination in the final section, ''Ody i poslaniia.'' In 1904, Briusov introduced a programmatic assertion of the idealistic aesthetic in the opening article, ''Kliuchi tain,'' of his new literary magazine *Apollon* and championed the prerogative of the intuitive throughout the essay:

> These gaps [in the prison of phenomena] are those
> moments of ecstasy, of pretersensual intuition which
> give other conceptions of worldly phenomena, pen-
> etrating more deeply beyond their surface to their

heart. The age-old task of art consists in recording these moments of insight, of inspiration.

Viacheslav Ivanov's, Andrei Belyi's, and Alexander Blok's adherence to the movement in this middle period contributed to the current atmosphere of elated expectancy more than did the reconsiderations of the decadents. All were Christians and Neo-Platonists. They believed in the spiritual basis of the apparently material world and in their own and mankind's capacity for mystical communion and attainment. Ivanov's philosophy as set forth in the essays of *Po zvezdam* (1909) is precisely the subject of the poems in his first two books, *Kormchie zvezdy* (1903) and *Prozrachnost'* (1904): the universe is a unity in multiplicity, nature is the receptacle of the divine, and art is an act of love, of aspiration, and a mystical power. The spirit which animates the world is symbolized either by Christ or the Eternal Feminine. He saw myths as the records of man's encounters with divinity and depicted pagan as well as Christian deities. The Dionysian mystery of attainment through death and resurrection particularly appealed to Ivanov. (pp. 273-74)

Belyi's first book of verse, *Zoloto v lazure* (1904), is characterized by a gentle melancholia that arises only from the elusiveness of the ineffable. He opened the book with an attentiveness to nature, especially to sunsets, questing after spiritual illumination through oneness with nature's deific essence. Elsewhere he displayed a nostalgia for the past beneath which can be sensed a longing for eternity. His playfully depicted folkloristic and legendary figures, such as giants and centaurs, seem to mask the presence of uncanny forces on earth. He ended the book on a note of mystical anticipation in the poem "Razdumie."

Blok, who was the most forthright and ardent mystic, recorded his chivalric devotion to Saint Sophia, the Holy Wisdom, as diary in *Stikhi o prekrasnoi dame* (1905). His mystical attainments and frequent anxieties may have either realistic or fanciful and legendary settings, but in his poems all the phenomena of nature, and all the cityscapes, share a portentousness lent by the rapt awareness of an anchorite and lover.

In these years, when metaphysical optimism was the reigning mood, decadence kept pace by assuming more dramatic and morally ominous forms, and signs of metaphysical perplexities appeared even among the mystics. When Bal'mont was concerned, as he was in some poems, with the inevitability of evil in the world order, his pantheism led him to identify with impulses to violence, corruption, shame, and ugliness. The tendency reaches demonic proportions in the section "Danses macabres" of *Budem kak solntse*. Sologub's melancholias and spleen found a new outlet in a resentful, sometimes rebellious, detestation of heaven for its alleged cruelties or emptiness. His spiteful poem "Kogda ia v burnom more plaval," in which he dedicates himself to Satan, appears in this context. Gippius was tempted to depart from Christian humility and charity into isolation, coldness, disdain, and pride. She hated banality, as is clear from the poem "Pyl'," yet she suspected that neither the world nor she was capable of rising above aridity. Briusov continued to depict the world as a senseless and lamentable juxtaposition of good and evil; hence his own notorious changeability, as expressed in the poem "Ia." His amorality allowed him to be flagrantly self-indulgent. He identified with historical instances of naked power and arrogance and took pride in all-consuming passions.

The appearance of decadence in the work of the youngest Symbolists was much rarer, but its forms were no less fright-

ening. In Belyi's *Zolotov v lazure*, his mystical doubts led to fears of insanity, to alarmed delusions of being Christ, and to a self-mockery conducted through the dreaded figure of the harlequin double. Certain poems show a horror of the vulgarities of contemporary life, and in the closing section, "Bagrianitsy v terniiakh," his mystical expectations are clouded by an undefined anguish. Blok's poems from 1902 to 1904 also show signs of fear: omens of spiritual loss, the appearance of the love triangle with its metaphysical disillusionments, and the figure of the clown. But these early failures of mystical attainment still seemed to Belyi and to Blok to be transient and not ideologically relevant. Only Ivanov displayed no philosophical fears. He did not resent the existence of suffering, but believed it to be a path to spiritual elevation.

During the period of the 1905 revolution and in its repressive aftermath, almost the entire Symbolist group was affected by the loss of the optimism which had earlier characterized its metaphysical outlook or expectations, with Ivanov again the sole exception. Bitterness, resentment, and irony became common manifestations in their work. Symbolists were now more impressed with the presence of evil, and some were more tempted by it. In Briusov's new work, *Stephanos* (1906), his former references to purity and the heavenly are absent, and his idealism is only residual. His general preoccupation with evil acquired a specific, even topical, application in his new concern with tyranny. Sologub published his most rancorous book, a small volume called *Zmii* (1907), in which the sun is vituperated as the source of earthly existence, and thus the origin of evil and suffering. In *Plammenyi krug* (1908) he depicted violent and cruel events and portrayed himself as turned aside in morbid dreams and barren solipsism. In the closing section, "Poslednee uteshenie," death appears as the only plausible solution to reality's dilemmas. Gippius continued to balance her religious yearning on the one hand with her guilty disdain for the material world and her equally guilty attraction to it on the other. Her second book contains the forceful poem "Neliubov'," in which she succumbs to the call of chaos.

Belyi's and Blok's new verse suggested a considerable emotional disorientation and a need for new and more tragic themes and imagery. Ideologically, they had not lost faith in idealism, but in the efficacy of mysticism and in the possibility of the embodiment of the ideal in any earthly phenomena. They were more aware of the material aspect of the world that limits human aspirations. Now they too had become splenetic, neuraesthenic, and, in brief, decadent. Blok's plunge into the world of the profane, the blasphemous irony with which he treated his former sanguine expectations, and his self-punishments for his "betrayals," have been adequately anthologized and described. Thus the heroines of his plays *Balaganchik* (1906) and *Neznakomka* (1906) appear as a cardboard bride and a fallen star, his poetic personae frequent taverns and banal social gatherings, and "Ia znaiu: istina v vine" concludes his poem "Neznakomka" as a sarcastic comment on intuitive perception. The entire cycle "Snezhnaia maska" (1907) is a struggle between his mystical nature and earthly passion. In the poem "Za grobom" (1910), the words "Literator modnyi / Tol'ko slov koshchunstvennykh tvorets. . ." ["A fashionable writer / Is a creator only of blasphemous words. . ."] obviously refer to himself. In a lecture delivered in 1910, Blok described his own experience of the lowering transformation of the sacred ideal that is necessarily caused by earthly perception:

> In other words, I had already made my own life into art (a tendency which quite clearly transverses all of

European *decadence*). Life became art and I pronounced an invocation, and before me finally arose that which I (personally) call "The Stranger": a beauty-doll, a blue specter, an earthly miracle.

In his poems Blok complained, as any decadent, of his own meanness, emptiness, and guilt. In the poem "Shagi komandora" (1912) he depicted a figure worthy of Don Juan's nemesis.

Belyi's disillusionment caused him to give funereal titles to his two books: *Pepel* (1909) and *Urna* (1909). In the former he gave a prominent place to his new social theme, the evils of provincial Russia, but he also adopted a theme familiar from the older decadent literature—the appalling vulgarity of reality. He pictured himself only in despair or with irony, only as an insane poet with messianic delusions, or as dead or doomed. He was again beset by his destructive double in his clownish domino ("Arlekinada").... Even more than Blok, he complained of a pervasive grief or emptiness. *Urna* is a calmer book, but one in which no hopes return. The very losses of which he speaks are merely personal and he pictures himself as spiritually cold.

The Symbolists dissociated themselves so stringently from utilitarian literature that the fact that, singly, each of them is known to have written engagé literature is never treated in a systematic way. But their societal themes can be related to their idealism and to their decadence. The Symbolists, in fact, inherited a disjointedness of snobbery on the one hand and involvement on the other from the Romantics, who espoused some social causes, such as democracy and political liberty. (pp. 274-77)

All of the major Russian Symbolists displayed signs of compassion for the suffering of humanity, and in many cases their abstract sympathy became manifest as a topical concern. Sologub was the earliest (in the 1890s) to publish verse sympathetic to the victims of social injustice. He began his career as a committed writer. The utopian aspirations apparent in his first novel, *Tiazhelye sny* (1896), were subsequently translated into arcadian imagery—in the fantasy world Oile, for example—in his metaphorical depictions of philosophical ideals. His social criticism was similarly heightened to a revolt against the cosmic tyranny of the heavens. Eventually his metaphysical and political rebellions fed each other. At the time of the 1905 revolution he contributed seditious satirical verse to clandestine magazines. He also attempted to voice the grief and alarm of the populace in a small book of verse called *Rodine* (1906), occasioned by the Russo-Japenese War. Sologub was never indifferent to current events and issues.

By contrast, Briusov's social themes grew out of his initial, generalized preoccupation with evil in the world. His contemporary and civic concern made its appearance in the "city poetry" of *Urbi et orbi* where he exposed in a naturalistic fashion the unfortunate and seamy side of human passions and amusements. In the section "Pesni" he imitated popular songs, in "Ballady" there are tales of violence, and in "Kartiny" he depicted the city as the site of moral corruption. The events of 1905 and the effects of political tyranny are the subjects of the section "Sovremennost'" in *Stephanos*. (pp. 277-78)

Bal'mont's revolutionary poems in *Pesni mstitelia* (1907), calling for the overthrow of the Russian monarch, appear to be unique among Symbolists in that they do not reveal any special connection to Symbolist theory. Zinaida Gippius, on the other hand, combined, like Sologub, political thought with philosophy. A constant undercurrent of her poetry was the desire to find a religious salvation for all humanity. Her political verse

appears to have derived from a related motivation. In the poem "14 dekabria" she pictured her generation as the heirs of the Decembrists.

The mystically inclined poets, Ivanov, Blok, and Belyi, are well known to have compounded the national image or populism itself with their metaphysical goals. All invested in the Russian people, and sometimes in the poets as their spokesmen, the capacity to change history through their mystical achievements, or conversely, to fail on a metaphysical plane. Ivanov's mystical anarchism, his response to the crises of 1905-7, was his own embodiment of the unlikely democratic Symbolism which he called for in his articles. In "Poet i chern'," he stated his view that the poet is the voice of his race, creating, through his intuitive access to the collective unconscious, symbols from which appear new myths:

> True symbolism must reconcile the Poet and the Rabble in a great, national art. The term of isolation is passing. We go by the path of the symbol to the myth. Great art is a myth-creating art. From the symbol will grow the myth, which has ever existed in potential, this pictorial discovery of the immanent spiritual truth of a national universal self-assertion.

Belyi also attached a transcendental meaning and a much more messianic role to the destiny of Russia. In 1905 he wrote in "Apokalipsis v russkoi poezii" that through the efficacy of Russian literature the Eternal Feminine would soon be made incarnate in the multiplicity of phenomena and thus solve the material metaphysical problems of European culture and bring about the end of "Universal History." Given these extravagant expectations, the failure of the 1905 revolution contributed to the collapse of his mystical aspirations. For Blok Russia became a hypostasis of the Eternal Feminine precisely after the repression of the revolution. He then sensed the coming of cultural strife, the magnitude of which he suggested by his extensive reference to medieval epics of the liberation from the Tatars in his own cycle "Na pole Kulikovom" (1908).... Thoroughly modern in this cycle is his notion of Russia as his own mystical bride, predicated on the omnipresence of the world spirit.

In the postrevolutionary era both Belyi and Blok wrote of Russia's squalor and poverty in pained and wrathful terms that resemble those used by the decadents to express their frustrations with universal evil. Both poets displayed a despairing love for the country while describing its taverns, stagnation, and meanness. Belyi's self-avowed contributions to the tradition of Nekrasov begin with the poem "Otchaian'e" which opens *Pepel*. Blok's own Nekrasov-like depressions are less visible because they are overshadowed by his rapt preoccupation with mythical Rus'. (pp. 278-79)

If it is true that some Russian Symbolists remind us most consistently of their idealism, preeminently Ivanov, and others more frequently of their decadence, especially Sologub, then it is also demonstrable that related waves of optimism and pessimism swept through the entire group in successive periods. Yet the two currents, idealism and decadence, were interdependent in the works of almost every poet. They functioned together, if only as a contrast, and often decadence was more specifically a vent for frustrations and their unwholesome consequences, diseases which served to unnerve the positivistically minded philistine. In the 1890s Bal'mont, Sologub, and Briusov posed as impotent and neuraesthenic personae, and Briusov exhibited his attraction to the themes of eroticism, violence, and death. It was little noticed, but Bal'mont and Briusov aspired to Platonic ideals and Sologub to social justice.

In the early years of the century, as the movement gathered momentum, its polarities became more visible. Bal'mont created a drama in his work by becoming an exultant pantheist. Sologub dedicated himself to a distant, ineffable ideal. Gippius made her appearance as a Christian longing for universal salvation. Briusov devoted himself to art as a sacred entity. Ivanov, Belyi, and Blok tipped the scales in favor of optimism when they appeared as mystics seeking manifestations of divinity, particularly at the Eternal Feminine or Saint Sophia. Ivanov and Belyi ascribed a mystical destiny to Russia. However, decadence could now more clearly be seen as an alternative to idealistic belief. Bal'mont, Sologub, and Briusov questioned the necessity and resented the very existence of evil. Bal'mont protested by identifying with violence, Sologub rebelled against heaven, Gippius succumbed to individualistic pride, and Briusov to amoralistic self-indulgence. In the aftermath of the 1905 revolution, these "poisons" again surfaced as the leading moods. No one abjured his faith in idealism or the sanctity of art, but the bitterness of the original decadents resulted in their less frequent aspirations to spiritual attainment. Sologub advocated the willing anticipation of death, and Briusov turned his attention to social evils and political tyranny. Ivanov alone remained optimistic. In their despair Belyi and Blok fell into the melancholias, amorality, and fantasies of death that had characterized the decadents since the 1890s. Their horror of Russia's social evils equaled the decadents' earlier despair over the universality of evil.

Symbolism as a movement did not survive the revolt of the Acmeists and Futurists against Platonic idealism, which had been its ideological core. But decadence had an existence of its own apart from the uses to which it was put by Symbolists. It can be seen both in the arrogant glamor of the Ego-Futurists and in the antibourgeois dandyism of the Cubo-Futurists. However, the Acmeists and Futurists inherited from Symbolism a nonmystical form of its idealism: the veneration of the artistic medium as the bearer in and of itself of some indefinable spiritual value. Idealism entered into a confluence with the flamboyant aspects of Futurism in this attenuated form, and a new literary movement was born. (pp. 279-80)

> *Evelyn Bristol, "Idealism and Decadence in Russian Symbolist Poetry," in* Slavic Review, *Vol. 39, No. 2, June, 1980, pp. 269-80.*

RUSSIAN SYMBOLIST THEATER

VALERY BRYUSOV

[*Bryusov initiated the Symbolist movement in Russian theater with his 1902 essay "Unnecessary Truth," in which he called for a rejection of the naturalistic style dominant in Russian theater at that time. In the following excerpt from his essay, he finds that attempts to simulate reality in the theater have failed and advocates the use of stylized stage sets that will direct the imagination of the audience toward spiritual truth rather than physical appearances.*]

It is three years now that the Art Theatre has been with us in Moscow. Somehow it was an immediate success with everyone—the public, the press, the partisans of the new art and the defenders of the old. Not long ago, it was the custom to cite the Maly Theatre as the model of the Russian stage; these days people only laugh at its routine. And this same Maly Theatre and another Moscow theatre—Korsh's—have begun to adopt the new methods. For Muscovites the Art Theatre has become a kind of idol; they are proud of it, and it is the first thing they hasten to show off to the visitor. When the Art Theatre visited Petersburg, it performed here to packed houses, arousing universal interest. The Art Theatre ventured to stage plays that had failed in other theatres—Chekhov's *Seagull*, for example—and was successful. Most surprising of all, it was the Art Theatre's experimental spirit, its innovations in decor and acting, its daring choice of plays, that won the sympathy of the crowd.

What is the Art Theatre, then? Is it really the theatre of the future, as some have called it? Has it made a step toward the spiritualization of art, toward the overcoming of the fatal contradictions between the essence and the surface of art? Simple probability says no. If the Art Theatre had set itself such tasks, it would hardly have won universal acclaim so quickly. Success attests that what the Art Theatre offers its audience is not the genuinely new, but the old refurbished, that it offers no threat to the deep-rooted habits of the theatregoer. It has only achieved with greater perfection what other theatres, including its rival the Maly, have aimed at. Together with the entire European theatre, with insignificant exceptions, it is on a false path.

Modern theatres aim at the utmost verisimilitude in their depiction of life. They think that if everything on the stage is as it is in reality, then they have worthily fulfilled their function. Actors endeavor to speak as they would in a drawing room, scene-painters copy views from nature, costume designers work in accordance with archaeological data. In spite of all this, however, there remains much that the theatre has not succeeded in counterfeiting. The Art Theatre has set itself the aim of reducing this "much." The actors there have begun to sit with their backs to the audience without constraint; they have begun to talk to each other instead of "out" to the audience. In place of the usual box set has appeared the room placed at an oblique angle: other rooms are visible through the open doors, so that an entire apartment is presented to the viewer's gaze. The furniture is arranged as it usually is in people's homes. If a forest or a garden is to be represented, several trees are placed on the forestage. If the play requires rain to fall, the audience is made to listen to the sound of water. If the play is set in winter, snow can be seen falling outside the windows. If it is windy, curtains flutter, and so on.

First of all, one has to say that these innovations are very timid. They are concerned with secondary matters and leave the essential traditions of the theatre undisturbed. And until these traditions, which comprise the essence of any stage production, are changed, no alteration of detail will bring the theatre closer to reality. All theatres, including the Art Theatre, try to make everything on stage visible and audible. Stages are lit by footlights and strip lights, but in real life light either falls from the sky, or pours in through windows, or is cast by a lamp or a candle. If there is a night scene, the Art Theatre has ventured to leave the stage in greater darkness than is customary, although it has not dared to extinguish all the lights in the theatre; however, if it were really night on stage, the audience would obviously be unable to see anything. Similarly, the Art Theatre is at pains to ensure that all stage conversation is audible to the auditorium. Even if a large gathering is represented, only one actor speaks at a time. When a new group begins to speak, the previous one "moves upstage" and begins gesticulating energetically—and this a quarter of a century after Villiers de l'Isle Adam in his drama *Le nouveau monde* bracketed two pages of dialogue with the direction "Everybody speaks at once!"

But even if the Art Theatre were more daring, it would still fall short of its purpose. To reproduce life faithfully on the stage is impossible. The stage is conventional by its very nature. One set of conventions may be replaced by another, that is all. In Shakespeare's day a board would be set up with the inscription "forest." Not so long ago we used to be content with a backdrop of a forest with side wings depicting trees with branches incomprehensibly intertwined against the sky. In time to come, forests will be constructed from artificial three-dimensional trees with foliage and rounded trunks, or even from living trees with roots hidden in tubs under the stage.... And all this, the last word in stage technique, will, like the Shakespearean inscription, be for the audience no more than a reminder, no more than a symbol of a forest. The modern theatregoer is not in the least taken in by a painted tree—he knows that a particular piece of lathe and canvas is intended to stand for a tree. In much the same way, a signboard meant "forest" to an Elizabethan audience and a stage sapling will mean a tree growing naturally to the audience of the future. The set is no more than a pointer to the imagination. In the Greek theatre, an actor playing someone who had just returned from foreign parts would enter from the left. At the Art Theatre, the actor is admitted to a small vestibule where he divests himself of sheepskin and galoshes as a sign that he has come from afar. But who among the audience is likely to forget that he arrived from the wings? In what way is the convention by which an actor removes his sheepskin more subtle than the one by which it is understood that if he enters from the left he is coming from foreign parts?

Not only the art of the theatre, but art of any kind cannot avoid formal convention, cannot be transformed into a re-creation of reality. Never, in looking at a picture by one of the great realist painters, will we be deceived like the birds of Zeuxis into thinking that before us are fruits or an open window through which we may glimpse a distant horizon. By infinitesimal gradations of light and shade, by the most elusive signals, the eye is able to distinguish reality from representation. Never will we bow to the marble bust of an acquaintance. It is unheard of that someone, on reading a story in which the author recounts in the first person how he came to commit suicide, should order a mass to be sung for the repose of his soul. And if there do exist reproductions of people and things that deceive the eye, such, for example, as bridges in a painted panorama or wax figures so convincing that they frighten children, we have difficulty in recognizing these creations as works of art. Not a single one of the spectators sitting in the orchestra and paying three or four roubles for his seat is going to believe that he is really looking at Hamlet, Prince of Denmark, and that in the final scene the Prince lies dead.

Each new technical device in art, be it that of the theatre or another, only arouses curiosity and suspicion in the spectator. A certain contemporary artist has, it is said, painted a new series of pictures in which the effect of moonlight is strikingly conveyed. When we see them, our first thought will be: how did he manage to do that? And then we will captiously seek out every discrepancy with reality. Only when we have satisfied our curiosity will we start looking at the picture as a work of art. When an avalanche of wadding descends on the stage, the members of the audience ask each other: how was that done?

If Rubek and Irene [characters in Henrik Ibsen's *When We Dead Awaken,* first produced by the Moscow Art Theater in 1901] simply walked off into the wings, the audience would believe more readily in their destruction than it does now, when before their eyes two strawstuffed dummies and armfuls of wadding go rolling over the boards. "It faded on the crowing of the cock," someone says of the Ghost in *Hamlet,* and this is enough for the audience to imagine the crowing of the cock. But in *Uncle Vanya* the Art Theatre has a cricket chirping. No one in the audience will imagine that the cricket is real, and the more lifelike the sound, the less convincing the illusion. In time, audiences will become used to the devices they now find so novel and will cease to notice them. But this will not come about because the audience will take wadding for snow in real earnest, or the rope that tugs at the curtains for wind, but because these devices will simply be numbered among the usual theatrical conventions. Would it not then be better to abandon the fruitless battle against the invincible conventions of the theatre, which only spring up with renewed strength, and rather than seeking to eradicate them, attempt to subjugate, to tame, to harness, to saddle them?

There are two kinds of convention. One kind arises from the inability to create successfully. A bad poet says of a beautiful woman: "She is as fresh as a rose." It may be that the poet really understood the vernal freshness of the woman's soul, but he was unable to express his feelings, substituting cliché for genuine expression. In the same way, people want to speak on the stage as they do in life but are unable to, stressing words unnaturally, pronouncing endings too emphatically and so on. But there is another kind of convention—that which is deliberately applied. It is a convention that statues of marble and bronze are left unpainted. They could be painted—at one time they even were—but it is unnecessary, since sculpture is concerned with form, not color. An engraving in which leaves are black and the sky striped observes certain conventions, but it nevertheless affords pure aesthetic enjoyment. Wherever there is art, there is convention. To oppose this is as absurd as to demand that science would dispense with logic and explain phenomena other than by their causal relationship.

It is time that the theatre stopped counterfeiting reality. A cloud depicted in a painting is flat, it does not move or change its form or luminiscence—but there is something about it that gives us the same feeling as a real cloud. The stage must provide everything that can most effectively help the spectator to recreate the setting demanded by the play in his imagination. If a battle is to be represented, it is absurd to send on stage a couple of dozen—or even a thousand—extras waving wooden swords: perhaps the audience will be better served by a musical picture from the orchestra. If a wind is called for, there is no need to blow a whistle and tug at the curtain with a rope: the actors themselves must convey the storm by behaving as people do in a strong wind. There is no need to do away with the setting, but it must be deliberately conventionalized. The setting must be, as it were, stylized. Types of setting must be devised that will be comprehensible to everyone, as a received language is comprehensible, as white statues, flat paintings and black engravings are comprehensible. Simplicity of setting will not be equivalent to banality and monotony. The principle will be changed, and there will be ample scope in particulars for the imagination of Messrs. set designers and technicians.

Dramatists too must in some degree perfect their artistic method. They are sovereign artists only when their work is read; on the stage their plays are only forms into which the actors pour their own content. Dramatists must renounce all superfluous, unnecessary and ultimately futile copying of life. Everything external in their work must be reduced to a minimum because it has little to do with the conduct of the drama. The drama can convey the external only through an intermediary—through the souls of the *dramatis personae*. The sculptor cannot take soul and emotion in his hands; he has to give the spirit bodily incarnation. The dramatist, on the contrary, should make it possible for the actor to express the physical in the spiritual. Something has already been achieved in the creation of a new drama. The most interesting attempts of this kind are the plays of Maeterlinck and the latest dramas of Ibsen. It is noteworthy that it is in the staging of these plays that the modern theatre has shown itself to be particularly ineffectual.

The ancient theatre had a single permanent set—the palace. With slight alterations it was made to represent the interior of a house, a square, the seashore. Actors wore masks and buckskins which forced them to put aside any thought of imitating everyday life. The chorus sang sacred hymns around the altar and also intervened in the action. Everything was at once thoroughly conventionalized and utterly alive; the audience devoted its attention to the action and not to the setting, "for tragedy," says Aristotle, "is the imitation not of men, but of action." In our day, such simplicity of setting has been preserved in the folk theatre. I chanced to see a performance of *Tsar Maximilian* [a popular Russian folk drama] given by factory workers. The scenery and props consisted of two chairs, the tsar's paper crown and the paper chains of his rebellious son Adolph. Watching this performance, I understood what powerful resources the theatre has at its disposal and how misguided it is in seeking the aid of painters and technicians.

The creative urge is the only reality that exists on earth. Everything external is, in the poet's words, "only a dream, a fleeting dream." Grant that in the theatre we may be partakers of the highest truth, the profoundest reality. Grant the actor his rightful place, set him upon the pedestal of the stage that he may rule it as an artist. By his art he will give content to the dramatic performance. Let your setting aim not at truth, but at the suggestion of truth. I summon you away from the unnecessary truth of the modern stage to the deliberate conventionalization of the ancient theatre. (pp. 25-30)

> *Valery Bryusov, "Against Naturalism in the Theatre," in* The Russian Symbolist Theatre: An Anthology of Plays and Critical Texts, *edited and translated by Michael Green, Ardis, 1986, pp. 25-30.*

MICHAEL GREEN

[*In the following excerpt, Green traces the development of Russian Symbolist theater and examines the Symbolists' dramatic and theatrical principles.*]

The late nineteenth century was a period of rebellion and renewal in the European theatre. Discontent with the mediocrity of the commercial stage with its "well-made plays" and comfortable moral assumptions had given rise to the New Drama. Less a unified movement than a useful banner to which all those who wished for change in the theatre could rally, the New Drama looked toward both Symbolism and naturalism— a dualism embodied in the work of such dramatists of the period as Ibsen, Strindberg, Hauptmann and Chekhov. Poets and philosophers too had their vision of the theatre of the future. Nietzsche dreamed of returning the theatre to its origins in Dionysian ritual and sweeping away the barrier between actor

and spectator. Wagner had looked back to the Athenian theatre and seen in it a profound union of poetry, music, drama, dance and design, the spirit of which he hoped to recapture in the modern *Gesamtkunstwerk*. In France, Mallarmé too called for a theatre that would lay all the arts under tribute to create a drama of mystery on a stage reduced to its barest elements. Maeterlinck announced that external action was dead and pleaded for a theatre of stillness and inner drama; his plays began to be taken up by the avant-garde as a sacred cause.

This ferment did not leave Russia untouched. With the first translations of Ibsen and Strindberg in the 1880s, the New Drama began to filter into the consciousness of cultured Russians; Maeterlinck and Hauptmann followed in the 1890s, and in the 1900s appeared a whole galaxy of new names that included Przybyszewski, Hofmannsthal, Wedekind, Hamsun, Schnitzler, D'Annunzio, Wilde and Shaw.

To a striking extent, the development of the Russian theatre at the turn of the century ran a similar course to that of the French theatre ten years earlier. In France, the naturalistic excesses of Antoine's Théâtre Libre (founded in 1887), which had specialized in painstakingly realistic productions of Ibsen and Hauptmann, had brought about a reaction in the shape of Paul Fort's Théâtre d'Art (1890) and its successor, Lugné-Poe's Théâtre de L'Oeuvre (1892), which introduced the dramas of Maeterlinck and staged Ibsen in a stylized "Symbolist" manner, bringing in artists of the Nabi school (Vuillard, Sérusier, Maurice Denis) to paint decorative backdrops. In Russia, the naturalism of Stanislavsky's Moscow Art Theatre (founded in 1898), which found effective vehicles in the plays of Ibsen, Hauptmann and Chekhov, was succeeded by the stylized theatre of Meyerhold, who produced plays by Maeterlinck, Ibsen and a number of Symbolists, both native and foreign, turning for decor to brilliant young painters from the ambience of the *World of Art*. There is, however, a factor that disturbs the neatness of the parallel—the ambiguous genius of Chekhov, whose relationship to the Symbolist theatre deserves some examination.

Chekhov has always been closely associated with the Moscow Art Theatre, which achieved its first significant success with its revival of *The Seagull* in 1898 and gave the premieres of all his major plays thereafter. Although Chekhov himself had reservations, the Art Theatre's naturalistic approach seemed ideally suited to Chekhov's plays, with the result that Chekhov has often been identified with naturalism in the theatre. Yet if Chekhov was a realist, he was a realist of a special kind who refined realism to the point where it threatened to become something else. Both realists and Symbolists sensed this in Chekhov. "Do you know what you're doing?" Gorky had expostulated, "You're killing realism." (pp. 9-10)

Chekhov's later plays convey a mysterious sense of something pressing beyond words to find expression in the multitude of pauses that Chekhov, unlike most dramatists, is wisely content not to fill with stage directions. Dialogue seems to rise out of a profounder silence and to sink back into it. It is here that we sense a kinship between Chekhov and Maeterlinck, whose writings on the theatre are full of observations that, in a curious way, seem even more applicable to Chekhov's dramas than to Maeterlinck's own. "It is idle," wrote Maeterlinck, "to think that, by means of words, any real communication can ever pass from one man to another." He had argued that "psychological action" was "infinitely loftier in itself than mere material action," maintaining that "side by side with the necessary dialogue" there was "another dialogue that seems superfluous,'' but really determines ''the quality and immeasurable range of the work.''

Chekhov was drawn toward Maeterlinck, just as he was repelled by Ibsen. A whole bouquet of uncomplimentary remarks about the great Norwegian may be gathered from Chekhov's conversation and correspondence: ''Listen, I tell you Ibsen is no dramatist,'' he wrote to Stanislavsky; to Andreyev he was even more unceremoniously dismissive—''Ibsen is an idiot.'' Ibsen, being, as Bernard Shaw admiringly observed in his *Quintessence of Ibsenism,* ''a moralist and a debater as well as a dramatist,'' had invented the play of discussion. Ibsen belongs to the old drama of communication, Chekhov to the new drama of non-communication, which is perhaps why he seems so ''modern'' to us today. No doubt it was just this polemical quality in Ibsen that Chekhov found unappealing. (pp. 10-11)

It is tempting to speculate on the direction Chekhov might have taken had he lived longer. *The Cherry Orchard*—''almost a farce,'' as Chekhov insisted—anticipates the harlequinade of the pre-revolutionary years. Stanislavsky tells in his memoirs of a projected play that suggests that Chekhov was moving toward a decisive break with the manner he had brought to such perfection. The play was to deal with two friends in love with the same woman who journey together to the North Pole; the set for the last act was to represent an enormous ice-bound ship, and the play was to end with the two friends having a vision of the ghost of the woman (who had died in the meantime) flitting across the snow. The icy remoteness of the setting recalls that Ibsen's last and most ''symbolic'' play, *When We Dead Awaken,* while both action and decor curiously anticipate Apollinaire's surrealist verse drama *Couleur du temps.* A jotting in Chekhov's notebook gives another hint of new departures: a play about a group of people waiting for someone who never arrives. (p. 11)

1902 was the year which saw the unmistakable emergence of new forces in the Russian theatre. In his article of that year, ''Unnecessary Truth,'' Valery Briusov, the leader of Russian Symbolism, for the first time called into question the achievement of the Moscow Art Theatre, then at the height of its success, and wondered whether naturalism was not opposed to the very nature of the stage [see excerpt above]. In 1902 Meyerhold resigned from the Art Theatre to form a company; eventually to take the name of ''The Fellowship of the New Drama''; with the young Aleksei Remizov as literary adviser, the troupe toured the provinces, including in its repertoire such unfamiliar names as Maeterlinck, Przybyszewski, Schnitzler and Hofmannsthal. In the same year the most popular actress of her generation, Vera Komissarzhevskaya, left the Alexandrinsky Theatre (where, in 1896, she had created the role of Nina in the original production of *The Seagull*), dissatisfied with the entrenched routine of the Imperial stage; by touring the provinces she raised enough money to open her own theatre in St. Petersburg in 1904. The later conjunction of these two searchers—Meyerhold and Komissarzhevskaya—was to bring about the brief flowering of the Symbolist theatre in Russia.

Stanislavsky's 1904 productions of Maeterlinck, though generally agreed to be disappointingly unimaginative, had shown him to be not unaware of the need for a change of direction if the Art Theatre was to retain its leading position. Deciding that the time was ripe for experiment, and even for ''novelty for novelty's sake,'' in 1905 he invited Meyerhold to take charge of an experimental ''Theatre-Studio'' attached to the Art Theatre. Briusov himself was to be in charge of the new theatre's

literary section, and two native Symbolist dramas, Briusov's *The Earth* and Viacheslav Ivanov's *Tantalus,* were planned for inclusion in the repertoire. For the Theatre-Studio's opening production, however, Meyerhold chose Maeterlinck's *La Mort de Tintagiles.* Under the influence of the Belgian dramatist's own theory of ''static theatre,'' Meyerhold matched the play's deathward drift and languid, hypnotic rhythms with a style of sparse, deliberate gesture that suggested the carefully composed groups of an antique bas-relief; formalized movement was complemented by formalized speech, each syllable falling, in Meyerhold's own memorable phrase, like a pebble into a deep well.

The Revolution of 1905 and Stanislavsky's dissatisfaction with the dress rehearsal of *Tintagiles* combined to bring about the premature demise of the Theatre-Studio, which never opened its doors to the public. Nevertheless, it had demonstrated during its brief, sequestered existence that a Symbolist theatre could exist outside the dreams of impractical poets. Moving now to St. Petersburg, Meyerhold became a frequenter of the famous Wednesday gatherings at the apartment of the erudite Symbolist poet Viacheslav Ivanov, where all that was liveliest in the artistic and intellectual life of the capital was to be encountered; apart from the host and his wife, the writer Lidia Zinovieva-Annibal, there was Blok, Bely, Sologub, Briusov, Berdiaev, Chulkov, Gippius and Merezhkovsky. The theatre of the future was a favorite topic of conversation at the Wednesdays. Imbued with Nietzschean ideas, Ivanov preached a theatre of religious communion and Dionysian ecstasy. The mood was one of expectancy. ''The idea of a symbolist theatre hung in the air,'' wrote the poet, dramatist and critic Georgii Chulkov. ''All that was lacking was a man of the theatre who would venture so risky an experiment. In those days only one director dreamed of a revolution in the theatre.'' That man was, of course, Meyerhold; together with Chulkov, he attempted to organize a new theatre: to be called ''Torches,'' it would—so went the gossip in theatrical circles—''be something like a Petersburg version of the ill-fated Moscow Studio.'' Although ''Torches,'' for want of financial backing, came to nothing, it did create conditions for an alliance between the new playwright and the new director, effectively bringing the poet into the theatre. It was for ''Torches'' that Blok, at Chulkov's suggestion, developed one of his lyrics into a short play of the same name— *The Puppet Show.*

In 1906 Komissarzhevskaya moved her theatre to new premises on Ofitserskaya Street and invited Meyerhold to be her director. An actress of great spiritual intensity who communicated to her roles something of her own tragic personality, Komissarzhevskaya won the hearts of poets (as Blok's touching obituary bears witness) no less than those of the theatregoing public; in the words of an admirer, ''all the restless longing of a catastrophic epoch found its expression in her, all the vague reaching out, the satiety with the visible material world, the thirst to penetrate the undiscovered secrets of the universe and of life.'' Her adherence to the cause of the Symbolist theatre helped to broaden its appeal and make it less of a coterie enterprise.

The very appearance of the theatre on Ofitserskaya Street made it clear that radical departures were to be expected. The keynote was a chaste and severe restraint: walls and columns were painted a stark white and the curtains were of a plain dark material. The only color was provided by Bakst's drop-curtain, on which a Greek temple in the depths of a mysterious forest suggested the theatre's aim of returning the theatre to its ancient ritual origins.

Meyerhold was director of Komissarzhevskaya's theatre for little more than a year (his first production, Ibsen's *Hedda Gabler,* opened on November 10, 1906, his last, Sologub's *The Triumph of Death,* on November 6, 1907). The partnership was an uneasy one and the break, when it came, bitter. If Meyerhold and Komissarzhevskaya were both explorers, their explorations were conducted in different regions: "She did not need the external contrivances of new acting techniques, but the possibility of expressing her soul"—what drew her to Symbolism was the movement's mystical and transcendental aspect; Meyerhold, on the other hand, was a scholar and a technician, fascinated by the stylization of past theatrical epochs and "theatre for theatre's sake." In a way, actress and director represented the division within Russian Symbolism itself.

The art of the Symbolist period was marked by a heightened awareness of developments in the west, a self-conscious return to the community of European culture. This internationalism of outlook was characteristic of the theatre on Ofitserskaya Street, which opened its doors with a defiantly anti-naturalistic production of a play by the Art Theatre's beloved Ibsen— *Hedda Gabler,* in which the heroine, attired in a gown that suggested some scaly creature of the deep, moved against the deep blue and orange of Sapunov's extravagant art nouveau set, a martyr to the aesthetic protest. Nevertheless, though another foreign plays were preponderant in the repertoire, the year of the Meyerhold-Komissarzhevskaya collaboration saw the premieres of such plays as Blok's *Puppet Show,* Andreyev's *Life of Man* and Sologub's *Triumph of Death*; the first of these was the occasion of a great theatrical battle of the order of the first night of *Hernani* or *The Rite of Spring* and marked a turning point in the history of the Russian theatre. After Meyerhold's departure, Komissarzhevskaya, with the aid of such brilliant directors as her brother, Fyodor Komissarzhevsky, and Nikolai Evreinov, continued her policy of staging Symbolist plays until the banning of Wilde's *Salome* in the autumn of 1908 forced her to close her theatre the following year. Russian dramas premiered during this period included Remizov's *Devil's Comedy,* Andreyev's *Black Maskers,* and Sologub's *Vanka the Steward and the Page Jehan.* With the closing of Komissarzhevskaya's theatre, the Symbolist drama was left without a theatre of its own. There was nothing to do but retreat to the little theatres and theatre-cabarets that were such a feature of the artistic life of St. Petersburg in the prerevolutionary years. This intimate atmosphere was well suited to such a master of chamber drama and *divertissement* as Kuzmin, and it also gave Meyerhold—since 1908 director of the Imperial Alexandrinsky Theatre—a chance to experiment with *commedia dell'arte* techniques in the guise of "Doctor Dapertutto." By 1912, when Leonid Andreyev in the first of his two "Letters about the Theatre," regretfully announced the demise of Symbolism in the theatre, Symbolism itself was fast on the wane as a movement. The only two native Symbolist dramas staged by Meyerhold at the Alexandrinsky—Sologub's *Hostages of Life* (1912) and Zinaida Gippius's *The Green Ring* (1915)—both represent a compromise with traditional realistic theatre. The most considerable late Symbolist drama, Blok's *The Rose and The Cross* (the carefully researched historical setting of which also, in a sense, represented a compromise), was never given the staging it deserved. (pp. 11-15)

[The] plays of the Symbolists were not, at their best, works intended, like the dramatic poems of the Romantics, for the study rather than the stage: they were highly theatrical creations in a new style that demanded a new style of production. Was it, then, a matter of a new theatre in search of a drama, or a new drama in search of a theatre? Meyerhold gave the primacy to literature: "The *New Theatre,*" he wrote in "Literary Intimations of the New Theatre" (1906), "has its roots *in literature.* Literature has always taken the initiative in breaking up dramatic forms. Chekhov wrote *The Seagull* before the Art Theatre came forward to stage it. Van Lerberghe and Maeterlinck existed before the theatre that staged them." Meyerhold added that by literature he meant not only "playwrights who create a new form demanding a different kind of technique," but also "critics who reject old forms." In both these capacities the Russian Symbolists helped Meyerhold to formulate the principles of his theatrical revolution. Briusov's rejection of stage naturalism in favor of stylization and Ivanov's demand for the abolition of the barrier between actor and spectator remained central to Meyerhold's thinking, while it would be difficult to overemphasize the key position that *The Puppet Show* occupied in his development. Meyerhold himself credited Blok's play with providing "the first impetus in finding the paths of my art," for it was here that he broke away from Maeterlinck's "static theatre" to create his own "grotesque theatre" of movement and surprise.

"The basis of the grotesque," wrote Meyerhold, "is the constant striving on the artist's part to thrust the spectator from a plane he has only just succeeded in comprehending to another for which he is utterly unprepared." Mystification, unease, ambiguity, a sense of the illusory and transient nature of things, a constant question of "reality," are at the very heart of the Symbolist drama. They spring inevitably from the dualism of the Symbolist vision, with its unresolved tension between transcendental and everyday reality. It is characteristic of Symbolist drama that its action proceeds on two or more intersecting but mutually uncomprehending planes, and that the transitions between these planes are abrupt, creating just that sense of dislocation envisaged by grotesque (in Meyerhold's sense) theatre. The method is most brilliantly deployed in Blok's *Puppet Show,* where the action attains a complex ambiguity far beyond the simpler binary opposition underlying most Symbolist drama. In Annensky's *Thamyris Kitharodos,* for example, the Apollonian world of high art represented by the ascetic protagonist co-exists with the Dionysian world of the Satyrs and Maenads. The lonely passion of Judas in Remizov's tragedy is counterpointed with the bizarre antics of Zif, Orif and the Monkey King. In the plays of Sologub, such as *The Triumph of Death* and *Vanka the Steward and the Page Jehan,* dualism is so all-pervasive as to assume the function of a constructive principle. Kuzmin's Count Stello in *The Venetian Madcaps* dwells in a world of pure aesthetic delight inaccessible to the play's *commedia dell'arte* characters. Misty Brittany, with its songs and legends, remains infinitely remote from the feudal realities of Languedoc in Blok's *The Rose and the Cross.*

These worlds co-exist rather than conflict, for there is no common ground between them on which conflict might take place. We might well say of these plays what Martin Esslin has said of the plays of the Theatre of the Absurd: that they reflect "one poet's most intimate and personal intuition of the human situation, his own *sense of being,* his individual vision of the world"; that each play "is a complex poetic image made of a complicated pattern of subsidiary images and themes, which are interwoven, like the themes of a musical composition, not, as in most well-made plays, to present a line of development, but to make in the spectator's mind a total, complex impression of a basic, and static, situation." This lack of dramatic conflict in the conventional sense is reflected in such terms as "Lyrical Drama" (as Blok designated his three playlets of 1906) or

Sologub's "Theatre of the Single Will." Yet while Sologub announced with unmixed satisfaction that all *dramatis personae* were but masks, transparent to a greater or lesser extent, behind which the face of their creator might be glimpsed, Blok (like Yeats and Hofmannsthal) came to distrust the lyrical, subjective element that was engulfing the stage, warning that "the subtle poisons of lyricism have eaten away the strong, simple chains that support the drama and hold it together." Condemning Maeterlinck, and with him Chekhov, "who has taken away from the Russian drama what Maeterlinck has taken away from the European drama," Blok proclaimed Ibsen to have been the last of the great European dramatists. Ironically, though, Blok's earliest and most purely lyrical plays remain his most convincing work for the theatre; even *The Rose and the Cross,* with all its beauties, has a slightly labored air beside the freshness of *The Puppet Show* and *The Stranger.*

Russian Symbolism not only anticipated the constructive principles of Absurdist drama, it was also capable of astonishingly prophetic insights into the function of the theatre in man's increasingly mechanized existence. "The Theatre of the Absurd," writes Martin Esslin, "forms part of the unceasing endeavor of the true artists of our time to breach this dead wall of complacency and automatism and to re-establish an awareness of man's situation when confronted with the ultimate reality of his condition"; it seeks "to instill in him again the lost sense of cosmic wonder and primeval anguish, to shock him out of an existence that has become trite, mechanical, complacent." In a letter to Meyerhold, written in 1906 under the immediate impression of a dress rehearsal of *The Puppet Show,* Blok used similar imagery to express virtually the same thought: "*Every* piece of buffoonery, including my own, seeks to become a *battering ram* to smash through all the deadness." The poet-buffoon, said Blok, may pretend to embrace the "crass and torpid" world of matter, but only in order to fool it; "at this point *the hour of mystery must strike*: matter has been fooled, disarmed and subdued; in this sense, I '*accept the world*'—the whole world with its stupidity, inertia and dead, dry colors—only in order to trick this bony old witch and make her young again. In the embrace of the Fool and the Buffoon the old world puts on youth and beauty, and its eyes become translucent, unfathomable."

The concept of the *Gesamtkunstwerk* haunted the synesthetic imagination of the Symbolists, and it is natural that the theatre, the meeting place of the arts, should have occupied a central place in their thinking. Rarely in the history of the arts have music, painting, poetry and dance entered into so fruitful a partnership as they did in Russia in these prerevolutionary years. The dominant art of the period was undoubtedly music—the condition to which, in Pater's well-known phrase, all art aspired. Andrei Bely, the leading theoretician of symbolism, had said that "music is the soul of all the arts," and that "music is the ideal expression of the symbol." If music could not occupy in the theatre of the word the supremacy it enjoyed in the ballet (which must be admitted the quintessential art form of these years), it is nevertheless a subtly pervasive element in the Symbolist drama, with its tendency toward the rhythmically organized language of verse and the dissolving of the action in song, mime and dance. Ivanov, Sologub and Annensky all envisage a theatre in which there would be a place for the dance, while Meyerhold wished to "subordinate acting to the rhythm of speech and the rhythm of plastic movement" in anticipation of a "rebirth of the dance."

In the Symbolist theatre the painter's role assumed an importance it had not had since the days of the great baroque dec-orators, such as Viviani and Gonzago, who had worked in Russia. Jettisoning with relief the laboriously constructed three-dimensional stage models demanded by the Moscow Art Theatre, the artists of the Symbolist theatre once again made scene painting a "music for the eyes" that merged with the rhythm of the production. Though far less well known, the decorative achievement of the Symbolist theatre bears comparison with that of Diaghilev's Ballets Russes, which indeed, it anticipated. In an article entitled "The Artist in V. F. Komissarzhevskaya's Theatre," Evreinov wrote: "It seems a ridiculous thing to say, but it is the truth: in the field of painting, backward Russia suddenly overtook all other countries in theatre design." The ambience of the *World of Art,* with its emphasis on technique, its cult of the theatre and its taste for the grand style in architecture, be it of St. Petersburg or Versailles, fostered a number of artists who were not only skilled decorators, but whose entire oeuvre is permeated by the spirit of the theatre. If Bakst and Benois devoted their talent mainly to the ballet at this period, there were others hardly less gifted—Dobuzhinsky, Roerich, Golovin, Sapunov, Sudeikin—to provide the atmospheric and brilliantly stylized settings demanded by the Symbolist theatre. This new kind of decorator, who united in himself the creative artist and the man of the theatre, assumed a position of power next only to that of the director himself, with whom he worked in the closest collaboration. Meyerhold spoke with reverence of Sapunov and Golovin—"those together with whom I joyously set out on a journey of exploration (. . .), before whom a secret door into Wonderland opened, as it did to me." (pp. 15-18)

The Symbolist theatre was close to the *World of Art* in another respect—its intense preoccupation with the styles and conventions of the past. The retrospectivism that marked Russian art at the turn of the century was not mere nostalgia or escapism; it was the result of a profound feeling that the way to the future lay through a recovery of the past. Diaghilev, the organizing force behind the *World of Art,* gave prophetic expression to this feeling in 1905, when, summing up what the movement had accomplished, he spoke of "a culture that has risen through us but will sweep us aside." The scholar-artist and the scholar-poet, versed in a variety of cultures and with a protean ability to recreate them in their own work, were typical of the age. "Stylization"—a word that Briusov had put forward with some caution in 1902—soon became something of a catchword in cultivated drawing rooms.

In an attempt to break with the "untheatrical" realism of the immediate past, the theatre turned to what Meyerhold called "the truly theatrical epochs." We read in Meyerhold's theatre magazine *The Love of Three Oranges* of an attempt "to write a light comedy directly continuing the traditions of the eighteenth century and bypassing the line of development upon which Russian drama entered in the nineteenth century." In 1907 the "Ancient Theatre," founded by Evreinov and Baron Drizen with the aim of staging plays in the style of the period in which they were written, opened a season of medieval miracles and mysteries with Blok's translation of Rutebeuf's *Le Miracle de Théophile*; a second season in 1911 was devoted to the seventeenth century Spanish drama. What then were the "truly theatrical epoch's that the anti-realists sought to revive? Classical Greece, the Middle Ages, Elizabethan England, the France of Molière; but above all the lost golden age was located in late eighteenth century Venice, where Gozzi had brought about a miraculous rebirth of the *commedia dell'arte* with his fantastic, semi-improvisatory fairytale plays. Gozzi became the object of a cult: the title of his first great theatrical triumph was adopted by Meyerhold for a magazine largely devoted to making available in Russian the Italian dramatist's plays and memoirs. Small wonder, then, if the masks of the *commedia dell'arte* haunt the drama of these years.

So powerful was the retrospective spirit in the years immediately preceding the Revolution that in his article "Russian Dramatists" of 1911, Meyerhold says nothing of the individual qualities of the representatives of the "New Drama," but contents himself with an approving enumeration of their links with past theatrical traditions: Viacheslav Ivanov is reviving the ancient Greek *orchestra*; Blok is following the tradition of Italian popular comedy, while his outlook is close to that of such German Romantics as Novalis and Tieck; Remizov is laying the foundation for a modern mystery, modeled on the mystery plays of the Middle Ages; Kuzmin writes plays in the spirit of the medieval drama, and is also "reconstructing" the French comic theatre; Bely is trying to create an original modern mystery; Sologub is drawn to the classical Greek theatre (*The Gift of the Wise Bees*) or to the great age of Spanish drama (*The Triumph of Death*). This is, of course, a one-sided view. Just as the figures in eighteenth century or eighteen thirties costume who move with slightly self-conscious theatricality in the shallow, stage-like picture-space of such *World of Art* affiliated artists as Somov, Sapunov and Sudeikin are clearly the artists' contemporaries playing at being aristocrats of the *ancien régime*, so the characters created by Symbolist playwrights reflect the sensibility of their own day. Count Stello in *The Venetian Madcaps* is really a St. Petersburg aesthete of the *fin de siècle*. Blok admitted that the men and women in his *The Rose and the Cross* were "modern people" and that "their tragedy is our tragedy." Annensky too conceded that, although he had "treated an ancient theme in an ancient form," his drama "very probably reflects the soul of modern man."

While Meyerhold looked to Gozzi and Tieck as the precursors of an absolute, self-sufficient theatre (though it is true that he also found links between Pushkin, Gogol, Lermontov and the great theatrical traditions of the past), it is possible to trace such an "anti-realistic" tradition—a minor one, to be sure—within the Russian theatre itself. Since Russian Symbolism was in many respects a return to the principles of Russian Romanticism, it is not surprising to find stirrings of discontent with the idea of verisimilitude as the basis of theatre in the writings of the Romantics. In a draft preface to *Boris Godunov*, Pushkin roundly declared that the very nature of drama excluded any such slavish copying of life: ". . . what kind of verisimilitude is there, for heaven's sake, in a room divided in two parts, one of which is occupied by two thousand people supposedly invisible to those on the stage?" Pushkin's friend, the Decembrist poet Küchelbecker, wrote a choric tragedy, *The Argives*, in which he attempted to return to the Greek theatre without the intermediacy of the French classicists. More startlingly, he recommended a revival of the mystery play, not on the model of Goethe's *Faust*, but in the style of "the artless allegorical popular spectacles of Hans Sachs, the *Frères de la Passion*, the English minstrels, the German mastersingers," and the *Sacramentales* of Calderon. He was attracted by the division of the medieval stage into two or three levels and also by the deliberate disruption of the theatrical illusion by direct appeals to the audience. All these features he attempted to incorporate into his own "Mystery," *Izhorsky* (1835).

Closer to the Theatre of the Absurd are the delightful nonsense plays of the comic team who wrote under the name of Kozma Prutkov. Not staged in their own day (with the exception of

the first of them, *Fantasia*, which was banned after, or—as its "author" proudly pointed out—*during* its first performance in 1851, when an unamused Nicholas I stalked out in disgust), Prutkov's plays were later to enjoy something of a vogue in the little theatres and cabarets of St. Petersburg, where they were staged by such directors as Evreinov and Komissarzhevsky. It would, however, be unwise to place to heavy an ideological weight on these *jeux d'espirit*; Aleksei Tolstoi, the most distinguished member of the Prutkov team, was, *in propria persona*, the author of worthy blank verse historical dramas and an advocate of the well-made play who objected to the "pointlessness" of Ostrovsky's dialogue. Close in spirit to Prutkov's plays, and like them an ancestor of Blok's *Puppet Show*, is Vladimir Soloviov's skit, *The White Lily*. Blok himself pointed to Sukhovo-Kobylin's extraordinary black farce, *Tarelkin's Death* (1869) as a play in which "the ancient lineaments of the symbolical drama may be discerned."

If the Russian Symbolist drama was not entirely without ancestors on native soil, neither was it without progeny. The "trans-rational" drama of early Futurism, Mayakovsky's expressionistic tragedy *Vladimir Mayakovsky* (certainly the ultimate example of the "Drama of the Single Will") and his later satirical grotesques, the Pirandello-like plays of Evreinov (whose earlier stage works, such as the harlequinade, *A Merry Death*, must be regarded as part of the Symbolist theatre), the tragi-comic farces of Bulgakov and Erdman, the allegorical fairytales of Evgenii Schwartz—not to mention verse dramas, such as those of Gumiliov and Tsvetaeva, that follow the lyrical rather than the grotesque line of Symbolist drama—are all in some measure indebted to the Symbolists' short-lived theatrical revolution. (pp. 18-21)

> *Michael Green, in an introduction to* The Russian Symbolist Theatre: An Anthology of Plays and Critical Texts, *edited and translated by Michael Green, Ardis, 1986, pp. 9-21.*

RUSSIAN SYMBOLISM AND THE FINE ARTS

JOHN E. BOWLT

[*In the following excerpt, Bowlt discusses the interrelationship of the Symbolist writers and the World of Art group and examines parallels in their artistic principles, focusing on their common interest in a synthesis of various art forms.*]

Over the last few years Russian and Western scholars have been giving long overdue attention to the history of Russian Symbolism, a move which has produced a variety of informative articles and books. These publications have been devoted, unfortunately, almost exclusively to the literary theory and practice of the Russian Symbolists, and the other arts, painting and music in particular, have received only marginal treatment. This disproportionate concentration on literature is especially lamentable in the context of Russian Symbolism since this movement was, as so many observers hasten to point out, a synthetic one, whose intellectual horizons extended far beyond the art of the written word. We have but to consult the work of the Russian Symbolist writers, such as A. Bely, A. Blok, V. Bryusov and V. Ivanov, to understand their deep concern with non-literary art forms and their common aspiration towards artistic wholism. In the late 1890s and early 1900s this aspiration was particularly evident within the framework of the St. Petersburg group known as the *World of Art,* which, as its name would imply, served as a common basis for many, varied, cultural activities. True, the *World of Art* favoured the visual arts, but it maintained the closest contact with writers and musicians and hence contributed to that deep interest in synthesism which became such an integral part of Modernist aesthetics both in Russia and in the West.

Essentially, the *World of Art* was a title applied to a cultural "club" of artists, literati, musicians and aesthetes, to a journal issued by them (1898-1904) and to a series of art exhibitions (1899-1906, 1910-1924). The organizational force behind many of the *World of Art*'s activities was S. Diaghilev who achieved subsequent renown in the West as the leader of the *Ballets Russes,* and it was through him that many of the *World of Art* artists, L. Bakst, A. Benois and N. Rerikh among them, also attained international repute from their stage and costume designs for his ballet productions; conversely, some of their colleagues, such as E. Lancéray, A. Ostroumova and K. Somov, did not assist in Diaghilev's enterprise and hence, unjustly, are not known by Western historians. The artistic sensibility which Diaghilev and his confrères cultivated was maintained, even intensified, by the contingent of literati, D. Filosofov, Z. Hippius, D. Merezhkovsky, N. Minsky, V. Rozanov, L. Shestov and, later, Bely and Bryusov. But despite the weight of such names, the *World of Art* remained oriented towards art and art history, rather than towards literature, an inclination which became especially pronounced during the last two years of the journal's existence. But outside of this basic division, the *World of Art* was not easily identifiable with one aesthetic principle. Certainly, it shared common ground with the so-called first generation of Russian Symbolist poets, led by K. Bal'mont and Bryusov, but its eclecticism allowed for a world-view broader than theirs alone could provide. Despite the *World of Art*'s tendency to regard art as "craft," rather than as "religion"—a tenet which distinguished the first from the second generations of Russian Symbolist writers—it sympathized with the later Symbolists such as Bely, Blok and V. Ivanov and, in turn, with the group of mystical painters, the *Blue Rose.* Indeed, the *World of Art* was in communication with the most diverse cultural figures of the time and served as a forum for the ceaseless discussion and interchange of aesthetic ideas. Hence, as a general rubric, the *World of Art* covered a multiplicity of artistic phenomena—the demonic art of M. Vrubel' and the stylized primitivism of V. Vasnetsov, the incisive graphics of Beardsley and the Art Nouveau designs of Mackintosh, the poetry of Bal'mont and the prose of Merezhkovsky, the individualism of Diaghilev and the historicism of Benois. Chronologically, however, the *World of Art* existed as a cohesive society during the hegemony of the first Russian Symbolist poets (late 1890s until c. 1904), and by the end of 1904, when a new wave of philosopher-poets had come to dominate the literary scene, it has lost its original physiognomy. Indeed, by then its place had been usurped by other publicist and artistic groups and, thenceforth, much of its energy was channelled into other activities, the theatre and the ballet among them.

The aestheticism of the *World of Art* artists, their alienation from social and political reality—reflected in their highly stylized, retrospective depictions of Versailles executed with unfailing technical finesse—indicated their tentative acceptance of "art for art's sake" and linked them to such adroit poets as Bal'mont and Bryusov. Just as the verse of the latter was opposed to the civic poetry of the 1860s and 1870s, so the artistic output of such painters as Benois and Somov was alien to the art of the Realists with their imitative presentations of

social disorders. The motto which appeared as an insignium on some *World of Art* publications epitomized their attitude towards the function of art: "Art is Free, Life is Paralyzed"—in other words, art was something too ethereal, too mobile to be anchored to depictions of the realities of life. Indeed, not until the 1905 revolution did some *World of Art* painters and writers turn their attention to the burning social questions of the day by contributing to satirical magazines, but even then, only a few worked at all effectively in this area. Most of the *World of Art* artists confined their political involvement to the signing of a joint communiqué or to private statements welcoming the 1905 revolution and criticizing the status quo. But, for the most part, their efforts were abortive and they retired to the calm world of their Epicurean dreams at least until 1917. This clarity of aesthetic vision distinguished them from the second generation of Russian Symbolists who treated art as a spiritual force by which to move *ab realia ad realiora* ["from one reality to a higher reality"]. Ultimately, however, this lack of a consistent and definite ideological system within the perimeter of the *World of Art* contributed to its own creative enervation.

The neglect of ideological and philosophical questions which we can identify with much of the *World of Art*'s artistic and literary output found a striking compensation in the resultant emphasis on intrinsic artistic properties, a move which connected many of the *World of Art* members with their Symbolist predecessors in France. The attention to the poetical fabric which Bal'mont and Bryusov, or, for that matter, Mallarmé and Verlaine, demonstrated in their verse, tended to reduce the

Cover by L. Bakst for Mir iskustva, *1902. From* Russian Literature Triquarterly, *No. 4, Fall, 1972. By permission of Ardis Publishers.*

poem to an independent arrangement of sounds, rhythms and visual images. This approach to the poem as something self-sufficient, although still associated semantically with concrete reality, found a figurative parallel in many of the paintings of the *World of Art* artists. Not only did such artists as Bakst, Benois and Somov concentrate on technical mastery and thence on specific painterly properties such as line, colour and mass, but also, quite deliberately, they confined the narrative content of the picture by resorting to a scenic format, i.e. by using equidistant trees or statues as theatrical wings and thereby forcing the eye to remain within the frame. . . . This theatricality was expressed, above all, by the artists' concentration on line—just as the poets tended to exaggerate sound—and this led, unexpectedly, to a partial syncretism, i.e. to "architectural painting" and to "musical poetry." In poetry the disruption of versification, noticeable especially in the early Bal'mont and Bely, can be compared therefore to the linear landscapes of Benois or Somov in which normal visual priorities are displaced. In other words, both in the poetry and in the painting of the time perceptual sequences are shifted: firstly we become aware of the formal devices employed and only then do we understand the action or narrative theme. In short, in both disciplines we see a tendency towards abstraction through technical and formal prerogatives. We can note a similar dislocation of traditional values within the framework of colour: the preponderance of white and blue in so much Symbolist verse not only symbolizes spiritual purity or, alternatively, "le grand néant" ["the great void"], but also presents an unnatural and abstracted conception of visual reality. The same is true of pictures by Puvis de Chavannes, Maurice Denis, V. Borisov-Musatov or Vrubel'—where highly subjective and exclusive colour schemes are applied regularly. In Vrubel's canvases, for example, the emphasis on blue, violet and purple reaches such extreme proportions that the subject becomes at times unrecognizable, a transformation which prompted poets to speak of the "poison" of Vrubel's painting.

The intense concern with formal ingredients experienced by the writers and artists of the *World of Art* anticipated the distinct orientation towards form peculiar to the Russian avant-garde after 1910. It was logical, therefore, that Bryusov could think subsequently in terms of "scientific poetry" or that Bely should have aspired to create an exact aesthetics, since both endeavours were the direct results of their preoccupation with poetical craft at the beginning of the century. Despite Bely's misleading statement that "we didn't trouble about form or style, but about inner vision," his very awareness of the need to revitalize poetical vocabulary and his deep interest in formal analyses pointed to the contrary. Even in the context of a profoundly philosophical and thematic poet such as Blok, the concern with poetical form is self-evident: for example, any examination of his famous poem, the *Stranger* (*Neznakomka*, 1906), reveals immediately its architectonic, hermetic composition founded on a rigid, triangular structure (first six verses—reality; seventh—reality/dream; last six—dream). In this, Blok and his colleagues shared common ground with Benois, Somov, etc., whose landscapes rested very often on a central axis within a symmetrical planear arrangement. Since in many cases the poems and paintings of the Symbolists reflected such general themes as moral disintegration and spiritual fatigue, this overt structuralization emerged as an ironic comment on the actual content. Ultimately, the intense concentration on one or more specific artistic elements contributed directly to a loss of methodological balance and hence to a loss of aesthetic totality. In poetry the emphasis on sound detracted automatically from the visuality of its imagery, in painting the cult of line weak-

ened the role of colour and in music the attention to the harmonic or vertical structure of the score overshadowed the value of the melodic or horizontal factor. It is because of this that, despite the formal accuracy described above, a certain dissonance or extremism is often identifiable with the *World of Art* and the Symbolist movement in general. But, in turn, it was the awareness of this failing and the wish to overcome it that contributed to the general synthetic tendency within the *World of Art* and inspired such remarkable essays as Blok's "Colours and Words" (1905).

The apolitical, asocial, even aphilosophical behaviour of many of the *World of Art* members should not allow us to apply the term "art for art's sake" as a blanket term for the aesthetic direction favoured by all of them. Indeed, together with its advocation of the Symbolist heroes, Ibsen, Nietzsche and the Russian philosopher, Vladimir Solov'ev, the *World of Art* tolerated, even publicized, such names as Dostoevsky, Repin, Ruskin and Tolstoi as well as the theurgic Symbolists, Bely and V. Ivanov. In this way, it acted as a junction of interests, rather than as the champion of a single trend. As Filosofov remarked: "The *World of Art* never had a definite programme. . . . It was a cult of dilettantism in the good and true sense of the word." But despite the confusion of artistic currents harboured by the *World of Art* we can detect certain rudimentary ideas whether in its literary or in its artistic output, and perhaps the most important of these was the whole concept of cultural integration.

The quest for artistic synthesism undertaken by so many of the *World of Art* painters and writers was particularly evident from their discovery and support of Wagner and the operatic drama. Although he was admired by all associates of the *World of Art,* the reasons for his popularity differed among them. In the case of Benois and Diaghilev it was admiration for the way in which Wagner had combined musical and visual forces to produce an expressive and emotive whole having little in common with the light Italian and French operas frequented by their forebears. Their appreciation, however, was not limited to passive observation: as early as 1893 Diaghilev had given a formal concert on the Filosofovs' estate when he had performed two arias from *Parsifal* and *Lohengrin* and in 1902 Benois realized one of his first stage sets by designing the Imperial Theatre's presentation of *Götterdämmerung*. In the case of both men Wagner remained a life-long interest and his name was mentioned frequently on the pages of the *World of Art* journal. The principal essay on the composer, G. Lichtenberger's "Wagner's Views on Art," expressed many thoughts similar to those of the Russian Symbolist philosophers: such statements as: "Drama is nothing but myth" or "Greek drama was 'collective' because it included not only many people, but also a union of the arts" were to find parallels in the writings of Bely and V. Ivanov. Just as Wagner, according to many of the *World of Art* members, had at times succeeded in creating a synthetic art, so Rimsky-Korsakov and Skryabin were regarded also in the same light. Rimsky-Korsakov's equation of notes with colours and his own mastery of operatic form endeared him to Diaghilev in particular who at one time received lessons from him and who propagated his works so successfully in the West. To Diaghilev, "heathen and hedonist," Skryabin's exotic and mystical music meant much, witness to which was his invitation to him to appear as a soloist at the season of Russian music in Paris in 1907. Skyrabin's efforts to draw distinct parallels between the seven colours of the spectrum and the seven notes of the European scale acted as a pseudo-scientific basis for his further investigation into the possibilities of total art; but in this Skryabin was not isolated, for he had affinities with N. Medtner, Rachmaninov and, above all, M. Chiurlienis.

When Chiurlienis moved from his home-land, Lithuania, to St. Petersburg in 1909 he was treated immediately as a long lost relative by the Symbolist fraternity, especially by V. Ivanov. For the Symbolists Chiurlienis was perhaps the most synthetic artist of all since his search for wholeness was undertaken on two levels: on the one hand his interest in folk-lore, both of the West and of the East, associated him with Bakst and V. Ivanov, on the other hand his attempts to "paint music," i.e. to unite two art forms in one whole, merited him comparison with Wagner and Skryabin. But it was not only his retrospectivism and visual music which linked him with the *World of Art* and post-*World of Art* intellectuals, but also his familiarity with the work of Beardsley, Puvis de Chavannes, Ibsen, Nietzsche and Wilde; structurally, too, his pictures had much in common with those of the St. Petersburg painters, particularly in their elements of linearity and symmetry. It was this which prompted V. Ivanov to speak of the "geometrical transparency" of Chiurlienis' pictures and another critic to observe that "one of the main peculiarities of Chiurlienis' compositions is the dominance of the vertical line. He is the poet of the vertical. . . . Every vertical is a denial of earthly life." The "transparency" of Chiurlienis' work, by which V. Ivanov must have meant the fusion of shapes and absence of strict delineation identifiable with the painter, was, however, a quality alien to the graphic clarity of Bakst, Benois or Somov; the ensuing tendency towards abstractivism in painting linked him more closely, in fact, with the second generation of Russian Symbolist painters, the *Blue Rose*.

The endeavours of Chiurlienis to "fuse time and space" and of Skryabin to raise musical performance into a grand *Poem of Ecstasy* in which all took part were, of course, seen by most of the Symbolists, especially Bal'mont and V. Ivanov, as experiments in artistic wholeness, pointing back to Greek drama: in the words of V. Ivanov, "the theatre must stop being 'theatre' in the sense of spectacle—zu schaffen, nicht zu schauen ["to create, not to observe"]. The crowd of spectators must fuse into a choral body, like the mystical community of ancient 'orgies' and 'mysteries'. . . ." Essentially, all the Russian Symbolist writers and artists regarded drama as the only medium which could guarantee direct communication between artist and spectator, one in which the word could become flesh. It was logical, therefore, that Bely should have advocated that the "author become a producer" ("rezhisser"), a desire fulfilled, albeit ironically, in such plays as Blok's *Fair Booth (Balaganchik)* and N. Evreinov's *Fourth Wall*. The *World of Art* painters were equally interested in the theatrical art, although they were still very conscious of artistic boundaries and of aesthetic canons peculiar to each artistic discipline within a dramatic performance. Paradoxically, it was their observation of these specific limitations and not their dismissal of them which contributed to the success of Diaghilev's presentations of ballet, surely like opera and drama, one of the most convincing examples of a synthetic art form. Diaghilev's opera and ballet productions remained purely artistic and, of course, had no religious or theurgical purpose: they remained in V. Ivanov's word, "spectacles," rejecting any notion of audience participation. The success of the *Ballets Russes* was the result very much of the general approach to art observed by Bakst, Benois and Diaghilev within the *World of Art*: that it was a supreme human expression which depended, nevertheless, on severe rules of technique, aesthetic balance and thematic resemblance. The attention to fine detail demanded by Diaghilev

in the dance, stage design and musical performance was therefore symptomatic of the *World of Art*'s emphasis on the "how" rather than on the "what," on technical precision, rather than on mimetic representation. In this respect, the *World of Art* painters shared the same conception of the theatre as Bal'mont and Bryusov, regarding it primarily as an exercise in the use of the intrinsic properties of a synthetic medium and not as a cosmic force of social unification.

The sense of form, composition and emotional restraint identifiable with much of the *World of Art* art—in Somov's watercolours or in Bryusov's verse—reached its creative apotheosis in the graphics of such masters as Bakst, Benois, Bilibin, M. Dobuzhinsky, Lancéray, A. Ostroumova and Somov. Their unfailing sense of line, in itself indicative of their innate artistic discipline, demonstrated a technical prowess so lacking in the Realist works of the preceding decades. Their technical mastery in graphics displayed itself in their many designs for stage productions as well as in miniatures, embroidery and fashion designs and, above all, in book illustration where an abundance of detail had to be included within strictly curtailed limits. Perhaps the greatest book illustrator of the time was Somov, whose love of the *Commoedia dell'arte* enabled him to produce such a striking cover to the first edition of Blok's dramatic works (1907, which Blok did not care for, as a matter of fact); in the same year, he executed his equally famous covers for V. Ivanov's *Cor Ardens* and Bal'mont's *Fire-bird*. Mention might be made also of Bilibin's exquisite covers and illustrations for a series of Russian fairy-tales published in 1901 onwards and the edition of Pushkin's *Queen of Spades* published in 1911 with illustrations by Benois. The graphic expertise encountered in the decorative and ornamental pieces of the *World of Art* artists might be seen, in broader terms, as the result of their non-philosophical approach to art, for without a definite ideological justification, their art was left to turn in on itself, to manipulate to the fullest extent its own properties of line, colour and mass. In this respect Bely's remark that schematization (stylization) pointed to the "inability to cope with reality" was particularly relevant, for the elegant, yet brittle examples of technical bravura encountered in much of Somov or the early Lancéray (or, for that matter, in Bryusov) speaks so ironically of the nothingness beyond. This philosophical vacuum was emphasized by the cyclical and hence insulatory structure of many poems and by the symmetrical arrangement evident in many portraits and landscapes: it was with meaningful irony, therefore, that V. Ivanov could have referred to such art as "flowers to cover the black void," for the highly contrived poetry of Bryusov or the refined 18th-century scenes of Somov were in direct opposition to the basic premise of the later Symbolists, i.e. that Symbolist art lay outside aesthetic categories. Bely, for his part, extended this argument to conclude that aestheticism was almost a synonym for creative insolvency and that "as a form of liberation from the will it was the consequence of the philosophy of a dying century"; in this respect, Bely considered Maeterlinck's dramas, so esteemed by the initial *World of Art* members, as the embodiment of an "ideology of sleep."

The tendency of the *World of Art* artists to "lightheartedly leave aside religious questions" was to a certain extent counteracted by their own intellectual curiosity. The "myth-making" and "god-searching" peculiar especially to the second generation of Russian Symbolists was identifiable also with the *World of Art* albeit on a less conscious level, and the reaction against Positivism which Merezhkovsky had sanctioned in his Symbolist manifesto of 1892, contributed substantially to the *World of Art*'s immediate interest in certain spiritual problems. Bakst, for example, while not stating his tenets in explicit terms, shared the *Zeitgeist* of eschatological mysticism as his famous picture, *Terror Antiquus,* indicated: the apocalyptic event which this picture harbingered was hence a visual parallel to the sunsets and falling stars described in so much of the early verse of the Russian Symbolist poets. Painters and poets shared common ground also in their mutual cultivation of the necrological, the demonic and the erotic; and what is important here is that both parties not only selected such themes, but also treated them stylistically in similar ways: just as the sensation of inescapability is transmitted in much verse of the time by frequent recourse to a uniform montage of blackness, to an insularized locale, to a process of dehumanization, to a circular poetical structure, etc., so in many *World of Art* pictures reality is reduced to a symmetrical nocturnal landscape, to a portrait of a lifeless figure against a hollow background or to an *intérieur* full of objects, but devoid of people. This desperate, pessimistic interpretation of life observed within the *World of Art* was not, however, exclusive. For example, we can recognize a less morbid, less negative attitude in some of Bryusov's urban verse where he presents the bourgeois city as a symbol of creative energy and not of moral and social disintegration. This conception was shared by Dobuzhinsky, whose remarkable graphic scenes of St. Petersburg, Riga and London betray the artist's admiration of human ingenuity and technological advance. In their tentative support of urban culture, both Bryusov and Dobuzhinsky anticipated the Futurists' advocation of industry and mechanical dynamism, although, of course, neither the poet nor the artist destroyed basic poetical or graphic conventions.

The association between representatives of art and literature within the *World of Art* led to the fine series of portraits of its members and contributors executed by such painters as Bakst and Somov. Among these figured Bakst's portraits of Bely and Hippius, Vrubel's unfinished portrait of Bryusov and, perhaps the most remarkable, Somov's portrait of Blok. Somov's small crayon and gouache rendering of Blok's head must surely rank as one of the most successful interpretations of a Symbolist character by a contemporaneous artist: Blok's head appears as if carved from a piece of stone, an impression emphasized by the symmetrical hairstyle, the Roman nose and the empty background; gazing out from this cold, pale montage are the eyes: "In Blok's eyes, so clear and seemingly beautiful, there was something lifeless—and it was this, probably, which struck Somov." It was a fortunate coincidence that both the poet and the painter should have shared a similar world-view at this time: Blok, plunged into despair and urban decadence, breathed the same vapid air as Somov, whose pictures of fireworks at Versailles and depictions of erotic play served only to hide the deep cynicism and sense of isolation felt by him throughout his life. His insertion of a pale vacuum as the background to the Blok portrait was therefore in keeping with the spiritual state of both and brought to mind immediately the ending of Blok's play, the *Fair Booth (Balaganchik):* "Harlequin jumps through the window. The distance visible through the window turns out to be drawn on paper. The paper burst. Harlequin flew head over heels into emptiness." Indeed, the profound awareness of the artificiality and farcicality of life, which dominated the whole Symbolist arena, permeated many levels of the *World of Art*. But nowhere did Blok and Somov share more closely the same absence of metaphysical values than in the terrible symmetry and weary sensuality of Somov's portrait of Blok.

The pessimistic conclusion both in Blok's play and in Somov's portrait was to a certain extent the direct result of an artistic style founded on morbid subjectivism (a transient mood with Blok, but constant with Somov), a faith of futility. Within the sphere of the *World of Art* several such parallel positions can be perceived, i.e. between writers and painters, and form specific aesthetic patterns within its overall prism. Somov's introspection and preoccupation with sex and death had much in common with Diaghilev's fundamental notion that art should be the summation of the ego: ". . . the meaning of [a work of art] consists of the highest manifestation of the creator's individuality and in the closest possible relationship between this individuality and that of the perceptor." At its face value such a statement was a virile, assertive plea for the artist's liberation from civic duty and, in turn, recalled the egocentric, yet dynamic and elemental verse of the early Bal'mont. But just as this conception turned "inward" and led directly to the emotional disintegration and contrived confusion of some of Bryusov's verse in the early 1900s or in much of Blok's work between c. 1904 and c. 1910, so, thematically, at least, much of Somov's work reflected the same *taedium vitae* and served as a practical extension of Diaghilev's argument. In contrast to Bakst, Benois or Rerikh who turned to past cultures as embodiments of social and moral cohesion, Somov regarded his subjects, normally from 18th-century France, with bitter irony depicting them as equally corrupt and artificial as his own age. In this way, he might be compared with Bryusov parodying Classical values in his cycle of verse, *Tertia Vigilia,* or with Blok raising the cardboard sword of the Middle Ages in his play, the *Rose and the Cross.* Somov's "People—ghosts playing at being people" were, however, the consequence of only one intellectual premise among several found within the *World of Art.* Benois, Diaghilev's closest colleague and, at one time, mentor, was opposed to such a philosophy of introspection as he indicated in a long and sensitive article, "Artistic Heresies": "Does not individualism, the cornerstone of contemporary artistic life, teach us that only that has value which has arisen freely in the artist's soul and has poured freely into his creation? . . . Artists have scattered into their own corners . . . and at all costs try to be only themselves. Chaos reigns, something turgid which has scarcely any value and which, strangest of all, has no physiognomy. . . . Individualism is heresy mainly because it denies communication." To a considerable extent it was this awareness which prompted Benois to look back to the rationality and integration of 17th- and 18th-century France and to Classical culture since for him they presented a panacea to social ills, a source of spiritual inspiration, which for Somov they were not. Benois' naive and often humorous depictions of Versailles emerged almost as evocations of some distant, yet fondly remembered childhood; his admiration for, and erudition in, this "enchanting lie" was matched only by V. Ivanov's love and knowledge of Greece and Rome.

The retrospectivism favoured by the *World of Art* was not confined to praise of specific historical periods such as Classical Greece or Versailles. A profound interest in popular myth and in the primordial state of Man also occupied painters such as Bakst as well as several writers. Indicative of this was the illustrated contribution on V. Vasnetsov to the first number of the *World of Art* journal, which, by its very presence, acted as a visual declaration of policy. Vasnetsov's work, like that of Vrubel', was seen by many of the *World of Art* members as the incarnation of an archaic, barbaric force, a world of ancient legend and elemental unity. In addition, Vasnetsov's interest in the traditions of the Russian Church attracted him to the images of the Virgin Mary and St. Sofia; and this, in turn, explained his popularity amongst Solov'ev, Blok and Bely with their earnest cult of the Eternal Feminine. As early as 1901, in his series of "Philosophical Conversations," the writer and thinker, Minsky, had defined the predicament of his contemporaneous culture as one which lacked the "wholeness and harmony of the child's soul," a statement which anticipated V. Ivanov or even the Neo-primitivists with their conscious recourse to naive art. V. Ivanov extended Minsky's thesis to conclude that "True Symbolism must reconcile the poet and the mob in a great, universal art. . . . We are taking the path of the symbol to the myth." Within such a world-view it was easy to accommodate the work of Bakst, Chiurlienis, Vasnetsov and Vrubel'. Bakst's depictions of Grecian landscapes which combined ethnographical accuracy and intense imagination were bound to appeal to the Hellenism of V. Ivanov and summarized in visual terms the Symbolists' belief in the need to return to a barbaric, elemental state. This concept Bakst developed later in his highly important article, "The New Paths of Classicism": "Painting of the future calls for a lapidary style, because the new art cannot endure the refined. . . . Painting of the future will crawl down into the depths of coarseness. . . ." Although this statement was relevant to the emergence of the Neo-primitivist painting of N. Goncharova, M. Larionov, *et al.*, it also had wider implications, especially when examined through the lense of V. Ivanov's terminology—"Dionysius . . . anarchy . . . the mob": for V. Ivanov and his fellow Symbolists the return to a primitive condition was to be a synthesizing factor, a process which would overcome the superstructure of rational and individualistic ideas created by Western Man and reach the pure essence of reality; for the Neo-primitivists, however, the return was only part of their endeavour to revitalize art and had none of the cosmic dimensions identifiable with the later Symbolists. This, as a matter of fact, was one of the main differences which separated the Russian Symbolists from the so-called literary and artistic avant-garde after c. 1908.

Apart from such general terms as synthesism, escapism and retrospectivism, the only definite philosophical system recognizable within the framework of the *World of Art* belonged to Bely. But since he established contact with the *World of Art* only during its last years, his statements must not be regarded as the general credo of the original *World of Art* group. Like Benois, Diaghilev, A. Nourok and W. Nouvel', Bely gave particular attention to the phenomenon of music, but he developed their basic concepts into an elaborate metaphysical system far removed from the ordinary tonal interpretation. In his article, "Forms of Art," Bely defined the essence of reality as music: "Movement is the basic feature of reality. . . . Only music goes to the heart of images, i.e. movement. Every artistic form has as its starting-point reality and as its finishing-point—music. . . . In music images are absent." While Bely considered music as the absolute of art forms, because it was based on temporal movement (and for him time was an inner, intuitive sensation), he did not reject poetry and painting out of hand. For Bely and for V. Ivanov poetry was the second most vital art form because of its prerequisites of rhythm and of sound, although painting for them contained "empirical" elements of colour and perspective. What Bely and V. Ivanov chose to ignore was that music, like painting, was based also to a large extent on perspective—i.e. the need to arrange orchestral instruments at a certain, predetermined distance in order to hear a certain sequence of sounds—and that painting, in turn, had its own equivalent of rhythm, namely line. If, for Bely and V. Ivanov, rhythm was the mobile and cohesive factor in a piece of music or poetry, then line should have been seen to play

the same role in a landscape or portrait. This is evident, for example, in any landscape of Bakst, Benois or Somov where the whole composition is constructed so as to transmit a sensation of rhythmic dynamism, especially by the "reflections" of verticals, horizontals and diagonals in various planes and by the rapid perspective achieved by a sequence of horizontals. Both in poetry and painting, therefore, we can interpret the emphasis on rhythm as an attempt to connect artistic units and thereby to gain artistic wholeness. Bely's comprehension of music as the fundamental and essential form of reality was but another symptom of the general aspiration towards monism within the *World of Art*, but his development of the basic concept into a theoretical premise—and hence his attribution of art with a philosophical purpose—was something alien to its original scale of values and closer to Blok or to the *Blue Rose*. In this respect, the fact that one of the last literary contributions to the *World of Art* journal was by Bely, creates a convenient bridge from the first Symbolist generation to the second. In this article, Bely continued to talk of the intensity of "musical symbols" and of the "approach of inner music to the surface of the consciousness": such mystical, abstracted thinking would explain his admiration for the musical canvases, evocative allusions of the *Blue Rose* painters, already far removed from the formal accuracy of the *World of Art* artists. In this context it is important to repeat Bely's specific ideas regarding painting, expressed on the pages of the *World of Art*: "In painting we are concerned with the projection of reality on to a plane. . . . It is not the picture itself which should come to the foreground, but the veracity of the emotions and moods being experienced which this or that picture of nature evokes in us." The idea that evocation of mood was more important in art than the representation of a given part of reality was especially relevant to the painting of the *Blue Rose* artists. Indeed, it was their reaction against the rigidity of the *World of Art* painting and their interfusion of mass, their subtle gradations of pastel colours and loss of contour which recalled the musicality of Chiurlienis' work and hence the cosmic artistic synthesism of such diverse figures as V. Ivanov, Kandinsky and Skryabin.

Bely's article of 1904, with its provocative ideas so contrary to the aesthetics of the original *World of Art* members, pointed to the decline of the *World of Art* as a cohesive, cultural centre: in the same year the journal ceased publication, Diaghilev turned his eyes Westward and new, progressive directions soon dominated the Russian cultural arena. Even if the *World of Art* had continued to exist as a society and as a journal, it would have been no match for the flamboyance and ebullience of the subsequent movements of Neo-primitivism and Futurism. For Benois, steeped in the traditions of the 18th century, the Futurists embodied the "cult of emptiness, of darkness and of nothingness." In point of fact, Benois failed to recognize that the new avant-garde, by destroying conventional disciplines, maintained the synthesist traditions of the *World of Art*—albeit in a different way—and united the arts even more closely. In this respect the *World of Art* set a valuable precedent for ensuing Modernist movements and despite the outward hostility between the aristocratic aesthetes of the *World of Art* and the radical leftists of the Futurists, both strove to renew cultural values by conceiving art as a total activity. This approach to art was manifest, above all, in Diaghilev's *Ballets Russes* which emerged as the fruition of the artistic principles practised by the *World of Art* at the turn of the century. But despite its admiration of Western culture, the *World of Art* remained at heart a Russian phenomenon. Witness to this was its very aspiration towards artistic synthesism, since this, in many ways, was the direct result of its members' reaction to the social and political fragmentation present during the last years of Imperial Russia. It is a sad paradox, therefore, that the grand, synthetic *Ballets Russes,* which owed so much to the *World of Art,* should have been seen and applauded only outside Russia. In this sense we might regard the *World of Art* not only as the progenitor of the *Ballets Russes,* but also, therefore, as the greatest, universal monument to the Russian Silver Age. (pp. 35-48)

> John E. Bowlt, "Synthesism and Symbolism: The Russian 'World of Art' Movement," in Forum for Modern Language Studies, *Vol. IX, No. 1, January, 1973, pp. 35-48.*

RALPH E. MATLAW

[*In the following excerpt Matlaw analyzes the works of the composer Alexander Scriabin, whose attempts to achieve mystical transcendence through music paralleled the goals of the Symbolist writers in literature.*]

When Boris Pasternak characterized the beginning of the twentieth century as the era of Scriabin, he restated in personal and poetic terms a phenomenon that had already been recognized by the public at large; by the leaders of an extraordinary flowering of the arts—musicians, poets, painters, theatrical giants; and by such elders and contemporaries of Scriabin's in the political arena as Lunacharsky and Plekhanov. "His music," the latter wrote, "was his era transposed into sound . . . it so fully expressed the mood of a very significant part of our intelligentsia at a particular period of its history." The memorial services, the funeral, the tributes, and the published and unpublished commemorations repeatedly demonstrate the feeling that Russia's leading figure in the arts had died, that in some quintessential way Scriabin was the epitome of his era, the incarnation of its tendencies and expressive modes as well as the most revolutionary composer of his time and one of its most popular pianists. (pp. 1-2)

Scriabin had an extraordinary effect not only through his music, though clearly that is the basis and ultimate guarantee of his fame, but also through his playing, which seems to have conveyed an electrifying sense of transport, and his personality, whose charm and infectious enthusiasm lent credence to his aims and dreams no matter how grandiose, mystical, or mad, so that he became an inspiration to others. While reports of Scriabin's conversations indicate that they lack the special quality of his musical performance, their contents invite comment like those of any other artist. Scriabin's writings seem at some points to be mystical ravings or less, and his poetry is largely derivative in content and inept in execution. Nevertheless, he was at the center of the modern movement in Russia, particularly symbolism, and was close to its leading theorists and practitioners, men like Vyacheslav Ivanov, Bryusov, Bal'mont, and Baltrushaitis, whom "he filtered through himself," according to the antagonistic Andrey Bely. He had ultimately a more grandiose and inclusive vision of art than the most extreme theurgists of Russian symbolism and mystics East and West, a *Gesamtkunstwerk* ["total art work"] made into a *Mysterium,* a work that was to be the last act of life and the race that exists and its transformation and transcendence into a higher life. This megalomanic and mystic fancy underlay and fed the production of his last ten years. He is thus also involved in the central notions of the theory and practice of a symbolist drama, ultimately, then, questions of aesthetics and religious messianism. He was concerned with perception and synes-

thesia, color and light, the import of astral and mythic visions, the cult of art and the creative personality. The demonic and titanic in his art, and the erotic in his life and his art, associated him with the decadents, while his concern for political realities (at one time he thought of an epigraph for the *Poem of Ecstasy:* "Arise, ye wretched of the earth!") associated him even more fully with the cultural climate of his time. (pp. 2-3)

Men of the theater who were concerned with a larger notion of its function and potential were particularly grieved by Scriabin's death. Evreinov, creator of the "theater in life," wrote of Scriabin's "Godlike colors, his majestic powers, heroic doubts." Meierhold, who had been taxed by Scriabin for eliminating the barrier between audience and stage—which, ironically, is precisely what Scriabin sought to do in the *Mysterium*—lamenting the loss and valuing Scriabin's achievements, uses the opportunity to castigate opposing views:

> The world of musicians and the world of poets has donned mourning, but why do we not see banners of mourning on the so-called "Theater-Temples"? Why do these people who fight against the "Theater-Spectacle" and mutter of some sort of Theater-Temple, why do these people who try from time to time to extract figures bearing charity from the "folds of Arlequin," why did they not cry out that the one person who held out so much for achievement in the realm of the Mysterium has died? Because the builders of these so-called "Theater-Temples" did not consider Scriabin one of themselves and did not dare to do so. The fact is that the whole idea of two paths in the realm of scenic action occurred to this unique person before it did to anyone else. The dilemma "Theater or Mysterium" occurred to Scriabin even in the early phase of his creativity. After the first symphony with its concluding hymn to art-religion Scriabin had started to write an opera but suddenly broke off his work and seemed to have sworn someone a strong oath to break with the theater once and for all. A man devoted to the great deed of creating a "Mysterium" could not and should not have served the Theater. The ways of the Theater and the ways of the Mysterium are not fused. That is the testament of the genius who created the sketches of the "Preliminary Action" who has so suddenly been taken from us.

Later Tairov makes a further distinction between Scriabin's ordered and prepared "initiates and the attempts of Evreinov, Meierhold, and Reinhardt."

Not all poets shared this view of the drama. The mercurial Andrey Bely had opposed Ivanov in 1907, when in "The Symbolist Theater" he had pointed out the impossibility of symbolism in the theater since it would destroy the barrier between viewer and actor. The true symbolist theater, Bely maintained, lay in the *Mysterium,* that is, the abolition of theater. Since that had not been attained, however, it had been replaced by stylization, whose first consequence is the destruction of the actor's individuality and the destruction of human traits in man—in short, the theater of marionettes and Chinese shadows, the theater of Meierhold, Kommisarzhevskaya, and Blok at that time. In October 1907 Bely questioned the entire notion of the true *Mysterium* and the religiosity of the act as presented by Ivanov. In "Theater and Contemporary Drama" he wrote: "The 'Temple' remains the Mariinsky Theater, as a restaurant remains a restaurant. We ought not to run to the theater in order to dance and sing over a dead tragic goat and then be astonished at what we have done when we return to ordinary life. That is how one escapes from Fate. . . . The symbolic drama is not a drama but the propagation of the great, constantly developing drama of humanity. It is the preaching of the imminence of the fatal denouement.''

As Scriabin drew closer to the *Mysterium* his concern with a synthesis of the arts became more pressing. But there had always been a peculiar synesthesia in him, an attempt to express himself in word and gesture and idiosyncratic concatenations of sensory images. Many of his compositions bear the title ''Poem''—not in that era's accepted designation of orchestral compositions as ''symphonic poems'' or ''tone poems,'' but substantively as *The Divine Poem, Poem of Ecstasy, Poem of Fire*. The middle and late piano works include titles like *Poème satanique* (op. 36), *Poème fantastique* (op. 45 no. 2), *Fragilité, Poème ailé* (op. 51 nos. 1 and 3), *Poème languide* (op. 52 no. 3), *Caresse dansée* (op. 57 no. 2), while others are not designated ''poems'' in their titles. He wrote that ''the majority of the 'poems' have a specific psychological content, but not all of them require a text,'' and referred to specific measures as ''the depths of tragedy,'' ''the flight of clouds,'' and the like. His apprehension of sensory data was not only sometimes mystically ecstatic, as in the sound of bells or light glancing off the golden cupolas of churches, but was also apparently mixed: he ''heard'' colors and perceived tonalities in hues. At first he used it to express himself verbally, later to augment the effect of the music. He was interested in the dance as plastic rhythm or symbolic gesture. He wanted to employ odors, both pleasant and unpleasant, to contribute to the total effect, not merely as a clever toy, as in Villiers de l'Isle-Adam's *Axël*. Touch and texture were also to contribute—the chorus of women at the beginning of the *Preliminary Action* would be robed in white and would move. The setting would also contribute to the total effect. Hence Scriabin's great interest in Gordon Craig's *Hamlet* in Moscow in 1910 and his attempt to discuss it with him. He was impressed by the fusion of scenic, architectural, and musical elements with the text, and especially the shimmering golden backdrops. He repeatedly went to Tairov's *Sakuntala* the following year, a production striking for its innovations in chants, processionals, body painting, stage levels, and more.

Before dealing with the verbal texts, then, we must briefly examine Scriabin's conceptions of color and movement. Scria-

Vyacheslav Ivanov in 1948. From Russian Literature Triquarterly, *No. 4, Fall, 1972. By permission of Ardis Publishers.*

bin saw colors for keys as well as individual notes. The phenomenon is not unique, even among composers: Rimsky-Korsakov possessed it, though for keys only, and his colors are slightly different from Scriabin's; other composers lack it entirely. Scriabin felt it so strongly that he was disturbed by Wagner's insensitivity to it, by his inconsistency in changing keys: ''Dawn'' in *Götterdämmerung* is in C-major (red) then in B-major (blue); the Firemusic in *Die Walküre* should be in G (orange), but that key is not used and the others are changed. Characteristically, Scriabin developed a complete system (the spectrum from red to violet corresponds to C G D A E B F-sharp); just as characteristically, system and practice diverge. Color is a means for conveying Scriabin's sensations and ideas. Thus early in the composing of *Prometheus* he reportedly said, ''You're right, it isn't for piano. It must be for orchestra. What marvelous colors! what a combination of colors in these zigzags, like tongues of flames. . . . I am getting it . . . these color sounds . . . I can see them,'' and he scored the second line of *Prometheus* for a light machine to produce a color for the root of the harmony indicated above it. But what Scriabin said about the colors of *Prometheus* and what they are supposed to represent does not, apparently, correspond to what is written. At first Scriabin wanted ''to augment sound with the parallelism of light. But *now,* I want counterpoint. The lights pursue melody and the music goes on with its own. Now I want a contrapuntalism of all the different lines of art.'' *Prometheus* begins with green and blue; after lights change and vanish it ends as it began, in blue mystery. At the culmination, marked *''avec un éclat éblouissant,''* Scriabin wanted the entire hall ''illuminated'' with blinding rays of white light.

The light machine was inadequate for concert performance but useful in other experiments. Scriabin worked for days with Alisa Koonen (Tairov's wife) to see how music could express itself in motion. Koonen first tried dance forms that might interpret the mood of the piece and finally came to understand how the music reveals its own shape, and how it may be expressed in motion. Scriabin not only played the accompaniment but operated a primitive version of Mozer's light machine in his darkened room to create shifting colors. Both artists seemed pleased with the achievement of uniting three forms of art.

Colors, after all, are a separation of light, and without recourse to Newtonian optics or Goethe's *Farbenlehre* the whole notion may in part be seen as a huge metaphor, in Scriabin's thinking, for fragmentation from unity to multiplicity and the possibility of reintegration. Light, and particularly the sun, is the single most important image associated with Scriabin, his work, and his thought. The most popular of the early symbolist poets, Konstantin Bal'mont, friend, champion, and favorite of Scriabin, had a similar penchant for the sun. He rhapsodized: ''Scriabin is the singing of a falling moon. Starlight in music. A flame's movement. A burst of sunlight. The cry of soul to soul. . . . A singing illumination of the air itself, in which he himself is captive child of the Gods. A strong tenderness; a mighty invincible sweetness . . . all his music is light itself.''

The importance of the sun in Scriabin's thought and music cannot be overestimated: it is the source of life, the symbol of creative energy, that toward which everything strives. He told Ivan Lipaev, ''When you listen to [the *Poem of Ecstasy*] you must look directly into the face of the sun.'' It may have been from his association with the theosophical ''Sons of the Flames of Wisdom'' that he garnered fire as the symbol of higher thought, as active energy, the creative principle, life, struggle, and so on. In Scriabin's own program notes to *Prometheus* we read, "Fire is light, life, struggle, increase, abundance, and thought." The theosophic ramifications are enormous. But there is a basis for it in orthodoxy as well, where gnosis is the awareness of spiritual life, ultimately the perfect knowledge of the Trinity. The first stage thereof is the experience of uncreated light, and light itself will become the experience since the "effulgence" is the visible quality of the divine. The basis of orthodox mysticism is a combination of the intellect and the senses, surpassing both when the body, the physical, finally becomes spiritualized into light. The contrary of gnosis, agnosis, is hell and darkness; tragedy may be conceived as the dark aspiring to light. Both elements coexist in Scriabin. The orphic and satanic, the emphasis on light, heat, stars, and dark flames is reflected throughout the music: the Seventh Sonata is the "White Mass," the Ninth is the "Black Mass"; *Vers la flamme* (op. 72) is opposed by *Flammes sombres* (op. 73 no. 2).

The contrast and the combination of spiritual and physical exultation is also reflected in Scriabin's dithyrambic and obscure philosophical jottings and poems published in 1919 in a volume also containing Pushkin's Lyceum Notebook. This conjunction testifies to the esteem and importance then accorded to Scriabin's writings and suggests a parallel that Osip Mandel'stam pursued in an essay, parts of which have been lost. Scriabin's writings show that even if he does work in the twin realms of poetry and music, as Ivanov wrote, his literary and musical expressions are independent, though related. They are two modes for expressing a single impulse, the verbal sometimes preceding the musical, as in the *Poem of Ecstasy,* sometimes following it, as in the Fourth Sonata. It is significant that Scriabin did not work on music and text simultaneously and that he changed his mind about the relationship and relative importance of text and music. It is still more significant that the two major texts, the early opera and the *Preliminary Action,* are unfinished and without music, though there are many sketches for the latter and Scriabin was obviously preparing to compose it.

In a letter to Belayev he writes that he has "resumed my music and literature," but he is also conscious of his literary inadequacies: "The text [of the *Preliminary Action*] is the only thing that troubles me. I feel myself a master (*vladikoj*) in music; there I am at ease, I do what I wish. But I must master the technique of verse completely. I cannot permit the text to be less than the music and I do not want my verse to be considered as the work of a musician who decided to write his own text to his music." He theorized in a confused way about his verse, which was to "disclose the cosmic sense of each personal experience. The history of a single feeling, of a single striving, is the history of the universe." He disliked philosophical verse and abstract thought in verse, and thought "my lyric must be an epic" by containing concrete images, not the ratiocination connected with the epic.

Again the texts do not correspond to the theory, though emotion, striving, and enthusiasm are crucial. The *Poem of Ecstasy* makes him ecstatic: "I have just written a monologue of the most divine beauty. . . . Again I am swept up by an enormous wave of creativity. I choke for bliss, but divinely. . . . I am working out a new style, and what joy it is to see it take shape so well! The very meter kindles the meaning. Sometimes the poem's effect is so potent that no content is needed. I am expressing what will be one and the same as the music." Those remarkable statements on meaning and rhythm were echoed

later, when he read the poem, which he loved, to friends: "I would not write it this way now, however; it was an experiment. But listen to its new rhythms." He thought the text explained the music, even though the text itself really needed a full commentary that he wanted to write. But he also thought the contrary: "Conductors who want to perform the *Poem of Ecstasy* can always be apprised that it has such a text, but in general I would prefer them to approach it first as pure music." In fact, there is little correspondence between text and music, the objective and subjective view of a single thing. Similar relationships exist between some of his other musical works and their texts.

We must distinguish between texts to be set to music and verbal poems, commentaries, or interpretations, whether written by Scriabin himself or with the mediation of Tatjana Schloezer or others, which occasionally appeared in program notes and have been republished with his piano works. Thus in the first movement of the Third Sonata "a free and wild soul passionately throws itself into the abyss of misery and struggle," the Fifth Sonata has an epigraph, and so on. But the Fourth Sonata has as text a poem "that was worked out on the basis of the music after the music was composed," involving his desire for and approach toward a distant, shimmering star that becomes a radiant sun, the expression of his desire, and is engulfed by him in a final frenzy. The text, unfortunately, is in French; it bears the influence and perhaps the formulations of Tatjana Schloezer, who is also responsible for formulating the program for the Third Symphony, to which the poem is related. Scriabin thought that music could be significant only if it was composed with a cogent world view, and the Third Symphony (the *Divine Poem*) is vital in attempting to unite philosophy with music. It contains many of Scriabin's basic notions and anticipates much of his later thought and music. It is therefore worthwhile to look at its program, even though it interposes others' views between Scriabin's formulations and the reader. Its three movements are *"Bor'ba"* (*"Luttes"*), *"Naslazhdenija"* (*"Voluptés"*), and *"Bozhestvannaja igra"* (*"Jeu divin"*), the three vital notions of overcoming obstacles in struggle, the delights of sensuality leading to the sublime, and the free godlike play of the liberated mind—the last a notion already present in stoic philosophy. The work as a whole represents, in Tatjana Schloezer's high-flown words, "the evolution of the human spirit which, freed from the legends and mysteries of the past which it has surmounted and overthrown, passes through Pantheism and achieves a joyful and exhilarating affirmation of its liberty and its unity with the universe." More succinctly, in Scriabin's *Notebooks* of a slightly later period, *"Zhizn'—dejatel'nost', stremlen'e, bor'ba"*—"Life is activity, striving, struggle." The second movement was called "Ecstasies" when the symphony was performed in New York in 1907. Its orgy leads to the *Poem of Ecstasy,* as the finale foreshadows the assertion theme of *Prometheus, "Ja esm'"* ("I am").

Scriabin's *Notebooks* help to provide the transition to the later works. He was terribly secretive about them, and with good reason: while they are devoted entirely to the development of his thought and "philosophy," they are at many times so orgiastic in their solipsistic expression of grandeur, joy, and power that one cannot be completely sure whether one is reading the diary of a deranged ecstatic, the beginning of a poem, or the text of an improbable opera. Thus the beginning of one of the earliest drafts reads: "I begin my tale, the tale of the world, the tale of the universe. I am (*Ja esm'*) and there is nothing outside me. I am nothing. I am everything, I am singular and in that is singular multiplicity. I wish to live, I am the trepidation of life, I am desire, I am the dream . . . I am flame. I am chaos.'' Further elaborations continue the series of anaphoric ''I's'' culminating in ''I am *God!*'' and an extension that perhaps indicates that this is part of a scenario: ''Nations, flourish, create, deny me and arise against me. Arise against me, you elements!'' There are also drawings of time and space, gyres of evolution and the world, and attempts at rational formulations that invoke ecstasy: ''A creative surge leads us into the realm of ecstasy, outside space and time. . . . Ecstasy is the highest surge of activity, ecstasy is the summit. . . . In the form of thought ecstasy is *the highest synthesis. In the form of feeling ecstasy is the highest bliss. In the form of space ecstasy is the highest flowering and destruction''* (Scriabin's italics). Various themes are stated—alarm, will, languor, self-assertion—the ''I'' becomes more and more titantic and exalted. This excitement carries over into the first outlines of the *Poem of Ecstasy,* Scriabin's only significant completed poetic text in Russian, a vital document among his creations and characteristic of his poetic style.

In the *Notebooks,* as in his correspondence, Scriabin refers to the *Poem of Ecstasy* as the ''*Poème orgiaque,''* which he means in a mystical and religious sense as well as a sexual sense (the score has a section marked ''*avec une volupté de plus en plus extatique''* [''with a voluptuousness more and more ecstatic''] whose approximate verbal equivalent in the poem is obviously sexual), and is the poetic expression of the explicit formulation ''as man during the moment of ecstasy in the sexual act loses *consciousness and his whole organism* experiences bliss at all points, so too God-man, experiencing ecstasy, fills the universe with bliss and kindles the flame. Man-God is the bearer of universal consciousness'' (Scriabin's italics). It was published May 30, 1906, under the more ambiguous but less shocking title of *Ecstasy.* The first prose outline is in four parts tracing spiritual struggle and the soul's final realization of its own God-likeness and the oneness of the universe. It is reminiscent of the *Divine Poem* and has similar programmatic indications, beginning ''the theme of the sweetness of dreams giving wings to the spirit, the desire to create, languor, thirst for the unknown.'' The first section ends with ''*relief in activity.''* The second introduces conflict (*bor'ba, luttes*), liberation through love, and the consciousness of oneness. The third is largely a gap, the fourth the final realization of oneness through the free play of the soul—again as in the *Divine Poem.* The outline repeats themes as if they were leitmotifs: Man is God, sweetness of dreams, love. It almost seems that this is a program for the symphony, which we know also started in four movements but, like the poem, turned into a single large movement. Also, the gaps in parts two and three are similar to omitted measures as Scriabin composed music. Yet we know also that the music was not written to the poem and that there is little if any correspondence between music and text. This suggests that Scriabin probably conceived the poem in a form approximating the sonata-allegro in music. Indeed, the statement of themes, transitions, restatements, and development betray their dependence on musical form and do not satisfactorily perform their literary counterpart: the poem presents ''The Spirit'' (''*Dukh''*), a neo-Lermontovian spirit of negation, hovering in a world of his imagination rather than over the Caucasus, with the opening section of eight lines repeated verbatim as the scene changes—the changes heralded by ''But suddenly,'' ''But again'' (''*No vnezapno,'' ''No snova''*)—and the variation of the second epithet in ''spirit playful, spirit desirous'' to ''spirit caressing, spirit suffering.'' Neither sensual pleasure nor the battle nor struggle suffice in themselves, though they lead ''the

spirit'' to the exalted realization of his ''divine free play.'' At the lower physical levels the process is ultimately unsatisfactory:

> But what casts gloom
> On that joyful moment?
> *Precisely that he has*
> *Attained his goal.*
> He regrets
> The former battle:
> And for a moment
> He feels
> Boredom, dejection, and emptiness.
>> (Scriabin's italics)

Voluptuousness is not life, nor is the penetration of the secret of evil. But the quickened rhythm of negating previously experienced forms creates a new meaning and leads to the spirit's concluding ecstatic monologue. The spirit calls hidden strivings into being; the world seeks its creator-God, who leads both spirit and world through ever more frenzied sexuality to the blissful ending:

> I am the instant that illuminates eternity
> I am affirmation
> I am Ecstasy . . .
> And the universe resounds
> With joyful shout
> I am! (*Ja esm'*)

Scriabin was surely correct when he noted the rhythms of the poem, for they are the most effective elements in an otherwise rather pedestrian work consisting largely of just the sort of abstractions Scriabin disliked in verse: assertions, abstract verbal adjectives (*-jushchij*), vague generalizations, and commonplace epithets. The meter is primarily choriambic . . . with a variety of anapestic and trochaic patterns and single bisyllabic or trisyllabic words; the illusion of acceleration is created more by the context than by the properties of the words themselves. The rhythms shift as quickly as the scenes and just as arbitrarily. Only in the orgiastic section of the monologue does Scriabin unite the light and fire of desire with a higher quest, a general synesthesia with a rhythmic frenzy that unfortunately remains merely sexual and decadent because of its ineptness, though it easily takes its place in the rich literature of the time:

> Then I shall fall upon you
> Like a shower of flowers,
> I will fondle and weary you
> With a whole gamut of aromas,
> With a play of fragrances
> Now tender, now sharp,
> With the play of touches
> Now soft, now striking.
>> And swooning
>> You will passionately
>> Whisper:
>> More,
>> Still more!
> Then I will throw myself on you
> Like a hoard of fearful monsters
> With fearful horror of torments,
> I will crawl on you like a seething herd of snakes
> And will sting and choke you!
> And you will desire
> Still more madly, more strongly.
> Then I shall fall on you
> Like a shower of marvelous suns
> And will burn you with the bolts
>> Of my passion,
>> The holy
>> Flames of desires

> The most delightful,
> The most forbidden,
> The most mysterious.

The poem differs from the dramatic texts which were designed to be set to music but never completed. It is curious that Scriabin's only successful use of the human voice is in the wordless sounds of *Prometheus* (suggesting a similar device in another theosophical work, Holst's *The Planets*); the only other use of the voice is in the finale of the First Symphony, an inept "Hymn to Art" embarrassing more for the poverty of its musical invention than for the triteness of its words: the soloists repeat several stanzas in which art restores and refreshes life, brings visions and feelings, and so on, before the choral conclusion:

> Come, all nations of the world,
> Let us sing glory to art.
> Glory to art,
> Eternal Glory.

In 1902 Scriabin resumed his literary efforts with a philosophical opera. Part of the text is extant, and the remaining plot is available in memoirs. It permits us to gauge some of the influences on Scriabin and some of his interests. Its hero, designated as the "philosopher-musician-poet," is clearly modeled on the Nietzschean superman. (Scriabin was attracted to *Zarathustra* as well as to *The Birth of Tragedy*.) The opera is built on two planes familiar to the symbolists, "the prose of life"—courtship, imprisonment, revolt—and "the poetry of the idea"—arias on ideals and visions. The plot involves the courtship of a king's daughter, a languid heroine who seeks someone who will conquer her by satisfying her imagination and quest for knowledge. This leads up to the hero's incarceration, the struggle for freedom, and the hero's leading the people to salvation. The unity of the two planes in the hero leads to the realization of the oneness of the whole world and the bliss that will later turn into ecstasy. The opera also shows that concern for social and political amelioration that Scriabin shared with his contemporaries. It presents "struggle" as political struggle and reflects Scriabin's deep political concern at the turn of the century. It is perfectly proper to present the opera's scheme, for Scriabin started out with an idea he wished to work out, rather than a creative impulse that happened to yield an idea. The opera, like the later *Preliminary Action*, indicates that the ideational ran ahead of the creational, and that the attempt to use a more or less traditional dramatic form led to insurmountable problems.

The libretto begins with a long narrative section describing and setting the mood of a fête at the palace. The scene is static. It is difficult to imagine how it might have been conveyed musically and dramatically. Since the material is divided among three guests, it suggests a rather lengthy introduction, perhaps something like the Nornen's opening *Götterdämmerung*, but the course of love between the princess and the hero is also conveyed in narrative. A dance and the heroine's *arioso* on the dance lead to her escape from the palace to the shore where her idol sits on a cliff. The rest of the material, in less finished state, consists of the hero's long monologues. Throughout there are echoes of Lermontov's *Demon* in setting and conception, as the hero entices the princess to a "feast of love" which, however, develops into an affirmation of the world and joy in existence: "I am so happy that if I could communicate one grain of my joy to the entire world, life would seem splendid to humanity."

Like all of Scriabin's heroic spirits this one, too, sees himself as "The apotheosis of creation / The goal of goals, the end of ends," but only after expressing his pity for the aimless life and the spiritual poverty and misery of others. He will bring meaning and joy with the triad of music, love, and wisdom:

> By power of the charms of heavenly harmony
> I will waft caressing dreams on mankind,
> And *by force* of limitless and wondrous *love*
> I will make their life a likeness of spring.
> I will give them long desired peace
> *By force* of my *wisdom*.
>
> 　　　　　　　　(Scriabin's italics)

The hero's strivings are poetically less inept than the earlier section where every noun is qualified by a vague emotion-laden modifier:

> Passionate breast of captivating night,
> Mysterious whisper of the warm wave,
> Magical splendor of anguished caress,
> Restless dreams of burning love.

Again, the most successful part of the text is the rhythmic *arioso* of the dance that uses the basic pattern . . . of *Ecstasy:*

Tanets prelestnyj	(Splendid dance
Daj mne zabven'ja,	Grant me oblivion,
Siloj chudesnoj	With your marvelous strength
Vyrvi muchen'ja.	Tear out the torments.
Zhizn'—stradan'e,	Life is suffering,
Zhizn—somnen'e,	Life is doubt,
Ty-zhe mechtan'e,	Yet you are a dream,
Ty—naslazhden'e.	You are delight.

It is fairly clear that Scriabin's grandiose conception was beyond his powers. The things heard in the mind are not, for Scriabin, expressible by the individual human voice, and the theatricality of the opera stage is not the medium for the transcendent purposes of his vision. But some of its music found its way into his piano compositions, and several elements of the opera were utilized in the *Preliminary Action*.

The *Preliminary Action* was the *Mysterium* greatly abridged and reduced, as it were, to a miniature. For the *Mysterium* was conceived as a grandiose liturgical act, lasting seven days or even longer, and culminating in an orgiastic dance and ecstasy that was to be the end of life and civilization as it exists, and its transformation into something higher. By its very nature the *Mysterium* could only be performed once. The *Preliminary Action*, however, was still in the realm of art and could be performed many times. It was to lead to a spiritual catharsis, uniting people and art in a mystical act that would prepare them for the final *Mysterium*. Indeed, at first Scriabin objected to the term "preliminary" (*predvaritel'nyj*) and preferred "preparatory" (*pregotovitel'nyj*).

Scriabin's *Mysterium* was all-inclusive. He believed that ancient rituals and mysteries used arts now forgotten or unknown to produce mystical catharsis, and that he might reintroduce them. He thought at first of writing the *Mysterium* in a universal synthetic language and of organizing special courses to prepare the mass of participants, for professional performers were not altogether suitable since inner spiritual preparation was as vital as technical competence. He wanted to found a special periodical to deal with problems of the *Mysterium*. He chose India, the country of miracles, the cradle of religion and homeland of prophets, as the locale, and special bells suspended from clouds in the Himalayas were to summon mankind to the event. The edifice for the *Mysterium* would be a semicircle of concentric arcs reflected in a pool of water to make a circle. Those at the edges would take a less active part in the *Mysterium* than those at the center, but there would be movement from one rank to the next. At the center an altar would be erected. Scriabin bought himself a pith helmet and a white suit and wrote in the blazing sun in preparation for the event. Later, as the *Mysterium* became the cantata-like *Preliminary Action,* he thought performers might be found, that *Action* would be performed and could even be given in an existing building of circular shape ("Only not a circus!"), and the language could be Russian. To accommodate the new conception the poetic text sacrificed the idea of inducing a creative transformation in the participants through images and symbols, resorting instead to a series of personifications, embodiments of ideas that would trace the history of mankind "as the process of distribution and immersion of the Spirit into matter and the counter return to unity, a process of cosmic evolution and involution, viewed by [Scriabin], of course, as a spiritual, or more precisely, a psychic process."

Approximately half of the text is in final form, the rest in the penultimate draft. The changes from one to the other consist largely of excision and regrouping with some improvement in poetic expression, but hardly enough to justify the purported approval of Ivanov and Baltrushaitis, particularly since Scriabin himself felt that much work remained to be done. The theme of *Action* is the creation of the world through the act of love and the dissolution of that world in an ecstasy of love into a new world and race: a rebirth through death, a movement from unity to multiplicity to a new unity, a process of materialization and spiritualization of the universe. The world emerges from the union of the male and female principles (a tenor and a contralto!), though the female insists that all is within the male: "I am not / Only you exist, / You fill all with yourself." But she describes herself as the bright joy of the ultimate achievement: "I am the ineffable bliss of dissolution / I am the joy of death, / I am freedom, I am ecstasy," and the male seeks to join her therein. It is a passage repeated near the end of the work, when death is imminent. Before reaching that blissful state of death, the male must pass through the variegated worlds separating them, the multi-colored expanses and disillusionments of life. In order to do so he must make three sacrifices, the first of which is the sacrifice of "the dream of the female" and all she represents. From their union emerge seven fire-bearing angels, creators of the new world. Now "The Waves of Life" emerge, materializations of the spiritual, the sought-for fragmentation and differentiation of unity, to imprint the face of God on the world. (The waves will remind every reader of Minsky's famous poem.) They in turn arouse "Feelings" with an *Ecstasy*-like erotic interlude and cause a new union, recognizing "A dual existence. / Henceforth I am the union / Of 'I' and a foreign 'not I'." The act of love creates the universe. Various natural and even inanimate objects chime in, the mountains describe themselves as congealed waves of stormy caresses, the deserts as the dry and sultry kiss of a light beam and the earth which banishes the living songs of streams; insects, birds, animals, and snakes join in. The rest of the text exists only in draft. A new temple is built from which the single law of eternal love and eternal humility (*smirenie*) is preached. Whoever transgresses it is excommunicate. Many succumb to false enticements and temptations from other forces. There is a dance-song of the fallen. The Eternal, it is explained, has permitted the fall in order to show the greater beauty where

> One may penetrate only through the spume of sensuality
> Into the realm of mystery where the treasure of the soul is,
> Where, having shed the agitated passions of the soul
> The saint is blissful in the shining calm.

When touch is lost with the heavens, mankind suffers battles and war and the coming of death, which is now seen as black, unlike the earlier desired death: "I am the God of hunger and destruction, / I am the scourge of nations, I am the God of Blood!" The outcast is victorious in battle but is ultimately found in the desert, alone with his wounds and his memories of passion. Death comes to him and in a dialogue clarifies his misapprehensions by claiming to be the delight of unity, the harmony in the temple of his soul, so that he apostrophizes her: "O Holy Virgin, charm of dreams, / Let me merge into you into perfected love." She orders him to serve his fallen brethren by bringing them the message, but they reject it, urging earthly blessings: "Mortals find bliss only in marriage."

We note here the Promethean and satanic nature of the hero (called both wanderer and sovereign, *strannik* and *vlastelin*), both in the romantic excess of his passionate rejections and in his theological revolt, his attempt to surpass God. At the same time, Scriabin repeats with minor changes a text that had earlier been given to the philosopher-poet-musician of his unfinished opera:

> Religion's charming deceit
> Has long ceased to captivate me . . .
> I am the sovereign of the universe!
> I am the cold God of observation.

His preaching arouses anger and he is put to torture, during which he prays for his tormentors and tries to persuade them to seek torments comparable to his own so that they may see the truth:

> You seek death, without admitting it,
> And love life only because
> Death's reflections, playing momentarily,
> Entice you toward it through life's darkness.

When at last he convinces them, "that temple—our life, our flowering, our ecstasy" bursts into the colors of all precious and semi-precious stones and prepares them to accept the Father, all-creating negation, the ultimate freedom. All merge ecstatically in a final dance with the Father and Death—who are one—and in a whirl of feelings are born into a single wave, the new unity:

> In unsheathed beauty
> Of shining souls
> We will disappear,
> We will melt.

Although the revision eliminated some excesses in anaphora, avoided repetition, changed meters (usually by doubling the length of lines), and made some poetically substantive changes, most of the changes involved the omission of long sections that were too explanatory and prosaic. The unfinished part is closer to a libretto and in several places resembles Scriabin's early attempt to write an opera. The action there, battle, torture, and so on, presents materials potentially more suitable for opera than for oratorio. It is difficult and perhaps pointless to speculate on Scriabin's score or the version created from his notes, but it is hardly likely that his grandiose vision could be communicated musically. There was always a discrepancy between those things Scriabin found in his music and described verbally—a process he frequently indulged in with his friends, so that, for example, the opening of the Seventh Sonata was "Perfumes, like clouds . . . this music already approximated the *Mysterium*"—and those things others heard in it. Whether that vision was communicable either in words or in music or by using all expressive means together is questionable, for what may work in small units cannot always be sustained. The poem moves discernibly to a statement of a higher unity but the music could not have done so, or could have done so only in a different way, just as *Ecstasy* has little to do with its program. Nevertheless Scriabin's enthusiastic and convincing presentation of the idea convinced others that he was working on something meaningful and feasible, whether seen mystically (as it ultimately must be) or symbolically (as it may be interpreted), and his contemporaries felt that he was on the verge of realizing their highest hopes: to convey, in a *Gesamtkunstwerk,* the aspirations of humanity and thereby to lead it to a higher existence. That it is based, in retrospect, on the apotheosis of the artist and the disguising of winged Eros as the angel of death places Scriabin all the more firmly among the Russian symbolists. (pp. 7-23)

> Ralph E. Matlaw, "Scriabin and Russian Symbolism," in Comparative Literature, *Vol. 31, No. 1, Winter, 1979, pp. 1-23.*

ADDITIONAL BIBLIOGRAPHY

Baer, Joachim T. "Symbolism and Stylized Prose in Russia and Poland: V. Brjusov's *Ognennyi angel* and W. Berent's *Żywekamienie.*" In *American Contributions to the Ninth International Congress of Slavists, Vol. II: Literature, Poetics, History,* edited by Paul Debreczeny, pp. 19-38. Columbus, Ohio: Slavica Publishers, 1983.
　　Stylistic analysis of two "outstanding examples of the Russian and Polish Symbolist tradition."

Basker, Michael. "Gumilyov's *Akteon:* A Forgotten Manifesto of Acmeism." *The Slavonic and East European Review* 63, No. 3 (October 1985): 498-517.
　　Demonstrates Gumilyov's drama to be an anti-Symbolist polemic.

Bely, Andrey. *Selected Essays of Andrey Bely,* edited and translated by Steven Cassedy. Berkeley: University of California Press, 1985, 311 p.
　　Includes nine theoretical essays, including "Symbolism as a World View" and "The Magic of Words," and an extensive critical introduction by Cassedy.

Carnicke, Sharon M. "Naturalism to Theatricalism: The Role of Symbolism." *Ulbandus Review* 1, No. 1 (Fall 1977): 41-58.
　　Discusses Russian Symbolist drama as a reaction againt the naturalistic style popularized by the Moscow Art Theater, examines Symbolist dramatic theory, and evaluates the artistic success of Symbolist theater.

Christa, Boris. "Andrey Bely and the Symbolist Movement in Russia." In *The Symbolist Movement in the Literature of European Languages,* edited by Anna Balakian, pp. 381-95. Budapest: Akadémiai Kiadó, 1982.
　　Examines Bely's writings in order to illustrate the importance of his contribution to the development of Symbolism.

Cioran, Samuel D. "In the Symbolists' Garden: An Introduction to Literary Horticulture." *Canadian Slavonic Papers* XVII, No. 1 (Spring 1975): 106-25.
　　Traces the garden motif in works by Russian Decadent and Symbolist poets. Noting that the "delicate fragrance, graceful forms, and subtle tenuous life" of flowers "reflected perfectly the concerns of both poetic mentalities," Cioran demonstrates how, "for the Decadents, flowers were exciters of the physical senses, whereas for the Symbolists they appeared to function as emblems of the other-worldly."

Elsworth, John. "Andrei Bely's Theory of Symbolism." In *Studies in Twentieth Century Russian Literature,* edited by Christopher J. Barnes, pp. 17-45. New York: Harper & Row, 1976.
　　Detailed analysis of Bely's theoretical writings on Symbolism.

Erlich, Victor. "Russian Symbolism and Polish Neo-Romanticism: Notes on Comparative Nomenclature of Slavic Modernism." In *American Contributions to the Seventh International Congress of Slavists, Vol. II: Literature and Folklore,* edited by Victor Terras, pp. 181-97. The Hague: Mouton, 1973.
　　Analyzes the terminology and nature of turn-of-the-century literary trends in Russia and Poland. While noting divergences between terms commonly used to denote developments in the two countries, Erlich demonstrates fundamental similarities between those developments.

Green, Michael, ed. and trans. *The Russian Symbolist Theater: An Anthology of Plays and Critical Texts.* Ann Arbor, Mich.: Ardis, 1986, 371 p.
　　Contains essays and dramas by Bryusov, Blok, Ivanov, Bely, Sologub, Kuzmin, Annensky, Remizov, and Andreyev.

Grossman, Joan Delaney. *Edgar Allan Poe in Russia: A Study in Legend and Literary Influence.* Würzburg, West Germany: Jal Verlag, 1973, 245 p.
　　Contains extensive discussion of Poe's influence on the Russian Symbolists.

Gumilev, Nikolai. *On Russian Poetry,* edited and translated by David Lapeza. Ann Arbor, Mich.: Ardis, 1977, 192 p.
　　Essays and reviews written between 1908 and 1921, including "Acmeism and the Legacy of Symbolism" (1913) and numerous reviews of Symbolist writings.

Hart, Pierre. "Time Transmuted: Merežkovskij and Brjusov's Historical Novels." *Slavic and East European Journal* 31, No. 2 (Summer 1987): 187-201.
　　Discusses the authors' adaptation of the historical novel for their own artistic purposes.

Janacek, Gerald, ed. *Andrey Bely: A Critical Review.* Lexington: The University Press of Kentucky, 1978, 222 p.
　　Contains nine critical essays on "Bely's Literary Legacy" and seven on "Bely and His Milieu." The latter category includes "Andrey Bely and the Modernist Movement in Russia" by Robert P. Hughes, "The Bely-Ivanov-Razumnik Correspondence" by Roger Keys, and "The Bely-Zhirmunsky Polemic" by Thomas R. Beyer, Jr.

Lossky, N. O. "Philosophical Ideas of Poet-Symbolists." In his *History of Russian Philosophy,* pp. 335-44. New York: International Universities Press, 1951.
　　Examines philosophical writings by Bely, Ivanov, Minsky, Merezhkovsky, and Rozanov.

Maslenikov, Oleg A. *The Frenzied Poets: Andrey Biely and the Russian Symbolists.* Berkeley: University of California Press, 1952, 234 p.
　　Biographical and critical study of Bely focusing on his personal and literary relationships with other members of the Symbolist movement.

——. "Russian Symbolists: The Mirror Theme and Allied Motifs." *The Russian Review* 16, No. 1 (January 1957): 42-52.
　　Examines the use of the mirror in Symbolist writings as a symbolic means to transcend both materialism and rationality.

Matlaw, Ralph E. "The Manifesto of Russian Symbolism." *The Slavic and East European Journal* XV, No. 3 (Fall 1957): 177-91.
　　Summary and analysis of Merezhkovsky's *On the Reasons for the Decline, and the New Currents, in Contemporary Russian Literature,* excerpted above. Noting that "to attack the idols and ideals of a militantly partisan reading public is a dangerous undertaking," Matlaw demonstrates that Merezhkovsky was deliberately circumspect in his denunciation of contemporary literature, being particularly careful not to "affiliate the new movement too closely with its French counterpart and its pejorative *décadence.*"

Mickiewicz, Denis. "*Apollo* and Modernist Poetics." *Russian Literature Triquarterly,* No. 1 (Fall 1987): 226-61.
　　Discusses the ideological and aesthetic principles of the journal *Apollo,* published between 1909 and 1917. Mickiewicz points out that the journal's editorial policies were not, as is often assumed,

"anti-Symbolist," but rather independent of all dogmatic literary schools.

Mirsky, D. S. Chapters IV and V. In his *Contemporary Russian Literature: 1881-1925*, pp. 151-80 and 181-240. New York: Alfred A. Knopf, 1926.
> History of the Russian Decadent and Symbolist movements, with separate sections devoted to the principal figures.

Pachmuss, Temira. "Women Writers in Russian Decadence." *Journal of Contemporary History* 17, No. 1 (January 1982): 111-36.
> Presents the history of Russian Decadence and examines works by Zinaida Hippius, Anastasiya Verbitskaya, Lidiya Zinovyeva-Annibal, Nadezhda Teffi, Mirra Lokhvitskaya, Poliksena Solovyova, Cherubina de Gabriak, and Adelaida Gertysk.

Peterson, Ronald E., ed. and trans. *The Russian Symbolists: An Anthology of Critical and Theoretical Writings*. Ann Arbor, Mich.: Ardis, 1986, 223 p.
> Excerpts of critical essays on Symbolism by Bryusov, Blok, Bely, Merezhkovsky, Hippius, Annensky, Sologub, Ivanov, and others. Also included are a brief history of the movement by Peterson and editorial statements from the Symbolist journals *Vesy, Zolotoe runo, Pereval,* and *Trudy i dni.*

Putnam, George F. "Viacheslav Ivanov on the Historical Role of the Symbolist Poet." *The Southern Review*, No. 3 (Winter 1967): 85-95.
> Analyzes Ivanov's theory of the relationship between the writer and society. Viewing Symbolist writings as the expression of "lost states of the folk soul," Ivanov believed that the intelligentsia and the people could be united by means of symbolic art.

Reeve, F. D. "Dobroljubov and Brjusov: Symbolist Extremists." *The Slavic and East European Journal* VIII (1964): 292-302.
> Discusses Bryusov and Dobrolyubov ("one famed for his esoteric idiosyncrasies, one for his anti-literary wildness") as examples of the dichotomy in the Symbolist movement between the aesthetes and the mystics.

Richardson, William. *"Zolotoe Runo" and Russian Modernism: 1905-1910*. Ann Arbor, Mich.: Ardis, 1986, 231 p.
> Detailed study of the journal through its five years of publication, including its contributors, editorial policies, and literary milieu.

Rosenthal, Bernice Glatzer. "The Transmutation of the Symbolist Ethos: Mystical Anarchism and the Revolution of 1905." *Slavic Review* 36, No. 4 (December 1977): 608-27.
> Analyzes the basic tenets of "mystical anarchism" and demonstrates that the doctrine "constituted a transmutation of the Symbolist ethos, one induced by the Revolution of 1905, . . . by explaining how elements of the pre-1905 Symbolist ethos were absorbed and transformed in mystical anarchism and by relating mystical anarchism's development to the course of the revolution."

Russian Literature Triquarterly, No. 4 (Fall 1972): 472 p.
> Issue devoted to Symbolism. Includes translated poetry, fiction, and criticism by thirteen Symbolist writers; essays by nine Western critics; previously unpublished letters, memoirs, and poems by Zinaida Hippius, Fyodor Sologub, and others; two humorous essays on Symbolism; a bibliography of criticism on Aleksandr Blok's *The Twelve;* and fifty illustrations.

Senelick, Laurence. "Vera Kommissarzhevskaya: The Actress as Symbolist Eidolon." *Theatre Journal* 32, No. 4 (December 1980): 475-87.

Attempts "to explore the curious interrelationship that existed between a hypersensitive, hyperkinetic actress and a shoal of idealistic poets, and to examine the influence they had on one another."

————. "Chekhov's Drama, Maeterlinck, and the Russian Symbolists." In *Chekhov's Great Plays: A Critical Anthology*, edited by Jean-Pierre Baricelli. New York: New York University Press, 1981.
> Traces affinities between Chekhov's dramas and works by Maurice Maeterlinck and the Russian Symbolists, and examines the largely unsympathetic reaction afforded Chekhov's works by the Symbolists.

————. *Russian Dramatic Theory from Pushkin to the Symbolists*. Austin: University of Texas Press, 1981, 336 p.
> Reprints essays by fourteen critics, including Andrey Bely ("The Cherry Orchard," "Theater and Modern Drama"), Fyodor Sologub ("The Theater of a Single Will"), Innokenty Annensky ("Drama at the Lower Depths"), Aleksandr Blok ("On Drama"), Valery Bryusov ("Realism and Convention on the Stage"), and Vyacheslav Ivanov ("The Essence of Tragedy").

Slonim, Marc. *Modern Russian Literature: From Chekhov to the Present*, pp. 79-210. New York: Oxford University Press, 1953.
> Traces the development of the Modernist movement in Russia from the militant aestheticism of the 1890s to the social and political consciousness of the prerevolutionary period.

Stone, Rochelle. "Aleksandr Blok and Bolesław Leśmian as Proponents and Playwrights of the New, Symbolist Drama: A Comparison." *Theatre Journal* 36, No. 4 (December 1984): 449-61.
> Analyzes stylistic, structural, and thematic similarities in dramas by Blok and Leśmian. Stone concludes that the two writers' protagonists are similar in their attempts "to free themselves, by means of metaphysics of the transcendental world, from the contradictions and chaos of reality," but notes that while Leśmian's heroes remain firm in their belief in transcendental forces, "Blok's dramas represent a negation and even a parody of this belief."

Strakhovsky, Leonid I. "The Silver Age of Russian Poetry: Symbolism and Acmeism." *Canadian Slavonic Papers* IV (1959): 61-87.
> Outlines salient characteristics of works by Merezhkovsky, Bryusov, Balmont, Ivanov, Sologub, Blok, Bely, Ellis, and the leaders of the Acmeist movement.

West, James. "The Poetic Landscape of the Russian Symbolists." In *Studies in Twentieth Century Russian Literature*, edited by Christopher J. Barnes, pp. 1-16. New York: Harper & Row, 1976.
> Relates the Symbolists' portrayals of the Russian landscape in their writings, as well as their appraisals of landscape painting, to their philosophic and aesthetic views.

Woronzoff, Alexander. *Andrej Belyj's "Petersburg," James Joyce's "Ulysses," and the Symbolist Movement*. Berne, Switzerland: Peter Lang, 1982, 211 p.
> Analyzes technical parallels in the novels, attributing their similarity to "the common heritage of the Symbolist aesthetic."

Zajda, J. I. "The Imagery of Love, Beauty, and Eternity in Russian Symbolist Poetry." *Melbourne Slavonic Studies*, No. 12 (1977): 47-62.
> Examines varying approaches to the Symbolists' shared belief in "the ideal and invisible world," demonstrating that "to Merezhkovsky it was essentially Neo-Christianity; to Balmont it was panaestheticism, and to Bryusov it was, above all, *a priori* rational mysticism."

Surrealism

INTRODUCTION

Surrealism was a literary and artistic movement whose adherents sought to revolutionize both art and life by utilizing the creative powers of the subconscious. The movement originated in France in 1922 as an outgrowth of Dadaism, a movement of artists and writers who responded to the horror and chaos of the First World War by creating chaotic and intentionally meaningless works. Led by André Breton, a Dadaist poet and medical student who was profoundly influenced by the theories of Sigmund Freud, the Surrealists broke with the nihilistic ideology of Dadaism in order to pursue the expression of a "superior reality" by means of compositional techniques that emphasized the role of the subconscious in the creative process. Openly expressing their contempt for all aesthetic traditions, the Surrealists attempted to reflect the suprarational workings of the subconscious in works characterized by bizarre juxtapositions of unrelated concepts and images. Since their goals were generally opposed to the artistic and ideological concerns of their contemporaries, the Surrealists were initially greeted with astonishment and even contempt. Yet as their importance in the art world gradually increased, their theories helped to inspire the freedom of expression that remains a primary feature of modern art.

The groundwork for Surrealism had been laid near the end of the nineteenth century by the iconoclastic plays of Alfred Jarry and the antibourgeois posture of the Symbolists, and in the early twentieth century by the stylistic innovations of poet Guillaume Apollinaire. Soon afterward the Dadaists, by rejecting the idea that art must carry some sort of meaning, made a decisive break with nineteenth-century aesthetics. Breton, however, quickly tired of the unrelenting meaninglessness of Dadaism and came to believe that humanity had fallen into a deplorable condition that demanded not a corresponding nihilism in art, but a more positive and constructive response. His experiences as an assistant physician in a neurological ward had convinced him that Freud was correct in his identification of a completely repressed level of consciousness within the human mind. Like Freud, Breton viewed human perception of reality not simply as a function of the logical, conscious mind, but as the result of a synthesis of conscious and subconscious awareness. He further assumed that by freeing the subconscious to participate more fully in the creation of art, an artist could more accurately reflect those processes by which human beings apprehend reality. This, then, was the essence of the Surrealists' optimism: the belief that through the use of Surrealist techniques, an artist could learn more about the nature of human existence and could communicate such knowledge to others. The ultimate goals of the Surrealists, however, reached far beyond even these broad parameters, since they viewed their techniques and products as a means of liberating humankind from the tyranny of rationalism.

When Breton left the Dadaists, he was followed by three writers: Benjamin Péret, Paul Eluard, and Louis Aragon, all of whom were inspired as much by the force of his intellect as by his nascent theories. These four were soon surrounded by a coterie that included writers Robert Desnos, Phillipe Sou-

pault, Pierre Naville, Antonin Artaud, Max Morise, and Tristan Tzara; artists Max Ernst, René Magritte, and Salvador Dali; and filmmakers Man Ray and Luis Buñuel. Such designations of genre were, however, extremely fluid, since all Surrealists experimented freely with various artistic forms. In 1924, two years after the break with the Dadaists, the group issued its first manifesto (written by Breton), began publishing the first of its several journals, and established the Bureau of Surrealist Research, where they conducted psychological and artistic experiments. By 1925 many members of the group had published individual or cooperative volumes of writings, while enough plastic art had been produced to stage an exclusively Surrealist exhibition at the Galerie Pierre in Paris. The Surrealist films *Un chien Andalou* and *L'âge d'or* appeared in 1928 and 1930, respectively.

Throughout the 1930s, the Surrealist movement continued to gain momentum despite internal disagreement and disaffections. The primary source of conflict lay in Breton's determination to control not only the direction of the movement, but also the activities of its individual members. Because of his contempt for all established literary and artistic authorities, he forbade any involvement with non-Surrealist publishers, theaters, or galleries, and he promptly expelled from the group any member who collaborated with those enemies. As a result of many such expulsions, Breton prefaced his second Surrealist manifesto with a lengthy denunciation of former members who had publicly expressed disapproval of his methods and theories. Nevertheless, as some artists left the group, many others joined, and by 1940 Surrealism had spread far beyond its original Parisian borders to the rest of Europe and to North America.

After the Second World War, the gradual attrition of the original Surrealist group—Desnos died in 1945, Eluard in 1952, Péret in 1959, and Breton in 1966—led not to the demise of Surrealism but to its mutation into new movements and styles. In France, Surrealist prose experiments led Alain Robbe-Grillet to propose the influential *nouveau roman,* or New Novel, which attempted to reflect human perception of reality as minutely and faithfully as possible. In England and the United States, the Surrealist influence was clearly manifested in postwar poetry, where free-form, highly personal, and psychologically complex verse became prevalent. More recently, renewed interest in Surrealism since the late 1960s has inspired the formation of several neo-Surrealist groups.

From the beginning, the techniques of Surrealist literature were based upon a single compositional principle known as psychic automatism. According to Breton, by surrendering oneself to a trancelike state resembling sleep, one could free the subconscious mind to participate in the creative process, and it was this "automatic writing" technique that the Surrealists used to create their distinctive texts. Poet Robert Desnos was thought to be the most adept practitioner of the technique until it was discovered that his trances had been facilitated by the frequent use of morphine; thereafter it was Benjamin Péret whose automatic writings were most widely respected. Critic Anna Balakian has noted that the most outstanding feature of poetry produced in this manner is its startling imagery, as in the following passage by Péret:

> There would be in the hollow of my hand
> a little lantern
> golden like a fried egg
> and so light that the soles of my shoes
>   would fly like a fake nose
> so that the bottom of the sea would be a
>   telephone booth
> and the phone would be forever out of order.

The Surrealists also invented games to create automatic texts; one of these, called Exquisite Corpse ("*cadavre exquis*") because its first use produced the line "the exquisite corpse will drink new wine," involved the composition of a sentence by a group of participants, each unaware of the others' contributions until the completed sentence was revealed. The element of random combination thus achieved produced writing which, like automatic poetry, contains startling and often bizarre images. A variation of Exquisite Corpse was played with one participant asking questions of others, who answered automatically. Although the Surrealists called these practices games, they were in reality designed primarily as research methods that could help to circumvent the conscious mind in order to secure information about the workings of the subconscious.

Surrealist painting and collage, on the other hand, were not generally the product of automatism. Instead, Surrealist artists utilized a variety of new techniques to reflect the random, nonrational images of the subconscious, particularly as exemplified in the dream state. One of the most frequently used techniques was the arrangement of objects in a fashion which mirrored the symbolic juxtaposition of seemingly unrelated images by the subconscious mind. Surrealist painters also used surprising combinations to create highly suggestive yet ultimately elusive images. Several Surrealists fashioned what they called "readymades," which were mass-produced articles that had been altered in such a way as to render them absurd, such as Meret Oppenheim's fur-covered teacup and Marcel Duchamp's bicycle wheel fixed atop a wooden stool. The significance of these creations remains somewhat obscure, except insofar as they represent a subversion of logic.

The success of the Surrealist endeavour can best be judged by its contribution to the individual arts. In literature, the Surrealists produced an abundance of highly regarded poetry, and several Surrealists are ranked among the major poets of the twentieth century. When they applied the principles of automatism to prose, however, the results were significantly less impressive. As a result, Surrealist novels and stories are considered important primarily for their experimental nature. Despite the fact that Breton originally applied his theories only to the creation of literature, critics generally agree that Surrealism made its most profound and enduring impact on the plastic arts. Throughout the mid-twentieth century, Surrealism dominated the art world, represented by such major figures as Salvador Dali, Max Ernst, Yves Tanguy, André Masson, and Joan Miró. Forms invented by the Surrealists, including the mixed media collage and the readymade, were quickly adopted by other artists and became important elements of modern art. Eventually, the Surrealist influence was carried into film, advertising, fashion, and interior design. Although the Surrealists were unable to achieve their ultimate goal—the liberation of humankind from all intellectual bonds—they did succeed in furthering the cause of human freedom in a limited way by liberating art from the constraints of rationality and tradition.

HISTORY AND FORMATIVE INFLUENCES

C. W. E. BIGSBY

[*Bigsby is a prominent Scottish critic and editor. In the following excerpt from an essay written in 1972, he traces the development of the Surrealist movement.*]

One evening in 1919 André Breton was struck by a phrase which "knocked at the window" of his consciousness. Though the sharpness of the image faded, he recalled the words, "there is a man cut in two by the window." This somewhat bizarre revelation was accompanied by a visual image and immediately followed by a number of equally gratuitous phrases which came into his mind without conscious volition. Familiar with the techniques of Freudian analysis Breton then attempted to give free rein to this arbitrary flow of images, unmediated by rational control. The written accounts of such experiences, the "automatic texts," which followed were instantly accepted by the Dadaists but they were in fact the first stirrings of a more determinedly experimental movement—surrealism.

Surrealism, as defined by Breton, was dedicated to revising our definition of reality. The means which it employed, automatic writing, accounts of dreams, trance narration, poems and paintings created as a result of random influences, art which pictured images of paradox and dream, were all devised to serve the same fundamental purpose—to change our perception of the world and hence to change the world itself. With such a messianic impulse at its heart it is scarcely surprising that it should have quickly enmeshed itself in political evangelism or that it should have been riven with sectarian dissension as its founder and chief prophet struggled to maintain the purity of what he saw as its central goal. But by the same token the sheer scale and effrontery of its objective guaranteed the enthusiastic commitment of writers and artists who increasingly felt that imagination alone could humanize a decadent art and decaying society.

André Breton was born in Normandy in 1896 which, by one of those coincidences so dear to the surrealists, was also the same year that Alfred Jarry was shocking Parisian audiences with his obscene and satirical fantasy, *Ubu Roi*. Of military age at the outbreak of hostilities he was mobilized first in the artillery and then in the medical corps. The war had a profound impact on him. It created a hatred for bourgeois chauvinism and a contempt for the writer who allowed his talent to be used to express the dangerous platitudes of what C. Wright Mills called the "power élite." His work with the wounded and shell-shocked introduced him to the new theories of Freud and brought him into contact with Jacques Vaché, who was to commit suicide in 1919, and Guillaume Apollinaire, whom Vaché derided. From the former, Breton derived an admiration for Jarry and the inspiration to regard himself as a poet; while the latter introduced him to the new literary and artistic movements of his day and later provided the name for the movement which swiftly eclipsed the achievements of Dada.

The word "surrealism" first made its appearance in Apollinaire's "absurdist" play, *Les Mamelles de Tirésias*, which was written in 1903 but first performed in 1917. The play was subtitled a "drame surréaliste" ["surrealist drama"]. For Apollinaire the word expressed an analogical way of conveying essential reality. As he pointed out, when man wished to imitate the action of walking he invented the wheel rather than mechanical legs. So, when the artist wishes to convey the fundamental truth of existence, he turns, not to the naturalist's slice of life but to the poet's evocative imagination. When Breton and Soupault looked for a name to describe their experiments it was natural that they should look to Apollinaire. Both men admired his work and in contriving his death to coincide with the celebration of Armistice Day he had assumed a further symbolic significance as a pivotal figure. (The writers of this time managed their deaths with masterly aplomb—Jacques Rigaut, for example, committing suicide at the age of thirty, having given himself a further decade of life ten years earlier.) In adopting Apollinaire's term, however, Breton imposed his own meaning on it, as he was to transform the meaning of everything he touched, from the headlines which he discovered in a newspaper and incorporated into a poem, to the objects which he found in the market-place and transmuted into mysterious symbols of the marvellous.

According to Hans Richter surrealism "jumped out of the left ear of Dada fully equipped and alive, making dada-ists = surrealists overnight." It is certainly true that men like Breton, [Paul] Éluard and [Louis] Aragon, who had constituted an important element of Paris Dada, did become the leaders of this new manifestation of revolt and freedom. Indeed as early as 1919 Breton and Soupault had published the first part of *Les Champs magnétiques* (published in full in 1922), which in retrospect, could be seen as the first truly Surrealist text. But the surrealists preferred to trace their heritage further back than Dada. They found their origin in the gothic novel, in the Marquis de Sade, and in the romantics and symbolists, although, as Breton later confessed, this search for ancestors was not without its irony for writers and artists who claimed to be iconoclasts.

The break with Dada came in 1922, following Breton's abortive conference to determine the course of modernism. If the influence of Dada was not to be so easily dismissed—provocation, for example, continuing to exert a powerful attraction—under the direction of Breton experimentation began to take a new direction. Automatic writing was followed by accounts of dreams and speeches made while under trance, the pursuit of the insights of the subconscious and a reliance on the nonrational which is the essence of surrealism. This was what Breton was later to call the "intuitive epoch" of Surrealism (and in more sanguine mood, the "heroic epoch") during which he believed that the mind could free itself of the restrictions of logic, rationality, and conscious control by its own efforts and that thought was "supreme over matter." It was this mood which was enshrined in the *Manifeste du Surréalisme,* published in 1924. From the standpoint of his later political commitment this seemed a rather naïve document which, if it accurately reflected the essence of surrealism as it existed at the time, failed to anticipate the radical shift which came in the following year. Nevertheless, the title of the group's first periodical, *La Révolution surréaliste,* which appeared in December 1924, did serve to indicate a commitment to radical change which soon came to embrace the political sphere as eagerly as it had the psychological, leading eventually to a new journal significantly called *Le Surréalisme au service de la révolution.*

In 1925 the new movement flexed its muscles and with a brashness and exuberance reminiscent of the Dadaists sallied forth to do battle with the forces of reaction, determined to assert its commitment to freedom in the face of conservatism. As Breton explained, "Nous vivons en plein coeur de la société moderne sur un compromis si grave qu'il justifie de notre part toutes les outrances." ["We live at the very center of modern society in a compromise so serious that it justifies all our

excesses."] They saw themselves as an irritant—but an irritant which was not purely destructive, for they were aware that the pearl is the end-product of an abrasive process, and such pearls, they insisted, were worth the death of a thousand divers. With this in mind they launched an attack on the Chancellors of Europe's universities for breeding men blind to the true mysteries of life, on the Pope, for distorting the human spirit, on Anatole France, for his conservatism, and on Paul Claudel, for his effrontery in denouncing them as pederasts.

Like the Dadaists they conducted public skirmishes with reactionary ideas in art and society. They opposed the literary bourgeoisie as they rejected the constrictions of conventional life. Breton ascribed the spiritual conformity and aridity of the middle class, intellectually to rationalism and logic, morally to the influence of church, state and family, and socially to the apparent necessity of work. The Surrealist thus placed himself in implacable opposition to the whole list—finding himself, somewhat to his surprise, a political as well as a spiritual revolutionary. Where the Dadaists had for the most part dissociated themselves from social and political activity, the surrealists came by degrees to extend their revolutionary activity from the potentially hermetic world of art to the more immediate political arena. Thus it is that the surrealists can be seen as providing a link between Baudelaire, on the barricades of 1848, and the dissident students, on the barricades of 1968; between the enthusiastic commitment of late romanticism and the expansive aims of a group of students who, in the middle of social revolt, could declare, "Forget all you have learnt, begin dreaming"; "Down with socialist realism. Long live surrealism." Surrealism, after all had announced the most revolutionary of policies. Annexing from Marx a commitment to change the world and from Rimbaud a determination to change life, they set themselves the task of altering reality—no less.

To an extent this shift towards political involvement implied a revision of the principles outlined in the First Manifesto. There Breton seemed to allocate an essentially passive role to the writer and artist. They should, he insisted, regard themselves simply as instruments. Continuing the analogy, he had denounced even such writers as Poe, Mallarmé, Jarry, and Reverdy, and such painters as Matisse, Picasso, Picabia, Chirico and Ernst because they "did not want to serve simply to orchestrate the marvellous score. They were instruments too full of pride, and this is why they have not always produced a harmonious sound." True surrealists, on the other hand, made "no effort whatsoever to filter" and regarded themselves as "simple receptacles of so many echoes, modest recording instruments." But, as the first issue of *La Révolution surréaliste* suggested, surrealism refused to allow its future to be determined by its past. (Aragon later said that "I do not admit the right of anyone to re-examine my words, to quote them against me. They are not the terms of a peace treaty.") Thus the passivity implicit in the early experiments gave way in time to a more avowedly active stance. In 1925, according to Breton, surrealism had already "ceased to be content with the results (automatic texts, accounts of dreams, improvised speeches, poems, spontaneous drawings or acts) it had initially proposed." Although these methods were by no means abandoned, Breton insisting on their centrality in the Second Manifesto in 1929, they were seen more rigorously for the techniques which they were. The new political awareness, which typified many of the surrealists, meant that experimentation was now seen in a new context.

The events of the Moroccan war of 1925 precipitated an attempt at *rapprochement* between the surrealists and the group associated with the left-wing publication, *Clarté*. This resulted in a joint manifesto, *La Révolution d'abord et toujours,* which was in itself evidence of the radical shift of emphasis on the part of the surrealists. In a sense it marked the end of their initial innocence, for now, by adopting an openly political stance, they were embracing public responsibility of a kind shunned by the Dadaists and regarded by themselves, only a year earlier, as irrelevant or, at best, of secondary importance. This was the start of what Breton, paradoxically, called the "reasoning epoch." As he was to assert later, in *What Is Surrealism?* "today, more than ever before, *the liberation of the mind,* the express aim of surrealism, demands as primary condition, in the opinion of the surrealists, *the liberation of man,* which implies that we must struggle with our fetters with all the energy of despair; that today more than ever before the surrealists entirely rely for the bringing about of the liberation of man upon the proletarian Revolution." The revolution in consciousness, it seemed, was to be a consequence rather than a cause of social change.

The union with *Clarté,* which somewhat incredibly had the blessing of the Soviet Commissar for Education, was by no means total. While pledging themselves to the cause of the working class, Breton and his followers wished to retain complete freedom in their work, a contradiction which was never resolved either at this time or in their subsequent quarrels with the communist party. Not surprisingly *La Guerre civile,* intended to be a joint product of the *Clarté* group and the surrealists, failed to appear, although reportedly mutual respect was somehow sustained. The French Communist Party, on the other hand, was not so sanguine about its putative allies. Certainly *Humanité,* edited now by Henri Barbusse, had little time for a movement which seemed incapable of accepting the full implications of its alleged commitment. But, as Breton argued in a brief pamphlet called *Légitime Défense,* published in 1926, the idea of the surrealists' material and spiritual aims being in opposition made no sense to a group whose central purpose and strategy lay in the reconciliation of such contradictions. *Légitime Défense* was an adroit attempt at simultaneously meeting the nascent objections of the party and the dialectical uncertainty which existed among the surrealists themselves, for if the pamphlet attacked the party it was only to suggest that it was not revolutionary enough. Despite his criticism of the party and in particular of its failure to realize that revolution was not limited to the material world, Breton, together with Éluard, [Benjamin] Péret, [Pierre] Unik and Aragon, did join in the following year (1927). But while calling for revolution and endorsing, when possible, the party line, the surrealists seem to have had a somewhat vague idea of the new society for which they were calling and of its value to them as surrealists. Significantly, they saw their role as defending the "soul" of the party against attacks from outside. When party officials, who were not attuned to the notion of surrealist defenders of the faith, asked them to co-operate in practical schemes the new converts were aghast. The materialistic emphasis which lay behind this restructuring of society made little sense of their own calls for the release of the imagination. Thus we are faced with the irony that for a brief time the surrealists were virtually the only organized group of intellectuals playing a leading role in the affairs of a French Communist Party which could not begin to understand their philosophy and which they in turn suspected of uncomprehending philistinism. The attraction which the surrealists felt for communism lay in the fact that the party seemed to be the incarnation of revolt. In many ways they were responding to Trotsky's association of communism with the idea of an optimistic freedom—social and metaphysical. En-

tranced by this image they were, for a while, blind to the growing determinism of a movement which eventually came to see Trotsky as an enemy and intellectual freedom as a threat to the construction of socialist unity. Their flirtation should be seen as an endorsement of iconoclasm; their eventual renunciation as a rejection of determinism. The decision to join the party, therefore, was a gesture which indicated the extent of their commitment but which did nothing to conceal the contradictions which led eventually to the inevitable break.

Breton's failure to anticipate the intolerable pressures which were soon brought to bear on him is the more surprising when placed beside the position outlined in *Légitime Défense.* None the less for a time at least, he seems to have been genuinely convinced by the party sophistry which sought to present disagreement as radical disaffection and neutrality as opposition. Perhaps one explanation for his acceptance of party diktats lies in the corresponding fervour with which he insisted on protecting the purity of surrealist orthodoxy. With an almost religious zeal he ex-communicated all those who seemed to deviate from the true faith and who failed to show his own dialectical dexterity. Thus [Antonin] Artaud, [Robert] Desnos, and [Georges] Ribemont-Dessaignes were invited to leave because they did not follow Breton in pledging allegiance to the party, wanting instead to "maintain surrealism on a purely speculative level." At the same time he defended himself against what he regarded as heresy on the left wing, by dismissing Aragon and [Pierre] Naville for their "ill-conceived political militancy."

Despite the arguments and denunciations which dominated this "reasoning epoch" these years were incredibly productive. Aragon had published *Traité du style* and *Le Paysan de Paris,* Éluard, *L'Amour la poésie,* Breton, the surrealist novel *Nadja* (itself a contradictory gesture since he had attacked the novel form in his manifesto) and Naville, *La Révolution et les Intellectuals.* Surrealism also conquered new areas: Luis Buñuel's film, *Un Chien andalou* demonstrated the cinema's unique ability to stimulate the subconscious; the establishment of the Galerie Surréaliste in 1926 underlined the growing importance of surrealist art—a phenomenon which, in skirting problems of translation and conveying directly the visual element only obliquely reconstructed in the written text, proved far more suitable for export and, arguably, more effective in expressing the paradoxical images of the subconscious.

Buñuel's *Un Chien andalou* was a product of what he himself called "a conscious psychic automatism." Its paradoxical images, its verbal and visual puns together with the flexibility of a form which could create visual effects of a kind impossible for the writer or painter, explain the significance which the cinema came to assume for the surrealists. Because of the forbidding expense of filmmaking many surrealist projects came to nothing, scenarios by Artaud, Desnos and [J. B.] Brunius never getting beyond the printed page. But the work of Buñuel and [Salvador] Dali, and later of Wilhelm Freddie and Harold Muller, demonstrated the potential of the medium.

Buñuel's films, which exhibit a more clearly symbolic dimension than most surrealist material, have always been provocative. In *Un Chien andalou* a woman's eye is sliced in two by a razor blade while in *L'Age d'Or* de Sade's Duke of Blangis emerges from the Castle of Selliny, after one hundred and twenty days of orgies, in the guise of Jesus Christ—a gesture which, at the film's first showing, understandably provoked a violent response from a largely Catholic audience.

Man in these films is portrayed as distorted and burdened by a society which distrusts passion and despises spontaneity, but

Buñuel's caustic humour deflates the pomposity of those characters who choose to place convention before humanity. At the same time the anarchic freedom of Buñuel's technique stands as a strikingly effective example of a surrealist liberty whose dynamic force seems more perfectly expressed through the fluidity of a visual medium than through the necessarily static force of the written text.

Surrealism was at first the creation of writers. Indeed the possibility of surrealist art was called into question in the early editions of *La Révolution surréaliste*. Certainly, of the twenty-six signatories of the January Declaration in 1925, only three were painters. Yet, as if to refute this, the first exhibition of surrealist art was actually held in that same year. It was admittedly an eclectic affair which drew on the work of painters like [Jean] Arp, [Paul] Klee and [Pablo] Picasso as well as Man Ray, [Joan] Miró and Max Ernst. Chirico's work, which was also shown, was an obvious precursor of surrealism but, as Sarone Alexandrian has pointed out, the paintings which he produced during the mid-twenties were, for the most part, so far from being surrealist that when he mounted an exhibition in 1928 the surrealists set up a rival one at which they displayed his earlier work. Breton himself seemed confident of the possibility of surrealist art—an art which must concern itself with enlarging the scope of reality. He found partial evidence of such work in Chirico, [Marcel] Duchamp, Ray and Klee, but it was in the experiments of Max Ernst, and, more especially, in his collages, that he saw the surreal at work. The very technique of the collage, the deliberate juxtaposition of objects, the dissonance between object and context, was surrealist.

In 1925 Ernst discovered a process which he equated with automatic writing. Using a method similar to that which produces brass rubbings he secured a tracing of the texture of wooden floorboards. This in turn, rather like a Rorschach ink-blot test, suggested certain forms to him. He called the process *frottage* and, perhaps somewhat spuriously, saw the artist as displaying the passivity associated with automatic writing. In reality it is arguable that a great deal of conscious choice was required, from the selection of object, to the size and colour of the frottage itself. None the less Ernst's frottages, the first of which were published in 1926, effectively mark the birth of surrealism in art—an occasion celebrated by the establishment in the same year of a Surrealist Gallery which became the scene of a number of subsequent exhibitions of surrealist art.

The series of articles which Breton published in *La Révolution surréaliste* under the title, "La Surréalisme et la Peinture" and which was concluded in 1927, does not, however, reveal the coherence which typified the literary aspect of surrealism. As critics have pointed out the title itself seems to accept a distinction between surrealism and painting which reveals a fundamental lack of conviction on Breton's part. Thus, in spite of his own assertions to the contrary, there would at this moment still seem to be some doubt in his mind if not that surrealist painting was possible at least that it was possible to define its characteristics and achievements.

By 1929 Breton felt the need for a re-examination of the aims and objectives of a movement which in a decade had adopted a number of seemingly contradictory poses and which had suffered both defections and expulsions (the list now included Queneau, Miró and [Roger] Vitrac among many others) as well as the infusion of new blood (Buñuel and Dali). Accordingly he invited replies to a letter which he sent to all those associated with the movement. The ensuing discussion proved predictably

abortive from one point of view but succeeded in sorting out the surrealist sheep from the politically unreliable and aesthetically self-conscious goats. Breton then outlined his own position in the *Le Second Manifeste du Surréalisme*, which affirmed the central commitment to revolt and to an expanded sense of reality but which criticized early errors which had led to an assertion of historical justification and a confusion between method and purpose. The manifesto rejected the bad faith of those who had been guilty of various heresies (he indicted Artaud, [André] Masson and [Phillipe] Soupault among many others) and constituted a justification of his twin faiths—dialectical materialism and surrealism. It was apparently a plea to the party not to look on the surrealists as "strange animals," whimsical and defiant, but rather as allies operating in a field outside the province of the working-class revolution. But from the tone of despair with which he mentions the French Communist Party it is clear that the manifesto is more justification than supplication.

As time went by, indeed, it became increasingly difficult for either the French Party or the surrealists to regard each other with anything less than considerable suspicion. The communist attitude towards culture became more severe while political opportunism left many of its supporters in a moral dilemma. The surrealists, on the other hand, were largely of bourgeois origins and evidenced what, from a Marxist viewpoint, seemed élitist attitudes. Certainly their work had little to say to the proletariat and, judging by the automatic texts and dream narrations published during the twenties, little of any political worth to say at all. There was, too, a suspicion that involvement with the party was conferring a significance on the surrealists and granting them revolutionary credentials which they might otherwise have lacked. At any rate the alliance, such as it was, did not survive much longer.

In 1932 Aragon, together with a small group which included Pierre Unik and Luis Buñuel, not merely joined the party but made it clear that it, and not surrealism, now had their primary loyalty. Although the surrealists staunchly defended Aragon when he was charged with sedition for his polemical poem "Red Front," they did so in terms which were unacceptable either to Aragon or the party. Thus Aragon publicly broke with the surrealists, even denouncing them as counter-revolutionary—an ironical appellation for a group which regarded communism as merely a minimum programme.

Two years later the Soviet pronouncement of the dogma of socialist realism confronted the surrealists with the very spectre which they had denounced in the First Manifesto. But whatever their doubts the issue had already been resolved when in 1933, following an attack on puritanism in the new Russia, by Ferdinand Alquié, the surrealists, with two exceptions, were all expelled.

Despite this and despite the reversal of policies which brought about an alliance between the communists and the French socialists which left the communists supporting precisely that militarism which the surrealists had rejected by joining the party in 1927, the final break on the surrealist side did not come about until 1935. After Breton had been refused permission to speak at the International Congress for the Defence of Culture they issued a pamphlet, *Du temps que les surréalistes avaient raison*, denouncing the Soviet regime in general and Stalin in particular. The document ended with the surrealists shaking a metaphorical fist in the face of a movement which they had once seen as playing a leading role in the liberation of mankind.

But in rejecting the party the surrealists were not abandoning their commitment to revolt. Indeed their central association of the party was that it had betrayed its own revolutionary integrity. In *La Position politique du Surréalisme,* published in that same year, Breton attempted a more detailed denunciation of the party's inadequacy and announced the founding of a new publication, *Contre-Attaque,* which was to be the organ of those revolutionaries who found it impossible to comply with the expedient and largely philistine dictates of party orthodoxy. Breton found Marx's call for "more consciousness" finally irreconcilable with the petty dogmatism of party functionaries. Real advance for the surrealists lay, it seems, less in the arid and compromised assertions of the left than in the vivid experiments of the increasingly right-wing Salvador Dali. He had already established his credentials with his formulation of *paranoia-criticism,* the principle of subversion which underlies most of his paintings. But the most important advance for the surrealists in the mid-thirties was the primary importance accorded to the *surrealist object,* which was a natural outgrowth of the work of Dali and Magritte and which marked a return to the experimental mood of the early twenties. These "objects perceived only dreams" were selected for their evocative quality. In a sense they were extensions of Duchamp's ready-mades but their central purpose was to subvert the utilitarian—to disconcert the literal-minded observer, to disturb his sense of reality and grant him a glimpse of the "marvellous." Thus in the 1936 exhibition of surrealist objects, held in Paris, Meret Oppenheim exhibited a "Fur-Covered Cup, Saucer, and Spoon," while Dali, in the same year, created, "The Venus de Milo of the Drawers"—the famous statue adapted as a "chest" of drawers. Both mocked the merely functional, the one in daily life, the other in art.

The war took most of the surrealists to the United States, including Breton, Ernst, [Yves] Tanguy and Dali, although the latter's fascist leanings and commercial instinct had long since alienated him from Breton. They were well received in their exile, contributing to such magazines as *VVV* and participating in an exhibition organized in New York in 1942, before returning to Europe at the end of hostilities. The expatriate years had a two-fold effect. On the one hand the surrealists left behind in America an inheritance not merely of American surrealists, such as Robert Motherwell, or those drawing on surrealist method, such as Mark Rothko and Ashile Gorky, but most significantly a lingering influence on the work of Jackson Pollock and the abstract expressionists. As Pollock himself explained, "I accept the fact that the important painting of the last hundred years was done in France. American painters have generally missed the point of modern painting from beginning to end.... Thus the fact that good European moderns are now here is very important, for they bring with them an understanding of the problems of modern painting. I am particularly impressed with their concept of the source of art being the Unconscious." Though he went on to admit that "the idea interests me more than these specific painters do, for the two artists I admire most, Picasso and Miró, are still abroad" the influence was an important one. The other important effect of the expatriate years lay in the fact that it tended to create a gulf between the surrealists and France. Although Éluard, who stayed behind in his native country, had fought with the Resistance, and Breton had at least broadcast for the Voice of America, their failure to contribute directly to the war effort may to some extent account for their failure to re-establish their influence and importance on their return to France. It was Camus and Sartre, the latter directly opposed to the surrealists in many ways, who between them determined the nature of the post-

war dialectic in France—a dialectic which allowed little room for the surrealists. They continued to work and to stage exhibitions (the International Exhibition of 1947 had contributors from twenty-seven countries) but these increasingly had the air of retrospectives which were not entirely divorced from a kind of nostalgia which had little place in the surrealist canon. They did continue to strike public poses on the war in Algeria and on Gaullism, but although their influence was still apparent in poetry and art surrealism seemed to have aspired to the very status against which it had fought with such determination. It was increasingly regarded as a movement which could be conveniently contained by the two wars. In many ways the surrealists under-estimated the ability of society to absorb the subversive image and sustain the impact of anarchic imagination. As Dali demonstrated, the marvellous proved a thoroughly marketable commodity. It was not for nothing that Breton renamed him Avida Dollars. Over the years surrealism has acquired a potentially embarrassing respectability and, more disturbingly, assumed a definite position in the rational catalogue of twentieth-century art and letters.

Yet surrealism did not die with VE day. Not only had the germ been spread to the United States, to Latin America and the Caribbean, and a dozen European countries, but the insight which it offered and the method which it outlined has continued to be relevant. It was therefore hardly surprising that the events of 1968 in France should have been accompanied by surrealist slogans or that the logical application of military technology in Vietnam should have been accompanied by a renewal of the surrealist spirit in the United States.

England remained curiously unaffected by all this (see Paul C. Ray, *The Surrealist Movement in England* [in Additional Bibliography]). Partly because of a natural insularity, reinforced by a traditional and unashamed ignorance of foreign languages and suspicion of foreign ideas, the exuberant early years of a movement which rapidly spread throughout the world left English writers and artists largely unmoved. Despite a native tradition which included the fantastic absurdities of Lewis's *The Monk,* or, in another mood, the creations of Lewis Carroll and Edward Lear, as well as the visionary creations of Blake, there was little enthusiasm for a group which purported to despise literature and bourgeois society alike. The freedom of the surrealist poets seemed less radical from the perspective of English romanticism and modernism, while the anti-clericism, which so shocked the French public, failed to provoke much more than wry amusement in a society so lacking in Catholic fervour and so inherently distrustful of passion.

The English learnt about surrealism not from Breton's manifesto and the bitter disputes of the early years but from David Gascoyne's *A Short Survey of Surrealism,* published in 1935 [see Additional Bibliography], or from the International Surrealist Exhibition staged in London in 1936. In other words surrealism was more than a decade in reaching England and arrived when much of its vital force had been spent. The 1936 Exhibition did serve, however, to bring the Belgian painter E. L. T. Mesens to Britain where he established the London Gallery and published the *London Gallery Bulletin* which, during the four years of its existence, was perhaps the single most important means of propagating surrealism in England.

While there remains even today a vestigial surrealist group, with its own magazine, its energy is somewhat attenuated and it remains a minor and insignificant influence. Without the dominant personality of an André Breton to keep the blood coursing English surrealism was virtually still-born and if its heart did succeed in beating, however feebly, it did not prove capable of propagating itself when the time came. (pp. 39-55)

C. W. E. Bigsby, "Birth, Progress and Politics," in his Dada & Surrealism, *Methuen & Co. Ltd., 1972, pp. 39-55.*

WALLACE FOWLIE

[*Fowlie is among the most respected and comprehensive scholars of French literature. His work includes translations of major poets and dramatists of France (Molière, Charles Baudelaire, Arthur Rimbaud, Paul Claudel, Saint-John Perse) and critical studies of the major figures and movements in modern French letters (Stéphane Mallarmé, Marcel Proust, André Gide, the Surrealists, among many others). Broad intellectual and artistic sympathies, along with an acute sensitivity for French writing and a firsthand understanding of literary creativity (he is the author of a novel and poetry collections in both French and English), are among the qualities that make Fowlie an indispensible guide for the student of French literature. In the following excerpt from his* Age of Surrealism *(1950), a survey of the literary precursors and representative figures of the Surrealist movement, Fowlie discusses formative influences on Surrealism.*]

Surrealism, during the years which separate the two world wars, seemed particularly concerned with negation, with revolution and the demolishing of ideals and standards. The surrealists were "anti" everything, but especially anti-literature and anti-poetry. They were asking for not much less than a total transformation of life. The formula which they combatted the most relentlessly was that which called literature an expression of society. This they considered the goal of bourgeois self-satisfied literature, and in denouncing it they were attacking . . . a basic aspect of classicism.

However, long before the period of surrealist invective, there had been in France a marked shift of preferences, a shift away from the kind of literature which was a social expression and a sociological document to forms of writing in which the artist tries to be sincere with himself, to express his thoughts and experiences with maximum degree of candor and honesty. It was obvious from the beginning of the century on, that preference of younger writers and critics, only some of whom were to become literally surrealists, was moving toward a literature of absolute sincerity. The word *realism* had taken on offensive connotations. The realistic creed had worn itself out tiresomely and monotonously. The two leading examples in this shift of preference are, first, in poetry, the ascendancy of Baudelaire, whose art is preferred to the cold impeccably formed Parnassian documents and the worn-out exercises of second-rate symbolists; and secondly, in prose, the preference accorded to Stendhal over Balzac. Younger readers in France had become irritated with the clearly defined motivations and the over-simplified psychological formulas of Balzac and other realists. François Mauriac was able to record early in the century, that young men were protesting against the real: "les jeunes êtres se défendent contre le réel." The success in 1913, when it was first published, of such a novel as *Le Grand Meaulnes* by Alain-Fournier was proof of the eagerness with which the French public accepted a work dealing with the world of dreams and the strange attraction of irrationality. The first part of Proust's novel *Du Côté de chez Swann* was published in 1913, but it wasn't read until after the war.

The need for sincerity in literary expression, felt strongly in France during the first twenty years of the century, is really the belief that the conscious states of man's being are not sufficient to explain him to himself and to others. His subconscious contains a larger and especially a more authentic or accurate part of his being. It was found that our conscious speech and our daily actions are usually in contradiction with our true selves and our deeper desires. The neat patterns of human behavior, set forth by the realists, and which our lives seem to follow, were found to be patterns formed by social forces rather than by our desires or temperaments or inner psychological selves. This discovery or conviction that we are more sincerely revealed in our dreams and in our purely instinctive actions than in our daily exterior habits of behavior (tea-drinking or cocktailing, etc.) is of course basic to surrealism. It is admirably summarized in a sentence of André Gide's autobiography, *Si le grain ne meurt*, when he speaks of the difficulty of our knowing the real motivation of any of our actions: "le motif secret de nos actes nous échappe" ["the secret motive of our actions escapes us"].

Reality, then, as demonstrated by the realists and as seen by man's own limited conscious self, entered upon a period of disfavor when it was considered imperfect, transitory, impure. And many of the new writers are characterized by their refusal of reality. Refusal and denial, in terms of reality, become currently used words. This is negative, a movement of anti-realism, but contains, as most negations do, an overwhelming positive aspiration. A new kind of absolute is in sight, which,

Portrait of André Breton by Pablo Picasso. Copyright ARS, NY.

although it contains a refusal of what we usually call logical intelligence, is an elevation of the subconscious of man into a position of power and magnitude and (the word now forces itself on us) surreality.

Behind this discovery or elevation of surreality lies the denial or refusal of reality, and still farther behind that, lies a more permanent state of mind of modern man for which the French have an excellent word: *inquiétude,* which in its English translation of "restlessness" seems inadequate. The current explanation of this *inquiétude* is the fact that man in the 20th century is forced to live in a period of threatened warfare or literal wars of such increasing cosmic magnitude that his state of mind is anything but peaceful. War is the most obvious human experience which accentuates the instability of the world. It certainly explains to a large degree the urgency felt by artists of the 20th century to discover a philosophy and art forms which will express their permanent sentiments of instability and restlessness.

If what is usually called real life or realistic life, ceases to have meaning, or represents a trap or false ambiency for the human spirit, reaction against reality is to be expected. An entire literature has come into being whose avowed goal was to escape from the real, to create an antidote for the insufficiency of realism. It might be called a literature of evasion and escape, in which the hero undertakes, not an exploration of the world with which he is most familiar, but an adventure in a totally exotic land or an investigation of his dream world. The example of Rimbaud in Ethiopia served as a model for the creative artist who was able to cut loose from all the stultifying bourgeois habits of living. And Lafcadio, the hero of André Gide's *Caves du Vatican,* whose goal is to commit a gratuitous act, an act having no motivation and no reason, also epitomized much of the new literature. Rimbaud always remained one of the gods of the surrealists, and *Les Caves du Vatican* was the book they preferred to all others of Gide, the only one of his which they wholeheartedly accepted.

The new hero is the unadaptable man, the wanderer or the dreamer or the perpetrator of illogical action. He represents what psychologists would define as the schizoid temperament. His method, and even his way of life, is introspection. For any man to understand himself, he must analyze all the varying and contradictory elements which go to form his personality. The great prose masters of this method of introspection—Dostoievski, Proust, and Gide—were heeded and studied by the surrealists who continued their method and pushed it so far that what is simply introspection in a Proust became in surrealist art the dissociation of personality, the splitting apart of the forces of a human character.

In whatever century we study him, man seems to remain strangely the same and recognizable. We can discover in each period the same human problems. What does change is the emphasis and the importance of these problems. But no matter what particular problem emerges as central and characteristic of an age, whether it be political or religious, philosophical or psychological, the artist goes about his work in much the same way. Whatever the problem of his particular age is, the artist, by his very vocation, has to make himself into the articulate conscience of the problem. The artist does not create the problem of his age, but he does create the myth of the problem. That is, the form by means of which the problem may in some sense be understood and felt by his own age and by subsequent ages. The form given to a problem by an artist, which is a myth, is precisely that form which will permit the problem to

be understood in the general hierarchy of all human problems. The myth of surrealist art . . . may well turn out to be the myth of the subconscious. That is, the myth of knowledge derived from data of man's subconscious activity.

Three writers especially, one of whom was venerated by the surrealists, presided over the emergence of this myth. First, the philosopher Henri Bergson demonstrated by his lessons of intuition the need to exceed the bounds of logical intelligence. Then, André Gide promulgated his lyrical lessons on self-affirmation. One of his early books, his most persuasive statement of doctrine, *Les Nourritures Terrestres,* is a paean of liberation from the traditional standards of society. It is a program of search for self-realization, self-integration, for morality of self, and especially a sensuous rejuvenation and understanding of self. The third among these major thinkers of modernism is, of course, Freud, whose illuminations on the subconscious form the leading principle of the surrealist creed.

It would be inaccurate to consider Bergson, Gide, and Freud as forerunners of the specific school of surrealism. They have influenced, in France, especially, and in those countries which follow France as a civilizing force, almost every aspect of modern thought. But the surrealists have derived from them a kind of subterranean impetus and confirmation. They have contributed help to the tremendous problem of sincerity for the modern artist: Bergson, in his lessons on the sincerity of intuition; Gide, on the sincerity of individual morality; Freud, on the revelations of the subconscious mind. The intellect alone, or a life regulated by the fixed standards of society, or our conscious states of being considered the sole source of self-knowledge, became for such thinkers as Bergson, Gide, and Freud, three barriers to sincerity, three ways of leading man into contradictory and deceitful life where actions, sentiments, and thoughts would be uncoordinated and unfruitful. If the principal problem for a Stendhal around 1830 seemed to be: how should I act? what should I do?, the problem one hundred years later appears to be: what am I? how can I attain to the center and the reality of my being? The problem of action for the hero of 1830 became for the hero of 1930 the problem of personality. The surrealists riveted themselves to this problem and in order to attain to some approximation of it have not ceased interrogating subconscious states of man, hypnotic states, and echolalia.

The surrealist found himself preoccupied with a contemporary hamletism. If he found himself unadaptable to society, it was because the secret of his being had to be revealed before he could actively engage in life, before he could follow any familiar course of action. This hamletism, which is an excessive analysis and study of self, an effort to probe into the deep restlessness or *inquiétude* of modern man which results in immobility and inactivity, seems to be a new form of the *mal du siècle,* the romantic malady of the early 19th century. Proust has been the fullest recorder of this *inquiétude.* He has played the rôle of analyst for our world which Rousseau and Chateaubriand played for the 19th century.

This new *mal du siècle* or hamletism came into great prominence after the first World War. In fact dadaism, which is a violent expression of it, originated in 1916, in Zurich, before the end of the war. The movement of Dada was soon replaced in the early 20's by surrealism, but not before it had expressed its strongly negative emphasis on many respectable notions and activities. It rebelled against society, language, religion, intelligence, and especially literature. The shattering effect of the war—that is, the defeatism of the war, felt even after the

Armistice of 1918—explains to some degree and perhaps very considerably, the *inquiétude* of the young men in the post-war world, their sense of futility, and their attacks of open remonstrance which find their expression in early surrealism.

The direct experience with war accounts therefore somewhat for the sense of futility and the philosophy of nihilism apparent in much of the surrealist art and literature. André Malraux, not a surrealist, but one of the best prose writers of contemporary France, who in 1947 announced unexpectedly his affiliation with De Gaulle and right-wing politics, wrote in his early book, *Les Conquérants:* "Nous avons été formés dans l'absurde de la guerre." In this sentence, "We were formed in the absurdity of war," he expresses an underlying thought of his generation, which is that of the surrealists. The first surrealists were also the first dadaists, and they had all been affected and marked in some personal way by the war: Breton, Eluard, Aragon, Péret. It is significant that the genesis of surrealism, between 1916 and 1922, developed under the influence of the war and that the literary works most admired by the surrealists, the writings of Lautréamont and Rimbaud, came into being at the time of the other war, that of 1870, in a comparable spirit of defeatism, in a comparable urgency to destroy traditional values.

The new movement was named before the end of the war by Guillaume Apollinaire. In a letter to Paul Dermée, of March, 1917, Apollinaire stated that he preferred to adopt the word *surrealism* rather than *surnaturalism,* and added that *surrealism* wasn't yet in the dictionary. Apollinaire at this time was the main god among the living for the first surrealists: Breton, Eluard, Aragon, Péret, Soupault. They also admired Max Jacob and especially the painters: Picasso, Matisse, Laurencin, le douanier Rousseau, Derain, Braque, Fernand Léger. The four earlier writers whom they all read and studied and claimed as the first gods of surrealism, the real ancestors, were Nerval, Baudelaire, Lautréamont, and Rimbaud.

The initial destructive element of surrealism might be illustrated by the character and the tragic end of Jacques Vaché. Before the war Vaché had been an art student in Paris, of not too great promise. He was sent to war and at the front was wounded in early 1916. He was treated, for his leg wound, at the neurological center at Nantes where André Breton, who had begun his career as a medical student, was an interne. The meeting in 1916 at Nantes of Breton and Jacques Vaché was of capital importance for the history of surrealism. In applying the principles of his personal philosophy, Vaché was to become for Breton and for most of the young surrealists, the dramatic symbol of their revolt, the man who dared to live his principles, who dared to surpass the mere eccentricities of behavior with which most of them stopped.

When Vaché was released from the hospital, he spent his time unloading coal on the wharves of the harbor at Nantes, or, dressed in impeccable elegance, frequenting the lowest dives of the city. He used to wear alternately a British uniform or a French aviation uniform, and give himself invented titles or tell about himself totally imagined adventures. The word he was the most serious about defining was *humor,* which he called "un sens de l'inutilité théâtrale et sans joie de tout, quand on sait." Humor, thus defined as the "theatric uselessness of everything," is an admirable clue to the meaning of dadaism, over which Jacques Vaché seemed to preside as a kind of prophet. The seemingly senseless actions of Vaché were really perpetrated in order to create about himself a world of unreality. He tried quite literally to live within the realm of his imagination.

He left no work of importance, save a volume of letters, *Lettres de Guerre* (1919), published after his death. His importance was his effect on, first, André Breton, who said he owed the most to Vaché ("C'est à Jacques Vaché que je dois le plus"), and then on his many admirers for whom he was a lucid and brilliant exponent of a way of life, or rather a way of looking at art. There are passages in his letters of literary nihilism, which became the manifesto of dadaism: "We have no liking for art or for artists—down with Apollinaire!" ("Nous n'aimons ni l'art ni les artistes—à bas Apollinaire!") Such sentences as "Nous ignorons Mallarmé" ("We don't know who Mallarmé is") were said in a tone both of scorn and high seriousness. They came from his fundamental belief in the ludicrous or useless display of art, or at least what was traditionally admired as art.

Vaché pushed his philosophy to its logical conclusion by taking his own life, at the end of 1918 in Nantes. He was a tall red-headed fellow who easily attracted people by his physical appearance. His personality and personal convictions were so strongly felt by his friends and admirers that they not only accepted the idea of his suicide but also the fact that he took a friend's life at the same time. The means of his suicide was an overdose of opium and he gave the same amount of opium to a friend who had asked to be initiated to the drug. It is more than probable that Vaché knew what the result of the two doses would be. I mention this tragic story first to illustrate the sense of defeatism which was felt at the end of the war, and secondly to illustrate the attraction toward death and self-destruction which is apparent in much of surrealist art. Prophecy, doom, destiny, occultism, and suicide are all manifestations of the pessimistic or nihilistic aspects of surrealism. . . . Vaché's suicide was immediately interpreted as a kind of martyrdom. He was a martyr to the futility and the doom of life, and his action was celebrated as a poetic or surrealistic justification of selfhood.

Surrealism at all times seemed to offer suicide as one alternative. But its other alternative has fortunately been believed in and practiced more assiduously than the suicidal interpretation. Belief in suicide has been strongly counteracted by belief in the miracle of art, in the magical qualities and properties of the artist. Surrealism receives this belief as a heritage from the early romantics of the 19th century, from a conviction about the artist and his work which had steadily grown in force and clarity throughout the century. The rôle of the writer was seen as usurping more and more the prerogatives of the priest, of the miracle-worker, of the man endowed with supernatural vision. The work itself of the writer, and particularly of the poet, was seen more and more to be a magical incantation, an evocative magic or witchcraft whose creation and whose effect were both miraculous. The artistic work might be compared to the "host" of sacramental Christianity which contains the "real presence." The poet then is the priest who causes the miracle by a magical use of words, by an incantation which he himself does not fully understand. And the work, thus brought into being, is a mystery which can be felt and experienced without necessarily being comprehended.

For the most part, the surrealists were poets and hence specialists in language. Poetry was for them, as legitimately as science and philosophy were for others, the way of knowledge. In the deepest sense, surrealism is a way of life, a method by means of which we may accept the enigmas of existence and in daily living learn to transcend impotencies, defeats, contradictions, wars.

In this way of knowledge, by which we are defining surrealism, there is one primary precaution always stressed, and this precaution helps to distinguish surrealism from other ways of knowledge: in the poetic or artistic creation, the poet must not intervene too consciously. He must learn the method of making himself into an echo, the method of echolalia. To become the magician, or the seer (the *voyant,* as Rimbaud calls him), he must learn to follow his inner life, or his imagination, as if he were an observer. He must learn to follow his conscious states, as when asleep he observes his dreams. Freud taught the surrealists that man is primarily a sleeper. The surrealist must therefore learn how to go down into his dreams, as Orpheus descended into the underworld, in order to discover his treasure there.

One poet, more profoundly than all others, is the ancestor of the surrealists. The position occupied by Charles Baudelaire in the history of modern poetry is remarkably equidistant between the two extremes or two heresies of modern poetry: first, the theory usually referred to as the art for art's sake theory (*L'art pour l'art*) and stressing the independence of art from any occupation or preoccupation of man; and second, the utilitarian theory of art which stresses its use and application. Baudelaire's life-long avoidance of falling into either one or the other heresy of art, is so important and so remarkable that I think his position in art might be compared to that of St. Thomas Aquinas in theology, who especially in his articles on grace, always avoided falling into one of the two possible heresies: of determinism or predestination on the one side, and of total liberty and independence of man from God's help on the other side.

Baudelaire's lesson on the autonomy of the imagination was to become a principal article of surrealist faith. For Baudelaire, the work of art is essentially a work of the imagination and yet it is true and real at the same time. This is perhaps the best way of defining what is meant by the sincerity of a work of art: the fidelity with which it adheres to the imagination of the artist. Additionally, for Baudelaire, a work of the imagination comes from a very real kind of anguish. Not so much the impermanent and transitory anguish of daily living, of insecurity, of war and love, as the inner and deeply permanent anguish of man which is usually repressed and covered over with willful forgetfulness. As in the treatment of psychoanalysis, the poet has to go very far down into his past, into the significance of his childhood. Considerable heroism is demanded for this facing of oneself in one's past.

The supernatural heroism of Baudelaire, which is the outstanding mark of his genius, was never matched by any surrealist writer. But the method and the ritual of his heroism were used and imitated by the surrealists. Baudelaire's self-discovery in his anguish and his self-revelation in his writing were archetypal. The artists who followed him, and especially the surrealists, have reenacted his method almost as a religious mystery, with the conviction that if all aspects of the ritual be observed, the mystery will again be achieved. All literature is to some degree psychoanalytic. Baudelaire went so deeply into psychoanalytic exploration that he passed beyond the personal reminiscence into the universal. That moment when the poet arrives at the center of himself and therefore at the center of human destiny, when he participates in the consciousness of the world and there establishes a point of contact between himself and the world, would be claimed by the [Surrealists] as the supremely surrealistic moment.

Baudelaire, and the man he claimed as spiritual brother, Edgar Allan Poe, whose life paralleled in so many ways Baudelaire's, would offer in their literary works sufficient material to establish the origins of surrealism. The particular kind of heroic anguish which they had to go through before they could attain to what we have called their surrealistic moment, appears to us, as time goes on and we see more clearly, propitiatory. An artist like Baudelaire assumes in himself much of the evil of humanity and by projecting it in his work relieves humanity of its evil. When we read the flowers of evil of Baudelaire, poems whose subject is known to us in varying degrees, we are thereby purged of the very evil which was in us. One of the most precious concepts of our world is the cathartic principle of art, which we owe to the *Poetics* of Aristotle. The surrealists, with the example especially of Baudelaire, have given to the doctrine of catharsis a renewed and vigorous interpretation. The myth of psychoanalysis, or rather the myth of the subconscious, which would be one facile way of describing the myth created and recreated by the surrealists, was formed in the wake of invasions, wars, and revolutions, in company with neo-thomism and communism, as a way of integrating and uniting scientific determinism and poetic sublimation. When one knows oneself (science means knowledge), at the end, say, of the performance of a tragedy, or after the reading of a poem, or after contemplating the spectacle of a painting, one has lived through both a human experience and its absolution. Infinitely more than practices which might be called classical, or romantic, surrealism has emphasized the closeness of art to a certain kind of psychic human experience and the remedial effect which such an art has on the human spirit. (pp. 12-27)

Wallace Fowlie, "Origins," in his Age of Surrealism, *1950. Reprint by Indiana University Press, 1960, pp. 11-27.*

MANIFESTOS

ANDRE BRETON

[*In the following excerpt, which constitutes the first half of the 1924* Manifesto of Surrealism, *Breton establishes the goals and concerns of the movement. This section was followed by specific directions for utilizing Surrealist literary techniques such as automatic writing and composition games.*]

So strong is the belief in life, in what is most fragile in life— *real* life, I mean—that in the end this belief is lost. Man, that inveterate dreamer, daily more discontent with his destiny, has trouble assessing the objects he has been led to use, objects that his nonchalance has brought his way, or that he has earned through his own efforts, almost always through his own efforts, for he has agreed to work, at least he has not refused to try his luck (or what he calls his luck!). At this point he feels extremely modest: he knows what women he has had, what silly affairs he has been involved in; he is unimpressed by his wealth or poverty, in this respect he is still a newborn babe and, as for the approval of his conscience, I confess that he does very nicely without it. If he still retains a certain lucidity, all he can do is turn back toward his childhood which, however his guides and mentors may have botched it, still strikes him as somehow charming. There, the absence of any known restrictions allows him the perspective of several lives lived at once; this illusion becomes firmly rooted within him; now he is only interested in the fleeting, the extreme facility of everything. Children set off each day without a worry in the world. Everything is near at hand, the worst material conditions are fine. The woods are white or black, one will never sleep.

But it is true that we would not dare venture so far, it is not merely a question of distance. Threat is piled upon threat, one yields, abandons a portion of the terrain to be conquered. This imagination which knows no bounds is henceforth allowed to be exercised only in strict accordance with the laws of an arbitrary utility; it is incapable of assuming this inferior role for very long and, in the vicinity of the twentieth year, generally prefers to abandon man to his lusterless fate.

Though he may later try to pull himself together upon occasion, having felt that he is losing by slow degrees all reason for living, incapable as he has become of being able to rise to some exceptional situation such as love, he will hardly succeed. This is because he henceforth belongs body and soul to an imperative practical necessity which demands his constant attention. None of his gestures will be expansive, none of his ideas generous or far-reaching. In his mind's eye, events real or imagined will be seen only as they relate to a welter of similar events, events in which he has not participated, *abortive* events. What am I saying: he will judge them in relationship to one of these events whose consequences are more reassuring than the others. On no account will he view them as his salvation.

Beloved imagination, what I most like in you is your unsparing quality.

The mere word "freedom" is the only one that still excites me. I deem it capable of indefinitely sustaining the old human fanaticism. It doubtless satisfies my only legitimate aspiration. Among all the many misfortunes to which we are heir, it is only fair to admit that we are allowed the greatest degree of freedom of thought. It is up to us not to misuse it. To reduce the imagination to a state of slavery—even though it would mean the elimination of what is commonly called happiness—is to betray all sense of absolute justice within oneself. Imagination alone offers me some intimation of what *can be,* and this is enough to remove to some slight degree the terrible injunction; enough, too, to allow me to devote myself to it without fear of making a mistake (as though it were possible to make a bigger mistake). Where does it begin to turn bad, and where does the mind's stability cease? For the mind, is the possibility of erring not rather the contingency of good?

There remains madness, "the madness that one locks up," as it has aptly been described. That madness or another. . . . We all know, in fact, that the insane owe their incarceration to a tiny number of legally reprehensible acts and that, were it not for these acts their freedom (or what we see as their freedom) would not be threatened. I am willing to admit that they are, to some degree, victims of their imagination, in that it induces them not to pay attention to certain rules—outside of which the species feels itself threatened—which we are all supposed to know and respect. But their profound indifference to the way in which we judge them, allows us to suppose that they derive a great deal of comfort and consolation from their imagination, that they enjoy their madness sufficiently to endure the thought that its validity does not extend beyond themselves. And, indeed, hallucinations, illusions, etc., are not a source of trifling pleasure. The best controlled sensuality partakes of it, and I know that there are many evenings when I would gladly tame that pretty hand which, during the last pages of Taine's *L'Intelligence,* indulges in some curious misdeeds. I

could spend my whole life prying loose the secrets of the insane. These people are honest to a fault, and their naiveté has no peer but by own. Christopher Columbus should have set out to discover America with a boatload of madmen. And note how this madness has taken shape, and endured.

It is not the fear of madness which will oblige us to leave the flag of imagination furled.

The case against the realistic attitude demands to be examined, following the case against the materialistic attitude. The latter, more poetic in fact than the former, admittedly implies on the part of man a kind of monstrous pride which, admittedly, is monstrous, but not a new and more complete decay. It should above all be viewed as a welcome reaction against certain ridiculous tendencies of spiritualism. Finally, it is not incompatible with a certain nobility of thought.

By contrast, the realistic attitude, inspired by positivism, from Saint Thomas Aquinas to Anatole France, clearly seems to me to be hostile to any intellectual or moral advancement. I loathe it, for it is made up of mediocrity, hate, and dull conceit. It is this attitude which today gives birth to these ridiculous books, these insulting plays. It constantly feeds on and derives strength from the newspapers and stultifies both science and art by assiduously flattering the lowest of tastes; clarity bordering on stupidity, a dog's life. The activity of the best minds feels the effects of it; the law of the lowest common denominator finally prevails upon them as it does upon the others. An amusing result of this state of affairs, in literature for example, is the generous supply of novels. Each person adds his personal little "observation" to the whole. As a cleansing antidote to all this, M. Paul Valéry recently suggested that an anthology be compiled in which the largest possible number of opening passages from novels be offered; the resulting insanity, he predicted, would be a source of considerable edification. The most famous authors would be included. Such a thought reflects great credit on Paul Valéry who, some time ago, speaking of novels, assured me that, so far as he was concerned, he would continue to refrain from writing: "The Marquise went out at five." But has he kept his word?

If the purely informative style, of which the sentence just quoted is a prime example, is virtually the rule rather than the exception in the novel form, it is because, in all fairness, the author's ambition is severely circumscribed. The circumstantial, needlessly specific nature of each of their notations leads me to believe that they are perpetrating a joke at my expense. I am spared not even one of the character's slightest vacillations: will he be fairhaired? what will his name be? will we first meet him during the summer? So many questions resolved once and for all, as chance directs; the only discretionary power left me is to close the book, which I am careful to do somewhere in the vicinity of the first page. And the descriptions! There is nothing to which their vacuity can be compared; they are nothing but so many superimposed images taken from some stock catalogue, which the author utilizes more and more whenever he chooses; he seizes the opportunity to slip me his postcards, he tries to make me agree with him about the clichés:

> The small room into which the young man was shown was covered with yellow wallpaper: there were geraniums in the windows, which were covered with muslin curtains; the setting sun cast a harsh light over the entire setting. . . . There was nothing special about the room. The furniture, of yellow wood, was all very old. A sofa with a tall back turned down, an oval table opposite the sofa, a dressing table and a

mirror set against the pierglass, some chairs along the walls, two or three etchings of no value portraying some German girls with birds in their hands—such were the furnishings [Fyodor Dostoevsky, *Crime and Punishment*].

I am in no mood to admit that the mind is interested in occupying itself with such matters, even fleetingly. It may be argued that this school-boy description has its place, and that at this juncture of the book the author has his reasons for burdening me. Nevertheless he is wasting his time, for I refuse to go into his room. Others' laziness or fatigue does not interest me. I have too unstable a notion of the continuity of life to equate or compare my moments of depression or weakness with my best moments. When one ceases to feel, I am of the opinion one should keep quiet. And I would like it understood that I am not accusing or condemning lack of originality *as such*. I am only saying that I do not take particular note of the empty moments of my life, that it may be unworthy for any man to crystallize those which seem to him to be so. I shall, with your permission, *ignore* the description of that room, and many more like it.

Not so fast, there; I'm getting into the area of psychology, a subject about which I shall be careful not to joke.

The author attacks a character and, this being settled upon, parades his hero to and fro across the world. No matter what happens, this hero, whose actions and reactions are admirably predictable, is compelled not to thwart or upset—even though he looks as though he is—the calculations of which he is the object. The currents of life can appear to lift him up, roll him over, cast him down, he will still belong to this *readymade* human type. A simple game of chess which doesn't interest me in the least—man, whoever he may be, being for me a mediocre opponent. What I cannot bear are those wretched discussions relative to such and such a move, since winning or losing is not in question. And if the game is not worth the candle, if objective reason does a frightful job—as indeed it does—of serving him who calls upon it, is it not fitting and proper to avoid all contact with these categories? "Diversity is so vast that every different tone of voice, every step, cough, every wipe of the nose, every sneeze...." If in a cluster of grapes there are no two alike, why do you want me to describe this grape by the other, by all the others, why do you want me to make a palatable grape? Our brains are dulled by the incurable mania of wanting to make the unknown known, classifiable. The desire for analysis wins out over the sentiments. The result is statements of undue length whose persuasive power is attributable solely to their strangeness and which impress the reader only by the abstract quality of their vocabulary, which moreover is ill-defined. If the general ideas that philosophy has thus far come up with as topics of discussion revealed by their very nature their definitive incursion into a broader or more general area, I would be the first to greet the news with joy. But up till now it has been nothing but idle repartee; the flashes of wit and other niceties vie in concealing from us the true thought in search of itself, instead of concentrating on obtaining successes. It seems to me that every act is its own justification, at least for the person who has been capable of committing it, that it is endowed with a radiant power which the slightest gloss is certain to diminish. Because of this gloss, it even in a sense ceases to happen. It gains nothing to be thus distinguished. Stendhal's heroes are subject to the comments and appraisals—appraisals which are more or less successful—made by that author, which add not one whit

to their glory. Where we really find them again is at the point at which Stendhal has lost them.

We are still living under the reign of logic: this, of course, is what I have been driving at. But in this day and age logical methods are applicable only to solving problems of secondary interest. The absolute rationalism that is still in vogue allows us to consider only facts relating directly to our experience. Logical ends, on the contrary, escape us. It is pointless to add that experience itself has found itself increasingly circumscribed. It paces back and forth in a cage from which it is more and more difficult to make it emerge. It too leans for support on what is most immediately expedient, and it is protected by the sentinels of common sense. Under the pretense of civilization and progress, we have managed to banish from the mind everything that may rightly or wrongly be termed superstition, or fancy; forbidden is any kind of search for truth which is not in conformance with accepted practices. It was, apparently, by pure chance that a part of our mental world which we pretended not to be concerned with any longer—and, in my opinion by far the most important part—has been brought back to light. For this we must give thanks to the discoveries of Sigmund Freud. On the basis of these discoveries a current of opinion is finally forming by means of which the human explorer will be able to carry his investigations much further, authorized as he will henceforth be not to confine himself solely to the most summary realities. The imagination is perhaps on the point of reasserting itself, of reclaiming its rights. If the depths of our mind contain within it strange forces capable of augmenting those on the surface, or of waging a victorious battle against them, there is every reason to seize them—first to seize them, then, if need be, to submit them to the control of our reason. The analysts themselves have everything to gain by it. But it is worth noting that no means has been designated a priori for carrying out this undertaking, that until further notice it can be construed to be the province of poets as well as scholars, and that its success is not dependent upon the more or less capricious paths that will be followed.

Freud very rightly brought his critical faculties to bear upon the dream. It is, in fact, inadmissible that this considerable portion of psychic activity (since, at least from man's birth until his death, thought offers no solution of continuity, the sum of the moments of dream, from the point of view of time, and taking into consideration only the time of pure dreaming, that is the dreams of sleep, is not inferior to the sum of the moments of reality, or, to be more precisely limiting, the moments of waking) has still today been so grossly neglected. I have always been amazed at the way an ordinary observer lends so much more credence and attaches so much more importance to waking events than to those occurring in dreams. It is because man, when he ceases to sleep, is above all the plaything of his memory, and in its normal state memory takes pleasure in weakly retracing for him the circumstances of the dream, in stripping it of any real importance, and in dismissing the only *determinant* from the point where he thinks he has left it a few hours before: this firm hope, this concern. He is under the impression of continuing something that is worthwhile. Thus the dream finds itself reduced to a mere parenthesis, as is the night. And, like the night, dreams generally contribute little to furthering our understanding. This curious state of affairs seems to me to call for certain reflections:

1) Within the limits where they operate (or are thought to operate) dreams give every evidence of being continuous and show signs of organization. Memory alone arrogates to itself

the right to excerpt from dreams, to ignore the transitions, and to depict for us rather a series of dreams than the *dream itself*. By the same token, at any given moment we have only a distinct notion of realities, the coordination of which is a question of will. What is worth noting is that nothing allows us to pre-suppose a greater dissipation of the elements of which the dream is constituted. I am sorry to have to speak about it according to a formula which in principle excludes the dream. When will we have sleeping logicians, sleeping philosophers? I would like to sleep, in order to surrender myself to the dream-ers, the way I surrender myself to those who read me with eyes wide open; in order to stop imposing, in this realm, the conscious rhythm of my thought. Perhaps my dream last night follows that of the night before, and will be continued the next night, with an exemplary strictness. *It's quite possible,* as the saying goes. And since it has not been proved in the slightest that, in doing so, the "reality" with which I am kept busy continues to exist in the state of dream, that it does not sink back down into the immemorial, why should I not grant to dreams what I occasionally refuse reality, that is, this value of certainty in itself which, in its own time, is not open to my repudiation? Why should I not expect from the sign of the dream more than I expect from a degree of consciousness which is daily more acute? Can't the dream also be used in solving the fundamental questions of life? Are these questions the same in one case as in the other and, in the dream, do these questions already exist? Is the dream any less restrictive or punitive than the rest? I am growing old and, more than that reality to which I believe I subject myself, it is perhaps the dream, the difference with which I treat the dream, which makes me grow old.

2) Let me come back again to the waking state. I have no choice but to consider it a phenomenon of interference. Not only does the mind display, in this state, a strange tendency to lose its bearings (as evidenced by the slips and mistakes the secrets of which are just beginning to be revealed to us), but, what is more, it does not appear that, when the mind is func-tioning normally, it really responds to anything but the sug-gestions which come to it from the depths of that dark night to which I commend it. However conditioned it may be, its balance is relative. It scarcely dares express itself and, if it does, it confines itself to verifying that such and such an idea, or such and such a woman, has made an impression on it. What impression it would be hard pressed to say, by which it reveals the degree of its subjectivity, and nothing more. This idea, this woman, disturb it, they tend to make it less severe. What they do is isolate the mind for a second from its solvent and spirit it to heaven, as the beautiful precipitate it can be, that it is. When all else fails, it then calls upon chance, a divinity even more obscure than the others to whom it ascribes all its aberrations. Who can say to me that the angle by which that idea which affects it is offered, that what it likes in the eye of that woman is not precisely what links it to its dream, binds it to those fundamental facts which, through its own fault, it has lost? And if things were different, what might it be capable of? I would like to provide it with the key to this corridor.

3) The mind of the man who dreams is fully satisfied by what happens to him. The agonizing question of possibility is no longer pertinent. Kill, fly faster, love to your heart's content. And if you should die, are you not certain of reawaking among the dead? Let yourself be carried along, events will not tolerate your interference. You are nameless. The ease of everything is priceless.

What reason, I ask, a reason so much vaster than the other, makes dreams seem so natural and allows me to welcome unreservedly a welter of episodes so strange that they would confound me now as I write? And yet I can believe my eyes, my ears; this great day has arrived, this beast has spoken.

If man's awaking is harder, if it breaks the spell too abruptly, it is because he has been led to make for himself too impov-erished a notion of atonement.

4) From the moment when it is subjected to a methodical examination, when, by means yet to be determined, we succeed in recording the contents of dreams in their entirety (and that presupposes a discipline of memory spanning generations; but let us nonetheless begin by noting the most salient facts), when its graph will expand with unparalleled volume and regularity, we may hope that the mysteries which really are not will give way to the great Mystery. I believe in the future resolution of these two states, dream and reality, which are seemingly so contradictory, into a kind of absolute reality, a *surreality,* if one may so speak. It is in quest of this surreality that I am going, certain not to find it but too unmindful of my death not to calculate to some slight degree the joys of its possession.

A story is told according to which Saint-Pol-Roux, in times gone by, used to have a notice posted on the door of his manor house in Camaret, every evening before he went to sleep, which read: THE POET IS WORKING.

A great deal more could be said, but in passing I merely wanted to touch upon a subject which in itself would require a very long and much more detailed discussion; I shall come back to it. At this juncture, my intention was merely to mark a point by noting the *hate of the marvelous* which rages in certain men, this absurdity beneath which they try to bury it. Let us not mince words: the marvelous is always beautiful, anything mar-velous is beautiful, in fact only the marvelous is beautiful.

In the realm of literature, only the marvelous is capable of fecundating works which belong to an inferior category such as the novel, and generally speaking, anything that involves storytelling. Lewis' *The Monk* is an admirable proof of this. It is infused throughout with the presence of the marvelous. Long before the author has freed his main characters from all temporal constraints, one feels them ready to act with an un-precedented pride. This passion for eternity with which they are constantly stirred lends an unforgettable intensity to their torments, and to mine. I mean that this book, from beginning to end, and in the purest way imaginable, exercises an exalting effect only upon that part of the mind which aspires to leave the earth and that, stripped of an insignificant part of its plot, which belongs to the period in which it was written, it con-stitutes a paragon of precision and innocent grandeur. It seems to me none better has been done, and that the character of Mathilda in particular is the most moving creation that one can credit to this *figurative* fashion in literature. She is less a char-acter than a continual temptation. And if a character is not a temptation, what is he? An extreme temptation, she. In *The Monk,* the "nothing is impossible for him who dares try" gives it its full, convincing measure. Ghosts play a logical role in the book, since the critical mind does not seize them in order to dispute them. Ambrosio's punishment is likewise treated in a legitimate manner, since it is finally accepted by the critical faculty as a natural denouement.

It may seem arbitrary on my part, when discussing the mar-velous, to choose this model, from which both the Nordic literatures and Oriental literatures have borrowed time and time again, not to mention the religious literatures of every country. This is because most of the examples which these literatures could have furnished me with are tainted by puerility, for the simple reason that they are addressed to children. At an early age children are weaned on the marvelous, and later on they fail to retain a sufficient virginity of mind to thoroughly enjoy fairy tales. No matter how charming they may be, a grown man would think he were reverting to childhood by nourishing himself on fairy tales, and I am the first to admit that all such tales are not suitable for him. The fabric of adorable improbabilities must be made a trifle more subtle the older we grow, and we are still at the stage of waiting for this kind of spider. . . . But the faculties do not change radically. Fear, the attraction of the unusual, chance, the taste for things extravagant are all devices which we can always call upon without fear of deception. There are fairy tales to be written for adults, fairy tales still almost blue.

The marvelous is not the same in every period of history: it partakes in some obscure way of a sort of general revelation only the fragments of which come down to us: they are the romantic *ruins,* the modern *mannequin,* or any other symbol capable of affecting the human sensibility for a period of time. In these areas which make us smile, there is still portrayed the incurable human restlessness, and this is why I take them into consideration and why I judge them inseparable from certain productions of genius which are, more than the others, painfully afflicted by them. They are Villon's gibbets, Racine's Greeks, Baudelaire's couches. They coincide with an eclipse of the taste I am made to endure, I whose notion of taste is the image of a big spot. Amid the bad taste of my time I strive to go further than anyone else. It would have been I, had I lived in 1820, I "the bleeding nun," I who would not have spared this cunning and banal "let us conceal" whereof the parodical Cuisin speaks, it would have been I, I who would have reveled in the enormous metaphors, as he says, all phases of the "silver disk." For today I think of a *castle,* half of which is not necessarily in ruins; this castle belongs to me, I picture it in a rustic setting, not far from Paris. The outbuildings are too numerous to mention, and, as for the interior, it has been frightfully restored, in such a manner as to leave nothing to be desired from the viewpoint of comfort. Automobiles are parked before the door, concealed by the shade of the trees. A few of my friends are living here as permanent guests: there is Louis Aragon leaving; he only has time enough to say hello; Philippe Soupault gets up with the stars, and Paul Eluard, our great Eluard, has not yet come home. There are Robert Desnos and Roger Vitrac out on the grounds poring over an ancient edict on dueling; Georges Aurie, Jean Paulhan; Max Morise, who rows so well, and Benjamin Péret, busy with his equations with birds; and Joseph Delteil; and Jean Carrive; and Georges Limbour, and Georges Limbours (there is a whole hedge of Georges Limbours); and Marcel Noll; there is T. Fraenkel waving to us from his captive balloon, Georges Malkine, Antonin Artaud, Francis Gérard, Pierre Naville, J.-A. Boiffard, and after them Jacques Baron and his brother, handsome and cordial, and so many others besides, and gorgeous women, I might add. Nothing is too good for these young men, their wishes are, as to wealth, so many commands. Francis Picabia comes to pay us a call, and last week, in the hall of mirrors, we received a certain Marcel Duchamp whom we had not hitherto known. Picasso goes hunting in the neighborhood. The spirit of *demoralization* has elected domicile in the castle, and it is with it we have to deal every time it is a question of contact with our fellowmen, but the doors are always open, and one does not begin by "thanking" everyone, you know. Moreover,

the solitude is vast, we don't often run into one another. And anyway, isn't what matters that we be the masters of ourselves, the masters of women, and of love too?

I shall be proved guilty of poetic dishonesty: everyone will go parading about saying that I live on the rue Fontaine and that he will have none of the water that flows therefrom. To be sure! But is he certain that this castle into which I cordially invite him is an image? What if this castle really existed! My guests are there to prove it does; their whim is the luminous road that leads to it. We really live by our fantasies when we *give free rein to them.* And how could what one might do bother the other, there, safely sheltered from the sentimental pursuit and at the trysting place of opportunities?

Man proposes and disposes. He and he alone can determine whether he is completely master of himself, that is, whether he maintains the body of his desires, daily more formidable, in a state of anarchy. Poetry teaches him to. It bears within itself the perfect compensation for the miseries we endure. It can also be an organizer, if ever, as the result of a less intimate disappointment, we contemplate taking it seriously. The time is coming when it decrees the end of money and by itself will break the bread of heaven for the earth! There will still be gatherings on the public squares, and *movements* you never dared hope participate in. Farewell to absurd choices, the dreams of dark abyss, rivalries, the prolonged patience, the flight of the seasons, the artificial order of ideas, the ramp of danger, time for everything! May you only take the trouble to *practice* poetry. Is it not incumbent upon us, who are already living off it, to try and impose what we hold to be our case for further inquiry?

It matters not whether there is a certain disproportion between this defense and the illustration that will follow it. It was a question of going back to the sources of poetic imagination and, what is more, of remaining there. Not that I pretend to have done so. It requires a great deal of fortitude to try to set up one's abode in these distant regions where everything seems at first to be so awkward and difficult, all the more so if one wants to try to take someone there. Besides, one is never sure of really being there. If one is going to all that trouble, one might just as well stop off somewhere else. Be that as it may, the fact is that the way to these regions is clearly marked, and that to attain the true goal is now merely a matter of the travelers' ability to endure.

We are all more or less aware of the road traveled. I was careful to relate, in the course of a study of the case of Robert Desnos entitled *Entrée des médiums,* that I had been led to "concentrate my attention on the more or less partial sentences which, when one is quite alone and on the verge of falling asleep, become perceptible for the mind without its being possible to discover what provoked them." I had then just attempted the poetic adventure with the minimum of risks, that is, my aspirations were the same as they are today but I trusted in the slowness of formulation to keep me from useless contacts, contacts of which I completely disapproved. This attitude involved a modesty of thought certain vestiges of which I still retain. At the end of my life, I shall doubtless manage to speak with great effort the way people speak, to apologize for my voice and my few remaining gestures. The virtue of the spoken word (and the written word all the more so) seemed to me to derive from the faculty of foreshortening in a striking manner the exposition (since there was exposition) of a small number of facts, poetic or other, of which I made myself the substance. I had come to the conclusion that Rimbaud had not proceeded any differently. I was composing, with a concern for variety that deserved better, the final poems of *Mont de piété,* that is, I managed to extract from the blank lines of this book an incredible advantage. These lines were the closed eye to the operations of thought that I believed I was obliged to keep hidden from the reader. It was not deceit on my part, but my love of shocking the reader. I had the illusion of a possible complicity, which I had more and more difficulty giving up. I had begun to cherish words excessively for the space they allow around them, for their tangencies with countless other words that I did not utter. The poem "Black Forest" derives precisely from this state of mind. It took me six months to write it, and you may take my word for it that I did not rest a single day. But this stemmed from the opinion I had of myself in those days, which was high, please don't judge me too harshly. I enjoy these stupid confessions. At that point cubist pseudo-poetry was trying to get a foothold, but it had emerged defenseless from Picasso's brain, and I was thought to be as dull as dishwater (and still am). I had a sneaking suspicion, moreover, that from the viewpoint of poetry I was off on the wrong road, but I hedged my bet as best I could, defying lyricism with salvos of definitions and formulas (the Dada phenomena were waiting in the wings, ready to come on stage) and pretending to search for an application of poetry to advertising (I went so far as to claim that the world would end, not with a good book but with a beautiful advertisement for heaven or for hell).

In those days, a man at least as boring as I, Pierre Reverdy, was writing:

The image is a pure creation of the mind.
It cannot be born from a comparison but from a juxtaposition
     of two more or less distant realities.
The more the relationship between the two juxtaposed realities
     is distant and true, the stronger the image will be—the
     greater its emotional power and poetic reality. . . .

These words, however sibylline for the uninitiated, were extremely revealing, and I pondered them for a long time. But the image eluded me. Reverdy's aesthetic, a completely a posteriori aesthetic, led me to mistake the effects for the causes. It was in the midst of all this that I renounced irrevocably my point of view.

One evening, therefore, before I fell asleep, I perceived, so clearly articulated that it was impossible to change a word, but nonetheless removed from the sound of any voice, a rather strange phrase which came to me without any apparent relationship to the events in which, my consciousness agrees, I was then involved, a phrase which seemed to me insistent, a phrase, if I may be so bold, *which was knocking at the window.* I took cursory note of it and prepared to move on when its organic character caught my attention. Actually, this phrase astonished me: unfortunately I cannot remember it exactly, but it was something like: "There is a man cut in two by the window," but there could be no question of ambiguity, accompanied as it was by the faint visual image of a man walking cut half way up by a window perpendicular to the axis of his body. Beyond the slightest shadow of a doubt, what I saw was the simple reconstruction in space of a man leaning out a window. But this window having shifted with the man, I realized that I was dealing with an image of a fairly rare sort, and all I could think of was to incorporate it into my material for poetic construction. No sooner had I granted it this capacity than it was in fact succeeded by a whole series of phrases, with only brief pauses between them, which surprised me only slightly less and left me with the impression of their being so

gratuitous that the control I had then exercised upon myself seemed to me illusory and all I could think of was putting an end to the interminable quarrel raging within me.

Completely occupied as I still was with Freud at that time, and familiar as I was with his methods of examination which I had had some slight occasion to use on some patients during the war, I resolved to obtain from myself what we were trying to obtain from them, namely, a monologue spoken as rapidly as possible without any intervention on the part of the critical faculties, a monologue consequently unencumbered by the slightest inhibition and which was, as closely as possible, akin to *spoken thought.* It had seemed to me, and still does—the way in which the phrase about man cut in two had come to me is an indication of it—that the speed of thought is no greater than the speed of speech, and that thought does not necessarily defy language, nor even the fast-moving pen. It was in this frame of mind that Philippe Soupault—to whom I had confided these initial conclusions—and I decided to blacken some paper, with a praiseworthy disdain for what might result from a literary point of view. The ease of execution did the rest. By the end of the first day we were able to read to ourselves some fifty or so pages obtained in this manner, and begin to compare our results. All in all, Soupault's pages and mine proved to be remarkably similar: the same overconstruction, shortcomings of a similar nature, but also, on both our parts, the illusion of an extraordinary verve, a great deal of emotion, a considerable choice of images of a quality such that we would not have been capable of preparing a single one in longhand, a very special picturesque quality and, here and there, a strong comical effect. The only difference between our two texts seemed to me to derive essentially from our respective tempers, Soupault's being less static than mine, and, if he does not mind my offering this one slight criticism, from the fact that he had made the error of putting a few words by way of titles at the top of certain pages, I suppose in a spirit of mystification. On the other hand, I must give credit where credit is due and say that he constantly and vigorously opposed any effort to retouch or correct, however slightly, any passage of this kind which seemed to me unfortunate. In this he was, to be sure, absolutely right. It is, in fact, difficult to appreciate fairly the various elements present; one may even go so far as to say that it is impossible to appreciate them at a first reading. To you who write, these elements are, on the surface, *as strange to you as they are to anyone else,* and naturally you are wary of them. Poetically speaking, what strikes you about them above all is their *extreme degree of immediate absurdity,* the quality of this absurdity, upon closer scrutiny, being to give way to everything admissible, everything legitimate in the world: the disclosure of a certain number of properties and of facts no less objective, in the final analysis, than the others.

In homage to Guillaume Apollinaire, who had just died and who, on several occasions, seemed to us to have followed a discipline of this kind, without however having sacrificed to it any mediocre literary means, Soupault and I baptized the new mode of pure expression which we had at our disposal and which we wished to pass on to our friends, by the name of SURREALISM. I believe that there is no point today in dwelling any further on this word and that the meaning we gave it initially has generally prevailed over its Apollinarian sense. To be even fairer, we could probably have taken over the word SUPERNATURALISM employed by Gérard de Nerval in his dedication to the *Filles de feu.* It appears, in fact, that Nerval possessed to a tee the spirit with which we claim a kinship, Apollinaire having possessed, on the contrary, naught but *the letter*, still imperfect, of Surrealism, having shown himself powerless to give a valid theoretical idea of it. Here are two passages by Nerval which seem to me to be extremely significant in this respect:

> I am going to explain to you, my dear Dumas, the phenomenon of which you have spoken a short while ago. There are, as you know, certain storytellers who cannot invent without identifying with the characters their imagination has dreamt up. You may recall how convincingly our old friend Nodier used to tell how it had been his misfortune during the Revolution to be guillotined; one became so completely convinced of what he was saying that one began to wonder how he had managed to have his head glued back on.

> . . . And since you have been indiscreet enough to quote one of the sonnets composed in this SUPER-NATURALISTIC dream-state, as the Germans would call it, you will have to hear them all. You will find them at the end of the volume. They are hardly any more obscure than Hegel's metaphysics or Swedenborg's *Memorabilia*, and would lose their charm if they were explained, if such were possible; at least admit the worth of the expression. . . .

Those who might dispute our right to employ the term SUR-REALISM in the very special sense that we understand it are being extremely dishonest, for there can be no doubt that this word had no currency before we came along. Therefore, I am defining it once and for all:

> SURREALISM, *n*. Psychic automatism in its pure state, by which one proposes to express—verbally, by means of the written word, or in any other manner—the actual functioning of thought. Dictated by thought, in the absence of any control exercised by reason, exempt from any aesthetic or moral concern.

> ENCYCLOPEDIA. *Philosophy*. Surrealism is based on the belief in the superior reality of certain forms of previously neglected associations, in the omnipotence of dream, in the disinterested play of thought. It tends to ruin once and for all all other psychic mechanisms and to substitute itself for them in solving all the principal problems of life. The following have performed acts of ABSOLUTE SURREALISM: Messrs. Aragon, Baron, Boiffard, Breton, Carrive, Crevel, Delteil, Desnos, Eluard, Gérard, Limbour, Malkine, Morise, Naville, Noll, Péret, Picon, Soupault, Vitrac.

They seem to be, up to the present time, the only ones, and there would be no ambiguity about it were it not for the case of Isidore Ducasse, about whom I lack information. And, of course, if one is to judge them only superficially by their results, a good number of poets could pass for Surrealists, beginning with Dante and, in his finer moments, Shakespeare. *In the course of the various attempts I have made to reduce what is, by breach of trust, called genius, I have found nothing which in the final analysis can be attributed to any other method than that.*

Young's *Nights* are Surrealist from one end to the other; unfortunately it is a priest who is speaking, a bad priest no doubt, but a priest nonetheless.

Swift is Surrealist in malice,
Sade is Surrealist in sadism.
Chateaubriand is Surrealist in exoticism.
Constant is Surrealist in politics.
Hugo is Surrealist when he isn't stupid.
Desbordes-Valmore is Surrealist in love.
Bertrand is Surrealist in the past.

Rabbe is Surrealist in death.
Poe is Surrealist in adventure.
Baudelaire is Surrealist in morality.
Rimbaud is Surrealist in the way he lived, and elsewhere.
Mallarmé is Surrealist when he is confiding.
Jarry is Surrealist in absinthe.
Nouveau is Surrealist in the kiss.
Saint-Pol-Roux is Surrealist in his use of symbols.
Fargue is Surrealist in the atmosphere.
Vaché is Surrealist in me.
Reverdy is Surrealist at home.
Saint-Jean-Perse is Surrealist at a distance.
Roussel is Surrealist as a storyteller.
Etc.

I would like to stress this point: they are not always Surrealists, in that I discern in each of them a certain number of preconceived ideas to which—very naively!—they hold. They hold to them because they had not *heard the Surrealist voice*, the one that continues to preach on the eve of death and above the storms, because they did not want to serve simply to orchestrate the marvelous score. They were instruments too full of pride, and this is why they have not always produced a harmonious sound.

But we, who have made no effort whatsoever to filter, who in our works have made ourselves into simple receptacles of so many echoes, modest *recording instruments* who are not mesmerized by the drawings we are making, perhaps we serve an even nobler cause. Thus do we render with integrity the "talent" which has been lent to us. You might as well speak of the talent of this platinum ruler, this mirror, this door, and of the sky, if you like.

We do not have any talent; ask Philippe Soupault:

> Anatomical products of manufacture and low-income dwellings will destroy the tallest cities.

Ask Roger Vitrac:

> No sooner had I called forth the marble-admiral than he turned on his heel like a horse which rears at the sight of the North star and showed me, in the plane of his two-pointed cocked hat, a region where I was to spend my life.

Ask Paul Eluard:

> This is an oft-told tale that I tell, a famous poem that I reread: I am leaning against a wall, with my verdant ears and my lips burned to a crisp.

Ask Max Morise:

> The bear of the caves and his friend the bittern, the vol-au-vent and his valet the wind, the Lord Chancellor with his Lady, the scarecrow for sparrows and his accomplice the sparrow, the test tube and his daughter the needle, this carnivore and his brother the carnival, the sweeper and his monocle, the Mississippi and its little dog, the coral and its jug of milk, the Miracle and its Good Lord, might just as well go and disappear from the surface of the sea.

Ask Joseph Delteil:

> Alas! I believe in the virtue of birds. And a feather is all it takes to make me die laughing.

Ask Louis Aragon:

> During a short break in the party, as the players were
> gathering around a bowl of flaming punch, I asked
> the tree if it still had its red ribbon.

And ask me, who was unable to keep myself from writing the
serpentine, distracting lines of this [manifesto].

Ask Robert Desnos, he who, more than any of us, has perhaps
got closest to the Surrealist truth, he who, in his still unpublished works and in the course of the numerous experiments
he has been a party to, has fully justified the hope I placed in
Surrealism and leads me to believe that a great deal more will
still come of it. Desnos *speaks Surrealist* at will. His extraordinary agility in orally following his thought is worth as much
to us as any number of splendid speeches which are lost, Desnos
having better things to do than record them. He reads himself
like an open book, and does nothing to retain the pages, which
fly away in the windy wake of his life. (pp. 3-29)

> André Breton, "Manifesto of Surrealism," in his
> Manifestoes of Surrealism, *translated by Richard*
> *Seaver and Helen R. Lane, The University of Mich-*
> *igan Press, 1969, pp. 1-48.*

ANDRE BRETON

[*The following excerpt is taken from the* Second Manifesto of
Surrealism, *which was written in 1929 and published in book form
in 1930. Much of the second manifesto is devoted to the now-
legendary vilification of former members of the group and to a
defense of Breton's own involvement with the French Communist
Party, for which he was criticized because he had previously
declared the Surrealists' contempt for all existing institutions.
Breton also used this opportunity to reaffirm his belief in the
viability of Surrealism both as a means of creating literature and
as a portal to higher awareness.*]

In spite of the various efforts peculiar to each of those who
used to claim kinship with Surrealism, or who still do, one
must ultimately admit that, more than anything else, Surrealism
attempted to provoke, from the intellectual and moral point of
view, *an attack of conscience,* of the most general and serious
kind, and that the extent to which this was or was not accomplished alone can determine its historical success or failure.

From the intellectual point of view, it was then, and still is
today, a question of testing by any and all means, and of
demonstrating at any price, the meretricious nature of the old
antinomies hypocritically intended to prevent any unusual ferment on the part of man, were it only by giving him a vague
idea of the means at his disposal, by challenging him to escape
to some meaningful degree from the universal fetters. The
bugaboo of death, the simplistic theatrical portrayal of the
beyond, the shipwreck of the most beautiful reason in sleep,
the overwhelming curtain of the future, the tower of Babel,
the mirrors of inconstancy, the impassable silver wall bespat-
tered with brains—these all too gripping images of the human
catastrophe are, perhaps, no more than images. Everything
tends to make us believe that there exists a certain point of the
mind at which life and death, the real and the imagined, past
and future, the communicable and the incommunicable, high
and low, cease to be perceived as contradictions. Now, search
as one may one will never find any other motivating force in
the activities of the Surrealists than the hope of finding and
fixing this point. From this it becomes obvious how absurd it
would be to define Surrealism solely as constructive or destructive: the point to which we are referring is a fortiori that
point where construction and destruction can no longer be bran-

dished one against the other. It is also clear that Surrealism is
not interested in giving very serious consideration to anything
that happens outside of itself, under the guise of art, or even
anti-art, of philosophy or anti-philosophy—in short, of anything not aimed at the annihilation of the being into a diamond,
all blind and interior, which is no more the soul of ice than
that of fire. What could those people who are still concerned
about the position they occupy *in the world* expect from the
Surrealist experiment? Is this mental site, from which one can
no longer set forth except for oneself on a dangerous but, we
think, supreme feat of reconnaissance, it is likewise out of the
question that the slightest heed be paid to the footsteps of those
who arrive or to the footsteps of those who leave, since these
footsteps occur in a region where by definition Surrealism has
no ear to hear. We would not want Surrealism to be at the
mercy of the whims of this or that group of persons; if it declares
that it is able, by its own means, to uproot thought from an
increasingly cruel state of thralldom, to steer it back onto the
path of total comprehension, return it to its original purity—
that is enough for it to be judged only on what it has done and
what it still has to do in order to keep its promises. (pp. 123-24)

[It] is worthwhile to know just what kind of moral virtues
Surrealism lays claim to, since, moreover, it plunges its roots
into life and, no doubt not by chance, into *the life of this period,*

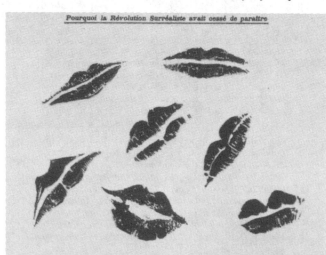

The first page of the Second Manifesto of Surrealism *as it
appeared in the December 15, 1929 edition of* La révolution
surréaliste. *Courtesy of Société Nouvelle des Editions Pauvert.*

seeing that I laden this life with anecdotes like the sky, the sound of a watch, the cold, a malaise, that is, I begin to speak about it in a vulgar manner. To think these things, to hold any rung whatever of this weatherbeaten ladder—none of us is beyond such things until he has passed through the last stage of asceticism. It is in fact from the disgusting cauldron of these meaningless mental images that the desire to proceed beyond the insufficient, the absurd, distinction between the beautiful and the ugly, true and false, good and evil, is born and sustained. And, as it is the degree of resistance that this choice idea meets with which determines the more or less certain flight of the mind toward a world at last inhabitable, one can understand why Surrealism was not afraid to make for itself a tenet of total revolt, complete insubordination, of sabotage according to rule, and why it still expects nothing save from violence. The simplest Surrealist act consists of dashing down into the street, pistol in hand, and firing blindly, as fast as you can pull the trigger, into the crowd. Anyone who, at least once in his life, has not dreamed of thus putting an end to the petty system of debasement and cretinization in effect has a well-defined place in that crowd, with his belly at barrel level. The justification of such an act is, to my mind, in no way incompatible with the belief in that gleam of light that Surrealism seeks to detect deep within us. I simply wanted to bring in here the element of human despair, on this side of which nothing would be able to justify that belief. It is impossible to give one's assent to one and not to the other. Anyone who should pretend to embrace this belief without truly sharing this despair would soon be revealed as an enemy. This frame of mind which we call Surrealist and which we see thus occupied with itself, seems less and less to require any historical antecedents and, so far as I am personally concerned, I have no objection if reporters, judicial experts, and others hold it to be specifically modern. I have more confidence in this moment, this present moment, of my thought than in the sum total of everything people may try to read into a finished work, into a human life that has reached the end of its road. There is nothing more sterile, in the final analysis, than the perpetual interrogation of the dead: did Rimbaud become converted on the eve of his death? can one find in Lenin's last will and testament sufficient evidence to condemn the present policy of the Third International? was an unbearable, and completely personal, disgrace the mainspring of Alphonse Rabbe's pessimism? did Sade, in plenary session of the National Convention, commit a counterrevolutionary act? It is enough to allow these questions to be asked to appreciate the fragility of the evidence of those who are no longer among us. Too many rogues and rascals are interested in the success of this undertaking of spiritual highway robbery for me to follow them over this terrain. When it comes to revolt, none of us must have any need of ancestors. I would like to make it very clear that in my opinion it is necessary to hold the cult of men in deep distrust, however great they may seemingly be. With one exception—Lautréamont—I do not see a single one of them who has not left some questionable trace in his wake. Useless to cite the example of Rimbaud again: Rimbaud was mistaken, Rimbaud wanted to fool us. He is guilty in our eyes for having allowed, for not having made completely impossible, certain disparaging interpretations of his thought, such as those made by Paul Claudel. So much the worse for Baudelaire too ("O Satan . . .") and that "eternal rule" of his life: "to say a prayer every morning to God, *source of all strength and all justice, to my father, to Mariette, and to Poe,* as intercessors." The right to contradict himself, I know, but really! To God, to Poe? Poe who, in the police magazines, is today so properly presented as the *master of*

scientific policemen (from Sherlock Holmes, in fact, to Paul Valéry . . .). Is it not a shame to present in an intellectually attractive light a type of policeman, *always a policeman,* to bestow upon the world a police *method?* Let us, in passing, spit on Edgar Poe. If, through Surrealism, we reject unhesitatingly the notion of the sole possibility of the things which "are," and if we ourselves declare that by a path which "is," a path which we can show and help people to follow, one can arrive at what people claimed "was not," if we cannot find words enough to stigmatize the baseness of Western thought, if we are not afraid to take up arms against logic, if we refuse to swear that something we do in dreams is less meaningful than something we do in a state of waking, if we are not even sure that we will not do away *with time,* that sinister old farce, that train constantly jumping off the track, mad pulsation, inextricable conglomeration of breaking and broken beasts, how do you expect us to show any tenderness, even to be tolerant, toward an apparatus of social conservation, of whatever sort it may be? That would be the only madness truly unacceptable on our part. Everything remains to be done, every means must be worth trying, in order to lay waste to the ideas of *family, country, religion.* No matter how well known the Surrealist position may be with respect to this matter, still it must be stressed that on this point there is no room for compromise. Those who make it their duty to maintain this position persist in advancing this negation, in belittling any other criterion of value. They intend to savor fully the profound grief, so well played, with which the bourgeois public—inevitably prepared in their base way to forgive them a few "youthful" errors—greets the steadfast and unyielding need they display to laugh like savages in the presence of the French flag, to vomit their disgust in the face of *every* priest, and to level at the breed of "basic duties" the long-range weapon of sexual cynicism. We combat, in whatever form they may appear, poetic indifference, the distraction of art, scholarly research, pure speculation; we want nothing whatever to do with those, either large or small, who use their minds as they would a savings bank. All the forsaken acquaintances, all the abdications, all the betrayals in the book will not prevent us from putting an end to this damn nonsense. It is noteworthy, moreover, that when they are left to their own devices, and to nothing else, the people who one day made it necessary for us to do without them have straightway lost their footing, have been immediately forced to resort to the most miserable expedients in order to reingratiate themselves with the defenders of *law and order,* all proud partisans of leveling via the head. This is because unflagging fidelity to the commitments of Surrealism presupposes a disinterestedness, a contempt for risk, a refusal to compromise, of which very few men prove, in the long run, to be capable. Were there to remain not a single one, from among all those who were the first to measure by its standards their chance for significance and their desire for truth, yet would Surrealism continue to live. (pp. 124-29)

Aragon and I were able to note, by the reception given our critical collaboration in the special number of *Varietés,* "Le Surréalisme en 1929," that the lack of inhibition that we feel in appraising, from day to day, the degree of moral qualification of various people, the ease with which Surrealism, at the first sign of compromise, prides itself in bidding a fond farewell to this person or that, is less than ever to the liking of a few journalistic jerks, for whom the dignity of man is at the very most a subject for derisive laughter. Has it really ever occurred to anyone to ask as much of people in the domain—aside from a few romantic exceptions, suicides and others—heretofore the least closely watched! Why should we go on playing the role of those who are fed up and disgusted? A policeman, a few gay dogs, two or three pen pimps, several mentally unbalanced persons, a cretin, to whose number no one would mind our adding a few sensible, stable, and upright souls who could be termed energumens: is this not the making of an amusing, innocuous team, a faithful replica of life, a team of men paid piecework, winning on points?

SHIT.

Surrealism's confidence cannot be well or ill placed for the simple reason that it is not placed. Neither in the palpable world, nor palpably outside of this world, nor in the perpetuity of mental associations which favor our existence with a natural demand or a superior whim, nor in the interest which the "mind" may have in sparing itself our transient clientele. And it is placed even less, it goes without saying, in the shifting fortunes of those who started out by putting their trust in Surrealism. It is not the man whose revolt becomes channeled and runs dry who can keep this revolt from rumbling, it is not any number of men you care to name—and history is hardly comprised of their ascent on their knees—who can keep this revolt from taming, in the great mysterious moments, the constantly renascent beast of "this is better." There are still today, in the lycées, even in the workshops, in the street, the seminaries and military barracks, pure young people who refuse to knuckle down. It is to them and them alone that I address myself, it is for them alone that I am trying to defend Surrealism against the accusation that it is, after all, no more than an intellectual pastime like any other. Let them in all objectivity try to ascertain what it is we have tried to do, let them lend us a hand, let them take our places one by one if need be. It is hardly worthwhile for us to refute the allegation that we ever were interested in constituting a closed circle, and the only persons who may derive any benefit from the propagation of such rumors are those who saw eye-to-eye with us for a brief moment and who were denounced *by us* for redhibitory defect. (pp. 131-33)

I have no idea whether there is any point in my replying here to the puerile objections of those who, calculating the possible conquests of Surrealism in the realm of poetry, where its initial efforts occurred, became worried when they saw it getting involved in the social struggle and maintain that it has everything to lose therein. This is unquestionably sheer laziness on their part, or a round-about way of expressing their desire to circumscribe us. "In the sphere of morality," we believe that Hegel has expressed the thought once and for all, "in the sphere of morality, insofar as it can be distinguished from the social sphere, one has only a formal conviction, and if we mention true conviction it is in order to indicate the difference and to avoid the confusion into which one can slip by considering conviction such as it is here, that is formal conviction, as though it were true conviction, whereas this latter occurs initially only in social life." (*Philosophy of Law.*)

No one needs any longer to be convinced of the adequacy of this formal conviction, and to desire to have us hold to it at all costs does no credit to the honor, to the intelligence, or to the sincerity of our contemporaries. Since Hegel, there is no ideological system that can, without risk of immediate collapse, fail to compensate for the void which would be created, in thought itself, by the principle of a will acting only for its own sake and fully disposed to reflect upon itself. Once I have reminded the reader that "loyalty" in the Hegelian sense of the term, can only be a function of the penetrability of subjective life by "substantial" life, and that, whatever their dif-

ferences may be in other respects, this notion has not met with any serious objection on the part of persons with as widely differing viewpoints as Feuerbach, who ultimately denies consciousness as a specific faculty; as Marx, entirely preoccupied with the need to modify the external conditions of social life from top to bottom; as Hartmann, who managed to derive from a basically pessimistic theory of the unconsciouss a new and optimistic affirmation of our will to live; as Freud, with his ever-increasing emphasis on the primacy of the superego—considering all this, I doubt that anyone will be surprised to see Surrealism turn its attention, in passing, to something other than the solution of a psychological problem, however interesting that problem may be. It is in the name of the overwhelming awareness of this necessity that I believe it impossible for us to avoid most urgently posing the question of the social regime under which we live, I mean of the acceptance or the non-acceptance of this regime. It is also in the name of this awareness that I take a certain degree of pleasure in condemning, by way of digression, those refugees from Surrealism for whom what I maintain is too difficult or too much beyond their reach. No matter what they do, no matter what false cry of joy accompanies their withdrawal, no matter what vulgar disappointment they may have in store for us—and with them all those who say that one regime is as good as another, since in any event man will be vanquished—they will not make me lose sight of the fact that it is not they, but, I trust, I who will enjoy the "supreme" irony which applies to everything, *and to regimes as well,* an irony which will be denied them because it is beyond, but presupposes a priori, the entire voluntary act which consists in describing the cycle of *hypocrisy, probabilism, the will which desires the good, and conviction.* (Hegel, *Phenomenology of the Mind.*)

Surrealism, although a special part of its function is to examine with a critical eye the notions of reality and unreality, reason and irrationality, reflection and impulse, knowledge and "fatal" ignorance, usefulness and uselessness, is analogous at least in one respect with historical materialism in that it too tends to take as its point of departure the "colossal abortion" of the Hegelian system. It seems impossible to me to assign any limitations—economic limitations, for instance—to the exercise of a thought finally made tractable to negation, and to the negation of negation. How can one accept the fact that the dialectical method can only be validly applied to the solution of social problems? The entire aim of Surrealism is to supply it with practical possibilities in no way competitive in the most immediate realm of consciousness. I really fail to see—some narrow-minded revolutionaries notwithstanding—why we should refrain from supporting the Revolution, provided we view the problems of love, dreams, madness, art, and religion from the same angle they do. (pp. 138-40)

It is unfortunate . . . that more systematic and sustained efforts, such as those Surrealism has consistently called for—have not been made in the sphere of automatic writing . . . and the description of dreams. In spite of our insistence that texts of this kind be included in Surrealist publications, and despite the prominent place they do occupy in certain works, we are forced to admit that the interest they arouse is not always sustained, or that they seem a little too much like "virtuoso pieces." The appearance of an obvious cliché in the middle of one of these texts is also completely prejudicial to the kind of conversion we wanted to bring about through them. The fault for this state of affairs stems from the rampant carelessness of the vast majority of their authors who were generally content to let their pens run rampant over the paper without making the least effort to observe what was going on inside themselves—this disassociation being nonetheless easier to grasp and more interesting to consider than that of reflected writing—or to gather together, more or less arbitrarily, oneirical elements with a view to emphasizing their picturesque quality rather than usefully revealing their interplay. Such confusion, of course, is of a kind calculated to deprive us of the full benefit that this sort of thing might provide us with. The main value they offer Surrealism, in fact, is that they are likely to reveal to us specific *logical* expanses, or more precisely those in which the logical faculty, hitherto exercised to the full extent of its powers in the realm of consciousness, does not act. What am I saying! Not only do these logical expanses remain unexplored, the fact is that we still know as little as we ever did about the origin of the *voice* which it is everyone's prerogative to hear, if only he will, a voice which converses with us most specifically about something other than what we believe we are thinking, and upon occasion assumes a serious tone when we feel most light-hearted or deals in idle prattle when we are unhappiest. This voice, moreover, does not submit to the simple need for contradiction.... While I am alone at my table, it talks to me about a man who emerges from a ditch without, of course, telling me who he is; if I become insistent, it will portray him for me fairly clearly: no, definitely, I do not know this man. The time it takes to note this fact, and already the man is lost. *I listen,* I'm far from the *Second Manifesto of Surrealism....* There's no point in offering a multitude of examples; it is the voice that speaks in this way.... Because the examples *drink* ... Sorry, I don't understand either. What would be truly interesting would be to know to what extent this voice is authorized, for example, to find fault with me: there's no point in offering a multitude of examples (and we know, since *Les Chants de Maldoror,* how unfettered and marvelous these critical intrusions can be). When the voice answers me that the examples drink (?) is this a way for the power which assumes it to conceal itself, and if this is true then why does it conceal itself? Was it on the verge of making itself clear at the moment I hastened to take it by surprise without grasping it? A problem such as this is not only of interest to Surrealism. No one, when he expresses himself, does anything more than come to terms with the possibility of a very obscure reconciliation between what he knew he had to say with what, on the same subject, he didn't know he had to say and nonetheless said. The most controlled thought is incapable of doing without this aid which, from the viewpoint of rigor, is undesirable. There really is torpedoing of the idea in the midst of the sentence which is articulating it, even if the sentence were to be free of any charming liberty taken with its meaning. Dadaism had especially wanted to draw attention to this torpedoing. We know that Surrealism, through its appeal to automatism, was involved in sheltering from this torpedoing a building of some sort: something like a Flying Dutchman (the image, which certain people thought they could use against me, however overused it may be, seems good to me, and I use it once again).

It is incumbent on us, I was therefore saying, to try to see more and more clearly what is transpiring unbeknownst to man in the depths of his mind, even if he should begin to hold his own vortex against us. We are, in all this, a far cry from wanting to reduce the portion of what can be untangled, and nothing could be farther from our minds than being sent back to the scientific study of "complexes." To be sure, Surrealism, which as we have seen deliberately opted for the Marxist doctrine in the realm of social problems, has no intention of minimizing Freudian doctrine as it applies to the evaluation of ideas: on the contrary, Surrealism believes Freudian criticism

to be the first and only one with a really solid basis. While it is impossible for Surrealism to remain indifferent to the debate which, in its presence, pits qualified practitioners of various psychoanalytical tendencies against one another—just as it is obliged to consider daily and with impassioned interest the struggle taking place within the leadership of the International—it need not interfere in a controversy which, it would seem, cannot long pursue a useful course except among practitioners. This is not the area in which Surrealism intends to point up the result of its personal experiments. But since by their very nature those individuals who are drawn to Surrealism are especially interested in the Freudian concept which affects the greater part of their deep concerns as men—the concern to create, to destroy artistically—I mean the definition of the phenomenon known as "sublimation," Surrealism basically asks these people to bring to the accomplishment of their mission a new *awareness,* to perform an act of self-observation, which in their case is of very exceptional value, to compensate for what is insufficient about the penetration of so-called "artistic" states of mind by men who for the most part are not artists but doctors. Moreover, Surrealism demands that, by taking a path opposite from the one we have just seen them follow, those who possess, in the Freudian sense, the "precious faculty" we are referring to, bend their efforts toward studying in this light the most complex mechanism of all, "inspiration," and, from the moment they cease thinking of it as something sacred, Surrealism demands that, however confident they are of its extraordinary virtue, they dream only of making it shed its final ties, or even—something no one had ever dared conceive of—of making it submit to them. There is no point in resorting to subtleties on this point; we all know well enough what inspiration is. There is no way of mistaking it; it is what has provided for the supreme needs of expression in every time and clime. It is commonly said that it is either present or it is not, and if it is absent, nothing of what, by way of comparison, is suggested by the human cleverness that interest, discursive intelligence, and the talent acquired by dint of hard work obliterate, can make up for it. We can easily recognize it by that total possession of our mind which, at rare intervals, prevents our being, for every problem posed, the plaything of one rational solution rather than some other equally rational solution, by that sort of short circuit it creates between a given idea and a respondent idea (written, for example). Just as in the physical world, a short circuit occurs when the two "poles" of a machine are joined by a conductor of little or no resistance. In poetry and in painting, Surrealism has done everything it can and more to increase these short circuits. It believes, and it will never believe in anything more wholeheartedly, in reproducing artificially this ideal moment when man, in the grips of a particular emotion, is suddenly seized by this something "stronger than himself" which projects him, in self-defense, into immortality. If he were lucid, awake, he would be terrified as he wriggled out of this tight situation. The whole point for him is not to be free of it, for him to go on talking the entire time this mysterious ringing lasts: it is, in fact, the point at which he ceases to belong to himself that he belongs to us. These products of psychic activity, as far removed as possible from the desire to make sense, as free as possible of any ideas of responsibility which are always prone to act as brakes, as independent as possible of everything which is not "the passive life of the intelligence"—these products which automatic writing and the description of dreams represent offer at one and the same time the advantage of being unique in providing elements of appreciation of great style to a body of criticism which, in the realm of art, reveals itself to be strangely helpless, of permitting a general reclassification of lyrical values, and of proposing a key capable of opening indefinitely that box of many bottoms called man, a key that dissuades him from turning back, for reasons of self-preservation, when in the darkness he bumps into doors, locked from the outside, of the "beyond," of reality, of reason, of genius, and of love. A day will come when we will no longer allow ourselves to use it in such cavalier fashion, as we have done, with its palpable proofs of an existence other than the one we think we are living. We will then be surprised to realize that, having come so close to seizing *the truth,* most of us have been careful to provide ourselves with an alibi, be it literary or any other, rather than throwing ourselves, without knowing how to swim, into the water, and without believing in the phoenix, plunging into the fire to reach this truth. (pp. 157-63)

André Breton, "Second Manifesto of Surrealism," in his Manifestoes of Surrealism, *translated by Richard Seaver and Helen R. Lane, The University of Michigan Press, 1969, pp. 117-87.*

PHILOSOPHIC, AESTHETIC, AND POLITICAL PRINCIPLES

HENRI PEYRE

[*Peyre is a French-born critic who has lived and taught in the United States for most of his career. One of the foremost American critics of French literature, he has written extensively on modern French literature in works that blend superb scholarship with a clear style accessible to the nonspecialist reader, most notably in* French Novelists of Today *(rev. ed. 1967). Peyre is a staunch defender of traditional forms of literature that examine the meaning of life in modern society and the role of individual destiny in an indifferent universe; he dislikes experimentalism for its own sake, noting that "many experimenters are the martyrs of a lost cause." Peyre particularly disagrees with critical trends that attempt to subsume literary analysis under the doctrines of restrictive theories, such as those of structuralism. Regarding his critical stance, Peyre has written that "there is no single approach that is infallible or systematically to be preferred when dealing with literature. Pluralism seems to me to be a far more fruitful attitude. . . . Any dogmatism, while it may provide the lover of systems with a cheaply acquired consistency and unity of point of view, soon proves detrimental to the most varied of human pursuits—the pursuit of beauty, truth, and 'greatness' in works of art. Fiction . . . sets everything in motion in us: our senses . . . , our sensibility, our intellect, our religious, philosophical, and social views, our aesthetic joys, our desire to know ourselves better and to penetrate other lives. Any approach to the novel, therefore, that is honest and intelligently sustained is valid if it draws us nearer to the work of art or its creator." For these reasons, Peyre has utilized several different approaches in his criticism—aesthetic, biographical, philosophical, political, and social. In the following excerpt from an essay written in 1964, he examines the Surrealists' philosophical tenets and literary goals in order to assess the importance of Surrealism as an intellectual movement.*]

Surrealism is likely to occupy a very considerable place in the intellectual history of the Western world in our century. Its significance as a literary phenomenon during the years 1920-1940 is unequalled. Ever since 1940, when powerful and occasionally unfair blows were dealt it by Sartre, as trenchant a polemicist as he is subtle a dialectician, Surrealism has staged a surprising comeback. It refused to concede victory to the Existentialist movement, which was impatient to bury it along with other hollow idols of an antediluvian or pre-Sartrian age. Breton returned from his American exile, shook his lion's mane in Montmartre, rallied new disciples, excommunicated others as he explained how only the mythical and magical ambitions of the Surrealists could bring any hope of salvation to a decrepit world. The release of Desire and the triumph of Love were the new levers which could move mountains of unbelief and hatred.

Several books appeared in the aftermath of World War II telling the history of the Surrealist group, delving into the intricacies of its successive negations and assertions, assessing the results of its pictorial and poetical achievements. A Surrealist exhibition at the Maeght Gallery in Paris in 1947 was more than a review of twenty-five years of Surrealist revolt; it brought home to many Parisians the tragic gravity which underlay most of the Surrealists' eccentricities and the bitter confirmation which their blasphemies had received from the war. Surrealism, which has received inadequate attention in this country, is one of the most far-reaching attempts at changing, not only literature and painting, but psychology, ethics, and man himself.

A span of fifteen years, *grande mortalis aevi spatium,* as Tacitus said of old, was enough to shift the emphasis from the turbulent aspect of the Surrealist movement to its deeper and lasting significance. In 1925, there were few indeed who saw in it anything more than a return to infantilism and nihilism. In 1940, its hoaxes and pranks were almost forgotten; one had to acknowledge that to Surrealism we owed one of the greatest prose writers of our age, André Breton; three or four of the purest poets—Eluard, Char and Desnos; and even an impure but occasionally brilliant one—Aragon; and several gifted painters. Surrealism was always more than a strictly literary and artistic movement; it influenced interior decoration and the film, our sensibility, our imagination, perhaps even our dreams. It left an imprint upon psychology and metaphysics; it spread to five or six European countries and to other continents. It may be that the adjective Surrealist will remain affixed to the whole era between the two World Wars as best describing its boldest ambition. It would be neither more nor less appropriate to that age than the word Symbolist as applied to the years 1880-1900.

For many a name may rightly be associated with Surrealism which never was actually on the select list of the initiates. Several of the early adepts broke away from the sanctum, or were rejected from it. Others, like Reverdy and Michaux, never actually joined the group. But posterity will disregard such fine distinctions. It calls "Romantic" men like Balzac and Michelet who never belonged to any Romantic *chapelle* ["school"], others like Delacroix who vehemently rejected the label and would have nothing to do with Balzac and Baudelaire, others still like Vigny who soon estranged themselves from the *cénacles* ["coteries"]. In spite of their probable protests, which death will some day silence, insuring the triumph of those modest but inevitable victors, the literary historians, we may consider as Surrealists the following men: Breton, Aragon, Soupault, Péret, Hugnet, Desnos, Crevel, Artaud, Naville, Tzara, Eluard, Michaux, Reverdy, Bataille, Prévert, Césaire, Gracq, Monnerot, Leiris. The list is far from exhaustive. . . . Among the painters are Miró, Max Ernst, Chirico, Tanguy, Picabia, Masson, Man Ray, Magritte, Matta, Arp, etc. And, of course, Salvador Dali—*quantum mutatus ab illo!* ["how changed from what he once was!"] He has, since the heroic age, become the butt of Breton's most venomous arrows and, among the faithful, has assumed the mock scrambled name of

Avida Dollars. Nonetheless, the number of other talents is impressive.

Iconoclasts, in France at least, take good care to find illustrious predecessors who posthumously sponsor their audacity. One of the most considerable achievements of Surrealism was its discovery that many writers and painters of the past had been Surrealists without knowing it: Sasseta, Hieronymus Bosch, Blake, Achim von Arnim, E. A. Poe, and others. They renovated the perspective in which some of the intercessors, or exciters, of Surrealism were henceforth to be viewed. It is now impossible, and hardly desirable, to deprive Sade, Nerval, Lautréamont, Rimbaud, Jarry and Apollinaire of the new stature that Surrealism has lent them. They will eternally remain as precursors of Surrealism, as Rousseau is a forerunner of Romanticism and Baudelaire a herald of Symbolist experiments.

Among the ancestors whom they worshipped, the first place belongs to Lautréamont; for, at the beginning, the Surrealists remained strangely reticent about Rimbaud. The rehabilitation of that forgotten prose-poet is one of their durable achievements. "To that man belongs probably the chief responsibility for the present condition of poetry," Breton declared, implying that the condition was Surrealist, hence admirable. Maldoror, Lautréamont's hero, was hailed as "the one name flung across the centuries as an unadulterated challenge to all that on earth is stupid, base, and sickening." From him they learned a lesson of courage, finding guidance perhaps in a statement he had prophetically announced in 1869 before his mysterious disappearance at the age of twenty-four: "At this very hour, new flashes of lightning race through the intellectual atmosphere; what is wanted is only the courage to face them steadily." With Lautréamont as their *duce e signore* ["lord and master"] they descended into vertiginous pits of hell, wandered among devilish nightmares, systematically cultivated monstrous hallucinations. Jarry's bitter buffoonery took on a new meaning when the Surrealists reinterpreted it as a derision of the old bourgeois ramshackle structure which collapsed with the war of 1914. Ubu Roi was, for Breton, "an admirable creation for which I would give all the Shakespeares and the Rabelais in the world." Apollinaire's message, expressed less in his verse than in his *Cubist Painters* and in a masterly article on "Poets and the New Spirit," published three weeks after his death in *Mercure de France* (1st December 1918), was bequeathed to the Surrealists who were the first to divine its significance. The role of the artist is to become inhuman; he must look for what in art has "most energy," scorn facile charm, leap forward and assert the claims of poetry and painting to explore the world of the future, claims which are prior to those of philosophy, psychology, and science. The enigmatic Jacques Vaché is the last patron saint of Surrealism; his influence on Breton was chiefly through conversation and the strangeness of his personality. For Vaché did not condescend to write anything, except a few striking war letters to his friend; he lived with a woman to whom he never said a word, only kissing her hand in noble silence after she had poured tea; he derided literature as a vain occupation ("aiming so conscientiously in order to miss the mark") and asserted that all was vain in life. He renounced it in 1919 when, along with two young Americans, he absorbed an inordinate dose of opium.

We shall not be concerned here with the history of the Surrealist sect, with its confused political affiliations, with its painters, nor with any attempt to define the claims of the Surrealists as they would themselves view them or wish to see them defined. We would rather, with the help of a few quotations and some acquaintance with the essential Surrealist texts, endeavor to point out the deeper significance of Surrealism. Eccentricities, excesses, childish mysticism, an obsession with fortuitous coincidences in life, and sheer mediocrity in paintings, films, and poems are to be found in abundance in Surrealism; they will be forgotten. The credit side of the movement is important enough for us to disregard some ephemeral littleness and to forgive some adolescent provocations.

Every literary or philosophical movement may be said to include a negative and a positive aspect. The two are developed simultaneously, but may be envisaged separately for clarity's sake. The young men who rally under some new banner agree with relative ease on what they negate; their hunger for destruction is all-embracing. They joyfully trample under their feet the legacy of previous generations. It is harder for them to find a common ground for their positive assertions. If they have any personality, they are likely to listen to their own temperaments and to plunge into heresy if a set of positive dogmas is proposed to their literary faith.

The negative side of the Surrealist revolt was stressed by the adepts of the group with a ferocious and systematic intransigence which, in the third decade of the century, caused the hair of many a bourgeois to stand on end. Yet even then it took no exceptional clearsightedness to sense that a desperate search for a new faith lay beneath the vehement blasphemies of Breton and his friends. Their uncommon energy would not long be satisfied by mere fist-shaking. The Surrealist revolt is to be compared to the Cartesian *tabula rasa,* or brushing aside of previous confused growth in order to lay new foundations for a sounder and more ambitious structure. There always remains much logic behind any French attempt at illogic and an almost immoral passion for morals behind any Gallic denunciation of conventional ethics. The Surrealists are no exception. They are logicians and moralists primarily.

Their revolt, which appeared to be undiscriminating and universal, differed in fact from the nihilism of Dada. It concentrated on three targets which we may define as ethics and religion, the social and political realm, and literary conventions.

In the matter of religion, Breton never wavered; and extremely few, if any, of the former Surrealists ever joined the ranks of Catholic converts. There was the curious conversion to Surrealism in 1926 of the priest, Gengenbach, which provides one of the most ludicrous episodes in the movement's history. Gengenbach had previously fallen in love with an actress and consequently been unfrocked by his bishop. But the actress found him no longer attractive when he ceased to wear a cassock; the former priest, in despair, went with suicidal intentions to the lake at Gerardmer where he glanced at a Surrealist review and saw the light. This curious individual attempted to reconcile Surrealism and Christianity. He failed, ended by denouncing Breton as Lucifer, and turned again to the faith of his childhood. He is not typical, for the Surrealists' unconcern with God is even more pronounced than that of the Existentialists.

In an interview, Breton even spurned the Nietzschean phrase "the death of God" as meaningless, since "to die, one should first have existence." Yet, like many adversaries of religion, like Nietzsche himself in his tragic *Ecce Homo,* Breton is an impious rival of Christ rather than a negator. His disciple Monnerot did not err when he asserted that Surrealism aims at a total transformation such as had only been attempted by religions; and Breton liked to quote Tolstoy's words: "What truth can there be, if there is death?" A religious critic, Michel

Carrouges, writing in the Dominican periodical *La Vie Intellectuelle* in November 1945, exemplifies the reactions of several latitudinarian French Catholics when he declares:

> Surrealism is no empty hoax; it is not necessarily
> demoniacal as is sometimes imagined; it is a great
> invention of the modern world still in its infancy. . . .
> It is perhaps the most extraordinary movement of the
> human spirit . . . the most terrible mental explosive
> in existence.

On the moral plane, too, the Surrealist pronouncements were calculated to shake our complacency; they were occasionally accompanied by determined and perverse attempts at demoralization of the youth—with lamentable success. "Morality, that weakness of the brain," a line of Rimbaud's *Season in Hell* had exclaimed. To the Surrealists, moral censorship practiced against the impulses of our unconscious had to be abolished in order that a new peace, according to Freudian therapeutics, might invade our being, and still more in order to liberate our imagination. Breton and Eluard acclaimed Sade as the prophet of the new ethical crusade. But they were soon to draw the lineaments of a new ethics, far removed from hedonist indulgence and resting on a lofty conception of desire and of love. When Breton broke with the Communists, it was clearly on moral grounds and because "moral sense was undeniably the human reality which their party trampled daily and most gleefully underfoot." Much earlier, in his volume *Les Pas perdus* (1924), that immoralist had confessed his love for all moralists, and added: "The moral question preoccupies me. . . . *La morale* is the great peacemaker. Even to attack her is to pay her a tribute. In her did I always find my most exalting inspiration."

In the field of politics, the fierceness of the Surrealist protest is best understood if one remembers that it originated during World War I. And in many ways that war shook the minds of men more powerfully than did World War II. For it burst out after a prolonged era of peace and material progress during which Europeans had become accustomed to celebrate civilization and science as undeniably beneficent. Suddenly they were faced with the glaring bankruptcy of science, of logic, and of their faith in progress, of philosophy and literature which failed to protest against the great massacre and often undertook to justify it. The Surrealists were impressed by the gaping abyss which separated man's power to change the world through science and his utter inability to change himself. They became convinced that there must exist, behind what we call reality or behind the conventional layers of our minds, forces which control us. Surrealism would attempt to discover those forces and to liberate them, if they could be harnessed for man's benefit.

To the Surrealists, and especially to Breton, we are indebted for some of the most moving and intelligent denunciations of war and its glamor. The cure for the monstrous evil is to be sought in the liberation of the imagination, in fulfilling by other means the boundless needs for childhood, for joy, for risk and for play, for intense emotions, which insidiously lead men to consent to collective murder. The Russian Revolution appeared to the Surrealists, as it did to many liberals in Europe, as the great hope for a new era of justice and fraternity. Their disillusion was all the more bitter when that Revolution turned to nationalism and the worship of Stakhanovist efficiency. Their sympathies went to Trotsky, who had proved understanding toward literature and had boldly announced that "the Revolution undertakes to conquer the right of all men, not only to bread, but to poetry." "Bread and also roses," Jaurès had,

before 1914, demanded for the working classes. From 1930 or thereabout, most of the Surrealists turned against Stalinist Communism and rejected a revolution deprived of idealism and "serving to improve that abominable thing, earthly comfort" (Breton). But they did not desist from their fight against any conservatism, whether it came from the right or from the left. "More than ever do I believe in the necessity of transforming the world in the direction of the rational (more exactly, of the surrational) and of justice," Breton declared in an important interview given to *Une Semaine dans le monde* (31st July 1948).

But it is easier in France to rise in revolt against political institutions, social and ethical conventions, and, of course, against any government, than to be a literary rebel. Most liberals, from Voltaire to P. L. Courier and Anatole France, most radicals, socialists, and anarchists had always remained the most orthodox guardians of the purity of the French language and timid conservatives in matters of taste. Breton, Aragon, and Éluard have not "twisted the neck" of the French language; they have paid frequent tribute to their predecessors and have at times revived among us the shades of the Troubadours or the cadences of seventeenth century prose. But they dared attack pitilessly realism and its platitudinous dullness, eloquence always lurking behind poetical writing, above all logic which, under the guise of the detective novel, has staged an insidious offensive in the last three decades; for the detective novel is naively based upon the assumption that there is a cause or an agent for all that happens, and it banishes the inexplicable and the gratuitous from our world. Against the novel and its attraction for money-minded writers of today Surrealism restored the claims of poetry. Breton saw the novel as a prosaic game of chess with a contemptible adversary, "man, whoever he is, being only a mediocre adversary." He added scornfully, "the ambition of novelists does not reach very far."

But Surrealism did more than restore poetry. It rebelled against the very notion of culture and revealed to many moderns the strange beauty of Negro sculpture and of African and Polynesian masks. It ridiculed the concept of good taste which tends to constitute a barrier to any innovation and systematically kills the annexation of provinces of ugliness to the realm of the beautiful. The Surrealists reveled in the epic monstrosities of bad taste—"in the bad taste of our age, I endeavor to go farther than anyone else," Breton once wrote—and extracted new flowers of evil from that horrifying paradise hitherto reserved for concierges, *pompiers* ["firemen"], and other philistines. The last stronghold of the élite, which is its conviction that its esthetic values would survive wars, revolutions, and financial loss of caste, that good taste is the one tyrannical evidence before which men will always bow, was stormed in the Surrealist ranks.

"Only the word liberty can still produce a state of exaltation in man." This famous cry of Breton provides a key to a just appreciation of the positive achievement of Surrealism. Liberty, or rather the pursuit of a total liberation, is the keyword of its doctrinal pronouncements.

Surrealism wanted to liberate the subconscious. Its direction was thus clearly parallel to that taken earlier or at the same time by Freud, Proust, and Joyce. Unlike Proust, however, it avoided superimposing a complex structure of didactic reasoning and of refined analysis upon an attempt to capture those mysterious moments when man, escaping the inexorable flow of time, reaches the "peak of sovereignty." Unlike Freud, to whom Breton owed much, the Surrealists did not advocate bringing to the light of clear consciousness, and dissipating eventually, the strange growth of complexes in our turgid depths. Much was made, in the early stages of Surrealism, of automatic writing, uncontrolled by reason or by critical spirit, which gave itself out as spoken and written thought seized in its spontaneous immediacy. In fact, the leading Surrealists never abused that perilous device. Their verse and their prose give evidence of elaborate composition, of skillful combination of effects, of a restrained choice made among the riches of the unconscious. But their originality lay precisely in having first proceeded to a courageous clearing of all that was worn out and effete in literature, and in having made a fresh selection from a new and vast accumulation of materials hitherto unexplored. Literature tends to utilize passively only the stones already quarried, hewn and polished by robust predecessors; it must periodically spurn such tempting and neatly arranged materials and carve out its own rock. In so doing, Surrealism occasionally hit upon sparkling gems. Its will to innovate was not a mere effort after originality; it was a resolute attempt to explore a virgin expanse in or under man's mind and to dig into the hidden layers in which the civilized creature cannot dissemble or lie, as he does in his so-called "rational," or diligently controlled life.

The second ambition of Surrealism was to open up to literature the domain of dreams, and even of insanity, strangely neglected but for a few feeble trials by classical and modern writers to depict dreams of tragic characters, Hamlet's, Hermione's, or Tasso's methodical madness. In the dream, the Surrealists respected what Reverdy called "a freer and more uninhibited form of thought." They reveled in its inconsistencies, in its capricious disregard of causality, in the vividness of its images. They explored its symbolic secrets as revealing remnants of a primitive mentality only imperfectly repressed in ourselves. Not a little of the beauty of Éluard's and Char's poetry is due to its dreamlike atmosphere. Breton went farther and resumed Nerval's century-old attempt to "direct his eternal dream instead of passively submitting to it." His volume, *Les Vases communicants,* contains the most splendid description of fantastic dreams written since Nerval's record of his madness in *Aurélia.* Dreams are no longer the privilege of sleep; daydreams are no longer mild, idyllic reveries. The realms of night and of day, sleep and wakefulness, hold a constant and fruitful interchange; the dream is respected and its luxuriance of images faithfully transcribed, while it is also interpreted and analyzed by a mystic trained in physiology and psychology. "I stand in the hall of a castle, a dark lantern in my hand, and I illuminate the sparkling armors one after the other." Thus Breton, the former medical intern, describes himself in the opening pages of his *Vases communicants.*

The twofold liberation of the subconscious and of the oneiric domain leads to a third: the unchaining of the imagination. The Surrealists are the faithful heirs of Baudelaire and Rimbaud and, beyond them, of Coleridge, Blake, Novalis, and Achim von Arnim. They have enthroned the "magical and synthetic power" as the goddess of their works; and to them, as to the English Romantics, the "renascence of wonder" became the highest achievement of the poet, recapturing the gifts of childhood in adult life.

Through an apparently spontaneous flow of images, Surrealism thaws the crust of blunted perceptions and of deductive reasoning which separates us from our deepest life and from the remnants of childhood buried in our subconscious. It maps out whole archipelagoes long submerged in a sea of dulled habit.

It plunges below our intellectual vision of the world and beyond our sensory data; it seems to "see into the life of things" and to forge new and closer links between ourselves and so-called inanimate objects. The normal translation of those uncharted lands into which Blake and Rimbaud had ventured is effected through a new metaphoric language. One of the chief claims to greatness of Surrealist poetry lies, in our opinion, in its imagery. That poery has replenished the threadbare stock of metaphors by which Hugo's successors and French Symbolists had long been content to live. Reverdy, a poet whom the Surrealists have always respected even though he did not join their ranks, wrote:

> An image is a pure creation of the mind. . . . It springs from the linking of two realities more or less distant. The more unexpected and just the relations between the two realities thus linked are, the more powerful the image, the greater its emotive force and its poetical truth.

The poetry of Breton and Eluard—and even that of minor figures like Tzara and Hugnet—abounds in rare and fresh images which seem to create the object anew for our blunted senses and to allow a dreamworld to glide gently into our consciousness, first shaken, then voluptuously lulled, by the discontinuous flow of Surrealist metaphors.

The Surrealists' endeavor to bring about a total renewal of the very mainsprings of literature has nowhere proved more courageous, and more startlingly successful, than in their treatment of love.

Love between man and woman had almost disappeared from literature after 1920. It happened that the leading figures of that literary era—Proust, Gide, Cocteau, and even Montherlant and Julien Green—were only slightly interested in heterosexual relations or in the "promotion of woman," as sociologists were pleased to call it. The war had, moreover, created many causes of friction or of misunderstanding between the sexes, and the "virile fraternity," cherished by Malraux and Saint-Exupéry, appeared nobler to many former or future soldiers than any sentimental and intellectual union with women, with whom young men often felt out of tune. An affectation of brutality and of cynicism had replaced the former rhetorical delusions of romantic love. Women, by winning new rights and meeting men on an equal footing in many a profession, seemed to have waived their former privilege as inspirers of artists and of poets.

Surrealism rehabilitated woman and love poetry in our midst. It would be naive to present the Surrealists as Platonic worshippers of spiritual beauty, or as hypocritical enough to conceal eroticism behind romantic adoration. They had read Sade even more than Musset. There is more Petrarchist inspiration, in Eluard especially, than there is Platonism. Yet they have ceased to exile woman from poetry, as Rimbaud and his followers had attempted to do, or to worship and abuse her alternately as a vessel for all the treacheries of Satan, in Baudelarian fashion. Aragon's war poetry, more faithful to the Surrealist creed than his former friends were willing to acknowledge, sang the most rapturous hymns chanted to woman since the Romantics. Eluard may well rank among the three or four supreme love poets in the French language. His theme is a continuous transfiguration of woman in her body and in her mysterious and dreamy charm.

> Toute tiède encore du linge annulè
> Tu fermes les yeux et tu bouges
> Comme bouge un chant qui naît
> Vaguement mais de partout

Odorante et savoureuse
Tu dépasses sans te perdre
Les frontières de ton corps

Tu as enjambé le temps
Te voici femme nouvelle
Révélée à l'infini.

[Fully warm still from discarded linen
You shut your eyes and stir
As stirs a song born
Vaguely but from all sides

Fragrant and redolent
You go without losing yourself beyond
The borders of your body

You have leaped beyond time
And are now a new woman
Infinitely revealed.—Translated by Henri Peyre]
("Une Longue Pensée amoureuse")

Breton's love poetry does not rise to such felicitousness of musical language, but one of his finest prose works, *L'Amour fou,* is devoted to a triumphant exaltation of love as the great constructive force. He does not indulge in any such mysticism of the flesh as do intoxicated Puritans like D. H. Lawrence and inverted woman-haters like Henry Miller. But he rarely chides men for stupidly despairing of love, for imagining, once their youth is over, that love lies behind them, in their brief adolescent years, while it is there "waiting for them, in front of them." Desire, or Eros, the old Hesiodic name of the earliest of the gods, must be emancipated and become the level which will achieve men's imaginative liberation from the mechanical forces which have made him a willing slave to tyranny and to war.

Surrealism, however, was more than an exploration of new literary realms or a rediscovery of the old theme of love. Beyond its literary or pictorial claims, it was and is a metaphysical perception of the tragic sense of human life and a desperate attempt to leap beyond the bounds usually assigned to human reason. In this respect, not only is it parallel to its jealous rival, Existentialism, but it must be linked, willy-nilly, with other significant movements of our age, whether religious (Kierkegaard) or para-religious (Kafka, Malraux, Camus), equally obsessed with the all-pervading tragedy of man's fate in a world from which man had vainly tried to banish tragedy.

The originality of the French Surrealists lies here in their insincerity. For, behind their youthful pranks and their delight in mischief and mystification, they were in truth passionately intense young men, venturing to the verge of insanity and suicide. One of their former members, Antonin Artaud, who died in 1948, spent years, as did Nerval, in an insane asylum; Eluard, always lucid and one of the most classical of poets, had to take refuge in another insane asylum and to pose as one of the deranged inmates in order to escape capture by the Germans for his activity in the French Resistance. Vaché, a precursor, had ended his life in 1919; one of the young Surrealist affiliates, Rigaut, killed himself in 1929, after writing a last message to his companions: "You are all poets and I am on the side of death." René Crevel, the gifted and promising author of a disturbing book, *Etes-vous fous?,* resorted to suicide in 1935 as "the most final of all solutions." Benjamin Péret, one of the earliest inspirers of the group, denounced modern society and lived in solitude. Breton tirelessly branded as cowardice the compromise which accepts the present conditions, social and metaphysical, of our existence. In "Poetic Evidence" (in *Donner à voir,* 1939), a remarkable essay, Eluard declared: "Somber are the truths which appear in the work of true poets; but truths they are, and almost everything else is lies."

But Surrealist literature does not wallow in pessimism. It never consents to despair, never delights in reviling man as naturalism and even Parnassian poetry had done. It plunges into the abysses of man's unconscious only in order to emerge with reasons for living more imaginatively, more authentically. It illuminates whatever may be sordid and animal in us with the rays of poetry and of dream. After opposing an inflexible *no* to the insidious temptation to accept man's fate as it is, it attempts to carry man far above his mediocre rational self into an impetuous dash of revolt. The crucial Surrealist assertion of this kind was made in 1930 in the second Surrealist manifesto [see excerpt above]. It asked man to think outside of and beyond the principle of contradiction, to break the shackles of logic, to bring out of opposite objects and contradictory concepts a deeper unity. Hegelian and Marxist dialectics was not unknown to Breton when he wrote these lines, but he leaped beyond their technical subtleties into the purer regions of poetical faith:

> Everything leads to the belief that there exists a certain point in the mind from which life and death, the real and the imaginary, the past and the future, what is communicable and what is incommunicable, the high and the low, cease to be perceived as contradictory. Vainly would one assign to Surrealist activity another ambition than the hope to determine this point.

Again, in *Les Vases communicants,* Breton proclaimed:

> The poet of the future will surmount the depressing idea of an irreparable divorce between dream and action. He will offer the magnificent fruit of the tree with tangled roots and will persuade those who taste it that there is no bitterness in it.

There, in our opinion, lies the deeper significance of Surrealism. On one side, the movement has staged an ardent revolt against all literary conventions, and chiefly against effete images and conventional rhetoric which encumber a great mass of nineteenth century literature. It has striven toward a language deprived of eloquence and of sumptuous draperies, closely molded on reality or surreality. In this sense, Surrealism is only one aspect of the most determined attempt of French literature since Rimbaud and Mallarmé: an attempt to pierce the screen of language and to render words so transparently lucid and pure as to let objects and feelings meet us directly. Eluard, Reverdy, and Char, the supreme poets of Surrealism, have accomplished what critics like Paulhan, Blanchot, and Picon would define as the great obsession of the moderns: the creation of a literature that is nonliterary. In its form, Surrealism is thus far remote from outdated Romanticism.

In its content, however, Surrealism must be regarded as a powerful Romantic offensive. Our age fondly imagines that it has buried the illusions of the Romantics beneath its own positive preoccupations, its cynicism, its resigned acceptance of man as a creature made up of animal impulses. It has only momentarily repressed its Romanticism and is unwittingly preparing a tidal wave of Romantic revolt, which is likely to put an end to all the pseudo-scientific claims of the novel, criticism, psychology, and sociology of the last few decades. The recent evolution of Surrealism is, in this connection, prophetic. Julien Gracq, celebrated by Breton as the most brilliant new recruit of Surrealism, has revived the Romantic novel of the English pre-Romantics. Eluard's late poetry delights in sensuous litanies in praise of woman which recall the Romantic bards even more than the metaphysical poets, for irony is not among the goddesses courted by the Surrealists. Péret proclaimed Romanticism as the first great revolutionary movement in poetry. And Breton has become the apostle of mystical union with nature as superior to any knowledge of nature:

> Scientific knowledge of nature can only be valuable if *contact* with nature through poetical, I would even say mythical, ways is re-established. (*Le Figaro*, October 1946).

Like the Romantics, the Surrealists, obsessed with frantic revolt, with the breaking of all moral and social conventions, occasionally attracted by suicide, have in truth aspired toward a total renewal of man. They have aimed at provoking first a grave intellectual and moral crisis in modern man, so as to shake him out of his complacency. Then they forced the locomotive of the human spirit off the rails of logic and reason and lured imagination to the heights where it can soar freely and meet the unknown, away from the mediocre and dull province of what is known and understood rationally. The impatience of Breton and his friends with ordinary, contented man springs from a boundless faith in the possibilities which man ignores or represses in himself. Their aim is not to create a Nietzschean superman, but to give noble and affirmative answer to the Nietzschean question echoed by M. Teste: "Of what is man capable?" "A man who has never tried to make himself equal to the gods is less than a man," said the creator of M. Teste. If he is right, the Surrealists have proved to be more than ordinary mortals. They have asserted most loudly in our century man's ability to change himself, and the extraordinary, almost magical, role that literature can play in effecting that change. To quote André Breton once more:

> Human life would not be for many of us the disappointment it is if we constantly felt ourselves capable of accomplishing acts above our strength. It seems that miracle itself can be within our reach.

(pp. 23-36)

Henri Peyre, "The Significance of Surrealism," in Yale French Studies, No. 31, May, 1964, pp. 23-36.

HERBERT S. GERSHMAN

[*Gershman was an American critic and educator who specialized in French literature of the nineteenth and twentieth centuries. In the following excerpt from his 1969 study* The Surrealist Revolution in France, *he examines the literary and extraliterary methods by which the Surrealists sought to attain spiritual revelation.*]

The surrealist aesthetic can be reduced to one theme: the attempt to actualize *le merveilleux* ["the marvelous"], the wonderland of revelation and dream, and by so doing to permit chance to run rampant in a wasteland of bleak reality. Not *le mystère* ["mystery"], the willful introduction of obscurity into art and life, which to Breton was a confession of weakness, but the lucidity that is a product of conviction and which will bind men together in a faith against which reason must falter and ultimately succumb. This private heaven could be attained in several ways, and the surrealists tried them all at different times. Taken together these several attempts help explain the evolution of the movement from the starveling, internecine revolt against Dada in the early twenties to its present Cheshire cat sleekness.

A penchant for the absolute is not peculiar to surrealism. Much of Baudelaire, for example, reflects this same longing for an

effortless beautitude—what T. S. Eliot called (with reference to Baudelaire) his "leave-taking poetry" or "waiting-room poetry." And whether this new land to which he is going, where "all is ordered and beautiful, / Luxurious, calm and voluptuous," is a heaven or a hell, we must of necessity "Dive to the depths of the abyss . . . in our never-ending search for *something new*." No sooner is the poet baffled by the maze of reality, no sooner does he succumb to the complexity, the irrationality (the absurdity) of existence, the so-called tragic sense of life, than there wells up the temptation to seek refuge in the trash cans of familiar myths, in the manner of Beckett. Where Baudelaire naively sought revelation "through forests of symbols," Rimbaud proposed a path through the forest, a technique—deliberate sensory confusion—which would permit the inspired poet to storm the gates of his Dionysian heaven. Mallarmé, despairing of locating a paradise beyond the blue, set out to create one, a purely formal, verbal one. Proust worked out his salvation in the past, in the realm of pure being where nothing changes, except as our memory (involuntary or other) so wills it. Valéry spied his amorphous will-o'-the-wisp heaven at each turn of a thought: could he but fix its shape, describe its relationship to man, then salvation, were it nothing more than dissolution in his own thought, would be his.

Surrealism is essentially a multi-faceted method for eliciting revelations, and as such it is indeed the prehensile tail of romanticism that Breton once termed it. There is, first in both time and importance, the much discussed and often mocked technique of automatic writing. The effort of choice, of decision, here gives way to the facility of free association—Protean chance bound by the silken threads of caprice, drowned in the inky well of unconscious objectivity. Where Valéry sought to observe his *Moi*, to enclose his thought in a coat of alexandrine mail, the surrealists became willing receptacles for the oracle, mimes of dark frenzy, to paraphrase Valéry. If the liberated (or tortured, if one prefers) syntax of the surrealists has no parallel in the 1920's, it has many parallels in the poetry of Mallarmé and his disciples. The element of mystery inherent in the surrealist world, where dreams fulfill wishes and words mean more than they seem to (charged as they are with emotional and erotic overtones), has only a distant analogy in the romantic wonder at the grandeur of the universe, but does recall the tales of Villiers and Lautréamont's enigmatic *Chants de Maldoror* (1869). It is therefore no great surprise that the surrealists, as passive toys of an other-world message, welcomed the aid of mediums. Given a choice between the limitations of reason and the calm conviction of spiritism, they opted for a mystic flight, one which would take them to the frontier where Being and Nothingness clasp uneasy hands and nonconformity touches on insanity. We have come a long way from the nihilism of Dada and its exuberant spoof of a prim, smug, and Prudhommesque society, one which could neither fight a just war nor win a decent peace. Now that the old tale of values had been smashed, thanks to Dada, new ones had to be found—or rather revealed, so as to give them their proper sacred character.

Yet as Breton himself admitted, neither automatic writing nor recourse to mediums was regularly effective or a sure way of inducing any persuasive series of oracles. What was required was a more intimate revelation, one that would passionately and eternally commit the small chosen clan of surrealists. Such was the role to be played by love, by the myth of the child-woman (*la femme-enfant*) and mad love (l'amour fou). To the surrealists love was an advanced form of automatism, the bolt from the blue canonized, normalized to a way of life, a vivid objectification of chance. It would free man from humdrum

*Photograph of Tristan Tzara taken in 1921 by Man Ray.
Copyright ARS NY/ADAGP.*

reality, lead to new discoveries, to the intimate possession of
new worlds; it ignores logic, encourages dreams, and rescues
the ideal from its season in hell, brings it to earth in an em-
braceable body and soul. In a word it fixes a goal for the *poésie
des départs* ["poetry of departures"], puts an end to that period
of waiting which is our life. But surrealism was destined to
remain millennial promise and the surrealists themselves seekers more than finders. In their search, however, lay their literary
salvation.

This new mythology, recalling the neo-Platonists more than
the romantics, had as its specific goal the conjuring up of an
earthly paradise. Between 1925 and 1935, the leaders of the
group, sporadically occupied with politics, had found little time
for the elaboration of earlier theoretical positions. The earthly
paradise, during the decade in question, was thought to be
attainable by essentially political means. But with Breton's
article "Revelation versus Mystery" (1936) and the more explicit *Mad Love* (1937) a new turning becomes manifest. Themes
little in evidence since "Here Come the Mediums" (1922) and
"Introduction to a Lecture on Reality and Its Limits" (1924)
are suddenly picked up and developed. Specifically love—not
simply love as the high point of life, the physical fusion of
dream and reality, but love as a myth, one of the exalting and
incredible myths which will send one and all to lay siege to
the unknown." The importance of love in literature is too
obvious to need illustration; its rejuvenating qualities and so-

cially revolutionary effects are equally evident, if less often
referred to specifically. This *amour fou*, as Breton called it,
invariably shatters the daily routine that society has so laboriously set up for the individual and implies that happiness,
the exaltation that gives a measure of value to life, can be
found beyond the traditional frame of family, work, and community effort. When the Beloved (*l'idole*), Dreams (*le rêve*),
and Poetry (*la poésie*) are deemed as necessary to life as the
air one breathes, then the divinization of love is a *fait accompli*.

This mythology of love is new in two important respects. It
differs from the neo-Platonic conception in fixing the idealization on earth: the party loved is of flesh and blood; there is
no beyond. On the other hand it differs from the Stendhalian
amour-passion in being something more than crystallized passion. The person loved has the attributes of the Bride of Saint
John of the Cross; she is the *idole*, as Mme Sabatier was to
Baudelaire, as Bouton de Chamilly was to the *religieuse por-
tugaise,* Maria Alcaforado. "All myths," as Péret said, "reflect man's ambivalence both with regard to the world and with
regard to himself. . . . The vital element in a myth is the striving
after happiness which one finds there. . . . They express, in
short, the feeling that there is a duality in nature, and in man,
duality and paradox which he is not likely to resolve in his
lifetime." When faced with an example of *amour sublime* (or
fou), society's initial reaction is normally condemnation, for
the two persons involved are capable of any action, however
antisocial, in the pursuance of their goal. Religion must of
necessity condemn it, for it tends to "replace God by man"
and make available to man a happiness in which religion has
had no part.

Having experienced little but deception in their attempts "to
change our way of life" and "to transform the world" by
militant political means, the surrealists hit upon another approach: rather than accept a political myth not of their own
making, they determined to refurbish one with deep roots in
poetry and in the world of dreams, the twin realms of language
and desire. That this myth of *l'amour fou* has often been confused by the public with eroticism is unfortunate. Not that the
surrealists were averse to eroticism or indeed to any exotic
attempt to arouse or reveal desire—one of their many international exhibitions was devoted to that very theme. But the
common elements are their unconscious origin and their anti-
social posture: *le merveilleux* and the almost religious moral
elevation of the one are completely absent from the other.
Neither, of course, should be confused with pornography, which
is eroticism travestied, the very antithesis of sublime love.

This conscious myth-making on the part of the surrealists (of
which *l'amour sublime* is but one example), this raising of the
femme-enfant to a position comparable to that held by Mary
in the Church, is not without its dangers. The surrealists have
long been manifest-happy, and were it not for the quality of
related literary productions—the poems of Eluard and Desnos,
the stories of Péret and Aragon, the longer works of Breton,
Crevel and others—these incurable pattern-makers would have
left no enduring mark on the intellectual slate. For a while it
was not clear that the movement had escaped the creeping
monadism that seemed to be overcoming it, that it had not
indeed taken refuge in a cloud of bogus mysticism, with talk
of magic, intoxicating exuberance, and hallucinatory throbbing
of misplaced heartstrings. But in the context of the aims of the
group, and these have evolved within guidelines that were clear
from the very beginning, the myth of *l'amour sublime* is seen
as a literary weapon designed to defend the individual at his

most intimate from a society become oppressively addicted to routine and, at the same time, to offer to society an illusion capable of both revivifying and liberating it. (pp. 1-5)

To the surrealists their method was their miracle, and as prophets glorying in the political gloom of the twenties and thirties, for whom all tenses paled save the future, they attracted an audience by proclaiming verities immune to logic, though not for that reason necessarily false: that free association was intrinsically superior to traditional, presumably commonplace association, and that the collage of intellectual debris, randomly ordered, was superior to a work produced by recourse to any traditional discipline. The conviction so common to the true believer, and which bobs uneasily in the wake of occult phenomena, lit their path. And so was born the original ash-can school of unconscious wits, one which became strikingly effective in incorporating into literature a domain previously (and illogically) excluded. Love was their latest and greatest mystery, a treasure trove of limitless surprises. Amenable neither to logic nor to common sense, resisting reality more efficaciously than even a medium's pronouncements, it led directly to heaven, violently on occasion, and with complete indifference to social norms. It is the one-man revolution, for the partner is of no great importance, any more than he (or she) is in the writings of the neo-Platonists. In a nutshell, it converts dream to reality without ever changing either.

If automatic writing, spiritism, and *l'amour fou* are the major surrealist weapons for releasing revelation from the wall of mystery surrounding us, they are not the only ones. Almost from the very beginning the surrealists devoted what must have seemed to onlookers as an inordinate amount of time to games. "Play," as Huizinga wrote in *Homo Ludens,* "is a function of the living, but is not susceptible of exact definition either logically, biologically or aesthetically." It is a voluntary activity, which removes it from the realm of the unconscious, but at the same time it serves to shut out reality as formal truths always shut out the world.

> Play is distinct from "ordinary" life both as to locality and duration. . . . It contains its own course and meaning. . . . Just as there is no formal difference between play and ritual, so the "consecrated spot" cannot be formally distinguished from the play-ground. The arena, the card-table, the magic circle, the temple, the stage, the screen, the tennis court, the court of justice, etc., are all in form and function playgrounds, i.e. forbidden spots, isolated, hedged round, hallowed, within which special rules obtain. All are temporary worlds within the ordinary world, dedicated to the performance of an act apart. . . . Play demands order absolute and supreme.

Huizinga then goes on to define the special position that play occupies in life: it requires that its rules, arbitrary though they are, be accepted without question; it promotes the formation of social groupings in its nonserious undertakings and, at the same time, serves to divorce each playful group from others surrounding it. Breton and his group could have served as models for that portrait.

To the surrealists games were a method by means of which they might detach themselves from the world, a gesture meaningless in the context of "ordinary" life, but pointing toward a social distinction and suggesting a distinctive metaphysical outlook. For many of the same reasons that the typical romantic wore his hair long (as did Breton) and the dandy, ever conscious of his role in the world, set himself apart by his foppish attention to his clothes, so the surrealists did not hesitate to

distinguish themselves by their numerous and often exotic games. These were a gesture of defiance directed at the world of reality, a thumbing of the nose at adult (utilitarian) logic, a retreat to a paradise where the liberty so loudly proclaimed in other spheres could not possibly obtain, for, to quote Huizinga again, the least deviation from the rules of the game "robs it of its character and makes it worthless." The beauty of a game lies in its being so clearly, so irrevocably ordered. No trespassing of the rules is permitted at the risk of denying the game, of breaking the magic circle, of opening the hothouse doors to the cold wind of the world beyond. The game, in short, is a formal construction which shuts out one reality while creating another, more nearly ideal one. (pp. 9-10)

The triumvirate of automatic writing, spiritism, and love stormed the gates of Wonderland directly. Play was more oblique. It created an artificial paradise closed to outsiders and, for the time of the game, within the rules of the game, gave free reign to chance, which no throw of the dice could ever abolish. Or perhaps it would be more accurate to say that automatic writing and its two avatars wooed *le merveilleux,* while play created it anew at each moment. Play, the art form of the rebel, is the rigid mask of the aesthete. It is liberty itself (always, however, within the confines of the game), for the real world is in no way involved. It relaxes the tense by displacing the tension. It frees the fool from the sentence of history, makes man a God and bloats his stomach with hope. It was, in a word, a divine artifice to which the surrealists were not insensitive.

The concept of total liberty, along with the practice of automatic writing and games, was of vital importance to the group: at any moment these pure spirits might have to demonstrate, either by word or deed, their detachment from things mundane. The *concept* of liberty, however, rather than its practice, was primary. If I think I am free then I am, and the irons which bind my body are unable to bind my thoughts, my soul. In a world in which everything is possible, even revelation, anything is possible, including freedom in slavery. The surrealists not only saw pie in the sky but insisted that they partook of it. "Only liberty still thrills me," wrote Breton in his first *Manifesto* [see excerpt above], the liberty to shut his eyes and, by so doing, annihilate the world, for, he implied, his imagination knew no limits. This is the freedom to make of one's life a work of art as did, say, the dandy in the nineteenth century, if only superficially, or the Sun-King in the seventeenth. Liberty, here, rejoins play and becomes pure form, a new version of the creative imagination. Bit by bit we see the elaboration not of a hoax, as is on occasion put forward, but of a myth, whether it be that of the pythoness in Breton's *Nadja* or of the *femme-enfant* in much of Eluard's poetry. Its goal is ever the same: to reorient reality. Will you play at being mad? There is *L'Immaculée conception* and its passages simulating the writings of those suffering from a variety of mental illnesses. Will you play at being God? The surrealists' refusal to recognize the world is matched only by Kafka's hunger artist caught in a web of his own creation, convinced that the game will indefinitely shut out reality. "Inspire me," says Breton, invoking a mythical Orient, "so that I may become he who has no shadow." So might have spoken the hunger artist had he a goal other than the crowd's admiration or a less finicky palate. If man's freedom is to be something more than a simple physical phenomenon, then it must include that part of him which dreams and is capable of flights of fancy which, for being wild, are nonetheless human. "The mind of the man who dreams," wrote Breton, "is at peace with its environment." The dream is as real as the other reality, and indeed has the additional advantage of permitting us to strut uninterrupted through the night. The terrors of the night become *ours* as those of our waking hours rarely can. One must be quite sensitive, or perhaps sensitized, to perceive the *incredible* which surrounds us—the very pattern of our existence—where others see only a mundane reality. For the surrealist there is no *fantastic*, there is only reality, and the stranger it seems the more revealing and valuable it becomes: "Revelation is always beautiful, every revelation is beautiful, indeed nothing but revelation is beautiful." It almost seems on occasion that the entire surrealist movement, its numerous theoretical positions and even more numerous collections of poetry, stories, and essays, has as its principal purpose the conquering of the romantic *ennui* by a *beau rêve* ["beautiful dream"] or a *beau geste* ["beautiful gesture"]: the never-ending embrace with the divine Lady of one's dreams, or the threat of wildly firing a revolver into a crowd. These formal dandies, delicate murderers, and exalted lovers lived naked on a stage performing rites designed to capture a harmony that could only have existed before the Fall. Their essence lay in their mask, in their play, and was the product of a glance.

Liberty, to the surrealists, has a pronounced negative aspect—or perhaps it would be more accurate to say that it recalls the principles and goals of [David] Riesman's inner-directed man. If it seeks martyrdom and oracular revelation, at the same time it denies the world and man's flesh and blood existence. How else can one explain the scorn for the innocent (though worldly) crowd, the scattered scandalous gestures which separate the surrealist elect from the *vulgus* ["rabble"], the numerous political interventions, but always as an independent force, except for their brief flirtation with the Communist Party? The surrealists were the elect, in their own eyes, if only by dint of frequent communion with the unconscious oracle; all others were to a greater or lesser extent compromised, crassly so, with the world. A gesture, however, regardless of its nobility, its disinterestedness, regardless even of its consequences, is futile in isolation, without a coherent doctrine to lend it meaning. In the battle for a better world it is what fireworks are to an artillery attack, illumination without substance.

In the crisis of sensibility which begins with romanticism, surrealism was but another attempt to resolve the logically irreconcilable, to fill by fiat the void of Being. Its most impressive conquest, according to Robbe-Grillet, was its ability to highlight, to bring to the attention of a blasé public, the wonder of daily life: "The most ordinary phenomena are therefore, in all probability, the most revelatory, the most striking." If indeed their most impressive conquest is

> To see a world in a grain of sand,
> And a heaven in a wild flower,
> To hold infinity in the palm of your hand,
> And eternity in an hour,

then we have not come far from Blake's *Auguries of Innocence*. But to Breton, "What is eye-opening about the fantastic is that there is no fantastic, there is only reality." The Englishman and the Frenchman here join hands.

Surrealism was born of a desire to wrest from the unknown knowledge born of revelation, *le merveilleux*. This was its origin and its aesthetic. Adding together the two axioms that nothing but *le merveilleux* is beautiful and that to be beautiful something must be *convulsive*, it seems clear that the intimate sense of the movement from its very beginnings has had extraliterary implications. When literature lost its ancient meaning, saw its function as servant to God and crown disappear,

its continued existence was called into question. For some, no class, no group or ideal merited their allegiance: hence the bacchanale that was Dada. The surrealists, however, recognized early the pointless and ultimately dreary circularity of spoofing the ridiculous, of parodying the pompous, of mocking society, themselves included. Had they been able, they would have pulled the trigger of Kirilov's gun, or Vaché's, tossed bombs as did Malraux's Chen and Desnos' anarchist friends. Instead their revolt was dissipated in two distinct directions: (1) toward the creation of new myths out of whole, if imaginary cloth, using Freudian techniques as a sort of springboard—and here they were well served by the cacophonous trio of automatic writing, mediumistic pronouncements, and the sensual anarchy, the *dérèglement de tous les sens* ["disorder of all the senses"] produced by a passionate commitment to love; (2) given the new social myths, they moved toward a radical Marxist interpretation of society, less for the purpose of elevating the proletariat, with which they had no extensive contact, than for bringing down, for casting into hell, their bourgeois brothers who were still untouched by surrealist grace.

Concomitant with the creation of new myths, or the refurbishing of old ones, came an ever-increasing reliance on games. These too could serve to elicit *le merveilleux* and so fill bleak reality with a pack of suggestive revelations. Man is a god in his games; they are his creation. Once in the game, however, his hands are tied, unless he is willing to be a spoil-sport and so destroy this thing of pure form. But the surrealists were not spoil-sports; games were to them a way of life:

> How many evenings did we spend lovingly creating a race of *cadavres exquis!* . . . All cares were banished, all thought of our poverty, our boredom, all thought of the outside world. We played with images and there were no losers. Everyone wanted his neighbor to win, and to continue winning ever more until he had everything. No longer was revelation an outcast. Its features disfigured by passion seemed far more beautiful to us as a group than when we are alone, for when we are alone we are struck dumb by our vision.

So wrote Eluard. The surrealists were actors on a mirrored stage, and were their roles sufficiently well played then the play itself would become life and life the shadow cast by the play. Each gesture counted, each word. Those who felt obliged to acknowledge the reality of the outside world, if only for the purpose of seeking employment without which they could not live, were soon excluded. Into the Ubu-like *trappe* went all those expelled, be it for literary, political, or financial reasons: Soupault, Desnos, Vitrac, Artaud, Aragon, Tzara, Eluard. No hunger artist, committed to his fast, can ever admit that existence may well precede essence in importance. Committed to a certain technique of revelation, the sole granting access to paradise, the true believer rarely can look kindly upon those who, once having seen the light, turn their backs upon it to follow other stars.

The belief in liberty, total and uncommitted liberty, subsumed everything the surrealists did or attempted. It was implicit in Dada, which saw the world as a scandal and itself as an irreverent gadfly or parodist. This liberty can never be assigned. It is the Church's free will and Gide's *disponibilité* ["availability"] combined and suggests that in life every act is gratuitous and every encounter meaningful. The world thus becomes a web of *hasards objectifs* ["objective chances"] in much the same way that for an earlier generation it was a forest of symbols. This sacred liberty, this "desire for *complete* freedom,'' whose shifting swamps are strewn with specters and soluble fish, prophecies of doom and at least a half-dozen suicides successful or attempted, is more a function than a thing and, alone, would be incapable of storming a heaven, even a surrealist heaven. For refusing to accept this limitation the surrealist adventure could not but end in a baroque failure, except paradoxically in the realms of art and literature, where its wonderland techniques blew up the desires innate in all of us into a shimmering balloon large enough to be easily recognized and gaudy enough to appeal. When the cardboard sphinx of traditional values was scornfully rejected, nothing was left to serve as a measuring rod, except perhaps a shadowy impressionism, which the Voltaires of all time have distrusted and the Rousseaus embraced. Surrealism brought the Unconscious into the world of letters, where it will likely remain long after the debate over the merits of the movement has subsided to an academic drone, or to paraphrase Philip Rieff, long after mortician professors conclude their attempt to let the blood out of its ideas. (pp. 10-15)

> Herbert S. Gershman, *"Toward a Definition of the Surrealist Aesthetic,"* in his The Surrealist Revolution in France, *The University of Michigan Press, 1969, pp. 1-15.*

J. H. MATTHEWS

[*Considered one of the foremost scholars of Surrealism, Matthews was a Welsh critic who wrote more than twenty-four books and numerous articles on that subject. In the following excerpt, he discusses the Surrealists' political involvement, finding the source of their revolutionary ideals in their iconoclastic aesthetic philosophy.*]

[From] the first, a pressing need to oppose a society built on reason, in which bourgeois values flourished, led the surrealists to promote revolutionary ideals by every means available. At the beginning, naturally, these ideals were not formulated with impeccable clarity in terms directly applicable to politics. Yet, although they remained vague initially, surrealist aspirations were openly and aggressively antagonistic to the existing social and political order. Publishing their first magazine, the Paris group called for ''a new declaration of the rights of man'' and titled the official organ of their movement *La Révolution surréaliste.* When *La Révolution surréaliste* (1924-29) was replaced by a second magazine, the latter's title also underscored surrealism's dedication to the cause of revolution: *Le Surréalisme au service de la Révolution* was to run between 1930 and 1933.

Even before 1930, the French surrealists had evidenced a strong attraction to the Left. (Of the first-generation members in France, Aragon, Breton, Eluard, Péret, and Unik joined the Communist Party in January 1927, but only Aragon and Eluard, in the end, were to choose in favor of communism.) However, so far as their dealings with the political opponents of the Right went, they manifested a certain amount of caution. More than one surrealist brought misgivings to discussions with the group that published the para-communist newspaper *Clarté.* This is to say that those who have recounted the history of surrealism's involvement with communism have placed insufficient emphasis upon the following fact. Idealism, rather than deficient foresight, prompted the Paris surrealists to look, despite obvious dangers, for common ground with those directing *Clarté* and, through them, with the Party. Conditioned by enthusiastic responsiveness to dialectical materialism, the surrealists, Breton was to remark in *Entretiens,* were guilty of ''too much pre-

cipitation.'' Schuster put it more forcefully when he attributed their behavior to naiveté. Whether naive or merely precipitate, the early surrealists in France gave dramatic proof of their sincere wish to parallel their efforts in favor of poetic liberation with participation in a movement having the declared purpose of advancing social and political emancipation.

Time has shown that since the twenties the surrealists have never attempted to propose a system of political thought all their own. Their interest in revolutionary endeavor on the plane of political and social militancy has been consistently proportionate to their belief that such an endeavor increases man's prospects of attaining complete freedom. Political and social oppression, at all events, is regarded in surrealist circles as the equivalent of the limitations imposed on poetic expression through verse by rationally controlled language and rules of prosody. Accordingly, liberty in the field of political self-determination is considered an accompaniment to the freedom that is an essential prerequisite for poetry in the widest sense entertained by surrealists.

As surrealists see it, conformity to imposed opinion in matters of politics is no less reprehensible than conformity, in verse, to accepted custom with regard to ethical, moral, or aesthetic issues. For this reason, whenever a member of the surrealist group has elected to place fidelity to some political cause before his obligations to surrealism, he either has found it advisable to part company with the surrealists of his own accord, or has found himself repudiated by them. The surrealists have remained adamant on this subject, ever since finding out for themselves the consequences of seeking compromise between their program of poetic liberation and that program of social and political revolution we know as the version of Marxism defended within the Communist Party.

Essentially, surrealists in France were victims of a misunderstanding upon which agreement with communism appeared, at first, both practical and efficacious. In two years of organized and purposeful activity, following the appearance of Breton's first manifesto [see excerpt above], members of the surrealist movement in France had concluded that poetry could not find complete liberation within the framework of complacent bourgeois society. So, in 1926, Breton's *Légitime Défense* asserted, ''There is not one of us who does not wish power to pass from the hands of the bourgeoisie into those of the proletariat.'' However, in his very next sentence, Breton went on to insist upon the need for preserving independence of action: ''In the meantime, it is no less necessary, in our opinion, for the experiments in inner life to go on, without any external control, naturally, even Marxist control.''

The line seemed to have been plainly drawn, to mark once and for all the point beyond which surrealists would refuse to be led. Yet when, the following year, Breton and several of his associates decided to enter the Party, the author of *Légitime Défense* took his text off the market, ''out of loyalty to the Communist Party,'' as *Entretiens* explains. Despite this and other tokens of their readiness to submit to Party discipline, the surrealists were regarded with suspicion by those in command, ever distrustful of the bourgeois origins of their new French recruits. Moreover, the surrealists were found guilty of distracting preoccupations that reduced their efficiency in advancing the immediate purposes of communism in France, when they did not impede these altogether. These preoccupations, needless to say, grew out of the surrealists' determination to pursue their own purposes—those of poetic liberation—in their own way. In consequence, dissension was inevitable, and not long delayed.

Having sought to escape the servitude imposed by the class-thinking to which they were born, the French surrealists found themselves facing the alternative of substituting for submission to bourgeois values unquestioning obedience to communist imperatives. Before long, they had learned a painful lesson they would never forget. While the *Second Manifeste du Surréalisme* [see excerpt above] reaffirmed faith in the principles of dialectical materialism, Louis Aragon's surrender of independent creative action to Party policies inspired horror in those who continued to be faithful to the author of both surrealist manifestoes. In 1932, Aragon's exclusion from the surrealist camp publicly marked the abandon of hopes of reaching an understanding with the communists. Within six years, André Breton had co-signed *Pour un Art révolutionnaire indépendant*.

Appearing for tactical reasons over the signatures of Breton and Diego Rivera in Mexico, on July 25, 1938, *For an Independent Revolutionary Art* was written by Breton and Leon Trotsky. It characterized true art as that which "tries to give expression to the inner needs of man and of humanity today," and as, by definition, revolutionary. Looked at this way, art becomes, in surrealist perspective, synonymous with poetry. For revolutionary art, said Breton and Trotsky, aspires to "a complete and radical reconstruction of society," incidentally "releasing intellectual creation from the chains that impede its activity." One observer has asked, "Can Trotsky really have signed this document?" But he quite rightly showed no surprise at Breton's having done so. The basis upon which the 1938 tract was erected is the one on which surrealists had wanted to build, from the first. Acknowledging that social revolution alone can "clear a path to a new culture," *Pour un Art révolutionnaire indépendant* expressed aversion for the ruling classes in contemporary USSR. The faith it went on to affirm is the one from which surrealist aspirations have never ceased to take flight—identification of the need for emancipating the spirit with "that primordial necessity," the need for emancipating man. And the conclusion drawn from this postulation is no less consistent with the surrealist posture: "It follows that art cannot consent without falling into decay to bend to any external directive and to fit meekly into the framework that some people believe they can assign it, for extremely short-sighted pragmatic ends."

Lest they be accused of indifference to political responsibility, Trotsky and Breton insisted they had no intention of pleading for so-called "pure" art, which they dubbed reactionary. "We consider that the supreme task of art in our time is to participate consciously and actively in preparing revolution." "Giving artistic incarnation to his inner world," the artist will make his contribution most effectively by emphasizing his individuality, they argued, not by stifling it in a cause to which he has abdicated the right to speak in his own name. All forms of artistic commitment, from social realism to Sartrian *engagement*, are rejected *a priori*. Meanwhile, confidence goes entirely to the revolutionary force that reflects individual poetic vision, such as gives the writings of Péret—an anarchist militant, as it happens, who took inspiration from Trotsky—a quality Breton and other surrealists have recognized very willingly as irreplaceable and inimitable.

The purpose behind *Pour un Art révolutionnaire indépendant* was clear enough to see: it appealed for promotion of revolution through art, or poetry, while guaranteeing art and poetry liberty in the face of "the usurpers of revolution." It marked the establishment of a Fédération internationale de l'Art révolutionnaire indépendant, more notable for its declared aims than for what it had the chance to accomplish in the short time before the war broke out in 1939: "*independence of art—for revolution; revolution—for the definitive liberation of art.*" In collaborating on the 1938 tract, Breton had reaffirmed that, as a surrealist, he identified political pragmatism and opportunism with rationalism, seeing them as equally limitative, so far as revolutionary action goes; just as rationalism appeared to him and his fellow surrealists to restrict thought, and to channel the poetic venture into unproductive byways. At the same time, he reaffirmed the surrealist belief that, if political and social freedom is a prerequisite for the liberation of the mind, it can never be the end to which all mental effort should be bent, since it does not, of itself, guarantee the mental freedom surrealists hope to see man attain thanks to poetry.

The collapse of France and the establishment of the Vichy Government, whose Censor deferred permission for Breton's poem *Fata Morgana* to be published, made it necessary for several of the surrealists to flee France. Upon his release from internment in Martinique, Breton made contact with Aimé Césaire in Fort-de-France, where in April 1941, Césaire had founded his magazine *Tropiques*. In the review edited by Césaire, his group's sympathies with surrealism were manifest from the first. As Suzanne Césaire explained, "Thus, far from contradicting, attenuating, or diverting our feeling for revolutionary living, surrealism trains it on its target." When we look back to the forties, most deserving of special attention, however, is that the surrealists then became fully convinced that political activism, aimed at ameliorating social structures and remedying or even eradicating their weaknesses, could not provide all the answers they were seeking. (pp. 138-44)

By the time Breton returned to France in 1946, it had become plain that reconciliation of the Marxist program, as summarized in the dictum "transform the world," with the ambition the surrealists had inherited from Rimbaud, "change life," could not be achieved simply by willingness on the surrealists' part to come to terms with this or that socio-political program for reform. As a result of their re-examination of the problem facing them, surrealists gave up their search for a solution in the political arena. They looked to another, alternative line of conduct, squarely faced in the catalog of the international surrealist exhibition of 1947, held in Paris to celebrate the reconstruction of the surrealist group in France.

In reality, no sudden change took place in surrealist policy with respect to the world about us. Looking back to 1935 and the preface Breton wrote then for his *Position politique du Surréalisme*, we can see he was already speaking of having been preoccupied for ten years with "bringing together surrealism as *a mode for creating a collective myth* with the much more general movement for liberating man which tends first of all to modify fundamentally the bourgeois form of property." Finding the price of this undertaking too high, the surrealists quite naturally fell back on their original program, underlined by Breton himself in the statement just cited. At almost twenty years' distance, two international surrealist exhibitions have offered their evidence of the surrealists' attempt to define a myth suited to our time. The article "Devant le Rideau," written by Breton to open the catalog of the 1947 exhibit, is of central importance in this connection. No less significant is the catalog *L'Ecart absolu*.

No reader of the French surrealist magazines could fail to notice how often reference is made to Saint-Simon, to the Abbé Constant, to Enfantin, and to Flora Tristan, during the fifties and sixties. Furthermore, Breton's last major poetic work was his *Ode à Charles Fourier* (1947), written in 1945. Prior to his stay in the United States, Breton had been interested in Fourier mainly as the advocate of social reform. Not until he purchased the 1846 edition of Fourier's complete works in New York, did he discover "the great poet of harmonious life" lauded in the *Ode*. For the next two decades, the influence of Fourier widened and deepened, not only upon Breton but also upon his entourage: the surrealist magazine which appeared only after Breton's death, *L'Archibras* (1967-68), was so called as a tribute to the author of *La Théorie des quatre Mouvements*.

The significance of surrealist revulsion before political activism and the surrealists' growing preference for the promises of nineteenth-century utopianism cannot be overestimated. Nor, though, must it be interpreted as a sign of the collapse of their hope of contributing, here and now, to improving man's situation. The specifically ideological tenor of the 1965 international exhibition, the surrealists insisted in a broadsheet, *Tranchons-en,* dated December 1965, was deliberately intended to "attack *directly* the most intolerable aspects of the society in which we live." Moreover, they pointed out, "Nothing having been able to reduce us by *assimilation* to a religious sect, to a political party or a literary coterie—or, over the years, to really break our unity and our capacity for renewal—those whom we disturb can no longer hope to drown surrealism in the confusion from which they derive profit and glory." (pp. 144-46)

> *J. H. Matthews, in his* Toward the Poetics of Surrealism, *Syracuse University Press, 1976, 241 p.*

ALBERT CAMUS

[*An Algerian-born French novelist, essayist, dramatist, and short story writer, Camus was one of the most important literary figures of the twentieth century. Throughout his varied writings, he consistently, often passionately, explored his major theme: the belief that people can be happy in a world without meaning. He defended the dignity and decency of the individual and asserted that through purposeful action one can overcome the apparent nullity of human existence. His notion of an "absurd" universe is premised on the tension between life in an irrational universe and the human desire for rationality. Although this worldview has led Camus to be linked with the Existentialists, he rejected this classification. In the following excerpt, Camus analyzes the intellectual rebellion inherent in Surrealist philosophy, noting in particular the internal contradictions that ultimately led to the failure of that creed as an ethical guide.*]

Absolute rebellion, total insubordination, sabotage on principle, the humor and cult of the absurd—such is the nature of surrealism, which defines itself, in its primary intent, as the incessant examination of all values. The refusal to draw any conclusions is flat, decisive, and provocative. "We are specialists in rebellion." Surrealism, which, according to Aragon, is a machine for capsizing the mind, was first conjured up by the Dadaist movement, whose romantic origins and anemic dandyism must be noted. Non-signification and contradiction are therefore cultivated for their own sakes. "The real Dadaists are against Dada. Everyone is a director of Dada." Or again: "What is good? What is ugly? What is great, strong, weak. . . .? Don't know! Don't know!" These parlor nihilists were obviously threatened with having to act as slaves to the strictest orthodoxies. But there is something more in surrealism than standard nonconformism, the legacy left by Rimbaud, which,

in fact, Breton recapitulates as follows: "Must we abandon all hope at that particular point?"

An urgent appeal to absent life is reinforced by a total rejection of the present world, as Breton's arrogant statement indicates: "Incapable of accepting the fate assigned to me, my highest perceptions outraged by this denial of justice, I refrain from adapting my existence to the ridiculous conditions of existence here below." The mind, according to Breton, can find no point of rest either in this life or beyond it. Surrealism wants to find a solution to this endless anxiety. It is "a cry of the mind which turns against itself and finally takes the desperate decision to throw off its bonds." It protests against death and "the laughable duration" of a precarious condition. Thus surrealism places itself at the mercy of impatience. It exists in a condition of wounded frenzy: at once inflexible and self-righteous, with the consequent implication of a moral philosophy. Surrealism, the gospel of chaos, found itself compelled, from its very inception, to create an order. But at first it only dreamed of destruction—by poetry, to begin with—on the plane of imprecation, and later by the use of actual weapons. The trial of the real world has become, by logical development, the trial of creation.

Surrealist irreligion is methodical and rational. At first it established itself on the idea of the absolute non-culpability of man, to whom one should render "all the power that he has been capable of putting into the word God." As in every history of rebellion, this idea of absolute non-culpability, springing from despair, was little by little transformed into a mania for punishment. The surrealists, while simultaneously exalting human innocence, believed that they could exalt murder and suicide. They spoke of suicide as a solution and Crevel, who considered this solution "the most probable, just, and definitive," killed himself, as did Rigaut and Vaché. Later Aragon was to condemn the "babblers about suicide." Nevertheless the fact remains that to extol annihilation, without personal involvement, is not a very honorable course. On this point surrealism has retained, from the "*littérature*" it despised, the most facile excuses and has justified Rigaut's staggering remark: "You are all poets, and I myself am on the side of death."

Surrealism did not rest there. It chose as its hero Violette Nozière or the anonymous common-law criminal, affirming in this way, in the face of crime, the innocence of man. But it also was rash enough to say—and this is the statement that André Breton must have regretted ever since 1933—that the simplest surrealist act consisted in going out into the street, revolver in hand, and shooting at random into the crowd. Whoever refuses to recognize any other determining factor apart from the individual and his desires, any priority other than that of the unconscious actually succeeds in rebelling simultaneously against society and against reason. The theory of the gratuitous act is the culmination of the demand for absolute freedom. What does it matter if this freedom ends by being embodied in the solitude defined by Jarry: "When I'll have collected all the ready cash, in the world, I'll kill everybody and go away." The essential thing is that every obstacle should be denied and that the irrational should be triumphant. What, in fact, does this apology for murder signify if not that, in a world without meaning and without honor, only the desire for existence, in all its forms, is legitimate? The instinctive joy of being alive, the stimulus of the unconscious, the cry of the irrational, are the only pure truths that must be professed. Everything that stands in the way of desire—principally society—must therefore be mercilessly destroyed. Now we can understand André Breton's remark about Sade: "Certainly man no longer consents to unite with nature except in crime; it remains to be seen if this is not one of the wildest, the most incontestable, ways of loving." It is easy to see that he is talking of love without an object, which is love as experienced by people who are torn asunder. But this empty, avid love, this insane desire for possession, is precisely the love that society inevitably thwarts. That is why Breton, who still bears the stigma of his declarations, was able to sing the praises of treason and declare (as the surrealists have tried to prove) that violence is the only adequate mode of expression.

But society is not only composed of individuals. It is also an institution. Too well-mannered to kill everybody, the surrealists, by the very logic of their attitude, came to consider that in order to liberate desire, society must first be overthrown. They chose to serve the revolutionary movement of their times. From Walpole and Sade . . . surrealists passed on to Helvétius and Marx. But it is obvious that it is not the study of Marxism that led them to revolution. Quite the contrary: surrealism is involved in an incessant effort to reconcile, with Marxism, the inevitable conclusions that led it to revolution. We can say, without being paradoxical, that the surrealists arrived at Marxism on account of what, today, they most detest in Marx. Knowing the basis and the nobility of the motives that compelled him, particularly when one has shared the same lacerating experiences, one hesitates to remind André Breton that his movement implied the establishment of "ruthless authority" and of dictatorship, of political fanaticism, the refusal of free discussion, and the necessity of the death penalty. The peculiar vocabulary of that period is also astonishing ("sabotage," "informer," etc.) in that it is the vocabulary of a police-dominated revolution. But these frenetics wanted "any sort of revolution," no matter what as long as it rescued them from the world of shopkeepers and compromise in which they were forced to live. In that they could not have the best, they still preferred the worst. In that respect they were nihilists. They were not aware of the fact that those among them who were, in the future, to remain faithful to Marxism were faithful at the same time to their initial nihilism. The real destruction of language, which the surrealists so obstinately wanted, does not lie in incoherence or automatism. It lies in the word *order*. It was pointless for Aragon to begin with a denunciation of the "shameful pragmatic attitude," for in that attitude he finally found total liberation from morality, even if that liberation coincided with another form of servitude. The surrealist who meditated most profoundly about this problem, Pierre Naville, in trying to find the denominator common to revolutionary action and surrealist action, localized it, with considerable penetration, in pessimism, meaning in "the intention of accompanying man to his downfall and of overlooking nothing that could ensure that his perdition might be useful." This mixture of Machiavellianism and Augustinism in fact explains twentieth-century rebellion; no more audacious expression can be given to the nihilism of the times. The renegades of surrealism were faithful to most of the principles of nihilism. In a certain way, they wanted to die. If André Breton and a few others finally broke with Marxism, it was because there was something in them beyond nihilism, a second loyalty to what is purest in the origins of rebellion: they did not want to die.

Certainly, the surrealists wanted to profess materialism. "We are pleased to recognize as one of the prime causes of the mutiny on board the battleship *Potemkin* that terrible piece of meat." But there is not with them, as with the Marxists, a

feeling of friendship, even intellectual, for that piece of meat. Putrid meat typifies only the real world, which in fact gives birth to revolt, but against itself. It explains nothing, even though it justifies everything. Revolution, for the surrealists, was not an end to be realized day by day, in action, but an absolute and consolatory myth. It was "the real life, like love," of which Éluard spoke, who at that time had no idea that his friend Kalandra would die of that sort of life. They wanted the "communism of genius," not the other form of Communism. These peculiar Marxists declared themselves in rebellion against history and extolled the heroic individual. "History is governed by laws, which are conditioned by the cowardice of individuals." André Breton wanted revolution and love together—and they are incompatible. Revolution consists in loving a man who does not yet exist. But he who loves a living being, if he really loves, can only consent to die for the sake of the being he loves. In reality, revolution for André Breton was only a particular aspect of rebellion, while for Marxists and, in general, for all political persuasions, only the contrary is true. Breton was not trying to create, by action, the promised land that was supposed to crown history. One of the fundamental theses of surrealism is, in fact, that there is no salvation. The advantage of revolution was not that it gives mankind happiness, "abominable material comfort." On the contrary, according to Breton, it should purify and illuminate man's tragic condition. World revolution and the terrible sacrifices it implies would only bring one advantage: "preventing the completely artificial precariousness of the social condition from screening the real precariousness of the human condition." Quite simply, for Breton, this form of progress was excessive. One might as well say that revolution should be enrolled in the service of the inner asceticism by which individual men can transfigure reality into the supernatural, "the brilliant revenge of man's imagination." With André Breton, the supernatural holds the same place as the rational does with Hegel. Thus it would be impossible to imagine a more complete antithesis to the political philosophy of Marxism. The lengthy hesitations of those whom Artaud called the Amiels of revolution are easily explained. The surrealists were more different from Marx than were reactionaries like Joseph de Maistre, for example. The reactionaries made use of the tragedy of existence to reject revolution—in other words, to preserve a historical situation. The Marxists made use of it to justify revolution—in other words, to create another historical situation. Both make use of the human tragedy to further their pragmatic ends. But Breton made use of revolution to consummate the tragedy and, in spite of the title of his magazine, made use of revolution to further the surrealist adventure.

Finally, the definitive rupture is explained if one considers that Marxism insisted on the submission of the irrational, while the surrealists rose to defend irrationality to the death. Marxism tended toward the conquest of totality, and surrealism, like all spiritual experiences, tended toward unity. Totality can demand the submission of the irrational, if rationalism suffices to conquer the world. But the desire for unity is more demanding. It does not suffice that everything should be rational. It wants, above all, the rational and the irrational to be reconciled on the same level. There is no unity that supposes any form of mutilation.

For André Breton, totality could be only a stage, a necessary stage perhaps, but certainly inadequate, on the way that leads to unity. Here we find . . . the theme of All or Nothing. Surrealism tends toward universality, and the curious but profound reproach that Breton makes to Marx consists in saying quite justifiably that the latter is not universal. The surrealists wanted to reconcile Marx's "let us transform the world" with Rimbaud's "let us change life." But the first leads to the conquest of the totality of the world and the second to the conquest of the unity of life. Paradoxically, every form of totality is restrictive. In the end, the two formulas succeeded in splitting the surrealist group. By choosing Rimbaud, Breton demonstrated that surrealism was not concerned with action, but with asceticism and spiritual experience. He again gave first place to what composed the profound originality of his movement: the restoration of the sacred and the conquest of unity, which make surrealism so invaluable for a consideration of the problem of rebellion. The more he elaborated on this original concept, the more irreparably he separated himself from his political companions, and at the same time from some of his first manifestoes.

André Breton never, actually, wavered in his support of surrealism—the fusion of a dream and of reality, the sublimation of the old contradiction between the ideal and the real. We know the surrealist solution: concrete irrationality, objective risk. Poetry is the conquest, the only possible conquest, of the "supreme position." "A certain position of the mind from where life and death, the real and the imaginary, the past and the future . . . cease to be perceived in a contradictory sense." What is this supreme position that should mark the "colossal abortion of the Hegelian system"? It is the search for the summit-abyss, familiar to the mystics. Actually, it is the mysticism without God which demonstrates and quenches the rebel's thirst for the absolute. The essential enemy of surrealism is rationalism. Breton's method, moreover, presents the peculiar spectacle of a form of Occidental thought in which the principle of analogy is continually favored to the detriment of the principles of identity and contradiction. More precisely, it is a question of dissolving contradictions in the fires of love and desire and of demolishing the walls of death. Magic rites, primitive or naïve civilizations, alchemy, the language of flowers, fire, or sleepless nights, are so many miraculous stages on the way to unity and the philosophers' stone. If surrealism did not change the world, it furnished it with a few strange myths which partly justified Nietzsche's announcement of the return of the Greeks. Only partly, because he was referring to unenlightened Greece, the Greece of mysteries and dark gods. Finally, just as Nietzsche's experience culminated in the acceptance of the light of day, surrealist experience culminates in the exaltation of the darkness of night, the agonized and obstinate cult of the tempest. Breton, according to his own statements, understood that, despite everything, life was a gift. But his compliance could never shed the full light of day, the light that all of us need. "There is too much of the north in me," he said, "for me to be a man who complies entirely."

He nevertheless often diminished, to his own detriment, the importance of negation and advanced the positive claims of rebellion. He chose severity rather than silence and retained only the "demand for morality," which, according to Bataille, first gave life to surrealism: "To substitute a new morality for current morality, which is the cause of all our evils." Of course he did not succeed (nor has anybody in our time) in the attempt to found a new morality. But he never despaired of being able to do so. Confronted with the horror of a period in which man, whom he wanted to magnify, has been persistently degraded in the name of certain principles that surrealism adopted, Breton felt constrained to propose, provisionally, a return to traditional morality. That represents a hesitation perhaps. But it is the hesitation of nihilism and the real progress of rebellion.

After all, when he could not give himself the morality and the values of whose necessity he was clearly aware, we know very well that Breton chose love. In the general meanness of his times—and this cannot be forgotten—he is the only person who wrote profoundly above love. Love is the entranced morality that served this exile as a native land. Of course, a dimension is still missing here. Surrealism, in that it is neither politics nor religion, is perhaps only an unbearable form of wisdom. But it is also the absolute proof that there is no comfortable form of wisdom: "We want, we shall have, the hereafter in our lifetime," Breton has admirably exclaimed. While reason embarks on action and sets its armies marching on the world, the splendid night in which Breton delights announces dawns that have not yet broken. . . . (pp. 91-9)

> *Albert Camus, "Metaphysical Rebellion: The Poets' Rebellion," in his* The Rebel: An Essay on Man in Revolt, *translated by Anthony Bower, revised edition, Vintage Books, 1956, pp. 81-99.*

ANTONIN ARTAUD

[*Artaud was a French dramatist, poet, and critic who influenced the development of modern drama with his theories of a Theater of Cruelty. Repudiating the traditions of Western theater, Artaud proposed the creation of antirationalist spectacles which would, through the incorporation of symbolic gestures, mime, incantations and nonreferential sounds, express humanity's anguished response to the cruelties of existence and to the implacable forces that control its fate. Although critics find his influence in the works of Eugene Ionesco and Jean Genet, his various theories have never been realized in a single production. Artaud worked closely with the Surrealists between 1924 and 1926, serving for a time as the director of the Bureau of Surrealist Research. In 1929, he was officially expelled from the group for engaging in proscribed literary activities, and while he and Breton later reestablished friendly relations, neither considered Artaud a Surrealist after the break. In the following excerpt, written shortly after his expulsion from the Surrealists, Artaud denounces the group's conversion to communism as naive optimism, asserting that the freedom they profess to value comes from spiritual rather than political change.*]

The question of whether the Surrealists drove me out or whether I walked out on their grotesque parody has long since ceased to be relevant. I withdrew because I had had enough of a masquerade that had gone on all too long. Besides, I was quite certain that in the new context they had chosen, just as in any other, the Surrealists would do nothing. Time and the facts have not failed to prove me right.

As to the question of whether Surrealism is in accord with the Revolution or whether the Revolution must be made outside the Surrealist adventure, one wonders what difference it can make to the world when one considers how little influence the Surrealists have managed to gain over the manners and ideas of the times.

Indeed, one wonders if there is still a Surrealist adventure, or if Surrealism did not die on the day when Breton and his adepts decided to join the Communist movement and to seek in the realm of facts and of immediate matter the culmination of an action that could normally develop only within the inmost confines of the brain.

They believe they can permit themselves to mock me when I speak of a metamorphosis of the interior conditions of the soul, as if I understood soul in the disgusting sense in which they understand it, and as if from the viewpoint of the absolute there could be the slightest interest in seeing the social armature of the world change or in seeing power pass from the hands of the bourgeoisie into those of the proletariat.

If, moreover, the Surrealists were really looking for this, they would at least be excusable. Their goal would be banal and limited, but at least it would exist. But have they the slightest goal toward which to undertake an action, and when did they ever give a damn about formulating one?

Are they even working toward a goal? Are they working with motives? Do the Surrealists believe they can justify their expectation by the mere fact that they are aware of it? Expectation is not a state of mind. When one does nothing, one runs no risk of falling on one's face. But this is not sufficient reason to get oneself talked about.

I have too much contempt for life to think that any sort of change that might develop in the realm of appearances could in any way change my detestable condition. What divides me from the Surrealists is that they love life as much as I despise it. To enjoy themselves on every occasion and through every pore, this is the center of their obsessions. But is not asceticism an integral part of the true magic, even the blackest, even the most foul? Even the diabolical hedonist has an ascetic side, a certain spirit of mortification.

I am not talking about their writings, which are brilliant, although negated by the point of view from which they are presented. I am talking about their central attitude, about the example of their lives as a whole. I do not hate them as individuals. I reject and condemn them as a group, giving each of them all the respect and even admiration he deserves for his works or for his mind. In any case I shall not, like them, be childish enough to execute a complete about-face and to deny them all talent the moment they cease to be my friends. But fortunately this is not the point.

The point is this displacement of the spiritual center of the world, this breaking up of appearances, this transfiguration of the possible which Surrealism was to help bring about. All matter begins with a spiritual deviation. To depend on things and on their transformations for guidance is the attitude of an obscene brute, of a metaphysical opportunist. Nobody has ever understood anything and the Surrealists themselves do not understand and cannot foresee where their desire for Revolution will lead them. Incapable of imagining, of conceiving a Revolution which did not evolve within the hopeless limitations of matter, they resort to fatality, to a certain accident of debility and impotence which is peculiar to them, in order to explain their inertia, their eternal sterility.

Surrealism has never meant anything to me but a new kind of magic. The imagination, the dream, that whole intense liberation of the unconscious whose purpose is to raise to the surface of the soul all that it is in the habit of keeping concealed, must necessarily introduce profound transformations in the scale of appearances, in the value of signification and the symbolism of the created. The whole of concrete reality changes its garb or shell and ceases to correspond to the same mental gestures. The beyond, the invisible, replace reality. The world no longer holds.

It is then that one can begin to screen out illusions, to eliminate frauds.

May the thick walls of the occult collapse once and for all on these impotent talkers who waste their lives in rebukes and empty threats, on these revolutionaries who revolutionize nothing.

These brutes whom it would suit me to be converted by. I would certainly need it. But at least I recognize that I am weak and impure. I aspire to another life. And all things considered, I would rather be in my position than in theirs.

What remains of the Surrealist adventure? Little besides a great disappointed hope, but in the domain of literature itself they may, in fact, have contributed something. This anger, this scathing disgust poured on the written word constitutes a fertile attitude and one which may be useful someday, later on. It has already purified literature, brought it closer to the essential truth of the brain. But that is all. Of positive conquests outside literature or images there are none, and yet this was the only thing that mattered. Out of the right use of dreams could be born a new way of guiding one's thought, a new way of relating to appearances. Psychological truth was stripped of all parasitic, useless excrescence, was much closer to being captured than before. We were alive then, to be sure, but pehaps it is a law of the spirit that the abandonment of reality can only lead to illusion. Within the narrow framework of our tangible domain we are pressured and solicited from every direction. We have seen this clearly in that aberration which has led revolutionaries on the highest possible level to literally abandon this level and to attach to this word "revolution" its utilitarian and practical meaning, the social meaning that is alleged to be the only valid one, since no one wants to be taken in by words. Curious reversal of position, curious leveling process.

Merely to advance a psychological attitude: does anyone believe that this can be enough, if this attitude is wholly characterized by inertia? The inner spirit of Surrealism leads it to Revolution. This is the positive fact. The only effective conclusion which is possible (so they say) and which a large number of Surrealists have refused to endorse; but as for the others, what has this espousal of Communism given them, what has it cost them? It has not made them take one step forward. This morality of becoming on which the Revolution is said to depend—never have I felt its necessity within the closed circle of my person. I place above any material necessity the logical exigencies of my own reality. This is the only logic that seems valid to me, and not some higher logic whose radiations affect me only insofar as they touch my sensibility. There is no discipline to which I feel forced to submit, however rigorous the reasoning that would persuade me to embrace it.

Two or three principles of life and death are for me higher than any precarious allegiance. And I have never encountered a logic that seemed to me anything but borrowed.

Surrealism has died of the idiotic sectarianism of its adepts. What remains is a kind of hybrid mass to which the Surrealists themselves are incapable of putting a name. Perpetually on the fringe of appearances, incapable of gaining a foothold on life, Surrealism is still at the stage of seeking its outlet, of marking time. Powerless to choose, to decide either totally in favor of the lie or totally in favor of the truth (the true lie of the illusory spiritual, the false truth of the immediate but destructible real), Surrealism hunts for that unfathomable, that indefinable interstice of reality in which to insert its one powerful lever, which has now fallen into the hands of eunuchs. But my well-known mental debility and cowardice refuse to take the slightest interest in upheavals which would affect only this external, immediately perceptible aspect of reality. External metamorphosis is, in my opinion, something which can only be given as a bonus. The social level, the material level toward which the Surrealists direct their pathetic attempts at action, their forever ineffectual hatreds, is for me no more than a useless and obvious illusion. (pp. 139-45)

> Antonin Artaud, *"In Total Darkness; or, The Surrealist Bluff,"* in his *Selected Writings, edited by Susan Sontag, translated by Helen Weaver, Farrar, Straus and Giroux, 1976, pp. 139-45.*

NAHMA SANDROW

[*In the following excerpt from her study of the diverse art forms produced by the Surrealists,* Surrealism: Theater, Arts, Ideas *(1972), Sandrow discusses the Surrealists' adaptation of traditional art forms to permit the expression of their nonrational worldview.*]

As the romantic tendency had always been, surrealist artists worked in traditional forms, which they shaped to their distinctive own uses. Surrealist philosophy bore very directly on surrealist art theories.

Surrealism's joyous embracing of chaos, for example, naturally made alien all classical structure. All art works had to reflect the universal dissolution of structure. Besides, formal patterns were impossible if art works were to emerge as the artist's spontaneous experiences. Finally, the distinction between content and treatment, which implies an orderly intellectual approach to creation, was discredited with all other theoretical distinctions, for pure nonrationality could not admit of it.

For all these reasons, association and repetition took the place of structure in surrealist literature and drama; in the latter, of course, the Aristotelian unities, with complications and denouement and characters behaving consistently, were obviously unacceptable to the surrealists. The characteristic extreme brevity of surrealist poems and plays and (Satie's) music made the shape imposed on them by their beginnings and ends seem to serve as structure. Art forms which seem to require a certain intellectual coherence and sustained control, such as the novel or the symphony, were rarely attempted by the surrealists; Breton's novel *Nadja* is an exception.

The universal nonrational chaos which the surrealists perceived led them to dismiss, along with structure, all rational distinctions but one: "my experience"—itself a nonrational entity—versus everything else (according to Freud, the infant's first distinction); and even this distinction dissolved at the level of surreality. The perception of general disintegration confirmed their concentration of all things and ideas in the individual experience. It also inevitably made all their art works chaotic as well. (pp. 49-50)

[All] surrealist art experience was centered in the artist. In other words mimesis, or imitation, of the world around the artist, the traditional goal of all the arts, was no longer tenable for the surrealists. Indeed mimesis as a goal of art seemed particularly absurd with the dissolution of confidence in the accuracy of mental and sensory perceptions, in the possibility of communicating such perceptions without distortion, and, finally, in the unlikelihood that the recipient's impression will ever be what you intended. It seemed impossible even to discover what that final impression was. Again, the absence of faith in rationality, the adoption in its place of nonrationality, is the prime motif in surrealist art.

In rejecting mimesis, surrealist art was firmly in the nineteenth-century line of development which put the artist, rather than imitation of an external subject, at the center of the art work. At the same time as the artist was coming to be popularly considered a special creature deserving honor for his role and life style as well as for the art works he produces, he was also attaining a kind of semi-divinity for his ability literally to create worlds according to his will. The surrealist self-image in life and art clearly fits this general pattern.

In nineteenth-century painting, for example, the picture was released from the tyranny of subject. We begin to trace, along with a continuing stream of Academy painters, a movement from the Impressionists, who applied their individual personalities to a landscape and simultaneously used the landscape to express their personalities, and culminating in Cézanne who went so far as actually to deform the landscape for the sake of the picture.

Another way of describing this tendency away from imitation is to say that art was not serving the artist's environment. It no longer aimed automatically to reflect the environment, realistically or symbolically; nor to elucidate it; nor to effect its social reform or spiritual uplift in the usual senses; nor simply to decorate it. All these traditional goals seemed particularly hopeless with the dissolution of confidence in the accuracy of mental and sensory perceptions, as well as in the possibility of communicating such perceptions to others rationally so that they may perceive them in exactly the same way. Instead, environment was at the service of art and the artist; and sur-

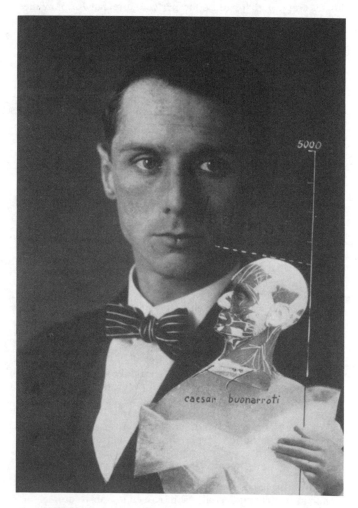

Self-portrait by Max Ernst. Copyright ARS NY/SPADEM.

realist art and artists, of course, were at the service of higher spiritual values.

The surrealists were not drawn by those art forms too inherently mimetic for reshaping. Novels, for example, have traditionally been mimetic, involving a subject which is, in Henry James's words, a "direct impression or perception of life." "Impression" presupposes the possibility of rationally communicating such an impression, and indeed the surrealists wrote very few novels. Perhaps the only real one, in fact, was *Nadja* by André Breton, which we have just mentioned. A free series of encounters between the author and a woman (apparently surrealist in life style) who is probably based on an acquaintance of the author's, it avoids imitating a real-life story as plot. This is quite different from the contemporaneous Joycean stream of consciousness, which imitates fictional minds reacting to an objective environment beneath a series of rational events—all presented so that the reader can even follow chronologically. Forty years later, novelists Marguerite Duras and Alain Robbe-Grillet seem to be wrestling to create nonmimetic novels, and they are both drawn to writing for films; Beckett (*Watt, Malone*) has probably come the closest to achieving that goal. Such novels are collages of passages of meticulously observed mimetic writing, put together so as to reflect nothing at all. In painting they resemble, for example, Magritte's close reproductions of impossibly juxtaposed objects.

Music ought perhaps to be the perfect surrealist form. Walter Sokel observes that whereas sculpture, with its imitation of natural forms, had always been the prototypical art of the West, music was now taking over: "the adoption of . . . principles of musical composition by the other arts is probably the single most dominant characteristic of all modernism." Surrealism was of course an expression of modernity. Music refers solely to the universe of the individual art experience. The conventional distinction between content and form cannot be applied to it. Music's unsuitability to function as a vehicle of intellection and its property of seeming to touch universals which elude logical verbalization seem to confirm surrealism's affinity with it. It is also possible to argue that musicalization occurred as men learned to manipulate abstractions and, in particular, to apply them to everyday life—as an aspect, in other words, of technological development.

Nevertheless, the Surrealist movement produced very little music. Erik Satie was the only well-known musician to be officially linked with the movement, although some of his disciples, Les Six (especially Auric, Poulenc, Milhaud, Tailleferre), occasionally contributed compositions to Dada or surrealist soirées, as did also Stravinsky. Aristotle called music the most mimetic of all arts, although he meant imitation of emotional states rather than of ideas or objective impressions. Perhaps music was prevented from conveying the artist's transformation from imitator to creator by the fact that it is a self-contained artificial universe which does not refer at all to its environment, and because it is purely sensory. Certainly rationality and irrationality are adjectives which are difficult to apply to music. Furthermore, music, like theater, requires performers to complete creatively the composer's creative impulse. Much of Satie's music is for solo piano, and the pianist was usually Satie himself. Indeed Satie's techniques approach music very much as surrealist artists in other media approached painting and other conventional forms, and the parallel with reappear.

On the other hand, the surrealists were drawn to those traditional art forms which could be practiced in nonstructured nonmimetic ways. Lyric poetry, for example, as a free expression

of the poet's feelings, was very congenial to the surrealists, almost all of whom wrote poems, at least sometimes, to express a love or a mood. . . . (pp. 50-4)

Surrealist painting, especially when it was the product of automatism, was sometimes purely nonmimetic. More often it was actively antimimetic. The surrealists used the art form to play with viewers' expectations of imitation; they reproduced certain features of the external world, but in unexpected, arresting arrangements which come from the artist and not from his impressions of the world. Surrealist paintings were cerebral rather than sensory, almost literary, almost verbal, so it was this arrangement of pictured objects and creatures rather than a retreat to abstractions in pure color or design which constituted surrealist nonmimetic tendencies in painting.

Similarly, surrealist sculptures, for the most part, neither represented human beings, nor distorted them according to a program. Rather they tended to be constructions: a whole new form . . . made of recognizable bits of the physical environment so combined as to stymie any attempt to correlate these bits rationally with that environment. They also differed from tradition in that they were rarely pleasing to the senses in design or texture.

Early surrealist experiments with film mostly avoided the abstract exercises in design and color—"pure film"—which were popular among other contemporary film makers, in favor of filming recognizable places or things but defying the spectator to construe the film as imitation of anything. In surrealist film, as much as possible, said a practitioner: "the story is nothing, but the vision is everything . . .": ". . . shadows and lights and their possibilities. . . ." Avant-garde French and Italian films of the last ten years seem to be following his dictum.

In drama the drive away from mimesis—from the story—impelled surrealist philosophy actually to fight the art form itself. Ever since Aristotle's *Poetics* named mimesis as the basis of tragedy, drama's conscious source has been imitation of life. The traditional ingredients of dramatic form integrally involve imitation of life and of lifelike thinking processes: characters with some psychological consistency; plots with some cause-and-effect logic progressing in time; and dialogue with some functional plausibility. All these were antithetical to surrealism, which thought of them, in Eugene O'Neill's contemptuous phrase of the same period, as merely "holding the family kodak up to nature."

Not surprisingly, two extreme categories of plays emerged from Dada and surrealism, according to the dramatists' attitudes toward retention of mimesis: one sort which was not really surrealistic, and another which was not really drama. Some playwrights of the first category simply violated surrealist principles. The art form here was too strong for the abstract principles. Many surrealist plays have traceable plots, and most of these even progress chronologically, if obscurely. Even when this progression is not logical, a story nevertheless seems to be unrolling on the stage, in the telling of which a time sequence is basically honored. And the characters in the story have some recognizable consistency.

It is true that, usually, even the plays which are dramaturgically most mimetic do exemplify surrealist life values and their dialogue resembles surrealist poetry. An example is *The Emperor of China* by Dadaist Georges Ribemont-Dessaignes, in which royal characters die violently after an incestuous love. Nevertheless the familiar material of domestic drama and conventional romance is not far off. Vitrac's play *The Mysteries of*

Love shows us the violent relationship between two lovers, Patrice and Léa; Tzara's *Cloud Handkerchief* is about a poet who has an affair with a banker's wife and later kills himself; Desnos' charming *La Place de l'Étoile* is about a young man and two women who perhaps love him; Apollinaire's *Sky Blue* is about three young spaceship adventurers who find their ideal embodied in a woman and destroy themselves over her; Neveux's *Juliette or the Key to Dreams* is about a young man who goes hunting for his once-glimpsed love; Goll's *Mathusalem* is about the marriage between a romantic middle-class girl (Mathusalem's daughter) and a revolutionary on the make; Aragon's *The Mirror Wardrobe One Fine Evening* is about a jealous husband.

The other extreme category of surrealist playwrights followed their principles right out of the theater. Clément Pansaers' *The Smack-smack on the Naked Negro's Ass*, with no action at all of any sort and no characters, is written in a sort of automatic-writing prose rather than dialogue. Roger Gilbert-Lecomte's *The Odyssey of Ulysses the Palimped*, with no plot or inter-acting characters, calls for a range of activities which defy staging. These are pieces to be read silently, as one reads a poem; Armand Salacrou actually called his *A Circus Story* a "play for reading." Like Gertrude Stein's contemporaneous *Turkey and Bones and Eating* and others, such plays have given up all connection with stage, performance, audience. Plays in name only, they are no longer drama and probably no longer theater events. Nevertheless, Tristan Tzara's *The Gas Heart*—three acts of repetitive nonsense inexplicably spoken by Nose, Ear, Neck, and other facial parts—did indeed give satisfaction of some sort when produced, as has Kenneth Koch's much more recent but similar effort *Bertha*.

The majority of surrealist playwrights compromised, retaining a story about certain characters but making it a dream-play of shifts, surprises, nonsense, violence, and laughter. "When man wanted to imitate walking," Apollinaire said in his Preface to *The Breasts of Tiresias,* "he created the wheel, which does not resemble a leg. In the same way he has created surrealism without knowing it." The surrealist version of conventional mimetic drama, with flexibility and verve, was intended to be to most plays as the wheel is to the leg: a better, more genuine way to do the same thing. In *La Place de l'Étoile,* starfish proliferate delightfully; throughout the second act characters talk about them: "salty, fat, fresh from the sea." Vitrac's *The Painter* begins with a surrealist imitation of an action: the action is surrealist in itself, and the imitation remains not quite a plot.

> (*. . . A painter is painting a door red. Enter a small boy carefully dressed in white. He approaches the painter and watches him painting.*)
>
> PAINTER. What's your name?
>
> CHILD. Maurice Parchment. (*Silence*) And yours?
>
> PAINTER. That's my name too.
>
> LITTLE MAURICE PARCHMENT. It's not true.
>
> PAINTER. It's not true? (*Silence*) You're right.
>
> (*He paints the child's face red.* LITTLE MAURICE PARCHMENT *goes out crying . . . The* PAINTER *goes on painting. Enter* MADAME PARCHMENT *. . . and little* MAURICE PARCHMENT, *cleaned up.*)
>
> MME. PARCHMENT. Sir, you are contemptible. What is your name?
>
> PAINTER. Maurice Parchment.
>
> MME. PARCHMENT. It's not true.

> PAINTER. It's not true? (*Silence*) You are right.
>
> (*He paints their faces red.* MME. PARCHMENT *and little* MAURICE PARCHMENT *go out crying. The* PAINTER *goes on painting. . . .*) [Much later in the action he will inexplicably look in the mirror, paint his own face red, and exit crying. Note, by the way, the pun; parchment is to be painted on.]

The compromise between the rejection of mimesis and the retention of dramaturgical conventions is similar to the effort to synthesize a "universal athlete" to produce an entire theater piece all by himself. Perhaps the tensions involved in such conflicts between the demand of form, of practice, and of aesthetic theory are responsible at least in part for the energy inherent in surrealist drama.

The surrealist ideal in drama had in fact been summed up in the Prologue to *The Breasts of Tiresias:*

> . . . the theatre should not be a copy of reality
> It is right that the dramatist should use
> All the mirages at his disposal. . . .
> It is right that he should let crowds speak inanimate objects
> If he so pleases
> And that he no longer should reckon with time
> Or space
> His universe is the play
> Within which he is God the Creator
> Who disposes at will
> Of sounds gestures movements masses colors
> Not merely in order
> To photograph what is called a slice of life
> But to bring forth life itself in all its truth. . . .

In practice, of course, it was difficult to accomplish all this on a stage.

One weapon against dramatic mimesis was sabotage of stage illusion. It was a Frenchman, Zola, who in the late nineteenth century called for a theater of perfectly reproduced naturalistic "slices of life." It was another Frenchman, Diderot, who in the mid-eighteenth century had described the perfect theatrical imitation of life as giving the illusion that one is looking into a real household's activities through its transparent fourth wall: the proscenium. Ever since Albert-Birot's *théâtre nunique,* projected in 1917, the French surrealists were intent on destroying that wall. The *théâtre nunique* had several revolving concentric circles for performers and audience. Similarly, Tzara's *Cloud Handkerchief* actually showed the actors making up in onstage dressing rooms and commenting on the play. In 1923 Kurt Schwitters began to sketch a Normalbühne Merz "for which he conceived a space stage in which the machinery constituted part of the visible aesthetic of the event."

Actors in surrealist stage plays did not attempt to believe a role in any sense nor to give audiences the illusion of the role's reality. In the 1960s Michael Kirby discussed this new kind of acting in connection with Happenings. He contrasted actors working from mimetic "matrices" of time-place-character with "nonmatrixed" actors like the Living Theater and Jerzy Grotowski's Polish Laboratory Theater, who are closer to dancers than to conventional actors, especially perhaps to dancers of such currently avant-garde groups as Merce Cunningham's. Especially in movies, where he was a marionette or "living sign" for the director, the actor's art lay for the surrealists in self-dramatization, as did the art of artists in other media. The pure power of presence, rather than impersonation, was the actor's gift. . . . Breton had a horror of role-playing.

Antonin Artaud's *Jet of Blood* and his scenarios give us a clue to the surrealist ideal in drama and are perhaps further evidence that the cinema was born with surrealism to be surrealism's element. The world which a film maker can create can be inconsistent beyond fantasy, beyond anthropomorphism. And since the audience sees not actions but pictures of actions, the mimetic illusion of reality is perhaps even less encouraged than onstage.

So the surrealists played with the usual arts. But in the process, their verve pushed and spilled out of the standard containers and was, as was fashionable for furniture at the time, "free form."

Language itself was escaping from old forms. "O mouths," the surrealists exulted, "man is in search of a new language / Which won't be the business of any grammarian in any tongue." For since neither logical thought nor orderly systems of expression seemed tenable any longer, language for the surrealists had lost its value as a vehicle of articulation. Rather, language was to serve, if at all, as a means of touching and sharing surreality.

We ought to get a sense of this language of chaos even before we enter the world of purely surrealist art forms, because all the surrealist arts are in a sense literary. Surrealism has been described as, simply, "a literary school," despite the presence of so many painters and sculptors as members. The movement's principal sources and founders were writers: Jarry and Apollinaire, Tzara (who remained faithful to Dada), Breton, Éluard, Aragon, and Soupault. Many of its members who were not primarily writers acknowledged their personal inspiration to have been literary in origin. Duchamp, for example, called Roussel's dramatized novel *Impressions of Africa* the greatest single influence on his work. (Apollinaire had taken him to see it.) Indeed Duchamp described surrealist painting in general as "intimately and consciously involved with literature." The surrealists expressed themselves collectively and individually through constantly issued manifestos, through speeches, and through a series of small literary magazines with picturesque names, such as *SIC, Littérature, La Révolution Surréaliste* (later to become the communist *Le Surréalisme au Service de la Révolution*), *Minotaure, Cannibale*, and *L'Oeuf dur* (*Hard-Boiled Egg*). This pervasive literary-ness may well be related to the movement's cerebral rather than sensual atmosphere and its origin in verbalized philosophical ideas.

Already in the nineteenth century Rimbaud had attempted to separate words from their intellectual functions and conventional meanings. His *Les Illuminations* (*Illuminations*) had tried to develop a language which would be truly "from the soul to the soul." Then Mallarmé, whom the surrealists often quoted (and who had championed the first scandalous performance of *King Ubu*), further liberated words from their conventional senses. Enormously influential in modern European literature, Mallarmé distinguished between "immediate speech"—for the rational uses of everyday existence—and "essential speech"— to deal with the essence of things. (pp. 54-61)

With the disintegration of logical thinking and articulation came disintegration of all the commonsense distinctions which are the basis of rational communication and traditional art. Perhaps the most basic conventional distinction to disappear was that between life and art. . . . [The] surrealists considered art different from life in degree rather than in kind. In *The Wedding on the Eiffel Tower,* The Dealer in Modern Paintings tries to sell the Collector of Modern Paintings the live ongoing wedding party, which he calls "a truly unique piece" entitled "The Wedding Party": "a kind of primitive," "one of the latest works of God," unsigned because "God does not sign" but ". . . look at that paint! What texture!" The Collector makes a deal and a large placard SOLD is propped against the merrymakers, who pay no attention. Their existence is art by arbitrary definition.

Thus an artist might find an art work entirely "ready-made" for him by his environment, simply waiting to be called an art work. Marcel Duchamp defined a ready-made, in fact, as "a usual object promoted to the dignity of art object by the simple choice of the artist." Perhaps the best-known example of this genre is the urinal which he displayed, upside down, at the New York Independents' Exhibition of 1917, entitled blandly "Fountain." Satie used bits of popular tunes in his compositions. Apollinaire used snatches of overheard conversations in his poems. Noise music, originated by the Italian Futurists but adopted by the Surrealists, consisted of machine noises, falling objects, and so on; Hugo Ball composed a complete "Noise music concert" and conducted it behind a screen at the Café Voltaire. (pp. 64-5)

The cabaret soirée, a Dada and surrealist institution . . . , can serve us now as an example of the way Dada and surrealist life and art reflected their world view of nonrational chaos. It was, in a way, the surrealist art form par excellence. It was also closer to theater than to any other single conventional category.

First of all, the soirée was both social and artistic in intent; Surrealism had after all abolished the distinction between these two spheres. It was a social occasion in the course of which art works were informally performed and exhibited. As in theory it was impossible to separate life and art, so it is impossible to isolate the art works which formed part of any soirée from their social context. Soirées were parties of friends and friendly enemies. Displaying and appreciating flamboyant behavior, greeting friends, eating and drinking—all were equally part of the experience, along with entertainment to be performed or watched with varying degrees of seriousness. Outsiders sometimes appeared at soirées, especially at those held in theaters or hired halls, and their presence added another amusing element.

At soirées, the conventional distinction between performers and audience was loose and shifting, since they were literally a single unified group of participants. They interchanged roles fluidly, acting and reacting. The spatial arrangement of the café floor encouraged this fluidity and influenced the surrealist theater experiments in which, as we have seen, the proscenium dissolves and stage and hall become confused. In Tzara's play *The Gas Heart*, presented as part of a soirée, there was even a speaker stationed over the audience's heads, facing the stage, and occasionally making on their behalf such blasé comments as "It's charming, your play, but one can't understand a word of it."

With the acceptance of chaos, the collage, which was not a new form, now gained the status of art. The soirée was a sort of collage of life situations. Bits of materials of all sorts— visual, verbal, and dramatic—combined in no perceptive pattern, reflected a universe arranged in the same way. Breton observed that collages assembled by chance "offer insight into a world where the distinction between necessity and accident had been lost."

The surrealists also repudiated formal distinctions between genres, which seemed to them no more valid than those between life and art or between waking consciousness and dreams. The soirée was a collage of art forms, too. It was composed of many parts, often haphazardly arranged. A Dada-Surrealist soirée entitled "Le Coeur à Barbe" ("The Bearded Heart"), held in Paris in 1923, included a brilliant variety of offerings in an environment designed for the occasion. The program included: films by Man Ray, Charles Cheeler, Paul Strand; poems by Cocteau, Tzara, Éluard, Zdanevitch, Soupault; musical compositions by Stravinsky, Milhaud, Auric; dances by Lizica Codreanu. It also included plays by Tzara and Ribemont-Dessaignes, which were in turn composed of poetry, acting, decor, costumes, dance.

Mixing of media was typical of surrealist art activities even outside the soirée. Apollinaire combined language and visual arts in witty poems arranged to form appropriate pictures in type: a mandolin, a necktie, stripes of falling raindrops. This was a popular seventeenth-century device which he adopted and named calligrammes; a recently fashionable name for it is "concrete poetry." Tzara included typographical decorations in the printing of his play *The Gas Heart*. Satie decorated his scores with marginal cartoons and clever comments. The Satie-Picabia ballet *Relâche* included a short film by René Clair, showing, among other scenes, Satie firing a cannon on a roof. Magritte wrote, "This is not a pipe" across the canvas of his straightforward painting of a pipe, whose original title was appropriately enough, *The Betrayal of Images*. Cocteau predicted a whole new mixed genre, heralded by his own *The Wedding on the Eiffel Tower*, "in the margin" between theater, ballet, and light opera. This "revolution which flings doors wide open . . . ," he continued, would allow the "new generation" to "continue its experiments in which the fantastic, the dance, acrobatics, mime, drama, satire, music, and the spoken word combine. . . ." *The Wedding on the Eiffel Tower*, moreover, includes a version of the classic chorus and the music-hall master of ceremonies, so that inconsistent styles and periods are jumbled together too.

A notable instance of the blending of media—as well as of the literary nature of the movement—is the invasion of surrealist art works in all media by literature in the form of title for paintings, sculpture, plays, and (Satie's) musical compositions. These titles were often long, or oblique, or outright nonsensical: *Why Not Sneeze?* for example, is the title for a cageful of marble ice cubes plus thermometer by Duchamp; and *Three Pear-shaped Pieces* and *Dried-out Embryos* for musical pieces by Satie; and *Please (S'il vous plaît)* for a play by Breton and Soupault. Rather than elucidating or describing the art work, these titles often combine with it, extend it, to produce an unexpected effect—or, indeed, to produce the finished work. Titles often made puns on the art work, like dreams, or they added a threat: Max Ernst's *Two Children Menaced by a Nightingale,* for example, or Yves Tanguy's *Mama, Papa Is Wounded.* These titles were not meant to transmit information; they were meant, said Duchamp, apropos of his *In Advance of a Broken Arm* (showing a snow shovel), to "create another form, as if using another color." Often, as in the case of the *Nightingale* (and like the above-mentioned "pipe"), the caption was written prominently right across the canvas so as to make words literally part of the painting. Magritte's paintings were often named for famous books, such as Poe's *The Domaine of Arnheim*, Rousseau's *Rêveries du promeneur solitaire*, and Sade's *La philosophie dans le boudoir*.

Conversely, the nonliterary imagery of surrealism tended to draw its strength from implied verbal formulations—again an instance of the blending of media. Literature was translated into visual form, as occurred when Dali actually built a "rainy taxi" (a popular surrealist verbal construction) for an exhibition in 1938. Magritte has been called a "painter of epigrams." In Apollinaire's play *The Breasts of Tiresias,* verbal puns slip from one medium to another. The play takes place in Zanzibar, for example, and the script calls for dice as a motif in the decor: *zanzibar* or *zanzi* is not only a place but also a dice game. Also, placards announce that, unlike the Seine, "notre scène" (our scene) is not at Paris (French pronunciation, which makes *Paris* sound like *pari*, or bet). Meanwhile two characters have just made a bet about where they are.

Since no traditional distinctions could be made in quality or kind, surrealist artists used materials not normally considered suitable for art, often in combination with conventional paints. Surrealism made happy use of the debris and waste products of society, the proliferating unlovely banal objects and mechanical relationships which were very often direct evidences of technology. Collages used ticket stubs, bottle labels, scraps of cloth and glass. Collages in an extra dimension, like sculptures, were called constructions. *Why Not Sneeze?* is an example. In 1936 Merle Oppenheim covered a cup, saucer, and spoon with fur and entitled the whole, appropriately enough, *Fur-Covered Cup, Saucer, and Spoon*. Constructions with moving parts and even live parts (tethered insects) appeared. Writers borrowed from life great masses of clichés and threw them whole into poems or plays. "Real" people such as Napoleon, Cleopatra, Mussolini, and Lloyd George appear as characters in otherwise totally fictional plays. Picasso's later play *Desire Caught by the Tail* has as characters Big Foot and Hunger. Noise music mixed with more conventional music in Satie's score for the ballet *Parade*. Kurt Schwitters put together inside his house constructions of wood and whatever else came to hand; he was building his environment, which he called *Merzbau* after some syllables which had once appeared by accident on a collage. (Eventually it took up the entire house, and he and his wife were forced to move out.) This is an example of mixing of materials and also of the refusal to distinguish between art to look at and art as an environment to live in.

Mixing of tone in all media is another evidence of the dissolution of all accepted categories in surrealist art. A play might include, for example, rhetorical philosophizing, nonsense doggerel, and conversational banalities, as does Rogert Vitrac's *The Mysteries of Love*. It might combine tragic romance and grotesque humor, as does Robert Desnos' *La Place de L'Étoile*.

Collages of all sorts also expressed another, related, concept which haunts critics in the arts today. If the universe is incoherent, composed of disparate phenomena of no intrinsic value, then all phenomena are equally valuable. Value judgments are impossible, at least in relation to art. It is impossible to weigh the quality of an object, or collection of objects, which claim to be nothing but an arbitrarily chosen artifact of someone's life. And furthermore, since every phenomenon can play its indispensable role as a key to surreality, every phenomenon is equally valuable. Here surrealist philosophy seems to be confirming the popular spirit of the times: the undiscriminating delight in accumulation of mass-produced things, the breakdown of social classes, and possibly the reaction to an increasingly stratified and complex society. (pp. 66-71)

In the light of the breakdown of genre distinctions, it is not surprising that most surrealist artists worked in more than one medium, refusing to classify themselves rigidly as a painter or poet. The poet Francis Picabia drew. Artaud . . . directed and designed costumes, Cocteau, who was only on the fringes of the movement, dabbled in all the arts. And all of them took part freely in performances and readings of each others' works; Duchamp, for example, appeared nude in the character of Adam in the ballet *Relâche*. Especially, confirming the essentially literary impulse of the movement, whatever their primary medium, almost all the surrealists wrote. Duchamp wrote poetry and prose. Henri Rousseau (not an actual member of the movement) wrote two delightful plays: a comedy entitled *A Visit to the Exposition of 1889* and an old-fashioned melodrama, performed recently for the first time, entitled *The Vengeance of a Russian Orphan Girl*.

In token of the breakdown of logical categories, individual surrealist art works generally had the quality called objectivation: they were composed of specific, clearly identifiable parts. Only in the manipulation of these parts was a possible abstraction, symbolic reference, or aesthetic value invoked. Similarly, Pronko speaks of more recent avant-garde playwrights' use of "concrete visual images to suggest a metaphysical bias" and suggests as examples the hats and tree in Beckett's *Waiting for Godot* and the doors in Ionesco's *The Chairs*. Furthermore, only in the juxtaposition or dislocation of these parts could surprising glimpses of surreality be attained. These fragments retained their individual concrete identities. They could be combined but not synthesized. It is the connection between the parts that operates; as in cinema it is the connection between the shots.

This chaos of fragments resisted unification; unity seemed to the surrealists too artificially rational a concept in the face of a chaotic universe. The unity of surrealist art works, like the definition of one object or another as surrealist art, is a matter of the artist's sole and arbitrary decision. Artaud observed that in film, it is the camera that imposes instantaneous temporary unity on whatever it frames, however arbitrary or uncontrolled the contents of the frame. Of course there is also unity insofar as the whole work came from one artist's subconscious. Apollinaire's concept of the internal frame in cubist paintings was, in effect, whatever element of the painting informed the rest— and was, besides, most characteristic of the individual painter. Closer to this concept is Tzara's description of ideal Dada poetry: ". . . a rhythm which one neither sees nor hears; beam from an interior arrangement toward a constellation of order." Again reference to the theater is illuminating, for this ideal rhythm seems like the "tragic rhythm" which Francis Fergusson analyzes as the heart and structure of classical tragedies.

One has the feeling, however, of a surrealist impulse to extract something positive, even definite, from chaos, and perhaps from the inescapable modern doubt over what constitutes a genuine perception. Nonrational and largely nonsensory and nonemotional, surrealist art operated through ideas, or perhaps through the single huge idea of idealessness. This seems connected with the literary or verbal quality which we noted earlier. Although the surrealists shunned abstractions, which are intellectual constructs, there is an abstract, cerebral quality to much of their art, even when the mood is angry or gay: a still place inside the chaos. As a critic said of Magritte's painted images: they have "intense affective import . . . with great immediacy but no sensuous correlative, just as in dreams the action is all in one's head." Perhaps this quality arises from the thrust of their artistic techniques, which move from principle toward experience. Perhaps it is their refusal to use symbolic images, which make coherent connections on several

levels simultaneously, that makes their art seem narrowed despite a commitment to chaos. Certainly this cerebral quality is related to the French classicism within which most of the surrealists were trained, no matter how hard they rebelled. It may be simply that the surrealists tried to exist at extremes whereas most people are used to a kind of ordinary middling human level of existence, and that this gives their art its rather cool, sometimes metallic, still, and almost ascetic quality. It offers experience purified of emotions and flesh.

The drive toward instantaneity which is revealed by every aspect of surrealist art is part of the same attempt to crystallize chaos. The surrealists seem to yearn to intensify existence rather than diffuse it: to gather up Bergson's duration-in-time into the present instant. A conspicuous evidence of this drive is that the majority of surrealist art works do not exist in ongoing time. They are paintings, constructions, or short poems. Presumably their creation was instantaneous; certainly their absorption . . . was to be instantaneous. Novels, which build in time and even use time as an element of content, were alien to surrealism. The surrealist urge toward theater which we have noted seems contradictory here, since plays inevitably progress in time. But, as one means of resolving the contradiction, surrealist plays (and musical compositions) were characteristically extremely short. Surrealist playwrights and Satie combated the cumulative nature of their media in several ways. They repeated words, sounds, musical or verbal phrases, so as to stay in the same place, as it were, and finally to negate any sense of ongoing time within the work; plays whose chronology can never be established do the same. They avoided developing themes of any sort; in any case, such development would have constituted a structure. It is also true, of course, that it is difficult to sustain an art work which refuses to develop—unless as a sort of collage of movements—and this circumstance may be a further factor in the marked brevity of most surrealist musical compositions and plays. We may speculate, in any case, that the tension between surrealism's will to negate time and the art form's will to progress in time is one more source of energy for surrealist drama.

We have already mentioned film's property of arresting time in connection with the film maker's absolute control. Although films do progress in time, the entire duration of the action can be compressed into a physical reel of film. They seem to synthesize, as it were vertically, all stimuli into an instant of effect. Also the film maker can use the medium to make time seem to go backwards or to stop entirely. Artaud wrote an unproduced scenario called *18 Seconds* whose whole purpose lies in this playing with time. We watch the hero watching eighteen seconds pass on a clock; meanwhile the film lasts an hour or two. In principle, the time difference consists of his fantasies; but this is never spelled out, and the focus of the film, as evidenced by its title, lies precisely in the relativity of time. Unlike surrealist plays, which tended to be brief so as not to dissipate their force and to exist only for a supreme instant, film made it possible to sustain the instant. Susan Sontag described film in words which we could use about surrealist theater and really about all the surrealist arts: "a compact theater-experience which approaches . . . the condition of painting"; and in this connection we might remember that many of the early film makers were painters.

Like the Eiffel Tower, surrealist art came from the disintegration of old aesthetics in the face of a fresh redefinition of art. Happy to be conspicuous, it advertised its own philosophical bases and its differences from everything that surrounded it.

Two exhibits from the 1938 International Exhibition of Surrealism in Paris. At left, Salvador Dali with his Window Dummy. *At right, his* Rainy Taxi. *Copyright Demart Pro Arte B.V.*

It also reveals, on analysis, attitudes which all Paris did in fact come to share. (pp. 72-7)

> *Nahma Sandrow, "Surrealist Art," in her* Surrealism: Theatre, Arts, Ideas, *Harper & Row, Publishers, 1972, pp. 49-77.*

POETRY

RICHARD STAMELMAN

[In the following excerpt, Stamelman discusses the unique use of language in Surrealist poetry.]

The absolute referral to the context of a poem and to the context alone is what distinguishes surrealist poetry from other kinds of poetry. A surrealist poem is a text without symbolic value. Absent from it are all meanings that might exist before the advent of writing of the text, namely those universal meanings traditionally assigned to words by men and catalogued in their dictionaries. Instead, its meanings depend on the relations that come into being during the act or process by which the text constitutes itself through time and space: that time during which the text develops and deploys itself and that space, namely the page, in which the poem's movement and self-deployment actually take place.

A word integrated into the organic structure of the surrealist poem is automatically divested of its traditional meanings; it is no longer a symbol for some thing existing in the world outside the poem. In linguistic terms, the poem attempts to divorce a *signifiant* ["signifier"] from those *signifiés* ["objects signified"] with which it has always been associated and to replace them with other *signifiés* that come into being as the poem unfolds temporally and spatially. The new meaning or meanings given the *signifiant* are coeval with the genesis of the poem. Words, by calling other words into being and maintaining a perpetual dialogue with them, generate innumerable existential meanings. . . . (pp. 561-62)

But words do not give up the semantic ghost easily; they do not willingly part with their symbolic meanings. These must be wrested away. When the word is inserted in a surrealist context, a wedge is driven between the word and the thing it denotes. When other meanings are then attached to the word, through the process of chance encounters by which words are juxtaposed to one another in startling ways, a tension forms between the familiar, symbolic meaning of the word and its new contextual meanings, as the following example from André Breton's poem "Amour parcheminé" reveals:

> J'appelle une fille qui rêve dans la maisonnette dorée; elle me rejoint sur les tas de mousse noire et m'offre ses lèvres qui sont des pierres au fond de la rivière rapide.
>
> ["'I call a girl who dreams in the golden cottage; she rejoins me on the heap of black moss and offers me her lips which are stones at the bottom of the rapid river.'"]

The dislocating transformation of the girl's lips into stones actually occurs; the lips do not simply resemble the stones found at the bottom of a river; they are the stones. Since a reader knows the things to which the word "lips" and the word "stones" refer, and since he knows that lips and stones cannot be transformed one into another, he finds Breton's poem difficult to accept because it contradicts his experience of the world and his use of language as well. It is the poet's intention, unconscious or otherwise, to juxtapose the words "lips" and "stones" so that their common, universally recognized meanings will be called into question and rendered problematic. Liberated from symbolic meanings the words can now develop new meanings in the text. In this manner, the surrealist de-symbolization of language unlocks the immense potential for creation which words possess; as the Mexican poet Octavio

Paz remarks, "Abolie la distance entre le nom et la chose; nommer c'est créer, et imaginer, naître" ["Abolish the distance between the name and the thing; to name is to create, and to imagine is to give birth"].

The surrealist poem constitutes a world literally apart, one that is generated by language. Within the poem, what language calls into being is the only reality. The poem does not recount or represent the birth and evolution of a world but is the very birth and evolution it presents. It is a cosmogony in the process of becoming. When in the opening line of one of his more famous poems from *L'Amour la poésie* Paul Eluard writes, "La terre est bleue comme une orange" ["The earth is blue like an orange"], he means for the reader to accept the words of the line literally, for, as he states in the next line of the poem, "Jamais une erreur les mots ne mentent pas" ["Never an error words don't lie"]. Since a surrealist poem invents a world that it alone can explain and since this world comes into being through the workings of a language in a state of perpetual motion, anything that can be revealed or expressed or presented in words truly exists. It is real, it happens, for words never lie. Expression in language guarantees the reality of whatever it is that is expressed. Expression is being. The surrealist poem, moreover, presents words in the act of creation; Breton's statement that "Les mots font l'amour" ["words make love"] is not hyperbole. Out of the silence and the vacuity that precede poetic creation—a state of nothingness incarnated by the blankness of the white paper staring back at the poet—there surges forth a word which, by projecting itself onto the page, initiates a succession of other words, an uninterrupted flow of language, which, when it finally does cease, has constituted a poem, created a self, invented a world: "Contre le silence et le vacarme, j'invente la Parole, liberté qui s'invente elle-même et m'invente, chaque jour" ["Against silence and cacophony, I invent the Word, liberty which invents itself and invents me, each day"].

In a surrealist poem language is experienced in the fullness of its materiality. What Francis Ponge calls "l'épaisseur sémantique des mots" ["the semantic density of words"] is found in surrealist poetry where words are objects that bump into one another by chance, where they take up positions in an environment of other word-objects, and where they are perpetually creating unusual relationships with one another. To read a surrealist poem is to place oneself in direct, first-hand contact with word-objects that exist nowhere else. Like the orange to which Eluard compared the earth, a word or an image in a surrealist poem has density, roundness, palpability, freshness; it even promises immense pleasure. The world constituted by the language of the surrealist poem is concrete, tangible, resolutely real. It is composed of letters, syllables, sounds, words, images, and sentences that must be regarded not as figures of speech but as speech itself, not as allusions to objects in the world beyond the poem but as the real, material things themselves, which invite the participation and the physical contact of a reader. . . . (pp. 562-64)

The substantiality of a word, its physical presence, has little ultimately to do with its meaning. . . . Rather it depends on the word's sensuous appeal as form, which is to say, as a series of black letters imposing themselves vertically, horizontally, and diagonally on the white surface of a page or as a series of differentiated sounds moving through the silent space of air. The word, seen from this point of view, becomes a body which occupies a space and fills a void; it is a three-dimensional object or what Ponge even calls "une personne à trois dimensions"

["a three-dimensional person"]. The word, by adopting the quality of substantiality or presence possessed by all things that occupy a space, can then offer itself to the contemplation of a reader. As an object capable of giving pleasure and enjoyment, as sensuous form, the word immediately appeals to the eyes or the ears of a reader, affecting his senses even before making contact with his intellect. The word first becomes an experience. And this is precisely what a surrealist poem gives: the experience of words, the feel of sensuous, living language, the enjoyment of what Eluard calls "les délices du langage le plus pur" ["the delights of the purest language"].

Since the relations and meanings created in the surrealist poem are born from the self-deployment of words that ultimately weave a poem, since these words have no rapports with anything outside the poem, but rather are related by contiguity to one another, and since language is ultimately being, then a surrealist poem is essentially non-mimetic. Words are accepted for themselves and not as signs or symbols for things. Imitation is no longer a factor because the surrealist poem envisions some thing—a world, an event, an adventure—that has never before existed. "Il n'y a pas de modèle pour qui cherche ce qu'il n'a jamais vu" ["There is no model for those who seek what they have never seen"], writes Eluard. A truly imaginative act is innovative, venturing into uncharted realms. And what it creates is automatic, spontaneous, instinctive, and beyond the power of reason to understand. . . . (pp. 565-66)

Richard Stamelman, "Surrealist Poetry: The Revolt Against Mimesis," in Kentucky Romance Quarterly, *Vol. 22, No. 4, 1975, pp. 561-71.*

ANNA BALAKIAN

[*Balakian is a critic of French literature who has written extensively on writers of the Symbolist, Surrealist, and Dadaist movements. In the following excerpt from her highly regarded study* Surrealism: The Road to the Absolute *(1970), she analyzes Surrealist poetic imagery.*]

In his first manifesto, published in 1924 [see excerpt above], André Breton, who remained all his life the principal generator of the surrealist movement, declared that surrealism was a new mode of expression, which he and his colleagues had discovered and wished to put at the disposal of others. When in the following year he took over the direction of the periodical, *La Révolution Surréaliste,* he stated that the principal aim of its founders was to raise the French language from the abject insignificance and stagnation to which it had been reduced under the influence of successful but mediocre authors like Anatole France. Six years later, in his second manifesto [see excerpt above], he once more contended that the chief activity of surrealism was in the field of verbal reconstruction, and that social and political questions were of secondary concern. In *Entretiens* (1952), considering surrealist activities in retrospect, Breton again asserted that their purpose was "essentially and before all else" to put language in "a state of effervescence."

Now linguistic innovations are an essential function of the *ars poetica*, whether we look back on the enrichments of vocabulary achieved by the Renaissance poets, the discriminate choice of words of the classicists, the emotional flexibility of language discovered by the romanticists, or the elasticity of connotation cultivated by the symbolists. As Shelley pointed out in his *Defense of Poetry,* the poet, through his use of language, establishes the analogies among life's realities, but every so often when these associations have grown stale and lost their power of conveying integral thought, it is up to him to refresh his imagery and thereby preserve the vitality of language.

Breton, together with Louis Aragon, Paul Eluard, Tristan Tzara, and some fifty other poets and artists (all under thirty), well versed in the history of literature, aesthetics, and philosophy, and possessed of a very strong capacity for convictions, felt that they had arrived at a crucial moment in the development of the French language. They considered literature at an *impasse* and called the manner of writing of their elders degrading and cowardly. But instead of confining themselves to a local renovation of the poetic form, they welcomed all poets of any nationality who wished to participate in their systematic cult of the latent possibilities of language. They believed that their linguistic revolution could not only revive literature but lead to a new understanding of the objects designated by language and thereby situate them at the center of a new *mystique*. (pp. 140-42)

The creative role of language was strongly stressed in the surrealists' concept of poetry. Poetry was no longer to be an expression of ideas or emotions but the creation of a series of images, which would not necessarily owe their existence to an a priori subject. "Images think for me," said Paul Eluard in "Défense de Savoir." And Aragon explained in the *Traité du Style:* "In our time there are no longer any ideas; they are as rare as smallpox, but it goes without saying that there are images caught, but, but for once well caught, real slaps in the face of any kind of good sense." Breton called ideas vain and ineffective compared to the force of the sudden, unexpected image. In his famous article, "Misère dela Poésie," he tried to come to the rescue of Aragon, accused of subversion in his poem, "Front Rouge." But as far as its aesthetic value was concerned, he dismissed the controversial poem as being a hundred years behind the times despite its so-called modern subject. The fact that it had a definite subject matter to develop belied the contemporary state of poetic evolution, which according to Breton banishes unity of subject matter from the poem. It is Breton's belief that the speed of thinking is not superior to that of linguistic expression, which, therefore, should not be subservient to logical thought. Words brought together by creative intuition could explode in a dynamic image which would be more provocative than are abortive thoughts seeking words to give them a countenance, he explains in his second manifesto. Images, then, are not to be *directed* by thoughts but should be conducive to them, and the function of the poem in regard to the reader is what Eluard called "donner à voir," *to give sight*. It is up to the reader to participate in the creative act of the author by deriving from his own pool of personal associations his particular stream of thought. And in order to allow the reader freedom of mental association there must be a compression of language and a minimum denominator of self-evident meaning.

Now the surrealists did not have in mind the type of imagery put into the French language by Verlaine and Mallarmé, i.e., terminology abstract in meaning and so undefined in connotation, in Verlaine's poetry, that it suggests moods rather than visions, or, in the case of Mallarmé, so hermetic as to remain in the Closed Book of one man's mind. On the contrary, their vocabulary is concrete in shape and color, in texture and intent, sometimes so precise as to be exclusive in use and technical in meaning. The words serving as stimuli or irritants to the senses were to produce their own images. Language was to be endowed with a hallucinogenic quality, and if expertly used, could grant pleasures beyond those induced by narcotics. Bre-

ton compares the spontaneity with which these images offer themselves and their habit-forming character to the stupefying state of mind produced by artificial paradises. In this state of subconscious stimulation the poet is alerted to the sensations that words can produce much in the manner that the painter is attracted to objects, which mean a different thing to each artist and speak a different language to each spectator. The surrealist poet in his use of words was approaching the painter's technique, and that is how a closer bond was established between poetry and art than ever before, and a greater gap between poetry and the literary forms that continued to have as their aim the expression of ideas.

A serious study of the quality and range of words was then, the *sine qua non* of poetry. . . . [A] generation before the surrealists, Guillaume Apollinaire had envisaged the possibility of experiments and investigations in this field. Breton and his colleagues went so far as to establish a Central Bureau of Surrealist Research to experiment with writing and to accept communications relative to their research from outside their ranks. In a chapter of *Les Pas Perdus*, characteristically called "Words without Wrinkles," Breton stated that the greatest poetic act was the understanding of the full destiny of words. He suggested ways of doing this: by studying the words themselves, the reaction of words to each other, the appearance of words and the effect of the figurative meaning on the literal. To such considerations could be attributed provocative surrealist titles as "Le Revolver à Cheveux Blancs" ("The White-haired Revolver"), "Clair de Terre" ("Earthshine"), "Les Yeux Fertiles" ("Fertile Eyes"), "L'Homme Approximatif" ("Approximative Man"), "Le Poisson Soluble" ("Soluble Fish"), "Le Paysan de Paris" ("The Peasant of Paris").

Breton explained that it took him six months to write his poem, "Forêt-noire" (of which the actual word count is *thirty*), for he virtually "coddled" the words to determine the space they permitted between each other, their tangency with innumerable other words which would not appear in the poem, but with which the written words came in contact in the author's mind during the process of composition. The most evident demonstration of the spontaneous suggestive power of words was the glossary composed by the surrealist poet, Michel Leiris, which consisted of basic words and the images they evoke, as for example: "humain—la main humide, moite. L'as-tu connue, cette main? ingénu—le génie nu; langage—bagage lent de l'esprit; révolution—solution de tout rêve; rumeur—brume des bruits qui meurent su fond des rues; suicide—idée sûre de sursis" ["human—the humid hand, moist. Have you known it, this hand? Ingenuous—the nude genie; language—sluggish baggage of the spirit; revolution—solution of every dream; rumor—fog of noises that die at the foot of streets; suicide—sure idea for surcease"]. Although seemingly playful, Leiris' verbal associations have as their basis a keen phonemic character and reveal his sensitivity to linguistic structures.

The poet's tolerance to words had to be increased; he could help himself by dismissing the wrong words from his mind. Which are the wrong words? Those that have wandered too far afield from their concrete specifications, those that have served too often to form rhymes, those that have received the tag "poetic" through excessive usage in poetry. Abused words can gain a new value if their primitive meaning is sought out. Sometimes it is even advisable to give a word the wrong meaning, for words do not really tell a lie, and if they come to the poet's mind at a given moment it is because they fulfill a poetic necessity. Breton discovered that he sometimes unwittingly used a word whose true meaning he had forgotten; looking it up later he would find that his use of the word was not etymologically incorrect.

For a more drastic interpretation of the meaning of words we can refer to Aragon's *Traité du Style,* in which he claims that dictionaries do not cover the full connotation of words; there is meaning contained in each syllable, according to him, and inherent in the very spelling of the words. Words are what another surrealist, Arpad Mezei, called "multidimensional," in an evaluation of surrealist accomplishments in *Le Surréalisme en 1947.* Etymology, which is only one of its dimensions, has unfortunately been overstressed and has become its dead weight, according to Breton. Michel Leiris considers it a perfectly useless science; the poet must look for the secret ramifications of words in the entire domain of language, the canals created by the association of sounds, of forms, and ideas. When this inner working of words is understood, language becomes prophetic and supplies a thread with which to guide us in the labyrinth of the mind, he explained in connection with his "Glossary."

To discover, then, what one might call the high voltage of words was to be the key to surrealist poetry. But in the composition of the poem, what is even more important than the right word is the happy marriage of words into illuminating (not elucidating) associations, which become the basic structure of the poetic image. The surrealists found in automatic writing a rich hunting ground for the capture of word associations. It assumed the same importance in the technical equipment of the surrealist as the practice of scales to the musician. In this quasi-hypnotic state the hand writes or draws (for the same thing can be done in art) almost alone, and the pen or pencil transcribes spontaneously the subconscious affiliations we feel between the words. These "Surrealist texts," as they are called, must not be taken for poems. They are just a means of developing or enriching poetic consciousness; they also break down traditional word associations which are too deep-set to be warded off consciously, and which are not only ineffective in imagery but even detrimental to the component words involved in the tedious alliance. Words should be drawn together not by emotional kinship but by what Baudelaire called "sorcellerie évocatoire" (incantatory bewitchment), or in the more recent terminology of Aragon, "puissance incantatorie" (power of incantation). Sometimes it is nothing more than assonance or alliteration, sometimes symmetry of appearance, sometimes antithesis. Of such nature are expressions like "femmes fugaces" (fugaceous females), "le très coquet caméléon de l'entendement" (the very flirtatious chameleon of understanding), "le désert vertical" (the vertical desert), "l'aigle sexuel" (the sexual eagle), "l'adorable déshabillé de l'eau" (the adorable deshabille of the water), "les arêtes des buissons et des navires" (the fishbones of the bushes and the boats), images taken at random from the poetry of Eluard and Breton, the effectiveness of which is entirely dependent on the rhythmic attuneness, generally impossible to carry over into direct translation.

To go one step further, this unexpected linking of words became the foundation of the new metaphor, which, instead of being based on analogy, is derived from divergence and contradiction. A more recent surrealist, Jean Brun, has put it somewhat emphatically in saying in "Le Problème de la Sensation et le Surréalisme": "The capital fact of the entire history of the mind lies perhaps in this discovery of surrealism: the word 'comme' ['like'] is a *verb* which does not signify 'tel que'

['such as']." The surrealist associates what we normally dissociate and the word "like" is inappropriate because the connections are nonsequential or psychic rather than rational. It is a principle to be remembered in reading almost any poem of Breton, Eluard, and most of the other surrealists; it is the trademark of authenticity. It renovates the entire notion of the metaphor, when for instance André Breton can say in "Le Revolver à Cheveux Blancs":

> The seasons like the interior of an apple from which
> a slice has been cut out.

> (Les saisons lumineuses comme l'intérieur d'une
> pomme dont on a détaché un quartier.)

Or in Péret's "Et les seins mouraient":

> He showed the north horizon
> and the horizon opened up like the door of a god
> stretched itself like the tentacles of an octopus

> (Il montra l'horizon du nord
> et l'horizon s'ouvrit comme le porte d'un dieu
> s'étendit comme less tentacules d'une pieuvre)

A number of years later the technique still persists in René Char's *Le Poème Pulvérisé* (1947) when he envisages that the soot of the poker and the crimson of the cloud are but one: "L'encre du tisonnier et la rouge du nuage ne font qu'un."

The metaphor used to be considered the most effective means of representing the *image*—which was preconceived in the writer's mind. Now the cart is placed before the horse, and it is the unusual metaphor that creates the even more extraordinary image, which is composed of two or more elements having no logical relationship with each other. One of the first to state the principle clearly was . . . the so-called cubist poet, Pierre Reverdy, whom the surrealists revered as their master. Breton quoted him in his first manifesto and praises him again in his 1952 review of surrealist outlook, *Entretiens,* for his "magie verbale." Reminiscing about Reverdy's discussions of the nature of the poetic image, Breton esteems him as an even more important theoretician than Guillaume Apollinaire. In *Le Gant de Crin* Reverdy had defined the image as the spontaneous meeting of two very distant realities whose relationship is grasped solely by the mind. Reverdy, moreover, observed that the more remote the relationship was between the two realities, the stronger became the resulting image. On the other hand, the power or even the life of the image was threatened if it were to be totally acceptable to the senses. Following this line of thinking, Breton finds that comparison is therefore a poor axis for the image, and that a radical modification is necessary in the very structure of the analogy. The surrealist image has to be a farfetched—or rather deep-fetched—chance encounter of two realities whose effect is likened to the light produced by the contact of two electrical conductors. In the ordinary image, the terms of which are chosen on the basis of similarity, the difference in potential between them is negligible and no spark results. The value of the surrealist image, therefore, consists not in an equivalence but in the subtraction of one set of associations from the other. The greater the disparity, the more powerful the light, just as in electricity the greater the difference in potential of the two live wires the greater the voltage. The resulting spark of imagery is first dazzling to the mind, which subsequently accepts and appreciates its reality. Thus by their inadvertent function the metaphors and resulting images increase the poet's scope of understanding of himself, and of the subtle relationships in the world about him. Says René Crevel:

"The writer makes his metaphor, but his metaphor unveils, throws light on its author."

Images constructed according to this notion contain a dose of absurdity and that element of surprise, which, in the opinion of Guillaume Apollinaire, was to be one of the fundamental resources of the modern mind. This type of poetic imagery rises on the same foundation as the "fortuitous meeting," in the words of Max Ernst, of two objects in a surrealist painting.... The effect that Dali created by placing a telephone and an omelette on the same range of vision in his painting, *Sublime Moment*, is a result of the same technique as the juxtaposition in a verbal image such as "un couvert d'argent sur une toile d'araignée" (a silver plate on a cobweb) in Breton's poem "Sur la Route qui monte et descend." Benjamin Péret's poery is the constant locale of strange encounters. More than anyone else among the surrealists he has practiced the rule of juxtaposition of distant realities, beginning with Lautréamont's famous formula: "beau comme" ["beautiful like"]. Describing the nudity of his mistress:

> Beautiful like a hole in a windowpane
> beautiful like the unexpected encounter of a cataract and
>   a bottle
> The cataract looks at you, beauty of bottle
> the cataract scolds because you are beautiful
> bottle
> because you smile at her and she regrets being a
>   cataract
> because the sky is shabbily dressed
> because of you whose nudity is the reflection of
>   mirrors.

(pp. 143-50)

Breton gave classifications for the surrealist image, for which examples can readily be found in his works and in those of other surrealists.

1. *Contradictions.* For instance in one of his earlier surrealist texts Breton plays on the linguistic contradiction caused by the simultaneous use of the past, present, and future tenses to create the impossible phenomenon of the movement of nonexistent curtains on the windows of future houses:

> Les rideaux qui n'ont jamais été levés
> Flottent aux fenêtres des maisons qu'on construira

> ["The curtains that were never put up
> Billow at the windows of the houses that will be built"]

In the much later poem, "Tiki" from the group called *Xénophiles*, the same sense of contradiction is conveyed by the combination of two adjectives incompatible in their original concrete meanings though having a junction in their extended connotation:

> I love you on the surface of seas
> Red like the egg when it is green

> (Je t'aime à la face des mers
> Rouge comme l'oeuf quand il est vert)

2. *One of the terms of the image is hidden.* This can be noticed in a section of Eluard's "La Rose Publique," consisting of a series of incomplete images:

> All along the walls furnished with decrepit orchestras
> Darting their leaden ears toward the light
> On guard for a caress mingled with the thunderbolt

> (Le long des murailles meublées d'orchestres décrepits
> Dardant leurs oreilles de plomb vers le jour
> A l'affût d'une caresse corps avec la foudre)

3. *The image starts out sensationally, then abruptly closes the angle of its compass.* Witness the following line from Breton's "La Mort Rose," in which he juxtaposes his dreams with the sound of the eyelids of water and suddenly finishes the image with an unsatisfactory "dans l'ombre":

> Mes rêves seront formels et vains comme le bruit
>   de paupières de l'eau dans l'ombre.

> ["My dreams will be formal and vain like the sound
>   of eyelids of water in shadow"]

Under this heading would come all the unsuccessful images which do not measure up to the expectations aroused by the beginning of the metaphor.

4. *The image possesses the character of a hallucination.* Typical of this is the entire poem, "L'Homme Approximatif," of Tristan Tzara with its agglomeration of animal, vegetable, and mineral words, coming every so often to a head in this strange refrain:

> For stony in my garments of schist I have dedicated my
>   awaiting
>   to the torment of the oxydized desert
>   and to the robust advent of the fire

> (Car rocailleux dans mes vêtements de schiste j'ai voué mon
>   attente
>   au tourment du désert oxydé
>   au robuste avènement du feu)

Or Michel Leiris' vision of the sun in his "Marécage du Sommeil":

> When the sun is but a drop of sweat
> a sound of bell
> the red pearl falling down a vertical needle

> (Quand le soleil n'est plus qu'une goutte de sueur
> un son de cloche
> la perle rouge qui tombe le long d'une aiguille verticale)

In an early prose writing of Benjamin Péret, *La Brebis Galante*, 1924, we appear to be witnessing the vision of a man in a barn watching the cows eat hay when suddenly the hallucination begins:

> the roof of the barn cracked from top to bottom. A white sheet appeared through the opening and was torn away by a wind that I could not feel. Then, slowly, it descended to the ground. Then the earth opened up. And I saw, along a strictly perpendicular line, a little red fish descend from the roof slipping down the sheet and sinking into the ground. It was followed by a second and a third. Finally their number grew as quickly as their dimension and the rarefaction of the air in the high atmospheric strata permitted it. The wind swelled and the barn slipped under the ground. When I say slipped . . . it sank or they flew away, for the barn had divided into two. One half left with the straw and the other half with the cows and each in a different direction, arriving at the same spot: the mountain of squirrel skin.

With the last dazzling image in which the mountain is compared with the skin of the squirrel Péret combines the most immovable entity with the most agile and mobile of creatures.

5. *The image lends to the abstract the mask of the concrete.* In this category would fall at least half of the surrealist images. They are numerous in Breton's poetry. Take for example simple transfers such as the following: eternity incorporated in a wrist watch, life in a virgin passport, thought becoming a white curve on a dark background, lightness shaking upon our roofs her

angel's hair. Or there are double-deckers such as in *Clair de Terre:*

> And in my handbag was my dream this smelling salt
> That had only been used by the godmother of God.
>
> (Et dans le sac à main il y avait mon rêve ce flacon de sels
> Que seule a respirés la marraine de Dieu.)

or his definition of life in *Fata Morgana:*

> Life might be the drop of poison
> Of non-sense injected into the song of the lark over the
>   poppies.
>
> (La vie serait la goutte de poison
> Du non-sens introduite dans le chant de l'alouette au-dessus
>   des coquelicots.)

(pp. 152-55)

6. *The image implies the negation of some elementary physical property.* Eluard will startle his reader by telling him that the earth is blue like an orange; and in Breton's poetry you might hear the sound of wet street lamps or of a bell made of straw, or find him wishing for the sun to come out at night, or be assured that the tree he has chopped down will forever remain green.

7. Finally there is the broad classification which would include *all images that provoke laughter;* such as in Benjamin Péret's "Au Bout du Monde":

> Stupid like sausages whose sauerkraut has already been eaten
>   away.
>
> (Bêtes comme des saucisses dont la choucroute a déjà été
>   mangée.)

The master of the "gay and acid" is of course Benjamin Péret. Drawing from the daily images their absurd and humoristic ingredients, Péret never reaches the pitch of black humor of Lautréamont. There is in him too much of what the French call "bonhomie," the healthy, exuberant sense of life, the inner sunshine of his own disposition:

> There would be in the hollow of my hand
> a little lantern
> golden like a fried egg
> and so light that the soles of my shoes would fly like a fake
>   nose
> so that the bottom of the sea would be a telephone booth
> and the phone would be forever out of order
>
> (Il y aurait dans le creux de ma main
> un petit lampion froid
> doré comme un oeuf sur le plat
> et si léger que la semelle de mes chaussures s'envolerait
>   comme un faux nez
> en sorte que le fond de la mer serait une cabine téléphonique
> d'où personne n'obtiendrait jamais aucune communication)

or in "Vive la Révolution":

> He was beautiful like fresh glass
> Beautiful like the smoke from his pipe
> Beautiful like the ears of a donkey that brays
> Beautiful like a chimney
> Which falls on the head of a policeman
>
> (Il était beau comme une vitre fraîche
> Beau comme la fumée de sa pipe
> Beau comme les oreilles d'un âne qui brait
> Beau comme une cheminée
> Qui tombe sur la tête d'un agent)

(pp. 156-57)

In sum, what essentially separates the surrealist way of writing from the poetry of the preceding generations is *not* its break and emancipation from metrical form; nor does the difference lie in any disregard for grammatical structure. It is, rather, in the use of words: an enrichment of the active vocabulary of poetry, a release from verbal inhibitions, a selection of word association beyond the barriers set up by logic, a new metaphor built upon these incongruous word groupings, and the images resulting from the association of one metaphor with another— which one might call the square of the metaphor. Finally, these images are cast into grammatically accurate sentences connected primarily on the basis of sensual synchronization.

What the surrealists have done is not to sacrifice clarity but to decide that this asset of prose was a liability in poetry. For French had assumed too long with M. Jourdain that what is not prose is verse. Poetry was discovered to be a different type of intellectual activity, consisting of what one might call mental deviation and linguistic alchemy.

It was a terrible test to which language was subjected, a veritable "trial of language" as Aragon had called it. That language which foreign critics have often condemned as unpoetic, as too specific, too rigid to express the ineffable dream vagueness necessary to true poetry, was now being destined to a plane of mystery and irrationalism beyond anything attempted in any of the so-called poetic languages. Recognizing this renaissance of poetry and the linguistic experimentation related to it, Apollinaire had made this challenging statement as early as 1918: "As far as can be seen there are hardly any poets today except of the French language."

It is too early yet to estimate the extent of the transformation surrealism will bring about in the French language, just as the effects of Du Bellay's sixteenth-century *Défense et Illustration de la Langue Française* were not crystallized until the seventeenth century. The surrealists have written too much, confused liberty with license at times, and probably made five unsatisfactory images for every successful one. There has been much trial and error, and unfortunately the surrealists consider every word that falls from their pen so sacred that they have freely published their errors. But the fact remains that their vociferous rejection of standard styles has affected nonsurrealists as well as surrealists and is beginning to have an effect on the poetic language of other countries as well. The surrealists consider their experimental work only the beginning of a tremendous upheaval which will test man's ability to integrate his perceptions over and above the miscellany of nature and thereby make of the poetic image not a representation of reality but an invention of the human mind directive of things to come.

It is evident that in coming into contact with this type of poetry words such as *understanding, explanation, expression* are inappropriate. *Knowledge, empathy, disturbance* are the type of terms that best convey the surrealist poet's aspirations and his relationship with the reader. "Beauty must be convulsive, or it is not beauty," said Breton in *Nadja.* In other words it has to shake up and shape up our reality.

The crucial difference between previous linguistic revolutions and the surrealist one is that this time the transformation of the word is not an end in itself or even a means to the more effective communication of what *is.* Rather, we see that language creates, it makes concrete the ineffable dream. For the surrealist poet, and . . . for the surrealist artist as well, the absolute and the infinite are within range of his pen or pencil, dependent on his power over words (or lines), on his ability to shuffle them, seizing their chance meetings, and on the variety of combinations he can produce with them. His mysticism constantly draws on this reservoir of language; and he finds that language is an inexhaustible reservoir. Through the word, the impossible is made possible, nature can be endowed with metaphysical properties, sensuality takes on new proportions: visions dispersed on the face of the earth, going abegging, undiscerned in their individual solitudes, are drawn to the new linguistic magnet and brought together into a new synthesis of imagery, which in turn creates a new synthesis of existence. (pp. 165-67)

> Anna Balakian, *"The Surrealist Image," in her* Surrealism: The Road to the Absolute, *revised edition, Dutton, 1970, pp. 140-69.*

NOVEL

GERMAINE BREE AND MARGARET GUITON

[*Brée is a French-born American critic and translator. Her critical works are devoted to modern French literature and include* Marcel Proust and Deliverance from Time *(1955) and* Gide *(1957). Concerning her work as a critic, Brée has written: "I do not consider myself a writer and should probably be classed among the 'academic' critics. . . . I have no particular critical method and am, in fact, an eclectic. Each writer seems himself to suggest to me the method of approach I should use as I attempt to elucidate the kind of book he has written. . . . I attempt, with a good deal of difficulty, to communicate what seems to me essential about each, rather than to prove, attack or praise." Guiton is the author of a critical study of the works of Jean de La Fontaine. In the following excerpt, the critics discuss André Breton's* Nadja *(1928;* Nadja*) and Louis Aragon's* Le paysan de Paris *(1926; Paris Peasant) as examples of the Surrealist novel.*]

During the year 1923-24 three writers who, to a large extent, had created the prewar novel—Pierre Loti, Maurice Barrès and Anatole France—happened to die. And during the same year André Breton, leader of the nascent surrealist movement, published his first manifesto [see excerpt above]. It was to be expected that the collision of these two events, the last rites of three respected literary veterans and the organization of the surrealist revolution, would produce sparks, but Breton's obituary of Anatole France surpassed all expectations:

> Loti, Barrès, France, let us at least put a beautiful festive banner on the year that did away with these three sinister simpletons: the idiot, the traitor and the policeman. With France, a bit of human servility has passed away. Let us celebrate the burial day of ruse, of traditionalism, of patriotism, of skepticism, and of heartlessness. . . . To incase his body let them empty, if they wish, a bookstall, such as is found along the *quais,* of those old books "that he loved so well," and let them throw the whole thing into the Seine. Now that he is dead, this man must not be allowed to make any more dust.

Today, when we look back on this benevolent old man, guilty of little more than an inflated literary reputation, we are surprised that he should have aroused such violent passions. Undoubtedly Breton was aiming for a scandal, a double scandal in the sense that he was deliberately offending both the literary standards of the day and a more general human respect for death. It is also true that to Breton, the benign and bearded figure of Anatole France, whose "delicate irony," "smiling

skepticism" and "hellenic graces" had so delighted his contemporaries, was guilty of a monstrous crime, that of calmly accepting the existing order of things. To a generation thirsting for fiery alcohols he had politely offered a dish of lukewarm camomile tea.

This camomile tea approach to life is strangely enough a powerful literary force. The reading public seldom refuses a pleasant sedative. Pehaps the only effective antidote to Anatole France was the irritant exploited so successfully by Breton and his disciples: an explosive and infuriating "so what?" The surrealist "so what?" is apparent in the scandal-mongering literary productions, lectures and art exhibits of the twenties. It helps explain the peculiar prestige of certain legendary figures of surrealism. It does not, however, account for the whole of surrealism. Indeed, had surrealism consisted entirely in the purely negative action of public scandals and private suicides, it would have been as short-lived as its predecessor, dadaism. The destructive "so what?" with which the surrealists battered the walls of practical necessity was backed by a positive faith in the deeper and more significant experience of life vaguely apprehended in childhood, in dreams, in occasional moments of heightened sensibility. And the surrealists themselves, these outwardly irresponsible *enfants terribles,* were aiming in deadly earnest at a total, if somewhat perverse, regeneration of the human race.

It was natural, given their literary aims and techniques, that they should have been attracted to the field of poetry rather than that of fiction. Indeed, for Breton, fiction was so irrevocably allied with the names of Bourget, Barrès and Anatole France that he considered the novel itself a hopeless product of "the realist attitude, born of positivism from St. Thomas to Anatole France"—an attitude that he defied with his habitual but in this case paticularly pertinent "so what?": "What I really cannot stand are these feeble discussions about this or that move when there is nothing to win or lose. When the game is not worth the candle." And yet to the very extent that they subordinated literature to life, that they earnestly attempted to understand and bring to light the hidden potentialities of the human imagination, these would-be poets were really unconscious novelists. They were not of course novelists in the traditional sense of the word, nor could the problems they investigated be handled with traditional instruments. They were innovators, and the special surrealist innovation lay in an adaptation of poetic techniques, in particular the technique of metaphor, to novelistic ends.

This development would no doubt have taken place even if the surrealists had never existed. Poetry, after Baudelaire, Rimbaud and Mallarmé, had become so rich in possibilities that the more gifted novelists naturally turned to it rather than to the exhausted novel for inspiration. Gide's novels are strongly influenced by the symbolist theories of late nineteenth century poetry. Proust, whom Breton unperceptively dismisses as another "analyst," had conceived his novel in terms of poetic analogy long before the surrealist manifesto ever saw the light of day. Yes—but no one, not even the surrealists themselves, had realized what was happening. Poetry, during the early years of this century, had been conceived as something utterly distinct from prose. It was consequently the minor, partial aspects of both Gide and Proust that stuck, and influenced, the secondary writers of the day. The surrealists, however inferior to Gide and Proust in literary talent, had thoroughly mastered the art of attracting public notice. By their writings, their manifestoes and the very violence of their methods, they succeeded in giving wide publicity to a literary tendency that in France, as elsewhere, has become an important aspect of contemporary fiction: the destruction of the barrier hitherto dividing poetry and prose into two watertight compartments.

The surrealists themselves, given their antipathy to the existing novel, never admitted that they were using the novel form. But how else can we describe Breton's *Nadja*, 1928, or Aragon's *Le Paysan de Paris* (*The Paris Peasant*), 1926? Neither one reveals that uncontrolled flow of the subconscious mind apparent in certain surrealist poems. Breton uses the tight and highly controlled prose style of his manifestoes. Aragon is intent on communicating an intelligible meaning. In each case we are offered, not simply the immediate expression of the poetic imagination, but a methodical investigation of the poetic imagination at work. The result is neither poetry nor criticism. The negative influence of the conventional novel form is frequently apparent, however, and this negative influence is a connecting link—of sorts. *Nadja* and *Le Paysan de Paris* are perhaps best defined as "anti-novels": a deliberate transgression of the established rules of the game.

The novel, by its very nature, is a fiction, an artificial reorganization of the raw materials of life. Much as the surrealists despised the "realist attitude," they were even more strongly opposed to "artifice." Speaking of Huysmans, Breton exclaimed: "How far I separate him from all the empiricists of the novel who attempt to bring forth characters distinct from themselves and situate them physically, morally, as they may desire, for the sake of one prefers not to know what cause!" The surrealist anti-novel is a direct transcription, not of the irrelevant routines, but of the surprising and unexpected shocks of life. Like Salvation Army converts, Breton and Aragon are giving personal evidence in favor of their creed, "le merveilleux du quotidien"—the miraculous quality of daily life.

This naked realism, unexpected, amusing, even slightly fantastic when kept in its place, becomes a serious bore when it degenerates into a childish insistence on "this is the way it really happened." Breton, in particular, often resembles the naïve storyteller who imagines that his story—whether this be of an unusual coincidence or a supernatural event—gains in interest and credibility by frequent and solemn guarantees as to its authenticity. But perhaps this is all part of the scheme. The surrealists believed that certain privileged people, objects and places have inexplicable psychic powers. For the individual imagination this certainly is true. We all have our personal fetishes. The collective fetish is possible only in hermetic and highly unified communities. And this exactly describes the surrealist group at its inception. Like the Brontë sisters living on their moors, Breton and his disciples invented a mythological kingdom in the heart of postwar Paris. Its headquarters was the Passage de l'Opéra of Aragon's *Le Paysan de Paris*, a covered arcade since destroyed to make room for the further expansion of the Boulevard Haussman. Its divinities were peculiar, marginal figures like Breton's Nadja, a mysterious "seeress" who ended up in an insane asylum. Both *Nadja* and *Le Paysan de Paris*, however personal in feeling, are thus supported by the wider framework of surrealist mythology. And Breton's insistent "this is the way it really happened" is no doubt intended to emphasize this aspect of his book.

Although many members of the surrealist clique knew Nadja, Breton was the only one who established any degree of personal intimacy with her. His resulting adventure, which shows the supernatural effects of certain emotional affinities, is no doubt a particular example of an over-all phenomenon generally classified as "love." Jules Romains, with his *Psyché*, once attempted something of the kind, but he made the mistake of naming the word, of analyzing the situation, of bringing grossly scientific instruments to bear on an intimate and inexplicable phenomenon. Breton's whole art lies in his refusal to analyze, explain or understand. He knows nothing of Nadja's past or present conditions of life; he meets her, quite by accident, in the street. And the exact nature of their relationship remains vague. This intentional silence on Breton's part liberates his heroine from the practical limitations of time and space, of cause and effect, so that she appears less a woman of flesh and blood than "a free genius, something like one of those spirits of the air which, through certain magical arts, we can momentarily attach to ourselves but which we never can enslave."

More important still, Breton's silence focuses our attention on the fact, not the external conditions and consequences, of his relationship with Nadja and helps to persuade us that this fact is not merely another example of the general phenomenon of love but a unique and miraculous "resonance" that momentarily transcends existing reality. An old theme thus recovers some of its inexplicable attributes, familiar enough in legends and fairy stories but conspicuously absent in any objective analysis of the emotion of love.

Aragon's *Le Paysan de Paris* "remagnetizes," to use surrealist language, another familiar theme, the magical influence of certain remembered scenes. The Passage de l'Opéra, already destroyed when Aragon wrote this book, has the nostalgic glamor of a thing remembered. "I do not make a step toward the past," he tells us, "without rediscovering this sense of strangeness that seized hold of me, when I was still wonder itself, in a scene where for the first time I became conscious of an inexplicable coherence and its radiations in my heart."

This introductory passage is reminiscent of the opening sentence of Barrès's *La Colline inspirée:* "There are certain places where the spirit breathes." But the surrealists, as Aragon proclaims, "no longer worship the gods on high places." Aragon's enchanted scene, in striking antithesis to the traditional concept of a sacred site, is the impermanent, illogical, unheroic and highly metropolitan Passage de l'Opéra. Nor is this scene, like Barrès's mountain top, merely a privileged setting for the unincarnate spirit of Christianity. It is an underground Olympus for the numerous apparitions of a modernized mythology.

A siren appears momentarily in the green, nocturnal light of a shop window. The eternal spirit of Don Juan glitters in the two-toned shoes of a Parisian pimp. An unknown and yet familiar woman steps lightly out of a beauty parlor:

"'Nana!' I exclaimed, 'but how you are gotten up in the latest fashion of the day!'"

"'I am,' she said, 'the very latest fashion of the day, and it is through me that all things breathe. Do you know the latest songs? They are so full of me one cannot sing them: one whispers them. Everything that lives on reflections, everything that glitters, everything that perishes follows me. I am Nana, the idea of time.'"

It is safer to speak of parallel developments than of influences, but these new gods and goddesses, half-human, half-divine, are familiar personages of the postwar novel. Already in Proust the fashionable ladies of Paris society hover on the edges of the animal and vegetable kingdoms. Giraudoux's young girls inherit the mysterious powers of nymphs and sybils. Cocteau's heartless adolescents are clearly related to the minor pagan deities. And presiding over the whole adventure, the venerable goddess of Time, Death, Change, the Passing of All Things, gravely acknowledges that she too is mortal as she glimpses her reflection in a fashionable dress, a popular song, the latest dance—some glittering facet of the modern world.

The only critical test that can be applied to *Nadja* or *Le Paysan de Paris* is the test that Breton and Aragon themselves apply to literature: Does the poetic reality coalesce? Is the spell sustained? Are we really transported into an enchanted surreality? The answer is both yes and no. Nadja is certainly an enchantress and the Passage de l'Opéra an enchanted scene. But the magical potential is never fully exploited in either case. Or, to put it differently, nothing ever happens. The promised surreality is always bypassed, the expected revelation always eluded. Just as he is standing on the threshold of an enchanted kingdom, Breton discovers that he is unworthy of Nadja. Aragon's excursions in the Passage de l'Opéra conclude, not, as he has led us to expect, with "an accession, beyond all my powers, to a still forbidden domain," but with another dose of theory about the "modern world." Past masters in the art of preparation, Breton and Aragon are continually opening magic casements on a perfectly blank wall. And in this respect the surrealist "anti-novel" might be described as something of an anticlimax.

In point of fact, the anticlimax is to be expected. Neither Breton nor the early Aragon is inclined to satisfy the reader, particularly in a genre for which each had so much contempt. Nor are they willing to accept the necessary artifice, if not of plot, at least of pattern and of composition—a unifying factory of some sort. None of the writers connected with surrealism— Aragon, Cocteau and Queneau, for example—matured as a novelist until he had broken with the movement. (pp. 134-40)

> *Germaine Brée and Margaret Guiton, "The Surrealist Anti-Novel," in their* An Age of Fiction: The French Novel from Gide to Camus, *Rutgers University Press, 1957, pp. 132-79.*

ARMAND HOOG

[In the following excerpt, Hoog discusses the contradiction between the themes of destruction and damnation that pervade Surrealist novels and the Surrealists' ambition to restore human innocence.]

In a scornful page of the first *Manifeste du surréalisme* [see excerpt above], André Breton has expressed his contempt for the novel: "Pure and simple expository style . . . is almost the only one used in novels. The authors do not aim very high. . . . I am not spared any hesitations concerning a character: will he be blond, what will be his name, shall we meet him in summer? . . . And the descriptions! Nothing is comparable to the void they offer; they are only an accumulation of catalogue pictures . . . etc." These words were written in 1924. Just what was happening at that time in French literature? A novel by the lamentable Thierry Sandre had just received the Goncourt prize. The French Academy was bestowing its literary award on Abel Bonnard's affected descriptions. An amusing reporter, who for a long time imagined himself a novelist, Paul Morand, had been granted the Prix de la Renaissance. Anatole France, and Barrès, and Loti had just died at the height of their fame; three enemies of surrealism, really three number one enemies, since they were of equal importance. It would be difficult to think that Breton's condemnation of the novel was not more

especially directed against certain novelists. Indeed on another page of the *Manifeste* he cites precedents in fiction, Lewis' *The Monk* for example. "The breath of the marvelous gives it life throughout." He adds, "There are tales to be written for grown-ups, tales that are still almost fairy stories." No contradiction exists between the two passages. The surrealist novel is a possibility. It will attain reality with greater certainty than can the novels called realistic, with their mass of documentation on objects, on fashions, and on furniture. The surrealist leader, as early as 1924, indicates the ultimate superiority of the imagination; really not imagination but the revelation of a higher reality. "The wonderful thing about the fantastic is that there is no longer the fantastic: there is only the real."

In the years to come we shall have to admit that painting and the novel are the most necessary forms of expression for surrealism, since plastic representation alone can offer the image of an overturned world. Overturned, that is to say, destroyed and rebuilt, a field of ruins or a place of transfiguration. The great intermediaries from preceding generations which surrealism has sought out are almost all novelists: Sade, Pétrus Borel, Huysmans, Lewis Carroll, Villiers de l'Isle-Adam. In 1924 Breton was as yet unable to name future masters of surrealist fiction, yet not many years had passed before their names and works were as important for us as the madness of poets and aggressiveness of painters. Aragon, Michel Leiris, Gisèle Prassinos, Scutenaire, Limbour, all were novelists. Breton himself, in spite of what he has said, was a novelist when he published *Nadja* in 1928. The second generation of the surrealist also offered the names of many novelists: Pieyre de Mandiargues, Julien Gracq, René Roger, Marcel Schneider, Maurice Fourré.

The great flame of surrealist protest ate its way into the world of living forms, the cities, the rural districts, trains, chateaux. It is probably true that the surrealist novel most often stops at the first indications of the conflagration and toppling walls, that it pauses to enjoy those cracks which completely span a universe which is turning to rubble. But the writers' ambitions, and especially is this true of André Breton, are directed toward rediscovery of new innocence, the golden age, and the hymns of liberated humanity. On a copy of *L'Amour fou*, André Breton wrote for the author of this essay (in spite of the fact that he considered him on the other side of the fence) these joyous words: "To leave no stone standing in the churches, beginning with the most beautiful ones. And then long live the new myth." Sentences perfectly in keeping with the will and the wonderful optimism of the author. The entire question is to find out whether the visionaries of the school will truly succeed in rebuilding innocence somewhere beyond the ruins. And supposing they do not succeed, how will their venture end? Answering these two questions implies following the trajectory of the surrealist novel.

In French literary history, no imagery in fiction has shown such demiurgical enthusiasm, such joyous and shattering will to change the conditions of existence. A total overthrow must be everywhere the initial step. Lautréamont was, says Julien Gracq, the "angelic dynamiter" whose fictional powers began the work. The time for demolishing is at hand.

I have only to leaf through these accounts in which is projected the surrealist vision, to find again the flaming ardor of destruction still intact. An infernal opera whose libretto is divided among several authors. More than any other, young Aragon, like a child prodigy intent on smashing everything, knew how to spread magic disorder and verbal revolt in his writings. (He will go much farther, and, having broken everything with immense skill, he will become a follower of Stalin.) In *Anicet* one reads, "Paris became a fine building game for me. I invented a sort of idiotic Cook Agency which, with a guide book in hand, was vainly trying to find its way in the labyrinth of eras and places where I moved about without any difficulty. The asphalt began to boil again under pedestrians' feet, houses fell to pieces; some climbed on top of those next door. . . . People led an untroubled existence in apartment houses with no fire, in gigantic aquariums. Suddenly a forest sprang up near the Opera."

I pause as I copy these sentences which are from Aragon's best period, from the time when the contractor in marvels had not yet sacrificed his liberty for the worst kind of conformity. With the passage quoted above had appeared for the first time in the surrealist novel a theme of geographical overthrow which was to enjoy great popularity. If the modern city with its petrified alignment of buildings, with its complex equipment, conceived over a long period of time by technical progress, with its tar and asphalt glued on the living epidermis of the soil, represents what the surrealists most detest, the alliance of industrialism and capitalism, commercial astuteness linked with the absurd pride of science—what a temptation there is for awakening the sleeping elements, for renewing their plot to release the wrath of water and forest on monuments of conceit and vanity! This avenging fiction continues to appear. Aragon uses it again a little farther on when the setting is a store window offering customers a display of exotic fruit. "From rose to red and violet, they take on the appearance of bluish meat, and the split figs bleed like pretty growths of cancer." A prolific miracle is unleashed. "The roots of the yams multiply, crawl, run, climb, and an entire virgin forest hatches in the glass egg. . . . From the taxidermist's shop, which I had not yet noticed, animals escape, filling the branches, the clumps, the vines. . . . The vegetation develops to such a degree, the animals become so numerous that I feel shut in, stifled, strangled. . . . Imagination fills me with fear. How can I get out of the forest? I don't know the magic words."

Here begins a long series of dreams. Fires, forests, tidal waves. Everything is contributing to upsetting the world. In *Aurora* by Michel Leiris there is a cataclysm at sea; a like spectacle occurs in *Le Diapason de l'orage* by René Roger. Léon-Paul Fargue, writing *Vulturne* under the influence of surrealism, shows trains emerging from the stations to lay waste the city of Paris. Pierre Mabille devotes a whole chapter of his *Miroirs du merveilleux* to celebrating catastrophe. "Cities swallowed up during a night, the slow descent of the lava; in the distance the oncoming tidal wave. . . ." This very rich vein has been continued in the novelists of the second generation. In Julien Gracq of *Un Beau Ténébreux:* "I often thought the trees were invading the suburbs, were enclosing the city with an impenetrable forest." In Pieyre de Mandiargues of the *Musée noir* which tells of the vegetal revolt of a jungle, invading the city, abetting the blows of the wreckers. Let us not be duped: if the jungle attacks the cities, it is because the cities must return to the jungle.

It is very easy to propose that this mania of destruction stems from strangely mixed feelings, sexual satisfaction, and doubtless the facile procedures of poetic compensation. Certainly. Why not? Above all it is proper to admit that the surrealist novel, in addition to its vocabulary of aggression and world destruction, utters a forceful "No" to existence as it is organized in this universe. "Existence is elsewhere," wrote Breton

in the last line of the first *Manifeste*. "What I like about *Aurora*," Michel Lieris said in 1946, "is the refusal, on almost every page, to accept the condition of mankind against which—no matter how sanely collective existence may one day be organized—a certain number of people will not cease rebelling." Joy in disorder and suffering, theatrical but pure refusal of man's condition, this goes farther than a mere orgy of colors or the assault of forests on the suburbs.

The clearly expressed intention of the first surrealist novelists was to traverse ruins and to build again, on the other side, what Breton called "the new myth." "It is time to promulgate a new myth capable of carrying man along to the last stage of his final destination . . . ," declare Breton, Joe Bousquet, Pierre Mabille, Jean Ferry, and others in the manifesto of *Rupture inaugurale*. The myth of innocence. Man become divine, creator of his liberty.

In *Le Libertinage* Aragon has expressed this. "The illusion of infinite power over the world. Events bent to my will. I was improving on God. Like a child let loose in a machine shop. I was lowering the levers to see what would happen. . . . Terrible sparks. . . ." And Benjamin Péret in *Main-forte:* "What is the use of being a man if you cannot change lead into cork and cork into lead. . . ." Demiurges—or machinists?

The weakness of the first surrealist novel was precisely in its preoccupation with machinery. And the secret of machinery is quickly discovered. Aragon was the first to become fed up with it. "Go on traveling, my dear friends, if such is your inclination. But as for me, let's think no more about it. You see, I know the secret of the most beautiful adventures." (*Le Libertinage*) He who wishes to destroy the world, and then rebuild it by means of marvels and humor, runs the risk of giving only the description of this strange apparatus. A comical form of artillery, ballistas which seem conceived by a mad engineering student, "objects that overthrow" or those "which function symbolically," and the eternal and tiresome umbrella photographed on the sewing-machine to serve as exegesis for a sentence from Lautréamont. Having set out to discover a myth, we most often have to be satisfied with a "musée noir" ["black museum"; an assemblage of the macabre] (as Pieyre de Mandiargues says), or with a catalogue of trick gadgets. Raymond Roussel's fictional work, in some respects so important, becomes much less interesting when it is concerned with feats of parlor magic. *Locus solus* offers a model of the novel which replaces the mythological impulse by mass production of tedious contrivances. The picture stories of Max Ernst, the unheard of landscapes arranged by J.M.A. Paroutaud, Gisèle Prassinos, Michel Fardoulis-Lagrange, and even, despite their dazzling skill, *Le Diapason de l'orage* by René Roger, the surprise novels of Audiberti which can be classified as quasi-surrealist, the stories collected by Mandiargues in his *Musée noir*—just so many stage sets in which the trick effects are too, too visible. Nothing is left except the fragments of a game.

They wished to give me back "the golden age." That is the title Henri Parisot found for a small contemporary collection which brings together the names of the minor surrealists, Jean Ferry, Georges Limbour, Louis Scutenaire, Paul Colinet, and others. In this collection greatest importance is given to the domain of dreams, that enticing and dangerous realm in which Marcel Béalu alone among the most recent writers has attained some mastery. I try to find the promised state of innocence and that Baudelairian tranquillity of previous existence, reigning over a world which had been cleared of obsessive goals and poisonous litigation. In almost all these authors I discover only a flimsy setting, provided with trap-doors for ghosts. The opera comes to an end in a provincial theater.

Just one exception. One day last year André Breton called together some fifty friends of surrealism in a Parisian hotel on the left bank. His purpose was to reveal to them Maurice Fourré, the author of *La Nuit du Rose-Hôtel*. An extraordinary novel, shining with "appeased" strangeness, it is all the more surprising in that its author is seventy-three years old. Perhaps for the first time a work linked with contemporary surrealism tries to express only reconciliation: of man and the individual, of man and his destiny, of man and the world. But the admiration I express for *La Nuit du Rose-Hôtel* does not make me forget that the author is not a genuine surrealist. The state of innocence which he has attained has not traversed revolt.

One cannot deny that Aragon, as a novelist, had a political turn of mind. Perhaps the first of any of them he sensed the impossibility of arriving at a new state of innocence by means of amusing contrivances and simulated exquisite corpses. Aragon's point of departure means, among other things, that surrealism must go beyond the stage of showmanship, even if the effects are "overwhelming." In Julien Gracq's novels surrealist revelation becomes metaphysical, bringing a sacrificial concept of man, situated between the world and God.

Black and desperate certainty of defeat. All is lost beforehand. That was not what Breton, the wonderful optimist, had imagined when he proposed salvation through "l'amour fou" ["mad love"]. Writers such as Leiris, Antonin Artaud, and Georges Bataille had already allowed personal inclination toward sacrifice and voluntary turning toward misfortune to appear in their works. With them, as with Julien Gracq today, the joyous or savage shout of man protesting against the world was becoming the rending cry of awaited and accepted torture. The demiurge is transformed into victim. He plunges into a kind of damnation. In order to avoid blameworthy recourse to religious vocabulary, let us call is "secular damnation."

In *Aurora* by Michel Leiris, that almost posthumous story which its author published some twenty years after writing it, what moves me—in spite of many trite procedures, in spite of recourse to the most facile display—is precisely that strange appetite for punishment, that strange vocation for perdition. If Leiris calls for Apocalyptic destruction of the world, he does not place himself outside of its reach. He is part of the terrible sacrifice: "blacker than a beast, somber and creaking as a rotten old barouche, you walk or rather you drag yourself through the outskirts of life, with your gnawed thumbs whose layers of skin you have been devouring for countless years. These fingers, which other people use for tender caresses, violent battles, or obstinate work, little by little you tear them, you lay them bare as if you wished to leave only the bone and to ransom, by the tithe of suffering which you thus inflict upon yourself, the threat of other greater, more dangerous pain hovering over you like a vampire." Of course the tone is not new. Lautréamont's influence is present here. But if surrealism has made Maldoror its principal intermediary, it is because, after a half century, it finds in him its own dizziness, its cruel metaphysics. He who holds the knife, as Baudelaire had devined, is the one who receives the wound.

Seen in this perspective, the importance of Julien Gracq becomes apparent. The most talented writer of the second surrealist generation is beyond doubt the one whose work, with that of Eluard and Breton, will be recognized some years hence as the most definite contribution by the school to contemporary

thought. In his 1942 lecture at Yale, André Breton expressed his high regard for *Au Château d'Argol* in which, he said, "surrealism pivots freely about itself." Gracq does not give surrealism anything which was not already there, but with lucidity not separated from inspiration he brings its tendencies to fulfillment. As early as 1938 Julien Gracq indicated quite clearly into what paths he was leading his readers: "There remained perhaps the elucidation of certain badly defined human problems, but ones which are of lasting interest, . . . in the first place that of salvation or more definitely—since the valid intermediary never apparently has been supposed to be left out unless all efficacy is removed from the state of grace achieved—that of the one who saves and the one who damns: the two forces being dialectically inseparable. . . ." Julien Gracq's heroes move and are slain on these metaphysical frontiers where the loss of the god, the sacrifice of Hercules on the pyre, is constantly renewed.

In the pages where Julien Gracq weaves the mystery of Argol, the author's plot will serve only to divide, between Albert Herminien and Heide, the share of malediction which goes to each character. So many wonders and surpassing of self (for example the extraordinary swim by the two youths and the woman toward the deep sea) end up with final defeat, as though agreed upon and accepted in advance. A significant sentence combines the intuitions of Baudelaire, of Sade, and of Freud concerning our *willed destiny*: "Only at that moment perhaps did he perceive that in every human being the instinct of his own destruction, of his own and devastating wasting away, was fighting, doubtless on equal terms, against care for his personal safety. . . ." Hasn't Freud shown that the instincts of death are as inherent in man as the instinct of preservation? In these extreme realms of the surrealist novel everything takes place as if the former, now and definitely, were winning over the latter.

The same cruel predestination is inscribed in the story of *Un Beau Ténébreux*. By his presence alone, Allan solidifies the mystery, causes men and women to utter their last cries in their most secret voices. He passes by, indifferent, somber, luminous, and in his wake the potential takes on definition; souls stuck with terror open or close. One night, the next day after a masked ball at which his mistress Dolores and he, as the lovers of Montmorency, painted blood stains over their hearts, he kills himself. And the marvelous expectation of the sacrifice, more and more unbearable in this being *born to die,* has become such that at the end of the book where the spell of temptation passes for some moments over Allan, it is the reader himself, as well as all the characters in the book, who makes Allan back up against the wall with the bottle of poison in his hand.

The ex-surrealist Georges Bataille, the philosopher of damnation, has paralleled Julien Gracq's fictional fatalism. In a book entitled *L'Expérience intérieure*: "The forces working to destroy us find such favorable complicity within us . . . that we cannot simply turn away from them as our self-interest dictates. We are led to making counterfires. . . . A dangerous region where destructive forces arise." When he has chosen to write novels, Bataille has attempted to establish in his narrative a kind of ascesis of downfall, ever more guilty and more voluntary. As a sociologist he is obsessed by the idea of sacrifice. The horror that Gabriel Marcel feels concerning these dark undertakings does not in any way detract from their authenticity.

At the end of a road strewn with easy victories and cruel defeats the surrealist novel appears to have arrived at its inevitable conclusion: the proud Promethean revolt ends on a black and bloody altar. That is not the least astonishing paradox of a school which began by demiurgic exaltation and belief in re-finding the shores of innocence. In his essay *André Breton* (1948), Julien Gracq himself has noted the apparent contra-diction of "Surréalisme noir" ["black Surrealism"]. "The despair of our epoch has come about because the poignant feeling of man's downfall has paradoxically outlasted and even feeds on the certainty of the *death of God*." Breton, for whom blasphemy, revolt, and blood lead to a kind of superior love of life, had wished something different. But already (according to Léon Bloy's phrase which Julien Gracq quotes) Lautréamont had come to announce "the gospel of damnation." This vo-cation for perdition, attested by Leiris, Artaud, Gracq, and Bataille, can be understood only if surrealism is placed back in its true metaphysical perspective: the defeat of the mythology of innocence. Surrealism, by its nature and with no outside help, slips toward the mysterious ritual of the holocaust through despair. "Are there then," asked Baudelaire, "souls doomed to the altar, anointed so to speak, and who must walk toward death and glory through a permanent sacrifice of themselves?" Incapable of reaching its goal, powerless to give man a su-perhuman law, surrealist conscience chose to become *bad* and martyred. To the very end the surrealist novel expresses the astonishing ambitions of the school as well as the hazards of destiny. (pp. 17-25)

Armand Hoog, "The Surrealist Novel," *in* Yale French Studies, *No. 8, 1951, pp.17-25.*

DRAMA

ANNABELLE HENKIN MELZER

[*In the following excerpt from her study of Dada and Surrealist theater,* Latest Rage the Big Drum, *Melzer examines the theory and techniques of Surrealist drama.*]

After Apollinaire's use of the word "sur-réalisme," in the program for *Parade* in 1917, and later as a subtitle for his own "drame surréaliste," *The Breasts of Tirésias*, the word floated in avant-garde circles vaguely present but hardly defined. In the August 1920 issue of *La Nouvelle Revue Française*, Breton, in his article, "For Dada," used the adjective "surréaliste" and referred to two of the areas which would soon concern the surrealist movement: the riches of the unconscious, and the essential nature of inspiration. In April 1922, Breton was shout-ing "Leave everything, leave dada." . . . (p. 163)

By 1924 . . . Breton and the group that surrounded him had evolved into a new movement.

The movement, however, proved a highly unstable one. By 1925, the "friendly group" had dissolved. Surrealism had en-tered the period of numerous arguments regarding philosophy and political action. By 1925, most of the plays that the mem-bers of the surrealist group were to write, had been written, and the group had ceased to function as an acting-producing unit. After 1925, those surrealist plays produced were done by avant-garde theatres outside the periphery of the group, by professional actors and often with the group's outspoken dis-approval. Aragon's *Au pied du mur*, scheduled for production at the Vieux-Colombier in June of 1925, was successfully sab-otaged by the surrealists, and the author's *The Mirror Ward-*

robe, One Fine Evening, was performed at the *Théâtre Art et Action* in March, 1926, after Aragon had specifically denied permission for its presentation. Vitrac's *The Mysteries of Love* opened the *Théâtre Alfred Jarry* in 1927 to the hoots and catcalls of the surrealists, while Vitrac along with Artaud had already been banished from the surrealist circle for yielding to what Breton considered commercial instincts in wanting to produce plays in the framework of a professional theatre.

The attempts of both the *Théâtre Art et Action* and the *Théâtre Alfred Jarry* to produce surrealist texts merits a full study of its own. After 1924, however, the surrealist group was no longer performance-oriented and the clique of young poets that had served its apprenticeship under Tzara fragmented and split. The "Office of Surrealist Research," which had been manned by Artaud, closed its doors. Soupault was expelled from the movement for engaging in "the stupid literary adventure," Breton became the sole editor of *La Révolution Surréaliste,* and the movement began to take a decidedly political turn. By 1925, then, the type of performance which had its beginnings with Tzara in Zurich had stopped to catch its breath. During the next 30 years, it would rear its head in the works of in-dividual theatre-people of the avant-garde: Artaud, for in-stance. Not until the late 1950s, however, would it again find the soil in which it could grow most fertilely—that of per-forming groups such as the communal Living Theatre, the Open Theatre with playwrights in residence, or the theatre of hap-pening created by an intimate group of artists and their friends.

Ludwig Wittgenstein, in the famous counsel set forth in his Philosophical Investigation, writes:

> Consider for example the proceedings that we call "games." I mean board-games, card-games, ball-games, Olympic games, and so on. What is common to them all?—Don't say: "There must be something common, or they would not be called 'games'"—but *look* and *see* whether there is anything common to all. For if you look at them, you will not see something that is common to all, but similarities, relationships, and a whole series of them at that . . . we see a complicated network of similarities over-lapping and criss-crossing; sometimes overall simi-larities, sometimes similarities of detail. . . .
>
> I can think of no better expression to characterize these similarities than "family resemblances"; for the various resemblances between members of a fam-ily: build, colour of eyes, features, gait, tempera-ment, etc. etc. overlap and criss-cross in the same way.—And I shall say: "Games" form a family.

It would be critically unproductive to make too narrow a def-inition of which poet/playwrights may be included in the family of the surrealist sketch. If, to name a poet/playwright "sur-realist," we simply accept exploration into the labyrinth of the unconscious, the reconciliation of dream and reality, the gen-erous list of precursors and contemporaries who at one time or another received acclaim from Breton and his followers, we obtain an understandable, though specious, vision of poetic creation. And what is to be done with the fearful stumbling block posed by Breton in his *First Manifesto of Surrealism* [see excerpt above], to the effect that the true surrealist will operate "in the absence of any control exercised by reason"? The domains offered the poet/playwright by the surrealist out-look were vast indeed: in method—automatic writing, simu-lated madness, games and violent provocation; in outlook—the realm of the unconscious, the power of dreams, the freeing of the psyche's menagerie, the revolt against the logical, the liberation from tradition. All these were some of its points of departure, its loci of inspiration. For some, reason was the great prostitute. For others, the greatest temptation was to try operating magically on things, first of all on one's own self.

The focus should remain, then, on the original nucleus of the surrealist group—that group of young writers who had lived the Paris-dada experience and were present at the founding of surrealism. This group immediately included André Breton, Philippe Soupault, Louis Aragon, Georges Ribemont-Dessaignes, Roger Vitrac, Jean Cocteau, Robert Desnos, Pierre Albert-Birot and Antonin Artaud. Tristan Tzara, though the acknowledged papa of dada, must also be included here. That Soupault remained more true to Tzara than to Breton, that Aragon left Breton's cenacle and that Cocteau staunchly denied ever having been part of it; that Ribemont-Dessaignes was considered one of the few true "dadas," and that Artaud has hardly been talked about in relation to surrealism—these are truths which do not infringe on the category I am proposing. For it is the nature of the theatre pieces written by these people, the models of performance chosen for their execution, the experience with performance in the early 1920s which shaped the authors and pieces alike, the cultural and theatrical milieu of the Parisian avant-garde which they shared, that allows the grouping of these people and labelling of them as the makers of the surrealist sketch.

In writing his "Project on contemporary literary history" in 1922, Louis Aragon included the names of almost all the people, works and events crucial to a performance history of the surrealist sketch:

> Futurism . . . The *Ballets Russes* . . . Nick Carter . . . The Duncans . . . Guillaume Apollinaire . . . The Movies, Charlie Chaplin and the Vampires . . . *SIC* . . . *Parade* . . . *The Breasts of Tirésias* . . . the influence of Jarry . . . Pierre Bertin . . . Madame Lara . . . *Art et Vie* becomes *Art et Action* . . . Dada . . . Cocteau takes shape . . . Raymound Radiguet . . . Fraenkel . . . Ivan Goll . . . *The Magnetic Fields* Picabia . . . Tzara . . . Ribemont-Dessaignes . . . Le premier vendredi de *Littérature* . . . period of Manifestations: *Grand Palais, Faubourg,* popular University, *Oeuvre* . . . the *Salle Gaveau* . . . *Le Boeuf sur le toît* and Cocteau's productions . . . the Barrès affair . . . André Breton separates from Dada . . . *Les Mariées de la Tour Eiffel* . . . Roger Vitrac . . . The Bearded Heart . . . Robert Desnos . . .

During the five years between Breton and Soupault's experiments in writing in *The Magnetic Fields* (*Les Champs Magnétiques,* 1919), and 1924, by which time surrealism became preoccupied with other things, the surrealist playwrights penned and mounted some 15 pieces for the theatre, among them: Breton and Soupault's *S'il vous plaît* (1919) and *Vous m'oublierez* (1920), Pierre Albert-Birot's *Le Bondieu* (1920), *L'homme coupé en morceaux* and *Les femmes pliantes* (1921), Raymond Radiguet's *Les Pélican* (1921), Jean Cocteau's *Les Mariés de la Tour Eiffel* (1921), George Ribemont-Dessaignes' *Le Sérin Muet, Zizi de Dada* and *Les partage des os* (1921), Tristan Tzara's *Le Coeur à Gaz* (1922), Roger Vitrac's *Entrée Libre* (1922), and *Les Mystères de l'Amour* (1923), Louis Aragon's *L'Armoire à glace un beau soir,* and *Au pied du mur* (1923), and Antonin Artaud's *le jet du sang* (1924).

The most striking of the family resemblances among these plays, and their most salient feature, is the dislocation of language from its usual function of rational communication. The surrealists gave precedence to the liberation of language, for,

as Breton had written in his *Second Surrealist Manifesto* [see excerpt above]:

> The problem of social action is . . . but one of the forms of a more general problem . . . which is that of human expression in all its forms. Whoever says expression, says, to begin with, language. You must not be surprised then, to see surrealism situated first of all almost exclusively on the plane of language.

The liberties the surrealists took in their relationship to a text were not, however, as with the dadas, expressions of hostility, or a stand against the academies, but were based on a new set of priorities. No longer would dialogue work essentially to support and develop plot. On the contrary, to the extent that plot would count at all in surrealist theatre, it would tend to function mainly as a support for dialogue—while the dialogue itself would be allowed to push forward on a level of exchange where common sense and normal sequence surrender their claim to attention.

J. H. Matthews, in his book *The Theatre in Dada and Surrealism* [see Additional Bibliography] states:

> The major discovery made in the name of surrealism, is that theatre is compatible with poetry, as surrealists understood this, but that on stage it is frequently necessary to liberate poetry through language at the expense of drama. Hence surrealism's impact upon playwriting rests mainly upon diversion of theatre from dramatic to poetic ends. This is the significance of plot discontinuity and inconsistency in character and behavior, called upon to play its part in setting the theatre free from its restricted role as mirror to reality.

But let there be no illusions. Surrealism had not sought to develop an aesthetic for the theatre, but rather had abducted a literary genre for its own purposes. Just as the surrealist text itself is often difficult to grapple with, on the theoretical level the reader will have to struggle with the absence of a consistent and consecutive approach to drama as well as the absence of a unified program for the stage. (pp. 164-67)

Breton's attitude to the theatre was ambivalent. In 1924, in his "Introduction au discours sur le peu de réalité," he wrote:

> O eternal theatre, you demand that not only to act the role of another, but even to dictate this role, we mask ourselves to resemble it, that the mirror before which we pass reflect a foreign image of ourselves. Imagination has every power except that of identifying us in spite of our appearance as a person other than ourselves.

Here, Breton seems to indicate a fear of so being taken in by the role as to be unable to separate the mask from the self. In *Nadja* (1928), he confided, "I have never been able to tolerate the theatre." Perhaps by this he means the theatre of convention, which takes itself seriously, for he is quite ready to say that the plays at the boulevard theatres such as the Théâtre Moderne (with the rudimentary acting of the performers who paid only the faintest attention to their parts and scarcely listened to one another—so busy were they making dates with the audience) "correspond perfectly" to his ideal. He goes out of his way to comment on *Les Détraquées* by Palau which, to him, was an extraordinary play because of the latent element of "strangeness" lurking within a totally naturalistic setting, and because of the intense impact of the play on his dream life. In his poem "Rideau, rideau," the poet's life is played out on the stage of a theatre, in a baroque spectacle which includes not only the actor playing Breton, but another man in a Breton mask and on a level below the stage, a silhouette of Breton, with a bullet in his heart, outlined in fire on a white wall. In *Les Vases Communicants,* he compares the dream's formal unity and integrity to that of a classical tragedy, while in *L'Amour fou,* he presents the reader with his own highly theatrical dream—costumes, stage directions and all. He speaks of having been possessed by a mental theatre in which he tried to construct the ideal play. He envisages a scene in which seven or nine symbolic men, dressed in black habits, participate in a mysterious rite. They are first perceived sitting on a bench engaged in an imperceptible dialogue, but always staring straight ahead. At dusk, they ritually wander to the shore in single file, skirting the waves. A further scene introduces seven or nine women clad in the most beautiful light clothing. Through the dream a juxtaposition of simultaneous monologues presents itself, completely disregarding the linguistic function of communication. It is here, in the potential for new uses of language, that theatre looms most attractive for Breton.

In his *First Manifesto of Surrealism* (1924), Breton states "The forms of surrealist language adapt themselves best to dialogue," and speaks of "dialogue" and "soliloquy" in a passage which is revealing to an understanding of the disordered conversations which tend to mark the surrealist plays:

> Poetic surrealism, which is the subject of this study, has focused in its efforts up to this point on re-establishing dialogue in its absolute truth by freeing both interlocutors from any obligations of politeness. Each of them simply pursues his soliloquy without trying to derive any special dialectical pleasure from it and without trying to impose anything whatsoever upon his neighbor. The remarks exchanged are not, as is generally the case, meant to develop some theses, however unimportant it may be; they are as disaffected as possible. As for the reply that they elicit, it is, in principle, totally indifferent to the personal pride of the person speaking.

To illustrate this surrealist dialogue, Breton quotes a conversation with a mental patient whose responses (which seem illogical and capricious) are actually triggered by sound mechanisms, poetic associations or dream musings and imagery:

> Q. "How old are you?"
>
> A. "You." (Echolalia)
>
> Q. "What is your name?"
>
> A. "Forty-five houses." (Ganser syndrome, or beside the point replies)

When he comes to writing *If You Please,* Breton, in collaboration with Soupault, records the following sequence:

> GILDA. Are your eyes really that color?
>
> MAXIME. Elbow on the tale like naughty children. The fruit of a Christian primary education, if books didn't lie, everything that is golden.
>
> GILDA. In the huts of fishermen one finds those artificial bouquets made up of periwinkle and even a bunch of grapes.
>
> MAXIME. The globe must be lifted up if it is not transparent enough. . . .

Here are the multiple "short-circuits" which Breton discusses in his *Second Manifesto of Surrealism,* here is the sabotaging of the usual "insanities" which form the realistic current of life.

Breton calls himself and Soupault "interlocutors," and although the most common definition of the word is someone who takes part in a conversation or dialogue, questions or cross-examines, the first dictionary definition of the word is, "the man in the middle of the line of performers of a minstrel troupe who carries on a conversation with the end men."

It is not surprising to find Breton writing with words from a theatre vocabulary, for theatricality had been a compelling part of the dada experience. His experiences at the major dada manifestations left him no longer afraid of boos and shouted expletives. He was used to painters and musicians, poets and ballet-masters, participating in a revue-type pastiche of movement, noise and assaulting activity. All theatrical stops were out. The body—clowning, naked, grotesquely sexual or reshaped by costumes and masks, took center stage. Activities absurd in their pointlessness or unrelatedness, defiant in their flaunting of stage as well as social custom, filled the playing time. Most striking perhaps was the "white" quality ("white" as in Satie's "white music," or the recent technological sedative, "white noise") of many of the pieces: that is, their absolute refusal to develop. This was perhaps dada's greatest legacy. Not merely were the unities dispensed with, but so was any consistent regard for characterization and any concept of sequence which might send one vaulting to a climax. . . . Dada theatrical schemas most nearly resembled the *cadavre exquis,* that collective collage so delighted in by the surrealists, in which they wrote down a word or drew a line, folded the paper, and passed it on for the next contribution.

Theatricality reigned above all. Beginning a lecture at the Ateneo in Barcelona on November 17, 1922, Breton said:

> In general I consider that a critical study is quite out of place in the present circumstances and that the smallest theatrical effect would serve my purposes better.

Dada had introduced the young surrealists to a new kind of relationship with the audience: the passive spectator must be converted to a hostile participant, beaten by the provocations of author and actors. And though occasionally they vacillated, the surrealists as performers or "claque" did not depart from this proscription. It was not until 1929 that Breton, in his *Second Manifesto of Surrealism,* recorded the departure of surrealism from this attitude towards the spectator: "We absolutely must stop the public entering if we want to avoid confusion."

André Breton and Philippe Soupault sat down to write *S'il vous plaît* in 1919, before Tzara's arrival in Paris. What was foremost then in their minds was the attempt to explore the potential of language by the methodology of automatic writing. Whatever the product, it would be acceptable. The models turned out to be the schemas of a traditional theatre, bending to the whims of the unconscious. By the time the two set out to write *Vous m'oublierez,* however, barely a year later in April of 1920, they had already been through the rodage of four dada months which had included performances at the *Palais des Fêtes,* the *Salon des Indépendants,* the *Club de Faubourg* and the *Université populaire.* Visions of Tzara-ian stage pictures danced in their heads and fragments of schemata of dada theatre had been imprinted on their consciousness. All that remained now was to join the mad rondel of dada performance and Philippe Soupault had made the willingness quite clear:

> *Vous m'oublierez* was written especially for a dada manifestation. We wanted to do something com-

A performance of Vous m'oublierez, *written by André Breton and Phillipe Soupault. Pictured are (clockwise from top left): Paul Eluard, Theodore Fraenkel, Breton, and Soupault. Editions Cahiers d'Art.*

pletely different from the regular theatre . . . to do something scandalous . . . against the academies.

Vous m'oublierez strikingly exhibits surrealism's attempt to assimilate dada performance. The qualities which link this sketch to the earlier *S'il vous plaît,* however, stand out just as clearly. They indicate the independent direction taken by the surrealist sketch, which even dada could not divert.

S'il vous plaît was written during the winter of 1919, and messages about it were quickly sent by Breton to Tzara, who was still in Zurich. On Friday, December 26, 1919, Breton wrote: "I have just completed, with Soupault, a play in four acts." On Wednesday, January 14, 1920, only three days before Tzara's arrival in Paris, Breton sent off: "I have just completed a play in collaboration with Soupault: "*S'il vous plaît,* a drama in four acts. We plan to perform it next spring."

The play itself is composed of four acts, divided into 25 scenes in the French manner, at the entrance or exit of any character. There are 30 characters none of whom appears in more than a single act of the play. Each act, then, is a self-contained unit with its own setting, characters, activities. There is a whore called Gilda, a husband and wife—Valentine and Françoise—Paul the lover, an office boy and an Algerian peddler. The characters kiss, they look in mirrors, knock on doors, shake hands and smoke cigarettes. They type, make phone calls and play cards. The characters are "like real people." The authors are writing relationships. What then is strange?

Each of the first three acts has a recognizable context, and is, in fact, modeled on one or another of the standard schemata of boulevard drama: Act I—the wife and lover interrupted by the husband; Act II—the heavy intrigue of an office linked with public affairs, the law, the police, the signing of papers; Act III—a whore and a gentleman meet in a cafe. From act to

act, however, there is no continuity. No act bears any relation to the other acts in the play. The build-up of intrigue associated with the well-made play, and anticipated by the audience because of the nature of the character-types and activities in the act, is effectively thwarted.

At the end of Act I, Valentine, the wife, is killed. The audience may think it has discovered the lover, Paul, as murderer in Act II, scene 10:

> LÉTOILE. (*To the policeman*) Arrest that man.
>
> THE YOUNG MAN. What's going on? You're out of your mind.
>
> LÉTOILE. Resistance is useless. (*To the policeman*) I make a formal accusation against this man for murdering his mistress, Madame Valentine Saint-Cervan.

but there is no mention of Paul in that scene, or afterwards in the act, or in the rest of the play—and the man accused is visibly younger than Paul and sports a blonde mustache. At the end of Act II, Létoile, in whose business office the act takes place, is himself arrested and in true anti-climactic fashion says "What does that matter to me." The curtain falls. His response is almost identical with that of Maxime, the gentleman, who, at the end of Act III, after being told by Gilda the whore that she has "the syph," responds "Who cares." Another curtain. What do Maxime and Gilda have to do with Létoile? What does Act II have to do with Act I? The answer seems to be—nothing.

Within the acts themselves, although the nature of the activity is recognizable, there is something new and confusing occurring with the energies of the characters. Roger Shattuck has pointed to three of Breton's favorite metaphors, all drawn from the language of physics: interference, the short circuit, and communicating vessels. All three are helpful in trying to pinpoint just what it is that gives these almost recognizable scenes their quality of being off-balance, and therefore unsettling. In the first segment of Act I, Paul and Valentine converse. The audience is set down on the frontier of a known language: I think I understand it, I must understand it for I understand all the words, but in fact I don't understand.

> PAUL. I love you. (*Long kiss*)
>
> VALENTINE. A cloud of milk in a cup of tea.

The level of frustration at almost-understanding is far greater than that of not understanding at all, and is one of the significant tensions which work through the surrealist sketch.

Here we are close to the world of the painting of Matisse and Masson whose works, no matter how abstract they become, always allude, however elliptically, to a subject. Masson and Matisse, spending a few weeks together in the country in 1932, explained to one another their manner of working. Masson described,

> I begin without any images or plan in mind, but just draw or paint rapidly according to my impulses. Gradually, in the marks I make, I see suggestions of figures or objects. I encourage these to emerge, trying to bring out their implications even as I now consciously try to give order to the composition.

Matisse replied,

> That's curious, with me it's just the reverse. I always starts with something—a chair, a table—but as the work proceeds, I become less conscious of it. By the

end, I am hardly aware of the subject with which I started.

For both painters, the subject is always present and Breton himself, in discussing surrealist painting, makes it quite clear that no matter how abstract the painting may appear, "it moves in favor of the subject."

What the painters did with their brush strokes to bring the subject into focus or allow it to fade to the edge of awareness, Breton and Soupault achieved with their verbal flights and the shaping of the scenes. Valentine and Paul never stop relating to one another, so that when the listener is buffeted by the juxtaposition of a sequence of dialogue such as:

> PAUL. Did you hear him come in?
>
> VALENTINE. Current morality: it makes me think of a current of water.
>
> PAUL. The charm lies in that lovely liquid song, the spelling out of the catechism by children.

he can still hang onto the "subject" of the scene. There is no doubt that the scene is a love-scene.

It is this balance between abstraction and an ever-present subject which is a striking quality of the surrealist sketch. It is this quality that gives the sense of the world-in-the-scene as being slightly unfocussed, a blurriness which provides an enticing tension. This lack-of-focus-tension, however, is extremely hard to maintain in the theatre, for everything that is put on stage cries for focus. What the playwrights resort to, therefore, to maintain this off-focus tension, are techniques of interference and short-circuiting. Valentine suddenly pushes the energies in the scene to a climax with "I dreamt that we were drowning"—a sexual image of identification. Paul's response is a short-circuit: "It's a long time since the charming statue on top of the Tour Saint-Jacques let fall . . . etc." Here are Breton's interlocutors, "freed from the obligations of politeness."

The short-circuiting in the second act (the only act performed at the *Théâtre de l'Oeuvre*) takes place between scenes, for within each scene, many lines proceed as in a boulevard play:

> LÉTOILE. (*Speaks heatedly; during the whole scene his eyes do not leave the other man*) Sir, I'm sorry to say I can't give you more than a few moments. I was about to go out when your card was sent in. Be so good as to take a seat. (*He remains standing.*)
>
> THE MAN. Yesterday evening my wife and I came home after having been to the theatre. I should tell you that the dressing room is quite some distance from our bedroom. Before undressing, my wife put her necklace and rings on the mantelpiece. I remained in the study.
>
> LÉTOILE. Excuse me, were you smoking?
>
> THE MAN. (*After taking time to reflect*) Yes. Several minutes later . . .
>
> LÉTOILE. Several minutes, you say.
>
> THE MAN. (*Troubled*) Well, about ten minutes. The jewels had disappeared.

It is from scene to scene that the major interference occurs. No pattern of energies is allowed to develop. Characters disappear never to be seen again. The concluding of activities begun is indefinitely postponed.

In Act III, it is possible to abstract from the running dialogue a 12-line text, more like an acting exercise, which gives the actors rather neutral lines on which to build characters:

> MAXIME. Aren't you bored?
>
> GILDA. Why?
>
> MAXIME. Aren't you waiting for someone?
>
> GILDA. No. (*She smiles*)
>
> MAXIME. (*Sitting down opposite her*) With your permission.
>
> (*A pause.*)
>
> GILDA. You haven't finished your letter . . . Someone has dared to sadden you.
>
> MAXIME. I don't think so; I've only just come in.
>
> GILDA. Are your eyes really that color? . . . Why do you laugh?
>
> (*A pause.*)
>
> GILDA. Call me Gilda.
>
> MAXIME. Where do you live?
>
> GILDA. (*Giving him her hand*) Let me leave alone . . . you'll regret it. I've got the syph.
>
> MAXIME. Who cares?
> (*They leave.*)

Any two actors could fill this skeleton scene with a hundred different people. But in between these lines, Breton and Soupault have filled in cloudy recollections of children ("I was dreaming I was still in boarding school"), a truth which two people know but seldom utter aloud ("I won't love you always"), with sentences whose syntax we understand but in whose noun-subject positions sit sensuous dream words ("Corridors and clouds are my whole life"). In the text the combination reads as follows:

> MAXIME. (*Sitting down opposite her*) With your permission.
> (*A pause.*)
>
> GILDA. I was dreaming that I was still in boarding school, I was wearing that lace collar one last time. They kept a sharp eye on my correspondence: an unknown man will climb over the garden wall this evening. He said to me: "You've been crying because of my mother of pearl cheeks." Night will fall. Soon there will be nothing but the windmills.
>
> MAXIME. You can take it or leave it. Interior elegance and the maddest acts of despair. To leave the church throwing candy around.
>
> GILDA. You're not like the others.
>
> MAXIME. How can one not say to oneself several times every day: that won't come back again!
> (*A pause.*)
>
> GILDA. You haven't finished your letter.
>
> MAXIME. What's the good forgiving a sign of life for too long a time.

The dialogue rests on the edge of the subliminal. The syntax is deceptive. What looks like a reassuringly logical succession of phrases collapses as sentences reach their conclusion or as one sentence follows another. The first three acts do, however, subscribe to the basically conventional theatrical acceptance of character, setting, subject and activity, and to the convention of a fourth wall as well.

Act IV is a fascinating study of a different kind. The first three Acts of *S'il vous plaît* were published in *Littérature* with the exhortation at their end "The authors of *S'il vous plaît* wish the text of the 4th Act not to be published." Benedikt, writing before the fourth act had been recovered, concluded that "This is one of the many outward signs of the then contemporary movement, Dada." But the act, discovered a number of years ago among Breton's papers, has since appeared in the Gallimard edition of *The Magnetic Fields.* Since it has not yet been translated into English, I quote it here in its entirety.

ACT IV

Scene 1:

(*The auditorium is plunged into a half-darkness. The curtain rises on a front door. Two insignificant characters, one with a cane in his hand, stop in front of the door.*)

X. (*Consulting his watch*) Look at the time, I'm leaving.

   (*They shake hands.*)

Y. (*Paces back and forth in front of the door without saying a word. He looks upwards, rubs his arms with his hands, blows his nose.*)

Scene II:

A SPECTATOR IN THE ORCHESTRA. "That's all?"

   (*The pacer on stage stops, looks at the interruptor with surprise, then lifts his eyes skyward and continues pacing.*)

THE SPECTATOR. Will you be finished soon?

One hears: Shhh!

A SECOND SPECTATOR. I don't understand anything. It's idiotic.

SOMEONE SHOUTS FROM THE BALCONY. Will you please shut up!

THE SECOND SPECTATOR. (*Standing*) I do have the right to say what I think.

FROM THE BALCONY. You have the right to leave.

   (*The actor is stopped.*)

THE SECOND SPECTATOR. I paid for my seat just like you.

THE WIFE OF THE SECOND SPECTATOR. Please, Edward, be quiet.

A VOICE FROM THE AUDIENCE. If at least it were amusing.

THE SECOND SPECTATOR. I repeat that I understand nothing. (*Applause*) It is probable that I'm not the only one. (*Standing on his seat*) For some time now, under pretext of originality and independence, our fine art has been sabotaged by a bunch of individuals, whose number increases every day and who are for the most part, strange types, lazy fellows or practical jokers. (*The curtain falls. Applause.*) It is easier to get yourself talked about in this fashion than to attain true glory at the cost of hard work. Are we going to put up with the most contradictory ideas and aesthetic theories, the beautiful and the ugly, talent and force without style being placed on the same footing? I appeal to our traditional good sense. It shall not be

said that the sons of Montaigne, Voltaire, Renan. . . .

THE SPECTATOR FROM THE BALCONY. Throw him out. Continue.

   (*The three knocks are sounded.*)

Scene III:

(*Same as the first scene. When Y pulls out his handkerchief, the second spectator stands.*)

THE SECOND SPECTATOR. Enough!

CRIES. Yes, enough, etc.

THE SECOND SPECTATOR. (*To his wife*) Let's go.

(*They exit noisily but before leaving the auditorium, the second spectator shakes his fist at the stage.*)

THE SECOND SPECTATOR. It's shameful.

   (*Tumult. The curtain falls. One hears cries of "Vive la France," "Continue," etc. One calls for the authors. Two actors bow in their stead. Curtain.*)

The fourth wall has crumbled and actors and audience join in a pre-dada jamboree. "Plants" have been placed in the audience, and the spectators argue among themselves as well as with the performers. The subject has disappeared, the performers have become "personal actors" and have extended to the audience, an invitation to chaos. Clearly, Breton and Soupault had sketched out for themselves a distinctive departure from conventional theatre before Tzara's arrival in Paris.

The critics who do approach the play are hard put to it to come to grips with the text. Sanouillet succumbs to calling it "play . . . composed of a series of sketches, constructed according to the best rules of dramatic art, but perfectly incoherent." Esslin dismisses it as "bizarre and largely improvised," while Béhar records its plot but generally avoids any further discussion. Even Michael Benedikt dismisses the author's attempts, by describing them merely as the desire to "flaunt the usual literary goal of homogeneity of style." It is only Matthews who agrees to see the structuring of the play as "willfully discontinuous." He writes:

> Intention, not incompetence . . . underlies the incoherent plot structure. . . . In aggressive fashion, Breton and Soupault demonstrate how proven ingredients can be arranged in a manner that shakes the stability of dramatic convention.

Tzara had come to Paris in 1920, carrying with him the text of *La Première aventure céleste de M. Antipyrine,* and the surrealists suddenly found themselves on stage in the roles of Pipi and CriCri, standing up to their necks in paper bags and singing "zdranga, zdranga, di, di, di." Tzara's play had no identifiable context at all. It was basically 239 lines divided among 9 characters and capped by a lengthy manifesto-monologue. It was filled with pseudo-Africanese, phonetic gibberish and simultaneous-poem-chants. In performance it brought down the house.

As their contribution to the *Salle Gaveau* manifestation (May 26, 1920) Breton and Soupault brought Tzara *Vous m'oublierez,* a sketch they had written especially for the occasion. Coming to the play with this knowledge, it is hard not to see the young poets' attempts to bring an offering which would please their "master," which would be acceptable to him and which he would include in his great manifestation rites. They had called their characters Umbrella, Sewing Machine, and Bathrobe, (the first two coming from that phrase of Lautréamont's which seemed to haunt the surrealists, about the fortuitous meeting of an umbrella and a sewing machine on a dissection table), in an attempt to bring them closer to M. Bleubleu than to Valentine and Paul. They had again and again repeated the meaningless question: "What then is that tree, that young leopard whom I caressed the other day upon coming home?" (four times within the first nine speeches), just to be provocative. They plotted non sequitur activities (Umbrella recalls a visit to a Chateau on the Loire; Bathrobe kneels down to pray) in an attempt to destroy context. But though Tzara's obfuscated dialogue in the *Antipyrine* plays and his energy-stunted schematic configurations had had their effect on Breton and Soupault, although *Vous m'oublierez* strikingly exhibits surrealism's attempt to work within criteria set up by dada performance, the qualities which link this sketch to the earlier *S'il vous plaît,* stand out just as clearly. They indicate the independent direction taken by the surrealist sketch, which even dada could not divert.

In moving so thoroughly to incorporate Lautréamont's psychosexual image into the sketch:

> The force of the image depends upon the fact that the umbrella cannot here but represent man, the sewing machine, woman (this is true in most cases of machines, except that here we deal with a machine frequently used by women, as we know for onanistic purposes), and the dissection table, the bed. . . .

Breton and Soupault are bowing in a direction other than Tzara's—a fervent tribute to Lautréamont and a step into a private esoteric enclave where the audience could not reach them.

> SEWING MACHINE. Explain it to me, and I'll leave.
>
> BATHROBE. No explanations.

Again, what is unique in this attempt at a dada text is that the characters relate to one another. Sewing Machine is decidedly female in the text. She says, "That means nothing to you, the honor of a woman," and one can trace her attempts to seduce Umbrella while brushing aside Bathrobe with an affectionate, "Shut up rabbit," "Shh! you red hooligan." Bathrobe is the odd man out in the love-triangle, an affectionate old geezer ("he is deaf and blue, with thunder on his hands, but in fact he's not a demanding old guy"), constantly rising from his search for some unknown object to ask "What?" as the conversation continues around him. The Lautréamont phrase and the repeated "What?" take on the rhythm of those repeated game-routines we recognize in the plays of Beckett and Ionesco, even to the mocking of theatre with "This play, will it ever be over?" and "my ears are buzzing, I beg of you, be quiet . . . This has gone on long enough."

Even in a play which they wrote under Tzara's tutelage, Breton and Soupault could not abandon the experiments they had begun in *S'il vous plaît,* and in *The Magnetic Fields.* The language of surrealism was to aim at reducing reason, at persuading the imagination to surrender before the enticing images of the marvellous. It allowed a new freedom "for" rather than the dada freedom "from." The customary bearings were gone, but here was a challenge to reason rather than mere provocation. Within the surrealist sketch, poetry abounds at the expense of dialogue continuity. Bizarre images reminiscent of Breton's "There is a man cut in two by the window" which first prompted him to investigate automatic writing, recur. Such dialogue steers the mind towards a much more ephemeral seeing of the "light of the image," to which it is infinitely sensitive. Automatism had left its indelible mark. Breton and Soupault were moving forward, faithful to their program of "giving language back its full purpose" and "making cognition take a big step forward." (pp. 164-82)

By 1924, the attraction of the dada manifestations and the dada variety of scandal had paled. With the departure of Tzara from the dada-surrealist cenacle, no one remained who was capable of revitalizing the realigned surrealists into a new performing unit, and the performing of plays was taken over by professional or semi-professional theatres. What had happened to the movement's strong theatrical bent? Perhaps Breton associated the general depression that afflicted him between 1921 and 1924 with the ranging series of performances he had compelled himself to participate in, all the while denying the many negative feelings the performances had raised in him.

By 1924 however, it no longer seemed that surrealism's inability or unwillingness to continue dada performance, or any performance at all, was simply a product of Breton's temperament. Nor was it even a decision made on artistic grounds, e.g. that something in the nature of dada-surrealist performance itself was self-defeating. With his shift into the political arena, Breton became more conscious of what he considered the compromising role *all* theatre assumed in relation to its audience. Theatre was the celebrant at society's feast and Breton, who was just beginning to crystallize his revolt against society, was unwilling to play lackey to any commercial venture. Artaud and Vitrac were bounced from the movement for dealing in tickets and auditoriums. Picasso was castigated for contributing (with his *Mercure*), to the evening-out of Maréchal Foch. And when Tzara himself had his most recent play performed before Paris high-society (*Mouchoir de Nuages,* 1924), Breton's rage knew no bounds. The revolt was not against dada performance, or against the medium of theatre itself, but rather against the theatre's parasitic need for society once that theatre had been taken out of the context of the "groupe amical"—Cocteau's "friendly group" which was capable of creating and maintaining a theatre without impresarios or box offices, without professional performers or a dependence upon an audience. Tzara had retreated from the Paris-dadas in 1923. Within a year of his departure the former dada group had splintered about Breton. Breton himself was incapable of fashioning a performance group, nor did he want to. As he watched his former performing colleagues taking their plays to professional theatres, he showered on them all the wrath of a young politician fiercely feeling the need to make his revolutionary politics visible.

By the end of 1924, then, the playing arena of surrealist performance had shifted. So had the attitudes of the surrealists towards performance itself. Whatever family resemblances there had been among the surrealist sketches blurred as the members of the family separated and moved on. (p. 195)

Annabelle Henkin Melzer, in her Latest Rage the Big Drum: Dada and Surrealist Performance, *UMI Research Press, 1980, 272 p.*

FILM

J. H. MATTHEWS

[*In the following essay, which was written in 1962, Matthews presents the history of Surrealist cinema, examining the Surre-*

alists' attitude toward the medium of film and the expression of their artistic philosophy in their cinematic experiments.]

It seems it is no longer fashionable to discuss surrealism. Evidently the novelty has worn off. A movement which once provoked irate incomprehension now is the occasion for conveniently trite critical judgements, which most of us are content to reiterate. Alarm has given place to patronizing indulgence—we have persistently refused to face up to the implications of the problems surrealism raises. Of course, it is much safer to accord surrealism some undefined degree of significance, to adopt a compromising position, than it is either to condemn it out of hand or to examine it closely. And so a critic like Marc Soriano, writing on *"Le Surréalisme au cinéma"* in *Formes et couleurs* in 1946, feels entitled to make a statement like "The quality of the surrealist films is beyond doubt," without feeling under any obligation to define this quality. It would appear that, when dealing with a group who deny the claims of logic, it is quite in order to continue with an illogical assertion, unsupported either by explanation or by evidence: "One may simply note that the words 'cinema' and 'surrealism' are contradictory." In the light of such a remark, we are left wondering what connection there can possibly be between surrealism and the cinema. If we are to hope to make any progress, we must start at the very beginning, seeking to establish what points of contact may exist between the aims of surrealism and what the cinema has to offer.

The founder of surrealism, André Breton himself, has made it clear that he believes such points of contact to exist. When, in 1951, *L'Age du cinéma* devoted a special number to the surrealist cinema, Breton contributed an article written for the occasion, under the title *"Comme dans un bois."* Breton establishes that the surrealists have always felt attracted to the cinema. During the 1914-18 war, for instance, he and Jacques Vaché would go to the movies every week. Their method of viewing films was quite distinctive, and very enlightening. It appears that they never consulted the week's program in advance, and always took care not to note the times of performances. Instead, they would choose a theater haphazardly, enter when they felt like, leave on a similar impulse, and hurry on to the next theater, where they behaved in the same way. It goes without saying that, within a few hours, they exhausted all the programs that the small town of Nantes had to offer, without however even knowing the names of the films from which they had seen fragments. Yet Breton comments, "I have never known anything more *magnetizing*. What was important was that we came out 'charged' for a few days." No one can deny that, if surrealism enters into this experience, it could only be to the extent that Breton's method *made use* of films. Appealing in the absence of premeditation to the law of chance, by which the surrealists have always set great store, the method he and Vaché followed is one that can turn any succession of films into surrealist material—regardless of what the film-maker had in mind. Their way of looking at movies transforms them into what Breton calls "lyrical substance," making the cinema, in René Clair's phrase, "an incomparable field of surrealist activity." It is obvious, though, that Breton's article tells us nothing precise regarding the surrealist cinema. It simply serves as proof that the surrealists felt, from the beginning, that the cinema was a medium with definite possibilities. And yet, when Breton admits that he has always admired, in the cinema, its *pouvoir de dépaysement*—its capacity to take man out of himself—he pinpoints the attraction which the films will never cease to hold for the surrealists.

Here is the essence of the surrealist's interest in the cinema, an inevitable consequence of his desire to transcend everyday reality and his willingness to avail himself of any means which seem to offer the opportunity to do so. We readily appreciate the hypnotic attraction of the lighted screen, viewed from a darkened auditorium. The very conditions of movie-going which seemed to Georges Duhamel to exert a baleful and alarming effect are those which encourage the surrealist to regard the cinema as a means both of release and of exploration. Watching a film is so much like experiencing a dream, one of those dreams in which we are at the same time involved and detached. Recalling that surrealism is, for Ado Kyrou writing in *Le Surréalisme au cinéma,* "the liberation of man by the search for and discovery of 'the real functioning of thought'," the destruction of "senile Cartesian ideas," in accordance with which "insurmountable boundaries are placed about the life of man," we can see why, for Breton, the cinema represents "the celebration of the only *absolutely modern myth*." For the surrealists, a visit to the movie theater constitutes a direct invocation of the marvelous, "the heart and nervous system of all poetry," as Benjamin Péret calls it. The surrealists' "appetite for the marvelous" could not but find satisfaction in a medium characterized by techniques perfectly suited to precipitating its audience into adventures entirely different from their own, to presenting images of infinite variety with remarkable intensity. The technical advantages of the cinema are of the greatest benefit to the film director intent on imposing his own pattern upon reality, submitted only to the limits of his own imagination. Editing, stop-action photography, parallel construction, montage—these are all means immediately available to the director who may use them to dominate reality and give it a new meaning, of his own devising. It is no wonder that Kyrou, writing from the surrealist standpoint, expresses the conviction that the cinema "can (and must) be the best spring board from which the modern world will plunge into the magnetic, brilliantly black waters of the subconscious, of poetry, and of the dream."

In *En Marge du cinéma français*, Jacques B. Brunius places *Entr'acte* and *Un Chien andalou* side by side, as films which most successfully represent their period. In doing so, he clearly implies a difference between them. And quite rightly. *Un Chien andalou* belongs indisputably to surrealism, whereas *Entr'acte*

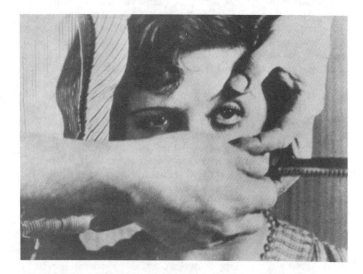

Scene from the surrealist film Un chien Andalou. *The Museum of Modern Art/Film Stills Archive.*

reflects an earlier period, and may best be regarded as an expression of dada. In spite of this, the organizers of the *"Journées surréalistes"* in Milan in 1959 felt entitled to include *Entr'acte* in their program of surrealist films. They did so, it seems, justifiably. For *Entr'acte* prepared the way for *Un Chien andalou,* pointing to the path authentic surrealist films were to follow.

Delighting at that time in the "marvelous barbarity" of the cinema, and confessing "I could easily resign myself to admitting in the world of images neither rules nor logic," René Clair welcomed the opportunity to collaborate with the dadaist editor of *391,* Francis Picabia, who supplied the scenario of *Entr'acte* (1924). Centered upon a complete disregard for habitual logic, and displaying the most violent humor—already, then, showing some of the qualities we associate with the surrealist cinema—*Entr'acte* offered a succession of apparently unrelated images of scandalous gratuitousness, culminating in the scene of the funeral procession, led by a hearse, bedecked with publicity posters and drawn by a camel, passing through a Parisian amusement park. The grotesque effect is heightened by appropriate—or rather, deliberately inappropriate—use of slow motion and speed-up, which prepares for the final effect: the corpse, bursting from his coffin, waves a wand which makes all his friends and relations disappear. Here the iconoclastic potentialities of the cinema are fully revealed. As Picabia wrote in the special number of *La Danse* devoted to the Swedish Ballet, "*Entr'acte* doesn't believe in much, in the pleasure of living perhaps; it believes in the pleasure of invention, it respects nothing unless it be the desire to *burst out laughing.*"

It is to the extent that *Entr'acte* deliberately departed from the conventional and demonstrated the role technical devices may play in this process that it invited the cinema to take a new direction.

Picabia had proposed to translate "the non-materialized dreams which take place in our brain." He posed the pertinent question, "Why relate what everyone sees or can see every day?" The same question is tacitly raised in the scenario which Antonin Artaud prepared for *La Coquille et le clergyman.* Publishing his text in *La Nouvelle revue française* in 1927, Artaud explained how it came to be written. He was searching, he said, for a type of film with "purely visual situations," in which the action, instead of being the adaptation in visual terms of a given text, comes from "a shock to the eye, drawn so to speak from the very substance of the eye." He was trying, then, to transpose action to a plane on which it makes its effect "almost intuitively on the mind." The direction Artaud was seeking is a significant one for those interested in the evolution of surrealism. The painter Chirico once commented, "What I listen to is worth nothing, there's only what my eyes see when they are open, and especially when they are closed." Echoing this remark, the surrealist poet Paul Eluard wrote: "One sees what one wishes only with one's eyes closed. . . ." The distinction Chirico and Eluard both make throws light upon Artaud's experiment. We listen with the mind—we evaluate what we have heard in terms of reason. On the other hand, the eye registers perception instinctively, without the interference of the mind. So it is worth noting that Artaud has stressed that his scenario is not the reproduction of a dream, and must not be considered as such. "I will not seek," he declared, "to find excuse for its apparent incoherence through the facile loophole of the dream." Interpreted as nothing more than the transcription of dream experience, *La Coquille et le clergyman*

would lose all its revolutionary force. Artaud wished to make his public realize that he was attempting rather to indicate the true purpose of the cinema as he conceived it: to display the motives of our actions "in their original and profound barbarity," and to transmit them visually.

Even today, *La Coquille et le clergyman* still communicates a remarkable impression of fluidity, of movement, of metamorphosis, in which all the advantages of the cinema are turned to disturbing account. The clergyman's coat-tails grow out of all proportion, and then, to demonstrate the instability of matter, change into darkness, into which he and the woman run. Their flight is interrupted by successive shots of the woman in various attitudes: now with a swollen, enormous cheek; now putting out her tongue, which stretches away endlessly—the clergyman hangs to it, as to a rope. Now her breasts balloon horribly. At the end of the race, we see the clergyman entering a corridor, while the woman is behind him "swimming in a sort of sky." The officer who stands between the hero and the object of his desire is similarly released from the control of gravity. When we first see him, he has the ability of a spider. Later, although destroyed by the clergyman, the officer reappears, transformed into a priest, interposing himself once more between the clergyman and the woman. Scorning the claims of logic, Artaud shows us the clergyman in two places at once, as, like the poet in Breton's *Vigilance,* he sees himself approach: absence and presence, as Breton has said, become one. *La Coquille et le clergyman* knows no laws but its own. When, aboard ship, a paroxysm takes possession of the clergyman, who reaches out to strangle the woman, her neck is miraculously transformed into phosphorescent landscapes, by an effect which announces the techniques of double image employed in Dali's surrealist canvases. We find the same effect produced by a close-up of the clergyman's head. The scenario reads:

> From inside his half-open mouth; in between his eyelashes something like shimmering smoke emanates, piling up in a corner of the screen, forming a town scene, or extremely illuminated landscapes. In the end the head disappears completely and houses, landscapes, towns, mingling and untangling, form into a sort of unbelievable celestial firmament, lagoons, grottos, with incandescent stalactites and beneath these grottos, among these clouds, in the middle of these lagoons we see the silhouette of the ship which passes back and forth, black against the white background of the towns, white against the backcloth of visions which suddenly turn black.

Leaving the ship—the image of chastity—the film abruptly enters a new phase: "But in all directions doors and windows open. Light floods into the room. Which room? The room with the glass ball. . . ." This is the ball which, as the film reaches its climax, the clergyman breaks, before drinking the blackish liquid to which his own head has melted.

It was Artaud's express wish that everything in this movie be translated in visual terms. As a consequence, not a word is spoken. Instead, symbolism is frequently used, taking the place of psychological commentary. The uniformed officer stands in strong contrast with the black-garbed clergyman, so that the phallic symbolism of the officer's great sabre cannot escape our notice. The initial scene, showing the clergyman filling phials of liquid and then smashing them, may be taken to image his frustration. At the same time, it suggests an ill-concealed violence which announces his sadistic conduct later on: in church, after praying by the woman's side, he throws himself upon her and tears away her clothing to be confronted with the symbol of his frustration—a carapace of oyster shells. The anguish he experiences as he awakens to sensual awareness is mirrored in a transposition of the birth process, as he crawls on all-fours up endless streets, and encounters the woman and the officer riding in a carriage drawn by four horses.

La Coquille et le clergyman represented a deliberate reaction against both the "pure" cinema—a concern with abstract forms and the exploitation of light and shade—and the "psychological" cinema, "which relates the development of a story, dramatic or otherwise." This movie was conceived as an experiment, an experiment in visual effects divorced from rational sequence, and devoid of narrative content. The aim was the examination of a state of mind by the evocation of a mood. The net result is one of *dépaysement* similar to what Breton has explained he was seeking in Nantes, some years previously.

The basic mood of revolt which marks Artaud's scenario and which gave Germaine Dulac's film its vitality distinguishes also Man Ray's *L'Etoile de mer* (1928). A cinematographic commentary and interpretation of a poem by Robert Desnos, *L'Etoile de mer* shows us Man Ray examining the potentialities of a medium which surrealism was to find so suited to its ends. Deformation and blurred images are here turned to poetic account, so that *L'Etoile de mer* confirms the surrealists' break with traditional approaches already made by Marcel Duchamp's *Anemic Cinema,* made almost exclusively of a record on film of its author's rotoreliefs in movement. The mood of rejection and iconoclasm which distinguishes surrealism in every field has found expression in the cinema as much as anywhere. We find it in *Un Chien andalou,* made by Luis Bunuel and Salvador Dali in 1929, where it commands attention from the very first shot, in which we see a woman's eye slashed with a razor.

And yet it would be limiting the purpose and scope of *Un Chien andalou* to say, as Arthur Knight does, that Dali and Bunuel had as their aim simply to shock and horrify their public. They wished to do more than this. They considered that the avant-garde cinema was, in Bunuel's phrase, directed exclusively to "the artistic sensibility and to the reason of the spectators." And so the directors of *Un Chien andalou* were, like Artaud, proposing a new conception of the cinema. Bunuel has assured us that, in working out the plot, they rejected as "irrelevant" every idea of a rational, aesthetic or technical nature. The result was a movie which Bunuel has qualified with some pride as "deliberately anti-plastic, anti-artistic."

We know that Artaud denied himself the justification he might have found in offering *La Coquille et le clergyman* as the reconstruction of a dream. Bunuel and Dali, if they did not seek simply to transcribe dream experiences, did find in dreams "a fruitful analogy." To the extent that the plot (for want of a better term) is the result of what Bunuel calls "a CONSCIOUS *psychic automatism*" it does not attempt to recount a dream. But, as Bunuel has remarked, it "profits by a mechanism analogous to that of dreams." Being freed from "the ballast" of reason and tradition, *Un Chien andalou* was intended to inspire in its audience both attraction and revulsion. Dramatic suspense, juxtaposition of images and of situations, a complete disregard for rational sequence and for the limitations of time and space—these are some of the elements of a film in which, Bunuel has admitted, the principle of free association was consciously applied, so that when an image suggested itself, it was "immediately discarded" if it had a "conscious association with another earlier idea." Denying, obviously, the restraint imposed by customary morality and reason, Bunuel and

Dali demonstrated in *Un Chien andalou* their fidelity to the fundamental principles of surrealism, in which irrational images are, by definition, more valid than rational ones, and for which those works which seek to reach out and explore the unknown are more valuable than those which are simply the record of past discoveries.

Nowhere is surrealism's attitude of deliberate protest and revolt better evidenced than in the films it has left us. And nowhere is the fundamental seriousness of the surrealist venture more in evidence. One of the earliest declarations of the surrealists' intentions announced as early as 1925: "Surrealism is not a new or easier means of expression, or even a metaphysics of poetry: It is a means for the total liberation of the mind and of all which resembles it." The full effect of the surrealist cinema depends as much upon the contribution of the audience as upon that of the film-maker. For, in surrealist terms, the principal role of the poet is, as Eluard has told us, "not to evoke, but to inspire"; his function is "not to be inspired, but to inspire." It was Louis Aragon who in *Le Paysan de Paris* defined "the vice called *surrealism*" as "the unreasoning and empassioned use of the stupefying image, for itself and for what it brings with it, in the domain of representation, of unforeseeable perturbation and metamorphosis: for each image every time forces you to revise the whole Universe." In both *La Coquille et le clergyman* and *Un Chien andalou* the use of unfamiliar imagery betokens a systematic denial of the claims of rational relationships and a determination not to submit to the dictates of accepted morality or good taste. *The Secret Life of Salvador Dali* reveals that its author has always considered good taste to be "one of the principal causes of the growing sterility of the French mind." Dali's attitude not only explains his preference for the work of Wagner, Gaudi and Bœcklin, but also the intention lying behind the scene in *Un Chien andalou* which shows rotting donkeys draped over a grand piano. The donkeys were, Dali has told us, "made up": pots of sticky glue were poured over them, their eye-sockets were enlarged with scissors, their mouths cut open "to make the white rows of their teeth show to better advantage." The donkeys were then ready to take their place in the sequence in which the hero of *Un Chien andalou,* about to attempt sexual assault upon a woman, crosses the room dragging after him the grand piano (with donkeys), and, among other symbols of childhood memories and inhibitive influences, two priests.

It is no surprise to find Bunuel denouncing in the twelfth number of *La Révolution surréaliste* "the imbecile crowd" which had praised *Un Chien andalou,* and which had found "fine and poetic what was, basically, nothing but a desperate, passionate call for murder." Now, as a consequence, he felt impelled to state his case more strongly, in *L'Age d'or* (1930). "It was surrealism," Bunuel has commented, "which revealed to me that, in life, there is a moral path man cannot refuse to take. Through surrealism I discovered for the first time that man isn't free." *L'Age d'or* is the fruit of that discovery.

In *La Coquille et le clergyman* and *Un Chien andalou* surrealism's protest had been translated in specifically cinematic terms. The shock was a visual one which exploited devices peculiar to the medium. In *L'Age d'or,* the protest is ethical rather than technical. Following the trend of surrealism during the early thirties, Bunuel formulated his rejection of society in social terms. So, for André Breton, writing in the eighth number of *Minotaure,* the incomparable value of this movie lies in its exaltation of "total love"—*l'amour fou*—which Bunuel shows to be in opposition to established social order. In this film, technical virtuosity takes second place to the evocation of the tragic fate of the individual in society. *L'Age d'or* stands as an act of defiance, epitomized in its recurring theme of eroticism, seen as a means of subversion. Bunuel once told Jacques Doniol-Valcrose that eroticism represents for him "the elements of struggle and violence." It is surely in the light of this statement that we must interpret the scenes of apparently pointless cruelty which accompany the main love theme of the film. Here, where love is continually thwarted by antagonistic society, cruelty is the reflection of the struggle which is the director's main preoccupation, and which leads him to conclude with a scene inspired by Sade's *Les Cent-Vingt journées de Sodome.*

Despite its somber picture of the human condition, *L'Age d'or* is not without its moments of humor. Among the things which the hero throws from an upstairs window is a giraffe, which clearly has no business being indoors. It is obvious that we are concerned here with the characteristic surrealist variety of humor, to which we owe the soluble fish, the white-haired revolver, the aphrodisiac dinner jacket and the arthritic grasshopper. According to Artaud, writing in *The Theater and Its Double,* the cinema "finds its moments of triumph in the most excessive humor." If this is the case, then we must regard the films of Wilhelm Freddie as triumphs indeed.

In Freddie's work, as in the films of Bunuel, eroticism plays an important role. It is so blatantly present in his painting that several of his canvases have found their way into the Copenhagen Criminological Museum. Those which were to have been shown at the International Surrealist Exhibition in London in 1935 were not allowed past the Customs. In his films, *Refus définitif d'une demande d'un baiser* (1949) and *Les Horizons mangés* (1950), as in certain passages of *L'Age d'or,* a disturbing eroticism is allied with that special brand of disconcerting surrealist humor. In *Les Horizons mangés* we see two men eating off a table. Their table—a surrealist object indeed—is a nude woman. When they put down a loaf of bread it proceeds to an intimate examination of the woman, and finally disappears from sight. The men then cut a hole in the woman and set about eating her with spoons. La Duca's comment is relevant here: "The hypocrisy of censorship, the inefficacy of morality, the stupidity of 'cinematographic art' are annihilated by the virulence of that primordial force, eroticism."

A noticeably long period of time separates the films of Freddie from those of Bunuel. Between whiles, Harold Muller's *It's a Bird* (1937) evidenced a continued interest in the cinema on the part of the surrealists. But the productive activity which *Un Chien andalou* and *L'Age d'or* seemed to announce at the beginning of the thirties never came. The conclusion which suggests itself would seem to be that, after an initial moment of enthusiasm, the surrealists lost interest in the cinema, abandoned their attempt to take advantage of its benefits. Then, apparently, they were enticed back, in the middle forties, when Hans Richter invited their collaboration when making *Dreams that Money Can Buy* (1944). Subsequently, surrealist elements reappear in Bunuel's *Los Olvidados* (1950) where, however, they are for the most part carefully insulated from the rest of the film by being confined to a dream sequence. It then appears that the early fifties saw a renewal of interest: Richter made *Not for Sale* (1952) and in the same year Michel Zimbacca and Jean-Louis Bebouin offered a surrealist experiment in the field of the documentary, entitled *L'Invention du monde.* At the same time, Jindrich Heisler and Georges Goldfayn inaugurated a series of *revues surréalistes*—short films in which the tra-

ditional relationships between image, sound-track, music and commentary are deliberately destroyed, in a technique similar to that of pictorial *collage.*

Faced with this evidence, we may feel inclined to wonder why so few surrealist movies have been made, since Artaud made the discovery of the potentialities of a medium well adapted to the aspirations of the surrealist group. We risk at this point some quite erroneous conclusions if we do not realize that, in reality, surrealism's enthusiasm for the cinema did not wane and then unaccountably revive again after about ten years. It is true that no surrealist movies were made. But there is still much to indicate that members of the group continued to be attracted to the medium. We find this, obviously, in the attention they have paid films like *King Kong,* in which Jean Levy, in *Minotaure,* discerned distinctly surrealist overtones, and *Shanghai Gesture,* which so caught their imagination that they made it the subject of one of their "inquiries." But we find their sustained interest even more clearly reflected in the scenarios which the surrealists have not ceased to write. Almost all of these have remained simply projects. B. Fondane, Joseph Cornell and Jean Ferry have printed theirs in book form. Others, like Léon Corcuff, Henry Storck, Jacques B. Brunius and Robert Desnos, have published their scenarios in reviews which are for the most part inaccessible.

The real reason for so little surrealist activity in the cinema is financial. When, in 1935, Breton, Paul Eluard and Man Ray began a film, they had to abandon it almost immediately in view of the absence of funds. So we are left with nothing more than a series of stills, reproduced in the *Cahiers d'art* under the title *Essai de simulation de délire cinématographique.* If it is true that Pierre Mabille's view may be regarded as typical of that of the surrealists—he considers that surrealism is better adapted to the cinema than it is to painting—it remains to be shown that surrealist methods and material have a market value. This is why the projects available to us are so worthy of our attention. They demonstrate conclusively that the surrealists' attitude towards the cinema has been much more consistent than is commonly believed. What is more, they stand as a salutary reminder that it is all too easy to misjudge that attitude, on the basis of insufficient evidence. Such a reminder is especially welcome when we are dealing with surrealism in the film. The first surrealist experiments in the medium are those by which the surrealist cinema is generally judged. Yet these films have not worn well. They reflect too faithfully the hectic atmosphere of the early years of surrealism for things to be otherwise. The brashness, the self-conscious straining for effect, even when the effect desired is not very clearly envisaged, give *Un Chien andalou* and *L'Age d'or* an uneven quality which cannot pass unnoticed and has provoked stern criticism. Meanwhile, the public has had little opportunity to correct its impressions. So far, *Les Horizons mangés,* shown at the Festival of Short Films in Paris in 1951, and *L'Invention du monde,* shown in Milan during the "*Journées surréalistes*" in 1959, have reached only a limited audience, while the early films are now available to film societies.

And so, before a fair assessment of the surrealist cinema can be reasonably attempted, due attention must be paid not only to all the films so far produced, but also to what surrealism would have liked to accomplish, if given the chance: careful consideration of the implications of existing scenarios is indicated. But here we must proceed with the greatest caution. Nothing has done more harm to the reputation of surrealism in the cinema than the attempt, on the part of critics genuinely

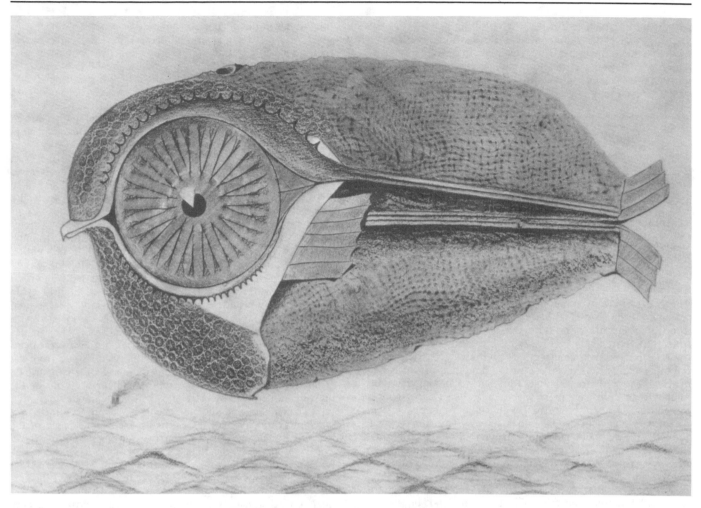

The Fugitive, *by Max Ernst. Copyright ARS, NY.*

seeking to determine the qualities of the surrealist films, to apply artistic criteria which can have no meaning for the surrealist. It is necessary to recall that surrealist movies, before they are anything else, are, like *Un Chien andalou,* anti-artistic. As Robert Desnos put it as early as 1930, in the first issue of *La Revue du cinema,* "When Réne Clair and Picabia made *Entr'acte,* Man Ray *L'Etoile de mer* and Bunuel his admirable *Chien andalou,* it was not a matter of creating a work of Art or of a new aesthetic, but of obeying profound, original impulses, consequently necessitating a new form." It would be a mistake to assume that the surrealists have had as their prime concern the enrichment of the cinema. They wish simply to make use of the possibilities it seems to offer. It is worth remembering that Fondane has confirmed that, in writing his *"ciné-poèmes"*—*Barre fixe, Paupières mûres* and *Mtasipoj*—he had no intention of trying to "correct" the cinema, to "improve" it. We would risk misconstruing the motives which lie behind the surrealist activity in the medium of films, and would consequently be misinterpreting the significance of these experiments, if we neglected to bear in mind that the surrealists have never regarded the cinema as an art-form, or even as an end in itself. They have always emphasized that they are not interested in art, but rather in finding means for exploring and revealing the surreal. So, for them, films are just a means of expression, valid like any other, but not necessarily more valid. The cinema, like painting and literature, is a medium to be exploited in directions which seem to promise man most. Zimbacca and Bédouin have explained, in the surrealist number of *L'Age du cinéma,* that their film *L'Invention du monde* was conceived as "an experiment carried out beyond the faddish classifications of ethnography and in complete indifference to aesthetic aspects." The hypothesis upon which *L'Invention du monde* rests is that there exist in the human mind certain forms of association which begin to function only when "poetic consciousness" is awakened. The heterogeneous collection of forms and symbols which this film presents owe their unity not to any technique of a cinematographic nature but to what the directors call "poetic influx" which, they claim, sets off a chain reaction.

The fact that, in the surrealist cinema, technical preoccupations are of secondary interest does not mean that it would be pointless to wonder what contribution surrealism, under the right conditions, could have made to the medium. And no one who feels impelled to do so can afford to disregard the hints given by surrealist criticism of the films of others. Nor should he forget the respect the surrealists have accorded the work of men like Tex Avery, Borowicz, Gras, Haanstra, Lenica and Polanska—to name only those who were represented in the program of films shown during the 1959-60 Surrealist Exhibition in Paris.

Despite attempts to declare the surrealist movement dead, its members continue to be active, eager to pursue their ends by any means available. Surrealism would long ago have lost its vitality, as its critics claimed it would, if it had not persistently looked to the future rather than to the past. In the circumstances, therefore, it does not seem idle speculation to ask if surrealism's most impressive and stimulating contribution to the medium of the cinema may not still be to come. (pp. 120-33)

*J. H. Matthews, "Surrealism and the Cinema," in
Criticism, Vol. 4, No. 2, Spring, 1962, pp. 120-33.*

PAINTING AND SCULPTURE

NORBERT LYNTON

[*In the following excerpt, Lynton discusses the role of artists in the Surrealist movement and analyzes varying approaches to Surrealism in works by the most prominent Surrealist painters and sculptors.*]

The Surrealist movement, like its immediate parent, Dada, rejected all the 'isms that had formed the story of modern art as artificial pursuits of no relevance to human existence at any time. The Surrealists' aim was to use the arts as a counter to the ordered and restricted ways of civilization by opening up the super-reality of fantasy, dream and imagination which, they claimed, is man's true habitat. More than Cubism, more obviously than Futurism, more specifically than Expressionism, the Surrealists were concerned with subject-matter and with the effects that subject-matter can have. Their aim being to subvert citizens from their good behaviour, they bombarded them with impolite and impolitic messages but also taught them the joys of anti-rational speculation. They were writers primarily, and their main focus was on literary problems. How, in writing, could they hope to capture true gobbets of irrationality? Merely to describe a dream would not be enough: conscious control would intervene. They experimented with drugs and hypnosis, partly to make themselves more at home in the unconscious. They adopted the Dadaists' game of using words in random sequence, exploiting their value as discrete and multivalent objects and also letting them send sparks of meaning to each other by imposing no intentional meaning on them. This could also be done with images, and they quoted repeatedly some words from the nineteenth-century poet, Lautréamont: "Beautiful as the accidental meeting of a sewing machine with an umbrella on an operating table." Both methods—verbal and visual—invited the reader's creative participation by stimulating his imagination to discover significance; the essential thing is to present him with data that will permit no commonsensical interpretations. To assist this process it would help to weaken the hold of logic on the spectator. Short of drugging him before submitting him to the Surrealist experience, the effective thing would be to disorientate him with shock. Thus Dadaists' tricks invented to show their rejection of civilized standards became essential strategies. Surrealism would liberate man by teaching him to live on a superior plane of natural freedom. Material constraints would become irrelevant as man shrugged off the bonds of rational order forged by the Greeks.

Poetry had always had this role. Its imagery had always been free to transcend the limits of practical discourse. In this sense Surrealism was merely asserting the primacy of the poetical faculty. But the Surrealists wrote in order to change society, overcoming their reluctance to risk losing their hold on what

they found in the unconscious in putting pen to cold paper. In 1923 André Breton, poet and leader of the Surrealist movement, considered giving up writing altogether; instead he and his colleagues pinned their faith on the shareability of irrational material and tended to disagree about how the sharing should be done. Egocentricity—the angler's intense gaze now fixed on to his own inner life—was the essential method of any Surrealist, but there would be no point in bringing one's catch to table unless it was nutritious to others. *The Surrealist Revolution,* the name they gave to the journal they published from 1924 to 1929 (it was succeeded by a journal with the even more pointed title, *Surrealism in the Service of the Revolution*), could not be confined to literature or the arts but would have to involve itself in the social struggle. For some years the Surrealists sought to ally themselves with international Communism but the alliance was uncomfortable and not wholeheartedly sustained on either side. The rise of Stalin, his triumph over Trotsky in 1928 and over Bukharin in 1929, brought an end to all tolerance of avant-gardism under Communism. As the doctrines of scientific materialism were pressed with growing dogmatism, Surrealists had to recognize the unbridgeable chasm that lay between those and their necessary belief in total freedom of thought and imagining. The artists associated with Surrealism participated little in the political work. Their names appear only rarely among the signatories of the several manifestos, statements and open letters that were issued from the Surrealist Research Office or printed in the Surrealist journals. Their relationship to the theoretical and literary core of the movement depended mostly on friendship with one or another of its members and did not necessarily imply more than a general sympathy with the Surrealist campaign. Some of the writers argued that Surrealist art was an impossibility; visual formulation of the irrational would destroy its authenticity. Others could not deny their interest in art and artists, and chief among them was Breton himself. Like his mentor, Apollinaire, Breton was stimulated by artists and responsive to their work, and he worked hard to prove that important contributions were to be made to Surrealism by visual means. In a series of articles that began in 1925 and were brought together in 1928 in the book *Surrealism and Painting* he defined some of these contributions and pointed to other artists as stimulating forerunners of Surrealist art.

On the whole he was to find artists unreliable colleagues. The automatism he proposed, in the first Surrealist Manifesto of 1924, as the essential means of exploring the unconscious regions was only of short-term interest to them. Instead, they departed on diverging, independent adventures; though Breton was often willing to give these public support, he was frequently disappointed by the result. Artists were also liable to accept involvement in activities Breton could not approve of. For example, he saw Ernst's and Miró's readiness to design the decor for *Roméo et Juliette* (music by Constant Lambert; choreographed by Nijinska) for Diaghilev's Russian Ballet company in 1926 as a major betrayal of Surrealist ideals, the company being a counter-revolutionary bourgeois institution. In a movement the history of which is full of resignations and expulsions, the artists tended to be the least constant elements. Yet the Surrealist spirit prospered in art: art notably enlarged its range of subject-matter, methods, and functions. We may wonder whether such growth would have occurred without Breton and Surrealism. The evidence suggests that much of it would have occurred independently in similar ways, but the fact remains that it did occur in and around Surrealism and came before the public mainly through Surrealist manifestations. There were major Surrealist exibitions in Paris in 1925,

1933, 1936, 1938, and 1947. A Surrealist Gallery opened in Paris in 1926; the Gradiva Gallery, run by Breton himself, opened in 1937; other galleries were sympathetic to Surrealism at various times. Individual artists involved in the movement had one-man exhibitions, and on several occasions Breton, Aragon or another of the Surrealist writers would produce supporting texts for the catalogues. Their own volumes, conversely, often appeared with illustrations done by the artists. Illustrations of recent work, as well as drawings or prints done specially for the occasion, appeared frequently in the Surrealist journals and gained international currency through them. In the thirties particularly Surrealim became an international phenomenon, with exhibitions in New York, London, Brussels, and elsewhere, and with local branches of the Surrealist movement.

Then the second world war came to outbid its often macabre findings. Much that was honored by the movement turned out to have been not so different from the clever but too charming confections with which Paris and the West had beguiled themselves while the storm clouds gathered. Hardly any of the major Surrealist artists whose work transcends the limits of the movement were French or thought of Paris as their home: in art at least, Surrealism seems to have been an incursion of non-Gallic forces upon the headquarters of French civilization.

Max Ernst . . . came to Paris [from Cologne] fully fledged in 1922. His work combined two elements that particularly appealed to Breton. It sprang from a positive response to the dream world of de Chirico and it relied for its essential method on what Breton had rightly isolated as modernism's chief gift to Surrealism, collage. Collage was an invitation to such stimulating juxtapositioning as Lautréamont had exemplified with words. De Chirico, in Breton's eyes, had recently lost his true path in confining himself increasingly to classical themes. In the young man from Cologne (only three years younger than de Chirico, but perennially youthful as well as highly articulate and gratifyingly untrammelled by any art training), Breton could see his ideal artist. Their relationship was not untroubled but Breton's regard for Ernst remained high. In 1929 he wrote of him that Ernst possessed "the most magnificently haunted brain at work today"; Ernst in return, was able to provide not only visual equivalents of atuomatism and productively unlinked images comparable to those of Surrealist writing, but also on occasion to paint detailed dream pictures and generally to retain remarkable mobility, constantly extending his own range and that of visual Surrealism.

His early interpretation of de Chirico was itself remarkable. Part of the pull of the Italian's characteristic paintings came from their pervading nostalgia. De Chirico's paintings exist in the past; we receive them as poignant recollections. In the early suite of lithographs *Fiat Modes* Ernst used de Chirico spaces and figures but turned his period effects into a tussle between yesterday and today whilst using references to dress-making as mocking metaphors for art. In one of the prints Chirico-esque perspective lines turn ambiguously into the wires or cables of a construction while an illogically inserted smaller image hints at the inverted scene offered by a plate camera. Ernst countermanded the bittersweet obsessiveness of de Chirico; the prints are critical where the Italian's paintings seem indulgent. By 1921-2 Ernst was experimenting with frottage—taking rubbings from floorboards and other surfaces in order to let the texture stimulate the imagination into discovering new images. He was to exploit this over some years, gradually adding other technical devices which would similarly trigger

the imagination in painting. In 1924, in Paris now, he made the picture-relief, *Two Children are menaced by a Nightingale*. Its painted portion, though mysterious and dreamlike, clearly echoes the Renaissance; to this he adds the Dada element of nonsensical assemblage. This has the effect of throwing doubt on any attempt to find a sensible interpretation of the pictorial drama and makes the Cubist trick of confronting us with different sorts of reality within one work into a painfully disruptive device. The title, written unceremoniously on to the inner frame, adds its dimension of derangement. Derangement of values, even: is that the way to label a work of art? Is that roughly affixed toy gate good enough for the frame? Is the whole thing worth putting in any frame? One almost forgets to ask oneself how a nightingale can threaten two "children," and who the third figure is.

In his pictorial novels—print sequences done from collaged graphics—Ernst extends our doubts in several directions. Other artists had been doing pictorial novels, high-minded, often rather sentimental works in which successive images told a comprehensible story. In Ernst's there is no story. Each turn of the page jolts our attention. Our minds leap and twist in an effort to catch and link up sparks of meaning. That meaning tends, not surprisingly, to focus on a few perennial human concerns, sex, death, the loss of identity. Ernst achieved the images that make up these novels by doctoring illustrations he took from nineteenth-century magazines and sales catalogues. Sometimes the resulting hybrids consist of many fragments; often only one or two fragments have been imposed on an existing image. The result is always astonishing. The images disrupt our normal reading habits. Before long we find ourselves distrustful even of the straightforward information carefully delineated for us by the original draughtsman.

In paintings Ernst often worked more abstractly, using a growing range of sources and devices, from early photographs recording air-flow patterns to the tracks made on a canvas by paint trickling from a can swinging above it. Often his paintings seem to record a creative dialogue between the painter and his visual and physical material. Seen in large quantity, Ernst's work is like a vortex. We look in vain for the man or his co-ordinating spirit in the many different kinds of images around us. "It is difficult," Ernst is reported to have said of women:

> for them to reconcile the gentleness and moderation of Ernst's expression with the calm violence which is the essence of his thought. They readily compare it to a gentle earthquake which does no more than rock the furniture yet does not hurry to displace everything. What is particularly disagreeable and unbearable to them is that they can almost never discover his *identity* in the flagrant (apparent) contradictions which exist between his spontaneous behavior and the dictates of his conscious thoughts.

(pp. 170-75)

Another artist associated with Surrealism who was to be of particular influence in America is Joan Miró. He divided his time between Spain and Paris. Here Spain means Catalonia and sometimes Majorca; most especially Barcelona ("I paint in the room where I was born") and a farm owned by his father at Montroig near by. Until the Spanish civil war and then the second world war distorted his life, Miró tended in the twenties and thirties to spend his summer months in Spain and the winter in Paris. His early (pre-Paris) work shows insistent detail raised to hypnotic power. In *The Farm* the cracks in the building, the utensils lying about, the contents of the outhouse, the forms of plants, animals, the soil itself—everything is stressed with the passion of urgent recollection; the empty blue sky answers with equal force. All is conscious design, incorporating hints from Cubism. The affidavit character of such a picture may remind us of Rousseau, but Miró was a thoroughly trained painter and his superrealism was a chosen style.

In Paris he was drawn to Surrealism principally through its poetry. In the first Surrealist exhibition of 1925 he showed *The Farm* but by that time he had pared down his style. He was now using the canvas as a large or small surface on which to make his statements. He stained and rubbed the surface to give it visual presence, and then he added signs and symbols of several sorts—many of them prepared for in *The Farm*—that hover in the ambiguous but shallow space created by his staining. We get the sense of a declaration issued by a particular person, the language and syntax of which are so idiosyncratic as intense inward focus can make them but the urgency of which compels our attention. The process may remind us of Malevich's Suprematist paintings, but these referred outwards, to cosmic space and to what the painter conceived as universal, impersonal truth. Also, difficult though it seems at first, Miró's sign language explains itself through familiarity with his work and by the recognition this brings of his ordinary, very human concerns. If Malevich's white surface is outer space, Miró's is a familiar wall and his marks are often like graffiti referring to all our personal lives. Miró's paintings look spontaneous and some of them probably were painted quickly. In any case they approximate to the "pure psychic automatism" Breton looked for, and it was this aspect of Miró's work that led Breton to welcome him to the Surrealist circle. But Miró rarely worked purely through automatism. His subsequent, very varied output (which includes sculpture and other three-dimensional objects and painted and ceramic murals as well as the normal range of production of a modern painter) shows him moving freely between consciously designed and composed images and more immediate, gestural work. The more thoroughly planned paintings tend to be those in which external thematic content dominates, as in *Still Life with Old Shoe*. This was painted from objects set up in the studio—bottle, apple with fork, broken loaf of bread, shoe. Working on the painting over five months, Miró transformed the realistic subject into a super-realistic one. It symbolizes Spanish peasantry under the shadow of the civil war. Abstract forms hover around the recognizable objects; their setting is the nauseating space of nightmares, and this sense is heightened by the electric or dark colours, the over-sharp or indeterminable forms. On other occasions Miró appears to work with completely abstract forms; these always function as symbols for something in his experience and rarely lack a hint of animal life. But on some occasions the marks and forms he uses are more detached. In 1930, for example, he produced a large horizontal painting that shows nothing but a small black disk and larger, softer red and yellow disks on a white field. This side of his work found its climax in three large paintings of 1962, intended to form a triptych. Each has its own ground colour, red, green, and yellow-orange. A few sparse marks on these grounds complement the colours in giving each painting its identity. Together they strike one as particularly naked paintings in which each element, formal or colouristic, has its greatest possible value. Such economical usage, combined with generosity of hue and size, suggests the art of post-war America. The Americans, Pollock, Rothko, and the others known as the Abstract Expressionists, were certainly affected by Miró's earlier work; it is likely that this triptych shows a return influence from the Americans on him.

The planning of Miró and Ernst, incorporating automatism but also presenting personal themes through signs and symbols,

was countered by another sort of Surrealist art, highly detailed paintings purporting to offer scenes brought up whole from the unconscious. The most elaborate and in many ways most persuasive of these are the work of another Spaniard, Salvador Dali. Until 1929 he practised several styles, ranging from naturalism of an old-master sort to Cubism and the Metaphysical Painting of de Chirico and Carrà. In 1928 he visited Paris. In 1929 he sent a group of paintings to Paris for a one-man exhibition which Breton saw and welcomed warmly. Dali's professed purpose, "to systematize confusion and thus to help discredit completely the world of reality," fitted well the Surrealist writers' programme, and his by then totally traditional methods of representation brought his pictures closer to the world of writing than were most of Ernst's and all of Miro's. Yet his means, at least the most effective of them, were visual, not literary. Dali has persistently exploited the ambiguities besetting our perceptual processes. We are always liable to misread what we see, especially so when we are in a state of diminished rationality owing to tiredness, illness, drugs or whatever. Dali's aim was to re-inforce such misreadings, until they throw doubt on the reading we call correct or normal. He also knew how to exploit to their utmost a whole range of distortions—of the human body (to which we respond with acute discomfort), of space (nauseating), of matter (as when a rock becomes flesh or watches go limp; nauseating again), and even of form itself (when negative forms become positive, hollows become solid, and so on; disorientating). In the second Surrealist Manifesto, written in 1929 when he had just been studying Dali's paintings, Breton wrote that there exists a mental point "at which life and death, real and imaginary, past and future, communicable and incommunicable, high and low, cease to be perceived in terms of contradiction." "It would be vain," he added "to examine Surrealist activity for any other motive than the hope of determining this point." This aptly describes the functioning of Dali's work at its best; it is at once destructive and constructive, disruptive and didactic. In purely pictorial terms it is, however, firmly reactionary. We observe his painted scene as a theatrical illusion prepared for us beyond the proscenium arch of the frame. His painting technique, admired by many, entirely lacks the grace of Raphael and the cool objectivity of Vermeer, his chosen heroes. These "hand-painted photographs," as Dali called his pictures, taste of nineteenth-century academic ponderousness. Only the brightness of his colours, echoing eighteenth-century painting and Impressionism, separates Dali's manner from that of a number of competent but timid painters of the age of Napoleon III. (pp. 176-80)

Many lesser talents were attracted to what is sometimes called naturalistic or veristic Surrealism. René Magritte was a naturalistic Surrealist in the sense that his paintings are representations of recognizable scenes or objects. The fantasy element in them seems, especially after Dali, modest and well-mannered. He lived quietly, in his native Belgium and in Perreux-sur-Marne near Paris from 1927 to 1930. Yet he struck at the traditional core of art, at the source of art's agreed value as communication: the convention by whch we identify an image with the thing it represents. More than any other Surrealist, more than any other artist except for Duchamp, Magritte was a painting philosopher. His usually very prosaic way of presenting images—in straightforward, frontal compositions, often painted rather heavily, as though with lard—disguises the edge of his paradoxes. *The Use of Words I* illustrates this. It is one of a number of pictures in which Magritte set words against representations. Here he accompanies a picture of a pipe, such as a signwriter might have produced, with the words "This is not a pipe.'' According to our expectations we might be taken aback by this declaration or accept it too readily. Of course this is not a pipe. It is paint on canvas, not to be filled with tobacco and lit. Yet our response to images rests on a suspension of such commonsense reading, and since images stir us emotionally it must be unrealistic to harp on the distinction between what is signified and what does the signifying. In some senses the painted pipe is more truly a pipe than the object in one's pocket: it is the pipe in general, not the pipe with this stem or that, with dirt in it or a chip out of the mouthpiece. It is the poet in the head that asserts the existence of a class of object we call ''pipe.'' Of course ''pipe'' will do for an Englishman, or a Frenchman, but not for an Italian, Red Indian or Chinese. Some people who see the picture will instantly recognize the object but not be able to read the words. What does this do to the message? Others may never have seen a pipe but be able to read French. What does this do to their knowledge of the world? In another painting, *The Key of Dreams,* Magritte showed four objects and set nouns against each: a bag, ''sky''; a penknife, ''bird''; a leaf, ''table''; a sponge, ''sponge.'' The last disconcerts us more than the others, and makes us wonder about names and titling. A picture of a naked woman may have a label ''Nude.'' Why? Magritte's title for that four-part picture suggests that wonder and fantasy, and also perplexity, arise out of naming and out of trust in names. Perhaps, after all, that leather container with handles should be called ''sky.'' Words are arbitrary, unreliable things, yet we tend to put more trust in them than in images even though we would agree that images can approximate to visual facts.

The Human Condition I leads us into a smaller conceptual maze without recourse to words. For a moment we do not know how to read the picture. Then we recognize that it shows a picture within a picture. Magritte has made the landscape painting he shows standing on the easel perfectly identical with the landscape outside the window, hence our momentary confusion. But how much do we know of the landscape outside the window? It is just possible that that picture has been set up in front of the window to stop us seeing what is really outside, something unbearable perhaps. There is an omnious silence in Magritte's paintings. We shall probably prefer the option of returning to our first explanation: the landscape on the easel is identical with the landscape beyond it, so much so that we can mistake one for the other. But why do we accept this even momentarily when we all know that few things are less like actual living landscape than even the most accurate paint-on-canvas rendering of a landscape? When we are hungry do we go into a gallery to satisfy ourselves with a still life? Why this pleasure in imitation, in self-deception? We call it art and treat it as treasure. And none of this even touches upon the curious light in the pictured room. The curtains cast shadows that suggest they are lit from above (like the picture would be in a gallery), which is odd. What produces the shadows cast by the legs of the easel? Whether we notice them consciously or not, such details are part of the picture's needling effect.

Neither Dali nor Magritte wanted to create new forms of painting as such. Ernst, Miró, and other Surrealists worked through new techniques and devices as much as through images and symbols. Neither Magritte's poker-faced manner nor Dali's bland stylishness could be mistaken for the product of any century but our own, yet there is no stylistic conflict between them and the academic inheritance that modernism had shed. In this sense their art was reactionary. Nevertheless we have to accept that, if Cubism established the freedom of artists from restraints of medium or technique, then one of the strat-

egies open to a painter was that of traditional illustrative painting. In asserting the efficacy of detailed representations Magritte and Dali were extending the life of late nineteenth-century Symbolism, on which de Chirico also had based himself; in using detailed illustration in order to question and to redirect the processes we employ in digesting the evidence of our eyes, they were themselves undermining the past. They went beyond the Cubist's questioning of a picture's relationship with reality. They were asking what use a man's perceptual and conceptual powers are to him, and what breaking the shackles of common sense would do to these powers. Like the Social Realists of the new Soviet and Mexican states, and like the New Objective painters in Germany, they were insisting on the primacy of meaning over aesthetic interest. Meaning, that is, in the old sense of discursive content partly or largely paraphrasable in words—not the latent meaning of a Mondrian or a Malevich where signs refer us to very general messages, nor that of a Kandinsky where intuitively assembled signs do not refer us to a body of ideas but are intended to transmit sensations through sensation. Kandinsky's programme of exteriorizing personal unconscious urges through forms and colours was close to Surrealist intentions, but his work is particularly inaccessible to literary analysis and was not recognized by the Surrealists as part of their world. (Significantly, the Surrealists were not interested in music either.) Klee's, on the other hand, was recognized. Ernst knew Klee personally and admired his work, and examples were included in the first Surrealist exhibition of 1925 and reproduced in *The Surrealist Revolution* in April the same year. Not only are there evidently fantastic elements in Klee's work; there is also something at least partly automatist about his way of letting images grow out of the marks he is making. Arp's presence in that 1925 exhibition may seem more surprising since his art lacks totally the convulsiveness that Breton said was the true beauty of modern times. Yet it is essentially metaphorical and springs from familiar human themes of the sort that motivated Miró's paintings. It contributed a benign, meditative aspect to the generally shriller body of Surrealist art.

The outsider who mattered most to the Surrealists was undoubtedly Picasso. They were right. During his long career Picasso adopted many roles but what links them all, what indeed goes some way towards explaining the hold that his flood of masterpieces, trifles and in-betweens has on our century, is his awe at the creative power of the imagination. He himself would not use such words. He was a deeply superstitious man, close to the primitive for whom an image is charged with spiritual powers and the environment is dense with omens. If one of the functions of Surrealism was to reawaken in man his ancient sense of dread and wonder, Picasso was its natural precursor. He had also been, of course, Apollinaire's prime artist-hero, and he was personally close to some of the poets who looked to Apollinaire as their master, especially Breton and Paul Eluard. It was Breton who, in or about 1921, persuaded the couturier Jacques Doucet to buy from Picasso the almost forgotten rolled-up *Demoiselles d'Avignon.* Breton wrote about Picasso in the July 1925 issue of *The Surrealist Revolution,* using him as the spearhead of his attack on those who held that Surrealism was out of reach of art. He illustrated his article with reproductions including the *Demoiselles* (which thereby became visibly part of the modern art world) and a new painting, *Three Dancers.* That November Picasso contributed to the Surrealist exhibition in spite of his general rule not to participate in mixed exhibitions.

''Beauty must be convulsive or cease to be,'' Breton had said. *Three Dancers* exemplifies that beauty. Its theme reflects Picasso's association, since 1917, with the Russian Ballet. He had designed decors for Diaghilev and had married a dancer in the company. Much of his graphic work of the early twenties was of dancers. By the mid-twenties he was tiring of the smart social life he had been leading and regretting his marriage. *Three Dancers* is the most emotionally charged painting he had done since the *Demoiselles*. The stylistic disarray of the earlier picture here becomes systematic. The distortion announced in the seated *demoiselle* but subsequently deflected by Cubist fragmentation, now takes full command. The *Demoiselles* became monstrous in the course of being painted; here dance itself is revealed in its primeval, Dionysiac role, frenzied and fierce action, not an entertainment. It recalls Matisse's *Dance* mural of 1910 (the raised foot of the dancer in the centre is a quotation from Matisse), and also the German Expressionists' harsh portrayals of dancers, Kirchner's especially. But the much greater extremes of distortion and movement that Picasso here allowed himself go beyond theirs, and are further extended by dislocations and duplications of anatomy that come from Cubism. This is most noticeable in the wild dancer on the left, multi-breasted and altogether riven by the obsessively ambiguous interaction of her body, dress, and background. This figure was the last of the three to be painted and involved a lot of reworking. Behind the dancer on the right looms a dark shadow. It stands for Picasso's friend Raymond Pichot, who died while the picture was in process. He plays St. John the Baptist to the Salomé of the girl on the left.

Les Demoiselles d'Avignon had been conceived as a moral allegory and had gradually become the less specific representation we know. *Three Dancers* has no subject beyond that announced by the title. The setting is a very ordinary French one, and even the intrusion of death does not result in a focused theme. Picasso was to wrestle at various points in his career with the problem of using art as a vehicle for particular messages; his innate tendency was towards generalized comments about life and death. In 1930 he painted, exceptionally, a picture with a defined subject, a historical and Christian one at that, a *Crucifixion*. It is small and intense, vivid in colouring, appalling in its use of distortion and conflicting scales, and stuffed with iconographical and stylistic references. Studies led up to it over the preceding three or four years, and in 1932 Picasso made a series of drawings after the Crucifixion from Grünewald's Isenheim altarpiece that shows he was still held by the subject. But his intention was not devotional. The drawings and the little painting (which Picasso kept by him and few people knew about) are thoroughly Expressionist in character. In 1929 he had painted a picture known as *Self-Portrait and Monster* in which a horrifyingly distorted head, which from other pictures we know to be female, seems to devour the painter's passive profile. In the *Crucifixion* monstrous heads crowd in on the innocent victim. A soldier-picador lances Christ's side and soldiers throw dice on a drum, while the Mother and Mary Magdalen bewail and also threaten the slight figure on the cross with their gaping jaws. That figure, we conclude, represents the artist; the traditional theme, ubiquitous in Roman Catholic countries, yields a private image of desperation. The picture formed part of a one-man show Picasso had in Paris in 1932. The Surrealists must have approved the use of an ancient myth as a personal statement.

The first issue of the journal *Minotaure*, launched in 1930 and interested primarily in Surrealism, featured thirty small Picasso images, drawn the previous year. Each was a female figure, paraphrased by means of assembled objects suggesting furniture and other utensils. About this time Picasso was also ex-

perimenting with constructed iron sculpture, which could involve a similar use of objects to suggest a figure or a head. Freud, the Surrealists' reluctant mentor, had referred much earlier to the "refashioning of ready-made and familiar material" as a means of conscious and also unconscious creation.

The essential autobiographical nature of Picasso's art distinguishes it from most Surrealist art in spite of the programme of self-examination. The Surrealist artist who comes closest to Picasso in this respect was Miró; we know that Picasso was positively interested in his work. We tend to expect such an autobiographical emphasis from German Expressionism but are often disappointed. Instead, we find critical or challenging poses, or external subject-matter coloured by personal experience, rather than intimate statements. (pp. 180-86)

Would sculpture be able to meet Surrealist aims? Surely the physical limitations and material substantiality of sculpture would not permit the full operation of fantasy and chance. Sceptics might have argued (they appear not to have done so) that sculpture is of its nature a surrealist activity, that one scarcely could go further than make a female figure 9 inches high for a mantelpiece or 40 feet high for a temple or 150 feet high for New York harbour, or to have a pair of anonymous lovers held for posterity in white marble, or a top-hatted mayor in black bronze. If sculpture is an art of physical, measurable fact, it is also the most mysterious of arts. Setting a sculpture on any sort of base, as until recently was almost always done, means refuting its actuality: like the stage and the picture frame, the base lifts the image on to a plane of unreality and therefore of special attention. Rilke called this special, removed space "a sculpture's circle of solitude"—and this of itself suggests why Cubists and others sought ways of breaking this convention. It was an obstacle to Cubism's mediation between the realities of art and of nature, to Futurism's attempt to draw the spectator into the work of art, to Constructivism's ambition to make art into an active element in daily industrial life. Picasso's 1912 *Guitar,* placed on a chair, Tatlin's *Counter Relief,* hanging in space, and certain Brancusis were attempts to overcome this problem—but how real is a functionless cluster of pieces of metal, let alone a metal paraphrase of a guitar encouraged to advertise its anthropomorphism by being invited to sit down? The best sculpture associated with Surrealism reflects three impulses, one of which is Picasso's playing with ambiguities of this sort. The other two are Duchamp's transmutation of values, achieved by removing objects from their normal habitat, and the enrolment of existing and specially made objects as things charged with supernatural powers as were those by African, Oceanic or American primitives. Indeed, primitive art was exemplary for all three. Through their regard for the primitive the Surrealists felt they were reconnecting the arts to their original function as necessary magic.

One way of making Surrealist sculpture was, of course, to make objects resembling goblins and fiends. Ernst did some of this sort in the thirties and forties; they are entertaining but of little interest as Surrealism. Another was to exploit, as Picasso had done already in the case of the *Guitar* and was doing in two and three dimensions during the twenties and after, our irrepressible human instinct for finding human images in everything. Another was to imitate Lautréamont's simile and bring together disparate objects to see what physical union would produce. The colanders that form part of Picasso's *Woman's Head* contribute to it a dimension of meaning that anonymous curved planes of metal could not have given it. But the process could be taken further at various levels of playfulness, as in Miró's *Poetic Object* or in Meret Oppenheim's agreeable disagreeable object, *Fur-Covered Cup, Saucer and Spoon*. Dali's *Rainy Taxi*, made for the 1938 International Surrealist Exhibition in Paris, was a disagreeable object on a larger scale. It consisted of a taxi occupied by a blonde female dummy and a dummy driver wearing goggles and a shark's snout. The taxi rained internally; ivy grew over it and the girl inside shared the back seat with lettuce and live snails. The main room of that exhibition was designed by Duchamp. Its floor was covered with dead leaves. Over a thousand dirty coal sacks hung from the ceiling. A lily pond towards one corner was flanked by an unmade double bed. Coffee roasters made their aromatic contribution to the complex of ideas and sensations set off by an environment which also included Surrealist paintings.

An exhibition shown two years earlier had done much to stimulate adventures in three-dimensional Surrealism. This was the Surrealist Exhibition of Objects held in Paris at the house of Charles Ratton. Politely arrayed on walls and on little pedestals, in showcases and on shelves, was a multitude of smallish objects: bits of nature (bones, stones, minerals) as found or after artistic adjustment, primitive artefacts including Oceanic and American Indian masks, Duchamps's *Bottlerack,* and a collection of "Surrealist objects" (thus distinguished in the catalogue) of past and present. Four pre-war sculptures by Picasso represented the past, including his *Still Life* of 1914, that remarkable parody of domestic trivia, as threatening as humorous, and a fine *Guitar* construction. The present was manifested in a large number of objects, many of them made specially for the occasion, by artists and writers of the Surrealist circle, among them Arp, Breton, Dali, Ernst, Magritte, the American artist and photographer Man Ray, the German-Swiss painter and sculpturess Oppenheim (with her furry object), Miró, and the English painter Roland Penrose. The different categories of object, old and new, Western and exotic, conscious art, unconscious art and nature's work, were jumbled together as equal in the sight of liberated man. This reminds us of the global embrace offered by the illustrations and text of the *Blaue Reiter* almanac. It should also make us aware of how much modern artists—as well as working their way more and more deeply into their professional and specialist concerns, away (it is often claimed) from anything they can share with the non-specialist world—have widened art's range of recognition and sympathy, turning art, in short, into a whole world of activities and objects of all regions and periods and of many disparate kinds.

Another contributor of Surrealist objects to the 1936 exhibition was Alberto Giacometti, from the Italian-speaking part of Switzerland. He had been in Paris since 1922, and had been influenced by Cubism as well as by primitive art. At the end of the twenties he found himself close to Surrealism. "For some years now," he said in 1933, "I have realized only such sculptures as presented themselves to my mind in a complete state; I have restricted myself to reproducing them in space without changing anything and without asking myself what they might signify." Earlier he had habitually worked from the model; now he was working from the imagination and, notably, from images that came into his head ready to be given three-dimensional material existence. In 1931 a spread in the December issue of *Surrealism in the Service of the Revolution* illustrated seven such "mute and movable objects" after Giacometti's drawings of them. They vary as sculptures, some involving a space frame, others an indeterminate plane or arena. Some look as though they should be touched, like the *Suspended Ball* or the long, spiky thing, or the *Object to be thrown away*. The

Suspended Ball (also known as *The Hour of Traces*) is not the first kinetic sculpture. Gabo had made a motorized sculpture in 1920 and in 1923 Man Ray had clipped a photograph of an eye to the pendulum of a metronome and called it *Object to be destroyed*. But Giacometti here introduced another function into sculpture, a new relationship between the art object and the spectator, bringing it painfully close to the attraction-repulsion experiences we know from life, wherein disgust and desire, pleasure and pain mingle inseparably. It is not the mobility of these things that matters but our urge to touch them and our fear of doing so. Like Picasso, Giacometti is unusually close to the roots of art. His work from nature too is charged with a primordial quality, as though he was the first man to turn formless matter into the image of a head or a figure. In 1935 he returned to working from the model, and found himself rejected by the Surrealists for doing so. They felt he had repudiated the imagination by turning to the visible world, and this demonstrates their shallow understanding of art. "I worked from the model throughout the day from 1935 to 1940. Nothing was like I imagined it to be." From 1950 he modelled figures from life as well as from memory; the results show no marked difference between one method and the other. As David Sylvester has pointed out: "Working from nature is working from memory: the artist can only put down what remains in his head after looking." There has also to be a period, however brief, of maturation: "our mind has to get outside the sensation before we can copy it." Neither does Giacometti see his sculptures as reflections of the world we call real. A work like *The Forest* shows that his sculptures, whether or not modelled from nature, and whether we find them lifelike or not, are part of his own poetic world. The dichotomy postulated by the Surrealists is a false one.

This may help us to understand the confusion and also the resistance that art movements produced during the last 150 years. Every launching of a new development in art exaggerates its differences from what was there before. It tends to emphasize, for the sake of differentiation, aspects that are not necessarily central. Slogans produced for a specific moment and purpose become a part of that development and distort our reading of it. Surrealist art was not everything Surrealists wished it to be, nor only what they wished it to be. Of its nature, it was a reiteration of preferences (rather than principles) voiced before, in the Romantic age particularly. In seeking to define itself more closely, to surmount the charge of being Romanticism or Symbolism revived, Surrealism tended to become dictatorial. In the name of liberation, like other revolutionaries, the Surrealists had to become exclusive and censorious. The essential matter of a movement may well make a deep impact, even while its externals are rejected. (pp. 190-96)

Norbert Lynton, "Calls to Order," in his The Story of Modern Art, *Cornell University Press, 1980, pp. 147-200.*

ACHIEVEMENT

MAURICE NADEAU

[Nadeau is a prominent French critic and the author of what many consider the definitive survey of Surrealism, Histoire du Surréalisme *(1946-48; The History of Surrealism). In the following excerpt from an afterword added to the 1957 revised edition of that work, Nadeau discusses the extent to which the Surrealists*

realized their dual ambition "to transform the world" and "to change life."]

Surrealism was based on a revolutionary conception of man and the world, in a period when the traditional conceptions of their relations had foundered in the Great War. Never before had man's submission to the world seemed so unendurable, that submission of which an intense awareness and a desire to bring it to an end are precisely what make the artist: it is because he seeks to put a stop to his alienation that the poet, the painter, the writer seeks to create new personal relations with that world. They succeed by their works, but without anything having changed around them. What they achieve is a personal adventure, often dramatic, sometimes tragic, an adventure which, for each, always begins over again at zero. Whether it finds its end in itself or leads to silence, on the essential point it is sealed by a defeat: books are added to books, canvases to symphonies without any other effect than to enchant a prison from which the artist escapes only ideally. There is no great writer, no matter how much he counts on posterity, who does not die in despair.

It was the ambition of surrealism to transcend the limits of subjectivity, and it did not mean to be content with words. For those who founded it, after the Dada experiment, it was no longer a question of everything beginning as before. Man was not that creature molded by a century of positivism, of associationism and "scientism," but a being of desires, instincts and dreams as psychoanalysis revealed him. In Russia, a society was being constructed on a new basis. Even more than Rimbaud or Lautréamont, those poets of inspired intuitions, Marx and Freud figured as the prophets of the new age. According to their particular modalities, the surrealists became Marxists and Freudians, putting the accent on the double evolution to be effected: "to transform the world," "to change life." They believed they could achieve this by a totalitarian activity of creation, starting from man himself taken as a totality and by means of an instrument, poetry, which was identified with the mind's very activity. This creative continuity was to be exercised in an unconditional freedom of feeling and action, beyond the compartmentalizations of life and art, in order to recuperate man as a whole. Whence the emphasis on the night side of being, on the imagination, on instinct, desire, and the dream, on the irrational or merely ludicrous forms of behavior, in order to have done with man mutilated, confined, alienated, reduced to categories of "doing" and "having." Surrealism opened a field of total renewal to man, by relation to his own life as much as to the life of men in groups, to the evolution of forms of thought, morality, art, and literature.

After the Second World War, surrealism's claims remained the same, and it is a sign of myopia to criticize it for having been unable to integrate new currents of sensibility or new forms of thought. The philosophy of the absurd, a certain romanticism of despair and even of existential commitment have long since been practiced by surrealism, and *all the way*— that is, to suicide (Rigaut, Crevel), to madness (Artaud), to revolutionary militancy (Aragon, Éluard, Péret), and for some, to a definitive "artistic" silence. If the surrealists suddenly seemed to be lacking in "presence" (I am thinking of the disappointing 1947 Exposition at the Galerie Maeght), it was because they had actually transcended the situation that was our own, because the movement had to a certain extent played its historic role. In the history of societies, there is no lack of those situations in which great movements and great men, whose urgent need they postulate, are at the same time afflicted

with statutory limitations. Babouvism vegetated over a century after Babeuf without influencing the labor movement; one of the two great artisans of the Russian Revolution was doomed to exile and then murdered in an age when his thought and action might have played a decisive role in the destiny of Soviet society. Indeed, this was the moral, intellectual, emotional situation after the Second World War, which did not show itself to be "equal to" surrealism.

After vainly seeking to make contact, Breton did not insist. He inflected the movement in a direction that had been one of its permanent temptations: the exploration of the sources of poetic activity, the inventory of its ways and means, the search for the metaphysical foundations of this particular form of knowledge. He recalled the existence of an "initiatory tradition" from which the great inspired creators down through history had to one degree or another derived: alchemists, occultists, magicians, and several poets, among whom were those most charged with mystery. To him it appeared of the greatest importance to reaffirm "the hieroglyphic key of the world which more or less consciously pre-exists all high poetry"; to follow "the paths of that internal revolution whose perfect achievement may well blend with that of the Great Work, as it was understood by the alchemists." Nicolas Flamel, Albertus Magnus, Fabre d'Olivet, Swedenborg, and among the poets, Hugo, Nerval, Baudelaire, Jarry, Roussel reasserted their stature as accursed seekers, nocturnal explorers, initiates. Modern poetry's mission was to continue their quest, to pursue the course they had taken, the trails they had blazed, toward that famous point where all contradictions are resolved. But were internal revolutions made in the market place, in groups, and by simple fiat or decree? Today surrealism is greedy for works which may serve us as landmarks.

How, nonetheless, can we help but envisage this falling back of surrealism onto its poetic minima, its transformation into a school of esotericism as the avowal of defeat? Do we not find at the very basis of its affirmation a hidden vice: the postulation that it is enough for thought to exist in order to become immediately operative, and for any task?

If poetry, which was to be freed of its artistic fetters, which was to function outside of any convention and any censorship, which was to become, according to Lautréamont's term, a common possession, is equivalent to the very activity of the mind, how can it find its point of impact in things, modify the reified world of social relations? Surrealism postulated the existence of a human order which it specifically proposed to sustain, and it came into conflict with an order that was chiefly economic, social, political, and artistic which thought alone was impotent to transform, because if this order is indubitably a human creation, it is also that of a man pinioned by history and time, exceeded by his own object which contains him and of which he is a prisoner. Between thought and action, there exists an indispensable mediation: the very history of men. Outside of a few attempts at political intervention (in the broadest sense), episodic and generally anarchic, surrealism did not possess the means for such intervention. It sought to compensate for this by preaching a greater and more radical revolution: the mind itself becoming the subject and the object of its own revolution. This was assuredly the only domain in which thought could become immediately operative.

Still, there exist certain societies situated precisely outside of time and history, in which thought becomes immediately operative: the shaman makes rain; the witch-doctor cures his patient by pronouncing certain formulas; game is killed not by the arrow but by the virtue of certain rites; the child born into the world does not always proceed from his fleshly mother. The mental universe of these societies is not thereby incoherent or illogical. It is a universe in which thought, carried by language, is substituted for facts and determines the event. Of little importance are the rational explanations which, we attempt to convince the men of these societies, are alone acceptable. All the experience of their daily life orders them to reject such explanations as inadequate, infinitely secondary. They live in a magical universe.

We may wonder if the present temptation of surrealism would not be to constitute—within our hyperlogical world that tends toward self-destruction by the very progress of a knowledge acquired with a view to its mere "utility"—the magic universe which would suit the men of this time, a universe based on the profound and generally unexploited resources of man, on the mysterious laws of a reality at whose threshold the conjectural explanations of science cease, on the desire to establish between microcosm and macrocosm a few essential "correspondences" whose inventory, verified in the form of laws, would serve to institute a new knowledge, and a new mastery. But then, in the fashion of the gnostic sects, of the Pythagorean schools or even of Saint-Simonism, the surrealist adherents would have to aim by every means (from the secret society to the political party) at directly influencing the government of men and things, we should have to believe them capable of educating scientists, philosophers, men of action, even militants.

Until further notice, we must resign ourselves to considering surrealism as a literary school, quite different from all those which have preceded it, and the most wonderful of those that have come into being since romanticism. Willy nilly, it must pass through all the stages, incarnate all the mediations by which a movement of thought ultimately determines, among other causes, and on condition that history lends it life, the consciousness of men.

Then after it will come, perhaps, those who will truly put an end to metaphors. (pp. 226-30)

> Maurice Nadeau, "Thirteen Years Later," in his The History of Surrealism, translated by Richard Howard, The Macmillan Company, 1965, pp. 226-30.

ADDITIONAL BIBLIOGRAPHY

Alquie, Ferdinand. *The Philosophy of Surrealism*. Ann Arbor: University of Michigan Press, 1965, 196 p.
  Analysis of the political, literary, and epistemological tenets of Surrealism by an adherent of the movement.

Balakian, Anna. *Literary Origins of Surrealism*. New York: New York University Press, 1947, 159 p.
  Examines the literary figures and movements that most influenced Surrealism, focusing in particular on the poetry of Arthur Rimbaud, Stéphane Mallarmé, and Charles Baudelaire.

Beck, William J. and Smith, Geneviève Brunet. "Images of Woman in Surrealist Literature: The French Connection." *The USF Language Quarterly* XXV, Nos. 3-4 (Spring-Summer 1987): 50-4.
  Discusses ambiguities in Surrealist images of women.

Block, Haskell M. "Surrealism and Modern Poetry: Outline of an Approach." *Journal of Aesthetics and Art Criticism* 18, No. 2 (December 1959): 174-82.

Contends that Surrealism can be best interpreted when considered not simply in terms of the manifestos, but also in the wider context of early twentieth-century literary trends.

Bohn, Willard. "From Surrealism to Surrealism: Apollinaire and Breton." *Journal of Aesthetics and Art Criticism* 36, No. 2 (Winter 1977): 197-210.
  Discusses the development of Apollinaire's concept of the surreal and relates it to that of Breton.

Bourassa, André G. *Surrealism and Quebec Literature*. Toronto: University of Toronto Press, 1984, 374 p.
  Study of Surrealist influence in Francophone Canadian literature using the broadest sense of the Surrealist classification, which includes themes and techniques used by artists from the Symbolists to the "beats."

Breton, André. *What Is Surrealism?: Selected Writings*, edited by Franklin Rosemont. New York: Pathfinder, 1978, 390 p.
  Excerpts from Breton's prose and poetry with an introduction by Rosemont, one of the primary spokesmen for contemporary Surrealists, which provides a "compact survey of the perspectives of international Surrealism as they have evolved through more than half a century."

Busi, Frederick. "Hegel and the Origins of Surrealism and the New Left." *Contemporary French Civilization* 2, No. 3 (Spring 1978): 379-95.
  Explores the influence of Hegelian theory in Surrealist revolutionary politics.

Carrouges, Michel. *André Breton and the Basic Concepts of Surrealism*. University: University of Alabama Press, 1974, 294 p.
  Study of Breton's thought written by an expelled Surrealist.

Caws, Mary Ann. "Motion and Motion Arrested: The Language of the Surrealist Adventure." *Symposium* 24, No. 4 (Winter 1970): 303-09.
  Discusses the central role of adventure in Surrealist poetry.

———. *A Metapoetics of the Passage: Architextures in Surrealism and After*. Hanover, N.H.: University Press of New England, 1981, 202 p.
  Study of structure and language in Surrealist poetry.

———. "The Meaning of Surrealism, and Why It Matters." In *Writing in a Modern Temper*, edited by Mary Ann Caws, pp. 146-63. Saratoga, Ca.: AMNA Libri, 1984.
  Examines the unique qualities of Surrealist literature.

Cook, Albert. "Surrealism and Surrealisms." In his *Figural Choice in Poetry and Art*, pp. 86-123. Hanover, N.H.: Brown University, 1985.
  Analyzes Surrealist poetry, concentrating in particular upon typical Surrealist imagery.

Duplessis, Yves. *Surrealism*. Westport, Conn.: Greenwood Press, 1962, 158 p.
  Examination and defense of Surrealist goals and techniques.

L'Esprit Créateur: Surrealist Literature VI, No. 1 (Spring 1966): 1-60.
  Special Surrealist issue which includes contributions by neo-Surrealists and prominent Surrealism scholars.

Gascoyne, David. *A Short Survey of Surrealism*. London: Frank Cass, 1970, 162 p.
  Traces the development of the Surrealist movement and reprints some translations of Surrealist writings.

Gershman, Herbert S. *A Bibliography of the Surrealist Revolution in France*. Ann Arbor: University of Michigan Press, 1969, 57 p.
  Most comprehensive English-language bibliography of Surrealism.

Grossman, Manuel L. "Jean Vigo and the Development of Surrealist Cinema." *Symposium* 27, No. 2 (Summer 1973): 111-25.
  Utilizes an analysis of Vigo's films to explain the nature of Surrealist film in general.

Hibbard, Tom. "Freedom by Chance: Dada and Surrealism." *Midwest Quarterly* XXVIII, No. 3 (Spring 1987): 364-77.

Examines the differences between Dada and Surrealism.

Ilie, Paul. *The Surrealist Mode in Spanish Literature*. Ann Arbor: University of Michigan Press, 1968, 242 p.
Analyzes the works of Spanish Surrealists, concluding that the Spanish group should be regarded as distinct from the Paris group because of its divergent aims and methods.

Jean, Marcel, ed. *The Autobiography of Surrealism*. New York: Viking, 1980, 472 p.
Collection of excerpts from various Surrealist writings, with historical background provided by editorial interpolations.

Josephson, Matthew. *Life among the Surrealists*. New York: Holt, Rinehart and Winston, 1962, 403 p.
Personal reminiscences by an English Surrealist who spent much time in the Paris group.

Kantarizis, Sylvia. "Surrealism, Communism, and Love." *Essays in French Literature*, No. 7 (November 1970): 1-17.
Studies the development of and reasons for the Surrealists' involvement in communism.

Kovács, Steven. *From Enchantment to Rage: The Story of Surrealist Cinema*. London: Associated University Press, 1980, 297 p.
Examines the Surrealists' ambitions in creating films and assesses the extent to which those ambitions were realized.

Lemaitre, Georges. *From Cubism to Surrealism in French Literature*. London: Geoffrey Cumberledge, 1947, 256 p.
Discusses historical aspects of Surrealism.

Levy, Julien, ed. *Surrealism*. 1936. Reprint. New York: Arno/Worldwide, 1968, 191 p.
Anthology of Surrealist works including film scenarios, extracts from the manifestos, poetry, and artwork.

Matthews, J. H. "Poetic Principles of Surrealism." *Chicago Review* 15, No. 4 (Summer-Autumn 1962): 27-45.
General discussion of Surrealist poetry.

————. "Literary Surrealism in France since 1945." *Books Abroad* 36, No. 4 (Autumn 1962): 357-64.
Discusses the activities of the surviving members of the Surrealist group after 1945.

————. *An Introduction to Surrealism*. University Park: Pennsylvania State University, 1965, 192 p.
Study which Matthews describes as an "attempt at explication" of Surrealist art.

————. *Surrealist Poetry in France*. Syracuse: Syracuse University Press, 1969, 240 p.
Analyzes the works of individual Surrealist poets.

————. *Surrealism and Film*. Ann Arbor: University of Michigan Press, 1971, 198 p.
Studies the films that inspired the Surrealists and those they subsequently produced.

————. *Theatre in Dada and Surrealism*. Syracuse: Syracuse University Press, 1974, 286 p.
Comprehensive study of Surrealist dramatists, including Breton, Artaud, Vitrac, and more recent adherents.

————. *The Imagery of Surrealism*. Syracuse: Syracuse University Press, 1977, 293 p.
Explores the expression of the Surrealists' aesthetic theories in their art.

————. *Surrealism, Insanity, and Poetry*. Syracuse: Syracuse University Press, 1982, 154 p.
Examines similarities between the irrationality of Surrealist imagery and various aberrant mental states.

————. *Languages of Surrealism*. Columbia: University of Missouri Press, 1986, 262 p.
Collection of essays on various topics, including considerations of Surrealist film, poetry, and painting.

Mead, Gerald. "Language and the Unconscious in Surrealism." *Centennial Review* XX, No. 3 (Summer 1976): 278-89.
Considers "the Surrealist position on the nature and dynamics of the unconscious and language."

Miller, Henry. "An Open Letter to Surrealists Everywhere." In his *The Cosmological Eye*, pp. 151-96. Norfolk, Conn.: New Directions, 1939.
Denounces the Surrealists for what Miller considers their lack of "guts and significance."

"Values in Surrealism." *New Directions in Poetry and Prose* (1940): 385-579.
Special Surrealist section which includes translations of Surrealist poetry and several critical articles.

Plottel, Jeanine. "The Mathematics of Surrealism." *Romantic Review* LXXI, No. 3 (May 1980): 319-29.
Discusses the Surrealists' manipulation of logic to create absurdity in their works.

Ray, Paul C. *The Surrealist Movement in England*. Ithaca: Cornell University Press, 1971, 331 p.
Study of the major figures of English Surrealism, including Herbert Read, David Gascoyne, Hugh Sykes Davies, and Ruthven Todd.

Read, Herbert, ed. *Surrealism*. London: Faber and Faber, 1936, 251 p.
Anthology of Surrealist writings and drawings which includes a restatement of the manifestos by Read.

Rhodes, S. A. "Candles for Isis: A Symposium of Poetic Ideas among French Writers." *Sewanee Review Quarterly* XLI (1933): 212-24, 286-300.
Includes an interview with Breton.

Sellin, Eric. "Aspects of Surrealism: Surrealist Aesthetics and the Theatrical Event." *Books Abroad* 43, No. 2 (Spring 1969): 167-72.
Discusses the technical and thematic characteristics of Surrealist drama and the extent to which the artistic goals of Surrealism are compatible with the medium of theater.

————. "Simultaneity: Driving Force of the Surrealist Aesthetic." *Twentieth Century Literature* 21, No. 1 (February 1975): 10-23.
Analysis of "relativity and the pluralistic consciousness" in Surrealist art.

Steel, David. "Surrealism, Literature of Advertising and the Advertising of Literature in France 1910-1930." *French Studies* XLI, No. 3 (July 1987): 283-97.
Describes the Surrealists' abundant use of standard publicity techniques.

Williams, Linda. *Figures of Desire: A Theory and Analysis of Surrealist Film*. Urbana: University of Illinois Press, 1981, 229 p.
Psychoanalytic approach to Surrealist film, concentrating on the work of Luis Buñuel, whose career as a Surrealist filmmaker spanned more than five decades.

Yale French Studies, Special Issue: Surrealism No. 31 (May 1964): 3-186.
Special Surrealism issue which includes essays by such notable scholars as Anna Balakian, Mary Ann Caws, and J. H. Matthews.

Zinder, David G. *The Surrealist Connection: An Approach to a Surrealist Aesthetic of Theatre*. Ann Arbor, Mich: University Microfilms International, 1976, 162 p.
Examines the Surrealists' rejection of artistic mimesis in their dramatic works.

Travel Writing in the Twentieth Century

INTRODUCTION

Accounts of travel have been part of world literature since its inception. Early travelers to little-known parts of the world, mindful that others might follow their paths, realized the vital importance of leaving a written record of their journeys. Maps, suggestions for modes of transportation, directions to lodging, analysis and evaluation of local inhabitants, food, and customs were the invaluable components of the earliest firsthand travel accounts. Concurrent with this instructive function was the tendency of travelers to recount in an entertaining manner the joys or hardships of their journey, to emphasize the strangeness of the foreign scenes they had observed, and to remark upon the differences between people of various lands. Thus, factual travel literature often incorporated elements of imaginative fiction, and the embroideries and fabrications of travel writers were welcomed as fanciful additions by readers of the genre, who enjoyed lively accounts of fabulous beasts, fantastically different yet recognizably human men and women, and the inevitable episodes of high adventure purportedly experienced by those returning from distant lands.

The early twentieth century is generally recognized as a prolific period of distinguished travel literature. At that time the geography of many parts of the world was imperfectly documented, lodging was scarce and often of dubious quality, and modes of transportation were slow, complicated, and sometimes dangerous, thus offering the determined traveler who wished to visit someplace new, "unspoiled," and uninhabited by other visitors from abroad a myriad of locations from which to choose. Many major figures in English and American literature traveled and wrote about their travels during this period. The complete works of Henry James, D. H. Lawrence, and Edith Wharton, for example, each contain several travel books of the same high literary quality as their renowned fiction. Some monumental works of travel literature, such as Charles M. Doughty's *Travels in Arabia Deserta*, stand as classics because they mark the first serious attempts to approach an understanding of a foreign land, culture, and people. In other instances, writers have undertaken journeys in the course of solving personal dilemmas, and an account of travel often becomes a revelation of the self. The introspective travel books of D. H. Lawrence, for example, offer insights that are not found elsewhere in his written works.

In his 1980 study of travel writing, *Abroad: British Literary Travel between the Wars*, Paul Fussell pronounced the early twentieth century the "great age" of travel, a statement which met with almost unanimous agreement by commentators on travel literature. However, Fussell's claim that travel literature has since become a moribund genre has been less widely supported. Going abroad, Fussell maintains, is now a highly organized industry involving package tours, strict itineraries, and homogenized local cultures, and he contends that the element of chance, opportunity for discovery, and latitude for the unexpected are not components of late twentieth-century travel. Existing conditions, Fussell contends, are not conducive to the writing of travel literature. In addition, the genre has suffered critical neglect in the latter part of this century, with much of the critical writing on travel literature focusing upon those works written earlier in the twentieth century. These are the classics of the genre, insightful works often of very high literary quality, written by some of the most notable authors of the age. Although literary quality is still a major component of travel books, the focus of contemporary travel writing has changed. In a thoroughly explored but still imperfectly understood world, contemporary travel literature is more and more concerned with people, history, and psychology than with elaborate descriptions of place. As fiction has become less concerned with representations of life, travel literature has taken on the role of social description once held by novelists who practiced a documentary realism. Changing the direction of their explorations, travel writers continue to seek insights and understanding, not among the world's places, but among its people.

THE TRAVEL BOOK: CONVENTIONS AND TRADITIONS

V. S. PRITCHETT

[*Pritchett is a highly esteemed English novelist, short story writer, and critic. Considered one of the modern masters of the short story, he is also one of the world's most respected and well-read literary critics. Pritchett writes in the conversational tone of the familiar essay, approaching literature from the viewpoint of a lettered but not overly scholarly reader. In his criticism, Pritchett stresses his own experience, judgment, and sense of literary art, rather than following a codified critical doctrine derived from a school of psychological or philosophical speculation. In the following essay, entitled "The Writer as Traveller," Pritchett discusses some differences between the European and the American "travelling writer," and outlines some characteristics of several English and American authors of travel books.*]

I distinguish first of all between the traveller who writes— Bates or Waterton on the Amazon, Doughty on Arabia—and the professional writer, the novelist, the critic, the poet who travels. And among these we can see the difference between the generations if we compare Maugham with Lawrence; or Lawrence with Auden, MacNeice, Isherwood and Graham Greene; and the difference in nationality when we compare Hemingway and Edmund Wilson with Aldous Huxley. In Edmund Wilson we have, in any case, the kind of travelling writer who is weightier than the man of letters, broader than the critic, which England does not now produce. He is—all American writers are—a continental. He is an alert voluminous American, in the rational fundamentalist tradition of William James. I do not put him among the travellers impelled from within, but among those who will themselves into movement with a strategic purpose, which is partly professional, partly temperamental.

The impelled writing-travellers are spasmodic in their appearances. Byronism was one impulse and we can see its roots in the Napoleonic war. There were the same motives in the neo-Byronism of the Thirties. There was Clough's travel-poem-notebook in 1848. Revolt against the modern cerebral world was D. H. Lawrence's case; and since his time, the travelling writers have broken out because the world has broken in. The modern educational journey is not the Grand Tour but the territories of the *Grand Débâcle:* Orwell in Spain, Auden and Isherwood in China. To have the talent of a Hardy or a Jane Austen and remain in one place would now require strength not to say obduracy of character; yet, in fact, if such writers could be found now they would probably be more "contemporary" and show as much fidelity to the realities of modern life as those made restless by the guilt of ignorance or the dread of being disengaged. For some it is proper to be restless in a restless world; it is not improper for others to record that there is no such person as "modern man" aware of all the tragedies of his time. We are also affected by what we are unaware of. It is a characteristic of our life that the imagination must fail; that there are insentient places called Buchenwald, Korea, Cyprus, the labour camps and—as Mr. Edmund Wilson was astonished to notice on his way to Haiti—the kind of thing that goes on in Miami: a scar grows over these things in our hardened minds.

Yet, to be on the move is the dominant characteristic of our civilisation. If they have done nothing more, millions of ordinary people have travelled out of their class or their forecastable lives; they have crossed frontiers in their own countries, and the appetite grows with eating. Lawrence's journey from Nottingham to Germany, Italy, Ceylon, Australia and New Mexico, springs from the dramatic loss of any faith to be found in his locality; it was a pilgrimage in search of a shrine which kept moving on. Perhaps too much has been made of that pilgrimage. British imperialism was one result of people breaking out from the claustrophobia and the littleness of this exquisite island which is over-endowed with the taste for authority and law. Again and again, the English travellers are the English rebels, the disestablishers, who have fought hard against the charm of conservative eccentricity and who have feared not to know the world. It is too odd not to have been continentalised at some period of one's life: today that means to accept a non-provincial training, to be considerably Russianised, Africanised, Americanised, or Asiaticised. All the same, it is a safe bet that any English village is packed with more people who have direct experience of other continents than any of the villages of the new, standardised mass societies which have, indeed, been carefully cut off from knowledge. In the long run, English madness has had its points.

The impelled-traveller depends as much upon the equipment that he takes with him as upon what he sees. To Africa, from Livingstone to Gide and Graham Greene, have gone the sin-eaters; in the tropics, the gross outrages of nature, the cannibal pools of stacked-up crocodile bellies, the poisonous tree, the whirligig of insect murder, have been matched by the outrages of man upon man. Conrad wrote of "the heart of darkness"; Graham Greene speaks of "the past from which one has emerged." We are back among the horrors of the womb. Africa, he says in *Journey without Maps,* is astonishing in that it is not strange:

> Freud has made us conscious, as we have never been before, of those ancestral threads which still exist in our unconscious minds to lead us back. The need, of course, has always been felt, to go back and begin again. Mungo Park, Livingstone, Stanley, Rimbaud, Conrad represented only another method to Freud's,

a more costly, less easy method, calling for physical as well as mental strength.

Did the explorers know "the nature of the fascination which worked on them, in the dirt, the disease, the barbarity and familiarity of Africa?" Greene's own real fascination is that of any *writer*: he idealises and wishes not to idealise the man of action. Writing stands between him and pilgrimage as a way of life. He is Hamlet, the reporter. From our point of view, these speculations of his, like the outcries of Lawrence, are chiefly important for what they provoke. Countries are well-described when they have become an intense experience in private life. He may be quite wrong, but the wrongness of human beings is their vivid distinction. We can be glad that Lawrence got the Mexicans wrong.

These impulses tell us more, of course, about the kind of country a man comes from than about the country he visits. What a burden has been lifted off man, Edmund Wilson felt, when he left the Zuñi Indians, with their collective life and their fulfilling of purgative religion, by simple, conscious, friendly American individuality. The American variant becomes clearer in Ernest Hemingway. Romantic, of course; liable to conversion; a seeker of alien people who know how to live; a Childe Harold of the bottle. We cannot doubt the effect of Spain on him. Yet his equipment is the technician's. He has the American instinct for being quick to seize the way things are done and marvels when he sees what they are done for. Hemingway, like many Americans, has been a user of countries. He travels to collect "know-hows." He used Spain to teach him the technique of bull-fighting and the utility of death; Africa to teach him how to hunt big game and the utility of the finer senses; the Caribbean to teach him how to fish and be idle. Practical action leads him to intimate experience of these places and, in his thoroughness, there is a sort of innocence and single-minded faith. It owes nothing to contemplation. He is not the spectator; he gravely participates. In this, he strangely approaches the naturalists, like Bates or Hudson. He has, unlike most travellers, something to do; and has, or affects to have, few opinions. One does not feel that there is the guilty shadow of the writer lying between him and his subject. He is relaxed. A natural traveller, he is thinking of more places.

He points to a fundamental difference between the European and the American travelling-writer, which is brought out most strongly by the contrasting cases of Aldous Huxley and Edmund Wilson. They are educated men, impelled by the new encyclopædic impulse. They are novelists, critics, historians, scholars, thinkers—whether original or not—their fields are wide. They are exceptional in being compendious and in this resemble Victorian writers who found no knowledge alien. But the Englishman is intense, effervescent, speculative, changeable, sweeping, individual and ego-centric; he has read up the Mexican cities, the population questions, the genetic questions, everything, in advance, and arrives on the scene assuming we must know what he knows and are as ready to speculate and assert as he is. He has capital enough to afford levity. He is even vulgar. He is inexhaustible, and when he sits down, it is to think of places where there is new knowledge to acquire. Turn to Edmund Wilson's *Red, Black, Blond and Olive,* four long accounts of the Zuñi Indians (New Mexico) in 1947, Haiti in 1949, Russia in 1935, Israel 1954 and we have a clear, deliberate, unemphatic, impersonal narrative. There is no intensity. Relaxed and with the care of the learned technician, Mr. Wilson takes one through the anthropological detail of the Zuñi religion, through the complexities of the life without colour bar in Haiti; in Russia he has the serious, documented fidelity of a phlegmatic diarist who tells precisely how things were done or were said, as close to fact as a Hogarth engraving the *Industrious Apprentice*. Critics have often complained—I do myself—that Mr. Wilson is careless about his style. This, I suspect, to be the pose of an extremely sensitive man, but it is also the habit of one whose great gift is for thinking, laying foundations, for the accumulating of evidence and for putting his finger sharply and dramatically on the important facts and issues. *To the Finland Station* and *The Wound and the Bow* are imaginative and expository works. Part of their exceptional effect comes from the disclosure, line by line, of the means of working. And there *is* intensity; but it is in the choice of subject and in the feeling behind the choice. When Huxley the traveller assumes we know, Wilson is seen in the process of clearing ground, finding out minutely, shrewdly and working up to his massive effect. A note of disparagement in his voice sharpens the edges; it is that note one has heard so often in the voice of the technician; but in his case it has another authority. It is the authority of his continuous impulse as a traveller and a writer, his concern with the growth of the idea of a collective society (Marx) and with the human disaster (Freud). He is the positive, rational, travelling-writer whose travels are not a search, but a statement of the excitement of the cumulative importance of research and the collecting of evidence. As time goes by, he has become the Johnsonian figure of Anglo-American letters. He is the only living critic with a sense of history. To travel with him is to see what will and method can do; to stoically dispense with the inspiration of personal distress. (pp. 693-94)

> *V. S. Pritchett, "The Writer as a Traveller," in* The New Statesman & Nation, *Vol. LI, No. 1318, June 16, 1956, pp. 693-94.*

VERNON YOUNG

[Young is an English-born American film writer and critic. In the following excerpt, he surveys some major twentieth-century travel books written by "educated observers who set out to visit countries very different from their own." Young maintains that the vast majority of such travellers are shocked by the apparent formlessness of life lived in unfamiliar ways and ultimately seek familiar analogies for their travel experiences.]

Elie Faure, whose five-volume *History of Art* no one outside France seems to read anymore, once claimed that we are united by our differences because we approach one another in order to study them. In a comprehensive view of modern history, this seductive inference is a double-edged sword. We have been approaching one another with accelerating frequency for more than two hundred years, but especially since the age of mass travel was initiated by the industrial revolution. Is it possible to say now that more people have been united by their differences than have been destroyed by them? A brash question and not one I am prepared to answer in haste. I have raised it because it has so often been the implicit subject, if not the main drift, in the uncertain category of literature with which I am here dealing: books of travel written in our day by dilettantes, that is to say, be writers who have not been primarily naturalists or missionaries or official explorers or big-game hunters or political journalists. I am exclusively concerned with educated observers who have gratuitously—many of them have so alleged—decided to visit countries as divergent as possible from their own and who have set down afterward, with varying degrees of candor and art, what it was like to be there.

The underlying motive of the articulate travelers who crowded the scene in the twenties and thirties has been critically defined by Paul Fussell in his admirable survey of British travelers between the wars, *Abroad*: "To the degree that literary travel between the wars constitutes an implicit rejection of industrialism and everything implied by the concept of 'modern Western Europe,' it is a celebration of a Golden Age. . . . One travels to experience the past, and travel is thus an adventure in time as well as in distance." This seems to me profoundly true and is supported by nearly every writer of distinction who has written a travel journal in this century.

Another important qualification presents itself whenever you scrutinize the conclusions of the several escapists who fled from the materialism of the western world into the jungle cultures of Africa and the Andes or to the plateaus of the Middle East. Eager as they sometimes were to recover the simplicities of a "Golden Age," they invariably rejected the premises when they came face to face with the labyrinthine evasions of the Asiatic mind or the poverty of concepts represented by the primitive mentality. Unconsciously, most of these high-minded fugitives agreed with E. M. Forster's Fielding in a *Passage to India* who, pausing in the Mediterranean on his way home from the East, recognized that for him there could be no true beauty without form, that the buildings of Venice "stood in the right place, whereas in poor India everything was placed wrong," and that "something more precious than [the] mosaics and marbles" of Saint Mark's spoke to him now: "The harmony between the works of man and the earth that upholds them, the civilization that has escaped muddle, the spirit in a reasonable form. . . . The Mediterranean is the human norm. When men leave that exquisite lake, whether through the Bosphorus or the Pillars of Hercules, they approach the monstrous and extraordinary."

Whatever reasons, conscious or subconscious, were advanced by European intellectuals for exploring the hinterlands of the globe, the shock of formlessness usually had the last word. André Gide's *Travels in the Congo*, written in 1929, is a case in point. Writing his day-by-day memoirs, Gide at first tries hard to take an intelligent interest in native customs, in the odd linguistic assumptions they reveal, in the fauna and the flora, in the manufacture of palm oil. As time goes by, however, he loses his grip on such details, overthrown by the unfamiliarity, the unselective life of man and plants, by homesickness for European clothes, the principle of cause and effect, Paris and literature and the fine arts. The reader senses that, before half his journey is done, Gide would much rather write essays on the paintings of Simone Margini, Benozzo Gozzoli, or Corot—with which he strives to compare swatches of the Congo landscape—or write letters to Roger Martin du Gard about Baudelaire and Goethe. Repeatedly Gide professes himself intimidated by the vegetation itself, a subaqueous paradigm of the subhuman scene.

> Beside me is a tuft of great papyri-like palm-trees rising out of the water, and exceedingly handsome, though the greater part of them are faded, and behind me the greatest mixture of grass and water that it is possible to imagine. Again I see the enormousness, the formlessness, the indecision, the absence of direction, of design, of organization, which so excessively disturbed me during the first part of our journey, which is indeed the chief characteristic of this country. But here the perplexity of nature, this wedding and welding of the elements this *blending* of grey and blue, of grass and water, are so strange and recall so little of anything in our countries (unless

perhaps certain pools in the Camargue or in the neighborhood of Aguesmortes) that I cannot stop gazing at it.

Even where most negative, Gide felt constrained to find a French analogy as a touchstone. At a spot called Maroua he notes his fourth rereading of Conrad's *Heart of Darkness*. "It is only after having seen the country that I realize how good it is." On the particular aspects of Conrad's novel that he found cogent he does not expatiate—it could scarcely have been the anti-imperialist theme, since his own observations on the subject of exploitation are neither passionate nor convincing. One could infer that the young M. Gide felt *d'accord* with Conrad's turgid visions of barbarism and the nameless rites that took possession of Mr. Kurtz—yet he suggests no atavistic stirrings of the elementary impulses. On the contrary, Gide restricts his impressions mainly to those of an aesthetic kind; confronted by the overlapping and prolific condition of everything, he affirmed that the necessity for *differentiation* among phenomena seemed to him the principal sensation with which he left the country.

For Graham Greene, five years later, Liberia was not so much a welcome reversal of civilization—which to his sense had *not* "escaped muddle"—as it was an indispensable reminder that since society at home was breaking down under the twin pressures of violence and ratified mediocrity, one could escape into a raw territory that was its mocking paraphrase. His journey through this dismal, infected country—he walked for four weeks to cover about 350 miles—was a *Journey without Maps* (the title of his book), which he fondly believed to be a psychoanalytic journey into the antecedent stages of human consciousness. What he, in fact, tramped through was a country whose native tribes had had imposed on them, a century before, a foreign body of freed slaves. Shortly before Greene's visit to this quasi-utopia, the regime in power had been found guilty of exporting slave labor. By Greene's description of the place, Liberia then consisted of a shabby and corrupt urban coastal area squatting at the edge of a primeval forest, with an unspeakable climate, abject superstitious natives, a few pathetically courageous missionaries living among the cockroaches and the guinea worms: a setting wholly compatible, of course, with Mr. Greene's compulsive interest in, and inexhaustible talent for, describing the hopeless and the seedy.

Greene arrived exhausted at a hut in the remote interior, without his native carriers, who had refused to cross a precarious bridge in the dark. Hence he had no beds, no mosquito nets, no lamps, no food, no air filter for the blanketing heat. "And suddenly," Greene tells us,

> I felt curiously happy and careless and relieved. One couldn't, I was sure, get lower than Duogobmai. I had been afraid of the primitive, had wanted it broken gently, but here it came on us in a breath, as we stumbled up through the dung and the cramped and stinking huts to our lampless sleeping place among the rats. It was the worst one need fear, and it was bearable because it was inescapable.

Few writers of any persuasion have anything like Greene's resources for conveying the nuances of gratification from self-punishment. Having completed his ostensible journey into the fears of childhood and returned to Grand Bassa on the coast, a third-rate mock-up of England at its dowdiest, he ruminated begrudgingly:

> We were all of us back in the hands of adolescence and I thought rebelliously: I am glad, for here is iced

beer and a wireless set which will pick up the Empire programme from Daventry, and after all it is home, in the sense that one has been taught to know home, where one will soon forget the finer taste, the finer pleasure, the finer terror on which one might have built.

Where? In the jungles of Liberia? Did Greene sense "finer terror" in the old man he saw "beaten with a club outside the poky little prison at Tappee Ta," or in "the naked widows at Tailahum covered with yellow clay and the wooden toothed devil swaying his raffia skirts between the huts," or in that "lampless sleeping place among the rats"? That we were at the zenith and the nadir simultaneously on a route from primitive Africa to twentieth-century Europe was, even as a figure of speech, a wild reading of history and ethnology. It was not in Africa where "we" lost our innocence! And the finer taste and pleasures on which we have built were still available to Mr. Greene; but, like many of the British intelligentsia of the twenties and thirties, he was so dismayed at the contradictions of a failing Christian society (revealed to him by the Fist World War, perhaps) that the gesture of repudiating that society entirely—at least within the confines of rhetoric—was as appealing to him as it has been to a legion of dissidents since.

A large part of Graham Greene's appeal as a novelist is the fascinated horror with which his unheroic heroes have stared into the bottom of the bottle and found it bearable because it was inescapable. This also may account for his personal conversion to Catholicism, his flirtation with communism, his nostalgia for the tawdry suburbs of the world, his snubbing, in general, of a society in which free choice may lead one to sorrow and madness. Unlike D. H. Lawrence, he did not go in search of a noble savage; he simply wanted to reassure himself that the ignoble one was within reach, there on the west coast of Africa. Certainly he had come closer than Gide to Conrad's heart of darkness. His description of its physical milieu is indelible; his attempt to incorporate it as a moral resource was largely histrionic.

Halfway, so to speak, between Conrad's Congo and Greene's Liberia, is H. M. Tomlinson's Amazon, the central presence of his splendid book *The Sea and the Jungle*. I have no hesitation in pronouncing this work a classic in the field of travel literature. Tomlinson was not your intrepid pioneer struggling on foot or muleback through malarial swamps and thickets, looking for primordial images of the self. On his voyage to the interior of Brazil during 1909 and 1910—those innocent years before the decline of the West was agreed upon—he functioned in the unglamorous role of purser (though few experiences were to him without glamor) on a tramp steamer from Swansea headed uncertainly, after Belém, by way of both the Amazon and Madeira rivers to San Antonio Falls, two thousand miles from the Amazon's mouth. He claimed to have met by chance, when boarding a commuter train to London, the skipper who later hired him. Probably the claim was an adroit fiction; it served the spirit of unabashed romance in which the enterprise was undertaken. To the captain's challenge, Tomlinson responded with alacrity: "It would be a noble journey. They would see Obydos and Santarem, and the foliage would brush their rigging at times, so narrow would be the way, and where they anchored at night the jaguars would come to drink." The ensuing pages are among the most evocative ever written, with an exotic landfall as their subject. Tomlinson saw the world—the ocean, the sky, America taking shape above the delta of that mighty flood, the wildlife and the tame life—with eyes totally fresh and with a mind so alert to wonder that you would believe him to be witnessing the dawn of creation on earth. There is not an unwritten sequence in his narrative; every paragraph is a cadence of discovery.

> I have been watching it for so long, this abiding and soundless forest, that now I think it is like the sky, intangible, an apparition; what the eye sees of the infinite, just as the eye sees a blue color overhead at midday, and the glow of the Milky Way at night. For the mind sees this forest better than the eye. The mind is not deceived by what merely shows. Wherever the steamer drives, the forest recedes, as does the sky at sea; but it never leaves us.
>
> The jungle gains nothing, and loses nothing, at noon. It is only a dubious thought still, as at midnight. It is still at noon so obscure and dumb a presence that I suspect the sun does not illuminate it so much as reveal our steamer in its midst. We are revealed instead. The presence sees us advancing into its solitudes, a small, busy, and impudent intruder. But the forest does not greet, and does not resent us. It regards us with the vacancy of large composure, with a lofty watchfulness which has no need to show its mind.

If Tomlinson somewhat insistently employed the pathetic fallacy to celebrate the mystery of that "abiding and soundless forest" gliding by for two thousand miles, "a shadow on the mind," he resisted the temptation to convert the river itself into anything like Conrad's "deceitful flow from the heart of an impenetrable darkness." He remained an interrogator with a poet's insatiable thirst for beauty and a scientist's decent respect for actuality.

Not unmindful of cruelty and death, Tomlinson italicized them no more than nature does in the cycle of things. In the ecology of the Amazon, headhunters are as welcome as butterflies. Dispassionately, he watches a praying mantis devouring its victim. "He eats it . . . as you do apples and the authentic mouthfuls of fly can be seen passing down his glassy neck. [He] is fragile as a new leaf in form, has the same delicate colour and has fascinating ways; but somehow he gives an observer the uncomfortable thought that the means to existence on this earth, though intricate and wonderfully devised, might have been managed differently." One of the most impressive interludes in the book is his discourse on "the power of the torrid sun" on a morning spent along a railway track near the hospital of Pôrto Velho (population 300). He felt the generative glow that spawned clouds of butterflies:

> a mother heat and light whose ardent virtues stained pinions crimson and cobalt, and made bodies strong and convulsive and caused the earth to burst with rushing sap. . . . You could hear the incessant low murmur of multitudinous wings. And I had been warned to beware of all this. I felt instead that I could live and grow forever in such a land.

Tomlinson's reverie was interrupted by a flatcar being pumped down the track toward the ship. As it passed, he saw "something under a white cloth; the cloth moulded a childish figure, of which only the hem of a skirt and the neat little booted feet showed beyond, and the feet swayed limply with the jolts of the car in a way curiously appealing and woeful." It was the body of the only white female in that community, a Brazilian girl from the coast who had been ailing and "wouldn't go home when told, poor thing."

Not the least notable feature of *The Sea and the Jungle* is that it is one of the few books in our time, written on a Latin-

American theme by an outsider, that might safely be called affirmative. Excepting the studies of naturalists such as Alexander von Humbolt, H. W. Bates, and W. H. Hudson, nearly every famous work—of fiction or fact—written by a northerner about Central or South America has been, at the heart, a history of sustained aversion. Both D. H. Lawrence's *The Plumed Serpent* and Malcolm Lowry's *Under the Volcano* are permeated with death and with the anomaly of the European consciousness in Mexico. Gusts of irritation sweep through Graham Greene's *Another Mexico* and Christopher Isherwood's *The Condor and the Cows,* but in these the vexation is mild if compared with Henri Michaux's *Ecuador* (1929). Animated by what he thought was a profound distaste for European civilization, Michaux escaped to the Andes and the sources of the Amazon where, traveling by foot, car, horseback, and canoe, he compounded the local miseries of travel—tropical weather, unfriendly natives, malaria, and jaundice—by taking opium and ether. Predictably he experienced Ecuador, Peru, and Brazil as a composite hell, and in his enraged outcry (the loudest before Paul Theroux's in 1979) there is nothing of the wit or the sardonic reverence that informs Michaux's later work, *A Barbarian in Asia.* (1933).

A creation of immense charm, nonetheless pejorative in sum, is Charles Macomb Flandrau's *Viva Mexico!,* first published in 1908 and regrettably out of print today. Conceivably Mexico has become so profitable as a destination for package tourism and so solicitous an object of mollifying sociology that Flandrau's unapologetic sketches are too filled with whimsical disdain to be tolerated. I have found them a pleasure to reread. Flandrau was an elegant stylist, a master of euphemism, and the lucid observer of a wide range of curiosa in a country he appears to have found fundamentally boring. Yet on Mexican children, on dirt eaters, on clerical routine, on the incense in Puebla Cathedral, on the complex art of coffee raising, on the tightrope question of Mexican honor, and on the dire character of American tourists he is unfailingly graphic and, if courtly, uncompromising. Years before Evelyn Waugh taught travelers how to damn with faint praise, Flandrau was writing sentences such as this: "Wealth, educaion and travel often combine to render unimportant persons who, had they stayed at home in a state of comparative poverty and ignorance, would perhaps have been worthy of one's serious consideration."

Waugh himself never wrote a better excursion, I think, than *Ninety-two Days* (1934), in which he recounted his arduous journey through British Guiana to Brazil, and back to the coast by another river route, for God knows what reason (and that's an appropriate idiom, surely)—certainly not for the reason he gave. "One does not travel, any more than one falls in love, to collect material. It is simply part of one's life." Even if this were true, it would not explain his choice of British Guiana— as dreary an acreage as any I know— from all the other journeys to forbidding interiors. The insouciance with which Evelyn Waugh had taken his fastidious sensibilities into outbacks and wildernesses where even rudimentary comfort is unknown was one of the more Mona Lisa aspects of his character. There is no evidence that he was looking for agony to convince himself, in the Graham Greene manner, that the ways of God are variously strange. He always kept his distance, he was seldom awed, never galvanized by impatience, never undermined by presences of evil or by spectacular states of exhaustion. Toward the end of *Ninety-two Days,* he expressed the fear that perhaps "too much of it [his account] has dealt with the difficulties of getting from place to place. But that," he concluded, "seems to me unavoidable for it is the preoccupation of two-thirds of the traveler's waking hours, and the matter of all his night-mares. It is by crawling on the face of it that one learns a country; by the problems of transport that its geography becomes a reality and its inhabitants real people." Then and there we are reminded that Waugh became a skilled commando in the Second World War; and there is no question that his Guiana expedition, every bit as grueling as Greene's walk in Liberia, if not as endangered as Michaux's in the Andean headwaters, must have been excellent preparation for the beaches of Normandy and the coast of Yugoslavia.

Even so, as convincing as he is when telling you how he walked or paddled or painfully rode from here to there, Waugh's métier is people—the only kind you can ever expect to meet in settlements as remote as the rivers of Guiana—weird people. He has insisted in a later, very dull, book (*Tourist in Africa*, 1960): "As happier men watch birds, I watch men. They are less attractive but more various." In Guiana he watched, and listened to with great trepidation, men whom he would subsequently use, with modifications, as characters in *A Handful of Dust*. At Boa Vista he was confined for weeks with a Father Alcuin, who spoke no English, and a Mr. Steingler, who spoke no language intelligibly. Early on he met Mr. Bain, an emaciated Creole commissioner for the Georgetown district, benign and garrulous, who "talked at large on every conceivable topic, eagerly, confidently, enthusiastically, not always accurately, sometimes scarcely coherently, inexhaustibly; with inspired imagination, with dizzy changes of thought and rather alarming theatrical effects, in a vocabulary compounded of the jargon he was accustomed to use among his subordinates and the longer, less habitual words he had noticed in print."

Peter Fleming's *Brazilian Adventure* (1934) is a more exciting book than Waugh's because it has, in its way, a plot. Fleming's reason for going to Brazil was to join a search party looking for a Colonel Fawcett who, with his son and a companion, had disappeared years before in an unexplored territory of the Matto Grosso. Fleming told a suspense story; for this reason and for the intrinsic interest of the setting—the Indian tribes, the alligator shooting, the seven-foot-long otters, the "harmless" piranha, forest fires, and ice-cold rain—the book was a best-seller in its day. Fleming wrote from the outside; he was not an anti-intellectual, but simply an empiricist who concentrated on telling a good story without the luxury of intellectual parentheses. He was perhaps the narrator par excellence of travel as physical adventure, of the fine art of living dangerously. *News from Tartary*, published only two years thereafter, is even more enthralling, to my taste at least, because the occasion engrossed by it took place on a stage immensely more significant in the history of mankind and more dramatic by reason of its spatial grandeur: the plateaus and mountains of central Asia where China, Russia, Tibet, and India converge. Fleming, as a special correspondent for the *Times*, was expected to find out what was taking place in the vast province of Sinkiang (Chinese Turkestan) which, since an outbreak of civil war in 1933, had been incommunicado. Nobody could get in; nobody could get out; rumors held that a "Foreign Power" was commandeering the province.

Fleming found himself leading a party of four with the unrevealed intention of proceeding from Peking to Kashmir by way of north Tibet and Sinkiang, a distance of nearly four thousand miles (by lorry, on foot, on camel, and on yak), with no passports for Sinkiang. As in *Brazilian Adventure*, Fleming made light of the difficulties involved ("great decisions and small deeds"), sometimes with a bit too much of the stiff-upper-lip act. But as he advances across wastes of waterless desert at altitudes above nine thousand feet, he rises to his subject; as they cross the so-called Tsaidam Marsh, their entry to Sinkiang, he confesses the awe with which his ordeal was informed.

> We took a certain pride in the very slowness and the primitive manner of our progress. We were travelling Asia at Asia's pace. . . . We had left the Twentieth Century behind with the lorries at Lanchow, and now we were up against the immemorial obstacles, the things which had bothered Alexander and worried the men who rode with Chinghis Khan—lack of beasts, lack of water, lack of grazing. We were doing the same stages every day that Marco Polo would have done if he had branched south from the Silk Road to the mountains.

Fleming's books are not works of art, but they are endlessly engaging to read; they transcend the pragmatic occasions that invoked them, they stimulate the imagination, and they leave you with the distinct feeling that you have been in the company of "a man for all seasons" who is cheerful, educated, courageous, and ethical. (In later years, Fleming enlisted his first-hand experience, his zeal for research and his balanced political sense in the service of recent and contemporary history: an outstanding example is his *Bayonets to Lhasa: The First Full Account of the British Invasion of Tibet in 1904*.)

That a woman—one Ella Maillart (nicknamed Kini), a special correspondent for a Paris newspaper—accompanied Fleming to the frontier of India is noteworthy to add. A Swiss-born journalist of remarkable attainments (among other feats she had sailed for Switzerland in the Olympics and walked across the Caucasus), she arouses admiration, if not incredulity, crossing half a continent on five barley loaves and two small fishes, as it were, with a man she had met once and briefly. Fleming never quite fills her in as a personality (she seems not to have been confiding) but he is gallant to a fault, vowing that she did everything more competently than he.

Woman in the Wilds. If Lady Hester Stanhope was the first of her English kind, a woman of aristocratic family who left it all behind her to wander in the Near East and finally become an autocrat among the tribes of Syria in the 1820s, perhaps Freya Stark was the last, although her resemblance to Lady Stanhope did not extend to imperial ambition or mystic delusion. She was the last, let us say, who wrote travel books. There is something altogether fey in the picture we get (in *The Valleys of the Assassins*, 1936) of this patrician: an erudite woman (an authority on the Lurs of Pusht-i-Kuh, she had learned "scanty Arabic and a little Persian, just for fun") riding a mule through the valleys and around the mountains of Persia, as if she were bewitched, in the company of a guide known as The Refuge of Allah, whose calm response to her materialistic explanations might be, "Anyone can see that it's an insect that eats the moon"; or traveling with a muleteer who complains, at her haste in rough country, "This bitterness, this roughness, for the sons of Adam!"; or being blandly asked to smuggle opium into Iraq on her return from Luristan; or encountering Kurds who, because she spoke Arabic, thought it was the language of Great Britain. Reading this enchanting book today, with the tribal life she recounts unchanged (in 1927) since the tenth century, we rub our eyes in wonder to realize that this is the country that, for over a year recently, was a standing outrage and one of the supreme banalities of the television networks, being obsessively identified with "the fate of the American hostages." Freya Stark eating sheep tongue, jam, and pomegranates while looking for hidden treasure in Luristan is somehow not an aspect of Iran's interior that you would expect to impose on the audience of Walter Cronkite.

I am baffled by Paul Fussell's refusal to include Freya Stark in his discussion of English travelers in *Abroad* on the ground that she was not a stylist of the first order. She meets the first obligation of the travel writer: she helps you *see*. Further, she meets the tacit obligation of such a writer, that is, to make fine distinctions.

> The tribesman in his heart knows that freedom, his own virtue, comes first in the order of things: it can in a pinch stand alone, while the beauty of law is of a secondary order, dependent for its excellence on the existence of the other as a basis. . . . He is an aristocrat. In our complicated lives the advantage of aristocracy is that of being able voluntarily to undergo those disciplines which are forced without choice on men less fortunately circumstanced: to eat bread and water from necessity has a depressing effect; to do so from choice is, in a reasonable measure, good for the soul; and the civilized use of riches is to become voluntarily independent of them. The nomad does not go so far: but he does prefer his lean emancipation to the flesh-pots of settled behaviour; and this makes him an insufferable neighbor but a gallant man.

The Second World War, beginning with the Spanish Civil War, and together with the incremental industry of mass tourism and the appearance of the ubiquitous refugee, destroyed or importantly vitiated the travel diary as a work of art and a chronicle of idiosyncratic discovery. As Fussell has noted, the travel book became the war book and then the sociological commentary, "setting people right about the situation here or there; it abandons subtlety and irony; it grows political . . . and self-righteous." Explorations of faraway places have not ceased, but masterpieces are fewer and farther between. As a substitute one is proffered the frequently astounding photographs of the *National Geographic* magazine, accompanied by texts so de-caffeinated and pulverized they can scarcely be defined as prose.

Standards of language and of critical intelligence have been admirably upheld in the travel lore of the past twenty years by that Brahmin among interpreters of the foreign strand, James (now Jan) Morris. She has not often been attracted to the faceless portions of the earth, for she is closer to being a cultural historian than an explorer of life in the raw. The culture she reports is normally urban, and her empirical enthusiasm is tempered by her institutional background: an Oxford education, service in the British army and, after the war, special assignments for the *Guardian,* the London *Times* and the *Arab News Agency.* For her insecure allegiance to the liberalism of the *Guardian* in earlier years, she has explained in her autobiography, *Conundrum:* "The elements I craved were fire, salt, laughter: the *Guardian's* specialties were fairness, modesty, and rational assessment. I liked a touch of swank; the *Guardian* shied from it like a horse from a phantom." Her several essays and books exhibit more fairness, modesty, and rational assessment than she concedes here. What, indeed, stamps her work is the scrupulous balance with which she researches and evaluates the numerous cities and countries she has elected to visit. (It may not be gratuitous to suggest that the dual sex she has experienced is reflected in her perpetual habit of qualifying her most conclusive judgments with "on the other hand. . . .") Sometimes you regret this rigorous impartiality. You find yourself hoping, as she gathers Singapore or Tangier or Los Angeles or Venice into her nutshell, that she will stop temporizing and give rein to her patent enthusiasm and "a touch of swank" or else surrender to her latent antipathy.

For that reason, I prefer *The Presence of Spain* (written in 1963 when she was still James) to all of Jan Morris's other books. Spain overwhelmed her, as it does most astute writers of North European and Protestant roots. Although she tried hard to report as many utilitarian and forward-looking prospects as she could find, she was more positively affected by the harsher face of things, omnipresent in the cities as well as in the villages. After contriving, in Andalusia, little scenarios of the stock characters of Spanish legend and of *Carmen,* she admits that Spain at its grassless foundation was "still a country, by and large, without running water, without lavatories, without enough schools and hospitals." And yet, despite the denuded soil, "the heat and the cold and the poverty and the ever-present abstractions of God, Death and the Inquisition," or perhaps because of these, Spain was greater than the sociology that found it backward. What stokes the eloquence of her best pages *is* the Spain of the Inquisition, of the crimson Renaissance, of Goya; the Spain embodied in the Dolorosa of Salamanca and in the Black Virgin of Montserrat; the Spain of the cities she differentiated so well: Madrid, Ávila, Valladolid, Tarragona, above all Toledo ("like one of those El Greco characters . . . in fact conceived here—towering, handsome, humourless, sad, a little bloodless"); the Spain of thirty-two thousand priests, twenty thousand monks, seventy-one thousand nuns, and twenty-five thousand seminarians.

Jan Morris feared that this clerical, reactionary Spain, if it improved the conditions that strike us as hopelessly retrograde, would by the same token lose the ferocious integrity that gives it a profile unique among the nations of Europe. Tourism, foreign investments, and progressive social reforms are humanly preferable to the stagnant condition of a country marked by provincial conceit, perennial dictatorship, and the *Guardia Civil.* It is a familiar question: How does a country liberate itself without importing the junk behavior that will debase it in another fashion? Jan Morris is always effective when she finds a reconciling metaphor. One of her most persuasive is found in the final paragraph of her book; as a rhetorical flourish, it is perhaps unsurpassed in the literature.

Seen from the ridge road between the Escorial and the Vale of the Fallen:

> There it all is, like a mirage in the morning: the space and the dust and the pride of it all, the chuffing steam trains on the high plateau, the tall golden towers beside the rivers of Spain, the storks and the priests and the policemen. It is the kind of high prospect that hermits look for, when they want to sit down with a skull on the table, and think about the future.

And in Spain, the last bastion of mystery and pride in Europe, is homogenized and obliterated by the great commonplaces of industrial democracy, what ceremony remains for the passionate pilgrim to relate except the low tide of poetry and the expansion of petit-bourgeois condominiums stretching across the savannas of Africa and all the beaches of the world? Sach-everell Sitwell mourned long ago, "When I think of how beautiful the world has been and how beautiful it could be, I could walk up and down and wring my hands and weep!" Wherever you investigate a backward country struggling to "catch up" or a torpid civilization of the East adopting Western customs, you can expect to find kitsch, corruption, and the kind of incongruity that has provoked the mirth of an Evelyn Waugh or the scorn of a Paul Theroux.

Any student of the cultural future in dominions outside our own might sober his prophecies by reading V. S. Naipaul on India. Calling upon the double advantage (and inhibition) of being an Indian brought up elsewhere, Naipaul speaks with sad authority in the book that records his homecoming to India from Trinidad, wherein he views his country with both the sentiment of a native and the conditioning of a colonial influenced by western psychology. *An Area of Darkness* (1964) is indeed a travel book; its geography extends from Kashmir to Madras, from Karachi to Calcutta. Ultimately it is a work of inferences, the particulars ruthlessly examined and brooded upon by an enlightened mind with an authentic respect for the precolonial past. Naipaul found a condition of schizophrenia everywhere in India. Speaking of the generic Anglo-Indian set, he wrote:

> That little corner of merry England which they have created in Bombay is also Druidical. It worships fire; its ways are narrow and protective, and at the end lie the Towers of Silence and the grim rites behind those walls whose main portals are marked with a symbol from the ancient world.
>
> The outer and inner worlds do not have the physical separateness which they had for us in Trinidad. They coexist; the society only pretends to be colonial; and for this reason its absurdities are at once apparent. Its mimicry is both less and more than a colonial mimicry. It is the special mimicry of an old country which has been without a native aristocracy for a thousand years and has learned to make room for outsiders, but only at the top. The mimicry changes, the inner world remains constant: this is the secret of survival. And so it happens that, to one whole area of India, a late seventeenth-century traveller like Ovington remains in many ways a reliable guide. Yesterday the mimicry was Mogul; tomorrow it might be Russian or American; today it is English.

What he usually called in this book "the medieval mind" he accounts for in his later work, *India: A Wounded Civilization* (1977), by employing the terminology of psychotherapy, which declares the Indian's confusion of disparity with continuity to be the expression of a fundamentally different perception of reality. This perception, compared with ours, "is closer to a certain stage in childhood when outer objects did not have a separate, independent existence but were intimately related to the self and its affective states." Hence, Naipaul believes that "it is more difficult, even unlikely, for an Indian to withdraw from experience and analyze it." Here it is not necessary for me to review Naipaul's postscript to a larger subject. But recalling Elie Faure's observation that we approach one another to study our differences, I ask myself how you can alter a perception of reality that is innate. We are back to E. M. Forster and we recapitulate with Paul Theroux.

If ever there was a man unprepared to be sympathetic with the casuistry of an Asiatic, or with the parlance of the tourist agency, that man is Paul Theroux. His two travel books to date, *The Great Railway Bazaar* (1975) and *The Old Patagonian Express* (1979) are anthologies of nausea through which, one must confess, there appears to run a distinct thread of sadomasochism. If you insist on traveling third class around Asia and from south of the United States border through the nether Americas, you can pretty well count in advance on being miserably accommodated, foully fed, and most of the time bored or revolted by your companions. Why would you expect on third-class trains in mainly Third World countries to meet any but third-class people? Theroux launches himself as if

trusting to fortune, then narrates an unceasing montage of dismal encounters, culinary disasters, idiotic inefficiency, conversational brainlessness, and abysmal hygiene. (Indeed, in *The Great Railway Bazaar* he is driven to calling it, at last, The Turd World.) This is not often depressing to read; it is too vituperative to be depressing, and it is sometimes even very funny. Although Theroux may well be accused of high-handedness, as when, for instance, he dismisses Japan in a few pages containing descriptions of sordid entertainments and dialogues with fatuous professors, where he has researched a subject, besides merely confronting it, his summarizing paragraphs can be unarguably damning.

> As Calcutta smells of death and Bombay of money, Bangkok smells of sex, but this sexual aroma is mingled with the sharper whiffs of death and money . . . a hugely preposterous city of temples and brothels.
>
> [Of Afghanistan] Formerly it was cheap and barbarous, and people went there to buy lumps of hashish—they would spend weeks in the filthy hotels of Herat and Kabul, staying high. But there was a military coup in 1973, and the kind (who was sunning himself in Italy) was deposed. Now Afghanistan is expensive but just as barbarous as before. Even the hippies have begun to find it intolerable. The food smells of cholera, travel there is always uncomfortable and sometimes dangerous, and the Afghans are lazy, idle, and violent.

Theroux has been justly criticized for ignoring or minimizing the history and traditions of the manifold places he has sped through. I find conspicuous in his breezy way of judgment the absence of any felt criterion, save that of creature comfort. We never know from what cultural ideal he is maintaining his perspective. What Theroux recites is what he experiences and, for purposes of reality (that is, the event one is called upon to cope with), he conveys with a tart flavor precisely what, at the moment, he is experiencing. I might add that he must be colossally indifferent to beauty, since I cannot suppose that the thousands of miles he covered, either in the East or in the southern Americas, were as devoid of scenic interest as he implies. Also, he must certainly have arranged his itinerary so that it would not conceivably intersect the life of the mind or of worldly society. Except for his interview with Jorge Luis Borges, he appears deliberately to have avoided having to confess that there is anyone anywhere in South America who thinks, creates, lays a chic table, conducts a respectable business, or smells fragrant.

> Limón looked like a dreadful place. It had just rained, and the town stank. The station was on a muddy road near the harbor, and puddles reflected the decaying buildings and over-bright lights. The smell of dead barnacles and a damp sand, flooded sewers, brine, oil, cockroaches and tropical vegetation which, when soaked, gives off the hot moldy vapor you associate with compost heaps in summer, the stench of mulch and mildew. It was a noisy town as well: clanging music, shouts, car horns.
>
> Visitors to Guayaquil are urged to raise their eyes, for on a clear day it is possible to see the snowy hood of Mount Chimborazo from the humid streets of this stinking city; and if you look down, all you see is rats.

Theroux's travel writing meets one important requirement of the genre. It convinces you that, after all, you had best stay at home.

Of Patagonia Theroux had little to say (perhaps by that time he was too exhausted to ratify his worst fears). Which is just as well, for it leaves a clear field in which to relish Bruce Chatwin's *In Patagonia* (1977), a polychrome, Flaubertian glimpse of that terminal country—region, to be accurate, since it is administered jointly by Argentina and Chile. Our primary impression of the place as landscape, by reference to Chatwin's hard, gem-like paragraphs, is of a thinly populated plateau (mountains to the west) into which various desperadoes have disappeared or in the valleys of which they have entrenched (''Butch'' Cassidy among them); where revolutions have ignited and been bloodily extinguished; and on the coasts of which stout men with a talent for mythomania have been wrecked. Here and there have settled snug little colonies of ranching immigrants from Wales, from England, from Germany, from Dutch South Africa, unassimilated and hugging the emblems— the solid mahogany, the teapots, the flowering shrubs, the sporting prints—of their native hearths, which they expect never to see again. A country, in brief, of castaways.

Bruce Chatwin is the latest inheritor of the British travel-writing tradition, but his art is of such a style and his succeeding work, *The Viceroy of Ouidah* (1890), is so inventively elaborated that the nature of his future contribution to literature is not to be too categorically decided. (pp.89-92)

Vernon Young, ''End of the Voyage,'' in The American Scholar, Vol. 51, No. 1, Winter, 1981-82, pp. 83-93.

PAUL FUSSELL

[*Fussell is an American educator and critic who has lived in the United States, England, France, Germany, Greece, and Spain. His* Abroad: British Literary Travelling between the Wars *is a highly regarded study of travel literature during what he calls ''the finest age of travel,'' from 1918 through 1939. Fussell advances the controversial thesis that the rise of tourism has meant the end of real travel and hence of travel writing. In* Abroad's *eclectic mixture of essay-like chapters, Fussell includes biographical sketches of travel book writers, criticism of travel literature, personal musings on passport photos, sex while travelling, reasons for travel, the impetus to write about travel, modes of transportation, and other topics related to travel and to travel literature. In the following excerpt, Fussell discusses travel literature as a literary genre.*]

Perhaps it is when we cannot satisfactorily designate a kind of work with a single word (*epic, novel, romance, story, novella, memoir, sonnet, sermon, essay*) but must invoke two (*war memoir, Black autobiography, first novel, picture book, travel book*) that we sense we're entering complicated territory, where description, let alone definition, is hazardous, an act closer to exploration than to travel. Criticism has never quite known what to call books like these. Some commentators, perhaps recalling the illustrated travel lectures of their youth or the travel films that used to be shown as ''short subjects,'' call them *travelogues*. Others, more literary, render that term *travel logs*, apparently thinking of literal, responsible daily diaries, like ships' logs. This latter usage is the one preferred by David Lodge, who says of 30's writing that ''it tended to model itself on historical kinds of discourse—the autobiography, the eyewitness account, the travel log: *Journey to a War, Letters from Iceland, The Road to Wigan Pier, Journey without Maps, Autumn Journal,* 'Berlin Diary,' are some characteristic titles.'' Even Forster is uncertain what to call these things. In 1941 he calls them *travelogues*, in 1949 *travel books*.

Let's call them travel books, and distinguish them initially from guide books, which are not autobiographical and are not sustained by a narrative exploiting the devices of fiction. A guide book is addressed to those who plan to follow the traveler, doing what he has done, but more selectively. A travel book, at its purest, is addressed to those who do not plan to follow the traveler at all, but who require the exotic or comic anomalies, wonders, and scandals of the literary form *romance* which their own place or time cannot entirely supply. Travel books are a sub-species of memoir in which the autobiographical narrative arises from the speaker's encounter with distant or unfamiliar data, and in which the narrative—unlike that in a novel or a romance—claims literal validity by constant reference to actuality. The speaker in any travel book exhibits himself as physically more free than the reader, and thus every such book, even when it depicts its speaker trapped in Boa Vista, is an implicit celebration of freedom. It resembles a poetic ode, an Ode to Freedom. The illusion of freedom is a precious thing in the 20's and 30's, when the shades of the modern prison-house are closing in, when the passports and queues and guided tours and social security numbers and customs regulations and currency controls are beginning gradually to constrict life. What makes travel books seem so necessary between the wars is what Fleming pointed to in *One's Company*, ''that lamb-like subservience to red tape which is perhaps the most striking characteristic of modern man.'' Intellectual and moral pusillanimity is another characteristic of modern man. Hence Douglas's emphasis on the exemplary function of the travel writer's internal freedom and philosophic courage:

> It seems to me that the reader of a good travel-book is entitled not only to an exterior voyage, to descriptions of scenery and so forth, but to an interior, a sentimental or temperamental voyage, which takes place side by side with the outer one.

Thus ''the ideal book of this kind'' invites the reader to undertake three tours simultaneously: ''abroad, into the author's brain, and into his own.'' It follows that ''the writer should . . . possess a brain worth exploring; some philosophy of life—not necessarily, though by preference, of his own forging—and the courage to proclaim it and put it to the test; he must be naif and profound, both child and sage.'' And if the enterprise succeeds, the reader's ''brain'' will instinctively adjust itself to accord in some degree with the pattern established by the author's travel, both external and internal: that is, it will experience an access of moral freedom. It is thus possible to consider the between-the-wars travel books as a subtle instrument of ethics, replacing such former vehicles as sermons and essays.

A fact of modern publishing history is the virtual disappearance of the essay as a salable commodity (I mean the essay, not the ''article''). If you want to raise a laugh in a publisher's office, enter with a manuscript collection of essays on all sorts of subjects. And if you want to raise an even louder laugh, contrive that your essays have a moral tendency, even if they stop short of aspiring to promulgate wisdom. The more we attend to what's going on in the travel book between the wars, the more we perceive that the genre is a device for getting published essays which, without the travel ''menstruum'' (as Coleridge would say), would appear too old-fashioned for generic credit, too reminiscent of Lamb and Stevenson and Chesterton. Thus the travel books of Aldous Huxley, a way of presenting learned essays which without exotic narrative support would find no audience. Thus also the performances of Douglas and of Osbert Sitwell, who, for all his defects, has thought long and hard about the essayistic element in the travel book and has coined for it the eccentric term *discursion,* as in his titles *Discursions on Travel, Art and Life* (1925) and *Winters of Content and Other Discursions on Mediterranean Art and Travel* (1950). "Discursions," he says, is "a word of my own minting, coined from *discourse* and *discursive,* and designed to epitomize the manner in which a traveler formulates his loose impressions, as, for example, he sits in a train, looking out [the] window, and allows the sights he so rapidly glimpses, one after another, to break in upon the thread of his . . . thoughts." *Discursions,* he goes on, "is an attempt . . . to find a new name for a particular kind of essay, that unites in the stream of travel . . . many very personal random reflections and sentiments. . . ." Thus in Sitwell's "travel books" we find a general essay on cabs, prompted by the cabs of Lecce, and one on the theory of bourgeois domestic architecture triggered by the sights of southern Germany. Neither essay could achieve a wide audience if detached from the sense data of the place abroad which has justified it. Alan Pryce-Jones's *The Spring Journey* (1931) is a good example of a travel book which functions as a mere framework for essays. The travel is to Egypt, Palestine, Syria, and Greece, but it is only a medium for inset Carlylean essays and discursive flourishes on the follies of modern education, the difference between Imagination and Fancy, the decay of contemporary civilization, and the superiority of music to "the other arts." An American counterpart is Hemingway's *Green Hills of Africa* (1935). Because of the public persona he has chosen, Hemingway can't plausibly write "essays" in the old schoolmasterly sense. He can get away with essays on bull-fighting if he connects his learned comments with memories of toreros he has known, and thus validates his remarks as memoir. But for him to discourse professorially about history and literature would seem unnatural—stuffy, pompous, very unoutdoors. He thus lodges his major essay on the character and history of American literature, his version of Lawrence's *Studies in Classic American Literature,* in a travel book, and presents it there as a conversation with a person encountered by chance, the character Kandinsky, an Austrian who is made to ask who the great writers are. "Tell me. Please tell me," he says, not very credibly. Hemingway responds with an essay of 1200 words, presented as dialogue, considering the merits of Poe, Melville, Emerson, Hawthorne, Whitier, James, Crane, and Twain. We easily remember his brilliant remark, one of the most acute critical perceptions any scholar or critic has uttered, that "all modern American literature comes from one book by Mark Twain called *Huckleberry Finn,*" but we may forget that it gets uttered at all because on the African veldt "under the dining tent fly" an Austrian has asked him about American writers. It is an open-air remark, a travel, not a library, remark.

Similarly, if one approached a publisher in 1940 with a collection of assorted ethical and historical essays one would have less chance of success than if one arranged them as "A Journey through Yugoslavia" and titled the whole immense work *Black Lamb and Grey Falcon,* as Rebecca West did. We recognize Lawrence's *Aaron's Rod* as akin to a travel book less, perhaps, because it goes to some lengths to describe abroad than because it provides a medium for promulgating essays. Lawrence will suddenly cast away his narrative pretences entirely, face his audience directly, and issue what we perceive is the "topic sentence" of an old-fashioned moral essay. On some of these occasions he sounds like a sort of Hilaire Belloc turned inside out: "The *idée fixe* of today," he will proclaim, "is that every individual shall not only give himself, but shall achieve the last glory of giving himself away." Or: "The David in the

Piazza della Signoria, there under the dark great Palace, in the position Michaelangelo chose for him, there, standing forward stripped and exposed and eternally half-shrinking, half-wishing to expose himself, he is the genius of Florence."

But to emphasize the presence of the essay element in the travel book is to risk not noticing sufficiently this genre's complex relation to adjacent forms which also require two words to designate them: *war memoir, comic novel, quest romance, picaresque romance, pastoral romance.* The memorable war memoirs of the late 20's and early 30's, by Graves and Blunden and Sassoon, are very like travel books and would doubtless show different characteristics if they'd not been written in the travel context of the period between the wars. They are ironic or parodic or nightmare travels, to France and Belgium, with the Channel ferries and the forty-and-eights replacing the liners and chic trains of real travel, with dugouts standing for hotel-rooms and lobbies and Other Ranks serving the travel-book function of "native" porters and servants. Curiously, at the end of the Second World War the war book has something of the same "travel" element attached to it, the same obsession with topography and the mystery of place, with even something like Lawrence's adhesions to the prepositional, like *into.* Recalling his first idea for *The Naked and the Dead,* Mailer says: "I wanted to write a short novel about a long patrol. . . . Probably [the idea] was stimulated by a few war books I had read: John Hersey's *Into the Valley,* Harry Brown's *A Walk in the Sun.*"

The element of the comic novel is visible not merely in the travel books of Byron and Waugh; it is in *Sea and Sardinia* as well, in much of Douglas, and even, if we can conceive the "seedy" as inherently comic, as a pathetic parody of a civilization not worth imitating, in much of Graham Greene. Anomaly is what unites comic novel and travel experience. A baron "traveling in cosmetics" and shaving in beer because the water in the wagons-lits has run out is an anomaly Anthony Powell met in Yugoslavia once. It fitted perfectly into his comic novel *Venusberg* (1933), where the baron is presented as Count Bobel. The comic novel between the wars would be an impoverished thing without its multitude of anomalous strangers—like Mr. Norris—encountered on actual trains and ships.

If as a form of prose fiction a "romance" is more likely than a novel to be set abroad or in an exotic place, then *romance,* whether "quest," picaresque, or pastoral, will suggest itself as a term to designate an indispensable element of the travel book. One could ask: aren't travel books really romances in the old sense, with the difference that the adventures are located within an actual, often famous, topography to satisfy an audience which demands it both ways—which wants to go adventuring vicariously, as it always has, but which at the same time wants to feel itself within a world declared real by such up-to-date studies as political science, sociology, anthropology, economics, and contemporary history? The proximity of the travel book to the thoroughly empirical picaresque romance, contrived from a multitude of adventures in non-causal series, can perhaps be inferred from Freya Stark's disappointment with Gertrude Bell's *Syria.* She felt the book let her down: "[Bell] did not have enough adventures." (On one of her Persian explorations in 1932 Stark took along *Pilgrim's Progress,* and in Brazil an item in Fleming's travel kit was "1 copy of *Tom Jones.*") As in a romance, the modern traveler leaves the familiar and predictable to wander, episodically, into the unfamiliar or unknown, encountering strange adventures, and finally, after travail and ordeals, returns safely. Somehow, we feel a travel book isn't wholly satisfying unless the traveler returns to his starting point: the action, as in a quest romance, must be completed. We are gratified—indeed, comforted—by the "sense of an ending," the completion of the circuit, as we are at the end of [Evelyn Waugh's] *Labels* or [Robert Byron's] *The Road to Oxiana* or [Graham Greene's] *Journey without Maps,* where the "hero" invites us to enjoy his success in returning home.

All this is to suggest that the modern travel book is what Northrop Frye would call a myth that has been "displaced"— that is, lowered, brought down to earth, rendered credible "scientifically"—and that the myth resembles the archetypal monomyth of heroic adventure defined by Joseph Campbell. The myth of the hero, Campbell explains, is tripartite: first, the setting out, the disjunction from the familiar; second, the trials of initiation and adventure; and third, the return and the hero's reintegration into society. Even if there is no return, the monomyth still assumes tripartite form, as in *Pilgrim's Progress,* whose title-page declares that the hero's "progress, from this world, to that which is to come" will be conceived in three stages: "The manner of his setting out; His Dangerous Journey; and Safe Arrival at the Desired Country." The first and last stages of the tripartite experience tend to be moments of heightened ritual or magic, even in entirely "secular" travel writings. Eliot understands this, and so does Auden. Witness stanza 4 of Auden's "Dover" (1937):

> The eyes of departing migrants are fixed on the sea,
>   Conjuring destinies out of impersonal water:
> "I see an important decision made on a lake,
> An illness, a beard, Arabia found in a bed,
>   Nanny defeated. Money."

Listening to the ship's engine as he sets out from Southampton for Spain, V. S. Pritchett writes in *Marching Spain* (1928), "Every man who heard those sounds must have seemed to himself as great a hero as Ulysses and pitted against as mysterious a destiny, the strange destiny of the outward bound." Starting on his Brazilian adventure, Peter Fleming notices something odd which he can describe only thus: "We were through the looking-glass." And returning is equally full of portent and mystery. We have seen Waugh throwing his champagne glass overboard, a gesture which, he says, "has become oddly important to me," somehow "bound up with the turgid, indefinite feelings of homecoming." Fleming would suggest that the magical feeling upon returning arises from moving from a form of non-existence back to existence, or recovering one's normal self-consciousness before one's accustomed audience. The traveler "who has for weeks or months seen himself only as a puny and irrelevant alien crawling laboriously over a country in which he has no roots and no background, suddenly [on returning] encounters his other self, a relatively solid and considerable figure, with . . . a place in the minds of certain people." Or, as Auden registers the magical act of reintegration in stanza 5 of "Dover,"

> Red after years of failure or bright with fame,
>   The eyes of homecomers thank these historical cliffs:
> "The mirror can no longer lie nor the clock reproach;
> In the shadow under the yew, at the children's party,
>   Everything must be explained."

Indeed, the stages of the classic monomyth of the adventuring hero cannot avoid sketching an allegory of human life itself. As Campbell notes, the "call to adventure" is a figure for the onset of adolescence; adult life is "the travel"; old age, the "return." For the literary imagination, says Auden, "It is

impossible to take a train or an airplane without having a fantasy of oneself as a Quest Hero setting off in search of an enchanted princess or the Waters of Life." That's why we enjoy reading travel books, even if we imagine we're enjoying only the curiosities of Liberia, British Guiana, Persia, or Patagonia. Even the souvenirs brought back so religiously by tourists are brought back "religiously." According to the anthropologist Nelson Graburn, tourists bring back souvenirs in unwitting imitation of the Grail Knight returning with his inestimable prize. Even for mass tourists, "the Holy Grail is . . . sought on the journey, and the success of a holiday is proportionate to the degree that the myth is realized."

But travel books are not merely displaced quest romances. They are also displaced pastoral romances. If William Empson is right to define traditional pastoral as a mode of presentation implying "a beautiful relation between rich and poor," then pastoral is a powerful element in most travel books, for, unless he's a *Wandervogel* or similar kind of layabout (few of whom write books), the traveler is almost always richer and freer than those he's among. He is both a plutocrat *pro tem* and the sort of plutocrat the natives don't mind having around. Byron and Waugh and Greene hire drivers and porters and bearers and pay outrageous prices for decrepit horses and cars; Lawrence pays bus and steamer fares; Norman Douglas keeps employed numerous waiters and *sommeliers*. If the cash nexus can be considered "a beautiful relation," the behavior of these characters is like the behavior of the court class in Renaissance pastoral, and there's a closer resemblance between Sidney's *Arcadia* and a modern travel book than is obvious on the surface. Consider the Lawrence of *Twilight in Italy*, attended by his aristocratic consort. Consider the affectionate patronizing of the Persian peasants in Byron's dialogue involving "The Caliph of Rum." And it is with the pastoral strain in travel books that we can associate the implicit elegiac tendency of these works. Pastoral has built into it a natural retrograde emotion. It is instinct with elegy. To the degree that literary travel between the wars constitutes an implicit rejection of industrialism and everything implied by the concept "modern northern Europe," it is a celebration of a Golden age, and recalling the Ideal Places of Waugh, Auden, and Priestley, we can locate that Golden Age in the middle of the preceding century. One travels to experience the past, and travel is thus an adventure in time as well as distance.

"The King's life is moving peacefully to its close," the BBC announced in January, 1936, invoking for this most solemn, magical moment of human imaginative experience, the figure of time rendered as space. If, as this essential trope persuades us, life is a journey (to the Eliot of the *Quartets*, a never-ending one), then literary accounts of journeys take us very deeply into the center of instinctive imaginative life. Like no other kinds of writing, travel books exercise and exploit the fundamental intellectual and emotional figure of thought, by which the past is conceived as back and the future as forward. They manipulate the whole alliance between temporal and spatial that we use to orient ourselves in time by invoking the dimension of space. That is, travel books make more or less conscious an activity usually unconscious. Travel books are special because the metaphor they imply is so essential. Works we recognize as somehow "classical" derive much of their status and authority from their open exploitation of this metaphor. Housman is an example:

> Into my heart an air that kills
>   From yon far country blows:
> What are those blue remembered hills,
>   What spires, what farms are those?

> That is the land of lost content,
> I see it shining plain,
> The happy highways where I went
> And cannot come again.

"When I was a young man," says Borges, "I was always hunting for new metaphors. Then I found out that good metaphors are always the same. I mean you compare time to a road, death to sleeping, life to dreaming, and those are the great metaphors in literature because they correspond to something essential." An Italian friend of Norman Douglas's, indicating that his fifteen-year-old son has died of tuberculosis, says, "He has gone into that other country."

And if living and dying are like traveling, so are reading and writing. As Michel Butor points out, [see Additional Bibliography], the eyes of the reader "travel" along the lines of print as the reader is "guided" by the writer, as his imagination "escapes" his own I Hate It Here world. Thus in reading, of all books, a travel book, the reader becomes doubly a traveler, moving from beginning to end of the book while touring along with the literary traveler.

> "O where are you going?" said reader to rider,

writes Auden in the Epilogue to *The Orators* (1931). His near-rhyme implies the parallelism between reading and riding, a parallelism as suggestive as the one Connolly instinctively falls into when designating the three things his Oxford crowd in the early 20's "had a passion for": "literature, travel, and the visual arts." And writing, as Butor perceives, is like traveling. Figures of travel occupy any writer's imagination as he starts out, makes transitions, digresses, returns, goes forward, divagates, pauses, approaches the subject from a slightly different direction, and observes things from various points of view (like Norman Douglas on his eminences). Thus, as Osbert Sitwell says, "To begin a book is . . . to embark on a long and perilous voyage," but to begin a travel book "doubles the sense of starting on a journey."

Thus to speak of "literary traveling" is almost a tautology, so intimately are literature and travel implicated with each other. Any child senses this, and any adult recalling his childhood remembers moments when reading was revealed to be traveling. Peter Quennell's first awareness that he had actually learned to read occurred at the age of four or five when he was looking through bound volumes of *The Boy's Own Paper* at home. "The story I scrutinized was . . . the work of some unknown author who described an African caravan, journeying to the sound of camel-bells from oasis to oasis. Suddenly, the printed words I painfully spelt out melted into a continuous narrative, whence a procession of fascinating images emerged and wound its way across my mental landscape." Gerald Brenan's mental landscape was formed, he reports, not just by the romances of William Morris, with their "descriptions of imaginary travel," but also by Elisée Reclus's *Universal Geography* in nineteen volumes, which he discovered at school. From Reclus he gathered that "foreign countries alone offered something to the imagination," and he filled notebooks with a plan for a tour of the world "which would last, with continuous traveling, some thirty years." As a boy Robin Maugham read all his uncle's short stories set in the Far East "and then determined," he says, "that one day I would visit the strange, exotic places about which he wrote. This I have done." A reading of Maugham also set Alec Waugh on his traveling career. "Were the South Seas really like that?" he wondered in the summer of 1926 after reading *The Moon and Sixpence* and *The Trembling of a Leaf*. "I had to find out for myself. I

bought a round the world ticket that included Tahiti," and "I have been on the move ever since."

Names like Brenan, Quennell, and the Maughams suggest the next question: how serious artistically and intellectually can a travel book be? Is there not perhaps something in the genre that attracts second-rate talents? Certainly the travel book will have little generic prestige in today's atmosphere, where if you identify yourself as a "writer," everyone will instantly assume you're a novelist. The genres with current prestige are the novel and the lyric poem, although it doesn't seem to matter that very few memorable examples of either ever appear. The status of those two kinds is largely an unearned and unexamined snob increment from late-romantic theories of imaginative art as religion-cum-metaphysics. Other kinds of works—those relegated to simple-minded categories like "the literature of fact" or "the literature of argument"—are in lower esteem artistically because the term *creative* has been widely misunderstood, enabling its votaries to vest it with magical powers. Before that word had been promoted to the highest esteem, that is, before the romantic movement, a masterpiece was conceivable in a "non-fictional" genre like historiography or memoir or the long essay or biography or the travel book. As recently as 1918 things were different. Fiction had not yet attained its current high status. *Ulysses* was waiting in the wings, not to appear until 1922. *Á la Recherche du Temps Perdu* had not been translated. *The Magic Mountain* hadn't been written, not to mention *Les Faux-Monnayeurs, The Sound and the Fury,* and *The Sun Also Rises*. In the *Century Magazine* for February, 1918, Henry Seidel Canby felt obliged to plead for the dignity and importance of fiction, which, as an editorial in the *New York Times Review of Books* commented, the reading public was accustomed to treat with "a certain condescension." But now a similar condescension is visited on forms thought to be non-fictional. Martin Green is one who doesn't think travel books are serious. They seem to him the natural métier of the dandy. "In *Work Suspended*," he says, "Waugh portrayed himself as a writer of detective novels; in *Brideshead Revisited*, as a painter of English country houses; these occupations, and writing travel books, were the métiers of the dandies. Notably lacking in anything large-scale, even in the dandy line—not to mention anything really serious, whether political or literary-critical." Yet between the wars writing travel books was not at all considered incompatible with a serious literary career. And who would not find *Sea and Sardinia* a better book than *The Plumed Serpent,* Forster's *Alexandria* a better book than *Maurice,* Ackerley's *Hindoo Holiday* better than the collected novels of Hugh Walpole? We can hardly condescend to the travel book when it is in that genre that Robert Byron wrote a masterpiece that (in England, at least) has outlived all but a half-dozen novels of its decade.

The problem for the critic is to resist the drowsy habit of laying aside his sharpest tools when he's dealing with things that don't seem to be fiction. It takes someone more like a common reader than a critic, someone like H. M. Tomlinson, to remind us of what's going on in these "non-fictional" genres. "We know that in the literature of travel our language is very rich," he writes; "yet as a rule we are satisfied with our certainty that these books exist. . . . We surmise vaguely that a book of travel must be nearly . . . all background. . . . We shrink from the threat of the vigilance it will exact; we shall have to keep all our wits about us." In short, "We have the idle way of allowing books of travel to pass without the test to which poetry must submit." That "test," we can assume, is the test both of a complicated coherence and of a subtle mediation between texture and form, data and significant shape. Like poems—and like any successful kind of literary performance—successful travel books effect a triumphant mediation between two different dimensions: the dimension of individual physical things, on the one hand, and the dimension of universal significance, on the other. The one is Coleridge's "particular"; the other, his "general." The travel book authenticates itself by the sanction of actualities—ships, trains, hotels, bizarre customs, odd people, crazy weather, startling architecture, curious food. At the same time it reaches in the opposite direction, most often to the generic convention that the traveling must be represented as something more than traveling, that it shall assume a meaning either metaphysical, psychological, artistic, religious, or political, but always ethical. A travel book is like a poem in giving universal significance to a local texture. The gross physicality of a travel book's texture should not lead us to patronize it, for the constant recourse to the locatable is its convention. Within that convention, as we have seen, there is ample room for the activities of the "fictionalizing" imagination. And an active, organic, and, if you will, "creative" mediation between fact and fiction is exactly the activity of the mind exhibited in the travel book, which Samuel Hynes has accurately perceived to be "a dual-plane work with a strong realistic surface, which is yet a parable." In the 30's, he understands correctly, two apparently separated modes of perception, reportage and fable, literal record and parable, tend to coalesce, and nowhere more interestingly than in the travel book. What distinguishes the travel books of the 30's from earlier classics like *Eothen* or even *Arabia Deserta* is the way, Hynes says, these writers between the wars "turned their travels into interior journeys and parables of their times, making landscape and incident [and, we must add, in Byron, architecture]—the factual materials of *reportage*—do the work of symbol and myth—the materials of fable." And since the journey is "the most insistent of 'thirties metaphors, . . . one might say that the travel books simply act out, in the real world, the basic trope of the generation." Acting out a trope, like perceiving the metaphor lodging always in the literal, is the essential act of poetry. It is also the essential act of both traveling and writing about it. (pp. 202-15)

> *Paul Fussell, in his* Abroad: British Literary Traveling between the Wars, *Oxford University Press, 1980, 246 p.*

BILLY T. TRACY

[*In the following excerpt, Tracy examines D. H. Lawrence's travel books in the context of travel literature traditions.*]

Over the years most of D. H. Lawrence's critics have found little more in his travel books than the rough materials of the novels and poems. *Twilight in Italy* (1916), *Sea and Sardinia* (1921), *Mornings in Mexico* (1927), and *Etruscan Places* (1923), have been considered primarily as notebooks in which Lawrence put aside ideas and characters that could be developed another time. Without doubt, an intimate connection exists between Lawrence's travel writings and fiction. Especially in the later works, landscapes and cultures so often have a symbolic significance that critics have found it profitable to examine the expository travel essays for an account of Lawrence's own response to a culture and terrain.

At the other extreme has been a small group of critics who praised Lawrence's travel books at the expense of the genre in which he chose to write. Evidently, they felt apologetic that

Lawrence should have written so well outside the respectable forms. Edward Nehls, for example, stated that "As one reads *Sea and Sardinia,* he comes increasingly aware of the indissoluble components of which the book is built—of Lawrence as an individual and as a world citizen, of Sardinia as an isolate island and as a stage on which the problems of an enormous world were being fought in miniature. One shies away, therefore, from the facile diction that makes of *Sea and Sardinia* a 'travel' book." R. E. Pritchard claimed that "*Twilight in Italy* (1916) is more than a series of travel sketches—though the quality of life in various places and people is brilliantly evoked—but embodies Lawrence's main concerns of the time. . . ." [*D. H. Lawrence: Body of Darkness* (1971)]. Louis Tenenbaum also wanted to take *Twilight in Italy* out of the category of travel literature and suggested this alternative designation: "Because ordinary books of travel depend upon a topicality which enables them only rarely to survive, one is tempted to describe Lawrence's descriptions of Italy as essays in comparative mores" ["Two View of the Modern Italian: D. H. Lawrence and Sean O'Faolain, *Italica* (1960)]. The consensus would seem to be that mediocre travel books are easily identifiable as travel books, but good ones must be something else.

It is time to bring Lawrence's travel books out from under the shadow of his fiction. Far from being just a supplement to the novels, each of the travel books can stand on its own as an independent and important work. Moreover, when read together, these books reveal a distinct pattern in Lawrence's spiritual autobiography: a search for Eden that begins in the real world and progresses to the world of his own imagination. (pp. 272-73)

Lawrence's reading in Charles Darwin, George Borrow, Henry Bates, George Dennis, Samuel Butler, Charles Doughty, and W. H. Hudson, among others, gave him a high regard for the travel genre. Expressing his admiration for Samuel Butler's *Erewhon*, Lawrence could think of no finer tribute than to say: "It begins like a book of travel. . . . You'd never dream it was a satire. It's so fresh, so romantic, such a sense of a new country." Near the end of 1913, when Henry Savage, the essayist, asked Lawrence to describe his reading habits, he replied: "I love travels and rather raw philosophy . . . books about Greek religions and the rise of Greek drama, or Egyptian influences—or things like that." If we delete "raw philosophy," for which he eventually lost all taste, and add novels, this list would be an accurate reflection of Lawrence's reading interests from youth till the time of his death. In his last novel, *Lady Chatterley's Lover* (1928), Lawrence endowed even Mellors with a fondness for books of travel; along with works on geology and Russian politics, they comprise the gamekeeper's library.

How large an impact did travel books have on Lawrence? Certainly they made him curious during his formative years about foreign cultures and impressed upon him the materialism of English life. His readings made him wonder whether he would not have been more at home in another culture of historical period than he was in twentieth-century Britain. It would be only a partial exaggeration to say that travel literature directly inspired him to become a traveller. By making him aware of the many alternatives to English conformity and domesticity, the writings of earlier travellers aroused in him the hope that he could find an Eden if only he looked hard enough.

But these writings provided him with no definite direction. Lawrence thought highly enough of Darwin's *The Voyage of the Beagle* (1839) and Doughty's *Arabia Deserta* (1888) to read each of these works twice, yet we have no indication that he ever planned seriously to follow in the footsteps of these travellers. In this respect Lawrence differed from W. H. Hudson and T. E. Lawrence, whose enthusiasm for Darwin and Doughty provided them with a calling as well as a destination. Lawrence rarely visited another country just because a writer had made it sound exciting. Perhaps only in the earliest, apprentice travel pieces, such as "A Chapel Among the Mountains" and "A Hayhut Among the Mountains," which were written in 1912, do we find Lawrence indebted to a predecessor for locale, method, and inspiration. The model for these sub-alpine sketches was Samuel Butler's *Alps and Sanctuaries* (1881), a work that set the standards for Edwardian writers on Northern Italy. Lawrence eventually chose the Lake of Garda, Sardinia, and Oaxaca as places that he would visit and write about. These spots were particularly attractive to him, not only because they lay off the usual tourist routes, but because English travel writers had hardly touched them.

Since many people are unacquainted with travel literature, it is proper to consider in some detail the following questions about this elusive genre. What distinctions can be made amongst travellers? For what audiences are travel books written? In what context should travel books be read? Do they chiefly have a biographical or a geographical significance? And, finally, why do some works in the genre attain the status of literature while others survive not at all?

Writers of travel books can be separated into adventurers, naturalists, esthetes, and ethnologists according to what concep-

Charles Montagu Doughty in Arab dress given him by the Sherif of Mecca.

tion they have of their primary function. To celebrate a discovery or a unique exploit motivated such men as Sir Richard Burton, John Hanning Speke, John L. Stephens, and Alexander Kinglake to record their travels. Naturalists, like explorers, seek out-of-the-way places, but emphasize zoological, botanical, and geological concerns, instead of the individual heroism demanded by exploration. In the nineteenth century, South America offered the most productive terrain for such naturalists as Henry Bates, Charles Darwin, Thomas Belt, and W. H. Hudson; Africa and the East, during the same period, provided the best field for adventurers. The esthetes—John Ruskin, Henry James, Norman Douglas, and Aldous Huxley come to mind—prefer more civilized areas, since their enthusiasms include art and history, as well as landscape. Whereas adventurers are succeeded by missionaries and traders, esthetes are followed by cultivated tourists. Ethnologists differ from esthetes in that they consider the daily life of a people more important than monuments and museums. George Borrow, Charles Doughty, Hilaire Belloc, and John Millington Synge, among others, visited cultures to find out how the common people thought, spoke, and acted. Both esthetes and ethnologists play the part of mediator between home and abroad, but esthetes analyze the high culture, and ethnologists explain the people.

These categories cannot be considered mutually exclusive; they are useful mainly in providing us with a broad outline. Burton, Stephens, and Douglas furnish descriptions of customs which rival those of the ethnologists. The travel narratives of Bates and Doughty are often as spirited as any explorer's. And George Borrow, who fit in so well with vagabonds, was one of the first writers on Spain to appreciate El Greco. The truth is that travel writing is a very open genre, and its practitioners rarely impose limits on themselves.

As a travel writer Lawrence belongs among the ethnologists. Even the archeological concerns of *Etruscan Places* did not prevent him from writing about the people he met in the Tuscan hill towns and the guides who took him to the painted tombs. That Lawrence should have rejected the role of the esthete, or literary traveller, does not surprise us, but it was a bit puzzling to some of his contemporaries. One reviewer of *Twilight in Italy,* for example, thought it "an unusual travel book in that it gives the impressions made upon the mind of the author by men and women, rather than by art monuments or natural scenery." The reviewer obviously expected the young novelist to follow in the path of the esthetic travellers. Lawrence did visit picture galleries during his pre-World War I travels, but his appraisals of Italian and German artists were included in his "Study of Thomas Hardy," not in *Twilight in Italy*. When he turned to the subject of art in the travel books, he emphasized folk art instead of high art. The crucifixes of the Tyrol, the Sicilian marionette theater, the Etruscan household pottery interested him not as artifacts for connoisseurship, but as expressions of the people's consciousness.

In *Twilight in Italy,* Lawrence wrote about the Lago di Garda region without once mentioning Catullus and Dante, two poets associated, if only in legend, with that area. He also refrained from commenting on the earlier trips of Goethe and Tennyson around that northern lake. *Sea and Sardinia* even more scrupulously avoided Baedeker-like capsulations of cultural and literary history. In fact, Sardinia appealed to Lawrence, both as a potential home and as a place to write about, because he believed that it had escaped the extensive heritage of the Mediterranean world. Halfway through the trip, Lawrence remained pleased that he had decided in favor of the island's lack of culture:

There is nothing to see in Nuoro: which, to tell the truth, is always a relief. Sights are an irritating bore. Thank heaven there isn't a bit of Perugino or anything Pisan in the place: that I know of. Happy is the town that has nothing to show. What a lot of stunts and affectations it saves! Life is then life, not museum-stuffing.

Lawrence's opposite is a traveller like Norman Douglas, for whom the very charm of travelling lay in the historical and literary associations of place. Whereas literature depended upon confrontations with inn-keepers, talks aboard trains, and observations of street life to provide the material for his travel books, the author of *Old Calabria* (1915) relied upon his own erudition and the resources of municipal libraries. "The number of monographs dealing with every one of these little Italian towns is a ceaseless source of surprise," Douglas wrote, seemingly undaunted by having to read them. A comparison of *Sea and Sardinia* and *Old Calabria* reveals that Lawrence surpasses Douglas in describing the terrain and peasants, while Douglas excels at revitalizing forgotten biographies and legendary material. It is a measure of the range possible within the travel genre that the two books succeed. Both Douglas's circuitous, scholarly route and Lawrence's more direct approach expose the southern Italian's character and the writers' own temperaments.

Although the careful portraits of Paolo and Maria in *Twilight in Italy,* the old roaster in *Sea and Sardinia,* and mozo in *Mornings in Mexico* justify Lawrence's inclusion with the ethnologists, his working methods were scarcely those of a field anthropologist. In fact, an indelible part of the myth surrounding Lawrence the traveller concerns the rapidity with which he would record his observations of a new place. W. H. Auden, in *Letters from Iceland* (1937), defined his own method of travel writing by comparing it with that of Lawrence: "I am no Lawrence who, on his arrival, / Sat down and typed out all he had to say." In "Elegy," Rebecca West recalled visiting Lawrence's room in Florence with Norman Douglas and Reggie Turner:

> So it was a small, mean room in which [Lawrence] sat tapping away at a typewriter. Norman Douglas burst out in a great laugh as we went in and asked if he were already writing an article about the present state of Florence; and Lawrence answered seriously that he was. This was faintly embarrassing, because on the doorstep Douglas had described how on arriving in a town Lawrence used to go straight from the railway station to his hotel and immediately sit down and hammer out articles about the place, vehemently and exhaustively describing the temperament of the people. This seemed obviously a silly thing to do, and here he was doing it.

Certainly, it was not always Lawrence's habit to establish a prolonged contact with a culture before he put his impressions on paper—*Kangaroo, Sea and Sardinia,* and the Florentine section of *Aaron's Rod* are evidence of this. But before we give too much weight to charges of a hasty impressionism or solipsism, we should remember that Lawrence lived among the peasants of the Lago di Garda for over a year, that his American sojourn lasted off and on for four years, and that the Etruscans interested him for the last ten years of his life and were the major preoccupation of two years. Besides, even though intimate knowledge of a country is a great help to a travel writer, time alone does not always confer it. Lawrence Durrell, who is perhaps the finest travel writer of our day, singled out *Sea and Sardinia, Twilight in Italy,* and *Fountains*

in the Sand (1912) by Norman Douglas as masterpieces which proved that it was not always essential for a traveller to have any special knowledge of a place.

Readers of travel books, generally speaking, can be divided into four groups: those whose familiarity with a foreign area makes them want to find out other responses to it; those who are planning a trip and seek aid in narrowing the choices; those who are fascinated by exotic places but (whether for lack of money, time, or energy) cannot go themselves; and those who begin with an interest in an author himself and want to read everything he wrote.

The travel books of D. H. Lawrence are read mostly by people in the last category. That these works are still in print and easily obtainable we can take as evidence of a continued, widespread interest in Lawrence the writer. Readers who approach the travel writings in this way seldom come away disappointed, for as selective, concentrated autobiography, Lawrence's travel books are of primary importance. *Twilight in Italy* provides one of the finest accounts we have of those exuberant first months with Frieda. When eight years later Lawrence began to feel threatened by the *Dea Mater,* whose spirit he saw reincarnated in Frieda, he recorded his rebellion against the female principle in *Sea and Sardinia.* The Southwestern essays of *Mornings in Mexico* and *Etruscan Places* are more nearly personal narratives of the imagination than transcripts of daily life, but they are no less revealing for that.

The story of Lawrence's search for a nourishing soil and a compatible culture is told more fully in the travel books than anywhere else. He could spend only so much time in the expatriate circles of Europe and America before he began to think as ill of them as of England. When the reaction started, he would move to less civilized spots where he inevitably became disgusted with the backwardness and brutishness of the inhabitants. Capri's cosmopolitan atmosphere drove him to remoter Sicily and eventually to Sardinia; and the Taos artist colony upset him enough to make the rugged, isolated life in the New Mexico mountains and Oaxaca seem wiser choices. Lawrence set such impediments in the way of finding an acceptable union of place and people that we are not surprised to see him finally adopting a mythical Etruria as his homeland.

Those readers for whom geographical and cultural concerns outweigh the claims of biography usually read a travel book in conjunction with related accounts by other travellers to the same area. Travel books profit by being placed in this light, because in a majority of cases travel writers themselves have this context uppermost in their minds. Doughty's *Arabia Deserta* has many revealing connections with his *The Dawn in Britain* (1906), but it should be read instead with Sir Richard Burton's *Personal Narrative of a Pilgrimage to El-Medinah & Meccah* (1855), W. G. Palgrave's *Narrative of a Journey Through Central and Eastern Arabia* (1865), and T. E. Lawrence's *Seven Pillars of Wisdom* (1926) as a major episode in that long-standing passion the English have had for the desert and its tribesmen.

Italophiles have never shelved *Twilight in Italy, Sea and Sardinia,* and *Etruscan Places* next to *Women in Love, The Lost Girl,* and *The Man Who Died.* Instead, they have placed Lawrence's Italian travels beside Goethe's *Italian Journey* (1816), Charles Dickens' *Pictures from Italy* (1846), Samuel Butler's *Alps and Sanctuaries,* and Norman Douglas's *Old Calabria* as works which both offer insights into the culture of the peninsula and explore the attraction Northern Europeans have always felt for the south. It is especially crucial to look at Lawrence's travel books from this perspective, since they have too often casually been tossed aside as peasant hunts by critics unsympathetic to the author's primitivism and unaware of the high place he commands in the extensive field of Italian travels.

But even topographically-oriented readers have to admit that a travel book's success depends to a large degree on the personality of its writer. Norman Douglas, in his essay on Charles Doughty, has commented that "it is not enough to depict, in however glowing hues, the landscape and customs of distant regions, to smother us in folklore, and statistics and history, and besprinkle the pages with imaginary conversations or foreign idioms by way of generating 'local color.' It is not enough. We want to take our share in that interior voyage and watch how these alien sights and sounds affect the writer" [see excerpt below]. The travel writer ought to be companionable, but not necessarily easy going. A list of pre-eminent travel writers, which would have to include Smollett, Borrow, Burton, and Doughty, reveals that almost all belong in the class of energetic eccentrics.

Lawrence retains in full the individual angle which enables the reader to become absorbed in the traveller as well as the tale. Like Dr. Johnson, George Borrow, Samuel Butler, and Hilaire Belloc, Lawrence often found his own character to be his choicest material. Wherever Lawrence went, he remained passionate and partial. By temperament, if not by stamina, he belongs with those earlier eccentric characters who wrote travel books. *Sea and Sardinia,* for example, reveals Lawrence as someone who trusted in the uniqueness of his perceptions and could say "the judgement may be all wrong: but this was the impression I got." Remaining in a state of hypersensitivity for much of this book, Lawrence is egotistical enough to assume that his minor preferences, if conveyed in a spirited manner, will be of general interest. A petulant temper is the main tale; fellow travellers, the local inhabitants, and the landscape are relegated often to the role of background provocateurs. At times the numerous incitements which fuel his ill humor happen too fast to be captured in complete sentences: "More and more people appear. More and more official caps stand about. It rains and rains. The train from Palermo and the train from Syracuse are both an hour late already, coming from the port. Fleabite."

By the time Lawrence began writing travel pieces, a change had occurred in the conception of the traveller as hero. According to John Alcorn, whose recent book, *The Nature Novel from Hardy to Lawrence,* argues that the Edwardian (or "naturist") travel book provided the model for the fictions of Forster, Douglas, and Lawrence, "the new travel hero . . . is the passive recipient of a wisdom which resides, not in the crafts of civilized man, but in physical nature itself" [see excerpt below]. Lawrence as a traveller is a direct descendant of the "naturist" group, which succeeded the swaggering, robust Victorian explorers. Instead of having the virtues of the adventurer—courage and resourcefulness—Lawrence possesses a sensitive awareness of life. His account of the old Sard roasting skewered meat over an inn's hearth and his appreciation of early bucchero ware in *Etruscan Places* show that Lawrence could endow daily activities and commonplace objects with a sense of wonder.

Ever since Laurence Sterne sent Yorick off on a Grand Tour, travel books have retained that freedom of form which allows for the intrusion of autobiographical, scientific and historical material, and even for frequent digressions and anecdotes. Alexander Kinglake's only excuse for providing history of Lady

Hester Stanhope in *Eothen* (1844) was his conviction that it would interest some readers. In *Mornings in Florence* (1877), Ruskin enlarged his appreciation of "The Descent of the Holy Spirit" (part of the fresco cycle in the Spanish Chapel, S. Maria Novella) to include a discussion of his own educational theories. W. H. Hudson quickly abandoned chronological continuity in *Idle Days in Patagonia* (1893) so that he could consider such topics as the vision of savages, atavistic memory, and the symbolism of whiteness in *Moby-Dick.* And in *Letters from Iceland,* Auden explained his choice of the travel genre:

> I want a form that's large enough to swim in,
> And talk on any subject that I choose,
> From natural scenery, to men and women,
> Myself, the arts, the European news. . .

Leaving aside the question of whether it is in the best tradition for travel writers to wander from the point, it is apparent that the travel book has a special appeal for riders of hobby horses and for those who value spontaneity over the strict logic of cause-and-effect.

Lawrence, too, valued the travel genre because of its open form. *Twilight in Italy,* the most loosely structured of the travel books, bears witness to the frequency with which Lawrence could exchange his walking stick for a lectern. Poet vignettes of peasant life give way often to discussions of the decline of Italian culture since the Renaissance and the theological significance of the Holy Ghost. Expressing opinion may be a flaw in a novelist, but it can be a virtue in a travel writer, if he has interesting ideas and can make them appear to flow effortlessly from his experiences. When Auden called Lawrence's travel books "essays on life prompted by something seen," he praised them for the same reason that earlier critics like Horace Gregory objected to them.

Travel writers have always flaunted their prejudices, fearing above all else that they should sink into being impersonal reporters. Accuracy pleases us when we find it in the travel reports of such naturalists as Bates, Darwin, and Hudson; but however authoritative a travel book may be, we rarely read it only as a source of information about a region or as an encyclopedia of another culture. The most famous exception was the dependence of Middle Eastern experts in World War I on *Arabia Deserta.* The most forgotten instance was a reviewer's suggestion that Lawrence's *Mornings in Mexico* be required reading for Congressmen seated on Latin American committees. These practical uses are high praise for the two books, yet mere accuracy is not enough to insure survival.

What is it that separates great travel books from the good ones which have only a short-lived appeal? Padraic Colum, the Irish travel writer and poet, came close to the answer when he said that they "have in them something more than the record of a journey into a country; in them is the journey into the writer's self, in them is the quest that is rarely spoken of—the secret quest." Using these criteria, Colum placed *The Bible in Spain, Arabia Deserta,* and *The Aran Islands* above Kinglake's *Eothen* and Pierre Loti's *Into Morocco.* Colum's first gauge of a superior travel book is undoubtedly accurate: travel narratives which are searches for identity as well as accounts of physical wanderings are the most compelling. His second measure, however, is quite cryptic. What does he mean by the "secret quest"? A passage from Lawrence's review of H. M. Tomlinson's *Gifts of Fortune* (1926) provides an explanation with which most travel writers from Doughty to Durrell, at least, would have agreed. Distinguishing between travellers and tourists, Lawrence says: "We do not travel in order to go from one hotel to another, and see a few side-shows. We travel, perhaps, with a secret and absurd hope of setting foot on the Hesperides, of running our boat up a little creek and landing in the Garden of Eden.''

The "secret quest" that pervades and controls the travel books of Doughty, Synge, Hudson, and Lawrence is the attempt to return to the beginnings of civilization. As John Alcorn has succinctly stated, "the story of the naturist travel book is, in fact, the story of a search for Eden." The naturist travel writers have journeyed to remote, or at least isolated, regions in the hope that existing traditional cultures still retained remnants of the life natural man enjoyed.

Throughout the nineteenth and twentieth centuries, the desire to investigate a more primitive consciousness remained a persistent reason both for travelling and for writing travel books. Borrow found his gypsies, Doughty his Bedouins, Synge his Aran Islanders, and Hudson, looking for birds in Patagonia, found himself. Following in this tradition, all of Lawrence's travel books explore earlier modes of awareness. *Twilight in Italy* shows Lawrence's fruitless search for a culture in which both the creative and sensual sides of man's nature remained active. Although initially attracted to what he called the Italians' "Pan-consciousness," he soon realized that their preoccupation with the physical was just as limiting as the northern glorification of the mind. In *Sea and Sardinia*, his next written travel book, Lawrence's atavistic pursuits were at their most extreme. His quest in this book was for a culture that in remaining outside of European civilization had never become conscious of historical process. In *Mornings in Mexico*, Lawrence attempted to find a society that did not have Northern Europe's tragic sense of dissociation from the cosmos. The Mexican and Pueblo Indians, he thought, might still possess a feeling of "pure relatedness" to the universe. More successful this time, he did find that the Indians' animistic awareness enabled them to stand in what Martin Buber would have called an "I:Thou" relation to the natural world. Lawrence's last travel book, *Etruscan Places*, attempted to reconstruct a civilization that lived very much as he himself would have liked to live. The vitality he discovered in the tomb scenes led him to exclaim: "There is more life in these Etruscan legs, fragments as they are, than in the whole bodies of men today." Lawrence attributed this vibrancy to the Etruscans' "symbolic consciousness," which permitted them to respond emotionally and imaginatively to the cosmos.

Lawrence's effort to recapture the older pagan world made his travels chronological as well as geographical. By travelling backwards in time, he attempted to answer questions similar to those Gauguin, another exile, posed on his most ambitious Tahitian canvas—"D'où venons nous? Que sommes nous? Où allons nous?" ["Where do we come from? What are we? And where are we going?"] Whereas Doughty tried to find aspects of the life of the Hebrew Patriarchs among the Bedouins, Lawrence wanted "to go back to old days, pre-Bible days, and pick up for us there what men felt like and lived by then." Lawrence intended to look a bit beyond the beginnings of western civilization; the final phase of what he called the "old order" was what really interested him.

Lawrence believed that the people of the "old order," besides having archaic forms of thought untouched by Judaic monotheism and Greek rationalism, maintained social organizations which allowed men to be free from economic bondage and the domination of women. The social structure most conducive to these liberties was, rather surprisingly, matriarchy. This earlier form of culture seemed to Lawrence superior to the later patriarchal systems founded upon division of labor, nuclear families, and individual ownership of property. (pp. 273-83)

The Indians of the Southwest in *Mornings in Mexico,* besides being champions of an older form of consciousness, had a matriarchal society which Lawrence found exemplary. Lawrence considered matriarchy to be equally rewarding for both sexes, but it is obvious that men benefit more. Released from the confinements of domestic obligations, the Pueblo males spend their time hunting, farming, and, above all, practicing religious rites with other males in the sacred meeting-house. Lawrence believed that it was "a social instinct in man to leave his wife and children safe home, while he goes out and foregathers with other men, to fulfill his deeper social necessities." The pattern of Indian life so impressed Lawrence that he advocated matriarchy as a way of saving the modern world from "the mess of industrial chaos and industrial revolt."

Matriarchy did not mean for Lawrence a gynaecocracy, or rule by women, but a society in which men willingly surrendered home, possessions, and children to women in return for the freedom to commune with other men. An equality of the sexes had no appeal for Lawrence; the domestic sphere seemed in his mind the appropriate place for women to use their talents. Thinking back on earlier days, Lawrence wrote: "Under the matriarchal system that preceded the patriarchal system of Father Abraham, the men seem to have been lively sports, hunting and dancing and fighting, while the women did the drudgery and minded the brats." Since women only have control over what men don't care about, Lawrence's version of matriarchy might be better called a "male civilization." The attraction of a "male civilization," beyond its correspondence to Lawrence's homosexual fantasies, was that the complete religious attention he found so commendable in Pueblo and Etruscan males would have been impossible under any other social arrangement.

In his quest for a spiritual home Lawrence sought a culture which retained all the virtues he associated with the pre-Christian world. The apparently interlocking "evidence" of theosophy, Frazer's *Golden Bough,* and Thomas Belt's geological theories aided his understanding of what he called, in the foreword to *Fantasia of the Unconscious,* "the great pagan world which preceded our own era." But esoteric religions and anthropological scholarship provided only partial disclosures of the lost Atlantean life. The real path back to the beginnings—as Lawrence learned first from the example of earlier travellers and later from his own experience—was through immersion in the spirit of place.

The student of Lawrence cannot help noticing the extreme importance of place in both travel writings and fiction. As Mark Schorer has perceptively stated, "often it [place] becomes the major character, as it were, Lawrence's arbiter disposing of human destinies in accordance with the response that human characters have made to itself, the non-human place." New Mexico's rugged landscape completely dominates the end of *St. Mawr,* assuming the role of Lou Carrington's superhuman lover, and thereby providing a potentially creative counterpart to the effete Rico. Similarly, in the story "Sun," Juliet's reaction to the erotic Sicilian coast is largely responsible for her near rebirth.

Lawrence put great confidence in the ability of landscape to change a person. His belief in this power has the importance of an article of faith in his personal religion. "There are a lot of me's,'' Rawdon Lilly, that high priest of the Lawrence cult, insisted in *Aaron's Rod*. ''I'm not only just one proposition. A new place brings out a new thing in a man.'' Although Lilly speaks for Lawrence in the novel, he would have been a little closer to the truth if he had said ''an ancient place brings out an old thing in a man.''

Lawrence was not unique in attributing so much power to the spirit of place. His predecessors in the travel book tradition were alert also to those moments when landscape transformed the consciousness of the observer. John Alcorn has even called the sensations of boundlessness and timelessness caused by a response to landscape ''the central subject of naturist travel literature.'' In particular, both John Millington Synge in *The Aran Islands* (1907) and W. H. Hudson in *Idle Days in Patagonia* (1893) anticipated Lawrence. Certain landscapes enabled the Irish playwright and the La Platan naturalist to shed their modern outlooks and enter a more primitive world.

While Lawrence and Hudson prized those times when experiencing a landscape would make them aware of hidden depths within the self, Synge was more frightened than delighted by the phenomenon. The rude curraghs which carried Synge to one of the last outposts of primitive life in Europe—he described Aran culture as a ''touch of the refinement of the old societies . . . blended, with singular effect, among the qualities of the wild animal''—perhaps took that former citizen of cosmopolitan Paris further than he wanted. If his response to place had produced waking revelations, he might have been as enthusiastic as Hudson and Lawrence. But he was less fortunate, and his atavistic insights surfaced in nightmares. ''Some dreams I have had in this cottage,'' the visitor to Aran wrote, ''seem to give strength to the opinion that there is a psychic memory attached to certain neighborhoods.'' (pp. 284-86)

The spirit of place made Lou Carrington, the heroine of ''Sun,'' and Lawrence the traveller come alive, and Lawrence intended that his evocations of place in the travel books would alert the reader to the revitalizing, curative powers of landscape. In the same manner that his analysis of the Indians' animistic awareness and the Etruscans' symbolic consciousness tried to make the reader recognize the depths of life within, his aim in capturing the spirit of place was to make the reader aware of the vital regions outside the self.

However personal the quest in his travel books may appear, Lawrence was searching on behalf of modern society as well as on his own. He regarded the primitive cultures that he investigated both as potential homes and as examples which might correct civilization. Edward Nehls has said that ''those readers who feel themselves alienated by Lawrence the prophet may still find a vast pleasure in Lawrence the traveller.'' But parts of the travel books would have to be carefully selected for such a reader. Only the earliest travel essays—''French Sons of Germany,'' ''Hail in the Rhineland,'' ''A Chapel Among the Mountains,'' and ''A Hayhut Among the Mountains''—lack philosophic and symbolic concerns. In truth, after 1913 no firm distinction can be made between Lawrence's travel and didactic writings: Lawrence the traveller and Lawrence the preacher are inseparable.

In this respect Lawrence's travel writings are of a piece with pseudotravel narratives like Montesquieu's *Persian Letters* and Swift's *Gulliver's Travels*, as well as the real travels of Doughty. For however far afield the real or imaginary travels go, one eye is always on the homeland. When Montesquieu has Usbek criticize French mores, or Swift makes the King of Brobding-nag reject Gulliver's offer of weaponry, or Doughty records the precise speech of the desert tribesmen, or Lawrence praises Indians for avoiding mechanical innovation, all of these writers are setting up cultural parallels in which the alien societies— whether aboriginal, non-western, or imaginary—demonstrate the way to a more humane and vital civilization at home. Lawrence's persistant use of antithesis to discuss the cultures that he visited reveals the instructional nature of the travel books. By contrasting one culture with another, Lawrence tried to convince the reader that one style of life or form of consciousness was superior.

As Lawrence knew from his readings, the didactic impetus behind travel literature at times involved something more than a cross-cultural dialogue. The lesson of *Arabia Deserta*, for example, did not lie in any contrast between the artificial civilization of Europe and the natural virtues of a primitive people. Doughty does admit a personal preference for the rugged desert life over England's softness: he says that ''lying to rest amidst wild basalt-stones under the clear stars . . . I have found more refreshment than upon beds and pillows in our close chambers.'' But, despite the Bedouins' retention of the same simple life that sustained Abraham and the patriarchs, Doughty readily concedes them to be ''a merry crew of squalid wretches, iniquitous, fallacious, fanatical.'' He was only too well aware that the Bedouins lived in a Hobbesian state of nature. The most that could be said in their behalf was that they escaped the evils attendant upon urbanization.

Doughty intended that Victorian society would benefit from the manner of the book, not from the example of noble Arabs. *Arabia Deserta* had, above all, a literary purpose: Doughty wanted to revitalize the English language by bringing it back into the main tradition of Chaucer and Spenser. Although his projected linguistic reform did not have the widespread effect he hoped, Doughty did broaden the possibilities of what could be attempted in the genre of travel literature. Lawrence also intended more in *Etruscan Places* than that the reader should recognize the sexual and religious deficiencies of English life as they were exposed by a loving look at Etruria. The primary didactic impulse behind Lawrence's last travel book consisted of nothing less than an attempt to transform the reader's consciousness—to reawaken mythopoeic thought in modern man.

It is beginning to be clear that a fair portion of Lawrence's reputation will come to rest on his merits as a travel writer. Emile Delavenay, the most recent biographer of Lawrence, has taken an initial step towards this revaluation by claiming [in *D. H. Lawrence: The Man and His Work* (1972)] that ''the numerous books of travel . . . stand high in Lawrence's total output.'' Instead of being only useful glosses on the novels, Lawrence's travel books often surpass the fiction in the way they treat two of his obsessive themes. Both the concern with primitive consciousness and the search for a male civilization are best expressed in the travel writings. Lawrence always had a lively curiosity about the beginnings of western culture, yet those sections of the novels which attempt to deal with such matters usually have a hollow ring. The comparisons of Birkin to stiff Egyptian Pharoahs, for example, have been embarrassments to admirers of *Women in Love*. Similarly, the leadership novels—*Aaron's Rod*, *Kangaroo*, and *The Plumed Serpent*—are weakest when their characters debate the virtues of male companionship. In *Sea and Sardinia* and *Mornings in Mexico*, however, Lawrence could describe cultures which already had a segregation of the sexes. It would seem that by its very nature the travel genre is better suited than fiction to handle explorations of earlier forms of consciousness and primitive ways of living.

Ciccio's home in the Alban mountains, Aaron's stay in Florence, Somers' visit to Australia, and Kate's journey down the lake make it hard in speaking of Lawrence to keep a rigid division between fiction and travels. A comprehensive study of Lawrence and travel would have to take into consideration *The Lost Girl, Aaron's Rod, Kangaroo,* and *The Plumed Serpent,* works that are strongest, in fact, when they come closest to travel writing. Lawrence's novels of the second rank mingle fiction, autobiography, and travels in a way that recalls the efforts of George Borrow, for whom he had an early and deep attachment. These lesser novels also share that persistent task of the travel books which Lawrence Durrell defined as isolating "the germ in the people which is expressed by their landscape."

Lawrence excelled at penetrating the connections between culture and place, and it is this ability ultimately that establishes him as a travel writer of the first order. He may have lacked the esthetic sensibility that John Ruskin took to Northern Italy, the knowledge of history that Norman Douglas took to Calabria, and the familiarity with the classics that George Dennis took to Etruria; but whatever he lost in accuracy, he made up for by being convincing. Other travel writers may be more esteemed by scholars, but no one has had a greater influence on the way non-specialist readers think of Italy, New Mexico, and Etruria than D. H. Lawrence. (pp. 288-91)

> *Billy T. Tracy, "D. H. Lawrence and the Travel Book Tradition," in* The D. H. Lawrence Review, *Vol. 11, No. 3, Fall, 1978, pp. 272-93.*

LAWRENCE DURRELL

[*Durrell is an Indian-born Anglo-Irish novelist and poet best known for the four-volume novel series* The Alexandria Quartet *(1957-1960). He has also written numerous travel essays and once listed travel as an avocational interest, although in 1960 he told an interviewer: "You know I'm so travel-stained with fifteen or sixteen years of it—the great anxiety of being shot at in Cyprus, being bombed, being tormented by the Marxists in Yugoslavia—that now for the first time I've a yen for my tiny roof. Staying put is so refreshing that it's almost anguish to go into town for a movie." In the following essay, Durrell discusses the significance of physical landscape in forming national character.*]

"You write," says a friendly critic in Ohio, "as if the landscape were more important than the characters." If not exactly true, this is near enough the mark, for I have evolved a private notion about the importance of landscape, and I willingly admit to seeing "characters" almost as functions of a landscape. This has only come about in recent years after a good deal of travel—though here again I doubt if this is quite the word, for I am not really a "travel-writer" so much as a "residence-writer." My books are always about living in places, not just rushing through them. But as you get to know Europe slowly, tasting the wines, cheeses and characters of the different countries you begin to realize that the important determinant of any culture is after all—the spirit of place. Just as one particular vineyard will always give you a special wine with discernible characteristics so a Spain, an Italy, a Greece will always give you the same type of culture—will express itself through the human being just as it does through its wild flowers. We tend to see "culture" as a sort of historic pattern dictated by the human will, for me this is no longer absolutely true. I don't believe the British character, for example, or the German has changed a jot since Tacitus first described it; and so long as

people keep getting born Greek or French or Italian their culture-productions will bear the unmistakable signature of the place.

And this, of course, is the target of the travel-writer; his task is to isolate the germ in the people which is expressed by their landscape. Strangely enough one does not necessarily need special knowledge for the job, though of course a knowledge of language is a help. But how few they are those writers! How many can write a *Sea and Sardinia* or a *Twilight in Italy* to match these two gems of D. H. Lawrence? When he wrote them his Italian was rudimentary. The same applies to Norman Douglas' *Fountains in the Sand*—one of the best portraits of North Africa.

We travel really to try and get to grips with this mysterious quality of "Greekness" or "Spanishness"; and it is extraordinary how unvaryingly it remains true to the recorded picture of it in the native literature: true to the point of platitude. Greece, for example, cannot have a single real Greek left (in the racial sense) after so many hundreds of years of war and resettlement; the present racial stocks are the fruit of countless invasions. Yet if you want a bit of real live Aristophanes you only have to listen to the chaffering of the barrow-men and peddlers in the Athens Plaka. It takes less than two years for even a reserved British resident to begin using his fingers in conversation without being aware of the fact. But if there are no original Greeks left what is the curious constant factor that we discern behind the word "Greekness"? It is surely the enduring faculty of self-expression inhering in landscape. At least I would think so as I recall two books by very different writers which provide an incomparable nature-study of the place. One is *Mani* by Patrick Leigh Fermor, and the other Miller's *Colossus of Maroussi.*

I believe you could exterminate the French at a blow and resettle the country with Tartars, and within two generations discover, to your astonishment, that the national characteristics were back at norm—the restless metaphysical curiosity, the tenderness for good living and the passionate individualism: even though their noses were now flat. This is the invisible constant in a place with which the ordinary tourist can get in touch just by sitting quite quietly over a glass of wine in a Paris *bistrot.* He may not be able to formulate it very clearly to himself in literary terms, but he will taste the unmistakable keen knife-edge of happiness in the air of Paris: the pristine brilliance of a national psyche which knows that art is as important as love or food. He will not be blind either to the hard metallic rational sense, the irritating *coeur raisonnable* of the men and women. When the French want to be *malins,* as they call it, they can be just as we can be when we stick our toes in over some national absurdity.

Yes, human beings are expressions of their landscape, but in order to touch the secret springs of a national essence you need a few moments of quiet with yourself. Truly the intimate knowledge of landscape, if developed scientifically, could give us a political science—for half the political decisions taken in the world are based on what we call national character. We unconsciously acknowledge this fact when we exclaim, "How typically Irish" or "It would take a Welshman to think up something like that." And indeed we all of us jealously guard the sense of minority individuality in our own nations—the family differences. The great big nations like say the Chinese or the Americans present a superficially homogeneous appearance; but I've noticed that while we Europeans can hardly tell one American from another, my own American friends will tease each other to death at the lunch-table about the intolerable misfortune of being born in Ohio or Tennessee—a recognition of the validity of place which we ourselves accord to the Welshman, Irishman and Scotsman at home. It is a pity indeed to travel and not get this essential sense of landscape values. You do not need a sixth sense for it. It is there if you just close your eyes and breathe softly through your nose; you will hear the whispered message, for all landscapes ask the same question in the same whisper. "I am watching you—are you watching yourself in me?" Most travellers hurry too much. But try just for a moment sitting on the great stone omphalos, the navel of the ancient Greek world, at Delphi. Don't ask mental questions, but just relax and empty your mind. It lies, this strange amphora-shaped object, in an overgrown field above the temple. Everything is blue and smells of sage. The marbles dazzle down below you. There are two eagles moving softly softly on the sky, like distant boats rowing across an immense violet lake.

Ten minutes of this sort of quiet inner identification will give you the notion of the Greek landscape which you could not get in twenty years of studying ancient Greek texts. But having got it, you will at once great all the rest; the key is there, so to speak, for you to turn. After that you will not be able to go on a shopping expedition in Athens without running into Agamemnon or Clytemnestra—and often under the same names. And if you happen to go to Eleusis in springtime you will come upon more than one blind Homer walking the dusty roads. The secret is identification. If you sit on the top of the Mena House pyramid at sunset and try the same thing (forgetting the noise of the donkey-boys, and all the filthy litter of other travellers— old cartons and Coca-Cola bottles): if you sit quite still in the landscape-diviner's pose—why, the whole rhythm of ancient Egypt rises up from the damp cold sand. You can hear its very pulse tick. Nothing is strange to you at such moments—the old temples with their death-cults, the hieroglyphs, the long slow whirl of the brown Nile among the palm-fringed islets, the crocodiles and snakes. It is palpably just as it was (its essence) when the High Priest of Ammon initiated Alexander into the Mysteries. Indeed the Mysteries themselves are still there for those who might seek initiation—the shreds and shards of the Trismegistic lore still being studied and handed on by small secret sects. Of course you cannot arrange to be initiated through a travel agency! You would have to reside and work your way in through the ancient crust—a tough one—of daily life. And how different is the rhythm of Egypt to that of Greece! One isn't surprised by the story that the High Priest at Thebes said contemptuously: "You Greeks are mere children." He could not bear the tireless curiosity and sensuality of the Greek character—the passionate desire to conceptualize things metaphysically. They didn't seem to be able to relax, the blasted Greeks! Incidentally it is a remark which the French often repeat today about the Americans, and it is always uttered in the same commiserating tone of voice as once the High Priest used. Yet the culture of Greece (so different from that of Egypt) springs directly from the Nile Valley—I could name a dozen top Greek thinkers or philosophers who were trained by Egyptians, like Plato, Pythagoras, Anaxagoras, Democritos. And the "tiresome children" certainly didn't waste their time, for when they got back home to their own bare islands the pure flower of Greek culture spread its magnificent wings in flights of pure magic to astonish and impregnate the Mediterranean. But just to hand the eternal compliment along they invented the word "barbarians" for all those unfortunate savages who lived outside the magic circle of Greece, deprived of its culture.

The barbarians of course were one day to produce Dante, Goethe, Bach, Shakespeare.

As I say the clue, then, is identification; for underneath the purely superficial aspects of apparent change the old tide-lines remain. The dullest travel poster hints at it. The fascinating thing is that Dickens characters still walk the London streets; that any game of village cricket will provide us with clues to the strange ritualistic mystery of the habits of the British. While if you really want to intuit the inner mystery of the island try watching the sun come up over Stonehenge. It may seem a dull and "touristic" thing to do, but if you do it in the right spirit you find yourself walking those woollen secretive hills arm in arm with the Druids.

Taken in this way travel becomes a sort of science of intuitions which is of the greatest importance to everyone—but most of all to the artist who is always looking for nourishing soils in which to put down roots and create. Everyone finds his own "correspondences" in this way—landscapes where you suddenly feel bounding with ideas, and others where half your soul falls asleep and the thought of pen and paper brings on nausea. It is here that the travel-writer stakes his claim, for writers each seem to have a personal landscape of the heart which beckons them. The whole Arabian world, for example, has never been better painted and framed than in the works of Freya Stark, whose delicate eye and insinuating slow-moving orchestrations of place and evocations of history have placed her in the front rank of travellers. Could one do better than *Valley of the Assassins?*

These ideas, which may seem a bit far-fetched to the modern reader, would not have troubled the men and women of the ancient world, for their notion of culture was one of psychic education, the education of the sensibility; ours is built upon a notion of mentation, the cramming of the skull with facts and pragmatic data which positively stifle the growth of the soul. Travel wouldn't have been necessary in the time (I am sure such a time really existed some time after the Stone Age) when there really was a world religion which made full allowance for the different dialects of the different races practising it: and which realized that the factor of variation is always inevitably the landscape and not the people. Nowadays such a psychic uniformity sounds like a dream; but already comparative anthropology and archaeology are establishing the truth of it. When we think about such formulations as "World-Government" we always think of the matter politically, as groups of different people working upon an agreed agenda of sorts; a ten-point programme, or some such set of working propositions. The landscape always fools us, and I imagine always will. Simply because the same propositions don't mean the same in Greek, Chinese and French.

Another pointer worth thinking about is institutions; have you ever wondered why Catholicism, for example, can be such a different religion in different places? Ireland, Italy, Spain, Argentina—it is theologically the same, working on the same premises, but in each case it is subtly modified to suit the spirit of place. People have little to do with the matter except inasmuch as they themselves are reflections of their landscape. Of course there are places where you feel that the inhabitants are not really attending to and interpreting their landscape; whole peoples or nations sometimes get mixed up and start living at right angles to the land, so to speak, which gives the traveller a weird sense of alienation. I think some of the troubles which American artists talk about are not due to "industrialization" or "technocracy" but something rather simpler—people not attending to what the land is saying, not conforming to the hidden magnetic fields which the landscape is trying to communicate to the personality. It was not all nonsense what D. H. Lawrence had to say in his communion with the "ghosts" in the New World. He was within an ace, I think, of making real contact with the old Indian cultures. Genius that he was, he carried too much intellectual baggage about him on his travels, too many preconceptions; and while the mirror he holds up to Mexico, Italy, England is a marvellous triumph of art, the image is often a bit out of focus. He couldn't hold or perhaps wouldn't hold the camera steady enough—he refused to use the tripod (first invented by the oracles in Greece!).

The traveller, too, has his own limitations, and it is doubtful if he is to be blamed . The flesh is frail. I have known sensitive and inquisitive men so disheartened by the sight of a Greek lavatory as to lose all sense of orientation and fly right back to High Street Clapham without waiting for the subtler intimations of the place to dawn on them. I have known people educated up to Ph.D. standard who were so completely unhinged by French plumbing that they could speak of nothing else. We are all of us unfair in this way. I know myself to be a rash, hasty and inconsiderate man, and while I am sitting here laying down the law about travel I feel I must confess that I also have some blind spots. I have never been fair to the Scots. In fact I have always been extremely unfair to them— and all because I arrived on my first visit to Scotland late on a Saturday evening. I do not know whether it is generally known that you can simply die of exposure and starvation in relatively civilized places like Inverness simply because the inhabitants are too religious to cut a sandwich or pour coffee? It sounds fantastic I know. Nevertheless it is true. The form of Sabbatarianism which the Scots have developed passes all understanding. Nay, it cries out for the strait-jacket. And sitting on a bench at Inverness Station in a borrowed deerstalker and plaid you rack your brains to remember the least pronouncement in the Old or New Testaments which might account for it. There is none—or else I have never spotted the reference. They appear to have made a sort of Moloch of Our Lord, and are too scared even to brush their teeth on the Sabbath. How can I be anything but unfair to them? And yet Scotland herself—the poetry, and the poverty and naked joyous insouciance of mountain life, you will find on every page of Burns's autobiographical papers. Clearly she is a queenly country and a wild mountainous mate for poets. Why have the Scots not caught on? What ails them in their craggy fastnesses? (But I expect I shall receive a hundred indignant letters from Americans who have adopted Scotland, have pierced her hard heart and discovered the landscape-mystery of her true soul. Nevertheless, I stand by what I say; and one day when I am rich I shall have a memorial plaque placed over that bench on Inverness Station platform—a plaque reading "Kilroy was here— but oh so briefly"!) But I must not fail to add that I have always admired the magnificent evocations of Scots landscape in the books of Stevenson; they are only adventure tales, but the landscape comes shining through.

So that I imagine the traveller in each of us has a few blind spots due to some traumatic experience with an empty tea-urn or the room-on-the-landing. This cannot be helped. The great thing is to try and travel with the eyes of the spirit wide open, and not too much factual information. To tune in, without reverence, idly—but with real inward attention. It is to be had for the feeling, that mysterious sense of *rapport*, of identity with the ground. You can extract the essence of a place once

you know how. If you just get as still as a needle you'll be there.

I remember seeing a photo-reportage in *Life* magazine once which dealt with the extraordinary changes in physique which emigrants to the U.S.A. underwent over such relatively short periods as two or three generations. Some of the smaller races like Chinese and Filipinos appeared to have gained almost eight inches in height, over the statutory period investigated, while their physical weight had also increased in the most extraordinary way. The report was based on the idea that diet and environment were the real answers, and while obviously such factors are worth considering I found myself wondering if the reporters were right; surely the control experiment would fail if one fed a group of Chinese *in China* exclusively on an American diet? I don't see them growing a speck larger myself. They might get fat and rosy on the diet, but I believe the landscape, in pursuit of its own mysterious purposes, would simply cut them down to the required size suitable to home-grown Chinamen.

One last word about the sense of place; I think that not enough attention is paid to it as a purely literary criterion. What makes "big" books is surely as much to do with their site as their characters and incidents. I don't mean the books which are devoted entirely to an elucidation of a given landscape like Thoreau's *Walden* is. I mean ordinary novels. When they are well and truly anchored in nature they usually become classics. One can detect this quality of "bigness" in most books which are so sited from *Huckleberry Finn* to *The Grapes of Wrath*. They are tuned in to the sense of place. You could not transplant them without totally damaging their ambience and mood; any more than you could transplant *Typee*. This has nothing I think to do with the manners and habits of the human beings who populate them; for they exist in nature, as a function of place. (pp. 156-63)

Lawrence Durrell, "Landscape and Character," in his Spirit of Place: Letters and Essays on Travel, *edited by Alan G. Thomas, Faber & Faber Limited, 1969, pp. 156-63.*

TRAVEL WRITING AND FICTION WRITING

JOHN ALCORN

[*In the following excerpt, Alcorn examines the conventions of the Edwardian travel book that relate to the development of the "travel novel," or naturist novel, in English literature.*]

Hardy's Via Iceniana, the great Western road which crossed Egdon Heath, was the product of a great imperialist power. So too was the road travelled by Englishmen, late in the reign of Victoria, to every part of her empire. But if Victorian travel literature owed its existence to a highly industrialized and civilized power, it provided an escape from that same power and that same civilization. It is not my purpose to survey that voluminous literature, but rather to indicate that travel books of the period 1895-1920 continue a well-established tradition that would include such Victorian travellers as Robert Louis Stevenson, John Addington Symonds, Lafcadio Hearn, and Sir Leslie Stephens.

Edwardian travel literature tends to focus on three geographical areas: Italy, South America, and the desert belt stretching from

Arabia across North Africa. Edwardian writers about Italy looked to Samuel Butler's *Alps and Sanctuaries* as a prototype; South American travellers found an authoritative precedent in Charles Darwin's *Voyage of the Beagle;* the desert school followed in the path of Charles M. Doughty's formidable *Travels in Arabia Deserta.* Of the first group, Norman Douglas and D. H. Lawrence are perhaps the outstanding examples; of the second, W. H. Hudson and H. M. Tomlinson; in the third—and by far the largest—group might be included Wilfrid Blunt, E. G. Browne, David Hogarth, R. B. Cunninghame Graham, T. E. Lawrence, and Norman Douglas. Yet the literature of the Arab world produced no important piece of English fiction—unless, that is, we wish to read T. E. Lawrence's *The Seven Pillars of Wisdom* as fiction, as some historians are inclined to do. It was the French novelist—Gide, in *The Immoralist,* or Camus, in *The Stranger* and *The Plague*—who exploited this vein. (p. 42)

[A] distinction might be made between the traveller as expatriate and as English citizen. Hudson and Tomlinson travel round-trip; their voyages begin and end in London, and this fact has an effect upon both the tone and structure of their books. But Douglas and Lawrence are wandering exiles: they convey the impression of having no home in England, no place to return, and thus the structure of their travel books—and novels—tends to have a serial quality whereby the movement of the traveller seems to extend beyond the limits of the story itself.

My purpose is to emphasize those conventions of travel literature which have to do importantly with the new "travel novel." This emphasis in no way carries the implication that Edwardian travel literature is not a delight and an end in itself: indeed, it might be argued that the travelogues of this period rank among the finest in all English literature. But if the Edwardian travel writer tends to succeed where the travel novelist fails, it is because the aims of the novelist are more ambitious and more difficult; and the Edwardian travel novel too has its origin in the age of Victoria; such romances as Rider Haggard's *King Solomon's Mines,* Stevenson's *Treasure Island,* and Anthony Hope's *The Prisoner of Zenda* have provided a precedent, at least in terms of locale. But the main channel of Victorian fiction has been urban and domestic, and merges from a point of view within English culture. With Hardy the English novel moves out of the Victorian parlor on to the open road; and the naturist novelist will follow that road to the outskirts of civilization.

The travel tale is hardly new to English literature: from Chaucer to Mandeville, from Hakluyt to Captain John Newton, from Nashe's Jack Wilton to Smollett's Roderick Random, from Stern's sentimental voyager to George Borrow's gypsy wanderer, the travel book—both as fiction and as reportage—had waxed and waned with an impressive durability. In each case the travel story had reflected the special values and aspirations of the time. so it was with the naturist travelogue: a traditional genre was transformed to meet a new and urgent need.

The earlier picaresque travel hero tends either to perpetrate (like Jack Wilton) or to suffer endlessly (like Roderick Random) from a series of those human deceptions and rogueries which have no geographical boundaries. The picaresque tale is a battle of wits among individuals, each seeking an identity within society. The new twentieth-century travel hero escapes the treacheries, not of individuals, but of society itself, and his goal is contemplative isolation rather than success in the world of men. When an eighteenth-century wayfarer like Rob-

inson Crusoe has the misfortune to be cast upon a lonely island, he overcomes the obstacles of his environment by means of his own vitality and ingenuity. The new travel hero, on the contrary, is the passive recipient of a wisdom which resides, not in the crafts of civilized man, but in physical nature itself. Geographical movement provides, for Roderick Random, a mechanical framework and a background for human action; in the new novel, the central human action is to see, to meditate, and to learn from landscape, which is the "principal personage" of the tale.

Hardy's prediction, in *Return of the Native,* that "the new Vale of Tempe may be a gaunt waste in Thule"—that the new tourist would find his mood reflected by landscapes of "sombreness" and "desolation"—proved during the following decades to be unusually prophetic. Samuel Butler's landscapes were, like Egdon, remarkable for their quality of barren grandeur, their lonely and solemn distance from civilization. Butler's "torrent pathway of desolation" to Erewhon remains a dominating image in *Alps and Sanctuaries,* for Butler's Italian Alps tend to surround, dominate, and almost hide his ecclesiastical sanctuaries. His fine pen-and-ink sketches betray his mood perhaps more than does his mercurial prose. His drawing, for example, of the Chapel of Saint Carlo, Piora, shows in the foreground a small stream with a tiny foot-bridge; a woman hobbles under a heavy load, a cane in her hand; a man is herding a few disconsolate cattle. In the center of the drawing is a tiny, toy-like building: it is the chapel. But the humans and their artifacts are utterly dwarfed by a line of bare Alpine peaks against an unending cloudless sky. Again, his sketch of Calonico church shows only a portion of roof and a low bell-tower, pinioned by bushes, trees, and mountainside. We can hear Butler exclaiming, with his Erewhonian narrator, "Oh wonderful, wonderful!"

These same qualities had already produced the same wonder in the heart of Charles Darwin when, during his early twenties, he had found in the plains of Patagonia his own "gaunt waste in Thule." Darwin would never forget that sight; it would hold a meaning for him which would become a common theme for the travel writers who would take Darwin's *Voyage of the Beagle* for a model. Darwin's self-questioning about his reaction to the "wretched and useless" Patagonian wastes marks the beginning of a special genre of travel book:

> . . . the plains of Patagonia frequently cross before my eyes; yet these plains are pronounced by all to be most wretched and useless . . . without habitations, without water, without trees, without mountains, they support only a few dwarf plants. Why, then—and the case is not peculiar to myself—have these arid wastes taken so firm possession of my mind?. . . I can scarce analyse these feelings, but it must be partly owing to the free scope given to the imagination. The plains of Patagonia are boundless, for they are scarcely practicable, and hence unknown . . . there appears no limit to their duration through future time. If, as the ancients supposed, the flat earth was surrounded by an impassable breadth of water, by deserts heated to an intolerable excess, who would not look at these last boundaries to man's knowledge with deep but ill-defined sensations?

These "ill-defined sensations" of boundlessness and timelessness become the central subject of naturist travel literature. W. H. Hudson, for example, recapitulates Darwin's theme at the beginning of *Idle Days;* and toward the end of the book, Hudson includes the passage from Darwin quoted above, a passage "which, for me, has a very special interest and significance.'' For Hudson's trip began with his reading of Darwin's *Voyage of the Beagle*. Patagonia took possession of Hudson's mind as it had Darwin's, and induced a state of ''suspense and watchfulness,'' where ''thought had become impossible.'' Hudson's language reminds us of Hardy's Egdon Heath, ''full of watchful intentness.'' And when H. M. Tomlinson later finds in the jungle a quality of ''vacancy of large composure, with a lofty watchfulness which has no need to show its mind'' (*Sea and Jungle*), we recognize a similarity of idiom which, if it is not the result of light plagiarism, is surely representative of a striking community of mind.

A like suspension of mind overtook Norman Douglas as he finished his travels through Old Calabria ''in the breathless hush of noon'' when ''the silence can be felt.'' ''Such torrid splendour,'' wrote Douglas, ''drenching a land of austerest simplicity, decomposes the mind into corresponding states of primal contentment and resilience.'' It is characteristic that this experience gave Douglas a glimpse of the better society of the future: ''There arises before our phantasy a new perspective of human affairs; a suggestion of well-being wherein the futile complexities and disharmonies of our age shall have no place.''

Hardy, Darwin, Hudson, Tomlinson, Douglas—all saw the same quality of landscape: a knowledge beyond that of man, greater, wiser, more mysterious. When they looked at brute matter, they saw what Darwin saw: the unknown. Thus for Tomlinson the landscape of Brazil contained ''the prescience of destiny, as though an eyeless mask sat at the table with us, but though it stays, makes no sign'' (*Sea and Jungle*). Thus for Hudson the landscape infused a receptivity of mind, a state of waiting for a message, ''a revelation of an unfamiliar and unsuspected nature hidden under the nature we are conscious of'' (*Idle Days*). Thus D. H. Lawrence wrote of a Tuscan hill: ''And immediately one feels: that hill has a soul, it has a meaning.''

This same feeling for the attractiveness of desolation was in large part responsible for a new and special branch of travel literature: the story of the desert. Doughty's *Arabia Deserta*, though it was not the first, was the best book on the subject, and it, along with Doughty's other books, was vastly admired at the turn of the century. Hudson praised *Arabia Deserta* to Garnett, whose abridgement of Doughty's work (*Wanderings in Arabia*, 1908) ran into several editions. Hudson also admired Doughty's *Dawn in Britain*, as did D. H. Lawrence. But Lawrence's favorite Doughty work was *Adam Cast Forth*, for in it he found an image which would become the central theme of his fiction. ''He sent me,'' wrote Jessie Chambers, ''Charles Doughty's *Adam Cast Forth*, and I was especially to note where Eve, after long separation, finds Adam, and he tells her to bind herself to him with the vine strands, lest they be separated again by the Wind of God.''

Certainly Doughty was one of those indomitable eccentrics who have always flourished in English culture. He attempted to outdo Milton, but no reader would wish Doughty's interminable epic to be any longer. Yet when Doughty shifts his attention and his imagination from poetry to geology, he becomes indeed poetic and creative. His *Arabia Deserta* is a highly original and powerful evocation of the spaces and contours of the desert land. Doughty sees, in these ''boundless and bare, lone and level sands,'' what others had ignored or found monotonous: the desert becomes alive in its desolation. Doughty's book inspired a generation of desert enthusiasts, of whom the most prominent was Doughty's young friend Lawrence of Arabia, who carried *Arabia Deserta* with him on his desert journeys.

Norman Douglas wrote a chapter on Doughty's *Deserta in Experiments;* and Tomlinson's choice of the two greatest writers of his time is startling and illuminating: Thomas Hardy and Charles M. Doughty. Tomlinson's pairing may seem odd, but Doughty's book was written with that same earth-reverence to be found in Hardy. Doughty's own description of his book is characteristic, for the description begins and ends, like *Return of the Native* and *Erewhon*, with earth and rocks, framing and diminishing humanity. Doughty describes *Arabia Deserta* as ''the Story of the Earth, Her manifold living creatures, the human generations and Her living rocks.'' Doughty's work is a story in two senses: it is both a pilgrimage-adventure and a topological-geological study. The mass of detail assembled by Doughty is framed and ordered by the author's own physical movement, his adventure. Thus tomlinson, writing in 1931, admired the book because for him it described a universal human experience: ''A poet's collected work, a novelist's series of tales, as well as the *Arabia Deserta*, may be classed as travel literature, whether or not we like the country.'' For the naturist, all good literature is travel literature: like D. H. Lawrence, Tomlinson saw even Whitman's book of poems as a kind of travelogue: ''Is not *Leaves of Grass* a survey of a new continent?'' But Tomlinson's highest tribute was reserved for Norman Douglas as a travel writer: ''He knows his earth, though it gives him a little less joy when we crowd the scene.'' ''To know his earth'' is the highest goal of the naturist travel writer: ''You could smell this good earth,'' Tomlinson would exclaim (*Sea and Jungle*); and Hudson would exult: ''And that was the life I desired—the life the heart can conceive—the earth life'' (*Far Away*).

Thus Norman Douglas chose, for his longest and best travel book, a region he calls ''the Sahara of Italy'' (*Old Calabria*), a land of ''austerest simplicity,'' beset with poverty and malaria. ''This corner of Magna Graecia,'' he wrote, ''is a severely parsimonious manifestation of nature. Rocks and waters!'' The reason for Douglas's loving and detailed description of these rocks and waters might well be taken as the credo of all the naturists: ''But these rocks and waters are actualities; the stuff whereof man is made. A landscape so luminous, so resolutely scornful of accessories, hints at brave and simple forms of expression; it brings us to the ground, where we belong.'' Douglas's contention that man is made of rocks and waters not only reflects his early zoological studies, it also betrays his deep indebtedness to Samuel Butler, for whom ''the body is everything.'' The writings of Douglas can in fact be seen as a twentieth-century extension of the spirit of Samuel Butler. The two men are strikingly akin temperamentally; both are passionate eccentrics, riders of hobby horses, collectors of trivia, antiquarians, expert biologists, inveterate travellers, and genteel rebels against prevailing mores. Butler's biological interests are echoed in Douglas's early writings; indeed Keith, in *South Wind*, urges young Denis to read only Butler: ''I took him up, I remember,'' Keith says, ''during my biological period.'' Douglas follows Butler's Lamarkian bias in his early scientific writings, and both writers display in their travel books a sharp sense of botanical gamesmanship that verges on pedantry. Butler discovers, for example, ''the rare English fern Woodsia hyperborea,'' and ''one specimen of Asplenium alternifolium''; (*Alps*), and Douglas, not to be outdone, notes in *Old Calabria* no less than thirteen types of fig: ''fico arnese, fico santillo, fico. . .'—and he continues ruthlessly to list all thirteen.

It might be said that Butler's *Alps and Sanctuaries* is based upon that same Rabelaisian motto honored by Havelock Ellis:

"Fays ce que vouldras," although Butler seems to prefer a Victorian version of the sentiment, quoting Disraeli: "There is nothing like will; everybody can do exactly what they like in this world, provided they really like it" (*Alps*). Butler's book is a model of caprice: it begins with a discussion of Handel and Shakespeare, and continues as a rambling, disconnected series of observations on every conceivable subject. The pages of *Alps* are filled with sketches and passages of music, usually of Handel; the sight of a young Italian peasant sketching leads Butler to a lengthy consideration of "primitive" art, illustrated with three sketches by untutored Italians.

Yet Butler's book is structured around a series of revelations not unlike that of Darwin in Patagonia, or that of the Erewhonian narrator at the sight of the "desolate torrent." Thus the sound of the "roar of the Ticino" river sets "a passage from the *Messiah* sounding in my ears"—and Butler unhesitatingly prints the bars from Handel, along with a sketch, as if to use every art to fix this moment of "ill-defined" recognition. It is in fact a mark of the progress—or retrogression—of the naturist movement that, where Butler resorts to Handel, Hudson abandons counterpoint for the simplicity of bird-song. Yet Butler is hardly immune to the charms of the bird-call: he notices that "there was one bird, I think it was the New Zealand thrush, but am not sure, which used to sing thus"—and he proceeds to print several bars of melody. Characteristically, Butler is angry with the bird: unlike Handel, the thrush fails to develop the opening melodic theme properly, and Butler unhesitatingly sets down several bars of music he *wishes* the thrush had sung. This Butlerian impatience with the artistic gaffes of the ornithological world is nowhere to be found in Hudson.

Butler's treatment of illness as a crime and crime as an illness, in *Erewhon,* receives a new expression in Douglas's contention about metaphysics: "You cannot refute a disease" (*Old Calabria*). Conversely, Douglas's abiding interest in food and its preparation reflects the Butlerian emphasis upon pleasures of the body. "Virtues and vices which cannot be expressed in physiological terms," writes Douglas, "are not worth talking about." But where Butler's hedonism is reserved and Victorian, Douglas adds a special scatological touch: of the southern Italians, he writes: "They have a proverb which runs 'sfoga o schiatta'—relive yourself or burst; our vaunted ideal of self-restraint, of dominating the reflexes, being thought not only fanciful but injurious to health." Above all, *Old Calabria* echoes Butler's firm belief in idleness and in the wisdom of child's-play, as does Douglas's charming and fanciful collection. *London Street Games.* Like Butler, Douglas is everywhere master of the *non-sequitur. Old Calabria* moves from a chat with a barber to thoughts about Byzantine art to discussions of Calabrian wine. In this Douglas is typical of the naturist travel writer: words such as "careless," "idle," "drifting," "curious," abound in these travel books. The book titles are themselves suggestive of this fascination with the unpremeditated, the gratuitous, the accidental: "Idle Days," "Experiments," "Mornings in Mexico."

Douglas typically insists that "childishness" is a matter of climatic influences; he pays special note to Calabrian children's games and childish superstitions. Idleness is the supreme good: "You may spend pleasant days in this city of Cosenza, doing nothing whatever." The art of doing nothing is a serious business for both Butler and Douglas. To be a "lotus eater" is a "moral duty" for Butler's Ernest Pontifex; and young Denis, at the conclusion of *South Wind,* learns the final lesson of the island from Keith: "He advised me to sit among the rocks at midnight and in the hot afternoons, conversing with the genii of earth and air." But such idle contemplation, such abandonment of mind and will to the earth-spirits, is the beginning of wisdom. The concluding sentence of *Old Calabria* is both an epitaph for Futler and an introduction to *South Wind:* "From these brown stones . . . he can carve out . . . some tonic philosophy that shall foster sunny mischiefs and farewell regret."

Beneath the apparent aimlessness of *Alps and Sanctuaries* and *Old Calabria* lies a serious purpose, an interior voyage of the heart. It is a journey that ends in an evolutionary beginning, when man emerged from the rocks and waters. This was the kind of voyage Douglas admired in Doughty's *Arabia Deserta:* "It seems to me," wrote Douglas about Doughty in *Experiments,* "that a reader of a good travel-book is entitled not only to an exterior voyage, to descriptions of scenery and so forth, but to an interior, a sentimental or temperamental voyage, which takes place side by side with that outer one."

Douglas's insight about Doughty's book is valid: *Arabia Deserta* derives unity from a sense of destination, just as Homer's Odysseus moves through a series of episodic adventures, but always with the purposeful pull towards Ithaca and Penelope. To compare Doughty with Homer is perhaps irreverent; yet Doughty's artistic sensibility worked inevitably in a pattern of epic. After completing *Arabia Deserta,* Doughty spent many years writing a six-volume epic entitled *The Dawn in Britain:* it was Milton's discarded subject for the poem that was to become *Paradise Lost.* Doughty wrote his own version of man's fall: *Adam Cast Forth* serves to remind us that always in the back of his mind was the myth of Eden, whether it was to be found in the story of Adam, or the story of Bonduca, or the "story of Earth" in Arabia. The immense popularity of both Doughty and Hudson during the Edwardian years rests primarily upon the fact that every one of their books is built around the myth of Eden. For the story of the naturist travel book is, in fact, the story of a search for Eden. D. H. Lawrence, reviewing Tomlinson's *Gifts of Fortune,* expressed the prevailing dream of travellers from Doughty to Lawrence himself: "We travel, perhaps, with a secret and absurd hope of setting foot on the Hesperides, of running our boat up a little creek and landing in the Garden of Eden" (*Phoenix*).

For modern man the search for Eden must be a movement backwards from paradise lost; thus Hudson's *Idle Days* opens with an exclamation which might be that of a fallen Adam: "'We are lost,' I heard one say; and another answer, "Aye, lost for ever!'." It is a line that might well be found in a tale by Joseph Conrad; but where Conrad's heroes usually remain "lost for ever," Hudson's line is a prelude to the story of paradise regained. Hudson's is the story of Lazarus rising from his sepulchre, not by means of the healing words of Christ, but by means of "Nature's voices":

> And we ourselves are the living sepulchres of a dead past . . . its old bones are slumbering in us dead, and yet not dead nor deaf to Nature's voices; the noisy burn, the roar of the waterfall, and the thunder of long waves on the shore, and the sound of rain and the whispering winds in the multitudinous leaves, bring it a memory of the ancient time; and the bones rejoice and dance in their sepulchre.

Hudson's *recherche du temps perdu* necessarily involves the image of Eden, and we are not surprised to find, in the depths of Patagonia, Eve's serpent of temptation. But there is a difference: where the snake of Eden is the cause of civilization, Hudson's anthropomorphized snake is its victim:

> Looking at a serpent of this kind, and I have looked at many a one, the fancy is born in me that I am regarding what was once a fellow-being, perhaps one of those cruel desperate wretches I have encountered on the outskirts of civilization, who for his crimes has been changed into the serpent form, and cursed with immortality.

This serpent-vision of Hudson's will reappear in "Snake," a poem written by Hudson's avid reader, D. H. Lawrence. Both writers' empathy for the serpent signals the fact that the way back to Eden is the way of regression, "a revelation of an unfamiliar and unsuspected nature hidden under the nature we are conscious of," which Hudson attributes to "an instantaneous reversion to the primitive and wholly savage mental conditions." The paradise that has been lost is, for Hudson, the lost happiness of childhood animality: "The return to an instinctive or primitive state of mind is accompanied by this feeling of elation, which, in the very young, rises to an intense gladness, and sometimes makes them mad with joy, like animals newly escaped from captivity." Here is the same "mad carousal" which Hardy's Mrs. Yeobright saw in the "wild ephemerons"; and years later Hudson would create, in Rima, an incarnation of the dream of the child-animal of freedom.

Naturism was related to the broad *fin-de-siècle* aesthetic movement known as primitivism. Gauguin's return to Tahiti in 1895 symbolized the primitivist impulse: seeking to escape the rationalism and dogmatism of his own culture, Gauguin discovered among the Tahitian natives a quality akin to the innocence of childhood. Hudson and Tomlinson located a similar aboriginal Eden in the jungle country of South America. It seemed indeed that Jean-Jacques Rousseau's ideal of "the noble savage" had come alive historically. The naturist movement is synchronous with the high-point of primitivism among painters from Gauguin and Henri Rousseau to the "Negro" periods of Vlaminck and Picasso.

Most of the naturists had read or been affected by Sir James Frazer's monumental and pioneering study of primitive societies, *The Golden Bough,* the first volume of which appeared in 1890, the last in 1915. Although Frazer himself was hardly free of imperial patronism toward "lesser breeds without the law," his treatise was part of a general reappraisal of "barbarian" cultures, and raised the question whether within the symbolic life of such cultures might be hidden a wisdom which the European white man had lost. Artists benefited immensely from the rapid growth of cultural anthropology—one of several new fields of social study based on Darwinism—for it suggested new subjects and new artistic styles. Most of the major painters and sculptors of the period—Gauguin, Rousseau, Van Gogh, Toulouse-Lautrec, Degas, Matisse, Vlaminck, Brancusi, Picasso—derived new shapes and colors from primitive artifacts and customs. *Ut pictura poesis:* the subject matter, the language, and the quality of description in naturist travel books and novels was, as we shall see, deeply indebted to the work of Frazer and his colleagues.

Naturism and primitivism alike reflected Darwin's (and anticipated Freud's) concern with the "unknown" within human nature in all places and times. But while there were primitivistic elements in naturism, the two movements were radically opposed in aesthetic practice. Where the primitivist typically seeks to reduce and distort nature into stylized abstract forms, the naturist prefers a realistic art of description; where the primi-

tivist painter contracts space into the two-dimensional surface of his canvas, the naturist writer (with few exceptions) prefers the old-fashioned perspective of Renaissance-inspired art. Primitivism leads directly from Cézanne towards cubism; but for the naturists, this primordial formalism constituted a rejection of the claims of nature in favor of totemism. In *Women in Love,* Loerke's primitivist bronze statue of a young girl on a horse provides a representative example of the naturist distaste for this aspect of primitivism. Gudrun exclaims: "*Look how stock and stupid and brutal it is. Horses are sensitive, quite delicate and sensitive, really.*" Loerke responds, after the manner of the moderns: "*. . . that horse is a certain form, part of a whole form . . . it is part of a work of art, it has no relation to anything outside that work of art.*" And Ursula then aptly summarizes the naturist objection to primitivism: "But why does he have this idea of a horse? I know it is his idea. I know it is a picture of himself, really—." Forms are ideas; ideas are pictures of ourselves. The naturist seeks simplicity, but recognizes that to simplify is not to reduce or to formalize; it is rather to catch, from the living organism, a glimpse of the possibility which Thoreau tried to make actual at Walden: "Let us spend one day as deliberately as nature."

Hudson's *Idle Days* moves, then, from the paradise lost of civilization to the regained life of nature. "Civilized life," for Hudson, "is one of continual repression," and the voyage to Patagonia is a movement toward "that feeling of relief, of escape, and absolute freedom which one experiences in a vast solitude, where man has perhaps never been, and has, at any rate, left no trace of his existence."

Tomlinson's *The Sea and the Jungle* follows the same pattern: the writer's eyes, even in the midst of the Amazonian jungle, are upon civilized England, which for him is symbolized in the image of a printed page: England is "a population of bundles of newspapers." Tomlinson's adventure begins, in fact, when he symbolically puts aside a book: "The waves were singing to themselves. A ray of light laughed in my eyes, playing hide and seek across the wisdom of my book. . . . I put the book down." In *Idle Days,* Hudson had written, "I had cast aside the unread newspaper"; and Tomlinson appropriates the image: "I put down the papers with their calls to social righteousness pitched in the upper register of the tea tray." Tomlinson's image recalls Butler's concluding sentence in *Alps and Sanctuaries:* "The science-ridden, art-ridden, culture-ridden, afternoon-tea-ridden cliffs of Old England rise upon the horizon." Tomlinson's opposition between tea-tray and "waves singing to themselves" is also the imagery of T. S. Eliot's Prufrock who, among the coffee spoons, hears "mermaids singing each to each." For Tomlinson, in 1912, they sing; for Prufrock, in 1916, they do not. Eliot's Prufrock might well be taken to mark the beginning of the end of the naturist dream of Eden. Even Lawrence would at long last agree that "the hope of running our boat up a little creek and landing in the Garden of Eden" was an impossible dream: "This hope is always defeated. There is no Garden of Eden, and the Hesperides never were. . . . There are no happy lands" (*Phoenix*).

Lawrence's recognition that there is no happy land does not alter the fact that he spent his life looking for it: his dream of Rananim, the colony he hoped to create with the Huxleys in Florida, remained a hope to the end. But Hudson and Tomlinson felt that they had found the "happy land" directly south of Rananim. Lawrence's remark serves to dramatize the vast difference between the naturists and their Christian humanist contemporaries, for whom Original Sin had destroyed forever all happy lands this side of heavenly paradise.

This difference is clearly illustrated in the contrast between Tomlinson's *The Sea and the Jungle* and Joseph Conrad's "The Heart of Darkness." A comparison between the two stories seem inevitable. Both are romantic tales of a journey up a river; both are expressions of a final vision of human nature. Conrad's story is fiction. Tomlinson is not. Yet *The Sea and the Jungle*, both in its dramatic structure and its exotic mood, approaches the boundaries of romantic fiction. But where Marlowe's trip up the Congo is a voyage to "the dark places of the earth," Tomlinson's voyage up the Amazon is a journey toward light and life: "I felt instead that I could live and grow for ever in such a land." In both cases the journey is a regression, a backward movement in time; but as Genesis approaches, Tomlinson's fascination is with the beauties of the Garden, Conrad's is with the terrors of the Serpent. "Going up that river," wrote Conrad, "was like travelling back to the earliest beginnings of the world, when vegetation rioted on the earth and the big trees were kings. An empty stream, a great silence, an impenetrable forest." But where, for Conrad, "there was no joy in the brilliance of sunshine," a similar intensity of light helps Tomlinson to see "the earth as a great and shining sphere." Conrad comes to rest with the moment of Original Sin, while Tomlinson pauses at that pristine moment on the seventh day of rest and rejoicing, after the glories of nature had been freshly created: ". . . we looked upon what was there for the first time since Genesis, where we might have been in the hush of the seventh day. . . ."

Tomlinson's careful description of landscape functions as part of a fiercely moral sensibility; his landscape is hardly less a *paysage moralisé* than Conrad's. But Tomlinson's faith of a naturalist allows him to dwell longer upon landscape, while Conrad's purpose is to transform, cast a spell, invest his landscape with a voodoo magic. In both cases, the jungle is a source of new knowledge, in the spirit of Darwin's remark about Patagonia: "Who would not look at these last boundaries to man's knowledge with deep but ill-defined sensations?"

Both stories provide the reader with a voyage of self-discovery. "The Heart of Darkness" represents a descent into the unconscious life of Marlowe whereby the inner core of his selfhood is revealed as isolated and irrevocably guilty. *The Sea and the Jungle* is equally an exploration of the unconscious; but here the self is identified with earth and physical nature, drawing strength and psychic health from an "ill-defined" bodily communion with sea and jungle and animal life. If Conrad's is a journey into exile, Tomlinson's is a voyage home.

Tomlinson's excursion into the regions of the unconscious involves the same lapse from rationality experienced by Darwin and Hudson. The process begins for Tomlinson as he watches the azure of sky and sea: "You feel your careless gaze snatched in the revolving hues speeding astern, and your consciousness is instantly unwound from your spinning brain, and you are left standing on the ship, an empty spool." But this experience of the sea is merely preparatory to the experience of the jungle, which has a mind of its own: "It regards us with the vacancy of large composure, with a lofty watchfulness which has no need to show its mind. I think it knows our fears of its domain. It knows the secret of our fate. It makes no sign." The primeval silence of the jungle prepares, in turn, for the stylized tableau—so like the Tahitian primitives of Gauguin—of the native women and children "negligent on the grass, sunning themselves." They are described in terms of sunlight and animality; their movements are slow, or arrested, as if their bodies were free from the tyrannical pressures of mind and will: "They were

as unconscious of their grace as animals. They looked round and up at us, and one stayed her hand, her comb half through the length of her hair. . . ."

Tomlinson's progress to this final vision of bodily integrity has been carefully prepared for. The trip across the sea was a process of unwinding the mind from the body; sensuous impressions of sea and sky have already won a victory over Tomlinson's brain. But the mind fights back; Tomlinson strains to fathom the meaning of the azure, and at last concludes that no meaning seems to be there: ". . . I can report no luck from my concentrated efforts on that symbol. The colour may have been its own reward."

Color is of primary importance to the naturist travel book. Hudson is an especially vivid colorist; and D. H. Lawrence—especially in *Women in Love*—further refines the color symbolism which is apparent throughout Hudson's writing. Hudson's landscape is itself a source of light, rather than a reflection of it. His plants and animals seem to burn with an intrinsic fire of vitality which is invariably portrayed in vivid primary hues. He notices, for example, "fully ripe cherries glowing like live coals amid the deep green foliage" (*Idle Days*). This same foliage becomes the presiding spirit and the "principal personage" of Hudson's novel, *Green Mansions*.

The naturists move from the muted twilight greys and siennas of Egdon Heath into the bright morning light—the crimsons, yellows and greens—of southern and tropical lands. Hudson is quite conscious of his use of color; his clearest exposition of his color symbolism occurs midway in *Idle Days*, where he pauses to meditate on the passage in *Moby Dick* where Melville discusses "whiteness" and its effect on the mind. Like Melville, Hudson is taken with the "mystique" of whiteness: the fear it inspires in humans, the sense of primitive magic in the lack of color. But he rejects Melville's "supernatural" explanation and substitutes his own theory of "animism," "the mind's projection of itself into nature."

In Hudson's work, this projection is never white; it is always prismatic, rainbow-colored. Hudson provides, both in theory and in practice, an interesting parallel to the school of French impressionists who are flourishing at the time of *Idle Days* (1893). Hudson is part of a broad movement in the arts to break away from nineteenth-century restraint in matters of color; and behind his continual use of a bright palette is a conscious and deliberate symbolism. One of the heavy costs of civilization, Hudson asserts, is our loss of visual power: we look, but we do not see. In a chapter of *Idle Days* entitled "Sight in Savages" (XI), he discusses this loss, and insists that "savages are our superiors in visual power." More specifically, our "defective color-sense is due to the inimical conditions of our civilization." The following chapter, "Concerning Eyes," is a discussion of this blurred color-sense in modern times. Hudson's landscapes are always bright; his eye falls immediately upon the most highly lighted parts of his picture. He sees, for example, a "magnetism" in a sunlit river, which has "the powerful effect of brightness, which fascinates us, as it does the moth, and the eye is drawn to it as to a path of shining silver." The moth analogy is characteristic: Hudson instinctively strives to ennoble human nature by means of a bird or insect simile, in the spirit of Hardy.

It follows that Hudson is fascinated by rainbows: he finds himself wondering why "the Incas were the only worshippers of the rainbow." For him it is the symbol of rejuvenation, of an "inward resurrection," for it possesses "a beauty that is not of the earth,'' a beauty that is transfigured. Hudson's symbol is appropriated by another worshipper who makes those same sunlit colors, ''arching in the blood,'' the culminating image of his most ambitious novel. Hudson's fellow-worshipper is D. H. Lawrence; the novel, *The Rainbow.*

But Hudson's most searching experiments in symbolism are attempts to transcend the limits of human vision. The key to this search is his assertion that ''sight, the most important of our senses, is the most intellectual.'' The word ''intellectual'' for Hudson denotes a limitation as well as an excellence; and he looks to the qualities of touch, sound, and odor to convey a dimension of experience impenetrable to the eye alone. *Idle Days* ends with a chapter called ''The Perfume of an Evening Primrose''; as Hudson writes the chapter, he holds a pen in one hand, a primrose in the other. His primrose, like Proust's madeleine soaked in tea, evokes ''many scenes and events of the past.'' Yet the smell of the primrose has the effect for Hudson, as for Proust, of annihilating the past, of destroying time, by incorporating it in a glowing present: ''I am no longer in an English garden recalling and consciously thinking about the vanished past, but during that brief moment time and space seem annihilated and the past is now.'' Hudson's visionary moment with primrose and bird-song is not unlike the imagery T. S. Eliot will later use in his *Four Quartets:* the rose and lotus will replace Hudson's primrose; Eliot's bird, like Hudson's, will speak—''Go, go, go, said the bird''—and Eliot's past and future, like Hudson's, will ''point to one end, which is always present.''

Hudson's experience with the primrose leads him to a long passage of speculation upon the difference between the olfactory and the visual in human experience; he wonders about the fact that the visual can be recalled, and thus can attain a permanence in the memory, but fragrance is transitory and evanescent, and all the more beautiful for being so. It is precisely this transitory intensity which D. H. Lawrence seeks continually to evoke until, at the end of his life, the Bavarian gentian represents a final unity of life and death in the moment, and final vision of the living beauty of darkness itself.

Hudson's search for a non-visual symbolism led him, as an ornithologist, inevitably to what he calls ''bird-music.'' In fact his only recorded complaint against Charles Darwin was that the great scientist wrote so little on the subject of bird-song (*Idle Days*). For Hudson, the attraction of bird-song is that ''there is no suggestion of human feeling in it.'' It is a language unto itself, and cannot be represented in human words: ''Bird music, and, indeed, bird sounds generally, are seldom describable.'' This attempt to describe the undescribable, to employ language to evoke a meaningful pattern of sounds, is a characteristic preoccupation of naturist writers. Hudson's attempt to find in bird-song a symbol of the wisdom of nature—which culminates in the character of Rima, in *Green Mansions*—is a key link between Hardy's ''language of nature'' and Lawrence's continual search for a non-verbal and non-visual musical symbolism. For Lawrence will share Hudson's ornithological impression of man's genesis in Eden: ''In the beginning,'' Lawrence will write in *Etruscan Places,* ''was not a Word, but a chirrup.''

The chirrup which resounds from the pages of *Idle Days* and becomes the crucial experience for Abel in *Green Mansions* may be taken as a symbol of the continuity between the travel book and the naturist novel. This continuity extends beyond questions of theme to matters of narrative style, descriptive technique, characterization, and story structure. In these travel books, spirit of place provides a platform and a perspective from which a narrator can look from the outside toward modern England and, by extension, toward modern civilization. These writers, following Hardy, have developed a kind of landscape description which itself contains an implicit critique of civilized society. This critical mood reflects a new historical sophistication and a revived interest in comparative studies of culture: Nietzsche's insight into Greek civilization, Burckhardt's revolutionary study of the Italian Renaissance, and Frazer's compilation of primitive myths have prepared the way for *Idle Days, Old Calabria, The Sea and the Jungle,* and *Etruscan Places.*

This abandonment to spirit of place is essentially a literary means of probing into non-conceptual and instinctive areas of human experience. The loose structure of the travel book itself expresses the naturist revolt against the tyranny of concepts. The plot of the travel book is a sequence of impressions, often rationally unconnected. This revolt against the machine of deterministic cause-and-effect is symbolized by a rejection of clock time and an abandonment to the accidents of the present moment, the here and now. Thus the unbuttoned mood of *Alps and Sanctuaries* leads directly to the relaxed dilettantism of the last half of *The Way of All Flesh;* Douglas's pleasant days in Cosenza, ''doing nothing whatever,'' prefigure *South Wind;* the impassioned geographical pursuit of the earth-life in *Sea and Sardinia* and *Etruscan Places* becomes a principle of story structure in *Aaron's Rod* and *Kangaroo.*

Idle Days and *The Sea and the Jungle* are constructed around a core of personal conversion: they build to and from moments of revelation. *Alps and Sanctuaries, Old Calabria,* and *Sea and Sardinia* are episodic, constructed around a series of momentary perceptions without any formal unity except the accidental unity of the journey itself. These moments of conversion become, in the naturist travel novel, the turning point of the plot: *South Wind* centers upon Bishop Heard's striking conversion to amorality as he accidentally witnesses a murder; *Where Angels Fear to Tread* is built around Lilia's romantic conversion in Monteriano; *The Lost Girl* rises to the moment when Alvina Houghton undergoes a spiritual rejuvenation in a desolate ''Place Called Califano''; *Green Mansions* builds slowly to Abel's revelatory vision of Rima.

Lawrence's travels have a profound effect upon the structure of his stories: after he begins his personal pilgrimage in 1915, his novels take on the *leitmotif* of place which characterizes *Women in Love, Aaron's Rod, Kangaroo,* and *The Plumed Serpent.* Aaron's journeys, for example, closely correspond to the movements of the first-person narrator in *Etruscan Places.*

These travelogues have provided an apprenticeship in landscape description; have created a new point of view identified with the genius of place; have brought to the novel a tradition of escape from mechanized time and industrialized place; have introduced a modern, Darwinian version of the myth of Eden. Lawrence gave the rallying cry for all naturist novelists, in his travelogue *Sea and Sardinia:* ''Comes over one an absolute necessity to move. And what is more, to move in some particular direction. A double necessity, then: to get on the move, and to know whither.'' The plot and the setting of the naturist novel was born out of the travel book. (pp. 43-59)

John Alcorn, ''Spirit of Place: The Travel Book,'' in his The Nature Novel from Hardy to Lawrence, *Columbia University Press, 1977, pp. 42-59.*

MORTON DAUWEN ZABEL

[*Zabel was an American poet, critic, and prominent scholar. From 1928 to 1937 he was associate editor, then editor, of Harriet Monroe's magazine* Poetry, *which was the only journal at that time devoted solely to contemporary poetry. Throughout this period he wrote extensively on English and American poetry. Later in his career, Zabel was influential in increasing the study of North American literature in South America. During the mid-1940s he held the only official professorship on North American literature in Latin America, and wrote two widely used American literary studies in Portuguese and Spanish. In the following excerpt, Zabel discusses Henry James's concern in both his fiction and his nonfiction writings with the "international subject" of travel and expatriation.*]

[Henry James] has been studied as an American, as a European, and as a man who could never successfully be either; as an aesthete, a social historian, a psychologist, and a religious allegorist; as the realist he claimed to be and as the idealist or abstract thinker he repudiated being; as a systematic moral critic and as a poet of metaphysical vision. If it is only the most dedicated who will follow him into the remote and perilous "country of the blue" of his ultimate values, there are less strenuous ways of gaining access to his work and discovering in it the clues to the history and character of the man who created it.

There has always been one clue particularly, one means of intimacy with James's mind and character, that few of his readers have ever missed or failed to respond to. It shows itself so pervasively in his pages, becomes so much the radical imagery and music of his fiction, that it has probably given most of his readers their clearest impression of what he represents in the art of the novel. A novelist as much as a poet is likely to be disguised by a characteristic vein of imagery. If he is the conscious artist James was, his imagery will run deep in his work—will persist, ramify, and enrich itself from book to book, and so become a key to his mind and to the revelation it seeks to impart. Only quotation can suggest it adequately, and since to quote is to be tempted to anthologize, quotation here must be brief.

> The early Roman spring had filled the air with bloom and perfume, and the rugged surface of the Palatine was muffled with tender verdure. . . . It seemed to him he had never known Rome so lovely as just then. He looked off at the enchanting harmony of line and colour that remotely encircles the city—he inhaled the softly humid odours and felt the freshness of the year and the antiquity of the place reaffirm themselves in deep interfusion. . . .

Thus an early visitor in Rome. Here is a later one:

> I may not attempt to report in its fulness our young woman's response to the deep appeal of Rome, to analyse her feelings as she trod the pavement of the Forum or to number her pulsations as she crossed the threshold of Saint Peter's. It is enough to say that her impression was such as might have been expected of a person of her freshness and her eagerness. She had always been fond of history, and here was history in the stones of the street and the atoms of the sunshine. She had an imagination that kindled at the mention of great deeds, and wherever she turned some great deed had been acted. . . . The sense of the terrible human past was heavy to her, but that of something altogether contemporary would suddenly give it wings that it could wave in the blue. . . . The herd of re-echoing tourists had departed and most of the solemn places had relapsed into solemnity. The

sky was a blaze of blue, and the plash of the fountains in their mossy niches had lost its chill and doubled its music. . . .

(pp. 3-4)

Where some novelists find their material and imagery in a given locality or fixed orbit of experience, others are impelled abroad to find the theater their imagination requires. James is classic in their company. Whatever else his work shows him to be—and it shows much—he is an artist and poet of travel. He became so by the requirements of his imagination, but he also became so by the special conditions and circumstances of his life—his origins, his nationality, his sense of history, and the moment of modern history he was given to record.

Travel was not the first condition of James's existence but it has a clear claim to having been the second. The popular legend of his career has for eighty years set him down as the classic example of the exile, expatriate, and voluntary fugitive of American literature; and of course his remains a pre-eminent case of the writer who finds his destiny and fulfills himself as an artist in foreign parts. But it is still necessary to take first things first in James's life, for without the fact of his origins and point of departure neither his travels, his expatriation, nor the art he made of them can be seen in their actual perspective and significance. The first condition of his career was his birth, as the second son of Henry James, Senior, and his wife, Mary Robertson Walsh, on Washington Place in New York City on April 15, 1843, and his thereby becoming enlisted at a stroke in a dual nationality—a citizen of the American republic and as what his brother William was to call his real nationality, "a native of the James family." That birth, with its double allegiance and division of loyalty, can be taken as basic to everything James was by origin, became by heredity and temperament, and remained by instinctive commitment to the end of his life. But the second portent of his history was soon to declare itself, and like the first it befell him, as he liked to say, "antecedent to choice." Six months had hardly elapsed before he was transported by his parents, an infant in arms, from the United States to Europe on the first of the journeys that were to become the habit and recurring feature of almost seventy years. He was initiated into travel before he was a year old.

The modern taste for finding symbolism at work in the lives of artists as much as in the products of their imagination need feel no scruple in reading into these two primary facts of James's career the clues to his destiny and vocation. It can be taken as no chance accident but as an ordained event that the elder Jameses delayed their voyage to France and England long enough for him to be born in America. It can be taken as an equal signal of his fate that he first crossed the Atlantic while he was still unconscious of the momentous displacement that interrupted the normal course of his American babyhood. Not wholly unconscious, however. It was to be James's boast seventy years later, when he came to write the account of his childhood in *A Small Boy and Others*, that the earliest "vibration of [his] very most infantine sensibility" which he could recall from his faraway infancy was the memory of having seen in Paris "as a baby in long clothes"—"while I waggled my small feet, as I definitely remember doing, under my flowing robe"—the "view, framed by the clear window of the vehicle as we passed, of a great stately square surrounded with high-roofed houses and having in its center a tall and glorious column," and thus of having "taken in, for all my time, the admirable aspect of the Place and the Colonne Vendôme." This precocious feat of observation, a "marvel" in after-years to his family and to himself a matter of boyish pride, was never forgotten as the first hint he caught of his destiny—a "mystic gage" of what the future held in store for him.

The signal was soon to be repeated. After returning with his family to America at the age of three, he was taken back to Europe at twelve, in 1855, for three years of schooling in Switzerland, England, and France with his brothers and sister, and for his first avid explorations of the foreign world that now opened itself to his curiosity in Geneva, London, Paris, and Boulogne-sur-Mer. He returned to New York and Newport in 1858, but another fifteen months found him back in Europe for a third time. His third homecoming fell in 1860; and for nine years New York, Newport, Cambridge, a short term at the Harvard Law School, and the deeply stirring experience of the Civil War stamped his American birthright on his mind and impelled him, by successive stages, into the career in letters he chose for himself. By the time he was ready to make his first adult journey to Europe in 1869, James approached her shores as a practiced traveler, already a seasoned cosmopolite of two continents.

The design of his future life had by that time assumed another dimension. The first story he succeeded in getting published, "A Tragedy of Error," in 1864, was a tale with a European setting, as his second, "The Story of a Year" in 1865, was, in appropriate antithesis, a tale of America and its Civil War. Other tales soon followed, with American themes alternating with dramas of Europe or European travel, some of them so elaborately equipped with scenic or touristic description— "Traveling Companions," "At Isella," "The Madonna of the Future"—as to give an impression of being travelogues with a story attached. When James was ready to publish his first book of fiction in 1875 its title announced one of the key phrases of his lifework, *A Passionate Pilgrim.* So did his second, *Transatlantic Sketches,* in the same year, with its account of his own pilgrimages, undisguisedly passionate in their emotion of homage and discovery in spite of the fact that they constituted not his first advent in Europe but his fourth and fifth, among the scenes and shrines of England, Switzerland, Holland, Belgium, Germany, and Italy.

When James's first long novel appeared in 1876 it was *Roderick Hudson,* the story of another passionate pilgrimage to Europe. Still another appeared in his next one, *The American,* in 1877. And both of them, like a dozen of the early tales, offered heroes who combined in their characters and fortunes two of the classic American types of the age, his own passionate pilgrim and the "innocent abroad" which another American of the time immortalized. When James was ready to publish his first book of essays in 1878 it was *French Poets and Novelists,* an account of what he had learned in the literary and aesthetic schools of Paris. His shorter tales up to this time had been roughly divided between American and European themes, but the two that won him his first popular success, *Daisy Miller* and *An International Episode* in 1878-79, were again tales of Americans—innocents or pilgrims—in Europe, and both their titles gave catchwords to the language of their day. *Confidence* in 1880 once more pictured the American abroad. So did *The Portrait of a Lady* in 1881, the theme now deepening into moral conflict and tragedy. *The Europeans* in 1878 had reversed the subject: it brought Europeans to America. It was not until *Washington Square* in 1880 that James applied his full strength (leaving aside the slighter effort of *Watch and Ward* ten years earlier) to the American scene and drama that were to engage him as a counter-subject intermittently in the

future. The central theme of his life-work, the "international subject," had defined itself as the special demesne and incentive of his imagination. He had established the basis and design of the huge creation that lay ahead. And that work was to include six further volumes and a continuous flow of essays on his travels.

James's account with travel was never to be closed. It appears, still a question for moral debate and inquisition, in the two novels he left unfinished at his death in 1916. He is notable among novelists in a number of the salient traits of his genius— in, among others, his union of the imaginative and the critical faculties in everything he wrote. But he is particularly marked among modern writers by the use to which he put the call and experience of travel. Marked, yet far from unique. Travel, displacement, quest, and exploration have become so pervasive in the literature of the modern age of restlessness and mobility, have so widely reasserted themselves in their ancient function as incentives to the personal and moral imagination, as to have become radical impulses in a host of writers. The novel of displacement has become a major genre in a century of unrest and dislocation. The opposite tradition will presumably always exist—the regionalists, local-colorists, and historians of a concentrated microcosm of human life, with Jane Austen, Balzac, Dickens, Manzoni, and Hardy among their masters. But those who have ranged abroad for their drama have come almost to outnumber them—Stendhal, Goethe, and Turgenev leading a procession that includes most of the nineteenth century Americans, from Irving, Cooper, and Melville to Howells, Fuller, Stephen Crane, and Edith Wharton; twentieth century writers of every rank and nationality—Gide, Malraux, Saint-Exupéry, and Camus; Mann and Kafka; Conrad, Lawrence, Forster, Greene, and Waugh; and again a troop of Americans: Fitzgerald, Lewis, Wolfe, Miller, Porter, Hemingway. But if James is far from alone or singular in his practice of the genre, he probably did more than anyone else to define and establish it, to make its claim and status recognized.

The point to be emphasized is that it was not from his personal experience alone that he took his incentive. It was from the age, moment, and situation in which he was born and lived, the pulse of one of whose radical necessities he felt with the accuracy of a diagnostician. Travel is not in his work a marginal matter of romantic atmosphere, arbitrary impulse, or escapist appeal. It is a cognate of the moral and historical drama to which he addressed himself; of the conflict of culture he saw as basic to his century; of the "complex fate" which he discovered "being an American," but being no less a man of full modern sensibility and responsible intelligence, imposed on him. (pp. 8-13)

He was, as we now look back on it across a century, enviably privileged in his opportunity. All the conditions of his liberal parentage, family circumstances, native temperament, as well as his age and nationality, joined to make him so. He was possessed as much as his father was by the "subjective passion" that endowed every action he took part in, every sight he beheld, with an incentive "largely educative," an emotion "supremely determinant." Even as a boy he saw his parents "homesick" for "the ancient order, and distressed and inconvenienced by many of the more immediate features of the modern, as the modern pressed about us, and since," as he said, "their theory of our better living was from an early time that we should renew the question of the ancient on the very first possibility I simply grew greater in the faith that somehow to manage that would constitute success in life." The "nostalgic cup,'' he recognized, had ''been applied to my lips before I was conscious of it''; and though he was later to call its potion a ''poison'' that ''had entered my veins,'' he drank from it without fear or foreboding. ''The sense of change'' had from the beginning rested ''with a most warm and comfortable weight on my soul.'' He knew from his earliest years that he had ''taken over, under suggestion and with singular infant promptitude, a particular throbbing consciousness'' of what travel and the past were to mean to him, and of ''the source at which it could best be refreshed''—a consciousness of ''certain impressions, certain *sources* of impression again, proceeding from over the sea and situated beyond it.'' The ''mild forces'' that had shaped his youth and temperament had done one thing for which he never ceased to be grateful. They had succeeded in ''pushing the door to Europe definitely open,'' and even as a youth he hoped it would never be closed to his access and exploration. It never was.

Moreover, the time and place of his birth were as propitious for his opportunity as the family into which he was born. James was an American in an age when it was one of the recognized duties of every cultivated American to recover and examine, weigh and estimate, his legacy of breed, culture, and tradition in the Old World. The impulse that had impelled Englishmen or Europeans of James's century—Goethe, Byron, Stendhal, Heine, Gautier—toward the classic lands of southern Europe in their search for a spiritual ancestry or inheritance became, among Americans of the nineteenth century, an even more urgent and comprehensive ambition. The past meant not only Italy and Greece. It meant England, France, Germany, Italy, Spain—every country that had fathered, sponsored, or initiated, in the discovery and settlement of America, the greatest human venture of modern times. The problem of defining the point at which America had arrived in her venture of nationhood—of determining her debt, responsibility, and relationship to the parent and rival civilizations of Europe—was one to which every serious American writer felt in one degree or another obligated to address himself. When James later said of himself that his problem ''was implied in every question I asked, every answer I got, and every plan I formed,'' he was speaking for almost every inquisitive member of his generation and for most of the major American writers of his time.

If it was not yet the moment for searching out a ''usable past'' in America itself, it was decidedly the moment for seeking such a past in the older world. Virtually every serious American writer of the age—Thoreau, Whitman, and Emily Dickinson are the obvious exceptions—was to make his journey overseas. The program of inquiry and assessment that had been initiated by Franklin, Adams, and Jefferson was continued under a variety of tenets—romantic, critical, skeptical, moralistic, inquisitive—by Irving, Cooper, and Poe, by Emerson, Hawthorne, Melville, Lowell, Mark Twain, Howells, and Henry Adams, and so by their followers in a new century: Henry B. Fuller, Stephen Crane, Edith Wharton, Willa Cather, Eliot, Pound, Lewis, Dos Passos, Fitzgerald—the list is a long one. But it was the nineteenth century traveler who had the advantage of a stronger compulsion, a more intimate personal need, and of a time when travel was still as much an opportunity for romantic education as for moral self-determination.

''The romance of travel'': James was to call it such when he retold this part of his life many years later in his memoirs. And as we now see it across the distance of a hundred years of reckless change and dislocation, it is the romance as much as the high-minded scruples of American travel in that age that gives cause for envy. Romantic travel was in its last great age. The tradition of the Grand Tour, though waning, was not yet spent. The cities and monuments of Europe still stood in their appointed places. Space had not yet been annihilated by engines, wires, wireless, and air flight. The sanctity of time and tradition still blessed the holy places of historical and aesthetic pilgrimage. Nations still lived in comparative friendship and mutual respect. Physically as much as spiritually, there still prevailed a sense of historical proportion in the conditions of the world, and in the relation of the New World to the Old. The traveler traced his steps slowly, methodically, and with a necessary deliberation of movement and intention. He was not yet hurtled across the ocean in a day or from one hemisphere to another in a night. His emotions and reflexes were not wrenched out of their normal habits and logic by scientific speed. History, except in minds like Rimbaud's, had not yet become ''foreshortened by violence.'' Whatever distortion of tradition or culture was in the making through machinery, industry, and commerce, the nations, cities, and shrines of the earth still respected the roles that had been assigned to them by long centuries of historic process and order. The conformities of standardization, the leveling destructiveness of scientific progress and warfare, were still biding their hour. It was, as James later called it, ''a moment of a golden age''—perhaps the last golden age the traveler will ever know.

When James wrote his biography of William Wetmore Story in 1903 he felt that that moment had already passed its zenith in his youth and slipped irrecoverably into the lost past. He opened the memoir by paying his tribute to the men of the earlier time who had prepared the way for his own generation—''the light skirmisher, the *éclaireurs*, who have gone before.'' He did so not only with a sense of his personal debt to them but with a sense of how much they did to preserve for their followers a feeling for the traditional continuities of European civilization which had already, when he himself began to travel, begun to disintegrate. ''Europe, for Americans, has, in a word, been *made* easy,'' he admitted. The ''old relation, social, personal, aesthetic, of the American world to the European'' had largely disappeared. The ''American initiation'' to the delights and lessons of travel had become darkened by ''a comparative historic twilight.'' ''The pure and precious time—the time of the early flowering—was the matter of a moment and lasted but while it could.''

It was the ''good faith'' of the old pilgrims that had supported them through the tribulations from which we are exempt, and their good faith thus becomes for us the constant key to their pleasure, or at least to their endurance.'' And while he argued that ''the dawn of the American consciousness of the complicated world it was so persistently to annex is the more touching the more primitive we make that consciousness,'' he was willing to admit that ''we must recognise that the latter can scarcely be interesting to us in proportion as we make it purely primitive.'' But he also felt that he had enjoyed an advantage soon to be lost to his successors when he touched the last moments of the romantic age of travel:

> I think of the American who started on his *Wanderjahre* after the Civil War quite as one of the moderns divided by a chasm from his progenitors and elder brothers, carried on the wave as they were not, and all supplied with introductions, photographs, travelers' tales, and other aids to knowingness. He has been, this child of enlightenment, very well in his way; but his way has not, on many sides, been equally well, save as we think of it all as the way of railroads and hotels.

Editorial cartoon that appeared at the time of Henry James's 1905 tour of the United States.

And, he concluded, "'a vanished society' is a label before which, wherever it be applied, the man of imagination must inevitably pause and muse":

> Do we know why it is we all ruefully, but quite instinctively, think of the persons grouped in such an air as having had, though they were not to know it, a better "time" than we? For we are surely conscious of that conviction, the source of which we perceive to be excess of our modern bliss. We have more things than they, but we have less and less room for them, either in our lives or in our minds; so that even if our taste is superior we have less the use of it, and thereby, to our loss, less enjoyment of our relations. The quality of these suffers more and more from the quantity, and it is in the quantity alone that we today make anything of a show. The theory would perfectly be workable that we have not time for friendships—any more, doubtless, than for enmities; luxuries, both, as to which time is essential. Friendships live on the possibility of contact, that contact which requires in some degree margin and space. We are planted at present so close that selection is smothered; contact we have indeed, but only in the general form which is cruel to the particular. That is logically the ground of our envy of other generations.

It is certainly the ground of our own envy of the nineteenth century traveler—of James himself, whose sense of shrunken zest and opportunity in his travels becomes almost incredible when we consider it in the light of the almost total disappearance of his kind of pleasure—the pleasure of "margin and space"—which has taken place during the forty years of progress, violence, and calamity since his death. What he defined when he wrote the above paragraph was an age he still had, whatever his regrets, the good fortune to share. The conditions for making travel a mode of civilized education were still available to him; he was still able to apply to his journeys the resources of his artist's intelligence.

Yet however much his age gave him that opportunity, his role as an American obliged him to be something more than a connoisseur of travel. The obligation of comparison, assessment, and judgment was as urgent in him as the prospect of delight. Europe might be a "threshold of expectation," a "scene for the reverential spirit," a world "immemorial, complex, accumulated." He could still approach it as a passionate pilgrim, an "heir of all the ages," a participator in "history as a still-felt past and a complacently personal future," in "society, manners, types, characters, possibilities and prodigies and mysteries of fifty sorts." He was free to discover that Europe meant "ever so many things at once, not only beauty and art and supreme design, but history and fame and power, the world in fine raised to the richest and noblest expression." But with whatever innocence or enthusiasm he approached the shrine, there worked in him another faculty, his "incurable critical impulse," which forced him both to identify himself with what he saw and to hold it under critical and moral scrutiny. To "criticise" meant by definition "to appreciate, to appropriate, to take intellectual possession, to establish in fine a relation with the criticised thing and make it one's own." That was what art of any kind meant to him. Which in turn leads us to ask what kind of artist of travel James was, what he made of his excursions at home or abroad, and what these count for in the sum of his achievement.

A distinction is needed at the outset, and one comes conveniently to hand. There is "the traveler who writes" and there is "the professional writer, the novelist, the critic, the poet, who travels." There are travelers "who will themselves into movement with a strategic purpose, which is partly professional, partly temperamental," and there are "the travelers impelled from within" [see essay above by V. S. Pritchett]. Both classes have been large, at times they overlap, and each has included famous chroniclers. The first begins with the ancient geographers and explorers, the scribes of conquistadors, discoverers, and empire builders; includes masters of adventure like Marco Polo, Hakluyt, Bernál Díaz, Fernão Mendes Pinto, and the historians of the *grandes peregrinaciones*; and continues down to Mungo Park, Livingstone, Darwin, Doughty, the men driven by later dreams of discovery, fervors of missionary zeal, schemes of conquest or scientific mastery, into the dark or waste lands of the earth, and whose successors are the specialists—biologists, anthropologists, and ethnologists—of the past hundred years. The second category shows an even longer descent and it has shaped a major department of modern literature—the legionary seekers and searchers of our own day.

Further distinctions follow. The traveler who writes either belongs to a primitive age or prefers an objective that is still primitive. The unknown exists for him either as *terra incognita* or as civilized ignorance. He is an explorer less in his own interests than in the interest of humanity at large. The unknown promises an extension of knowledge, new opportunities for conquest, trade, power, or moral influence, for the civilization of which he is the agent. The strange, the inaccessible, and the savage are his chosen territory: Asia, Africa, or America in their unconquered darkness, or regions of a later age still shrouded in primitive violence or unpenetrated mystery—Arabia, Amazonas, Antipodes, South Seas, the East, the Poles—the *Lawless Roads*, the *Enchafèd Flood*, *Journey without Maps*, *Journey to a War*, *Le Mystère bestial*, *L'Espace du Dedans*. "The modern educational journey is not the Grand Tour but the territories of the *Grand Débâcle*." Poets and novelists sometimes venture on it, but they take explorers and scientiests for their guides.

The writer who travels is less likely to choose virgin territory (though he may, like Melville, Conrad, Saint-Exupéry, or Michaux, make forays into it). He is not so much a discoverer as a rediscoverer. His values are as much those he brings with him as those he finds waiting for him. The profession or scientific traveler works under a great initial advantage. He profits by the unprejudiced truth of his material, the objective reality of the life he encounters. If he happens to have an artist's skill in reporting it, as Park, Doughty, and Parkman had, his expressive powers will be strengthened by the objective truth he deals with. Imaginative writers sometimes draw on that kind of strength also. But it is now his first business to create or impose. It is to observe and impart.

The writer who travels may enjoy greater advantages of access, transport, preparation, and comfort, but his task, whether as poet, novelist, or chronicler, is a much more complex one. He comes as a predisposed, purposive, and highly subjective sensibility, a prepared and sensitized instrument. He brings with him a complicated conditioning and a prepared insight, to which he must remain faithful. But he encounters phenomena of place and time, history and society, culture and achievement, and the values they embody, and he has to be faithful to these likewise. He travels under a double responsibility. He must bring into single focus two aspects of reality—his own truth and the truth of what he sees. He owes a duty to his phenomena but he also owes a duty to himself. It is not every writer, however gifted, who is capable of sustaining the dual honesty of the reporter and of the man of creative insight and imagination. (pp. 17-26)

When Henry James wrote his earlier travel essays he put himself in the middle ground where the journalist and the artist are expected to collaborate. Though already fully aware of which of these two roles he had dedicated himself to, he took on the office of the traveler who writes, and as such he sent his reports to the *Nation*, the *New York Tribune*, and the *Atlantic Monthly*. (It is significant that almost none of his travel writings were done for English periodicals. Though some enjoyed circulation among continental tourists in the Tauchnitz editions, until 1900 only one of his travel books, *Portraits of Places*, was published in England. He wrote about his travels expressly for Americans and only incidentally or until his last years for the English.) He made himself as efficient a journalist as it lay in his capacity to do. But he was never wholly comfortable in this role, least of all when journalism put pressure on his prose and required it to be simple or newsworthy. When he engaged to write Paris letters for the *New York Tribune* in the 1870's, he made his one effort to become a systematic reporter of public events and history, and to do his duty by French politics, social news, and theatrical events; it was not to be until many years later, when he made his first return journey in twenty-one years to the United States in 1904-05 and produced *The American Scene*, that he applied himself to anything resembling systematic critical or social observation. But when Whitelaw Reid, the editor of the *Tribune*, complained that his reports were not the lively topical article his readers wanted, James was quite willing to throw up the game.

James, in fact, was not prepared to treat history in motion, or, outside his fiction, life in action. How far he was from being an active sociologist or systematic reporter can be seen if one compares all but his last travel writings with some of the classics of systematic observation in the nineteenth century—Tocqueville's *La Démocratie en Amérique*, Taine's *Notes sur l'Angleterre*, or Livingstone's *Journals*, just as his distance from the efficient topical journalism of his time can be seen by any comparison of his essays with the flood of contemporary reporting and history that poured from the presses of his day, to a large share of which he at one time gave his attention as a reviewer. James preferred his history and subject matter fixed for scrutiny, composed for observation, arrested so far as possible in their moment of time for his study or diversion. In one or two of his English essays—"An English Easter," "London at Midsummer," both of 1877, and in a few paragraphs of his long London study of 1888—he touches briefly on the social undercurrent, the life of the working class and the poor, but any attempt at a serious portrayal of that life such as he undertook in writing *The Princess Casamassima* is soon skirted. When he found himself surrounded by the Roman carnival in 1873 ("A Roman Holiday"), he found it to be a distraction from his Roman preferences. ("I turned my back accordingly on the Corso and wandered away to the grass-grown quarters. . . . I have been keeping Carnival by strolling perversely along the silent circumference of Rome. . . . The place has passed so completely for the winter months into the hands of the barbarians that that estimable character the passionate pilgrim finds it constantly harder to keep his passion clear.") Arriving on another journey in Genoa ("Italy Revisited"), he saw the spectacle of toil and poverty in the palatial streets as a round intrusion on his pleasure:

> A traveler is very often disposed to ask himself whether it has been worth while to leave his home—whatever his home may have been—only to see new forms of human suffering, only to be reminded that toil and privation, hunger and sorrow and sordid effort, are the portion of the great majority of his fellow-men. To travel is, as it were, to go to the play, to attend a spectacle; and there is something heartless in stepping forth into the streets of a foreign town to feast upon novelty when the novelty consists simply of the slightly different costume in which hunger and labour present themselves.

France gave him a stronger challenge and a richer opportunity for social analysis: he made a fairly serious effort to provide it in his *Tribune* dispatches; but it was at a place like the Théâtre Français that he found French civilization best displayed: "a copious source of instruction as to French ideas, manners, and philosophy." Even when, thirty years later, he returned to the United States to observe the new energy at work in his native land, whatever the zest, astonishment, or fascination he applied to studying the teeming forces of the New World—the business, commerce, immigrant life, and headlong progress of New York and other cities—they were exercised under a kind of protest. "The huge American rattle of gold," the "'business' field," the "movement of a breathless civilization," the "whole play of wealth and energy and untutored liberty"—these, he confessed, offered "a line of research closed to me, alas, by my fatally uninitiated state." The push and thrust of the "ubiquitous American force," the stir of aggressive life, the turbulence of sheer animal energy, stimulated him to the most acute social observation he ever arrived at, and they helped to make *The American Scene* a masterpiece of its kind; but they were not the stimulus his own kind of vision most required or best could use. On certain occasions they served him importantly in his fictions; in his travels they confused his purpose and distracted his contemplation. The kind of book Taine and Engels wrote about England, or Tocqueville, Dickens, and the Trollopes about America, was beyond his capacity and outside his purpose. "Such failures of opportunity and of penetration, however, are but the daily bread of the visionary tourist," he admitted. He looked in another direction for his success.

A "visionary tourist"—it was by some such term that he habitually called himself: sometimes a "sentimental tourist," frequently a "seeker of aesthetic pleasure" or a "lover of the picturesque," often a "cosmopolite," most characteristically a "passionate pilgrim." He belongs in fact to a distinctly nineteenth century race of travelers. The race has largely disappeared today. If they survive they seek their subjects in places as remote from the harassed West as possible—Claudel in China, Freya Stark in Asia Minor, Isak Dinesen in Africa. Their high moment fell between the strain and danger of early exploration and the scientific inquiry or political engagement of our own age. Their century was the century of the *genius loci,* and their bibles were Murray, Baedeker, and the *Guide Joanne.* Goethe, Byron, Chateaubriand, Stendhal, and Browning were the heroes in whose wake a large class of lesser wanderers and seekers of the place spirit trailed—Clough with the *Amours de Voyage*; Gissing with a masterpiece, *By the Ionian Sea*; Symonds, Hearn, Howells, Loti, Vernon Lee; with Norman Douglas as one of the last of the line. (pp. 26-31)

When James presented himself as a devotee of "constituted beauty"; when he made it his business to discover "the classic quality of the French nature"; when he said that among England's abbeys and castles "you feast upon the pictorial, you inhale the historic"; when he asked with some uneasiness "How far should a lover of old cathedrals let his hands be tied by the sanctity of their traditions?"; when he felt in American resorts of pleasure "the absence of serious associations"; when he asserted that "the flower of art blooms only where the soil is deep" and that "it takes a great deal of beauty to produce a little literature"; when he began his elaborate evocation of the history and splendors of Venice by saying, "I write these lines with the full consciousness of having no information whatever to offer," and added that "I hold any writer sufficiently justified who is himself in love with his topic," he set himself down as a member of that company.

To steep himself in "the tone of time," to cultivate and nourish his "sense of the past," was his constant and ruling passion; and the one discomfort he seems to have felt in indulging it came from the fact that, as a tourist at least partially disabled by the romantic fallacy inseparable from the role of the spectator, he could not more completely identify himself with what he saw. "Our observation in any foreign land is extremely superficial," he more than once confessed; and the hero of one of his early stories, "Travelling Companions," beholding the "palpable, material sanctity" of a great Italian church, exclaims to his companion: "What a real pity that we are not Catholics; that that dazzling monument is not something more to us than a mere splendid show! What a different thing this visiting of churches would be for us, if we occasionally felt the prompting to fall on our knees. I begin to grow ashamed of this perpetual attitude of bald curiosity."

Curiosity, bald or furtive, successfully concealed or not, was nevertheless the first incentive of James's explorations, and he never discarded his native American passion or innocence sufficiently to disguise it. But the mind that directed it could never

let it remain curiosity and nothing more. Conscious as he admitted himself to be of "missed occasions and delays overdone," much as he could "regret that [he] might not, first or last, have gone farther, penetrated deeper, spoken oftener—closed, in short, more intimately with the great general subject," he was fully aware that "from the moment the principle of selection and expression, with a tourist, is not the delight of the eyes and the play of fancy, it should be an energy in every way much larger," and that "there is no happy mean . . . between the sense and the quest of the picture, and the surrender to it, and the sense and the quest of the constitution, the inner springs of the subject—springs and connections social, economic, historic."

> There are relations that soon get beyond all merely showy appearances of value for us. Their value becomes thus private and practical, and is represented by the process—the quieter, mostly, the better—of absorption and assimilation of what the relation has done for us.

Such value was bound to be a critical value for him: it was what his role as a traveling American and native of the James family required him to seek. It was as a traveling critic and observer preparing himself for a professional career in writing that he always felt himself obliged to justify his foreign sojourns and indulgences, both to his uneasy family back home and to his editors and readers in America. But rigorous critical application was never the whole duty of travel to him. Criticism might mean something better than systematic analysis and dissection. "To appreciate, to appropriate, to take intellectual possession," and to make the criticized thing "one's own," as well as "the quest of the constitution, the inner springs of the subject," were important. Without them he would have considered himself a spendthrift of time and opportunity and a failure in his task. But James emphasizes equally the necessity of "surrendering" to the picture before him, of making it his own in more than an energetic or possessive sense. He may have traveled as a critic but he also traveled as a seeking spirit and an artist in sensations, an explorer of "a world of reflection and emotion." When he undertook to write his sketches he might try his best to sit down to journalism; he invariably rose from authorship.

And it was more than sketches he made of his travels. He made tales and novels of them as well. Delightful, charming, amusing, and instructive as his essays are—for pure pleasure and grace of writing they have few equals in English—the greater value and profit of his explorings shows itself in his fiction. There his images of travel take on their deepest insight and resonance; there his experience in the landscape, cities, monuments, and history of Europe and America joins most profoundly with his sense of human fate and character, with the comedy and tragedy of life, and with the dramas of conflict, evil, or spiritual triumph he created from the age he witnessed and the wide international stage he took for his province. (pp. 32-5)

How essential to his experience James's travels were; how much they gave his genius its appropriate voice and opportunity; how necessary a part he made them of his achievement and of the moment of history that made the achievement possible—all this becomes apparent as soon as his character as an artist is realized and his work is experienced in its full meaning. All achievement in art, once its authority and truth are clear, takes on a retrospective logic. It is one of the functions of art to do so. We profit in our own lives by seeing the use to which a talent puts the opportunity that is given it, and every feature of that opportunity—good fortune or bad, privilege or privation, success or failure—counts in the sum.

James's opportunity was a rich one and he met it fully prepared. He came to it as an American, as a man of the nineteenth century, as a member of the James family; as a product of the "sensuous education" his father provided him and as a nature schooled from childhood in enthusiasm, curiosity, and a sense of the past. It was this equipment that he brought with him into his excursions at home and abroad; and, as we see what he made of it, it is impossible to think of his life or his work apart from the great scene in which they were tested and fulfilled. Dubious as he might sometimes feel about yielding to "the baleful spirit of the cosmopolite" or of "seeing many lands and feeling at home in none"; much as he might warn one friend of the "drawback" of "not having the homeliness and the inevitability and the happy limitation and the affluent poverty of a Country of your Own," or confess to another that "the mixture of Europe and America which you see in me has proved disastrous," there could have been for him, as there can be for his readers today, no question of the fitness to his character and purpose which he made of these conditions of his life. He was given a subject to record, a moment of history to dramatize, and a penetrating sense of past and present to express. For their faithful expression no other stage was possible than the international scene he chose as the theater of his imagination.

Nor was it possible for him, however widely he ranged through the scenes and nations that gave him the settings and characters of his drama, to disown the endowment of spirit and curiosity his origins had given him. This remained his point of vantage and departure in everything he wrote. It came of being born in 1843 in New York City, the son of his particular parents, a child of his century, and the heir not merely "of all the ages" but of what must always count as a greater advantage for a writer who puts his talent to the service of realism and justice— a specific, concrete, and imperative moment in time. There could be little risk of such a character losing itself abroad. There was only the severe task for that character of proving itself worthy of its opportunity as the chosen instrument of the moment, subject, and experience that were given it to record.

James was right in thinking of his as a "given" case. So is everyone's case, and failure or success are measured by the degree to which a man is able to prove the justice of it. Few men have exposed themselves more fully than James did to the tests of such an assignment, and few have confessed their exposure by a more complete exercise of consciousness and perception. He changed his skies. He did not and could not change the character or spirit he took with him. These remained the animus of his explorings of the world of his time, and the art by which he fulfilled them testifies as much to the truth of insight and imagination he carried into that world as to the truth of the revelation with which the world repaid him. His travel writings, with their acuteness of observation, integrity of interest, and brilliance of detail and expression, share with his writings on literature and art the resources of intelligence, sympathy, and imagination that produced the greater art of his fiction. They are part and substance of that art, and they are an indispensable share of James's gift to his inheritors. (pp. 46-8)

> *Morton Dauwen Zabel, in an introduction to* The Art of Travel *by Henry James, edited by Morton Dauwen Zabel, Doubleday & Company, Inc., 1958, pp. 1-48.*

MARY SUZANNE SCHRIBER

[*In the following excerpt, Schriber contends that American novelist Edith Wharton's travel literature may be interpreted as part of a process of self-discovery that Wharton went through in order to resolve personal conflicts.*]

Between 1907 and 1910, Edith Wharton came to a momentous decision. She chose to reverse the pattern of her life, to make France her home and America a place to visit. She had travelled so frequently in Europe between the ages of five and twenty-one that, according to the estimate of R. W. B. Lewis, she had lived a total of eight of her first twenty-one years abroad. After her marriage to Teddy Wharton in 1885, she made an annual pilgrimage to the continent. Having rented the Paris apartment of the George Vanderbilts on the Rue de Varenne in 1907 and 1908, and having spent the entire year of 1909 in Europe without returning at all to America, she determined to settle more or less permanently in the Faubourg. In early 1910 she did so, selling her New York apartment and leasing a flat in Paris. Although she had various reasons for her decision, precisely why or how she reached it by 1910 is not yet clearly understood.

Wharton herself attributed her expatriation to her husband's health. While Teddy Wharton required a climate more mild than that of New York, she longed for "the kind of human communion," she wrote in her autobiography, that aimless wanderings about the French and Italian Rivieras in search of warm weather for Teddy did not provide. Teddy's condition alone, however, does not account for her decision to live abroad permanently. She unquestionably loved the art, the architecture, the history, the entire texture of the past that Europe offered. Further, she was generally uneasy in America. She found that her Parisian friends—the Paul Bourgets, the Comtesse Robert de Fitz-James, the Comte d'Haussonville, Paul Hervieu, Henri de Régnier, the Marquis de Ségur and a host of others—were interested in her as a professional writer while her literary success, she wrote, "puzzled and embarrassed my old friends [in America] far more than it impressed them." Moreover, she fell in love with Morton Fullerton at this time. Having met him in 1907, she saw him at public gatherings in Paris during the first months of 1908, and had become intimate with him that spring. Although she began to see the complexities of Fullerton's life and relationships as early as 1909 and had terminated her liaison with him by 1910, her sexuality had been awakened, and with it she experienced "an upsurge of initiative," phenomena that often occur concurrently, as Cynthia Wolff points out. All of these factors, together with Wharton's increasing difficulties with her husband and American attitudes toward divorce, must have influenced her desire to have done with America. Though Percy Lubbock's observation—that Wharton came to Europe "by degrees and stages" rather than being propelled by a great decision—is partially true, it is also the case that several currents in her life converged between 1907 and 1910 to make expatriation deeply attractive to her.

Still, from another perspective, the timing of Wharton's decision was somewhat risky. It jeopardized a recently established but essential aspect of her identity: her self as a recognized, professional writer whose popularity and recognition were tied to American, not European, materials. *The House of Mirth* (1905) and *The Fruit of the Tree* (1907) had made her reputation as a critic of American society, and had won for her a popular success that she thoroughly enjoyed. Her decision to remove herself from the American scene, the source of her materials, was thus a serious professional, as well as personal, decision. In her autobiography, Wharton makes it unmistakably clear that writing was crucial to her; she reports that she discovered her soul, her vocation, her personality with the publication of her first volume of short stories in 1899. Further, she is equally clear about the importance of success to her; it was "recognition as a writer," she declares, that had "transformed" her life. While life in France apparently fostered rather than impeded her work (witness the publication of *Madame de Treymes* and *The Fruit of the Tree* in 1907 and *The Hermit and the Wild Woman and Other Stories* in 1908), expatriation might eventually—if not immediately—diminish that success and the sense of self associated with it. Yet nothing in the biographies of her nor in her autobiography suggests that Wharton took this serious risk into account. Perhaps she was so confident in her craft, at long last, and so preoccupied with personal matters—ranging from her affair with Fullerton to divorce from Teddy—that the potential professional cost did not surface in her mind. Perhaps her continued productivity made it seem highly unlikely to her that her creative powers, only recently recognized, could be threatened so soon.

Even if the professional consequences of her decision did not disturb her, Wharton's affair was on the wane by 1909, her marriage had been failing for a number of years, and—what's more—she had fallen in love with Europe long before 1910. Why did she make her decision at this particular time? I believe the answer lies in her travel writings and the process of self-discovery they initiated. When Wharton lists in her autobiography the "absorbing" work of the period before her permanent move to Paris, she includes a travel record of her early motor journeys entitled *A Motor-Flight Through France*. Published in 1908, *Motor-Flight* is a revision of a series of travel essays originally published in the *Atlantic Monthly* in 1906 and 1907. Having begun to dabble in travel writing as early as 1894, Wharton published in 1905 her first travel book, *Italian Backgrounds,* including an essay on Parma that had appeared in *Scribner's Magazine* in 1902. In short, Wharton had applied her considerable craft and reflective powers to the writing of European travel narratives during the very years she most certainly was considering her decision to live permanently in France, and she had in fact revised her French travel narrative shortly before actually making that decision. Her travel essays, as a consequence, provide a significant bridge between her experience of Europe and her decision to expatriate. They set in motion a sequence of writing followed by action that occurs on other occasions in her life: her design of The Mount in Lenox, Massachusetts, was preceded by *The Decoration of Houses* (1897); her horticultural expertise was accompanied by *Italian Villas and Their Gardens* (1904); and her divorce from Teddy Wharton in 1913 was foreshadowed by a number of short stories devoted to questions of marriage and divorce. Wharton seems to be a textbook case of writing as a process of discovery, and her travel essays make up a chapter of the text.

When submitted to the art of composition, a number of journeys and a melange of esthetic, cultural, and geographical exploits became an act of self-discovery in which Wharton identified the intensity of her engagement with Europe and the degree to which Europe stimulated, excited, and energized her. Far from being a kind of detritus thrown off to satisfy her publishers as painlessly as possible, her travel essays demonstrate the awareness of genre and devotion to craft that mark her fiction. Just as she had earlier ridden the crest of the popularity of the historical romance with *The Valley of Decision* (1902), so she wrote narratives of her Italian and French travels with her rhetorical situation in mind. Nineteenth-century American travellers from Cooper to Stowe to James to Story had religiously published accounts of their travels, making it essential for their successors not only to combat the banality that inevitably threatened books of European lore but also to satisfy the genre expectations of readers. Wharton was aware of this. Her travel narratives refer to Joanne and Baedeker and "the sight-seer's accepted 'curriculum,'" to "the stock phrase of the stock tourist" and the fear that the charm of a painting will be lost "when it has become a star in Baedeker." Working in a genre associated with the exploration of the unknown at a time when the horizon of the unknown in Europe was rapidly receding, she attempts to avoid banality by concentrating on relatively obscure places: a little church in Chauvigny, for example, as well as the romanesque mecca of Poitiers. Or she fastens on the significant detail or the background that other travel writers ignore: in a relief at Amiens, the bishop's dog rather than the bishop; in a bank of choirstalls at Poitiers, the winsome face of a lonely bat rather than the predictable faces of monks.

Wharton deployed the same selectivity and craft in the construction of her travel books that had served her so well in her fiction. Her travel books can reasonably be understood as a kind of fiction. As Charles Batten and William Spengemann have amply demonstrated in their studies of travel literature [*Pleasurable Instruction* (1978) and *The Adventurous Muse* (1977)], the equation between fact and travel writing is complex; the difference between fact and fiction in this most eclectic of genres would be difficult to fix if there were a reason to attempt it. The process by which Wharton composed her travel prose illustrates the relationship. Following her actual travels, she would gather her recollections of Europe and set them down in a narrative form. She would fabricate a narrator, introduce suspense, and generate drama through metaphors and personifications. After a passage of time, she would make further revisions. But this process is not different from the process of fictional storytelling that Wharton describes in her autobiography. There she recounts how some of her "novels happened to" her, "how each little volcanic island shot up from the unknown depth, or each coral-atoll slowly built itself." Sometimes, she claims, a fictional situation occurs to her first and "sometimes a single figure suddenly walks into my mind. If the situation takes the lead, I leave it lying about, as it were, in a quiet place, and wait till the characters creep stealthily up and wriggle themselves into it. All I seem to have done is to say, at the outset: 'This thing happened—but to whom?' Then I wait, holding my breath, and one by one the people appear and take possession of the case." These "people" come to Wharton with a destiny, but, she says, they "walk to it by ways unrevealed to me beforehand." Similarly, in her travel essays one sees that Europe is the "situation" that is left "lying about" for a number of years until "a single figure" walks into it and "takes possession of the case." But in these writings, that figure is not a "character" but an earlier Wharton, the one who between 1891 and 1905 travelled with various people, such as the Paul Bourgets and Henry James, to various places in Europe. She is a character much like those that populate other, more obviously fictional narratives. As such a figure, this other "Wharton" has a destiny, but her nature will unfold for her creator only in the process of self-discovery that writing can provide.

The travel narratives thus provided the means by which Wharton met an avatar in the character of her narrator, and this character—happily—turned out to be an inveterate and engaging storyteller. This other self transforms humdrum travel from one place to another into exciting adventures. Engrossed in her tales, she omits mention of anything as mundane as food and lodging, and turns such practical matters as one's means of transportation into accomplices in adventure. Her travels in France, for example, open with a hymn to "the motor-car," for it has, she claims "restored the romance of travel." She paces her telling to create anticipation and suspense. Instead of taking us directly to Orcival, for instance, she describes herself and her companions as going in search of "the *remote village* of Orcival," which turns out to be but one of a "*strange group* of Auvergnat churches." Building suspense, the narrator focuses on obstacles to be overcome; "misleading directions [are] plentifully bestowed" on the narrator and her companions and result in "endless doublings through narrow lonely glens." Finally and blessedly, they arrive: "Here it was *at last*—and our first glance told us how well worth the search we had made for it" (italics mine). This teller of tales gives over more of her narrative to happenings and reflections on the way than she gives to her destination, but the happy effect of this shift of focus is to convert a destination into an object of desire. The narrator's verb choices intensify the sense of adventure. The road to Rouen "flings" itself and "swept us on," the travellers "flashed" through villages and "fled" ever upward. Buildings and towns are cast as actors in the drama of travel. A building is "arrogant" and a castle that "insolently dominates" the Etrurian plain is "threatening" and "predatory." No Quixote encountering trees that turn into dragons or castles that house fair ladies, this thoroughly modern narrator projects life and personalities into towns that testify to the impact of Europe on her imagination.

Wharton's narrator conceives of her travels as more than mere adventure, however. She lifts her experience of Europe beyond the ordinary, converting her travels into a sacred quest that anticipates travel books of the Twenties and Thirties. She invests her travels with the air of a pilgrimage requiring "faith" but promising "the pilgrim" the reward of "fortune." Like other pilgrims who set out on spiritual quests, she must make certain sacrifices. "Yearning" to climb the Puy de Dôme, the narrator decides that "renunciation" is necessary. Long runs in the motor-car demand "the sacrifice of much that charms and arrests one. . . . We suffered, I remember, many pangs by the way." Yet to bypass any sites or shrines borders on sin, for the narrator and her companions think "remorsefully" of the "wonders we had missed." These travellers are surely in search of the Grail and must suffer a serial ordeal if they are to win salvation. Thus, as they pass along the Loire on a "morning's flight across country to Orléans," they are beset: "Boreas was up with all his pack, and hunted us savagely across the naked plain, now behind, now on our quarter, now dashing ahead to lie in ambush behind a huddled village, and leap on us as we rounded its last house." Or again, this time in search of Cerveno, the travellers drive "in a light country carriole up the stony mulepath, between vines and orchards, till the track grew too rough for wheels; then we continued the ascent on foot."

Obstacles, adventure, trials, the quest for the Grail—the character who narrates Wharton's travels enlists all of these as metaphors associated with the ultimate pilgrimage, life itself. "Every wanderer through the world," she rather sententiously declaims, "has these pious pilgrimages to perform." Her metaphors turn the discovery and assimilation of Europe into a religious imperative. The adventure is a "call," an invitation to the development and exercise of her God-given talents in order to be perfect, fulfilled, redeemed. The narrator goes so far as to cast herself as the woman in Luke 8:43 who touches the fringe of Christ's cloak and is cured of a hemorrhage. For

Wharton's woman, however, a place such as Milan replaces the Savior, and the unredeemed pilgrim who follows certain wanderings through Milan has but to touch "the hem of her garment." The art, architecture, and history of Europe, in other words, offer salvation, a promise of life to the avatar of Wharton created in her travel narratives.

The metaphors of pilgrimage, vocation, salvation, and quest draw into their system another feature of the narrative, the occasional interjection of dialogue that brings irresistibly to mind, in the context of these metaphors, miracle plays staged outside the medieval piles such as Vezelay and Poitiers. Describing the square of Splügen, the narrator notes its "absurd resemblance to a stage-setting." As "figures pass and repass in a kind of social silence, they suggest the leisurely opening of some play composed before the unities were abolished, and peopled by types with generic names—the Innkeeper, the Postmistress, the Syndic—some comedy of Goldoni's, perhaps, but void even of Goldoni's simple malice." Wharton's narrator introduces dialogue into her rendition of a visit to the chateau of George Sand, thereby heightening significantly the drama of a visit to a sister artist of especial importance to Wharton. "Is one permitted to visit the house of George Sand?" "*Le château de George Sand?*" (A pause of reflection. "*C'est l'écrivain, n'est-ce pas?*" ["That is the writer, correct?"] (Another pause.) "*C'est à Nohant, le château? Mais, Madame, je ne saurais vous le dire*" ["The chateau is in Nohant? But, Madam, I would not have known to tell you that"]. In these small dramas within the larger drama of European adventures, the miraculous sacred object is Europe, the sought-after cure is the discovery of an identity, a history, in the sense of the past that Europe offers.

The narrator who journeys through Wharton's travel books is an enormously learned pilgrim who displays a formidable knowledge of political, literary, and art history. She understands Correggio in relation to Zucchero and the town of La Châtre in the light of the novels of George Sand. In creating and speaking through her narrator, Wharton must have assumed an audience steeped not only in travel books about Europe and acquainted with the predictable European shrines, but highly educated in literature and art as well. Even beyond assumptions about her audience, however, Wharton allows her narrator to layer her adventures with so many learned allusions that, ultimately, the allusions draw attention to themselves. They seem to be valued for their own sake, as if Wharton seizes the occasion of these travel narratives not simply to use but to revel in her considerable erudition. [In *Edith Wharton's Argument with America* (1980)], Elizabeth Ammons points out that in 1902, Wharton defended the right of George Eliot and all women to write about science, politics, and history, all in the "domain of intelligent adults," and in that same year made the mistake of "presenting her superb intellectual credentials" in the low-brow genre of historical romance in *The Valley of Decision*. But here, in her travel writing, Wharton need not apologize for her intelligence and learning any more than would other writers of travel volumes, whether Pater or Symonds, Lee or Bourget, whom Wharton admired. Travel writing thus freed Wharton to write with unabashed intellectual abandon, to indulge the exercise of a mental prowess frowned upon in women in America but accepted and sometimes even celebrated in Europe.

In keeping with the conventions of other travellers who recounted their experiences before her, Wharton's narrator enlists the known—America—to assist her audience in envisioning the unknown, the hitherto neglected treasures of Europe. The comparisons the narrator draws, however, almost invariably cut two ways, denigrating America as they are clarifying Europe. In Tirano, Italy, for example, the narrator finds "an architectural dignity which our great cities lack"; at Amiens she feels a reverence for the past that is "the cathedral's word to the traveller from a land which has undertaken to get on without the past"; of Dourdan she writes: "to taste the full flavour of such sensations, it is worth while to be of a country where the last new grain-elevator or office building is the only monument that receives homage from the surrounding architecture." As the narrator comes to life under Wharton's pen, Europe becomes a means by which to assess America, to set it in relief, to identify its deficiencies, to resurrect Wharton's feelings toward her homeland. Europe intensifies the negative impact of America, as Wharton's correspondence, also, makes unmistakably clear. Returning in 1903 from the trip to Italy that provided much of the material for *Italian Backgrounds*, she wrote to Sara Norton: "My first weeks in America are always miserable, because the tastes I am cursed with are all of a kind that cannot be gratified here . . . my first sight of American streets, my first hearing of American voices, and the wild, dishevelled backwards look of everything when one first comes home! You see, in my heart of hearts, a heart never unbosomed, I feel in America . . . out of sympathy with everything." Driving home the comparison between Europe and America in her early drafts of the travel writing and, then, in the revisions three or four years later, Wharton could hardly escape the implications such feelings must have for her life.

When Wharton undertook in 1908 the revisions that became *A Motor-Flight Through France*, she did so with a care and attentiveness that underscore the process of writing and revision as the occasion of self-discovery, of recognition of an authentic self who came to light as Wharton asked "to whom" Europe had "happened" and listened as the character "actually [began] to speak within me" with her own voice. The 200 pages in the book edition of *Motor-Flight* incorporate some 150 changes from the original text in the *Atlantic Monthly*. Some of the changes are simply editorial, upper replacing lower case letters, commas added or deleted. Other changes serve the interest of accuracy: a *palais de justice* is changed to a *hôtel de ville*; Langeais replaces Carcassonne in a list of castles. A number of changes, however, are matters of finding just the right nuance. In a description of a cathedral, for example, in which contemplation would "fortify" a conviction, Wharton replaces "deeply fortify" with "strongly fortify" because "strongly" harmonizes with "fortify" as "deeply" does not. Other changes create drama, as when she places "from the last hill of" in front of "the Viterbo road," heightening the sense of the length and the labor of a descent into Rouen. Thus tending to her craft in 1908, she came into intimate contact once again with the character who had earlier undertaken these travels, the latter-day medieval pilgrim who had travelled to sacred places in search of a new life.

By 1909, then, Wharton could no longer resist the desire to immerse herself continually in the history and culture that energized her. In the process of writing and revising her travel essays, she because convinced as never before that the geographical balance of her life must change, that it must correspond to her own psychological and intellectual balance, that Europe was in fact her home and America an alien land. Having set out first on physical journeys and then on imaginative reconstructions of them, Wharton recognized in the narrative version of herself a woman who had undertaken a spiritual

quest and had found her most authentic self. Her experience anticipates that of the speaker of T. S. Eliot's "Little Gidding": "the end of all our exploring / Will be to arrive where we started / And know the place for the first time." (pp. 257-67)

Mary Suzanne Schriber, "Edith Wharton and Travel Writing as Self-Discovery," in American Literature, *Vol. 59, No. 2, May, 1987, pp. 257-67.*

COMPARATIVE ESSAYS ON TRAVEL WRITERS

MARION A. THOMAS

[*In the following excerpt, Thomas compares two works of travel literature, Graham Greene's* Journey without Maps *(1936) and Bernard Dadié's* La ville où nul ne meurt *(1969), finding that in the case of both writers, "self-affirmation is deepened in proportion to contact with others," and that the travels of both writers meet the twofold purpose of allowing them to examine the present and search for the past.*]

The English writer Graham Greene and Bernard Dadié of the Ivory Coast both concern themselves with real problems of contemporary society. The two books selected here are Greene's *Journey without Maps* (1936) and Dadié's *La Ville où nul ne meurt* (1969). They are particularly valuable as they not only reflect a particular society but also a variety of problems: international cultural relationships, social discrimination and materialism. Personal reflections are woven among the comments on the journey, and tend to demonstrate that self-affirmation is deepened in proportion to contacts with others, provided that these contacts are engaged in with an open-minded attitude. Both books also reflect the increasing interest during the twentieth century in psycho-analysis and cultural anthropology. They are good examples of the various functions of the travel book as a literary form—suitable as a contribution to a more objective observation both of oneself and of one's own culture, as an encouragement to international contacts, and leading to the evaluation of the diverse contributions of different cultures towards the enrichment of our twentieth-century cosmopolitan way of life. Condemnation, scorn and fear of others are to be replaced by a sincere discernment. The difficulty of this open-mindedness, however, is not to be underestimated, as prejudice and exploitation have long histories. (p. 1)

The journeys made by Graham Greene and Bernard Dadié in these books are both an examination of the present and a search for the past. Writing in the first person, the authors attempt to "whisper in the reader's ear." This engaging of the reader's close attention is an attempt to have him participate in the experience of the journey, identifying with the "double" or "persona" of the story. Dadié speaks in a personal, subjective way in parts of the book, and as a more distant narrator in other parts. This anonymous narrator includes the ancestors, and provides a more objective view of events. The alternation between subjectivity and objectivity explains the choice and personification of cultural, historic objects (such as the statue of Caesar Augustus), and allows a greater freedom of imaginative creativity.

A similar role in Greene's book is played by the references to the unnamed cousin who follows and accompanies him. The technique of double articulation also helps to express the fact that there is both a sense of being in one place and a sense of movement, which is very important in both books. In this connection also, the regularity of the rhythm is very meaningful, and a slowing of the pace occurs at moments of ease and relaxation of tension, or of deliberate heavy stress. An accelerated pace occurs to convey either urgency or lightness of mood. The pace of the journey is therefore skilfully used to intensify the meaning and mood of the reflections.

Graham Greene's choice of Liberia as a place to visit and write about in 1935 was initially the result of his reading a government report about conditions there. He noted that the interior forest region had not yet been developed industrially at all, and a trip there was an opportunity to explore the darkness and mystery of the unknown, as well as a return to a primitive stage of civilization: like returning to the innocence of early childhood. He does not hesitate to refer to cannibalistic societies as follows:

> That afternoon the doctor came in to talk about the bush societies. . . .
>
> I am not an anthropologist and I cannot pretend to remember very much of what Dr Harley told me: a pity, for no white man is closer to that particular "heart of darkness," the secret societies being more firmly rooted in Liberia than in any other country on the West Coast. . . . Everyone in Ganta knew they were there, with their ritual need of the heart, the palms of the hands, the skin of the forehead, but no one knew who they were. The Frontier Force were active, searching for strangers. Presently the fear passed. The Manos round Ganta knew what the men were seeking, for they have their own cannibalistic societies, and though I said nothing of this to my boys and there were no Manos among the carriers, Laminah and Amedoo knew all about it. Laminah said to me one day, 'These people bad, they chop men', and they were happy to leave the Manos behind. This is the territory the United States map marks so vaguely and excitingly as "Cannibal."

Of the commericialization developed by the French, he says, "Perhaps even the cannibals on the Ivory Coast were now chiefly occupied in manufacturing baits for tourists."

Greene was aware that the American rubber company Firestone had plantations around Monrovia, and he planned to enter Liberia via an inland route through Sierra Leone, in a forest region he was to call "the green tunnel." From this perspective, the journey was to make possible an exploration of his own unconscious and of mankind's past, a subject which was just becoming popular at the time. (pp. 2-3)

The search for the past in Dadié's book takes the form of an account of a trip to Rome at Easter, 1959. Rome is regarded as the seat of European culture as well as of the Roman Catholic Church, and the deep significance for Dadié of this concept of "seat" or "source" of religious and cultural traditions can best be understood by those who are aware of the importance of the seat, or throne, of Krinjabo in the Agni society in which Dadié was brought up. It is central to traditional ceremonies, and has conferred the general idea of "guardian of traditions" upon the family seat throughout that ethnic group.

As Dadié observes people, places, and vestiges of ancient Roman culture around Rome, he becomes more and more aware of his African perspective and value system, and yet also of certain positive aspects he can use from the learning acquired from European teachers.

Both writers make some attempt to improve the images that Europeans and Africans have of each other and to lessen prejudices, although it will be seen that Dadié's more cosmopolitan outlook leads him to greater progress in this direction. The ambivalent attitudes prevalent in both cultures have been described by Richard Bonneau in these words (my translation):

> Indeed, for the European, Africa is on the one hand the sea-coast and its palm-trees, the pleasures of hunting, and on the other hand the "Green Hell"; but for the African, the West, both feared and admired, appears as the worst and the best of things.

Despite falling into the stereotyped images already noted (darkness, cannibals, etc.), Graham Greene does try to make his English reader think more deeply about such words as "civilization," explaining how it had become synonymous with exploitation in Sierra Leone, and describing its effect:

> Neither ILP nor Communist Party urges a strike in England because the platelayers in Sierra Leone are paid sixpence a day without their food. Civilization here remained exploitation; we had hardly, it seemed to me, improved the natives' lot at all, they were as worn out with fever as before the white man came, we had introduced new diseases and weakened their resistance to the old, they still drank polluted water and suffered from the same worms. . . . Civilization so far as Sierra Leone was concerned was the railway to Pendembu, the increased export of palm-nuts; civilization, too, was Lever Brothers and the price they controlled; civilization was the long bar in the Grand, the sixpenny wages. It was not civilization as we think of it, a civilization of Suffolk churches and Cotswold manors, of Crome and Vaughan.

Greene had, of course, been strongly influenced by Joseph Conrad's books, as well as by hearing his aunt's stories of her life in South Africa. J. Koyinde Vaughan spoke out, in a well-documented article which appeared in the review *Présence Africaine* against Greene's perpetuation of the image of Africa as a place of darkness. It must be noted, however, that Greene's use of the image extends to broader horizons: it becomes in this book a symbol of the moral decadence of England, and as such, contributes greatly to the importance of the work.

Greene also takes a real interest in some of the local customs, and especially in the personal role of the "priest devil" Landow. He compares the atmosphere of the bush school with a public school in England, and emphasizes the element of fear involved in both situations:

> Most natives . . . will attend a bush school, of which the masked devil is the unknown head. Even the Christian natives attend. . . . The school and the devil who rules over it are at first a terror to the child. It lies as grimly as a public school in England between childhood and manhood. He has seen the masked devil and has been told of his supernatural power; no human part of the devil is allowed to show.

In this, he clearly reflects his own childhood attitudes towards his father and the school where the family had its home: Greene's father was the headmaster. He relates more of these experiences in *A Sort of Life*, 'The Lost Childhood' in *Collected Essays*, and in his other travel book, *The Lawless Roads*.

Dadié shows a comparable interest in folklore and legends, and his use of African proverbs is an important aspect of his book, accentuating the West African perspective in spite of using the language brought to his homeland by the European colonialists. The social significance of the use of the proverb has been explained by the Nigerian writer Emenyonu, who quotes the Igbo's description of it as "the palm oil with which words are eaten.'' Dadié's style is alert and lively, with a humor which brings an attractive freshness to the criticism of social evils and injustices. In sharp contrast to Greene's slow, groping trek through the forest, Dadié flies by jet aircraft to Rome and beholds with astonishment the city which contains so many centuries of civilization and represents so much of western culture. This flight is an image of the rapid changes brought about by European colonization in Africa, and the astonishment translates the bewilderment with which the African may face the confusion of old and new ways of life.

Observations by the two writers on their respective journeys are noted in relation to personal recollections, both elements are skilfully combined and certain symbols selected. The images and symbols used merit some detailed consideration. There will be no attempt here to present an exhaustive interpretation of all the symbols used in the two books, but the following remarks should serve to demonstrate their multiple meanings and their relation to the social perspective of the two writers.

The symbols are the most striking and the riches single element in the structure of the works. Mircea Eliade has described the symbol as revealing the most profound aspects of reality which cannot be communicated in any other way. Usually, a symbol cannot be explained because it appeals beyond its context to the observer's experience. It can serve an important social goal by facilitating communication and co-operation, as has been noted in a recent study by Altizer, Beardslee and Young [*Truth, Myth, and Symbol* (1962)]. As these writers have explained, the symbol's effectiveness depends largely on the skill of its user, as the object itself is relatively arbitrary. The symbol's main role is evocation, and it achieves this by connecting aspects or areas of experience which are different, and even sometimes in opposition.

In Greene's book, rats and insects feature prominently. Among the information that Greene had acquired before leaving England for the journey to Liberia was the following:

> The rat population may fairly be described as swarming, the wood and corrugated iron houses lend themselves to rat harbourage. . . .
>
> The great majority of all mosquitoes caught in Monrovia are of a species known to carry yellow fever.

A native hut was regarded as synonymous with rats and insects by the character referred to in the book as ''Daddy,'' who had spent twenty-five years in Freetown, and who advised Greene against the trek through the forest region. Greene's own observations of the ants and bats begin when he stays at a hotel in Freetown, and from that point on, various insects and rats are mentioned with increasing, obsessive intensity. However, there is some humour in his descriptions of his host's efforts to rid the house of moths, cockchafers and beetles during the evening Greene spends at the border of Sierra Leone and French Guinea. Later, in Bolahun, he expresses admiration for the Catholic missionaries' courage as they constantly face the risk of fever and the abundance of snakes, worms and rats.

As swarms of moths fly round the paraffin lamps lit for the funeral ceremony of the Tailahun chief, Greene acknowledges not only a fear of moths which he says is inherited from his mother, but also his habitual reaction of avoiding any idea which is unpleasant to him, such as the concept of eternal life and damnation: ''But in Africa one couldn't avoid them any more than one could avoid the supernatural.''

However, just as it was impossible to avoid the insects of the forest, he is obliged to learn to face up to them, and he compares this with a psychoanalytical process. As the trek progresses, the descriptions of the various insects, spiders and rats accompany his expressions of nervousness, boredom and frustration. When the path gets difficult, every living thing seems to be a snake or insect, and his reaction to the difficulty of the trek is reflected by the various emphases on them.

After walking for more hours of the day than usual to reach Duogobmai, and reaching that village ahead of his porters, he realizes that he will have to sleep without his equipment, and again, the observations on the rats reflect his disgust and frustration. He accepts the conditions he finds simply because they are unavoidable, but he is still afraid of catching malaria in a place so remote from any medical help. This leads to his recognition of how dependent he is on the willingness of his porters not to abandon him in the middle of the forest, and he yields to their requests for a rest day. However, this rest day at Duogobmai is full of problems and frustrations, expressed in two pages about the rats. Clearly, the descriptions of the rats are connected with the intensity of his mood of disgust.

At Zigita, he was disappointed at the non-appearance of the sorcerer, and he again writes about his impressions of disturbance by rats, although he finds that nothing in the hut was actually disturbed during the night at all.

The mood of rottenness is somewhat different at the Zorzor mission: there are beetles instead of rats, and this difference could indicate Greene's notion that evil in religious communities may take on a different expression from that in secular society. Later, he notes that the presence of insects is a sign of the absence of the corrupt and corrupting civilization such as he had observed on the coast of Sierra Leone and Senegal, as well as in Europe.

Using a rest house allotted to him at Bamakama (in French Guinea), he finds the hut full of insects and the smell of a dead rat under the floor. This, however, finally leads him to bury his fear of rats, and he arrives safely at Ganta to meet Dr Harley. Disagreeable conditions later on mostly give rise to comments on the destructiveness of invading goats or the presence of large spiders. Towards the end of the long trek through the forest region, where Greene notes the reappearance of signs of the decadent coastal civilization, the spiders represent the decay and the futility of progress, as well as his personal depression and fatigue.

Greene's trek as a whole is an image of man's struggle for survival in a decadent world. The rats, mosquitoes and other insects that disturbed him are not only physical realities, but also symbols of everything that torments and destroys man in today's world. Like the jigger that penetrated into his foot during the trek, and which he mentions repeatedly, evil is also within man. Jacques Madaule commented on this aspect of all Greene's writing, when he said in 1949: ''We are constantly aware of the catastrophes that assail us, and which show, in various ways, that evil is in man'' [*Graham Greene*, 1949]. Madaule comments that Greene's literary talent harmonizes with his Catholic view of the world.

There are rare moments in Greene's book when one catches a glimpse of beautiful aspects of the forest, the sight of butterflies, a waterfall, or other sign of freshness and vivid colour; these reflect a very momentary pleasure or sense of relief, but are significant because they lighten the pervading oppressiveness of the other elements. Greene's moral and spiritual perspective has been indicated by Madaule: "The world in which we live, which has been corrupted by our sin, is a world in which there is a superabundance of evil, and it will continue that way until the end of time."

Bernard Dadié, also a Roman Catholic, perceives a similar malaise of civilization, but his manner of describing it differs considerably from Greene's. The spider is a popular character in regional folk-tales in the Ivory Coast, and not mentioned by Dadié in his travel book. When he refers to the flies and insects of the tropical forest, he uses them cleverly to connect in a humorous way two thoughts on anthropology and materialism which conclude thus: "Donc la mouche est une nouvelle espèce de créature humaine qui vient, discute avec vous, et ensuite le ventre bien gros de nouvelles, s'envole se dégorger chez ceux qui le paient pour cette récolte," which I roughly translate as: "Therefore the fly is a new species of human being who comes to converse with you, and when he has had his fill of news, flies off to spill it out to those who pay him for these tit-bits."

When Dadié mentions rats, the tone again contrasts with that used by Greene. On seeing a young Jewish woman during his journey, Dadié mentions the death of rats in a violent bush fire as an illustration of the atrocious torture of Jews in Europe.

Repeatedly throughout the book, Dadié attributes most manifestations of aggressiveness to the accumulation of wealth, and observes that the spiritual influence of the Christ who was born in poverty is hardly apparent in a world controlled by the power of money. He reminds his reader that money came to his homeland along with European trade and colonization. And he includes a striking warning to young people against a thoughtless acceptance of the attraction to get richer, which easily leads to aggressive behaviour.

Among Dadié's symbols are two objects representative of degenerate human enterprise: the Bank of the Holy Spirit which he sees in Rome, and the Cinzano advertisement board. The fact that Dadié has chosen objects made by man is meaningful. Man is the agent who spreads evil by his egoistic activities. The metal and stone of which these objects are built are neither good nor bad in themselves; that depends on the use made of them by man. The Bank of the Holy Spirit is the object selected by Dadié as the seat and symbol of the generalized usurpation of spiritual areas by materialism. He says:

> Men have progressed. God the Father, remaining in heaven, God the Son, nailed on the Cross, the very astute Romans, wishing to reconcile the irreconcilable, considered it opportune, beneficial, and good politics, to house God the Holy Spirit in a bank, the house of Mammon. . . . Has money become a holy spirit?

Dadié notes the power of the wealthy with irony, and points to what could be achieved by a fairer distribution of wealth:

> Does this mean that, from now on, money, the spirit of the modern world, could play a more human rôle? Unite men, families, peoples, nations, instead of dividing them into the poor and the rich? Act as a leaven and not a brake?

Both in Rome and at home, "money is the liquor that goes most easily to the head." His sharp criticism is softened at some points: "When there are so many ruins around and within one, one reaches the point of trying to reconcile the irreconcilable: Rome is at that point."

He aims his criticism more directly at the élite of the new young nations, referring to the fact that they are able to keep wealth from their countrymen by placing it in "a mountainous, inaccessible place called Switzerland." Nor does the Papal estate escape sharp irony:

> Over there, in the distance, one can distinguish a powerful dome bearing a globe with a cross on it. It is the residence of the Pope, God's representative on earth. . . . Jesus Christ must have been born in a poverty they are ashamed of. Fortunately the Bank of the Holy Spirit was born.

During the visit to the Vatican described towards the end of the book, Dadié repeats the word "golden" over and over again, and finally concludes: "Take away the gold, and wouldn't that take from them all reason for living?" Dadié's sharpest criticisms are often expressed in this interrogative form, to provoke his reader's reflection rather than merely to express his own condemnation. It also allows for the humorous effect. His cool remark after the Pope's appearance may be quoted as a final comment on his satire: "Besides, he is infallible."

His criticism is directed not only towards leaders of the church and heads of government, but towards all who hold economic power and participate in the overturning of moral values. His adept juxtaposition of ideas and his well-turned phrases emphasize contrasts and achieve a penetrating, humorous effect.

His second symbol is the Cinzano advertisement board, the significance of which extends to all means of propaganda which influence other people's minds. Dadié mentions this advertisement board as soon as he leaves the airport in Rome, and he also associates with it his regret that the Romans seem to confuse their situation of "holy city" with cultural superiority, and seem to dominate others with the approval of the Church.

The Roman ruins have a double function in this book: they are the symbol of ancient culture as well as of decadence. In devoting most of forty pages to the Roman history which he is reminded of by the ruins, statues and other monuments, Dadié not only demonstrates his wealth of knowledge of the details of this history, but also exercises his gift for rendering these historical accounts interesting to his readers by using a light tone, inserting amusing anecdotes, playing on words, and quoting proverbs. He interprets the presence of the ruins as meaning that Rome has not wanted to break with her past, a past which can still teach modern generations. The decadence indicated is an absence of gratitude to illustrious ancestors such as Caesar Augustus, whose statue seems to serve only as a tourist attraction and as a source of lucrative gain—a materialistic, egoistic attitude observed in a modern Rome as well as in modern African cities. Dadié is aware that modern industrialization has often been achieved at the cost of a lowering of moral values, and his is one of the prophetic voices greatly needed for today's world.

Commercialization of religious traditions is criticized by both writers. For Greene, it is an aspect which spoils the effect of the "devil's dance." And he is reminded of an occasion during his childhood when missionaries visiting his school had impressed him by their preoccupation with money. In Dadié's book, there is at first a note of surprise at the preoccupation with the sale of religious objects in Rome which he refers to in this way: "Fetichism in this country is spread around ostentatiously in the streets." Then a note of impatience: "Is there anywhere in this city where they don't sell religious trinkets?" and he refers to the sale of portraits of the Pope as a flourishing industry, constituting most of the articles for sale in some places. For both writers, a real religious piety does not involve this kind of commercialization. For Greene, there is also a more vaguely described sense of the supernatural, expressed in descriptions of the witch, the priest-devil, and the missionary doctor, and these harmonize with his themes of darkness and mystery.

Dadié's book includes a fourth symbol: the butterfly, although it is only mentioned four times. Butterflies had been his childhood favourites during carefree hours at play, and this aspect may be noted in his pseudo-autobiographical novel, *Climbié*. Now, after long arduous efforts towards his country's independence, freedom is expressed by this symbol of the butterfly: freedom to be himself, just as on those days when he could forget the restrictions of school life and wander about daydreaming. The butterfly which appears in Rome, a spirit of youthful spontaneity, promises him a happy, flourishing future. Only a very small part of the great city is filled with such laughter and song: the "Song of the Butterfly" resounds in a small restaurant. Light and fanciful, the butterfly represents hope, and poetic inspiration. It gives Dadié's book a note of hope for the future. (pp. 3-11)

> Marion A. Thomas, "*Graham Greene Travels in Africa and Dadié Travels in Europe*," *in* African Literature Today, *No. 14, 1984, pp. 1-11.*

ALASTAIR NIVEN

[*Niven is a Scottish educator and critic. In the following excerpt, he examines two travel narratives: Nirad Chaudhuri's* Passage to England *(1960) and V. S. Naipaul's* An Area of Darkness *(1964). Niven characterizes the recounted trips as exercises in self-discovery, journeys made on the part of each writer to test the reality of India against long-held personal conceptions.*]

In 1955 Nirad Chaudhuri made his first visit outside India and in 1962 V. S. Naipaul went to India for the first time. Both men were established writers, practiced in human observation and yet possessing an innately patrician sense of their own distinction. In viewing their own societies they had been trenchant when not caustic, at all times provocative and sometimes perverse. After their journeys abroad they brought the same qualities to the books they wrote about their visits, Chaudhuri in *A Passage to England* and Naipaul in *An Area of Darkness*. Their methods were similar: to write in portrait form a series of short essays analysing what they saw and accounting for their own reactions to it. Chaudhuri was fifty-seven when he left India for the first time for an eight-week visit to Europe, five weeks in England, two in Paris and one in Rome. In the "Plea for the Book", as he charmingly christens the preface to *A Passage To England,* he tells us that he celebrated the three-thousandth week of his life at the end of his tour. Naipaul was only thirty when he traced his ancestral footsteps back to India, an islander in a sub-continent, and it may be that their contrasting ages has much to do with the different attitudes with which they approached their new experiences. A comparison between the two writers, masters both of the imperially endowed language in which they write, has more than a tenuous racial vindication, for if their casts of mind are often different they share an abiding awareness of their cultural origins. Both are obsessed with the fact of empire, neither is impressed by modish points of view, and together they have provided not just in their travel writings but in the body of their work a collection of observations which make them unsurpassed among contemporary Indian essayists.

That Naipaul descends from indentured Indian labour brought to Trinidad in the early part of the century, that Brahmin *hauteur* affects every statement he makes, is elementary to any regular reader of his fiction, his journalism or his documentaries. Naipaul's dissociation from Trinidad and corresponding incapacity to find a spiritual home elsewhere has been the basis for almost all his writings and has made him suspicious of any kind of commitment to causes that may prove illusory. Chaudhuri, on the other hand, has always worked within a framework of personal certainties. His brand of Hinduism may not be orthodox, his suspicion of social radicalism is scarcely fashionable, and he has at times a veneration for European excellence that, if not carefully weighed against his sense of the folly and failure of their empires, can at least embarrass one with its affection and at its worst seem monstrous in its assertion of a distinctive Aryan purity. For both writers their journeys abroad were exercises in self-discovery. Both wished to test the realities they encountered against long-imbibed notions of the societies they visited and both admit implicitly that they undertook their travels with preconceptions so strong that only revolution could have changed them. And revolution, as they make clear, was not in the air either in the Europe of 1955 or the India of 1962.

By the time he visited India Naipaul's disenchantment with the West Indies had been apparent both in satires like *The Suffrage of Elvira* and in the bitter affection with which he had painted the vulnerable Mr. Biswas. At the root of that disenchantment lay his distress at being an actor in a charade when he profoundly desired to be real. Metaphors of stage, film, puppetry and mimesis recur throughout all Naipaul's work for they best express his desolate sense of having inherited nothing which he can decently call his own. The colonial mentality ensured that mirrors of England were set up throughout the world, before whose reflection the minions would prance in eager emulation. This policy created a new reality in which all was imitation, a culture of the derivative and phoney. A way of life that was already in decline in England was recreated abroad with nothing to nourish it: a cardboard and canvas world peopled by actors who were hemmed in by the rules of their craft and the dictates of their lines. Even the language they uttered was all sound and no conviction.

The paradox, of course, was that Naipaul showed in everything he wrote the weaknesses of his case. A wittier writer than the author of *The Mystic Masseur* or a more poised one than the consummate stylist who has emerged since *The Mimic Men* would be hard to find. Like James Baldwin, who had once felt condemned to the prison-cell of another man's language, Naipaul has learned to fashion that language to his own ends and has become, in the process, outraged when others less fastidious than he abuse it. In *An Area of Darkness* he is concerned centrally with the handling of language:

> As soon as our quarantine flag came down and the last of the barefooted, blue-uniformed policemen of the Bombay Port Health Authority had left the ship, Coelho the Goan came aboard and, luring me with a long beckoning finger into the saloon, whispered, "You have any cheej?"

This is a novelist's opening *par excellence*, establishing a Greene-like Oriental seediness. Our moral antennae are alerted to what kind of graft or corruption "cheej" can be. Contraband it is, though mispronounced: cheese, an Indian delicacy. Naipaul has at once established a linguistic standard of exactness both in expression and accent: To depart from it, as every Indian he encounters seems to do, is to confuse meaning and therefore

Evelyn and Alec Waugh at Villefranche. By permission of Weidenfeld & Nicolson Archives.

to violate communication. Naipaul's thesis of colonial mimicry ensures that every time an Indian speaks English he parodies his former masters. Yet how fastidious is this master of cadence and irony himself? "Imports were restricted," he goes on to say, "and Indians had not yet learned how to make cheese, just as they had not yet learned how to bleach newsprint." Calculatedly offensive and obviously patronising, the statement is also untrue. Indians have "learned" to make cheese and to bleach newsprint but have not chosen to practice the skills on a state-wide scale. Such pedantic details matter when a writer presents honesty of observation as his *raison d'être*.

Throughout *An Area of Darkness* Naipaul maintains his concern for the accuracy of language not just in writing but in pronunciation. His one positive recommendation to the India of to-morrow is to abandon English: he insists that a nation which conducts a large part of its official business in an imported language must inevitably blur the subtleties of nuance necessary to a sensitive society. Naipaul knows that Engish is but one

of several imported languages in India—"Every other conqueror bequeathed a language to India," he admits, but "English remains a foreign language." That his generalisation will not hold can be evidenced in the range of Indian writing written in English since the 1930's: Mulk Raj Anand's compassion, R. K. Narayan's intimate objectivity, Raja Rao's clarity of metaphysical enquiry, Kamala Markandaya's poise, Nissim Ezekiel's agility, Nehru's commanding rhetoric, Chaudhuri's witty intelligence. What does Naipaul's word "foreign" mean used of the English employed by writers such as these? But apart from a glancing acknowledgement of Chaudhuri himself Naipaul does not read them. His one analysis of a modern Indian novel, Manohar Malgonkar's *The Princes*, conspicuously lacks the context of reading necessary to deal with the book. He makes no mention of Forster's *The Hill of Devi* or Anand's *Private Life of an Indian Prince*. "Nowhere," says Naipaul of Malgonkar's novel, "do I see the India I know: those poor fields, those three-legged dogs, those sweating red-coated railway porters carrying heavy tin trunks on their heads."

But where in *An Area of Darkness* is the political acuteness of *The Princes* or any comparable attempt to speak of the death of the Raj as it affected the indigenous Indian *élite*? All writers are selective, Malgonkar in his way and especially Naipaul in his. Anniah Gowda's reaction to *An Area of Darkness* is representative of many Indian critics who saw in Naipaul's book too partial a view of their country: "Naipaul, in his reminiscences, has chosen to shut his eyes to the India which is not defecating." He closed his ears, too, to the India which did not mispronounce English.

Part of the trouble is that Naipaul sees in pre-colonial India only a vast historic darkness. Chaudhuri, on the other hand, draws upon Indian history with every breath he takes. Indeed, he makes what for him is the profound discovery that only in England have the scars of earlier colonisations been effectively eradicated.

> Neither in London nor in the country was I able, by looking at the faces, figures, and clothing of the people, to guess that there had been invasions of England and spells of foreign rule for its inhabitants. In respect of India, this is one of the easiest things to do even in one street in Delhi.

Chaudhuri has seen evidence of conquest everywhere he looks in India. In England a massive fusion of cultures has taken place which results in an aesthetic and temperamental unity he has never experienced on a national scale before. But that does not make him see his own people as philistine or imitative. He could never share Naipaul's epithet, "a sense of history, which is a sense of loss" (*An Area of Darkness*), nor really endorse his view of the inevitable obfuscation of English when handled by Indians. This, after all, is the writer who delights in noting that the English refer to Indian independence as a "gift" whereas his own people look upon it as a "victory." The change of word asserts a world of national difference, with self-respect enlisted on both sides. Neither word is wrong and neither is complete. Chaudhuri, unlike Naipaul, relishes the verbal imprecision of both sides while being never less than precise himself.

Naipaul and Chaudhuri embarked on their journeys to find out more about themselves. Both readily concede that they had well-formed notions of what they would find and were looking for confirmation of their preconceptions. Naipaul expected disenchantment, Chaudhuri expected enchantment, and neither was confounded. "I saw how close in the past year I had been to the total Indian negation," Naipaul writes at the end of *An Area of Darkness*, "how much it had become the basis of thought and feeling." Chaudhuri concludes in a different vein altogether: "Never before, except in the intimacy of my family life, had I been so happy as I was during my short stay in England. It was the literal truth, and the happiness has lasted." Though these summaries are quite opposite, Naipaul and Chaudhuri journeyed with two similar intentions, to know themselves more fully and to discover what they could about the imperial inheritance as it conditions the minds and psyches of those who have been affected by it. Both writers, for example, share with E. M. Forster a conviction that distinctions of temperature have moulded the different outlooks of the eastern and the western personality. Naipaul swelters throughout his stay in India; Chaudhuri learns early on how not to freeze in London. For both of them there exists an immutable alienation between east and west for which the implacable universe no less than human perversity is responsible.

Naipaul, though, has the racial appearance of the people he is among, Chaudhuri does not. When a Paris worker asks Chaudhuri if he is English he chuckles at the absurdity of the question. "I was taken aback by his idea of the size and looks of an Englishman." Naipaul admits with honest vanity that his visit to India was the first occasion in his life when he had not been ethnically conspicuous and that he did not altogether like being an anonymous face in the crowd. Naipaul's point goes beyond egotism, though, for there is pathos in the complete separation of body and spirit which he feels in India—a skin which fits, a soul which rejects, all that he encounters, Naipaul's dissociation derives from historic sources, as a work like *The Loss of El Dorado* tesitifies, no less than from his personal temperament. Nonetheless, he is repelled by almost everyone he meets in India whereas Chaudhuri loves the conversational vitality of even the most trivial dinner-party in England.

The greatest fear of any writer is that he will cease to respond to life and therefore cease to write. India has this anaesthetizing quality in abundance, so Naipaul asserts, and early in the book we find that the incapacity to handle language properly is beginning to affect him too. "I was finding it hard to spell and to frame simple sentences." A sense of dread accompanies him everywhere. He knows before he sets out on a pilgrimage that he cannot have access to the mysteries of religion: he can only observe others' ecstacies. He approaches the village of his forebears certain that the visit is pointless. "I had learned my separateness from India, and was content to be a colonial, without a past, without ancestors." He discovers an India no more alive than the calendar pictures of it which he remembered from his Trinidad childhood. Chaudhuri's view of England is quite opposite. From the moment he looks out of the plane to the clear landscape below he finds a three-dimensional solidity to European life which he missed at home, though that is not to make of Chaudhuri's India the same wasteland as Naipaul's. In India he is aware of "a sensation of extension in space . . . I cannot remember any historic building in northern India, with the exception of the Taj at dawn, which conveys the feeling of mass. . . . Hues always seem to flow and run into the surrounding atmosphere, as dyes which are not fast do in water." We see India, Chaudhuri claims, in a "rarefied" way; Europe we see in a "concrete" way.

> Another striking effect of the light is seen in the English landscape, which seemed decidedly more stereoscopic to me than any visual reality I had been familiar with previously. I thought I was looking at everything through a pair of prismatic binoculars. In India any landscape tends to resolve into a silhouette, with a side-to-side linking of its components, in the West it becomes a composition in depth, with an into-the-picture movement, a recession, which carries the eye of the onlooker, wherever any opening is left, to the vanishing point on the horizon.

Chaudhuri converts this sense of the concreteness of European life into an aesthetic theory whereby to talk of English painting, architecture and literature. "There is a curious solidity and into-the-space movement in them too." Of course, when Chaudhuri talks of this density in English life as a tangible physical reality he is beginning to talk the same language as Naipaul, for whom the tragedy of colonial territories lies in their attempt to reconstruct England using flimsy materials. The difference is that Naipaul believes the colonial imitator has a fantasy England in his mind, one that never properly existed. Chaudhuri finds evidence of its existence wherever he goes. London really is for him "the Great Mother of modern cities," with

Calcutta among her children, whereas Naipaul, when he visits a Calcutta palace, feels that

> this is how a film might begin; the camera will advance with us, will pause here on this broken masonry, there on this faded decoration.

India as a large film-set inhabited by actors and extras: a view which denies the reality of India. One would have more confidence in Naipaul's view if he had known enough about India when he went there in 1962, but despite naming several books he has read he displays no intimate understanding of the country's literature, art or philosophy. He admits as much when discussing the Hindu ceremonies he witnessed as a child in Trinidad. "The images didn't interest me; I never sought to learn their significance." Such a *blasé* attitude surely indicates a deadness in Naipaul, not in the religion he implicitly belittles. Chaudhuri, by contrast, opens his book with a response to the "belief in the West that we Hindus regard the world as an illusion." Naipaul certainly believes this: "The world is illusion, the Hindus say." "We do not," Chaudhuri continues, "and indeed cannot, for the only idea of an after-life accepted by a Hindu—the unconscious assumption behind all that he does—is that he will be born again and again in the same old world and live in it virtually for eternity. . . . A people who have learnt to believe in that way are not likely to be the persons most ready to dismiss the world as insubstantial." Now it may be claimed that the author of *The Continent of Circe*, with its thesis that Hindus are of European origin and that their Aryanism provides them with an instinctive consciousness of being superior to other peoples, is not the best person to represent the typical Hindu metaphysic and that Naipaul's understanding of Hinduism approximates more closely to the norm. But none can dispute Chaudhuri's depth of reading in Indian philosophy and in the epics; however solitary his conclusions are about Hinduism in *The Continent of Circe*, in *A Passage to England* or in the more recent analysis of Indian family life, *To Live or Not to Live!* they are based on a lifetime's study. It is greatly significant that Chaudhuri did not publish his first work, *The Autobiography of an Unknown Indian*, until 1951 when he was fifty-four years old and that his first trip abroad should not be until his fifty-eighth year. He needed the time before then for a maturing of wisdom and range of reading in both the Indian and the European arts. In his sixties and seventies he has published much, most recently his acclaimed biographies of Max Müller and Robert Clive, but he held back until he was ready.

Point for point Naipaul and Chaudhuri so often stand close together yet on opposite sides that it would be wearisome to list each instance. Where, for example, Naipaul claims that "It is still through European eyes that India looks at her ruins and her art," Chaudhuri only half agrees. "Even in regard to Hinduism most Hindus prefer to go to an English book," he says, much in the spirit if not the tone of Naipaul, yet he indicts the Hindu view of art not for the weakness of its influence but for its strength. It has made it, he argues, "impossible to look at a nude without a leer, it has resolved flesh to its most fleshly elements; the Europeans have made it the expression of the spiritual in man." Chaudhuri distinguishes between two different sets of aesthetic imperatives in his book; Naipaul denies that India has any kind of creative spirit, so aesthetic definitions do not arise.

Yet it is in the matter of definition that the two writers come closest to each other. Naipaul's desire for an absolutely scrupulous use of language suggest that he himself is as obsessed with definition as those he castigates, but he does not notice this paradox. Certainly his Indian, and Chaudhuri's also, is engaged on a massive labyrinthine exercise of definition and distinction. "To define is to begin to separate oneself," so every Indian, with an almost Calvinistic zeal to prove his status morally and socially, sets out to show off his rôle by the cut of his beard, the type of his caste mark, the style of his clothes. Appearance has not just become more important than inner reality, it subsumes it. A nation develops interested only in the form of things.

> These forms had not developed over the centuries. They had been imposed whole and suddenly by a foreign conqueror, displacing another set of forms, once no doubt thought equally unalterable, of which no trace remained.

Chaudhuri, too, sees an India obsessed by forms.

> For the Indian minister or official the mere discussion of his plans with an Occidental in an air-conditioned room is equivalent to execution.

The occasion for action becomes the action itself. Naipaul's book is full of similar moments in which intention is substituted for achievement with no sense of their difference. It is enough that Gandhi spoke. To implement what he advised becomes irrelevant. Perhaps there is truth in this thesis. Within a week of taking virtually absolute powers in an unprecedented constitutional shake-up Indira Gandhi was able to insist that there was no crisis in India. Ignore the obvious—"In India the easiest and most necessary thing to ignore," says Naipaul—and, if it won't exactly go away, it may not matter much.

The writers share, too, the same experience of Indian attitudes to work. The clerk who will not bring a glass of water to Naipaul's companion when she faints because it is not part of his duty to do such a thing is matched by Chaudhuri's table-duster whose obligations do not extend to sweeping the floor. Both see in India a society petrified by far greater class distinctions than exist in England, but it is hard to imagine Chaudhuri converting the reality of what he sees around him into the kind of ultimate James-ism of Naipaul when, on the pilgrimage, he feels that "Now indeed, in that valley, India has become all symbol."

Chaudhuri divides *A Passage To England* into four sections, "The English Scene," "The English People," "Cultural Life" and "State of the Nation." Sometimes his observation is acute, as in his account of the "traditional and even venerable ritual" he witnesses in the House of Commons (Chaudhuri, too, can recognize mimicry when he sees it). Sometimes he risks absurdity: do dark faces really reflect light less evenly than pink ones? Occasionally he is sheerly provocative, with a kind of naughty glee:

> . . .The history of love in Bengali Hindu society is fairly well established. It was introduced from the West much later than tobacco or potatoes, but has neither been acclimatized as successfully, nor has taken as deep roots, as these two plants.

At other times he displays a patrician intellect which will never endear him to Third World radicals. "Now, it is a good thing to do away with the caste system by birth, also by wealth, but a deadly mistake to tamper with the natural caste system of the mind." Naipaul would surely endorse that, at least. Finally, Chaudhuri can be provocative in a more searching way than any yet quoted. His view of the Welfare State, which he admires for its compassion, nevertheless raises issues to do with social anxiety and bored leisure which British society has only recently started to investigate.

At the heart of Chaudhuri's study of England, however, lies his sense of history. He cannot believe in a dying England if a theatre at Stratford-upon-Avon plays *Twelfth Night* to capacity. Such an audience is in touch with its civilization. He is shocked by a party of tourists in Canterbury Cathedral who appear not to have heard of Thomas à Becket, rather as Naipaul reacts to the attitude of the tourists at the fort of the Pandavas: "this rubble, no longer of use to anyone. Well, it was time to eat, time for the puris and the potatoes." But such people are not the rule in Chaudhuri's Europe as they are in Naipaul's India. Chaudhuri discovered in Englishmen, Frenchmen and Italians a living communion with their past such as he already had with his own past. Had he stayed longer in Europe and mixed with a wider social cross-section he might have modified this view but he would surely not have changed it thoroughly.

India was his companion on his passage to England, but so was his deep understanding, which few English people could rival, of European culture. Embedded in his prose we find constant evidence of an educated sensibility, often blended with self-mockery. "What I was seeing in England was making such an impression on me that, though neither dying nor drunk, I was incessantly babbling on green fields and suchlike." That kind of intimacy with English and its literature simply contradicts Naipaul's view of a mimic India with no capacity to understand the language it has adopted. Nor does Naipaul avoid stereotyped reactions himself. When he receives an invitation to go away he exclaims, "A weekend in the country! The words suggest cool clumps of trees, green fields, streams." Do they? Only to someone whose use of English has become an Englishman's. When Aziz, his guide, is introduced he has "something of the Shakesperian mechanic": Naipaul instinctively reaches for a wholly English likeness. Yet a few pages later he notes ironically that scones, tipsy pudding, trifle and apple tart are on offer in the heart of Kashmir. Englishness, it would appear, is funny in other people, fastidious in himself.

In all Chaudhuri's and all Naipaul's work one comes back to the central fact of empire. They share a view of the offensiveness of Anglo-Indian society, though they differ in their assessment of its most remarkable chronicler, Rudyard Kipling. For Naipaul Kipling renders a journey to India virtually unnecessary, for the society he records eighty years ago is the society still parroted up and down the sub-continent. "It is as if an entire society has fallen for a casual confidence trickster." "It was all there in Kipling, barring the epilogue of the Indian inheritance." For Chaudhuri, though, the epilogue cannot be so lightly dismissed. It is, after all, the era in which he lives, Kipling's view, however brilliant, is dated and partial: "the Indian sojourn made him incapable of loving any Indian with a mind, and led him to reserve all his affection for what could be called the human fauna of the country." Both writers attest the ease with which Britain has sloughed off her empire, barely remembering that she had one only a generation ago. The difference, however, is that whereas Naipaul sees this as further evidence of a decomposing civilization Chaudhuri, maybe with a touch of sentimentality, see it as proof of British resilience and even British grace.

An Area of Darkness and *A Passage to England* could only have been written by men fascinated with Britain, with India, with the links between them and the language one bestowed upon the other. At the end, however, one comes back to the men themselves. For both of them their journeys were essential stages in self-knowledge. William Walsh has spoken of Nirad Chaudhuri as a man with "an intense fascination with himself" and all V. S. Naipaul's prose contains a major element of autobiography, even when it is the subjectivity of detached observation. Theoretically, though one never believes it could have been so in practice, India might have been the cause which Naipaul at once craves and condemns in his writing. His visit confirmed him in his wariness of commitment and that, far more than the trenchancy or partiality of any particular observation, will always be the fascination of *An Area of Darkness*. In *A House for Mr. Biswas* Naipaul had already declared himself a major novelist. That promise has been amply confirmed in *The Mimic Men, In a Free State* and *Guerillas*. But no study of his fiction would be complete without the complement of his other work and amongst that his account of the Indian sojourn has a special pathos. Nor would it be fair to leave *An Area of Darkness* without noting that some of the sourness there has been replaced by a harsh compassion in the essays on India published in *The Overcrowded Barracoon* as a result of other visits. That book contains many tributes to Chaudhuri, whose *Autobiography*, Naipaul says, "may be the one great book to have come out of the Indo-English encounter." As for Chaudhuri himself, his scholarship and his capacity to examine two cultures simultaneously undoubtedly make him the foremost man of letters in modern India. Not lacking in irony or scepticism he nevertheless establishes in *A Passage to England* a note of uncynical enthusiasm which testifies not only to the enduring inheritance of empire but to his own grandness of heart. (pp. 21-35)

> Alastair Niven, "*Crossing the Black Waters: Nirad C. Chaudhuri's 'A Passage to England' and V. S. Naipaul's 'An Area of Darkness'*," in Ariel *(The University of Calgary), Vol. 9, No. 3, July, 1978, pp. 21-36.*

NORMAN DOUGLAS

[*Douglas was a cosmopolitan man of letters who wrote scientific monographs, memoirs, and novels, but is best remembered for his vivid, lively travel books. Born in Austria to Scottish and German parents, he travelled widely and lived abroad most of his life, producing books about those foreign locations that particularly captivated him. His* Fountains in the Sand: Rambles Among the Oases of Tunisia *(1912) is considered one of the finest English-language travel books ever written. Douglas's most famous novel,* South Wind *(1917), is a typical product of his peripatetic career: planned and written in England and Italy, it is set on an imaginary Mediterranean island and peopled by pleasure-seeking Europeans who discover the tendency of the Mediterranean atmosphere to "open the moral pores." Ralph D. Lindeman has written of* South Wind *that "Douglas the novelist is still Douglas the travel writer. The descriptive power is there, the ability to create atmosphere, the carefully composed canvas, the clearly defined line and masses moving across mosaics of bright colors in a stylized, almost artificial effect." In the following excerpt from a favorable review of Charles Montague Doughty's* Travels in Arabia Deserta *(1888), Douglas compares and contrasts the works of French and English travel writers, as well as the travel books of professional and nonprofessional writers, contending that the innocent, enthusiastic amateur is best able to convey the freshness and excitement necessary to an interesting travel narrative. He concludes with some general insights on travel writing.*]

Not long ago there was sent me a recently-published French book about Morocco—*Marrakech*, by the brothers Tharaud, then already in its twenty-fifth edition. What did I think of it? And why could we not write such things in English?

Well, I thought it good, despite that unseasonable military atmosphere—decidedly good of its kind; the story grows livelier and impressive towards the end. Moreover, thank Heaven, it exhales but faintly the familiar odour of Parisian patchouli; there are some luminous and suggestive metaphors, and a moment of real tragedy. For the rest: head-work, self conscious glitter, a virtuosity bordering on the precious. One detects only the frailest link of human sympathy between the authors and the scenes they describe. A wealth of outlandish customs and figures has been noted down by the pen of a scrupulous journalist and then distilled into elaborately-tinted phrases. It is almost wearisome, all this material, where so much is seen, so little felt. I recall, for instance, that suffocating chapter "La Place Folle." 'Qu'il est donc malaisé," say the authors in one place, "de peindre avec justesse le charme de l'Orient! A inventorier ces beautés . . . on a l'air d'un pédagogue" ["How difficult it is . . . to accurately describe the charm of the Orient! Cataloguing those splendors . . . makes one seem like a pedagogue"]. Exactly! An artist should never "inventorier" ["catalogue"]. Why therefore this endless cataloguing in *Marrakech*? Why? Because the authors, as Frenchmen, were unable to do what they should have done—unable to make their readers really feel the life they depict. Your Gaul is a centripetal fellow, a bad nomad. His affinities with foreign folk are only skin-deep—aesthetic rather than constitutional. One suspects that, while gadding abroad, he is pretty frequently homesick. One knows it. He will tell you so himself.

As to writing such things in English, the feat is not impossible. We must try, first and foremost, to be more logical, to rid ourselves of that lamentable haziness, of those iridescent flashes of thought and feeling that can be struck out of a single word; we must learn, in short, to content ourselves with a vocabulary such as our neighbours possess. Cut down to a quarter of its size that preposterous dictionary of ours, throw on the scrapheap all those mellow verbal forms, and consign the residue into the hands of a conscience-stricken Academy that shall stereotype the meaning and prescribe the proper usage of every time—the thing is done. There will be no more half-tones, no more interplay of shades. We shall step from twilight into sunshine. For what is the chief secret of French precision? Lack of words. To be sure, their writers are mostly professionals—*gens du métier* ["professionals"]; they know how to handle those few words.

That is why, generally speaking, they produce such mediocre travel-books.

The *homme de lettres* ["man of letters"], of whatever nationality, is handicapped in this department; he can never more attain to a jovial heedlessness of expression. His schooling militates against it; he knows for whom he writes; he has learnt to play to the gallery. The personal note (an impersonal travel-book is a horror) becomes him ill; there is apt to be something spectacular and meretricious in the work. This applies particularly to Frenchmen. Having an old-established literary tradition of what is good and bad—how to compass the one and avoid the other—they shine at objective narrative. Whey they write, as they sometimes do, in the first person, they often fail to ring true; art decays into artifice; it is as if, accustomed to producing fictional characters in their tales and romances, they would now read fictitious characters into themselves. Or else, as in *Marrakech,* they leave a mere blur so far as personality is concerned. The ideal author of travel-books is the inspired,

or at least enthusiastic, amateur. One would not take it amiss, furthermore, were he obsessed by some hobby or grievance, by idiosyncrasies and prejudices not common to the rest of us. And it goes without saying that he must be gloriously indifferent to the opinions of his fellow-creatures. Can professionals ever fulfil these conditions? No! They should therefore never attempt to write travel-books.

They have lost their innocence.

It was at a friend's house near a green English village, in the heart of a green English summer long ago—years before the abridged edition of *Arabia Deserta* appeared—that I became acquainted with the original Doughty. And these, you may instantly divine, are the conditions most favourable to an appreciation of his merits. That gaunt Odyssey reads mighty well in comfortable England. Amid verdant fields and streamlets, an opulence for the body, and a sense of immemorial tranquillity, how pleasant it is to conjure up visions of the traveller's marches under the flaming sky and of all his other hazards in a land of hunger and blood and desolation! I opened the first volume not quite at the commencement, and remember taking some little credit to myself (one was younger, in the middle 'nineties) for persisting to read to the last word of the second.

A tough, elemental, masculine performance. *Man muss sich hineinlesen* ["one must read oneself into it"], as the Germans say. The author himself calls his book "not milk for babes." Far from it! Stuff to be humbly and patiently masticated—an unwelcome occupation to our democratic age which, among other symptoms of senility, has lost the use of its teeth and now draws sustenance, ready chewed and half digested, pepsinized, out of the daily Press. Open *Arabia Deserta* where you please, and you find yourself stumbling among thought-laden periods that might have been hacked out of Chaos by some demoniac craftsman in the youth of the world. Strange, none the less, how that sense of anfractuosity evaporates. The theme, by subtle alchemy, justifies the style. Those harsh particles of language—so it seemed to me—were wondrously adapted to mirror the crudeness of Arabian landscape and character.

Be that as it may, I felt, on closing the book, as one who has been forcefully led through all the harassments of a dream; a weary, lingering dream; one of those that refuse to relax their hold upon the imagination, haunting our daylight moments with a vague presentiment of danger and disquietude. Here is no glint of mirth, no mockery; a spirit of sombre truthfulness broods over the scene. The book is oppressive by weight of thought and length of text. That might well be appropriate from an artistic point of view. Nothing short of eleven hundred pages could do justice to this toilsome, nightmarish epic. "I passed this one good day in Arabia; and all the others were evil because of the people's fanaticism." One good day in two years! Nor is it a featureless monster, like Pallas' Russian travels. A well-jointed monster, on the contrary, of spiky carapace and deliberate gait—pensively alert, harmonious.

Of one thing I was soon convinced: Doughty's outlook was not mine. Never could I have attained to his infinite capacity of suffering fools gladly. My days would have been short among those empty and elvish creatures whose only inducement (as often as not) to offer their far-famed hospitality is that they count on you to feed them another day—which would be almost impossible if they had obeyed their consciences and cut your throat. Dangers of rock or ice or desert may well be tempting, but such fuddled fanaticism grows insupportable. Can there be a greater torture of mind than to travel month after month among peevishly ferocious bigots, repressing an altogether praiseworthy inclination to laugh at them or hit them on the head? In default of being murdered I should have succumbed to cerebral congestion. Doughty's feat calls for quite a peculiar temper:

> The mad sherîf had the knife again in his hand! and his old gall rising, "Show me all thou hast," cries he, "and leave nothing; or now will I kill thee."— Where was Maabûb? whom I had not seen since yester-evening; in him was the faintness and ineptitude of Arab friends.—"Remember the bread and salt which we have eaten together, Sâlem!"—"Show it all to me, or now by Ullah I will slay thee with this knife." More bystanders gathered from the shadowing places: some of them cried out, "Let us hack him in morsels, the cursed one! what hinders?—fellows, let us hack him in morsels!"—"Have patience a moment, and send these away." Sâlem, lifting his knife, cried, "Except thou show me all at the instant, I will slay thee!" . . .

Charming people!

Endeavouring at this distance of time to recall my first impression of *Arabia Deserta*—to delve, that is, through multiple layers of experience which have accumulated since those green summer days of long ago—I remember being vastly pleased with the motives which allured Doughty into these stricken regions. He went not in search of disused emerald mines or to open up commercial markets; he took with him no commission from the home authorities, no theories to air, no gospel to preach. His purport is refreshingly anti-utilitarian. What drove him, besides a Homeric love of adventure, to undergo these hardships was pure intellectual curiosity, the longings of a brain that feeds on disinterested thought. "Other men," said the Arabs to him, "jeopardy somewhat in hope of winning, but thou wilt adventure all, having no need." He hoped, he now tells us, "to add something to the common fund of Western knowledge." A certain Mahmud, describing the rock-hewn sculptures of Median Salih, "was the father of my painful travels in Arabia." All thanks to Mahmud! Burckhardt's discovery of Petra may have helped to ignite the train; and also the Bible, full as it is of lore and legends of those more reasonable Semites who lived here in olden times, who revered letters and song, and planted the vine, and built cities of stone, before the blight of Islam fell upon the land. That mysterious and romantic background of the past cannot but appeal to the imagination. Doughty's book, so dispassionately worded, is a truthful indictment of Mahomet turning his country into a wilderness. What a creed can do! So Borrow's account of Spanish savagery reflects the achievement of those inquisitors who, in the name of a kindly God, brought to withering-point the kindliness of nature and of man.

And I likewise remember saying to myself, "*Hoec olim meminisse* . . . who would not envy this man his memories?"

Ideas such as these will have flitted through the minds of all the early admirers of Doughty. They must have realised that his volumes do provoke thought in no common degree. Here is not only information; here is character, a human document. The image of the poet-traveller is no blur. Doughty has etched his lonely figure against this desolation of sand and lava-crag, and we are glad to see how the thing has been accomplished; it does one good to be in contact with a companion full of natural resources and listen to his tale; one leaves him with

regret, as one bids farewell to some friend of robust and well-stored mind, perceiving that, all unconsciously, his words have been of use in revealing us to ourselves. They have helped us to rectify and clarify our own perspective. (Can anything be called a book unless it forces the reader by one method or another, by contrast or sympathy, to discover himself?) So *Arabia Deserta* is the antithesis of the purely pictorial *Marrakech*, inasmuch as therein we enjoy that feeling of intimacy for which every sensitive person must crave, while wandering with his author through strange places. It seems to me that the reader of a good travel-book is entitled not only to an exterior voyage, to descriptions of scenery and so forth, but to an interior, a sentimental or temperamental voyage, which takes place side by side with that outer one; and that the ideal book of this kind offers us, indeed, a triple opportunity of exploration—abroad, into the author's brain, and into our own. The writer should therefore possess a brain worth exploring; some philosophy of life—not necessarily, though by preference, of his own forging—and the courage to proclaim it and put it to the test; he must be naïf and profound, both child and sage. Who is either the one or the other in these days, when the whole trend of existence makes for the superficial and commonplace, when a man writes with one eye on his publisher and the other on his public?

This may account for the insipid taste of many travel-books printed just now: lack of personality on the part of their authors. It is not enough to depict, in however glowing hues, the landscape and customs of distant regions, to smother us in folklore and statistics and history, and besprinkle the pages with imaginary conversations or foreign idioms by way of generating "local colour." It is not enough. We want to take our share in that interior voyage and watch how these alien sights and sounds affect the writer. If he lacks that compulsion of the spirit which is called character, or lets his mind linger on contingencies hostile to frank utterance, he will be unable to supply that want and leave us dissatisfied. Doughty is rich in character, self-consistent, never otherwise than himself. Press him to the last drop, it has the same taste as the first; whereas Palgrave, for instance, who traversed some of these same regions, is by no means always Palgrave; and Burton—what of Burton? A driving-force void of savour or distinction; drabness *in excelsis*; a glorified Blue Book. A man who could write at one and the same time ten (was it ten?) different volumes on as many different subjects. . . .

The modern author of travel-literature one suspects to be a greyish little person, uncommonly wide awake, perky and plausible, but somewhat deficient in humanity—a kind of reporter, in fact, ready to adopt anybody's philosophy or nobody's in particular. Those earlier ones were not of this sort. They derived, to begin with, from another stock, for voyages used to be costly undertakings; they were gentleman-scholars who saw things from their own individual angle. Their leisurely aristocratic flavour, their wholesome discussions about this or that, their waywardness and all that mercurial touch of a bygone generation—where is it now? How went it? An enquiry which, rightly solved, might explain the rarity of types like Doughty.

That mercurial touch disappears naturally when the conditions which gave it birth are at an end. We have ceased to be what we were, that is all. Year by year our hard-won domestic privileges have been gnawed or lopped away; the recent history of the English citizen is one long wail of liberties forfeited; we are being continentalised, standardised—a process which cannot but reflect itself in life and literature. It blunts our peculiar edges. Singularly, the hall-mark of that older Anglo-Saxon, is hardly perceptible in our modern bearing or writing. We have ceased to be "mad"; none but a flatterer would still call us eccentric. All kinds of other factors have contributed to this result, such as improved world-communications. Dr. Arnold, again, that merciless pruner of youthful individualism, has wrought a miracle of destruction so far as originality is concerned, for his energies hit hardest the very class from whom those sturdy and idiomatic, and sometimes outrageous, opinions used to come.

Doughty seems to have escaped the contagion; he goes so far as to call the Universities "shambles of good wits." Hid edges are intact. He sees clearly, and feels deeply, and warily chooses his words. There is a morning freshness in that gift of investing the ordinary phenomena of life with an extraordinary interest—a kind of bloom, I should call it.

> No matins here of birds; not a rock partridge-cock, calling with blithesome chuckle over the extreme waterless desolation. Grave is that giddy heat upon the crown of the head; the ears tingle with a flickering shrillness a subtle crepitation it seems, in the glassiness of this sun-stricken nature: the hot sand-blink is in the eyes, and there is little refreshment to find in the tents' shelter; the worsted booths leak to this fiery rain of sunny light. Mountains looming like dry bones through the thin air, stand far around about us: the savage flank of Ybba Moghrair, the high spire and ruinous stacks of el-Jebâl, Chebàd, the coast of Helwàn! Herds of weak nomad camels waver dispersedly, seeking pasture in the midst of this hollow fainting country, where but lately the swarming locusts have fretted every green thing. This silent air burning about us, we endure breathless till the assr: when the dozing Arabs in the tents revive after their heavy hours. The lingering day draws down to the sun-setting; the herdsmen, weary of the sun, come again with the cattle, to taste in their menzils the first sweetness of mirth and repose. . . .

Now what do Frenchmen think of such language? And why cannot they convey these shades of meaning in their own?

Well, even Fromentin will give you a taste of that dumb ache which rends and racks the human frame under a sun-drenched sky. But one has only to name him—and that is precisely and soley why I am referring to these folk—in order to appraise Doughty at his right worth. Or glance into another of them: Loti's *Désert*. What of it? A cloying and tinkling performance; as voiceless, almost as voiceless, as a picture on a wall. Where, you ask, where is the shrewd wit, the insight, the humanity of Montaigne? And that other one about Constantinople, or about Morocco: how prettily constructed, how unconvincing! Yet Loti is a writer of renown; there is no gainsaying those exquisite gifts. What militates against his, and his countrymen's, veracity in a personal relation like *Le Désert* is professionalism—and one or two other little things. Lack of humility, for instance; or call it simple imperviousness to foreign languages and ideals. They are curiously incurious, again, as to matters non-human; even the Goncourts' *Journal* is full of queer blunders of observation; they seem to have inherited somewhat from those old Troubadours to whom the human element was everything, and who would now utilise nature as a mere scenic decoration against which to display their emotions, their "sensations d'Orient" or whatever it might be. French schooling, too, does not encourage the seeing eye. Their children are saturated with Racine and other full-mouthed rhetoricians; the taint clings to them in later years, vitiating their outlook and

making them unduly concerned about stage-effect—a preoccupation which ruins the intimate note essential to every good travel-book.

To carry off that intimate note demands independence; what we call cussedness. Think of the cussedness of Doughty in doing what he did among those stark, God-struck zelots; note the cussedness in every word he writes. Such a man, strong in reserves, can afford to be veracious, and himself. His charm resides in sincerity, and you feel that, however much he gives, he is witholding still more. Latin authors of the subjective variety seldom produce that sense of reserve. Their personalities are less marked, their mutual divergencies fewer, and their reserves, if they have any, are apt to be blown into stylistic fireworks.

Their personalities are less marked: here lies, maybe, the core of the matter. The Anglo-Saxon has a laxer literary discipline, commendable distrust of authority, a language that lends itself gaily to the unburdening of extremest individualism; and not only that. His educational system (despite the efforts of that old disciplinarian and prayer-monger) and the very laws of his country induce him to break away from the parent-stock. He is centrifugal. Without abdicating an ounce of self-respect he can merge himself into anything and assimilate what you please. He makes a good nomad. His sympathies with alien races are broad and deep; there is, at times, something intuitional or prophetic about them. Could any foreigner have written *Haji Baba*? Which of them has looked clean through the Spaniard like Mr. Havelock Ellis or through the Neapolitan as did Charles Grant in his *Stories of the Camorra*? And there occurs to me, at this moment, a volume by Mr. Lowes Dickinson—I forget its title; quite an unpretentious little thing; notes, I fancy, from a travelling diary. Unpretentious, but symptomatic; one questions whether anybody but an Anglo-Saxon could have achieved such a point of view. It is to the credit of our race that, knowing itself to be the Salt of the Earth, it can yet survey strange people in so benign and intelligent a fashion. Doughty is another example of this artlessly sublime detachment. Whether a French Doughty will ever appear?

The phenomenon is not inconceivable. Borne on the wings of opium, or tossed over the sea by some black fury of despair, a certain one of them may presently unveil for us the throbbing heart of the Far East. There, among those steamy forests and many-hued native folk, he may cut the cable that binds him to the boulevards; there he may learn to squeeze new and glamorous colour-effects out of that old mother-tongue, provided—provided he forgets the solemn Academy everlastingly engaged upon its blithe topiarian tactics. Must language, a child of necessity, be clipped and groomed like a box hedge? Must a living organism be at the mercy of a pack of dismal gentlemen in frock coats? Why not let it grow freely under the sun and stars, to thrive or suffer with the rest of them, throwing out buds and blossoms, bending to the winds, and discarding outworn members with painless ease? (pp. 1-15)

> *Norman Douglas, "'Arabia Deserta,'" in his Experiments, Robert M. McBride & Company, 1925, pp. 1-22.*

ADDITIONAL BIBLIOGRAPHY

Akiyama, Masayuki. "The American Image in Kafu Nagai and Henry James." *Comparative Literature Studies* XVIII, No. 2 (June 1981): 95-103.

Contrasts the books that Kafu Nagai and Henry James wrote about their respective visits to the United States: Kafu's from 1903 to 1907 (his first trip to the United States) and James's 1904 return after twenty-two years abroad.

Auden, W. H. Introduction to *The American Scene,* by Henry James, edited by W. H. Auden, pp. v-xxvi. New York: Charles Scribner's Sons, 1946.
Discusses James's travel writing.

Bering-Jensen, Henrik. "Evelyn Waugh: The Last Tourist." *The National Review* XXXVI, No. 21 (2 November 1984): 56-7.
Lively appreciation of Waugh's travel writing.

Birkerts, Sven. "On Mandelstam's *Journey to Armenia.*" *Secret Destinations: Writers on Travel,* edited by Mark Rudman, pp. 79-92. New York: New York University, 1985.
Assigns a symbolic meaning to Osip and Nadezhda Mandelstam's 1930 trip to Armenia, and discusses the brilliant, poetic prose of Mandelstam's *Journey to Armenia.*

Bishop, Peter. "The Geography of Hope and Despair: Peter Matthiessen's *The Snow Leopard.*" *Critique* XXVI, No. 4 (Summer 1985): 203-16.
Discusses both the actual and symbolic journeys described in Matthiessen's *The Snow Leopard.*

Butor, Michel. "Travel and Writing." *Mosaic* VIII, No. 1 (Fall 1974): 1-16.
Analyzes both the literary nature of travel and the ways in which writing and reading resemble travel.

Gay, Ruth. "Charles Doughty—Man and Book." *The American Scholar* 50, No. 4 (Autumn 1981): 527-35.
Appreciation of Doughty's *Travels in Arabia Deserta,* which Gay praises as one of the few English-language travel books that "can enmesh the reader so entirely in the remote and dreamlike fabric of an Arabian journey. All clocks stop; history disappears; there is only the seamless present of the sun, the tribe, and the voice of the narrator in our ear."

Gendron, Charisse. "Lucie Duff Gordon's *Letters from Egypt.*" *Ariel* 17, No. 2 (April 1986): 49-61.
Biographical and critical examination of "one of a number of lively, personal books of travel to the East that delighted Victorian readers," which Gedron finds still valuable for the insights it offers into the "archetypal theme of the journey" as interpreted by writers of the British empire.

Grace, Jane Opper. "Geography as Metaphor: Larbaud's Fiction Revisited." *Romanic Review* LXVII, No. 4 (November 1976): 300-07.
Contrasts Valéry Larbaud's use of geographical description in his nonfiction and fiction, finding that portrayal of landscape in the fiction usually has symbolic rather than merely descriptive value.

Janik, Del Ivan. *The Curve of Return: D. H. Lawrence's Travel Books.* Victoria, Canada: University of Victoria, 1981, 119 p.
Considers Lawrence's four travel books—*Twilight in Italy, Sea and Sardinia, Mornings in Mexico,* and *Etruscan Places*—important for what they reveal about his development as a thinker and an artist, and intrinsically valuable as well-written travel narratives.

Johnson, Stuart. "American Marginalia: James's *The American Scene.*" *Texas Studies in Language and Literature* 24, No. 1 (Spring 1982): 83-101.
Examines "the problem of the writer's relation to his experience" in James's travel narrative *The American Scene.*

Lawrence, T. E. Introduction to *Travels in Arabia Deserta,* by Charles M. Doughty, pp. 17-28. New York: Random House, 1921.

Praises *Travels in Arabia Deserta* as the finest book of its kind and finds that continual study of the book and its topic increases his "respect for the insight, judgment, and artistry of the author."

Lyons, Richard S. "'In Supreme Command': The Crisis of the Imagination in James's *The American Scene.*" *The New England Quarterly* 55, No. 4 (December 1982): 517-39.
Identifies the real subject of *The American Scene* as James's "imaginative effort to give shape and meaning" to the American culture he was observing firsthand after an absence of two decades.

Meckier, Jerome. "Philip Quarles' Passage to India: *Jesting Pilate, Point Counter Point,* and Bloomsbury." *Studies in the Novel* 9, No. 4 (Winter 1977): 445-67.
Discusses the relationship between Aldous Huxley's travel narrative *Jesting Pilate,* based upon his 1925-26 trip to India, and his novel *Point Counter Point,* which incorporates aspects of Huxley's Indian travels.

Reitt, Barbara A. "'I Never Returned As I Went In': Steinbeck's *Travels with Charley.*" *Southwest Review* 66, No. 2 (Spring 1981): 186-202.
Interprets Steinbeck's crosscountry excursion that formed the basis of *Travels with Charley* as a personal symbol of the writer's regained command and control of his personal life and artistic independence.

Smith, Carl J. "James's Travels, Travel Writings, and the Development of His Art." *Modern Language Quarterly* 38, No. 4 (December 1977): 367-80.
Explores the role of James's travel writing in his intellectual and artistic growth.

Spengeman, William C. "The Poetics of Adventure." In his *The Adventurous Muse: The Poetics of American Fiction, 1789-1900,* pp. 6-67. London: Yale University Press, 1977.
Describes the effect of travel writing on the development of American fiction.

Stout, Janis P. *The Journey Narrative in American Literature: Patterns and Departures.* Westport, Conn.: Greenwood Press, 1983, 272 p.
Discusses the pervasiveness of travel as a thematic concern and recurrent symbolic action in American fiction and identifies basic patterns of journey narratives in American fiction.

Tomlinson, H. M. *Norman Douglas.* New York: Haskell House Publishers, 1974, 63 p.
Affectionate and approbatory critical and biographical study. Tomlinson praises Douglas's contributions to many literary genres and includes *Siren Land, Old Calabria,* and *Fountains in the Sand* among the world's best books of travel.

Ulyaslov, Pavel. "The Whole World Is a Man's Home: Grigori Baklanov and His Essays About His Trips Abroad." *Soviet Literature* 4, No. 257 (1986): 168-70.
Identifies the interdependence of all humankind as the central theme of Baklanov's travel essays.

Von Hallberg, Robert. "Tourists." In his *American Poetry and Culture: 1945-1980,* pp. 62-92. Cambridge: Harvard University Press, 1985.
Surveys the careers of American poets who lived abroad in the 1940s and 1950s and wrote poetry with travel themes, reflecting the increase in overseas travel by Americans in those decades.

Waterston, Elizabeth. "Travel Books (1880-1920)." In *Literary History of Canada: Canadian Literature in English,* pp. 347-63. Toronto: University of Toronto Press, 1965.
Surveys Canadian travel literature of the late nineteenth and early twentieth centuries.

Woodcock, George. "Many Solitudes: The Travel Writings of Margaret Lawrence." In his *The World of Canadian Writing,* pp. 63-78. Vancouver: Douglas & McIntyre, 1980.

Demonstrates the interdependence of themes in Lawrence's fiction and concepts she explored in her travel writings.

Zorach, Cecile Cazort. "Two Faces of Erin: The Dual Journey in Heinrich Böll's *Irishes Tagebuch*." *The Germanic Review* LIII, No. 3 (Summer 1978): 124-31.
    Examines the "artistic subtleties" and "dualistic structure" of the *Irishes Tagebuch*, a comparative discussion of Böll's native German culture and that of Ireland.

———. "Geographical Exploration as Metaphor in Recent German Narrative." *The German Quarterly* 59, No. 4 (Fall 1986): 611-27.
    Explores some reasons that modern German authors are drawn to geographical exploration as subject matter.

Appendix

The following is a listing of all sources used in Volume 30 of *Twentieth-Century Literary Criticism*. Included in this list are all copyright and reprint rights and acknowledgments for those essays for which permission was obtained. Every effort has been made to trace copyright, but if omissions have been made, please let us know.

THE EXCERPTS IN TCLC, VOLUME 30, WERE REPRINTED FROM THE FOLLOWING PERIODICALS:

African Literature Today, n. 14, 1984. Copyright 1984 by Heinemann Educational Books Ltd. All rights reserved. Reprinted by permission of Africana Publishing Corporation, New York, NY.

Amateur Correspondent, November-December, 1937.

American Literature, v. 59, May, 1987. Copyright © 1987 Duke University Press, Durham, NC. Reprinted by permission of the publisher.

The American Scholar, v. 32, Summer, 1963; v. 51, Winter, 1981-82. Copyright © 1963, 1981 by the United Chapters of Phi Beta Kappa. Both reprinted by permission of the publishers.

Ariel: A Review of International English Literature, v. 9, July, 1978 for "Crossing the Black Waters: Nirad C. Chaudhuri's 'A Passage to England' and V. S. Naipaul's 'An Area of Darkness' " by Alastair Niven. Copyright © 1978 The Board of Governors, The University of Calgary. Reprinted by permission of the publisher and the author.

The Bookman, New York, v. L, November & December, 1919.

Commentary, v. 84, November, 1987 for "The New York (Jewish) Intellectuals" by Ruth R. Wisse. Copyright © 1987 by the American Jewish Committee. All rights reserved. Reprinted by permission of the publisher and the author.

Comparative Literature, v. 31, Winter, 1979 for "Scriabin and Russian Symbolism" by Ralph E. Matlaw. © copyright 1979 by University of Oregon. Reprinted by permission of the author.

The Conch, v. V, 1973. © 1973 Conch Magazine Limited (Publishers).

Criticism, v. 4, Spring, 1982 for "Surrealism and the Cinema" by J. H. Matthews. Copyright 1962, Wayne State University Press. Reprinted by permission of the publisher and the Literary Estate of J. H. Matthews.

The D. H. Lawrence Review, v. 11, Fall, 1978. © 1978 James C. Cowan. Reprinted with the permission of *The D. H. Lawrence Review.*

The Dial, v. 38, June 1, 1905.

Evening News, April 17, 1931.

THE EXCERPTS IN TCLC, VOLUME 30, WERE REPRINTED FROM THE FOLLOWING BOOKS:

Alcorn, John. From *The Nature Novel from Hardy to Lawrence*. Columbia University Press, 1977. Copyright © 1977 John Alcorn. All rights reserved. Used by permission of the publisher.

Artaud, Antonin. From *Selected Writings*. Edited by Susan Sontag, translated by Helen Weaver. Farrar, Straus and Giroux, Inc., 1976. Translation copyright © 1976 by Farrar, Straus and Giroux. All rights reserved. Reprinted by permission of Farrar, Straus and Giroux, Inc.

Babalola, Adeboye. From "A Survey of Modern Literature in the Yoruba, Efik and Hausa Languages," in *Introduction to Nigerian Literature*. Edited by Bruce King. Evans Brothers, 1971, Africana Publishing Corporation, 1972. © University of Lagos and Evans Brothers Limited, 1971. All rights reserved. Reprinted by permission of Holmes & Meier Publishers, Inc., 30 Irving Place, New York, NY 10003. In Canada by Unwin Hyman Ltd. and the author.

Balakian, Anna. From *Surrealism: The Road to the Absolute*. Revised edition. Dutton, 1970. Copyright © 1959, 1970 by Anna Balakian. All rights reserved. Reprinted by permission of the author.

Bigsby, C. W. E. From *Dada & Surrealism*. Methuen, 1972. © 1972 C. W. E. Bigsby. Reprinted by permission of Methuen & Co. Ltd.

Bloom, Alexander. From *Prodigal Sons: The New York Intellectuals & Their World*. Oxford University Press, 1986. Copyright © 1986 by Alexander Bloom. All rights reserved. Reprinted by permission of Oxford University Press, Inc.

Booth, James. From *Writers and Politics in Nigeria*. Africana Publishing Company, 1981. Copyright © 1981 James Booth. All rights reserved. Reprinted by permission of Holmes & Meier Publishers, Inc., 30 Irving Place, New York, NY 10003.

Bowen, Elizabeth. From an introduction to *The Second Ghost Book*. Edited by Lady Cynthia Asquith. J. Barrie, 1952.

Brée, Germaine, and Margaret Guiton. From *An Age of Fiction: The French Novel from Gide to Camus*. Rutgers University Press, 1957. Copyright © 1957 by Rutgers, the State University. Renewed 1985 by Germaine Brée and Margaret Otis Guiton. Reprinted by permission of the publisher.

Breton, André. From *Manifestoes of Surrealism*. Translated by Richard Seaver and Helen R. Lane. University of Michigan Press, 1969. Copyright © The University of Michigan 1969. All rights reserved. Reprinted by permission of the publisher.

Briggs, Julia. From *Night Visitors: The Rise and Fall of the English Ghost Story*. Faber, 1977. © 1977 by Julia Briggs. All rights reserved. Reprinted by permission of Faber & Faber Ltd.

Bristol, Evelyn. From "From Romanticism to Symbolism in France and Russia," in *American Contributions to the Ninth International Congress of Slavists: Literature, Poetics, History, Vol. II*. Edited by Paul Debreczeny. Slavica, 1983. Copyright © 1983 by Evelyn Bristol. All rights reserved. Reprinted by permission of the publisher and the author.

Briusov, Valery. From "Against Naturalism in the Theatre," in *The Russian Symbolist Theatre: An Anthology of Plays and Critical Texts*. Edited and translated by Michael Green. Ardis, 1986. Copyright © 1986 by Ardis Publishers. All rights reserved. Reprinted by permission of the publisher.

Caeiro, Oscar. From "Profile of German and Spanish Exile Poets in Latin America," in *Latin America and the Literature of Exile: A Comparative View of the 20th-Century European Refugee Writers in the New World*. Edited by Hans-Bernhard Moeller. Carl Winter Universitätsverlag, 1983. © 1983. Carl Winter Universitätsverlag, gegr. All rights reserved. Reprinted by permission of the editor.

Camus, Albert. From *The Rebel: An Essay on Man in Revolt*. Translated by Anthony Bower. Revised edition. Vintage Books, 1956. Copyright © 1956, renewed 1984 by Alfred A. Knopf, Inc. All rights reserved. Reprinted by permission of the publisher.

Cazden, Robert E. From *German Exile Literature in America, 1933-1950: A History of the Free German Press and Book Trade*. American Library Association, 1970. Copyright © 1965 by the American Library Association. All rights reserved. Reprinted by permission of the publisher.

Clark, John Pepper. From *The Example of Shakespeare*. Northwestern University Press, 1970. © J. P. Clark 1970. Reprinted by permission of the publisher.

Cooney, Terry A. From *The Rise of the New York Intellectuals: "Partisan Review" and Its Circle*. The University of Wisconsin Press, 1986. Copyright © 1986 The Board of Regents of the University of Wisconsin System. All rights reserved. Reprinted by permission of the publisher.

De la Mare, Walter. From an introduction to *They Walk Again: An Anthology of Ghost Stories*. Edited by Colin de la Mare. E. P. Dutton & Co., Inc., 1931. Copyright 1931, renewed 1959 by Colin de la Mare. Reprinted by permission of the publisher, E. P. Dutton, a division of NAL Penguin Inc.

Donchin, Georgette. From *The Influence of French Symbolism on Russian Poetry*. Mouton & Co., 1958.

Douglas, Drake. From *Horror!* The Macmillan Company, 1966. Copyright © 1966 by Drake Douglas. All rights reserved. Permission granted by Bertha Klausner International Literary Agency, Inc.

Willett, John. From "The Emigration and the Arts," in *Exile in Great Britain: Refugees from Hitler's Germany*. Edited by Gerhard Hirschfeld. Berg, 1984. © The German Historical Institute 1984. All rights reserved. Reprinted by permission of Berg Publishers Ltd.

Wilson, Edmund. From *Classics and Commercials: A Literary Chronicle of the Forties*. Farrar, Straus and Giroux, 1950. Copyright 1950 by Edmund Wilson. Renewed 1977 by Elena Wilson. All rights reserved. Reprinted by permission of Farrar, Straus and Giroux, Inc.

Young, Peter. From "Tradition, Language and the Reintegration of Identity in West African Literature in English," in *The Critical Evaluation of African Literature*. Edited by Edgar Wright. Heinemann Educational Books Ltd., 1973. © in this selection Edgar Wright 1973. Reprinted by permission of the publisher.

Zabel, Morton Dauwen. From an introduction to *The Art of Travel*. By Henry James, edited by Morton Dauwen Zabel. Doubleday & Company, Inc., 1958. Copyright © 1958 by Morton Dauwen Zabel. Renewed 1986 by Marguerite Dauwen. All rights reserved. Reprinted by permission of Doubleday, a division of Bantam, Doubleday, Dell Publishing Group, Inc.